Liberating Faith

Liberating Faith

Religious Voices for Justice, Peace, and Ecological Wisdom

Edited by
Roger S. Gottlieb

ROWMAN & LITTLEFIELD PUBLISHERS, INC.
Lanham • Boulder • New York • Toronto • Oxford

ROWMAN & LITTLEFIELD PUBLISHERS, INC.

Published in the United States of America
by Rowman & Littlefield Publishers, Inc.
A wholly owned subsidiary of The Rowman & Littlefield Publishing Group, Inc.
4501 Forbes Boulevard, Suite 200, Lanham, Maryland 20706
www.rowmanlittlefield.com

PO Box 317
Oxford
OX2 9RU, UK

British Library Cataloguing in Publication Information Available

Library of Congress Cataloging-in-Publication Data

Liberating faith : religious voices for justice, peace, and ecological wisdom / edited by
Roger S. Gottlieb.
    p. cm.
  Includes bibliographical references.
  ISBN 0-7425-2534-1 (alk. paper)—ISBN 0-7425-2535-X (pbk. : alk. paper)
  1. Religion and justice.   2. Peace—Religious aspects.   3. Environmentalism—Religious aspects.
4. Liberalism—Religious aspects.   5. Religious ethics.   I. Gottlieb, Roger S.
  BL65.J87L53   2003
  291.1′7—dc21   2003011947

Printed in the United States of America

⊗™ The paper used in this publication meets the minimum requirements of American
National Standard for Information Sciences—Permanence of Paper for Printed Library
Materials, ANSI/NISO Z39.48-1992.

To All Those Who

Find God in Compassion

and

Spiritual Wisdom

in

the Search for Justice

What does the Lord require of you but to do justice, and to love kindness, and to walk humbly with your God?

—Micah 6:8

True religion is real living; living with all one's soul, with all one's goodness and righteousness.

—Albert Einstein

Contents

❧

Preface

❧

This book explores the connections between religious traditions and progressive politics, the ways in which a religious sensibility can join with—and learn from—theories of and movements for social justice, peace, and ecological wisdom.

It is a very large book, but easily could have been twice as long. Many wonderful writers, institutional statements, and movements have been left out. And, at the same time, while there is a wealth of material from a truly global range of sources, I am aware that my own background, as well as the predominant setting for the use of the book, privileges a Western point of view. There is something of a tilt toward concerns with justice over those of community, and there are more selections from Western religions than Eastern or indigenous ones. However, a close look at the table of contents should reassure readers that there is indeed something for everyone here.

In any event, neither of these limitations is critical: Any volume of this kind will reflect the cultural, political, and religious presuppositions of its editor, and anyone taken with the ideas expressed here will have no trouble finding a wide range of resources on both these topics and related ones.

Though I have organized Parts IV through VIII according to particular themes, readers should realize that there is necessarily some overlap among their respective concerns. New theologies will often include or make reference to new rituals; religious responses to injustices of class, race, gender, or species cannot easily be separated. For a historical sensibility, the book might well be read from beginning to end. However, it can also be perused thematically, in terms of the particular tradition that calls to the reader, or by reference to analytic pieces, institutional statements, or accounts of real-world struggles.

There is a great wealth of ideas here, because so many people of faith have taken seriously Jesus' command to love their neighbors, the prophet Amos's instruction to "let justice roll down like the waters," or the Buddhist goal of saving all beings from unhappiness. It is my hope that these voices will instruct, inspire, and prompt us all to act.

Acknowledgments

❧

This book would not have been possible without the help and advice of many people.

Numerous colleagues and strangers were kind enough to suggest selections and comment on my own contributions. I am grateful to Bob Atkins, Nick Baker, David Barnhill, Miriam Greenspan, Stephanie Kaza, Jim Langford, Holmes Rolston, Judith Scoville, John Sanbonmatsu, Thomas Shannon, Ruth Smith, and Les Sponsel.

The staff of the Humanities and Arts Department of Worcester Polytechnic Institute helped with many chores of copying, typing, and collecting material.

Rowman & Littlefield has been a real pleasure to work with throughout: Terri Boddorff did the near insurmountable job of getting permissions; Erin McKindley managed the production of a large and complicated manuscript.

A special appreciation to my editor and now friend, Brian Romer, who has always been helpful, reassuring, supportive, and (when necessary) critical.

Most of all, to the writers, theologians, activists, scholars, and poets collected here—thank you for your work.

Introduction

༄

Those who say religion has nothing to do with politics do not know what religion is.

—Gandhi

RELIGION, POLITICAL MOVEMENTS, AND THE FATE OF THE WORLD

We live in a dark time. The world seems increasingly polarized between the soulless bureaucrats of globalization, modernization, and instant Internet service, and the passionate carnage of ethnic, national, or religious hostility. And many people think religion is one of the major sources of that darkness. From the September 11 murders to the endless conflict between Palestinians and Israelis, from the hate-filled rhetoric of some of the religious right to the savage hostilities between Hindus and Moslems, we are now (and have been for some time) confronted almost daily with the specter of religious violence, arrogant proclamations that "we alone" possess the "one true faith," and an often brutal attachment to male privilege.

Yet for all their self-proclaimed ownership of the "true faith," the fundamentalists' violent, premodern form of devotion is not the only religion in town. Religious values have taken other forms, adopting democratic, liberal, progressive, or even radical ways of thinking about and seeking to change some of society's most basic institutions and values. Such efforts have been increasingly widespread in the last fifty years or so, but they did not begin in the mid-twentieth century. Rather, there has always been an aspect of religious life that seeks not only God, Enlightenment, and personal morality, but also the ethical transformation of society as a whole. From Biblical injunctions to care for the stranger and allow the ox to eat while he works, to Indian Buddhist emperor Ashoka's edicts emphasizing tolerance for different religions and care for the poor, religion has exhibited—along with its many cruel excesses—a profound impulse to collective forms of justice and reconciliation. In recent decades, groups defined by religious faith have sought peace in the midst of ethnic violence, supported women's equality, resisted the human costs of the triumphant global economy, and joined hands with environmentalists. And they have done so not only in support of secular justice, but also as an expression of God's will and of spiritual wisdom.

From Gandhi and Martin Luther King to feminist peaceniks and Green defenders of the rainforest, from Jewish Renewal and Catholic Liberation Theology to the Quaker Peace Fellowship and Engaged Buddhism, spiritual social activists claim that authentic religion must be an activist, transforming presence in the political world; that the moral and psychological insights of religion are of enormous value for those seeking progressive social change; and that liberating political theories and movements can have important lessons for religions. These religious voices are the focus of this book.

Interestingly it is sometimes hard, if not impossible, to neatly distinguish the history of religion from that of liberal or even radical secular politics. On the one hand, Enlightenment ideals of democracy and equality, and subsequent social movements that tried to make those ideals real, have touched religious life deeply. Secular political movements have transformed a good deal of the world's religious community, as well as many of those freelance believers self-defined as "spiritual but not religious." Spiritual social activists have been moved by their encounters with ideals of political rights, rational inquiry, justice for those marginalized by race, gender, ethnicity, religion, or sexuality, and care for all of earth's creatures. As the Christian churches of the eighteenth and nineteenth centuries had to come around to the basic democratic idea that common people could determine who would have political power, so some religious groups in the twentieth century have had to confront racism, sexism, anti-Semitism, ecological devastation, and oppression of those with disabilities.

At the same time, however, segments of the religious community have been integral parts of the very movements and accomplishments we often think of as "secular." For many the very idea of human rights was rooted in a vision of human beings as all equal in the sight of God.[1] Struggles to abolish slavery and apartheid, isolated groups resisting the siren song of war, religious calls to respect the dignity of the working class, visionaries who proclaimed the sacredness of the earth and the sin of pollution—in these encounters and more, religious voices have been part of our collective efforts to steer civilization toward a moral and fulfilling form of life. The historical record tells us that progressive politics and religion have not only been enemies, but also comrades; have not only at times flat out rejected each others' perspectives, but also at times learned from them, embraced them, and lent a hand.

As in the past, religious voices are needed to achieve the goals of justice, community, and a rational society. This need becomes increasingly clear, I think, if we realize that the happy Enlightenment prediction that democracy plus science would produce freedom and happiness has been, at best, only minimally fulfilled. While in select parts of the world the last two hundred years have produced significant increases both in material standard of living and political rights, much of the rest of the world seems resistant to economic development and downright rejecting of doctrines of democracy and rights. Equally important, even in the United States, Europe, Japan, and the newly emerging capitalist centers such as Brazil or Thailand, deep questions are being raised about the ultimate value of secular modernity. From the deadly efficiency of Nazi gas chambers to the deadly threat of global warming, unrestrained technology seems to be as much a danger as a blessing. Constant expansion of consumption leads to environmental devastation and an addiction to shopping. A culture devoted to infinite shades of personal "lifestyle" choice creates a population riddled with boredom, drug addiction, and an indefinable sense that life has little meaning outside of the next escape or distraction. The idea that religion should be a purely private affair, if it exists at all, has been challenged by a growing realization that without a sense of the sacred we will be left with nothing but uncontrolled economic growth and cultural despair.

Further, there is the often dismal track record of radical political movements. We have seen the decline of Marxian socialism into Communist tyranny, endless organizational splits and infighting, initially powerful movements like feminism becoming marginalized, and the right capturing important social issues. These failings suggest that secular political movements might benefit from an infusion of the best that religion has to offer: an understanding of peacemaking, a commitment to social values beyond higher wages and benefits, and an ability to connect to a broad range of the population.

CHURCH AND STATE

Yet if religion is to be an active presence in the public square, it cannot do so in a way that demands adherence to one single faith or that marginalizes unbelievers. How is this to be accomplished?

Long, dark centuries of religious wars and persecutions in Europe created a traumatic background to the doctrine that Church and State should be fundamentally separated. Each faith would be free to believe and practice its own vision; the government would support each one equally by supporting none. In this way individuals or groups could pursue faith in any way they chose, much as they were to be able to choose their profession, marriage partner, or zip code. Religious life, in short, would become part of private life.

This doctrine has been enshrined in law, embodied in social practice, and struggled over for centuries in virtually all modernized countries. Furthermore, the reawakening of religious passions throughout the world over the last two decades has so frightened some contemporary thinkers that they view any prospect of "religious politics" as a dangerous threat. Religious resistance to women's rights, the murder of abortion providers, putting the Bible on an equal footing with Darwin, justification of physical abuse (for example, female genital mutilation)—these and other practices lead some critics of religion to wish to isolate not only religious authority but even religious values and forms of understanding behind the sanitized wall separating church and state. Public discourse about democracy, social policy, and our common life, these thinkers suggest, should be free of religious reasoning.[2] Only in this way can we protect the accomplishments of rational democracy from the dangers of irrational faith. If such secularism is valid, what room is there for religious voices in the political realm? This is a key question, for unless the right answer is found, the whole enterprise of spiritual social activism is rendered suspect—or illegitimate—from the outset.

I do think ways out of the dilemma can be found. On the one hand it is as true now as it was when the Constitution was written that in a secular democracy only those directly elected or their delegates should hold political power. Nothing else makes sense in a society comprised of a wide variety of faiths and unfaiths. The Bishop and the Rabbi no more deserve to make laws or set public policy because of their religious position than I do because I've managed to get tenure at my university. Being a member of the clergy, just like being a professor, is outside of the boundaries of the political process. That is the foundation of the political meaning of a secular, "multicultural" society. In just this way a key element of the separation of church and state is established. And certainly the religious advocates of human rights, peace, and ecological wisdom are all agreed on this point. Democracy is as much a bedrock value for them as it is for the secular left.

On the other hand, however, it is morally unfair and psychologically impossible to expect religious citizens to check their values at the door when they enter the town meeting of democracy. Religious authority must not directly translate into political authority, but a religious perspective has as much—or as little—of a role to play in shaping our vision of our common life as any other. If some would appeal to Thomas Jefferson, Ralph Nader, the National Organization of Women, or Ronald Reagan for their political values, others can just as legitimately appeal to Moses, Jesus, the Buddha, or Gandhi. All of these sources have provided broad visions of what social life should be like, and each of their philosophies can be argued for.

The key element, I believe, is willingness to dialogue with other people, and this shoe fits secular and religious feet in exactly the same way. Secular political groups cannot simply say

"Do it this way *because* FDR [or Marx, or George Washington] said so." And spiritual social activists cannot simply quote the Bible, the Pope, or their local Rabbi. Rather, anyone who seriously wishes to influence the community, the nation, or the world must offer serious reasons to support their values and beliefs. Thus when religious activists address the morality of abortion or the rights of homosexuals, the size of our defense budget or our stand on global warming, they have to explain their moral principles and tell us in detail what society would be like if people followed their lead. Those of a different mind-set can see what sense the religious vision makes, evaluate the moral track record of religious authorities, and determine to what degree their own moral ideals are in harmony or conflict with those who have a faith with a different label.

The crucial point is that this process of assertion and evaluation, quite simply, is the same for all those who would seek to influence our common life. *Every* person who comments on public policy does so from the vantage point of some large-scale perspective on morality, the goal of social life, the nature of human existence, and our place in the universe. If we argue about whether the Brand New Mall should take the place of the Soggy Old Wetland, we have to choose between a "religion" of development, technology, and profits, and one that includes devotion to the sacredness of the wild. I doubt if there is a definitive justification for either of these religions, or for any other comprehensive worldview. All that the developer and the spiritual deep ecologist, the disciple of growth and the devotee of stewardship for God's creation, can do is to explain as fully as possible what a world would be like in which their values triumphed—and let the rest of us think it over. In just this way a "separation of church and state" in which religious values are not publicly brought forward is simply impossible.

Of course there are many, far too many, religious fanatics who would cheerfully shoot abortion providers, lock women in the kitchen, and condemn homosexuals to hell (or worse!). For them, ideas are not to be brought forward for democratic discussion but imposed by force. While this book celebrates the many religious voices for justice, peace, and ecological wisdom, there are (sadly) also many for oppression, exploitation, and war. Yet does this moral heterogeneity in any way distinguish religious social activists from secular ones? I think not. If for every Martin Luther King Jr. there is a Jerry Falwell, for every Thomas Merton an Ayatollah, then for every Franklin Delano Roosevelt there is a Richard Nixon, and for every Abraham Lincoln a George Lincoln Rockwell. Secular institutions from Wall Street to the World Bank, not to mention the world's collective Departments of Defense, have as much blood on their hands as any group of fanatical fundamentalists. When a secular politician resigns in disgrace, or brutal nationalists wage bloody wars, we do not call for an end to "secular" politics—but for better, more humane, more rational politics. The same response is justified in the face of religious actors who are corrupt, violent, or oppressive. Religion has not cornered the market on sin, nor the secular on virtue. If we want a better world, or even to preserve the one we've got, we had better accept the positive contributions we can get from all sources, and be very aware of the dangers confronting us from all sides.

A NEW RELIGIOUS ORDER

Thus the bewildering fact is that some religious voices are making the world better and some worse; some are ready to recognize the basic principles of democracy and human rights, and others long for the days when the religious authorities could order heretics burned at the stake. These differences are not random, but systematic. For a *faith* to be *liberating*, it must change, develop, and progress: in a sense, it must become liberated *itself.* This process develops in six essential ways.

First, a liberating faith must be rooted in its own traditional ethical teachings. As I will try to show through the selections in Part I, both the world's large-scale institutionalized religions and small indigenous groups have an ethical dimension that can be a powerful basis for active political engagement in the today's political struggles. When God tells the Israelites not to oppress their workers because the Egyptians oppressed them, we can make connections with the need to unionize migrant farm workers. When Buddhists are instructed to seek peace and curb their anger, then injunctions against war of all kinds, especially the enormously destructive wars of the modern age, can be found. Indigenous worldviews that center on communion with the wisdom of other species are irreplaceable resources for helping us respond to the environmental crisis.

Second, this commitment to religious ethics must in some ways come to take precedence over commitment to particular religious institutions and to other aspects of religious doctrine. This change, I believe, is one of the characteristic and profound moves of modern religion. In the eighteenth century some Christians argued that an authentic faith simply could not be compelled, and therefore toleration of different beliefs was essential to religious life. In the nineteenth century, Protestant Existentialist Søren Kierkegaard emphasized that personal, subjective passion was more essential to Christianity than an explicit belief in Jesus. Reform Judaism has for over 150 years stressed the ethical content of the Prophets over the detailed religious laws of the Talmud. Countless interfaith dialogs have taught members of one faith community how to share wisdom with other faith communities. Even the concept of the "spiritual," which some people criticize as signaling a lack of real commitment to anything religiously serious, was initially invoked in the United States to emphasize the shared ethical aspirations of different forms of Christianity. In these and countless other cases we find an increased concentration on the ethical and on the importance of holding religious beliefs subjectively, personally, and passionately, and a corresponding lessening of concern over agreements about religious doctrines or (pseudo) rational arguments for the "truth" of a particular faith.

Third, to liberate faith spiritual social activists must learn to connect their passionately held ethical beliefs to our collective political situation and to collective movements to change that situation. "Politics," in this context, reaches far beyond the conventional dismissal of a program or statement as "Oh, he's just being political." It is not simply about the way a small elite cynically manipulates bored or browbeaten populations; rather, in this context, "politics" refers to the pursuit of collective forms of justice, reason, and well-being. It is the politics of the American Revolution, of the movements to end segregation, give women the vote, or end the Vietnam War.

In our highly interconnected and interdependent societies, it is simply impossible to follow *religious* ethics without being aware of, or contributing to, *political* life. We cannot love our neighbor, refrain from theft, or pursue nonviolence without being conscious of and trying to reshape our social relationships. The neighbor whom we are to love, after all, might be a resident of a faraway country whose trees are dying because of the acid rain from our factories. Theft might be taking a village's land to make a plantation for agribusiness. The issue of peace might arise not because of our angry feelings, but because money is automatically deducted from our paycheck to pay taxes to support a military machine. As South African archbishop and antiapartheid activist Desmond Tutu wondered: "How anyone having read the prophets could say, 'Do not mix religion with politics' is quite baffling. Which Bible had they read?"[3] If our religious ethics would tell us—and which one would not?—that we should help someone starving at our feet, we need to be aware of those starving one mile or ten thousand miles away. All the more so because such starvation may be connected to a process of globalization that our country and its major economic institutions are supporting.

Fourth, religion must reach outside itself for conceptual tools to understand the social world in which ethical lives unfold. In many of the selections that follow, religious voices often seamlessly interweave political analysis with moral instruction. Further, when global economic, political, and technological conditions change, each faith is tested by its ability to understand and respond. As Catholic priest and pioneering ecotheologian Thomas Berry has warned: "The future of the Catholic church in America, in my view, will depend above all on its capacity to assume a religious responsibility for the fate of the earth."[4]

This interweaving is necessary because, for the most part, traditional religious teachings are inadequate to understanding the crucial contexts of the rise of capitalism, the confusing and dangerous contours of globalization, the interpersonal complexities of personal relationships under patriarchy, or the many ways in which the disabled are marginalized. As faiths move toward liberation, they have benefited from the democratic theories of the late eighteenth centuries, which argued for the rights of "man"; from varieties of socialist teachings which analyzed the destructive and irrational features of capitalism and challenged its prerogatives; from feminism and environmentalism which have analyzed structures of domination between genders and species. If the interpersonal world of the village was the moral universe of the original tradition, liberated faiths now realize that their morality is truly a global affair. Vast impersonal bureaucracies and evermore sophisticated technologies connect us to people thousands of miles away.

Fifth, and perhaps hardest: faithful adherents of rich traditions who wish to practice a liberating faith must be willing to break with the past. They need to see the ways in which some long-established religious beliefs, traditions, and practices reflect neither God's will nor a path to sacred wisdom. Rather, arrangements of power and historically limited forms of understanding have led the faiths they love into blind alleys of oppressive relationships.

Perhaps the most dramatic recognition of a fault of this kind is embodied in the profound change that feminism has wrought throughout the world of religion. Long-standing teachings have been rejected or interpreted in very different ways. New theologies that honor women's gifts and undermine male supremacy have been devised and are being taught. Women have become rabbis, priests, and meditation teachers; and our very images of God's gender (or lack of it) have been altered. In a process of deep learning from secular feminism, those women (and their male allies) who "stayed and fought" rather than left their "churches" completely, have made a dramatic change in religion in a breathtakingly short amount of time. Feminists in world religion do not seek to abandon the faiths of their fathers—or mothers—but to make them more holy. Judith Plaskow, perhaps the most widely respected Jewish feminist theologian, tells us she went through "a gradual process of refusing to split between a Jewish and a feminist self. I am not a Jew in the synagogue and a feminist in the world. I am a Jewish feminist and a feminist Jew in every moment of my life."[5]

Of course the view that religions are improved when they accept democracy, the equal value of women, and environmentalism is one view among many and some may wonder what gives me the right to define religion's proper course. My answer is that conflicting views about what religion *should be* are simply part of what religion *is*; just as arguments about justice, beauty, knowledge, and objectivity have been essential to law, art, education, and science.[6] Debates about God, the true church, revelation, and the nature of authentic devotion permeate the history of all faiths. Consequently, there is just as much—probably more—deep disagreement about religion among believers themselves than there is criticism of religion from the secularists. Each person has the right to say what is or is not authentic religion because each person has a mind, a spirit, and a need to make sense of life and the world.

Sixth, a liberating faith that moves into the world to make society more moral is not just the handmaiden of secular politics, but has a unique and precious contribution to social change. If political activists can *teach* religion lessons about strategies for social change and the political dimensions of spiritual concepts, they can *learn* from religions something about how to be human and moral in the midst of political turmoil.[7] Alongside the political understanding of people as bearers of social roles resisting or inflicting injustice, religious values (at their best) offer a sense of the moral worth of people as individuals and as victims of collective emotional trauma. Progressive political movements that want more than individualistic democracy, a free market, and group entitlement can use religious resources to construct a substantive vision of a just social order. And religious practices of prayer, meditation, self-examination, and collective celebration can support the emotional—and thus inevitably the political—lives of activists. As Evangelical Christian and progressive political voice Jim Wallis tells us, "Central to any new politics will be a new spirituality—indeed, a renewal of some of our oldest spirituality—creating a moral sensitivity that refuses to separate political ideas from their consequences for human beings and for the rest of the creation."[8]

ABOUT THIS BOOK

I believe that the religious pursuit of social justice is rooted in traditional moral teachings. Therefore *Liberating Faith* begins with sources that indicate the range and content of those teachings. To bring Christianity to bear on poverty, Buddhism on peace, or even Islam on the rights of women is not, I believe, to abandon those traditions but to simultaneously preserve and reinterpret them. Examples of what we must preserve and reinterpret are the subject matter of Part I.

While the major focus of *Liberating Faith* is on writers, groups, and movements after World War II, Part II includes a range of material from religious political critics and activists before that time, writings that bridge the gap between traditional religious morality and the full-fledged response to and participation in the political struggles of the twentieth century. Here we find religious voices responding to the overweening power of the state, capitalist development, slavery, and the situation of women. This material is exclusively Western, because it was in the combined context of modern nationalism, the Reformation's challenge to established religious authority, and the Enlightenment project of human rights that religious political activism first emerged.

Part III is devoted to Gandhi's enduring and preeminent legacy for religiously motivated political actors. From Americans like Martin Luther King and Cesar Chavez to South Africa's Desmond Tutu and Burma's Aung San Suu Kyi, Gandhi is acknowledged as a central inspiration.[9] This acknowledgment does not suggest—for them or for me—that Gandhi was a perfect role model or clearly understood every single issue of our day. But the size of the movement he led, his ecumenical attitude toward other religions, his persistent commitment to a positive social alternative to modernity, and his emphasis on nonviolence within his movement as well as against the British, still serve as a benchmark and a source of insight for those who bring religious ideals into the public realm.

The writings in Part IV provide a wide variety of views on the central theme of this book: the manner in which a full-fledged religious identity requires involvement in social change, and the way movements for social change can themselves benefit from that involvement. The remarkable convergence of these authors' conclusions coexists with a remarkable diversity in background and style of thought. Jew and Christian, Buddhist and Moslem, from North and

South America, Europe and Asia—all believe that the voice of God or Enlightenment must be heard in social struggles for justice, peace, and environmental wisdom. This section reveals the basic orientation of spiritual social activism, an orientation which is made concrete in the several different contexts explored in the rest of the book.

Part V focuses on the broad category of social justice. This area encompasses struggles for racial freedom, economic democracy, human rights, cultural survival for indigenous peoples, and issues of disability. As in the following two sections, the selections came from a broad spectrum of theologians, religious institutions, organizations, and activists. One of the most striking aspects of Parts V through VIII is the range of issues in which religious voices have played an important role. Ending segregation in America and resisting repression in Latin America, economic development in Sri Lanka and rights of the poor in the United States—in these and many other areas secular appeals for political and economic justice have been supported and encompassed by their connection to religious values.

Since the material in Part VI addresses gender justice, it could well have been included in Part V. Yet the changes initiated by the feminist transformation of world religion are so significant I think it is reasonable to give gender its own section. Given that virtually all of the world's religions have been patriarchal to some degree or other, the issue of gender often centers on the rights of women. Yet by implication, the challenges to existing norms of gender confront our understanding of masculinity as well as femininity, and reach toward a fundamental change in our attitudes toward homosexuality. Thus Part VI includes abstract challenges to basic religious concepts in the creation of feminist theology; accounts of the religious witness to male violence against women; new spiritual understandings of masculinity; and position papers from a number of denominations concerning the rights of and the full acceptance of all forms of sexual identification.

Part VII points toward what I believe to be religion's special vocation of peacemaking. Secular movements often suffer from a collective inability to realize that political struggles frequently include two dimensions. Along with concerns with justice and oppression, there are also histories of collective antagonism and victimization without a neat division between oppressor and oppressed. In the dimension of justice we ask: who is right and who is wrong? What must be done to overthrow the powerful in favor of the weak? In the dimension of endless reciprocal violence and war we implore: tell me about your pain, and please listen to mine. We try to remember that parents on both sides love their children, want to live in peace, and carry painful memories that prompt collective hatred; and we dare to hope that our common suffering and hope might bring us together. While everyone concerned with social life may hate war and violence, a religious presupposition that we are all children of God or are all suffering beings who seek happiness and have deep faults, has given spiritual social activists a particular ability to pursue peace.

If much of *Liberating Faith* is about encounters between religious ethics and political activism, Part VIII reveals that, in environmental politics and ecological spirituality, they are often virtually fused. Modern environmentalism has challenged and changed religion throughout the world. Simultaneously, awakened by environmental activists, religious institutions have addressed in detail the politics, economics, and policy dimensions of pollution, climate change, endangered species, resource depletion, and overpopulation. Religious leaders, theologians, local clergy, and bands of the faithful have recognized that the earth as a whole is in an unprecedented predicament and are responding accordingly. At its most developed form, this response is a beautiful integration of spiritual aspiration and political critique. There is deep concern with the world's pain and a deep ecological understanding that "the world" is more than human beings. There is a familiar political ability to critique the sins of the powerful and a searching religious self-examination of how we all participate in the ruin of the earth—and thus how our pursuit of ecojustice must be framed with humility, compassion, and self-awareness.

Religious life, and this is part of its genius, encompasses more than beliefs, organizations, and actions. Part of its power is its emotional technology of ritual, and thus *Liberating Faith* concludes with examples of how concerns with justice, peace, and ecological wisdom can be reflected in prayers, services, forms of meditation, new interpretations of old rituals, and completely new rituals. Paradoxically, these characteristically religious creations are part of religion's distinctive contribution to political life. They engage parts of the psyche and soul that are often left out of manifestos, treatises, and mass action. And they help make both our religious life and our political struggle something to involve and reflect the whole self on both the personal and the collective levels.

HOPE AND FAITH

Given the darkness of the hour, does it make sense to think that the religious attempt to remake the world in the image of God and compassion has any chance of success? Ultimately, in a time such as ours, don't both religion and politics require a kind of hope or faith? I believe they do, as long as we recognize that hope is very far from certainty. The hope that is needed is not the dogmatic confidence with which a religious true believer knows that he will go to heaven because he followed the rules. Neither is it the old Marxist certitude that the laws of history would ensure the triumph of the working class. Certainty of heaven breeds contempt for the Earth and for those who are not saved. Certainty of revolution breeds contempt for anyone who gets in the way.

The kind of hope I have in mind has to do with willingness to act in the face of sorrow and loss, to look clearly at what must be changed and act without surety of success. The crucial role of hope is, perhaps, simply to admit that one doesn't know what will happen. Clearly, after a century that included the Holocaust, the nuclear arms race, two world wars, and the devastation of nature, cheerful optimism may be a little out of place. Yet history is nothing if not ambiguous. The same century saw the end of colonialism, successful struggles for democracy, and a worldwide movement for women's rights. Humanity produced an international environmental movement as well as evermore deadly weapons, Gandhi and King as well as Stalin and Sadaam Hussein. If looking at the past is supposed to tell us whether or not we can hope, the answer is clear: yes and no.

That ambiguity and a fundamental ignorance about the future may be our richest source of hope and faith. All we can be sure of is that in living out what is most sacred to ourselves we choose the path that is most likely to take us all to that new world, the one in which, in the words of the prophet Amos, "justice and righteousness well up like a never-ending stream," and where human beings, together, heal both the earth and their own hearts.

NOTES

1. Michael Perry argues that without God, ideals of human rights are literally incoherent, because if we are not equally related to God, there is no reason *why* we should be treated equally and with respect. Jeremy Waldron has claimed that John Locke, perhaps the preeminent philosopher of political equality,

bases his position on a particular understanding of Christianity. See Michael Perry, *The Idea of Human Rights* (New York: Oxford University Press, 2000); Jeremy Waldron, *God, Locke, and Equality: Christian Foundations in Locke's Political Thought* (New York: Cambridge University Press, 2002).

2. America's most influential political philosopher, John Rawls, has argued this position. It can also often be found in secular publications from the leading newspapers to icons of the left such as *The Nation*.

3. Desmond Tutu, foreword to *The Hebrew Prophets: Visionaries of the Ancient World*, by Lawrence Boadt (New York: St. Martins, 1997), 8.

4. Thomas Berry, "Ecology and the Future of Catholicism," in *Embracing Earth: Catholic Approaches to Ecology*, ed. Albert P. LaChance and John E. Carroll (Maryknoll, N.Y.: Orbis, 1994), xi.

5. Judith Plaskow, *Standing Again at Sinai: Judaism from a Feminist Perspective* (New York: Harper-SanFrancisco, 1990), xii.

6. Some readers may recognize the influence of Alasdair MacIntyre here. Beyond MacIntyre, there is a book that influenced us both: W. B. Gallie, *Philosophy and the Historical Understanding* (London: Chatto and Windus, 1964).

7. This double motion is described in detail in my book *Joining Hands: Politics and Religion Together for Social Change* (Cambridge, Mass.: Westview Press, 2002).

8. Jim Wallis, *The Soul of Politics: Beyond "Religious Right" and "Secular Left"* (New York: Harcourt Brace, 1995), xviii.

9. Thus, more than thirty years after his death, Catherine Ingram could title her volume of interviews with leading contemporary spiritual social activists *In the Footsteps of Gandhi* (Berkeley: Parallax Press, 1991).

I

TRADITION: ETHICAL ROOTS OF SPIRITUAL SOCIAL ACTIVISM

The Holy God is sanctified through righteousness.

—Isaiah 5:16

Does religious tradition itself call for religiously motivated political action? Can a strong identification with Christianity, Islam, or Buddhism, for instance, be a springboard for commitment to changing fundamental political institutions and challenging commonplace social norms—and doing so in a way that furthers social justice, community, human rights, peace, and ecological wisdom?

Not surprisingly, my answer to this question is an unambiguous "yes!" The selections of basic moral teachings in Part I support that answer. I believe that moral instruction is basic to religion, and that such instruction provides a clear basis for social involvement and political activism.

Of course I cannot pretend that the tradition is completely unambiguous on morality or politics. Every tradition provides a basis for many *different* styles of social involvement. Even the devil (or perhaps especially the devil!) can quote scripture to his purposes. No original teaching by itself can justify any particular form of life or set of values because all contemporary religious postures depend on the way tradition is interpreted. In these interpretations some teachings are given more weight than others, and a narrative is created which connects the history of the faith to histories of political movements and social forces leading up to the present.

Yet my argument is simply that present-day spiritual activists can be as rooted in tradition as present-day religious fundamentalists and conservatives, and the selections of Part I, even though brief, bear out this claim.

These selections reveal some shared and familiar themes. First, religious traditions insist on the values of reciprocity, justice, and community. The value of "loving your neighbor as yourself," of learning to see the world through the experiences and needs of others, is absolutely essential. The movement from these values to criticisms of political oppression is easy indeed. Later selections throughout *Liberating Faith* will constantly refer back to the passages quoted here, or to similar ones, when offering religious reasons to participate in movements for justice or equality.

Second, we can find here a deep questioning of society's nonreligious powers and values. Secular kingship is seen as subsidiary to the lordship of God—and the values God instructs us to follow. Wealth and social position are devalued in comparison to wisdom and personal spiritual

1

development. In these teachings there are profound resources for criticisms of materialism, social convention, and false hierarchies of social value. They cast doubt on unrestricted technological development without moral purpose, the acquisition of wealth without wisdom, or the addictive pursuit of pleasure.

A critique of unjust power and a critique of false values—these two aspects of religious tradition are the twin supports of contemporary social activism. Yet if, in outline, those supports are not unexpected, there are details in what follows that may surprise some readers. Islam, for instance, is not widely thought of as an environmentally oriented religion, yet the Koran tells us (6:38) that "No kind of beast is there on earth nor fowl that flieth with its wings, but is a folk like you: nothing have we passed over in the Book: then unto their Lord shall they be gathered." Judaism, similarly, restricts not just the activity of human beings on the Sabbath, but of their beasts of burden as well. ("No one is to work on that day—not you, your children, your slaves, your animals, or the foreigners who live in your towns." Exodus 20:10) Similarly, Confucianism, often (with some accuracy) described as a religion based more in reverence for the past and for community than respect for individuals, repeats in its own idiom essential teachings of Judaism and Christianity: "Tsekung asked, 'Is there one word that can serve as a Principle for life?' Confucius replied, 'The word 'shu,' reciprocity: Do not do to others what you do not want them to do to you.'" (15.23)

The religions of the world's indigenous peoples are much less defined by classic texts than faiths such as Judaism, Islam, or even Buddhism. Yet they, no less than text-based traditions, carry supports for social and political alternatives to the prevailing "common sense" of global society. Therefore, I conclude Part I with an excerpt from Native American writer Luther Standing Bear's account of the Lakota relation to nature, for contained in that relation is wisdom that can be the basis not only for environmental wisdom, but also for a wide-ranging critique of many of our culture's ways of life.

Judaism

❧

from The Tanach—the Hebrew Bible

EXODUS 20

[8]Remember that the Sabbath Day belongs to me. [9]You have six days when you can do your work, [10]but the seventh day of each week belongs to me, your God. No one is to work on that day—not you, your children, your slaves, your animals, or the foreigners who live in your towns. [11]In six days I made the sky, the earth, the oceans, and everything in them, but on the seventh day I rested. That's why I made the Sabbath a special day that belongs to me.

[12]Respect your father and your mother, and you will live a long time in the land I am giving you.

[13]Do not murder.

[14]Be faithful in marriage.

[15]Do not steal.

[16]Do not tell lies about others.

[17]Do not want anything that belongs to someone else. Don't want anyone's house, wife or husband, slaves, oxen, donkeys or anything else.

EXODUS 23

[1]Don't spread harmful rumors or help a criminal by giving false evidence.

[2]Always tell the truth in court, even if everyone else is dishonest and stands in the way of justice.

[3]And don't favor the poor, simply because they are poor. [4]If you find an ox or a donkey that has wandered off, take it back where it belongs, even if the owner is your enemy.

[5]If a donkey is overloaded and falls down, you must do what you can to help, even if it belongs to someone who doesn't like you. [6]Make sure that the poor are given equal justice in court. [7]Don't bring false charges against anyone or sentence an innocent person to death. I won't forgive you if you do.

[8]Don't accept bribes. Judges are blinded and justice is twisted by bribes.

[9]Don't mistreat foreigners. You were foreigners in Egypt, and you know what it is like.

LEVITICUS 19

[1]The LORD told Moses [2]to say to the community of Israel:

I am the LORD your God. I am holy, and you must be holy too! [9]When you harvest your grain, always leave some of it standing along the edges of your fields and don't pick up what falls on the ground. [10]Don't strip your grapevines clean or gather the grapes that fall off the vines. Leave them for the poor and for those foreigners who live among you. I am the LORD your God.

[11]Do not steal or tell lies or cheat others.

[12]Do not misuse my name by making promises you don't intend to keep. I am the LORD your God.

[13]Do not steal anything or cheat anyone, and don't fail to pay your workers at the end of each day. [14]I am the LORD your God, and I command you not to make fun of the deaf or to cause a blind person to stumble.

[15]Be fair, no matter who is on trial—don't favor either the poor or the rich.

[16]Don't be a gossip, but never hesitate to speak up in court, especially if your testimony can save someone's life. [17]Don't hold grudges. On the other hand, it's wrong not to correct someone who needs correcting. [18]Stop being angry and don't try to take revenge. I am the LORD, and I command you to love others as much as you love yourself.

[33]Don't mistreat any foreigners who live in your land. [34]Instead, treat them as well as you treat citizens and love them as much as you love yourself. Remember, you were once foreigners in the land of Egypt. I am the LORD your God.

[35–36]Use honest scales and don't cheat when you weigh or measure anything.

I am the LORD your God. I rescued you from Egypt, [37]and I command you to obey my laws.

DEUTERONOMY 24

[10]When you lend money to people, you are allowed to keep something of theirs as a guarantee that the money will be paid back. But you must not go into their house to get it.

[11]Wait outside, and they will bring out the item you have agreed on.

[12]Suppose someone is so poor that a coat is the only thing that can be offered as a guarantee on a loan. Don't keep the coat overnight.

[13]Instead, give it back before sunset, so the owner can keep warm and sleep and ask the Lord to bless you. Then the LORD your God will notice that you have done the right thing.

[14]If you hire poor people to work for you, don't hold back their pay, whether they are Israelites or foreigners who live in your town. [15]Pay them their wages at the end of each day, because they live in poverty and need the money to survive. If you don't pay them on time, they will complain about you to the Lord, and he will punish you.

[16]Parents must not be put to death for crimes committed by their children, and children must not be put to death for crimes committed by their parents. Don't put anyone to death for someone else's crime.

[17]Make sure that orphans and foreigners are treated fairly. And if you lend money to a widow and want to keep something of hers to guarantee that she will pay you back, don't take any of

her clothes. ¹⁸You were slaves in Egypt until the LORD your God rescued you. That's why I am giving you these laws.

¹⁹If you forget to bring in a stack of harvested grain, don't go back in the field to get it. Leave it for the poor, including foreigners, orphans, and widows, and the LORD will make you successful in everything you do.

²⁰When you harvest your olives, don't try to get them all for yourself, but leave some for the poor. ²¹And when you pick your grapes, go over the vines only once, then let the poor have what is left. ²²You lived in poverty as slaves in Egypt until the LORD your God rescued you. That's why I am giving you these laws.

ISAIAH 1

¹⁰You are no better
than the leaders and people
of Sodom and Gomorrah!
So listen to the LORD God:
¹¹Your sacrifices
mean nothing to me.
I am sick of your offerings
of rams and choice cattle;
I don't like the blood
of bulls or lambs or goats.
¹²Who asked you to bring all this
when you come to worship me?
Stay out of my temple!
¹³Your sacrifices are worthless,
and incense is disgusting.
I can't stand the evil you do
on your New Moon Festivals
or on your Sabbaths
and other times of worship.
¹⁴I hate your New Moon Festivals
and all others as well.
They are a heavy burden
I am tired of carrying.
¹⁵No matter how much you pray,
I won't listen.
You are too violent.
¹⁶Wash yourselves clean!
I am disgusted
with your filthy deeds.
Stop doing wrong
¹⁷and learn to live right.
See that justice is done.

Defend widows and orphans
and help those in need.
¹⁸I, the LORD, invite you
to come and talk it over.
Your sins are scarlet red,
but they will be whiter
than snow or wool.
¹⁹If you willingly obey me,
the best crops in the land
will be yours.
²⁰But if you turn against me,
your enemies will kill you.
I, the LORD, have spoken.
²¹Jerusalem, you are like
an unfaithful wife.
Once your judges were honest
and your people lived right;
now you are a city
full of murderers.
²²Your silver is fake,
and your wine
is watered down.
²³Your leaders have rejected me
to become friends of crooks;
your rulers are looking
for gifts and bribes.
Widows and orphans
never get a fair trial.
²⁴I am the LORD All-Powerful,
the mighty ruler of Israel,
and I make you a promise:
You are now my enemy,
and I will show my anger
by taking revenge on you.
²⁵I will punish you terribly
and burn away everything
that makes you unfit
to worship me.
²⁶Jerusalem, I will choose
judges and advisors
like those you had before.
Your new name will be
"Justice and Faithfulness."
²⁷Jerusalem, you will be saved
by showing justice; Zion's people who turn to me
will be saved
by doing right.

ISAIAH 58

¹Shout the message!
Don't hold back.
Say to my people Israel:
You've sinned! You've turned
against the LORD.
²Day after day, you worship him
and seem eager to learn
his teachings.
You act like a nation
that wants to do right
by obeying his laws.
You ask him about justice,
and say you enjoy
worshiping the LORD.
³You wonder why the LORD
pays no attention
when you go without eating
and act humble.
But on those same days
that you give up eating,
you think only of yourselves and abuse your workers.
⁴You even get angry
and ready to fight.
No wonder God won't listen
to your prayers!
⁵Do you think the LORD
wants you to give up eating
and to act as humble
as a bent-over bush?
Or to dress in sackcloth
and sit in ashes?
Is this really what he wants
on a day of worship?
⁶I'll tell you
what it really means
to worship the LORD.
Remove the chains of prisoners
who are chained unjustly.
Free those who are abused!
⁷Share your food with everyone
who is hungry;
share your home
with the poor and homeless.
Give clothes to those in need;

don't turn away your relatives.
8Then your light will shine
like the dawning sun,
and you
will quickly be healed.
Your honesty will protect you as you advance,
and the glory of the LORD
will defend you from behind.
9When you beg the LORD for help,
he will answer, "Here I am!"
Don't mistreat others
or falsely accuse them
or say something cruel.
10Give your food to the hungry
and care for the homeless.
Then your light will shine
in the dark;
your darkest hour will be
like the noonday sun.

AMOS 5

21I, the Lord, hate and despise
your religious celebrations
and your times of worship.
22I won't accept your offerings
or animal sacrifices—
not even your very best.
23No more of your noisy songs!
I won't listen
when you play your harps.
24But let justice and fairness
flow like a river
that never runs dry.

MICAH 4

1In the future, the mountain
with the Lord's temple
will be the highest of all.
It will reach above the hills,
and every nation
will rush to it.
2People of many nations

will come and say,
"Let's go up to the mountain
of the LORD God of Jacob
and worship in his temple."
The LORD will teach us his Law
from Jerusalem,
and we will obey him.
³He will settle arguments
between distant
and powerful nations.
They will pound their swords
and their spears
into rakes and shovels;
they will never again make war
or attack one another.
⁴Everyone will find rest
beneath their own fig trees
or grape vines,
and they will live in peace.
This is a solemn promise
of the LORD All-Powerful.
⁵Others may follow their gods,
but we will always follow
the LORD our God.

Christianity

❧

from The New Testament

MATTHEW 5

[1]When Jesus saw the crowds, he went up on the side of a mountain and sat down. Jesus' disciples gathered around him,
[2]and he taught them:
[3]God blesses those people
who depend only on him.
They belong to the kingdom
of heaven! [4]God blesses those people
who grieve.
They will find comfort!
[5]God blesses those people
who are humble.
The earth will belong
to them!
[6]God blesses those people
who want to obey him more than to eat or drink.
They will be given
what they want!
[7]God blesses those people
who are merciful.
They will be treated
with mercy!
[8]God blesses those people
whose hearts are pure.
They will see him!
[9]God blesses those people
who make peace.
They will be called
his children!
[10]God blesses those people
who are treated badly

for doing right.
They belong to the kingdom
of heaven.

[21]You know that our ancestors were told, "Do not murder" and "A murderer must be brought to trial." [22]But I promise you that if your are angry with someone, you will have to stand trial. If you call someone a fool, you will be taken to court. And if you say that someone is worthless, you will be in danger of the fires of hell. [23]So if you are about to place your gift on the altar and remember that someone is angry with you, [24]leave your gift there in front of the altar. Make peace with that person, then come back and offer your gift to God.

[38]You know that you have been taught, "An eye for an eye and a tooth for a tooth." [39]But I tell you not to try to get even with a person who has done something to you. When someone slaps your right cheek, turn and let that person slap your other cheek. [40]If someone sues you for your shirt, give up your coat as well. [41]If a soldier forces you to carry his pack one mile, carry it two miles. [42]When people ask you for something, give it to them. When they want to borrow money, lend it to them.

[43]You have heard people say, "Love your neighbors and hate your enemies." [44]But I tell you to love your enemies and pray for anyone who mistreats you. [45]Then you will be acting like your Father in heaven. He makes the sun rise on both good and bad people. And he sends rain for the ones who do right and for the ones who do wrong. [46]If you love only those people who love you, will God reward you for that? Even tax collectors love their friends. [47]If you greet only your friends, what's so great about that? Don't even unbelievers do that? [48]But you must always act like your Father in heaven.

MATTHEW 7

[1]Don't condemn others, and God won't condemn you. [2]God will be as hard on you as you are on others! He will treat you exactly as you treat them.

MATTHEW 25

The Final Judgment

[31]When the Son of Man comes in his glory with all of his angels, he will sit on his royal throne. [32]The people of all nations will be brought before him, and he will separate them, as shepherds separate their sheep from their goats.
[33]He will place the sheep on his right and the goats on his left. [34]Then the king will say to those on his right, "My father has blessed you! Come and receive the kingdom that was prepared for you before the world was created. [35]When I was hungry, you gave me something to eat, and when I was thirsty, you gave me something to drink. When I was a stranger, you welcomed me, [36]and when I was naked, you gave me clothes to wear. When I was sick, you took care of me, and when I was in jail, you visited me."

[37]Then the ones who pleased the Lord will ask, "When did we give you something to eat or drink? [38]When did we welcome you as a stranger or give you clothes to wear [39]or visit you while you were sick or in jail?"

[40]The king will answer, "Whenever you did it for any of my people, no matter how unimportant they seemed, you did it for me."

LUKE 6

[27]This is what I say to all who will listen to me:

Love your enemies, and be good to everyone who hates you. [28]Ask God to bless anyone who curses you, and pray for everyone who is cruel to you. [29]If someone slaps you on one cheek, don't stop that person from slapping you on the other cheek. If someone wants to take your coat, don't try to keep back your shirt. [30]Give to everyone who asks and don't ask people to return what they have taken from you. [31]Treat others just as you want to be treated.

[32]If you love only someone who loves you, will God praise you for that? Even sinners love people who love them. [33]If you are kind only to someone who is kind to you, will God be pleased with you for that? Even sinners are kind to people who are kind to them.

[34]If you lend money only to someone you think will pay you back, will God be pleased with you for that? Even sinners lend to sinners because they think they will get it all back.

[35]But love your enemies and be good to them. Lend without expecting to be paid back. Then you will get a great reward, and you will be the true children of God in heaven. He is good even to people who are unthankful and cruel.

[36]Have pity on others, just as your Father has pity on you.

[37]Jesus said:

Don't judge others, and God won't judge you. Don't be hard on others, and God won't be hard on you. Forgive others, and God will forgive you. [38]If you give to others, you will be given a full amount in return. It will be packed down, shaken together, and spilling over into your lap. The way you treat others is the way you will be treated.

1 CORINTHIANS 13

[1]What if I could speak
all languages
of humans
and of angels?
If I did not love others,
I would be nothing more
than a noisy gong
or a clanging cymbal.
[2]What if I could prophesy
and understand all secrets
and all knowledge?

And what if I had faith
that moved mountains?
I would be nothing,
unless I loved others.
[3]What if I gave away all
that I owned
and let myself
be burned alive? I would gain nothing,
unless I loved others.
[4]Love is kind and patient,
never jealous, boastful,
proud, or [5]rude.
Love isn't selfish
or quick tempered.
It doesn't keep a record
of wrongs that others do.
[6]Love rejoices in the truth,
but not in evil.
[7]Love is always supportive,
loyal, hopeful,
and trusting.
[8]Love never fails!
Everyone who prophesies
will stop,
and unknown languages
will no longer
be spoken.
All that we know
will be forgotten.
[9]We don't know everything,
and our prophecies
are not complete.
[10]But what is perfect
will someday appear,
and what isn't perfect
will then disappear.
[11]When we were children,
we thought and reasoned
as children do.
But when we grew up,
we quit our childish ways.
[12]Now all we can see of God
is like a cloudy picture
in a mirror.
Later we will see him
face to face.

We don't know everything,
but then we will,
just as God completely
understands us.
[13] For now there are faith,
hope, and love.
But of these three,
the greatest is love.

Islam

❧

from The Koran

Those who believe, those who follow Jewish scriptures, the Christians, the Sabians, and any who believe in God and the Final Day, and do good, all share their rewards with their Lord and they will not come to fear and grief. 5:69; 2:62.

To each of you God has prescribed a Law and Way. If God would have willed, He would have made you a single people, But God's purpose is to test you in what he has given each of you, so strive in the pursuit of virtue, and know that you will all return to God, and He will resolve all the matters in which you disagree. 5:49

My mercy embraces all things. 7:156

It is not piety that you turn your faces in prayer to the East and to the West. True piety is this: to believe in God, and the Last Day, the angels, the Book, and the Prophets, to give of one's goods, however cherished, to kinsmen, and orphans, the needy, the traveler, beggars, and to ransom the slave, to perform the prayer, to pay the alms. 2:177

Be good to your parents. Kill not your children on a plea of want. We provide sustenance for you and for them. Approach not lewd behavior whether open or in secret. Take no life, which God has made sacred, except by way of justice and law. This He commands you, that you may learn wisdom. And approach not the property of the orphan, except to improve it, until he attains the age of maturity. Give full measure and weight, in justice. No burden do We play on any soul but that which it can bear. And if you give your word, do it justice, even if a near relative is concerned; and fulfill your obligations before God. 6:151–3

We created you from a male and female, and made you into peoples and tribes so that you might come to know each other. The noblest among you in God's sight is that one of you who best performs his duty. 49:13

Those who disbelieve filled their hearts with fanatical rage—the fanatical rage of the Time of Ignorance—and God sent down serenity to His Messenger and to the believers, and obliged them to respect the formula of heedfulness which they had most right to and were most entitled to. God has knowledge of all things. 48:26

Then when the Trumpet is blown, no ties of kinship will exist between them on that day, nor may they question one another. 23:101

A good action and a bad action are not the same. Repel the bad with something better and, if there is enmity between you and someone else, he will be like a bosom friend. 41:34

. . . if someone kills another person—unless it is in retaliation for someone else or for causing corruption in the earth—it is as if he had murdered all mankind. And if anyone gives life to another person, it is as if he had given life to all mankind. . . . 5:32

There are only grounds against those who wrong people and act as tyrants in the earth without any right to do so. Such people will have a painful punishment. 2:42

Those who give in times of both ease and hardship, those who control their rage and pardon other people—God loves the good-doers. 3:134

There is no good in much of their secret talk, except in the case of those who enjoin charity, or what is right, or putting things right between people. If anyone does that, seeking the pleasure of God, We will give him an immense reward. 4:114

O ye who believe! Stand out firmly for justice, as witnesses to Allah, even as against yourselves, or your parents, or your kin. . . . 4:135

If your enemy incline towards peace, then you should seek peace and trust in God. 8:61

Greater surely than the creation of man is the creation of the heavens and of the earth: but most men know it not. 40:57

No kind of beast is there on earth nor fowl that flieth with its wings, but is a folk like you: nothing have we passed over in the Book: then unto their Lord shall they be gathered. 6:38

Jainism

❧

ACARANGASUTRA. FIRST BOOK. FOURTH LECTURE.
CALLED RIGHTEOUSNESS.

First Lesson

The Arhats and Bhagavats of the past, present, and future, all say thus, speak thus, declare thus, explain thus: all breathing, existing, living, sentient creatures should not be slain, nor treated with violence, nor abused, nor tormented, nor driven away. (1)

This is the pure, unchangeable, eternal law, which the clever ones, who understand the world, have declared: among the zealous and the not zealous, among the faithful and the not faithful, among the not cruel and the cruel, among those who have worldly weakness and those who have not, among those who like social bonds and those who do not: "that is the truth, that is so, that is proclaimed in this (creed)." (2)

ACARANGASUTRA 5.101–2

One who you think should be his is no one else but you. One who you think should be governed is none else but you. One who you think should be tortured is none else but you. One who you think should be enslaved is none else but you. One who you think should be killed is none else but you. A sage is ingenuous and leads his life after comprehending the parity of the killed and the killer. Therefore, neither does he cause violence to others nor does he make others do so.

SUTRAKRITANGA 1.11.33

A man should wander about treating all creatures as he himself would like to be treated.

TATTVARTHASUTRA 5.21

Rendering help to another is the function of human beings.

Hinduism

LAW OF MANU 10.63

Nonviolence, truthfulness, no stealing, purity, control of the senses—this, in brief, says Manu, is the Dharma for all the four castes.

GARUDA PURANA 112

The vile are ever prone to detect the faults of others, though they be as small as mustard seed, and persistently shut their eyes against their own, though they be as large as Vilva fruit.

RAMAYANA, YUDDHA KANDA 115

A superior being does not render evil for evil; this is a maxim one should observe; the ornament of virtuous persons is their conduct. One should never harm the wicked or the good or even criminals meriting death. A noble soul will ever exercise compassion even toward those who enjoy injuring others or those of cruel deeds when they are actually committing them—for who is without fault?

BAGAVAT GITA, FROM CHAPTERS 3 AND 4

Every selfless act, Arjuna, is born from Brahman, the eternal, infinite godhead. He is present in every act of service. All life turns on this law, O Arjuna. Whoever violates it, indulging his senses for his own pleasure and ignoring the needs of others, has wasted his life. But those who realize the Self are always satisfied. Having found the source of joy and fulfillment they no longer seek happiness from the external world. They have nothing to gain or lose by any action; neither people nor things can affect their security. Strive constantly to serve the welfare of the world for by devotion to selfless work one attains the supreme goal of life. Do your work with the welfare of others always in mind. True sustenance is in service, and through it a man or woman reaches the eternal Brahman. But those who do not seek to serve are without a home in this world.

BASAVANNA, VACAN 248

Why sir, do you get angry at someone who is angry with you? What are you going to gain by it? How is he going to lose by it? Your physical anger brings dishonor on yourself; Your mental anger disturbs your thinking. How can the fire in your house burn the neighbor's house without engulfing your own?

Buddhism

~❧~

AVOIDING THE TEN EVILS

The Buddha said: "All acts of living creatures become bad by ten things, and by avoiding the ten things they become good. There are three evils of the body, four evils of the tongue, and three evils of the mind.

"The evils of the body are, murder, theft, and adultery; of the tongue, lying, slander, abuse, and idle talk; of the mind, covetousness, hatred, and error.

"I exhort you to avoid the ten evils: 1. Kill not, but have regard for life. 2. Steal not, neither do ye rob; but help everybody to be master of the fruits of his labor. 3. Abstain from impurity, and lead a life of chastity. 4. Lie not, but be truthful. Speak the truth with discretion, fearlessly and in a loving heart. 5. Invent not evil reports, neither do ye repeat them. Carp not, but look for the good sides of your fellow-beings, so that ye may with sincerity defend them against their enemies. 6. Swear not, but speak decently and with dignity. 7. Waste not the time with gossip, but speak to the purpose or keep silence. 8. Covet not, nor envy, but rejoice at the fortunes of other people. 9. Cleanse your heart of malice and cherish no hatred, not even against your enemies; but embrace all living beings with kindness. 10. Free your mind of ignorance and be anxious to learn the truth, especially in the one thing that is needful, lest you fall prey either to scepticism or to errors. Scepticism will make you indifferent and errors will lead you astray, so that you shall not find the noble path that leads to life eternal."

THE EIGHTFOLD PATH

It is the Noble Eightfold Path, the way that leads to the extinction of suffering, namely: 1. Right Understanding, 2. Right Mindedness, which together are Wisdom. 3. Right Speech, 4. Right Action, 5. Right Living, which together are Morality. 6. Right Effort, 7. Right Attentiveness, 8. Right Concentration. What, now, is Right Mindedness? It is thoughts free from lust; thoughts free from ill-will; thoughts free from cruelty. This is called right mindedness.
What, now, is Right Speech? It is abstaining from lying;
abstaining from tale-bearing; abstaining from harsh language;
abstaining from vain talk.
What, now, is Right Action? It is abstaining from killing;
abstaining from stealing; abstaining from unlawful sexual intercourse.

FROM THE DAMMAPADA

1. The Twin-Verses

What we are is the result of what we have thought,
is built by our thoughts, is made up of our thoughts.
If one speaks or acts with an impure thought,
suffering follows one,
like the wheel of the cart follows the foot of the ox.
What we are is the result of what we have thought,
is built by our thoughts, is made up of our thoughts.
If one speaks or acts with a pure thought,
happiness follows one,
like a shadow that never leaves.
"They insulted me; they hurt me;
they defeated me; they cheated me."
In those who harbor such thoughts,
hate will never cease.
"They insulted me; they hurt me;
they defeated me; they cheated me."
In those who do not harbor such thoughts,
hate will cease.
For hate is never conquered by hate.
Hate is conquered by love.
This is an eternal law.
Whoever lives only for pleasures,
with senses uncontrolled,
immoderate in eating, lazy, and weak,
will be overthrown by Mara,
like the wind throws down a weak tree.
Whoever lives not for pleasures,
with senses well controlled,
moderate in eating, has faith and the power of virtue,
will not be overthrown by Mara,
any more than the wind throws down a rocky mountain.

9. Good and Bad

A person should hurry toward the good
and restrain one's thoughts from the bad.
If a person is slow in doing good,
one's mind will find pleasure in wrong.
If a person does what is wrong, let one not do it again.
Let one not find pleasure in wrong.
Painful is the accumulation of bad conduct.

If a person does what is good, let one do it again.
Let one find joy in it.
Happiness is the result of good conduct.
Whoever does wrong to an innocent person
or to one who is pure and harmless,
the wrong returns to that fool
just like fine dust thrown against the wind.

15. Joy

Let us live in joy, not hating those who hate us.
Among those who hate us, we live free of hate.
Let us live in joy, free from greed among the greedy.
Among those who are greedy, we live free of greed.
Let us live in joy, though we possess nothing.
Let us live feeding on joy, like the bright gods.
Victory breeds hate, for the conquered is unhappy.
Whoever has given up victory and defeat
is content and lives joyfully.

17. Anger

Overcome anger by love; overcome wrong by good;
overcome the miserly by generosity, and the liar by truth.
Speak the truth; do not yield to anger;
give even if asked for a little.
These three steps lead you to the gods.

19. The Just

Whoever settles a matter by violence is not just.
The wise calmly considers what is right and what is wrong.
Whoever guides others by a procedure
that is nonviolent and fair
is said to be a guardian of truth, wise and just.

SIKSHASAMUCCAYA, 280–281

A bodhisattva resolves: I take upon myself the burden of all suffering. I am resolved to do so, I will endure it. I do not turn or run away, do not tremble, am not terrified, nor afraid, do not turn back, or despond.

And why? At all costs I must bear the burdens of all beings.... I have made the vow to save all beings. All beings I must set free. The whole world of living beings I must rescue, from the terrors of birth, of old age, of sickness, of death and rebirth, of all kinds of moral offence, of all states of woe, of the whole cycle of birth-and-death, of the jungle of false views, of the loss of wholesome dharmas, of the concomitants of ignorance—for all these terrors I must rescue all beings.

Confucianism

❧

FROM THE ANALECTS OF CONFUCIUS

1:14 Confucius said: "When the Superior Man eats he does not try to stuff himself; at rest he does not seek perfect comfort; he is diligent in his work and careful in speech. He avails himself to people of the Tao and thereby corrects himself. This is the kind of person of whom you can say, 'he loves learning.'"

1:15 Tzu Kung asked: "What do you think of a poor man who doesn't grovel or a rich man who isn't proud?" Confucius said, "They are good, but not as good as a poor man who is satisfied and a rich man who loves propriety."

2:1 Confucius said: "If you govern with the power of your virtue, you will be like the North Star. It just stays in its place while all the other stars position themselves around it."

2:22 Confucius said: "If a person lacks trustworthiness, I don't know what s/he can be good for. When a pin is missing from the yoke-bar of a large wagon, or from the collar-bar of a small wagon, how can it go?"

4:5 Confucius said: "Riches and honors are what all men desire. But if they cannot be attained in accordance with the Tao they should not be kept. Poverty and low status are what all men hate. But if they cannot be avoided while staying in accordance with the Tao, you should not avoid them. If a Superior Man departs from jen, [the source of all virtue] how can he be worthy of that name? A Superior Man never leaves jen for even the time of a single meal. In moments of haste he acts according to it. In times of difficulty or confusion he acts according to it."

4:11 Confucius said: "The Superior Man cares abut virtue; the inferior man cares about material things. The Superior Man seeks discipline; the inferior man seeks favors."

4:14 Confucius said: "I don't worry about not having a good position; I worry about the means I use to gain position. I don't worry about being unknown; I seek to be known in the right way."

4:16 Confucius said: "The Superior Man is aware of Righteousness, the inferior man is aware of advantage."

4:17 Confucius said: "When you see a good person, think of becoming like her/him. When you see someone not so good, reflect on your own weak points."

15.23 Tsekung asked, "Is there one word that can serve as a Principles for life?" Confucious replied, "The word 'shu' reciprocity: Do not do to others what you do not want them to do to you."

FROM MENCIUS

1A:4 King Hui of Liang said: "I would like to quietly receive your instruction."

Mencius said: "Is there any difference between killing a man with a stick or a sword?"

The King replied: "No difference."

Mencius said: "Is there any difference between doing it with a sword and doing it with government?"

"No difference" was the reply.

Mencius said: "There are loads of fat meat in your kitchen while the people in the country-side are dying of starvation. Animals are even eating people. Now, men despise animals who feed on each other. And you say you want to be 'the parent of the people.' But in the actual handling of your government, you cannot even prevent animals from feeding on men. How can you be regarded as a 'parent of the people?'"

"Confucius said: 'Wasn't the first fellow who made wooden images for burial with the dead remembered forever?' This is because he made images of men and used them for such a purpose. What memory shall there be of the man who made his people die of starvation?"

2A:6 Mencius said: "All people have a heart which cannot stand to see the suffering of others. The ancient kings had this heart which could not stand to see the suffering of others, and, with this, operated a government which could not stand to see the suffering of the people. If, in this state of mind, you ran a government which could not endure people's suffering, you could govern the realm as if you were turning it in the palm of your hand." "Why do I say all human beings have a heart which cannot stand to see the suffering of others? Even nowadays, if an infant were about to fall into a well, anyone would be upset and concerned. This concern would not be due to the fact that the person wanted to get in good with the baby's parents, or because s/he wanted to improve his/her reputation among the community or among his/her circle of friends. Nor would it be because he/she was afraid of the criticism that might result from a show of non-concern."

"From this point of view, we can say that if you did lack concern for the infant, you would not be human. Also, to lack a sense of shame and disgust would not be human; to lack a feeling of humility and deference is to be "in-human" and to lack a sense of right and wrong is to be inhuman."

"The sense of concern for others is the starting point of jen. The feeling of shame and disgust is the starting point of Righteousness. The sense of humility and deference is the starting point of Propriety and the sense of right and wrong is the starting point of Wisdom."

"People's having these four basic senses is like their having four limbs. Having these four basic senses and yet claiming inability to act on them is to cheat yourself. To say that the ruler doesn't have them is to cheat the ruler. Since all people have these four basic senses within themselves, they should all understand how to enhance and develop them. It is like when a fire just starts, or a spring first bubbles out of the ground. If you are able to develop these four basic senses, you will be able to take care of everybody within the four seas. If you do not develop them, you won't even be able to take care of your own parents."

Taoism

~

from the Tao Te Ching

1. To conduct one's life according to the Tao,
is to conduct one's life without regrets;
to realize that potential within oneself
which is of benefit to all.

3. By retaining his humility,
the talented person who is also wise,
reduces rivalry.
The person who possesses many things,
but does not boast of his possessions,
reduces temptation, and reduces stealing.
Those who are jealous of the skills or things
possessed by others,
most easily themselves become possessed by envy.
Satisfied with his possessions,
the sage eliminates the need to steal;
at one with the Tao,
he remains free of envy,
and has no need of titles.
By being supple, he retains his energy.
He minimizes his desires,
and does not train himself in guile,
nor subtle words of praise.
By not contriving, he retains
the harmony of his inner world,
and so remains at peace within himself.

8. Like water, the sage abides in a humble place;
in meditation, without desire;
in thoughtfulness, he is profound,
and in his dealings, kind.
In speech, sincerity guides the man of Tao,
and as a leader, he is just.

In management, competence is his aim,
and he ensures the pacing is correct.
Because he does not act for his own ends,
nor cause unnecessary conflict,
he is held to be correct
in his actions towards his fellow man.

9. The sage works quietly,
seeking neither praise nor fame;
completing what he does with natural ease,
and then retiring.
This is the way and nature of Tao.
The ordinary man seeks honour, not dishonour,
cherishing success and abominating failure,
loving life, whilst fearing death.
The sage does not recognize these things,
so lives his life quite simply.
The ordinary man seeks to make himself
the centre of his universe;
the universe of the sage is at his centre.
He loves the world, and thus remains unmoved
by things with which others are concerned.
He acts with humility, is neither moved nor moving,
and can therefore be trusted in caring for all things.

18. When the way of the Tao is forgotten,
kindness and ethics need to be taught;
men learn to pretend to be wise and good.
All too often in the lives of men,
filial piety and devotion
arise only after conflict and strife,
just as loyal ministers all too often appear,
when the people are suppressed.

19. It is better merely to live one's life,
realizing one's potential,
rather than wishing
for sanctification.
He who lives in filial piety and love
has no need of ethical teaching.
When cunning and profit are renounced,
stealing and fraud will disappear.
But ethics and kindness, and even wisdom,
are insufficient in themselves.
Better by far to see the simplicity
of raw silk's beauty
and the uncarved block;

to be one with onself,
and with one's brother.

24. He who boasts
is not enlightened,
and he who is self-righteous
does not gain respect
from those who are meritous;
thus, he gains nothing,
and will fall into disrepute.
Since striving,
boasting and self-righteousness,
are all unnecessary traits,
the sage considers them excesses,
and has no need of them.

30. When leading by the way of the Tao,
abominate the use of force,
for it causes resistance, and loss of strength,
showing the Tao has not been followed well.
Achieve results but not through violence,
for it is against the natural way,
and damages both others' and one's own true self.

"Nature"

༺༝

Luther Standing Bear

Luther Standing Bear was chief of the Oglala, Lakota from 1905 to 1939. This excerpt is taken from his classic account of Native American life, *Land of the Spotted Eagle*.

༺༝

The Lakota was a true naturist—a lover of Nature. He loved the earth and all things of the earth, the attachment growing with age. The old people came literally to love the soil and they sat or reclined on the ground with a feeling of being close to a mothering power. It was good for the skin to touch the earth and the old people liked to remove their moccasins and walk with bare feet on the sacred earth. Their tipis were built upon the earth and their altars were made of earth. The birds that flew in the air came to rest upon the earth and it was the final abiding place of all things that lived and grew. The soil was soothing, strengthening, cleansing, and healing.

This is why the old Indian still sits upon the earth instead of propping himself up and away from its life-giving forces. For him, to sit or lie upon the ground is to be able to think more deeply and to feel more keenly; he can see more clearly into the mysteries of life and come closer in kinship to other lives about him.

The earth was full of sounds which the old-time Indian could hear, sometimes putting his ear to it so as to hear more clearly. The forefathers of the Lakotas had done this for long ages until there had come to them real understanding of earth ways. It was almost as if the man were still a part of the earth as he was in the beginning, according to the legend of the tribe. This beautiful story of the genesis of the Lakota people furnished the foundation for the love they bore for earth and all things of the earth. Wherever the Lakota went, he was with Mother Earth. No matter where he roamed by day or slept by night, he was safe with her. This thought comforted and sustained the Lakota and he was eternally filled with gratitude.

From Wakan Tanka there came a great unifying life force that flowed in and through all things—the flowers of the plains, blowing winds, rocks, trees, birds, animals—and was the same force that had been breathed into the first man. Thus all things were kindred and brought together by the same Great Mystery.

Kinship with all creatures of the earth, sky, and water was a real and active principle. For the animal and bird world there existed a brotherly feeling that kept the Lakota safe among them. And so close did some of the Lakotas come to their feathered and furred friends that in true brotherhood they spoke a common tongue.

The animal had rights—the right of man's protection, the right to live, the right to multiply, the right to freedom, and the right to man's indebtedness—and in recognition of these rights the Lakota never enslaved the animal, and spared all life that was not needed for food and clothing.

This concept of life and its relations was humanizing and gave to the Lakota an abiding love. It filled his being with the joy and mystery of living; it gave him reverence for all life; it made a place for all things in the scheme of existence with equal importance to all. The Lakota could despise no creature, for all were of one blood, made by the same hand, and filled with the essence of the Great Mystery. In spirit the Lakota was humble and meek. "Blessed are the meek: for they shall inherit the earth," was true for the Lakota, and from the earth he inherited secrets long since forgotten. His religion was sane, normal, and human.

Reflection upon life and its meaning, consideration of its wonders, and observation of the world of creatures, began with childhood. The earth, which was called *Maka,* and the sun, called *Anpetuwi,* represented two functions somewhat analogous to those of male and female. The earth brought forth life, but the warming, enticing rays of the sun coaxed it into being. The earth yielded, the sun engendered.

In talking to children, the old Lakota would place a hand on the ground and explain: "We sit in the lap of our Mother. From her we, and all other living things, come. We shall soon pass, but the place where we now rest will last forever." So we, too, learned to sit or lie on the ground and become conscious of life about us in its multitude of forms. Sometimes we boys would sit motionless and watch the swallow, the tiny ants, or perhaps some small animal at its work and ponder on its industry and ingenuity; or we lay on our backs and looked long at the sky and when the stars came out made shapes from the various groups. The morning and evening star always attracted attention, and the Milky Way was a path which was traveled by the ghosts. The old people told us to heed *wa maka skan,* which were the "moving things of earth." This meant, of course, the animals that lived and moved about, and the stories they told of *wa maka skan* increased our interest and delight. The wolf, duck, eagle, hawk, spider, bear, and other creatures, had marvelous powers, and each one was useful and helpful to us. Then there were the warriors who lived in the sky and dashed about on their spirited horses during a thunder storm, their lances clashing with the thunder and glittering with the lightning. There was *wiwila,* the living spirit of the spring, and the stones that flew like a bird and talked like a man. Everything was possessed of personality, only differing with us in form. Knowledge was inherent in all things. The world was a library and its books were the stones, leaves, grass, brooks, and the birds and animals that shared, alike with us, the storms and blessings of earth. We learned to do what only the student of nature ever learns, and that was to feel beauty. We never railed at the storms, the furious winds, and the biting frosts and snows. To do so intensified human futility, so whatever came we adjusted ourselves, by more effort and energy if necessary, but without complaint. Even the lightning did us no harm, for whenever it came too close, mothers and grandmothers in every tipi put cedar leaves on the coals and their magic kept danger away. Bright days and dark days were both expressions of the Great Mystery, and the Indian reveled in being close to the Big Holy. His worship was unalloyed, free from the fears of civilization.

I have come to know that the white mind does not feel toward nature as does the Indian mind, and it is because, I believe, of the difference in childhood instruction. I have often noticed white boys gathered in a city by-street or alley jostling and pushing one another in a foolish manner. They spend much time in this aimless fashion, their natural faculties neither seeing, hearing, nor feeling the varied life that surrounds them. There is about them no awareness, no acuteness, and it is this dullness that gives ugly mannerisms full play; it takes from them natural poise and stimulation. In contrast, Indian boys, who are naturally reared, are alert to their surroundings; their senses are not narrowed to observing only one another, and they cannot spend hours seeing nothing, hearing nothing, and thinking nothing in particular. Observation was certain in its rewards; interest, wonder, admiration grew, and the fact was appreciated that life was more than mere human manifestation; that it was expressed in a multitude of forms. This appreciation enriched Lakota existence. Life was vivid and pulsing; nothing was casual and commonplace. The Indian lived—lived in every sense of the word—from his first to his last breath.

The character of the Indian's emotion left little room in his heart for antagonism toward his fellow creatures, this attitude giving him what is sometimes referred to as "the Indian point of view." Every true student, every lover of nature has "the Indian point of view," but there are few such students, for few white men approach nature in the Indian manner. The Indian and the white man sense things differently because the white man has put distance between himself and nature; and assuming a lofty place in the scheme of order of things has lost for him both reverence and understanding. Consequently the white man finds Indian philosophy obscure—wrapped, as he says, in a maze of ideas and symbols which he does not understand. A writer friend, a white man whose knowledge of "Injuns" is far more profound and sympathetic than the average, once said that he had been privileged, on two occasions, to see the contents of an Indian medicine-man's bag in which were bits of earth, feathers, stones, and various other articles of symbolic nature; that a "collector" showed him one and laughed, but a great and world-famous archeologist showed him the other with admiration and wonder. Many times the Indian is embarrassed and baffled by the white man's allusions to nature in such terms as crude, primitive, wild, rude, untamed, and savage. For the Lakota, mountains, lakes, rivers, springs, valleys, and woods were all finished beauty; winds, rain, snow, sunshine, day, night, and change of seasons brought interest; birds, insects, and animals filled the world with knowledge that defied the discernment of man.

But nothing the Great Mystery placed in the land of the Indian pleased the white man, and nothing escaped his transforming hand. Wherever forests have not been mowed down; wherever the animal is recessed in their quiet protection; wherever the earth is not bereft of four-footed life—that to him is an "unbroken wilderness." But since for the Lakota there was no wilderness; since nature was not dangerous but hospitable; not forbidding but friendly, Lakota philosophy was healthy—free from fear and dogmatism. And here I find the great distinction between the faith of the Indian and the white man. Indian faith sought the harmony of man with his surroundings; the other sought the dominance of surroundings. In sharing, in loving all and everything, one people naturally found a measure of the thing they sought; while, in fearing, the other found need of conquest. For one man the world was full of beauty; for the other it was a place of sin and ugliness to be endured until he went to another world, there to become a creature of wings, half-man and half-bird. Forever one man directed his Mystery to change the world He had made; forever this man pleaded with Him to chastise His wicked ones; and forever he implored his Wakan Tanka to send His light to earth. Small wonder this man could not understand the other.

But the old Lakota was wise. He knew that man's heart, away from nature, becomes hard; he knew that lack of respect for growing, living things soon led to lack of respect for humans too. So he kept his youth close to its softening influence.

II

PRECURSORS OF A LIBERATING FAITH

That the sweat and tedious labour of the farmer, early and late, cold and hot, wet and dry, should be converted into the pleasure of a small number of men—that continued severity should be laid on nineteen parts of the land to feed the inordinate lusts and delicate appetites of the twentieth, is so far from the will of the great Governor of the world, . . . [it] is wretched and blasphemous.

—William Penn, 1669

All Friends everywhere, who are dead to carnal weapons, and have beaten them to pieces, stand in that which takes away the occasions of wars, in the power which saves men's lives, and destroys none.

—George Fox, *Epistle 177*

While the main focus of this book is on religious participation in progressive political movements of the twentieth century, Part II helps us recognize that precursors of contemporary movements for social change have existed for centuries.

These precursors take their inspiration from, and are shaped by, three different kinds of social forces. First, their origins can be found partly in religious history itself. As Sheila Rowbotham makes clear, the protofeminism of women preachers in the seventeenth century stemmed directly from ideas of personal integrity that were the hallmark of the Protestant Reformation. Once the established authority of the Catholic Church could be challenged, all other forms of authority might be challenged as well. Yet for the women writers in Part II this resistance to male authority in religious matters was not a rejection of religion, but a new interpretation of it. Like the religious feminists in Part V, these are women who believed the church belonged as much to them as it did to those who said they had no right to speak. Margaret Fell and Lucretia Mott do not see themselves as offering *secular* reasons for the rejection of male religious authority, but rather as offering *religious* reasons as to why specifically male religious authority is unjustified, or at least grossly exaggerated. Evelyn Higginbotham's fascinating account of feminism among black Baptist women in late-nineteenth-century America reveals a similar dynamic.

Second, religious social activism was at times sparked by a direct encounter with secular history. This is nowhere more clear than in the movement to abolish slavery. As the selections from Theodore Wright and Elizur Wright show, the religious basis of abolition was a clear case of religious values attempting to make the secular world more moral—or at least less grossly immoral. For the religious abolitionist, slavery was not simply some secular error, but a sin. It violated God's will as well as the rights of human slaves.

As we shall see throughout this book, the encounter between religion and secular politics typically involves a double movement, either side of which may be more important in any particular instance. On the one hand, religious moral values (such as those contained in Part I) go forth to transform the world. On the other hand, progressive political movements influence tradition, altering collective interpretations of just what religion, morality, and holiness mean.

This last dynamic is evident in the selections from Walter Rauschenbusch and Pope Leo XIII. Rauschenbusch was perhaps the foremost exponent of the "social gospel," a movement which proclaimed the necessity of applying religious values and insights to the social conflicts and crises of late-nineteenth-century America; in particular, to an emerging industrial capitalist society in which class conflict, urban poverty, and the concentration of wealth had become widespread. Like Rauschenbusch, Leo III is responding to comparable developments in Europe, as well as the presence of large, well-organized, and multinational socialist and trade union movements. In both cases, we have religious spokespersons being influenced by, and seeking to distinguish themselves from, secular particular movements. How to relate to secular political movements—whether to accept, reject, or do both partially—is a permanent theme of religious social action. Alternatively, we may find that social movements—for instance, the pursuit of democracy—may be initially rejected and then, as in Leo III's statement below, taken for granted.

Finally, we have in a brief selection from John Locke's *Letter Concerning Toleration*, a premonition of the ecumenical spirit that animates relations between progressive believers in our own day. This text is an important moment in the centuries-long process (still underway in certain parts of the world) by which the faithful come to realize that passionate adherence to one's own religion can coexist with respect for the different beliefs of others. In order for religious social activists to function on the terrain of democracy and human rights, this journey is absolutely necessary.

from *Women, Resistance and Revolution*

❧

Sheila Rowbotham

British socialist feminist theorist Sheila Rowbotham is best known for her groundbreaking *Women's Consciousness, Man's World*. The following selection is taken from her historical overview of women's relation to radical and revolutionary movements. Interestingly, this overview from a self-consciously secular author must begin with women's relation to religion.

❧

Beginnings are hard to find. People don't see themselves as beginners. How are they to know what comes ahead? They can see behind them, not in front. There is no "beginning" of feminism in the sense that there is no beginning to defiance in women. But there is a beginning of feminist possibility—even before it is conceived as such. Female resistance has taken several historical shapes.

"You have stepped out of your place," the Calvinist church fathers in the Massachusetts Bay colony told Anne Hutchison in the mid-seventeenth century. "You have rather been a husband than a wife, and a preacher than a hearer, and a magistrate than a subject, and so you have thought to carry all things in Church and Commonwealth as you would and have not been humbled for it."[1]

They worked hard at humbling her. She had gathered round her a group of followers, mostly women. They met together and Anne Hutchison preached on texts, criticized some of the ministers, and became respected for her knowledge of scripture and of healing herbs. She believed every individual should aspire to direct communion with God and that God dwelt in every human being. She upset Calvinist dogma, political differentiation, and masculine superiority. She was accordingly tried by both civil and religious authority. Pregnant and ill, at one stage while she was being questioned she almost collapsed, but they wouldn't let her sit down. The governor of the colony merely noted tersely in his record of the trial: "Her countenance disclosed some bodily infirmity." Finally she faltered and confessed to heresy. But they were still not satisfied. "Her repentance is not in her countenance." She was banished from the colony. Her fearlessness, her knowledge of scripture, her eloquence infuriated them all the more because she was a woman.

Anne Hutchison was not alone in her insubordination; Richard Hubberthorne, a Quaker, was a more tolerant man than the governor of Massachusetts Bay in the 1650s. But the most tolerant of men know where to draw the line. Travelling through England Richard drew it rather firmly when he encountered Mildred, one of the group called ranters who emphasized uncompromisingly the direct communion of true believers to God. He called her "an impudent lass that said she was above the apostles."[2]

It is apparent that Anne and Mildred were far from being the first women to question their place in the world and aspire to something better. However, the context and language in which they expressed their aspirations represented the beginning of completely new ways of proceeding. Ideas of insubordination fell on fertile ground in the seventeenth century. People were finding new footholds and climbing at a great pace. Puritanism could give their presumption a justification and confidence which made it much more dangerous to all those who cherished the established state of things. Time and industry appeared every day to produce new knowledge, Jonah came crying out of the belly of the whale—Nature, Reason, Justice, Rights, Liberty, Property, and Freedom! There were changes in the organization of work, in the scope of trade, in the rhythm of industry. There was a protracted struggle in parliament, a civil war, a series of republican experiments. People used old principles only to find them transformed by touching this impatient reality. Anne and Mildred were just part of a much wider revolution. The growth of early capitalism, of puritanism and of new ideas of reason and science caused people to see many questions in a new light. This was true not only of religious and political ideas of order and unity, of economic ideas about poverty and idleness; it also allowed the expression of doubt about the nature of relationships between men and women, parents and children, the family and society, which the Aristotelean and Old Testament traditions had kept buried for centuries. The fact of revolution gave them a new authority. While a succession of heresies had challenged the hierarchy of clearly defined authorities—God, king, priest, husband, father, master—they had never presumed legitimacy before. They had lurked only in by-ways, murmured in taverns, whipped the crowd up at fairs, crept slyly into the universities, been defrocked, sought communion with nature, heard the music of the spheres, worshipped the sun, pursued the millennium and been hanged, drawn and quartered or burned at the stake for prophesying the possibility of heaven on earth.

Now the prophets of heaven had emerged, tempered, stern, serious and bitter, killed a king and set themselves up as the rightful government of the Commonwealth, thus upsetting the establishment and certainty of order, subordination and authority forever. They provided the prophetesses with an amazing justification for impudence. Thus, just when the ground was being taken from under everyone's feet and a man needed a bit of peace and privacy in his own home, who should start spouting texts and interpreting God's word but the women. This seemed a preposterous and unnatural development to the man. Women's subordination was apparently part of the immutable order of things. It was well known that with a woman, a dog and a walnut tree, the more you beat 'em the better they be. Equally "natural" was the duplicity of women. According to proverbial wisdom they were saints in the church, angels in the streets, devils in the kitchen and apes in bed. Sexual "greediness" was a common theme in seventeenth-century drama. The preachers warned men to take heed of young women and of prophetesses. Sexuality and female theorizing combined dangerously.

[. . .]

Simultaneous with the breakdown of the traditional social structures which had contained the aspirations of women, the forces which promised a new potentiality grew stronger. When in the seventeenth century the puritan revolution unleashed so many heretics, babblers and talkers upon the world, it would have been indeed surprising if some impudent lasses, like Mildred, who had been forced to keep their place, sit in silence, obey with humility, and bide their time, had not decided to join in. While impatient and radical thinkers challenged so many authorities, judged their betters, expected to be able to consent before being governed and even taught that all were equal, women tentatively started to take some of these ideas to themselves. Within the self-governing religious communities of the puritan sect they found a certain limited equality and a larger scope for self-expression. Here the Lord could pour out his spirit to all alike. The poor lace-maker could become God's handmaiden. Having got rid of the priest and proclaimed the priesthood of all believers, why confine divine inspiration to men? Anna Trapnel fasted, prophesied, and in "The Cry of a Stone" declared that "Whom the Son makes free, they are free indeed."[3] If the only criterion was individual conscience why couldn't women challenge their husbands' and fathers' right to instruct them in what to believe and their power to control how they behaved. To the horror of Anglicans and Presbyterians, for whom it was anathema that those "who lie in the same bed . . . should yet be of two churches,"[4] puritan women not only chose their own beliefs but actually divorced their husbands for spiritual deviation. The notion that the authority of fathers and husbands should rest on agreement like the authority of the state, that the husband had no more right to control the wife's conscience than the magistrate had to coerce the man's, persisted. Though by no means popular with many supporters of the Protectorate it was to outlast the Commonwealth of the seventeenth century and in many legal guises find itself chased through the courts in subsequent centuries. Like the Quaker George Fox's idea that male domination belongs to sin and that in the new life men and women will be equals, it has still to be fully realized.

[. . .]

Puritanism effected a species of moral improvement in the position of women. Within a very confined sense it allowed women a certain restricted dignity. It provided an impetus for a more humane concept of relationships between the sexes, protesting against wife-beating and opposing rituals like churching which had emphasized the uncleanness and animal baseness of women. By regarding morality as an affair of the inner spirit rather than the opinion of the world or the apparatus of government, it provided a means of challenging the double standard of sexual morality. Essential to radical-puritan democracy was the idea of the individual as the independent owner of his own person and capacities, with the right to resist invasion and violation. This had obvious implications for women. Within puritan democratic thinking too was the assumption that women, as human beings, had certain inalienable rights to civil and religious liberty.

NOTES

1. Charles Francis Adams, ed., *Antinomianism in the Colony of Massachusetts Bay, 1636–1638* (Boston: Prince Society, 1894), 329.
2. Elisabeth Brockbank, *Richard Hubberthorne* (London: Friends' Book Centre, 1929), 90–91.
3. Quoted in Keith Thomas, "Women in the Civil War Sects," *Past and Present* 13 (1958): 48.
4. Thomas, "Women in the Civil War Sects," 52.

from "Women's Speaking"

&

Margaret Fell

Margaret Fell was married to George Fox, and with him helped originate the Quakers. This sermon, from 1666 or 1667, expresses the classic Quaker resistance to established authority and extends that resistance to some of the conventional forms of male authority.

&

Justified, Proved, and Allowed of by the Scriptures, *All such as speak by the Spirit and Power of the Lord Jesus.*

And how Women *were the first that Preached the Tidings of the Resurrection of* Jesus, *and were sent by Christ's own Command, before he Ascended to the Father,* John 20. 17.

Whereas it hath been an Objection in the Minds of many, and several times hath been objected by the Clergy, or Ministers and others, against Women's speaking in the Church; and so consequently may be taken, that they are condemned for medling in the things of God: The ground of which Objection is taken from the Apostle's Words, which he writ in his first Epistle to the Corinthians, Chap. 14. Vers. 34, 35. And also what he writ to Timothy in the first Epistle, Chap. 2. Vers. 11, 12. But how far they wrong the Apostle's Intentions in these Scriptures, we shall shew clearly when we come to them in their course and order. But first let me lay down how God himself hath manifested his Will and Mind concerning Women, and unto women.

And first, when *God created Man in his own Image, in the Image of God created he them, Male and Female; and God blessed them, and God said unto them, Be fruitful and multiply: And God said, Behold, I have given you of every Herb,* &c. Gen. 1. Here God joyns them together in his own Image, and makes no such Distinctions and Differences as Men do; for though they be weak, he is strong; and as he said to the Apostle, *His Grace is sufficient,* and his *Strength is made manifest in Weakness,* 2 Cor. 12. 9. And such hath the Lord chosen, even *the weak things of the World, to confound the things which are mighty; and things which are despised, hath God chosen, to bring to nought things that are,* 1 Cor. 1. And God hath put no such difference between the Male and Female, as Men would make.

It is true, The Serpent, that was more subtle than any other Beast of the Field, came unto the Woman with his Temptations, and with a Lye; his Subtlety discerning her to be the weaker Vessel, or more inclinable to hearken to him, when he said, *If ye eat, your Eyes shall be opened;*

and the Woman saw, *that the Fruit was good to make one wise:* There the Temptation got into her, and she did eat, and gave to her Husband, and he did eat also; and so they were both tempted into the Transgression and Disobedience; and therefore God said unto *Adam,* (who hid himself when he heard his Voice) *Hast thou eaten of the Tree, which I commanded thee that thou should'st not eat?* And *Adam* said, *The Woman which thou gavest me, she gave me of the Tree, and I did eat. And the Lord said unto the Woman, What is this that thou hast done? And the Woman said, The Serpent beguiled me, and I did eat.* Here the Woman spoke the Truth unto the Lord. See what the Lord saith, Vers. 15, after he had pronounced Sentence on the Serpent, *I will put Enmity between thee and the Woman, and between thy Seed and her Seed; it shall bruise thy Head, and thou shalt bruise his Heel,* Gen. 3.

Let this Word of the Lord, which was from the beginning, stop the Mouths of all that oppose Women's Speaking in the Power of the Lord; for he hath put Enmity between the Woman and the Serpent; and if the Seed of the Woman speak not, the Seed of the Serpent speaks; for God hath put Enmity between the two Seeds; and it is manifest, that those that speak against the Woman and her Seed's Speaking, speak out of the Envy of the old Serpent's Seed. And God hath fulfilled his Word and his Promise, *When the fulness of time was come, he sent forth his Son, made of a Woman, made under the Law, that we might receive the Adoption of Sons,* Gal. 4. 4, 5.

Moreover, the Lord is pleased, when he mentions his Church, to call her by the Name of Woman, by his Prophets, saying, *I have called thee as a Woman forsaken, and grieved in Spirit, and as a Wife of Youth,* Isai. 54. Again, *How long wilt thou go about, thou back-sliding Daughter? For the Lord hath created a new thing in the Earth, a Woman shall compass a Man,* Jer. 31. 22. And *David,* when he was speaking of Christ and his Church, he saith, *The King's Daughter is all glorious within, her Cloathing is of wrought Gold, she shall be brought unto the King; with gladness and rejoicing shall they be brought; they shall enter into the King's Pallace,* Psal. 45. And also King Solomon in his Song, where he speaks of Christ and his Church, where she is complaining and calling for Christ, he saith, *If thou knowest not, O thou fairest among Women, go thy way by the Footsteps of the Flock,* Cant. 1. 8. c. 5. 9. And John, when he saw the Wonder that was in Heaven, he saw *a Woman cloathed with the Sun, and the Moon under her feet, and upon her Head a Crown of twelve Stars; and there appeared another Wonder in Heaven, a great red Dragon stood ready to devour her Child.* Here appears the Envy of the Dragon, Rev. 12.

Thus much may prove, that the Church of Christ is represented as a Woman; and those that speak against this Woman's speaking, speak against the Church of Christ, and the Seed of the Woman, which Seed is Christ; that is to say, Those that speak against the Power of the Lord, and the Spirit of the Lord speaking in a Woman, simply by reason of her Sex, or because she is a Woman, not regarding the Seed, and Spirit, and Power that speaks in her; such speak against Christ and his Church, and are of the Seed of the Serpent, wherein lodgeth Enmity. And as God the Father made no such difference in the first Creation, nor ever since between the Male and the Female, but always out of his Mercy and Loving-kindness, had regard unto the Weak. So also his Son, Christ Jesus, confirms the same thing; when the Pharisees came to him, and asked him, *if it were lawful for a Man to put away his Wife? He answered and said unto them, Have you not read, That he that made them in the beginning, made them Male and Female; and said, For this Cause shall a Man leave Father and Mother, and shall cleave unto his Wife, and they twain shall be one Flesh; wherefore they are no more twain, but one Flesh? What therefore God hath joyned together, let no Man put asunder,* Mat. 19.

Again, Christ Jesus, when he came to the City of Samaria, where Jacob's Well was, where the Woman of *Samaria* was, you may read in John 4 how he was pleased to preach the Everlasting

Gospel to her; and when the Woman said unto him, *I know that when the Messiah cometh* (which is called Christ) *when he cometh, he will tell us all things.* Jesus saith unto her, *I that speak unto thee am he.* Also he said unto Martha, when she said, *she knew that her Brother should rise again in the last day.* Jesus said unto her, *I am the Resurrection and the Life; he that believeth on me, though he were dead, yet should he live; and whosoever liveth and believeth, shall never die. Believest thou this?* She answered, *Yea, Lord, I believe thou art the Christ, the Son of God.* Here she manifested her true and saving Faith, which few at that day believed so on him, John 11. 25, 26.

Also that Woman, that came unto Jesus with an Alabaster Box of very precious Ointment, and poured it on his Head as he sat at meat; it is manifest that this Woman knew more of the secret Power and Wisdom of God, than his Disciples did, who were filled with Indignation against her; and therefore Jesus saith, *Why do ye trouble the Woman, for she hath wrought a good Work upon me? Verily, I say unto you, Wheresoever this Gospel shall be preached in the whole World, there shall also this that this Woman hath done, be told for a Memorial of her,* Mat. 26. Mark 14. 3. Luke saith farther, *She was a Sinner,* and that *she stood at his Feet behind him weeping, and began to wash his Feet with her Tears, and did wipe them with the Hair of her Head, and kissed his Feet, and annointed them with Ointment.* And when Jesus saw the Heart of the Pharisee that had bidden him to his House, he took occasion to speak unto Simon, as you may read in Luke 7 and he turned to the Woman, and said, *Simon, seest thou this Woman? Thou gavest me no Water to my Feet; but she hath washed my Feet with Tears, and wiped them with the Hair of her Head: Thou gavest me no Kiss; but this Woman, since I came in, hath not ceased to kiss my Feet: My Head with Oil thou didst not annoint; but this Woman hath annointed my Feet with Ointment: Wherefore I say unto thee, her Sins, which are many, are forgiven her; for she hath loved much,* Luke 7. 37. to the End.

Also, there was many Women which followed Jesus from Galilee, ministering unto him, and stood afar off when he was Crucified, Mat. 28. 55. Mark 15. Yea even the Women of Jerusalem wept for him, insomuch that he said unto them, *Weep not for me, ye Daughters of Jerusalem; but weep for your selves, and for your Children,* Luke 23. 28.

And certain Women which had been healed of Evil Spirits and Infirmities, Mary Magdalen, and Joanna the wife of Chuza, Herod's Steward's Wife; and many others which ministered unto him of their Substance, Luke 8. 2, 3.

Thus we see that Jesus owned the Love and Grace that appeared in Women, and did not despise it: and by what is recorded in the Scriptures, he received as much Love, Kindness, Compassion, and tender Dealing towards him from Women, as he did from any others, both in his lifetime, and also after they had exercised their Cruelty upon him; for Mary Magdalene, and Mary the Mother of James, beheld where he was laid; *And when the Sabbath was past, Mary Magdalene, and Mary the Mother of James, and Salom, had brought sweet Spices, that they might annoint him: And very early in the Morning, the first Day of the Week, they came unto the Sepulchre at the rising of the Sun; and they said among themselves, Who shall roll us away the Stone from the Door of the Sepulchre? And when they looked the Stone was rolled away, for it was very great,* Mark 16. 1, 2, 3, 4. Luke 24. 1, 2. *And they went down into the Sepulchre,* and as Matthew saith, *The Angel rolled away the Stone, and he said unto the Women, Fear not, I know whom ye seek, Jesus which was Crucified: He is not here, he is risen,* Mat. 28. Now Luke saith thus, That *there stood two Men by them in shining Apparel, and as they were perplexed and afraid, the Men said unto them, He is not here, remember how he said unto you when he was in Galilee, That the Son of Man must be delivered into the Hands of sinful Men, and be Crucified, and the third Day rise again; and they remembered his Words, and returned from the Sepulchre, and told all these things to the Eleven, and to all the rest.*

It was Mary Magdalene, and Joanna, and Mary the Mother of James, and the other Women that were with them, which told these things to the Apostles, and their Words seemed unto them as Idle Tales, and they believed them not. Mark this, ye despisers of the Weakness of Women, and look upon your selves to be so wise: But Christ Jesus doth not so; for he makes use of the weak: For when he met the Women after he was risen, he said unto them, *All Hail!* And they came and held him by the Feet, and worshipped him; then said Jesus unto them, *Be not afraid, go tell my Brethren that they go into Galilee, and there they shall see me,* Mat. 28. 10. Mark 16. 9. And John saith, when Mary was weeping at the Sepulchre, that Jesus said unto her, *Woman, why weepest thou? what seekest thou? And when she supposed him to be the Gardener, Jesus said unto her, Mary; she turned her self, and said unto him, Rabboni, which is to say, Master; Jesus saith unto her, Touch me not, for I am not yet ascended to my Father; but go to my Brethren, and say unto them, I ascend unto my Father, and your Father, and to my God, and your God,* John 20. 16, 17.

Mark this, you that despise and oppose the Message of the Lord God that he sends by Women; What had become of the Redemption of the whole Body of Mankind, if they had not cause to believe the Message that the Lord Jesus sent by these Women, of and concerning his Resurrection? And if these Women had not thus, out of their Tenderness, and Bowels of Love, who had received Mercy, and Grace, and Forgiveness of Sins, and Virtue, and Healing from him; which many Men also had received the like, if their Hearts had not been so united and knit unto him in Love, that they could not depart as the Men did; but sat watching, and waiting, and weeping about the Sepulchre until the time of his Resurrection, and so were ready to carry his Message, as is manifested, else how should his Disciples have known, who were not there?

Oh! Blessed and Glorified be the Glorious Lord; for this may all the whole Body of Mankind say, though the Wisdom of Man that never knew God, is always ready to except against the Weak; but the Weakness of God is stronger than Men, and the Foolishness of God is wiser than Men, 1 Cor. 1. 25.

And in Acts 18 you may read how Aquilla, and Priscilla, took unto them Apollos, and expounded unto him the way of God more perfectly, who was an Eloquent Man, and mighty in the Scriptures; yet we do not read that he despised what Priscilla said, because she was a Woman, as many now do.

And now to the Apostle's Words, which is the Ground of the great Objection against Women's Speaking. And first, 1 Cor. 14. Let the Reader seriously peruse that Chapter, and see the end and drift of the Apostle in speaking these Words: For the Apostle is there exhorting the Corinthians unto Charity, and to desire Spiritual Gifts, and not to speak in an unknown Tongue; and not to be Children in Understanding, nor to be Children in Malice; but in Understanding to be Men. And that the Spirits of the Prophets, should be subject to the Prophets; for God is not the Author of Confusion, but of Peace: And then he saith, *Let your Women keep Silence in the Church,* &c.

Where it doth plainly appear, that the Women, as well as some others that were among them, were in Confusion: For he saith, *How is it Brethren? when ye come together, every one of you hath a Psalm, hath a Doctrine, hath a Tongue, hath a Revelation, hath an Interpretation? Let all Things be done to Edifying.* Here is no Edifying, but Confusion speaking together: Therefore he saith, *If any Man speak in an unknown Tongue, let it be by two, or at most by three, and that by course, and let one Interpret: But if there be no Interpreter, let him keep Silence in the Church.* Here the Man is Commanded to keep Silence, as well as the Woman, when in Confusion and out of order.

from "Abuses and Uses of the Bible"

Lucretia Mott

Quaker Lucretia Mott was intensely involved in struggles to end slavery and to advance the rights of women. She attended a world antislavery meeting (and was refused seating because she was a woman) and led the historic Seneca Falls Convention of 1848, which issued a dramatic call for women's social equality.

SERMON, DELIVERED AT CHERRY STREET MEETING, PHILADELPHIA, NOVEMBER 4, 1849

What are the abuses and what are the proper uses of the Bible and of this day of the week? This question is of some importance for us to seek to answer aright lest we should fall into the popular error that prevails upon this subject. Mingling as we do in religious society generally, adopting some of its forms and some of its theories, we have need to be upon our guard lest we fall into the superstition and error and before we are aware become bigoted in our opinions and denunciatory in our conduct. We know well that in Christendom generally it is assumed that the Bible is the word of God, while we from the earliest date of our religious society have declared and believe we have been sustained by Scripture testimony in the view that the word of God is a quickening spirit or as beautifully expressed in what are called the apocryphal writings: "Thine incorruptible spirit Oh Lord filleth all things. Therefore chastiseth thou them by a little and little that offend, and warnest them by putting them in remembrance wherein they have offended, that leaving their wickedness they may return unto thee O Lord." A portion of this blessed, this divine and all pervading spirit of which there is an acknowledgment to a greater or less extent everywhere, is found wherever man is found, darkened to be sure and clouded by very many circumstances. This divine and holy spirit which is a quickening spirit and has even been believed to be by this Society the word of God and the only word of God; that it has been through the operation and inspiring power of this word that the testimony to the truth has been borne in various ages of the world; that this testimony wherever it be found either in Scriptures or out of them is but a corroboration of the word and not the word itself and that word of God, which is quick and powerful, which showeth the thoughts and intent of the heart, that engrafted word which is able to serve the soul, we find so spoken in the Scriptures, but we no where find the Scriptures called the word of God by themselves. We read of one of the ancient Hebrew writers who after being converted to a purer faith, commended the Scriptures as being able to give knowledge of that which is to come, being able to make wise into salvation; giving knowledge of a purer way, but only through the faith of Jesus Christ. What is this faith of Jesus Christ; not as theologians define it, faith in the Trinity and a vicarious atonement, not faith in a system, a mere scheme of salvation, a plan of redemption? Faith of Jesus Christ is faith in the truth, faith in God and in man. The life that I now live in the flesh, said the Apostle, I live by the faith of the son of God, who loved me and gave himself for me. Well what is this other than a faith similar to that which Jesus held, the faith of the Son of God. How many chosen sons of God are there who have not loved their lives unto death, who have given themselves for their brethren even as the Apostle recommended; that as he, Jesus, laid down his life for the brethren so do we also lay down our lives one for another. This then perhaps is the more intelligent reading of these Scriptures and of what is spoken of as the word of God and as the saving faith of the Christian. The great error in Christendom is that the Bible is called the word, that it is taken as a whole, as a volume of plenary inspiration and in this way it has proved one of the strongest pillars to uphold ecclesiastical power and hireling priesthood. What has been the power of this book? Is it not uniformly taken among all the professors to establish their peculiar creeds, their dogmas of faith and their forms of worship, be they ever so superstitious? Is not the Bible sought from beginning to end for its isolated passages wherewith to prove the most absurd dogmas that ever were palmed off upon a credulous people; dogmas doing violence to the divine gift of reason with which man is so beautifully endowed; doing violence to all his feelings, his sense of justice and mercy with which the Most High has seen fit to clothe him? The Bible has been taken to make man from his very birth a poor corrupt sinful creature, and to make his salvation depend upon the sacrifice of Jesus in order that he should be saved. When his understanding has been imposed on by a Trinity and Atonement in the manner that it has, well may we say that the abuse of the Bible has been a means of strengthening priestcraft, and giving sanction to sectarian ordinances and establishments. We find the religionist, especially those whose greater interest it is to build up sect than to establish truth and righteousness in the earth, and probably many of these in the main idea that by this means they shall do the other more effectually, ready to flee to the Bible for authority for all their mysteries, their nonsensical dogmas, that have been imposed as articles of belief, as essential doctrines of Christianity. But also my friends has there not been an unworthy resort to this volume to prove the rightfulness of war and slavery, and of crushing woman's powers, the assumption of authority over her, and indeed of all the evils under which the earth, humanity has groaned from age to age? You know as well as I do how prone the sectarian has been to flee to the Bible to find authority for war, and indeed in the very existence of war, and there is a disposition because of the undue veneration of these records, to regard our God, even now as a God of battles. We do not duly discriminate between that comparatively dark age, when they set up their shouts of victory for their successes in their wars, whether aggressive or defensive, and the present. There is not sufficient allowance for the state that they were in at that time. Because of the veneration paid to the Bible, we find, even down to the present time, the overruling providence of God is claimed as giving countenance to the most barbarous and horrid wars, that are even in this day, cursing and disgracing the nations of the earth. Slavery, you know how ready the apologists for slavery and these apologists, to the shame of the church be it spoken, have been abundantly found in the pulpit, have screened themselves behind their imaged patriarchal institution and what sanction has been given to this greatest of all oppressions, this most wicked system which the English language furnishes no words wherewith rightly to depict the enormity of its cruelty. And this is done even at the present time by these priests of sect, these monopolizers of the pulpit. These ecclesiastics of our day have sought authority from the Bible and made it the plea for the sabbath, by quotations there from, that it was of God's sanction, that it was a patriarchal institution. You know as regards sensual indulgence the great obstacles that were thrown in the way of the temperance reformation by the use that was made of the Bible, by authority sought, for indulging in the intoxicating cup. We may rejoice that truth has been found stronger than all these, that thus the great efforts that have been made in our day for peace, for human freedom, for temperance, for moral purity, for the removal of all oppressions and monopolies that are afflicting mankind, have been to a considerable extent successful notwithstanding such obstacles as a popular priesthood, a popular clergy and a popular belief and the use of the Bible, have placed in the way of these great reformations. See now the resort to the Bible to prove the superstitious observances of a day. The manner in which this day is observed is one of the strongholds of priestcraft. It forms one of the pillars which must be broken down and which will be broken down, before an enlightened Christian faith. But then it needs that there should be boldness to declare this faith. It needs there should be faith to act in accordance with this and to declare the abuse that is now made of the Bible, in seeking to establish forms of worship which long since should have passed away. Superstitions, baptism, communion tables and devotions of various kinds and orders, have there found their sanction by improper reference to this volume. Thus by taking the examples of the ancients, even though they may have been comparatively modern, though they may have been disciples of Jesus in his day, yet I believe there is no rightful authority, no Scripture authority, for taking their example as sufficient authority for the continuance of the practice in the present day. We are not thus to use the example or practice of the ancients. It may have been well for them, coming from under the cloud of superstition formerly. They may still have needed their outward school master to bring them to a higher position, a higher sphere, a higher understanding, a higher dispensation, but are we because we find that they continued their type under the law, or their baptism which was of John, because they continued in their Sabbath observances, are we to do these things? I tell you nay. This divine word which we believe to be our sufficient teacher, draws us away from a dependance upon books, or everything that is outward, and leads us onward and upward in the work of progress toward perfection. Were we to come to the light we should have less need of the ordinance, for it would lead us away from customs of the religious world. If we have come as a babe, like stated in the language of the Apostle, what need he says have we any more of these ordained; touch not, taste not, handle not for all are designed to punish with the using but the substance is of Christ. And if ye come to this then let no man judge you as regards meats and drinks or new moons, or Sabbath days.

Remember the Sabbaths are but a shadow of things to come but the substance is of Christ. Those whose dependance is upon apostolic authority cannot find it, but there is notwithstanding a superstitious veneration put in the clerical explanation of that authority which has led many most mournfully to pin their faith upon ministers sleeves. Therefore we see the religious world gone on satisfying itself with its mysteries, with its nice theories of religion. These they regard as useful but which are really anything but true religion. We see them going out satisfied with their forms and devotions, taking comparatively little interest in the great subject of truth and humanity.

"Feminist Theology, 1880–1900"

☙

Evelyn Brooks Higginbotham

Evelyn Brooks Higginbotham is professor of Afro-American studies and African American religious history at Harvard University. Here she examines Baptist women's emerging feminist consciousness in the late nineteenth century.

☙

What if I am a woman; is not the God of ancient times the God of these modern days: Did he not raise up Deborah, to be a mother and a judge in Israel [Judges 4:4]? Did not queen Esther save the lives of the Jews? And Mary Magdalene first declare the resurrection of Christ from the dead?

—Maria Stewart, "Farewell Address," September 21, 1833

Boston black minister Peter Randolph cited gender proscriptions among the "strange customs" that he confronted when he returned to his Virginia birthplace soon after the Civil War to assume the pastorate of Richmond's Ebenezer Baptist Church. Randolph noted the segregated seating for men and women and the men's refusal to permit women at the business meetings of the church. Charles Octavius Boothe, a black Baptist minister in Alabama, recalled that in the early years of freedom women were not accustomed to the right to pray publicly.[1] Even as late as the 1880s in Tennessee and in Arkansas, black women met with virulent hostility in their efforts to establish separate societies.

During the last two decades of the nineteenth century black Baptist women increasingly challenged such examples of gender inequality. Working within the orthodoxy of the church, they turned to the Bible to argue for their rights—thus holding men accountable to the same text that authenticated their arguments for racial equality. In drawing upon the Bible—the most respected source within their community—they found scriptural precedents for expanding women's rights. Black women expressed their discontent with popular conceptions regarding "woman's place" in the church and society at large. They challenged the "silent helpmate" image of women's church work and set out to convince the men that women were equally obliged to advance not only their race and denomination, but themselves. Thus the black Baptist women developed a theology inclusive of equal gender participation. They articulated this viewpoint before groups of men and women in churches, convention anniversaries, and denominational schools, and in newspapers and other forms of literature.

The religious posture of black Baptist women was contextualized within a racial tradition that conflated private/eschatological witness and public/political stand. Saving souls and proselytizing the unconverted were integral to black women's missions, but their work was not limited to the private sphere of spiritual experience. The public discourse of church leaders and members, both male and female, had historically linked social regeneration, in the specific form of racial advancement, to spiritual regeneration. According to the ethicist Peter Paris, the principle of human freedom and equality under God constituted the "social teaching" of the black churches. This social teaching survived as a "nonracist appropriation of the Christian faith" and as a critique of American racism. The social teaching of human equality distinguished black churches from their white counterparts and represented a liberating principle "justifying and motivating all endeavors by blacks for survival and transformation."[2]

While the "nonracist" principle called attention to a common tradition shared by black churches, it masked the sexism that black churches shared with the dominant white society. Black women reinterpreted the church's social teaching so that human equality embraced gender as well. In the process, they came to assert their own voice through separate women's societies and through their recognition of an evangelical sisterhood that crossed racial lines. Within a female-centered context, they accentuated the image of woman as saving force, rather than woman as victim. They rejected a model of womanhood that was fragile and passive, just as they deplored a type preoccupied with fashion, gossip, or self-indulgence. They argued that women held the key to social transformation, and thus America offered them a vast mission field in which to solicit as never before the active participation of self-disciplined, self-sacrificing workers.[3] Through the convention movement, black Baptist women established a deliberative arena for addressing their own concerns. Indeed, one could say that the black Baptist church represented a sphere for public deliberation and debate precisely because of women.

ORTHODOXY'S GENDERED VISION

The feminist theology in the black Baptist church during the late nineteenth century conforms to Rosemary Ruether's and Eleanor McLaughlin's concept of a "stance of 'radical obedience.'" Referring to female leadership in Christianity, Ruether and McLaughlin distinguished women's positions of "loyal dissent" that arose within the mainline churches from women's positions of heresy that completely rejected the doctrines of the traditional denominations. They argued for the wider influence of women inside rather than outside the denominations, since women in the "stance of 'radical obedience'" seized orthodox theology in defense of sexual equality.[4]

If black Baptist women did not break from orthodoxy, they clearly restated it in progressive, indeed liberating language for women. In many respects their gendered vision of orthodoxy was analogous to the progressive racial theology already espoused by black ministers. In the Jim Crow America of the late nineteenth century, the Reverend Rufus Perry's *The Cushites, or the Descendants of Ham as Found in the Sacred Scriptures* (1893) dared to interpret the Bible as a source of ancient black history—as the root upon which race pride should grow.[5] Nor was a progressive, liberating theology new to blacks. For generations under slavery, African Americans rejected scriptural texts in defense of human bondage. Despite the reluctance of the slavemaster to quote the biblical passage "neither bond nor free in Christ Jesus," the slaves expressed its meaning in their spirituals and prayers. However, in the black Baptist church of the late nineteenth century, the women in the leadership called attention to the verse in its more complete form: "Neither bond nor free, neither male nor female in Christ Jesus."

By expounding biblical precedents, black women presented the intellectual and theological justification for their rights. But they expressed, too, a gendered interpretation of the Bible. The multivalent religious symbols within the Bible had obviously caused slavemasters and slaves, whites and blacks to invoke "orthodoxy" with meanings quite different from one another. It is perhaps less obvious that the Bible served dually to constrain and liberate women's position vis-à-vis men's in society. Caroline Bynum acknowledges gender differences in the way people appropriate and interpret religion in its symbolic and practical forms, inasmuch as people are gendered beings, not humans in the abstract. Bynum calls attention to the radical potential in this acknowledgment: "For if symbols can invert as well as reinforce social values . . . if traditional rituals can evolve to meet the needs of new participants . . . then old symbols can acquire new meanings, and these new meanings might suggest a new society."[6]

Even more important than the multivalent character of biblical symbolism are the very acts of reappropriation and reinterpretation of the Bible by black women themselves. As interpreters of the Bible, black women mediated its effect in relation to their own interests. Rita Felski asserts this point in her discussion of the social function of textual interpretation: "Radical impulses are not inherent in the formal properties of texts; they can be realized only through interactions between texts and readers, so that it becomes necessary to situate the . . . text in relation to the interests and expectations of potential audiences."[7]

The black Baptist women's advocacy of a new social order combined a progressive gendered and racialized representation of orthodoxy. However, their biblically based arguments were neither new nor unique. During the first half of the nineteenth century, black women such as Maria Stewart, Jarena Lee, and Sojourner Truth were precursors in adopting a scriptural defense of women's rights. In 1832 Maria Stewart, a free black in Massachusetts, was the first woman— black or white—to stand before an audience of men and women and offer biblical precedents in denunciation of sexism, slavery, the denial of adequate education to blacks, and other forms of oppression. Her social consciousness was molded by private religious conviction, which figured centrally in her public pronouncements. Marilyn Richardson has observed: "Resistance to oppression was, for Stewart, the highest form of obedience to God."[8] In her farewell address to the people in Boston in 1833, Stewart called forth names of biblical women who, with divine sanction, led the ancient Hebrew people. She then posed to the women of her own time: "What if such women as are here described should rise among our sable race?"[9]

During the 1880s and 1890s black women in the Baptist and Methodist churches, and such Protestant Episcopal women as Anna J. Cooper, posed a similar question. It is conceivable that all were influenced by Stewart's speeches, since she lived to publish her collected works in 1879. Stewart's influence notwithstanding, the public discourse of black women formed part of a broader trend in liberal theology, which sought to bring the Bible into greater harmony with values and assumptions related to women's changing status and a variety of other social and scientific developments.

WOMEN'S THEOLOGIZING

Women members of the male-dominated American National Baptist Convention, forerunner of the National Baptist Convention, U.S.A., were the first to question the illusory unity of the convention as the voice of all its people. Within this national body, Virginia Broughton of Tennessee and Mary Cook and Lucy Wilmot Smith of Kentucky were the most vocal in defense of women's rights. Broughton, Cook, and Smith were active in organizing separate Baptist women's conventions in the face of varying levels of male support and hostility. They spoke for an expanding public of women who stood in opposition to exclusive male power and dominance.

All three women were born in the South during the last years of slavery, but Broughton's background was the most privileged. She described her father as an "industrious man" who hired out his time from his master and subsequently bought his wife's and his own freedom. Raised as a free black, Broughton enrolled in a private school taught by a Professor Daniel Watkins during her adolescent years. She graduated from Fisk University in 1875—claiming to be the first woman of any race to gain a collegiate degree from a southern school. She was married to John Broughton, a lawyer active in Republican Party politics in Memphis, although she continued to work as a teacher and full-time missionary throughout her married life. In 1885, Broughton's feminist attitude surfaced when she challenged the appointment of a less experienced, black male teacher over herself. Supported by her husband, she eventually won her case as head teacher in the Kortrecht school—the only black public school in Memphis to have one year of high school instruction.[10]

After working for twelve years as a teacher in the public school system and as a part-time missionary for at least five of those years, Broughton left the school system to become a full-time missionary. She was immensely popular among southern black and northern white Baptist women. Her stature as a national figure among black Baptists continued to rise in the upcoming century.[11] Broughton's gendered appropriation of biblical symbols shaped her understanding of the women of her own day; she traced the Baptist women's movement and its providential evolution to Eve in the Garden of Eden. In *Women's Work, as Gleaned from the Women of the Bible* (1904), Broughton summed up the ideas that had marked her public lectures, correspondence, and house-to-house visitations since the 1880s, and she sought to inspire the church women of her day "to assume their several callings."[12]

Mary Cook was born a slave in Kentucky in 1862. Raised in a very humble environment, she was able to acquire a college education partly through the philanthropy of white Baptist women in New England and partly through the support of the Reverend William J. Simmons, black Baptist minister and president of the State University at Louisville. Cook graduated from the Normal Department of the State University at Louisville in 1883 and subsequently taught Latin and literature at her alma mater.[13] Like Broughton, Cook worked closely with the black Baptist women of her state and enjoyed communication with northern white Baptist women. In 1898 she married the Reverend Charles H. Parrish, a leader among black Baptists in Kentucky. She was active in the national convention of black Baptist women, which was founded in 1900, and also in secular black women's clubs, especially the National Association of Colored Women.

Cook, the most scholarly of the three women, expressed her views in the black press, in an edited anthology, and in speeches before various groups, including the American National Baptist Convention. She served on the executive board of the ANBC and was honored by being selected to speak on women's behalf in the classic statement of black Baptist doctrine, *The Negro Baptist Pulpit* (1890). In often militant language, Cook strove to enlarge women's power in the church. She termed the Bible an "iconoclastic weapon" that would destroy negative images of her sex and overcome the popular misconceptions of woman's place in the church and society. Like Broughton, Cook derived her position from the "array of heroic and saintly women whose virtues have made the world more tolerable."[14]

Although it is not clear whether Lucy Wilmot Smith was born a slave, she is reported to have grown up in a very poor household. Born in 1861, Smith was raised by her mother, who as a sole provider struggled to give her daughter an education. Smith graduated from the Normal Department of the State University at Louisville, taught at her alma mater, and also worked as a journalist. She never married. At the time of her premature death in 1890, she was principal of the Model School at the State University at Louisville. A leader in the Baptist Woman's Educational Convention of Kentucky, she sat on its Board of Managers and served as the secretary of its children's divisions. Like Cook, she was one of the very few women to hold an office in the male-dominated American National Baptist Convention. She served as Historian of the ANBC, wrote extensively in the black press, and delivered strong feminist statements at the annual meetings of the ANBC.[15] She ardently supported women's suffrage. Her death in 1890 prevented her from joining Broughton and Cook in the later movement to organize a national women's convention. Cook eulogized her: "She was connected with all the leading interests of her race and denomination. Her pen and voice always designated her position so clearly that no one need mistake her motive."[16]

None of the women was a theologian in any strict or formal sense, and yet their theocentric view of the world in which they lived justifies calling them theologians in the broad spirit that Gordon Kaufman describes:

> Obviously, Christians are involved in theologizing at every turn. Every attempt to discover and reflect upon the real meaning of the Gospel, of a passage in the Bible, of Jesus Christ, is theologizing; every effort to discover the bearing of the Christian faith or the Christian ethic on the problems of personal and social life is theological. For Christian theology is the critical analysis and creative development of the language utilized in apprehending, understanding, and interpreting God's acts, facilitates their communication in word and deed.[17]

As Kaufman implies, the act of theologizing was not limited to the formally trained male clergy. Nor did it extend only to college-educated women such as Broughton, Cook, and Smith. Scriptural interpretation figured significantly in the meetings of ordinary black women's local and state organizations. Virginia Broughton noted a tremendous groundswell of black women engaged in biblical explication in their homes, churches, and associational meetings.[18] In 1884 Lizzie Crittenden, chairman of the board of managers of the women's convention in Kentucky, identified the women's gendered interpretation of orthodoxy as revelation of their continued organizational growth: "It has really been marvelous how much has been found in the sacred word to encourage us that before had been left unsaid and seemed unheeded."[19] The reports of northern white missionaries in southern black communities confirmed these observations. Mary O'Keefe, a white missionary in Tennessee, wrote to her Chicago headquarters that black women in Bible Bands recited and interpreted passages of Scripture at their meetings. O'Keefe was fascinated by their black expressive culture. One elderly black woman, interpreting a scriptural text, became louder and louder in her delivery. "The last word came out with a whoop," O'Keefe recounted, "which was echoed and re-echoed by the others until it was quite evident that her view was accepted."[20] Mary Burdette, a leader of white Baptist women in the Midwest, also found black Baptist women engaged in biblical study during her tour of Tennessee. The women discussed ancient role models in justification of current demands for participatory parity within the denomination. Burdette described their round-table discussion: "Six sisters added to the interest by brief essays and addresses relating to women's place and work in the church as illustrated by the women of the Bible. Mrs. Broughton spoke of Eve, the mother of us all and the wife given to Adam for a help-meet, and following her we heard of Deborah, and that from her history we could learn that while men might be called to deliver Israel, they could not do it without the presence and assistance of Christian women."[21]

The enthusiasm with which black women of all educational backgrounds and ages claimed their right to theological interpretation was characterized by Virginia Broughton as part of the "general awakening and rallying together of Christian women" of all races. There were other black women who joined Broughton, Cook, and Smith in voicing gender concerns. Black women interpreters of the Bible perceived themselves as part of the vanguard of the movement to present the theological discussion of woman's place.[22] They used the Bible to sanction both domestic and public roles for women. While each of the feminist theologians had her own unique style and emphasis, a textual analysis of their writings reveals their common concern for women's empowerment in the home, the church, social reform, and the labor force. The Baptist women invoked biblical passages that portrayed positive images of women and reinforced their claim to the public realm. This realm, according to the literary critic Sue E. Houchins, provided black religious women like Broughton and others an arena in which they could transcend culturally proscribed gender roles and "could 'function as person[s] of authority,' could resist the pressures of family and society . . . and could achieve legal and structural support from the church for their work as spiritual advisors, teachers, and occasional preachers."[23]

THE GOSPEL ACCORDING TO WOMAN

The feminist theologians of the black Baptist church did not characterize woman as having a fragile, impressionable nature, but rather as having a capacity to influence man. They described woman's power of persuasion over the opposite sex as historically positive, for the most part, although they also mentioned a few instances of woman's negative influence, notably, the biblical stories of Delilah and Jezebel. But even this discussion emphasized man's vulnerability to woman's strength, albeit sometimes pernicious, and never recognized an innate feminine weakness to fall to temptation. Mary Cook asserted that woman "may send forth healthy, purifying streams which will enlighten the heart and nourish the seeds of virtue; or cast a dim shadow, which will enshroud those upon whom it falls in moral darkness."[24]

According to the feminist theologians, while the Bible depicted women in a dual image, it also portrayed good and evil men, and thus only affirmed woman's likeness to man and her oneness with him in the joint quest for salvation. Virginia Broughton insisted that the Genesis story explicitly denied any right of man to oppress woman. Her interpretation of woman's creation stressed God's not having formed Eve out of the "crude clay" from which he had molded Adam. She reminded her readers that God purposely sprang Eve from a bone, located in Adam's side and under his heart, for woman to be man's companion and helpmate, and she noted that God took the bone neither from Adam's head for woman to reign over him, nor from his foot for man to stand over her. Broughton observed that if woman had been Satan's tool in man's downfall, she was also God's instrument for human regeneration, since God entrusted the germ for human redemption to Eve alone. By commanding that "the seed of woman shall bruise the serpent's head," God had linked redemption inseparably with motherhood and woman's role in the physical deliverance of the Redeemer.[25]

Feminist theologians praised and took pride in the mothers of Isaac, Moses, Samson, and other greater or lesser heroes of the Old Testament. They described the women of the Old Testament as providing far more than the bodily receptacles through which great men were born into the world. They were responsible for rearing and molding the sons who would deliver Israel from its oppressors. The mother's determining hand could extend as far back as the child's prenatal stage—or so concluded Virginia Broughton in a reference to Samson's mother: "An angel appeared to Manoah's wife, told her she should have a son and instructed her how to deport herself after the conception, that Samson might be such a one as God would have him be, to deliver Israel from the oppression of the Philistines."[26]

Since motherhood was regarded as the greatest sanctity, Mary the mother of Jesus personified the highest expression of womanhood. Of all biblical mothers, she assumed the position of the "last and sublimest illustration in this relation."[27] Hers was motherhood in its purest, most emphatically female form, for it was virginal and thus without the intercession of a man. To the feminist theologians of the black Baptist church, Jesus, conceived from the union of woman and the Angel of God, became the fruition of God's commandment in Genesis. Mary Cook used her knowledge of ancient history and the Latin classics to add further insight concerning the virgin mother theme: she revealed its roots in antiquity by calling attention to the concept of virgin mother as a literary motif. Citing parallels with the story of the twins, Remus and Romulus, the mythical founders of Rome, Mary Cook posited, "Silvia became their mother by the God Mars, even as Christ was the son of the Holy Ghost."[28]

Although motherhood remained the salient image in their writings and speeches, Broughton, Cook, and Smith did not find their own personal lives consumed with maternal responsibilities. Lucy Wilmot Smith never had a husband or child, nor did Mary Cook during the period when she wrote her feminist theological texts. Broughton, on the other hand, was married with five children, and even lectured on the subject of "the ideal mother." Yet she spent little time in the actual role of mothering. She admitted taking her son periodically with her on missionary trips, but more often the care of the younger children fell to older siblings, other family members, and a number of "good women secured from time to time." In fact Broughton noted that all her children were taught domestic duties at an early age. The eldest daughter, Elizabeth, fixed suppers for the family and "was always solicitous about her mother's comfort."[29] Although she wrote lovingly of her children in her autobiography, Broughton undoubtedly valued her missionary work above every other responsibility. This is clearly revealed in the case of her daughter's illness. Broughton canceled a missionary engagement to join her sick daughter Selena, who died a few days after her mother's return home. She never again canceled a missionary engagement, for her daughter's death had taught her that "she could stay home and sit by the bedside of her children and have all the assistance that medical skill could render, and yet God could take her children to himself if he so willed it."[30] What may seem callous by today's standards was not viewed as such by Broughton's household. Broughton describes her last hours with her daughter as loving spiritual moments that influenced all of the family members to "think seriously of heavenly things." Her single-minded devotion to missions did not result in censure or condemnation by her community. Broughton commanded the respect of the women in her community and black Baptist women across the nation.

In addition to motherhood, the feminist theologians referred to the roles of wife, sister, and daughter in order to complete the larger picture of woman's participation in the home. They frequently attributed a man's conversion or a minister's righteous lifestyle to a mother's influence, a sister's guidance, or to the tender persuasion of a devoted wife or daughter. Marriage was presented as "a holy estate." Speaking before the American National Baptist Convention in 1888 on the subject "Women in the Home," Mrs. G. D. Oldham of Tennessee asserted: "The home is the first institution God established on earth. Not the church, or the state, but the home." To Oldham, woman's domestic role was of supreme importance and represented her "true sphere," since within the home, woman exercised her greatest influence of all; there she reigned "queen of all she surveys, her sway there is none can dispute, her power there is none can battle." Although Oldham acknowledged that exceptional women would seek work outside the home and indicated her hope that they not be excluded from careers in government and the natural sciences, she firmly believed that most women would confine their activities to domestic duties. She exhorted women to be the ministers, not the slaves of their homes. Woman as homemaker should provide her husband with an atmosphere of comfort and bliss. Oldham's image of marriage and home life romanticized woman's ability to create a refuge from worldly pressures and problems. Home life was to resemble the "center of a cyclone where not even a feather is moved by the hurricane that roars around it."[31]

For feminist theologians such as Cook and Broughton, the image of woman as loyal, comforting spouse transcended the husband-wife relationship to embrace that of Jesus and woman. They were quick to point out that no woman betrayed Jesus and noted that a woman had bathed his feet with her tears and wiped them with her hair, while Mary and Martha had soothed him in their home after his long, tiring journey. Biblical women had expressed their faith through acts of succor and kindness much more than had men. Yet Cook and Broughton coupled woman's domestic image as comforter with the public responsibility of prophesying and spreading the gospel. Cook remarked that in Samaria, Jesus engaged in conversation with the woman at the well, "which was unlawful for a man of respect to do," and by so doing set a new standard for encouraging woman's intellect and permitting "her to do good for mankind and the advancement of His cause."[32]

Their emphasis on woman's relationship with Jesus ironically, albeit subtly, shifted women's duties outside the home, since woman's primary obligation was interpreted to be to God rather than husband. This was evident in Virginia Broughton's own marriage. Broughton resisted pressures of family and society by proclaiming her allegiance to God above family. She boldly alluded to her work as independent of her husband's wishes. Not yet converted when she began mission work, Broughton's husband demanded that she cease this endeavor, since it took her away from home and family for several days at a time. When he asked, "When is this business going to stop?" Broughton replied with what she termed a divinely inspired answer. "I don't know," she hurled at him, "I belong to God first, and you next; so you two must settle it." According to Broughton, her husband eventually came around to her way of thinking, "after a desperate struggle with the world, the flesh, and the devil." Broughton was able to convince her husband that she was called by God for missionary work and that "to hinder her would mean death to him."[33]

During the late nineteenth century, feminist theology turned to the example of women leaders in the Old and New Testaments as sanction for more aggressive church work. Both Cook and Broughton reinterpreted biblical passages that had traditionally restricted woman's role—particularly Paul's dictum in the book of Corinthians that women remain silent in church. For Cook, an analysis of the historical context of Paul's statement revealed that his words were addressed specifically "to a few Grecian and Asiatic women who were wholly given up to idolatry and to the fashion of the day." Her exegesis denied the passage universal applicability. Its adoption in the late nineteenth century served as merely a rationalization to overlook and minimize the important contribution and growing force of woman's work in the church. Both Cook and Broughton argued that Paul praised the work of various women and, at times, depended upon them. The feminist theologians particularly enjoyed citing Paul's respect for Phoebe, the deaconess of the church at Cenchrea. Having entrusted Phoebe with an important letter to Rome, Paul demanded that everyone along her route lend assistance if needed. The Baptist women added the names of others who aided Paul, for example, Priscilla, Mary, Lydia, and "quite a number of women who had been co-workers with the apostle."[34]

In a speech before the male-dominated American National Baptist Convention in 1887, Mary Cook praised ministers such as William J. Simmons, who took a progressive stand toward women and included them in the convention's programs. She acknowledged the traditional roles of assisting pastors and working in Sunday Schools, but noted the increasing interest of women in business meetings and other church affairs. Alerting the men that this was only the beginning of women's denominational activity, Cook expressed the rising expectations of black Baptist women for organizational work when she declared that women would play a vital role in the work of the Baptist church in the future. This would require many changes, which Cook interpreted as a holy mandate from God: "God is shaking up the church—He is going to bring it up to something better and that too, greatly through the work of the women."[35]

From a perspective slightly different from Cook's, Virginia Broughton also rejected a literal interpretation of Paul's injunction to silence women in church. As she had done in her own home life, Broughton insisted that a woman's allegiance to God transcended her more conventional and earthbound responsibilities. Paul, Broughton argued, was well aware that mankind was both carnal and spiritual. But Christians distinguished themselves by their spirituality; they served not Mammon but God through the spirit. Paul's meaning was clear to Broughton: "Woman according to the flesh is made for the glory of man; but when recreated in Christ or born of the Spirit, she is recreated for such spiritual service as God may appoint through the examples given in his Word." She added that Peter had affirmed Joel's prediction that both sons and daughters would prophesy. Despite the broad number of roles that Broughton believed the Bible authorized and her rather unusual autonomy within her own household, she explicitly warned women against the danger of aspiring to roles that had no female precedents in the Bible. She denied that women should have access to the clergy or perform the clergy's role of establishing new churches, baptizing converts, and administering the Eucharist. Notwithstanding these proscriptions, Broughton argued for the presence of women on the executive boards of both state and national conventions of the denomination.[36]

The black feminist theologians also found biblical precedent for leadership outside the church in charitable philanthropic work. Olive Bird Clanton, wife of the Reverend Solomon T. Clanton of New Orleans, addressed the American National Baptist Convention in 1887 and maintained that Christian doctrine "has placed the wife by the side of her husband, the daughter by the side of her father, the sister by the side of her brother at the table of the Lord, in the congregation of the sanctuary, male and female met together at the cross and will meet in the realms of glory." Unlike Broughton and Cook, Olive Clanton's northern upbringing made her sensitive to the plight of foreign immigrants and to the squalid conditions in urban tenements. She had little faith in ameliorative legislation if unaccompanied by the activity of women in social reform, especially female education, the care of children, and the cause of social purity. Clanton advocated an aggressive, outgoing Christianity to reach the oppressed and needy class of women and children who did not go to church and thus remained outside the purview of the minister. These types could be helped by women, whose kindness and compassion uniquely qualified them for uplift work. In Clanton's opinion, "the wearied wife, and anxious mother, the lonely woman, often feeling that she is forgotten by the world and neglected by the church will open her heart and life to the gentle Christian woman that has taken the trouble to visit her." She encouraged women to organize social purity societies, sewing schools, and other types of unions in order to uplift the downtrodden.[37] The tireless work of Dorcas, who sewed garments for the needy, became a standard biblical reference for women's charitable work.

Mary Cook proclaimed the unique capability of women to cleanse immorality, indecency, and crime "in the face of the government which is either too corrupt to care, or too timid to oppose." For Cook, Baptist women represented much more than the hope of the church. They represented the hope of the world, inasmuch as their influence would have greater moral than political sway. Since Cook perceived social ills as primarily a moral issue, she did not trust their eradication to legislation alone. Mary Cook pictured the ideal wife of a minister as a good homemaker, an intellectual, and at the forefront of social reform causes. She encouraged women to engage actively in charitable work in orphanages, hospitals, and prisons.[38]

Proponents of a feminist theology endeavored to broaden employment opportunities for women. Lucy Wilmot Smith, Historian of the American National Baptist Convention, put the issue squarely before her predominantly male audience in 1886 when she decried the difference in training between boys and girls. She noted that the nineteenth-century woman was dependent as never before upon her own resources for economic survival. Smith believed that girls, like boys, must be taught to value the dignity of labor. She rejected views that considered work for women disdainful, or temporarily necessary at best—views that conceded to women only the ultimate goal of dependency on men. "It is," she wrote, "one of the evils of the day that from babyhood girls are taught to look forward to the time when they will be supported by a father, a brother, or somebody else's brother." She encouraged black women to enter fields other than domestic service and suggested that enterprising women try their hand at poultry raising, small fruit gardening, dairying, bee culture, lecturing, newspaper work, photography, and nursing.[39]

Mary Cook suggested that women seek out employment as editors of newspapers or as news correspondents in order to promote women's causes and to reach other mothers, daughters, and sisters. She advocated teaching youths through the development of juvenile literature and urged women in the denomination's schools to move beyond subordinate jobs by training and applying for positions as teachers and administrators. Cook praised women with careers as writers, linguists, and physicians, and she told the gathering of the American National Baptist Convention in 1887 that women must "come from all the professions, from the humble Christian to the expounder of His word; from the obedient citizen to the ruler of the land."[40]

Again, the Baptist women found biblical precedents to bolster their convictions and to inspire the women of their own day. Cook and Broughton pointed to the biblical woman Huldah, wife of Shallum. Huldah studied the law and interpreted the Word of God to priests and others who sought her knowledge. In the Book of Judges another married woman, Deborah, became a judge, prophet, and warrior whom God appointed to lead Israel against its enemies. Depicting Deborah as a woman with a spirit independent of her husband, Cook asserted: "Her work was distinct from her husband who, it seems, took no part whatever in the work of God while Deborah was inspired by the Eternal expressly to do His will and to testify to her countrymen that He recognizes in His followers neither male nor female, heeding neither the 'weakness' of one, nor the strength of the other, but strictly calling those who are perfect at heart and willing to do his bidding."[41]

Biblical examples had revealed that God used women in every capacity and thus proved that there could be no issue of propriety, despite the reluctance of men. Mary Cook urged the spread of women's influence in every cause, place, and institution that respected Christian values, and she admonished her audience that no profession should be recognized by either men or women if it lacked such values. She concluded her argument with an assertion of women's "legal right" to all honest labor, as she challenged her sisters in the following verse:

Go, and toil in any vineyard
Do not fear to do and dare;
If you want a field of labor
You can find it anywhere.[42]

[. . .]

The feminist theology of the black Baptist church never altered the hierarchical structure of the church by revolutionizing power relations between the sexes, nor did it inhibit ministers from assuming men's intellectual and physical superiority over women.[43] To the ire of black women, the black newspaper *Virginia Baptist* in 1894 presented a two-part series that adopted biblical arguments for restricting women's church work to singing and praying. The newspaper claimed divine authority in denying women the right to teach, preach, and vote.[44] Although the black feminist theologians opposed this line of thought, they did not challenge the basis for male monopoly of the clergy, nor did they demand equal representation in conventions in which both men and women participated. But feminist theology stirred women to find their own voice and create their own sphere of influence.

Throughout the last two decades of the nineteenth century, black women doubtless encouraged greater male appreciation for their potential contribution to the race and the denomination. Within the American National Baptist Convention, black feminist theology won outstanding male converts. It gained the respect of such ardent race leaders as William J. Simmons and Charles H. Parrish of Kentucky, Walter H. Brooks of Washington, D.C., and Harvey Johnson of Maryland.[45] In 1899 *The National Baptist Magazine,* the official organ of the National Baptist Convention, indicated women's growing influence. In the lead article of the magazine, the Reverend J. Francis Robinson supported "human rights for every individual of every race, of every condition, regardless of sex." Introducing biblical texts to illustrate the historical importance of women's church work and charitable activity, Robinson concluded that women should be allowed to reign not only in the home, but in the political world as well. He endorsed woman's suffrage and admitted his preference for the ballots of women as opposed to those of saloon-keepers and ward bosses. He urged women's equality in the name of progress and enlightened thought by stating:

> The slaves have been emancipated; now let us emancipate women! The unconditional and universal and immediate emancipation of womanhood is the demand of the age in which we live; it is the demand of the spirit of our institutions; it is the demand of the teachings of Christianity; it is her right, and, in the name of God, let us start a wave of influence in this country that shall be felt in every State, every county, every community, every home and every heart.[46]

The progressive aspects of feminist theology, as part of the liberal theological impulse of the age, appear most clearly when counterposed to the image of women and the church presented in Ann Douglas's *The Feminization of American Culture* (1977). Douglas portrays the disestablished, non-evangelical clergy of the Northeast as anti-intellectual and misogynist. The clergy, like the predominantly female laity, occupied a position marginal to government and to an increasingly industrialized and urbanized America. According to Douglas, the clergy and the female laity worked together to feminize religion and to produce an ever-growing number of ministers who preferred to read fiction and poetry rather than think and develop theological scholarship. Worse yet, Douglas found women in these northeastern churches unable and also disinclined to provide a polemical theology to counter the sentimentalism and consumerism that finally engulfed them all.[47]

Late nineteenth-century feminist theological writings call into question generalizations of an insipid, anti-intellectual religious tradition. The contribution of black Baptist women is especially noteworthy, for they were farthest removed from the American political-economic structure. Yet it was through the church, and specifically the black Baptist convention movement, that they established an arena for discussion, debate, and implementation of their social, economic, and political agenda vis-à-vis white America.[48] If the National Baptist Convention symbolized a deliberative arena for people denied access to electoral and other strong secular institutions, black women were most responsible for expanding the true meaning of its "representative" character.

Feminist theology had significant implications for black Baptist women's future work. It buttressed their demand for more vocal participation and infused their growing ranks with optimism about the dawning twentieth century. It also encouraged women to establish and control their own separate conventions at the state and national levels. Black Baptist women did not, in the end, demand a radical break with all the sexist limitations of their church, but they were surely ingenious in fashioning the Bible as an "iconoclastic weapon" for their particular cause. The feminist theologians had operated "from a stance of 'radical obedience.'" And indeed it was this vantage of orthodoxy that compelled the brethren to listen.

NOTES

1. Peter Randolph, *From Slave Cabin to the Pulpit: The Autobiography of Rev. Peter Randolph* (Boston: James H. Earle, 1893), 89. Charles O. Boothe, *The Cyclopedia of the Colored Baptists of Alabama* (Birmingham: Alabama Publishing, 1895), 252; also see Jacqueline Jones, *Labor of Love, Labor of Sorrow: Black Women, Work, and the Family from Slavery to the Present* (New York: Random House, 1985), 67.

2. Peter J. Paris, *The Social Teaching of the Black Churches* (Philadelphia: Fortress Press, 1985), 11–13.

3. Mary V. Cook, "Work for Baptist Women," in *The Negro Baptist Pulpit*, ed. Edward M. Brawley (Philadelphia: American Baptist Publication Society, 1890), 271–85; American National Baptist Convention (hereafter ANBC), *Journal and Lectures of the Second Anniversary of the 1887 American National Baptist Convention, Held with the Third Baptist Church, Mobile, Ala., August 25–28, 1887* (n.p., n.d.), 57.

4. Rosemary Ruether and Eleanor McLaughlin, eds., *Women of Spirit: Female Leadership in the Jewish and Christian Traditions* (New York: Simon and Schuster, 1979), 19; also see this argument applied to white women during the Second Great Awakening in Carroll Smith-Rosenberg, "The Cross and the Pedestal: Women, Anti-Ritualism, and the Emergence of the American Bourgeoisie," in *Disorderly Conduct: Visions of Gender in Victorian America* (New York: Oxford University Press, 1986), 129–64.

5. Rufus Perry traced the ancestry of black Americans to the biblical Cushites, who were the descendants of Cush, Ham's eldest son. According to Perry, the Cushites were the ancient Ethiopians and indigenous Egyptians whose history exemplified prowess in medicine, war, art, and religious thought. Identifying the Cushite leaders of the Bible, Perry considered the greatness of the African past to be the foundation stone of the African American's future. See Rufus L. Perry, *The Cushites, or the Descendants of Ham as Found in the Sacred Scriptures and in the Writings of Ancient Historians and Poets from Noah to the Christian Era* (Springfield, Mass.: Willey, 1893), 17–18, 158–61.

6. Caroline Walker Bynum, Stevan Harrell, and Paula Richman, eds., *Gender and Religion: On the Complexity of Symbols* (Boston: Beacon Press, 1986), 15–16.

7. Caroline Bynum argues similarly with regard to the appropriation and interpretation of symbols: "Even when men and women have used the same symbols and rituals, they may have invested them with different meanings and different ways of meaning." *Gender and Religion*, 16; also Rita Felski, *Beyond Feminist Aesthetics: Feminist Literature and Social Change* (Cambridge, Mass.: Harvard University Press, 1989), 161–62, 179.

8. Marilyn Richardson, ed., *Maria W. Stewart: America's First Black Woman Political Writer* (Bloomington: Indiana University Press, 1987), 9.

9. Richardson, *Maria W. Stewart*, 70.

10. See Kathleen Berkeley's discussion of the Broughton case. Berkeley argues that the case was more than simply one of gender discrimination, but a power struggle between the white superintendent of

schools and a black member of the school board. Kathleen C. Berkeley, "The Politics of Black Education in Memphis, Tennessee, 1868–1891," in *Southern Cities, Southern Schools: Public Education in the Urban South,* ed. Rick Ginsberg and David N. Plank (Westport, Conn.: Greenwood Press, 1990), 215–17.

11. Broughton was elected to office in the Woman's Convention, Auxiliary of the National Baptist Convention, U.S.A., when it was organized in 1900. She held the office of recording secretary in this organization, which represented more than one million black women across the United States. See National Baptist Convention, *Journal of the Twentieth Annual Session of the National Baptist Convention, Held in Richmond, Virginia, September 12–17, 1900* (Nashville: National Baptist Publishing Board, 1900), 195–96. See also Thomas O. Fuller, *History of the Negro Baptists of Tennessee* (Memphis: Haskins Print–Roger Williams College, 1936), 238.

12. Virginia Broughton, *Women's Work, as Gleaned from the Women of the Bible, and Bible Women of Modern Times* (Nashville: National Baptist Publishing Board, 1904), 3, 23, 36.

13. I. Garland Penn, *The Afro-American Press and Its Editors* (Springfield, Mass.: Willey, 1891), 367–74; G. R. Richings, *Evidences of Progress among Colored People,* 12th ed. (Philadelphia: Geo. S. Ferguson, 1905), 224–27; Charles H. Parrish, ed., *Golden Jubilee of the General Association of Colored Baptists in Kentucky* (Louisville: Mayes, 1915), 284–85; State University Catalogue, 1883–1884, Simmons University Records, Archives Department, University of Louisville.

14. Brawley, ed., *The Negro Baptist Pulpit,* 271–86; ANBC, *Journal and Lectures, 1887,* 49.

15. Penn, *The Afro-American Press,* 376–81.

16. See Mary Cook's eulogy of Lucy Wilmot Smith in *Home Mission Echo* (January 1890): 4–5; Penn, *Afro-American Press,* 378–81; Woman's American Baptist Home Mission Society (hereafter WABHMS), *Twelfth Annual Report of the Woman's American Baptist Home Mission Society with the Report of the Annual Meeting, Held in the First Baptist Church, Hartford, Connecticut, May 7–8, 1890* (Boston: C. H. Simonds, 1890), 26.

17. Gordon D. Kaufman, *Systematic Theology: An Historicist Perspective* (New York: Charles Scribner's Sons, 1968), 57.

18. Virginia W. Broughton, *Twenty Years' Experience of a Missionary* (Chicago: Pony Press, 1907), 32.

19. *Minutes of the Baptist Women's Educational Convention of Kentucky. First, Second, Third, Fourth, Fifth Sessions, 1883–1887* (Louisville: National Publishing, 1887), 13.

20. Miss M. O'Keefe to Mary Burdette, 4 April 1891, Mary Burdette File, Correspondence 1891–1898, WABHMS Archives, American Baptist Archives Center, Valley Forge, Pa.

21. See report of Mary Burdette, "Our Southern Field," *Tidings* (January 1894): 9.

22. Mary Cook stated: "As the Bible is an iconoclastic weapon—it is bound to break down images of error that have been raised. As no one studies it so closely as the Baptists, their women shall take the lead." ANBC, *Journal and Lectures, 1887,* 49.

23. See introduction by Sue E. Houchins, *Spiritual Narratives* (New York: Oxford University Press, 1988), xxxii. *Spiritual Narratives* includes Virginia Broughton's autobiography, *Twenty Years' Experience of a Missionary,* along with those of Maria Stewart, Jarena Lee, Julia A. J. Foote, and Ann Plato.

24. ANBC, *Journal and Lectures, 1887,* 53–54; also see the evaluation of woman's influence by black Baptist minister William Bishop Johnson, editor of *The National Baptist Magazine,* when he stated: "Man may lead unnumbered hosts to victory, he may rend kingdoms, convulse nations, and drench battlefields in blood, but woman with heavenly smiles and pleasant words can outnumber, outweigh, and outstrip the noblest efforts of a generation." William Bishop Johnson, *The Scourging of a Race, and Other Sermons and Addresses* (Washington, D.C.: Beresford Printer, 1904), 78.

25. Broughton, *Women's Work,* 5–7.

26. Broughton, *Women's Work,* 11–16.

27. Broughton, *Women's Work,* 25.

28. Mary Cook described Mary, the mother of Jesus, as "non-excelled maternal devotion." See ANBC, *Journal and Lectures, 1887,* 47–48.

29. Broughton, *Twenty Years' Experience,* 48–51.

30. Broughton, *Twenty Years' Experience,* 42–45, 48.

31. Representative of the cult of domesticity, Oldham's version of home life advocated woman's complete attentiveness to her husband's needs. See ANBC, *Journal, Sermons, and Lectures of the Third Anniversary of*

the American National Baptist Convention, Held with the Spruce Street Baptist Church, Nashville, September 23–24, 1888 (n.p., n.d.), 88, 90.

32. ANBC, *Journal and Lectures, 1887,* 48; Broughton, *Women's Work,* 31–32; Brawley, ed., *Negro Baptist Pulpit,* 273.

33. Broughton, *Twenty Years' Experience,* 46–47. Sue Houchins argues that Broughton and women like her drew confidence to transcend prescriptive gender roles from belief in the "privileged nature of their relationship with God." See introduction by Houchins, *Spiritual Narratives,* xxxiii.

34. The argument that attempted to restrict Paul's words exclusively to "immoral" women of Corinth was used by both black and white advocates of greater church roles for women. See, for example, Frances Willard, *Women in the Pulpit* (Boston: D. Lothrop, 1888), 159, 164; ANBC, *Journal and Lectures, 1887,* 48–50.

35. ANBC, *Journal and Lectures, 1887,* 49–50.

36. Broughton restricted women in these three cases since none of the twelve apostles had been women. Otherwise, she sought to encourage women by noting that of the seventy who followed Jesus, "we are not sure they were all men." A classic rejoinder to those who shared Broughton's view on the twelve apostles was Frances Willard's statement that no black or Gentile had been among the twelve, but this did not restrict men of either group from seeking ordination to the ministry. See Broughton, *Women's Work,* 39–41; Broughton, "Woman's Work," *National Baptist Magazine* (January 1894): 35; Willard, *Woman in the Pulpit,* 35.

37. Olive Bird Clanton was raised in Decatur, Illinois, where she obtained a high school education. Her husband was elected secretary of the American National Baptist Convention in 1886. In a biographical sketch of Solomon Clanton, William J. Simmons, then president of the American National Baptist Convention, described Olive Clanton as "one of the most discreet, amiable, and accomplished women in the country." See William J. Simmons, *Men of Mark: Eminent, Progressive and Rising* (Cleveland: Geo. M. Rewell, 1887), 419–21; ANBC, *Journal and Lectures, 1887,* 56–57.

38. ANBC, *Journal and Lectures, 1887,* 46, 55.

39. ANBC, *Minutes and Addresses of the American National Baptist Convention, Held at St. Louis, Mo., August 25–29, 1886 in the First Baptist Church* (Jackson, Miss.: J. J. Spelman, 1886), 68–74.

40. ANBC, *Journal and Lectures, 1887,* 50–53, 55–56.

41. ANBC, *Journal and Lectures, 1887,* 47; Broughton, *Women's Work,* 27–28.

42. ANBC, *Journal and Lectures, 1887,* 55–56.

43. Anthony Binga does not describe women outside the role of homemaker; William Bishop Johnson contended that men did not give women their proper estimation in society, and yet he also assigned to man the qualities of "understanding" and "mind," and to woman, "will" and "soul." See Binga, *Sermons,* 293; Johnson, *Scourging of a Race,* 76.

44. See the response of black club women to the *Virginia Baptist* articles in "Editorial—Woman's Place," *The Woman's Era,* 1 (September 1894).

45. Penn, *Afro-American Press,* 370, 378; Brawley, *Negro Baptist Pulpit,* 279–81; Simmons, *Men of Mark,* 39–63, 729–32, 1059–63; Richings, *Evidences of Progress,* 222–24.

46. J. Francis Robinson, "The Importance of Women's Influence in All Religious and Benevolent Societies," *National Baptist Magazine* (November-December 1899): 117, 120–21.

47. Douglas, *Feminization of American Culture,* 3–48, 130–39, 168–81.

48. Boothe, *Cyclopedia of the Colored Baptists,* 252; Simmons, *Men of Mark,* 730; DeBaptiste, "Ministerial Education," 243–46; Brawley, ed., *Negro Baptist Pulpit,* 5–9, 19–23.

"Prejudice against the Colored Man"

❧

Theodore S. Wright

Reverend Theodore S. Wright was an African American minister in New York City and an active Abolitionist. This address was delivered before the New York Antislavery Society in 1837.

❧

Mr. President, with much feeling do I rise to address the society on this resolution, and I should hardly have been induced to have done it had I not been requested. I confess I am personally interested in this resolution. But were it not for the fact that none can feel the lash but those who have it upon them, that none know where the chain galls but those who wear it, I would not address you.

This is a serious business, sir. The prejudice which exists against the colored man, the free man is like the atmosphere, everywhere felt by him. It is true that in these United States and in this State, there are men, like myself, colored with the skin like my own, who are not subjected to the lash, who are not liable to have their wives and their infants torn from them; from whose hand the Bible is not taken. It is true that we may walk abroad; we may enjoy our domestic comforts, our families; retire to the closet; visit the sanctuary, and may be permitted to urge on our children and our neighbors in well doing. But sir, still we are slaves—everywhere we feel the chain galling us. It is by that prejudice which the resolution condemns, the spirit of slavery, the law which has been enacted here, by a corrupt public sentiment, through the influence of slavery which treats moral agents different from the rule of God, which treats them irrespective of their morals or intellectual cultivation. This spirit is withering all our hopes, and ofttimes causes the colored parent as he looks upon his child, to wish he had never been born. Often is the heart of the colored mother, as she presses her child to her bosom, filled with sorrow to think that, by reason of this prejudice, it is cut off from all hopes of usefulness in this land. Sir, this prejudice is wicked.

If the nation and church understood this matter, I would not speak a word about that killing influence that destroys the colored man's reputation. This influence cuts us off from everything; it follows us up from childhood to manhood; it excludes us from all stations of profit, usefulness and honor; takes away from us all motive for pressing forward in enterprises, useful and important to the world and to ourselves.

In the first place, it cuts us off from the advantages of the mechanic arts almost entirely. A colored man can hardly learn a trade, and if he does it is difficult for him to find any one who will employ him to work at the trade, in any part of the State. In most of our large cities there are associations of mechanics who legislate out of their society colored men. And in many cases where our young men have learned trades, they have had to come to low employments for want of encouragement in those trades.

It must be a matter of rejoicing to know that in this vicinity colored fathers and mothers have the privileges of education. It must be a matter of rejoicing that in this vicinity colored parents can have their children trained up in schools—at present, we find the colleges barred against them.

I will say nothing about the inconvenience which I have experienced myself, and which every man of color experiences, though made in the image of God. I will say nothing about the inconvenience of traveling; how are we frowned upon and despised. No matter how we may demean ourselves, we find embarrassments everywhere.

But sir, this prejudice goes farther. It debars men from heaven. While sir, slavery cuts off the colored portion of the community from religious privileges, men are made infidels. What, they demand, is your Christianity? How do you regard your brethren? How do you treat them at the Lord's table? Where is your consistency in talking about the heathen, traversing the ocean to circulate the Bible everywhere, while you frown upon them at the door? These things meet us and weigh down our spirits.

And, sir, the constitution of society, molded by this prejudice, destroys souls. I have known extensively, that in revivals which have been blessed and enjoyed in this part of the country, the colored population were overlooked. I recollect an instance. The Lord God was pouring out His Spirit. He was entering every house, and sinners were converted. I asked, Where is the colored man? Where is my brother? Where is my sister? Who is feeling for him or her? Who is weeping for them? Who is endeavoring to pull them out of the fire? No reply was made. I was asked to go round with one of the elders and visit them. We went and they humbled themselves. The Church commenced efficient efforts, and God blessed them as soon as they began to act for these people as though they had souls.

And sir, the manner in which our churches are regulated destroys souls. Whilst the church is thrown open to everybody, and one says come, come in and share the blessings of the sanctuary, this is the gate of heaven—he says to the colored man, *be careful where you take your stand*. I know an efficient church in this State, where a respectable colored man went to the house of God, and was going to take a seat in the gallery, and one of the officers contended with him, and said, "You cannot go there, sir."

In one place the people had come together to the house of the Lord. The sermon was preached—the emblems were about to be administered—and all at once the person who managed the church thought the value of the pews would be diminished if the colored people sat in them. They objected to their sitting there, and the colored people left and went into the gallery, and that, too, when they were thinking of handling the memorials of the broken body and shed blood of the Savior! And, sir, this prejudice follows the colored man everywhere, and depresses his spirits.

Thanks be to God, there is a buoyant principle which elevates the poor down-trodden colored man above all this—it is that there is society which regards man according to his worth; it is the fact, that when he looks up to Heaven he knows that God treats him like a moral agent, irrespective of caste or the circumstances in which he may be placed. Amid the embarrassments which he has to meet, and the scorn and contempt that is heaped upon him, he is cheered by the hope that he will be disenthralled, and soon, like a bird set forth from its cage, wing his flight to Jesus, where he can be happy, and look down with pity on the man who despises the poor slave for being what God made him, and who despises him because he is identified with the poor slave. Blessed be God for the principles of the Gospel. Were it not for these, and for the fact that a better day is dawning, I would not wish to live. Blessed be God for the antislavery movement. Blessed be God that there is a war waging with slavery, that the granite rock is about to be rolled from its base. But as long as the colored man is to be looked upon as an inferior caste, so long will they disregard his cries, his groans, his shrieks.

I rejoice, sir, in this Society; and I deem the day when I joined this Society as one of the proudest days of my life. And I know I can die better, in more peace today, to know there are men who will plead the cause of my children.

Let me, through you, sir, request this delegation to take hold of this subject. This will silence the slaveholder, when he says where is your love for the slave? Where is your love for the colored man who is crushed at your feet? Talking to us about emancipating our slaves when you are enslaving them by your feelings, and doing more violence to them by your prejudice, than we are to our slaves by our treatment. They call on us to evince our love for the slave, by treating man as man, the colored man as a man, according to his worth.

"The Sin of Slavery and Its Remedy"

Elizur Wright

Elizur Wright was a professor of science and mathematics at Western Reserve College, and for many years he was active in the Abolitionist movement. This selection is excerpted from a pamphlet published in 1833.

INTRODUCTION

The American revolution was incomplete. It left one sixth part of the population the victims of a servitude immeasurably more debasing than that from which it delivered the rest. While this nation held up its Declaration of Independence—its noble bill of human rights, before an admiring world, in one hand; it mortified the friends of humanity, by oppressing the poor and defenseless with the other. The progress of time has not lessened the evil. There are now held in involuntary and perpetual slavery, in the southern half of this republic, more than two million men, women, and children, guarded with a vigilance, which strives, and with success appalling as it is complete, to shut out every ray of knowledge, human and divine, and reduce them as nearly as possible to a level with the brutes. These miserable slaves are not only compelled to labor without choice and without hire, but they are subjected to the cruelty and lust of their masters to an unbounded extent. In the northern states there is very generally a sympathy with the slaveholders, and a prejudice against the slaves, which shows itself in palliating the crime of slaveholding, and in most unrighteously disregarding the rights, and vilifying the characters of the free colored men.

At the same time, slavery, as a system, is (in a certain sense) condemned. It is confessed to be a great evil, "a moral evil," and when the point is urged, *a sin*. The slaves, it is admitted, have rights—every principle of honesty, justice, and humanity, *"in the abstract,"* calls aloud that they should be made free. The word of God is in their favor. Indeed, there is no ground claimed by the abettors of slavery, on which they pretend to justify it for a moment, but a supposed—a begged—*expediency*, baseless as the driven clouds. I say baseless, for while not a single fact has ever been produced, going to show the danger of putting the slaves, all at once, under the protection of law, and employing them as free laborers, there have been produced, on the other side, varied and fair experiments showing, that it is altogether safe and profitable.

IMMEDIATE ABOLITION

Under the government of God, as exhibited in this world, there is but one remedy for sin, and that is available only by a *repentance,* evidenced by reformation. There is no such thing as holding on to sin with safety. It is not only to be renounced, but the very occasions of it are to be avoided at whatever sacrifice. If thy right hand cause thee to offend, cut it off—if thy right eye, pluck it out. The dearest human relationships are to be broken through when they interfere with the relation which a man bears to God, and through him to his rational creatures. This being the case, we might naturally expect that the entire agency which God has provided to reclaim the world should be adapted to produce *immediate repentance.* It certainly is so if we take the testimony of the Bible. . . . The doctrine of the immediate abolition of slavery asks no better authority than is offered by scripture. It is in perfect harmony with the letter and spirit of God's word.

The doctrine may be thus briefly stated. It is the duty of the holders of slaves immediately to restore to them their liberty, and to extend to them the full protection of law, as well as its control. It is their duty equitably to restore to them those profits of their labor, which have been wickedly wrested away, especially by giving them that moral and mental instruction—that education, which alone can render any considerable accumulation of property a blessing. It is their duty to employ them as voluntary laborers, on equitable wages. Also, it is the duty of all men to proclaim this doctrine—to urge upon slaveholders *immediate emancipation,* so long as there is a slave—to agitate the consciences of tyrants, so long as there is a tyrant on the globe.

Though this doctrine does not depend, in regard to the slaveholder, upon the safety of immediate emancipation, nor, in regard to the nonslaveholder, on the prospect of accomplishing any abolition at all, but upon the commands of God, yet I shall attempt to establish it upon those lower grounds. I am willing to rest the cause on the truth of the following propositions.

1. The instant abolition of the whole slave system is safe, and the substitution of a free labor system is safe, practicable and profitable.
2. The firm expression of an enlightened public opinion, on the part of nonslaveholders, in favor of instant abolition, is an effectual, and the only effectual means of securing abolition in any time whatsoever.

from *Christianity and the Social Crisis*

❧

Walter Rauschenbusch

Walter Rauschenbusch, 1861–1918, was a Baptist clergyman and later professor of church history. His understanding of social problems and their relation to religion was partly stimulated by encounters with European socialist movements. These selections come from his widely read 1907 book *Christianity and the Social Crisis,* a book which influenced, among many others, Martin Luther King and Reinhold Niehbuhr.

❧

SOLIDARITY AND COMMUNISM

It is assumed as almost self-evident in popular thought that communism is impracticable and inefficient, an antiquated method of the past or a dream of Utopian schemers, a system of society sure to impede economic development and to fetter individual liberty and initiative. Thus we flout what was the earliest basis of civilization for the immense majority of mankind and the moral ideal of Christendom during the greater part of its history. Communistic ownership and management of the fundamental means of production was the rule in primitive society, and large remnants of it have survived to our day. For fifteen centuries and more it was the common consent of Christendom that private property was due to sin, and that the ideal life involved fraternal sharing. The idea underlying the monastic life was that men left the sinful world and established an ideal community, and communism was an essential feature of every monastic establishment. The progressive heretical movements in the Middle Ages also usually involved an attempt to get closer to the communistic ideal. It is a striking proof how deeply the ideas of the Church have always been affected by the current secular thought, that our modern individualism has been able to wipe this immemorial Christian social ideal out of the mind of the modern Church almost completely.

The assumption that communistic ownership was a hindrance to progress deserves very critical scrutiny. It is part of that method of writing history which exalted the doings of kings and slighted the life of the people. For the grasping arm of the strong, communistic institutions were indeed a most objectionable hindrance, but to the common man they were the strongest bulwark of his independence and vigor. Within the shelter of the old-fashioned village community, which constituted a social unit for military protection, economic production, morality, and religion, the individual could enjoy his life with some fearlessness. The peasant who stood alone was at the

64

mercy of his lord. Primitive village communism was not freely abandoned as an inefficient system, but was broken up by the covetousness of the strong and selfish members of the community, and by the encroachments of the upper classes who wrested the common pasture and forest and game from the peasant communities. Its disappearance nearly everywhere marked a decline in the prosperity and moral vigor of the peasantry and was felt by them to be a calamity and a step in their enslavement.

But we need not go back into history to get a juster verdict on the practicability and usefulness of communism. We have the material right among us. Ask any moral teacher who is scouting communism and glorifying individualism, what social institutions today are most important for the moral education of mankind and most beneficent in their influence on human happiness, and he will probably reply promptly, "The home, the school, and the church." But these three are communistic institutions. The home is the source of most of our happiness and goodness, and in the home we live communistically. Each member of the family has some private property, clothes, letters, pictures, toys; but the rooms and the furniture in the main are common to all, and if one member needs the private property of another, there is ready sharing. The income of the members is more or less turned into a common fund; food is prepared and eaten in common; the larger family undertakings are planned in common. The housewife is the manager of a successful communistic colony, and it is perhaps not accidental that our women, who move thus within a fraternal organization, are the chief stays of our Christianity. Similarly our public schools are supported on a purely communistic basis; those who have no children or whose children are grown up, are nevertheless taxed for the education of the children of the community. The desks, the books to some extent, the flowers and decorations, are common property, and it is the aim of the teachers to develop the communistic spirit in the children, though they may not call it by that name. Our churches, too, are voluntary communisms. A number of people get together, have a common building, common seats, common hymnbooks and Bibles, support a pastor in common, and worship, learn, work, and play in common. They are so little individualistic that they fairly urge others to come in and use their property. Private pews and similar encroachments of private property within this communistic institution are now generally condemned as contrary to the spirit of the Church, while every new step to widen the communistic serviceableness of the churches is greeted with a glow of enthusiasm.

Thus the three great institutions on which we mainly depend to train the young to a moral life and to make us all good, wise, and happy, are essentially communistic, and their success and efficiency depend on the continued mastery of the spirit of solidarity and brotherhood within them. It is nothing short of funny to hear the very men who ceaselessly glorify the home, the school, and the church, turn around and abuse communism.

It can fairly be maintained, too, that the State, another great moral agent, is communistic in its very nature. It is the organization by which the people administer their common property and attend to their common interests. It is safe to say that at least a fourth of the land in a modern city is owned by the city and communistically used for free streets and free parks. Our modern State is the outcome of a long development toward communism. Warfare and military defense were formerly the private affair of the nobles; they are now the business of the entire nation. Roads and bridges used to be owned largely by private persons or corporations, and toll charged for their use; they are now communistic with rare exceptions. Putting out fires used to be left to private enterprise; today our fire departments are communistic. Schools used to be private; they are now public. Great men formerly had private parks and admitted the public as a matter of favor; the people now have public parks and admit the great men as a matter of right. The right of jurisdiction was formerly often an appurtenance of the great landowners; it is now controlled by the people. The public spirit and foresight of one of the greatest of all Americans, Benjamin Franklin, early made the postal service of our country a communistic institution of ever-increasing magnitude and usefulness. In no case in which communistic ownership has firmly established itself is there any desire to recede from it. The unrest and dissatisfaction is all at those points where the State is not yet communistic. The waterworks in most of our cities are owned and operated by the community, and there is never more than local and temporary dissatisfaction about this great necessity of life, because any genuine complaint by the people as users of water can be promptly remedied by the people as suppliers of water. On the other hand, the clamor of public complaint about the gas, the electric power and light, and the street railway service, which are commonly supplied by private companies, is incessant and increasing. While the railway lines were competing, they wasted on needless parallel roads enough capital to build a comfortable home for every family in the country. Now that they have nearly ceased to compete, the grievances of their monopoly are among the gravest problems of our national life. The competitive duplication of plant and labor by our express companies is folly, and their exorbitant charges are a drag on the economic welfare and the common comfort of our whole nation. This condition continues not because of their efficiency, but because of their sinister influence on Congress. They are an economic anachronism.

Thus the State, too, is essentially a communistic institution. It has voluntarily limited its functions and left many things to private initiative. The political philosophy of the nineteenth century constantly preached to the State that the best State was that which governed least, just as the best child was that which moved least. Yet it has almost imperceptibly gathered to itself many of the functions which were formerly exercised by private undertakings, and there is no desire anywhere to turn public education, fire protection, sanitation, or the supply of water over to private concerns. But the distinctively modern utilities, which have been invented or perfected during the reign of capitalism and during the prevalence of individualistic political theories, have been seized and appropriated by private concerns. The railways, the street railways, the telegraph and telephone, electric power and light, gas—these are all modern. The swift hand of capitalism seized them and has exploited them to its immense profit. Other countries have long ago begun to draw these modern public necessities within the communistic functions of the State. In our country a variety of causes, good and bad, have combined to check that process; but the trend is manifestly in the direction of giving state communism a wider sweep hereafter.

Private ownership is not a higher stage of social organization which has finally and forever superseded communism, but an intermediate and necessary stage of social evolution between two forms of communism. At a certain point in the development of property primitive communism becomes unworkable, and a higher form of communism has not yet been wrought out; consequently men manage as best they can with private ownership. To take a simple illustration: on the farm or in a country village the creek is common property for bathing purposes; the "swimmin'-hole" is the communistic bathtub for all who want to refresh their cuticle. As the village grows, the march of the houses drives the bathers farther out; the pervasiveness of the "eternally feminine" robs the boys of their bath; the primitive communism of the water ceases. Some families now are wealthy enough to install private bathtubs and have the increased privilege of bathing all the year around. The bulk of the people in the cities have no bathing facilities at all. At last an agitation arises for a public bath. A beginning is made with enclosed river-baths, perhaps, or with shower-baths. At last a plunge-bath is built and opened summer and winter. The bathing instinct of the community revives and increasingly centers about the public bath. The communism of the water has returned. From the communistic swimming hole to the marble splendor of the communistic bath the way lay through the individualistic tub of the wealthy and the unwashed deprivations of the mass. In the same way there is no need of parks in primitive society, because all nature is open. As cities grow up, the country recedes; a few are wealthy enough to surround their homes with lawns and trees; the mass are shut off from nature and suffocate amid brick and asphalt. Then comes the new communal ownership and enjoyment of nature: first the small square in the city; then the large park on the outskirts; then the distant park on the seashore or by the river and lake; and finally the state or national reservation where wildlife is kept intact for those who want to revert to it. Thus we pass from communism to communism in our means of enjoyment, and that community will evidently be wisest which most quickly sees that the old and simple means of pleasure are passing, and will provide the corresponding means for the more complex and artificial community which is evolving. The longer it lingers in the era of private self-help, the longer will the plain people be deprived of their heritage, and the more completely will the wealthy minority preempt the means of enjoyment for themselves.

Everywhere communism in new forms and on a vaster scale is coming back to us. The individualistic pump in the backyard is gone; the city waterworks are the modern counterpart of the communistic village well to which Rebekah and Rachel came to fill their water jar. The huge irrigation scheme of our national government in the West is an enlarged duplicate of the tanks built by many a primitive community. The railway train carrying people or supplies is a modernized form of the tribe breaking camp and carrying its women and children and cattle and tents to better grazing or hunting grounds. Compared with the old private vehicle, the railway carriage is a triumphant demonstration of communism. Almost the only private thing about our railways is the dividends. The competitive individualism of commerce is being restricted within ever-narrower limits. State supervision and control is a partial assertion of the supremacy of communistic interests. It is probably only a question of time when the private management of public necessities will be felt to be impossible and antiquated, and the community will begin to experiment seriously with the transportation of people and goods, and with the public supply of light and heat and cold.

How far this trend toward communistic ownership is to go, the common sense of the future will have to determine. It is entirely misleading to frighten us with the idea that communism involves a complete abolition of private property. Even in the most individualistic society there is, as we have seen, a large ingredient of communism, and in the most socialistic society there will always be a large ingredient of private property. No one supposes that a man's toothbrush, his love letters, or the shirt on his back would ever be common property. Socialists are probably quite right in maintaining that the amount of private property *per capita* in a prosperous socialist community would be much larger than it is now. It seems unlikely even that all capital used in production will ever be communistic in ownership and operation; a socialistic State could easily afford to allow individuals to continue some private production, just as handicraft lingers now amid machine production. It will never be a question of having either private property absolute or communism absolute; it will always be a question of having more communism or less.

The question then confronts Christian men singly and the Christian Church collectively, whether they will favor and aid this trend toward communism, or oppose it. Down to modern times, as we have seen, the universal judgment of Christian thought was in favor of communism as more in harmony with the genius of Christianity and with the classical precedents of its early social life. Simultaneously with the rise of capitalism that conviction began to fade out. Protestantism especially, by its intimate alliance with the growing cities and the rising business class, has been individualistic in its theories of Christian society. The question is now, how quickly Christian thought will realize that individualism is coming to be an inadequate and antiquated form of social organization which must give place to a higher form of communistic organization, and how thoroughly it will comprehend that this new communism will afford a far nobler social basis for the spiritual temple of Christianity.

For there cannot really be any doubt that the spirit of Christianity has more affinity for a social system based on solidarity and human fraternity than for one based on selfishness and mutual antagonism. In competitive industry one man may profit through the ruin of others; in cooperative production the wealth of one man would depend on the growing wealth of all. In competitive society each man strives for himself and his family only, and the sense of larger duties is attenuated and feeble; in communistic society no man could help realizing that he is part of a great organization, and that he owes it duty and loyalty. Competition tends to make good men selfish; cooperation would compel selfish men to develop public spirit. The moral and wholesome influences in society today proceed from the communistic organizations within it; the divisive, anarchic, and destructive influences which are racking our social body today proceed from those realms of social life which are individualistic and competitive. Business life today is organized in growing circles within which a certain amount of cooperation and mutual helpfulness exists, and to that extent it exerts a sound moral influence. Insofar as it is really competitive, it engenders covetousness, cunning, hardness, selfish satisfaction in success, or resentment and despair in failure. It is a marvelous demonstration of the vitality of human goodness that a system so calculated to bring out the evil traits in us, still leaves so much human kindness and nobility alive. But the Christian temper of mind, the honest regard for the feelings and the welfare of others, the desire to make our life serve the common good, would get its first chance to control our social life in a society organized on the basis of solidarity and cooperation.

It would seem, therefore, that one of the greatest services which Christianity could render to humanity in the throes of the present transition would be to aid those social forces which are making for the increase of communism. The Church should help public opinion to understand clearly the difference between the moral qualities of the competitive and the communistic principle, and enlist religious enthusiasm on behalf of that which is essentially Christian. Christian individuals should strengthen and protect the communistic institutions already in existence in society and help them to extend their functions. For instance, the public schools can increasingly be made nuclei of common life for the district within which they are located, gathering the children for play out of school hours, and the adults for instruction, discussion, and social pleasure in the evenings. The usefulness of the public parks as centers of communal life can be immensely extended by encouraging and organizing the play of the children and by holding regular public festivals. Simply to induce the crowd listening to a band concert in the park to join in singing a patriotic song, would convert a mass of listening individuals into a social organism thrilled with a common joy and sensible of its cohesion. Public ownership of the great public utilities would be desirable for the education it would give in solidarity, if for no other reason. Even if a street railway should be run at a loss for a time under city management, it would at least draw the people closer together by the sense of common proprietorship and would teach them to work better together to overcome the trouble. Every step taken in industrial life to give the employees some proprietary rights in the business, and anything placing owners and employees on a footing of human equality, would deserve commendation and help.

The Christian spirit of fraternity should create fraternal social institutions, and the fraternal institutions may in turn be trusted to breed and spread the fraternal spirit. It is a most hopeful fact that the communistic features of our government are awakening in some public officials a wholehearted and farseeing devotion to the public welfare. A number of our public health officers have thrown themselves into the crusade against tuberculosis and infant mortality with a zeal more farsighted and chivalrous than is usually called out in the ordinary doctor who cures patients on the individualistic plan. When men at the head of some department of city government realize the immense latent capacity of their department to serve the people, they are fired with ambition to do what they see can be done. Their natural ambition to make themselves felt, to exert power and get honor, runs in the same direction with the public needs. Such men are still scarce, but they are a prophecy of the kind of character which may be created in a communistic society and of the power of enthusiastic work which may hereafter be summoned to the service of the people. The vast educational work done by some departments of our national government, for instance the Department of Agriculture, furnishes similar proof of what may be done when we abandon the policeman theory of government and adopt the family theory. Certainly it would be no betrayal of the Christian spirit to enter into a working alliance with this great tendency toward the creation of cooperative and communistic social institutions based on the broad principle of the brotherhood of men and the solidarity of their interests.

THE UPWARD MOVEMENT OF THE WORKING CLASS

In asking for faith in the possibility of a new social order, we ask for no Utopian delusion. We know well that there is no perfection for man in this life: there is only growth toward perfection. In personal religion we look with seasoned suspicion at anyone who claims to be holy and perfect, yet we always tell men to become holy and to seek perfection. We make it a duty to seek what is unattainable. We have the same paradox in the perfectibility of society. We shall never have a perfect social life, yet we must seek it with faith. We shall never abolish suffering. There will always be death and the empty chair and heart. There will always be the agony of love unreturned. Women will long for children and never press baby lips to their breast. Men will long for fame and miss it. Imperfect moral insight will work hurt in the best conceivable social order. The strong will always have the impulse to exert their strength, and no system can be devised which can keep them from crowding and jostling the weaker. Increased social refinement will bring increased sensitiveness to pain. An American may suffer as much distress through a social slight as a Russian peasant under the knout. At best there is always but an approximation to a perfect social order. The kingdom of God is always but coming.

But every approximation to it is worthwhile. Every step toward personal purity and peace, though it only makes the consciousness of imperfection more poignant, carries its own exceeding great reward, and everlasting pilgrimage toward the kingdom of God is better than contented stability in the tents of wickedness.

And sometimes the hot hope surges up that perhaps the long and slow climb may be ending. In the past the steps of our race toward progress have been short and feeble, and succeeded by long intervals of sloth and apathy. But is that necessarily to remain the rate of advance? In the intellectual life there has been an unprecedented leap forward during the last hundred years. Individually we are not more gifted than our grandfathers, but collectively we have wrought out more epoch-making discoveries and inventions in one century than the whole race in the untold centuries that have gone before. If the twentieth century could do for us in the control of social forces what the nineteenth did for us in the control of natural forces, our grandchildren would live in a society that would be justified in regarding our present social life as semibarbarous. Since the

Reformation began to free the mind and to direct the force of religion toward morality, there has been a perceptible increase of speed. Humanity is gaining in elasticity and capacity for change, and every gain in general intelligence, in organizing capacity, in physical and moral soundness, and especially in responsiveness to ideal motives, again increases the ability to advance without disastrous reactions. The swiftness of evolution in our own country proves the immense latent perfectibility in human nature.

Last May a miracle happened. At the beginning of the week the fruit trees bore brown and greenish buds. At the end of the week they were robed in bridal garments of blossom. But for weeks and months the sap had been rising and distending the cells and maturing the tissues which were half ready in the fall before. The swift unfolding was the culmination of a long process. Perhaps these nineteen centuries of Christian influence have been a long preliminary stage of growth, and now the flower and fruit are almost here. If at this juncture we can rally sufficient religious faith and moral strength to snap the bonds of evil and turn the present unparalleled economic and intellectual resources of humanity to the harmonious development of a true social life, the generations yet unborn will mark this as that great day of the Lord for which the ages waited, and count us blessed for sharing in the apostolate that proclaimed it.

from *Rerum Novarum: "The Condition of Labor"*

❧

Pope Leo XIII

Leo XIII was pope from 1878–1903. In this 1878 document he stakes a ground for Catholic concern with the rights and conditions of working people, which is far in advance of the Church's medieval focus on issues of poverty and charity, yet explicitly distinct from the militant socialist movements of his time. In the twentieth century some Catholic thinkers and activists came much closer to socialist and Marxist perspectives, and relations to social radicalism became a divisive issue with the Church hierarchy itself.

❧

1. It is not surprising that the spirit of revolutionary change, which has long been predominant in the nations of the world, should have passed beyond politics and made its influence felt in the cognate field of practical economy. The elements of a conflict are unmistakable: the growth of industry, and the surprising discoveries of science; the changed relations of masters and workmen; the enormous fortunes of individuals and the poverty of the masses; the increased self-reliance and the closer mutual combination of the working population; and, finally, a general moral deterioration. The momentous seriousness of the present state of things just now fills every mind with painful apprehension; wise men discuss it; practical men propose schemes; popular meetings, legislatures, and sovereign princes, all are occupied with it—and there is nothing which has a deeper hold on public attention.

Therefore, venerable brethren, as on former occasions, when it seemed opportune to refute false teaching, we have addressed you in the interests of the Church and of the commonwealth, and have issued letters on political power, on human liberty, on the Christian constitution of the State, and on similar subjects, so now we have thought it useful to speak on

THE CONDITION OF LABOR

It is a matter on which we have touched once or twice already. But in this letter the responsibility of the apostolic office urges us to treat the question expressly and at length, in order that there may be no mistake as to the principles which truth and justice dictate for its settlement. The discussion is not easy, nor is it free from danger. It is not easy to define the relative rights and the mutual duties of the wealthy and of the poor, of capital and of labor. And the danger lies in this, that crafty agitators constantly make use of these disputes to pervert men's judgments and to stir up the people to sedition.

2. But all agree, and there can be no question whatever, that some remedy must be found, and quickly found, for the misery and wretchedness which press so heavily at this moment on the large majority of the very poor. The ancient workmen's guilds were destroyed in the last century, and no other organization took their place. Public institutions and the laws have repudiated the ancient religion. Hence by degrees it has come to pass that workingmen have been given over, isolated and defenseless, to the callousness of employers and the greed of unrestrained competition. The evil has been increased by rapacious usury, which, although more than once condemned by the Church, is nevertheless, under a different form but with the same guilt, still practiced by avaricious and grasping men. And to this must be added the custom of working by contract, and the concentration of so many branches of trade in the hands of a few individuals, so that a small number of very rich men have been able to lay upon the masses of the poor a yoke little better than slavery itself.

3. To remedy these evils the *socialists*, working on the poor man's envy of the rich, endeavor to destroy private property, and maintain that individual possessions should become the common property of all, to be administered by the State or by municipal bodies. They hold that, by thus transferring property from private persons to the community, the present evil state of things will be set to rights, because each citizen will then have his equal share of whatever there is to enjoy. But their proposals are so clearly futile for all practical purposes, that if they were carried out the workingman himself would be among the first to suffer. Moreover they are emphatically unjust, because they would rob the lawful possessor, bring the State into a sphere that is not its own, and cause complete confusion in the community.

JUSTICE TOWARD ALL

To the State the interests of all are equal whether high or low. The poor are members of the national community equally with the rich; they are real component parts, living parts, which make up, through the family, the living body; and it need hardly be said that they are by far the majority. It would be irrational to neglect one portion of the citizens and to favor another; and therefore the public administration must duly and solicitously provide for the welfare and the comfort of the working people, or else that law of justice will be violated which ordains that each shall have his due. To cite the wise words of Thomas Aquinas: "As the part and the whole are in a certain sense identical, the part may in some sense claim what belongs to the whole."[1] Among the many and grave duties of rulers who would do their best for their people, the first and chief is to act with strict justice—with that justice which is called in the schools *distributive*—toward each and every class.

But although all citizens, without exception, can and ought to contribute to that common good in which individuals share so profitably to themselves, yet it is not to be supposed that all can contribute in the same way and to the same extent. No matter what changes may be made in forms of government, there will always be differences and inequalities of condition in the State. Society cannot exist or be conceived without them. Some there must be who dedicate themselves to the work of the commonwealth, who make the laws, who administer justice, whose advice and authority govern the nation in times of peace, and defend it in war. Such men clearly occupy the foremost place in the State, and should be held in the foremost estimation, for their work touches most nearly and effectively the general interests of the community. Those who labor at a trade or calling do not promote the general welfare in such a fashion as this; but they do in the most important way benefit the nation, though less directly. We have insisted that, since it is the end of society to make men better, the chief good that society can be possessed of is virtue. Nevertheless, in all well-constituted States it is by no means an unimportant matter to provide those bodily and external commodities, "the use of which is necessary to virtuous action."[2] And in the provision of material well-being, the labor of the poor—the exercise of their skill and the employment of their strength in the culture of the land and the workshops of trade—is most efficacious and altogether indispensable. Indeed, their cooperation in this respect is so important that it may be truly said that it is only by the labor of the workingman that States grow rich. Justice, therefore, demands that the interests of the poorer population be carefully watched over by the administration, so that they who contribute so largely to the advantage of the community may themselves share in the benefits they create—that being housed, clothed, and enabled to support life, they may find their existence less hard and more endurable. It follows that whatever shall appear to be conducive to the well-being of those who work should receive favorable consideration. Let it not be feared that solicitude of this kind will injure any interest; on the contrary it will be to the advantage of all; for it cannot but be good for the commonwealth to secure from misery those on whom it so largely depends.

THE FIRST LAW OF GOVERNMENT

28. We have said that the State must not absorb the individual or the family; both should be allowed free and untrammelled action as far as is consistent with the common good and the interests of others. Nevertheless, rulers should anxiously safeguard the community and all its parts; the community, because the conservation of the community is so emphatically the business of the supreme power, that the safety of the commonwealth is not only the first law, but is a government's whole reason of existence; and the parts, because both philosophy and the Gospel agree in laying down that the object of the administration of the State should be not the advantage of the ruler, but the benefit of those over whom he rules. The gift of authority is from God, and is, as it were, a participation of the highest of all sovereignties; and it should be exercised as the power of God is exercised—with a fatherly solicitude which not only guides the whole but reaches to details as well.

Whenever the general interest of any particular class suffers, or is threatened with, evils which can in no other way be met, the public authority must step in to meet them.

29. Now, among the interests of the public, as of private individuals, are these: that peace and good order should be maintained; that family life should be carried on in accordance with God's laws and those of nature; that religion should be reverenced and obeyed; that a high standard of morality should prevail in public and private life; that the sanctity of justice should be respected, and that no one should injure another with impunity; that the members of the commonwealth should grow up to man's estate strong and robust, and capable, if need be, of guarding and defending their country. If by a strike, or other combination of workmen, there should be imminent danger of disturbance to the public peace; or if circumstances were such that among the laboring population the ties of family life were relaxed; if religion were found to suffer through the workmen not having time and opportunity to practice it; if in workshops and factories there were danger to morals through the mixing of the sexes or from any occasion of evil; or if employers laid burdens upon the workmen which were unjust, or degraded them with conditions that were repugnant to their dignity as human beings; finally, if health were endangered by excessive labor, or by work unsuited to sex or age—in these cases there can be no question that, within certain limits, it would be right to call in the help and authority of

the law. The limits must be determined by the nature of the occasion which calls for the law's interference—the principle being this, that the law must not undertake more, nor go further, than is required for the remedy of the evil or the removal of the danger.

THE RIGHT OF PROTECTION

Rights must be religiously respected wherever they are found; and it is the duty of the public authority to prevent and punish injury, and to protect each one in the possession of his own. Still, when there is question of protecting the rights of individuals, the poor and helpless have a claim to special consideration. The richer population have many ways of protecting themselves, and stand less in need of help from the State; those who are badly off have no resources of their own to fall back upon, and must chiefly rely upon the assistance of the State. And it is for this reason that wage earners, who are, undoubtedly, among the weak and necessitous, should be specially cared for and protected by the commonwealth.

30. Here, however, it will be advisable to advert expressly to one or two of the more important details.

It must be borne in mind that the chief thing to be secured is the safeguarding, by legal enactment and policy, of private property. Most of all it is essential in these times of covetous greed, to keep the multitude within the line of duty; for if all may justly strive to better their condition, yet neither justice nor the common good allows anyone to seize that which belongs to another, or, under the pretext of futile and ridiculous equality, to lay hands on other people's fortunes. It is most true that by far the larger part of the people who work prefer to improve themselves by honest labor rather than by doing wrong to others. But there are not a few who are imbued with bad principles and are anxious for revolutionary change, and whose great purpose it is to stir up tumult and bring about a policy of violence. The authority of the State should intervene to put restraint upon these disturbers, to save the workmen from their seditious arts, and to protect lawful owners from spoliation.

THE WORKMAN'S RIGHTS

31. When workpeople have recourse to a strike, it is frequently because the hours of labor are too long, or the work too hard, or because they consider their wages insufficient. The grave inconvenience of this not uncommon occurrence should be obviated by public remedial measures; for such paralysis of labor not only affects the masters and their workpeople, but is extremely injurious to trade, and to the general interests of the public; moreover, on such occasions, violence and disorder are generally not far off, and thus it frequently happens that the public peace is threatened. The laws should be made beforehand, and prevent these troubles from arising; they should lend their influence and authority to the removal in good time of the causes which lead to conflicts between masters and those whom they employ.

32. But if the owners of property must be made secure, the workman, too, has property and possessions in which he must be protected; and, first of all, there are his spiritual and mental interests. Life on earth, however good and desirable in itself, is not the final purpose for which man is created; it is only the way and the means to that attainment of truth, and that practice

of goodness in which the full life of the soul consists. It is the soul which is made after the image and likeness of God; it is in the soul that sovereignty resides, in virtue of which man is commanded to rule the creatures below him, and to use all the earth and ocean for his profit and advantage. "Fill the earth and subdue it; and rule over the fishes of the sea and the fowls of the air, and all living creatures which move upon the earth."[3] In this respect all men are equal; there is no difference between rich and poor, master and servant, ruler and ruled, "for the same is Lord over all."[4] No man may outrage with impunity that human dignity which God himself treats with reverence, nor stand in the way of that higher life which is the preparation for the eternal life of heaven. Nay, more; a man has here no power over himself. To consent to any treatment which is calculated to defeat the end and purpose of his being is beyond his right; he cannot give up his soul to servitude; for it is not man's own rights which are here in question, but the rights of God, most sacred and inviolable.

From this follows the obligation of the cessation of work and labor on Sundays and certain festivals. This rest from labor is not to be understood as mere idleness; much less must it be an occasion of spending money and a vicious excess, as many would desire it to be; but it should be rest from labor consecrated by religion. Repose united with religious observance disposes man to forget for awhile the business of this daily life, and to turn his thoughts to heavenly things and to the worship which he so strictly owes to the Eternal Deity. It is this, above all, which is the reason and motive for the Sunday rest; a rest sanctioned by God's great law of the ancient covenant, "Remember thou keep holy the Sabbath day,"[5] and taught to the world by his own mysterious "rest" after the creation of man, "He rested on the seventh day from all his work which he had done."[6]

HOURS OF LABOR

33. If we turn now to things exterior and corporal, the first concern of all is to save the poor workers from the cruelty of grasping speculators, who use human beings as mere instruments for making money. It is neither justice nor humanity so to grind men down with excessive labor as to stupefy their minds and wear out their bodies. Man's powers, like his general nature, are limited, and beyond these limits he cannot go. His strength is developed and increased by use and exercise, but only on condition of due intermission and proper rest. Daily labor, therefore, must be so regulated that it may not be protracted during longer hours than strength admits. How many and how long the intervals of rest should be will depend upon the nature of the work, on circumstances of time and place, and on the health and strength of the workman. Those who labor in mines and quarries, and in work within the bowels of the earth, should have shorter hours in proportion, as their labor is more severe and more trying to health. Then, again, the season of the year must be taken in account; for not infrequently a kind of labor is easy at one time which at another is intolerable or very difficult. Finally, work which is suitable for a strong man cannot reasonably be required from a woman or a child.

CHILD LABOR

And in regard to children, great care should be taken not to place them in workshops and factories until their bodies and minds are sufficiently mature. For just as rough weather destroys the buds of spring, so too early an experience of life's hard work blights the young promise of a child's powers, and makes any real education impossible. Women, again, are not suited to certain trades; for a woman is by nature fitted for home work, and it is that which is best adapted at once to preserve her modesty, and to promote the good bringing up of children and the well-being of the family. As a general principle, it may be laid down that a workman ought to have leisure and rest in proportion to the wear and tear of his strength; for the waste of strength must be repaired by the cessation of work.

In all agreements between masters and workpeople, there is always the condition, expressed or understood, that there be allowed proper rest for soul and body. To agree in any other sense would be against what is right and just; for it can never be right or just to require on the one side, or to promise on the other, the giving up of those duties which a man owes to his God and to himself.

JUST WAGES

34. We now approach a subject of very great importance and one on which, if extremes are to be avoided, right ideas are absolutely necessary. Wages, we are told, are fixed by free consent; and, therefore, the employer when he pays what was agreed upon has done his part, and is not called upon for anything further. The only way, it is said, in which injustice could happen would be if the master refused to pay the whole of the wages, or the workman would not complete the work undertaken; when this happens the State should intervene, to see that each obtains his own, but not under any other circumstances.

This mode of reasoning is by no means convincing to a fair-minded man, for there are important considerations which it leaves out of view altogether. To labor is to exert one's self for the sake of procuring what is necessary for the purposes of life, and most of all for self-preservation. "In the sweat of thy brow thou shalt eat bread."[7] Therefore, a man's labor has two notes or characters. First of all, it is *personal;* for the exertion of individual power belongs to the individual who puts it forth, employing this power for that personal profit for which it was given. Secondly, a man's labor is *necessary;* for without the results of labor a man cannot live; and self-conservation is a law of nature, which it is wrong to disobey. Now, if we were to consider labor merely so far as it is *personal,* doubtless it would be within the workman's right to accept any rate of wages whatever; for in the same way as he is free to work or not, so he is free to accept a small remuneration or even none at all. But this is a mere abstract supposition; the labor of the workingman is not only his personal attribute, but it is *necessary;* and this makes all the difference. The preservation of life is the bounden duty of each and all, and to fail therein is a crime. It follows that each one has a right to procure what is required in order to live; and the poor can procure it in no other way than by work and wages.

Let it be granted, then, that, as a rule, workman and employer should make free agreements, and in particular should freely agree as to wages; nevertheless, there is a dictate of nature more imperious and more ancient than any bargain between man and man, that the remuneration must be enough to support the wage earner in reasonable and frugal comfort. If through necessity or fear of a worse evil, the workman accepts harder conditions because an employer or contractor will give him no better, he is the victim of force and injustice. In these and similar questions, however—such as, for example, the hours of labor in different trades, the sanitary precautions to be observed in factories and workshops, etc.—in order to supersede undue interference on the part of the State, especially as circumstances, times and localities differ so widely, it is advisable that recourse be had to societies or boards such as we shall mention presently, or to some other method of safeguarding the interests of wage earners; the State to be asked for approval and protection.

WORKMEN'S ASSOCIATIONS

36. In the first place—employers and workmen may themselves effect much in the matter of which we treat, by means of those institutions and organizations which afford opportune assistance to those in need, and which draw the two orders more closely together. Among these may be enumerated: societies for mutual help; various foundations established by private persons for providing for the workman, and for his widow or his orphans, in sudden calamity, in sickness, and in the event of death; and what are called "patronage," or institutions for the care of boys and girls, for young people, and also for those of more mature age.

The most important of all are workmen's associations; for these virtually include all the rest. History attests what excellent results were effected by the artificer's guilds of a former day. They were the means not only of many advantages to the workmen, but in no small degree of the advancement of art, as numerous monuments remain to prove. Such associations should be adapted to the requirements of the age in which we live—an age of greater instruction, of different customs, and of more numerous requirements in daily life. It is gratifying to know that there are actually in existence not a few societies of this nature, consisting either of workmen alone, or of workmen and employers together; but it is greatly to be desired that they should multiply and become more effective. We have spoken of them more than once; but it will be well to explain here how much they are needed, to show that they exist by their own right, and to enter into their organization and their work.

37. The experience of his own weakness urges man to call in help from without. We read in the pages of Holy Writ: "It is better that two should be together than one; for they have the advantage of their society. If one fall he shall be supported by the other. Woe to him that is alone, for when he falleth he hath none to lift him up."[8] And further: "A brother that is helped by his brother is like a strong city."[9] It is this natural impulse which unites men in civil society; and it is this also which makes them band themselves together in associations of citizen with citizen; associations which, it is true, cannot be called societies in the complete sense of the word, but which are societies nevertheless.

These lesser societies and the society which constitutes the State differ in many things, because their immediate purpose and end is different. Civil society exists for the common good, and, therefore, is concerned with the interests of all in general, and with the individual interests in their due place and proportion. Hence, it is called *public* society, because by its means Thomas Aquinas says, "Men communicate with one another in the setting up of a commonwealth."[10] But the societies which are formed in the bosom of the State are called *private*, and justly so, because their immediate purpose is the private advantage of the associates. "Now, a private society," says St. Thomas again, "is one which is formed for the purpose of carrying out private business; as when two or three enter into partnership with the view of trading in conjunction."[11]

38. Particular societies, then, although they exist within the State, and are each a part of the State, nevertheless cannot be prohibited by the State absolutely and as such. For to enter into a

"society" of this kind is the natural right of man; and the State must protect natural rights, not destroy them; and if it forbids its citizens to form associations, it contradicts the very principle of its own existence; for both they and it exist in virtue of the same principle, viz., the natural propensity of man to live in society.

There are times, no doubt, when it is right that the law should interfere to prevent association; as when men join together for purposes which are evidently bad, unjust, or dangerous to the State. In such cases the public authority may justly forbid the formation of association, and may dissolve them when they already exist. But every precaution should be taken not to violate the rights of individuals, and not to make unreasonable regulations under the pretense of public benefit. For laws only bind when they are in accordance with right reason, and therefore with the eternal law of God.[12]

NOTES

1. Thomas Aquinas, 2a 2æ Q. lxi. art. 1 and 2.
2. Thomas Aquinas, *De Regimine Principum,* I, cap. 15.
3. Gen. 1:28.
4. Rom. 10:12.
5. Exod. 20:8.
6. Gen. 2:2.
7. Gen. 3:1.
8. Eccles. 4:9, 10.
9. Prov. 18:19.
10. Thomas Aquinas, *Contra impugnantes Dei cultum et religionem,* cap. II.
11. Aquinas, *Contra impugnantes.*
12. "Human law is law only in virtue of its accord with right reason: and thus it is manifest that it flows from the eternal law. And insofar as it deviates from right reason it is called an unjust law; in such case it is not law at all but rather a species of violence." Thomas Aquinas, *Summa Theologiae* 1a 2æ Q. xciii. art. iii.

from *A Letter Concerning Toleration*

❧

John Locke

John Locke was the greatest English philosopher of the seventeenth century. His work on the theory of knowledge and the foundations of political equality are central to the development of a modern world view emphasizing scientific rationality and human rights. He wrote *A Letter Concerning Toleration* in 1689 in response to religious conflict between the Church of England, English Catholics, and dissenting Protestant sects.

❧

Honoured Sir,

Since you are pleased to inquire what are my thoughts about the mutual toleration of Christians in their different professions of religion, I must needs answer you freely that I esteem that toleration to be the chief characteristic mark of the true Church. For whatsoever some people boast of the antiquity of places and names, or of the pomp of their outward worship; others, of the reformation of their discipline; all, of the orthodoxy of their faith—for everyone is orthodox to himself—these things, and all others of this nature, are much rather marks of men striving for power and empire over one another than of the Church of Christ. Let anyone have never so true a claim to all these things, yet if he be destitute of charity, meekness, and good-will in general towards all mankind, even to those that are not Christians, he is certainly yet short of being a true Christian himself. "The kings of the Gentiles exercise leadership over them," said our Saviour to his disciples, "but ye shall not be so." The business of true religion is quite another thing. It is not instituted in order to the erecting of an external pomp, nor to the obtaining of ecclesiastical dominion, nor to the exercising of compulsive force, but to the regulating of men's lives, according to the rules of virtue and piety. Whosoever will list himself under the banner of Christ, must, in the first place and above all things, make war upon his own lusts and vices. It is in vain for any man to usurp the name of Christian, without holiness of life, purity of manners, benignity and meekness of spirit. "Let everyone that nameth the name of Christ, depart from iniquity." "Thou, when thou art converted, strengthen thy brethren," said our Lord to Peter. It would, indeed, be very hard for one that appears careless about his own salvation to persuade me that he were extremely concerned for mine. For it is impossible that those should sincerely and heartily apply themselves to make other people Christians, who have not really embraced the Christian religion in their own hearts. If the Gospel and the apostles may be credited, no man can be a Christian without charity and without that faith which works, not by force, but by love. Now, I appeal to the consciences of those that persecute, torment, destroy, and kill other men upon pretence of religion, whether they do it out of friendship and kindness towards them or no? And I shall then indeed, and not until then, believe they do so, when I shall see those fiery zealots correcting, in the same manner, their friends and familiar acquaintance for the manifest sins they commit against the precepts of the Gospel; when I shall see them persecute with fire and sword the members of their own communion that are tainted with enormous vices and without amendment are in danger of eternal perdition; and when I shall see them thus express their love and desire of the salvation of their souls by the infliction of torments and exercise of all manner of cruelties. For if it be out of a principle of charity, as they pretend, and love to men's souls that they deprive them of their estates, maim them with corporal punishments, starve and torment them in noisome prisons, and in the end even take away their lives—I say, if all this be done merely to make men Christians and procure their salvation, why then do they suffer whoredom, fraud, malice, and such-like enormities, which (according to the apostle) manifestly relish of heathenish corruption, to predominate so much and abound amongst their flocks and people? These, and such-like things, are certainly more contrary to the glory of God, to the purity of the Church, and to the salvation of souls, than any conscientious dissent from ecclesiastical decisions, or separation from public worship, whilst accompanied with innocence of life. Why, then, does this burning zeal for God, for the Church, and for the salvation of souls—burning I say, literally, with fire and faggot—pass by those moral vices and wickednesses, without any chastisement, which are acknowledged by all men to be diametrically opposite to the profession of Christianity, and bend all its nerves either to the introducing of ceremonies, or to the establishment of opinions, which for the most part are about nice and intricate matters, that exceed the capacity of ordinary understandings? Which of the parties contending about these things is in the right, which of them is guilty of schism or heresy, whether those that domineer or those that suffer, will then at last be manifest when the causes of their separation comes to be judged of He, certainly, that follows Christ, embraces His doctrine, and bears His yoke, though he forsake both father and mother, separate from the public assemblies and ceremonies of his country, or whomsoever or whatsoever else he relinquishes, will not then be judged a heretic. . . .

That any man should think fit to cause another man—whose salvation he heartily desires—to expire in torments, and that even in an unconverted state, would, I confess, seem very strange to me, and I think, to any other also. But nobody, surely, will ever believe that such a carriage can proceed from charity, love, or goodwill. If anyone maintain that men ought to be compelled by fire and sword to profess certain doctrines, and conform to this or that exterior worship, without any regard had unto their morals; if anyone endeavour to convert those that are erroneous unto the faith, by forcing them to profess things that they do not believe and allowing them to practise things that the Gospel does not permit, it cannot be doubted indeed but such a one is desirous to have a numerous assembly joined in the same profession with himself; but that he principally intends by those means to compose a truly Christian Church is altogether incredible. It is not, therefore, to be wondered at if those who do not really contend for the advancement of the true religion, and of the Church of Christ, make use of arms that do not belong to the Christian warfare. If, like the Captain of our salvation, they sincerely desired the good of souls, they would tread in the steps and follow the perfect example of that Prince of Peace, who sent out His soldiers to the subduing of nations, and gathering them into His Church, not armed with the sword, or other instruments of force, but prepared with the Gospel of peace and with the exemplary holiness of their conversation. This was His method. Though if infidels were to be converted by force, if those that are either blind or obstinate were to be drawn off from their errors by armed soldiers, we know very well that it was much more easy for Him to do it with armies of heavenly legions than for any son of the Church, how potent soever, with all his dragoons.

The toleration of those that differ from others in matters of religion is so agreeable to the Gospel of Jesus Christ, and to the genuine reason of mankind, that it seems monstrous for men to be so blind as not to perceive the necessity and advantage of it in so clear a light. I will not here tax the pride and ambition of some, the passion and uncharitable zeal of others. These are faults from which human affairs can perhaps scarce ever be perfectly freed; but yet such as nobody will bear the plain imputation of, without covering them with some specious colour; and so pretend to commendation, whilst they are carried away by their own irregular passions. But, however, that some may not colour their spirit of persecution and unchristian cruelty with a pretence of care of the public weal and observation of the laws; and that others, under pretence of religion, may not seek impunity for their libertinism and licentiousness; in a word, that none may impose either upon himself or others, by the pretences of loyalty and obedience to the prince, or of tenderness and sincerity in the worship of God; I esteem it above all things necessary to distinguish exactly the business of civil government from that of religion and to settle the just bounds that lie between the one and the other. If this be not done, there can be no end put to the controversies that will be always arising between those that have, or at least pretend to have, on the one side, a concernment for the interest of men's souls, and, on the other side, a care of the commonwealth.

III

GANDHI, THE EXEMPLAR

I have no message to give except this: that there is no deliverance for any people on this earth or for all the people on this earth except through truth and nonviolence in every walk of life without any exception.

—M. K. Gandhi, 1937

In a book covering so much material, and from which (alas!) so many vital voices have had to be left out, why an entire unit on one person?

Gandhi was the first person with a primarily religious perspective to lead a mass movement the central aim of which—national independence from colonial control—is an essential value of modern progressive politics. He showed that religious values could enter the public world in a way that was not only compatible with values of democracy and human rights, but which furthered those values. In a time of political turmoil and ferment, he organized a nationwide movement, attracted the attention of the world, and combined several of the critical elements of a liberating faith.

Gandhi's understanding of the relation between religion and social action is, I believe, the most important single inspiration for religious social activists who have come after him. Martin Luther King, Thomas Merton, Cesar Chavez, Joanna Macy, Thich Nhat Hanh, Ang San Suu Kyi, Sulak Sivaraksa, James Lawson—these and countless others cite Gandhi as their teacher: an exemplar of the reasoned, humane, and inspired entry of religious values into the public sphere.

Gandhi's writings run to thousands of pages, and his life in public to countless campaigns, struggles, and actions. The full reality of his life far exceeds this space. I believe, however, that even these brief selections reveal the four essential and distinctive principles that guided his engagement with political life.

First, he understood political action in religious terms and demanded that it be governed by religious values. The goal of life was the search for truth, the realization of our own divine nature. Pursuit of this goal meant recognizing our own limitations, the essentially holy nature of all human beings, and the necessity of nonviolence in the pursuit of justice. Because we are essentially holy we should not permit injustice to exist; because all other people are also essentially holy, we must engage in that pursuit nonviolently.

Second, however, Gandhi's approach to religious tradition is critical as well as faithful. Influenced by secular concepts of equality and rights, he firmly rejected Hinduism's practice of untouchability; and moved during his life toward a position of women's equality.

Third, just as he was unafraid to challenge religious tradition, he refused to accept the dogmas of modernity uncritically. As alternatives to individualism, affluence, and unreflective technological innovation, he proposed a model of rich community life, the dignity of labor, and spiritual development.

Fourth, in his synthesis of religion and politics, Gandhi was explicitly open to and respectful of other religious traditions. He frequently praised the wisdom of Judaism, Christianity, Islam, and Buddhism, offering an interpretation of what was essential to all religions of which cooperation and mutual respect were natural consequences.

In varying degrees, these four characteristics mark virtually all the ideas expressed in Parts IV through VIII. That they were combined so clearly and forcefully in one person is remarkable. This does not mean that Gandhi was the perfect man or that the beliefs of someone who died in 1948 are fully adequate to social change today. His positions on the caste system and women's full equality were far from complete, and along with his religious ecumenicalism he could also manifest a more narrow cultural nationalism. He was, in short, a man, not a messiah. But he taught—and lived—the lessons of a liberating faith more completely than anyone before him.

Gandhi's central ideas were articulated in thousands of very small pieces, often connected topically to some historical situation or moment of the struggle in India, or in correspondence with people all over the world. The following selections indicate the range of his concerns, and the central values and beliefs he held. The first five express his basic commitment to religious truth and the value of nonviolence. "The Jews" and "Atomic Warfare" embody his characteristic response to two of the twentieth century's greatest calamities: the Holocaust and the advent of nuclear weapons. "Fellowship and Toleration" indicates the depth of his commitment to religious cooperation, and "Potency of Prayer" reaffirms his belief that spiritual discipline and principled political action are inseparable.

Selections from His Writings

❧

Mohandas Gandhi

THE DOCTRINE OF AHIMSA

Literally speaking, Ahimsa means "non-killing." But to me it has a world of meaning, and takes me into realms much higher, infinitely higher. It really means that you may not offend anybody; you may not harbor an uncharitable thought, even in connection with one who may consider himself to be your enemy. To one who follows this doctrine there is no room for an enemy. But there may be people who consider themselves to be his enemies. So it is held that we may not harbor an evil thought even in connection with such persons. If we return blow for blow we depart from the doctrine of Ahimsa. But I go farther. If we resent a friend's action, or the so-called enemy's action, we still fall short of this doctrine. But when I say we should not resent, I do not say that we should acquiesce: by the word "resenting" I mean wishing that some harm should be done to the enemy; or that he should be put out of the way, not even by any action of ours, but by the action of somebody else, or, say, by divine agency. If we harbor even this thought we depart from this doctrine of nonviolence. Those who join the Ashram have literally to accept that meaning.

This does not mean that we practice that doctrine in its entirety. Far from it. It is an ideal which we have to reach, and it is an ideal to be reached even at this very moment, if we are capable of doing so. But it is not a proposition in Geometry; it is not even like solving difficult problems in higher mathematics—it is infinitely more difficult. Many of us have burnt the midnight oil in solving those problems. But if you want to follow out this doctrine you will have to do much more than burn the midnight oil. You will have to pass many a sleepless night, and go through many a mental torture, before you can even be within measurable distance of this goal. It is the goal, and nothing less than that, which you and I have to reach, if we want to understand what a religious life means.

A man who believes in the efficacy of this doctrine finds in the ultimate stage, when he is about to reach the goal, the whole world at his feet. If you express your love—Ahimsa—in such a manner that it impresses itself indelibly upon your so-called enemy, he must return that love. Under this rule there is no room for organized assassinations, or for murders openly committed, or for any violence for the sake of your country, and even for guarding the honor of precious ones that may be under your charge. After all, that would be a poor defense of their honor. This doctrine tells us that we may guard the honor of those under our charge by delivering our own lives into the hands of the man who would commit the sacrilege. And that requires far greater courage than delivering of blows. If you do not retaliate, but stand your ground between your charge and the opponent, simply receiving the blows without retaliating, what happens? I give you my promise that the whole of his violence will be expended on you, and your friend will be left unscathed. Under this plan of life there is no conception of patriotism which justifies such wars as you witness today in Europe.

THE THEORY AND PRACTICE OF SATYAGRAHA

[The following is taken from an article by Gandhiji contributed to the Golden Number of Indian Opinion which was issued in 1914 as a souvenir of the eight years' Satyagraha in South Africa.]

Carried out to its utmost limit, Satyagraha is independent of pecuniary or other material assistance; certainly, even in its elementary form, of physical force or violence. Indeed, violence is the negation of this great spiritual force, which can only be cultivated or wielded by those who will entirely eschew violence. It is a force that may be used by individuals as well as by communities. It may be used as well in political as in domestic affairs. Its universal applicability is a demonstration of its permanence and invincibility. It can be used alike by men, women, and children. It is totally untrue to say that it is a force to be used only by the weak so long as they are not capable of meeting violence by violence. This superstition arises from the incompleteness of the English expression, *passive resistance*. It is impossible for those who consider themselves to be weak to apply this force. Only those who realize that there is something in man which is superior to the brute nature in him and that the latter always yields to it, can effectively be Satyagrahis. This force is to violence, and, therefore, to all tyranny, all injustice, what light is to darkness. In politics, its use is based upon the immutable maxim, that government of the people is possible only so long as they consent either consciously or unconsciously to be governed. We did not want to be governed by the Asiatic Act of 1907 of the Transvaal, and it had to go before this mighty force. Two courses were open to us: to use violence when we were called upon to submit to the Act, or to suffer the penalties prescribed under the Act, and thus to draw out and exhibit the force of the soul within us for a period long enough to appeal to the sympathetic chord in the governors or the lawmakers. We have taken long to achieve what we set about striving for. That was because our Satyagraha was not of the most complete type. All Satyagrahis do not understand the full value of the force, nor have we men who always from conviction refrain from violence. The use of this force requires the adoption of poverty, in the sense that we must be indifferent whether we have the wherewithal to feed or clothe ourselves. During the past struggle, all Satyagrahis, if any at all, were not prepared to go that length. Some again were only so-called Satyagrahis. They came without any conviction, often with mixed motives, less often with impure motives. Some even, whilst engaged in the struggle, would gladly have resorted to violence but for most vigilant supervision. Thus it was that the struggle became prolonged; for the exercise of the purest soul-force, in its perfect form, brings about instantaneous relief. For this exercise, prolonged training of the individual soul is an absolute necessity, so that a perfect Satyagrahi has to be almost, if not entirely, a perfect man. We cannot all suddenly become such men, but if my proposition is correct—as I know it to be correct—the greater the spirit of Satyagraha in us, the better men will we become. Its use, therefore, is, I think, indisputable, and it is a force, which, if it became universal, would revolutionize social ideals and do away with despotisms and the ever-growing militarism under which the nations of the West are groaning and are being almost crushed to death, and which fairly promises to overwhelm even the nations of the East. If the past struggle has produced even a few Indians who would dedicate themselves to the task of becoming Satyagrahis as nearly perfect as possible, they would not only have served themselves in the truest sense of the term, they would also have served humanity at large. Thus viewed, Satyagraha is the noblest and best education. It should come, not after the ordinary education in letters, of children, but it should precede it. It will not be denied, that a child, before it begins to write its alphabet and to gain worldly knowledge, should know what the soul is, what truth is, what love is, what powers are latent in the soul. It should be an essential of real education that a child should learn, that in the struggle of life, it can easily conquer hate by love, untruth by truth, violence by self-suffering.

THE DOCTRINE OF THE SWORD

In this age of the rule of brute force, it is almost impossible for anyone to believe that anyone else could possibly reject the law of the final supremacy of brute force. And so I receive anonymous letters advising me that I must not interfere with the progress of noncooperation even though popular violence may break out. Others come to me and, assuming that secretly I must be plotting violence, inquire when the happy moment for declaring open violence will arrive. They assure me that the English will never yield to anything but violence secret or open. Yet others, I am informed, believe that I am the most rascally person living in India because I never give out my real intention, and that they have not a shadow of doubt that I believe in violence just as much as most people do.

Such being the hold that the doctrine of the sword has on the majority of mankind, and as success of noncooperation depends principally on absence of violence during its pendency, and as my views in this matter affect the conduct of a large number of people, I am anxious to state them as clearly as possible.

I do believe that where there is only a choice between cowardice and violence I would advise violence. Thus when my eldest son asked me what he should have done, had he been present when I was almost fatally assaulted in 1908, whether he should have run away and seen me killed or whether he should have used his physical force which he could and wanted to use, and defended me, I told him that it was his duty to defend me even by using violence. Hence it was that I took part in the Boer War, the so-called Zulu rebellion and the late War. Hence also do I advocate training in arms for those who believe in the method of violence. I would rather have India resort to arms in order to defend her honor than that she should in a cowardly manner become or remain a helpless witness to her own dishonor.

But I believe that nonviolence is infinitely superior to violence, forgiveness is more manly than punishment. Forgiveness adorns a soldier. But abstinence is forgiveness only when there is the power to punish; it is meaningless when it pretends to proceed from a helpless creature. A mouse hardly forgives a cat when it allows itself to be torn to pieces by her. I therefore appreciate the sentiment of those who cry out for the condign punishment of General Dyer and his ilk. They would tear him to pieces if they could. But I do not believe India to be helpless. I do not believe myself to be a helpless creature. Only I want to use India's and my strength for a better purpose.

Let me not be misunderstood. Strength does not come from physical capacity. It comes from an indomitable will. An average Zulu is any way more than a match for an average

Englishman in bodily capacity. But he flees from an English boy, because he fears the boy's revolver or those who will use it for him. He fears death and is nerveless in spite of his burly figure. We in India may in a moment realize that one hundred thousand Englishmen need not frighten three hundred million human beings. A definite forgiveness would therefore mean a definite recognition of our strength. With enlightened forgiveness must come a mighty wave of strength in us, which would make it impossible for a Dyer and a Frank Johnson to heap affront upon India's devoted head. It matters little to me that for the moment I do not drive my point home. We feel too downtrodden not to be angry and revengeful. But I must not refrain from saying that India can gain more by waiving the right of punishment. We have better work to do, a better mission to deliver to the world.

I am not a visionary. I claim to be a practical idealist. The religion of nonviolence is not meant merely for *rishis* and saints. It is meant for the common people as well. Nonviolence is the law of our species as violence is the law of the brute. The spirit lies dormant in the brute and he knows no law but that of physical might. The dignity of man requires obedience to a higher law—to the strength of the spirit.

I have therefore ventured to place before India the ancient law of self-sacrifice. For Satyagraha and its offshoots, noncooperation and civil resistance, are nothing but new names for the law of suffering. The *rishis,* who discovered the law of nonviolence in the midst of violence, were greater geniuses than Newton. They were themselves greater warriors than Wellington. Having themselves known the use of arms, they realized their uselessness and taught a weary world that its salvation lay not through violence but through nonviolence.

Nonviolence in its dynamic condition means conscious suffering. It does not mean meek submission to the will of the evildoer, but it means the pitting of one's whole soul against the will of the tyrant. Working under this law of our being, it is possible for a single individual to defy the whole might of an unjust empire, to save his honor, his religion, his soul, and lay the foundation for that empire's fall or its regeneration.

And so I am not pleading for India to practice nonviolence because she is weak. I want her to practice nonviolence being conscious of her strength and power. No training in arms is required for realization of her strength. We seem to need it because we seem to think that we are but a lump of flesh. I want India to rcognize that she has a soul that cannot perish and that can rise triumphant above every physical weakness and defy the physical combination of a whole world. What is the meaning of Rama, a mere human being, with his host of monkeys, pitting himself against the insolent strength of ten-headed Ravana surrounded in supposed safety by the raging waters on all sides of Lanka? Does it not mean the conquest of physical might by spiritual strength? However, being a practical man, I do not wait till India recognizes the practicability of the spiritual life in the political world. India considers herself to be powerless and paralyzed before the machine guns, the tanks, and the airplanes of the English. And she takes up noncooperation out of her weakness. It must still serve the same purpose, namely, bring her delivery from the crushing weight of British injustice if a sufficient number of people practice it.

I isolate this noncooperation from Sinn Feinism, for, it is so conceived as to be incapable of being offered side by side with violence. But I invite even the school of violence to give this peaceful noncooperation a trial. It will not fail through its inherent weakness. It may fail because of poverty of response. Then will be the time for real danger. The high-souled men, who are unable to suffer national humiliation any longer, will want to vent their wrath. They will take to violence. So far as I know, they must perish without delivering themselves or their country from the wrong. If India takes up the doctrine of the sword, she may gain momentary victory. Then India will cease to be the pride of my heart. I am wedded to India because I owe my all to her. I believe absolutely that she has a mission for the world. She is not to copy Europe blindly. India's acceptance of the doctrine of the sword will be the hour of my trial. I hope I shall not be found wanting. My religion has no geographical limits. If I have a living faith in it, it will transcend my love for India herself. My life is dedicated to service of India through the religion of nonviolence which I believe to be the root of Hinduism.

Meanwhile I urge those who distrust me not to disturb the even working of the struggle that has just commenced, by inciting to violence in the belief that I want violence. I detest secrecy as a sin. Let them give nonviolent noncooperation a trial and they will find that I had no mental reservation whatsoever.

MY FAITH

[Extract from Gandhiji's Presidential Address at the 39th Session of the Indian National Congress, Belgaum, Dec. 1924.]

Noncooperation and civil disobedience are but different branches of the same tree called Satyagraha. It is my *Kalpadruma*—my *Jam-i-Jam*—the Universal Provider. Satyagraha is search for Truth; and God is Truth. *Ahimsa* or nonviolence is the light that reveals that Truth to me. Swaraj for me is part of that Truth. This Satyagraha did not fail me in South Africa, Kheda, or Champaran and in a host of other cases I could mention. It excludes all violence or hate. Therefore, I cannot and will not hate Englishmen. Nor will I bear their yoke. I must fight unto death the unholy attempt to impose British methods and British institutions on India. But I combat the attempt with nonviolence. I believe in the capacity of India to offer nonviolent battle to the English rulers. The experiment has not failed. It has succeeded, but not to the extent we had hoped and desired. I do not despair. On the contrary, I believe that India will come to her own in the near future, and that only through Satyagraha. The proposed suspension is part of the experiment. Noncooperation need never be resumed if the program sketched by me can be fulfilled. Nonviolent noncooperation in some form or other, whether through the Congress or without it, will be resumed if the program fails. I have repeatedly stated that Satyagraha never fails and that one perfect Satyagrahi is enough to vindicate Truth. Let us all strive to be perfect Satyagrahis. The striving does not require any quality unattainable by the lowliest among us. For Satyagraha is an attribute of the spirit within. It is latent in every one of us. Like Swaraj it is our birthright. Let us know it.

MY FAITH IN NONVIOLENCE

[From a talk after the evening prayer on board the ship at Suez on the way to London for the Round Table Conference.]

I have found that life persists in the midst of destruction and, therefore, there must be a higher law than that of destruction. Only under that law would a well-ordered society be intelligible and life worth living. And if that is the law of life, we have to work it out in daily life. Wherever there are jars, wherever you are confronted with an opponent, conquer him with love. In a crude manner I have worked it out in my life. That does not mean that all my difficulties are solved.

I have found, however, that this law of love has answered as the law of destruction has never done. In India we have had an ocular demonstration of the operation of this law on the widest scale possible. I do not claim therefore that nonviolence has necessarily penetrated the three hundred millions, but I do claim that it has penetrated deeper than any other message, and in an incredibly short time. We have not been all uniformly nonviolent; and with the vast majority, nonviolence has been a matter of policy. Even so, I want you to find out if the country has not made phenomenal progress under the protecting power of nonviolence.

It takes a fairly strenuous course of training to attain to a mental state of nonviolence. In daily life it has to be a course of discipline though one may not like it, like for instance, the life of a soldier. But I agree that, unless there is a hearty cooperation of the mind, the mere outward observance will be simply a mask, harmful both to the man himself and to others. The perfect state is reached only when mind and body and speech are in proper coordination. But it is always a case of intense mental struggle. It is not that I am incapable of anger, for instance, but I succeed on almost all occasions to keep my feelings under control. Whatever may be the result, there is always in me a conscious struggle for following the law of nonviolence deliberately and ceaselessly. Such a struggle leaves one stronger for it. Nonviolence is a weapon of the strong. With the weak it might easily be hypocrisy. Fear and love are contradictory terms. Love is reckless in giving away, oblivious as to what it gets in return. Love wrestles with the world as with the self and ultimately gains a mastery over all other feelings. My daily experience, as of those who are working with me, is that every problem lends itself to solution if we are determined to make the law of truth and nonviolence the law of life. For truth and nonviolence are, to me, faces of the same coin.

The law of love will work, just as the law of gravitation will work, whether we accept it or not. Just as a scientist will work wonders out of various applications of the law of nature, even so a man who applies the law of love with scientific precision can work greater wonders. For the force of nonviolence is infinitely more wonderful and subtle than the material forces of nature, like, for instance, electricity. The men who discovered for us the law of love were greater scientists than any of our modern scientists. Only our explorations have not gone far enough and so it is not possible for everyone to see all its working. Such, at any rate, is the hallucination, if it is one, under which I am laboring. The more I work at this law the more I feel the delight in life, the delight in the scheme of this universe. It gives me a peace and a meaning of the mysteries of nature that I have no power to describe.

THE JEWS

The German persecution of the Jews seems to have no parallel in history. Can the Jews resist this organized and shameless persecution? Is there a way to preserve their self-respect, and not to feel helpless, neglected, and forlorn? I submit there is. No person who has faith in a living God need feel helpless or forlorn. Jehovah of the Jews is a God more personal than the God of the Christians, the Mussalmans or the Hindus, though, as a matter of fact, in essence, He is common to all and one without a second and beyond description. But as the Jews attribute personality to God and believe that He rules every action of theirs, they ought not to feel helpless. If I were a Jew and were born in Germany and earned my livelihood there, I would claim Germany as my home even as the tallest gentile German may, and challenge him to shoot me or cast me in the dungeon; I would refuse to be expelled or to submit to discriminating treatment. And for doing this, I should not wait for the fellow Jews to join me in civil resistance but would have confidence that in the end the rest are bound to follow my example. If one Jew or all the Jews were to accept the prescription here offered, he or they cannot be worse off than now. And suffering voluntarily undergone will bring them an inner strength and joy which no number of resolutions of sympathy passed in the world outside Germany can. Indeed even if Britain, France, and America were to declare hostilities against Germany, they can bring no inner joy, no inner strength. The calculated violence of Hitler may even result in a general massacre of the Jews by way of his first answer to the declaration of such hostilities. But if the Jewish mind could be prepared for voluntary suffering, even the massacre I have imagined could be turned into a day of thanksgiving and joy that Jehovah had wrought deliverance of the race even at the hands of the tyrant. For to the God-fearing, death has no terror. It is a joyful sleep to be followed by a waking that would be all the more refreshing for the long sleep.

It is hardly necessary for me to point out that it is easier for the Jews than for the Czechs to follow my prescription. And they have in the Indian Satyagraha campaign in South Africa an exact parallel. There the Indians occupied precisely the same place that the Jews occupy in Germany. The persecution had also a religious tinge. President Kruger used to say that the white Christians were the chosen of God and Indians were inferior beings created to serve the whites. A fundamental clause in the Transvaal Constitution was that there should be no equality between the whites and colored races including Asiatics. There too the Indians were consigned to ghettoes described as locations. The other disabilities were almost of the same type as those of the Jews in Germany. The Indians, a mere handful, resorted to Satyagraha without any backing from the world outside or the Indian Government. Indeed the British officials tried to dissuade the Satyagrahis from their contemplated step. World opinion and the Indian Government came to their aid after eight years of fighting. And that too was by way of diplomatic pressure, not of a threat of war.

But the Jews of Germany can offer Satyagraha under infinitely better auspices than the Indians of South Africa. The Jews are a compact, homogeneous community in Germany. They are far more gifted than the Indians of South Africa. And they have organized world opinion behind them. I am convinced that if someone with courage and vision can arise among them to lead them in nonviolent action, the winter of their despair can in the twinkling of an eye be turned into the summer of hope. And what has today become a degrading manhunt can be turned into a calm and determined stand offered by unarmed men and women possessing the strength of suffering given to them by Jehovah. It will be then a truly religious resistance offered against the godless fury of dehumanized man. The German Jews will score a lasting victory over the German gentiles in the sense that they will have converted the latter to an appreciation of human dignity. They will have rendered service to fellow-Germans and proved their title to be the real Germans as against those who are today dragging, however unknowingly, the German name into the mire.

ATOMIC WARFARE

There have been cataclysmic changes in the world. Do I still adhere to my faith in truth and nonviolence? Has not the atom bomb exploded that faith? Not only has it not done so but it has clearly demonstrated to me that the twins constitute the mightiest force in the world. Before it the atom bomb is of no effect. The two opposing forces are wholly different in kind, the one moral and spiritual, the other physical and material. The one is infinitely superior to the other which by its very nature has an end. The force of the spirit is ever progressive and endless.

Its full expression makes it unconquerable in the world. In saying this I know that I have said nothing new. I merely bear witness to the fact. What is more, that force resides in everybody, man, woman, and child, irrespective of the color of the skin. Only in many it lies dormant, but it is capable of being awakened by judicious training.

It is further to be observed that without the recognition of this truth and due effort to realize it, there is no escape from self-destruction. The remedy lies in every individual training himself for self-expression in every walk of life, irrespective of response by the neighbors.

RELIGION AND SOCIAL SERVICE

[About January 23, 1935]

I have been asked by Sir S. Radhakrishnan to answer the following three questions:

(1) What is your religion?
(2) How are you led to it?
(3) What is its bearing on social life?

My religion is Hinduism which, for me, is the religion of humanity and includes the best of all the religions known to me.

I take it that the present tense in the second question has been purposely used instead of the past. I am being led to my religion through Truth and nonviolence, i.e., love in the broadest sense. I often describe my religion as religion of Truth. Of late, instead of saying God is Truth I have been saying Truth is God, in order more fully to define my religion. I used at one time to know by heart the thousand names of God which a booklet in Hinduism gives in verse form and which perhaps tens of thousands recite every morning. But nowadays nothing so completely describes my God as Truth. Denial of God we have known. Denial of Truth we have not known. The most ignorant among mankind have some truth in them. We are all sparks of Truth. The sum total of these sparks is indescribable, as-yet-Unknown Truth, which is God. I am being daily led nearer to it by constant prayer.

The bearing of this religion on social life is, or has to be, seen in one's daily social contact. To be true to such religion one has to lose oneself in continuous and continuing service of all life. Realization of Truth is impossible without a complete merging of oneself in and identification with this limitless ocean of life. Hence, for me, there is no escape from social service; there is no happiness on earth beyond or apart from it. Social service here must be taken to include every department of life. In this scheme there is nothing low, nothing high. For all is one, though we *seem* to be many.

FELLOWSHIP AND TOLERATION

[Before January 15, 1928]

In order to attain a perfect fellowship,[1] every act of its members must be a religious act and an act of sacrifice. I came to the conclusion long ago, after prayerful search and study and discussion with as many people as I could meet, that all religions were true and also that all had some error in them, and that whilst I hold by my own, I should hold others as dear as Hinduism, from which it logically follows that we should hold all as dear as our nearest kith and kin and that we should make no distinction between them. So we can only pray, if we are Hindus, not that a Christian should become a Hindu, or if we are Mussalmans, not that a Hindu or a Christian should become a Mussalman, nor should we even secretly pray that anyone should be converted, but our inmost prayer should be that a Hindu should be a better Hindu, a Muslim a better Muslim and a Christian a better Christian. That is the fundamental truth of fellowship. That is the meaning of the wonderful passion, the story of which Andrews read out to you, of the song and verses that Khare, Shastri, and Imam Saheb recited. If Andrews invited them to give their song and verses for mere courtesy or by way of patronizing toleration, he was false to the fellowship. In that case, he should not have done so, but I have known Charlie Andrews too well, and I know that he has given the same love to others as he has for his own, and thereby broadened his Christianity, as I broaden my Hinduism by loving other religions as my own.

If however there is any suspicion in your minds that only one religion can be true and others false, you must reject the doctrine of fellowship placed before you. Then we would have a continuous process of exclusion and found our fellowship on an exclusive basis. Above all I plead for utter truthfulness. If we do not feel for other religions as we feel for our own, we had better disband ourselves, for we do not want a wishy-washy toleration. My doctrine of toleration does not include toleration of evil, though it does the toleration of the evilminded. It does not therefore mean that you have to invite each and every one who is evilminded or tolerate a false faith. By a true faith I mean one the sum total of whose energy is for the good of its adherents, by a false I mean that which is predominantly false. If you, therefore, feel that the sum total of Hinduism has been bad for the Hindus and the world, you must reject it as a false faith.

I would not only not try to convert but would not even secretly pray that anyone should embrace my faith. My prayer would always be that Imam Saheb should be a better Mussalman, or become the best he can. Hinduism with its message of *ahimsa* is to me the most glorious religion in the world—as my wife to me is the most beautiful woman in the world—but others may feel the same about their own religion. Cases of real honest conversion are quite possible. If some people for their inward satisfaction and growth change their religion, let them do so. As regards taking our message to the aborigines, I do not think I should go and give my message out of my own wisdom. Do it in all humility, it is said. Well, I have been an unfortunate witness of arrogance often going in the garb of humility. If I am perfect, I know that my thought will reach others. It taxes all my time to reach the goal I have set to myself. What have I to take to the aborigines and the Assamese hillmen except to go in my nakedness to them? Rather than ask them to join my prayer, I would join their prayer. We were strangers to this sort of classification— "animists," "aborigines," etc.,—but we have learned it from English rulers. I must have the desire to serve and it must put me right with people. Conversion and service go ill together.

The next day early morning the friends met for an informal conversation with Gandhiji when again the same question was asked by many of them.

"Would you have a ruling of such a character that those who had a desire to convert should not be eligible for membership?"

Personally, I think they should not be eligible. I should have framed a resolution to that effect as I regard it as the logical outcome of fellowship. It is essential for interreligious relationship and contact.

"Is not the impulse to proselytize God-given?" inquired another friend.

I question it. But if all impulses are God-given, as some of our Hindus believe, He has also given us discrimination. He will say, "I have given you many impulses so that your capacity to face temptation may be tested."

"But you do believe in preaching an economic order?" inquired one of the fair sex.

I do, as I believe in preaching laws of health.

"Then why not apply the same rule in religious matters?"

It is a relevant question. But you must not forget that we have started with the fundamental principle that all religions are true. If there were different but good and true health laws for different communities, I should hesitate to preach some as true and some as false. I am positive that, with people not prepared to tolerate one another's religious belief, there can be no international fellowship.

Moreover, physical analogies when applied to spiritual matters are good only up to a certain point. When you take up an analogy from Nature, you can stretch it only to a certain point. But I would take an illustration from the physical world and explain what I mean. If I want to hand a rose to you, there is definite movement. But if I want to transmit its scent, I do so without any movement. The rose transmits its own scent without a movement. Let us rise a step higher, and we can understand that spiritual experiences are self-acting. Therefore, the analogy of preaching sanitation, etc., does not hold good. If we have spiritual truth, it will transmit itself. You talk of the joy of a spiritual experience and say you cannot but share it. Well, if it is real joy, boundless joy, it will spread itself without the vehicle of speech. In spiritual matters we have merely to step out of the way. Let God work His way. If we interfere, we may do harm. Good is a self-acting force. Evil is not, because it is a negative force. It requires the cloak of virtue before it can march forward.

"Did not Jesus Himself teach and preach?"

We are on dangerous ground here. You ask me to give my interpretation of the life of Christ. Well, I may say that I do not accept everything in the gospels as historical truth. And it must be remembered that he was working amongst his own people, and said he had not come to destroy but to fulfill. I draw a great distinction between the Sermon on the Mount and the Letters of Paul. They are a graft of Christ's teaching, his own gloss apart from Christ's own experience.

POTENCY OF PRAYER

There is little doubt that India is about to reach her cherished goal of political independence. Let the entrance be prayerful. Prayer is not an old woman's idle amusement. Properly understood and applied, it is the most potent instrument of action.

Let us then pray and find out what we have meant by nonviolence, and how we shall retain the freedom gained by its use. If our nonviolence is of the weak, it follows that we shall never be able, by such nonviolence, to retain freedom. But it follows also that we shall not, for some length of time, at any rate, be able to defend ourselves by force of arms, if only because we have neither them nor the knowledge of their use. We have not even the requisite discipline. The result is that we shall have to rely upon another nation's help, not as equals, but as pupils upon their teachers, if the word "inferiors" jars upon our ears.

Hence there is nothing but nonviolence to fall back upon for retaining our freedom even as we had to do for gaining it. This means exercise of nonviolence against all those who call themselves our opponents. This should not mean much for a man who has used himself to nonviolence for nearly three decades. It is summed up in "die for your honour and freedom" instead of "kill if necessary and be killed in the act." What does a brave soldier do? He kills only if necessary and risks his life in the act. Nonviolence demands greater courage and sacrifice. Why should it be comparatively easy for a man to risk death in the act of killing, and almost superhuman for him to do so in the act of sparing life? It seems to be gross self-deception to think that we can risk death, if we learn and practice the art of killing, but cannot do so otherwise. But for the hypnotism induced by the repetition of an untruth we should not grossly deceive ourselves.

But the critic or the scoffer will ask, why bring in prayer if the matter is so simple as you put it. The answer is that prayer is the first and the last lesson in learning the noble and brave art of sacrificing self in the various walks of life culminating in the defense of one's nation's liberty and honor.

Undoubtedly prayer requires a living faith in God. Successful *satyagraha* is inconceivable without that faith. God may be called by any other name so long as it connotes the living Law of Life—in other words, the Law and the Lawgiver rolled into one.

NOTE

1. Members of the Council of International Federation and their friends stayed in the Ashram and held discussions on "the fundamental objective of the fellowship."

"Gandhi in the Twenty-First Century"

❧

Ronald J. Terchek

Ronald J. Terchek is professor of politics at the University of Maryland. He writes on issues in liberalism and political theory and here critically addresses the question of Gandhi's continuing relevance to political life.

❧

The opinions I have formed and the conclusions I have arrived at are not final. I may change tomorrow; I have nothing new to teach to the world. Truth and nonviolence are as old as the hills. All I have done is to try experiments in both on as vast a scale as I could do. In doing so, I have sometimes erred and learnt by my errors. Life and its problems have thus become to me so many experiments in the practice of truth and nonviolence.[1]

On its face, Western democratic societies have seldom been stronger. Their dangerous totalitarian opponents have been vanquished; their technology continues to move at a dizzying pace; their citizens are living longer, are more literate, and generally enjoying a higher standard of living than earlier generations; their models of the economy and polity have become dominant; and their culture is becoming globalized. The West has put its stamp on the world: modernity and modernization provide the standards by which we understand success and failure. But the themes of several recent books published in the West signal that for some, at least, all is not well. Agnes Heller writes about the dissatisfied society; Jeffrey Goldfarb offers us *The Cynical Society;* Daniel Bell detects the cultural contradictions of capitalism; Norbitto Bobbio talks about the broken promises of democracy; David Marquand finds *The Unprincipled Society;* Ronald Beiner asks, *What's the Matter with Liberalism?;* and Alan Bloom laments *The Closing of the American Mind.*[2] There are other signs of trouble and discontent. Political participation is declining while cynicism is increasing; hard choices assert themselves between full employment and a generous state; drugs and crime climb to troubling levels; the family is under siege; people live longer but many seem neither secure nor satisfied; and the environment is degraded while the world's population increases.

Special problems await the two largest groups in the world, the young and the poor. The young are likely to have some education, live in urban areas, move away from the traditions of their parents, accept cosmopolitan norms of identity and of the good, be less deferential to authority, and be part of a changing, mobile environment. At the same time, very large numbers will be underemployed or unemployed, finding that the promises of modern culture have been broken and that they have no worth in their own society.[3] Where this leads is uncertain. Strong, disciplinary governments may check unrest with harsh police measures that are not respecters of basic rights; political leaders may manipulate loneliness and frustration into ugly, violent, nativist movements; crime and social disorganization may intensify; internal civil strife may explode; or the poor may be intimidated and humiliated in the harsh realities of their urban slums. From a Gandhian perspective, such outcomes are neither imaginary nor inevitable. They are not imaginary because severe dislocations, the intense demands of individualism, a decayed tradition, a continued devaluation of persons in the economy, and a host of other dislocating moves are bound to have an effect, sometimes leading to violence, always involving some measure of domination, and invariably sacrificing autonomy. However, Gandhi thinks this state of affairs can be challenged in two different but related ways. In the first place, he wants to show that injustice can be confronted nonviolently. Secondly, he insists that a different imperative—one that emphasizes the cosmological interdependence of everyone— and different institutional arrangements can foster (though not guarantee) a society that resists these assaults on autonomy. In this way he speaks to those at the margin, admonishing them to discard their lethargy, reject fatalism, and claim their own dignity through public, nonviolent assertion.

I have argued that one of Gandhi's great contributions as a political theorist of the twentieth century comes with his invitation to think freshly about the future, and he does this by reaching for both the past and present. If the future is as menacing as Gandhi fears it can become, then his importance increases with his reminders of what we risk losing and his claim that people can nonviolently challenge modern versions of fatalism.

His sweeping challenge to modern expressions of fatalism makes Gandhi distinctive in the late-modern era. By questioning the inevitability and intractability of modernity, he wants to expose it as a construction that can be resisted. He is not interested in replacing everything that is modern, but in contextualizing the modern temper within a cosmological framework that guards autonomy. Moreover, he sets out to defend and nourish local traditions where individuals live and work and which, Gandhi believes, provide them with purpose and dignity. To do this, he confronts modern versions of fatalism; some hold that we cannot escape complexity, that we cannot avoid centralization, that we cannot resist the globalization of modern culture, that we cannot repeal the inevitability of violent conflict, or that we cannot challenge the growing impersonality of a world that judges the good in terms of its economic contribution.

Although it is impossible to return to an earlier cosmos, Gandhi means to fill in some of the blank spaces left by modernity. He does this by continually applying ethical standards to contemporary practices and institutions. For him, the earlier cosmic harmony promised that the autonomy of everyone would be assured, and he wants to make this the ultimate standard for judgment in the modern world. Therefore, he constantly asks about the status of autonomy and all that he thinks autonomy requires.

Gandhi challenges the contemporary tendency to see modernity embodying progress, reason, and liberation and to believe that alternative standards and practices that stand in its way can be eliminated without costly consequences. Should this attitude prevail, Gandhi fears that an increasing number of persons will become obsolescent, seen as having no worth and nothing to contribute in the modern world. For him, the modern tendency to make economic criteria the standard for judging persons and institutions reduces human beings to means; with such an outlook, talk about their dignity is beside the point.

As society becomes increasingly complex, there is an accelerating tendency for greater centralization, coordination, and hierarchy and the increasing dominance of the specialist. Deeply troubled by these encroachments on autonomy, Gandhi is especially alarmed at the prospect of the centralized state. His specific proposals for the panchayat raj may not offer much guidance in the crowded polity of the late modern world, but his political critique signals what has traditionally been at the heart of the democratic project, namely that people ought to govern themselves. Accordingly, he wants to show the dangers of concentrated power and the need to disperse power and encourage participation throughout society.

Gandhi warns about the globalization of the modernized economy, not only because of its economic effects but also because it is accompanied with the globalization of culture. He continually celebrates the diversity he sees in India and fears that such globalization is reducing what is distinctive and fostering what is uniform. Local cultures are critical to Gandhi's project because he sees each providing a concrete, not abstract, sense of identity and meaning apart from productivity and consumption. To defend autonomy and resist domination, Gandhi argues that persons must be equipped with a standard and that standard typically comes from tradition. However, one cannot rely on a tradition that has grown tired and corrupt, and so Gandhi continually revisits tradition and, where he finds it necessary, challenges it. For him, a revitalized and reformed tradition represents the best moral resource to question the efficiencies of the age.

GANDHI'S CIVIC REALISM

Although it seems strange to think of Gandhi as a political realist, much of his work is infused with a rich understanding of power and he shares much with conventional political realists, such as Machiavelli[4] in the West and Kautilya in India. In the realist account, power is unavoidable, seductive, and important. Whether we like it or not, power surrounds us; for realists, including Gandhi, the issue is not whether we can avoid power by ignoring it but how we understand and respond to its nature and uses. Realists share the views that power cannot be completely tamed, that it frequently carries dangerous consequences, and that it can never be fully exonerated by a comprehensive morality. To the realist, power itself is ubiquitous, unpredictable, and often hazardous. It provides us with the means to achieve some goal or overcome obstacles, but our quest for power often blinds us to its dangers. Realists see us frequently inflating our capacity to direct and control power and failing to appreciate its limits. Entering the fluid, unpredictable world of power, we frequently harm others and unintentionally injure ourselves. For all of the problems associated with it, realists find people continually searching for more power, often to keep pace with their competitors.[5]

For someone such as Machiavelli, the power of any person or state is always problematic, subject to the wiles of *fortuna*. Even though one actor has ostensibly greater power than its opponents at any given moment, it can be undermined by unexpected changes or unconventional power.[6] One reason is that power takes many forms, and what seems to be an overwhelming expression of power in a particular setting can be inexplicably undermined by alternative modes of power.[7]

Gandhi's realism follows from his reading of power as unavoidable, dangerous, and coveted. For him, power needs to be understood more expansively than it generally is, not to repackage in new containers that deny its hazards or inevitability, but to show people its many locations and forms. Although Gandhi does not hold the bleak view of conventional realists that people are constantly driven by ambition and ready to dominate others, he finds that any society is open to this possibility. For this reason, Gandhi wants to domesticate power by dispersing it throughout society to avoid monopolistic or oligopolistic concentrations.

Gandhi's civic realism departs from conventional realism in several important ways. One reflects his argument that politics is about more than power and must address the purposes for which it is employed and how it is used. He intends to direct it in ways that speak to the dignity, freedom, and equality of persons. For him, the way power is applied has profound effects, and often unintended ones. In arguing that violent applications of power undermine even generous principles, Gandhi insists that people pay attention to the kind of power they employ and the means they use to mobilize it. If the purpose of power is to foster mutuality and autonomy, he means to show that violence only subverts these goals.

Gandhi's civic realism is also reflected in the attention he gives to the institutions of civil society which are critical to his understanding of power. The ways they organize and distribute power serve to facilitate or diminish individual self-governance, and he calls attention to the ways that institutions reward, ignore, and penalize particular forms of behavior. Some arrangements signal to people that they can protect their own economic well-being and security only by transferring their self-governance elsewhere. For these reasons, Gandhi leaves a conventional political realism that is preoccupied with state power and moves to a wider understanding of power which pays attention to how civil society is organized and what happens there.

The very features of politics that Gandhi makes a central part of his understanding of power and politics, namely love and conversion, seem to disqualify Gandhi as a realist, but I think not. He finds that lasting change does not come through coercion; that support born of good economic times often falters when the economy grows sour; that appeals to conscience often have a profound effect—if not immediately, then over time; and that some of the most intractable issues are not settled by violence but require dialogue and understanding. He takes his readers beyond conventional meanings of power to show what an expanded version can accomplish. Gandhi's civic realism, for all of its emphasis on love, speaks more directly to power than a political realism purporting to be scientific, a realism trying to mimic economic markets, or a realism that makes efficient management its center. In presenting a multidimensional understanding of power and its effects on individuals, Gandhi leaves a crude realism and attempts to teach a civic realism in order to reach ethical conclusions about political life.

GANDHI'S FUTURE

Although many support autonomy and decentralization and the postmodernist impulse to question is extensive, these positions—along with Gandhi's—do not seem to be the priorities of the late modern world. It is not so much that the twenty-first-century promises to be hostile to Gandhi's theories and his idiom; more likely, it will be unconcerned. The metaphors of the future are apt to revolve around globalization and its kin uniformity; the market and its kin consumerism; instrumental rationality and its kin order and predictability; and none of these metaphors has need of Gandhi. Where Gandhi wants diversity, modernity covets regularity; where he sees politics as struggle, it sees politics as administration; where he looks to a reformed tradition, it concentrates on current satisfactions; where he reaches for localism, it revels in universalism; and when he joins his voice with the periphery, it is indifferent. Gandhi's walk into the twenty-first century, then, may be a lonely one.

Although the modern temper is preoccupied with matters far removed from much that Gandhi promotes and although some of his specific proposals are anachronistic in our complex, troubled society, his ideals continue to speak to the late modern world. It is a world that seems fragmented and incoherent and where control seems elusive, and Gandhi means to challenge this state of affairs. Tying together disparate themes, he abandons the usual specializations that conventionally mark modern thinking. Politics, economics, morality, religion, tradition, and the household are interwoven into his frame of thinking in an effort to see how they can cohere in ways that speak to freedom and equality.

In his efforts to recover coherence and control, he raises questions to unsettle and disturb both those who carry formal power and those who do not in order to challenge the former and energize the latter. In upsetting what has been thought to have been decided in the modern era, he seeks to show his readers that they do not have to assume the world can be no other way than it is now; that current standards used to judge success and failure are constructions which do not necessarily speak to the best in them and sometimes address the weakest in them. For him, politics, economics, and tradition are not separate, discrete phenomena but are interlocking and carry significant consequences for men and women.

Even though Gandhi's call to limit wants may seem utopian and the likelihood of its being accepted remote, the urgency of his message becomes all the more pressing with each passing year. The environment is degraded, waterways assaulted, nonrenewable resources depleted, and the atmosphere corrupted. Today's consumer society has little sense of obligation to the environment, and Gandhi wants to challenge this kind of moral apathy. He finds that modern consumption rests on a hubris that threatens to destroy both consumers and those who serve them. However, the ethic of limited consumption Gandhi wants to encourage seems to have little prospect of succeeding today. Recognizing the magnitude of the task, he believes a voluntary limitation of consumption is more likely to thrive if people have a cosmological outlook rather than a narrowly individualistic one. Persons who see interconnectedness and interdependency are more likely to recognize the need to limit their consumption than someone whose sole point of reference is the isolated, "independent" self.

Another area of concern in the late modern world that Gandhi addresses is violence. Although the great threat of global thermonuclear destruction has lessened in the post–Cold War period, other forms of armed conflict continue unabated, and the traffic in weapons intensifies. In this setting, Gandhi is a clear voice about the dangers of accepting violence as inevitable, whether local or international. He invites us not only to address the ways conflict can be settled without violence but also to see how civil society, with its patterns of domination and humiliation, can be reconstituted in order to avoid the conditions that give rise to violence in the first place.

If Gandhi speaks to the future, what political language is equipped to translate his teachings to the modern ear? The twenty-first century is likely to be a time when some form of liberalism is the dominant language of politics. What should be noticed is that there is not a single liberalism but many forms, and some are more open to much that Gandhi says just as some are antagonistic. Gandhi's frequent attacks on many basic principles in much liberal thinking should not obscure his many affinities with liberalism. True, he is impatient with a liberalism that spawns a narrow individualism, disregards tradition and community, and equates economic growth with morality. At the same time, he borrows heavily from a liberalism that speaks of civil liberties, the need to separate church and state, and representative democracy. To acknowledge Gandhi's kinship with aspects of a generous liberalism that raises questions about poverty, racism, sexism, and violence and that celebrates autonomy is to make him accessible and familiar to liberals who share his distemper with violence and domination and his commitment to self-governance.

PROBLEMATIZING GANDHI

Reading Gandhi as a problematizer of violence and modernity also serves to problematize Gandhi. The defender of tradition turns out to be one of its harshest critics; his self-conscious attacks on modernity cannot conceal his own reliance on many of its central concepts, such as equality, freedom, and reason; his assault on modernization is always coupled with a sense of what it promises and what it fails to deliver; and his opposition to violence is accompanied by repeated calls for struggle and resistance. Gandhi's harsh criticisms of tradition, violence, modernity, and modernization are not meant to offer a metanarrative of despair, and his morality tales about a simple economy and polity are not presented as a metanarrative of nostalgia. If Gandhi has something to say to the late modern world, it is surely not found in his specific proposals for spinning or a rural economy. His legacy comes with the issues he raises about autonomy, democracy, economic security, participatory communities, and the nonviolent resolution of conflict. For Gandhi, these issues need a home in the late modern world and ought not become remainders.

He is particularly concerned about the ways efforts to dominate continue to appear and reappear in any society. Fearing that many individuals often accept domination as necessary, as beyond challenge, or even as legitimate, Gandhi sees people becoming complicit in the way power is employed. Should we expect Gandhi to offer more than struggle to live an autonomous life? Although he continually holds out ideals and repeatedly talks about the need to find a harmony in one's life and community, in the end he thinks that such goods can only be approached through struggle. Efforts to picture him building a regime and community that are perpetually peaceful and harmonious misread Gandhi.

If Gandhi is to have a voice in the twenty-first century, then not all of his texts can be approached literally. Texts do not entirely speak for themselves, particularly those that teach and admonish, often by reaching to practices, problems, and opportunities whose original home is much different than that of later readers. In responding to his own immediate world, Gandhi not only calls up specific solutions that do not address the late modern world, he also reaches for resources—such as a rural economy and a simple society—that have weakened in our own time. Anyone in the late modern world who is interested in addressing the issues Gandhi raises earlier about autonomy and nonviolence needs to interrogate him to understand how his commitments are transported to a different world and translated into their own idiom.

Because this often means accepting Gandhi's invitation to experiment and because the results are unpredictable, many find this is one of the most discordant aspects of his theories.[8] They lead, as Joan Bondurant observes, "to solutions as yet unknown."[9] And they must, given Gandhi's views that no one possesses the whole truth, that truth emerges in the encounters agents have with one another, and that to approach the truth, struggle is often necessary.

NOTES

1. Gandhi, *Harijan*, March 28, 1936.
2. See Agnes Heller and Ferenc Feher, *The Postmodern Political Condition* (Cambridge: Polity Press, 1988); Jeffrey Goldfarb, *The Cynical Society* (Chicago: University of Chicago Press, 1991); Daniel Bell, *The Cultural Contradictions of Capitalism* (New York: Basic, 1976); Norberto Bobbio, *Future of Democracy;* David Marquand, *The Unprincipled Society* (London: Fontana Press, 1988); Ronald Beiner, *What's the*

Matter with Liberalism? (Berkeley: University of California Press, 1992); and Alan Bloom, *The Closing of the American Mind* (New York: Simon and Schuster, 1987).

3. I am indebted to Rajni Kothari's discussion of the impact of the consequences of a blind technological imperative. See his *Footsteps into the Future*, particularly 90–94.

4. See Anthony Parel, "Gandhian *Satyagraha* and Machiavellian *Virtu*" in *The Meanings of Gandhi*, ed. Paul Powers (Honolulu: University Press of Hawaii, 1971).

5. To temper the destructive aspect of pride, Kautilya and Machiavelli counsel prudence; for Niebuhr, the solution comes with humility.

6. Gandhi also recognizes that power does not necessarily respond to our rational plans or best efforts.

7. Gandhi works with this kind of reasoning to mobilize unconventional power from below in order to confront formal, institutional power with his civil disobedience.

8. Those who particularly value order find remarks by Gandhi on experimentation disturbing. "Evolution is always experimental. All progress is gained through mistakes and their rectification. . . . This is the law of individual growth. The same law controls social and political evolution also. The right to err, which means the freedom to try experiments, is the universal condition of all progress." Gandhi, *Truth Is God* (Ahmedabad: Navajivan, 1990), 135.

9. Joan Bondurant, *Conquest of Violence*, 194.

IV

OVERVIEWS OF TRANSFORMATION: THE SACRED, THE SOCIAL, AND THE POLITICAL

To try to preach without referring to the history one preaches in is not to preach the gospel. Many would like a preaching so spiritualized that it leaves sinners unbothered and does not term idolaters those who kneel before money and power. A preaching that says nothing about the sinful environment in which the gospel is reflected upon is not the gospel.

—Archbishop Oscar Romero, *The Violence of Love*

Only our religious institutions, among the mainstream organizations of Western, Asian, and indigenous societies, can say with real conviction, and with any chance of an audience, that there is some point to life beyond accumulation.

—Bill McKibben, *Daedelus*, fall 2001

What was the "prophetic dimension" of the church supposed to be about if not the concerns of the prophets?—the widows, the orphans, the foreigners, and the broken, vulnerable of every society.

—Joan Chittister, "The Power of Questions to Propel"

By what right, with what interests and concerns, and with what distinctive contributions, does religion enter the public realm? Selections in this part provide comprehensive answers to these critical questions. While there is necessarily some overlap with other sections of the book, the distinct point of these essays is to describe in general terms why and how a liberating faith is both possible and indispensable.

Through the richness, complexity, and diversity of these authors, a number of central themes emerge.

First, there is the need to reread tradition: to see it, as Jewish Renewal leader Rabbi Michael Lerner puts it, as containing *both* the voice of God and the repetitive messages of oppression and pain. Farid Esack and Carter Heyward develop this theme in terms of a liberating theology for Islam and the critical edge of feminism. The message here is that a liberating faith is one necessarily always in critical connection with its own past.

Second, my essay, and those by Dorothee Soelle, Reinhold Niebuhr, and Walpola Rahula, challenge the familiar religious tendency to withdraw from the world, or to see spiritual concerns as separate from the realm of politics. By contrast, we believe that holiness requires politics, that the moral values that lie at the heart of tradition cannot be realized, or even approached, without an understanding of and an involvement in political life. Philip Berryman's essay describes in concrete terms how such a process might occur. Finally, Tu Weiming addresses the distinctive contributions that religion—or what we might call "religious culture"—can bring to politics. Writing from the standpoint of traditional Chinese thought, Weiming reminds us that if individualism, personal freedom, and material consumption come to define the goal of social life, interpersonal conflict and ecological damage will result. The pursuit of politics should not rest with human rights for atomized individuals, but seek the creation and maintenance of sustaining communities.

"The Struggle between Two Voices of God in Torah"

❧

Michael Lerner

Rabbi Michael Lerner has written *Spirit Matters*, edits *Tikkun Magazine*, and has long been actively involved in movements for peace and social justice. He seeks to combine religious passion with social change, joining a religious sense of wonder and awe with a hardheaded understanding of oppression.

❧

THE VOICE OF CRUELTY IS NOT THE VOICE OF GOD

Torah is filled with the voice of God as I have tried to describe, a voice of compassion and transcendence. But it is also filled with another voice, which mirrors human distortions and accumulated pain. Just as Abraham had trouble getting the land of Haran out of him, so the Jews had deep trouble getting the spiritual, ethical, and emotional legacy of Egypt out of them.

If, as I have argued, the accumulated pain and cruelty is passed from generation to generation, reinforced by the dynamics of nonrecognition and the desperate attempt to achieve connection by acting in ways that stay loyal to what our parents have taught us, then the people of Israel, like all peoples, will be hearing the voice of God in ways that are often mixed with the voices of pain and distortion. Our job is to distinguish the one from the other. To the extent that we are ready to hear God's voice, we can find it in Torah. But to the extent that we are morbidly drawn to our own tendencies toward cruelty and pain, those will be the resonant voices we respond to in Torah. How could it be otherwise?

Torah itself gives us some hints at the limited nature of the receivers of the revelation—as though perhaps it were partly conscious of the problem. From the moment that we understood the revelation, we began running from it. According to Exodus 20:15–16, the people were trembling and distanced themselves (*amdu m'rachok*), and then turned to Moses and said, "You speak to us and we will listen; but God should not speak with us because we will die." It is simply too much to stay in the full presence of what is being asked of us; and so we retreat. Let it be turned into language that is mediated through the limited consciousness of another human being.

The tradition says that "this is the Torah which Moses put before the children of Israel, by the mouth of God, by the hand of Moses." God may have transmitted, but it was Moses who received. Moses was a limited human being like every other human being. So what he heard was a limited revelation, the revelation receivable through the conceptual apparatus of a remarkable person, but a person born and raised in Egypt, looking at the world through its assumptions and its language even as he rebelled against those assumptions and that language.

In addition to Moses' limitations, we have another set of distortions: those imposed by virtue of trying to make a Torah that would be applicable to the specific realities of the people. The medieval Jewish philosopher Maimonides was alert to this issue in his own interpretation of many of the rituals that were developed by God. Moses is up on Sinai for forty days, but when he tarries to return a few hours late, the children of Israel lose faith that he will return, and demand of Aaron as follows: "Up, make us gods that will go before us . . ." (Exodus 32:1). So Aaron makes a calf from their gold rings, and the people say, "These are your gods, Israel, which brought you up out of the land of Egypt."

The people are hungry for the ways of Egypt. They are limited beings, and they can make only so much of a leap in one generation. Maimonides believed that many of the detailed rituals within the Torah were given by God in order to elevate our historically conditioned needs by placing them within the liberatory context of the fundamental insights of Judaism. The rituals are accommodations to the historical limitations of the people—they are not wanted by God as ends in themselves, but as a means to make it possible for limited human beings to "get" the fundamental points by teaching it to them through ritual behaviors that satisfy their needs. They give the people some degree of being "regular," with a "regular" religion that doesn't *only* demand that they stay true to the message of transcendence, but *also* gives them some less overwhelming tasks.

But there are more serious limitations to the message of transcendence, moments in which Torah seems to propagate ancient social practices and attitudes that embody the pain and cruelty of existing social systems. Sexism is the most striking and upsetting example.

This distortion shows through most clearly in the passage in which God tells Moses to prepare the people for the revelation. "And the Lord said unto Moses: 'Go to the people, and sanctify them today and tomorrow, and let them wash their garments, and be ready against the third day; for the third day the Lord will come down in the sight of all the people upon Mount Sinai. And you shall set bounds to the people around about, and say: Take heed to yourselves, that you do not go up into the mount, or touch the border of it; whoever touches the mountain shall surely be put to death; no hand shall touch him, but he shall surely be stoned, or shot through; whether it be beast or man, it shall not live; when the ram's horn sounds long, they shall come up to the mount.' And Moses went down from the mount to the people, and sanctified the people; and they washed their garments. And he said unto the people: 'Be ready against the third day; come not near a woman'" (Exodus 19:10–15).

Where does this "come not near a woman" come from? Not from God, according to the text; Moses simply understands from the standpoint of his conceptual apparatus that when God asks the people to sanctify themselves, this must mean that the injunction is addressed to the men and not to the women; and that contact with women undermines this sanctity.

It's quite clear in this instance that these are assumptions Moses brings into the communication—Moses receives God's command through his own sexist framework.

If we understand the "we" to be the community of males, thereby excluding and marginalizing women, then we can say that the primary form of distortion within the Torah is the distortion of exclusion, lack of concern for, and intuitive sympathy with the other. And the tension exists as a contradiction within the text itself. On the one hand, there is the recognition that we are all equally created in the image of God. The revolutionary implications are there in the text: "male and female created He them." And the rabbis of the Talmudic period, commenting on the notion of *tzelem Elohim*, the image of God, say explicitly that the purpose of this emphasis is precisely to communicate that everyone is equal, that no nation could possibly say that it is on a higher plane or closer to God.

And yet the text itself continues to reflect a different voice and sensibility as well, one that embodies the fear and denigration of the other, and the desire to pass on to others the violence that has been done to us, the common practice for those living in a world of oppression. The children of Israel are enslaved and then subjected to genocide as Pharaoh orders the death of every newborn Jew. The degradation and humiliation that this causes us as a people is deeply embedded, and though Torah does its best to undermine the process, it is at the same time, and in important ways, a product of that very process. So at times Torah externalizes anger at the other, falling into the pattern of nonrecognition that it itself most seeks to transcend.

The Israelites had gotten at least as far as anyone else in their contemporary world in overcoming cruelty and recognizing the other. The Torah tells us that when the Israelites left Egypt, it was not simply the blood descendants of Abraham, Isaac, and Jacob who became part of the people—it was "a mixed multitude." The Jewish people are not composed, then, of people who were racially pure or born Jewish—we are composed of this mixed multitude that wandered together in the desert. The great challenge of transcendence is specifically focused on the relationship to the non-Israelite, the *ger*, the person who is the outsider. Over and over again, Torah shows us an ethos of caring and concern for the other, for the powerless, for those who are in no position to defend themselves. Moreover, the revolutionary claim that Torah makes about human nature, that we are *all* created in the image of God, is the locus classicus of the politics of inclusion. Counter to every document of exclusion, there is in Torah a voice that insists on the sanctity of the other.

And yet there is another voice that we can hear clearly in Torah. It is precisely in regard to the other, the outsider, the non-Israelite, that the legacy of pain and cruelty acted out against us reasserts itself and is heard by some as the voice of God. The book of Deuteronomy, claiming to be recounting Moses' speech to the Israelites in accord with the will of God, makes clear that one of the tasks is to dispossess and destroy the peoples of the land to which they are coming, the land that God promised them.

In one sense, to come to the new place, to create a new reality, it was necessary to uproot the old way of life, to make no compromise with the oppressive world that already existed. One might hear this notion as a revolutionary demand: Make no deals; don't allow yourself to flirt with the dominant culture; create something totally different. But when that kind of insight gets translated, as it does in the Torah, to the demand that the peoples of the land be utterly destroyed, then we have, under the guise of fighting for a righteous cause, the reemergence of the cruelty and pain that had been inflicted upon the Jewish people in Egypt.

THE VOICE OF CRUELTY IN TORAH: "SHOW NO MERCY"

The triumphalist tone of Moses' account of the march of the people of Israel toward the Promised Land already marks this deterioration in moral sensibility. Sihon, the king of Heshbon, would not allow the people of Israel to pass through nor sell food or water to them, but instead fought against them. "And the Lord our God delivered him up before us; and we smote him, and his sons, and all his people. And we took all his cities at that time, and utterly destroyed every city, the men, and the women, and the little ones; we left none remaining; only the cattle we took for a prey unto ourselves, with the spoil of the cities which we had taken" (Deuteronomy 2:33–35).

But lest we think that this is a momentary aberration flowing from the passion of the battle and the anger at having been attacked, Moses goes on in Deuteronomy to tell the people exactly what they are expected to do to the Hittite, the Girgashite, the Amorite, the Canaanite, the Perizzite, the Hivite, and the Jebusite—the seven nations that live in the land that God is now giving to the Jewish people: "Thou shalt smite them; then thou shalt utterly destroy them; thou shalt make no covenant with them, nor show mercy unto them" (Deuteronomy 7:2). *Loe techanem*—thou shalt show no mercy.

The Book of Joshua carries forth this spirit, rejoicing in the defeats and destruction of the people of the land, assuring us that this is really the spirit of God and the continuation of the legacy of Moses. And that same spirit manifests itself again when Samuel, prophet of God, turns in fury on King Saul, who has failed to kill Agag, the king of the Amalekites, despite the allegedly clear command of God that he do so. Samuel picks up the sword and himself beheads the Amalekite—supposedly showing thereby his vigilance and commitment to God. It is an action that recalls a similar act of violence in the Torah itself, when Pinchas kills an Israelite and the Midianite woman with whom he is having sexual relations—to show that the Israelites are not to have sexual contact with "the enemy"—and is rewarded by God with the right to have his branch of the Levite family become the high priests.

It matters little for the sake of the present argument if all this was written much later than other parts of the Torah tradition, written so much in the style of the late prophets that some people believe that the whole book of Deuteronomy was a creation of Jeremiah or his followers. Or if it was written by a people of Israel who were becoming enslaved and defeated by those around them, or by people in Babylonian exile, or by people recently returned from exile in the time of Ezra. It matters little if the whole story of the conquest was a later fabrication, as has been forcefully argued by some historians, an attempt to give strength and a sense of purpose to a people who were experiencing themselves as powerless and unable to defend themselves.

Actually, these considerations *would* matter if our task were to judge *them*, the people who put this book together, or the people who heard God's revelation in this way. But that is not my purpose in raising this issue. I confront these passages and the entire "Joshua tradition" not to judge those who adopted it, but to say in the most unequivocal terms: *This is not the voice of God*, but the voice of pain and cruelty masquerading as the voice of God.

There is no point in trying to hide from ourselves the cruelty and insensitivity in these passages. Nor is there any point in pretending that it was a momentary aberration. All through Jewish history some people have been hearing God's voice in this way, building on these passages their own understanding of the essence of Judaism. Furious at their vulnerability and powerlessness, outraged at the immorality of those non-Jews who periodically murdered, raped, and pillaged them, some Jews adopted a Torah of cruelty that distorted the Torah of love and compassion. Unable to imagine that the non-Jew was himself or herself a victim of oppression, seeing only their power and the hurtful and destructive way that power was used against the Jewish people, some Jews embraced those strands of the tradition that refused to recognize the non-Jew as really deserving of the dignity that Torah seemed to confer on them in claiming that we were *all* created in the image of God. So, for example, the sixteenth-century compendium of Jewish law, the Shulchan Aruch (Yoreh Deah 158), reasserts a talmudic injunction forbidding Jews to save the life of an idolater or of a Jew who brazenly rejects the kosher dietary laws or someone who does not believe that the dead will be resurrected someday. It's not hard to see how nonrecognition of the other as created in the image of God is a slippery slope: one starts with the idolater, and it is only a few steps to taking nonobservant or nonbelieving Jews to be the enemy as well. Right-wing Israelis who have physically attacked peace activists continue this distorted process.

This sensibility, this denial of the other, really is in the text. The text really does record two different kinds of voices of God. The redactors or composers of the Torah, like the halakhic authorities of later ages, reflect both those voices in the text and do not recognize, or at least do not tell us that they are recognizing, the conflict between these two voices.

Those who redacted the Torah and the Joshua tradition incorporated this cruelty into the revelation as they understood it, because when they listened to the voice of God, part of what they heard was the transcendent message of Sinai, and part of what they heard was the distorting influence of the legacy of pain that infused their consciousness. By the time we get to later elaborations of Jewish law, there are some who argue that Jews do not have an obligation to save the life of a non-Jew. The voice of cruelty appeared at some moments and within some sectors of the Jewish world to be more powerful than the voice of healing and compassion.

Jews in subsequent generations have built on this tradition of anger and denigration of the other, used it as their own basis of fantasied compensation for the actual experience of powerlessness and humiliation in their daily lives. They were responding to the voice of pain and cruelty within, not to the call of God. Through the ages, and culminating in the religious Right wing in Israel today, these passages from Deuteronomy, Joshua, and Samuel have given the voice of cruelty an apparent divine seal of approval. The massacre of twenty-nine Muslims at prayer in Hebron in February 1994 by an Orthodox Jew was an outgrowth of a culture of violence among some "Modern Orthodox" Jews that builds on these texts, using them as their own historical precedent to legitimize the way that they too can identify their own inner cruelty with the voice of God.

FINDING THE "NICE" QUOTES

The approach of many of the rabbis throughout Jewish history and of many of the more humane religious voices in Israel today has been to try to counter these quotes with other quotes, to find textual bases in which to root a more humane and sensitive attitude toward others. For example, countering rightists who cite the injunctions to kill the inhabitants of the land as justification for contemporary policies toward Palestinians, they've pointed to those interpreters of Halakha who claim that "idolaters" refers only to the original seven tribes of Canaan, and hence that there really isn't anything to worry about in injunctions against idolaters since none exists anymore.

Religious rightists, on the other hand, have accused these religious humanists of ignoring the texts, and they have a legitimate argument. If you accept the defining position of contemporary orthodoxy, that the texts are themselves holy and the embodiment of God's will and word, then you must take seriously the parts of the text that seem to be in conflict with your sensibilities. The religious Right makes this point when it says that the religious humanists are really embodying a set of Western ideas and parading them as Judaism. It would be more accurate to say that there are conflicting voices and strands within the tradition. The voice of cruelty and fanaticism and intolerance and oppression sometimes *can* be heard in our holy texts, alongside the voice of transcendence and compassion. The religious Rightists, in emphasizing one strand, are no more or less "authentic" than Jewish renewalists who emphasize the other. What is a distortion sometimes engaged in by the Right, however, is to attribute the ideas of compassion and caring for others to Western humanism or post-Enlightenment optimism, when these values so clearly come from the Torah.

INEVITABLE DISTORTIONS

Talking about the struggle within our tradition between the voice of transcendence and the voice of accumulated cruelty is not meant to be any denigration of Torah. If Torah embodies this struggle between two voices, if some of what is identified as God in Torah is really the voice of accumulated pain, it is nevertheless a document which provides us with a way of hearing the voice of God and, from that insight, being able to learn to critique the voice of accumulated pain. The extraordinary thing about Torah is not that it contains a voice of pain—after all, it was limited and distorted human beings, we and our forefathers and foremothers, who *received* Torah, so naturally we would receive it through our limited and distorted receptors—but that it is not *only* the voice of pain, and that for the first time in human history a human community consciously acknowledges itself to be hearing, commanded by, and committed to a different kind of voice, a voice of love, justice, and transcendence. Respond to *that* voice!

HOW DO YOU RECOGNIZE THE VOICE OF GOD?

The voices of God can be found in those parts of Jewish tradition—Torah; Midrash; the stories; the Halakha; the humor; the way of being human in the world—that tend to lead you to believe that the world can be changed from one dominated by pain, oppression, patriarchy, and evil to one in which human beings can live together in love and justice.

Whatever parts of the tradition help you to connect with the recognition of the other as created in the image of God, whatever tends to give you confidence and hopefulness about the possibility of joining as partners with God in the task of healing and repair of the universe, those are the parts of the tradition that have been revealed, that have the mark of God in them. Every part of the tradition, the Halakha, the stories, the humor, or the ways of being in the world that tend to make you doubt the possibility of human beings living that way is *not* the voice of God, but the voice of the accumulated pain of history, masquerading and parading as wisdom or profundity, but reflecting only our collective disappointment and impatience that the healing of humanity is taking so long.

The antireligious secularist makes a powerful challenge at this point in the argument: "Once you've abandoned the notion that God's revelation is responsible for the entire Torah, aren't you simply reduced to picking what you like from the Torah? And if you are doing that, in what sense are you rooted in the Torah? Moreover, why even bother with the Torah in the first place; why not just start from your own insights about what you like?" My answer: because in Torah we find God.

I've tried to argue that the Torah can best be understood as the record of human beings' encounter with the Divine, including the record of the ways that our understanding of that encounter has been limited by who we are and who the people were who first had that encounter. The struggle between our capacity for transcendence and compassion, on the one hand, and our tendency to embody and pass on the pain and cruelty of the past, on the other, is the central drama of human life and human history. That it finds expression in the Torah should be no surprise, nor necessarily a basis for discounting the divinity and holiness of the Torah tradition.

There's a part of many liberals that would have been more comfortable with a Torah that manifested only transcendence and compassion, and that had no pain and cruelty. Yet such a book would have had little to do with the reality of the human experience. The Torah is a useful guide to life because it is both a record of grappling with reality from the standpoint of God, and a record of the way that we are still in the struggle. To be Israel, the very word implies, is to *yisra* (struggle with) *El* (God). That wrestling is never a finished product, but a path which a people has chosen to be on.

Some people yearn for a Torah that would feel more like the completed teachings of "a perfect master," along the lines of various Eastern religious gurus. But we have a Torah that is an ongoing process, in which each generation unpacks its meaning by allowing itself to hear the voice of God within it in the way that that generation can hear. Some generations merely accept the texts as the received tradition, and to the extent that they treat these texts as "holy" fetishes that can't be struggled with, they transform them into idols. The essence of the process of renewal built into the Torah is to take these words, *va'chie ba'hem*, and *live* through them, which is to say, make them alive and life-giving and life-nurturing. Jewish renewal is a central part of the process through which this takes place.

This is very different from a guru's enlightenment. Many who relate to the guru traditions exhibit a certain passivity, a willingness to let others do the interpreting, a waiting for others to provide the meaning and suggest the roads with which to find the highest truths. The over-reliance on authority, be it the authority of a given explicator of the Torah or a given Hasidic spiritual master, has always engendered resistance in the Jewish world. The Jewish world has been characterized by a degree of contentiousness and disagreement that has guaranteed a spirit of independence of thought and action. Although the contentions often take place within the normative framework of Jewish religious tradition, the spirit of that contention, embodied in a long history of disputes about what exactly the tradition *is*, has created much space for alternative ways of looking at the world. But in the process, the tradition must not be radically discontinuous with the world it seeks to transform. "*Loe bashamayim hee,*" says a verse of the Torah about the Torah—it is not in heaven, but very close to us. And that very closeness permits for distortion.

But if there is distortion built into the Torah, then aren't we better off relying on our own intuitions and not basing ourselves on a tradition that encompasses the voice of pain and cruelty?

Any liberatory tradition will necessarily incorporate the distortions and limitations of its period. There is no Archimedean point from which one can build a solidly healthy and transformative vision: every vision is necessarily partial and partially distorted. Consider some other liberatory traditions, such as psychoanalysis, Marxism, and feminism, to name a few that have been recent contenders. When one looks at each of these closely, one will find a set of distortions in some of the founding literature, based in part on the historically conditioned limitations of the people who were the initial theorists and founders. Moreover, each tradition has been used at various points as an instrument to repress rather than liberate by at least some of its practitioners.

Our Torah documents the history of human efforts at transcendence, and records the interaction between those attempts and the distortions that emerged in their midst. We may not yet have a total vision of the good, but we do have a vision of what has been bad, and we do have some solid intuitions that have been gleaned through the history of the human race and have contributed to the emergence of a liberatory perspective. We as a human race know that it is wrong to create needless suffering, and though we do not fully agree on what is needless at any particular historical moment, we nevertheless feel confident that there is some substantial content to this insight.

What the Torah also gives us is not a single criterion for determining what is God's word, but a sense of how people heard that word in the past, and evokes in us the confidence to criticize the Torah in the name of Torah. And that, in fact, has been precisely what three thousand years of Jewish commentary has been about—the critique of the Torah from the perspective of Torah, but done in the form of commentary.

DOES THIS ACCOUNT GIVE HUMANS TOO MUCH AUTHORITY?

If we say that two voices are contending in Torah, don't we ultimately leave the whole matter up to human beings to determine what is the voice of God and what is the voice of accumulated evil?

Yes. But that is not a new situation. We always have had to rely on human beings when understanding the Torah. We had to rely on human beings to determine where God wanted the Temple, and when an action is killing and not murder, and which are the real prophets and which the false. We had to rely on human beings to tell us that when the Temple was destroyed what God really wanted was prayer instead of sacrifice, in defiance of the plain meaning of the words of the text. The rabbis of the talmudic period understood what they were doing, and they spent a great deal of their time trying to find "prooftexts," however stretched the interpretations of them, upon which they could hang their own particular approach. Yet they understood that what they were doing was giving *their* interpretation, not *the* interpretation. When they changed the laws requiring sacrifices into the basis for a requirement of prayer, they knew that this didn't appear in the text. Perhaps they might have been tempted to claim that they were prophets, hearing a new revelation. But they made no such claim. They were changing the plain meaning of the text based on their best ability to understand, in light of their own intellects and spiritual intuition, what would be the best way to keep the enterprise of Torah alive in their own circumstances. Hundreds of years later, those who followed these talmudic rabbis attributed to them and their work a holiness that at least many of the talmudic rabbis would have dismissed as silly, pretentious, or idolatrous. In imagining that these rabbis were on some higher plane, later generations could excuse themselves of the responsibility of opening their own ears to the call of God and to the need to reunderstand the text. Yet that attribution of a higher status to previous generations, and the selective process of choosing *which* of the interpreters of the past will be the ones we choose to respond to, *is* an act of interpretation every bit as subjective as the talmudic rabbis'.

We are always interpreting what God really wants, selecting which interpreters and which texts of the past to find decisive, and no set of written words is ever going to explain itself. So the notion of relying on fallible human beings is a shock only to those who have hid from themselves the degree to which even the most orthodox of the Orthodox rely on a long set of interpretations that seem to go directly counter to the obvious meaning of the texts.

And this is why the objection to the enterprise that says, "You are merely reading your own set of values into the text rather than really responding to what is there," is always either a deep misunderstanding or bad faith. The moment one chooses a rabbi, a *yeshiva*, a *posek*, a theory of literary interpretation, a hermeneutic style, one is already approaching texts from a particular discourse or framework. Read the Midrash and its frequent attempts to prove that the patriarchs were really observing Torah laws before they were given to Moses (e.g., that Abraham's serving butter and lamb together to the visiting three angels wasn't really a violation of *kashrut*) and you get a dramatic demonstration of how very ancient is this process of rereading texts.

Coming to the text with one's own set of conceptions, questions, language, and needs is inevitable. Attention is always and necessarily selective. All that exist are the Torah scrolls, scribbles on the page, and then interpretations of those scribbles into words, and interpretations of those words into meanings. The *ta'amey hamkirah*, the symbols that taught us how to sing a sentence and where that sentence actually ends (because the text has no punctuation, no commas or periods or question marks), was the first interpretive venture, and ever since there has always been selective attention in constructing the meaning of the text. Biblical scholars often imagine themselves as merely detached and objective readers unpacking the nuances, complexities, and contradictory elements of the text. Yet this style of reading is itself a political choice. All too often, the enterprise of Bible scholarship becomes the enterprise of taming the Bible so that it no longer sizzles with revolutionary power. The ability of one group of interpreters to portray its reading as objective scholarship, apolitical, and a rejection of "selective attention," is a fact about power, not about Torah.

Every position is inevitably shaped by interests and cultural baggage—but that doesn't preclude serious grappling with the text. I've often found myself astounded by what I've discovered as I've tried to uncover the complexities and nuances of a particular formulation—the clever wordplays, the economy of language, the playfulness, the hidden meaning in poetry, the layers of meaning—and this is part of the joy of studying the Torah. There is much pleasure and excitement in studying the texts—and though one always brings one's self, no matter how pious or Orthodox a self it is, one can find within the text formulations and insights that challenge and argue with that self.

Just as the answer to the question "Who is to say what we are to do when the Temple gets destroyed?" must be answered, *"We are,"* so too a similar answer for the question "Who is to decide which is the voice of cruelty and which the voice of God?" *We*, the people who accept the Torah; who hear in it the voice of God; who feel ourselves commanded by Torah; and who accept the responsibility for preserving, observing, and passing on the tradition to the next generation; *we*, who in this process become the current historical embodiments of the people of Israel, are the ones to say which is the voice of cruelty and which is the voice of God, using our best efforts to understand the tradition, ourselves, our distortions, our historical epoch and *its* distortions.

Could we be mistaken? Sure. But when you attune your ear carefully and open your heart appropriately, it doesn't seem so very hard to discover which texts seem to speak to the most loving and other-affirming places in your being, and which texts seem to speak to the angriest, hurt or hurtful, vengeful, and oppressive parts of your being. The more profoundly we become aware of the ways that our own past, our own inner distortions, and our own loyalties to past ways of thinking and feeling are currently shaping us, the more we are able to distinguish between the parts of what we hear when we listen for God's voice that are shaped by our own personal legacy, and the parts that seem actually to represent a voice of love, caring, compassion, and holiness. The value of what we have learned through psychoanalytic thought, Marxist thought, feminist thought, critical theory, music, art, poetry, and meditation is that these methodologies assist us in detaching ourselves from our conditioned psychological inheritance, distancing ourselves from the chains of anger and cruelty that are passed from generation to generation.

So here is how we listen to the voice of God: using every intellectual and emotional and spiritual tool at our disposal; refracting what we think we are hearing through the community of others similarly committed to hearing God's voice, constantly engaged in prayer and meditation to help us recognize new forms of self-deception; reminding ourselves in humility that no matter how hard we try, we are self-deceptive in the way we apprehend reality, asking for God's guidance, aware of the ways that others who have honestly asked for this guidance have nevertheless been shaped by their own inner legacies of anger and cruelty; and doing our best to stay true to what we hear or what we get as we open ourselves to God's presence in the universe. Using those intellectual and spiritual tools, and retaining the deep humility of knowing that what we hear is likely to be only a partial getting of what God wants us to get, we then approach the texts to listen to where we hear the voice of God and where we do not. If not everyone agrees with what we have gotten or the way we've identified God's voice in the text, that doesn't make us any worse off than anyone else who has ever approached these texts and this tradition.

"No, you *are* worse off, because your Jewish renewal is saying that some parts of Torah are not the voice of God, whereas in the past the founders of Rabbinic Judaism did not say that any part of the tradition wasn't really God's word; they only changed the interpretation or meaning of God's word." A reasonable objection, but it doesn't hold. Because what they were doing, in effect, was saying that they had gotten a new revelation of God's word that gave them the right to change the original meaning to their own meaning. And that was at least as dangerous an assumption as saying, as I do, that the original voice was not the voice of God, but only the way God's voice was heard by somewhat limited human beings, and that we, another group of very limited human beings, must try to hear God's voice as best *we* can—and that will entail, in part, determining for ourselves where in Torah we really think we are hearing the voice of God.

This is not to deny the holiness of the text. The Torah is holy precisely because it so strikingly preserves for us both voices, shows us the contrast, forces us to choose. In the very process of coming to grips with the voice of God and the voice of cruelty, we become sensitized to the fact that this same struggle is going on inside us at all times, and that at every moment we are forced to make choices about which part of our being we are going to give priority. Choosing how to read the Torah, and where in it to find the word of God, becomes a central part of our own inner *tikkun*.

Ultimately there is no escaping this obligation to put our full selves into the process. If we think we've escaped this by trusting some *rebbe* or authoritative teacher or *posek*, we've merely deceived ourselves, because in making the choice of *which rebbe* or authoritative teacher or *posek* to pay attention to, we have made the same intuitive choice.

Maybe we are distinguishing the voice of God from the voice of pain on the basis of our contemporary Western values: democracy, egalitarianism, feminism, etc., and hence simply picking and choosing on a contemporary Western value-basis what we like and dislike in the Torah. If that's true, it doesn't distinguish our actions from those in any other moment in Jewish history. What people heard at previous moments as the voice of God was based on the contemporary values of *those* times as well. What else were the rabbis doing, for example, when they decided to modify the elimination of loans during the sabbatical year? When they used their own understanding of what the Torah was trying to accomplish, and decided that their methods were better than those described in the Torah itself, they could just as easily have been accused of substituting the values of *their* contemporary society for the values of Torah. They thought they knew what would be best, and they read the Torah to conform to their judgment. Doing just this, using one's best possible judgment, *is the tradition*. It is obvious from reading the Talmud that they selected texts to justify the interpretive choices they had already made—choices that in their own minds were totally consistent with Torah—but choices that were not articulated in the Torah itself.

How do we decide which is the voice of God? This is a many-sided process. In part, this judgment emerges from our intuition or our ability to tune in to the reverberations of Sinai that remain available to us. But it is not intuition or listening alone. God created us with rational capacities and as part of a community of rational communicators, and so whatever we intuit must be subject to challenge, argument, and doubt. And we must do our best to overcome those factors that might distract or modify our choices. As Rabbi Israel Salanter and a wide variety of Hasidic teachers have insisted, we have to be aware that our own egos may distort our perceptions. We have to overcome what Jewish tradition calls *negiah*, the way that our own interests may touch on a matter in ways that make us unable to see it clearly. We can go through therapy to clear up the ways in which we may still be dominated by the legacy of cruelty from our own past. We can study with those who seem to us to have made progress in their own inner struggles against accumulated pain and anger. We can study the long history of Jewish interpreters and look for the ways in which they tried to interpret texts to highlight what they thought was God's voice and what they thought was the voice of distortion. We can engage in acts of kindness and compassion to deepen our own sensitivity to the pains of others. We can put forward tentative assessments of what we hear in the text that we think is holy and what we hear that we think is not so holy, and then compare them with the assessments of others. We can decide to join with others in an interpretive community and abide by the judgments of that community (but first we have to make the decision about which community to join or *which* people share enough of our sense of spiritual sensitivity to God to want to build such a community with them).

We must always keep ourselves open to rational questioning and rational critique, and we must insist that all people, created in the image of God, are part of the community of discourse whose concerns and critiques of the way we distinguish the voice of God from the voice of cruelty must be taken seriously. It is within this context of ongoing intellectual and spiritual struggle, always open to new doubts about our own possible distortions, always sensitive to and trying to compensate for the complex psychological, social, and ideological factors that may be inclining us in a particular direction, that we make what may be called a leap of faith, as we decide which is in fact the voice of God and which is in fact the voice of cruelty.

Does this leave us with a charismatic religion based solely on individual judgments, personal intuitions, and claims to direct access to God? If so, we might soon be indistinguishable from the crackpots on the corner who are constantly telling us that they hear the voice of God and who use that to validate every possible nonsense. What distinguishes us, as Rabbi Tzvi Blanchard points out, is precisely that our listening to the voice of God is always done within the context of a tradition that we accept, an interpretive community whose historical and current realities provide a framework for assessing our current encounters with God's voice. Faith does not isolate us from the demands of reason or self-doubt, nor from the responsibility of engaging in ongoing rational dialogue with the community of rational communicators. Abraham Joshua Heschel once said to me that he knew the Bible was sacred because he could hear God's voice in the texts. To know that, he *already* had some sense of who God was. Yet that sense was not something that popped into his head whole cloth, but rather was a product of a life enmeshed in a particular community of discourse, of study, and of *mitzvot*.

So when people object to this enterprise and say, "Who are you to say what is the voice of God and what is the voice of cruelty?" the only possible reply is: "A member of the Jewish people; part of a community that has been struggling with these texts for thousands of years; a contemporary inheritor of the wisdom and the techniques and the passion and the experience of our people; a community of people that developed psychoanalysis and Marxist analysis in part to deepen our abilities to recognize and compensate for our own distortions, now engaged in trying to do in this generation what Jews have done in every generation: open our ears to God's revelation, whose sound waves are still pulsating through the universe, and our eyes to God's Torah and to the interpretive community that grapples with Torah, that takes it seriously, and that will try not to allow it to be hijacked either by the legacy of cruelty or by the arrogance of those who think they have all the answers."

We confront this task with humility and a prayerful request to God, repeated in the Shachreet service each morning: "Enlighten our eyes in Your Torah, and cause our hearts to cleave to You, and unify our hearts to love and stand in awe of Your Name."

Prayer is no afterthought. Throughout this book I have argued that God is the Force that makes possible our ability to transcend our history and to recognize one another. And it is the God energy within us, the way that we are created in God's image, that gives us the ability to recognize God's voice.

It is this same God who is constantly pulling us toward transcendence of our own constituted ways of being and understanding reality. We move toward our newer conceptions of God *not* because we wish to be chic and modern, but because we are pulled in that way by God. Thus, Jewish renewal in every generation is made possible because of God's energy in the world.

"The Justice of Transcendence and the Transcendence of Justice"

❧

Roger S. Gottlieb

In this essay I explore some of the social and political dimensions of mysticism, and the contributions a contemporary form of mysticism may make to social life.

❧

Humanity's responses to the perils and pains of existence give rise to many attempts to see the sources of our suffering, to escape or transcend our limits, and to form or recognize communities of solidarity—both with other people and other beings. The cry of the heart has gone out to gods and goddesses, to totem animals and sacred mountains, and to those with whom we would join on the barricades. In the desperate time of the present, as cynics celebrate the end of alternatives to global capitalism, global industrialism, and global technoaddiction, those of us who are not entranced by the prospect of a fully administered society search for something else. Sensing the bleak and poisonous prospects around us, we shrink from pollution that is physical, psychic, and moral. Surely, we believe, (as people have always believed) that there is some other choice we can make. Surely we can find some wisdom with which to confront the soulless intelligence of modernity and the amoral cyberchic of postmodernity. Surely we can touch with our living hearts the Heart of the World and listen to the secret revelations of its unending beat. Surely, at least as individuals, we do not have to be bound by the endless commodification of the living world. Surely, if we cannot defeat or change, then we can *transcend* that which surrounds us.

One name for that transcendence is mysticism. It has for thousands of years signified the attempt to move beyond the confines of society and history, to break the bounds of normal human interaction, normal consciousness, and normal physical reality. It has been, or has been claimed to be, the foundation for a wisdom beyond—or hidden beneath—"this world." Yet, as we shall see in relation to the present, the world has a way of persisting in the face of the most transcendent of wisdoms. The struggle between transcendence and the social world, and the dangers that attend each, are the subjects of this essay.

117

MYSTICISM

This term is used to describe a variety of at times overwhelming, often life-defining, experiences, encounters that give rise to fundamental shifts in how we sense the nature of both the universe and our own personal identity. For many, those experiences are the heart of the world's religions. Beyond details of dogma, institutional organization, or even ethical teachings, the direct encounter with the divine seems to make possible a temporary release from the boundaries of the social ego and the socially constructed understanding of the body. This encounter provides an alternative to constricted forms of self-definition and challenges merely local claims about who we are, what we owe each other, and what we can be. The truth contained in mystical experiences seems to dwarf parochial understandings. People see them as "perennial" (as in "the perennial wisdom"), to be hidden from people not mature enough to grapple with the insights that mystical experience can confer, and even containing a hint of danger if misunderstood or misappropriated (as in the yogic warnings about the perils of developing psychic powers without the appropriate ethical development).

Mystical experiences are celebrated in every religious tradition. Consider, for example, the "Arhat," the type of the Sage in the original form of Buddhism that has come to be known as "Theravada." In his religious practices the Arhat seeks an end to the psychic confinement caused by mistaken identification with a self bound to desires and attachments. Intellectually, the Arhat has come to believe that this identification is the source of great pain (as the Buddha taught in the first of the Four Noble Truths). Yet intellectual acceptance of the first Noble Truth does not necessarily produce a sense of self (or "non-self") that is actually free of attachment. The question arises: is it in fact possible to be alive as a human being and *not* identify with a conventionally understood self, a collection of desires, aversions, etc? This question is answered—and what we might call mystical wisdom arises—when the student directly experiences a state of mind in which identification with self dissipates. As one early practitioner is reputed to have said, when questioned by a fellow seeker: "During my meditation I reached a point where I had no thought that 'I am this; this is mine; this is my self.'"[1]

Or consider the prophet Elijah. Fleeing for his life from Jezebel's wrath after he put to death the prophets of Baal, he encounters God not in a mighty wind, an earthquake, or a fire but in a "still, small voice" (I Kings 19:11–12). The voice is "inside him." It is a source of ultimate knowledge, or, in the case of what is typically stressed in Jewish scriptures, of ultimate moral responsibility—a responsibility that takes precedence over all merely social, merely conventional, customs or forms of authority. The experience of God's voice provides an ultimate ethical arbiter that releases us from any conflicting obligations to social powers.

Consider how the poet William Blake saw Christ suspended in air, dancing outside his window; or the states of ecstatic no-self produced by Sufi dancing or tribal chanting; or the transformations of consciousness that come on a Native American Vision Quest, prepared for by days of fasting and isolation. Or consider the feminist image of a divine interconnection and sharing and mingling of mind, emotion, and body—an interconnection in which God does not speak from the heavens or even within our hearts but emerges in the sacred spaces that both separate and connect us.[2]

In all these (and the legion more that could be discussed) we find the wisdom of mysticism. This wisdom provides an end, or at least a temporary alternative to, the ego's twisted identification with a psychic condition of permanent dissatisfaction, insecurity, and violence. From attachment to a particular social role we move to an identification with a cosmic harmony for which possessions, status, or social group become merely relative, merely historical, essentially contingent. From attachment to our particular, personal, self-owned pains and pleasures we move to a celebration of the infinite fields of energy that move through us. As in the case of Elijah, we develop a deeply altered and often highly critical sense of the meaning and validity of social life, of its teaching about what is important, of its norms of human interaction, of its models of success or adequacy.

Perhaps most important: while the intensity of the experience fades and may be hard even to remember at times (it is said that Pascal, having had an experience of God, sewed an image of the sun or a phrase beginning "fire, fire" into his clothes to remind himself), the wisdom of mysticism opens the receiver up to a clarity of understanding about what is of lasting importance in the realms of everyday, nontranscendent life. Variously known as love, grace, peace, or care, the wisdom of mysticism releases us from bondage to patterns of emotion that ultimately serve neither ourselves nor others. The demands that we earn a lot of money, be beautiful, make war on our "enemies," believe the government, manage to be successful at being "men" or "women"—these snarling dogs of desire ("fires" the Buddha called them) become the tame lapcats of tamed desire. We escape—initially only for a moment but then for much longer if we are able to maintain the power of the memory of that moment—the demands, evaluations, and definitions of our social existence. Maintaining this memory requires stern but rewarding discipline, described in detail in the mystical traditions. If we follow these paths of prayer, meditation, fasting, study, retreat, knowledge, and/or service, the traditions promise, we will be evermore released from the bondage of false attachments.

And it is in just this promise that the danger lies: the place where mysticism can betray itself and deteriorate into self-deception, folly, and escapism. For mysticism can be and has been used simply to evade that which is frightening, confusing, or difficult *in* the social realm. In such cases it is motivated by an inability to face what is threatening in the world-as-it-is, and what the mystic really seeks is escape. In such cases the mystic claims to have experienced—and at times to offer to others—the Truth of the Whole; but he is really simply avoiding what is distasteful.

For instance, we become entranced by, even addicted to, the *experience* of the mystical state. It is so lofty, so sweet, such a relief from how awful we feel most of the time. And when we are under it or in it or up to it, we do not have to take seriously our suffering, anyone else's suffering, or the ways in which it is not only what Buddhists would call the folly of individual attachment but also social evil that causes that suffering.

This danger of mysticism is that it becomes in Kierkegaard's sense merely "aesthetic": merely a series of experiences that do not contribute to the formation of an ethical and spiritual character. Merely something that, in the end, is another titillation, another object of desire, another way to pacify a self that has not been transformed but merely thrilled or sedated. Put another way, the danger of mysticism is that it can become an escape from concerns about other people. Entranced by the cosmic oneness of it all, we end up forgetting or ignoring the other people in the room, on our block, or on our globe. Feeling cared for by an infinite source of love, we forget (inadvertently? to some extent intentionally?) that it is up to us to manifest as well as receive that love. And that, if we do not, our own access to the source will become increasingly strained, desperate, and attenuated.

Many years ago a teacher of yoga and meditation instructed me: "Do not be distracted by sounds in your practice, but use them. For instance, if you are meditating and you hear a loud siren outside your window, instead of feeling interrupted you can simply take in that energy, move it up your spine to your crown chakra and use it to further your practice." A useful tip I thought at first. But then I thought further, and asked him: "Sir, this sounds a fine idea if, for instance, the siren is simply from an ambulance on its way to a nearby hospital. But what if it is the siren of the police vans that in Amsterdam took Jews to be transported to the death camps? When is the sound a source of energy to be incorporated into the meditation and when is it an indication that we need to end the meditation, look outside ourselves, and act in resistance to help innocent people who are being murdered? And what is the source of an ability to distinguish between the two?"

I am not trying to discredit mysticism. Although I do have some sympathy with Marx's and Nietzsche's critiques of religion, I do not accept their fundamental antagonism to spiritual life. Unlike them, I believe that mystical experience contains the possibility of Great Truth. *But* I am suggesting that it also contains the chance of Real Error. In fact, it is just because mystical experience contains the Powers of Truth—relief from suffering, transcendence of social limitations, insights into Connectedness, Grace, Gaia, or God—that we can use those experiences as distractions, painkillers, or excuses to Look the Other Way.

The danger that mysticism may become (merely) aesthetic or serve as a spiritual bypass of the moral and the political is not unknown in religious culture. In traditional Judaism people do not approach the mysticism of the Kabbalah until they are established in family and community, typically, not until the age of forty. The entire history of Buddhism is marked by a split over precisely the nature of mystical enlightenment and the role of the enlightened person in the community. While Theravada Buddhism saw the Sage as ultimately no more than a person who provides an example to others that Enlightenment is possible, Mahayana Buddhism arose partly out of the critique of what it took to be the selfish and ultimately self-defeating character of that ideal. In its place the Mahayana offered the image of the Bodhisattva, who refuses ultimate Enlightenment in order to help all other sentient beings to achieve it. Such a person is like a strong young man who, when his household is lost in a dangerous forest, stays with the group to help them all to safety rather than making his own way home.

Yet the awareness of these traditions is itself suspect in part because of the duality of all mystical encounters: at once a communion with energies that transcend society *and also* experiences processed, understood, and described in words by socially situated human beings. The pervasive sexism of even the most mystically founded traditions should remind us that while God or Goddess may touch us directly, our response to that touch will necessarily bear some imprint of our contingent selves. For example, it was not, in fact, "people" who, when suitably mature, were allowed by the Rabbis to study Kabbalah. It was always and only men. Women were told that they had other things to do. In this and countless other examples the claim to know a Truth Beyond Question has too often been a strategy for Power Over the Uninitiated.

In our time the dangers of mysticism are especially real, because much of mysticism in the advanced industrial societies is disconnected from tradition, community, and personal responsibility. It was, after, all, in great measure the widespread use of psychedelic drugs that brought an interest in ecstatic states back into a society defined by professionalism, technology, and television. The power of these drugs—for many people an instant revelation—was precisely their impotence. Since nothing had prepared us for what they offered—and we had not seriously prepared ourselves—the next day's psychic life was often no more holy than the day before. At best, the drug experience was a signal that there was more to life than was dreamed of at Harvard Business School or the National Science Foundation. At best, it served only as a beginning to a long and difficult search.

Further, since the cavalier cultural raids on ancient and tribal traditions of the 1980s, one can learn the secrets of a South American Shaman for the cost of a weekend's time and a few hundred dollars. (This will be a wonderful experience. And next month we can learn witchcraft. Or perhaps the mysteries of the Druids.) The consequence is that far from becoming an alternative to the limitations of social life, mystical experience becomes one more commodity—with no more ultimate spiritual meaning than anything else that can be bought or sold.

In short, while the actual Truths disclosed by mystical experience may, in fact, be just what all of us need to know, our access to them has always been (and perhaps, given the depth and extent of the presence of society, are now even more so) conditioned by the social setting in which they unfold.

DEEP ECOLOGY

In our own social setting our collective violence towards the environment has led to a return— on something approaching a mass scale—of a mysticism that takes the earth and all its life as an ultimate truth. The crucial fact is that we may be destroying the very support systems that make human life possible. With less uncertainty we can say that we have *already* extinguished countless species, poured millions of tons of toxic wastes into the air, earth, and water, and altered the earth's atmosphere and climate.

A variety of environmental movements and philosophies have arisen in response to this crisis. From the heart of the spiritual impulse and the memories of countless generations in which forest and grassland, bird and wolf and salmon were our home and family and intimate enemy, comes Deep Ecology. The Deep Ecology of which I speak here is not the version presented in the technical language of philosophical ethics, where debates about varieties of intrinsic as opposed to instrumental value take place. Rather, I speak of a passionate, spiritually oriented, mystical communion with the earth and its many beings, a recognition of kinship with those beings that no more requires philosophical justification than does the connection we feel with our parents, pets, or lovers. As such, Deep Ecology is a spiritual philosophy; and the deepest experiences that animate its adherents are profoundly mystical.[3] What is "deep" about this perspective is the experience—and the conviction—that our surroundings are essential to who we are. And this not just because they are useful, but because we are indeed tied to them by invisible threads of longing, teaching, learning, connection, struggle for existence, and memory. Sky and earth, bird and fish, each leaf on each tree—all these mirror who and what we are; indeed, without them we could not be ourselves.

This Deep Ecology is not, nor could it possibly be, a recent creation. As humans have evolved physically, cognitively, culturally, and spiritually in a setting bounded by beings who are not people, so a recognition of our delight in them and affinity with them has been present throughout all human cultures.

There is a Midrash (a Jewish spiritual story which aims to enlighten rather than legislate) that speaks of trees: "When a tree that bears fruit is cut down, its moan goes round the world. Yet no sound is heard." Or even more poignantly, in the words of the eighteenth-century Hasidic Rebbe Nachman: "If a person kills a tree before its time, it is like having murdered a soul." The medieval Catholic Hildegaard of Bingen saw God in the physical world: "I, the fiery life of divine essence, am aflame beyond the beauty of the meadows, I gleam in the waters, and I burn in the sun, moon, and stars. . . . I awaken everything to life." The *Koran* was confident that "the creation of the heavens and the Earth is greater than the creation of humankind; yet most people understand not." And the World Council of Indigenous Peoples stated in 1977 that in their past "The earth was our nurturing mother, the night sky formed our common roof, the Sun and the Moon were our parents. . . ."[4]

This recognition is also found in nondenominational, often explicitly nonreligious, nature writing that celebrates a luminous moment of seeing in which the natural world speaks to us. In her celebrated essay "Living Like Weasels" Annie Dillard describes a moment when, face-to-face with a weasel, "our eyes locked, and someone threw away the key. Our look was as if two lovers, or deadly enemies, met unexpectedly on an overgrown path when each had been thinking of something else" (14). Similarly, Aldo Leopold, one of the inspirations of the deep ecological turn in contemporary environmental ethics, speaks of seeing a "fierce green fire" in the eyes of a dying wolf he had himself shot, and of never again thinking of wolves, or mountains, or wilderness in the same way.

Considered as a form of spirituality—as a way of moving beyond the conventional social understanding of the self or of the social construction of the body—Deep Ecology articulates a powerful and pervasive sensibility. It unifies and expands our childhood love for an animal, the times as adolescents when only the woods or fields seem to understand us, the moments of grace we feel watching a sunrise, or light glinting over ice-covered branches, or hearing birds sing on a surprisingly warm day in March. Knitting together these moments, a Deep Ecological perspective simply says: "You are more than your profession and race and religion and even gender. In your cells and sinews and even your atoms there is a tie to all this which surrounds you. Open yourself up to this source of grace and peace and love. More important, open yourself up to the love you feel for it."

As Joanna Macy observes, Deep Ecology also signals something of our capacity to love and the reality of our connections to other beings across space and time. Our sadness for the burning rainforests and casually eliminated species is a sign that, despite everything, we can still love—and mourn. As Deep Ecology sings of the joy we feel in our delight of nature, so it must also have us join in the requiem for what we have ourselves helped to kill. Our pain is not simply that things will be inconvenienced: that recreation will be interfered with because the forest has been clearcut; that a potential cancer cure has been lost as the rainforest burns; that forty thousand people in Newfoundland's fishing communities have lost their jobs because mechanized trawlers stripmined the cod fishery. The earth is not just being polluted, Deep Ecology suggests, it is being *desecrated*. Something more than useful, more than physically pleasing, something *holy* is being torn to bits for what are too often the most trivial, thoughtless, or downright cruel reasons. Thus, Deep Ecology highlights the limitations of a purely instrumental attitude toward nature, an attitude that reduces nonhuman nature to quantities of stuff to be measured, mastered, and commodified. As a philosophy based in powerful emotional experiences, Deep Ecology expresses simply and directly what many people feel: a love and concern for the natural world. As more familiar mystical experiences might alter our attitudes toward death, our fear of the unknown, or our petty insecurities, realization of our kinship with the earth confirms the need to question any unquestioned trashing of what surrounds us. Its insights can teach us to see the familiar in a new way, challenging our taken-for-granted beliefs, practices, and institutions.

Deep Ecology, like all forms of mysticism, comprises knowledge as well as emotionally meaningful experiences. It reminds us of truths that industrial civilization and many forms of patriarchy have obscured, for example, that we are physical beings, made of the same stuff as earth and stream and air, or that we need wilderness because, as Edward Abbey observed, we ourselves are wild animals. Paul Shepard argued that we develop a good deal of our language, our sense of ourselves, our understanding of morality, and our very sensory apparatus from direct or symbolic lessons from the natural world. David Abram has suggested that the boundaries between the human and the more-than-human are the sources of knowledge about balance and integrity for the human community; and for time out of mind wisdom was sought beyond those boundaries and seen as vested in the shamans, priestesses, and prophets who journeyed there.

Finally, an identification with nature can be the source of deep pleasure and deeper calm. Just as people who hear the voice of God may feel a little differently about a flat tire or being passed over for a promotion, so a felt connection with a tree or a bird can soothe the anxieties and relieve the sense of overwhelming pressure to achieve or possess in the social realm. Such a connection might even, if we let it, help us learn not to be quite so (desperately, compulsively) busy. Experiencing ourselves as natural as well as social, part of a cosmos as well as a community, we can find a remedy for the kinds of neurosis that typically are not part of the lives of ants, birches, or elks.

Even my anxiety over the fate of the environment can be soothed by the experience of connection with it. I can, for instance, see the rainforest not only as an object I am trying to save, but, in John Seed's words: "See myself as *part* of the rainforest trying to save itself" (Seed, Macy, and Fleming:8). And I can then realize that even desperation to save nature need have no place in my life. As the leaves on the trees that I love, I can only do my bit, then drift gently down to the forest floor and make way for more life. And, once again, here is where the dangers arise. For Deep Ecology (just as other forms of mysticism) can slide too easily into the attempt to escape society, or attempt to bring into the social realm one of the more pernicious forms of religious ideology and practice. There are, in fact, at least four central dangers that face Deep Ecology in this regard.

First, there is the problem that mystical experience can give rise to fundamentalism. In the face of the long history—and the present resurgence—of religiously motivated violence and narrow-mindedness, this is a bleak prospect indeed. While Deep Ecology is a powerful critic of modernist scientific and economic reductionism, it is, as Michael Zimmerman has argued, always quite difficult to transcend the limitations of the Enlightenment while simultaneously keeping its accomplishments. We see the consequences of the rejection of those accomplishments in religious totalitarianism of all stripes. Political notions of individual rights and a spiritual understanding that mystical knowledge is essentially metaphorical are both foreign to any form of fundamentalism. The mullahs of whatever faith are sure they know what God wants, and they have the whips and chains to put that knowledge into practice.

Of course, Deep Ecology remains too institutionally marginal for it to face an exactly comparable danger. However, its form of fundamentalism, I believe, would take the shape of attempting to escape society, to see "nature" as a realm in which people are absent and in the celebration of which people can be ignored. Yet if it is truly nature we love, we must not forget people, for they too are born of the earth.[5] If we would commune with plants, we must not (as Aldo Leopold himself suggested) forget the weeds in a city vacant lot. And we must also show some concern for those kids playing in the city lot—at risk from broken glass, drug dealers, and the lack of economic or cultural access to the wilderness we seek to preserve.

In another area, we can recognize that the special virtue of nonfundamentalist contemporary spirituality is its ability to synthesize spiritual insights across traditions. Buddhists talk to Jews; Christians study yoga; and everybody wants to know a little bit about shamanism. The wonderful opportunities of this openness are obvious, but the danger is that certain principles will be lost. While every tradition can be clearly seen for its virtues and powers, spiritual Deep Ecologists will lose their way if they let certain clarities be obscured: the equal value of men and women, a recognition of the past and present effects of racial domination, the need to frame spiritual truths in the context of a worldwide economy and culture. If these are neglected, the integrity of Deep Ecology will diminish, and it may devolve into a sect of spiritually, and thus socially, irrelevant bird-watchers.

Third: All attachment to truth provides the opportunity to hate Error. There is thus the possibility—which at times has been realized in practice—of Deep Ecologists erecting a sharp divide between themselves and other kinds of environmentalists. Yet, surely there are grounds for alliance with those who (merely) think of the world as deserving of care because it is God's creation and not in itself sacred. Surely the Deep Ecologists have enough in common with the stewards of nature and the moderate conservationists to make common cause with them against the pure despoilers. On a practical level, only a mass movement can motivate the government to constrain global capital and demand international, national, and local programs to recover what we've lost and clean up the mess we've made. Such a movement will require environmentalists of all stripes, and participation will necessitate a long view in which tactical compromise with less radical elements will be necessary to secure the basis of an ongoing collective, and effective, movement. As they relate to others in the struggle to protect nature, spiritual Deep Ecologists should remember that in our own time we encounter the wilderness with the accomplishments of our society riding on our back. As E. O. Wilson observed, no matter how much the naturalist loves the jungle, he had better be very well equipped, or before long a host of jungle dwellers will break him down into his constituent amino acids. Every Deep Ecologist goes to the wilds with his vibram boots on his feet, his nylon back pack, and his Swiss army knife. With all that stuff along, there is little room for arrogance.

What all this adds up to is that, just as we experience the mystical touch of God as socially situated existing individuals, so we come to "nature" through social life. We bring our historically defined expectations and needs. We have a concept of nature (as benign or threatening, comfortable or forbidding, infinitely powerful or dangerously at risk) that is very much the product of our own society's level of technological development.

Thus, there is, fourth, also the problem that at times the bland images of nature that emerge from Deep Ecology distort what "nature" really is like. For example, our mystically based love of life will not extend to the AIDS virus, and our wariness at tampering with the sacred character of nature may well be suspended when it comes to using genetic engineering to cure cystic fibrosis. Ghetto rats will probably escape the purview that holds all of life as sacred, as might the black flies that cause widespread blindness in Africa. Adopting a Deep Ecological perspective will not eliminate the hard choices we face—choices about how much to take for ourselves and how much to leave for others; how much to exercise the control we increase day by day, and how much to surrender. And it will not turn the real world into a PBS special on butterflies or dolphins. The love we feel for the more-than-human is not a love that can erase the realities of struggle and conquest—of nature as one long and frequently quite painful food chain.

There is an old Buddhist tale about two monks who stand on top of a mountain, surveying all of nature. "How horrible!" says one, with tears in his eyes, "they are all eating each other." "Don't be so upset," the other comforts him, "really, they are feeding each other." The point, of course, is that both are correct.

SOCIAL TRANSFORMATION

In human history the long counterpoint to ecstasy that takes us out of our social setting is the longing for justice within it. Morality and transcendence are the twin axes along which authentic personal and communal existence develops, and our success at both is the measure of a truly humane form of life. This longing for a more just social order can be found in the cautionary words of prophets, social reformers, and revolutionaries. In contrast to the claims of mysticism the pursuit of justice is very much an awareness of just how socially situated we are and how our concerns with making things better center on the alteration and improvement of this situation that defines us, grounds us, and sets our tasks.

This pursuit of justice exists, among other things, as a needed corrective to the ahistorical pretensions of mystical traditions—their claims to provide doctrines that originate outside of the social order. From a viewpoint that originated in politics rather than spirituality we are able, for instance, to critique the sexist teachings of early Buddhism. While the Buddha may have seen his way clear of the imposed caste system and the empty formalities of ritual sacrifices, he could not escape his own attachment to patriarchy. For all its self-understanding as a source of truth beyond the ego, early Buddhism maintained the idea of women's social and spiritual inferiority. What source could there be for even recognizing this failing except a socially based political critique? Such a source only rarely emerges from transcendent visions but rather typically stems from the cries of the oppressed themselves. Ultimately, as I mentioned above, the danger here is that mystical *experience* is used as a support for *social authority*. It is then that, inevitably, veracity must be claimed not only for the experience but also for one particular discursive and institutional expression of it. And this expression will *always* give rise to structures of power and privilege—which will be defended with the typical violence and deceit that hierarchies of power always employ.

In our own time Deep Ecology in particular and the conservation movement in general have by this time been the subject of extensive critiques: for ignoring the social basis of their own perspectives; for emphasizing wilderness while forgetting toxic waste dumps; for love of trees and lack of concern for children. These criticisms have helped move Deep Ecologists toward an understanding that environmentalism needs to embrace the concerns of environmental justice: an awareness of and resistance to the unfair distribution of responsibility for and suffering from humanity's attacks on the environment. The uranium mines on native lands, the toxic wastes flowing into poor neighborhoods, the outlawed chemicals exported to the Third World—can we really love nature if these things escape our vision?[6]

Finally, it must be stressed that for many the struggle for justice is *itself* a form of connection that can break the bonds of the ego. While social movements too often have devolved into the brutal tyrannies of a Stalin or the crass appeal to group hatred of a Farrakan, at their best they provide experiences where political solidarity blossoms into a kind of selfless love. At times people struggling for justice are freed from the usual petty isolations, jealousies, and fears. In the very struggle they find the joy of service and the spiritual clarity that comes from knowing the ultimate rightness of what they are doing.

AND YET...

Too often confidence in one's ultimate rightness has led political movements into dogmatic violence. The history of too many revolutions is the history of the replacement of one autocracy by another. The history of too many Left groups reveals sectarianism, verbal violence, and exclusion of others who deserve solidarity. We have seen the fundamental wisdom of the struggle for justice be obscured by rage, pompous posturing, or simple careerism.[7] And, thus, as the political perspective is necessary for both a grounding and a critique of mysticism and Deep Ecology, so its spiritual insights and resources can be a corrective to the excesses of politics.

Mysticism in general can offer relief from identification with theories, rigidly held "positions," and the pursuit of institutional power. An emphasis on compassion, on empathy even for the guilty, on service rather than on the acquisition of personal status within the "movement"—these are values that can be forthcoming from a direct experience of the holy. For from that experience, once again, we may learn that the ego-bound concerns that motivate us toward arrogance and violence, even in the service of justice, are not the only realities. To make the point we need only compare Lenin's practice of threatening to expel any party leader who disagreed with him to Gandhi's insistence that comrades vote against him if that was what their own inner wisdom dictated. Coercion is clearly a product of any kind of fundamentalism, whether of a religious or a secular kind. Control or cooperation, manipulation or trust, the Grand Inquisitor and Lenin or Gandhi and Ang San Suu Kyi—these choices face any collection of human beings, any institutional structure, any attempt to bring truth into the world.

From Deep Ecology in particular the world of conventional human-oriented politics also has much to learn. For one thing, Deep Ecology's emphasis on the value of the nonhuman offers a measure and a limit of what we are seeking when we pursue an improved "standard of living." The notion of a "sustainable" form of life begins to condition what we are after, becoming an essential defining element along with "justice" and "freedom." And (as difficult as it is to find the right way of putting this) we have before us the prospect that the true subjects of political life are not just people but people, animals, plants, ecosystems, and perhaps the biosphere itself. Thus, for social activities of all kinds new questions arise: What is the ultimate worth of this construction project, these jobs, this or that commodity? Whose needs or wants deserve to be satisfied? And which should be altered?

In the same vein, a mystical identification—or deep relationship—with the natural world allows us to orient political struggle away from entitlement and rage—and in a direction not tied (or at least less tied) by a psychic addiction to the very social system that destroys us. As Marcuse observed, consumer society binds its subjects to the principles of ever-increasing production and consumption by rooting personal identity in the ownership of things. The recognition of spiritual values in general and the value(s) of nature in particular gives us a way out of the ecocidal cul-de-sac of the endless mall. We develop, in short, an alternative sense of self. This alternative allows the possibility of a withdrawal of psychic energy from a cultural and economic system that threatens all those subject to it.

In more strategic political terms concern for nature is a value that can provide the basis for a new kind of solidarity. We might remember that whatever else divides us as human beings, we all need to breathe. And virtually all of our hearts rejoice to the sounds of spring. These commonalties may save us when the divisions of race, class, gender, ethnicity, or sexuality leave us deeply suspicious of each other.

While those getting very rich off of pollution are not likely to be convinced, as well as many of those whose most immediate livelihood depends on exploitation of their surroundings, we have already seen multiclass, multirace, and multinationality coalitions doing serious political work. An enormous dam project slated for India—supported by the World Bank and liable to destroy the habitat of endangered species and indigenous people alike—was stopped by a transcontinental alliance of local people, environmental activists, lawyers, and concerned citizens from India, Switzerland, and the United States (Rich: 44–47). In Wisconsin white activists have helped Native Peoples fend off multinational mining interests (Gedicks). These are but a few examples of arenas of cooperation based on the joint concern for the human and the nonhuman worlds.

It may actually be that care for the environment will continue and flourish as one of the main motivating forces of politics in the twenty-first century. The abatement signaled in the

United States by the Republican victories of the mid-1990s was, I believe, a temporary development. The attempt to dismantle environmental regulations was defeated. In any event, the "working class," as Andre Gorz (218) observed many years ago, is not likely to mount a serious challenge to the established social order to get a 10 percent increase in pay. Concern for the environment—a concern motivated both by "self-interest" and as interest for nature that we love and long for—*could* be a significant element in a major social transformation. If people can truly see what is at stake, they may yet rise to the challenge. And the spiritual understanding of this concern has been and will continue to be an essential element in the process. We have seen it already in the spiritual motivation of the radical ecology group Earth First!; in the convention-challenging claims of the new, earth-oriented ecotheology coming out of mainstream religious; and in the politicized versions of spiritual ecofeminism.

Finally, and perhaps most surprisingly, there is in a general "Deep Ecological" orientation a cognitive corrective to the distortions of centralized, reductionist, commodified knowledge, and social practice. In agriculture, for instance, the belief that modernized science and technology can replace the fertility of the earth or the expertise of local groups has led to a series of disasters. As Vandana Shiva has described it, the imposition of "advanced," commodity-oriented monocultures has erased a wide variety of crops, seeds, productive uses (for food, fodder, herbs, local consumption, etc., as well as sale), and ultimately peoples. The result has been polluted soils, drastically increased water consumption, less productive land use, and violent social dislocation. In commodified monoculture there is respect neither for the earth nor for the people who have sustainably managed their fields and forests for centuries. A perspective that sees communion with nature as having spiritual as well as instrumental value might look very carefully at any attempt to supplant either natural processes or long-established local forms of culture and practice. Thus, as a spiritual view of the ultimate value of persons can provide an orientation for social life (though clearly not a simple way to resolve its conflicts and contradictions), so a spiritual view of nature can offer at least the beginning of an orientation toward production, consumption, and development.

And so, paradoxically, the wisdom of a mystical Deep Ecology can augment the powers and promises of the secular drive for just social transformation. They must work together if the environmental crisis is not to erode the conditions for human life on earth and simultaneously erode our very confidence in our right to exist on it. If we are to be truly touched by the Holy Spirit, our own spirit of holiness must reach out to the enormous family of life that surrounds us, shapes us, and gives us our own particular place in the vastness of time and space.

CONCLUSION

The vision of mysticism offered here will not satisfy everyone. It is a particularly *nonmetaphysical* view in which ultimate reality is pretty much exhausted by "ordinary" reality. Of course, when illuminated by the sparks of mystical experience, "ordinary" reality can shine quite brightly—as in the old Zen story that identifies true enlightenment with simply seeing "a mountain as a mountain and a river as a river." But what is absent here is any confidence that the pains of injustice and loss will be compensated for by any Grand Plan, Protecting All-Powerful Source, or Cosmic Pattern of Growth and Development. Speaking quite personally, I never could feel any of those; I believe we just have what we have. Mysticism, in my view, does not mean transcendence but illumination: not to believe in Something Else but to See More Clearly (and more brightly) Who We Are. In the end, the work of mysticism is to join us to what we have—in delight, in grief, in life, and in death. Sometimes that joining will have the force and pleasure of a sexual climax, sometimes the utter peace of spring flowers, or the caress of a child's hand. Sometimes it will be the knowledge that only by resisting evil can we join with what is and that "acceptance" of our lives requires that we struggle for justice. In the end, we can fully realize our desire to transcend the falseness of our social world not by finding some other realm but—through acts of solidarity and resistance—by transforming it.[8]

NOTES

1. For these and other accounts of Buddhism in this paper see, for example, the works by Conze and Stryk.
2. For a feminist account, see Heyward.
3. There are many sources here, e.g., Macy; Devall and Sessions.
4. For these quotations, as well as many sources on contemporary and traditional writings on religion and nature, see Gottlieb 1996.
5. This critique is developed more extensively in Gottlieb 1995.
6. Two accounts of these matters are in Gedicks; Bullard.
7. For an extensive critique of these defects in the history of European and U.S. Left movements, see Gottlieb 1987 and 1992.
8. This approach to spiritual life is developed in Gottlieb 1999. It obviously shares values with many other writers, from the biblical prophets to twentieth-century figures such as Martin Luther King, Gandhi, Dorothy Day, and Cesar Chavez.

REFERENCES

Abbey, Edward. 1977. *The Journey Home*. New York: Penguin.

Abram, David. 1996. *The Spell of the Sensuous*. New York: Pantheon.

Bullard, Robert D., ed. 1994. *Unequal Protection: Environmental Justice and Communities of Color*. San Francisco: Sierra Club.

Conze, Edward. 1951. *Buddhism: Its Essence and Development*. New York: Harper.

Devall, Bill, and George Sessions. 1985. *Deep Ecology: Living as if Nature Mattered*. Salt Lake City, Utah: Peregrine Smith.

Dillard, Annie. 1982. *Teaching a Stone to Talk*. New York: HarperCollins.

Gedicks, Al. 1993. *The New Resource Wars: Native and Environmental Struggles against Multinational Corporations*. Boston: South End Press.

Gorz, Andre. 1990. "Socialism and Revolution." In *An Anthology of Western Marxism: From Lukacs and Gramsci to Socialist-Feminism*, ed. Roger S. Gottlieb. New York: Oxford University Press.

Gottlieb, Roger S. 1987. *History and Subjectivity: The Transformation of Marxist Theory*. Philadelphia: Temple University Press.

———. 1992. *Marxism 1844–1990: Origins, Betrayal, Rebirth*. New York: Routledge.

———. 1995. "Spiritual Deep Ecology and the Left." *Capitalism, Nature, Socialism: A Journal of Socialist Ecology* 6, no. 4: 1–21. Reprinted in Gottlieb 1996.

———. 1999. *A Spirituality of Resistance: Finding a Peaceful Heart and Protecting the Earth*. New York: Crossroad.

Gottlieb, Roger S., ed. 1996. *This Sacred Earth: Religion, Nature, Environment*. New York: Routledge.

Heyward, Carter. 1992. *Touching Our Strength*. San Francisco: Harper.

Leopold, Aldo. 1949. *A Sand County Almanac*. New York: Oxford University Press.

Macy, Joanna. 1994. *World as Lover, World as Self*. San Francisco: Parallax.

Marcuse, Herbert. 1967. *One-Dimensional Man.* Boston: Beacon Press.

Rich, Bruce. 1994. *Mortgaging the Earth: The World Bank, Environmental Impoverishment and the Crisis of Development.* Boston: Beacon Press.

Seed, John, Joanna Macy, and Pat Fleming. 1991. *Thinking Like a Mountain: Towards a Council of All Beings.* Philadelphia: New Society.

Shepard, Paul. 1983. *Nature and Madness.* San Francisco: Sierra Club.

Shiva, Vandana. 1993. *The Violence of the Green Revolution.* London: Zed Press.

Stryk, Lucien, ed. 1969. *World of the Buddha.* New York: Anchor.

Wilson, E. O. 1983. *Biophilia.* Cambridge, Mass.: Harvard University Press.

Zimmerman, Michael. 1995. *Contesting Earth's Future: Radical Ecology and Postmodernity.* Berkeley: University of California Press.

from *The Silent Cry: Mysticism and Resistance*

❧

Dorothee Soelle

Dorothee Soelle, an activist in peace and ecological movements, has taught theology in the United States and Germany. This excerpt explores mysticism's connections to political resistance.

❧

OUT OF THE HOME INTO HOMELESSNESS

"Mysticism *is* resistance." Years ago, a friend said this to me and I wanted to know how to picture the relationship between mysticism and resistance. The experiences of unity in the midst of commotion—hearing the "silent cry"—necessarily puts us in radical opposition to what is regarded as a normal way of life.

At the theological seminary in New York where I used to teach, we were once asked about our religious experiences. There was an embarrassed silence; it was as if we had asked our grandmothers about their sex life. A young woman eventually spoke up and offered to present, in a week's time, an extensive report on her experiences. Accordingly, she told us that as a very young girl in the American Midwest, she had spent many hours reading in bed at night, without permission. One winter's night, she woke up at four in the morning, went outside, and looked at the stars in the clear, frosty sky. She had a once-in-a-lifetime feeling of happiness, of being connected with all of life, with God; a feeling of overwhelming clarity, of being sheltered and carried. She saw the stars as if she had never seen them before. She described the experience in these words, "Nothing can happen, I am indestructible, I am one with everything." This did not happen again until about ten years later when, in a different context, something similar took place. The new context was a huge demonstration against the Vietnam War. There, too, she knew that she was sheltered, a part of the whole, "indestructible," together with the others. Struggling for words and with her own timidity, she brought both experiences together under the rubric of religious experience.

Suppose that this young woman had lived in fourteenth-century Flanders; she would have had at her disposal other traditions of language allowing her to say, "I heard a voice" or "I saw a light brighter than everything else." Our culture confines her to sobriety, self-restriction, and scholarly manners of expression. How she fought these constraints and the very fact that she did so makes her unforgettable.

Mystical experience is bliss and simultaneously it makes one homeless. It takes people out of the home they have furnished for themselves into homelessness, as it did to young Gautama, known later as the Buddha. I sensed a bit of this ascetic homelessness in the student's report and in her feeling of being drawn more and more into a nonviolent life. The least that can be said is that being touched by religion produces a condition that evokes alienation; in terminology that conveys a degree of loathing, the New Testament specifies it as alienation from "this world." Distance from everyday reality does not necessarily legitimate the big word "resistance," but it does point to a different life. Bliss and homelessness, fulfillment and quest, God's presence and the bitterness of God's absence in the everyday, violence-riddled reality belong together.

Is mysticism necessarily connected with this resistance? The thesis can be questioned from two different positions. Observers far removed from mysticism will look upon mysticism more as a flight from the world, an introversion and concentration on the well-being of one's soul. To them the privatization of religion will seem to be the essential aspect within mysticism. They will find the many examples of conflicts included in the first two parts of this book to be beside the point, even though such conflicts arose from mystical sensitivity. Such interpretation strangely flattens out the dimension of the love of God that is essential to every form of religion—as if ritual and being consoled were all there is! Most of the great men and women of mystical movements have also spoken clearly in their theory against a complete withdrawal from the world. For a time being, they indeed practiced the contemplative "way inwards," but their aim was consistently the unity of the contemplative and the active life, of *ora et labora* (work and prayer). The notion of mysticism as a flight from the world is much more a result of the bourgeois idea that religion is a private affair.

But there is also a very different objection to the idea that mysticism is resistance. It comes from a context that is quite far removed from religion and much closer to what political ethics calls resistance. It is represented by postreligious thinkers who concede that in the course of history, mysticism may have on occasion played a part in resisting the numerous forms of barbarism. However, for such thinkers, rational arguments can now provide sufficient support for the refusal to go along obediently with any further barbarization of society. The apparent persuasiveness of this view seems to arise from a certain overestimation of rationality, usually associated with the Left. To me it expresses a kind of naive faith in the goddess Reason.

I am personally acquainted with many groups that practice pacifist and ecological resistance and, above all in the world's poorest countries, economic resistance. I learn from them ever anew that experience, analysis, and insight alone are too weak to bring us out of the prison in which we are asleep. We need a different language that keeps awake and shares the memory of liberation and the promise of freedom for all. We need a different hope than that of political strategies and scientific prediction.

For Martin Buber, the difference between secular and religious movements striving for a renewal of society lies in how they relate themselves to what he called the foundational substance of tradition. Is that substance rejected in principle? Is the "axe to be laid at the root" of the existing order, or is there a relation to tradition that does not eliminate tradition as such? In his view, revolutionary movements work with the knowledge of "how it was meant to be; they begin with the hidden spark in every human being and want to wipe clean the mirror of its distortions, bring back again what was lost and repair again what was destroyed."[1] The category of "again" promises liberation from the compulsion to win.

The failure of state socialism perhaps has an in-depth relationship to the totality of its repudiation of received culture, tradition, and religion. It did not invoke the time "when Adam delved and Eve span," nor any memory of the good story of the beginning of life in creation. The new elites were always the authors of their own being; there was no good beginning. They wanted something completely different and not the *renovation* and the renewal of the face of the earth that is promised in Psalm 104:30. What mysticism can contribute today to the substance of resistance movements is this relation to the origin of life that is often expressed in a phrase like "surely, this is not all there is to it, it wasn't meant to be like this." Whoever desires the new needs the memory and the feast that, even now, celebrate the renewing.

The concept of resistance that meets us in many places of mystical tradition is broad and diverse. It begins with our not being at home in this world of business and violence. Abstention, disagreement, and dissent lead on to simple forms of nonconformist behavior. The American Quakers who helped black slaves escape to the North often got into trouble for their love of truth and their deeply rooted preference for plain speech. When asked whether they had seen a slave pass by on the road, they did not say "No," for that would have transgressed the commandment of truthfulness. Instead, they said, "I saw no slave," staying with the truth that the black person they had seen was a child of God and nothing else. They did not share the implicit belief that such a person could be named a slave. Children of Quakers were sometimes entrusted with hiding refugees so that their parents could truthfully say that they knew nothing about illegal guests.

It is not always easy to keep up this relation between love of truth and protecting the persecuted. In many forms of resistance, there was and is a necessity for secrecy. Whenever possible, the early Quakers preferred to confuse their persecutors "with truth rather than with lies." During the years of the Cold War, Quakers traveled to Poland with aid supplies and were asked by American secret agents what ships they had seen in the harbor. They would reply, "If we had seen any, we would not tell you. It would be deceiving the Polish government to say that we came to help and then spied for the U.S.A." This principle of open and honest talk and disclosure of intentions plays an important role in nonviolent actions. Several Quakers informed the authorities of their acts of civil disobedience, but only after the asylum-seeking refugees had safely crossed the borders.

The broadest notion of resistance assumed here arises from the distance established from what is regarded as the normal world, a world founded on power, possession, and violence. Consequently, in different situations the notion varies between evasion, dissent, abstinence, refusal, boycott or strike, reform or counterproposal, dialogue, or mediation. Yet, however radically mystical consciousness practices and strives for changes in conditions based on possessions and violence, the connection to those who think otherwise is steadfastly maintained. No one is excluded or eliminated. Such consciousness is deeply marked by "revolutionary patience" that sets out from the experience of what has always been good.

I remember an act of civil disobedience when we occupied a nuclear weapons facility in the Hunsrück Mountains in Germany. We spoke the Lord's Prayer together. About forty people faced the huge military vehicles that drove in and out and we said, "Your kingdom come." Never had I heard that petition as I heard it then. Never had I known as clearly how different the kingdom would look without the instruments of death. Never had I felt as I did then what it means to pray. The mysticism of the good beginning and of its reestablishment and resistance against the terror of violence were present to all of us at that moment as genuine forms of life. We knew something that we could not clearly name at the time. Thanks to Jewish mysticism, I see more plainly now. "Every individual in Israel who calls on God in prayer places a crown on God's head, for prayer is an act of crowning God, of acknowledging God as king."[2] The image of the coronation of one who, according to orthodox Christian opinion, needs no coronation and certainly not at the hands of ordinary, sinful people shows how far mystics can proceed especially in a situation of resistance.

I have long thought about what verbs go with mysticism and resistance. Which verbs can we can utilize in order to express mysticism and resistance as a unity? Is there such a thing at all as mystical activities? Is praying also a kind of fighting, like weeping, smiling, keeping silent? Years ago, young people in Zürich wrote an ironic mystical slogan on the walls of their city: "We have enough reason to cry even without your tear gas." In this sentence, crying is a mystical activity, a response to the "silent cry."

NOTES

1. Martin Buber, *Werke III: Schriften zum Chassidismus* (Heidelberg: Verlag Lambert Schneider, 1963), 803.

2. Gershom Scholem, *Von der mystischen Gestalt der Gottheit: Studien zu Grundbegriffen der Kabbala* (Frankfurt, 1995), 16.

from *Qur'an, Liberation, and Pluralism:*
An Islamic Perspective of Interreligious Solidarity against Oppression

⤜⤛

Farid Esack

Farid Esack, an internationally known South African Muslim scholar and activist, has been called "Islam's first liberation theologian." Esack's focus on interreligious dialogue and cooperation is rooted in his experience of the struggles against apartheid. He served as a commissioner for gender equality in Nelson Mandela's government.

⤜⤛

It is not uncommon for religious believers in the struggle to discover that they have more in common, theologically speaking, with comrades from very different religious traditions than they have with members of their own communities who are not involved in the struggle. This religious commonalty in the struggle demands a theological framework which can give it expression and explain it. (Gross 1990, 2)

WHAT BAGGAGE DOES THIS INTERPRETER CARRY?

"God's word is revealed to the searcher." Which comes first, the word or the searcher? At first glance this is a seemingly innocuous question. Not so when dealing with a text such as the Qur'an which most Muslims believe to be coeternal with God (in other words, it has existed as long as God has). So where does one commence a work on qur'anic hermeneutics, the text or the context? Alas, the slip will show right from the beginning. Given that every literary production is inescapably autobiographical, I shall locate the birth of my ideas in my personal, social, and ideological history.

I have always been deeply moved by humankind's seemingly inexhaustible capacity to inflict injustice upon the "Other"—religious, racial, or sexual—and for long have I estimated my own humanity—or lack thereof—in terms of my willingness to react against it or my inability, unwillingness, or refusal to do so.

My father abandoned our family when I was three weeks old. My mother was left with six sons of whom three were from a previous marriage where her first husband had abandoned her when the third son was three months old. (Enough to drive anyone to Trinitarianism!) I was raised in Bonteheuwel, a colored township on the Cape Flats to which our family was forcibly moved under the Group Areas Act. This apartheid law, promulgated in 1952, set aside the most barren parts of the country for Blacks, Indians, and Coloreds.[1] Long periods passed during which we had no shoes and I recall running across frost-covered fields to school so that the frost could not really bite into my feet. Slightly more painful were the many times when my brother and I went around knocking on the doors of neighbors to ask for a piece of bread or scavenging in the gutters for discarded apple cores and the like.

This poverty was but one manifestation of apartheid South Africa. Here, in the 1980s, Whites, who constituted one-sixth of the total population, earned almost two-thirds of the national income while Blacks, who made up nearly three-quarters, earned only one quarter (Wilson and Ramphele 1989, 20). As for the millions who did not even fall in the category of wage earners, the unemployed: "We just sleep in the wilderness. You sleep without having eaten and you get up without having eaten. Tomorrow you go and look for a job. If you don't get it, you come back. When you come back, you go about uncovering rubbish bins thinking: 'Could it be there is something that has been thrown in here, just a little something that I can chew?'" (Wilson and Ramphele, 100).

My mother was an underpaid worker in a factory where she slogged from can't see to can't see—from early in the morning when it was still dark until late when it was dark already. My early life as a victim of apartheid and poverty, seeing my mother finally succumb under the burden of economic exploitation and patriarchy, filled me with an abiding commitment to a comprehensive sense of justice.

A Land of Many Faiths

In both Wynberg and Bonteheuwel we had Christian neighbors on both sides of our house, and in our school we were subjected to Christian National Education, a conservative religious ideology meant to make us obedient and God-fearing citizens of the apartheid state. Besides Christians, the only recollection I have of the religious Other are of Mr. Frank, a kind debt collector who was a Jew and of Tahirah, a Bahá'i girl at primary school whose parents prohibited her discussing her faith with anyone.

South African society has for long been multireligious. The now virtually decimated Khoikhoin, the Nguni, the San, and other indigenous groups are known to have held diverse religious beliefs and practices. The arrival of Dutch Christian settlers, Muslim slaves, and political exiles from the Indonesian Archipelago in the middle of the seventeenth century accentuated this religious diversity. More recent numerically significant additions to this diversity are the Hindus who arrived in the second half of the nineteenth century from India and the East European Jews who made their way to South Africa at the turn of this century.[2]

On our Christian neighbors we depended for "a cup of sugar," "a rand until Friday," and a shoulder to cry on—and on the kindness of Mr. Frank we depended for extensions on the repayment of the never-ending hire-purchase agreements. The fact that our oppression was made bearable by the solidarity, humanity, and laughter of our Christian neighbors made me suspicious of all religious ideas that claimed salvation only for their own and imbued me with a deep awareness of the intrinsic worth of the religious Other. How could I possibly look Mrs. Batista and Aunty Katie in the eye while believing that, despite the kindness that shone from every dealing which they had with us, they were destined for the fire of hell? This acceptance of the Other, the core of religious pluralism, did not come naturally however, to the township dwellers. Even as people suffered together they upheld notions of exclusive paradises for Christians or Muslims; even as they shared their humble meals with each other, they did so serving the religious Other out of specially reserved marked plates and cups.

Religion plays a major role among all classes in South African society. In the ghettoes the first community project is invariably the building of a mosque or a church. In the face of dislocation from a stable community under the Group Areas Act, religion or alcohol—more often than not, both—became important factors in the struggle for survival. In my family, Islam as a cultural anchor was an important tool in the struggle for survival among the sandy dunes and Port Jackson trees of Bonteheuwel. We bonded quickly with our Muslim neighbors—and "neighbors" could conceivably include those living thirty or forty houses away from ours. While my family was not unusually religious, the mosque-in-progress was, nevertheless, an important focal point. Here I played after school and weekends, pushed wheelbarrows of sand as a child, and ended up as secretary of the society that controlled the mosque and as *madrassah* teacher when I was still a kid at school.

Service in Return for Justice

I was strangely and deeply religious as a child, with a deep concern for the suffering which I experienced and witnessed all around me. I dealt with these two impulses by holding on to an indomitable belief that for God to be God, God had to be just and on the side of the marginalized. More curious was a logic, based on a text in the Qur'an, "If you assist Allah then He will assist you and make your feet firm" (47:7). For me this meant that I had to participate in a struggle for freedom and justice and, if I wanted God's help in this, then I had to assist Him.[3] "Him" was interpreted as "His religion" and so I persisted with the Tablighi Jama'ah, an international Muslim revivalist movement, that I had joined at the age of nine.

I was still at school when I was first detained by the Special Branch, as the security police were then known, as a result of my work in National Youth Action and the South African Black Scholars Association. Both of these organizations were committed to radical sociopolitical change and were housed in the buildings of the Christian Institute before its banning in 1973. There we enjoyed the warm hospitality and solidarity of its director, the Reverend Theo Kotze, and his staff. Theo offered the Muslims in these organizations prayer facilities and came to visit our families after our release from detention, to console them and to assure them that "getting mixed up" with the police was actually a privilege. (A poster on the wall of the Christian Institute read: "Where there's growth there's a branch; where there's special growth, there's bound to be a special branch.")

Pakistani Women and Christians as Black South Africans

After school I spent eight years on a scholarship in Pakistan doing my theological training, much of it in a frightfully conservative institute where everything "this-worldly" was frowned upon. I remember a twelve-year-old, Abdul Khaliq Allie, being rushed to the hospital one night and undergoing an emergency operation lasting a couple of hours. Adil Johaar stayed with him the morning, while I trod along to classes after having spent the night in hospital. In class the following morning Mawlana Baksh enquired where Adil was. Upon being told that Adil was watching over Abdul Khaliq in the hospital, he said: "Did you people come here to study or to look after sick people?"

I marvel at how I survived the place; a combination of courage, cunning, and the Grace of God I suppose.

Much as I came to love Pakistan, my coming from a Muslim family in a minority situation alerted me to the religious and social persecution of the Christian and Hindu minority communities. Derrick Dean, a young Christian activist, was visiting me one night in the *madrassah* room I shared with six others. Haji Bhai Padia, the South African leader of the Tablighi Jama'ah, put in a surprise appearance. Upon discovering that Derrick was not a Muslim he asked him to recite the *kalimah*, the Muslim formula of faith. I had a deep respect for Derrick as he was, and much love for Bhai Padia, and felt somewhat embarrassed. What was happening here was that my simplistic logic of "If you help God, He will help you" was becoming unstuck. The gap between my inherently conservative theology and progressive praxis was becoming exposed and choices had to be made.

I frequented the discussions of the Student Christian Movement, later renamed Breakthrough and witnessed how they tried to make sense of living as Christians in a fundamentally unjust and exploitative society. The most inspirational figure of the group, Brother Norman Wray, a La Salle brother, invited me to come and teach Islamic Studies at a school where he was the principal. I subsequently worked with him and the group on a number of different projects, which included paramedical work in the Karachi Central Prison, teaching in Hindu and Christian ghettoes for sweepers, and working in a home for abandoned children. Later I was to repeat all of the lessons of marrying belief and praxis in South Africa.

In Pakistan, I also became vividly aware of the many similarities between the oppression of women in Muslim society and that of Blacks in apartheid South Africa. The inescapable convergence between sexist and racist discourse has, consequently, come to form a permanent backdrop to my own concerns and commitment.

As if all of this were not enough.

Soon after my return to South Africa in 1982 I was called into a room by Omar, one of my brothers and the door was closed. "Farid, we have a sister; she's the eldest of all of us." My mother had had a daughter before marrying her first husband and the baby was handed over to her father seven days later. The pain of living an entire life carrying this secret must have been unbearable. Society stigmatizes women who fall pregnant outside marriage, as if these pregnancies were all phantom-induced, with no men ever involved. Later I learnt from Sharifah, my sister, now sixty years old, of the unbearably sad spectacle of an utterly lonely woman standing on the side of the road, watching from a safe distance the funeral procession of her mother—whom she had never known—passing, not daring to go near in fear of rejection by six brothers.

In 1983 resistance to a new constitution began. The preamble of this widely rejected tricameral constitution commenced with "In humble submission to the Almighty God" and then proceeded with the details of an elaborate system of entrenching the racial divisions among God's people. While the then state president, P. W. Botha, invoked the biblical narrative of the prodigal son to plead for apartheid South Africa's reentry into the community of nations, the vast majority of South Africans of diverse religious persuasion were making plans, in the name of the same Almighty God, to intensify that isolation and to destroy that same constitution as the first step of the last stage in the liberation struggle.

RELIGION AS CONTESTED TERRITORY

South Africa was entering the beginning of the last stage of our struggle against apartheid and I could not bear being safely tucked away in a seminary. The discomfort I first experienced when Bhai Padia wanted Derrick to recite the *kalimah* had turned full circle. Along with three friends, I spearheaded the founding of the Call of Islam in 1984. This affiliate of the United Democratic Front (UDF, established in 1983), the major internal liberation movement, soon became the most active Muslim movement, mobilizing nationally against apartheid, gender inequality, threats to the environment and to interfaith work. In the UDF itself, the Call was one of many religiously based organizations engaged in "the struggle." For these organizations, religion had always been contested terrain and the struggle was as much about regaining ideological territory from religious conservatism and obscurantism as it was about political freedom.

Much of the suffering inflicted on the people of South Africa was committed in the name of, and sometimes with, the scriptural support of a religious tradition, more specifically, that of Christianity. However, the subjugation and oppression of South Africa's people did not proceed with the general support of all Christians. Organizations such as the Christian Institute and individuals such as Beyers Naudé and Theo Kotze show that, even among Christians who came from privileged backgrounds, there were always dissident voices calling for justice and human rights. These voices were often marginalized and smothered, but always coherent and principled. They invoked the same sacred scriptures, often even the same textual references to sustain their arguments, as their fellow Christians to denounce the exploitation and suffering of black people.

Religion and scripture as contested territory were also evident in the responses among the exploited and oppressed. The vast majority of Blacks and a small, but significant, number of Whites viewed the entire social structure of South Africa as irredeemably racist, exploitative, and desperately in need of radical changes. Given the significance of religion in the lives of South Africans, it was not surprising that many made a connection between religion and liberation. (Even if some did it rather simplistically, wanting to help God's religion if He helped them bring about freedom!) There were, however, also many who argued that politics should be kept apart from religion. Among Blacks, the "apolitical" Zionist Christian Church, with a membership numbering a few million, attracted hundreds of thousands to their annual gathering at Moria. The Charismatic and Pentecostal churches, which claimed to confine themselves to "spiritual" concerns, attracted people from all race groups and experienced tremendous growth in the urban areas during the 1980s (Gifford 1988; 1989).[4]

All the main political players in South Africa invoked religion as the ultimate proof of self-correctness. In 1985, from his prison cell on Robben Island, Nelson Mandela wrote a moving letter to the Muslim Judicial Council (MJC, established in 1945), wherein he spoke about the spiritual solace he derived from his visits to the shrine of Shaikh Madura, a Muslim saint imprisoned on the island until his death in 1742. In that letter he also reaffirmed his commitment to his Methodist roots and spoke glowingly about the role of religion, not just Christianity, in shaping the ideals of the African National Congress (ANC, established in 1912). Meanwhile, in the KwaZulu Bantustan capital of Ulundi, Gatsha Buthelezi, the Bantustan's leader, at his annual prayer breakfasts, lamented the political role which religious leaders were increasingly playing against homeland governments.

In the 1980s especially, the conflict between two expressions of religion, accommodationist and liberatory, was increasingly evident. In a context of oppression, it seems that theology, across religious divisions, fulfills one of two tasks: it either underpins and supports the structures and institutions of oppression or it performs this function in relation to the struggle for liberation. Accommodation theology tries to accommodate and justify the dominant status quo "with its racism, capitalism and totalitarianism. It blesses injustice, canonizes the will of the powerful and reduces the poor to passivity, obedience and apathy" (*The Kairos Document* 1985, 13). It focuses on questions of personal conversion and salvation while it ignores or denies the role which socioeconomic structures play in the shaping of personal values. In a sociological investigation into this model of religiousness conducted in 1969, Milton Rokeach reported that

> the general picture that emerges is that those who place a high value on salvation are conservative, anxious to maintain the status quo and unsympathetic or indifferent to the plight of the black or the poor. Considered all together, the data suggest a portrait of the religious minded as a person having a self-centred preoccupation with saving his own soul, an other worldly orientation, coupled with indifference toward or even a tacit endorsement of a social system that would perpetuate social inequality and injustice. (Cited in Stott 1984, 8)

In South Africa manifestations of this theological model were witnessed both in the so-called mainstream religious structures such as the Anglican and Dutch Reformed Churches and the Majlisul Ulama, and in numerous groups such as Christians for Peace, Christ for All Nations, the Zionist Christian Council, the United Christian Reconciliation Council, the Tablighi Jama'ah and the Islamic Propagation Centre.

In contrast to accommodation theology, liberation theology is the process of praxis for comprehensive justice, the theological reflection that emerges from it, and the reshaping of praxis based on that reflection. In South Africa, liberation theology was manifested in the growing numbers of religious figures and organizations who confessed the sin of silence in the face of oppression, acquiescence in the face of exploitation, and power in the face of want. They sought a God who is active in history, who desires freedom for all people and the simultaneous conversion of hearts and social structures, a God whose own unity was reflected in the oneness of people.

The tension between these two expressions of theology was not confined to Christianity; Islam, Hinduism, Judaism, and African Traditional Religion, in various degrees, saw new forms of contextual theology and religious structures emerging to challenge apartheid. In resisting the ideology of apartheid and its resulting injustices, adherents of all faiths increasingly discovered each other as companions in the struggle for justice. In the Muslim community the most significant area where this battle over interpretations of religion was being waged was the discourse of solidarity with the religious Other in the struggle against apartheid.

When the Self Engages the Other

Interfaith solidarity, particularly during the 1980s, was an intrinsic part of the South African struggle for justice. It also remains an important dimension of the vision for a just and nonracial society held by all of those who were a part of that struggle. The often bitter debate around interfaith solidarity against apartheid featured prominently in Muslim discourse in the 1980s. With the emergence of a nonracial and democratic South Africa, it is timely to examine some of the theological dimensions of this debate and their wider hermeneutical implications.

How did political activism, or the lack of it, shape the Muslim community's understanding of the Qur'an and their perception of the Other? How did a conscious desire to recognize and respect righteousness in religiously Other comrades compel progressive Islamists to reinterpret qur'anic texts which, at a superficial glance, may be regarded as uncharitable, even unjust, to the Other? What led these Islamists regularly to invoke some "revolutionary texts" while quietly passing over other texts? And what led the accommodationist clerics[5] to invoke the "spiritual texts" while ignoring other texts? How was Islam affected by its use as a means of liberation? What does this question of Islam being "affected" say about deeply held beliefs in the Muslim community of a faith which has a timeless essence and which transcends history? These were some of the questions confronting, and being confronted, by progressive Islamists who have been engaged in what has cryptically been known as "the struggle."

My present search for a South African qur'anic hermeneutic of pluralism for liberation was rooted in the fusion of our nation's crucible and in my own commitment to comprehensive justice. While this work primarily focuses on rethinking approaches to the Qur'an and to the theological categories of exclusion and inclusion rooted in a struggle for freedom from economic exploitation and racial discrimination, its application is intended to be broader than these two forms of injustice. I believe that the ideas I put forward can have a wider application to all categories of social and political injustice, ranging from the obvious oppression of women in Muslim society to discrimination against left-handed people.

WHOSE JUSTICE? WHICH MORALITY?

But "whose 'injustice'?" one may well ask. In the same way, in the expression "In humble submission to the Almighty God," one may also ask: "but which God?" More than most societies, South Africans have a particularly acute sense of the consequences of living with competing realities and, consequently, rival injustices. The task of judging between competing and incompatible rationalities and justices is exceptionally difficult, because one cannot pose a point of view which is free from any one particular conception of rationality or justice (MacIntyre 1988, 1–18).

Contemporary hermeneutics alerts us to the false pretensions of objectivity or neutrality and the need to rehabilitate "the concept of prejudice and a recognition of the fact that there are legitimate prejudices" (Gadamer 1992, 261). The present work, like all literary productions, takes sides. While not denying my personal commitment to the struggle against injustice and the public role I have played in this regard, I strive to make the best use of some contemporary developments in the human sciences to explain the phenomenon of qur'anic interpretation among contemporary South African progressive Islamists.

People with a religious commitment may choose to believe that truth is exclusively an eternal and preexisting reality beyond history. However, people also make truth. Modernity has increased our awareness that the human mind is not a blank slate covered with facts entirely imported through cognitive or spiritual senses, or through the authority of religiointellectual traditions. Increasingly, we are beginning to understand that, whatever else it may be, the essential awareness of one's mind is as "the tissues of contingent relations in language" (Aitken 1991, 1). Language, we now know, plays a significant role in shaping us and our consciousness. Language though, much as it shapes history, is also a prisoner of history. Yet, according to Muslims, God is utterly beyond history. It is this utter beyondness and its use of an inevitably history-bound mechanism, language, which provides a central dilemma for the Muslim who also seeks to live contemporaneously and in complete awareness of the baggage of prejudices.

More than the elaboration of intellectual modernity and postmodernity in the West, it was the South African crucible that confronted progressive Islamists with the "truth" that people bring their indispensable baggage of race, class, gender, and personal history along when they engage the qur'anic text.

My Baggage of Theological Assumptions

I believe that the Transcendent, God, has intervened and is intervening in history. This intervention, however, can make no sense other than within the framework of humankind's existence here on earth. The religious legacy of South African Muslims, and our ongoing commitment to that legacy, compel us to find new ways of describing the way God may address a world in which human beings constantly change.

In South Africa the world in which Muslims live is also being shaped by others who struggle to survive, who suffer, despair, and hope; by others who do not share their religious beliefs. The progressive Islamists could not deny the joys of a shared existence and the moral compulsion of a common struggle against apartheid. Yet we had to live in faithfulness to a text—the Qur'an—that seemed to be harsh toward the Other, suffering along with us in the quest for liberation and justice. To become creatively engaged alongside the Other, risked being transformed. Given that religiosity was an intrinsic part of the identity of progressive Islamists, it was inevitable that our understanding of religious tradition and scripture would also be transformed.

What was, in effect, happening among us closely resembles the use of the "hermeneutic circle" in liberation theology. Juan Luis Segundo, a liberation theologian from Uruguay, defines the hermeneutic circle as "the continuing change in our interpretation of the Bible which is dictated by the continuing changes in our present-day reality, both individual and societal," (Segundo 1991, 9).[6] He suggests two preconditions for creating a hermeneutic circle. First, profound and enriching questions and suspicion about one's real situation. Second, a new interpretation of scripture that is equally profound and enriching.

The fundamental difference between Segundo's circle and the methodology proposed by Fazlur Rahman (d. 1988), one of this century's most profound modernist Islamic scholars, whose ideas are examined in some detail in the second chapter, is the conscious decision to enter the circle from the point of liberative praxis which is decidedly political. "The hermeneutic circle," says Segundo, "is based on the fact that a political option in favour of liberative change is an intrinsic element of faith" (Segundo 1991, 97).

I believe that a Muslim's task of understanding the Qur'an within a context of oppression is twofold. First, it is to expose the way traditional interpretation and beliefs about a text function as ideology in order to legitimize an unjust order. A text dealing with *fitnah*—(literally, "disorder") would, for example, be critically reexamined in order to see how the word has come to be broadly interpreted as challenges to the dominant political status quo, however unjust that status quo may be. Second, it is to acknowledge the wholeness of the human being, to extract the religious dimensions within that situation of injustice from the text and utilize these for the cause of liberation. (One would, for example, ask questions about the relationship of God to hunger and exploitation.) These theological dimensions simultaneously shape and are being shaped by the activity of those Islamists engaged in a struggle for justice and freedom.

To search for the religious dimensions of a particular socioeconomic situation and to highlight them may open one to charges of the selective and arbitrary appropriation of certain texts, to the exclusion of others. There are two responses to this problem. First, freedom from starvation and exploitation paves the way for a more authentic popular embrace of a comprehensive theology. You cannot truly submit to God when you are under the yoke of hunger. Such submission is a form of coercion. The *hadith* (saying of Muhammad), "I am in the hands of Allah with regards to poverty and *kufr* (rejection/denial/ingratitude)" (Ibn Hanbal 1978, vol. 2, 101) is a significant indicator of the relationship between lack of faith and hunger. The Qur'an, in dealing with the encounter of the Israelites and Pharaoh, does not refer to sins of "personal morality" which may have occurred among the Israelites because their dominant reality was that of oppression; nor does the Qur'an dwell at length on the feebleness of their faith in God; it deals with Pharaoh's claims to divinity and emphasizes the political consequences of those claims for the enslaved Israelites (10:83–5, 90). This is not to suggest that belief in the unity of God was not an important requirement of the Israelites when they were enslaved; it is only to argue that all dimensions of faith do not have to enjoy an equal measure of attention at all times. Furthermore, if sociopolitical burdens serve as obstacles to faith, then in the present historical circumstances, the struggle for their removal must be the dominant aspect of a believer's activity. The second response is that a search for the theological dimensions in a particular political context does not imply that one views politics as the only dimension of faith and that the text is valuable only insofar as it addresses immediate political concerns. It only emphasizes this dimension as the most crucial one in the here and now "where people are crushed under the weight of oppression and wandering in search of bread and human dignity" (Boff and Boff 1985, 104). That the Qur'an does, in fact, deal with these sociopolitical burdens on numerous occasions is undisputed. These qur'anic texts have, however, been used to legitimize the burden and to provide comfort to those responsible for its imposition. Accommodationist Islam's use of these texts has done nothing to enhance the dignity of the victims of structural injustice, nor to facilitate their freedom.

The beliefs outlined above lead to a number of ideas that both underpin my investigation and are confirmed by it. They also support my advocacy of a South African qur'anic hermeneutic of religious pluralism for liberation.

1. One cannot escape from the personal or social experiences which make up the sum of one's existence. Therefore, any person reading a text or viewing any situation does so through the lenses of his or her experiences.

2. Anyone's attempts to make sense of anything read or experienced take place in a particular context. Because every reader approaches the Qur'an within a particular context it is impossible to speak of an interpretation of the qur'anic text applicable to the whole world. Meaning is always tentative and biased.

3. According to the Qur'an, one arrives at correct beliefs (orthodoxy) through correct actions (orthopraxis) (29:69). The latter is the criterion by which the former is decided. In a society where injustice and poverty drive people to say "Even God has left, no one cares anymore," orthopraxis really means activity which supports justice, i.e., liberative praxis. A qur'anic hermeneutic of liberation therefore emerges within concrete struggles for justice and derives its authenticity from that engagement.

4. Formal statements of doctrine, whether "true" or not, and no matter how intensely the believer clings to them, are, in the first instance, the results of intellectual labor that has often endured for centuries. This labor is invariably accompanied by religiopolitical disputes, which inevitably impact upon theological developments and the way these statements are shaped.

5. Islamic theology in general, and qur'anic studies specifically, have consistently become increasingly rigid in a process that followed the systematization of theology.

Accompanying this process was the growing inability to deal with all forms of Otherness, within the historical community of Muslims and outside it.

6. Both the revelation of the Qur'an within specific contexts, as well as acceptance of the righteous and just Other are intrinsic to the Qur'an (2:281; 3:23–4; 16:111; 4:40, 85; 10:44; 12:56, etc.). It is Muslim conservatism[7] that persistently narrowed the theological base for defining *iman, islam,* and widened the base for *kufr.*[8] As the basis of conservatism gradually narrowed, the categories of the Other widened so that fewer and fewer were regarded as belivers and more and more as *kafir.*

7. Muslims are confronted with a variety of urgent questions: What is an "authentic" appreciation of the qur'anic message today? What makes and shapes "authenticity"? How legitimate is it to produce meaning, rather than extracting meaning, from qur'anic texts? These are some of the issues, which hermeneutics does not create (they have always been with us) but which demand to be addressed. They are part and parcel of the search for a qur'anic response to the challenges confronting humankind today.

NOTES

1. It should be noted that ethnic descriptions in South Africa often bear little or no resemblance to reality. The term "Arab," for example, was used to describe some Indians in Natal during the late nineteenth century. European Jews were described as "Peruvians" between 1888 and 1914, and in the 1850s even white converts to Islam were referred to as "Malays" (Chidester 1991, 14). In the case of the description "African," absurd as it may sound, the Khoikhoin, the earliest known inhabitants of South Africa, would be excluded. "Blacks" is an ethnic description employed for those usually referred to as "Africans." The word "black" may also be a political description referring to all non-Caucasians in this area. "Coloreds" refers to those of "mixed parentage"—and aren't all of humankind?—while "Whites" refers to people of Caucasian origin.

2. According to the 1991 population census, 70.4 percent of South Africans indicated a religious affiliation: 66.5 percent regarded themselves as Christians, 1.3 percent as Hindus, 1.1 percent as Muslims, and 1.2 percent indicated that they had no religion, while 29.6 percent did not answer the question or objected to doing so. Christianity is the dominant religion among all "racial" groups except the Indians.

3. I do not believe in a masculine Deity and endeavor to use gender-inclusive language wherever possible. In some cases though, particularly when dealing with texts such as the Qur'an, one is constrained to employ the masculine.

4. Recently revealed information indicates that these groups were the recipients of substantial state funds from the apartheid regime in order to counter the influence of liberation theology.

5. In theory, Sunni Islam does not have an *ecclesia* and has therefore no clerics. In practice though, the "*ulama*" (literally, "scholars"), to all intents and purposes, fulfill a similar function and are often organized as a formal and institutionalized body. A secondary reason why I prefer the term "clerics" to "*ulama*" in the South African context is that the group which exercises religious leadership in South Africa comprises individuals with both scholarly and nonscholarly backgrounds. It is, for example, not uncommon for the *mu'adhdhin* (caller to prayer) to successfully succeed the *imam* upon the latter's demise.

6. I am unaware of any of the progressive Islamists, including myself, having read any work on liberation theology during the 1980s. A vague awareness of it and its significance in Latin America and some parts of Asia was, however, common in liberation struggle circles.

7. I use the word "conservative" to refer to "those who wish and think that it is possible to preserve society substantially as it is and who deprecate the significance of social change (Cantwell-Smith 1963, 377).

8. Aware that all translation is also a form of interpretation, I prefer using the Arabic terms throughout until the act of interpretation is conscious and intentional.

REFERENCES

Aitken, Richard. 1991. "Did Those Mortal Beings Imagine that Allah Talked with the Quakers' God: Reflections on a Woodbrookean Conversation." Paper Delivered at President's Seminar, Selly Oak Colleges, September.

Boff, Leonardo, and Clodovis Boff. 1985. *Salvation and Liberation: In Search of a Balance between Faith and Politics.* Maryknoll, N.Y.: Orbis.

Cantwell-Smith, Wilfred. 1963. *Modern Islam in India.* Lahore: Sh. Muhammad.

Chidester, David. 1991. *Shots in the Streets: Violence and Religion in South Africa.* Boston: Beacon Press.

Gadamer, Hans Georg. 1992. *The Historicity of Understanding,* in *The Hermeneutics Reader,* ed. K. Meuler-Volmer. New York: Continuum, 261–67.

Gifford, Paul. 1988. *The Religious Right in Southern Africa.* Harare: Jongwe.

———. 1989. "Theology and Right Wing Christianity." *Journal of Theology for Southern Africa* 69: 28–39.

Gross, Selwyn O. P. 1990. "Religious Pluralism in Struggles for Justice." *New Blackfriars* 71(841): 377–86.

Ibn Hanbal, Ahmad. 1978. Musnad al-Imam Ahmad bin Hanbal, ed. 'Abbas Ahmad al-Baz 6 vols. Mecca: Dar al-Baz li al-Nashr wa al-Tawzi'.

The Kairos Document. 1985. Braamfonteing: The Kairos Theologians.

MacIntyre, Alisdaire. 1988. *Whose Justice? Which Rationality?* London: Duckworth.

Segundo, Juan Luis, S. J. 1991. *The Liberation of Theology.* Maryknoll, N.Y.: Orbis.

Stott, John. 1984. *Issues Facing Christians Today: A Major Appraisal of Contemporary Social and Moral Questions.* Hants: Marshalls, Morgan and Scott.

Wilson, Francis, and Ramphele, Mamphela. 1989. *Uprooting Poverty: The South African Challenge.* Cape Town: David Phillip.

"The Social Teachings of the Buddha"

◈

Walpola Rahula

Walpola Rahula was an enormously influential Buddhist monk from Sri Lanka. Scholar and teacher, the first Buddhist monk to hold a university professorship in the United States, Rahula's ideas helped prompt Buddhist monks to bring their faith into the modern age of religious pluralism, modern technology, and political engagement.

◈

The common belief that to follow the Buddha's teaching one has to retire from life is a misconception. It is really an unconscious defense against practicing it. There are numerous references in Buddhist literature to men and women living ordinary, normal family lives who successfully practiced what the Buddha taught, and realized Nirvana. Vacchogatta the Wanderer once asked the Buddha straightforwardly whether there were laymen and women leading the family life, who followed his teaching successfully and attained to high spiritual states. The Buddha categorically stated that there were not one or two, not a hundred or two hundred or five hundred, but many more laymen and women leading the family life who followed his teaching successfully and attained to high spiritual states.[1]

It may be agreeable for certain people to live a retired life in a quiet place away from noise and disturbance. But it is certainly more praiseworthy and courageous to practice Buddhism living among your fellow beings, helping them and being of service to them. It may perhaps be useful in some cases for a person to live in retirement for a time in order to improve his or her mind and character, as preliminary moral, spiritual, and intellectual training, to be strong enough to come out later and help others. But if someone lives an entire life in solitude, thinking only of their own happiness and salvation, without caring for their fellow beings, this surely is not in keeping with the Buddha's teaching which is based on love, compassion, and service to others.

Those who think that Buddhism is interested only in lofty ideals, high moral and philosophical thought, and that it ignores the social and economic welfare of people, are wrong. The Buddha was interested in the happiness of people. To him happiness was not possible without leading a pure life based on moral and spiritual principles. But he knew that leading such a life was hard in unfavorable material and social conditions.

Buddhism does not consider material welfare as an end in itself: it is only a means to an end—a higher and nobler end. But it is a means which is indispensable, indispensable in achieving a higher purpose for human happiness. So Buddhism recognizes the need of certain minimum material conditions favorable to spiritual success—even that of a monk engaged in meditation in some solitary place.[2]

The Buddha did not take life out of the context of its social and economic background; he looked at it as a whole, in all its social, economic, and political aspects. His teachings on ethical, spiritual, and philosophical problems are fairly well known. But little is known, particularly in the West, about his teaching on social, economic, and political matters. Yet there are numerous discourses dealing with these scattered throughout the ancient Buddhist texts. Let us take only a few examples.

The *Cakkavattisihanada-sutta* of the *Digha-nikaya*[3] clearly states that poverty (*daliddiya*) is the cause of immorality and crimes such as theft, falsehood, violence, hatred, cruelty, etc. Kings in ancient times, like governments today, tried to suppress crime through punishment. The *Kutadanta-sutta* of the same *Nikaya* explains how futile this is. It says that this method can never be successful. Instead the Buddha suggests that, in order to eradicate crime, the economic condition of the people should be improved: grain and other facilities for agriculture should be provided for farmers and cultivators; capital should be provided for traders and those who are engaged in business; adequate wages should be paid to those who are employed. When people are thus provided for with opportunities for earning a sufficient income, they will be contented, will have no fear or anxiety, and consequently the country will be peaceful and free from crime.

Because of this, the Buddha told laypeople how important it is to improve their economic condition. This does not mean that he approved of hoarding wealth with desire and attachment, which is against his fundamental teaching, nor did he approve of each and every way of earning one's livelihood. There are certain trades like the production and sale of armaments, which he condemns as evil means of livelihood.

A man named Dighajanu once visited the Buddha and said: "Venerable Sir, we are ordinary laymen, leading the family life with wife and children. Would the Blessed One teach us some doctrines which will be conducive to our happiness in this world and hereafter."

The Buddha tells him that there are four things which are conducive to a man's happiness in this world: First: he should be skilled, efficient, earnest, and energetic in whatever profession he is engaged, and he should know it well (*utthana-sampada*); second: he should protect his income, which he has thus earned righteously, with the sweat of his brow (*arakkha-sampada*); (This refers to protecting wealth from thieves, etc. All these ideas should be considered against the background of the period); third: he should have good friends (*kalyana-mitta*) who are faithful, learned, virtuous, liberal, and intelligent, who will help him along the right path away from evil; fourth: he should spend reasonably, in proportion to his income, neither too much nor too little, i.e., he should not hoard wealth avariciously, nor should he be extravagant—in other words he should live within his means (*samajivikata*).

Then the Buddha expounds the four virtues conducive to a layman's happiness hereafter: *Saddha*—He should have faith and confidence in moral, spiritual, and intellectual values. *Sila*—He should abstain from destroying and harming life, from stealing and cheating, from adultery, from falsehood, and from intoxicating drinks. *Caga*—He should practice charity, generosity, without attachment and craving for his wealth. *Panna*—He should develop wisdom which leads to the complete destruction of suffering, to the realization of Nirvana.[4]

Sometimes the Buddha even went into details about saving money and spending it, as, for instance, when he told the young man Sigala that he should spend one fourth of his income on his daily expenses, invest half in his business and put aside one fourth for any emergency.[5]

Once the Buddha told Anathapindika, the great banker, one of his most devoted lay disciples who founded for him the celebrated Jetavana monastery at Savatthi, that a layman who leads an ordinary family life has four kinds of happiness. The first happiness is to enjoy economic security or sufficient wealth acquired by just and righteous means (*atthi-sukha*); the second is spending that wealth liberally on himself, his family, his friends and relatives, and on meritorious deeds (*bhoga-sukha*); the third is to be free from debts (*anana-sukha*); the fourth happiness is to live a faultless and a pure life, without committing evil in thought, word, or deed (*anavajja-sukha*). It must be noted here that three of these kinds of happiness are economic, and that the Buddha finally reminded the banker that economic and material happiness is "not worth one-sixteenth part" of the spiritual happiness arising out of a faultless and good life.[6]

From these few examples, one can see that the Buddha considered economic welfare as requisite for human happiness, but that he did not recognize progress as real and true if it was only material, devoid of a spiritual and moral foundation. While encouraging material progress, Buddhism always lays great stress on the development of the moral and spiritual character for a happy, peaceful, and contented society.

The Buddha was just as clear on politics, war, and peace. It is too well known to be repeated here that Buddhism advocates and preaches nonviolence and peace as its universal message, and does not approve of any kind of violence or destruction of life. According to Buddhism there is nothing that can be called a "just war"—which is only a false term coined and put into circulation to justify and excuse hatred, cruelty, violence, and massacre. Who decides what is just or unjust? The mighty and the victorious are "just," and the weak and the defeated are "unjust." Our war is always "just," and your war is always "unjust." Buddhism does not accept this position.

The Buddha not only taught nonviolence and peace, but he even went to the field of battle itself and intervened personally and prevented war, as in the case of the dispute between the Sakyas and the Koliyas, who were prepared to fight over the question of the waters of the Rohini. And his words once prevented King Ajatasattu from attacking the kingdom of the Vajjis.

In the days of the Buddha, as today, there were rulers who governed their countries unjustly. People were oppressed and exploited, tortured and persecuted, excessive taxes were imposed and cruel punishments were inflicted. The Buddha was deeply moved by these inhumanities. The *Dhammapadatthakatha* records that he, therefore, directed his attention to the problem of good government. His views should be appreciated against the social, economic, and political background of his time. He had shown how a whole country could become corrupt, degenerate, and unhappy when the heads of its government, that is the king, the ministers, and administrative officers become corrupt and unjust. For a country to be happy it must have a just government. How this form of just government could be realized is explained by the Buddha in his teaching of the "Ten Duties of the King" (*dasa-ra-jadhamma*), as given in the *Jataka* text.[7]

Of course the term "king" (*Raja*) of old should be replaced today by the term "Government." "The Ten Duties of the King," therefore, apply today to all those who constitute the government, such as the head of state, ministers, political leaders, legislative and administrative officers, etc.

The first of the "Ten Duties of the King" is liberality, generosity, charity (*dana*). The ruler should not have craving and attachment to wealth and property, but should give it away for the welfare of the people.

Second: A high moral character (*sila*). He should never destroy life, cheat, steal and exploit others, commit adultery, utter falsehood, and take intoxicating drinks. That is, he must at least observe the Five Precepts (*Panca-sila*), the minimum moral obligations of a lay Buddhist—(1) not to destroy life, (2) not to steal, (3) not to commit adultery, (4) not to tell lies, (5) not to take intoxicating drinks.

Third: Sacrificing everything for the good of the people (*pariccaga*), he must be prepared to give up all personal comfort, name and fame, and even his life, in the interest of the people.

Fourth: Honesty and integrity (*ajjava*). He must be free from fear or favor in the discharge of his duties, must be sincere in his intentions, and must not deceive the public.

Fifth: Kindness and gentleness (*maddava*). He must possess a genial temperament.

Sixth: Austerity in habits (*tapa*). He must lead a simple life, and should not indulge in a life of luxury. He must have self-control.

Seventh: Freedom from hatred, ill-will, enmity (*akkodha*). He should bear no grudge against anybody.

Eighth: Nonviolence (*avihimsa*), which means not only that he should harm nobody, but also that he should try to promote peace by avoiding and preventing war, and everything which involves violence and destruction of life.

Ninth: Patience, forbearance, tolerance, understanding (*khanti*). He must be able to bear hardships, difficulties, and insults without losing his temper.

Tenth: Nonopposition, nonobstruction (*avirodha*), that is to say that he should not oppose the will of the people, should not obstruct any measures that are conducive to the welfare of the people. In other words he should rule in harmony with his people.[8]

The Buddha says: "Never by hatred is hatred appeased, but it is appeased by kindness. This is an eternal truth."[9] "One should win anger through kindness, wickedness through goodness, selfishness through charity, and falsehood through truthfulness."[10]

There can be no peace or happiness for a man as long as he desires and thirsts after conquering and subjugating his neighbor. As the Buddha says: "The victor breeds hatred, and the defeated lies down in misery. He who renounces both victory and defeat is happy and peaceful."[11] The only conquest that brings peace and happiness is self-conquest. "One may conquer millions in battle, but he who conquers himself, only one, is the greatest of conquerors."[12]

Buddhism aims at creating a society where the ruinous struggle for power is renounced; where calm and peace prevail away from conquest and defeat; where the persecution of the innocent is vehemently denounced; where one who conquers oneself is more respected than those who conquer millions by military and economic warfare; where hatred is conquered by kindness, and evil by goodness; where enmity, jealousy, ill-will, and greed do not infect men's minds; where compassion is the driving force of action; where all, including the least of living things, are treated with fairness, consideration, and love; where life in peace and harmony, in a world of material contentment, is directed toward the highest and noblest aim, the realization of the Ultimate Truth, *Nirvana*.

NOTES

1. *Majjhima-nikaya*, I (Pali Text Society edition), 30–31.

2. *Majjhima-nikayatthakatha, Papancasudani*, I (Pali Text Society), 290ff. Buddhist monks, members of the order of the *Sangha*, are not expected to have personal property, but they are allowed to hold communal (*Sanghika*) property.

3. No. 26.

4. *Anguttara-nikaya*, ed. Devamitta Thera (Colombo, 1929) and Pali Text Society edition, 786ff.

5. *Digha-nikaya*, III, ed. Nanavasa Thera (Colombo, 1929), 115.

6. *Anguttara-nikaya*, ed. Davamitta Thera (Colombo, 1929) and Pali Text Society edition, 232–33.

7. Jataka I, 260, 399; II, 400, 274, 320; V, 119, 378.

8. It is interesting to note here that the Five Principles or *Pancha-sila* in India's foreign policy are in accordance with the Buddhist principles which Asoka, the great Buddhist emperor of India, applied to the administration of his government in the third century B.C.E. The expression *Pancha-sila* (Five Precepts or Virtues), is itself a Buddhist term.

9. *Dhammapada*, ed. K. Khammaratana Thera (Colombo, 1926), I 5.

10. *Dhammapada*, XVII 3.

11. *Dhammapada*, XV 5.

12. *Dhammapada*, VIII 4.

from *Moral Man and Immoral Society*

❧

Reinhold Niebuhr

Reinhold Niebuhr was one of the last great public intellectuals in America. Prolific author and teacher, his ideas on religious social engagement, his critical connections to socialist thought, and his realism about the limitations of any religious tradition or political movement (including his own) influenced thinkers as diverse and important as Thomas Merton and Martin Luther King.

❧

Essentially religion is a sense of the absolute. When, as is usually the case, the absolute is imagined in terms of man's own highest ethical aspirations, a perspective is created from which all moral achievements are judged to be inadequate. Viewed from the relative perspectives of the historic scene, there is no human action which cannot be justified in terms of some historic purpose or approved in comparison with some less virtuous action. The absolute reference of religion eliminates these partial perspectives and premature justifications. There is no guarantee against the interpretation of the absolute in terms of faulty moral insights; and human vice and error may thus be clothed by religion in garments of divine magnificence and given the prestige of the absolute. Yet there is a general development in the high religions toward an interpretation of the divine as benevolent will, and a consequent increase of condemnation upon all selfish actions and desires. In investing the heart of the cosmos with an ethical will, the religious imagination unites its awe before the infinitude and majesty of the physical world with its reverence for the ethical principle of the inner life. The inner world of conscience, which is in constant rebellion against the outer world of nature, is made supreme over the world of nature by the fiat of religion. Thus the Bechuana regarded thunder as the accusing voice of God and cried: "I have not stolen, I have not stolen, who among us has taken the goods of another?"[1] And Jesus, in the sublime naïveté of the religious imagination at its best, interprets the impartiality of nature toward the evil and the good, which secular reason might regard as its injustice, as a revelation of the impartial love of God. The religious imagination, seeking an ultimate goal and point of reference for the moral urges of life, finds support for its yearning after the absolute in the infinitude and majesty of the physical world. The omnipotence of God, as seen in the world of nature, invests his moral character with the quality of the absolute and transfigures it into holiness. Since supreme omnipotence and perfect holiness are incompatible attributes, there is a note of rational absurdity in all religion, which more rational types of theologies attempt to eliminate. But they cannot succeed without sacrificing a measure of religious vitality.

The religious conscience is sensitive not only because its imperfections are judged in the light of the absolute but because its obligations are felt to be obligations toward a person. The holy will is a personal will. Philosophers may find difficulty in transferring the concept of personality, loaded as it is with connotations which are derived from the sense limitations of human personality, to the absolute. But these difficulties are of small moment to the poetic imagination of religion. It uses the symbols derived from human personality to describe the absolute and it finds them morally potent. Moral attitudes always develop most sensitively in person-to-person relationships. That is one reason why more inclusive loyalties, naturally more abstract than immediate ones, lose some of their power over the human heart; and why a shrewd society attempts to restore that power by making a person the symbol of the community. The exploitation of the symbolic significance of monarchy, after it has lost its essential power, as in British politics for instance, is a significant case in point. The king is a useful symbol for the nation because it is easier for the simple imagination to conceive a sense of loyalty toward him than toward the nation. The nation is an abstraction which cannot be grasped if fitting symbols are not supplied. A living person is the most useful and potent symbol for this purpose. In religion all the higher moral obligations, which are lost in abstractions on the historic level, are felt as obligations toward the supreme person. Thus both the personality and the holiness of God provide the religious man with a reinforcement of his moral will and a restraint upon his will-to-power.

If religion be particularly occupied with the absolute from the perspective of the individual, it is nevertheless capable of conceiving an absolute society in which the ideal of love and justice will be fully realized. There is a millennial hope in every vital religion. The religious imagination is as impatient with the compromises, relativities, and imperfections of historic society as with the imperfections of individual life. The prophet Isaiah dreamed of the day when the lion and the lamb would lie down together, when, in other words, the law of nature which prompts the strong to devour the weak would be abrogated. The religious idealists of both Egypt and Babylon had their visions of an ideal reign. Sometimes the contrast between the real and the ideal is drawn so sharply that the religious man despairs of the achievement of the ideal in mundane history. He transfers his hopes to another world. This is particularly true of religion influenced by Platonic idealism, in which the ideal world is always above and not at the end of human history. It was the peculiar genius of Jewish religious thought, that it conceived the millennium in this-worldly terms. The gospel conception of the kingdom of God represents a highly spiritualized version of this Jewish millennial hope, heavily indebted to the vision of the Second Isaiah. Wherever religion concerns itself with the problems of society, it always gives birth to some kind of millennial hope, from the perspective of which present social realities are convicted of inadequacy, and courage is maintained to continue in the effort to redeem society of injustice. The courage is needed; for the task of building a just society seems always to be a hopeless one when only present realities and immediate possibilities are envisaged. The modern communist's dream of a completely equalitarian society is a secularized, but still essentially religious, version of the classical religious dream. Its secularization is partly a reaction to the unrealistic sentimentality into which the religious social hope degenerated in the middle-class religious community; partly it is the inevitable consequence of the mechanization of modern life and the destruction of religious imagination. Though it is a secularized version of the religious hope, its religious quality is attested by its emphasis upon catastrophe. It does not see the new society emerging by gradual and inevitable evolutionary process. It is pessimistic about the present trends in society and sees them driving toward disaster; but its hope, as in all religion, grows out of its despair, and it sees the new society emerging from catastrophe. Evolutionary millennialism is always the hope of comfortable and privileged classes, who imagine themselves too rational to accept the idea of the sudden emergence of the absolute in history. For them the ideal is in history, working its way to ultimate triumph. They identify God and nature, the real and the ideal, not because the more dualistic conceptions of classical religion are too irrational for them (though they are irrational); but because they do not suffer as much as the disinherited from the brutalities of contemporary society, and therefore do not take as catastrophic a view of contemporary history. The more privileged proletarians turn catastrophic Marxism into evolutionary socialism for the same reason. Religion is always a citadel of hope, which is built on the edge of despair. Men are inclined to view both individual and social moral facts with complacency, until they view them from some absolute perspective. But the same absolutism which drives them to despair, rejuvenates their hope. In the imagination of the truly religious man, the God who condemns history will yet redeem history.

Both the resources and the limitations of religion in dealing with the social problem, are revealed even more clearly in its spirit of love than in its sense of contrition. Religion encourages love and benevolence, as we have seen, by absolutising the moral principle of life until it achieves the purity of absolute disinterestedness and by imparting transcendent worth to the life of others. This represents a permanent contribution to the moral life which, despite limitations revealed in the more intricate and complex social relations, must be gratefully accepted as an extension and enlargement of the moral attitudes, usually expressed only in the more intimate relations. "If ye love them that love you, what reward have ye?" declared Jesus; and in the logic of those words the whole social genius of the Christian religion is revealed. The transcendent perspective of religion makes all men our brothers and nullifies the divisions, by which nature, climate, geography and the accidents of history divide the human family. By this insight many religiously inspired idealists have transcended national, racial, and class distinctions.

The great seers and saints of religion have always placed their hope for the redemption of society in the possibility of making the love-universalism, implicit in religious morality, effective in the whole human society. When Celsus accused the early Christians of destroying the integrity of the empire by their moral absolutism, Origen answered: "There is no one who fights better for the king than we. It is true that we do not go with him to battle, but we fight for him by forming an army of our own, an army of piety, through our prayers to the Godhead. Once all men have become Christians then even the barbarians will be inclined to peace."

NOTE

1. Quoted by W. E. Hocking, *The Meaning of God in Human Experience* (New Haven, Conn.: Yale University Press, 1924), 235.

from "Jesus of Nazareth/Christ of Faith: Foundations of a Reactive Christology"

༄

Carter Heyward

Carter Heyward, passionate lesbian Episcopal priest, was among the first women ordained in that tradition. She is professor at the Episcopal Divinity School in Cambridge, Massachusetts, and author of widely read books on religion, politics, sexuality, and resistance to patriarchy.

༄

WRONG RELATION IN CHRISTOLOGICAL EPISTEMOLOGY: FALSE KNOWING

Let me examine briefly the connection between dualism and nonrelationality in Christological epistemology. Dualism is steeped in an assumption of opposition: whether in relation to the knowledge of God or Christ, of ourselves or the world, we can know something only insofar as we are unlike it. Man is unlike woman. Spirit is unlike flesh. Light is unlike darkness. Heaven is unlike earth. God is unlike humanity. In a dualistic praxis, "the other" is always better or worse, more or less, than oneself or one's people. Identity is forged and known by contrast and competition, not by cooperative relation. Dualism is cultivated in a praxis of alienation between men and women, rich and poor, light and dark, and, in the image of such oppositions, divinity and humanity.[1]

The prevailing shape of Christian anthropology is linked causally and effectively to this problem: in our fallen (sinful) condition, human being is less, and worse, than divine being. In fact, in relation to divinity, we human beings are *bad*. The Christological solution to this problem has been historically to assume that in the person of Jesus, divine and human being overcame the dualism generated by the fall. The split was healed, the brokenness made whole, and now, in the spirit of Jesus, which is Christ, all human beings are called to participate in this continuing redemptive process.

The problem with this scenario is a double one: in worshipping Jesus as *the* Christ, *the* Son, *the* Savior, we close our eyes to the possibility of actually seeing that the sacred liberating Spirit is *as* incarnate here and now among us as She was in Jesus of Nazareth. We cannot recognize that redemption is an ongoing process which was neither begun nor completed, historically, in the life, death, and resurrection of Jesus. Reflecting this same tendency is the similarly exclusivistic assumption that Christians are *the* people with *the* way, *the* truth, and *the* life. Thus, as Christians, we learn to recognize ourselves primarily as unlike "the world," "pagans," "heretics," Jews. . . .

Dualism is wrong relation. A dualistic epistemology is steeped in a wrong way of knowing and thus generates false knowledge and lies, about ourselves, others, that which we believe to be divine, and the significance of the Jesus story. To do Christology, as most men have done it, on the basis of wrong relation, is to begin on the assumption that Christians alone are in right relation to God and, as such, have a monopoly on the knowledge and love of God. Another assumption is that it is more important, morally, spiritually, and liturgically, for Christians to preserve a right relation with our own religious heritage than with sisters and brothers who currently inhabit the earth with us. A wrong relational epistemology, rooted in dualism, causes us to imagine that some of us or our people (in whose interests we work) know it all—about Jesus Christ, redemption, God, or ourselves.

Theological narcissism, the preoccupation with oneself and one's god in one's image—or in the image of one's racial, gender, cultural, or religious roots—is a foundational component of the theological structure of ruling class (read white affluent Christian male) privilege. This privileged narcissism has been basic to the development of dominant Christological models in Europe and the United States, in which God comes out looking like Charlton Heston and Jesus like Jeffrey Hunter.

We should recognize that this tendency to create divinity in our own image is, to some degree, universal. It is not wrong to create theological and Christological images of ourselves. In fact, it is vital to our well-being and to our taking responsibility for what we are doing in the name(s) of God. But more than abstractly wrong, it is destructive of the created/creative world we share to leave the matter there—stuck on one's own "Jesus" or "Christ" image. It is wrong to close the canons at the end of one's own story or that of one's people. This is the epistemological fallacy that has given us the dominant Christological image of the blue-eyed, fair-haired Jesus as Lord of all. It is also the twist that provokes Christian objections to the Christa, the sculpted image of a full-bodied, nude female Christ on a cross.[2] The reification of one's own experience has, as its cause, a wrong relational, dualistic epistemology and as its consequence a Christology in which the Christian Redeemer with the most salvific power in any situation is the one who comes wrapped in the neatest conceptual package. This Christology best serves those who are holding the social, political, and ecclesial power in place.

Both the Jesus-of-history and the Christ-of-faith models of redemption have been constructed historically to combat such narcissism—to challenge, for example, the arrogance of ecclesiastical authorities or the obsessive preoccupation of many Christians with their own interior lives as the beginning and end of spirituality. But in attempting to correct such mistakes, both Christ-of-faith and historical Jesus images have served primarily to move the debate in a circle, back again into a self-defensive posturing which signals the drawing of Christological wagons around our own sacred icons—be they privatized spirituality or the readily misleading notion that where the bishop is, there is the church.[3]

What has been missing in the dominant structures of Christian faith and discourse has been *a praxis of relational particularity and cooperation*. In this praxis theological knowing might cease to be a matter of discovering *the* Christ and would become instead a matter of generating together images of what is redemptive or liberating in particular situations. In a praxis of relational particularity, we might discover that what is *not* Christic—frequently is that which the Christian churches have associated most closely with Jesus/Christ. What is not liberating is any relationship or system which is closed to discovery, new truths, and self-criticism; unwelcoming of new or different people, ideas, and possibilities. Creative, liberating interpretations of the Jesus story cannot take root in wrong relation. Such distorted power claims prevent Christians from finding creative and liberating Christic meanings in either the Jesus story or their own.

NOTES

1. *Alienation* is a term in Marxist theory which denotes "negation of productivity." Erich Fromm writes,

Alienation (or "estrangement") means, for Marx, that man does not experience himself as the acting agent in his grasp of the world, but that the world (nature, others, and he himself) remain alien to him. They stand above and against him as objects, even though they may be objects of his own creation. Alienation is essentially experiencing the world and oneself passively, receptively, as the subject separated from the object (Erich Fromm, *Marx's Concept of Man* [New York: Ungar, 1961], 44).

2. Reference is specifically to the bronze sculpture "Christa" by English artist Edwina Sandys.

3. The development of this idea was initiated in the third century by Cyprian, bishop of Carthage, a student of Tertullian. Trying to secure the *unity* of the church in an era of its persecution by the Roman state, Cyprian identified the presence of the church with the person of the bishop. *Letters*, 66.8, in *The Fathers of the Church (A New Translation)*, vol. 51 (Washington, D.C.: Catholic University of America, 1964), 228–29.

"How Christians Become Socialists"

❧

Philip Berryman

Writer and translator Philip Berryman has written on liberation theology, particularly in Central America. He served as a priest in Guatemala (1965–1973) and as American Friends Service Committee Central America representative (1976–1980).

❧

The "how" is meant in two senses: the process by which Christians come to see themselves as socialists, and what sort of socialists they tend to become. They are socialists not in the sense of having a blueprint for society—especially that of the United States—but in having a profound sense that our ills are systemic and that the system is called capitalism. (That does not mean, however, that capitalism necessarily subsumes patriarchy or racism.)

Of course there were Christian socialists around the turn of the century, and Karl Barth, Paul Tillich, and Reinhold Niebuhr all regarded themselves as socialists, at least during significant periods in their lives. Here, however, I want to focus on a growing sympathy with socialism among significant groups of Christians since the 1960s, outlining first the process that leads in that direction and then the reinterpretation of Christianity it involves. An underlying question here is whether there is an underlying affinity between Christianity and socialism.[1]

RADICALIZATION

To come to a profound critique of capitalism while living in the midst of capitalist society one somehow needs to step out of it, to have some experience of being alienated and estranged from it. For some Christians, living in other countries has provided such an experience. I have in mind particularly church people who have gone to Latin America since the 1960s.

Some went to do pastoral or missionary work, while others went to aid in development projects (seen as an expression of the church's mission). Many sought to come closer to the poor by moving away from the traditional parish house, convent, or mission compound and into modest homes or even shacks in villages or barrios. Although they could not share the ultimate insecurity of poverty, they could share some of its conditions.

This sharing the condition of the poor was itself aimed at entering into real dialogue with them. The starting point was often a Bible discussion or a concrete problem in the village or barrio, or simply an effort to bring people together to consider their situation. Two things could

156

happen: people could develop a greater critical awareness of their situation and the reasons for their problems, and they could develop ties among themselves and so become something of a community. If their motive for meeting was explicitly religious, they could become a *communidad eclesial de base,* or "Christian base community," with their own lay leadership. At the local level they could start a cooperative, or lobby the government to build a school, set up a health post, or get them drinking water.

Yet such activity soon ran up against limits. People began to see that the real problems were not due to their own "backwardness," but to inequality in wealth and power, especially as manifested in land tenure systems. They often became more militant. Before too long they ran up against the power structure, whether in the form of the local landholding class or the army and police, which threatened them or actually used violence against them.

In this process, church workers themselves experienced first-hand the anguish of the poor. For example, a priest might be called on to baptize infants who were dying, either because of a lack of elementary health services or of illnesses caused by undernourishment. Those church workers got a widening sense of the problem and saw, for example, that local landholders, the army, and the police were simply part of a larger class structure—and that the nation's whole agroexport system was itself part of a world economic system.

In the late 1960s and early 1970s such church personnel might have been "slow learners." The process sketched out often took years and considerable experience. In other words, people were radicalized by living with poor people and seeing what happened when those people tried to organize and pressure for change; they were not radicalized by reading Marx or Marxists. If they did any such reading, however, it tended to reinforce what they had experienced and intuited, and bring it into sharper focus.

Overseas experience led many people to question their previous assumption that the United States was the world's benefactor. They became aware of U.S. intervention, whether subtle or overt, to maintain its hegemony, and of the U.S. role in maintaining the world capitalist system. Such an experience led to a feeling of estrangement vis-à-vis the United States and to conflict. I recall how, during a visit home in California in 1969, I was invited to address some "mission circles" in an Orange County parish. After I showed some slides and gave a talk, someone began the question period by asking, "What can we do for those people down there—perhaps send clothes?" I tried to explain the Latin American perspective on "underdevelopment," and suggested that rather than sending clothing they might examine U.S. foreign policy. As the evening wore on, I encountered an increasing hostility breaking through the surface cordiality. Obviously I had touched on something very deep—their own identity as Americans. It struck me that these people were much more offended by my criticism of the United States than they would have been if I had suggested that the doctrine of the Trinity be revised to include a Fourth Person. In other words, there was something "religious," something of ultimate value, in their attachment to their country. By the same token, the experience brought home to me how estranged I was becoming from mainstream America.

Some church personnel have been close to highly politicized and conflictive events, such as Chile during the Unidad Popular years, or under repressive military governments, or in the struggles of Central America. Under such conditions the radicalization process can be much quicker.

In the United States, many church people undergo a comparable, though perhaps less dramatic, experience without going overseas. Entry points have included direct grassroots contact with the poor, involvement in the civil rights, feminist, anti–Vietnam War, and antinuke struggles. The crucial step is recognition of the systemic nature of these things. (Again, I am leaving open the question of how patriarchy, racism, and capitalism intersect.) The process also involves the recognition of the contradictions within the churches themselves and how they function to provide religious legitimation to existing society.

The political practice inherent in this radicalization process can vary enormously. Church workers in Latin America have generally not become directly involved in leftist politics, but they have defended people's right to organize and supported them when they did so. In some cases they have come into direct contact with revolutionary organizations, sometimes collaborating with those organizations, occasionally even becoming militant members.

An option for socialism often makes sense for people who have been exposed to Latin America, who have seen genuinely revolutionary organizations and have a rough idea of what a socialist revolution could look like. In the United States, on the other hand, things are much less clear. No society in the world offers anything like a model for a transition to socialism—not even of what to avoid; nor is there much sense of what kind of process could lead the United States beyond capitalism.

Christians in the United States may sense that profound changes are needed and may have an intuition that what is required is a new kind of order, which may be called "socialism." But since socialism is far from the agenda of mainstream politics, their everyday political practice will continue to be working on a set of issues and struggles. Here they will find themselves side by side with those whose route into those struggles was not religious. In other words, in their political practice, the criteria they use, the organizations they join, and the struggles they engage in, they will be "secular."

A NEW UNDERSTANDING OF CHRISTIANITY

Those whose radicalization process has been nonreligious can nevertheless find familiar land-marks in what I have just described: experience with the poor, the violence used by power structures, the growing awareness of systemic connections. Those Christians I have in mind, however, also see this process as a "conversion." The word may conjure up a dramatic emotional event—St. Paul struck on the way to Damascus, or revival participants "repenting and declaring for Jesus"—but the biblical word refers to a basic shift in mind-set, attitude, and life-orientation. That is what the experience I have been outlining is all about. As such it calls for a new and deeper understanding of Christianity.

The claim of Christianity is that God has acted in human life in the whole series of events contained in the scriptures, and particularly in Jesus Christ. As embodied in the churches, that conviction has taken cultural forms throughout history and has gone through periods of reformation or renewal. Every such reform movement has been in some sense a retrieval of something in the scriptures, e.g., Francis of Assisi seeking to return to the poverty of Jesus and his first followers.

A key biblical symbol being retrieved today is the Exodus. Whatever the original event was—apparently the escape of a group of slaves from Egypt under circumstances that would, at least later, be recalled as miraculous (plagues, passage through the Red Sea)—the Exodus became a paradigm for faith, that the true God hears the cry of his oppressed people, sends them a liberator named Moses, and goes before them, leading them to freedom. All the events, their wandering in the desert, fidelity/infidelity/repentance, the covenant, etc., became paradigmatic for what Israel should be as a people.

In Latin America, at least, people can make a direct translation of the Exodus, seeing themselves under oppression—whether the Pharaoh has a name like Somoza or is an entire oppressive system—and they yearn for liberation. Similarly, the voice of the Hebrew prophets sounds very contemporary, even down to the denunciation of how the wealthy take land from the poor or cheat them with crooked scales.

At first glance the Christian scriptures (the New Testament) might seem less "political" than the Hebrew scriptures. It is true that Jesus did not advocate revolution (in the modern sense) against the Romans—it would be anachronistic to expect him to have done so. Yet the experience of repression today, especially in Latin America, has alerted people to the conflictive aspect of Jesus' life. From the very start, the gospels present Jesus as standing in conflict with the authorities. His message is one of hope for the poor and the outcast, and that message eventually brings his own death—by an execution in which both "church" and state have a hand. The Resurrection can then be seen as God's vindication of the truth of Jesus' life and message.

Inspired by their faith, many Latin American Christians have indeed given up their lives out of commitment to an ideal of a more just society, a commitment that frequently began with the kind of village-level pastoral work mentioned above. In the serious life-and-death context of Latin America today, many find a deep meaning in the Christian conviction of resurrection—that God is on the side of life and evil cannot ultimately stamp it out. Archbishop Oscar Romero of San Salvador said, "If I die, I will rise in the Salvadorean people." His belief was orthodox—that is, he regarded the resurrection as something real and not simply a metaphor for the memory of posterity—but he also linked his faith in resurrection to the people's struggle.

I could go on at some length giving examples of the kinds of reinterpretation of the scriptures arising out of experience today. However, rather than assembling further examples, it seems more important to point out what this new kind of interpretation means.

In the first place, it is a reading from the situation of the poor. In fact, it is often the poor themselves who are looking at the scripture and giving their own reading. Liberation Theology seeks to grasp the message of scripture from the side of the poor. Part of the conversion process of church pastoral workers is that they find themselves being "evangelized by the poor," that is, the poor teach them the meaning of the Christian gospel.

It is a reading that takes the material world and human society seriously. Until roughly a generation ago religion and religious symbols essentially affirmed the existing order, including the class system. Although many versions of Christianity continue to do that, this new reading subjects existing societal arrangements to a critique whose standard is how it affects the welfare of the poor. Not only does this reading not see the existing order as fixed by God, but it sees human beings as responsible for the earth, including the societal arrangements they live under.

In this sense we can speak of a "transformative" (in William Tabb's term) way of reading the scriptures, and indeed of understanding Christian faith. In Latin America one frequently hears the notion that human beings are called to be "subjects of their own destiny," "co-creators in history." Although such language may sound Promethean or naively overconfident in the United States, it expresses something central in the new religious vision developing in Latin America.

An option for socialism may make certain symbols or images in the scriptures take on new meaning. I am thinking particularly of all the scriptural images about unity. To begin with, the Bible itself has a very "corporate" understanding of humanity: it seems far more interested in the fate of the "people" (both Israel and the church) than the fulfillment of individuals in our modern Western sense. Various analogies are applied to the church: Paul speaks of the church and Christ being joined into one body, so that if one member suffers, all do. John has Jesus say, "I am the vine, you are the branches" in the same discourse in which he repeatedly urges his followers to love one another.

Throughout the history of Christianity these startlingly collective symbols of unity have either been ignored, or have been applied to the church as institution, or have been given a mystical interpretation, namely that we are united in Christ, despite our apparent differences. A "transformative" reading of the scripture holds not only that there is a mystical unity in Christ, but that we human beings must work to make it something real in human history.

The intuition, then, is that the ideals sketched in the New Testament, including the "primitive communism" described in the Acts of the Apostles (early Christian communities that held their possessions in common), not only express a mystical truth—that despite appearances we are one in Christ—but are an affirmation that human beings can live as sisters and brothers, and that Christians must work to make that possible.

This intuition was not the original understanding of the New Testament authors. They were thinking primarily of the Christian community, the church, although there are some hints of a wider—even cosmic—interpretation. However, their horizon was limited by their conviction that the Lord was due to return soon. They could not have envisioned the transformation of society as a task flowing from the gospel.

Thus a radical or socialist reading of the Bible no doubt goes further than what the original authors consciously intended. Yet it need not be regarded as simply a product of fancy or imagination. The New Testament sees the Spirit as present in the church, providing the basis for new interpretations for new situations.

It is clear that such a reading was impossible at the time of the New Testament, as well as during most of the history of Christianity. It became possible only when material conditions began to make it conceivable. To a great extent it was Marx who signaled a shift in human consciousness. In that sense, what we are talking about amounts to a theological paraphrase of Marx's Eleventh Thesis on Feuerbach: "The theologians have only interpreted the world in various ways; the point is to change it."

ANARCHISM OR SOCIALISM?

Perhaps we can see that there is some affinity between some strands in Christianity and socialism. Not all radicalized Christians become socialists, however. Some believe that what the gospel demands is radical witness to the Kingdom now, with no direct concern for societal transformation. Moreover, they may believe that it is normal for Christians to be in tension with all forms of power—perhaps interpreting this in terms of what the epistle to the Ephesians calls "principalities and powers." Being a Christian then becomes a matter of standing in a small community of faithful witnesses against the world.

In political terms, such an option can be called anarchism. People who make such an option emphasize the purity of witness and not political effectiveness as such. They would regard an option for socialism as an illusion. For them political power and how it is exercised is the problem, not the solution. They may believe that the example of "really existing socialism." bears out their position.

CHURCH INSTITUTIONS

So far we have been describing a radicalization that has affected a small but significant minority in the churches. These are lay people, priests, sisters, and pastors, whose experience and reflection lead them to the conviction that today Christianity itself calls for structural change in society. At one point, in the immediate aftermath of Vatican II, people who were thus radicalized tended to transfer that radicalism to the institutional church itself, and to assume that their option inevitably meant a head-on confrontation with church authorities. And indeed, many actions within the church institution, such as the Vatican's assault on Liberation Theology, seem to bear that out.

Nevertheless, things are not quite so simple. Many of the church people who have been radicalized themselves occupy positions in the church structures. For example, those who deal with missions or with issues of international justice have had frequent occasion to meet with people from the third world or representatives from sister churches, and have been able to get something of a third world–view of issues. Consequently, ordinary churchgoers in the pews are often more conservative than church bureaucrats. That is not because those officials take on an a priori Left mentality, but because they have had to confront the issues directly and repeatedly.

In Latin America and elsewhere, at the institutional level, churches have often taken positions against the worst abuses, especially against governments that violate human rights (e.g., in Brazil, Pinochet's Chile, Central America, South Africa, the Philippines, South Korea). This has not always been the case—the Argentine Catholic hierarchy preferred to ignore the "dirty war" of the later 1970s and is now largely discredited. In some instances Catholic hierarchies have not simply condemned abuses, such as murder, abduction, and torture, but have gone on to point out the structural cause of violence in the unjust distribution of wealth and power.

The stumbling block seems to come over the question of formulating alternatives, that is, the possibility of other economic and political systems, as well as political struggle involved in bringing about change. A most eloquent example was furnished by Pope John Paul II in 1983: in Haiti, where there were no prospects for change on the horizon, he said boldly, "This has to change!" while in Nicaragua he could not accept change when it was staring him in the face. Fear of Marxism (due partly to the experience of the church under Marxist regimes) impels church hierarchies into advocating some sort of vague hypothetical model for society that will avoid the negative features of both capitalism and communism. Hence the great attraction of Christian Democracy, which seems to promise the best of all worlds but which in practice is simply capitalism paved with good intentions.

The pastoral letter of the U.S. Catholic bishops on nuclear weapons (1983) and the final draft of the letter on the economy (forthcoming) are another illustration. The peace pastoral expressed clear opposition to Reagan administration policies and devoted considerable attention to pacifism as a legitimate option for Christians. Nevertheless, its general policy framework remained well within establishment liberal parameters. Similarly, the letter on the economy, which some thought might raise fundamental questions about the capitalist system, again remains liberal, although somewhat to the left of the Democratic Party mainstream. What is most intriguing about its first draft is the insistence that the criterion for judging an economic system should be its impact on the poor.

Radicalized Christians are aware of the many ways the churches are a part of the existing order—from investment portfolios, to the partriarchy and racism in their own practice, to the legitimating power of Christian symbols. Yet they believe that the churches offer important political space, as well as symbols that form the basis for a critique of that order. Most important—from the viewpoint of faith—they believe the church itself can, and must, be converted if it is to be faithful to its own message.

FAITH AND POLITICAL COMMITMENT

During the 1960s there were a number of Christian-Marxist dialogues, often between well-known theologians and prominent Marxist thinkers. The aim was to find points of convergence and outline areas of difference. Such a type of dialogue seemed to imply that persons holding two more or less integral world views were meeting across the table.

What has happened recently in Latin America and elsewhere is rather different. As a result of the process sketched above, Christians have moved toward a systemic understanding of injustice and also a kind of political practice that fits their new understanding. In Latin America, at least, that practice is Marxist to some degree. However, Marxism is viewed not as a world view but as an "instrument of analysis," a kind of engaged social science, and as a method for political struggle.

Consequently, faith and politics operate at different levels. Politics, even when it is about a dreamed-of future society that is in no way on the horizon, is somehow concerned with means, while faith deals with the ultimate grounding and final end. If this is true, there should be no real basic conflict between Christianity and politics—even Marxist politics. Political strategies and tactics should be judged primarily on the basis of whether they offer the means whereby people can achieve justice and peace and expand freedom.

Faith has little to say directly about criteria for political struggle, e.g., about whether it makes sense to work toward socialism within the Democratic Party. Any criterion is primarily secular. In that respect, radicalized Christians are as secular in their political options as their nonreligious colleagues. Like those colleagues, they may be perplexed about how a genuine broad mass movement for change can be built, and despite their own intuitional sense that systemic change is needed, they put their energies into those particular issues they feel called to work on: against intervention in Central America, for a nuclear freeze, against apartheid, etc.

What their religious conviction supplies is a sense of ultimacy, something that goes deeper than any particular issue, and indeed than political struggle as a whole. As an ultimate frame of reference, it can provide a basis for a critical attitude toward Marxism—which is not regarded as an ultimate frame of reference but rather as a heuristic framework, a method that is fruitful but always open to testing and revision. Some Christians may make options that do not seem to make sense in terms of sheer political calculus but do make sense in terms of faith, e.g., opting to work with people simply because they are poor, even disregarding to what extent they may or may not be a "proletariat" and therefore potential agents for change.

Hence a final question: If Christians who become radicalized are essentially "secular" in their political positions and options, is it possible that those who see themselves as nonreligious, or secular, nevertheless have as their ultimate grounding not simply a world view or a method for critique and political action, such as Marxism, but something akin to a faith? I will not presume to put a name on it, but I would like to know whether they would.

NOTE

1. I have preferred to remain within my own Christian, and specifically Roman Catholic, tradition. The question of whether there is an underlying affinity between socialism and other religions, especially Judaism, is obviously of great interest but will not be addressed here.

"Beyond the Enlightenment Mentality"

⚘

Tu Weiming

Tu Weiming, professor of Chinese history and philosophy at Harvard University, is the author of *NeoConfucian Thought in Action,* and *Way, Learning and Action.* He is a fellow of the American Academy of Arts and Sciences and president of *Contemporary,* an intellectual journal published in Taiwan. This essay brings Confucian values to bear on the problems of contemporary world civilizations.

⚘

The Enlightenment mentality underlies the rise of the modern West as the most dynamic and transformative ideology in human history.[1] Virtually all major spheres of interest characteristic of the modern age are indebted to or intertwined with this mentality: science and technology, industrial capitalism, market economy, democratic polity, mass communication, research universities, civil and military bureaucracies, and professional organizations. Furthermore, the values we cherish as definitions of modern consciousness—including liberty, equality, human rights, the dignity of the individual, respect for privacy, government for, by, and of the people, and due process of law—are genetically, if not structurally, inseparable from the Enlightenment mentality. We have flourished in the spheres of interest and their attendant values occasioned by the advent of the modern West since the eighteenth century. They have made our life-world operative and meaningful. We take for granted that, through instrumental rationality, we can solve the world's major problems and that progress, primarily in economic terms, is desirable and necessary for the human community as a whole.

We are so seasoned in the Enlightenment mentality that we assume the reasonableness of its general ideological thrust. It seems self-evident that both capitalism and socialism subscribe to the aggressive anthropocentrism underlying the modern mind-set: man is not only the measure of all things but also the only source of power for economic well-being, political stability, and social development. The Enlightenment faith in progress, reason, and individualism may have been challenged by some of the most brilliant minds in the modern Western academy, but it remains a standard of inspiration for intellectual and spiritual leaders throughout the world. It is inconceivable that any international project, including those in ecological sciences, not subscribe to the theses that the human condition is improvable, that it is desirable to find rational means to solve the world's problems, and that the dignity of the person as an individual ought to be respected. Enlightenment as human awakening, as the discovery of the human potential for global transformation, and as the realization of the human desire to become the measure and master of all things is still the most influential moral discourse in the political culture of the

163

modern age; for decades it has been the unquestioned assumption of the ruling minorities and cultural elites of developing countries, as well as highly industrialized nations.

A fair understanding of the Enlightenment mentality requires a frank discussion of the dark side of the modern West as well. The "unbound Prometheus," symbolizing the runaway technology of development, may have been a spectacular achievement of human ingenuity in the early phases of the industrial revolution. Despite impassioned reactions from the romantic movement and insightful criticisms of the forebears of the "human sciences," the Enlightenment mentality, fueled by the Faustian drive to explore, to know, to conquer, and to subdue, persisted as the reigning ideology of the modern West. It is now fully embraced as the unquestioned rationale for development in East Asia.

However, a realistic appraisal of the Enlightenment mentality reveals many faces of the modern West incongruous with the image of "the Age of Reason." In the context of modern Western hegemonic discourse, progress may entail inequality, reason, self-interest, and individual greed. The American dream of owning a car and a house, earning a fair wage, and enjoying freedom of privacy, expression, religion, and travel, while reasonable to our (American) sense of what ordinary life demands, is lamentably unexportable as a modern necessity from a global perspective. Indeed, it has now been widely acknowledged as no more than a dream for a significant segment of the American population as well.

An urgent task for the community of like-minded persons deeply concerned about ecological issues and the disintegration of communities at all levels is to insure that both the ruling minorities and cultural elites in the modern West actively participate in a spiritual joint venture to rethink the Enlightenment heritage. The paradox is that we cannot afford to accept uncritically its inner logic in light of the unintended negative consequences it has engendered on the life-support systems; nor can we reject its relevance, with all of the fruitful ambiguities this entails, to our intellectual self-definition, present and future. There is no easy way out. We do not have an "either-or" choice. The possibility of a radically different ethic or a new value system separate from and independent of the Enlightenment mentality is neither realistic nor authentic. It may even appear to be either cynical or hypercritical. We need to explore the spiritual resources that may help us to broaden the scope of the Enlightenment project, deepen its moral sensitivity, and, if necessary, transform creatively its genetic constraints in order to realize fully its potential as a worldview for the human condition as a whole.

A key to the success of this spiritual joint venture is to recognize the conspicuous absence of the idea of community, let alone the global community, in the Enlightenment project. Fraternity, a functional equivalent of community in the three cardinal virtues of the French Revolution, has received scant attention in modern Western economic, political, and social thought. The willingness to tolerate inequality, the faith in the salvific power of self-interest, and the unbridled affirmation of aggressive egoism have greatly poisoned the good well of progress, reason, and individualism. The need to express a universal intent for the formation of a "global village" and to articulate a possible link between the fragmented world we experience in our ordinary daily existence and the imagined community for the human species as a whole is deeply felt by an increasing number of concerned intellectuals. This requires, at a minimum, the replacement of the principle of self-interest, no matter how broadly defined, with a new Golden Rule: "Do not do unto others what you would not want others to do unto you."[2] Since the new Golden Rule is stated in the negative, it will have to be augmented by a positive principle: "in order to establish myself, I have to help others to enlarge themselves."[3] An inclusive sense of community, based on the communal critical self-consciousness of reflective minds, is an ethico-religious goal as well as a philosophical ideal.

The mobilization of at least three kinds of spiritual resources is necessary to ensure that this simple vision is grounded in the historicity of the cultural complexes informing our ways of life today. The first kind involves the ethico-religious traditions of the modern West, notably Greek philosophy, Judaism, and Christianity. The very fact that they have been instrumental in giving birth to the Enlightenment mentality makes a compelling case for them to reexamine their relationships to the rise of the modern West in order to create a new public sphere for the transvaluation of typical Western values. The exclusive dichotomy of matter/spirit, body/mind, sacred/profane, human/nature, or creator/creature must be transcended to allow supreme values, such as the sanctity of the earth, the continuity of being, the beneficiary interaction between the human community and nature, and the mutuality between humankind and Heaven, to receive the saliency they deserve in philosophy, religion, and theology.

The Greek philosophical emphasis on rationality, the biblical image of man having "dominion" over the earth, and the Protestant work ethic provided necessary, if not sufficient, sources for the Enlightenment mentality. However, the unintended negative consequences of the rise of the modern West have so undermined the sense of community implicit in the Hellenistic idea of the citizen, the Judaic idea of the covenant, and the Christian idea of fellowship that it is morally imperative for these great traditions, which have maintained highly complex and tension-ridden relationships with the Enlightenment mentality, to formulate their critique of the blatant anthropocentrism inherent in the Enlightenment project. The emergence of a communitarian ethic as a critique of the idea of the person as a rights-bearing, interest-motivated, rational economic animal clearly indicates the relevance of an Aristotelian, Pauline, Abrahamic, or Republican ethic to current moral self-reflexivity in North America. Jürgen Habermas's attempt to broaden the scope of rational discourse by emphasizing the importance of "communicative rationality" in social intercourse represents a major intellectual effort to develop new conceptual apparatuses to enrich the Enlightenment tradition.[4]

The second kind of spiritual resource is derived from non-Western, axial-age civilizations, which include Hinduism, Jainism, and Buddhism in South and Southeast Asia, Confucianism and Taoism in East Asia, and Islam. Historically, Islam should be considered an essential intellectual heritage of the modern West because of its contribution to the Renaissance. The current practice, especially by the mass media of North America and Western Europe, of consigning Islam to radical otherness is historically unsound and culturally insensitive. It has, in fact, seriously undermined the modern West's own self-interest as well as its own self-understanding. Islam and these non-Western ethico-religious traditions provide sophisticated and practicable resources in worldviews, rituals, institutions, styles of education, and patterns of human-relatedness. They can help to develop ways of life, both as continuation of and alternative to the Western European and North American exemplification of the Enlightenment mentality. Industrial East Asia, under the influence of Confucian culture, has already developed a less adversarial, less individualistic, and less self-interested modern civilization. The coexistence of market economy with government leadership, democratic polity with meritocracy, and individual initiatives with group orientation has, since the Second World War, made this region economically and politically the most dynamic area of the world. The significance of the contribution of Confucian ethics to the rise of industrial East Asia offers profound possibilities for the possible emergence of Hindu, Jain, Buddhist, and Islamic forms of modernity.

The Westernization of Confucian Asia (including Japan, the two Koreas, mainland China, Hong Kong, Taiwan, Singapore, and Vietnam) may have forever altered its spiritual landscape, but its indigenous resources (including Mahāyāna Buddhism, Taoism, Shintoism, shamanism, and other folk religions) have the resiliency to resurface and make their presence known in a new synthesis. The caveat, of course, is that, having been humiliated and frustrated by the imperialist and colonial domination of the modern West for more than a century, the rise of industrial East Asia symbolizes the instrumental rationality of the Enlightenment heritage with a vengeance. Indeed, the mentality of Japan and the Four Mini-Dragons (South Korea, Taiwan, Hong Kong, Singapore) is characterized by mercantilism, commercialism, and international competitiveness. The People's Republic of China (the motherland of the Sinic world) has blatantly opted for the same strategy of development and has thus exhibited the same mentality since the reform was set in motion in 1979. Surely the possibility for these nations to develop more humane and sustainable communities should not be exaggerated; nor should it be undermined.

The third kind of spiritual resource involves the primal traditions: Native American, Hawaiian, Maori, and numerous tribal indigenous religious traditions. They have demonstrated, with physical strength and aesthetic elegance, that human life has been sustainable since Neolithic times. The implications for practical living are far-reaching. Their style of human flourishing is not a figment of the mind but an experienced reality in our modern age.

A distinctive feature of primal traditions is a deep experience of rootedness. Each indigenous religious tradition is embedded in a concrete place symbolizing a way of perceiving, a mode of thinking, a form of living, an attitude, and a worldview. Given the unintended disastrous consequences of the Enlightenment mentality, there are obvious lessons that the modern mind-set can learn from indigenous religious traditions. A natural outcome of indigenous peoples' embeddedness in concrete locality is their intimate and detailed knowledge of their environment; indeed, the demarcations between their human habitat and nature are muted. Implicit in this model of existence is the realization that mutuality and reciprocity between the anthropological world and the cosmos at large is both necessary and desirable. What we can learn from them, then, is a new way of perceiving, a new mode of thinking, a new form of living, a new attitude, and a new worldview. A critique of the Enlightenment mentality and its derivative modern mind-set from the perspective of indigenous peoples could be thought-provoking.

An equally significant aspect of indigenous lifeways is the ritual of bonding in ordinary daily human interaction. The density of kinship relations, the rich texture of interpersonal communication, the detailed and nuanced appreciation of the surrounding natural and cultural world, and the experienced connectedness with ancestors point to communities grounded in ethnicity, gender, language, land, and faith. The primordial ties are constitutive parts of their being and activity. In Huston Smith's characterization, what they exemplify is participation rather than control in motivation, empathic understanding rather than empiricist apprehension in epistemology, respect for the transcendent rather than domination over nature in worldview, and fulfillment rather than alienation in human experience. As we begin to question the soundness or even sanity of some of our most cherished ways of thinking—such as regarding knowledge as power rather than wisdom, asserting the desirability of material progress despite its corrosive influence on the soul, and justifying the anthropocentric manipulation of nature even at the cost of destroying the life-support system—indigenous perspectives emerge as a source of inspiration.

Of course, I am not proposing any romantic attachment to or nostalgic sentiments for "primal consciousness," and I am critically aware that claims of primordiality are often modernist cultural constructions dictated by the politics of recognition. Rather, I suggest that, as both beneficiaries and victims of the Enlightenment mentality, we show our fidelity to our common heritage by enriching it, transforming it, and restructuring it with all three kinds of spiritual resources still available to us for the sake of developing a truly ecumenical sense of global community. Indeed, of the three great Enlightenment values embodied in the French Revolution, fraternity seems to have attracted the least attention in the subsequent two centuries. The representation of the *Problematik* of community in recent years is symptomatic of the confluence of two apparently contradictory forces in the late twentieth century: the global village as both a virtual reality and an imagined community in our information age and the disintegration and restructuring of human togetherness at all levels, from family to nation.

It may not be immodest to say that we are beginning to develop a fourth kind of spiritual resource from the core of the Enlightenment project itself. Our disciplined reflection, a communal act rather than an isolated struggle, is a first step toward the "creative zone" envisioned by religious leaders and teachers of ethics. The feminist critique of tradition, the concern for the environment, and the persuasion of religious pluralism are obvious examples of this new corporate critical self-awareness. The need to go beyond the Enlightenment mentality, without either deconstructing or abandoning its commitment to rationality, liberty, equality, human rights, and distributive justice, requires a thorough reexamination of modernity as a signifier and modernization as a process.

Underlying this reexamination is the intriguing issue of traditions in modernity. The dichotomous thinking of tradition and modernity as two incompatible forms of life will have to be replaced by a much more nuanced investigation of the continuous interaction between modernity as the perceived outcome of "rationalization" defined in Weberian terms and traditions as "habits of the heart" (to borrow an expression from Alexis de Tocqueville), enduring modes of thinking, or salient features of cultural self-understanding. The traditions in modernity are not merely historical sedimentation passively deposited in modern consciousness. Nor are they, in functional terms, simply inhibiting factors to be undermined by the unilinear trajectory of development. On the contrary, they are both constraining and enabling forces capable of shaping the particular contour of modernity in any given society. It is, therefore, conceptually naïve and methodologically fallacious to relegate traditions to the residual category in our discussion of the modernizing process. Indeed, an investigation of traditions in modernity is essential for our appreciation of modernization as a highly differentiated cultural phenomena rather than as a homogeneous integral process of Westernization.

Talcott Parsons may have been right in assuming that market economy, democratic polity, and individualism are three inseparable dimensions of modernity.[5] The post–Cold War era seems to have inaugurated a new world order in which marketization, democratization, and individualism are salient features of a new global village. The collapse of socialism gives the impression that market rather than planned economy, democratic rather than authoritarian polity, and individualist rather than collectivist style of life symbolize the wave of the future. Whether or not we believe in the "end of history," a stage of human development in which only advanced capitalism—characterized by multinational corporations, information superhighways, technology-driven sciences, mass communication, and conspicuous consumption—dominates, we must be critically aware of the globalizing forces which, through a variety of networks, literally transform the earth into a wired discourse community. As a result, distance, no matter how great, does not at all inhibit electronic communication and, ironically, territorial proximity does not necessarily guarantee actual contact. We can be frequent conversation partners with associates thousands of miles apart, yet we are often strangers to our neighbors, colleagues, and relatives.

The advent of the global village as virtual reality rather than authentic home is by no means congenial to human flourishing. Contrary to the classical Confucian ideal of the "great harmony" (*ta-t'ung*), what the global village exhibits is sharp difference, severe differentiation, drastic demarcation, thunderous dissonance, and outright discrimination. The world, compressed into an interconnected ecological, financial, commercial, trading, and electronic system, has never been so divided in wealth, influence, and power. The advent of the imagined, and even anticipated, global village is far from a cause for celebration.

Never in world history has the contrast between the rich and the poor, the dominant and the marginalized, the articulate and the silenced, the included and the excluded, the informed and the uninformed, and the connected and the isolated been so markedly drawn. The rich, dominant, articulate, included, informed, and connected beneficiaries of the system form numerous transnational networks making distance and, indeed, ethnic boundary, cultural diversity, religious exclusivism, or national sovereignty inconsequential in their march toward domination. On the other hand, residents of the same neighborhood may have radically different access to information, ideas, tangible resources (such as money), and immaterial goods (such as prestige). People of the same electoral district may subscribe to sharply conflicting political ideologies, social mores, and worldviews. They may also experience basic categories of human existence (such as time and space) in incommensurable ways. The severity of the contrast between the haves and the have-nots at all levels of the human experience—individual, family, society, and nation—can easily be demonstrated by hard empirical data. The sense of relative deprivation is greatly intensified by the glorification of conspicuous consumption by the mass media. Even in the most economically advanced nations, notably North America, the Scandinavian countries and other nations of Western Europe, and Japan and the Mini-Dragons, the pervasive mood is one of discontent, anxiety, and frustration.

If we focus our attention exclusively on the powerful megatrends that have exerted shaping influences on the global community since the end of the Second World War—science, technology, communication, trade, finance, entertainment, travel, tourism, migration, and disease—we may easily be misled into believing that the world has changed so much that the human condition is being structured by newly emerging global forces without any reference to our inherited historical and cultural praxis. One of the most significant fin-de-siècle reflections of the twentieth century is the acknowledgment that globalization does not mean homogenization and that modernization intensifies as well as lessens economic, political, social, cultural, and religious conflict in both inter- and intranational contexts. The emergence of primordial ties (ethnicity, language, gender, land, class, and faith) as powerful forces in constructing internally defensive cultural identities and externally aggressive religious exclusivities compels practical-minded global thinkers to develop new conceptual resources to understand the spirit of our time. The common practice of internationalists, including some of the most sophisticated analyzers of the world scene, of condemning the enduring strength of primordial ties as a parochial reaction to the inevitable process of globalization is simple-minded and ill-advised. What we witness in Bosnia, Africa, Sri Lanka, and India is not simply "fragmentization" as opposed to global integration. Since we are acutely aware of the explosive potential of ethnicity in the United States, language in Canada, and religious fundamentalism in all three major monotheistic religions, we must learn to appreciate that the quest for roots is a worldwide phenomenon.

Nowadays we are confronted with two conflicting and even contradictory forces in the global community: internationalization (globalization) and localization (communization). The United Nations, which came into being because of the spirit of internationalization, must now deal with issues of rootedness (all those specified above as primordial ties). While globalization in science, technology, mass communication, trade, tourism, finance, migration, and disease is progressing at an unprecedented rate and to an unprecedented degree, the pervasiveness and depth of communal (or tribal) feelings, both hidden and aroused, cannot be easily transformed by the Enlightenment values of instrumental rationality, individual liberty, calculated self-interest, material progress, and rights consciousness. The resiliency and explosive power of human-relatedness can be better appreciated by an ethic mindful of the need for reasonableness in any form of negotiation, distributive justice, sympathy, civility, duty-consciousness, dignity of person, sense of intrinsic worth, and self-cultivation.

In the Confucian perspective, human beings are not merely rational beings, political animals, tool-users, or language-manipulators. Confucians seem to have deliberately rejected simplistic reductionist models. They define human beings in terms of five integrated visions:

1. Human beings are sentient beings, capable of internal resonance not only between and among themselves but also with other animals, plants, trees, mountains, and rivers, indeed nature as a whole.
2. Human beings are social beings. As isolated individuals, human beings are weak by comparison with other members of the animal kingdom, but if they are organized to form a society, they have inner strength not only for survival but also for flourishing. Human-relatedness as exemplified in a variety of networks of interaction is necessary for human survival and human flourishing. Our sociality defines who we are.
3. Human beings are political beings in the sense that human-relatedness is, by biological nature and social necessity, differentiated in terms of hierarchy, status, and authority. While Confucians insist upon the fluidity of these artificially constructed boundaries, they recognize the significance of "difference" in an "organic" as opposed to "mechanic" solidarity—thus the centrality of the principle of fairness and the primacy of the practice of distributive justice in a humane society.
4. Human beings are also historical beings sharing collective memories, cultural memories, cultural traditions, ritual praxis, and "habits of the heart."
5. Human beings are metaphysical beings with the highest aspirations not simply defined in terms of anthropocentric ideas but characterized by the ultimate concern to be constantly inspired by and continuously responsive to the Mandate of Heaven.

The Confucian way is a way of learning, learning to be human. Learning to be human in the Confucian spirit is to engage oneself in a ceaseless, unending process of creative self-transformation, both as a communal act and as a dialogical response to Heaven. This involves four inseparable dimensions—self, community, nature, and the transcendent. The purpose of learning is always understood as being for the sake of the self, but the self is never an isolated individual (an island); rather, it is a center of relationships (a flowing stream). The self as a center of relationships is a dynamic open system rather than a closed static structure. Therefore, mutuality between self and community, harmony between human species and nature, and continuous communication with Heaven are defining characteristics and supreme values in the human project.[6]

Since Confucians take the concrete living human being here and now as their point of departure in the development of their philosophical anthropology, they recognize the embeddedness and rootedness of the human condition. Therefore, the profound significance of what we call primordial ties—ethnicity, gender, language, land, class, and basic spiritual orientation—which are intrinsic in the Confucian project, is a celebration of cultural diversity (this is not to be confused with any form of pernicious relativism). Often, Confucians understand their own path as learning of the body and mind (*shen-hsin-chih-hsüeh*) or learning of nature and destiny (*hsing-ming-chih-hsüeh*). There is a recognition that each one of us is fated to be a unique person embedded in a particular condition. By definition, we are unique particular human beings, but at the same time each and every one of us has the intrinsic possibility for self-cultivation, self-development, and self-realization. Despite fatedness and embeddedness as necessary structural limitations in our conditionality, we are endowed with infinite possibilities for self-transformation in our process of learning to be human. We are, therefore, intrinsically free. Our freedom, embodied in our responsibility for ourselves as the center of relationships, creates our worth. That alone deserves and demands respect.

In discussing the "spirit" of the Five Classics in the concluding section of *The World of Thought in Ancient China,* Benjamin Schwartz, referring to the central issue of the Neo-Confucian project, observes:

> In the end the root problem was to be sought where Confucius and Mencius had sought them— in the human heart/mind. It is only the human heart/mind . . . which possesses the capacity to "make itself sincere" and having made itself sincere to extend this transcendent capacity to realize the *tao* within the structures of human society. When viewed from this perspective, this is the essential gospel of the Four Books. At a deeper level, the Four Books also point to an ontological ground for the belief in this transcendental ethical capacity of the individual in the face of the ongoing challenge of a metaethical Taoist and Buddhist mysticism.[7]

The ontological grounding of the Neo-Confucian project on the learning of the heart-and-mind enabled Confucian intellectuals in late imperial China, premodern Vietnam, Chosŏn Korea, and Tokugawa Japan to create a cultural space above the family and below the state. This is why, though they never left home, actively participated in community affairs, or deeply engaged themselves in local, regional, or "national" politics, they did not merely adjust themselves to the world. Max Weber's overall assessment of the Confucian life-orientation misses the point. The spiritual resources that sustained their social activism came from minding their own business and included cultivating themselves, teaching others to be good, "looking for friends in history," emulating the sages, setting up cultural norms, interpreting the Mandate of Heaven, transmitting the Way, and transforming the world as a moral community.

As we are confronted with the issue of a new world order in lieu of the exclusive dichotomy (capitalism and socialism) imposed by the super powers, we are easily tempted to come up with facile generalizations: "the end of history,"[8] "the clash of civilizations,"[9] or "the Pacific century." The much more difficult and, hopefully, in the long haul, much more significant line of inquiry is to address truly fundamental issues of learning to be human: Are we isolated individuals, or do we each live as a center of relationships? Is moral self-knowledge necessary for personal growth? Can any society prosper or endure without developing a basic sense of duty and responsibility among its members? Should our pluralistic society deliberately cultivate shared values and a common ground for human understanding? As we become acutely aware of our earth's vulnerability and increasingly wary of our own fate as an "endangered species," what are the critical spiritual questions to ask?[10]

Since the Opium War (1840–1842), China has endured many holocausts. Prior to 1949, imperialism was the main culprit, but since the founding of the People's Republic of China, erratic leadership and faulty policies must also share the blame. Although millions of Chinese died, the neighboring countries were not seriously affected and the outside world was, by and large, oblivious to what actually happened. Since 1979, China has been rapidly becoming an integral part of the global economic system. More than 30 percent of the Chinese economy is tied to international trade. Natural economic territories have emerged between Hong Kong and Chuan Chou, Fujian and Taiwan, Shantung and South Korea. Japanese, European, and American, as well as Hong Kong and Taiwanese, investments are present in virtually all Chinese provinces. The return of Hong Kong to the PRC, the conflict across the Taiwan Straits, the economic and cultural interchange among overseas Chinese communities and between them and the motherland, the intraregional communication in East Asia, the political and economic integration of the Association for Southeast Asian Nations, and the rise of the Asia-Pacific region will all have substantial impact on our shrinking global community.

The revitalization of the Confucian discourse may contribute to the formation of a much needed communal critical self-consciousness among East Asian intellectuals. We may very well be in the very beginning of global history rather than witnessing the end of history. And, from a comparative cultural perspective, this new beginning must take as its point of departure dialogue rather than clash of civilizations. Our awareness of the danger of civilizational conflicts, rooted in ethnicity, language, land, and religion, makes the necessity of dialogue particularly compelling. An alternative model of sustainable development, with an emphasis on the ethical and spiritual dimensions of human flourishing, must be sought.

The time is long overdue to move beyond a mind-set shaped by instrumental rationality and private interests. As the politics of domination fades, we witness the dawning of an age of communication, networking, negotiation, interaction, interfacing, and collaboration. Whether or not East Asian intellectuals, inspired by the Confucian spirit of self-cultivation, family cohesiveness, social solidarity, benevolent governance, and universal peace, will articulate an ethic of responsibility as Chinese, Japanese, Koreans, and Vietnamese emigrate to other parts of the world is profoundly meaningful for global stewardship.

We can actually envision the Confucian perception of human flourishing, based upon the dignity of the person, in terms of a series of concentric circles: self, family, community, society, nation, world, and cosmos. We begin with a quest for true personal identity, an open and creatively transforming selfhood which, paradoxically, must be predicated on our ability to overcome selfishness and egoism. We cherish family cohesiveness. In order to do that, we have to go beyond nepotism. We embrace communal solidarity, but we have to transcend parochialism to realize its true value. We can be enriched by social integration, provided that we overcome ethnocentrism and chauvinistic culturalism. We are committed to national unity, but we ought to rise above aggressive nationalism so that we can be genuinely patriotic. We are inspired by human flourishing, but we must endeavor not to be confined by anthropocentrism, for the full meaning of humanity is anthropocosmic rather than anthropocentric. On the occasion of the international symposium on Islamic-Confucian dialogue organized by the University of Malaya (March 1995), the Deputy Prime Minister of Malaysia, Anwar Ibrahim, quoted a statement from Huston Smith's *The World's Religions*. It very much captures the Confucian spirit of self-transcendence:

> In shifting the center of one's empathic concern from oneself to one's family one transcends selfishness. The move from family to community transcends nepotism. The move from community to nation transcends parochialism and the move to all humanity counters chauvinistic nationalism.[11]

We can even add: the move toward the unity of Heaven and humanity (*t'ien-jen-ho-i*) transcends secular humanism, a blatant form of anthropocentrism characteristic of the Enlightenment mentality. Indeed, it is in the anthropocosmic spirit that we find communication between self and community, harmony between human species and nature, and mutuality between humanity and Heaven. This integrated comprehensive vision of learning to be human serves well as a point of departure for a new discourse on the global ethic.

The case against anthropocentrism through the formulation of an anthropocosmic vision embodied in the Neo-Confucian learning of the heart-and-mind is succinctly presented by

Wang Yang-ming. Let me conclude with the opening statement in his *Inquiry on the Great Learning:*

> The great man regards Heaven and Earth and the myriad things as one body. He regards the world as one family and the country as one person. . . . That the great man can regard Heaven, Earth, and the myriad things as one body is not because he deliberately wants to do so, but because it is natural to the humane nature of his mind that he do so. Forming one body with Heaven, Earth, and the myriad things is not only true of the great man. Even the mind of the small man is no different. Only he himself makes it small. Therefore when he sees a child about to fall into a well, he cannot help a feeling of alarm and commiseration. This shows that his humanity (*jen*) forms one body with the child. It may be objected that the child belongs to the same species. Again, when he observes the pitiful cries and frightened appearance of birds and animals about to be slaughtered, he cannot help feeling an "inability to bear" their suffering. This shows that his humanity forms one body with birds and animals. It may be objected that birds and animals are sentient beings as he is. But when he sees plants broken and destroyed, he cannot help . . . feeling . . . pity. This shows that his humanity forms one body with plants. It may be said that plants are living things as he is. Yet even when he sees tiles and stones shattered and crushed, he cannot help . . . feeling . . . regret. This shows that his humanity forms one body with tiles and stones. This means that even the mind of the small man necessarily has the humanity that forms one body with all. Such a mind is rooted in his Heaven-endowed nature, and is naturally intelligent, clear and not beclouded. For this reason it is called "clear character."[12]

For Confucians to fully realize themselves, it is not enough to become a responsible householder, effective social worker, or conscientious political servant. No matter how successful one is in the sociopolitical arena, the full measure of one's humanity cannot be accommodated without a reference to Heaven. The highest Confucian ideal is the "unity of man and Heaven," which defines humanity not only in anthropological terms but also in cosmological terms. In the *Doctrine of the Mean (Chung yung)*, the most authentic manifestation of humanity is characterized as "forming a trinity with Heaven and Earth."[13]

Yet, since Heaven does not speak and the Way in itself cannot make human beings great—which suggests that although Heaven is omnipresent and may be omniscient, it is certainly not omnipotent—our understanding of the Mandate of Heaven requires that we fully appreciate the rightness and principle inherent in our heart-minds. Our ability to transcend egoism, nepotism, parochialism, ethnocentrism, and chauvinistic nationalism must be extended to anthropocentrism as well. To make ourselves deserving partners of Heaven, we must be constantly in touch with that silent illumination that makes the rightness and principle in our heart-minds shine forth brilliantly. If we cannot go beyond the constraints of our own species, the most we can hope for is an exclusive, secular humanism advocating man as the measure of all things. By contrast, Confucian humanism is inclusive; it is predicated on an "anthropocosmic" vision. Humanity in its all-embracing fullness "forms one body with Heaven, Earth, and the myriad things." Self-realization, in the last analysis, is ultimate transformation, that process which enables us to embody the family, community, nation, world, and cosmos in our sensitivity.

The ecological implications of the Confucian anthropocosmic worldview are implicit, yet need to be more carefully articulated. On the one hand, there are rich philosophical resources in the Confucian triad of Heaven, Earth, and human. On the other hand, there are numerous moral resources for developing more comprehensive environmental ethics. These include textual references, ritual practices, social norms, and political policies. From classical times Confucians were concerned with harmonizing with nature and accepting the appropriate limits and boundaries of nature. This concern manifested itself in a variety of forms cultivating virtues that were considered to be both personal and cosmic. It also included biological imagery used for describing the process of self-cultivation. To realize the profound and varied correspondences of the person with the cosmos is a primary goal of Confucianism: it is a vision with vital spiritual import and, at the same time, it has practical significance for facing the current ecological crisis. This volume itself begins to chart a course for realizing the rich resources of the Confucian tradition in resituating humans within the rhythms and limits of the natural world.

NOTES

1. I wish to acknowledge, with gratitude, that Mary Evelyn Tucker and John Berthrong were instrumental in transforming my oral presentation into a written text. I would also like to note that materials from three published articles of mine have been used in this paper: "Beyond the Enlightenment Mentality," in *Worldviews and Ecology: Religion, Philosophy, and the Environment,* ed. Mary Evelyn Tucker and John A. Grim (Maryknoll, N.Y.: Orbis, 1994), 19–28; "Global Community as Lived Reality: Exploring Spiritual Resources for Social Development," *Social Policy and Social Progress: A Review Published by the United Nations, Special Issue on the Social Summit, Copenhagen, 6–12 March 1995* (New York: United Nations Publications, 1996), 39–51; and "Beyond the Enlightenment Mentality: A Confucian Perspective on Ethics, Migration, and Global Stewardship," *International Migration Review* 30 (spring 1996): 58–75.

2. *Analects,* 12:2.

3. *Analects,* 6:28.

4. Jürgen Habermas, "What Is Universal Pragmatics?" in his *Communication and the Evolution of Society,* trans. Thomas McCarthy (Boston: Beacon Press, 1979), 1–68.

5. Talcott Parsons, "Evolutionary Universals in Sociology," in his *Sociological Theory and Modern Society* (New York: Free Press, 1967), 490–520.

6. See Thomé H. Fang, "The Spirit of Life," in his *The Chinese View of Life: The Philosophy of Comprehensive Harmony* (Taipei: Linking, 1980), 71–93.

7. Benjamin I. Schwartz, *The World of Thought in Ancient China* (Cambridge, Mass.: Belknap Press of Harvard University Press, 1985), 406.

8. Francis Fukuyama's use of this Helena expression may have given the misleading impression that, with the end of the Cold War, the triumph of capitalism necessarily led to the homogenization of global thinking. Dr. Fukuyama's recent emphasis on the idea of "trust" by drawing intellectual resources from East Asia clearly indicates that, so far as shareable values are concerned, the West can hardly monopolize the discourse.

9. Samuel P. Huntington, "The Clash of Civilizations?" *Foreign Affairs* 72, no. 3 (summer 1993): 22–49.

10. These questions are critical issues for my course, "Confucian Humanism: Self-Cultivation and the Moral Community," offered in the "moral reasoning" section of the core curriculum program at Harvard University.

11. Quoted by Anwar Ibrahim in his address at the opening of the international seminar entitled "Islam and Confucianism: A Civilizational Dialogue," sponsored by the University of Malaya, 13 March 1995. It should be noted that Huston Smith's remarks, in this particular reference to the Confucian project, are based on my discussion of the meaning of self-transcendence in Confucian humanism. If we follow my "anthropocosmic" argument through, we need to transcend "anthropocentrism" as well. See Huston Smith, *The World's Religions* (San Francisco: Harper, 1991), 182, 193, and 195 (notes 28 and 29).

12. *A Source Book in Chinese Philosophy,* trans. Wing-tsit Chan (Princeton, N.J.: Princeton University Press, 1963), 659–60.

13. *Chung yung* (Doctrine of the Mean), chap. 22. For a discussion of this idea in the perspective of Confucian "moral metaphysics," see Tu Wei-ming, *Centrality and Commonality: An Essay on Chung-yung* (Honolulu: The University Press of Hawaii, 1976), 100–141.

V

"JUSTICE, JUSTICE YE SHALL PURSUE"

The poor still cannot find one liter of water to drink while these others have thousands of liters in which to swim. We don't want to reach where they are. Instead we believe in a spiritual foundation, moral relationships, and small economic and political organizations in a highly decentralized but highly coordinated way.

—A. T. Ariyaratne, "Waking Everybody Up"

In a community in which the sacred manifests through inner integrity rather than external authority, the integrity of every self is valued—yours as well as mine.

—Starhawk, *Dreaming the Dark*

God is hiding in the world. Our task is to let the divine emerge from our deeds.
—Abraham Joshua Heschel, *God in Search of Man*

A concern for social justice can be found in all the world's religions, and is perhaps the dominant moral theme of western monotheism. The core of this idea is that people deserve certain kinds of treatment because each person has a spiritual identity based in an absolute and unchangeable relation to God. Therefore, collective social relationships between rich and poor, dominant and subordinate social groups, and the coercive power of the government and unarmed citizens can be evaluated by unshakable moral standards.

Of course few will disagree with the call for justice in the abstract. The devil, as usual, is in the details. In religious tradition the absolute *equality* of human beings (we are all, it is said, "made in the image of God") coexists with acceptance of various kinds of traditional or customary *inequality* and *oppression*. Several questions then arise: when do social arrangements violate the religious commandment to pursue justice? When has the religious tradition *itself* contradicted its own professed ideals and condoned or ignored injustice? What would a more just society—and a more just religion—look like? And how should we accomplish the needed changes?

The selections in Part V address these concerns from a variety of contexts. We begin with perhaps the most famous piece of writing from an American spiritual social activist, Martin Luther King Jr.'s "Letter from a Birmingham Jail." Inspired by the tradition of nonviolent religious social action, King has (justifiably, in my view) taken his place as America's most respected exemplar of the principled connection of religion and politics. When we talk of "religion's" positive role in the civil rights movement, however, it should be remembered that King's letter was composed in response to a public statement by eight local clergy from a variety of faiths, a letter counseling him to go slow, be patient, and avoid civil disobedience.

This encounter shows something of the full range of religious responses to social problems. James Cone continues the discussion of the civil rights movement, reflecting on his own earlier groundbreaking connections between black theology and black power; and examining the thorny problem of violence in social change.

Perhaps the boldest and most passionate religious cry for social justice has come from the broad and varied movement known as "liberation theology." Initially rooted in poor Catholic communities in Latin America, liberation theology proposed to identify with the condition and needs of poor and repressed peasants, and freely borrowed from Marxist movements to comprehend the social forces and interests which perpetuated the peasants' enormous suffering. Selections from Gustavo Guitierrez, Mark Engler, and Daniel Berrigan reveal the essential ideas of liberation theology, and demonstrate that life and death issues are at stake in its pursuit. Dozens of church members have been murdered by repressive regimes for the pursuit of justice that they believe is their religious duty.

While liberation theology was typically the province of local priests and individual theologians, the spirit of the institutional church, following the historic meetings known as Vatican II in the early 1960s, became increasingly committed to social transformation, human rights, and concern for the poor as an issue of justice rather than charity. This concern is evidenced in documents from Vatican II, U.S. Catholic bishops, and the National Catholic Rural Life Conference.

Such concern always exists in dialogue with secular social movements. As Catholic lay activist Dorothy Day makes clear, a prevailing anticommunism in society as a whole and in the Church in particular should not obscure the common bonds that can join the secular and the religious in the pursuit of social justice. That pursuit, in turn, may be evidenced more by lives than by words. Murray Polner and Jim O'Grady's short sketch of Daniel and Philip Berrigan, leading radical Catholic activists for forty years, provides a small indication of what such lives are like, while Rich Barlow's news story describes the positive role religion played in a contemporary struggle for a living wage for janitors. Michael Bourdeaux reminds us of the important part performed by organized religion in the fall of communism, and of how freedom of worship is an essential part of any just society.

Racial justice, workers' rights, resistance to government repression—these are familiar concerns of religious social action. In recent years, however, the force of globalization and the advent of a world culture of spectacle and consumption have challenged spiritual social activists to expand their understanding of justice: from a guarantee of individual rights to a concern with the humanly fulfilling character of society as a whole. Essays by Mary John Mananzan and Harvey Cox offer deep criticisms of the political and cultural structures of globalization. Joanna Macy, Sulak Sivaraksa, and Rami G. Khouri demonstrate how religious traditions and contemporary movements that use them offer at their best a positive alternative to globalization's unrestrained market and destruction of community, and can expand the resources of the secular Left. Religious thinkers from regions outside the West in particular are more likely to think in terms of the community and its collective needs, than in terms of the individual and his or her freedoms.

The selections from indigenous peoples and from Michael Dodson remind us that in their case issues of justice, community value, respect for nature, and spirituality are inescapably intertwined. For these groups, cultural survival and religious fulfillment go hand in hand, along with a concern for simple justice—something indigenous groups continue to be denied.

Finally, Nancy Eiesland's essay extends theology into territory only recently explored, as secular movements and progressive religious activists alike begin to face the question of disability. The disability rights movement poses serious questions for conventional understandings of God, human nature, social justice, and our responsibility to love and care for one another.

"Letter from a Birmingham Jail"

❧

Martin Luther King Jr.

Martin Luther King Jr. received the Nobel Peace Prize in 1966 for his courageous and principled leadership of the African American struggle against racial segregation. King joined a passionate Christianity with an affirmation of basic democratic rights, and was an articulate critic of American imperialism and class inequality as well as an adherent of nonviolent and activist civil disobedience. This essay was written while King was in jail during a civil rights struggle.

❧

My Dear Fellow Clergymen,

While confined here in the Birmingham city jail, I came across your recent statement calling our present activities "unwise and untimely." Seldom, if ever, do I pause to answer criticism of my work and ideas. If I sought to answer all of the criticisms that cross my desk, my secretaries would be engaged in little else in the course of the day, and I would have no time for constructive work. But since I feel that you are men of genuine good will and your criticisms are sincerely set forth, I would like to answer your statement in what I hope will be patient and reasonable terms.

I think I should give the reason for my being in Birmingham, since you have been influenced by the argument of "outsiders coming in." I have the honor of serving as president of the Southern Christian Leadership Conference, an organization operating in every southern state, with headquarters in Atlanta, Georgia. We have some eighty-five affiliate organizations all across the South—one being the Alabama Christian Movement for Human Rights. Whenever necessary and possible we share staff, educational and financial resources with our affiliates. Several months ago our local affiliate here in Birmingham invited us to be on call to engage in a nonviolent direct-action program if such were deemed necessary. We readily consented and when the hour came we lived up to our promises. So I am here, along with several members of my staff, because we were invited here. I am here because I have basic organizational ties here.

Beyond this, I am in Birmingham because injustice is here. Just as the eighth-century prophets left their little villages and carried their "thus saith the Lord" far beyond the boundaries of their hometowns; and just as the Apostle Paul left his little village of Tarsus and carried the gospel of Jesus Christ to practically every hamlet and city of the Graeco-Roman world, I too am compelled to carry the gospel of freedom beyond my particular hometown. Like Paul, I must constantly respond to the Macedonian call for aid.

Moreover, I am cognizant of the interrelatedness of all communities and states. I cannot sit idly by in Atlanta and not be concerned about what happens in Birmingham. Injustice anywhere is a threat to justice everywhere. We are caught in an inescapable network of mutuality, tied in a single garment of destiny. Whatever affects one directly affects all indirectly. Never again can we afford to live with the narrow, provincial "outside agitator" idea. Anyone who lives in the United States can never be considered an outsider anywhere in this country.

You deplore the demonstrations that are presently taking place in Birmingham. But I am sorry that your statement did not express a similar concern for the conditions that brought the demonstrations into being. I am sure that each of you would want to go beyond the superficial social analyst who looks merely at effects, and does not grapple with underlying causes. I would not hesitate to say that it is unfortunate that so-called demonstrations are taking place in Birmingham at this time, but I would say in more emphatic terms that it is even more unfortunate that the white power structure of this city left the Negro community with no other alternative.

In any nonviolent campaign there are four basic steps: (1) collection of the facts to determine whether injustices are alive, (2) negotiation, (3) self-purification, and (4) direct action. We have gone through all of these steps in Birmingham. There can be no gainsaying of the fact that racial injustice engulfs this community.

Birmingham is probably the most thoroughly segregated city in the United States. Its ugly record of police brutality is known in every section of this country. Its unjust treatment of Negroes in the courts is a notorious reality. There have been more unsolved bombings of Negro homes and churches in Birmingham than any city in this nation. These are the hard, brutal and unbelievable facts. On the basis of these conditions Negro leaders sought to negotiate with the city fathers. But the political leaders consistently refused to engage in good faith negotiation.

Then came the opportunity last September to talk with some of the leaders of the economic community. In these negotiating sessions certain promises were made by the merchants—such as the promise to remove the humiliating racial signs from the stores. On the basis of these promises Rev. Shuttlesworth and the leaders of the Alabama Christian Movement for Human Rights agreed to call a moratorium on any type of demonstrations. As the weeks and months unfolded we realized that we were the victims of a broken promise. The signs remained. Like so many experiences of the past we were confronted with blasted hopes, and the dark shadow of a deep disappointment settled upon us. So we had no alternative except that of preparing for direct action, whereby we would present our very bodies as a means of laying our case before the conscience of the local and national community. We were not unmindful of the difficulties involved. So we decided to go through a process of self-purification. We started having workshops on nonviolence and repeatedly asked ourselves the questions, "Are you able to accept blows without retaliating?" "Are you able to endure the ordeals of jail?" We decided to set our direct-action program around the Easter season, realizing that with the exception of Christmas, this was the largest shopping period of the year. Knowing that a strong economic withdrawal program would be the by-product of direct action, we felt that this was the best time to bring pressure on the merchants for the needed changes. Then it occurred to us that the March election was ahead and so we speedily decided to postpone action until after election day. When we discovered that Mr. Connor was in the run-off, we decided again to postpone action so that the demonstrations could not be used to cloud the issues. At this time we agreed to begin our nonviolent witness the day after the run-off.

This reveals that we did not move irresponsibly into direct action. We too wanted to see Mr. Connor defeated; so we went through postponement after postponement to aid in this community need. After this we felt that direct action could be delayed no longer.

You may well ask, "Why direct action? Why sit-ins, marches, etc.? Isn't negotiation a better path?" You are exactly right in your call for negotiation. Indeed, this is the purpose of direct action. Nonviolent direct action seeks to create such a crisis and establish such creative tension that a community that has constantly refused to negotiate is forced to confront the issue. It seeks so to dramatize the issue that it can no longer be ignored. I just referred to the creation of tension as a part of the work of the nonviolent resister. This may sound rather shocking. But I must confess that I am not afraid of the word *tension*. I have earnestly worked and preached against violent tension, but there is a type of constructive nonviolent tension that is necessary for growth. Just as Socrates felt that it was necessary to create a tension in the mind so that individuals could rise from the bondage of myths and half-truths to the unfettered realm of creative analysis and objective appraisal, we must see the need of having nonviolent gadflies to create the kind of tension in society that will help men to rise from the dark depths of prejudice and racism to the majestic heights of understanding and brotherhood. So the purpose of the direct action is to create a situation so crisis-packed that it will inevitably open the door to negotiation. We, therefore, concur with you in your call for negotiation. Too long has our beloved Southland been bogged down in the tragic attempt to live in monologue rather than dialogue.

One of the basic points in your statement is that our acts are untimely. Some have asked, "Why didn't you give the new administration time to act?" The only answer that I can give to this inquiry is that the new administration must be prodded about as much as the outgoing one before it acts. We will be sadly mistaken if we feel that the election of Mr. Boutwell will bring the millennium to Birmingham. While Mr. Boutwell is much more articulate and gentle than Mr. Connor, they are both segregationists, dedicated to the task of maintaining the status quo. The hope I see in Mr. Boutwell is that he will be reasonable enough to see the futility of massive resistance to desegregation. But he will not see this without pressure from the devotees of civil rights. My friends, I must say to you that we have not made a single gain in civil rights without determined legal and nonviolent pressure. History is the long and tragic story of the fact that privileged groups seldom give up their privileges voluntarily. Individuals may see the moral light and voluntarily give up their unjust posture; but as Reinhold Niebuhr has reminded us, groups are more immoral than individuals.

We know through painful experience that freedom is never voluntarily given by the oppressor; it must be demanded by the oppressed. Frankly, I have never yet engaged in a direct action movement that was "well-timed," according to the timetable of those who have not suffered unduly from the disease of segregation. For years now I have heard the word "Wait!" It rings in the ear of every Negro with a piercing familiarity. This "Wait" has almost always meant "Never." It has been a tranquilizing thalidomide, relieving the emotional stress for a moment, only to give birth to an ill-formed infant of frustration. We must come to see with the distinguished jurist of yesterday that "justice too long delayed is justice denied." We have waited for more than 340 years for our constitutional and God-given rights. The nations of Asia and Africa are moving with jet-like speed toward the goal of political independence, and we still creep at horse and buggy pace toward the gaining of a cup of coffee at a lunch counter. I guess it is easy for those who have never felt the stinging darts of segregation to say, "Wait." But when you have seen vicious mobs lynch your mothers and fathers at will and drown your sisters and brothers at whim; when you have seen hate-filled policemen curse, kick, brutalize and even kill your black brothers and sisters with impunity; when you see the vast majority of your twenty million Negro brothers smothering in an airtight cage of poverty in the midst of an affluent society; when you suddenly find your tongue twisted and your speech stammering as you seek to explain to your six-year-old daughter why she can't go to the public amusement park that has just been advertised on television, and see tears welling up in her little eyes when she is told that Funtown is closed to colored children, and see the depressing clouds of inferiority begin to form in her little mental sky, and see her begin to distort her little personality by unconsciously developing a bitterness toward white people; when you have to concoct an answer for a five-year-old son asking in agonizing pathos: "Daddy, why do white people treat colored people so mean?"; when you take a cross-country drive and find it necessary to sleep night after night in the uncomfortable corners of your automobile because no motel will accept you; when you are humiliated day in and day out by nagging signs reading "white" and "colored"; when your first name becomes "nigger" and your middle name becomes "boy" (however old you are) and your last name becomes "John," and when your wife and mother are never given the respected title "Mrs."; when you are harried by day and haunted by night by the fact that you are a Negro, living constantly at tiptoe stance never quite knowing what to expect next, and plagued with inner fears and outer resentments; when you are forever fighting a degenerating sense of "nobodiness"; then you will understand why we find it difficult to wait. There comes a time when the cup of endurance runs over, and men are no longer willing to be plunged into an abyss of injustice where they experience the blackness of corroding despair. I hope, sirs, you can understand our legitimate and unavoidable impatience.

You express a great deal of anxiety over our willingness to break laws. This is certainly a legitimate concern. Since we so diligently urge people to obey the Supreme Court's decision of 1954 outlawing segregation in the public schools, it is rather strange and paradoxical to find us consciously breaking laws. One may well ask, "How can you advocate breaking some laws and obeying others?" The answer is found in the fact that there are two types of laws: there are *just* and there are *unjust* laws. I would agree with Saint Augustine that "An unjust law is no law at all."

Now what is the difference between the two? How does one determine when a law is just or unjust? A just law is a man-made code that squares with the moral law or the law of God. An unjust law is a code that is out of harmony with the moral law. To put it in the terms of Saint Thomas Aquinas, an unjust law is a human law that is not rooted in eternal and natural law. Any law that uplifts human personality is just. Any law that degrades human personality is unjust. All segregation statutes are unjust because segregation distorts the soul and damages the personality. It gives the segregator a false sense of superiority, and the segregated a false sense of inferiority. To use the words of Martin Buber, the great Jewish philosopher, segregation substitutes an "I-it" relationship for the "I-thou" relationship, and ends up relegating persons to the status of things. So segregation is not only politically, economically and sociologically unsound, but it is morally wrong and sinful. Paul Tillich has said that sin is separation. Isn't segregation an existential expression of man's tragic separation, an expression of his awful estrangement, his terrible sinfulness? So I can urge men to disobey segregation ordinances because they are morally wrong.

Let us turn to a more concrete example of just and unjust laws. An unjust law is a code that a majority inflicts on a minority that is not binding on itself. This is difference made legal. On the other hand a just law is a code that a majority compels a minority to follow that it is willing to follow itself. This is sameness made legal.

Let me give another explanation. An unjust law is a code inflicted upon a minority which that minority had no part in enacting or creating because they did not have the unhampered right to vote. Who can say that the legislature of Alabama which set up the segregation laws was democratically elected? Throughout the state of Alabama all types of conniving methods are used to prevent Negroes from becoming registered voters and there are some counties without a single Negro registered to vote despite the fact that the Negro constitutes a majority of the population. Can any law set up in such a state be considered democratically structured?

These are just a few examples of unjust and just laws. There are some instances when a law is just on its face and unjust in its application. For instance, I was arrested Friday on a charge of parading without a permit. Now there is nothing wrong with an ordinance which requires a permit for a parade, but when the ordinance is used to preserve segregation and to deny citizens the First Amendment privilege of peaceful assembly and peaceful protest, then it becomes unjust.

I hope you can see the distinction I am trying to point out. In no sense do I advocate evading or defying the law as the rabid segregationist would do. This would lead to anarchy. One who breaks an unjust law must do it *openly, lovingly* (not hatefully as the white mothers did in New Orleans when they were seen on television screaming, "nigger, nigger, nigger"), and with a willingness to accept the penalty. I submit that an individual who breaks a law that conscience tells him is unjust, and willingly accepts the penalty by staying in jail to arouse the conscience of the community over its injustice, is in reality expressing the very highest respect for law.

Of course, there is nothing new about this kind of civil disobedience. It was seen sublimely in the refusal of Shadrach, Meshach and Abednego to obey the laws of Nebuchadnezzar because a higher moral law was involved. It was practiced superbly by the early Christians who were willing to face hungry lions and the excruciating pain of chopping blocks, before submitting to certain unjust laws of the Roman Empire. To a degree academic freedom is a reality today because Socrates practiced civil disobedience.

We can never forget that everything Hitler did in Germany was "legal" and everything the Hungarian freedom fighters did in Hungary was "illegal." It was "illegal" to aid and comfort a Jew in Hitler's Germany. But I am sure that if I had lived in Germany during that time I would have aided and comforted my Jewish brothers even though it was illegal. If I lived in a Communist country today where certain principles dear to the Christian faith are suppressed, I believe I would openly advocate disobeying these anti-religious laws. I must make two honest confessions to you, my Christian and Jewish brothers. First, I must confess that over the last few years I have been gravely disappointed with the white moderate. I have almost reached the regrettable conclusion that the Negro's great stumbling block in the stride toward freedom is not the White Citizens Counciler or the Ku Klux Klanner, but the white moderate who is more devoted to "order" than to justice; who prefers a negative peace which is the absence of tension to a positive peace which is the presence of justice; who constantly says, "I agree with you in the goal you seek, but I can't agree with your methods of direct action"; who paternalistically feels that he can set the timetable for another man's freedom; who lives by the myth of time and who constantly advised the Negro to wait until a "more convenient season." Shallow understanding from people of good will is more frustrating than absolute misunderstanding from people of ill will. Lukewarm acceptance is much more bewildering than outright rejection.

I had hoped that the white moderate would understand that law and order exist for the purpose of establishing justice, and that when they fail to do this they become dangerously structured dams that block the flow of social progress. I had hoped that the white moderate would understand that the present tension of the South is merely a necessary phase of the transition from an obnoxious negative peace, where the Negro passively accepted his unjust plight, to a substance-filled positive peace, where all men will respect the dignity and worth of human personality. Actually, we who engage in nonviolent direct action are not the creators of tension. We merely bring to the surface the hidden tension that is already alive. We bring it out in the open where it can be seen and dealt with. Like a boil that can never be cured as long as it is covered up but must be opened with all its pus-flowing ugliness to the natural medicines of air and light, injustice must likewise be exposed, with all of the tension its exposing creates, to the light of human conscience and the air of national opinion before it can be cured.

In your statement you asserted that our actions, even though peaceful, must be condemned because they precipitate violence. But can this assertion be logically made? Isn't this like condemning the robbed man because his possession of money precipitated the evil act of robbery? Isn't this like condemning Socrates because his unswerving commitment to truth and his philosophical delvings precipitated the misguided popular mind to make him drink the hemlock? Isn't this like condemning Jesus because His unique God-consciousness and never-ceasing devotion to his will precipitated the evil act of crucifixion? We must come to see, as federal courts have consistently affirmed, that it is immoral to urge an individual to withdraw his efforts to gain his basic constitutional rights because the quest precipitates violence. Society must protect the robbed and punish the robber.

I had also hoped that the white moderate would reject the myth of time. I received a letter this morning from a white brother in Texas which said: "All Christians know that the colored people will receive equal rights eventually, but it is possible that you are in too great of a religious hurry. It has taken Christianity almost two thousand years to accomplish what it has. The teachings of Christ take time to come to earth." All that is said here grows out of a tragic misconception of time. It is the strangely irrational notion that there is something in the very flow of time that will inevitably cure all ills. Actually time is neutral. It can be used either destructively or constructively. I am coming to feel that the people of ill will have used time much more effectively than the people of good will. We will have to repent in this generation not merely for the vitriolic words and actions of the bad people, but for the appalling silence of the good people. We must come to see that human progress never rolls in on wheels of inevitability. It comes through the tireless efforts and persistent work of men willing to be co-workers with God, and without this hard work time itself becomes an ally of the forces of social stagnation. We must use time creatively, and forever realize that the time is always ripe to do right. Now is the time to make real the promise of democracy, and transform our pending national elegy into a creative psalm of brotherhood. Now is the time to lift our national policy from the quicksand of racial injustice to the solid rock of human dignity.

You spoke of our activity in Birmingham as extreme. At first I was rather disappointed that fellow clergymen would see my nonviolent efforts as those of the extremist. I started thinking about the fact that I stand in the middle of two opposing forces in the Negro community. One is a force of complacency made up of Negroes who, as a result of long years of oppression, have been so completely drained of self-respect and a sense of "somebodiness" that they have adjusted to segregation, and, of a few Negroes in the middle class who, because of a degree of academic and economic security, and because at points they profit by segregation, have unconsciously become insensitive to the problems of the masses. The other force is one of bitterness and hatred, and comes perilously close to advocating violence. It is expressed in the various black nationalist groups that are springing up over the nation, the largest and best known being Elijah Muhammad's Muslim movement. This movement is nourished by the contemporary frustration over the continued existence of racial discrimination. It is made up of people who have lost faith in America, who have absolutely repudiated Christianity, and who have concluded that the white man is an incurable "devil." I have tried to stand between these two forces, saying that we need not follow the "do-nothingism" of the complacent or the hatred and despair of the black nationalist. There is the more excellent way of love and nonviolent protest, I'm grateful to God that, through the Negro church, the dimension of nonviolence entered our struggle. If this philosophy had not emerged, I am convinced that by now many streets of the South would be flowing with floods of blood. And I am further convinced that if our white brothers dismiss as "rabble-rousers" and "outside agitators" those of us who are working through the channels of nonviolent direct action and refuse to support our nonviolent efforts, millions of Negroes, out of frustration and despair, will seek solace and security in black nationalist ideologies, a development that will lead inevitably to a frightening racial nightmare.

Oppressed people cannot remain oppressed forever. The urge for freedom will eventually come. This is what happened to the American Negro. Something within has reminded him of his birthright of freedom; something without has reminded him that he can gain it. Consciously and unconsciously, he has been swept in by what the Germans call the *Zeitgeist,* and with his black brothers of Africa, and his brown and yellow brothers of Asia, South America and the Caribbean, he is moving with a sense of cosmic urgency toward the promised land of racial justice. Recognizing this vital urge that has engulfed the Negro community, one should readily understand public demonstrations. The Negro has many pent-up resentments and latent frustrations. He has to get them out. So let him march sometime; let him have his prayer pilgrimages to the city hall; understand why he must have sit-ins and freedom rides. If his repressed emotions do not come out in these nonviolent ways, they will come out in ominous expressions of violence. This is not a threat; it is a fact of history. So I have not said to my people "get rid of your discontent." But I have tried to say that this normal and healthy discontent can be channelized through the creative outlet of nonviolent direct action. Now this approach is being dismissed as extremist. I must admit that I was initially disappointed in being so categorized.

But as I continued to think about the matter I gradually gained a bit of satisfaction from being considered an extremist. Was not Jesus an extremist in love—"Love your enemies, bless them that curse you, pray for them that despitefully use you." Was not Amos an extremist for justice—"Let justice roll down like waters and righteousness like a mighty stream." Was not Paul an extremist for the gospel of Jesus Christ—"I bear in my body the marks of the Lord Jesus." Was not Martin Luther an extremist—"Here I stand; I can do none other so help me God." Was not John Bunyan an extremist—"I will stay in jail to the end of my days before I make a butchery of my conscience." Was not Abraham Lincoln an extremist—"This nation cannot survive half slave and half free," Was not Thomas Jefferson an extremist—"We hold these truths to be self-evident, that all men are created equal." So the question is not whether we will be extremist but what kind of extremist will we be. Will we be extremists for hate or will we be extremists for love? Will we be extremists for the preservation of injustice—or will we be extremists for the cause of justice? In that dramatic scene on Calvary's hill, three men were crucified. We must not forget that all three were crucified for the same crime—the crime of extremism. Two were extremists for immorality, and thusly fell below their environment. The other, Jesus Christ, was an extremist for love, truth and goodness, and thereby rose above his environment. So, after all, maybe the South, the nation and the world are in dire need of creative extremists.

I had hoped that the white moderate would see this. Maybe I was too optimistic. Maybe I expected too much. I guess I should have realized that few members of a race that has oppressed another race can understand or appreciate the deep groans and passionate yearnings of those that have been oppressed and still fewer have the vision to see that injustice must be rooted out by strong, persistent and determined action. I am thankful, however, that some of our white brothers have grasped the meaning of this social revolution and committed themselves to it. They are still all too small in quantity, but they are big in quality. Some like Ralph McGill, Lillian Smith, Harry Golden and James Dabbs have written about our struggle in eloquent, prophetic and understanding terms. Others have marched with us down nameless streets of the South. They have languished in filthy roach-infested jails, suffering the abuse and brutality of angry policemen who see them as "dirty nigger-lovers." They, unlike so many of their moderate brothers and sisters, have recognized the urgency of the moment and sensed the need for powerful "action" antidotes to combat the disease of segregation.

Let me rush on to mention my other disappointment. I have been so greatly disappointed with the white church and its leadership. Of course, there are some notable exceptions. I am not unmindful of the fact that each of you has taken some significant stands on this issue. I commend you, Rev. Stallings, for your Christian stance on this past Sunday, in welcoming Negroes to your worship service on a non-segregated basis. I commend the Catholic leaders of this state for integrating Springhill College several years ago.

But despite these notable exceptions I must honestly reiterate that I have been disappointed with the church. I do not say that as one of the negative critics who can always find something wrong with the church. I say it as a minister of the gospel, who loves the church; who was nurtured in its bosom; who has been sustained by its spiritual blessings and who will remain true to it as long as the cord of life shall lengthen.

I had the strange feeling when I was suddenly catapulted into the leadership of the bus protest in Montgomery several years ago that we would have the support of the white church. I felt that the white ministers, priests and rabbis of the South would be some of our strongest allies. Instead, some have been outright opponents, refusing to understand the freedom movement and misrepresenting its leaders; all too many others have been more cautious than courageous and have remained silent behind the anesthetizing security of the stained-glass windows.

In spite of my shattered dreams of the past, I came to Birmingham with the hope that the white religious leadership of this community would see the justice of our cause, and with deep moral concern, serve as the channel through which our just grievances would get to the power structure. I had hoped that each of you would understand. But again I have been disappointed. I have heard numerous religious leaders of the South call upon their worshippers to comply with a desegregation decision because it is the *law*, but I have longed to hear white ministers say, "Follow this decree because integration is morally *right* and the Negro is your brother." In the midst of blatant injustices inflicted upon the Negro, I have watched white churches stand on the sideline and merely mouth pious irrelevancies and sanctimonious trivialities. In the midst of a mighty struggle to rid our nation of racial and economic injustice, I have heard so many ministers say, "Those are social issues with which the gospel has no real concern," and I have watched so many churches commit themselves to a completely otherworldly religion which made a strange distinction between body and soul, the sacred and the secular.

So here we are moving toward the exit of the twentieth century with a religious community largely adjusted to the status quo, standing as a taillight behind other community agencies rather than a headlight leading men to higher levels of justice.

I have traveled the length and breadth of Alabama, Mississippi and all the other southern states. On sweltering summer days and crisp autumn mornings I have looked at her beautiful churches with their lofty spires pointing heavenward. I have beheld the impressive outlay of her massive religious education buildings. Over and over again I have found myself asking: "What kind of people worship here? Who is their God? Where were their voices when the lips of Governor Barnett dripped with words of interposition and nullification? Where were they when Governor Wallace gave the clarion call for defiance and hatred? Where were their voices of support when tired, bruised and weary Negro men and women decided to rise from the dark dungeons of complacency to the bright hills of creative protest?"

Yes, these questions are still in my mind. In deep disappointment, I have wept over the laxity of the church. But be assured that my tears have been tears of love. There can be no deep disappointment where there is not deep love. Yes, I love the church; I love her sacred walls. How could I do otherwise? I am in the rather unique position of being the son, the grandson and the great-grandson of preachers. Yes, I see the church as the body of Christ. But, oh! How we have blemished and scarred that body through social neglect and fear of being nonconformists.

There was a time when the church was very powerful. It was during that period when the early Christians rejoiced when they were deemed worthy to suffer for what they believed. In those days the church was not merely a thermometer that recorded the ideas and principles of popular opinion; it was a thermostat that transformed the mores of society. Wherever the early Christians entered a town the power structure got disturbed and immediately sought to convict them for being "disturbers of the peace" and "outside agitators." But they went on with the conviction that they were "a colony of heaven," and had to obey God rather than man. They were small in number but big in commitment. They were too God-intoxicated to be "astronomically intimidated." They brought an end to such ancient evils as infanticide and gladiatorial contest.

Things are different now. The contemporary church is often a weak, ineffectual voice with an uncertain sound. It is so often the arch-supporter of the status quo. Far from being disturbed by the presence of the church, the power structure of the average community is consoled by the church's silent and often vocal sanction of things as they are.

But the judgment of God is upon the church as never before. If the church of today does not recapture the sacrificial spirit of the early church, it will lose its authentic ring, forfeit the loyalty of millions, and be dismissed as an irrelevant social club with no meaning for the twentieth century. I am meeting young people every day whose disappointment with the church has risen to outright disgust.

Maybe again, I have been too optimistic. Is organized religion too inextricably bound to the status quo to save our nation and the world? Maybe I must turn my faith to the inner spiritual church, the church within the church, as the true *ecclesia* and the hope of the world. But again I am thankful to God that some noble souls from the ranks of organized religion have broken loose from the paralyzing chains of conformity and joined us as active partners in the struggle for freedom. They have left their secure congregations and walked the streets of Albany, Georgia, with us. They have gone through the highways of the South on tortuous rides for freedom. Yes, they have gone to jail with us. Some have been kicked out of their churches, and lost support of their bishops and fellow ministers. But they have gone with the faith that right defeated is stronger than evil triumphant. These men have been the leaven in the lump of the race. Their witness has been the spiritual salt that has preserved the true meaning of the gospel in these troubled times. They have carved a tunnel of hope through the dark mountain of disappointment.

I hope the church as a whole will meet the challenge of this decisive hour. But even if the church does not come to the aid of justice, I have no despair about the future. I have no fear about the outcome of our struggle in Birmingham, even if our motives are presently misunderstood. We will reach the goal of freedom in Birmingham and all over the nation, because the goal of America is freedom. Abused and scorned though we may be, our destiny is tied up with the destiny of America. Before the Pilgrims landed at Plymouth we were here. Before the pen of Jefferson etched across the pages of history the majestic words of the Declaration of Independence, we were here. For more than two centuries our foreparents labored in this country without wages; they made cotton king; and they built the homes of their masters in the midst of brutal injustice and shameful humiliation—and yet out of a bottomless vitality they continued to thrive and develop. If the inexpressible cruelties of slavery could not stop us, the opposition we now face will surely fail. We will win our freedom because the sacred heritage of our nation and the eternal will of God are embodied in our echoing demands.

I must close now. But before closing I am impelled to mention one other point in your statement that troubled me profoundly. You warmly commended the Birmingham police force for keeping "order" and "preventing violence." I don't believe you would have so warmly commended the police force if you had seen its angry violent dogs literally biting six unarmed, nonviolent Negroes. I don't believe you would so quickly commend the policemen if you would observe their ugly and inhuman treatment of Negroes here in the city jail; if you would watch them push and curse old Negro women and young Negro girls; if you would see them slap and kick old Negro men and young boys; if you will observe them, as they did on two occasions, refuse to give us food because we wanted to sing our grace together. I'm sorry that I can't join you in your praise for the police department.

It is true that they have been rather disciplined in their public handling of the demonstrators. In this sense they have been rather publicly "nonviolent." But for what purpose? To preserve the evil system of segregation. Over the last few years I have consistently preached that nonviolence demands that the means we use must be as pure as the ends we seek. So I have tried to make it clear that it is wrong to use immoral means to attain moral ends. But now I must affirm that it is just as wrong, or even more so, to use moral means to preserve immoral ends. Maybe Mr. Connor and his policemen have been rather publicly nonviolent, as Chief Pritchett was in Albany, Georgia, but they have used the moral means of nonviolence to maintain the immoral end of flagrant racial injustice. T. S. Eliot has said that there is no greater treason than to do the right deed for the wrong reason.

I wish you had commended the Negro sit-inners and demonstrators of Birmingham for their sublime courage, their willingness to suffer and their amazing discipline in the midst of the most inhuman provocation. One day the South will recognize its real heroes. They will be the James Merediths, courageously and with a majestic sense of purpose facing jeering and hostile mobs and the agonizing loneliness that characterizes the life of the pioneer. They will be old, oppressed, battered Negro women, symbolized in a seventy-two-year-old woman of Montgomery, Alabama, who rose up with a sense of dignity and with her people decided not to ride the segregated buses, and responded to one who inquired about her tiredness with ungrammatical profundity: "My feet is tired, but my soul is rested." They will be the young high school and college students, young ministers of the gospel and a host of their elders courageously and non-violently sitting-in at lunch counters and willingly going to jail for conscience's sake. One day the South will know that when these disinherited children of God sat down at lunch counters they were in reality standing up for the best in the American dream and the most sacred values in our Judeo-Christian heritage, and thusly, carrying our whole nation back to those great wells of democracy which were dug deep by the Founding Fathers in the formulation of the Constitution and the Declaration of Independence.

Never before have I written a letter this long (or should I say a book?). I'm afraid that it is much too long to take your precious time. I can assure you that it would have been much shorter if I had been writing from a comfortable desk, but what else is there to do when you are alone for days in the dull monotony of a narrow jail cell other than write long letters, think strange thoughts, and pray long prayers?

If I have said anything in this letter that is an overstatement of the truth and is indicative of an unreasonable impatience, I beg you to forgive me. If I have said anything in this letter that is an understatement of the truth and is indicative of my having a patience that makes me patient with anything less than brotherhood, I beg God to forgive me.

I hope this letter finds you strong in the faith. I also hope that circumstances will soon make it possible for me to meet each of you, not as an integrationist or a civil rights leader, but as a fellow clergyman and a Christian brother. Let us all hope that the dark clouds of racial prejudice will soon pass away and the deep fog of misunderstanding will be lifted from our fear-drenched communities and in some not too distant tomorrow the radiant stars of love and brotherhood will shine over our great nation with all of their scintillating beauty.

Yours for the cause of Peace and Brotherhood,

Martin Luther King Jr.

from *Black Theology and Black Power*

જ

James H. Cone

James Cone, one of America's best-known radical theologians, teaches at the Union Theological Seminary in New York. His widely read attempts to connect black power and liberation theology have been recognized as classics for three decades. Here he looks back at his earlier work, and also reflects on the place of violence in social change.

જ

VIOLENCE

To raise the question of revolution is to raise the question of violence. Revolution always involves coercion. Is Black Theology a theology of violence? Does it advocate guerrilla warfare against the white adversary? These questions are not new. They are the kinds of theoretical questions that we expect from those who sit in the grandstand of middle-class Western morality untouched by the stings of oppression. They are also existential questions which the oppressed themselves are forced to think through as the oppressors continue to tighten the rope. When the oppressed first come to the recognition of their humanity and their treatment as things by the societal structures, the response usually consists of spontaneous, undisciplined outbursts of violence, saying, "We can't stand any more of this." But the masters are always silent on injustice, saying, "Justice will come only in a stable orderly society"—which means at the good pleasure of the white overlords. Therefore, if Black Theology is to speak to the predicament of the oppressed, it must deal honestly with the question of violence.

First, we must realize that to carve out a theology of black revolution which does not sidestep the question of violence is difficult. It is normal, with a Western view of morality, to think that any expression of violence, at least by the disfranchised, is unchristian. By contrast it is quite normal to think that a nation has a right to defend its national interests with violence, especially if it happens to be a part of the "free" world. It is interesting that so many advocates of nonviolence as the only possible Christian response of black people to white domination are also the most ardent defenders of the right of the police to put down black rebellion through violence. Another interesting corollary is their defense of America's right to defend violently the government of South Vietnam against the North. Somehow, I am unable to follow the reasoning.

Our chief difficulty with Black Theology and violence, however, arises from the New Testament itself. The New Testament picture of Jesus seems to suggest that he was against violence as a proper redress. He certainly never resorted to violence. In fact, he seemed to have avoided the term "Messiah" as a personal designation because of its political (violent) implications. Also his constant references to love and the turning of the other cheek seem to indicate that the Christian life cannot be one characterized by an "eye for an eye and a tooth for a tooth." Does not Jesus clearly say that his ministry is for the meek and helpless precisely because they are without an advocate? And even if we agree that love, as suggested in Chapter II, includes power, does this mean the power of violence? Is it not true that the power of love as expressed in the life and death of Jesus eschews the use of violence and emphasizes the inward power of the Christian man to accept everything the enemy dishes out? Is this not what he meant when he said, "Father forgive them, for they know not what they do"? Can we then, by any strength of the imagination or clever exegesis, interpret his command to turn the other cheek to mean a turning of the gun?

These questions are not easy to answer. The real danger of these questions is the implied *literalism* in them. Like the fundamentalist who stressed the verbal inspiration of Scripture, this view suggests that ethical questions dealing with violence can be solved by asking: "What would Jesus do?" We cannot solve ethical questions of the twentieth century by looking at what Jesus did in the first. Our choices are not the same as his. Being Christian does not mean following "in his steps" (remember that book?). His steps are not ours; and thus we are placed in an existential situation in which we are forced to decide without knowing what Jesus would do. The Christian does not ask what Jesus would do, as if Jesus were confined to the first century. He asks: "What is he doing? Where is he at work?" And even though these are the right questions, they cannot be answered once and for all. Each situation has its own problematic circumstances which force the believer to think through each act of obedience without an absolute ethical guide from Jesus. To look for such a guide is to deny the freedom of the Christian man. His only point of reference is the freedom granted in Christ to be all for the neighbor. Therefore, simply to say that Jesus did not use violence is no evidence relevant to the condition of black people as they decide on what to do about white oppression.

"The first task of Christian ethics," writes Bonhoeffer, "is to invalidate this knowledge" (the knowledge of good and evil).[1] Bonhoeffer is referring here to the Pharisaic and philosophical assumption that there is a guide, an absolute standard to right and wrong.

> For the Pharisee every moment of life becomes a situation of conflict in which he has to choose between good and evil. For the sake of avoiding any lapse his entire thought is strenuously devoted night and day to the anticipation of the whole immense range of possible conflicts, and to the determination of his own choice.[2]

The Pharisee is a man who figures out on the basis of law what is the right and wrong course of action. If asked why he chose this action rather than that, he can rationally defend himself. Essentially the Pharisee is not a doer of good or evil; he is basically one who judges the actions of others. But to assume that one has knowledge of good and evil is to ignore the fall of man. It assumes that doing the will of God means obeying a system of rules, a pattern of life. It fails, according to Dietrich Bonhoeffer, to recognize that

> The knowledge of Jesus is entirely transformed into action, without any reflection upon a man's self. A man's own goodness is now concealed from him. It is not merely that he is no longer

obliged to be judge of his own goodness; he must no longer desire to know of it at all; or rather he is no longer permitted to know of it at all. . . . His deed has become entirely unquestioning; he is entirely devoted to his deed and filled with it; his deed is no longer one possibility among many, but the one thing, the important thing, the will of God.[3]

In dealing with the question of violence and black people, Black Theology does not begin by assuming that this question can be answered merely by looking at the Western distinction between right and wrong. It begins by looking at the *face* of black America in the light of Jesus Christ. To be Christian means that one is concerned not about good and evil in the abstract but about men who are lynched, beaten, and denied the basic needs of life. It is not enough to know that black people make up a high percentage of the poor; that white complacency forces them to live in rat-infested apartments; that despite the gains of civil rights laws, police brutality is on the increase; that the appeal to love and nonviolence is a technique of the rich to keep the poor poor. These facts must be translated into human beings. While America is the richest country in the world as a result of the involuntary servitude of blacks and the annihilation of Indians, this country persists in expecting black people to accept their ideals of freedom and democracy. This country expects black people to respect law and order while others beat them over the head. It is this perspective which Black Theology must face before it can deal with the question of violence.

It is not that black Americans suffer more than any other people in the world, or even more than some whites in America. We may even safely assume that the blacks of America suffered more physically in the past than today. As the adversary would say: "Blacks never had it so good." Black suffering is not new. But what is new is "black consciousness." Black people know who they are; and to know who you are is to set limits on your being. It means that any act of oppression will be met with an almighty Halt! Any act of freedom will be met with an almighty Advance! This is the mood of black America which gives rise to Black Theology.

It does not matter how many gains are made in civil rights. Progress is irrelevant. The face of the black revolutionary will always be there as long as white people persist in defining the boundary of black being. It is the price one pays for oppression. The System, symbolized in the words "law and order," can only mean injustice for black people as long as the structure operates on the basis of racism. The appeal to democracy becomes a façade behind which the white hierarchy defends its right to rule over blacks. In any case the majority of black people see no relationship between the democratic process and their attempt to be free.

It is in this situation that Black Theology must speak the Word of God. How does it begin to deal with the face of the black revolutionary? Black Theology says, with José Bonino, that "A Christian must think through the question of revolution on the basis of his faith and he must express this interpretation in the concrete situation and translate it into action."[4] This means that the Christian is placed in a situation in which he alone makes the choice. The dichotomy between "good and evil," "right and wrong" is a false one. The Christian man

has not to simply decide between right and wrong and between good and evil, but between right and right and between wrong and wrong. . . . Precisely in this respect responsible action is a free venture; it is not justified by any law; it is performed without any claim to a valid self-justification, and therefore also without any claim to an ultimate valid knowledge of good and evil. Good, as what is responsible, is performed in ignorance to good and in surrender to God of the deed which has become necessary and which is nevertheless, or for that very reason, free.[5]

Black Theology realizes that violence per se is not the primary question. Violence is a "subordinate and relative question."

> It is subordinate because it has to do with the "cost" of desired change—the question of the legitimacy of revolution is not decided on the basis of the legitimacy of violence and vice versa! Violence is a cost that must be estimated and pondered in relation to a particular revolutionary situation. It is "relative" because in most revolutionary situations . . . violence is already a fact constitutive of the situation: injustice, slave labor, hunger and exploitation are forms of violence which must be weighed against the cost of revolutionary violence.[6]

It is this fact that most whites seem to overlook—the fact that violence already exists. The Christian does not decide between violence and nonviolence, evil and good. He decides between the less and the greater evil. He must ponder whether revolutionary violence is less or more deplorable than the violence perpetuated by the system. There are no absolute rules which can decide the answer with certainty. But he must make a choice. If he decides to take the "nonviolent" way, then he is saying that revolutionary violence is more detrimental to man in the long run than systemic violence. But if the system is evil, then, revolutionary violence is both justified and necessary.

Whether the American system is beyond redemption we will have to wait and see. But we can be certain that black patience has run out, and unless white America responds positively to the theory and activity of Black Power, then a bloody, protracted civil war is inevitable. There have occasionally been revolutions—massive redistributions of power—without warfare. It is passionately to be hoped that this can be one of them. The decision lies with white America and not least with white Americans who speak the name of Christ.

NOTES

1. Dietrich Bonhoeffer, *Ethics,* ed. Eberhard Bethge and trans. N. H. Smith (New York: Macmillan, 1955), 17.
2. Bonhoeffer, *Ethics*, 27. Used with permission.
3. Bonhoeffer, *Ethics*, 34–35. Used with permission.
4. José Bonino, "Christians and the Political Revolution," *The Development Apocalypse,* special U.S. edition of *Risk,* ed. Stephen Rose and Peter Vav Lelyveld (1967), 114–15.
5. Bonhoeffer, *Ethics*, 249. Used with permission.
6. Bonino, "Christians and the Political Revolution," 116. Used with permission.

PREFACE TO THE 1989 EDITION OF BLACK THEOLOGY AND BLACK POWER

Black Theology and Black Power was a product of the Civil Rights and Black Power movements in America during the 1960s, reflecting both their strengths and weaknesses. As an example of their strengths, this book was my initial attempt to identify *liberation* as the heart of the Christian gospel and *blackness* as the primary mode of God's presence. I wanted to speak on behalf of the voiceless black masses in the name of Jesus whose gospel I believed had been greatly distorted by the preaching and theology of white churches.

Although Martin Luther King, Jr., and other civil rights activists did much to rescue the gospel from the heresy of white churches by demonstrating its life-giving power in the black freedom movement, they did not liberate Christianity from its cultural bondage to white, Euro-American values. Unfortunately, even African-American churches had deviated from their own liberating heritage through an uncritical imitation of the white denominations from which they separated. Thus, it was hard to distinguish between the theologies of white and black churches and the images of God and Jesus they used to express them. African-Americans, it seemed to me at the time, had assumed that, though whites did not treat them right, there was nothing wrong with whites' thinking about God.

It was the challenging and angry voice of Malcolm X that shook me out of my theological complacency. "Christianity is the white man's religion," he proclaimed, again and again, as he urged African-Americans to adopt a perspective on God that was derived from their own cultural history. He argued:

> Brothers and sisters, the white man has brainwashed us black people to fasten our gaze upon a blond-haired, blue-eyed Jesus! We're worshiping a Jesus that doesn't even *look* like us! Oh, yes! . . . Now just think of this. The blond-haired, blue-eyed white man has taught you and me to worship a *white* Jesus, and to shout and sing and pray to this God that's *his* God, the white man's God. The white man has taught us to shout and sing and pray until we *die*, to wait until *death*, for some dreamy heaven-in-the-hereafter, when we're *dead*, while this white man has his milk and honey in the streets paved with golden dollars here on *this* earth!

Since I was, like many African-American ministers, a devout follower of Martin King, I tried initially to ignore Malcolm's cogent *cultural* critique of the Christianity as it was taught and practiced in black and white churches. I did not want him to disturb the theological certainties that I had learned in graduate school. But with the urban unrest in the cities and the rise of Black Power during the James Meredith March in Mississippi (June 1966), I could no longer ignore Malcolm's devastating criticisms of Christianity, particularly as they were being expressed in the articulate and passionate voices of Stokely Carmichael, Ron Karenga, the Black Panthers, and other young African-American activists. For me, the burning theological question was, how can I reconcile Christianity and Black Power, Martin Luther King, Jr.'s idea of nonviolence and Malcolm X's 'by any means necessary' philosophy? The writing of *Black Theology and Black Power* was the beginning of my search for a resolution of that dilemma.

Considered within the sociopolitical context of the sixties, I still believe that my answer was correct: "Christianity . . . is Black Power." Since theology is *human* speech and *not* God speaking, I recognize today, as I did then, that *all* attempts to speak about ultimate reality are limited by the social history of the speaker. Thus, I would not use exactly the same language today to speak about God that I used twenty years ago. Times have changed and the current situation demands a language appropriate for the problems we now face. But insofar as racism is still found in the churches and in society, theologians and preachers of the Christian gospel must make it unquestionably clear that the God of Moses and of Jesus makes an unqualified solidarity with the victims, empowering them to fight against injustice.

As in 1969, I unfortunately still see today that most white and black churches alike have lost their way, enslaved to their own bureaucracies—with the clergy and staff attending endless meetings and professional theologians reading learned papers to each other, seemingly for the exclusive purpose of advancing their professional careers. In view of the silence of the great majority of white theologians when faced with the realities of slavery and segregation, the white churches' preoccupation with "academic" issues in theology and their avoidance of the issue of justice, especially in the area of race, do not surprise me. What does surprise and sadden me, however, is a similar situation among many African-American churches and their theologians, especially those who claim to speak and act in the name of a black theology of liberation. In view of Sojourner Truth and Fannie Lou Hamer, Martin King and Malcolm X and the tradition of resistance that they and others like them embody, African-American ministers and theologians should know better than lose themselves in their own professional advancement, as their people, especially the youth, are being destroyed by drugs, street gangs, and AIDS. More black youth are in jails and prisons than in colleges and universities. Our community is under siege; something must be done before it is too late. If there is to be any genuine future for the black church and black theology, we African-American theologians and preachers must develop the courage to speak the truth about ourselves, saying to each other and to our church leaders what we have often said and still say to whites: *Enough is enough! It is time for this mess to stop!* Hopefully, the re-issuing of *Black Theology and Black Power* will contribute to the development of creative self-criticism in both black and white churches.

An example of the weakness of the 1960s black freedom movement, as defined by *Black Theology and Black Power,* was its complete blindness to the problem of sexism, especially in the black church community. When I read my book today, I am embarrassed by its sexist language and patriarchal perspective. There is not even one reference to a woman in the whole book! With black women playing such a dominant role in the African-American liberation struggle, past and present, how could I have been so blind?

The publication of the twentieth-anniversary edition tempted me to rid *Black Theology and Black Power* of its sexist language (as I did in the revised edition of *A Black Theology of Liberation* [Orbis, 1986] and also insert some references to black women. But I decided to let the language remain unchanged as a reminder of how sexist I once was and also that I might be encouraged never to forget it. It is easy to change the language of oppression without changing the sociopolitical situation of its victims. I know existentially what this means from the vantage point of racism. Whites have learned how to use less offensive language, but they have not changed the power relations between blacks and whites in the society. Because of the process of changing their language, combined with the token presence of middle-class African-Americans in their institutions, it is now even more difficult to define the racist behavior of whites.

The same kind of problem is beginning to emerge in regard to sexism. With the recent development of womanist theology, as expressed in the articulate and challenging voices of Delores Williams, Jackie Grant, Katie Cannon, Renita Weems, Cheryl Gilkes, Kelly Brown, and others, even African-American male ministers and theologians are learning how to talk less offensively about women's liberation. Many seem to have forgotten that they once used exclusive language. Amnesia is an enemy of justice. We must never forget what we once were lest we repeat our evil deeds in new forms. I do not want to forget that I was once silent about the oppression of women in the church and the society. Silence gives support to the powers that be. It is my hope that by speaking out against sexism other male African-American preachers and theologians, especially in the historic black churches, will also lift their prophetic voices against this enemy of God in the black church community. So far, too few of us have spoken out in our own denominations.

Black Theology and Black Power is also limited by the Western theological perspective that I was fighting against. After spending six years of studying white theology in graduate school, I knew that the time had come for me to make a decisive break with my theological mentors. But that was easier said than done. I did not know much about my own theological tradition which had given rise to my rebellion. I was struggling to become a *black radical* theologian without much knowledge of the historical development of African-American religion and radicalism. I had studied a little "Negro History" in high school and college, but no text by a black author had been included in my theological curriculum in graduate school. That was one of the things that made me so angry. I had been greatly miseducated in theology, and it showed in the neo-orthodox, Barthian perspective of *Black Theology and Black Power*.

"How can you call what you have written 'black theology,'" African-American theologians pointedly asked me, "when most of the theological sources you use to articulate your position are derived from the white theology you claim to be heretical?" "Your theology," they continued, "is black in name only and not in reality. To be black in the latter sense, you must derive the sources and the norm from the community in whose name you speak." That criticism was totally unexpected, and it shook me as nothing else had. I had expected my black brothers and sisters to support me in my attacks on white theology. But it seemed to me at the time that they were attacking me instead of our enemies. In time, however, I came to see the great value of their criticism. My effort to correct this cultural weakness in my theological perspective has been an on-going process since the publication of *The Spirituals and the Blues* (1972).

As I began to reflect more deeply upon my own cultural history, tracing it back to the African continent, I began to see the great limitations of Karl Barth's influence upon my Christological perspective. Barth's assertion of the Word of God in opposition to natural theology in the context of Germany during the 1930s may have been useful. But the same theological methodology cannot be applied to the cultural history of African-Americans in the Americas or to Africans and Asians on their continents. Of course, I knew that when I wrote *Black Theology and Black Power*, but my theological training in neo-orthodoxy hindered my ability to articulate this point.

As in 1969, I still regard Jesus Christ today as the chief focus of my perspective on God but not to the exclusion of other religious perspectives. God's reality is not bound by one manifestation of the divine in Jesus but can be found wherever people are being empowered to fight for freedom. Life-giving power for the poor and the oppressed is the primary criterion that we must use to judge the adequacy of our theology, not abstract concepts. As Malcolm X put it: "I believe in a religion that believes in freedom. Any time I have to accept a religion that won't let me fight a battle for my people, I say to hell with that religion."

Another weakness of *Black Theology and Black Power* was my failure to link the African-American struggle for liberation in the United States with similar struggles in the Third World. If I had listened more carefully to Malcolm X and Martin King, I might have avoided that error. Both made it unquestionably clear, especially in their speeches against the U.S. government's involvement in the Congo and Vietnam, that there can be no freedom for African-Americans from racism in this country unless it is tied to the liberation of Third World nations from U.S. imperialism.

"You can't understand what is going on in Mississippi if you don't understand what is going on in the Congo." Malcolm told a Harlem audience. "They're both the same. The same interests are at stake. The same sides are drawn up, the same schemes are at work in the Congo that are at work in Mississippi." During the last year of his life, Malcolm traveled throughout the Middle East and Africa as he sought to place the black freedom struggle in the United States into an international context. When African-American leaders questioned the value of his international focus, Malcolm said: "The point that I would like to impress upon every Afro-American leader is that there is no kind of action in this country ever going to bear fruit unless that action is tied in with the overall international struggle."

Martin King shared a similar concern. Against the advice of many friends in the civil rights movement, churches, and government, he refused to separate peace and civil rights issues. His condemnation of his government's involvement in the war in Vietnam, referring to "America as the greatest purveyor of violence in the world today," alienated many supporters in both the white and black communities. Martin King contended that the black freedom struggle and the struggle of the Vietnamese for self-determination were tied together because "injustice anywhere is a threat to justice everywhere."

My failure to link black liberation theology to the global struggles for freedom contributed to my blindness regarding the problem of classism. Class privilege was (and still is) a dominant reality in the white community of the United States as well as in the African-American community. In fact, the problem of oppression in the world today is defined not exclusively in terms of race but also in terms of the great economic gap between rich and poor nations and the haves and havenots within them. Again, if I had listened more attentively to Martin King and Malcolm X, I might have seen what I did not see at the time I wrote *Black Theology and Black Power*. Both turned toward economic issues during their later lives. They saw the great limitations of capitalism and, while rejecting the anti-democratic and atheistic principles of the Soviet Union, Martin and Malcolm began to search for the human, democratic side of socialism. What was clear to both of them, and clear to me now, is that we need to develop a struggle for freedom that moves beyond race to include all oppressed peoples of the world. As Malcolm X told a Columbia University audience a few days before his assassination: "It is incorrect to classify the revolt of the Negro as simply a racial conflict of black against white or as a purely American problem. Rather, we are today seeing a global rebellion of the oppressed against the oppressor, the exploited against the exploiter."

Despite its limitations, I hope that *Black Theology and Black Power* will remind all who read it that good theology is not abstract but concrete, not neutral but committed. Why? Because the poor were created for freedom and not for poverty.

from *A Theology of Liberation*

❧

Gustavo Gutiérrez

Gustavo Gutiérrez, a founder of liberation theology, studied medicine and literature in Peru and psychology and philosophy in Europe. In 1993 he was awarded the Legion of Honor by the French government for his tireless work for human dignity. This essay sketches some of the key ideas of Liberation Theology, as they emerged from Latin American theologians' responses to the liberalization of the Church following Vatican II and to the persistence of repressive and economically unjust social and economic regimes.

❧

FAITH AND SOCIAL CONFLICT

The council led us onto a new path on which there is no turning back: openness to the world. The history in which the Christian community, the church, plays a part today is marked by various kinds of opposition among individuals, human groups, social classes, racial groupings, and nations. In addition, the situation gives rise to confrontations that lead to various kinds of violence. Meanwhile, a choice was made at Medellín that has been a decisive one for the church during the years since then: the preferential option for the poor. By "the poor" I mean here those whose social and economic condition is the result of a particular political order and the concrete histories of countries and social groups.[1]

At this point challenging questions arise: How are we to live evangelical charity in the midst of this situation? How can we reconcile the universality of charity and a preferential solidarity with the poor who belong to marginalized cultures, exploited social classes, and despised racial groups? Furthermore, unity is one of the essential notes of the church. How, then, are we to live this unity in a history stamped by social conflict? These are questions we cannot avoid. They hammer at the Christian conscience everywhere but are especially acute in Latin America, the only part of the world in which the majority is both poor and Christian. The problem is especially urgent in the pastoral sphere in which the church lives its everyday life; it is therefore a challenge to any theology that endeavors to serve the proclamation of the gospel.

If we are to face these challenges in the right way, we must first see the real world without evasion, and we must be determined to change it. Let me say at the very outset that none of us can accept with unconcern, much less with satisfaction, a situation in which human beings

196

live in confrontation with one another. This is not acceptable to us either as human beings or as Christians. This state of affairs is doubtless one of the most painful aspects of human life. We would like things to be different and must therefore try to overcome the oppositions at work. But we must not fail to see the situation as it is and to understand the causes that produce it. Social conflict—including one of its most acute forms: the struggle between social classes—is a painful historical fact.[2] We may not decide not to look at it in light of faith and the demands of the kingdom. Faith in the God who is love is the source of light and energy for Christian commitment in this situation.

1. The claim that conflict is *a social fact* does not imply an unqualified acceptance of it as something beyond discussion.[3] On the contrary, the claim is subject to scientific analysis, and science is in principle always critical of its own claims. The various social sciences, to say nothing of simple empirical observation, tell us that we are faced today with an unjust social situation in which racial groupings are discriminated against, classes exploited, cultures despised, and women, especially poor women, are "doubly oppressed and marginalized."

Situations such as the one in South Africa display a cruel and inhuman racism and an extreme form of conflictual confrontation that is also to be found, even if in less obvious forms, in other parts of the world. It raises difficult questions for Christians living in these countries. These and other situations, such as those in Northern Ireland, Poland, Guatemala, and Korea, show us that in addition to economic factors others of a different character play a part in oppositions between social groups.

Acknowledgment of the facts of social conflict, and concretely of the class struggle, is to be seen in various documents of the church's magisterium. There are passages in the writings of Pius XI that are clear in this regard. He says, for example, in *Quadragesimo Anno:* "In fact, human society now, because it is founded on classes with divergent aims and hence opposed to one another and therefore inclined to enmity and strife, continues to be in a violent condition and is unstable and uncertain" (no. 82). A few lines later, he speaks of how far the struggle can go: "As the situation now stands, hiring and offering for hire in the so-called labor market separate persons into two divisions, as into battle lines, and the contest between these divisions turns the labor market itself almost into a battlefield where, face to face, the opposing lines struggle bitterly" (no. 83). The class struggle is a fact that Christians cannot dodge and in the face of which the demands of the gospel must be clearly stated.[4]

In 1968 the French episcopal commission on the working classes issued a statement that said, among other things:

> Oppression of the workers is a form of class struggle to the extent that it is carried on by those managing the economy. For the fact of class struggle must not be confused with the Marxist interpretation of this struggle. *The class struggle is a fact* that no one can deny. If we look for those responsible for the class struggle, the first are those who deliberately keep the working class in an unjust situation, oppose its collective advancement, and combat its efforts at self-liberation. Its actions do not indeed justify hatred of it or violence directed against it; it must nevertheless be said that the "struggle for justice" (to use Pius XII's expression), which is what the struggle of the working class is, is in itself conformed to the will of God.[5]

This statement is still primarily concerned with saying that the class struggle is a fact. At the same time, however, it points to those chiefly responsible for it, while also rejecting "hatred of them or violence directed against them."[6]

In his encyclical on human work John Paul II has dealt extensively and in depth with this difficult point. In the section "Conflict between Labor and Capital in the Present Phase of

History" the pope writes:

> Throughout this period, which is by no means yet over, the issue of work has of course been posed on the basis of the *great conflict* that in the age of, and together with, industrial development emerged between "capital" and "labor"—that is to say, between the *small* but highly influential *group* of entrepreneurs, owners or holders of the means of production, and the *broader multitude* of persons who lacked these means and who shared in the process of production solely by their labor [*Laborem Exercens*, 11; emphasis added].

The conflict has its origin in exploitation of workers by "the entrepreneurs . . . following the principle of maximum profit" (*Laborem Exercens*). A few pages later, the pope repeats his point that behind a seemingly abstract opposition there are concrete persons:

> It is obvious that, when we speak of opposition between labor and capital, we are not dealing only with abstract concepts or "impersonal forces" operating in economic production. Behind both concepts there are persons, *living, actual persons:* on the one side are those who do the work *without being the owners* of the means of production, and on the other side those who act as entrepreneurs and *who own these means* or represent the owners. [*Laborem Exercens*, 14; emphasis added].

This fact enables him to conclude: "Thus *the issue of ownership or property* enters from the beginning into the whole of this historical process" (*Laborem Exercens*). What we have, then, is an opposition of *persons* and not a conflict between abstract concepts or impersonal forces. This is what makes the whole matter so thorny and challenging to a Christian conscience.

2. This harsh and painful situation cannot be ignored.[7] Only if we acknowledge its existence can we give a *Christian evaluation* of it and find ways of resolving it. This second step should of course be the most important thing for us. These situations are caused, after all, by profound injustices that we cannot accept. Any real resolution requires, however, that we get to the causes that bring about these social conflicts and that we do away with the factors that produce a world divided into the privileged and dispossessed, into superior and inferior racial groupings. The creation of a fraternal society of equals, in which there are no oppressors and no oppressed, requires that we not mislead others or ourselves about the real state of affairs.

Earlier in this book I said that awareness of the conflict going on in history does not mean acceptance of it and that the important thing is to struggle "for the establishment of peace and justice amid all humankind."[8] The connection of peace with justice is an important theme in the Bible. Peace is promised along with the gift of the kingdom, and it requires the establishment of just social relationships. Drawing inspiration from some words of Paul VI, which it cites, Medellín begins its document on peace by saying: "'If development is the new name for peace,' Latin American underdevelopment, with its own characteristics in its different countries, is an unjust situation promoting tensions that conspire against peace" ("Peace," 1).

These tensions, which can develop into very sharp conflicts, are part of everyday life in Latin America. Moreover, they often place us in disconcerting situations in which theological reflection can advance only gropingly and in an exploratory way.[9] But the trickiness of the subject does not justify an approach that forgets the universalist demands of Christian love and ecclesial communion. On the other hand, these demands must be shown to have a necessary connection with the concrete situations mentioned above if we are to give adequate and effective answers to the Christians who face them.

The gospel proclaims God's love for every human being and calls us to love as God loves. Yet recognition of the fact of class struggle means taking a position, opposing certain groups of persons, rejecting certain activities, and facing hostilities. For if we are convinced that peace indeed supposes the establishment of justice, we cannot remain passive or indifferent when the most basic human rights are at risk. That kind of behavior would not be ethical or Christian. Conversely, our active participation on the side of justice and in defense of the weakest members of society does not mean that we are encouraging conflict; it means rather that we are trying to eliminate its deepest root, which is the absence of love.[10]

When we thus assert the universality of Christian love, we are not taking a stand at an abstract level, for this universality must become a vital energy at work in the concrete institutions within which we live. The social realities to which I have been referring in this section are difficult and much debated, but this does not dispense us from taking sides. It is not possible to remain neutral in the face of poverty and the resulting just claims of the poor; a posture of neutrality would, moreover, mean siding with the injustice and oppression in our midst.[11] The position we take under the inspiration of the gospel must be real and effective.

In his encyclical on work John Paul II acknowledges that the reaction of workers in the nineteenth century to the exploitation from which they suffered "was justified from the point of view of social morality." He goes on to mention the validity of the solidarity movements now being formed in the world of work, and he says that "the church is firmly committed to this cause, for it considers it its mission, its service, a proof of its fidelity to Christ, so that it can truly be the 'church of the poor'" (no. 8).[12]

Given the experience of Latin America, it is not difficult to see the importance of this solidarity with worker movements and with those who suffer "the scourge of unemployment" (*Laborem Exercens*, 8). We know the price that many Christians have had to pay for this solidarity. We know, too, that in it "our fidelity to Christ is proved." I am obviously not identifying the preferential option for the poor with any ideology or specific political program. Even if they represent legitimate options for the Christian laity, they do not at all satisfy fully the demands of the gospel.

The universality of Christian love is, I repeat, incompatible with the exclusion of any persons, but it is not incompatible with a preferential option for the poorest and most oppressed. When I speak of taking into account social conflict, including the existence of the class struggle, I am not denying that God's love embraces all without exception. Nor is anyone excluded from our love, for the gospel requires that we love even our enemies; a situation that causes us to regard others as our adversaries does not excuse us from loving them. There are oppositions and social conflicts between diverse factions, classes, cultures, and racial groupings, but they do not exclude respect for persons,[13] for as human beings they are loved by God and are constantly being called to conversion.

The conflict present in society cannot fail to have repercussions in the church, especially when, as is the case in Latin America, the church is, for all practical purposes, coextensive with society. Social tensions have effects within the church itself, which I understand here as the totality of its members—that is, as the people of God.

These tensions are reflected in statements the Latin American episcopate has been addressing with some frequency to Christians who occupy position of economic or political power. The bishops reproach these individuals for using their position to marginalize and exploit their brothers and sisters. The censure has in some cases taken the form of excommunications issued by episcopal conferences and individual bishops (for example, in Paraguay, Brazil, and Chile) against Christians who deliberately ignore the demands of ethics and the gospel concerning respect for the life, physical integrity, and freedom of others. These may seem to be extreme cases, but they demonstrate the seriousness of the situation. Without going as far as excommunication, other bishops have issued calls to order that, though less severe, are of a similar kind. The sternness shown in these statements and in the actions taken does not, however, prevent our also seeing in them the love that the bishops have for brothers and sisters who have strayed from the right path.

If the church is really present in the world, it cannot but reflect in its own life the events disturbing the world. But in the face of social divisions in which even Christians are involved, the affirmation of unity as the fundamental vocation of the church is increasingly necessary. Even within the church's own precincts it is important and even absolutely necessary that we see things as they really are, for otherwise we distort the Lord's summons to unity. The fact that there are oppositions among members of the Christian community does not negate the principle of the church's essential unity, but they are indeed an obstacle on the church's historical journey toward this unity, an obstacle that must be overcome with lucidity and courage.

The promise of unity is at the heart of Christ's work; in him human beings are sons and daughters of the Father and brothers and sisters to one another. The church, the community of those who confess Christ as their Lord, is a sign of unity within history (*Constitution on the Church*, 1). For this reason, the church must help the world to achieve unity, while knowing that "unity among human beings is possible only if there is real justice for all."[14] In a divided world the role of the ecclesial community is to struggle against the radical causes of social division. If it does so, it will be an authentic and effective sign of unity under the universal love of God.

Jesus does not ask the Father to take us from a world in which the forces of evil seek to divide his disciples. He asks only that we may be one as he and the Father are one. This prayer of Jesus springs from the conviction that grace is stronger than sin; he does not deny the presence of sin in the world, but believes that it will not conquer love (see John 17).

One important and pressing task of the church in Latin America is to strengthen this unity—a unity that does not conceal real problems but brings them to light and evaluates them in the light of faith. The deeper unity of a community that is on pilgrimage in history is a unity that is never fully achieved.[15] The unity of the church is first and foremost a gift of the Lord, an expression of his unmerited love; but it is also something built up, something freely accepted within time; it is our task and a victory we win in history.

This call to unity certainly reaches beyond the boundaries of the Catholic Church. It extends to all Christians and is the wellspring of the ecumenism to which Vatican II gave such an important stimulus. The paths of ecumenism may not be quite the same in Latin America as in Europe. Among us, as experience has shown, the commitment to proclaiming the love of God for all in the person of the poorest is a fruitful meeting ground for Christians from the various confessions. At the same time, we are all trying to follow Jesus on the path leading to the universal Father.

NOTES

1. In his opening address to the Puebla Conference John Paul II spoke of "mechanisms that . . . lead on the international level to the ever increasing wealth of the rich at the expense of the ever increasing poverty of the poor" (III, 4).

2. In a famous letter Marx says: "As for me, mine is not the merit of having discovered either the existence of classes in modern society or the struggle between them. Long before me bourgeois historians

described the historical development of this class struggle and bourgeois economists studied its economic anatomy." Marx considered that his own contribution was to have shown the connection between this reality and economic factors (and the dictatorship of the proletariat) (letter to J. Weydemeyer, March 5, 1852, in Karl Marx and Friedrich Engels, *Etudes philosophiques* [Paris: Editions Sociales, 1951], 151). Economic factors are often described as historically determined. I am not interested here in the important debate to which this view has given rise, or the interpretations it has produced even within Marxism; it is enough to say that the determinist approach based on economic factors its completely alien to the kind of social analysis that supplies a framework for the theology of liberation.

3. It was for this reason that I said at a meeting sponsored by CELAM in 1973: "The problem facing theology is not to determine whether or not social classes are in opposition. That is in principle a matter for the sciences, and theology must pay careful attention to them if it wishes to be au courant with the effort being made to understand the social dimensions of the human person. The question, therefore, that theology must answer is this: If there is a class struggle (as one, but not the only, form of historical conflict), how are we to respond to it as Christians? A theological question is always one that is prompted by the content of faith—that is, by love. The specifically Christian question is both theological and pastoral: How are Christians to live their faith, their hope, and their love amid a conflict that takes the form of class struggle? Suppose that analysis were to tell us one day: 'The class struggle is not as important as you used to think.' We as theologians would continue to say that love is the important thing, even amid conflict as described for us by social analysis. If I want to be faithful to the gospel, I cannot disregard reality, however harsh and conflictual it may be. And the reality of Latin America is indeed harsh and conflictual!"(*Dialogos en el Celam* [Bogotá 1974], 89–90).

4. Further on, when discussing socialism and the differences between it and communism, Pius XI maintains that "*if the class struggle* abstains from enmities and mutual hatred, it gradually *changes into an honest discussion* of differences founded on a desire for justice, and if this is not that blessed social peace we all seek, it can and ought to be the point of departure from which to move forward to the mutual cooperation of the industries and professions" (*Quadragesimo Anno,* 114; emphasis added). The claim is a far-reaching one, for it is not limited to a description of facts but indicates a possible development: when the class struggle is approached in a way that takes into account the basic Christian requirement of the exclusion of hatred, it can change into "an honest discussion."

5. Letter signed by Alfred Ancel, auxiliary bishop of Lyons, in *Documentation Catholique* 65, no. 1528 (November 17, 1968): 1950.

6. When Medellín describes the social tensions at work in Latin America, it says that the opposition is more intense "in those countries characterized by a *marked biclassism,* where a few have much (culture, wealth, power, prestige), whereas the majority has very little" ("Peace," 3; emphasis added). Following the lead of John Paul II, Puebla speaks of structural conflict.

7. We are indeed faced with a "social fact," and it is precisely as a fact that I speak of it. For this reason, what I say has nothing to do with a more philosophical approach that talks of social conflict, and specifically of class struggle, as "the force that drives history" or "the law of history."

8. Camilio Torres, *Revolutionary Writings* (New York: Harper & Row, 1972), 163–64.

9. The history of theological reflection on war, that deadly scourge of humanity, is an eloquent example of what I mean. European theologians have an extensive and direct experience in this area, which persons in other parts of the world do not always understand in all its details. Even so, European theological thinking on the subject has never been entirely satisfactory, because of the sensitivity and slipperiness of the subject itself. Theological reflection on war is always tentative and in process. The divergent and in some ways opposed positions recently taken by the North American and European episcopates on nuclear weapons are examples of what I am saying.

10. In this area John Paul II has made a clarifying distinction. Speaking of social conflict, the pope says: "This conflict, interpreted by some as a socio-economic *class conflict,* found expression in the *ideological conflict* between liberalism, understood as the ideology of capitalism, and Marxism, understood as the ideology of scientific socialism and communism, which professes to act as the protagonist for the working class and the worldwide proletariat. Thus the real conflict between labor and capital was transformed into *a systematic class struggle,* conducted not only by ideological means but also and chiefly by political means" (*Laborem Exercens,* 11). The "real conflict" is one thing, its ideological transformation into "a systematic

class struggle" as the sole political strategy is quite another. In my approach I refer to the former, not to the latter.

11. Worth citing in this context is an interesting passage from Karl Lehmann, theologian and now archbishop of Mainz: "Situations can undoubtedly arise in which the Christian message allows only one path to be followed. In these cases, the church has an obligation to take sides in a decisive way (think, for example, of the experience of Nazi dictatorship in Germany). In these circumstances, an attitude of unqualified neutrality in political matters contradicts the commandment of the gospel and can have deadly consequences" ("Problemas metodológicos y hermeneúticos de la teología de la liberación," in International Theological Commission, *Teológia de la liberación* [Madrid: BAC, 1978], 37).

12. For an analysis of this point, see my "El Evangelio del trabajo," in *Sobre el trabajo humano* (Lima: CEP, 1982).

13. There are times in the struggle for justice when opposition seems to exclude respect for others. Speaking of labor unions, John Paul II says: "They are indeed involved in the struggle for social justice, for the just rights of workers in accordance with their individual professions. However, this struggle should be seen as a normal endeavor 'for' the just good: in the present case, for the good that corresponds to the needs and merits of workers associated by profession; but it is not a struggle 'against' others." He goes on to say: "Even if in controversial questions the struggle takes on an *aspect of opposition* toward others, this is because it aims at the good of social justice, not for the sake of 'struggle' or in order to eliminate the opponent" (*Laborem Exercens*, 20; emphasis added). In these difficult situations there may in fact be opposition among individuals, but even then the Christian response is to reject any hatred.

14. Peruvian Episcopate, *Justicia en el mundo* (August 1971), 24.

15. See Lucio Gera, "Reflexión teológica," in *Sacerdotes para el tercer mundo* (Buenos Aires, 1970), 125: "As long as the church is on pilgrimage in this world, it is indeed one, but it nonetheless always does penance for the imperfection of its unity and strives for greater unity. Unity, like peace, is something that must be continually achieved."

"Toward the 'Rights of the Poor': Human Rights in Liberation Theology"

❧

Mark Engler

Mark Engler is a writer and activist living in Brooklyn, New York. He has worked for the Arias Foundation for Peace and Human Progress in San Jose, Costa Rica, as well as the Public Intellectuals Program at Florida Atlantic University. This essay examines some of the difficulties of applying concepts of human rights to the world's poor, especially when those concepts are formulated and applied by first-world countries.

❧

With the reforms of the Second Vatican Council and the release of the encyclical *Pacem in Terris*, the Roman Catholic church began a profound embrace of human rights. Although this moral language grew increasingly important to the social mission of Roman Catholicism during the 1960s and 1970s, it garnered only minimal attention in the emerging theology of liberation that was to transform the Latin American Catholic church in these times. While many expected the radical theologians, engaged priests, and activist laypeople associated with the "liberationist" Christianity to be at the forefront of the new human rights crusade, their abstention from use of this discourse was marked. When Latin American liberation theologians finally did approach the subject, beginning in the late 1970s, they surprised even more people: José Comblin, for example, has argued that "the mission of defending human rights has run out of steam" (Comblin 1992, 435), and Juan Luis Segundo stated, more severely, that the concept constituted an "ideological trap" for those struggling in the developing world (Segundo 1978/1993, 64). Even in their more recent, more conciliatory adoption of human rights, liberationists insistently contrasted the ostensible "universalization" of these ideals with the daily violation lived by the poor. They demanded that rights theory be reformulated to focus on the experience of society's most economically and politically oppressed.

In this article, I trace how a Latin American liberationist position on human rights has emerged in several distinct stages over the past thirty years, developing from an initial avoidance of the concept, to an early critique, and then to a nuanced theological appropriation. I contend that liberation theology, in the end, brings a thoroughgoing concern for the poor to human rights and demands that this moral discourse be accountable to historical praxis. My argument counters those who assume that liberationist views have been derived, without substantial alteration, from earlier schools of rights theory. This article also challenges analyses that address the interaction

203

between liberation theology and human rights without reference to historical shifts, or that consider it only in the final "rights of the poor" adaptation.

While my purpose is to clarify the position of human rights within a specific Christian religious movement in a particular geographical region, my examination of the liberationists' outlook is necessarily immersed in larger questions about the role of human rights language. Because these theologians simultaneously drew on the philosophical and programmatic frameworks of liberal, Marxist, and Catholic thinkers, they were distinctively situated to evaluate the relevance of human rights in the world: they considered carefully what unique contributions this discourse might bring to, and what limits it might impose upon, their political and theoretical work. As scholars and activists, they grappled concretely with the divisions among different "generations" of rights, among various proposed declarations, and among diverse options for rights advocacy.

The changes in the liberationist attitude toward human rights, I argue, reflected not only the contours of theological debate but also important political and historical shifts affecting the climate for this discourse in Latin America. Thus, I attempt to connect the intellectual history of human rights within liberation theology with major stances taken by actors outside the movement—those advanced by insurgent socialist groups of the late 1960s and early 1970s, by the Carter administration in the United States in the late 1970s, and by burgeoning human rights organizations in the 1980s. But ultimately this article aims to describe liberation theologians' distinctive criticisms, adaptations, and applications of the concept and language of human rights—for their approaches have influenced the wider Christian understanding of this discourse, have helped to shape political movements in Latin America, and continue to provide compelling challenges to those working for human rights today.

1. THE EARLY AVOIDANCE OF RIGHTS DISCOURSE

The first major works of liberation theology did not take up human rights as a theological theme.[1] Gustavo Gutiérrez's *A Theology of Liberation* mentioned human rights very few times.[2] The work's index offered no entry for the concept, an absence made conspicuous by the fact that it was first published in 1971, eight years after the Catholic Church endorsed human rights with *Pacem in Terris,* an encyclical in which Pope John XXIII gave theological justification to a long list of rights that virtually mirrors those set forth in 1948 in the United Nations Universal Declaration of Human Rights. I would argue that this neglect was not simple oversight, for a distinctive theme in these early liberation theology texts was an implicit critique of human rights; by focusing on the development of a "new humanity" or "new society," liberation theologians avoided investing themselves in a conventional liberal anthropology of human rights.

A sense of hope and of transformative potential permeated *A Theology of Liberation,* in which Gutiérrez proposed liberative praxis as the means to a "new society" of emancipated human beings (Gutiérrez 1971/1988, 56). Theologically, he fortified this vision by constructing an eschatology that focused on the importance of historical action in the construction of a utopian Kingdom of God. Gutiérrez remarkably included himself and his audience in the company of Ernesto "Che" Guevara, who argued that "We revolutionaries often lack the knowledge and intellectual audacity to face the task of the development of a new human being by methods different from the conventional ones, and the conventional methods suffer from the influence of the society that created them."[3]

The language of building a "new humanity" reflected the historical moment from which early liberation texts arose. The 1960s and early 1970s saw a resurgence in the prominence of the radical Left in Latin America, a trend most visibly demonstrated by the persistence of the Cuban revolution and the rise of Salvador Allende in Chile. Socialist movements provided vocal and seemingly viable opposition to many Latin American regimes. A sizable group of theologians felt it necessary to contribute their unique perspective to these vibrant movements in order to articulate a role for Christians in the development of a new society. In this context, forming a theology of liberation was not a methodical or patiently wrought academic affair, but rather a most urgent project. The early liberationist engagement with Marxism was intellectual as well as practical; the use of Marxist terminology and conceptual categories (class struggle, alienation, ideology, praxis, revolution) abounded in their dialogue, and a very substantial number of early texts were partially or wholly devoted to advancing a Christian-Marxist dialogue (Míguez Bonino 1976; Miranda 1974; Miranda 1980).

Many Marxists fashioned an opposition to human rights language from the theory of dialectical materialism. In his "Critique of the Gotha Program" (1891), Karl Marx argued that "right can never be higher than the economic structure of society and its cultural development which this determines" (Marx 1994, 321).[4] Human rights, from this point of view, were to be understood in superstructural terms, as ideas arising from a particular set of alienating economic arrangements. As instruments of critique, these ideas were thought to be limited by an inability to conceptualize the role played by economic factors in human exploitation. Ideologically, they were considered both to conceal the particular interests of the bourgeoisie and to expose the limits of this class's liberal revolution (Marx 1994; Haughey 1982, 102–41). Once a new society, based upon the people's control of the economic means of production, was established, the apparatus of rights, which functioned primarily to justify bourgeois possession of private property, would become unnecessary.

Though subsequent socialist movements developed varied positions on the potentials and dangers of human rights, the spirit of Marx's historicist insight lived to influence the discussion among Latin American revolutionaries in the early 1970s. Here, too, there was widespread agreement that human rights continue to "suffer" from their origins in elite first-world liberalism and that a "new humanity" would have to transcend the limited visionary possibilities that this tradition had offered. In liberationists' early grappling with Marxist thought and in Gutiérrez's dramatic use of Che Guevara, one sees in secularized, inchoate form several of the ideas that will mature with the subsequent theological critique and later appropriation of human rights language: There is the unmasking of "universal" human rights to reveal "the society that created them," the society whose ideological biases they contain; there is the sense of intellectual challenge, a drive to create not only new concepts, but also a new "method"; and there is the vibrant emphasis on agency, on the formation of a "we" that is poised to demand its rightful place in the making of history.

2. EMERGING CRITICISM: HUMAN RIGHTS AND THE LOGIC OF IMPERIALISM

It was not until a full decade after the foundational Medellín conference that human rights emerged as a major theme in liberationist dialogue.[5] The new attention to human rights, like the previous avoidance, had much to do with historical circumstances. The end of the 1970s saw the rise of human rights discourse in the foreign policy of the United States under President Jimmy Carter. Liberation theologians, however, were not convinced that the behavior of the United States had truly changed. They saw themselves in a continuing struggle against neo-imperialism in the form of exploitative first-world economic policies. For this reason, Latin American liberationists were drawn into debate about the theory and practice of human rights: the new rhetoric of morality being used by the United States demanded explicit response. This response soon came—in the form of Hugo Assmann's *Carter y la lógica del imperialismo* (1978). This broad, two-volume work collected over fifty essays from prominent theologians and secular analysts, integrating diverse sources into a powerful explanation of the political situation that liberationists faced.

2.1 Criticism of the United States

The collection was most centrally concerned with issuing a direct critique of the Carter administration's newly defined foreign policy; contributing authors sought to uncover the practical meaning and consequence of "trilateralism," "national security," and "new democracy." Carter's use of human rights was described by the liberationists in hostile terms, as an "ideological trap" (Segundo 1978/1993, 64) or, alternately, as a "specific ideological weapon" of imperialism (Petras 1977, 43). Liberation theologians argued that the "new morality" was not new at all, but merely the most recent of the duplicitous attempts by which the U.S. government sought to put a human face on its domination of the third world. Similarly, the "new democracy" being promoted through the U.S. State Department, they explained, was new only in that it abandoned all but the pretense of the universal ideals of democracy and liberalism (Hinkelammert 1977/1986, 116–19). The essays in the Assmann volumes together formed a detailed defense of these rhetorical claims, documenting the arguments with ample historical observation and acute analysis.[6]

Though *Carter y la lógica del imperialismo* focused on the specifics of U.S. foreign policy, a substantial number of the essays were devoted to the broader discussion of human rights. In fact, we find, here, the first concerted reflection on the concept to be found in the corpus of liberation theology. Most powerfully expressed in Segundo's "Human Rights, Evangelization, and Ideology," a deep suspicion about human rights language appeared in several of the essays, as well as in other liberationist texts of this period. Though the Assmann volumes did not represent a single, unified position on human rights, a cogent commentary can be compiled from the collection as a whole. I would like to draw out this position with some care for two reasons: first, because it has been largely forgotten by contemporary advocates of human rights (first-world analyses of liberation appropriations of the concept are especially prone to ignore it)[7] and, second, because the points articulated in this critique will ground my examination of later responses to human rights language. My goal will be to present as clear and cohesive an argument as possible, given the diverse sources; I will, however, interject critical comments that will point to ambiguities in the discussion and highlight problems that will become relevant later.

2.2 Criticism of the Notion of Universal Human Rights

The critique of human rights that emerges in the Carter period is based on an interrogation of the "universal" nature of human rights. The liberationist argument rests on a twofold premise, that rights are effectively limited to political and civil spheres and that respect for different rights is prioritized on the basis of foreign concerns. As a consequence of these two conditions, the interests of the Latin American poor have, in fact, been frustrated by use of the concept, even though guarantees of human rights ostensibly apply to the poor.

To begin, liberationists argue that human rights, loyal to their liberal origins, fail to extend beyond the protections of first-generation rights.[8] Segundo argues this point on juridical grounds. Human rights as "rights," he explains, rely on a legal apparatus of enforcement. Courts, however, are only equipped to adjudicate cases involving a certain type of rights, the civil and political rights of an individual. These same institutions have a profound inability to enforce rights relating to basic survival. With few exceptions, "no court, national or international, will entertain a complaint of hunger" (Segundo 1978/1993, 61).[9]

Not surprisingly, the juridical limits of human rights closely coincide with the concerns of elites. When some of the varied "inviolable" rights of individuals come into conflict with one another, especially in the third world, those valued by the ruling classes and foreign interests are given priority. Franz Hinkelammert points to the fact that one of the few economic rights actually respected in liberal capitalist societies, the "unconditional recognition of the right to private property," makes the guarantee of the right to work a relative one. Indeed, maintaining an absolute right to private property deprioritizes virtually all social rights, creating conditions of massive poverty, in which the rights "to satisfy basic needs in food, shelter, medical attention, education, and social security" are inaccessible for the majority of human beings (Hinkelammert 1977/1986, 120). Here, the liberationists propose, one sees human rights "suffering" from the legacy of their liberal conception.

Given these juridical limits and this ideological prioritization, it cannot be said that human rights are extended with impartiality to all persons; rather, they are accorded in a manner that shows deference to certain groups of people. Clearly, since basic social human rights are not genuinely respected, those who face constant violation of these rights can take little solace in the pretentious language of universality. This is especially true if they compare themselves with those who benefit from the rights that are actually enforced, those who have substantial private property in need of protection. It is with this argument that the charge of "ideology" acquires a more precise meaning; liberationists echo the Marxist insight that, in the succinct words of Peter Railton, "dominant ideas . . . not only reflect the experience of the dominant class," in this case including both elite and bourgeois elements, "but also serve its interests" (Railton 1995).[10] The juridical enforcement of human rights is ideological in this sense.

Liberation theologians, thus, begin to interrogate human rights in ways that on the surface seem paradoxical. Defying the assumption that human rights are universal they ask, with José Míguez Bonino, "Whose Human Rights?" (Míguez Bonino 1977, 222). Not only do the biases of human rights have a theoretical basis, liberationists emphasize, they have a long operative history. This is a history that pinpoints the particular social group from which liberalism emerged and to which the liberal conception of rights is traditionally partial, a history whose pernicious legacy lives in entrenched structures of racism, patriarchy, and imperialism.

2.3 Four Dangers

Working from this general critique of the universality of human rights, I would like to draw out four important practical dangers that liberationists attribute to the use of human rights language. The warnings about this discourse are closely intertwined, but each brings into view a slightly different emphasis, and each adds a distinctive nuance to our understanding of human rights.

The first danger revealed by the liberationist critique is that human rights, on their own, lack a systemic vision. Segundo passionately indicts the limits of rights discourse as he affirms the ethical mandate not to "lose sight of the great proportion of human beings who lead a subhuman life and to whom no one pays any attention, let alone affords the juridical instruments ... to mount an effective attempt to claim their rights" (Segundo 1978/1993, 64). Human rights language does not provide the conceptual tools with which one could even understand oppression in institutional, rather than individual, terms. The very structure of a "violation" that can be isolated and acted upon presumes the existence of a basically orderly politico-economic system in which such an event would be an aberration. By focusing on the occasional, ugly, individually directed assault on human dignity, human rights theory prescribes a myopic practice that is blind to the basic needs of two-thirds of humanity. Hinkelammert observes that in Latin America the "guarantee" of human rights is replaced with a "campaign" for such rights; the fundamental injustice of capitalism is ignored, and only its most abusive excesses are regulated (Hinkelammert 1977/1986, 120). These moves are particularly important because, by calling into question the lexicon of human rights discourse, liberation theologians raise two important questions about the relationship between theory and practice: To what extent do the terms attached to human rights prescribe a particular (and perhaps dubious) practice? What is the significance of a theoretical "guarantee" if such a guarantee is neither absolute nor universal?[11]

Some liberation theologians take this argument a step further and opt for an even stronger criticism: not only does human rights discourse lack a systemic vision, it actually condones methodical violation of human dignity by legitimating the societies and systems responsible for making the fulfillment of basic human needs inaccessible to the majority of the people. This is the second danger that liberationists attribute to human rights discourse, and it reflects the practical limits on the scope of human rights. Human rights discourse makes the capitalist first world into a model of global citizenship, absolving it of the guilt of the oppression it perpetrates. Hinkelammert explains that "criticizing human rights violations becomes a way of praising the Trilateral countries, even though they are at the source of those violations. They seem to be islands of respect for human rights that can offer their example to others, when in reality they are the centers of a worldwide empire in which the violation of human rights is the rule" (Hinkelammert 1977/1986, 124). In turn, through what Segundo identifies as the most "inhumane and anti-evangelical element in the defense of human rights," the third world is depicted as a savage, morally undeveloped land (Segundo 1978/1993, 65). Latin America is seen as a set of countries whose leaders do not grasp the enlightened virtue of universal human rights and who have the unfortunate tendency of sponsoring military dictatorships that violate these rights. All too often, institutional churches in Latin America accept their predetermined roles in this scheme, pleading guilty in the face of international rebuke and adopting an abstract ministry of universal human rights that is far removed from the reality of the majority.[12] This may involve advocating the formal restoration of democratic rights—the creation of procedural or "restricted democracies"—while ignoring economic systems of exploitation (see Gutiérrez 1983, 87).

The third danger revealed in unmasking the implicit prioritization of human rights is the way in which rights language is used to condemn genuine attempts to guarantee the fulfillment of the basic human needs that are supposedly protected under second-generation rights provisions. Those who fail to respect the individual rights valued by elites, "even if they do so only in order to protect people from greater evils, or to attain more effectively the ideals contained in rights," are morally detested and legally punished as violators of human rights (Segundo 1978/1993, 65). The right to unlimited private property is central to this paradox; although it is at the root of many systemic violations, it cannot be challenged because of its privileged, inviolable status.

Thus, if the Latin American Catholic church is to avoid a position that would be divisive or conflictual, it must defend property rights over those rights that are more central to the well-being of its impoverished people whenever these different rights come into conflict, which they inevitably do.

Liberation theologians have long recognized the trap that is inherent in this compromise, and they have identified the avoidance of conflict as an outward sign of "ghetto-like withdrawal" from the church's true obligations (Assmann 1973/1975, 65). Enrique Dussel, in his Philosophy of Liberation, contends that liberationist action, if it truly favors the poor and oppressed, will necessarily be condemned by the powerful few who benefit from the world's inequality; "if it criticizes the system, then this system must criticize it, persecute it" (Dussel 1980/1985, 180). The oppressed who effectively claim their human dignity are named the violators of human rights; in the minds of elites, the view of the third world as a bastion of human rights violators is reinforced with these condemnations. Associating this danger with the use of human rights language, liberation theologians raise crucial questions about who has authority over this discourse. They ask, "Who is allowed to make claims against human rights, and who adjudicates their claims?" Not only do these questions become important to the later appropriation of human rights by liberation theologians, but they also point to the fourth danger that liberation theologians see arising from the false universality of these concepts.

The final danger risked in the use of human rights language concerns the denial of the agency of the poor.[13] Liberation theologians argue that a concept of human rights that reflects the experience of the bourgeoisie necessarily relies on the action of this class for its realization. The defense of human rights tends to be managed by government bureaucrats, by humanitarian groups, and by those who have access to the legal system. In this context, as Hugo Villela explains, "the popular classes do not have the character of actors, but of secondary beneficiaries" (Villela 1978, 2:403). Brazilian Bishop Helmut Frenz warns that by taking up the banner of traditional, liberally formulated human rights, the institutional church loses its ability, necessary for liberation, to be an institution with the poor, rather than for them. The invocation of human rights further erodes the agency of those struggling for intellectual self-determination in the third world insofar as these thinkers are denied the opportunity to conceive their own vision of justice, one appropriate to their experience. They are instead expected to adopt the ideal of universal human rights and to accept the legitimacy of its liberal sources. There is some sense in Latin American liberation theology of the need for indigenous and non-European voices in the dialogue about the nature of human rights; interestingly, however, one generally does not find, here, the charges of cultural relativism that are more common in Asian contexts.[14]

Carefully drawing this multifaceted argument from the various contributors to Assmann's collection, one sees clearly the foundations of a skepticism that has been important to liberationist thought about human rights. Most basically, liberation theologians charge both that human rights are structured so as to protect only political and civil rights and that rights are implicitly prioritized in accordance with elite interests. More specifically, they fault human rights advocates for lacking systemic vision and for excluding the poor as potential agents of change; they point to the ways in which human rights have been invoked in order to legitimate first-world governments and to condemn attempts at resistance.

It is important to note that their critique of human rights discourse in Carter's foreign policy functions at two levels. First, there is an immanent practical critique. Here, liberation theologians accept the validity of human rights as an ideal or concept, and they prophetically decry the U.S. government's hypocritical violation of these rights. However, there is also a second, more theoretical level of criticism. Segundo, Hinkelammert, and Assmann, in particular, contend that there may be something flawed and dangerous about human rights themselves—that the received conception of universal human rights may contain too many of the problematic biases of liberalism and capitalism to be reclaimed fruitfully by those working for liberation. Human rights discourse may serve to mask and implicitly justify the systems of oppression that deprive the poor of the most basic means of subsistence. Failing to place second- and third-generation rights in a context of systemic oppression may effectively limit attempts to realize the ideals that stand behind the conception of such rights.

Liberation theologians themselves do not clearly distinguish these two levels, and this often muddles their analysis. I would argue, however, that this lack of distinction is not wholly unintentional, but reveals an important theoretical predisposition. In concluding this article, I will suggest that by focusing on praxis, liberation theologians force a reexamination of the connections between the two levels of critique that I have just outlined. Before turning to that, however, I wish to examine and evaluate the approach to human rights that liberation theologians have developed on the basis of the "rights of the poor."

3. THE SHIFT TO APPROPRIATION

Despite this initial avoidance and early critique, liberation theology has now begun to appropriate human rights discourse; indeed, an approach focusing on the "rights of the poor" has risen to prominence and now holds a dominant place in liberationist discourse on the subject. This is clearly evidenced by the 1989 publication of a volume entitled *Derechos humanos, derechos de los pobres* in the influential Theology and Liberation series (Aldunate et al. 1989/1993). Naturally, this shift invites questions: What brought the "rights of the poor" to such prominence? What are the theoretical merits and shortcomings of this position, especially in comparison with the prior critique?

Just as early liberationist criticisms of human rights were rooted in historical trends, so, too, I would contend, is this more recent appropriation. Although the causes of the shift in liberation theology away from both a dialogue with Marxism and an emphasis on a "new humanity" are complex and contested, I want to outline a few factors that have undoubtedly been important. By the close of the 1970s, the influence of Marxist groups was waning in many parts of Latin America, a trend correlated, not surprisingly, with the rise of repressive "national security" regimes supported by the United States.[15] Increasingly, Christian groups defined their independence from these movements. Meanwhile, the strength of liberal, predominantly first-world, and internationally focused human rights organizations increased greatly. An engagement with the likes of Human Rights Watch and Amnesty International, as well as with United Nations commissions, became a matter of great importance for groups struggling in Latin America, especially when they were faced with the many military regimes that rose during this period—regimes whose "national security" ideology led to massive violations of civil and political rights. While stressing this practical motivation for the liberationist adoption of human rights language, Salvadoran theologian Jon Sobrino has insisted that the move was not merely "pragmatic" in the pejorative, opportunistic sense of the term; instead, many of those reckoning with the daily struggle of the poor saw appeals to human rights as a potentially effective means of saving lives (Sobrino 1998). In this way, the shift reflected the continued urgency and relevance of the liberationist endeavor.

Liberation theologians were influenced not only by political changes but also by ecclesial and theological considerations. Several first-world theologians and human rights advocates, such as Jürgen Moltmann, admonished liberation theologians to look for the good in philosophical liberalism. They charged those who were unwilling to do so with throwing the baby of human rights out with the bathwater of imperialism. Within the Latin American Catholic Church, furthermore, conservative elements (notably Alfonso López Trujillo, a Colombian bishop and chief of the Latin American Episcopal Council) organized resistance to liberation theology, which put Leftist theologians on the defensive.[16] Papal criticisms paralleled this resistance (which focused largely on the Marxist overtones of liberation theology) and were expressed in the papal "instructions" of 1984 and 1986 (Congregation 1984, 1986). For all of these reasons, the period between the mid-seventies and late eighties saw liberation theology move from a revolutionary moment to a more conciliatory one.

As Sobrino stressed in his defense of "pragmatism," one of the most important factors in the liberationist appropriation of human rights was the early recognition of the usefulness of the concept in religious ministry. It is important to note that the various themes in the liberationist discussion of human rights did not follow one another in an easy chronology. Though the rights of the poor achieved theological prominence only later, it had a strong precedent. An appropriation of human rights discourse was, early on, an important pastoral theme, appearing in bishops' statements and local documents throughout the 1960s and 1970s. Most prominent among these were the documents produced at the two General Conferences of Latin American Bishops, organized by the Latin American Episcopal Council (CELAM) in 1968 and 1979; the Medellín documents spoke of the church's role in defending the "rights of the poor and the oppressed"; those from Puebla also referred to this idea several times.[17]

The legacy of the Carter administration presented a dual challenge to liberation theologians: at the same time that liberationists sought to unmask the ideological dangers of human rights language, they also felt compelled to use this critical awareness to "find the proper roots of a Christian defense of human rights" (Míguez Bonino 1977, 222). This second undertaking was especially important to those who felt that the increased attention to human rights demanded a uniquely Latin American expression of the concept. Even as early as the Assmann collection, a number of theologians had offered such a reformulation, Míguez Bonino being perhaps the most prominent among them. Moreover, Assmann's collection concluded with the "Universal Declaration of the Rights of Peoples [Pueblos]," a third-generation document drafted by representatives from countries recently freed from colonialism, as well as representatives of various socialist parties.

Finally, it is important to note that later theological reflections on the rights of the poor did not emerge in direct engagement with the critique of human rights that I have already examined, a fact that often works to their detriment. For example, in the work of Leonardo Boff, a leading advocate of rights of the poor, one can often see a failure to recognize the complex dangers associated with human rights discourse (Boff 1985, 22–46).[18] For this reason, examining this appropriation in explicit comparison with the earlier critique remains a promising task—one to which I now turn.

4. APPRAISING THE RIGHTS OF THE POOR

It is not surprising that the "preferential option for the poor," perhaps liberation theology's key tenet, would eventually come to guide a liberationist approach to human rights.[19] As I will now argue, one can consider the rights of the poor to be an application of the preferential option, one that allowed liberation theologians to bring the principle of "partiality" to bear on the claims to "universality" that they previously found so problematic in human rights. But before comparing rights-of-the-poor language with Carter-era liberationist criticisms of human rights discourse, I want to emphasize the extent to which both the early criticisms and the later appropriations constitute theological arguments.

In section 2, I presented the liberationist critique of human rights in secular, social-scientific terms, but this criticism had a theological dimension as well. Liberation theologians asked whether human rights, even as noble concepts, could be truly connected with the good news of God's reign as it manifests itself in history. Here, they used the theological language of idolatry in a way similar to the way they used the secular language of ideology. First, liberationists drew on a Catholic grounding of human rights in the belief that people are made in the image of God. Then, just as they had asked questions about whose interests were ideologically represented in various articulations of human rights, liberation theologians interrogated the conception of God that would be latent in these different theories. Taking this idea to its ethical conclusion, liberation theologians condemned as idolatrous those systems that held private property or the laws of the market to be sacred and inviolable. These systems, they argued, represented the false god of consumer capitalism, and their worshippers were sinful.[20] Thus, theological language helped make explicit the normative, moral force of early liberationist criticisms of human rights.

With the emergence of the positive project of formulating a liberative Christian expression of human rights, concern with the theological grounding of these rights has become still more pronounced. In general, as the Catholic church has embraced human rights, it has been very concerned that its adoption reflect core religious principles and not be a mere concession to secular values. As Alois Müller and Norbert Greinacher have explained, "The Church's contribution must be genuinely her own. She must produce concrete proposals from the heart of the Gospel" (Müller and Greinacher 1979, x; emphasis in original). Thus, as liberation theologians began to adopt human rights, it was logical that they, too, would return to their core religious principles in creating a distinctive stance. Since the preferential option for the poor, "a prophetic and comradely commitment to the life, cause, and struggle of these millions of debased and marginalized human beings" (Boff and Boff 1987, 3), had guided so much liberationist reflection on theological systematics, it naturally became a critical point of departure for appropriating human rights.

4.1 Partiality for the Poor

Most basically, the preferential option arises from a concrete, lived encounter with the injustice inflicted upon "the poor"—an encounter that serves as the very foundation of liberation theology. Not surprisingly, a large body of liberationist work explores the extent, nature, and moral significance of poverty. To convey a sense of the profound deprivation that exists in the developing world, many texts employ statistics such as those provided by the United Nations Development Programme (UNDP). This agency reported in 1998 that "of the 4.4 billion people in developing countries, nearly three fifths lack access to safe sewers, a third have no access to clean water, a quarter do not have adequate housing, and a fifth have no access to modern health services of any kind" (Crossette 1998). Moreover, 1.3 billion people live on incomes of less than one dollar a day (UNDP 1999).

These are the people to whom liberation theologians refer when they speak of "the poor." However, liberationists also define the category in more general terms. Leonardo Boff and Clodovis Boff, for example, explain that

[b]y "poor" . . . we mean a collective poor, the "popular classes," which is a much wider category than the "proletariat" singled out by Karl Marx. . . . The poor are also the workers exploited by the capitalist system; the underemployed, those pushed aside by the production process—a reserve army always at hand to take the place of the employed; they are the laborers of the countryside, and migrant workers with only seasonal work [Boff and Boff 1987, 3–4].

As this passage suggests, liberation theologians understand the poor as a social class, a group whose destitute circumstances are the product, not of chance misfortune, but of systematic exploitation. Using a combination of social-scientific analysis, religious reflection, and practical activity, liberationists attempt to fully understand this oppression, to appreciate the structural causes of poverty as well as the power of the poor to transform the situation (see McGovern 1989, 30–46, 105–94). They argue that in a world that presents such stark inequality—in a system of winners and losers—one is ethically obligated to struggle on the side of the losers, to assert a "preference" for the poor. Putting this in religious terms, Boff and Boff write, "How are we to be Christians in a world of destitution and injustice? There can be only one answer: we can be followers of Jesus and true Christians only by making common cause with the poor and working out the gospel of liberation" (Boff and Boff 1987, 7).

Looking more closely at the preferential option for the poor, one finds that this idea can readily be applied in the realm of human rights theory. Ultimately, human rights presented liberationists with a dilemma very similar to one they had already tackled in conventional theology: How can a "universal" value also have a "partial" character? To a large extent, the preferential option is an argument about why God's universal love should necessarily translate into a partiality for the poor. North American theologian Stephen Pope describes the threefold reasoning behind this position: Morally, Christians are called to the side of the poor not because of any special ability this group may have, but because of the special need for liberation that accompanies tremendous poverty. Religiously, biblical exegesis reveals a God who affirms a love for all human beings through attentive care for those who are most dehumanized. Cognitively, Christians are called to acknowledge "a 'perspectivism' rooted in the sociology of knowledge, i.e. a recognition that social location profoundly influences our sensibilities, attitudes, priorities, moral commitments, etc." (Pope 1993, 247). Acknowledging that all thought reflects the experience of a particular group, liberation theologians explicitly advance the situated viewpoint of the poor as the most appropriate for a Christian approach to God and to worldly action.

Pope's differentiation of moral, religious, and cognitive dimensions of partiality is helpful in understanding how the liberationists' adherence to a preferential option for the poor structures their transformation of conventional human rights theory. Cognitively, the option for the poor leads liberation theologians to a hermeneutical suspicion of any human rights theology that goes only so far as to assert the universal endowment of these rights to all humans—that is, of any theology that stops with stressing that all of humanity is created in God's image and thus fails to recognize that this broad proposition itself grows from a particular social location. The religious partiality that comes from the preferential option leads liberationists to contend that human rights, if indeed God-given, must contain an explicit concern for the downtrodden. Here, biblical exegetes like Leonardo Boff reveal a "God of Life" that "takes the part of the poor and oppressed, whose lives are threatened" (Boff 1988, 61).[21] He argues that "the rights spoken of in the Bible belong to the orphan, the widow, the pauper, the immigrant, and the alien. There is no sidestepping that fact that biblical rights, especially in the Prophets, the Wisdom literature, and the New Testament, are the rights of the oppressed" (Boff 1988, 59). Finally, expressing a moral partiality, liberationists prioritize the basic needs of the poor over the liberties of the rich, and in doing so, they affirm foremost the foundational right to life. Since the rights and dignity of the rich and powerful have always been respected, an emphasis on universal human rights for their benefit makes no sense. Rather, as Comblin makes clear, it is in defense of the poor, who are in need and whose rights have never been respected as such, that a language of human rights gains meaning: "The defense of human rights consists in publicly asserting that laws are valid for the poor, too, that the poor, too, have rights" (Comblin 1990, 57). Here, Comblin argues that the language of human rights requires a preference, because it is unnecessary to defend the rights of those whose rights are not at risk. As liberationists assert the wider validity of the rights that only elites currently enjoy, these rights truly become human rights, rather than merely some particularized type of moral rights. Thus, universality is affirmed as these rights are extended beyond the exclusive possession of a privileged class.

4.2 The Four Dangers Reconsidered

With the preferential option guiding their emphasis on the rights of the poor, liberationists can effectively address the concerns raised in the earlier critique, which expressed skepticism about the "universality" of human rights. Indeed, their previous unmasking of the elite bias built into human rights as they have traditionally been conceived allows liberation theologians to consciously place themselves as advocates of a different group, the poor and oppressed. This shift represents a radical challenge to traditional rights theory, as it demands that theorists reevaluate their views about rights from the perspective of those whom human rights practice has, so far, largely failed—those who have not been afforded the protections of the social contract, those who make up the "greatest number" but have never received their part of the "greatest good," and those whose "God-given" nature has not appeared self-evident to many oppressors. Liberationists who have appropriated human rights discourse do not regard commitment to the protection of human rights as the social status quo which governments must be pressed to maintain and to which agents of the state must be held accountable. From their perspective, such protection has yet to be achieved. Assertions of these rights become, instead, urgent demands for social transformation. In religious terms, the rights of the poor are a theodicy, an attempt to show God working on the side of those who have seen the reality of evil. It is through their realization that God will be shown to be the liberator of the poor rather than their betrayer.[22]

The focus on the rights of the poor also allows liberationists to reckon with each of the dangers that are associated with the more conventional liberal formulation of human rights: the lack of systemic vision, the moral absolution of the first world, the condemnation of conflict, and the dependence on bourgeois conceptions of agency. I will now reexamine these in turn, exploring the resources that an emphasis on the rights of the poor might bring to the discussion of each, but I will also explore the extent to which these four concerns might continue to confound liberationists who employ human rights language.

Centralizing the rights of the poor addresses the systematic violation of human rights in several ways. First, it enables theologians to frame human rights as a set of "claims in conflict." David Hollenbach explains how this liberationist insight has influenced a wider Catholic understanding of human rights: "(1) the needs of the poor take priority over the wants of the rich. (2) The freedom of the dominated takes priority over the liberty of the powerful. (3) The participation of marginalized groups takes priority over the liberty of the powerful" (Hollenbach 1979, 204–7, quoted in Hennelly 1989, 99). Not only do these guidelines force consideration of how some claims to rights may be validated more fully than others, but they also allow theorists to revalue rights that fit poorly within traditional individualistic forms of liberal rights theory. Liberation theologians, thus, highlight rights of the poor that force people to interrogate systems—rights such as the right to work, the right to participate in political and economic systems, and the right to transform society, as well as the right to equality. Furthermore, liberation theologians stress the importance of using this discussion to break down the established dichotomies of rights discourse: the rights of the poor are both in personam, as poor individuals are able to demand relief from specific abuses, and in rem, as society must create structures that can provide this relief more generally. They are both concrete, a set of actual substantive entitlements that the poor can demand, and abstract, providing ethical norms to guide public discourse (Aldunate 1989/1993, 106–12).

Although the assertion of a broad range of system-oriented, second- and third-generation rights is an innovative strategy for challenging the limits of traditional liberal conceptions of human rights, it remains uncertain whether the category of "rights" can bear the burden of this move. Many of the rights that liberation theologians affirm remain theoretically underdeveloped. A key example of this is the "right to equality." Joaquín Undurraga argues that the poor can claim not only equality of right, "equality before God or before the law," but also equality of hecho (act) (Undurraga 1989/1993). It is very unclear, however, what this second form of the right to equality entails—Undurraga's article refers variously to a right to equal opportunity to command scarce resources, to equal distribution of such resources, and (most awkwardly) to equal access to one of the different unalienating means by which to subsist economically and culturally. Moreover, the *Derechos de los pobres* volume never questions the extent to which "equality" constitutes a category of entitlement, or liberty, to which a "right" could viably refer. Thus, the question remains as to what practical impact second- and third-generation rights can have, given their theoretical indeterminacy.

In connection with the next two dangers associated with use of human rights language, the rights of the poor provide an important tool for challenging both first-world claims to moral purity and first-world condemnations of resistance. Situating oneself with the poor forces one to examine the systems of dependency and inequality that the first world perpetuates. From this perspective, one inevitably asks whose rights are being affirmed by the ostensibly universally minded policies of the United States and whose rights are being denied. Furthermore, a liberationist view of rights as "claims in conflict" is innovative in two ways. First, it affirms the necessity of conflict among the different moral demands made in the name of rights. Second, it helps reshape the lexicon of rights language to preclude facile condemnations of those defending the rights of the poor; since conflicting claims necessarily mean that not all rights will be equally honored at a given time, individual "violations" must be put in a larger social context. This new conceptualization of human rights discourse does not presume a egalitarian system that is functioning well; rather, it keeps the real misery of so much of humanity at the center of discussion. As Gutiérrez explains, adopting the rights of the poor "is not merely a matter of words. This alternative language represents a critical approach to the laissez-faire, liberal doctrine to the effect that our society enjoys an equality that in fact does not exist" (Gutiérrez 1983, 87).

Finally, while affirming the importance of the juridical and legislative function of human rights, a focus on the rights of the poor also draws attention to other uses of "rights" that better allow the poor to become agents in the making of history. Human rights can function as utopian norms at the root of a vision of just relations and as a set of demands that mandate immediate historical action by many persons and groups working with the poor for a better society. They are variously recommended as tools for political consensus building and for base community consciousness raising. Perhaps most importantly, human rights, in their liberationist formulation, become a strong reason for Christian churches to take the side of the poor and to make their moral and material resources available to engaged parishioners.

5. HISTORICIZING ETHICAL ANALYSIS

A conception of human rights that focuses on the rights of the poor is now firmly established in the corpus of liberation theology, and it has been variously employed in different countries over the past two decades. Nevertheless, some remain skeptical about the use of human rights, and several of the critical insights from the Carter era remain trenchant. Having examined the rights of the poor in light of the earlier liberationist critique of human rights, one can ask which of the original concerns may still be relevant today. Can the language of universal human rights be successfully co-opted or appropriated by liberation theologians? Can economic and social ideals truly be accommodated as rights? Will the definition and defense of human rights remain the prerogative of legal officials, policymakers, and monitoring specialists, or will the force of popular movements give this work a new context, a new direction, and a new meaning? Can human rights discourse be a force for progressive change today, or will it rather serve as a rationalization for complacency?

Liberation theologians hold that these questions cannot be resolved through abstracted contemplation. In their analysis of human rights, as in their theoretical work more generally, liberationists advance a strong methodological contention: they stress that intellectual analysis should be informed by an active engagement with the poor, by a practical commitment to challenging the systems of oppression at work in our world today. They see their academic work not as removed and speculative, but instead as "critical reflection on praxis" (Gutiérrez 1983, 87)—an activity designed not just to understand the world, but to change it. Thus, to effectively address questions about the philosophical validity of human rights claims, we must know how these questions have previously been answered in historical struggle, and we must try to discern what potential there may be for changes in the use of human rights in the future.

Advancing this position, Salvadoran liberationist Ignacio Ellacuría calls for a "historicization" of ethical analysis. As John Hassett and Hugh Lacey explain:

> Central to Ellacuría's methodology is the view that the meanings of such key terms of moral theory as "property," "democracy," "human rights," and "violence" cannot be comprehended abstractly or dissociated from their uses in concrete historical circumstances and what they apply to within different socio-economic structures. Their meanings are variable, and they are shaped and refined ... in response to actual events [Hassett and Lacey 1991, 10].

Ellacuría further stresses the gap that can exist between the principles that are rhetorically affirmed in the abstract and the practical use made of this rhetoric. The irony of human rights, he states, is that "as abstract and universal, everyone assents to them and they stand for realities which, as they operate in history, are however the negation of what they claim to be" (Ellacuría 1991, 109).

In their political thought, liberation theologians argue that any process of reform is dangerous when the changes it effects are merely announced and accepted in theory, without the necessarily conflictive engagement that accompanies real change. Along these lines, Assmann denounces "changes [that] are evoked in proclamation, 'believed' in utopian and ideological fashion, not won in the fight"; such reforms, he proposes, are "justifications for leaving things as they are" as often as they are genuinely emancipatory acts (Assmann 1973/1975, 99). The widespread adoption of human rights language risks being such a pseudoreform. A "human rights revolution," liberationists suggest, cannot come about simply through deliberation in the diplomatic proceedings of the United Nations or in philosophical journals; such a revolution, instead, must be lived by the majority in our world whose human rights are constantly violated and by those who would deprive them of these rights. Ellacuría's challenge to historicization not only echoes Assmann's warning but also offers a way for scholars to reckon with it; he demands that ethicists study concepts like human rights in a new way, one that involves "demonstrating [their] impact . . . within a particular context" (Ellacuría 1991, 109).

In their insistence both on historicizing human rights and on grounding intellectual work in practical struggle, liberation theologians point to the analytical limits inherent in this article's traditional theoretical inquiry. But even while a survey of liberationist approaches to human rights cannot be an end unto itself, such analysis nevertheless gives insight into the perennial questions that surround the very notion of human rights, allowing for deeper understanding and strategic thinking about these ideals. Especially for those committed to developing a full vision of human rights in their work for a more just society, the distinctive understanding that emerges from liberation theology can provide an important guide. Focusing on the rights of the poor is a way of making explicit the perspectives, concerns, and values that inform liberationist work. It calls into question the latent prioritizations of human rights that so often make their enforcement coincide with elite interests. It also proposes a manner in which human rights can take effect in the world in a new way, showing explicit partiality toward the most oppressed members of our society.

Ultimately, liberation theologians force us to recognize that human rights are not established and intransigent ideals. Rather, they are concepts continually being shaped and defined in historical struggle. The argument for the rights-of-the-poor appropriation is not that human rights are inherently positive and their acceptance uncontroversial. The argument, instead, is that human rights have conceptual value and practical usefulness, and that, in a world of persistent injustice, the emergent meaning and mandate of these rights may greatly influence the course of social development for the better. The argument, in short, is that the idea of human rights is an idea worth fighting for.

NOTES

1. To document my generalizations in this section about early thought in liberation theology, I will rely primarily on Gustavo Gutiérrez's *A Theology of Liberation*, which is now most often cited as the central text of the liberation canon. Similar use could be made of Assmann 1973/1975, Míguez Bonino 1975, or Segundo 1976.

2. Contrary to common belief, even in this early text Gutiérrez did not entirely avoid using "rights" or "human rights." In fact, he used this language in the important capacity of describing who was to be included among the "poor," pointing to those "struggling for the most basic rights," and also in describing activities that generate hope (Gutiérrez 1971/1988, 64, 97, 111, 125, 159, 173).

3. Guevara 1968, 396, as quoted in Gutiérrez 1971/1988, 56 (emphasis added); also see 1971/1988, 202 n. 47, where Gutiérrez further cites the theological vision of a "new man" advanced by Bolivian Néstor Paz.

4. Marx was specifically referring to a section of the Gotha Program of the German Workers Party that asserted the "equal right" of all members of society to "the proceeds of labor."

5. The Second General Conference of Latin American Bishops, organized by the Latin American Episcopal Council (CELAM), took place in 1968 in Medellín, Colombia. The bishops, in reflecting on how the teachings of Vatican II would apply to Latin America, produced a collection of documents that greatly helped to spread and popularize liberation theology in the region.

6. Noam Chomsky and Edward Herman, whose work was included in Assmann's collection, meticulously evidenced the trends that "should be obvious to any student of recent third world history" (Chomsky and Herman 1977, 29–31). Both before and during Carter's presidency, the distressingly persistent results of U.S. involvement were an increase in the numbers of human rights abuses and of political prisoners. These increases, furthermore, had a suspicious correspondence with the development of a more "favorable climate" for business investment. Liberationists charged that the United States maintained its repressive activities in Latin America during Carter's administration but masked them with the language of human rights.

7. One notable exception (which is very perceptive, if cursory) is Berryman 1987, 111–24; also notable is the earlier substantial analysis in Berryman 1984, 320–30.

8. Now widely used, the concept of rights evolving in successive "generations" can be attributed to Vasak 1982. Civil and political claims constitute a first generation of human rights; social and economic entitlements, a second; and cultural or "solidarity" rights, a third.

9. It is worth noting that Segundo himself points to a separate role of human rights as "human ideals," paralleling a traditional distinction in rights theory between moral rights, which are the just claims of a person or group, and legal rights, which are actualized by the force of law. We are, therefore, left to speculate about other uses of rights that would transcend a limited legalistic program.

10. Marx originally developed the concept in "The German Ideology" (Marx 1994, 102–56).

11. See Huber 1979 for an outline of the different "guarantee procedures" that separate first-generation and second-generation rights.

12. The Chilean Catholic Church is held up as the clearest example of an institution that follows this pattern, and it is repeatedly condemned in Assmann's collection. In Segundo's words, "paradoxically, but also symptomatically, the very Chilean episcopate that had been the most explicit and incisive in refusing the historical option [for the poor], is now perhaps the most committed to the defense of human rights" (Segundo 1978/1993, 65).

13. Agency is invoked here in the sense of who will be the agents of social change and philosophical production. Thus, this discussion of agency should not be confused with the examination of agency in the work of philosopher Alan Gewirth or "will theorists" of rights, who ground human rights in the broader sphere of human action. Further exploration of these different uses of "agency" may be an interesting project, but it is outside the scope of this article. In general, concern with the class status or social position of those who would implement human rights policy seems foreign to mainstream, and especially liberal, rights theory.

14. Indeed, the most forceful liberationist statement on the cultural issues involved in the international use of human rights discourse comes from one working to develop an Asian theology of liberation; see Pieris 1989.

15. During the 1980s there remained a number of notable exceptions, including movements in Nicaragua and El Salvador. However, this trend continued and was strongly confirmed during the following decade, especially with the end of Soviet communism and the fall of the Eastern bloc.

16. For an excellent analysis of the changing power dynamics within the Latin American Catholic Church, see Smith 1991.

17. Medellín 1968/1990, par. 22, 27; see also Assmann 1994, 72; Puebla 1979, par. 1217; Boff 1988, 63–64 and references, par. 320, 324, 711, and 1119.

18. Boff's thought on rights has evolved considerably. Although his essay "Rights of the Poor: Rights of God" showed little appreciation of earlier critiques, his more recent "El Dios defensor de los derechos del pobre" offers a more thorough review of potential pitfalls (Boff 1988; Boff 1989/1993). It is also important to note the diversity within expressions of the rights of the poor, and appropriations range from the explicitly Marxist "Derechos de los Pueblos" document (Assmann [ed.] 1978, 2:471–75) to the more conservative affirmations written at Puebla.

19. This particular formulation of liberation theology's consistent solidarity with the poor achieved prominence when adopted as part of the official document produced at Puebla in 1979. For

significant primary articles on the preferential option for the poor, see Gutiérrez 1993; Boff and Elizondo 1986.

20. Indeed, liberation theologians have especially developed the theme of idolatry in terms of the marketplace. Assmann's recent thought on human rights evaluates the relevance of the "cry of the poor" to an idolized economic god that is deaf to this cry (Assmann 1994).

21. Though I focus on the theologically conceived option here, Boff elsewhere chronicles the "christo-logical, eschatological, apostolic, and ecclesiological" foundations of a preference (see Boff and Boff 1987, 44–46).

22. See Gutiérrez 1987, 101–3, for a prominent liberationist attempt to reckon with the question of theodicy, asserting "a right to complain and protest" for "those who suffer unjustly" and identifying denunciation of abuses as a crucial Christian prerogative. See Sobrino 1985 for a more explicit discussion of the power of human rights language to reveal the character of God.

REFERENCES

Aldunate, José, et al., eds. 1993. *Derechos humanos, derechos de los pobres.* 1989. Theology and Liberation Series. Santiago, Chile: Rehue.

Assmann, Hugo, 1975. *Theology for a Nomad Church.* 1973. Translated by Paul Burns. Introduction by Frederick Herzog (copyright 1976). Maryknoll, N.Y.: Orbis. This translation was published in Great Britain as *Practical Theology of Liberation.* London: Search Press.

———. 1994. "El clamor de los pobres en America Latine y El Caribe." In *Economía y religión,* 61–100. San José, Costa Rica: DEI (Departamento Ecuménico de Investigaciones).

Assmann, Hugo, ed. 1978. *Carter y la lógica del imperialismo.* 2 vols. San José, Costa Rica: EDUCA (Editorial Universitaria Centro Americana).

Berryman, Phillip, 1984. *The Religious Roots of Rebellion: Christians in Central American Revolutions.* Maryknoll, N.Y.: Orbis.

———. 1987. *Liberation Theology: Essential Facts about the Revolutionary Movement in Latin America—and Beyond.* Philadelphia, Pa.: Temple University Press.

Boff, Leonardo, 1985. *Church, Charism and Power: Liberation Theology and the Institutional Church.* Trans-lated by John W. Diercksmeier. New York: Crossroad.

———. 1988. "Rights of the Poor: Rights of God." In *When Theology Listens to the Poor.* Translated by Robert R. Barr, 50–64. Cambridge, Mass.: Harper and Row.

———. 1993. "El Dios defensor de los derechos del pobre." 1989. See Aldunate, et al., 1993, 84–100.

Boff, Leonardo, and Clodovis Boff, 1987. *Introducing Liberation Theology.* Translated by Paul Burns. Maryknoll, N.Y.: Orbis.

Boff, Leonardo, and Virgil Elizondo, 1986. "Editorial: Theology from the Viewpoint of the Poor." In *Option for the Poor: Challenge to the Rich Countries,* Concilium Series, vol. 187, ix–xii. Nijimegen, Holland: Stichting Concilium.

Chomsky, Noam, and Edward S. Herman, 1977. "The United States versus Human Rights in the Third World." *Monthly Review* 29, no. 3 (July/August): 22–45.

Comblin, José, 1990. "Person and Body." In *Retrieving the Human,* 44–58. Maryknoll, N.Y.: Orbis.

———. 1992. "The Church and Defense of Human Rights." In *The Church in Latin America, 1492–1992,* edited by Enrique Dussel, 435–54. Maryknoll, N.Y.: Orbis.

Congregation for the Doctrine of the Faith, 1984. "Instruction on Certain Aspects of Liberation Theol-ogy." *National Catholic Reporter,* September 21.

———. 1986. "Instruction on Christian Freedom and Liberation." Origins: NC Documentary Service 15 (April 17): 713–28.

Cooper, John, 1988. "Liberation Theology, Human Rights, and U.S. Security." In *The Politics of Latin American Liberation Theology,* edited by Richard L. Rubenstein and John K. Roth, 288–305. Washington, D.C.: The Washington Institute Press.

Crossette, Barbara, 1998. "Kofi Annan's Astonishing Facts!" *New York Times,* September 27, sec. 4.

Dussel, Enrique D., 1985. *Philosophy of Liberation*. Translated by Aquilina Martinez and Christine Morkovsky. 1980. Maryknoll, N.Y.: Orbis.

Ellacuría, Ignacio, 1982. "Human Rights in a Divided Society." See Hennelly and Langan 1982, 52–65.

———. 1990. "Historización de los derechos humanos desde los pueblos oprimidos y las mayorías populares." *Estudios Centroamericanos* 45, no. 502 (August): 589–96.

———. 1991. "The Historicization of the Concept of Property." Translated by Phillip Berryman. See Hassett and Lacey 1991, 105–37.

Garrett, William, 1988. "Liberation Theology and the Concept of Human Rights." In *The Politics of Religion and Social Change*, edited by Anson Shupe and Jeffrey Hadden, 128–40. New York: Paragon House.

Guevara, Ernesto, 1968. "Man and Socialism in Cuba." In *Venceremos! The Speeches and Writings of Ernesto Che Guevara*, edited by John Gerassi. New York: Macmillan.

Gutiérrez, Gustavo, 1983. *The Power of the Poor in History*. Translated by Robert R. Barr. Maryknoll, N.Y.: Orbis.

———. 1987. *On Job: God-talk and the Suffering of the Innocent*. Translated by Matthew J. O'Connell. Maryknoll, N.Y.: Orbis.

———. 1988. *A Theology of Liberation: History, Politics, and Salvation*. 1971. Translated and edited by Caridad Inda and John Eagleson. Maryknoll, N.Y.: Orbis.

———. 1993. "Option for the Poor." In *Mysterium liberationis: Fundamental Concepts of Liberation Theology*, edited by Jon Sobrino and Ignacio Ellacuría, 235–50. Maryknoll, N.Y.: Orbis.

Hassett, John, and Hugh Lacey, 1991. "Introduction: Comprehending Reality from the Perspective of the Poor." See Hassett and Lacey 1991, 1–15.

Hassett, John, and Hugh Lacey, eds., 1991. *Towards a Society that Serves Its People: The Intellectual Contribution of El Salvador's Murdered Jesuits*. Washington, D.C.: Georgetown University Press.

Haughey, John, 1982. "Individualism and Rights in Karl Marx." See Hennelly and Langan 1982, 102–41.

Hennelly, Alfred T., 1989. *Theology for a Liberating Church*. Washington, D.C.: Georgetown University Press.

Hennelly, Alfred, ed. and trans., 1990. *Liberation Theology: A Documentary History*. Maryknoll, N.Y.: Orbis.

Hennelly, Alfred, and John Langan, eds., 1982. *Human Rights in the Americas: The Struggle for Consensus*. Washington, D.C.: Georgetown University Press.

Hinkelammert, Franz, 1986. *The Ideological Weapons of Death*. 1977. Maryknoll, N.Y.: Orbis.

———. 1995. *Cultura de la esperanza: Una sociedad sin exclusión*. San José, Costa Rica: DEI.

Hollenbach, David, 1979. *Claims in Conflict*. New York: Paulist Press.

———. 1982. "Global Human Rights: An Interpretation of the Contemporary Catholic Understanding." See Hennelly and Langan 1982, 9–24.

Huber, Wolfgang, 1979. "Human Rights—A Concept and Its History." Translated by Martin Kitchen. See Müller and Greinacher (eds.) 1979, 1–9.

John XXIII, 1963. *Pacem in Terris* (Peace on Earth). Encyclical letter. Washington, D.C.: United States Catholic Conference.

Johnstone, Brian, 1989. "Human Rights, Justice and Theology." In *Culture, Human Rights, and Peace in Central America*, edited by George McLean, et al., 193–208. Lanham, Md.: University Press of America.

Marx, Karl, 1994. *Selected Writings*, edited by Simon Lawrence. Indianapolis, Ind.: Hackett.

McGovern, Arthur, 1989. *Liberation Theology and Its Critics*. Maryknoll, N.Y.: Orbis.

[Medellín] Second General Conference of Latin American Bishops, 1990. "Document on Peace." 1968. See Hennelly (ed.) 1990, 106–14.

Míguez Bonino, José, 1975. *Doing Theology in a Revolutionary Situation*. Philadelphia, Pa.: Fortress.

———. 1976. *Christians and Marxists: The Mutual Challenge to Revolution*. Grand Rapids, Mich.: Eerdmans.

———. 1977. "Whose Human Rights?" *International Review of Mission* 66: 220–24.

Miranda, José Porfirio, 1974. *Marx and the Bible: A Critique of the Philosophy of Oppression*. Translated by John Eagleson. Maryknoll, N.Y.: Orbis.

————. 1980. *Marx against the Marxists: The Christian Humanism of Karl Marx.* Translated by John Drury. Maryknoll, N.Y.: Orbis.

Müller, Alois, and Norbert Greinacher, 1979. "Editorial." See Müller and Greinacher (eds.) 1979, vii–x.

Müller, Alois, and Norbert Greinacher, eds., 1979. *The Church and the Rights of Man.* Concilium Series, vol. 124. New York: Seabury; Edinburgh: T & T Clark, Ltd.; Nijmegen, Holland: Stichting Concilium.

Petras, James, 1977. "President Carter and the 'New Morality.'" *Monthly Review* 29, no. 2 (June): 43.

Pieris, Aloysius, 1989. "Human Rights Language and Liberation Theology." In *The Future of Liberation Theology,* edited by Marc Ellis and Otto Maduro, 299–310. Maryknoll, N.Y.: Orbis.

Pope, Stephen, 1993. "Proper and Improper Partiality in the Preferential Option for the Poor." *Theological Studies* 54, no. 1: 242–71.

[Puebla] Third General Conference of the Latin American Episcopate, 1979. "Evangelization in Latin America's Present and Future." In *Puebla and Beyond,* edited by John Eagleson and Philip Scharper, translated by John Drury, 122–285. Maryknoll, N.Y.: Orbis.

Railton, Peter, 1995. "Ideology." In *The Oxford Companion to Philosophy,* edited by Ted Honderich, 392–93. Oxford: Oxford University Press.

Segundo, Juan Luis, 1976. *Liberation of Theology.* Translated by John Drury. Maryknoll, N.Y.: Orbis.

————. 1993. "Human Rights, Evangelization, and Ideology." 1978. Translated by Alfred T. Hennelly. In *Signs of the Times: Theological Reflections,* 53–66. Maryknoll, N.Y.: Orbis.

Smith, Christian, 1991. *The Emergence of Liberation Theology.* Chicago: University of Chicago Press.

Sobrino, Jon, 1985. "Lo divino de los derechos humanos." *Diakonía* 9, no. 33 (March): 38–51.

————. 1998. Interview by author. San Salvador, 22 August.

Undurraga, Joaquín, 1993. "El derecho de los pobres a la igualidad." 1989. See Aldunate, et al., 1993, 123–27.

United Nations Development Programme (UNDP), 1999. "A Balance Sheet of Human Development, 1990–1997." In *Human Development Report 1999.* New York: Oxford University Press.

United Nations General Assembly, 1948. Universal Declaration of Human Rights. Adopted December 10. Text annexed to U.N. General Assembly Resolution 217 (III).

Vasak, Karel, 1982. *The International Dimensions of Human Rights.* Westport, Conn.: Greenwood.

Villela, Hugo, 1978. "La defensa de los derechos humanos como 'solidaridad' con los oprimidos." See Assmann (ed.) 1978, 2: 381–407.

"The Martyrs' Living Witness: A Call to Honor and Challenge"

Daniel Berrigan

Daniel Berrigan, prolific poet and essayist, was trained in the Society of Jesus and ordained in 1952. Since the 1960s he has worked tirelessly and bravely for civil rights, nuclear disarmament, and social justice, and he has frequently been jailed for civil disobedience. Here he describes the moral and spiritual implications of the murder of church activists in El Salvador.

In San Salvador, on the 16th of November 1989, as is known around the world, six Jesuit priests, together with their cook and her daughter, were dragged from their beds and murdered. The event was hardly unforeseen or even unchosen by the priests.

For at least four years, they had dwelt under the livid threat that at length broke through their doors and called in a debt of blood. At one point several years ago, an ultimatum was issued against them; 30 days to leave the country or be killed. They chose to remain and take their chances. The word of the Spirit, one concludes, was: Remain.

Instead of leaving, the Jesuits sent a modest appeal to their brothers around the world. Please be apprised of our predicament. Please come if possible to El Salvador. International attention is our only hope. A slight interference, the presence of outsiders, might, just might, delay discharge of guns already cocked and aimed.

It was at this point that another New York Jesuit and I resolved to go. In the course of our visit, we met all those who were subsequently murdered. It occurred to me at the time that it might also be useful to publish a small account of the journey, of the friendships we formed, of the dangers and complications of life in that tormented country. I did so. But nothing we could do availed, as we were to learn to our horror and grief.

The reality of the situation of the Jesuits required neither drama nor dramaturge. Day after day, year after year, as the guns resounded to and fro like mad metronomes, the mortal danger wherein the priests stood—what form the end might take—could hardly have been made more vivid to them. Certainly not by their unclairvoyant visitors from *el Norte*.

The priests had no need of a drama, a play within their play. Why should someone seize the cincture of one among them, bind himself over, and so declare their plight? The Spirit, one might conclude, had spoken to them; a circuit of doom and glory bound them, each to each. One in life and work and consequence: Remain.

Agabus declared through the symbolic binding certain boundaries of knowledge of the future and its form (Acts 21:10–11). The prospective binding of Paul could only signify the drastic curtailing, if not the end, of his extraordinary mission. The response of the community to this dire likelihood is a spontaneous outcry, it is beyond bearing that Paul be taken prisoner. Yet again, friends are appalled. They beg him to stay free, while he is yet able, from bonds whose very prospect is a throttling of hope.

And he will not. He will counter their dread by introducing a larger, more awful threat and embracing that. "Why these tears, why try to weaken my resolution? I am ready not only to be bound, but to die in Jerusalem for the name of the Lord Jesus" (Acts 21:13).

What friend willingly consents in mind to the suffering of a friend, no matter the nobility of the cause? The office of friendship, we think, is to act counter to intemperate heroism. And in discharging that office with all one's might, as the heart drums insistently, the friend acts all the more nobly. Friendship cries in protest, weakens, warns, declares null and void the hot will of the one who runs to death. "Let this cross be far from you."

The outburst of Peter in the face of Jesus' announcement of his death—so heartfelt and altruistic, so right (and so wrong), so in accord with the heart's deep welling, so weakening and delaying what must be—is coldly received, perceived only as an assault on invincible will. And it is rejected in tones brusque, final, scandalous: "Stand aside, Satan."

Thus the friend, protesting, impeding, standing athwart, is locked in combat with the beloved one. "Simon, son of John, do you love me?" Friendship, and then vocation. How shall a sedulous friend resolve the dilemma? How do we stand with the other, and still pay respect to the friend's vocation?

The solution is hardly a relief, it is a multiplying of sorrow. It implies agreement with the determination of a friend, that he go where he must go, where he is quite literally and beforehand "bound." And then the new agreement is sealed in blood. It is the blood of an all but unimaginable pact.

The friend imagines, then leaps the void that lies between friendship and vocation. It is quite simple and final. He joins his friend in death. "In very truth I tell you, . . . when you are old you will stretch out your arms and a stranger will bind you fast and bring you where you have no wish to go" (John 21:18).

They all came to this in the early gathering. One, their friend, preceded them; the others were tardy, but eventually grew hardy in purpose. It was a gathering of death and rising from death.

"So, as Paul would not be dissuaded, we gave in and said, 'The Lord's will be done. . . .'" (Acts 21:14). Now we have something more than friendship, as the world would understand it. We have a community standing on the shore, not in farewell but in an accompanying spirit. The wind in his sails bears them along in a gale; all are bent on the same errand, the journey toward Jerusalem. Friend and friends, they are bound over. They stretch forth their hands and feet in one direction. More, they bend their necks to Paul's will, "To die in Jerusalem for the name of the Lord Jesus."

The members are well advised not to doubt the worst, to embrace the darkness of their own foreboding. And this for Paul's sake, that he not go alone on his dolorous way. And for their own also. The journey is theirs, and the binding over; and eventually, in likely prospect, the martyrdom as well.

The martyrs test the church. The church knows itself, which is to say it has mapped its journey toward Jerusalem and calculated the consequence of the journey. But this only insofar as it knows, embraces, honors, exonerates the martyrs.

This attitude and activity in regard to our own can only be called crucial. It implies at the same time that the church rejects the ideology which the state invariably, for its own perverse delight and to cover its crimes, attaches to the believers whom it marks for martyrdom. This is an insulting tag attached to a noble corpse: ideologue, or troublesome priest, or disturber of public order.

Thus the sequence: The state executes the martyrs, then denigrates their deaths behind a meticulous (or foolish) scrim of duplicity and doubt.

It was thus in the case of Jesus. He must not only die, but Roman law must be vindicated in his death (and he dishonored, his memory smirched) by charges of subversion, threats of destruction of the temple, endangerment of law and order.

In his death we have something more shameful even. We have the classic instance of religion abandoning the martyr, joining the vile secular chorus of dishonor. Worse and worse, it supplies out of its own foxy canons a philistine logic to conceal its implication in the crime: "One of them, Caiaphas, who was high priest that year, said, 'You have no grasp at all of the situation; you do not realize this: It is more to your interest that one man should die for the people than that the whole nation should be destroyed. . . .'" (John 11:49–50).

Martyrdom is included in the church's catechesis, for the church knows why martyrs die, and says so. More, in certain circumstances, the church makes it clear that such death is the only honorable witness and outcome.

Then, their deaths accomplished, the church's task continues. It raises them to the altar for holy emulation. For they are, after Christ and Mary, the church's chief glory. The church knows it and at least sometimes says it boldly, sternly defending the martyrs. The defense is risky. Often guns again are lowered, the terror continues, and others are placed at danger. The mere declaration of how and why the martyrs perished heightens the immemorial struggle between the church and the worldly powers—a struggle that the martyrs personify to the highest and noblest degree.

In San Salvador as elsewhere, noble tongues are silenced, but the truth must continue to be told. The truth of their death, the cruelty and injustice of it, the precious connection between their death and the integrity of the gospel. This is judgment, the heavy tolling, not of a passing bell, but a presentiment of the last day itself. The bell tolls for the defeat here and now of the violent victors, for the triumph of the victims.

The martyrs, all said, have stood surrogate for Christ and the church. Their crime is their firm withstanding on behalf of an irresistible word of love. In this they have spoken for the whole body of Christ.

Then, death accomplished, their community takes up the task, not solely to justify the innocent death, nor to seek justice. That's an impossible task in most cases, since the unjust and violent sit also in the courts. The task is otherwise: to confront the powers with judgment and a call to repentance. Even murderers, and the powers that impel them, must be salvaged. Even those who are furthest from the saving truth, from the mercy and compassion they have sought to extinguish.

This is the consonance between church and martyr: the martyr standing witness for the church, the church vindicating and honoring the martyr.

An ordination photo of Father Ellacuria, murdered Jesuit of El Salvador, shows him vested, prostrate on the sanctuary floor while the litany of saints is chanted over the new priests. A photo dated Thursday, November 16, 1989, shows Father Ellacuria murdered, prostrate outside the Jesuit house. He is in exactly the position of his ordination rite.

The church from time to time (and wondrously in our own time) earns the name church of martyrs. It does not mean, obviously, that all the faithful perish, it signifies the living consonance between the witness of those who die and those who survive. Both speak up, both pay dearly; some in blood, some in the bearing of infamy and danger.

This continuing burden of truth telling is, it would seem (and here one speaks with trepidation), mainly a matter laid upon the local church. The situation could hardly be called ideal. When the highest authorities of the church refuse to vindicate our martyrs, and thus refuse to confront the powers clearly and unequivocally, only the local community of faith can supply for the moral deficit.

The situation implies a kind of vexed and sorrowful logic. A given community has nourished the faith of the martyr with word and sacrament. A kind of holy ampelopsis has joined the holy one to the body of Christ. It seems only fitting (though regrettable as well) that after death, both the good repute of the martyr and the continuing witness against the powers should lie in the hands of those (invariably the poor) who survive and mourn. Let the great be silent, or mouth platitudes, or introduce absurd political innuendo. It is the humble who know, who speak; their tears are eloquent.

In the great world, and the great worldly church, other concerns are in the air. The blood and torment are distant. They are carried on the airwaves and tubes, a phenomenon known fatuously as "international news." There the images of the dead are seized, impeded, manipulated, shuffled about.

Add to this the political and economic interests of ecclesiastical headquarters. Suppose for a moment (one need not suppose!) that those who died perished for speaking on behalf of inarticulate, powerless Christians and others. Their deaths occurred in a minor, indeed inconsiderable, land, worlds distant from the highly "developed" church and its special concern and interest in the "developed" superstates.

The situation does not invite moral clarity. A conclusion is reached in exalted circles (and this in fact is the rub) that the murdered Christians defended no recondite or required dogma. They did not die for the integrity of, say, the doctrine of Eucharist, the virginity of Mary, the bodily resurrection of Christ. A mutter is heard from influential lips. The victims died in a politically volatile situation; it is reported that they took sides, that they were defenders of one ideology or another.

It could be conceded perhaps that they died for the sake of the powerless and poor. But this hardly suffices to grant them the entitlement of martyrs. So it is thought and said. Or is not said, but the silence wears a frown of thunder.

Let us be as clear as might be. Innumerable sisters and brothers have died in our lifetime for the sake of the powerless and poor. Let us think in consequence of this of a scriptural teaching baptized again and again in a sea of blood. A teaching, let it be added, generally neglected in high ecclesiastical circles—the teaching of the body of Christ.

Paul writes of the mutuality and integrity of all members of the body, the consonance of the lowliest with the most honored. "So that there might be no division in the body, but that all its parts might feel concern for one another. If one part suffers, all suffer together; if one flourishes, all rejoice together" (I Corinthians 12:25–26).

Bishops and others, we beg you, take notice of this passion for the integrity of the body, this rejection of the rejection of the lowly. Behold the scripture on behalf of which a host of martyrs in your lifetime and mine have staked their lives.

In the face of the ambivalent speech (and the even more ambivalent silence) of authorities, the harmless pieties, the intertwining of profane and church interests, are we not justified in insisting that those appointed to speak for the universal church speak clearly, passionately, in defense of our martyrs? That they clarify issues of faithful political witness, that their words resound with the same truth that at a crack of gunfire turned mortal bodies to pentecostal flame?

This is unpleasant and, to the mind of many, unfortunate; and, all said, true. Faith is a political matter, inevitably. So is martyrdom, in most cases. The task is to separate out, in mind and heart, the political content of a given death (one's dying for the poor, who themselves are joined to political parties of revolution, thus means taking sides). This political implication must be separated from another lurking issue—that of ideology: high and low, ecclesiastical or secular; the itch and appetite of special interest pursuits, hankerings; and, above all, the appetite for power, control, secrecy, nonaccountability.

Thus the death of the martyrs urges a scrutiny of conscience on the part of all. This includes a self-scrutiny of authority, of its ideology and behavior—especially an ideology that inhibits speaking the truth concerning the murder of our sons and daughters, the honor and dishonor of their deaths.

Let us, for Christ's sake, hear loud and clear, let the assassins hear, and let the faceless politicos and oligarchs hear why our martyrs stood where they did ("the standpoint is the viewpoint"), why in consequence they, known and anonymous, were eliminated. Let us hear praise of the martyrs. Let us hear an unambiguous call to the faithful, that the holy dead be emulated by the living.

IMITATING THE MARTYRS: VOICES FOR PEACE

A Call to Action

I remember the living quarters of the murdered Jesuit priests and the two women—the blood-stained walls, the shattered glass, the bullet holes in the concrete walls. The blood-stained floors of the individual rooms were a stark contrast to the sitting room of the living area, where rocking chairs still encircled a table that held cups of unfinished coffee and ashtrays with crushed-out cigarette butts, representing an evening of conversation and closing evening prayer.

For me, it was in those moments of hearing the detailed story of the night of murder and violence that the impact of those eight murders—and the 75,000 other murders—finally was stored in my heart and soul.

I'd seen death, pain, and destruction in many other situations; but this, in a place of peace broken by the horror of evil, was once again a reminder of people's inhumanity to people. Yet it was also a reminder of the incredible power of the gospel message of freedom and liberation.

As I struggled to control the throbbing in my heart, someone showed me one of the bullets that investigators had found at the site—and on it was stamped "Made in the U.S.A."

Maybe it was later, or maybe it was at that moment, but I was struck by the depth of responsibility that we as U.S. citizens and as U.S. churches carry in this bloody conflict—and the need for us as church people to call for repentance for our complicity in the ongoing terror, death, and destruction of the Salvadoran people.

It is a call that comes from the understanding that out of the depths of great pain and human destruction come life, celebration, and salvation. Yet often when we in the First World call for repentance, we repent, we weep, we are sorrowful; and just as quickly we move on to celebration and salvation. We often forget the final step which is the call to action.

At a commemoration service for the martyred, which also marked the first time the ecumenical community in El Salvador had been together since the deaths of the Jesuits and the women, I heard stories of persecution interwoven with words of hope and celebration. After all the moving stories and uplifting music, a teen-age woman representing the youth of the Lutheran Church in El Salvador got up and said, "All has been said, all stories have been told. I cannot tell any more, but I do have one final reflection. I have learned and believe the words 'Do not weep for the martyrs, but rather imitate them.'"

It is these simple words that are a call to action for us. This is our call in the United States to become witnesses for the martyred, our opportunity to imitate them, to imitate the witness of the churches in El Salvador.

We need to be clear to our government officials so that they know that the religious community does not define itself by national boundaries, and that the persecution of one body of the community is felt by the whole. It's as if we were all under that persecution.

Now is the time. We—the powerful religious communities of the North—are called to be imitators of the prophetic churches serving the poor in the South. We are called to use all of our resources to stop our country from supplying military aid, and call for a politically negotiated settlement.

We are called to use all of our resources to speak out against the persecution of the church, to demand that justice be served in violations of human rights and the innocent deaths of thousands. We are called, as imitators of our brothers and sisters in El Salvador, to accompany them whenever they ask and whenever is needed.

The question for us, my friends, is, Are we ready to repent and be forgiven? For, indeed, it is in that forgiveness that we are free to respond to this call for action.

—Christine Grumm

Christine Grumm, vice president of the Evangelical Lutheran Church of America, accompanied Lutheran Bishop Medardo Gomez on a trip to El Salvador in January 1990. This reflection was offered at a convocation of U.S. and Salvadoran religious leaders in Washington, D.C., on January 23, 1990.

The Promise of the Resurrection

I am daily inspired by the words of a Salvadoran friend and union leader. I asked him once if he never felt despair, never felt like giving up. After some thought he turned to me and said, "No, Karen; because despair is a First World luxury."

It is our responsibility as the world's wealthy, my friend Oscar pointed out, not to despair, but to have the sufficient imagination to walk in the struggle with our brothers and sisters for whom justice is an issue of life and death. Not to give up until they do—and they will never give up. For they know that justice is inevitable, that unjust structures cannot forever withstand a people's hunger for freedom and dignity.

We of the First World are simply left with a choice: We can turn our backs and walk away from a challenge, or we can have the imagination to walk with the Salvadorans to the end of their struggle.

Our presence may bring that closer and lessen the suffering and the blood spilled. But with or without us, it is inevitable—that *is* the promise of the resurrection.

—Karen Ridd

Karen Ridd, a Canadian volunteer for Peace Brigades International in El Salvador, was deported from the country after being picked up during a November raid on a church shelter by Salvadorian security forces.

Go and Tell Them. . . .

The persecution against the church became very strong after the rebel offensive began in November, but many church leaders who had been targeted did not want to leave our country. The experience of being away makes us very sad, because we are very far away from our people.

We resisted having to leave. But it was even our own people that came to us and begged us to leave. They said, "Save your life; we need you later." But probably what convinced us most is when they said, "Go and tell people in the United States our message: We beg of you, we want peace."

On another occasion I visited the refugee camp of Mesa Grande in Honduras. Our brothers and sisters had prepared a great reception, with large banners that read: "Welcome Bishop Gomez. We want peace."

I asked the brothers and sisters at Mesa Grande, "Why do you ask me to bring peace if I am not the one to bring peace?" But they said, "No, you can bring us peace."

I said, "I don't know how to do that. Tell me, what can I do to bring peace?" And they said, "You can travel, Brother Gomez. You can travel to the United States. Go there and tell our brothers and sisters that we want peace."

Peace in our country means simply the following: No to the military aid. Peace in our country means a more humane policy than the current U.S. policy. And this peace can be constructed with your accompaniment.

Peace means that delegations of your groups would come to El Salvador, that you would become closer to us, more knowledgeable of our reality. Peace means all of the prayer and the solidarity actions that you carry out for us.

I am very grateful to God for each one of you. The Bible, the Word of God, continues to be written. And the scripture is written with all of the solidarity actions that are carried out on our behalf. May God bless you, brothers and sisters, for your great love.

—Medardo Gomez

Medardo Gomez, bishop of the Salvadoran Lutheran Church, was forced into exile last November. This reflection was offered at a convocation of U.S. and Salvadoran religious leaders in Washington, D.C., on January 23, 1990.

We Have Right on Our Side

We are a hard-working people, and our children deserve a better today and a much better tomorrow. Yet our rivers, our lakes, and our mountains are stained with blood.

We are a people who want liberty, who want an authentic democracy. We are against the forces of death, and we want a truly prosperous country that we construct with the work of all. For all these reasons, my brothers and sisters, in the name of the Salvadoran people, and in the name of our Lord Jesus Christ, I urge you to continue your struggle together until we have peace with social justice in El Salvador.

Until we tear down and destroy that position which has been shown to have failed over the last 10 years—the position of a military victory—we must turn to the only possible alternative. Now with moral strength, with all that we are, we say no more war. We want negotiation, and we want peace.

And that, beloved brothers and sisters, we will achieve as one part of the body of Christ; because we have right on our side. This is what we believe, because we believe that the reign of God has come down, through the efforts of the Lord and through our own efforts. Let us continue on in the struggle.

—Edgar Palacios

Edgar Palacios is pastor of Shalom Baptist church in San Salvador and the coordinator of the Permanent Commission of the National Debate for Peace in El Salvador. This reflection was offered at a vigil of U.S. and Salvadoran religious leaders on the steps of the U.S. Capitol on January 29, 1990.

Those Who Long for Peace

Peace should not be left in the hands of those for whom party interests are more important than the needs of the people, but should be in the hands of those who truly long for peace. We need a humanization of peace.

We need to work for peace from the perspective of the suffering of the orphans and widows, and the tragedy of the assassinated and disappeared. We must keep our eyes on the God of Jesus Christ, the God of life, the God of the poor, and not on the idols, or the gods of death, that devour everything.

More compelling than spoken words, the reality of El Salvador—the 75,000 dead, the 7,000 disappeared, the widows and the orphans, the 1.5 million displaced people and refugees, and the millions of impoverished Salvadorans—cries out for peace.

—Ignacio Ellacuría

Ignacio Ellacuria, the rector of the Central American University in San Salvador, was one of the six Jesuit priests murdered by Salvadoran armed forces in November. These comments were made at a march for peace in San Salvador on March 4, 1989, and are included in El Salvador: A Spring Whose Waters Never Run Dry.

All of Us Can Do Something

We have been told by the faithful of El Salvador to weep no more, and instead to imitate the actions of the martyrs. And yet we've discovered that sometimes we cannot stop the tears.

At times like this, we remember not only our brothers and sisters who have lost their lives, but those who are being deprived of freedom right now. Parish workers from my community were tortured for 15 days at the hands of the security forces before they were allegedly handed over to the civil judiciary system.

While President Cristiani talks about a judicial system in El Salvador that works, in reference to the case of the murdered Jesuits, hundreds and hundreds of political prisoners in El Salvador right now are outside of any legal system. They have never been charged. So part of our weeping is not only for those deceased, those who have been murdered, but for those who continue to suffer in the prisons and the barrios of El Salvador.

To those of you who have seen the pain of the Salvadoran people, you cannot wait until the tears are no more; you march with your tears. You don't wait until you have conquered your fear; you walk with the fear. You don't wait until the anger has subsided; you speak with the anger.

The day that he was assassinated, Archbishop Oscar Romero, in his last sermon, spoke at a memorial service for a woman who had died the previous year. In that service he told stories about what this simple woman had done. And then he said, "All of us can do something."

Whether this day we are doing civil disobedience, speaking with truth and anger to congressional representatives, praying and fasting, or writing still another letter—all of us can do something; all of us can do something; all of us can do something.

—Jim Barnett

Jim Barnett, a Dominican priest, served four and a half years in a parish of displaced people near San Salvador. He left the country last November under threat of death. This reflection was offered at a vigil of U.S. and Salvadoran religious leaders on the U.S. Capitol steps on January 23, 1990.

from *Gaudium et Spes: Pastoral Constitution on the Church in the Modern World*[1]

❧

Second Vatican Council, 1965

The Second Vatican Council opened under Pope John XXIII in 1962 and was closed by Pope Paul VI in 1965. Its goal was to bring the church up to the demands of the modern world, and it has long been identified with an increase in Catholic commitment to ecumenism and social justice.

❧

PREFACE

The Intimate Bond between the Church and Mankind

1. The joys and the hopes, the griefs and the anxieties of the men of this age, especially those who are poor or in any way afflicted, these too are the joys and hopes, the griefs and anxieties of the followers of Christ. Indeed, nothing genuinely human fails to raise an echo in their hearts. For theirs is a community composed of men. United in Christ, they are led by the Holy Spirit in their journey to the kingdom of their Father and they have welcomed the news of salvation which is meant for every man. That is why this community realizes that it is truly and intimately linked with mankind and its history.

For Whom This Message Is Intended

2. Hence this Second Vatican Council, having probed more profoundly into the mystery of the Church, now addresses itself without hesitation, not only to the sons of the Church, and to all who invoke the name of Christ, but to the whole of humanity. For the Council yearns to explain to everyone how it conceives of the presence and activity of the Church in the world of today.

Therefore, the Council focuses its attention on the world of men, the whole human family along with the sum of those realities in the midst of which that family lives. It gazes upon that world which is the theater of man's history, and carries the marks of his energies, his tragedies, and his triumphs; that world which the Christian sees as created and sustained by its Maker's love, fallen indeed into the bondage of sin, yet emancipated now by Christ. He was crucified and rose again to break the stranglehold of personified Evil, so that this world might be fashioned anew according to God's design and reach its fulfillment.

The Service to Be Offered to Humanity

3. Though mankind today is struck with wonder at its own discoveries and its power, it often raises anxious questions about the current trend of the world, about the place and role of man in the universe, about the meaning of his individual and collective strivings, and about the ultimate destiny of reality and of humanity. Hence, giving witness and voice to the faith of the whole People of God gathered together by Christ, this Council can provide no more eloquent proof of its solidarity with the entire human family with which it is bound up, as well as its respect and love for that family, than by engaging with it in conversation about these various problems.

The Council brings to mankind light kindled from the gospel, and puts at its disposal those saving resources which the Church herself, under the guidance of the Holy Spirit, receives from her Founder. For the human person deserves to be preserved; human society deserves to be renewed. Hence the pivotal point of our total presentation will be man himself, whole and entire, body and soul, heart and conscience, mind and will.

Therefore, this sacred synod proclaims the highest destiny of man and champions the godlike seed which has been sown in him. It offers to mankind the honest assistance of the Church in fostering that brotherhood of all men which corresponds to this destiny of theirs. Inspired by no earthly ambition, the Church seeks but a solitary goal: to carry forward the work of Christ himself under the lead of the befriending Spirit. And Christ entered this world to give witness to the truth, to rescue and not to sit in judgment, to serve and not to be served.[2]

INTRODUCTORY STATEMENT: THE SITUATION OF MEN IN THE MODERN WORLD

Hope and Anguish

4. To carry out such a task, the Church has always had the duty of scrutinizing the signs of the times and of interpreting them in the light of the gospel. Thus, in language intelligible to each generation, she can respond to the perennial questions which men ask about this present life and the life to come, and about the relationship of the one to the other. We must therefore recognize and understand the world in which we live, its expectations, its longings, and its often dramatic characteristics. Some of the main features of the modern world can be sketched as follows:

Today, the human race is passing through a new stage of its history. Profound and rapid changes are spreading by degrees around the whole world. Triggered by the intelligence and creative energies of man, these changes recoil upon him, upon his decisions and desires, both individual and collective, and upon his manner of thinking and acting with respect to things and to people. Hence we can already speak of a true social and cultural transformation, one which has repercussions on man's religious life as well.

As happens in any crisis of growth, this transformation has brought serious difficulties in its wake. Thus while man extends his power in every direction, he does not always succeed in subjecting it to his own welfare. Striving to penetrate farther into the deeper recesses of his own mind, he frequently appears more unsure of himself. Gradually and more precisely he lays bare the laws of society, only to be paralyzed by uncertainty about the direction to give it.

Never has the human race enjoyed such an abundance of wealth, resources, and economic power. Yet a huge proportion of the world's citizens is still tormented by hunger and poverty, while countless numbers suffer from total illiteracy. Never before today has man been so keenly aware of freedom, yet at the same time, new forms of social and psychological slavery make their appearance.

Although the world of today has a very vivid sense of its unity and of how one man depends on another in needful solidarity, it is most grievously torn into opposing camps by conflicting forces. For political, social, economic, racial, and ideological disputes still continue bitterly, and with them the peril of a war which would reduce everything to ashes. True, there is a growing exchange of ideas, but the very words by which key concepts are expressed take on quite different meanings in diverse ideological systems. Finally, man painstakingly searches for a better world, without working with equal zeal for the betterment of his own spirit.

Caught up in such numerous complications, very many of our contemporaries are kept from accurately identifying permanent values and adjusting them properly to fresh discoveries. As a result, buffeted between hope and anxiety and pressing one another with questions about the present course of events, they are burdened down with uneasiness. This same course of events leads men to look for answers. Indeed, it forces them to do so.

Profoundly Changed Conditions

5. Today's spiritual agitation and the changing conditions of life are part of a broader and deeper revolution. As a result of the latter, intellectual formation is ever increasingly based on the mathematical and natural sciences and on those dealing with man himself, while in the practical order the technology which stems from these sciences takes on mounting importance.

This scientific spirit exerts a new kind of impact on the cultural sphere and on modes of thought. Technology is now transforming the face of the earth, and is already trying to master outer space. To a certain extent, the human intellect is also broadening its dominion over time: over the past by means of historical knowledge; over the future by the art of projecting and by planning.

Advances in biology, psychology, and the social sciences not only bring men hope of improved self-knowledge. In conjunction with technical methods, they are also helping men to exert direct influence on the life of social groups. At the same time, the human race is giving ever-increasing thought to forecasting and regulating its own population growth.

History itself speeds along on so rapid a course that an individual person can scarcely keep abreast of it. The destiny of the human community has become all of a piece, where once the various groups of men had a kind of private history of their own. Thus, the human race has passed from a rather static concept of reality to a more dynamic, evolutionary one. In consequence, there has arisen a new series of problems, a series as important as can be, calling for new efforts of analysis and synthesis.

Changes in the Social Order

6. By this very circumstance, the traditional local communities such as father-centered families, clans, tribes, villages, various groups and associations stemming from social contacts experience more thorough changes every day.

The industrial type of society is gradually being spread, leading some nations to economic affluence, and radically transforming ideas and social conditions established for centuries.

Likewise, the practice and pursuit of city living has grown, either because of a multiplication of cities and their inhabitants, or by a transplantation of city life to rural settings.

New and more efficient media of social communication are contributing to the knowledge of events. By setting off chain reactions, they are giving the swiftest and widest possible circulation to styles of thought and feeling.

It is also noteworthy how many men are being induced to migrate on various counts, and are thereby changing their manner of life. Thus a man's ties with his fellows are constantly being multiplied. At the same time "socialization" brings further ties, without, however, always promoting appropriate personal development and truly personal relationships ("personalization").

This kind of evolution can be seen more clearly in those nations which already enjoy the conveniences of economic and technological progress, though it is also astir among peoples still striving for such progress and eager to secure for themselves the advantages of an industrialized and urbanized society. These peoples, especially those among them who are attached to older traditions, are simultaneously undergoing a movement toward more mature and personal exercise of liberty.

Psychological, Moral, and Religious Changes

7. A change in attitudes and in human structures frequently calls accepted values into question. This is especially true of young people, who have grown impatient on more than one occasion, and indeed become rebels in their distress. Aware of their own influence in the life of society, they want to assume a role in it sooner. As a result, parents and educators frequently experience greater difficulties day by day in discharging their tasks.

The institutions, laws, and modes of thinking and feeling as handed down from previous generations do not always seem to be well adapted to the contemporary state of affairs. Hence arises an upheaval in the manner and even the norms of behavior.

Finally, these new conditions have their impact on religion. On the one hand a more critical ability to distinguish religion from a magical view of the world and from the superstitions which still circulate purifies religion and exacts day by day a more personal and explicit adherence to faith. As a result many persons are achieving a more vivid sense of God.

On the other hand, growing numbers of people are abandoning religion in practice. Unlike former days, the denial of God or of religion, or the abandonment of them, is no longer unusual and individual occurrences. For today it is not rare for such decisions to be presented as requirements of scientific progress or of a certain new humanism. In numerous places these views are voiced not to a deeper understanding of the laws of social life which the Creator has written into man's spiritual and moral nature.

Since rather recent documents of the Church's teaching authority have dealt at considerable length with Christian doctrine about human society,[3] this Council is merely going to call to mind some of the more basic truths, treating their foundations under the light of revelation. Then it will dwell more at length on certain of their implications having special significance for our day.

God's Plan Gives Man's Vocation a Communitarian Nature

24. God, who has fatherly concern for everyone, has willed that all men should constitute one family and treat one another in a spirit of brotherhood. For having been created in the image of God, who "from one man has created the whole human race and made them live all over

the face of the earth" (Acts 17:26), all men are called to one and the same goal, namely, God himself.

For this reason, love for God and neighbor is the first and greatest commandment. Sacred scripture, however, teaches us that the love of God cannot be separated from love of neighbor: "If there is any other commandment, it is summed up in this saying, Thou shalt love thy neighbor as thyself. . . . Love therefore is the fulfillment of the Law" (Rom. 13:9–10; cf. 1 John 4:20). To men growing daily more dependent on one another, and to a world becoming more unified every day, this truth proves to be of a paramount importance.

Indeed, the Lord Jesus, when he prayed to the Father, "that all may be one . . . as we are one" (John 17:21–22) opened up vistas closed to human reason. For he implied a certain likeness between the union of the divine Persons, and in the union of God's sons in truth and charity. This likeness reveals that man, who is the only creature on earth which God willed for itself, cannot fully find himself except through a sincere gift of himself.[4]

The Interdependence of Person and Society

25. Man's social nature makes it evident that the progress of the human person and the advance of society itself hinge on each other. For the beginning, the subject, and the goal of all social institutions is and must be the human person, which for its part and by its very nature stands completely in need of social life.[5] This social life is not something added on to man. Hence, through his dealings with others, through reciprocal duties, and through fraternal dialogue he develops all his gifts and is able to rise to his destiny.

Among those social ties which man needs for his development, some, like the family and political community, relate with greater immediacy to his innermost nature. Others originate rather from his free decision. In our era, for various reasons, reciprocal ties and mutual dependencies increase day by day and give rise to a variety of associations and organizations, both public and private. This development, which is called socialization, while certainly not without its dangers, brings with it many advantages with respect to consolidating and increasing the qualities of the human person, and safeguarding his rights.[6]

But if by this social life the human person is greatly aided in responding to his destiny, even in its religious dimensions, it cannot be denied that men are often diverted from doing good and spurred toward evil by the social circumstances in which they live and are immersed from their birth. To be sure, the disturbances which so frequently occur in the social order result in part from the natural tensions of economic, political, and social forms. But at a deeper level they flow from man's pride and selfishness, which contaminate even the social sphere. When the structure of affairs is flawed by the consequences of sin, man, already born with a bent toward evil, finds there new inducements to sin, which cannot be overcome without strenuous efforts and the assistance of grace.

Promoting the Common Good

26. Every day human interdependence grows more tightly drawn and spreads by degrees over the whole world. As a result the common good, that is, the sum of those conditions of social life which allow social groups and their individual members relatively thorough and ready access to their own fulfillment, today takes on an increasingly universal complexion and consequently involves rights and duties with respect to the whole human race. Every social group must take

account of the needs and legitimate aspirations of other groups, and even of the general welfare of the entire human family.[7]

At the same time, however, there is a growing awareness of the exalted dignity proper to the human person, since he stands above all things, and his rights and duties are universal and inviolable. Therefore, there must be made available to all men everything necessary for leading a life truly human, such as food, clothing, and shelter; the right to choose a state of life freely and to found a family; the right to education, to employment, to a good reputation, to respect, to appropriate information, to activity in accord with the upright norm of one's own conscience, to protection of privacy, and to rightful freedom in matters religious too.

Hence, the social order and its development must unceasingly work to the benefit of the human person if the disposition of affairs is to be subordinate to the personal realm and not contrariwise, as the Lord indicated when he said that the Sabbath was made for man, and not man for the Sabbath.[8]

This social order requires constant improvement. It must be founded on truth, built on justice, and animated by love; in freedom it should grow every day toward a more humane balance.[9] An improvement in attitudes and widespread changes in society will have to take place if these objectives are to be gained.

God's Spirit, who with a marvelous providence directs the unfolding of time and renews the face of the earth, is not absent from this development. The ferment of the gospel, too, has aroused and continues to arouse in man's heart the irresistible requirements of his dignity.

Reverence for the Human Person

27. Coming down to practical and particularly urgent consequences, the Council lays stress on reverence for man; everyone must consider his every neighbor without exception as another self, taking into account first of all his life and the means necessary to living it with dignity,[10] so as not to imitate the rich man who had no concern for the poor man Lazarus.[11]

In our times a special obligation binds us to make ourselves the neighbor of absolutely every person, and of actively helping him when he comes across our path, whether he be an old person abandoned by all, a foreign laborer unjustly looked down upon, a refugee, a child born of an unlawful union and wrongly suffering for a sin he did not commit, or a hungry person who disturbs our conscience by recalling the voice of the Lord: "As long as you did it for one of these, the least of my brethren, you did it for me" (Matt. 25:40).

Furthermore, whatever is opposed to life itself, such as any type of murder, genocide, abortion, euthanasia, or willful self-destruction, whatever violates the integrity of the human person, such as mutilation, torments inflicted on body or mind, attempts to coerce the will itself; whatever insults human dignity, such as subhuman living conditions, arbitrary imprisonment, deportation, slavery, prostitution, the selling of women and children; as well as disgraceful working conditions, where men are treated as mere tools for profit, rather than as free and responsible persons; all these things and others of their like are infamies indeed. They poison human society, but they do more harm to those who practice them than those who suffer from the injury. Moreover, they are a supreme dishonor to the Creator.

Reverence and Love for Enemies

28. Respect and love ought to be extended also to those who think or act differently than we do in social, political, and religious matters, too. In fact, the more deeply we come to understand

their ways of thinking through such courtesy and love, the more easily will we be able to enter into dialogue with them.

This love and good will, to be sure, must in no way render us indifferent to truth and goodness. Indeed love itself impels the disciples of Christ to speak the saving truth to all men. But it is necessary to distinguish between error, which always merits repudiation, and the person in error, who never loses the dignity of being a person, even when he is flawed by false or inadequate religious notions.[12] God alone is the judge and searcher of hearts; for that reason he forbids us to make judgments about the internal guilt of anyone.[13]

The teaching of Christ even requires that we forgive injustices,[14] and extends the law of love to include every enemy, according to the command of the New Law: "You have heard that it was said, 'Thou shalt love thy neighbor, and shalt hate thy enemy.' But I say to you, love your enemies, do good to those who hate you, and pray for those who persecute and calumniate you" (Matt. 5:43–44).

The Essential Equality of Men; and Social Justice

29. Since all men possess a rational soul and are created in God's likeness, since they have the same nature and origin, have been redeemed by Christ, and enjoy the same divine calling and destiny, the basic equality of all must receive increasingly greater recognition.

True, all men are not alike from the point of view of varying physical power and the diversity of intellectual and moral resources. Nevertheless, with respect to the fundamental rights of the person, every type of discrimination, whether social or cultural, whether based on sex, race, color, social condition, language, or religion, is to be overcome and eradicated as contrary to God's intent. For in truth it must still be regretted that fundamental personal rights are not yet being universally honored. Such is the case of a woman who is denied the right and freedom to choose a husband, to embrace a state of life, or to acquire an education or cultural benefits equal to those recognized for men.

Moreover, although rightful differences exist between men, the equal dignity of persons demands that a more humane and just condition of life be brought about. For excessive economic and social differences between the members of the one human family or population groups cause scandal, and militate against social justice, equity, the dignity of the human person, as well as social and international peace. Human institutions, both private and public, must labor to minister to the dignity and purpose of man. At the same time let them put up a stubborn fight against any kind of slavery, whether social or political, and safeguard the basic rights of man under every political system. Indeed human institutions themselves must be accommodated by degrees to the highest of all realities, spiritual ones, even though meanwhile, a long enough time will be required before they arrive at the desired goal.

More Than an Individualistic Ethic Is Required

30. Profound and rapid changes make it particularly urgent that no one, ignoring the trend of events or drugged by laziness, content himself with a merely individualistic morality. It grows increasingly true that the obligations of justice and love are fulfilled only if each person, contributing to the common good, according to his own abilities and the needs of others, also promotes and assists the public and private in situations dedicated to bettering the conditions of human life.

Yet there are those who, while professing grand and rather noble sentiments, nevertheless in reality live always as if they cared nothing for the needs of society. Many in various places even make light of social laws and precepts, and do not hesitate to resort to various frauds and deceptions in avoiding just taxes or other debts due to society. Others think little of certain norms of social life, for example those designed for the protection of health, or laws establishing speed limits. They do not even avert to the fact that by such indifference they imperil their own life and that of others.

Let everyone consider it his sacred obligation to count social necessities among the primary duties of modern man, and to pay heed to them. For the more unified the world becomes, the more plainly do the offices of men extend beyond particular groups and spread by degrees to the whole world. But this challenge cannot be met unless individual men and their associations cultivate in themselves the moral and social virtues, and promote them in society. Thus, with the needed help of divine grace, men who are truly new and artisans of a new humanity can be forthcoming.

[. . .]

CHAPTER 3: SOCIOECONOMIC LIFE

Some Aspects of Economic Life

63. In the socioeconomic realm, too, the dignity and total vocation of the human person must be honored and advanced along with the welfare of society as a whole. For man is the source, the center, and the purpose of all socioeconomic life.

As in other areas of social life, modern economy is marked by man's increasing domination over nature, by closer and more intense relationships between citizens, groups, and countries and by their mutual dependence, and by more frequent intervention on the part of government. At the same time progress in the methods of production and in the exchange of goods and services has made the economy an apt instrument for meeting the intensified needs of the human family more successfully.

Reasons for anxiety, however, are not lacking. Many people, especially in economically advanced areas, seem to be hypnotized, as it were, by economics, so that almost their entire personal and social life is permeated with a certain economic outlook. These people can be found both in nations which favor a collective economy as well as in others.

Again, we are at a moment in history when the development of economic life could diminish social inequalities if that development were guided and coordinated in a reasonable and human way. Yet all too often it serves only to intensify the inequalities. In some places it even results in a decline in the social status of the weak and in contempt for the poor.

While an enormous mass of people still lacks the absolute necessities of life, some, even in less advanced countries, live sumptuously or squander wealth. Luxury and misery rub shoulders. While the few enjoy very great freedom of choice, the many are deprived of almost all possibility of acting on their own initiative and responsibility, and often subsist in living and working conditions unworthy of human beings.

A similar lack of economic and social balance is to be noted between agriculture, industry, and the services, and also between different parts of one and the same country. The contrast between the economically more advanced countries and other countries is becoming more serious day by day, and the very peace of the world can be jeopardized in consequence.

Our contemporaries are coming to feel these inequalities with an ever-sharper awareness. For they are thoroughly convinced that the wider technical and economic potential which the modern world enjoys can and should correct this unhappy state of affairs. Hence, numerous reforms are needed at the socioeconomic level, along with universal changes in ideas and attitudes.

Now in this area the Church maintains certain principles of justice and equity as they apply to individuals, societies, and international relations. In the course of the centuries and with the light of the gospel she has worked out these principles as right reason demanded. In modern times especially, the Church has enlarged upon them. This sacred Council wishes to reinforce these principles according to the circumstances of the times and to set forth certain guidelines, primarily with regard to the requirements of economic development.[15]

SECTION 1: ECONOMIC DEVELOPMENT

In the Service of Man

64. Today, more than ever before, progress in the production of agricultural and industrial goods and in the rendering of services is rightly aimed at making provision for the growth of a people and at meeting the rising expectations of the human race. Therefore, technical progress must be fostered, along with a spirit of initiative, an eagerness to create and expand enterprises, the adaptation of methods of production—in a word, all the elements making for such development.

The fundamental purpose of this productivity must not be the mere multiplication of products. It must not be profit or domination. Rather, it must be the service of man, and indeed of the whole man, viewed in terms of his material needs and the demands of his intellectual, moral, spiritual, and religious life. And when we say man, we mean every man whatsoever and every group of men, of whatever race and from whatever part of the world. Consequently, economic activity is to be carried out according to its own methods and laws but within the limits of morality,[16] so that God's plan for mankind can be realized.[17]

Under Man's Control

65. Economic development must be kept under the control of mankind. It must not be left to the sole judgment of a few men or groups possessing excessive economic power, or of the political community alone, or of certain especially powerful nations. It is proper, on the contrary, that at every level the largest possible number of people have an active share in directing that development. When it is a question of international developments, all nations should so participate. It is also necessary for the spontaneous activities of individuals and of independent groups to be coordinated with the efforts of public authorities. These activities and these efforts should be aptly and harmoniously interwoven.

Growth must not be allowed merely to follow a kind of automatic course resulting from the economic activity of individuals. Nor must it be entrusted solely to the authority of government. Hence, theories which obstruct the necessary reforms in the name of a false liberty must be branded as erroneous. The same is true of those theories which subordinate the basic rights of individual persons and groups to the collective organization of production.[18]

Citizens, for their part, should remember that they have the right and the duty, which must be recognized by civil authority, to contribute according to their ability to the true progress of their own community. Especially in underdeveloped areas, where all resources must be put to urgent use, those men gravely endanger the public good who allow their resources to remain unproductive or who deprive their community of the material and spiritual aid it needs. The personal right of migration, however, is not to be impugned.

Removing Huge Differences

66. If the demands of justice and equity are to be satisfied, vigorous efforts must be made, without violence to the rights of persons or to the natural characteristics of each country, to remove as quickly as possible the immense economic inequalities which now exist. In many cases, these are worsening and are connected with individual and group discrimination.

In many areas, too, farmers experience special difficulties in raising products or in selling them. In such cases, country people must be helped to increase and to market what they produce, to make the necessary advances and changes, and to obtain a fair return. Otherwise, as too often happens, they will remain in the condition of lower-class citizens. Let farmers, especially young ones, skillfully apply themselves to perfecting their professional competence. Without it, no agricultural progress can take place.[19]

Justice and equity likewise require that the mobility which is necessary in a developing economy be regulated in such a way as to keep the life of individuals and their families from becoming insecure and precarious. Hence, when workers come from another country or district and contribute by their labor to the economic advancement of a nation or region, all discrimination with respect to wages and working conditions must be carefully avoided.

The local people, moreover, especially public authorities, should all treat them not as mere tools of production but as persons, and must help them to arrange for their families to live with them and to provide themselves with decent living quarters. The native should also see that these workers are introduced into the social life of the country or region which receives them. Employment opportunities, however, should be created in their own areas as far as possible.

In those economic affairs which are today subject to change, as in the new forms of industrial society in which automation, for example, is advancing, care must be taken that sufficient and suitable work can be obtained, along with appropriate technical and professional formation. The livelihood and the human dignity of those especially who are in particularly difficult circumstances because of illness or old age should be safeguarded.

NOTES

1. The pastoral constitution *De Ecclesia in Mundo Hulus Temporis* is made up of two parts; yet it constitutes an organic unity.

By way of explanation: the constitution is called "pastoral" because, while resting on doctrinal principles, it seeks to express the relation of the Church to the world and modern mankind. The result is that, on the one hand, a pastoral slant is present in the first part, and, on the other hand, a pastoral slant is present in the second part.

In the first part, the Church develops her teaching on man, on the world which is the enveloping context of man's existence, and on man's relation to his fellow men. In part two, the Church gives closer consideration to various aspects of modern life and human society; special consideration is given to those questions and problems which, in this general area, seem to have a greater urgency in our day. As a result, in part two the subject matter which is viewed in the light of doctrinal principles is made up of diverse elements. Some elements have a permanent value; others, only a transitory one.

Consequently, the Constitution must be interpreted according to the general norms of theological interpretation. Interpreters must bear in mind—especially in part 2—the changeable circumstances which the subject matter, by its very nature, involves.

2. Cf. Jn. 18:37; Mt. 10:28; Mk. 10:45.

3. Cf. John XXIII, encyclical letter *Mater et Magistra,* May 15, 1961: AAS 53 (1961), 401–64, and encyclical letter *Pacem in Terris,* Apr. 11, 1963: AAS 55 (1963), 257–304; Paul VI, encyclical letter *Ecclesiam Suam,* Aug. 6, 1964: AAS 54 (1964), 609–59.

4. Cf. Luke 17:33.

5. Cf. St. Thomas, 1 Ethica Lect. 1.

6. Cf. John XXIII, encyclical letter *Mater et Magistra:* AAS 53 (1961), 418. Cf. also Pius XI, encyclical letter *Quadragesimo Anno:* AAS 23 (1931), 222ff.

7. Cf. John XXIII, encyclical letter *Mater et Magistra:* AAS 53 (1961).

8. Cf. Mk. 2:27.

9. Cf. John XXIII, encyclical letter *Pacem in Terris:* AAS 55 (1963), 266.

10. Cf. Jas. 2:15–16.

11. Cf. Lk. 16:18–31.

12. Cf. John XXIII, encyclical letter *Pacem in Terris:* AAS 55 (1963), 299, 300.

13. Cf. Lk. 6:37–38; Mt. 7:1–2; Rom. 2:1–11; 14:10–12.

14. Cf. Mt. 5:43–47.

15. Cf. Pius XII, address on Mar. 23, 1952: AAS 44 (1952), 273; John XXIII, allocution to the Catholic Association of Italian Workers, May 1, 1959: AAS 51 (1959), 358.

16. Cf. also Pius XI, encyclical letter *Quadragesimo Anno:* AAS 23 (1931), 190ff; Pius XII, address on Mar. 23, 1952: AAS 44 (1952), 276ff; John XXIII encyclical letter *Mater et Magistra:* AAS 53 (1961), 450; Vatican Council II, *Decree Inter Mirifica* (On the Instruments of Social Communication), chapter 1, art. 6: AAS 56 (1964), 147.

17. Cf Mt. 16:26; Lk. 16:1–31; Col. 3:17.

18. Cf. Leo XIII, encyclical letter *Libertas, in Acta Leonis XIII;* t. VIII, 220ff; Pius XI, encyclical letter *Quadragesimo Anno:* AAS 23 (1931), 191ff; Pius XI, encyclical letter *Divini Redemptoris:* AAS 29 (1937), 65ff; Pius XII, Christmas message, 1941: AAS 34 (1942), 10ff; John XXIII, encyclical letter *Mater et Magistra:* AAS 53 (1961), 401–64.

19. In reference to agricultural problems, cf. especially John XXIII, encyclical letter *Mater et Magistra:* AAS 53 (1961), 341ff.

from *Economic Justice for All*

❧

U.S. Catholic Bishops, 1986

U.S. Catholic bishops meet twice a year and frequently issue statements on social issues, including unemployment, racism, war, popular culture, and the environment.

❧

PRINCIPAL THEMES OF THE PASTORAL LETTER

12. The pastoral letter is not a blueprint for the American economy. It does not embrace any particular theory of how the economy works, nor does it attempt to resolve the disputes between different schools of economic thought. Instead, our letter turns to Scripture and to the social teachings of the Church. There, we discover what our economic life must serve, what standards it must meet. Let us examine some of these basic moral principles.

13. *Every economic decision and institution must be judged in light of whether it protects or undermines the dignity of the human person.* The pastoral letter begins with the human person. We believe the person is sacred—the clearest reflection of God among us. Human dignity comes from God, not from nationality, race, sex, economic status, or any human accomplishment. We judge any economic system by what it does *for* and *to* people and by how it permits all to *participate* in it. The economy should serve people, not the other way around.

14. *Human dignity can be realized and protected only in community.* In our teaching, the human person is not only sacred but also social. How we organize our society—in economics and politics, in law and policy—directly affects human dignity and the capacity of individuals to grow in community. The obligation to "love our neighbor" has an individual dimension, but it also requires a broader social commitment to the common good. We have many partial ways to measure and debate the health of our economy: gross national product, per capita income, stock market prices, and so forth. The Christian vision of economic life looks beyond them all and asks, Does economic life enhance or threaten our life together as a community?

15. *All people have a right to participate in the economic life of society.* Basic justice demands that people be assured a minimum level of participation in the economy. It is wrong for a person or group to be excluded unfairly or to be unable to participate or contribute to the economy. For example, people who are both able and willing, but cannot get a job are deprived of the participation that is so vital to human development. For, it is through employment that most individuals and families meet their material needs, exercise their talents, and have an

opportunity to contribute to the larger community. Such participation has a special significance in our tradition because we believe that it is a means by which we join in carrying forward God's creative activity.

16. *All members of society have a special obligation to the poor and vulnerable.* From the Scriptures and church teaching, we learn that the justice of a society is tested by the treatment of the poor. The justice that was the sign of God's covenant with Israel was measured by how the poor and unprotected—the widow, the orphan, and the stranger—were treated. The kingdom that Jesus proclaimed in his word and ministry excludes no one. Throughout Israel's history and in early Christianity, the poor are agents of God's transforming power. "The Spirit of the Lord is upon me, therefore he has anointed me. He has sent me to bring glad tidings to the poor" (Lk. 4:18). This was Jesus' first public utterance. Jesus takes the side of those most in need. In the Last Judgment, so dramatically described in St. Matthew's Gospel, we are told that we will be judged according to how we respond to the hungry, the thirsty, the naked, the stranger. As followers of Christ, we are challenged to make a fundamental "option for the poor"—to speak for the voiceless, to defend the defenseless, to assess life styles, policies, and social institutions in terms of their impact on the poor. This "option for the poor" does not mean pitting one group against another, but rather, strengthening the whole community by assisting those who are most vulnerable. As Christians, we are called to respond to the needs of *all* our brothers and sisters, but those with the greatest needs require the greatest response.

17. *Human rights are the minimum conditions for life in community.* In Catholic teaching, human rights include not only civil and political rights but also economic rights. As Pope John XXIII declared, "all people have a right to life, food, clothing, shelter, rest, medical care, education, and employment." This means that when people are without a chance to earn a living, and must go hungry and homeless, they are being denied basic rights. Society must ensure that these rights are protected. In this way, we will ensure that the minimum conditions of economic justice are met for all our sisters and brothers.

18. *Society as a whole, acting through public and private institutions, has the moral responsibility to enhance human dignity and protect human rights.* In addition to the clear responsibility of private institutions, government has an essential responsibility in this area. This does not mean that government has the primary or exclusive role, but it does have a positive moral responsibility in safeguarding human rights and ensuring that the minimum conditions of human dignity are met for all. In a democracy, government is a means by which we can act together to protect what is important to us and to promote our common values.

19. These six moral principles are not the only ones presented in the pastoral letter, but they give an overview of the moral vision that we are trying to share. This vision of economic life cannot exist in a vacuum; it must be translated into concrete measures. Our pastoral letter spells out some specific applications of Catholic moral principles. We call for a new national commitment to full employment. We say it is a social and moral scandal that one of every seven Americans is poor, and we call for concerted efforts to eradicate poverty. The fulfillment of the basic needs of the poor is of the highest priority. We urge that all economic policies be evaluated in light of their impact on the life and stability of the family. We support measures to halt the loss of family farms and to resist the growing concentration in the ownership of agricultural resources. We specify ways in which the United States can do far more to relieve the plight of poor nations and assist in their development. We also reaffirm church teaching on the rights of workers, collective bargaining, private property, subsidiarity, and equal opportunity.

20. We believe that the recommendations in our letter are reasonable and balanced. In analyzing the economy, we reject ideological extremes and start from the fact that ours is a

"mixed" economy, the product of a long history of reform and adjustment. We know that some of our specific recommendations are controversial. As bishops, we do not claim to make these prudential judgments with the same kind of authority that marks our declarations of principle. But, we feel obliged to teach by example how Christians can undertake concrete analysis and make specific judgments on economic issues. The Church's teachings cannot be left at the level of appealing generalities.

21. In the pastoral letter, we suggest that the time has come for a "New American Experiment"—to implement economic rights, to broaden the sharing of economic power, and to make economic decisions more accountable to the common good. This experiment can create new structures of economic partnership and participation within firms at the regional level, for the whole nation, and across borders.

22. Of course, there are many aspects of the economy the letter does not touch, and there are basic questions it leaves to further exploration. There are also many specific points on which men and women of good will may disagree. We look for a fruitful exchange among differing viewpoints. We pray only that all will take to heart the urgency of our concerns; that together we will test our views by the Gospel and the Church's teaching; and that we will listen to other voices in a spirit of mutual respect and open dialogue.

[. . .]

CHAPTER 1: THE CHURCH AND THE FUTURE OF THE U.S. ECONOMY

1. Every perspective on economic life that is human, moral, and Christian must be shaped by three questions: What does the economy do *for* people? What does it do *to* people? And how do people *participate* in it? The economy is a human reality: men and women working together to develop and care for the whole of God's creation. All this work must serve the material and spiritual well-being of people. It influences what people hope for themselves and their loved ones. It affects the way they act together in society. It influences their very faith in God.[1]

2. The Second Vatican Council declared that "the joys and hopes, the griefs and anxieties of the people of this age, especially those who are poor or in any way afflicted, these too are the joys and hopes, the griefs and anxieties of the followers of Christ."[2] There are many signs of hope in U.S. economic life today:

- Many fathers and mothers skillfully balance the arduous responsibilities of work and family life. There are parents who pursue a purposeful and modest way of life and by their example encourage their children to follow a similar path. A large number of women and men, drawing on their religious tradition, recognize the challenging vocation of family life and child rearing in a culture that emphasizes material display and self-gratification.
- Conscientious business people seek new and more equitable ways to organize resources and the workplace. They face hard choices over expanding or retrenching, shifting investments, hiring or firing.
- Young people choosing their life's work ask whether success and security are compatible with service to others.
- Workers whose labor may be toilsome or repetitive try daily to ennoble their work with a spirit of solidarity and friendship.

    🙟 New immigrants brave dislocations while hoping for the opportunities realized by the millions who came before them.

3. These signs of hope are not the whole story. There have been failures—some of them massive and ugly:

    🙟 Poor and homeless people sleep in community shelters and in our church basements; the hungry line up in soup lines.

    🙟 Unemployment gnaws at the self-respect of both middle-aged persons who have lost jobs and the young who cannot find them.

    🙟 Hardworking men and women wonder if the system of enterprise that helped them yesterday might destroy their jobs and their communities tomorrow.

    🙟 Families confront major new challenges: dwindling social supports for family stability; economic pressures that force both parents of young children to work outside the home; a driven pace of life among the successful that can sap love and commitment; lack of hope among those who have less or nothing at all. Very different kinds of families bear different burdens of our economic system.

    🙟 Farmers face the loss of their land and way of life; young people find it difficult to choose farming as a vocation; farming communities are threatened; migrant farmworkers break their backs in serf-like conditions for disgracefully low wages.

4. *And beyond our own shores, the reality of 800 million people living in absolute poverty and 450 million malnourished or facing starvation casts an ominous shadow over all these hopes and problems at home.*

5. Anyone who sees all this will understand our concern as pastors and bishops. People shape the economy and in turn are shaped by it. Economic arrangements can be sources of fulfillment, of hope, of community—or of frustration, isolation, and even despair. They teach virtues—or vices—and day by day help mold our characters. They affect the quality of people's lives; at the extreme even determining whether people live or die. Serious economic choices go beyond purely technical issues to fundamental questions of value and human purpose.[3] We believe that in facing these questions the Christian religious and moral tradition can make an important contribution.

    [. . .]

196. a. *The first line of attack against poverty must be to build and sustain a healthy economy that provides employment opportunities at just wages for all adults who are able to work.* Poverty is intimately linked to the issue of employment. Millions are poor because they have lost their jobs or because their wages are too low. The persistent high levels of unemployment during the last decade are a major reason why poverty has increased in recent years.[4] Expanded employment especially in the private sector would promote human dignity, increase social solidarity, and promote self-reliance of the poor. It should also reduce the need for welfare programs and generate the income necessary to support those who remain in need and cannot work: elderly, disabled, and chronically ill people, and single parents of young children. It should also be recognized that the persistence of poverty harms the larger society because the depressed purchasing power of the poor contributes to the periodic cycles of stagnation in the economy.

197. In recent years the minimum wage has not been adjusted to keep pace with inflation. Its real value has declined by 24 percent since 1981. We believe Congress should raise the minimum wage in order to restore some of the purchasing power it has lost due to inflation.

198. While job creation and just wages are major elements of a national strategy against poverty, they are clearly not enough. Other more specific policies are necessary to remedy the institutional causes of poverty and to provide for those who cannot work.

199. b. *Vigorous action should be undertaken to remove barriers to full and equal employment for women and minorities.* Too many women and minorities are locked into jobs with low pay, poor working conditions, and little opportunity for career advancement. So long as we tolerate a situation in which people can work full-time and still be below the poverty line—a situation common among those earning the minimum wage—too many will continue to be counted among the "working poor." Concerted efforts must be made through job training, affirmative action, and other means to assist those now prevented from obtaining more lucrative jobs. Action should also be taken to upgrade poorer paying jobs and to correct wage differentials that discriminate unjustly against women.

200. c. *Self-help efforts among the poor should be fostered by programs and policies in both the private and public sectors.* We believe that an effective way to attack poverty is through programs that are small in scale, locally based, and oriented toward empowering the poor to become self-sufficient. Corporations, private organizations, and the public sector can provide seed money, training and technical assistance, and organizational support for self-help projects in a wide variety of areas such as low-income housing, credit unions, worker cooperatives, legal assistance, and neighborhood and community organizations. Efforts that enable the poor to participate in the ownership and control of economic resources are especially important.

201. Poor people must be empowered to take charge of their own futures and become responsible for their own economic advancement. Personal motivation and initiative, combined with social reform, are necessary elements to assist individuals in escaping poverty. By taking advantage of opportunities for education, employment, and training, and by working together for change, the poor can help themselves to be full participants in our economic, social, and political life.

202. d. *The tax system should be continually evaluated in terms of its impact on the poor.* This evaluation should be guided by three principles. First, the tax system should raise adequate revenues to pay for the public needs of society, especially to meet the basic needs of the poor. Secondly, the tax system should be structured according to the principle of progressivity, so that those with relatively greater financial resources pay a higher rate of taxation. The inclusion of such a principle in tax policies is an important means of reducing the severe inequalities of income and wealth in the nation. Action should be taken to reduce or offset the fact that most sales taxes and payroll taxes place a disproportionate burden on those with lower incomes. Thirdly, families below the official poverty line should not be required to pay income taxes. Such families are, by definition, without sufficient resources to purchase the basic necessities of life. They should not be forced to bear the additional burden of paying income taxes.[5]

203. e. *All of society should make a much stronger commitment to education for the poor.* Any long-term solution to poverty in this country must pay serious attention to education, public and private, in school and out of school. Lack of adequate education, especially in the inner city setting, prevents many poor people from escaping poverty. In addition, illiteracy, a problem that affects tens of millions of Americans, condemns many to joblessness or chronically low wages. Moreover, it excludes them in many ways from sharing in the political and spiritual life of the community.[6] Since poverty is fundamentally a problem of powerlessness and marginalization, the importance of education as a means of overcoming it cannot be overemphasized.

204. Working to improve education in our society is an investment in the future, an investment that should include both the public and private school systems. Our Catholic schools have

the well-merited reputation of providing excellent education, especially for the poor. Catholic inner-city schools provide an otherwise unavailable educational alternative for many poor families. They provide one effective vehicle for disadvantaged students to lift themselves out of poverty. We commend the work of all those who make great sacrifices to maintain these inner-city schools. We pledge ourselves to continue the effort to make Catholic schools models of education for the poor.

205. We also wish to affirm our strong support for the public school system in the United States. There can be no substitute for quality education in public schools, for that is where the large majority of all students, including Catholic students, are educated. In Catholic social teaching, basic education is a fundamental human right.[7] In our society a strong public school system is essential if we are to protect that right and allow everyone to develop to their maximum ability. Therefore, we strongly endorse the recent calls for improvements in and support for public education, including improving the quality of teaching and enhancing the rewards for the teaching profession.[8] At all levels of education we need to improve the ability of our institutions to provide the personal and technical skills that are necessary for participation not only in today's labor market but also in contemporary society.

206. f. *Policies and programs at all levels should support the strength and stability of families, especially those adversely affected by the economy.* As a nation, we need to examine all aspects of economic life and assess their effects on families. Employment practices, health insurance policies, income security programs, tax policy, and service programs can either support or undermine the abilities of families to fulfill their roles in nurturing children and caring for infirm and dependent family members.

207. We affirm the principle enunciated by John Paul II that society's institutions and policies should be structured so that mothers of young children are not forced by economic necessity to leave their children for jobs outside the home.[9] The nation's social welfare and tax policies should support parents' decisions to care for their own children and should recognize the work of parents in the home because of its value for the family and for society.

208. For those children whose parents do work outside the home, there is a serious shortage of affordable, quality day care. Employers, governments, and private agencies need to improve both the availability and the quality of child care services. Likewise, families could be assisted by the establishment of parental leave policies that would assure job security for new parents.

209. The high rate of divorce and the alarming extent of teenage pregnancies in our nation are distressing signs of the breakdown of traditional family values. These destructive trends are present in all sectors of society: rich and poor; white, black, and brown; urban and rural. However, for the poor they tend to be more visible and to have more damaging economic consequences. These destructive trends must be countered by a revived sense of personal responsibility and commitment to family values.

210. g. *A thorough reform of the nation's welfare and income-support programs should be undertaken.* For millions of poor Americans the only economic safety net is the public welfare system. The programs that make up this system should serve the needs of the poor in a manner that respects their dignity and provides adequate support. In our judgment the present welfare system does not adequately meet these criteria.[10] We believe that several improvements can and should be made within the framework of existing welfare programs. However, in the long run, more far-reaching reforms that go beyond the present system will be necessary. Among the immediate improvements that could be made are the following:

211. (1) *Public assistance programs should be designed to assist recipients, wherever possible, to become self-sufficient through gainful employment.* Individuals should not be worse off economically

when they get jobs than when they rely only on public assistance. Under current rules, people who give up welfare benefits to work in low-paying jobs soon lose their Medicaid benefits. To help recipients become self-sufficient and reduce dependency on welfare, public assistance programs should work in tandem with job creation programs that include provisions for training, counseling, placement, and child care. Jobs for recipients of public assistance should be fairly compensated so that workers receive the full benefits and status associated with gainful employment.

212. (2) *Welfare programs should provide recipients with adequate levels of support.* This support should cover basic needs in food, clothing, shelter, health care, and other essentials. At present only 4 percent of poor families with children receive enough cash welfare benefits to lift them out of poverty.[11] The combined benefits of AFDC and food stamps typically come to less than three-fourths of the official poverty level.[12] Those receiving public assistance should not face the prospect of hunger at the end of the month, homelessness, sending children to school in ragged clothing, or inadequate medical care.

213. (3) *National eligibility standards and a national minimum benefit level for public assistance programs should be established.* Currently welfare eligibility and benefits vary greatly among states. In 1985 a family of three with no earnings had a maximum AFDC benefit of $96 a month in Mississippi and $558 a month in Vermont.[13] To remedy these great disparities, which are far larger than the regional differences in the cost of living, and to assure a floor of benefits for all needy people, our nation should establish and fund national minimum benefit levels and eligibility standards in cash assistance programs.[14] The benefits should also be indexed to reflect changes in the cost of living. These changes reflect standards that our nation has already put in place for aged and disabled people and veterans. Is it not possible to do the same for the children and their mothers who receive public assistance?

214. (4) *Welfare programs should be available to two-parent as well as single-parent families.* Most states now limit participation in AFDC to families headed by single parents, usually women.[15] The coverage of this program should be extended to two-parent families so that fathers who are unemployed or poorly paid do not have to leave home in order for their children to receive help. Such a change would be a significant step toward strengthening two-parent families who are poor.

NOTES

1. Vatican Council II, *The Pastoral Constitution on the Church in the Modern World,* 33. [Note: This pastoral letter frequently refers to documents of the Second Vatican Council, papal encyclicals, and other official teachings of the Roman Catholic Church. Most of these texts have been published by the United States Catholic Conference Office of Publishing and Promotion Services; many are available in collections, though no single collection is comprehensive. See Selected Bibliography.]

2. *Pastoral Constitution,* 1.

3. See *Pastoral Constitution,* 10, 42, 43; Congregation for the Doctrine of the Faith, *Instruction on Christian Freedom and Liberation* (Washington, D.C.: USCC Office of Publishing and Promotion Services, 1986), 34–36.

4. Sheldon Danzinger and Peter Gottschalk, "The Poverty of Losing Ground," *Challenge* 28, no. 2 (May/June 1985): 32–38.

5. The tax reform legislation of 1986 did a great deal to achieve this goal. It removed from the federal income tax rolls virtually all families below the official poverty line.

6. Jonathan Kozol, *Illiterate America* (New York: Anchor Press/Doubleday, 1985).

7. Pope John XXIII, *Peace on Earth*, 13.

8. These reports and studies include: E. Boyer, *High School: A Report on Secondary Education in America* (Princeton: Carnegie Foundation for the Advancement of Teaching, 1983); P. Cusick, *The American High School and the Egalitarian Ideal* (New York: Longman, 1983); J. L. Goodlad, *A Place Called School: Prospects for the Future* (New York: McGraw Hill, 1983); The National Commission on Excellence in Education, *A Nation at Risk: The Imperative for Educational Reform* (Washington, D.C.: U.S. Department of Education, 1983); D. Ravitch, *The Troubled Crusade: American Education, 1945–1980* (New York: Basic, 1983); T. R. Sizer, *Horace's Compromise: The Dilemma of the American High School* (Boston: Houghton Mifflin, 1984); Task Force on Education for Economic Growth, *Action for Excellence: A Comprehensive Plan to Improve Our Nation's Schools* (Denver: Education Commission of the States, 1983); and The Twentieth Century Fund Task Force on Federal Elementary and Secondary Education Policy, *Making the Grade* (New York: Twentieth Century Fund, 1983). For a discussion of the issues raised in these reports see *Harvard Educational Review* 54, no. 1 (February 1984): 1–31.

9. The Vatican, Charter of the Rights of the Family (Washington, D.C.: USCC Office of Publishing and Promotion Services, 1983). See also *On Human Work*, 19; *Familiaris Consortio*, 23, 81; and "Christian Solidarity Leads to Action," in Address to Austrian Workers (Vienna, September 1983) in *Origins* 13, no. 16 (September 29, 1983): 275.

10. H. R. Rodgers Jr., *The Cost of Human Neglect: America's Welfare* (Armonk, N.Y.: W. E. Sharpe, 1982); C. T. Waxman, *The Stigma of Poverty*, 2d ed. (New York: Pergamon Press, 1983), esp. ch. 5; and S. A. Levitan and C. M. Johnson, *Beyond the Safety Net: Reviving the Promise of Opportunity in America* (Cambridge, Mass.: Ballinger, 1984).

11. Congressional Research Service and Congressional Budget Office, *Children in Poverty* (Washington, D.C., May 22, 1985).

12. U.S. House of Representatives Committee on Ways and Means, *Background Materials and Data on Programs within the Jurisdiction of the Committee on Ways and Means* (Washington, D.C., February 22, 1985), 345–46.

13. Committee on Ways and Means, *Background Materials and Data on Programs*, 347–48.

14. In 1982, similar recommendations were made by eight former Secretaries of Health, Education, and Welfare (now Health and Human Services). In a report called "Welfare Policy in the United States," they suggested a number of ways in which national minimum standards might be set and strongly urged the establishment of a floor for all states and territories.

15. Committee on Ways and Means, *Background Materials and Data on Programs*.

"Love Is the Measure" and "Our Brothers, the Communists"

⮜⮞

Dorothy Day

Dorothy Day adopted Catholicism after being a Communist activist. She founded the Catholic Worker movement and its newspaper and was long active in service to the poor and in movements for peace and social justice. These short pieces explore the relationship between religious activism and communism and identify the central principles of her own work.

⮜⮞

LOVE IS THE MEASURE

We confess to being fools and wish that we were more so. In the face of the approaching atom bomb test (and discussion of widespread radioactivity is giving people more and more of an excuse to get away from the philosophy of personalism and the doctrine of free will); in the face of an approaching maritime strike; in the face of bread shortages and housing shortages; in the face of the passing of the draft extension, teenagers included, we face the situation that there is nothing we can do for people except to love them. If the maritime strike goes on there will be no shipping of food or medicine or clothes to Europe or the Far East, so there is nothing to do again but to love. We continue in our fourteenth year of feeding our brothers and sisters, clothing them and sheltering them, and the more we do it, the more we realize that the most important thing is to love. There are several families with us, destitute families, destitute to an unbelievable extent, and there, too, is nothing to do but to love. What I mean is that there is no chance of rehabilitation, no chance, so far as we see, of changing them; certainly no chance of adjusting them to this abominable world about them—and who wants them adjusted, anyway?

What we would like to do is change the world—make it a little simpler for people to feed, clothe, and shelter themselves as God intended them to do. And to a certain extent, by fighting for better conditions, by crying out unceasingly for the rights of the workers, of the poor, of the destitute—the rights of the worthy and the unworthy poor, in other words—we can to a certain extent change the world; we can work for the oasis, the little cell of joy and peace in a harried world. We can throw our pebble in the pond and be confident that its ever-widening circle will reach around the world.

We repeat, there is nothing that we can do but love, and dear God—please enlarge our hearts to love each other, to love our neighbor, to love our enemy as well as our friend.

June 1946

OUR BROTHERS, THE COMMUNISTS

Women think with their whole bodies. More than men do, women see things as a whole.

Maybe I am saying this to justify myself for my recent protest of the refusal of bail to the eleven Communists, a protest which was published in the *Daily Worker,* the *American Guardian,* and other papers, much to the horror of many of our Catholic fellow workers.

It is necessary to explain if we do not wish to affront people. We sincerely want to make our viewpoint understood.

First of all, let it be remembered that I speak as an ex-Communist and one who has not testified before congressional committees, nor written works on the Communist conspiracy. I can say with warmth that I loved the people I worked with and learned much from them. They helped me to find God in His poor, in His abandoned ones, as I had not found Him in Christian churches.

I firmly believe that our salvation depends on the poor with whom Christ identified Himself. "Inasmuch as you have not fed the hungry, clothed the naked, sheltered the homeless, visited the prisoner, protested against injustice, comforted the afflicted . . . you have not done it to Me." The Church throughout the ages in all its charities, in the person of all its saints, has done these things. But for centuries these works were confined to priests, brothers, and nuns. Pius XI called on everyone to perform these works when he called for Catholic Action. The great tragedy of the century, he said, is that the workers are lost to the Church. All this has been repeated many times.

But I must speak from my own experiences. My radical associates were the ones who were in the forefront of the struggle for a better social order where there would not be so many poor. What if we do not agree with the means taken to achieve this goal, nor with their fundamental philosophy? We do believe in "from each according to his ability, to each according to his need." We believe in the "withering away of the State." We believe in the communal aspect of property, as stressed by the early Christians and since then by religious orders. We believe in the constructive activity of the people, "the masses," and the mutual aid which existed during medieval times, worked out from below. We believe in loving our brothers, regardless of race, color, or creed and we believe in showing this love by working, immediately, for better conditions, and ultimately, for the ownership by the workers of the means of production. We believe in an economy based on human needs, rather than on the profit motive.

Certainly we disagree with the Communist Party, but so do we disagree with the other political parties, dedicated to maintaining the status quo. We don't think the present system is worth maintaining. We and the Communists have a common idea that something else is necessary, some other vision of society must be held up and worked toward. Certainly we disagree over and over again with the means chosen to reach their ends, because, as we have repeated many a time, the means become the end.

As for their alleged conspiracy to overthrow the government by force and violence, I do not think that the State has proved its case. Of course, the Communists believe that violence will come. (So do we when it comes down to it, though we are praying it won't.) They believe it will be forced upon the worker by the class struggle which is going on all around us. This class war is a fact, and one does not need to advocate it. The Communists say it is forced on them and when it comes they will take part in it. In the meantime they want to prepare the ground and win as many as possible to their point of view. And where will we be on that day?

If we spend the rest of our lives in slums (as I hope we will, who work for and read *The Catholic Worker*), if we are truly living with the poor, helping the poor, we will inevitably find ourselves on their side, physically speaking. But when it comes to activity, we will be pacifists—I hope and pray—nonviolent resisters of aggression, from whomever it comes, resisters to repression, coercion, from whatever side it comes, and our activity will be the Works of Mercy. Our arms will be the love of God and our brother.

But the Communists are dishonest, everyone says. They do not want improved conditions for the workers. They want the end, the final conflict, to bring on the world revolution.

Well, when it comes down to it, do we of *The Catholic Worker* stand only for just wages, shorter hours, increase of power for the workers, a collaboration of employer and worker in prosperity for all? No, we want to make "the rich poor and the poor holy," and that, too, is a revolution obnoxious to the pagan man. We don't want luxury. We want land, bread, work, children, and the joys of community in play and work and worship. We don't believe in those industrial councils where the heads of United States Steel sit down with the common man in an obscene *agape* of luxury, shared profits, blood money from a thousand battles all over the world. No, the common good, the community must be considered.

During the first seven months of this year, 412 miners were killed at work. And as for crippling and disabling accidents there were 14,871 during these same months.

What has all this to do with signing protests, advocating bail for convicted Communists?

If people took time to think, if they had the zeal of the C.P. for school and study and meeting and planning, and with it all the thirst for martyrdom, and if Catholics delved into the rich body of Catholic liturgy and sociology, they would grow in faith and grace and change the world.

I believe we must reach our brother, never toning down our fundamental oppositions, but meeting him when he asks to be met with a reason for the faith that is in us. "We understand because we believe," St. Anselm says, and how can our brothers understand with a darkened reason, lacking this faith which would enlighten their minds?

The bridge—it seems to me—is love and the compassion (the suffering together) which goes with all love. Which means the folly of the Cross, since Christ loved men even to that folly of failure.

St. Therese said her aim was to make God loved. And I am sure that we pray to love God with an everlasting love, and yearn over our fellows in desire that He should be loved. How can they hear unless we take seriously our lay apostolate and answer them when they speak to us? We believe that God made them and sustains them. It is easier sometimes to see His handiwork here than in the Pecksniffs and Pharisees of our capitalist industrial system. We must cry out against injustice or by our silence consent to it. If we keep silent, the very stones of the street will cry out.

from *Disarmed and Dangerous: The Radical Life and Times of Daniel and Philip Berrigan*

❧

Murray Polner and Jim O'Grady

Murray Polner is the chair of the Jewish Peace Fellowship and was founder and editor in chief of *Present Tense* magazine (1972–1990). He has written for many publications including *The N.Y. Times, Washington Monthly, The Nation,* and the *Village Voice.* Jim O'Grady, activist, writer, and reporter, has worked in the antinuclear, AIDS, and homeless movements. He has written a biography of Dorothy Day. This essay provides a brief glimpse of the lives of two of America's most important religious social activists.

❧

"HOW DO THEY KEEP GOING?"

We taste the spices of Arabia, yet never feel the scorching sun which brings them forth.

—Sir Dudley North

Toward the end of Lent, on a spring day under a faltering sun, Daniel Berrigan walks a Manhattan sidewalk on a routine errand that will end, as he intends, with his arrest. Actually, he processes. He is one among some 2,000 solemn Catholics performing the Stations of the Cross along the Via Dolorosa of Forty-second Street on Good Friday. Around him, Latin chants lift on a breeze that flutters pennants bearing painted crosses swaying above the marchers' heads, in what looks and sounds like a medieval pilgrimage during rush hour. This "Peace Walk," crossing the city from the United Nations to the offices of a Pentagon defense contractor, is a traditional enactment of the Passion and Death of Christ. But unlike common observances of the rite, each Station is linked to a controversial social justice issue. For example, "Jesus Is Stripped of His Garments," the Ninth Station, is held on a block near Times Square crammed with commercial pornography. It is all very much in the Berrigan style of public demonstration: a fusion of venerated Catholic ritual with acutely modern concerns, with an emphasis on the redemptive power of sacrificial suffering. And, in the Berrigan vein, it is grandly cinematic, concluding with time spent in a precinct with several followers and friends.

It is 1995: forty-three years since Berrigan's ordination, at age thirty-one, as a Jesuit priest; twenty-seven years—including eighteen trying months in federal prison—after his arrest for burning Vietnam War draft files with eight others in Catonsville, Maryland; and fifteen years from the morning that he, his brother Philip, and six others strolled through the front doors of a General Electric plant in King of Prussia, Pennsylvania, hammered and poured human blood on an unarmed nuclear warhead, then prayed aloud while awaiting arrival of the FBI and state and county police.

He wears these credentials lightly, but unmistakably. His weathered face is amply creased and his lips are primly pursed, like a Confucian mulling a paradox, as he leaves the crowd to cross the street with thirteen fellow activists. At seventy-three years old, he has skipped the greater part of the Peace Walk (starting at 8:30 A.M. and lasting four hours, it is something of an endurance test), joining it near the end. He appeared around the time someone mounted a flatbed truck, the procession's portable stage, and recited into a microphone, *"Eloi, Eloi, lama sabachtani?"*—Christ's famous wail to heaven, "My God, my God, why have you forsaken me?"—a signal for the thousands to fall to their knees in a dirty parking lot near the Port Authority Bus Terminal, observing a moment of silence to complete the Twelfth of Fourteen Stations, "Jesus Dies on the Cross."

The crowd has now moved a hundred yards farther west in the direction of Ninth Avenue, and cheers as Berrigan and his group walk into a green granite building at 330 West Forty-second Street. They are headed for the ground-floor offices of the Riverside Research Institute, commonly labeled a "Star Wars Think Tank" by people opposed to it. (Riverside claims this may have been true in the past when it did some work for the Strategic Defense Initiative, but not anymore, though it does admit to still conducting systems support for Defense Department weapons programs.[1]) The thirteen cross a dim lobby to the institute's thick glass doors, then sit in a knot on the floor. Berrigan, in the middle of them, looks collected. He's been through this before.

The protesters are immediately surrounded by the New York City police, who have been expecting them, and the building's security officers, walkie-talkies cackling. Either by chance or by tacit agreement between the organizers and the cops, the protesters get a couple of minutes to explain their unlawful presence. Anna Brown, a young instructor at St. Peter's College in Jersey City, stands up next to the centerpiece prop, a podium bearing a brilliant white Easter lily. She reads from "A Devout Meditation in Memory of Adolf Eichmann," an essay by the Trappist monk Thomas Merton, who before his death in 1968 had been one of Berrigan's closest friends. The passage she chooses reiterates Hannah Arendt's observation that the majority of the century's many mass murderers have had much in common with the mental and emotional makeup, even the behavior, of the citizenry that produced them: Dutiful, "sane," and "without anxiety," they win public respect for active devotion to the state-sanctioned cause of the day—which, of course, in Nazi Germany meant assembly-line genocide. Lenny Bruce used to mock the pretensions of blind authoritarianism by reading this same Merton essay in a thick German accent at the end of his nightclub act; Brown means it to reflect similarly on the government research going on behind the glass doors.

> The sanity of Eichmann is disturbing. We equate sanity with a sense of justice, with humaneness, with prudence, with the capacity to love and understand other people. We rely on the sane of the world to preserve it from barbarism, madness, destruction. And now it begins to dawn on us that it is precisely the sane ones who are the most dangerous.

Brown doesn't get very far before the officer-in-charge breaks in with a warning that she and the others are "trespassing at the present time on private property and will be duly arrested if you do not leave the premises." Nobody moves; Brown continues.

Eichmann was sane. The generals and fighters on both sides, in World War II, the ones who carried out the total destruction of entire cities, these were the same ones. Those who have invented and developed atomic bombs, thermonuclear bombs, missiles; who have planned the strategy of the next war; who have evaluated the various possibilities of using bacterial and chemical agents: these are not the crazy people, they are the sane people. The ones who coolly estimate how many millions of victims can be considered expendable in a nuclear war, I presume they do all right with Rorschach ink blots too. On the other hand, you will probably find that the pacifists and the ban-the-bomb people are, quite seriously, just as we read in *Time,* a little crazy.[2]

A command is given and the police—who have also been through this before—move in to harvest these ban-the-bomb people in groups of five and four. Berrigan stands and cooperatively places his hands behind his back so his arresting officer can bind him with plastic cuffs. He is led outside to a police wagon where he steps up and in and wedges with the others onto one of two steel benches. Once everyone is loaded, the back doors slam and lock. Two cops enter the driver's cab and discuss the situation, but decide not to close the sliding door that would separate them from their prisoners—there aren't that many of them. During past Good Fridays—in the mid-1980s, say, when President Reagan was joking about nuclear first strikes—more than 120 people would come at the Riverside offices in waves, to be busted and escorted into overflowing wagons, then driven in total darkness through the streets, many standing pressed against other bodies they could feel but couldn't see, singing disjointed hymns, rocking in the claustrophobic space.

Not today. The group sits meekly as the wagon pulls into traffic. For a moment, through a corner of the windshield, one glimpses the crowd across the street as they strain at the blue police barricades, urging on their surrogates being carted off to jail. In seconds the sight is replaced by the weaving, oblivious midtown traffic.

Even contorted in handcuffed posture, Berrigan looks stylish. His fashion theme is basic black: pants, jacket, and rakish cotton cap, with an informal purple stole slung around his neck like an avant-garde flying ace. Protruding from the zipper of his jacket is a daisy. The demonstration organizers had arranged for the group to approach the lab with flowers in their fists. The others have dropped theirs in a pile on Riverside's steps, but Berrigan, with typical flair—or display, depending on one's attitude, and he inspires strong and disparate attitudes—has used one to garnish himself.

He has spent a lot of time in the second half of his life taking rides to precinct houses in dented and graffiti-marred wagons like this one, with blasts of depressing chatter piercing the static on the dashboard's two-way radio: "We've got four shots fired on an anonymous 911." Car horns blare as Berrigan listens politely to one of his comrades, an elderly woman with unruly hair, who addresses him incoherently on a subject that would seem to relate to vegetarianism; at the same time the officer near him waxes rapturously on the kill capacity of his newly issued 9-millimeter handgun. Some days it must take an act of faith just to show up for one of these things. But Berrigan also must see in the several young faces around him a sign that the ranks of the so-called nonviolent Christian resistance that he and his brother Philip have worked so long and hard to build—often in the midst of painful disagreements and defections—will be replenished, if only in trickles. And besides, when it comes to his favorite subject of the proper relation of religion to politics, this is his milieu.

One of the cops pokes his head back into the wagon. Like a steward on a cruise ship, he is expansive. "You all right? You doing OK? Is everybody happy?" he asks the perpetrators of alleged disorderly conduct. Berrigan smiles and answers with emphasis, "*I feel right at home.*" The protesters near him indulge the joke with a round of knowing chuckles.

Disgorged into a waiting area of the Midtown South police precinct, the protesters surrender IDs in return for desk appearance tickets, which assign them various court dates for arraignment. The process normally takes a couple of hours and moves smoothly, but for Berrigan there is one hitch: While running a routine check on him, the police have found outstanding warrants. This is serious enough to delay his release while they consider whether to "put him through the system," a fairly dreadful prospect. It means Berrigan will spend a long day and night in Corrections Department custody, including transfer from the precinct to a detention center holding cell while his paperwork is churned through Central Booking. The warrants are for previous acts of civil disobedience in New York. They have probably been attached to his computer file by mistake—the records don't always keep up with the disposal of cases in court, especially for frequent offenders like Daniel Berrigan.

He is calm, though, and sits patiently at an absurdly undersized school desk, one of those oddball furnishings found in the warrens of municipal bureaucracies, before a cardboard American flag tacked to a corkboard. The protesters huddle around to lend support. His daisy has begun to wilt, and he seems to be resigning himself to a possibly rotten fate. Then, after forty minutes, his arresting officer struts across the room to announce that they have kindly decided to drop the warrants—the recidivist reverend can go home.

Berrigan brightens at the news. "My debt's been paid to society," he proclaims, as if to some vast assembled throng. Were this twenty years ago, when his and Phil's portraits made the cover of *Time,* and almost everyone in America had an opinion on the two, there would be a crush of supporters on the steps outside, among them photographers, documentary crews, and reporters straining to capture his every incendiary utterance. Today, he addresses a clutch of beaming allies in a desultory patrol room. "I'm a free man," he declares. Then, cracking an impish grin, he ends with a sly impromptu paradox, delivered on a note of self-conscious bravura: "I'm wearing an Easter smile on Good Friday!"

NOTES

1. From a July 28, 1995, interview with an employee, who refused to be identified, in the financial department of the Riverside Research Institute (RRI) at 330 West Forty-second Street in New York City. Citing the institute's biomedical and electromechanical projects, the employee complained that the Berrigans and the Catholic peace group, Pax Christi, "picket us all the time, but they have no idea what we're really involved in." However, RRI's president, Marvin King, made no effort to shed light on his company's work, refusing comment. Nor did the chief of security, William Jackson, who would only say, "We don't comment one way or the other about the demonstrators or any project having to do with the Berrigans." Interviews with King and Jackson, August 8, 1995.

2. Thomas Merton, *Thomas Merton: The Nonviolent Alternative,* rev. ed. of *Thomas Merton on Peace,* ed. Gordon Zahn (New York: Farrar, Straus & Giroux, 1980), 160–61.

"Faith Takes a Seat at the Bargaining Table"

❧

Rich Barlow

Rich Barlow is a reporter for the *Boston Globe*.

❧

One morning last summer, the Rev. David Carl Olson led more than 200 people in prayer, alternately facing the four compass points and reflecting on the symbolic meaning of east (morning and birth), west (sunset and rest), south (the heat of midday when we work), and north ("The pole star that draws us," Olson recalls saying, "Our faith, the ethics that we bear.")

For Olson, a Unitarian Universalist minister and president of the Greater Boston Interfaith Organization, such prayerful meditation is as natural as breathing. But his usual forum is the Community Church of Boston, the congregation in Copley Square he leads.

But that July day he was in a hotel room, offering an opening prayer at collective bargaining talks between Boston janitors and cleaning companies. Neither the praying nor the bargaining averted the janitors' strike. Still, labor-management negotiations normally aren't ecclesiastical exercises.

"I can tell you that doesn't happen very often," said the Rev. Robert Francis Murphy, minister of the Unitarian Universalist Fellowship of Falmouth.

From a Nation of Islam minister rallying workers at a demonstration to the state's Episcopal bishops declaring that the corporate culture served by the janitors bears primary responsibility for their low wages, many religious leaders are throwing their weight behind the strike. For janitors involved in the two-week-old strike, the visible presence and support from various denominations has given their cause moral weight. The alliance also marks an important moment for religious leaders and activists. "The explicit involvement of clergy is certainly far more significant than I have seen before," says the Rev. Edward Boyle, a Jesuit active in Boston-area labor issues for 33 years.

What's changed?

Last year's fight by Harvard University workers for a living wage was a "wake-up call for a lot of the religious community," says Murphy, underscoring the struggle that Greater Boston's low-income workers face.

Then came the janitor's strike, which featured a largely minority workforce struggling with low wages and inadequate health care, causes that are important to many religious activists.

The religious activism goes well beyond walking picket lines and offering prayers (such as Cardinal Bernard Law's special Mass Tuesday for the strikers). The Greater Boston Interfaith

Organization clergy and organizers have met with owners of buildings affected by the strike and with Steven Kletjian, chief executive of Unicco, one of the two biggest cleaning companies in the area. Some denominations have invited janitors to address their congregations and have raised money to replace lost pay. Ministers attend contract negotiations as observers.

A Unicco negotiator has called the clergy's involvement a case of good intentions trumping clear understanding of the issues.

Churches have long sided with workers. Pope Leo XIII issued Rerum Novarum, an encyclical supportive of labor rights, in 1891. But the labor-church alliance in the United States frayed during the Vietnam War, which many clergy opposed and the more conservative labor leaders backed.

In the mid-1990s, however, unions, weakened by decades of atrophying membership and public support, realized that coalitions with social activists could lend their causes greater legitimacy, says Gary Chaison, a professor at Clark University in Worcester and coauthor of the book *Unions and Legitimacy.*

"Nowadays, they're forming coalitions with their old friends, the clergy," he added.

Boyle says that two organizations founded during the Great Depression—the Archdiocese of Boston's Labor Guild, of which he is executive secretary, and the Jewish Labor Committee—were for many years the pivotal religious groups focused on local workplace issues. Now, their ranks have grown with the addition of groups such as the Massachusetts Interfaith Committee for Worker Justice, formed in 1997.

Chaison contrasts the janitors' strike with another labor story in the news, the lockout—recently halted by a presidential decree—of West Coast longshoremen over a contract dispute. That conflict involves workers better-off than the janitors agitating to protect their jobs, he argues. The janitors' strike, framing its cause as one of basic rights, has evolved from economic action into moral crusade.

"You could frame the janitors' dispute as a civil rights movement. You have a hard time making that case for a longshoreman," Chaison says.

The support of religious leaders and denominations might leverage broader public sympathy. The national president of the Unitarian Universalist Association has asked church members to honor picket lines.

Rabbi Jonah Pesner of Temple Israel in Boston says some in his congregation who own buildings have not only committed to providing their janitors a living wage but have supported his siding publicly with the strikers. "One guy thanked me for standing for the same Temple Israel principles that he learned here as a child."

"Religion and the Fall of Communism"

✧

Michael Bourdeaux

Michael Bourdeaux, founder of Keston College in England, is a scholar-activist who has focused on the systematic destruction of religion in Iron Curtain nations during the Cold War.

✧

People say that if you take one slab out of a dam it can never be put back, and eventually the whole structure will collapse. So it certainly was with the Berlin Wall. I have often been asked, "Was there ever a time before the wall came down when the demise of Communism seemed certain to you?" My answer is Yes. I had predicted this more than once in public.

So when did I first know that Communism could not survive? By the time of the election of Pope John Paul II, in October 1978, I had more than an inkling. When I experienced the aftermath of his first visit back to Poland in 1989 I was certain, after seeing the reaction to him in several different places. But there were a series of events—not by themselves individual happenings of dramatic content—which began to sow seeds of doubt before then.

From 1961, with incredible fortitude and organization, Russian Baptists began to gather systematic information about their opposition to Nikita Khrushchev's renewed persecution. This was under the very noses of the KGB, who dumped any activists they caught straight into prison. Already these evangelicals exhibited an indomitable spirit. Tragically for them, the official Baptist leaders in Moscow denied the facts of the persecution and impugned the integrity of those who reported it (and even of those few in the West who listened to the voice of the oppressed).

Beginning in 1965 a few isolated voices within the Russian Orthodox Church began to make themselves heard; the issue of religious persecution and opposition to it began to edge itself onto the agenda of international Christian organizations, and into international political debate. However, the reaction of the key bishops and officials of the Moscow patriarchate was identical to that of the Baptist leaders: information about persecution was dismissed as fiction, its purveyors were characterized as malcontents who wanted only the destruction of the Soviet system.

Only with the collapse of the Soviet system did it become possible to prove that this whole campaign was inspired and funded by the KGB, which had subverted a significant number of spokesmen for the Russian Orthodox Church. It is noteworthy that the Catholic bishops in the Soviet Union, few and isolated though they were, did not add their propagandistic voices to this campaign.

It was about ten years later, in the mid-1970s, that it first became obvious that the Catholic Church in the Soviet Union, about which so little was known, would play a key role in the emergent human-rights movement.

Information began to filter through to Keston from Lithuania. That country, though ten times smaller in population than Poland, had been just as solidly Catholic before its subjugation to Communism. Lithuanians began translating some of their most important documents into Russian; when I read them I was bowled over by their detail and the vigor of their defense of religious liberty.

Perhaps one factor more than any other had impressed me: that children, educated entirely under the Communist system and never having experienced the freedom their parents had enjoyed before 1939, were as ready to sacrifice themselves for their country and their church as their parents. The abiding loyalty of these Lithuanians to Rome, the symbol of their faith, shone out in many documents.

And at the very time that the Lithuanian protest began to gather momentum, there was a new political initiative involving North America and both Eastern and Western Europe: the Helsinki Agreement. When the Agreement was published in the Soviet press (as was required under its own terms), that "Helsinki monitors" were born. In almost every republic of the Soviet Union these groups emerged, determined to take the Agreement at its face value. The KGB stepped in and arrested almost everyone involved— but already there was sustenance for those who were now fighting Soviet oppression with increasing conviction.

In 1988, when the Russian Orthodox Church celebrated its millennium and I was able to witness, during those unforgettable summer weeks in Russia, the religious fervor that gripped a nation after seven decades of persecution. That there was almost no bloodshed in Eastern Europe was due in no small measure to the almost universal hatred of Communism, which proved to be more deep-seated and widespread than even I had envisaged.

However, this was not the time for triumphalism. There was immediate work to be done. Perhaps even we did not appreciate the full extent to which the blight of Communism had poisoned the very core of Christian life in so many places: among Protestants in East Germany, for example, just as seriously as within the Russian Orthodox Church or among the Baptists of what would soon be the "former" Soviet Union. The Catholic Church in many countries was not untainted, but nevertheless was able rapidly to put in train the process of reform.

A special case was the emergence into the open of the Ukrainian Catholic Church of the Eastern Rite (they now call themselves Greek Catholics). This was the largest single religious group to have been totally suppressed under the Soviet system. In 1946 Stalin's henchmen left not even a vestige above ground, as the Moscow Patriarchate enforced an absorption into its ranks of those clergy who were not complaisant to the Soviet system. The Gorbachev era saw increasingly open activity by clergy and laity of this underground Church. The eventual legalization of the Ukrainian Catholic Church, coinciding with Gorbachev's visit to Rome in December 1989, was to be one of the key events in Soviet church life during this period, presaging as it did the imminent secession of Ukraine from the USSR.

The West was amazingly apathetic to the challenge which all this represented. The notion that "Communism has collapsed, so there aren't any more problems," was a naive view, but it was endemic.

In a curious way, since information became freely available with the collapse of the Communist system it is less accessible than it used to be. When there was censorship, believers of all kinds used every possible means of sending information to us. Now that they can publish freely, it is quite rightly their concern to do so, but it has become much less imperative to communicate with the West.

Political events of the last year, with elections to the Duma last December and the choice of a president more recently, underline the continuing instability of the Soviet system, despite the progress in democracy. Even the religious liberty currently guaranteed under the Russian law is under threat from retrogressive elements, not least those in the Russian Orthodox Church itself. Therefore the efforts of those in the West who support religious freedom—not only monitoring new developments, but also engaging directly with Russian believers on a broad ecumenical front—are high priorities. Seven years after the collapse of the Wall, many opportunities are still to be taken, but the vistas opened up are exciting and the potential spiritual rewards great.

"A Catholic Rural Ethic for Agriculture, Environment, Food, and Earth"

⁓

The National Catholic Rural Life Conference

This statement was written in 1998 in response to a request from the Catholic Bishops of Kansas. It applies and summarizes Catholic social teaching to food, agriculture, land use, and the environment.

⁓

The National Catholic Rural Life Conference applies the following principles when considering economic, social, and environmental policies on behalf of agriculture and rural communities:

Human Dignity
Subsidiarity
Solidarity
Universal Destination of Goods
The Common Good
Integrity of Creation
Option for the Poor

These principles, adapted to rural life in the twentieth century, are drawn from the Scriptures, church traditions, and philosophical ethics. By these principles we are led as a faithful people to the care of Creation and the care of Community by the loving care of Christ.

PRINCIPLE 1: HUMAN DIGNITY

Human beings are created in the image of God. In this image, we human beings have worth and value by virtue of our existence, and that our dignity shall not be taken away from us nor diminished in any way. It is never permissible to use a human being to attain some proscribed end or purpose. The rightful purpose of an economic system, therefore, is to serve the human person; people are not meant to serve the economy or to be slaves to the economy. Any reduction of the human person to increase commodity production violates that dignity.

262

In a system of factory farms or debt-laden contract production, farmers and farmworkers are turned into modern-day serfs. This goes against the principle of human dignity. We as a society sometimes refuse to see the dignity of a farmer when he clings dearly to his land even as market forces work against him. We may be led to believe that such farmers are poor operators. They may also begin to see themselves no longer as farmers, but as failures. As fellow human beings, we should not tolerate this lowering of others. Human dignity is not meant to be defined by market forces and manipulators of the market.

PRINCIPLE 2: SUBSIDIARITY

In harmony with dignity, human beings hold the natural right to organize, to associate with one another, and to exercise responsible self-governance in their communities and local regions. No higher political authority—no state—should strip a person or local community of their capacity to judge and act on their own behalf.

Subsidiarity means local control and democratic participation, as long as people within the locality are willing and able to fulfill their necessary functions. Opposite to subsidiarity is centralized bureaucracies or economic concentration which rob people of their ability to act freely. Subsidiarity creates attachment to a real place—a person's town or city—which in turn creates strong feelings to the preservation of the nation and our constitutional republic.

In respect to the international situation and appeals to global authorities, any intervention to solve economic, political, social, and cultural problems should be applied to correct imbalances, but then fade away as responsible local control regains its rightful place. The World Trade Organization, for example, can create rules and regulations that supersede national laws; for purposes of global trade, labor, and environmental laws are pushed to the side. In many rural areas here and abroad, the land is turned into an endless stretch of commodity production for global export rather than a natural landscape of community imbued with rights. This we fight against in solidarity.

PRINCIPLE 3: SOLIDARITY

The virtue of solidarity propels individuals and communities to go beyond their narrow self-ishness or enclave mentality, and to care for their neighbors, their regions, even the world. Solidarity moves us beyond blind self-interest and private advantage; solidarity reminds us that we are social beings. In solidarity, we are joined in a greater body of being and the fruitful sharing of common desires.

For rural life, the principle of solidarity motivates us to care for the earth and the greater bio-community in which we ourselves are just a part. Solidarity in this sense means a stewardship of the land as we recognize that creation is a web of life in which we all cling together. What does not fall into the web of life? What is not a part of creation? We confess that all things are a part of creation, and solidarity extends this to say that all people and all living things are part of one community, the community of Christ—the new creation we seek in our modern lives.

To this end, the farmer and the consumer need to be in solidarity. They should know and understand one another since they are sharing in the very goods of the earth which sustain us as human beings. The American farmer also needs to be in solidarity with farmers around the world, each providing food for communities around them rather than ruinously competing with one another for a share of the global market.

PRINCIPLE 4: UNIVERSAL DESTINATION OF GOODS

The earth is God's and has been created for the well-being of all. Creation and all its goods are simply for the good of all. We also teach and accept that private ownership of goods is a natural right. So what is the best mechanism to distribute the goods of the earth? What is our measure of social equality that limits economic concentration of wealth and reduces the causes of poverty?

We say that on every private ownership there is a social mortgage: If bread is good for me, then bread for all is a goal worthy of us as dignified human beings in solidarity. Greed, excess profits, control by a few of the goods meant for many—these are contrary to God's desire that creation is for the good of all.

The universal destination of goods is clear: all of us, each person in the world, is meant to receive enough to eat and drink, enough to clothe and house themselves, and enough to live in human dignity. In rural life, all of us should realize that farmers continue to be squeezed by those who control farm inputs and supplies and by those who farmers must sell to. In some cases, farmers are caught in the grip of a single firm both supplying inputs and receiving the food or fiber produced, leaving the farmer vulnerable to monopolistic practices.

The destination and accessibility of goods today is skewed by our society's fascination with bigness and technology. The big operator or producer is favored over the small family farmer—scales are weighed against the common good as global corporate interests win political and financial favors. What might be called the "common good" is lost in the abyss between winners and losers, those who grow big and those who get pushed out.

PRINCIPLE 5: THE COMMON GOOD

The common good encourages individuals and communities to act on behalf of the good of all. "What is the good of all?" Surely the fundamental common good is the vital goods of human sustenance—food, water, the air we breathe, the right to life. The common good is also social, which means that each of us finds comfort and happiness when we belong to others around us and when we are accepted for who we are. Do we extend this to rural life and the many farming communities which are dying? In our modern lives, have we put the burden of proof upon farmers—and everyone else—to convince us that we should care about them?

The common good is cultural, which gives meaning to our lives by allowing us to act in concert with others and leading us to build a way to live, work, play, and believe together. Do we include farmers and farmworkers in how we bring meaning to our lives? Does rural life no longer retain a place in our modern world except as an idealized countryside image on a package of food?

Finally, we say as Catholics that the common good is religious, which deepens us as individuals and as a people in the sublime harmonies of the universe. The common good is at once a basic need and an ultimate end, the sharing of life's necessities and the love of one another and creation which flows from our love of God and God's love for us. Where the common good is ignored or disdained, we should not be surprised by the social, economic, personal, and ecological disharmonies which will grow like choking weeds around us.

PRINCIPLE 6: INTEGRITY OF CREATION

As Catholics we believe that the earth belongs to the Lord. If this is true, then creation has an integrity and an inherent value beyond its utility or usefulness for human beings. Human beings are meant to be responsible stewards of creation, and indeed we can say that we work in harmony with God as co-creators. Just as God is One, the web of life is one. What is not a part of creation?

How we live on the land with creation cannot be disconnected to how we live in community as social beings. If we are to sustain ourselves in community, we must maintain a healthy environment, we must develop a beneficial economy, and we must build a just society. When we say "support the family farm," we are claiming that a proper habitat for the family is on a farm. Here nature and human beings can live integrally and share the benefits of creation.

PRINCIPLE 7: OPTION FOR THE POOR

A fundamental moral measure of any society is to ask how the poor and vulnerable are faring. We say that the poor are those who suffer from lack of basic goods and necessities. But following all I have said so far, the poor includes our degraded lands, spoiled waters, confined livestock, and threatened wildlife. The poor bring before us a profound question about the order of the world, and whether this order is good. The option for the poor means that we should act—as individuals and as members of community—to overcome the structural injustice of social and world orders.

The National Catholic Rural Life Conference assists by helping to analyze structural problems in our food and agricultural system. As consumers, each of us can decide to end our support of certain foods and food processes that favor large global corporations over small farmers. At the political level, we can fight against social injustice by contacting our local, state, and federal representatives and voicing our concern for the rights of farmers and farmworkers, the safety and security of our food, and a greater protection of the environment.

Finally, the option for the poor in rural life means to design realistic alternatives to how we currently produce food in an intensively industrial way. The preferential option for the poor is a commitment to transforming society into a place where human rights and the dignity of all are respected. So this returns us to our initial principles of human dignity, solidarity, and the common good. Let us begin to build a new earth based on our new creation as the faithful followers of Christ.

ADDENDUM: WHAT MORE CAN WE DO?

As part of a broad-based effort, Catholic parishes can facilitate a greater understanding of—and response to—the issues affecting family-based and owner-operated farms. It is important that these issues be included as part of parish-based catechesis and adult education activities. Besides relating farm issues to parish interests, there is also a need to raise awareness on food and consumer topics, such as the corporate structure of our food system, the quality and safety of food products, and community-supported agriculture (i.e., direct marketing between farmers and consumers). Encourage parish-based meetings to facilitate outside speakers, video presentations, and group discussions.

Rural parishes have a unique role to play in the lives of farm and ranch families. Often, the parish is also a focal point of social and emotional support as well as spirituality. Parishes have a special responsibility for seeing to it that hurting individuals and families are assisted and, when necessary, directed to proper resources, such as farm crisis hotlines or mental health and financial counseling. Equally important is that hurting individuals and families need to stay involved in parish and community life, especially through effective outreach and attention toward affected children and youth.

Whether farmer or consumer, it can be overwhelming for anyone to understand and deal with powerful economic forces that are creating difficult circumstances for family-based, owner-operated farms. There is a great sense of helplessness about a person's ability to withstand and change these forces, many of which are of a global dimension. Nonetheless, it is important for us as members of the Church to let family farmers know that we are aware, at least in part, of the difficulties they face in production agriculture today.

The Jubilee Year 2000 offered an opportunity for parishes to pursue their concern for the land and farm communities. Here was an opportunity to reconsider the meaning of the gift of the earth and the use we make of God's creation. During the twenty-first century, parishes can work toward turning the scarred land back into a sacred land according to Catholic social teachings and the seven principles of a Catholic rural ethic.

Some specific actions to foster sound agriculture in your community or region:

- Oppose concentrated animal feeding operations and "factory farms."
- Encourage Church leadership and grassroot organizations to advocate family-sized, owner-operated farms and to act on behalf of family farmers.
- Educate yourself and others about sustainable agriculture.
- Support an alternative food system: Use parish kitchens, church halls, and other church institutions as local processing centers and incubators for local food production.
- Use church halls and parking lots for farmer markets and direct agricultural marketing.
- Join in a National Period of Prayer for Family Farms, beginning on World Food Day (October 16) and continuing until Thanksgiving Day.
- Support the call of a Agricultural Summit for Bishops, in concert with staff from the Pontifical Council on Peace and Justice.
- Ask civic and governmental institutions to buy locally and support a regional food system.
- Help schools develop garden projects for children—to eat their own produce or to share with the poor.
- Support policies which prevent the loss of prime farmland, control urban sprawl, and develop balanced approaches to growth.
- Produce cookbooks for your local community which contain recipes using local foods and which celebrate special days, seasons, and events expressive of the connection between spirituality and the food and fiber produced on the land.
- Frequent restaurants which buy food from local, sustainable, family farms.

- ☙ Support pasture poultry, pasture pork and beef, and locally-produced vegetables.
- ☙ Demand labeling which tells us who produced the food, where it was produced, and how it was produced.
- ☙ Engage in networks and practice solidarity with like-minded organizations in your locality. Support each other at local, state, regional, and national levels. Plan regular meetings and contracts with other social action and social justice advocates.
- ☙ Think about feeding neighbors and local communities as much as feeding the world!

"Globalization and the Perennial Question of Justice"

❧

Mary John Mananzan

Mary John Mananzan is a missionary Benedictine sister and the president of St. Scholastica's College, Manila. She has written *Challenges to the Inner Room* and *The Woman Question in the Philippines*. Here she describes the realities of globalization from the standpoint of its victims.

❧

INTRODUCTION

After reflecting on the question posed by the editor of this *Festschrift*, "What is the most important spiritual question of our time?" I have come to the conclusion that it still is the question of justice. I also find it fitting to write on this topic because this *Festschrift* is in honor of a woman passionately committed to justice. For a long time justice has been the preoccupation of the church and yet it is as urgent now as ever before. In our times this question of justice is, for me, tied up with a global phenomenon—globalization. In this essay I propose to clarify this elusive term, discuss its impact on the peoples of the third world, especially Asia, particularly the Philippines. I would then make some theological and ethical conclusions and see its impact on one's spirituality.

WHAT IS GLOBALIZATION?

It is very necessary to say exactly what we mean by the word "globalization," because so many things are meant by it. It can mean the worldwide development of technology that makes the world into the so-called global village. As such, we have nothing against this development. Some people will take it to mean the networking going on internationally in all fields, and if this is all that is meant, we also have nothing against it, because true international solidarity cannot but be positive. I would like to define it, however, in the context in which it arose—in its economic *Sitz im Leben*. In the 60s and 70s, activists (including me) went into the streets to denounce "foreign control of the economy," "economic imperialism," and so on. Today, these words have become unpopular and yet the reality they describe is still very much with us but decked with the euphemistic word "globalization."

So generically, globalization means the integration of the economies of the world into the liberal market economy of the West controlled by the G8. Here are some of its main features:

1. *Borderless economy.* It advocates the elimination of protective tariffs and gives free play to the market.
2. *Import liberalization.* This is a corollary of the borderless economy. Goods from all other countries can enter our country. This may seduce us as consumers to think that it is good because then we have many choices and the competition can bring down the prices. But this will also kill local industries, and when they are killed we will be dependent for our basic needs on other countries and this certainly will not ensure, for example, food security. This is not sustainable consumption.
3. *Free play of the market.* This advocates less control from the state and making the market forces the main criteria of activities. This will make profit and market demand the supreme values. Everything else will be sacrificed to these—consumers, labor, and so on. This does away with social and ethical concerns.
4. *Privatization.* All productive enterprises will be put into private hands, and in our case, mostly foreign hands. This effectively entrenches the foreign control of our economy (Calabarzone controlled by Taiwanese, Lotto by Malaysians, textiles by Germans, and so on). This will also put basic services, such as energy, into private hands, whose motive is profit. Therefore, subsidies will have to be taken away and prices of basic services will soar.
5. *Financial capitalism.* Today, there is actually not much productivity going on in our country. What is going on is financial speculation. So even production is done not to serve needs but for speculation. The only two productions happening are textiles and electronics, but these depend upon imports for 80 percent of their components.

The result of this is an export-oriented, import-dependent, foreign-investment-controlled, and debt-ridden economy.

THE IMPACT OF GLOBALIZATION ON PEOPLES

Globalization is not a new phenomenon. As mentioned above, it is the euphemistic term for what we have fought against for many years: the foreign control of our economy—in short, economic imperialism. But the new word is seductive because it promises so many things that would make a heaven on earth. And yet, when we look at the actual consequences of globalization, it is just the opposite.

Consider the crisis we are suffering in Asia. Barely five years ago Asian countries were supposed to be "tigers" and "cubs." Now, no Asian country, not even Japan, is spared a currency crisis, stock market crisis, food crisis, energy crisis, employment crisis, and so on.

Janet Bruin aptly observes,

Instead of spreading wealth around, "globalization" and current macro-economic policies in both North and South are concentrating wealth in fewer hands. Unemployment and the number of people living in poverty are increasing in many countries. Workers are being forced into low paying jobs and women are being forced into unsafe workplaces, into the unprotected informal economy where social security and other benefits do not apply, or into prostitution. Children are forced to leave school for work in carpet factories, farms or in the streets to help support their families, and people are forced to leave their countries in search of paid labor elsewhere, provoking an international backlash against immigrants as economic and security threats. Both migration and anti-immigrant xenophobia are expected to intensify as population pressures, unemployment, and economic disparities between countries become ever more acute.[1]

This has lately been confirmed by the United Nations Development Programme (UNDP), which has come up with a comprehensive report involving many countries of the third world, pointing to one uncontested fact: globalization has widened the gap between the rich and the poor.[2]

In the Philippines and in Asia conversion of fertile lands into golf courses and industrial complexes has reduced the land available for the cultivation of staple food. Some cultivated lands are reserved for cash crops like asparagus and cut flowers. This not only reduces lands available for cultivation of staple food for local consumption, but also causes adverse effects on soil fertility because of the massive use of fertilizers and pesticides. The Philippines now imports rice, whereas it provided that staple sufficiently for itself in the past. Lack of subsidy and technological help to farmers renders agriculture a nonsustainable activity and reduces farmers to amassing continuous debt. The proliferation of prawn farms and fishing pens for growing prawns and fish for export has allotted marine resources, which form part of the peoples' daily fare, to the export business.

Deregulation of the oil companies has caused them to raise the price of oil arbitrarily and, in a domino effect, that of all basic commodities. All this, plus the recent devaluation of the Philippine peso, has caused housewives to stretch their marketing money to the breaking point. Import liberalization tries to convince the consumer that this would mean more choices and cheaper prices in competition. But this eventually destroys local industries and local businesses, leading to the loss of food security because the consumers become dependent on foreign producers. The Chernobyl incident underlined the dependence of a lot of countries with regard to dairy products.

The Center for Women Resources study on the General Agreement of Tariffs and Trade (GATT) concludes,

> As our economy is oriented more and more towards producing "cash crops" and depending more and more on imports for basic staples such as rice and corn, sources of our daily food consumption become unstable, putting the very survival of the Filipinos at stake.[3]

So are we saying that no one is benefiting from globalization? Of course not! But the question is, Who benefits from it? The upper 2 percent who have capital. Maybe it trickles down to the 10 percent who are used in the management of the enterprises. And basic sectors are not only excluded from the gains of the economic activities going under globalization, but are also negatively affected by it. Homes of urban poor were violently demolished during the last Asia-Pacific Economic Cooperation (APEC) meeting hosted by the Philippines. Due to land conversions, thousands of Filipino farmers have been dispersed and have lost the lands they till. Indigenous people are suffering the loss of their ancestral lands due to mining. Further, the strip mining has polluted their rivers and seas, depriving them of still another source of living. Workers who are supposed to be the main beneficiaries of industrialization are now suffering the loss of job security because of contractual labor practices. And in all these sectors, women are the most adversely affected because of the feminization of poverty.

Globalization has not respect for the uniqueness of peoples' culture. It has successfully "macdonalized" or "cocalized" the world. Urban youth culture is a monoculture of discos, malls, and jeans. Indigenous culture is exploited and bastardized for tourists. So the effect of globalization is not only on our economic life but also on our culture. It also has political implications because the decision makers of international agencies like the IMF-WB, WTO, and GATT are not elected by people, yet their decisions adversely affect the lives of so many. Nicanor Perlas writes, "The posture of GATT is totalitarian and radically arrayed against any notion of sovereignty and self-determination."[4]

THEOLOGICAL AND ETHICAL REFLECTIONS

When one looks at the effects of globalization on the majority of excluded peoples, one can conclude that it has unleashed forces of death. Pope John Paul II writes in *Solicitudo Rei Socialis,*

> In today's world, including the world of economics, the prevailing picture is one destined to lead us more quickly toward death rather than one of concern for true development which would lead all toward a "more human world" as envisaged by the encyclical *Populorum Progressio.*[5]

The Ecumenical Association of Third World Theologians (EATWOT) has drawn this same conclusion. Thus, it has made globalization its main concern in its last general assembly in December 1996 in Tagaytay, Philippines, with its theme "Search for a New Just World Order: Challenges to Theology." Moreover, it has adopted as its theological theme for the next five years, "Towards a Fullness of Life: Theology in the Context of Globalization."

In all the national, continental, and intercontinental meetings of EATWOT the members are urged to continue the theological reflection begun in the general assembly. In some theological reflections EATWOT members see globalization as a sort of "new religion." It has its God: profit and money. It has its high priests: GATT, WTO, IMF-WB. It has its doctrines and dogmas: import liberalization, deregulation, and so on. It has its temples: the super megamalls. It has its victims on the altar of sacrifice: the majority of the world—the excluded and marginalized poor.

In the face of globalization EATWOT sees the need for a prophetic theology

> that will critique prince and priest, market and mammon, multinationals and war merchants and all hegemony and all plunder of the poor. It will call into question the silence of religions and churches as children die of hunger in Iraq, in Orissa, due to imperialist policies of superpowers or local magnates. It will call into question the centuries old oppression of women at home and in society. And it will seek to serve people's dreams and struggles for a beautiful tomorrow.[6]

The values of globalization are also ethically questionable. Its foremost value of profit and market is definitely an example of "serving mammon." It has commodified people, treating workers as merely factors in production. This is shown by its policies of "flexibilization of labor" and "labor-only contracting." Women and children are likewise commodities to be used in child labor or in sex trafficking. Its practice of cutthroat competition, which even prevents governments from protecting their fledgling industries, is an economic survival of the fittest. This leads to the economic dictatorship of the rich and powerful, who become even richer and more powerful. For globalization, people such as the urban poor, who do not have capital or skills to be in the playing field, are totally expendable. Globalization promotes consumerism by its aggressive advertising techniques and by luring consumers with megamalls and supermarkets. It convinces people that their wants are needs and that they have the right to buy anything as long as they can afford it. This leads to surplus production, which has not only depleted our irreplaceable natural resources, but also has caused ecological disasters such as deforestation, pollution, thinning of the ozone layer, global warming, and, with these, the consequent "natural" calamities.

One ethically questionable issue that is connected with globalization is biotechnology or genetic engineering. Nicanor Perlas describes it this way:

> This science and technology package is based on the belief that there is nothing sacred in life, that life is simply a bunch of chemicals (DNA and related compounds) and their interactions and that all traits—from chemical properties, outer appearance, and behaviour—can be understood and reconstructed on the basis of studies of the DNA and its manipulation. Human beings could now play God, disassembling, decoding, recombining all life forms on the planet.[7]

At present, tens of thousands of genetic experimentations are going on. Life forms have been patented, animals have been cloned, and both open the ominous possibility of cloning human beings. With GATT, activities of biopirates have been legitimized. Multinational companies go all over the world collecting precious plants and animal species, interfere with their genetic makeup, and patent them to the detriment of the peoples who had been using these for centuries for their livelihood. For the sake of profit, seeds are tampered with so that they cannot reproduce, forcing farmers to buy more seeds. Furthermore, science and technology are producing food products that are harmful, such as irradiated food, pesticide-laden products, and biotech food. Indeed, never before has the assault to life been as massive as in our times. Economics cannot continue to be immune from moral and ethical scrutiny. The tremendous injustice, exclusion of peoples, and assault to life resulting from globalization must be morally judged and condemned. The opposite values of sharing, service, compassion, equity, interdependence, and solidarity must be reemphasized.

SPIRITUALITY FOR OUR TIMES

In order to face the challenges of today, we need to develop a spirituality attuned to our times. There are several characteristics of this spirituality.

1. It is a *prophetic spirituality*. It is a spirituality that is convinced of the good news it has to announce and has the courage to denounce what it considers as the bad news. There are many people who are more convinced that God wants us to suffer than that God wants us to be happy. We somehow have to convey to people that God wants them to be truly happy in an integral way, meaning body and soul. When we see obstacles to this integral salvation of peoples, we must not hesitate to take a stand, even if this would mean risks or inconveniences for us. In other words, it is a committed spirituality. In our times it is a commitment to economic justice, gender and racial equality, and ecological activism.

2. It is an *integral spirituality*. Just as we proclaim an integral salvation, we also have to develop an integral spirituality that transcends dichotomies such as body-soul, sacred-profane, contemplation-action, heaven-earth, and so on. We need to integrate our

relationships with God, with ourselves, with others, and with the planet. It is inclusive and resists exclusion of peoples for any reason, be it class, race, gender, or any other.

3. It is a spirituality that is characterized by *simplicity of lifestyle*. In contrast to consumerism, it strives to do without superfluities, mindful that the earth's resources are limited and that these have to be shared by all.

4. It is an *empowering spirituality*. It is self-affirming, aware, and grateful for God's gifts to us giving us a healthy self-esteem. It is also mutually empowering, affirming other people and facilitating their blossoming.

5. It is a *healing spirituality*. It is a process of healing one's own wounds and using one's own experiences to heal others.

6. It is a *contemplative spirituality*. It emphasizes moments of reflection, meditation, and contemplation—being present to the Presence, a constant awareness of the absolute within us, who is the inexhaustible source of joy, love, and energy and makes us committed but carefree.

7. It is an *Easter spirituality*. It is a spirituality that transcends Good Friday, that is infected with the fearless joy of Easter. It resists the forces of death and promotes the enhancement of life. It feasts more than it fasts. It is not so much control as surrender. It is not cold asceticism but a celebration of life.

CONCLUSION

The need is urgent to restore justice and harmony in human relationships at all levels and the relationship of human beings to the whole of creation. The continuing resistance of peoples' organizations against the forces of death in our society is a sign of hope. Christians have options. They can be obstacles to these efforts, bystanders, and let history move without them. Or, they can accompany the struggling peoples on their journey to the new Jerusalem, and together with them build a new heaven and a new earth.

NOTES

1. Janet Bruin, *Root Causes of the Global Crisis* (Manila: Institute of Political Economy, 1996), 11.

2. *Human Development Report* (New York: Oxford University).

3. "The GATT," in *Piglas Diwa* (Manila: Center for Women Resources, 1995), 8.

4. Nicanor Perlas, *Elite Globalization and the Attack on Christianity* (Quezon City, Philippines: Center for Alternative Development Initiatives, 1998), 44.

5. Pope John Paul II, *Solicitudo Rei Socialis* (Rome: Vatican Press, 1987), 40.

6. K. C. Abraham, ed., *Search for a New Just World Order: Challenges to Theology* (Bangalore, India: Voices Publication of EATWOT), 207.

7. Perlas, *Elite Globalization*, 31.

"Mammon and the Culture of the Market: A Socio-Theological Critique"

❦

Harvey Cox

Harvey Cox, professor at Harvard Divinity School, is an American Baptist minister and a leading American theologian. He writes a column for www.belief.net and authored the influential books *The Secular City* and *The Feast of Fools*. This essay offers a vision of religious value that contrasts with the dominant values of globalization.

❦

Just as a truly global market has emerged for the first time in human history, that market is functioning without moral guideposts and restraints, and it has become the most powerful institution of our age. Even nation-states can often do little to restrain or regulate it. More and more, the idea of "the market" is construed, not as a creation of culture ("made by human hands," as the Bible says about idols), but as the "natural" way things happen. For this reason, the "religion" the market generates often escapes criticism and evaluation or even notice. It becomes as invisible to those who live by it as was the religion of the preliterate Australians whom Durkheim studied, who described it as just "the way things are."[1] My thesis is that the emerging global market culture—despite those who do not, or choose not, to see it—is generating an identifiable value-laden, "religious" worldview. I would also hold that a truly critical theology should make people aware of these religious values and of how they coincide with or contradict Christian values.

There is much disagreement today about the global world market and its culture. But these also display some characteristics about which both advocates and critics agree. For example:

1. Global market culture uproots traditional forms of work, family, and community. In doing so, it also undermines traditional belief systems and moral norms. Some welcome these changes as contributing to "progress." Others lament the erosion of "traditional values." But all agree that the process is universal and apparently inevitable wherever global market culture spreads. Indeed, such changes are often believed to be prerequisite to the development of a genuinely market-oriented culture.

2. Global market culture produces enormous new wealth but tends to polarize populations between a relatively small group who reap the benefits of this wealth and a much larger group who are excluded from its bounty. For example, in June 1996 the U.S. Census Bureau reported that the gap between affluent Americans and everyone else in the nation was wider than at any time since the end of World War II, and steadily increasing. On a global scale, the disparity was

even wider. The result is that as we begin the twenty-first century, in Central America as well as in Africa the "quality of life" levels today are lower than those experienced by the indigenous peoples of Central America and Africa five hundred years ago. There are many who consider this to be *the* scandal of our age. More than 70 percent of the people of Central America live in poverty, 50 percent in economic misery, and these percentages continue to rise each year.

There is relatively little disagreement about the scope of this disparity. But advocates and opponents of the global market economy tend to disagree on how long the polarization will last and how best to overcome it. Advocates claim it is only a temporary phase and that at some future point everyone will be drawn into the benefits. Opponents say this is a false promise, that an unregulated, "free" market economy will always produce enormous inequalities that will only grow worse over time. They also warn that if the entire population of the earth, now about six billion people, were in fact to reach the level of consumption enjoyed today by the elites in industrially developed countries, the planet's resources would be exhausted even faster than they are being depleted now.

3. All agree that an economy is closely related to the possibilities of political democracy. But the nature of the relationship is a highly disputed point. Its advocates say that by dissolving traditional, semifeudal, and corporate-state structures and command economies, the "free market" makes political freedom possible as well. Others claim that when the market becomes this powerful it "marketizes" politics, with the result that the democratic idea of "one person one vote" is replaced by "one dollar one vote." Then, what appears to be a democracy becomes in fact a plutocracy, where the wealthiest groups exert undue influence on the electoral process.

The recurrent debate over campaign finance reform in the United States highlights this dispute. Some defend virtually unlimited contributions as a constitutionally protected exercise of free speech. Others disagree and point out that although theoretically anyone can be elected to the Senate, in actuality only people with private fortunes or who are financially supported by special interest groups with considerable financial resources have much of a chance. Consequently, a majority of U.S. senators are millionaires.

These are all complex debates that will undoubtedly continue for some time. My goal in this essay, however, is to explore the *mainly* implicit value-and-meaning system that market capitalism engenders, sustains, and, in fact, requires. My contention is that, however these debates proceed, the discourse *within which* they are argued (a highly value-laden one) is rarely probed and that the myths that carry these values are scarcely examined at all.[2]

Although, as will soon become evident, I am highly critical of many (not all) of the values of market culture, I do not use the term "myth" here in a polemical sense. I use it, as phenomenologists of religion have for decades, to characterize the empirically nonverifiable assumptions—often stated in narrative fashion—that constitute the worldview of market culture. I realize that others have done this before. What I wish to add is that this worldview is itself grounded in a system of beliefs—sometimes, but not often, stated—that add up to a functioning religion grounded in a doctrine of God.

THE GOD OF THE MARKET AND THE MARKET AS GOD

The religion of market culture exhibits all the qualities of a more classical religion. It has:

A story ("myth") about the origin and course of the human enterprise. The current worldwide "Market Revolution" is seen as the culmination of this history.

An interpretation, often quite explicit, of the inner meaning of human history. It is the story of freedom, with human freedom of choice as its climax.

A doctrine of sin and redemption—what is wrong and how to fix it. More about this will be said below.

An array of sacraments—that is, rituals for delivering the salvific power to those in need of it. This sacramental system focuses on the central act of exercising the freedom to choose by making market decisions: "I shop therefore I am."[3]

A vast catechetical network by which to convey teachings to those who require enlightenment. Advertising is the systematic self-explication of the market faith.

An eschatology (a teaching about the "last things"). This was recently described by Fukuyama in his book *The End of History and the Last Man.*[4]

A pantheon of exemplary heroes—the risk-taking, informal, relaxed, but tough and realistic new breed of enterpreneurs—who inspire emulation as did the saints and martyrs of old.

Most important, the market culture's "god," under whose benevolent, if sometimes mysterious guidance, all things eventually work together for the good. These divine qualities the market culture attributes to the *Market itself* (which I shall, from here on, capitalize to indicate its "divine" status).

THE MARKET GOD

Different religions have, of course, somewhat different—although sometimes quite similar— views of the formal qualities of God. In Christianity, God has traditionally been seen as omnipotent, omnipresent, and omniscient, although these characteristics are partially hidden from human eyes by sin and by the transcendent mystery of the Divine. The Market God also exhibits all these "divine attributes," but, analogously, they are also not always completely evident and must often be affirmed by faith.

1. The Market Is Omnipotent

From the earliest stages of human history there have been markets. But in previous eras the Market was not "God" because there were other centers of value, other "gods." The market functioned within a complex set of traditions and institutions that restrained and guided it. As Karl Polanyi has demonstrated in his classical *The Great Transformation,* only in the past two centuries has the Market been cut loose from these social and ethical restraints and allowed to become the culturally determinative institution it is today.[5]

At first, the Market's ascent to Olympic supremacy replicated the gradual emergence of Zeus above all the other divinities of the ancient Greek pantheon.[6] But recently the Market has become more like the Yahweh of the Old Testament, not just one superior deity contending with others, but the Supreme Being, the only "true" deity, a "jealous God" whose reign must be universally recognized and who brooks no rivals.

In the American school of "process theology" advocated by followers of Alfred North Whitehead, God is *not yet* fully omnipotent but wills to be and is *becoming* so. This would seem true for the Market God. The true, accomplished omnipotence of the Market God would mean that everything was for sale. This is not quite the case. Not yet. But in the logic of the Market, there is no humanly conceivable limit to the infinite reach of consumer choice, the profit motive, and the transformation of creation into commodities. Land is the key example. For millennia of human history, land has held multiple meanings for human beings—as soil, resting place of the ancestors, holy mountain or enchanted forest, tribal homeland, aesthetic inspiration, sacred turf. The Market transforms all these complex meanings into one: land becomes real estate; there is no land that is not theoretically for sale, at the right price. This change radically alters the human relationship to land. The same, of course, is true of water and air and presumably of space and the heavenly bodies. In theological terms, this process appears to be similar to the miracle of transubstantiation in which the ordinary bread and wine of the Eucharist are changed into vehicles of sacred power—only in reverse. Sacred elements are now transformed into saleable products.

The human body itself is the latest, but surely not the last, object of this reverse transubstantiation by the Market. Beginning with blood, but now all organs—including kidneys, skin, bone marrow, eyes, and the heart itself—are being moved into the expanding realm of the commodity. Fathers' sperm cells and mothers' wombs are for sale and rent. But this transformation is not proceeding without opposition. A considerable battle is shaping up in the United States about the effort to market human genes. For the first time in memory, virtually every religious institution in the country, including so-called conservative and liberal ones, have banded together to oppose this new extension of the power of the Market God into the human body that persons of faith believe was created "in the image of God." Many nonreligious people also oppose this extension of the Market, on other grounds.

Occasionally some people try to bite the hand of the deity that allegedly feeds them. On October 26, 1996, the German government, with no previous notice to its 350 residents, ran an advertisement offering the entire village of Liebenberg—in what was previously East Germany—for sale. Its citizens—many of them elderly and retired or unemployed—loudly protested. They had certainly not liked communism, but when they opted for the market economy that reunification would bring, they had hardly expected this. The town, however, includes a thirteenth-century church, a baroque castle, a lake, a hunting lodge, two restaurants, and three thousand acres of meadow and forest. Once a favorite site for boar hunting by the old German nobility, it was obviously entirely too valuable a piece of real estate to overlook. Besides, having once been expropriated by the former East German communist government, it was now legally eligible for sale under the terms of German reunification. The outraged *burghers* of Liebenberg were finally granted a postponement. But everyone realized that in the long run theirs was a losing battle. The Market may lose a skirmish, but, *sub specia aeternitatis*, it always wins.

Lakes, meadows, church buildings—everything now carries its sticker price. But this practice exacts a cost. As everything in creation is transformed into a commodity, human beings inevitably internalize this cultural ethos and look upon the world, nature, each other, and themselves as bearing a colored tag with numbers on it. The inherent worth of things and persons disappears as their sale value defines them. Money and income become the determinants of worth. According to the inscrutable logic of the Market God, if a child is born severely handicapped, and has little to contribute to the gross national product, there is no logical reason to expend valuable resources to keep him alive, unless the value derived from sale of medicines, leg braces, and the CAT scan equipment is figured into the equation. A careful cost analysis might conceivably conclude that it would be economically worthwhile to keep the child alive, but the inherent value of the child's life is not part of the calculation. The same costing out is applicable to older people who have lost their productive utility, but might become customers for nursing homes and geriatric medical suppliers. Health and life itself change before our eyes on the Market altar, and once the God of the Market's rule is complete, everything will be for sale and nothing will be sacred.

In fact, it seems that already not even the sacred is sacred. Recently a sharp controversy erupted in Great Britain when a Railway Pension Fund that had owned the small jeweled casket in which the remains of Saint Thomas à Becket are said to have rested decided to auction it off through Sotheby's. The casket dates from the twelfth century and is thought of both as a sacred relic and as a national treasure. A bid by the British Museum was not high enough, however, and the casket was sold to a Canadian. Only feverish last minute measures by the British government prevented the removal of a national relic from the U.K. In principle, however, and according to the logic of the Market God, there is no reason why any relic, coffin, body, or other national monument—including the Statue of Liberty or Westminster Abbey—should not be for sale.

2. The Market Is Omniscient

Current thinking about the global "free market" attributes to it a comprehensive wisdom that in the past only the gods have known. The Market, it is alleged, is able to determine not just how much things should sell for but also what genuine human needs are, what raw materials and capital should cost, and how much workers should be paid. In days of old, seers entered a trance state and then informed seekers what mood the gods were in and whether it was advisable to begin a journey or enter into a marriage. The prophets of Israel repaired to the desert and then returned to announce whether Yahweh was feeling benevolent or wrathful. Today, the Market God's fickle will is clarified by the daily reports that emanate from Wall Street and by the other sensory organs of finance. Thus we can learn on a day-to-day basis that the Market was "apprehensive," "relieved," "nervous," or even at times "jubilant." On the basis of this information, the faithful make critical decisions about whether to buy or sell. Like one of the devouring gods of old, the Market—aptly personified as a bull or a bear—must be fed and kept happy under all circumstances.

The prophets and seers of the Market God's whims and moods are the high priests of the Market religion. To act against their admonitions is to risk excommunication and possibly damnation. Today, for example, if any government's policy displeases the Market God, those responsible for such irreverence will be made to suffer. The fact that the Market is not at all displeased by rising unemployment or a decline in the living standards of workers, or can be gleeful about the expansion of cigarette sales to Asian young people, does not cause anyone to question the Market's unfathomable omniscience. Like Calvin's inscrutable God, the Market's ways may be mysterious but It knows best.

But the Market God's omniscience seeks further knowledge. The traditional God of Christianity is described as One "unto whom all hearts are open, all desires known, and from whom no secrets are hid." The Market God too wants to see the deepest secrets and darkest desires of our hearts. By knowing our fears and desires, and then by offering commodities-for-sale as the remedy, the reach of the Market can be extended infinitely. Like the gods of the past, whose priests offered up the prayers and petitions of the people, the Market God relies on its own intermediaries: market researchers. Trained in the advanced arts of psychology, which has replaced theology as the true "science of the soul," market researchers—like the confessors of the medieval Catholic Church—probe the fears and fantasies, the insecurities and hopes, of the populace. They are also the Market's soothsayers. But instead of examining bird entrails, they rely on thematic perception profiles, depth interviews, field surveys, and focus groups. Then, by devising powerful images (once mainly the artifacts of the priests, now the favored medium of the marketeers), they link whatever deep human aspiration they uncover to a commodity that has the power, they assure us, to assuage it.[7]

Advertising is both the catechumenate and the confessional of the Market Religion. The penitent is first urged to become aware of his or her failure. Is someone lonely, unattractive, insecure, in need of love and respect? The cure of the soul can heal the most painful flaw. This new item of apparel, houseware, jewelry, software, perfume, tobacco, food, or drink will restore both body and spirit. The proof that the product for sale does provide satisfaction is that we see it replete with icons of carefree, healthy, vigorous people—young, nubile, joyously interracial, and almost always at the beach—and so can be sure of its universal redemptive properties. Now, go and buy, and sin no more.

In the cold light of day it may seem like sheer nonsense to claim that a perfume can bring anyone serenity, that a laundry detergent can solidify anyone's family ties, or that swallowing a mixture of carbonated water, sweetener, and synthetic flavoring can initiate you as a full member of the rollicking fellowship of those who live life to the hilt. But to dare to question the omniscience of the Market is to question the inscrutable wisdom of God. People continue to buy these things, it is argued, and so it is clear they are exercising sovereign consumer choice. Consequently, even things that seem patently absurd must be believed—if only to make sure the mechanism keeps rolling. As the early Christian theologian Tertullian once remarked, "Credo quia absurdum est" (I believe because it is absurd). It seems that the real venue of the *sacrificum intellectum* today is not the church but the mall. It is no longer God but the Market that—by definition—knows all and knows best.

3. The Market Is Omnipresent

The latest trend in Market economics is the attempt to apply market principles to areas that once appeared to be exempt, such as courtship, family life, marital relations, and child rearing. Henri Lepage, an enthusiastic advocate of the world market culture, speaks now about a "total market." Just as Saint Paul reminded the Corinthians that their own poets sang of a God "in whom we live and move and have our being," so now the Market is not only around us but inside us, informing our senses and our feelings. There seems nowhere left to flee from Its insatiable maw. Like the Hound of Heaven, It now pursues us home from the marketplace itself and into the nursery and the bedroom. Once Zeus becomes supreme, he can bear no rivals. Once the logic of the Market is enthroned as omniscient, it demands our devotion in all realms of life. Finding a wife or husband becomes just another example of comparing what is in the showcase and engaging in some carefully calculated shopping. Of course, like other consumer choices, if the customer is not satisfied, then—since there is nothing intrinsic or unique about the item sold—a return-and-exchange policy must be understood as part of the original transaction. Perhaps soon every marriage, not just some, will be preceded by a documented prenuptial agreement—the not-to-be-mislaid sales slip required with returned or exchanged goods.

It used to be thought that at least the inward, or spiritual, dimension of life was resistant to market values. But as the markets for material goods become increasingly glutted, such previously nonmarketable phenomena as adventure, serenity, personal growth, and spirituality are appearing in the catalogs. Since buyers already have all the wardrobe, automotive, and audiovisual gear they can absorb, the eternally creative Market offers personal growth, exotic experiences in unspoiled regions, ecstasy, and "spirituality"—now available in a convenient generic form. In this way, the Market makes available the religious benefits that used to come from prayer and fasting but can now be acquired without the awkward particularity that once limited their accessibility. All can be handily purchased, without unrealistic demand on one's time, as a weekend workshop package on an island resort (with a psychological consultant taking the place of a retreat master).

Advertising is both the basic catechism and the mass evangelism of the religion of the Market God. It is the medium through which the Market shows us what to think and feel abut ourselves, and what the Market tells us to do to become what it tells us to be. Like any Christian evangelist, the advertiser is not content with making the message known. He or she presses for a decision. "Act now . . . tomorrow this offer may be over." I believe that theologians should study the images and messages of advertising with great care. These images spell out just what the Market God, the main rival to Christianity in our time, wills and wants. Advertising tells us what is wrong with us (sin) and what we need to do to correct it (redemption). The reason we do not recognize the catechetical evangelism of the Market God for what it is, is that it surrounds us every day. It envelops us so completely in its omnipresent messages that we fail to identify the values, worldviews, and ways of life it promotes.[8]

CHRISTIANITY AND THE GOD OF GLOBAL MARKET CULTURE

The early Christians lived within a complex relationship to the global culture of their time, just as we do today. On the one hand, they took advantage of the *pax romana* to carry the Gospel across the empire. They wrote in *koine* Greek, the lingua franca of the day. But they also found themselves in conflict with the imperial religion and the market culture of their time. This is why they caused such a "a great disturbance," as the Bible reports, at Ephesus. An "idol" is any human creation made into a value that displaces the preeminence of God. Also, an idol, in the biblical view, is hollow. It poses as something it is not. It makes promises it cannot possibly fulfill. The first-century Christians exposed the false promises of the idols. They saw that the idols of their time were promising people life and community, salvation and well-being, but that those idols were in reality completely powerless. They were "not gods at all." So Paul and his followers proclaimed, in the name of the God revealed in Jesus Christ, that gods made of human hands could not deliver on their promises. There was bound to be a great disturbance.

Today the relationship between the now much larger Christian movement and the Global Market God with all its promises is even more complex. One could argue that the emergence of a global technological culture has made a truly global Christian movement possible for the first time. Christians use the hardware and software of the global culture to make the Gospel known. Just as Paul made use of ships, letters, and his Roman citizenship to travel with the good news, so Christians benefit from the worldwide travel and communications technologies of today. Just as the *pax romana* guaranteed by the emperor cult and by the Roman legions provided the space for the expansion of the early church, so today's global village makes possible a global church.

But while the first-century Christians said both "yes" and "no" to the global culture of their time, today's Christians mainly just say "yes."[9] Occasionally, however, here and there Christians challenge the hegemony of the Global Market God. The churches of the United States of America have insisted that human genes should not be marketed. Christians have advocated a simplification of lifestyle so that the goods of the Earth can be shared more equitably. Christians in Latin America and elsewhere have strenuously opposed imposition of an international market economy on their more traditional ways of living. Both the World Council of Churches and the pope have issued statements reminding Christians that there are important virtues the market does not nurture—indeed, mostly discourages—virtues Christians value such as compassion, cooperation, and tenderness. In many churches pastors warn their people against being swept away by the empty promises of consumerism and acquisition.

But frequently Christian churches are reluctant to cause any "disturbance" about the Market God, and even contribute to its growing power. Most often, they do this by simply trying to ignore the Market God and all Its patently non-Christian values. They concentrate on the "spiritual" and leave the "material" to others. What they forget is that Christianity is a radically embodied, and even in one sense "material," faith. God created the material world and found it originally good. Also, the Bible has much to say about economics. The Jewish law protects the poor and those without families from the cruelty of the rich. The prophets issue stern warnings against the privileged and powerful. In Jesus Christ, God actually enters the material world and clearly casts his lot with those on the bottom of the social and economic hierarchy. The Bible is anything but a merely "spiritual" book. It repeatedly warns against the terrible dangers of following after the gods of the market. There may be some religions in which it would be acceptable to ignore the economy, the ways in which the goods of the Earth are produced and distributed; or there may be religions in which one might not take any interest in the culture spawned by an economy, that is, the values it celebrates and the worldviews it promotes. But Christianity cannot ignore these things and remain true to the Bible.[10]

At worst, certain Christian movements actually promote and even sacralize the false values of the Market. In a church in America, I once heard a minister tell people that if they were rich and successful it meant that God had looked with favor on them, and that poor people were poor because they lacked sufficient faith. In a church in Brazil, I once heard a woman give a testimony in which she thanked God that although she once did not have a color television, now she owned one. Rather than help her to question the consumer way of life, which is the main rival of Christian faith today, her church seemed to strengthen and undergird consumerism's values. It is hard to reconcile this woman's testimony, however sincere, with the values announced by Jesus in the Sermon on the Mount.

Christianity and the religion of the global Market also have different views of nature. For Christians, "the earth is the Lord's and the fullness thereof, the sea and all that is therein." God is the only real owner of the earth, the sea, the sky. God makes human beings his stewards and gardeners. But God, as it were, retains title to the Earth. The logic of the Market religion is quite different. Human beings, more particularly those with the money to do so, own anything they buy (and everything is for sale), and they can dispose of it as they choose. But a terrible collision awaits the human race if the religion of the Market God continues to go unchallenged, a future quite different from the rosy one predicted in the promises of the global market forecasts. There is an absolute contradiction when an economic system whose inner logic is based on infinite growth continues to dominate a finite planet. The Market God literally knows no limits. But the Earth's supply of clean air, drinkable water, arable soil, and minerals and fossil fuel is limited. Infected by the pathology of the Market logic, which celebrates "growth" above all else, some Christian groups point to their growth, rather than their faithfulness to the Gospel, as the hallmark of their success.

The Market God strongly prefers individualism and mobility. It needs to be able to move people wherever production requires. It is only hampered when individuals have deep ties to families, local traditions, particular places. Therefore, It wishes to dissolve these ties. In the Market's eyes, all places—and indeed all persons—are interchangeable. The Market prefers a uniform, homogenized world culture with as few inconvenient particularities as possible. We can discern a foreshadowing of what the Market God has in store for us in the indistinguishable airports, luxury hotels, and glistening downtown business areas of the major cities of the global culture. Even food and music and dress, which used to the exhibit distinct local cultural qualities, are becoming uniform. Where particularities survive, they are rapidly becoming merely folkloristic, exotic reminders of what used to be. Parodies of local custom are preserved to lend a pseudo-"authentic" flavor to places that have been transformed into commodities in the world travel market.

But Christianity need not become a mere acolyte in the temple of the Global Market God. The early Christians did not shrink from telling the Ephesians that their gods were no gods at all. They did not hesitate to announce and demonstrate a way of life based on sharing, not vicious competition. Acts 4:32 to 5:12 describes the common purse Christians required, and the sorry fate of Ananias and Sapphira, who preferred to accumulate rather than share. In a blow against all leveling and homogenizing, the descent of the Spirit at Pentecost in Acts showed how people could respect and affirm cultural particularities, including different languages, and still live together in a vibrant Spirit-filled community. Although they were not always completely consistent, they were usually unwilling to make compromises with the corrupt religious culture of their day. Paul and Peter and many others died rather than allow Christianity to become yet one more subcult in the imperial religious system, which at that time spanned the known globe. The result of this early Christian resistance was that when the global culture of Rome cracked and fell, Christians were ready to build a new culture to replace it.

Christians are not against a world culture as such. The vision of a single world family stems from the biblical teaching that we are all descended from the same ancestors, and that Jesus Christ died to redeem the whole world, not just one class or nation or race. Christianity, however, envisions a world culture built from the bottom up by the gentle action of the Holy Spirit, not a culture imposed from the top down by an imperial religion or a wealthy elite. The Gospel clearly requires a "preferential option for the poor," not an economic system that rewards the few and excludes the many. Christianity is not against markets, but it is unalterably opposed to allowing the Market ethic to dictate the meaning of life; and the Gospel stands in dramatic opposition to the dominant values of the currently reigning Market Religion.

But will Christians in this global economy manage to resist it as the early Christians resisted theirs? The question is still an open one. If Christians ignore the obvious fact that the global economy has spawned not just a new kind of society but a new Market culture with its characteristic religion, then Christianity will fail in its prophetic task. But Jesus said, "You cannot serve God and Mammon." And what is "Mammon" but Money (as it is translated in the New English Bible) that is growth and productivity and consumption raised to the level of a religious system?

In this new century, Christians will have to develop ways of living marked by communal sharing, not by individualistic accumulation. Christians will have to speak out for the integrity of the Creation against its despoilers. And we will have to expose the false claims of the "gods that are no gods," in the religion of the global market. If we can be faithful to this calling, God may permit us to create something new, just, and beautiful in place of the religious culture of the present world age, when it finally collapses, as it one day surely will.

NOTES

It was under the imaginative eye of Robert N. Bellah that, as a doctoral student at Harvard in the late 1950s, I was first exposed to Max Weber and Emile Durkheim. The influence of all three is evident in this chapter and is gratefully acknowledged. A shortened version of this piece appeared in *The Atlantic*, March 1999.

1. Emile Durkheim, *The Elementary Forms of Religious Life*.

2. There are important exceptions to this obliviousness. See, for example, Michael Taussig, *The Devil and Commodity Fetishism in South America;* Mary Douglas and Baron Isherwood, *The World of Goods*.

3. On ritual, see Edmund Leach, "Ritualization in Man in Relation to Conceptual and Social Development"; Victor Turner, *From Ritual to Theater: The Human Seriousness of Play;* Sally Falk Moore and Barbara Myerhoff, eds., *Secular Ritual*.

4. Francis Fukuyama, *The End of History and the Last Man*.

5. Karl Polanyi, *The Great Transformation*.

6. E. R. Dodds, *The Greeks and the Irrational*.

7. For a historical overview of this phenomenon, see Piero Camporesi, *Bread of Dreams: Food and Fantasy in Early Modern Europe*.

8. See Jackson Lears, *Fables of Abundance*.

9. For a fascinating account of how Christians in the first five centuries of Christianity both used and were used by the prevailing cultural and religious symbolism of the day, see Thomas F. Matthews, *The Clash of the Gods*.

10. Kathryn Tanner, *The Politics of God*.

"Sarvodaya"

❧

Joanna Macy

Joanna Macy, internationally known Buddhist and Deep Ecologist, pioneered in exploring the connections between emotional life and the state of the world. She has written *Despair and Empowerment in a Nuclear Age* and *World as Lover, World as Self*. Her essay describes a contemporary movement for social change rooted in spiritual values.

❧

We Build the Road and the Road Builds Us.

—Sarvodaya slogan

"Real development is not free trade zones and mammoth hydroelectric dams," the young trainer told us. "It's waking up to our own needs and our own power."

I was sitting in an open-walled classroom with two dozen Sri Lankan village workers, absorbing the principles of a movement that promised to revolutionize Third World development. "This awakening happens on different levels. It's personal and spiritual as well as economic and cultural. These aspects of our lives are all interdependent." I wished planners at the World Bank could hear him.

A Buddhist-inspired people's self-help movement, Sarvodaya Shramadana Sangamaya was the largest nongovernmental organization in Sri Lanka, active in several thousand villages. It modeled a different kind of development than that preached and promoted by the industrialized countries. I had encountered it three years earlier on a trip to South Asia while I was still at Syracuse University. Throughout my graduate studies, I had sustained a strong interest in the potential for social change to be found in Asian religions, especially Buddhism. "Go talk to Ari," a community organizer in Bodh Gaya had advised me. He was referring to Sarvodaya's founder and president, A. T. Ariyaratne, a former high school teacher. "Some call him the Gandhi of Sri Lanka."

I did as I was told, and on that same trip in 1976, flew to Sri Lanka. When I walked into Ariyaratne's crowded little office in the Sarvodaya complex outside Colombo, it took me no more than two minutes to know that I wanted to stay and learn from his movement. For in this voluble, diminutive dynamo I found a scholar-activist who took the social teachings of the Buddha seriously and dared to believe that they could inspire change in the modern world. He had banked his life on that conviction, drawing from ancient traditions to empower what he called "the poorest of the poor."

When I completed my dissertation two years later in 1978, Ari invited me to come live with Sarvodaya for a year and study how it worked. And so, as soon as Peggy, my daughter, graduated from high school, I took off. I came equipped with a typewriter, a modest grant from the Ford Foundation, and half a year's instruction in Sinhalese from the kind monks at the Washington Buddhist Vihara.

Gandhi had taken the term *sarvodaya* from the Sanskrit word which means the "upliftment of all." Ari brought it to Buddhist Sri Lanka and recast it in terms of awakening. He explained that that's what the Buddha did under the Bodhi tree. He woke up. And that is what we all can do—awaken to our innate wisdom and power to act. Ari added the word *shramadana*, "gift of labor," so the movement's full name means, in effect, "everyone wakes up by working together." I listened with growing excitement. Here was the "liberation Buddhism" that I had imagined might be realized some day, with luck and the blessings of all the bodhisattvas.

My fascination with the shramadanas grew. From the start, these village work camps had constituted the movement's central organizing strategy. When Ari was still teaching high school, he heard about church-sponsored work camps in postwar Europe. He immediately saw how that kind of service could fit with the Buddha Dharma and how it could generate self-reliance and solidarity. But he didn't say, "Here's a great idea from the West, let's adopt it and imitate it." He said, "Let's draw from our own traditions and our own strengths." Using the word Gandhi had coined for the maintenance of his ashram and the cleaning of its latrines—"shramadana," gift of labor—Ari took the concept much further.

Sarvodaya's slogan was "We build the road and the road builds us." The process started early. A movement organizer would invite villagers to gather, perhaps in their temple's preaching hall, to discuss their needs and to deliberate on the choice of a project. Should they first dig some public latrines, or clear the weed-choked irrigation canal, or open a shortcut to the nearest by route? Then they considered where tools would be found and who would do what. This process was slow, involving more and more people, from elders to children. By the time the actual shramadana began, a good part of its purpose—to get the community working together—had already been achieved.

Teenagers were lugging out car batteries and hanging loudspeakers from the trees when I arrived at my first road-building shramadana. "You can't work without music!" they informed me. Huge cooking pots appeared as well, along with baskets of food that the children had collected from every household. Older women scolded and laughed as they cleaned rice, chopped pumpkin, and scraped coconut for curries. I joined one of the eight work teams, and we counted off to see who would be our leader for the first shift. The lot fell to a thirteen-year-old who made sure we each got *a mamoty*—a heavy Dutch hoe—and led us to our work site.

Much of my research entailed interviewing Sarvodaya monks, for the more progressive ones offered vivid examples of the role that clergy can play in social change. They opened their temple precincts to Sarvodaya preschools and literacy and sewing classes for adults. They drew from old Dharma stories to teach courage and self-respect. They used their status to draw villagers together in "family gatherings," recruited school dropouts to help organize shramadanas, and encouraged the young women and girls to take part. By their very presence they stilled any disapproving gossip about village daughters mixing with boys.

As I called on these monks and we spoke of village plans and scripture passages, what I loved most was the scent of courage. I never heard a word of complaint from Sarvodaya monks, but I began to realize the price they paid for engaging in community development work. It was more than the time it took, added on to hours of *puja* (rituals), temple care, and pastoral duties. It was more than the physical exertions involved: leaving the tranquil comforts of the temple for the wattle and daub shacks of the poorest families, or suffering the brain-addling sun of a shramadana, or trying to navigate the daunting bureaucratic labyrinths of government. The harshest cost was in reputation and prestige. One was not applauded by the larger, traditional Sangha, nor by the larger, conservative laity. On the contrary. The forest-dwelling monks in meditative retreat and the scholarly ones in their libraries received the most reverence. Their kind of renunciation did not rock the boat. When I had the nerve to raise the topic outright, the Sarvodaya monks responded with a calm yes. "Yes, that is true, by a lesser kind of monk. But it doesn't matter. It makes no difference."

Ethnic conflict between Hindu Tamils, residing largely in the North and East, and the majority Buddhist Sinhalese erupted into civil war in 1983: blood-letting that continues to this day. Sick at heart, I wondered for years how the violence and polarization was affecting Sarvodaya. Returning for short visits, I found the movement heavily engaged in relief and rehabilitation work, along with occassional marches for peace. Its most distinctive contribution to easing hostilities lay, I soon realized, in the way it embodies the tolerance and nonviolence the Buddha taught, and his rejection of dogmatism. This stands in sharp contrast to the nationalism and anti-Tamil chauvinism displayed by the powerful Buddhist clergy.

Today in Sri Lanka Sarvodaya plays a critical role in modeling an understanding of the Dharma that is consonant with a pluralistic society. At a time when the Buddhist majority finds itself in a narrowly defensive posture, acting as if Sri Lanka were by right a Buddhist Sinhalese state, Sarvodaya demonstrates the tolerance and respect for diversity that is integral to the Buddha's teachings. To Gautama, the notion of possessing an absolute truth or exclusive historical privileges was a dangerous delusion, leading to attachment, aversion, and suffering. Hence, the inclusivity he taught, which Sarvodaya exemplified from its outset by engaging with people of all faiths, showed a way of being true to the Dharma while working actively for the needs and rights of all, and not falling prey to Buddhist nationalism.

"Alternatives to Consumerism"

❦

Sulak Sivaraksa

Sulak Sivaraksa is a prominent Thai social critic and activist, and one of the major sources of contemporary engaged Buddhism. He has been nominated for the Nobel Peace Prize and received the Right Livelihood award in 1995. This essay illustrates the particular sensibility someone from an Eastern tradition can bring to criticisms of globalization.

❦

Consumerism can be defined as the religion of consumption—attributing ultimate meaning to purchasing power. Economic growth at the cost of the poor has become the driving force of globalization even though world leaders try to hide this fact with cosmetic measures and rhetoric.

Undeniably, the fuel that keeps the capitalist engine running is profit: the more of it, the better, the argument goes. Hence, corporations must be free to pursue it—at all costs. The ends justify the means. It is also argued that the profit generated by the system will eventually trickle down to benefit the mass of humanity. The available evidence points otherwise. To be fair, capitalism does generate some benefits to humanity, but they are largely unintended byproducts of the system.

Capitalism works by exploiting labor and natural resources in order to concentrate wealth in the hands of an elite group. For maximum results, capitalism alienates humans from their communities, families, and ultimately, their spiritual selves by attributing worth solely in terms of economic value. The atomistic individual, rather than a larger community, is at the center of the capitalist system. Consumerism is able to dominate much of contemporary society because individuals have become alienated from their culture and from each other. The sense of community that led people to share scarce resources and work cooperatively has been supplanted by an anger, competitiveness, and fear that cause people to seek acquisitions at the expense of their neighbors. In sum, consumerism is a consequence of using greed and violence to regulate socioeconomic relations.

At the most profound level, consumerism owes its vitality to the delusion of the autonomous individual self; a self that exists independently of social relations and of human relations with nature—a human person thrown into the world. For the Buddha it was clear that the "self" constituted only a pattern of persistently changing experiences that had no more substance or permanence than those experiences.

We are deluded into seeking some transcendental subject; something that defines experience yet lies beyond the experience. We are exhorted to know ourselves and yet the "self" in this dualistic system remains unknowable. For the Buddhists, this delusion is the fundamental cause of suffering. Ontologically, we become estranged aspects of our experiences of others and ourselves. Hence we are precluded from any meaningful conception of identity.

Consumerism provides an artificial means to define our existence by suggesting that identity is realized through the process of acquisition. Put differently, consumerism is a perverse corollary of the Cartesian proof of personal existence: "I shop, therefore I am." Insatiable consumption is equated with ultimate happiness, freedom, and self-realization. As David Arnott, a British Buddhist and human rights activist, explains:

> By participating in the sacrament of purchase, sacrificing money, you can buy an object that is not so much an object as a focus of images which grants you a place in the system of images you hold sacred. For a while when you buy a car you also buy the power, prestige, sexuality, and success which the advertisements have succeeded in identifying with the car, or whatever the commodity is. Consumerism works by identifying the sense of unsatisfactoriness or lack (*dukkha*) we all hold at a deep level of mind . . . and then [by corporations] producing an object guaranteed to satisfy that "need."[1]

Corporatization depends on greed, delusion, and hatred in order to become entrenched in the global society and in the individual and is thus an anathema to the goals of Buddhism. When an individual places self-interest above all and negates the relational idea of "self," the result is greed and selfishness. Neoliberalist rhetoric deludes people and international organizations into believing that profits from multinational corporations will be fairly distributed in society and that any improvement in material conditions is an absolute gain for society. The ideology of consumerism deludes people into believing that constant acquisition of goods and power will lead to happiness. Lastly, competitive consumerism depends on callousness and hatred to prevent people from forming coalitions to challenge the existing system. Hatred is a force that paralyzes and prevents self-transformation and cooperative strategies.

In Buddhism, prosperity is defined as "more being." As such, it cannot be realized atomistically, only collectively, and with an emphasis on spirituality. Buddhism denounces and renounces greed, because it is seen as leading one down the perfidious road of aggression and hatred—in a word, of suffering. Greed can never lead to satisfaction, individually or collectively. Thus Buddhism seeks to show how to be content with changing oneself—that is, self-cultivation— and emphasizes the importance of caring about, promoting, and benefiting from one another's well-being. Whereas capitalism treats a person as only half-human—the economic dimension (e.g., greed, hatred, and selfishness) is cultivated to the exclusion of other considerations— Buddhism approaches a human person holistically. The mind and heart must be cultivated, and diversity must be nourished in social relations and in human relations with nature. A human person is an "interbeing" existing within a web of relations that includes all sentient beings.

In contrast to the modern notion of frantic, ceaseless consumption, the Buddha said that tranquility is the most important prerequisite for self-cultivation and self-criticism, for the true understanding (*prajña*) of the self. It should be pointed out that understanding is different from intellectual knowledge, since it is filtered through both the heart and the mind. Understanding helps the individual to recognize his or her limits and to be more humble. At the same time, it promotes loving kindness and compassion: the individual will be in a better position to witness the suffering of others and to help eliminate the cause of suffering. Of course, when one tackles the cause of suffering, particularly in an oppressive social system, one usually gets hurt. Here *bhavana* (mindfulness) facilitates the understanding of such danger as well as the forgiving of the oppressor. The oppressive system is hated and will be destroyed, but the oppressor will neither be despised nor executed. If one is aware of one's anger, then one can envelop it with mindfulness, thereby transforming it into compassion. Thich Nhat Hanh says that anger is like a closed flower; the flower will only bloom when deeply penetrated by the sunlight of bhavana. The constant radiation of compassion and understanding will eventually crack anger, enabling one to perceive its depth and roots. Likewise, bhavana will fully open the flower buds of greed, hatred, and delusion.

Compassion and competition are not mutually exclusive. His Holiness the Dalai Lama says, "Any human activity carried out with a sense of responsibility, a sense of commitment, a sense of discipline, and a wider vision of consequence and connections, whether it be involved with religion, politics, business, law, medicine, science, or technology—is constructive." The emphasis is on the motivation for action. Given that motivation is deeply connected to worldview, a change in worldview, such as an understanding of interdependence or the universality of suffering, will lead to a change in motivation. As motivation shifts and the sense of responsibility and commitment are strengthened, broader changes can take place. For example, when a motivation for profit shifts to a sense of concern for the well-being, economic and spiritual, of the employees of a corporation, a cooperative relationship can start to replace a formerly exploitative one.

Similarly, competition is not a singularly negative force. In moderation and with a sense of direction it can be used to push us to become more generous and kind. His Holiness makes the distinction between two kinds of competition when he says that one kind of competition is only for individual glory and the other kind of competition includes an awareness that other people must also be fostered to succeed. Competition can be beneficial if it inspires us to be the best we can in order to serve others. Rituals and games are often built on competition but can serve also to strengthen the spirit. This discussion of competition and achievement parallels the discussion among Buddhist scholars about the purpose of nirvana. For some, spiritual enlightenment is a personal quest. For others, such as those in the Engaged Buddhist community, enlightenment is built upon wisdom and compassion and is intrinsically connected with the well-being of all others. The Mahayana tradition is particularly emphatic that all beings must be liberated before the bodhisattva can attain enlightenment. These discussions about the nature of competition and nirvana highlight how a seemingly minor difference in focus can shift the focus from an ego-centered attitude to a community-centered philosophy.

Instead of basing all interpersonal relations on social obligation or an economic calculation about what we can gain from another person, Buddhism uses the principles of *metta* (loving kindness), *karuna* (compassion), *mudita* (sympathetic joy), and *upekkha* (equanimity) to be the guiding forces in interpersonal relations. These Four Sublime Abodes (*Brahma Vihara*) are as follows:

1. Metta or loving kindness toward oneself and others. Yes, we all desire to be happy and have every right to do so. Nevertheless, through practicing the precepts and meditation, a different state of happiness can be achieved. It is a state of happiness where the mind is in harmony with oneself as well as with others. It renders assistance and benefits without ill will and without the malice of anger and competition. Once one is tranquil and happy, these qualities will be spread to others as well.

2. Karuna or compassion can only be cultivated when one recognizes the suffering of others and, consequently, is driven to bring that suffering to an end. Undoubtedly a rich person who does not care about the miserable conditions of the poor lacks this quality. It is terribly difficult for him or her to develop into a better person. All those

who lock themselves up in ivory towers in the midst of a shockingly unjust world cannot be called compassionate. In Mahayana Buddhism, one vows to become a bodhisattva and forgoes one's own nirvana until all sentient beings are free from suffering. In other words, one cannot remain indifferent; rather, one must endeavor to help others and alleviate or mitigate their suffering as much as one can. The essential characteristic of any healthy community/society is its principle of inclusion. As we become more attuned to compassion as the instrumentality of social organization, we can embrace the community.

3. Mudita or sympathetic joy is a mental condition whereby one genuinely rejoices when others are happy or successful in a number of ways. One feels this without the flame of envy even when a competitor gets ahead.

4. Upekkha or equanimity refers to the state in which the mind is cultivated until it becomes evenly balanced and neutral. Whether one faces success or failure, whether one is confronted with prosperity or adversity, one is not "moved" by it.

The Four Sublime Abodes are to be developed step by step from the first to the last. Even when one is not perfect, one must set one's mind toward this goal. Otherwise, in one way or the other, one's dealing with the self or with others will tend to be harmful. Moving toward happiness and tranquility rather than toward worldly success and material progress, a Buddhist is then in a position to develop his or her community—the family, neighborhood, village, etc. An individual who is awakened by these realities is called *purisodya*. When this awakening is shared with others, ultimately the whole nation may be awakened to the threats posed by capitalism, including its ethos.

Moreover, in a time of moral emergency like the present, the Buddhist teaching of the Four Wheels may serve as a useful antidote to the detrimental values of corporatization. As a cart moves steadily on four wheels, likewise human development should rest—and this point cannot be overemphasized—on the four dhammas, namely, Sharing, Pleasant Speech, Constructive Action, and Equality.

1. One must Share (*dana*) what one has with others—be it goods, wealth, knowledge, time, labor, etc. Corporatization, on the other hand, in Adam Smith's telling phrase, upholds the dictum "all for [ourselves] and nothing for other people." Powerful transnational corporations control access to essential commodities such as food, drugs, and technology. Yes they are all made available to us—for a high sum of course. To a large extent, dana is still practiced in most village cultures. We should strengthen the concept of dana and spread it to counteract the invasion of materialism and the ethos of competition by sharing, and by leading less commercialized lifestyles.

2. Pleasant Speech (*piyavaca*) not only refers to polite talk but also to speaking truthfully and sincerely. Its basic assumption is that everyone is equal. On the contrary, consumerism or the culture of corporatization posits that less commercialized lifestyles are inferior. People must be *deceived* to consume goods and services that they do not really need in the name of a "high standard of living."

3. Constructive Action (*atthacariya*) means working for one another's benefit. Here again it is antithetical to the dynamics of the corporation. A corporation does not work to benefit its employees or the town or city it is situated in. Rather, it is only geared toward enriching the large shareholders. For instance, it seems that every time a corporation

"downsizes," the price of its shares skyrockets. Thereby new rules must be promulgated whereby investors who have high stakes in the well-being of their localities are rewarded.

4. And finally, Equality (*samanattata*) means that Buddhism does not recognize classes or castes, does not encourage one group to dominate or exploit the other. The global economy however creates a small caste of "winners" and mass hordes of "losers." The winners take all, and their action is deemed perfectly legitimate under the banner of "free trade" and "free competition." Hence, we urgently require "fair trade," not free trade.

The Four Sublime Abodes and the four dhammas are meant to act as guidelines for living a life consistent with a Buddhist understanding of freedom, drastically apart from a capitalistic notion of choice as the ultimate expression of freedom. Merely having a wealth of choices is not freedom. We must make the right choices—choices that show compassion for all and which are not motivated by greed. For Buddhists, the ideal of freedom is threefold: the first freedom is the freedom to be free from insecurities and the dangers of poverty, disease, famine, etc. The second freedom is social freedom and the freedom from human oppression and exploitation; such a state presupposes tolerance, solidarity, and benevolence. Lastly is the freedom of the inner life, the freedom from mental suffering, from impurities of the mind that people to commit all kinds of evil.

Engaged Buddhism (or "buddhism with a small b") has become a living alternative movement within Buddhism to put into practice the ideals of Buddhism and allow more people to have access to an alternate conception of freedom. We must let our common goal of creating an alternative guide us toward greater collaborative alliances. A fresh common effort to shape interreligious education—especially in the context of education reform now common in many countries, as well as joint outreach of emancipatory and community-based education fully involving the poor and underprivileged—should be undertaken without delay.

NOTE

1. See David Arnott, "Sri Lanka—Victim of a Deep Colonialism" (unpublished paper, 1984).

"Islamic Banking"

☙

Rami G. Khouri

Rami G. Khouri is a well-known Jordanian journalist whose work is syndicated around the world. He writes on issues of peace, war, the Israel–Palestine conflict, Arab nationalism, and cultural conflict.

☙

Al–Barr: the Source of All Goodness, the messenger of Allah (Peace and Blessings of Allah be upon him) has said, "Allah does not take into account your figures or your wealth. He looks and values your hearts and deeds."

Millions of people avoid banks as institutions. Some are simply wary of organizations not rooted in their own villages. But many are professional and business people, and it is not suspicion, but Islamic beliefs that bar them from financial dealings they define as usurious. Yet Muslims need banking services as much as anyone. Nor are they averse to legitimate profit: the Prophet Muhammad himself was a successful businessman. But today's financial world is tightly knit, linking Muslim and non-Muslim. In this world, can Muslims find room for the principles of their religion? The answer comes with the rise of international Islamic banking.

As oil prices increased after 1974, a number of Arab and Muslim countries experienced a rise in income and became dissatisfied with the rigid requirements of commercial banks (mostly Western) and the banks' view of interest-earning activities as their central reason for being. The best response, for both individuals and communities, seemed to be reinvigoration of the principles of Islam.

Several Qur'anic passages admonish the faithful to shun *riba,* or fixed interest payments: "Fear God and give up what remains of your demand of usury, if ye are indeed believers." Riba is prohibited on the tenet that money is only a medium of exchange, a way of defining value; it has no value in itself, and should not give rise to more money simply by being put in a bank or lent. The human effort, initiative, and risk involved in a venture are more important than the money used to finance it.

According to the Shari'a, or Islamic law, the provider and the user of capital should equally share the risk of business ventures. Translated into banking terms, the depositor, the bank, and the borrower should all share the risks and rewards of business ventures, unlike the interest-based commercial banking system where all the pressure is on the borrower, who must pay back the loan and the agreed interest regardless of the success or failure of the venture. Islamic economics also requires investments to support only practices or products that are not forbidden or discouraged by Islam. Trade in alcohol or arms, for example, would not be financed by an Islamic bank. Nor could money be lent to other banks at interest.

Islamic banks have devised creative, flexible variations on the risk-sharing, profit-sharing principle. A group in Jordan, for example, had the land for a community college, but not the money to build it. An Islamic bank built the college and agreed to be repaid with 30 percent of tuition fees. But after the school opened, the government raised admission standards; the number of students—and the college's cash flow—fell to half of predicted levels. The bank responded by stretching out the repayment period. Another Islamic bank finances individuals' car or taxi purchases by *murabaha*, buying the vehicle and transferring ownership to the client, who repays the cost over thirty-six to forty months. If the client cannot repay on the original, or a revised schedule, the bank agrees with the client to sell the car secondhand, whether or not the proceeds cover the outstanding balance of the original debt.

The public's acceptance of Islamic banking has been quicker and greater than its advocates had anticipated. The banks initially attracted depositors whose religious beliefs had caused them to shun commercial banks' interest-bearing savings accounts. (Islamic banks also offer a full spectrum of the normal services of modern banking that do not involve interest payments.) Once they had proved their viability and safety, the Islamic banks attracted others who preferred the less pressured style of profit-sharing dealings, or who shared the precept that wealth should be invested in socially and economically productive ventures rather than idly earning money in interest-bearing accounts.

The first of the contemporary Islamic banks, the Dubai Islamic Bank, was founded in 1975. Between that year and 1983 most new Islamic banks were established in Arab countries. In the past four years Islamic banking has spread more widely, to Asia, Africa, and Europe. Today there are more than one hundred Islamic banks and financial institutions throughout the world, and several multinational banking companies. In countries other than Iran and Pakistan, which have required their banking systems to apply Islamic practices, Islamic and interest-based commercial banks operate side by side; increasingly, they cooperate with one another on principles acceptable to both.

In most cases, Islamic banks have paid dividends and profits that compare well with the rates of commerical banks. Islamic bankers shun this sort of comparison, insisting that their clients consider both financial criteria and the satisfaction of conducting their business in accord with religious dictates and ethical traditions. Indeed, some Islamic banking practices are not designed to make a profit, such as *gard hassan*, or social-purpose loans, extended to poor or needy individuals at no charge. "Our clients are not motivated solely by financial gain," General Manager Musa Shihadeh, of the Jordan Islamic Bank, said in a recent interview, "Their two main criteria are to honor their deeply-held religious beliefs, and to deal with banks that offer confidence and minimum risk."

"Statement of Indigenous Nations, Peoples, and Organizations"

∝

In 1992 leaders from twenty cultures of North, Central, and South America, the Pacific Rim, Eurasia, and the polar regions brought their message to the United Nations for the first time, inaugurating the International Decade of the World's Indigenous Peoples.

∝

Gucumatz, Condor, Father Sun, Eagle, Anahuac, Mother Earth. INVOKING the spirits of our ancestors and acting in our tradition of resistance in the defense of Mother Earth, asserting our fundamental and historical rights,

ASSERTING all the millions of brothers and sisters who have sacrificed their lives in defense of our millennial culture, In the name of the more than 300 million indigenous people which inhabit the Earth, and the efforts over the years of work by indigenous peoples and NGO's, we, the members of the INDIGENOUS NATIONS AND ORGANIZATIONS, gathered in New York City, from the 8th to the 10th of December of 1992,

WE CONSIDER:

I. That all indigenous peoples have the right to self-determination as expounded in the principles of the Universal Declaration of the Rights of Indigenous Peoples. Accordingly, indigenous peoples have the right to determine all matters relating to our political, economic, social, spiritual and cultural affairs. We call for the immediate adoption of the above declaration.

II. The struggle for our territorial rights is common to all indigenous nations and peoples, and this right is persistently denied by governments and dominant societies.

III. Economic development practices of Nation States are destroying the natural resources which have been protected within indigenous territories. As a consequence, the survival of all species is threatened.

IV. The indigenous peoples' contribution to the social, intellectual and cultural diversity of the world, particularly to the ecology and harmony of Mother Earth must be valued and supported by Nation States and international agencies.

V. The human rights of indigenous peoples to our culture, identity, religions and languages are inalienable. These rights continue to be sacrificed in the programs, policies and budgets of the Nation States and international agencies.

VI. While democracy is heralded by dominant societies, what this means to indigenous peoples is repression, genocide and misery in the Americas and in the rest of the world. As an example, [in] the process by which the dialogue for peace is taking place in Central and South

America, there is no direct participation by indigenous organizations and nations in spite of the fact that indigenous peoples are directly affected by the conditions of the wars.

VII. The survival of indigenous sovereign governments continues in spite of the oppressive actions and programs of the Nation States and the dominant society.

VIII. Governments continue to desecrate and appropriate religious and sacred places and objects, depriving indigenous nations around the world of their basic spiritual ways of life.

THEREFORE: The International Year of the World's Indigenous People, 1993, must not be merely celebrations or paternalistic declarations, but rather, the resolution of the above requires that the United Nations and its member-states take the following actions:

1. Recognize indigenous rights to indigenous territories, including the recovery and demarcation of such territories.

2. Recognize, honor, and document under international law all treaties, compacts, accords and other formal agreements concluded with indigenous peoples of the world. Additionally the Study on Indigenous Treaties delegated to the Human Rights Commission must be given priority attention by the United Nations and its member-states.

3. Recognize and honor indigenous forms of government when such governments are practiced according to traditional laws and customs.

4. Promote and strengthen indigenous intellectual and cultural property rights under International Law and principles. Additionally, the study on intellectual and cultural property rights undertaken by the United Nations Commission on Human Rights should be given priority.

5. Consult with indigenous organizations and nations regarding the ratification of Covenant 169 of the International Labor Organization.

6. Provide legal assistance and technical training to the indigenous organizations and nations.

7. Promote at the national and international levels the reform of laws and policies such that they recognize the sovereign rights of the indigenous peoples.

8. Promote and strengthen indigenous education, culture, art, religion, philosophies, literature and sciences of indigenous nations.

9. Return historic places and sacred sites and objects to the indigenous nations to whom they belong.

10. Demonstrate sincere commitment to the new partnership with indigenous peoples by making adequate financial resources available to implement actions presented herein. Furthermore, make significant donations to the Voluntary Fund so that future projects be realized, and assure that the indigenous peoples have direct input into the management of said fund.

11. That the United Nations Secretary General and its specialized agencies, commissions and programs convene special consultations with indigenous peoples of the world at the most local level practical.

12. That the Secretary General of the United Nations create immediately a specific indigenous program to be administered and executed with direct participation of indigenous organizations.

Written in the City of New York, December 9, 1992

"Voices of the Peoples—Voices of the Earth: Indigenous Peoples—Subjugation or Self-Determination?"

෨

Michael Dodson

Michael Dodson is Aboriginal and Torres Strait Social Justice Commissioner for Australia. His essay provides an account of some of the particular features of the oppression of native peoples throughout the world, an oppression in which physical suffering and cultural genocide are closely tied.

෨

In the tradition of my people, I would like to begin by thanking the traditional owners of this country for having me here on their land. Those of you who have a taste for irony may wish to contemplate the broad context of my visit. In 1643 indigenous people in Australia witnessed the arrival of Dutch explorers "discovering" their "South Pacific Continent." In the supreme "Eurocentrism" which characterized their time, these strangers called our country "New Holland." Although they were not to be the ones to ultimately claim sovereignty over that land, their fellow "colonizers in crime," the British, did so a century and a half later.

Today, after 350 years of subjugation, indigenous peoples are making the return journey. The late twentieth century is the time for us, the first peoples, to reassert the ancient truth that our countries are not "New Holland," "New England," or "New Anywhere-Else."

When your European forefathers came to us, they were deaf to our voices and contemptuous of our rights. For this we seek no admonitions of guilt. What we seek is the justice of recognition. We make no claims for charity or for the creation of special privileges. But we do call for the justice of restoring our preexisting rights.

If the injustices of history are grievous, then of even greater gravity are the injustices which remain entrenched in the attitudes, practices, and laws of contemporary states.

To be touched by the stark reality of what I am talking about, you must abandon the technical niceties of laws, instruments, and concepts, and come back to the human experience of devastation, brutalization, and subjugation. As we speak, the rights of indigenous peoples all over the world are being systematically violated. We continue to suffer discrimination and marginalization. Our lands and cultures continue to be stolen, destroyed, and exploited. It is a sobering experience to cross the planet hearing this same story with haunting regularity.

296

While the Wik people of the far north of Australia seek justice for the mining of their land, the burning of their homes, and displacement of their communities, the Yanomami Indians of Brazil seek protection from the invasion of their territories by 45,000 gold miners whose activities have led to the poisoning of their entire river system, the death of 15 percent of their population, and the destruction of entire villages. Simultaneously, the Jumma people of the Chittagong Hill tracts of Bangladesh, the Udege of far east Russia, the Alutiiq of Alaska, the Lumad of the Philippines, and countless others from every corner of the earth fight to prevent their lands and peoples from being sacrificed at the hands of ever-encroaching multinational companies seeking new sources of profit. This total disregard for the integrity, survival, or will of the indigenous peoples is going ahead with overt or tacit approval from the state.

In the face of this global, *state sanctioned* genocide, indigenous peoples have no other option than to rediscover the strength of our own voices and our own authority, and through our voices to demand of the international community that the decimation of our people and cultures no longer be the price of someone else's "development."

I believe that as we stand perched on the verge of the twenty-first century, there has never been a more critical time for the governments and peoples of the world to open their ears, minds, and hearts to those voices which have been silenced and overpowered for so long.

I say this not just in view of the violation of the rights of indigenous peoples, but also in the shadow of the environmental and social crises which this planet is facing. It is now all too evident that dominant political, social, and land management practices of modern nation-states are failing. The detrimental effects which progress has had on the environment are no longer escapable, nor is the suffering of an ever-growing number of people who have been the victims of the "great dreams of development."

I believe that the dignity and perhaps even the survival of the human race hinges on the revival of the voices and cultures of the earth. We are, after all, the peoples who have lived for millennia with the land without bringing it, or ourselves to the state of simmering crisis which the world now faces. Our cultures offer a source of opportunity for a more equal, just, and sustainable future. It is my hope that we will have the vision and respect to give ourselves that opportunity.

It is with a sense of cautious optimism that I say that there has been a shift in recent years. The fact that 1993 was declared the International Year of the World's Indigenous Peoples indicates that indigenous issues have emerged from the invisible margins and made a mark on the international conscience.

Only a hopeless idealist could have expected the year to restore substantive justice and achieve the full enjoyment of human rights for indigenous peoples. What we had hoped was: that our plight would come to the forefront of the consciousness of all peoples and governments; that our voices would emerge from the margins, and; that in hearing our just claims all nations would make a commitment to laying the groundwork for the realization of justice.

Now that we have entered the last month of that year, we are asking what the real impact on the international agenda for action will be?

On the positive side, the year has certainly resulted in a growth in awareness amid the broader community. At least, this has certainly been the case in Australia. However, it is sadly indicative of the distance we still have to go that the year received minimal support from the international community, including the agencies of the United Nations and token, if any, support from most nations.

The proposal for an "International Decade of the World's Indigenous Peoples" will soon be put to the UN General Assembly, and has already received the support of the Vienna World Conference on Human Rights.[1]

I, too, offer my support for this proposal, but with the several qualifications. It must be adequately funded, coordinated at the international level, and substantive. Even more importantly it must be planned, organized, and implemented in genuine partnership with indigenous peoples. Nothing would be worse than to see our proposals cheapened into an "international circus" organized for us, or even worse, to put us on display.

Having attracted the attention of the international community, now is the time that indigenous and nonindigenous peoples must sit together, as we will be doing during this conference, to negotiate the way forward. We have certainly needed, and still need, to tell the stories of violation and oppression which will inspire compassion and action. But we must now formulate the practical programs which will translate concepts of justice into meaningful experience.

The title of this conference, "Voices of the Earth," touches deeply on the two aspects which are most essential to indigenous peoples: our distinct voices and identities, and our connection with our traditional territories.

These two elements are also at the very core of the degradation of our lives and the violation of our rights. The destruction of indigenous societies essentially began with two simultaneous forms of abuse: forced removal from our lands, and the desecration of our sovereign right to control our lives, live according to our own laws and determine our own futures.

It is thus the recognition of these two fundamental rights, the right to live on our lands and the right to self-determination, which have been at the forefront of indigenous struggles.

The most immediate impact of colonial expansion on indigenous peoples was our removal from our traditional lands. As more and more of our lands proved to be attractive sources of wealth, the encroachment expanded. To legalize the theft and dispossession, the alien cultures devised and imposed self-justifying laws and institutions.

In Australia the justification took the form of the legal doctrine of *terra nullius,* which declared that at the time of so-called "discovery," the country belonged to no one. This fiction effectively nullified the land rights of the indigenous inhabitants and allowed all other forms of land title to run rampant over those rights.

It was only in 1992 that the High Court of Australia debunked that fiction, and thereby recognized the validity of traditional indigenous law and indigenous land title.

To understand the profound implications of the violation of indigenous land rights, you need to go outside the Western paradigm. It is nearly impossible to use a nonindigenous language to describe the nature of the connection we indigenous peoples have to our traditional lands.

In English at least, the words "land" and "earth" have become barren, and have all too often been stripped down to signify little more than an exploitable resource. In an indigenous language, the one word may mean country, hearth, everlasting home, totem, place, life source, spirit center and much more. When I speak of the earth, I may also be speaking of my shoulder or side, of my grandmother or brother. Removed from our lands, we are literally removed from ourselves.

This is the context for our demands for the full recognition of our fundamental, inherent and inalienable rights to our land.

The fact that imposed states have constructed systems which are based on the nonrecognition of our rights can no longer be used to justify that nonrecognition. We are not seeking the dispossession of other peoples, or the invalidation of their interests. The moral bankruptcy which underpins many of those interests however, must be exposed. People must begin to ask: "Whose loss underwrites my gain?"

From that point we can start to negotiate agreements which will allow for all peoples to enjoy their rights over land and resources, in ways which do not structurally discriminate against one group of peoples.

If the physical dimension of dispossession was removal from our lands, the procedural dimension was the violation of our right to control our own lives. When foreign states claimed sovereignty over our lands, we were denied our freedom and independence, and deprived of the inherent right as peoples to determine the course of our own lives. Until the middle of this century the treatment of indigenous Australians was comparable only to that of orphans or the insane; the only difference being that orphans were allowed to grow up, and the insane at least had the opportunity of proving their sanity. Indigenous peoples were not permitted the right to vote, freedom of movement or access to the fundamental civil, political and economic rights that were the due of all adult citizens.

It is genocide to destroy a people; so, too, is it genocide to destroy that people's distinctive identity. The tyranny, insecurity, and blindness of dominant colonizing cultures have led to nothing less than policies designed to obliterate the essential difference of indigenous peoples. We were subject to racist policies ranging from eradication to protection, integration, and assimilation.

It is from within this context of profound disrespect for our culture, identity difference, and integrity, that our call for self-determination is uttered with such a passionate sense of urgency.

Indigenous peoples from all over the world have made it perfectly clear that the right to self-determination is the most fundamental of our rights as peoples. "Self-determination is to peoples what freedom is to individuals; the very basis of their existence."[2]

During the great French and American revolutions of the eighteenth century, the world witnessed the power of the call for individual freedom; perhaps the great revolution of the late twentieth century is that of peoples as we call for self-determination.

The paramount nature of this right has been strenuously argued by indigenous peoples during the twelve years of meetings with the UN Working Group on Indigenous Populations. Despite constant opposition from states, and for many years from the members of the Working Group itself, we have continued to assert that there can be no compromise or derogation from that right, and that the unqualified right must be a fundamental element of any declaration articulating our rights.

To understand the crucial position of this right you need to look at a number of factors. At the most fundamental level, self-determination is "deeply rooted in the ultimate goal of human dignity."[3] It is an inherent right of peoples which is indivisible, nonnegotiable and cannot be erased through nonrecognition. At a more pragmatic or instrumental level, the enjoyment of the right to self-determination is essential to our survival as peoples. It is the pillar which supports all other rights; a right of such a profound nature that the integrity of all other rights depends on its observance.

Indigenous peoples are the most oppressed and subjugated peoples in the world. In almost every country, we are radically deprived of our fundamental human rights. We have the shortest life expectancy, highest infant mortality, poorest living conditions, least access to education or employment, and highest rates of incarceration, and we suffer the most severe discrimination.

Recognition of the right to self-determination will be a fundamental prerequisite to correcting this shameful state of affairs.

Furthermore, international law has recognized the axiomatic place of this right. In 1919 U.S. President Woodrow Wilson, introducing the concept to the League of Nations, already described self-determination as:

> the right of every people to choose the sovereign under which they live, to be free from alien masters, and not to be handed about from sovereign to sovereign as if they were property.[4]

Almost seventy-five years later the words have lost none of their poignancy.

The right to self-determination is clearly recognized in the UN Charter and is the very first right established in both international human rights covenants. In the very words of the resolutions of the UN General Assembly on this matter we find repeated vehemence. I quote:

> The effective exercise of a peoples' right to self-determination [is] an essential condition or prerequisite... for the genuine existence of other rights and freedoms. Only when self-determination has been achieved can a people take the measures necessary to ensure human dignity, [and] the full enjoyment of all rights,... without any form of discrimination. Human rights and fundamental freedoms can only exist truly and fully when the right to self-determination also exists.[5]

Member states of the United Nations have made explicit commitments under international law to abide by the human rights standards set out in United Nations instruments, including respect for the right of all peoples to self-determination. Surely they have an overdue obligation to ensure that indigenous peoples fully enjoy the rights which are our entitlement as members of the human race. It is a commitment to which they must be held.

The powerful conviction which underlies the protection of the right to self-determination is evident in statements of the international community concerning the status of colonies. Colonization has been condemned outright as denying peoples' freedom and independence, exploiting them and their resources, violating their human rights, and discriminating against them.[6] The United Nations made clear that the recognition of justice for colonized peoples required their freedom to assert the right to be their own rulers and be free from subjugation to alien masters.

If you apply the same ethical standards to the situation of indigenous peoples, there can be no other conclusion than that we have been subject to the same alien subjugation, and that our present position is due to exactly the same type of colonization and oppression. The effects are equally heinous, and we should thus be subject to the same right to liberation from oppression. The fact that we are colonized within the geographical borders of existing states makes no difference to the experience. The facts about the lives of indigenous peoples I outlined above make it all too evident that our human rights are not being respected by the states in which we live. In addition, these states do not support or affirm our cultural and spiritual development, and at the most profound level, their organization and institutions are alien to our cultures.

Between indigenous peoples and states there are fundamental conflicts in basic principles of nationhood, the structure of government, and the shaping and sharing of power, wealth, and national resources. It cannot be assumed that we can be part of an aggregate of peoples who exercise their right to self-determination as a whole. A framework which explicitly recognizes our unique status as first peoples is the minimal condition which must be met for us to be said to be exercising our right to self-determination within existing nations.

Against this background, it is the cause of the greatest irony and distress to indigenous peoples that positive international law excludes us from the peoples entitled to enjoy the right to self-determination.

By any reasonable definition, indigenous peoples are unambiguously "peoples." We are united by common territories, cultures, traditions, histories, languages, institutions, and beliefs. We share a sense of kinship and identity, a consciousness as distinct peoples and a political will to exist as distinct peoples. What then could be the justification for our exclusion from this right? The answer is quite simply "power." The hard reality is that states decide what will and will not be recognized and incorporated into international law. And states only wish to recognize the rights of indigenous peoples insofar as they do not defeat or diminish the powers which are currently enjoyed by the state. Effectively, that means that international law only recognizes our rights to the extent that they can be accommodated within the interests of states.

States reject the application of the right of self-determination to indigenous peoples because they fear that the consequences of the application would lead to the violation of their territorial integrity. Self-determination for indigenous peoples is seen as a potential "nation wrecker" with the ability to violate a state's claims to absolute sovereignty and political unity.

What we see is an inversion of logic where the decision about which peoples in fact have the right to self-determination is not derived from recognition of what a people is. The true meaning of "peoples" is in practice of very little importance for how things really work. The answer as to what *actually* determines what a people is results from a backward process. The interests of present nation-states are first priority, thereby excluding those peoples whose application for the right to self-determination could entail consequences inconsistent with these interests. In other words, the desired outcome is first determined and the facts created secondly. The underlying tension is between the preservation of the territorial integrity and power monopoly of the existing states, and the respect for the human rights of indigenous peoples.

Here is the catch: the existing status quo is predicated on the violation of our sovereign rights, so it can hardly be expected to be the source of disinterested criteria for who should enjoy which rights. At the end of the day, no right to self-determination is recognized where it clashes with the rules of the system. As the great African-American freed slave, Frederick Douglass once said, "power concedes nothing without a demand, it never did and it never will."[7]

This leaves us with nothing less than an ethically bankrupt law infected with hidden and morally suspect interests.

Do we look to international law to promote universal values, to reflect the highest order of morality and to further dignity and justice for all peoples? Specifically, can indigenous peoples see international law as a source of support for our *continued survival and flourishing*? Or will we tolerate a situation where international law "makes might right"?

States have argued that protection of their territorial integrity is necessary for security and that self-determination would lead to instability. Quite apart from questioning whether repressive stability is a desirable condition, a quick glimpse at what is happening in the world today makes it obvious that this equation is simply a fallacy. The vehemence, passion, and commitment with which people fight for freedom bear witness to the adage that regardless of what you do, people who are not truly free will continue to fight for that freedom until it is theirs. Strict enforcement of territorial integrity at the expense of human rights promotes disorder, whereas the right to self-determination could well lead to future stability and peace. Perhaps states' fears of dispossession conceal a recognition that the ground of their own sovereign integrity, built on the dispossession of others, is fundamentally unstable. They fear that our claims will inevitably result in their demise and the disintegration of their political power, because this is exactly what they did to us.

We really need to come back to the truths which underlie the different interests. Despite their claims to the contrary, the fact is that *states* are not sovereign. *Peoples* are sovereign. *States* do not have rights. *Peoples* have rights. Contemporary state boundaries, although legal in one sense, do not reflect what people in those countries actually value or feel about their identities. By that I am not suggesting that the only solution is monoethnic or monocultural states. But there must be the space for peoples within states to assert their rights to self-determination, and for that right not to be trumped by the dominant voice of the state.

So what might the exercising of the right to self-determination look like? Essentially, self-determination is an expression of the aspiration to be free to rule one's self, and not be ruled by others.[8] It is in fact a right of process, and as such implies no predetermined outcome. The application will depend on what is considered appropriate by different indigenous peoples. All that is essential is that the people be free to determine their own political organization and future in forms which will respect and support their integrity. The great fear of states is that the application of the right to self-determination will inevitably lead to secession. I do not believe that this is the case. The right does not necessarily imply anything about territoriality or disintegration of the state system. It simply implies a system of government where indigenous peoples will be free from the oppression of others. This could range from full statehood to autonomy in some areas of competence in the state system or to full integration.

Indigenous people are most likely to choose full independence where there has been a consistent failure on the part of the state to respect their fundamental human rights. As such, states could be acting proactively to avoid the conditions which would provoke secession.

In any case, the right to self-determination is indivisible. Freedom can have no qualification, and it must be open to us to freely determine our best options.

In conclusion, I would like to look briefly at the situation in Australia to give a practical illustration of some of the concepts I have touched upon. As I mentioned, in 1992 the High Court of Australia brought down a decision which overturned the racist doctrine of *terra nullius,* and gave common law recognition to Native title, the original land title of indigenous peoples. The decision is significant for a number of reasons.

First of all, it lays the foundation for the recovery of land for some indigenous peoples where they can prove a continuing connection to the land and their title has not been extinguished by an act of the crown. For others, past extinguishment of Native title may give rise to compensation.

Secondly, it changes the basis of the claims of indigenous peoples. While we have always seen our claims as a matter of rights and justice, others preferred to relegate them to the realms of welfare. The latter perception trapped us in a powerless position which is destructive to our sense of worth and dignity. This is no longer possible. The High Court Native title decision gave credibility to our assertion that we have rightful claims to land. Now when we assert our rights we can stand with our dignity and relate to nonindigenous peoples from a position of strength. In terms of the theme of the international year, "a new partnership," this transformation has been crucial. To speak of a partnership is meaningless if one partner has no bargaining power. And while it would be naive to suggest that indigenous peoples are now equal partners in Australia, we now have the strength of legal recognition. It is also meaningless to speak of a partnership where the parties cannot communicate. In this sense the decision has also been transformative.

The High Court judgment brought together formerly alien and estranged legal systems. It recognized that Native title gives rise to rights, valid and enforceable within the common law system. But it also recognized that Native title can *only* be defined by reference to the indigenous traditional law which is its *fundamental,* original source of validity. It thus opened the space for a dialogue between the voice of indigenous and nonindigenous laws.

Finally, the decision has significant implications regarding self-determination. When James Cook arrived in Australia in 1788, he was given explicit instructions that in acquiring land, he was to obtain "the consent of the Natives." This he never did, and thereby set the pattern for the next 200 years. We were not consulted because in the eyes of the colonizing culture, we were not there, in the sense of peoples with a right to have any influence over the development of our country, let alone our own lives.

It is now law that in matters concerning our land we must be consulted. Sadly, the result of history is that we have lost much of that land, and thus the possibility of asserting our rights is limited. But the principle has broader implications than the literal enjoyment of rights of control over specific land. By acknowledging the preexisting rights of indigenous peoples, and the validity of indigenous law, the decision provided recognition of our inherent rights as distinct peoples. While it did not recognize our sovereignty nor explicitly touch upon the matter of self-determination, it did acknowledge the competency of indigenous law, and the fact that as peoples we did not automatically lose our rights when the British claimed sovereignty. Which of those rights we will be able to exercise is yet to be worked out through a negotiated settlement.

At this stage, the signs are reasonably positive. The federal government has negotiated closely with indigenous representatives and has indicated that its proposed legislation will ensure the protection of many of the rights established by the High Court decision. Certainly, indigenous peoples have had to compromise significantly on what we would have ideally sought, but we recognize that partnerships, like marriages, must involve compromises.

However, I have to say that to assert a just solution, the Australian government had to take a strong stand against some of the most shameful, explicitly hostile, and racist proposals. These have included repealing Australia's antiracism laws, moving all aboriginal people to one area, and prohibiting all past and possible future claims by indigenous peoples. Such proposals were justified by various claims by racists to the effect that any recognition of indigenous rights would inevitably plunge the country into economic chaos and social warfare. Indigenous people, it was claimed, not having invented the wheeled cart, were of a lower caliber anyway, and their dispossession was inevitable if not desirable. It went on to state that any assertion of indigenous rights discriminated against all other Australians. Even as I speak, one state in Australia is putting through separate reactionary rebel legislation designed to remove any remnant rights which the High Court decision may have protected.

The conflict in Australia is of exactly the same character as other struggles I described earlier; staunch defense of morally bankrupt interests in the name of stability, versus a compassionate recognition of the inherent dignity of all peoples. Put that way, you may wonder how the choice can be anything but perfectly obvious.

I spoke earlier of the opportunity available to everyone on this planet to listen to the "voices of the earth," and thereby to salvage our home and our dignity. I urge you also to listen to the voice of the earth which exists in each of you, indigenous or nonindigenous. The connection is there if you choose to heed it.

NOTES

1. The UN General Assembly proclaimed the UN Decade for the World's Indigenous People, commencing on 10 December 1994, in its resolution 48/163 of 21 December 1993.

2. Nasser Addine Ghazali, Opposition to violations of human rights, in UNESCO, *Violations of Human Rights, 1984,* quoting in part Karel Vasak, "Human Rights: As a Legal Reality," in *The International Dimensions of Human Rights,* ed. Karel Vasak (Paris/Westport, Conn.: UNESCO/Greenwood Press, 1982), 3.

3. Lung-Chu Chen, "Self Determination as a Human Right," in *Toward World Order and Human Dignity: Essays in Honour of Myres McDougal,* ed. W. Michael Reisman and Burns H. Weston (New York: Free Press, 1976), 198–241.

4. Quoted in Deborah Z. Cass, "Rethinking Self-Determination: A Critical Analysis of Current International Law Theories," *Syracuse Journal of International Law and Commerce* 18 (spring 1992).

5. Hector Gross Espiell, "The Right To Self Determination: Implementation of UN Resolutions," para 59, UN Doc. E/CN. 4/Sub. 2/405/Rev. 1 (1980).

6. See Preamble to the Declaration on the Granting of Independence to Colonial Countries and Peoples.

7. Frederick Douglass, quoted in Studs Terkel, *Race* (London: Minerva, 1992).

8. See Dov Ronen, *The Quest for Self-Determination,* (New Haven, Conn.: Yale University Press, 1979), 7.

from *The Disabled God: Toward a Liberatory Theology of Disability*

❧

Nancy L. Eiesland

Nancy L. Eiesland is associate professor of sociology of religion at Candler School of Theology. She coedited *Human Disability and the Service of God* and has lectured on disabilities worldwide. Here she explores some implications of disability for our conception of God and spiritual life.

❧

> *We have seen signs which shall not be cut off. The branches shall not be cut off from the vine. Our power will not be diminished or rendered ineffective. The sacrament of life shall not be withheld—the body, the blood, the sensuality of God's presence on earth.*
>
> —Carter Heyward, *Our Passion for Justice*

For me, epiphanies come too infrequently to be shrugged off as unbelievable. Like a faithful Jew who had conscientiously opened the door for Elijah each Seder and spun images of the majestic beauty of a Messiah who would shout out an order and the universe would tremble, I had waited for a mighty revelation of God. But my epiphany bore little resemblance to the God I was expecting or the God of my dreams. I saw God in a sip-puff wheelchair, that is, the chair used mostly by quadriplegics enabling them to maneuver by blowing and sucking on a strawlike device. Not an omnipotent, self-sufficient God, but neither a pitiable, suffering servant. In this moment, I beheld God as a survivor, unpitying and forthright. I recognized the incarnate Christ in the image of those judged "not feasible," "unemployable," with "questionable quality of life." Here was God for me.

After glimpsing this hidden image of God, I began to think and to share my contemplations with friends in the disability rights movement. Making sense of our fascination with and appreciation of that image has been a driving force for this book. This theology of liberation emerged from those conversations, our common labor for justice, and corporate reflection on symbol. Although this work cannot represent the experience of all people with disabilities who seek justice and God with equal fervor, it is a beginning and an invitation to emancipatory transformation for both people with disabilities and others who care. By beginning with the experience of persons with disabilities, recounting our history of the disability rights movement, examining models for understanding disability, and naming the injustice wrought in the name of Christian goodwill, I have engaged in the theological task of describing as accurately as possible how things are for people with disabilities. Yet the method used here attempts not only to unmask our real, lived experience, making our multifaceted body knowledge a resource for "doing theology," but also to offer a vision of a God who is for us and a church that is for that God and persons with disabilities as the people of God.

In this chapter, I explore a liberatory theology of disability that incorporates both political action and reconception of symbols. Emancipatory transformation must be enacted not only in history, but also in imagination and language. Liberatory theology of disability is the work of the bodily figuration of knowledge.[1] As embodied theology, it is both the struggle of resistance and the revelation of our long-masked knowledge and images. It is not an abstract theory, but is grounded in the bodies and actions of people with disabilities and others who care. To speak of a liberatory proclamation for people with disabilities is to recognize, as Nancy Mairs maintains, that a voice is the creature of the body that produces it. A liberatory theology of disability begins with our bodies and keeps faith with our hidden history. This liberatory theology recognizes biblical revelation and truth in those texts and interpretative models that transcend their able-bodied frameworks—which isolate and stigmatize people with disabilities—and that permit a vision of people with disabilities as theological subjects and historical actors. One locus of such revelation and truth is embodied in the image of Jesus Christ, the disabled God.

ON INCARNATING LIBERATION

In exploring the relationship between physical embodiment and religious symbols, two fundamental insights must be acknowledged. First, all human beings are embodied. Feminists have directed our attention to the gender of those bodies as fundamental to our understanding of religious experience. They note that the experiences of men and women are seldom the same socially or religiously. People with disabilities have contended that embodiment includes physical ability as well. By focusing on the physical status of individuals, people with disabilities have questioned the use of "normal" bodies as the basis for scholarly study of religion or practice of religious ritual.

Second, religious symbols point individuals beyond their ordinary lives. Religious symbols not only prescribe or reproduce social status, but they also transform it. The power of symbols and myths is in the motive force they engender. Clifford Geertz, an anthropologist, maintains that symbols have performative power for societies and individuals because they establish and maintain beliefs and values—a cultural ethos. "Religion is a system of symbols which acts to produce powerful, pervasive, and long-lasting moods and motivations in [people] by formulating conceptions of a general order of existence."[2] By "moods," Geertz means psychological dispositions, such as self-confidence, awe, or trust. "Motivation" is the tendency to act or feel a particular way. Symbols create normative standards for human interaction. They legitimate social structures, political arrangements, and attitudinal inclinations, constitute our cultural toolkits, and offer visions of what can be. Carol Christ argues that it is because of this performative power that oppressive symbol systems cannot simply be repudiated, but must be replaced. She writes, "Where there is not any replacement, the mind will revert to familiar structures at times of crises, bafflement, or defeat."[3]

Empowering symbols are vital for any marginalized group. Yet if thoroughgoing transformation is the aim, those reconceived symbols must be linked to the dominant social-symbolic order. That is, not only must they change the way that people with disabilities conceive of our experiences and, in particular, our relationships to God, they must also alter the regular practices, ideas, and images of the able-bodied. The obstacles that confront us in our daily lives are held in place by the images, ideas, and emotional responses of an able-bodied society. Hence a separatist symbol system for people with disabilities would perpetuate the segregation that is already too often our practical reality. Furthermore, separatism would deny our real interdependence with able-bodied persons. We need symbols that affirm our dignity in relation not only to other people with disabilities, but also to able-bodied persons. We need symbols that call both people with disabilities and the able-bodied to conversion.

My focus on symbols as crucial for emancipatory transformation is a strategic judgment about the power of religious symbols with reference to disability. The importance of visibility in the stigmatization of people with disabilities and discourse about disability, suggests that a liberatory theology of disability must create new images of wholeness as well as new discourses. Furthermore, the bodily rituals of stigmatization and exclusion that are a significant form of oppression of people with disabilities must be supplanted by bodily practices of ordinary inclusion.

The stigmatization of people with disabilities is not simply a matter of rationalized and deliberate institutional and individual discrimination, though it is unquestionably that; it is also a condition of the modern human psyche and a physical stance of being. Iris Marion Young states,

> Group oppressions are enacted in this society not primarily in official laws and policies but in informal, often unnoticed and unreflective speech, bodily reactions to others, conventional practices of everyday interactions and evaluations, aesthetic judgments, and the jokes, images, and stereotypes pervading the mass media.[4]

For people with disabilities, the bodily reactions of the able-bodied are often particularly oppressive. Goffman calls them rituals of degradation.[5] For example, people who use wheelchairs endure physical debasement when people refuse to meet their eyes or stand beside the chair to talk instead of before the person. Deep seated unconscious aversion to people with disabilities is typically enacted and upheld by attitudinal barriers and physical avoidance. Stigmatization sometimes also takes the form of inappropriate fascination with the bodies of people with disabilities. Often strangers in elevators ask me what I did to myself. This inappropriate curiosity, defended as charitable goodwill, is a ritual enactment of patterns of social power in which able-bodied people assume an exceptional access to the bodies of people with disabilities.

As asserted in chapter 4, these attitudinal barriers are funded by foundational Christian themes such as the conflation of sin and disability, virtuous suffering, and segregationist charity. The social-symbolic order that these Christian theologies help to establish perpetuates the belief that disability is inherently "un(w)holy" and that the suffering of people with disabilities is the natural outcome of our impairments. Institutional practices also dissipate our yearning for justice, substituting instead self-pity and the isolating charity of others. These Christian theologies defraud people with disabilities by undercutting our self-empowerment and frustrating our liberatory work. They sometimes seduce people with disabilities into sharing the prejudices about ourselves and others held by the able-bodied community, leading to feelings of self-rejection and shame. The symbols also promote the mood and motivation of charity, which sanctions dependency as an appropriate Christian virtue.

The most promising model for addressing this real institutional discrimination and submerged cultural imperialism, that is, "the universalization of a dominant group's experience and culture, and its establishment as the norm,"[6] is through a liberatory theology of disability that includes both political action and resymbolization. Emancipatory transformation must include not only an examination of dominant practices and beliefs and the ways in which they maintain or challenge structures of stigmatization and marginalization, but also a search for and proclamation of alternative structures and symbols of religious life that can effectively challenge oppressive beliefs and values. Rebecca S. Chopp writes:

> Until we change the values and hidden rules that run through present linguistic practices, social codes, and psychic orderings, women, persons of color, and other oppressed groups will be forced—by language, discourses, and practices available to them—into conforming to ongoing practices, to babbling nonsense, or to not speaking at all.[7]

In changing the symbol of Christ, from that of suffering servant, model of virtuous suffering, or conquering lord, toward a formulation of Jesus Christ as disabled God, I draw implications for the ritual and doctrine of the Eucharist based on this new symbol. This two-step theological construction intends constitutive change and the creation of new symbols and rituals whereby people with disabilities can affirm our bodies in dignity and reconceive the church as community of justice for people with disabilities. Thus the truth of these theological statements is in their ability to transform reality, not necessarily for all people at all times, but for particular people in particular situations of oppression and pain. The truth of this liberatory theology of disability is in its ability to enable transformation for people with disabilities within the church and in its adaptability to addressing our ever-emerging challenges and opportunities. In order to accomplish these goals, the thoroughgoing transformation of institutional, bureaucratic, and theological foundations of the Christian church is essential.

ACTING OUT AND HOLDING OUR BODIES TOGETHER

This theological method joins political action and resymbolization. Political action is the work of "acting out" and "holding our bodies together" in the struggle against the overt discrimination endemic in society and the church. Political action includes increasing the visibility and authority of people with disabilities, promoting face-to-face interaction between people with disabilities and the able-bodied, and emphasizing the communal benefit afforded by the inclusion of a minority viewpoint. These activities question and disrupt able-bodied society's stance toward people with disabilities. As Iris Marion Young asserts, "Encounter with the disabled person again produces the ambiguity of recognizing that the person whom I project as so different, so other, is nevertheless like me."[8] "Acting out" means refusing to acquiesce to the acceptable role for people with disabilities; it is the revolutionary work of resistance. "Holding our bodies together" is the work of solidarity with our own bodies, other people with disabilities, and other marginalized groups.

Acting out involves being willing to expend our sometimes flagging store of energy on the struggle for justice. It is risking acknowledgment of how weary we are of oppression. Fatigue is a double-edged sword for people with disabilities. Often our bone-weariness with living a difficult life made more difficult by stigmatizing social systems necessitates that we rebel. Yet people with disabilities cannot afford to ignore or underestimate the real work of liberation. We must and have learned to pick our battles carefully. Though we do not necessarily opt only for winnable campaigns, we must always be aware of the implications of any one struggle for advancing our common cause.

Fatigue can also cut us off from our corporate energy. We must tend to our families and friends and generate the requisite quantity and quality of labor at our jobs, as well as put our bodies on American Disabled for Attendant Programs Today (ADAPT) protest lines, write letters to legislators, organize ourselves, and attend our meetings. Hence actual liberation requires that our liberatory practices incorporate our need for health and survival. Displacing the notion of virtuous suffering from the church, only to reinstitute it as revolutionary practice is not emancipatory for people with disabilities. Our physical and communal survival requires that a first-order priority of a liberatory theology is the creation of positions that enable people to work full time for liberation within the disability community and within the church.

Second, acting out and holding our bodies together requires coming to terms with our own bodies—bodies that sometimes throw us to the pavement simply for placing our feet carelessly, and bodies that twitch and pitch, searching for an ever-elusive comfortable position. Embodiment is not a purely agreeable reality; it incorporates profound ambiguity—sometimes downright distress. There is simply no denying it. We concede the precarious position of living a difficult life and affirming our bodies as whole, good, and beautiful. In this incongruity, the revolutionary act of accepting our bodies as "survive-able," not deficient or deformed, is vital. "Survive-able" bodies are painstakingly, honestly, and lovingly constructed, not, according to Nancy Mairs, "heroic figure[s], wounded but still defiant."[9] Instead of flagellating ourselves or aspiring to well-behaved "perfect" bodies, we savor the jumbled pleasure-pain that is our bodies. In a society where denial of our particular bodies and questing for a better body is "normal," respect for our own bodies is an act of resistance and liberation.

Further, holding our bodies together denotes attention to our sexuality as a resource for solidarity with one another and with ourselves. We maintain that knowledge is fundamentally relational. Hence it is dynamic, rather than static. Audre Lorde attends to this notion of the body as erotic.

> The erotic . . . provides the power which comes from sharing deeply any pursuit with another person. The sharing of joy, whether physical, emotional, psychic, or intellectual, forms a bridge between the sharers which can be the basis for understanding much of what is not shared between them, and lessens the threat of their difference.[10]

This erotic understanding is revealed in Diane DeVries's description of her relation with her sister and her embodiment of Debbie's body. The power of this interconnection is its genesis in shared bodies and lives and its synergistic pleasure. Among people with disabilities, holding our bodies together touches the "joy we know ourselves to be capable of"[11] and emerges from a complex and concrete love of life. This erotic power draws us out of our physical isolation; it is the "laying on of hands" that releases the embodied power of God on earth.

Holding our bodies together also means placing ourselves in solidarity with other people with disabilities. It means not distinguishing between "good" and "bad" disabilities, refusing to stigmatize people with intellectual disabilities as inherently more impaired than those with ambulatory disabilities, for example. For those very few "token" individuals who are allowed to succeed in the able-bodied system, it means refusing to be flattered into believing that our "extraordinary" achievements are the result of our atypical intelligence and talent. By holding our bodies together, we turn our backs on a social system that institutionalizes horizontal violence as the toll charge of inclusion.

Finally, holding our bodies together means uniting with other marginalized peoples in resistance. A liberatory theology of disability is in solidarity with other liberation theologies, though it incorporates unique emphases and perspectives. Structures and attitudes that keep women, people of color, and the poor marginalized also stigmatize people with disabilities as their "normal" practice. Hence the consciousness-raising efforts of other marginalized people have provided both motivation and models for people with disabilities. A liberatory theology of disability shares with feminist theology a valuation of the body as a theological resource. It, too, challenges the patriarchal image of God. Following Latin American liberation theologians, a liberatory theology of disability calls for justice for the poor. Only institutionalized violence and systemic torture can explain why malnutrition is the primary cause of disability worldwide. It is estimated that there are at least 600 million people worldwide who have disabilities. Malnutrition accounts for approximately 20 percent of that disablement.[12] Bearing witness for peace and struggling against the weapons trade, a liberatory theology of disability calls for an end to the violence which tears at bodies and multiplies refugees, who often suffer undernourishment and inadequate care for injuries. With those who resist not-so-subtle racism in educational practices that conceal potent resistance narratives, a theology of disability seeks to uncover and expound the history of resistance to oppression.

Although acting out and holding our bodies together are essential liberatory tactics, they are not enough. While I hope with Pat Wright, once director of the Disability Rights Education and Defense Fund, who writes, "You can't legislate attitudes, but the attitudinal barriers will drop the more disabled people are employed, the more they can be seen on the street and when we become not just a silent minority, but fully participating members of society,"[13] I am less confident that the presence of our bodies in public will displace the pervasive belief structure that thrives on our subjugation. As the history of the disability rights movement demonstrates and as marginalized people already know, political action does not thoroughly alter the attitudes that underlie discrimination. A liberatory theology of disability must also incorporate resymbolization aimed at these attitudinal supports. It must create new symbols of wholeness and new embodiments of justice.

Resymbolization entails the deconstruction of dominant symbolic meanings and a reconstitution of those symbols, making them both liberatory for the marginalized group and unsettling for the dominant group. Resymbolization is radical symbol sedition. Following Paul Ricoeur's proposition that the symbol gives rise to thought, I maintain that the symbol can also give rise to subversive thought and action.[14] A symbol can be reclaimed as part of a hidden history. It is this decentering of the dominant symbolic order that resists "normal" attitudes and unconscious prejudice. It is this paradoxical coexistence of difference and sameness incorporated into familiar symbols that infiltrates the misleading mystifications of disability and demythologizes the mythic archetypes of suffering and heroic survival. Although this process recognizes that people with disabilities are not at home within the Christian tradition and the social-symbolic order it has engendered, it suggests that we are not as estranged as the able-bodied church and society portrays us. We have been hidden, but we haven't gone away. Our hidden history is latent within the Christian symbols, and we will not be cut off.

THE DISABLED GOD

A reconception of the symbol of Jesus Christ, as disabled God, is developed here as a contextualized Christology. It is contextualized in that the disabled God emerges in the particular situation in which people with disabilities and others who care find themselves as they try to live out their faith and to fulfill their calling to live ordinary lives of worth and dignity. Contextualization is an authentic process of perceiving how God is present with people with disabilities and of unmasking the ways in which theological inquiry has frequently instituted able-bodied experience as the theological norm. The theological lenses through which we have traditionally viewed our own and others' bodies distort the physical presence not only of people with disabilities but also of the incarnate God. To contextualize then is both to engage the past and present of a biblical text or a religious symbol in light of the past and present of its readers and hearers and to look to the future and the transformative effect that such a reading can have upon those who will come into contact with it.

Christology is the natural domain of contextualization since the Incarnation is the ultimate contextual revelation. Orlando E. Costas writes, "Biblical contextualization is rooted in the fact that the God of revelation can only be known in history. Such a revelation comes to specific peoples in concrete situations by means of particular cultural symbols and categories."[15] God became flesh in a particular time and place. Through centuries of theological abstractions, the power of that very physical reality of God present in human flesh has sometimes been obscured. Yet Christology is fundamentally about human experience and human bodies as partially constitutive of God. God is with us: Emmanuel (Matt. 1:22–23). As Nancy Mairs writes:

> A God who put on a body and walked about in that body and spoke to us from that body and died as that body and yet somehow did not die then or ever but lives on in our bodies which live in God. It's not the easiest story to swallow.[16]

The coming of Emmanuel was understood by the early church in terms of the death and resurrection.[17] At the Resurrection, the disciples understood the person Jesus for who he really was. Only through the lens of resurrection could they understand the meaning and significance of the life of Jesus on earth. In the resurrected Jesus Christ, they saw not the suffering servant for whom the last and most important word was tragedy and sin, but the disabled God who embodied both impaired hands and feet and pierced side and the imago Dei. Paradoxically, in the very act commonly understood as the transcendence of physical life, God is revealed as tangible, bearing the representation of the body reshaped by injustice and sin into the fullness of the Godhead. Luke 24:36–39 relates an appearance of this resurrected Jesus:

> While they were talking about this, Jesus himself stood among them. . . . They were startled and terrified, and thought that they were seeing a ghost. He said to them, "Why are you frightened, and why do doubts arise in your hearts? Look at my hands and my feet; see that it is I myself. Touch me and see; for a ghost does not have flesh and bones as you see that I have."

Here is the resurrected Christ making good on the incarnational proclamation that God would be with us, embodied as we are, incorporating the fullness of human contingency and ordinary life into God. In presenting his impaired hands and feet to his startled friends, the resurrected Jesus is revealed as the disabled God. Jesus, the resurrected Savior, calls for his frightened companions to recognize in the marks of impairment their own connection with God, their own salvation. In so doing, this disabled God is also the revealer of a new humanity. The disabled God is not only the One from heaven but the revelation of true personhood, underscoring the reality that full personhood is fully compatible with the experience of disability.

THEOLOGICAL IMPLICATIONS OF THE DISABLED GOD

The symbol of Jesus Christ, the disabled God, has transformative power. It is the experience of Christ from below as a corporeal experience. The power of the disabled God is the seemingly inherent contradiction this God embodies. This revelation of God disorders the social-symbolic order, and God appears in the most unexpected bodies. The disabled God does not engage in a battle for dominance or create a new normative power, God is in the present social-symbolic order at the margins with people with disabilities and instigates transformation from this de-centered position.

The disabled God repudiates the conception of disability as a consequence of individual sin. Injustice against persons with disabilities is surely sin; our bodies, however, are not artifacts of sin, original or otherwise. Our bodies participate in the imago Dei, not in spite of our impairments and contingencies, but through them. The conflation of sin and disability causes problems for the interpretation of the resurrected Jesus Christ. What is the significance of the resurrected Christ's display of impaired hands and feet and side? Are they the disfiguring vestiges of sin? Are they to be subsumed under the image of Christ, death conqueror? Or should the disability of Christ be understood as the truth of incarnation and the promise of resurrection? The latter interpretation fosters a reconception of wholeness. It suggests a human-God who not only knows injustice and experiences the contingency of human life, but also reconceives perfection as unself-pitying, painstaking survival.

The resurrected Jesus Christ in presenting impaired hands and feet and side to be touched by frightened friends alters the taboo of physical avoidance of disability and calls for followers to recognize their connection and equality at the point of Christ's physical impairment. Christ's disfigured side bears witness to the existence of "hidden" disabilities, as well. Historically, inter-pretations of the "pierced" side of Jesus have emphasized the tragedy of innocent suffering. But understanding the internal damage wrought by hacking swords as part of God's eternal existence necessitates a deromanticization of interpretations of Christ's impaired body and a recognition of the population of people who identify with Christ's experience of disabilities, hidden and displayed, as part of our hidden history. For many people whose hidden disabilities keep them from participating fully in the church or from feeling full-bodied acceptance by Christ, accept-ing the disabled God may enable reconciliation with their own bodies and Christ's body the church. Hence, disability not only does not contradict the human-divine integrity, it becomes a new model of wholeness and a symbol of solidarity.

Feminist criticisms of the symbolism of Jesus as the male Galilean and lordly Christ—a problematic image for women—notwithstanding, the image of Jesus Christ, the disabled God, is not inherently oppressive for women, particularly women with disabilities. The disabled God provides a new way of identifying with the physical reality of Jesus. Clearly feminists and marginalized people cannot continue to support an

> image of Christ [which] is manipulated in the praxis of privilege (by those on the top, repre-
> sentatives of white male gentry) not only to symbolize the suffering servant, with whom those
> on the bottom can identify in terms of passive acceptance of suffering; but also, because Christ
> is God, to symbolize the rulership of all that is established, the guardian and custodian of all
> human and "natural" resources.[18]

Nonetheless, one need not move from a rejection of this image of Christ to a negation of either the physical presence or the divinity of Jesus Christ. Jesus Christ, the disabled God, is not a suffering servant or a conquering lord. Rather this contextualization of Jesus enables that "the Christ understood as the stranger, the outcast, the hungry, the weak, the poor, [and I would add person with disabilities] makes the traditional male Christ (Black and White) less significant."[19] The significance of the disabled God is not primarily maleness, but rather physicality. Jesus Christ the disabled God, is consonant with the image of Jesus Christ the stigmatized Jew, person of color, and representative of the poor and hungry—those who have struggled to maintain the integrity and dignity of their bodies in the face of the physical mutilation of injustice and rituals of bodily degradation.

Jesus Christ the disabled God, is not a romanticized notion of "overcomer" God. Instead here is God as survivor. Here language fails because the term "survivor" in our society is contaminated with notions of victimization, radical individualism, and alienation, as well as with an ethos of virtuous suffering. In contradistinction to that cultural icon, the image of survivor here evoked is that of a simple, unself-pitying, honest body, for whom the limits of power are palpable but not tragic. The disabled God embodies the ability to see clearly the complexity and the "mixed blessing" of life and bodies, without living in despair. This revelation is of a God for us who celebrates joy and experiences pain not separately in time or space, but simultaneously.

The disabled God is God for whom interdependence is not a possibility to be willed from a position of power, but a necessary condition for life. This interdependence is the fact of both justice and survival. The disabled God embodies practical interdependence, not simply willing to be interrelated from a position of power, but depending on it from a position of need. For many people with disabilities, too, mutual care is a matter of survival. To posit a Jesus Christ who needs care and mutuality as essential to human-divine survival does not symbolize either humanity or divinity as powerless. Instead it debunks the myth of individualism and hierarchical orders, in which transcendence means breaking free of encumbrances and needing nobody and constitutes the divine as somebody in relation to other bodies.

This disabled God makes possible a renewal of hope for people with disabilities and others who care. This symbol points not to a utopian vision of hope as the erasure of all human contingency, historically or eternally, for that would be to erase our bodies, our lives. Rather it is a liberatory realism that maintains a clear recognition of the limits of our bodies and an acceptance of limits as the truth of being human. This liberatory realism also calls for a realization of the necessity of a social and interpersonal transformation that does not surrender to cynicism and defeatism any more than the limits of our bodies suggest that we should do nothing. It locates our hope in justice as access and mutuality, a justice that removes the barriers which constrain our bodies, keep us excluded, and intend to humiliate us. It also situates our hope in the reality of our existence as ones with dignity and integrity. Hope is the recollection and projection that even our nonconventional bodies, which oftentimes dissatisfy and fail us, are worth the living. It is knowing that the so-called curses sometimes feel like blessings.

The image of the disabled God proceeds from Jesus Christ's embodied commitment to justice as rightly ordered interpersonal and structural relations. This is the God who indicts not only deliberate injustice, but unintended rituals of degradation that deny the full personhood of marginalized people. Moreover, Jesus Christ, the disabled God, disorders the social-symbolic orders of what it means to be incarnate—in flesh—and confirms that "normal" bodies, like impaired bodies, are subject to contingency. And it is a contingency born not of tragedy or sin but of ordinary women and embodied unexceptionably. This representation of God does not gloss over the suffering enacted against bodies as the consequence of injustice; rather it posits that our bodies cannot be subsumed into injustice or sin.

The disabled God defines the church as a communion of justice. Jesus Christ, the disabled God, is as Jürgen Moltmann writes:

> The one who is to come is then already present in an anticipatory sense in history in the Spirit and the word, and in the miserable and the helpless. His future ends the world's history of suffering and completes the fragments and anticipations of his kingdom which are called the church.[20]

Thus the church, which depends for its existence on the disabled God, must live out liberating action in the world. The church finds its identity as the body of Christ only by being a community of faith and witness, a coalition of struggle and justice, and a fellowship of hope. This mission necessitates that people with disabilities be incorporated into all levels of participation and decision making.

Jesus Christ as the disabled God provides a symbolic prototype and opens the door to the theological task of rethinking Christian symbols, metaphors, rituals, and doctrines so as to make them accessible to people with disabilities and remove their able-bodied bias. In chapter 6, the Eucharist is explored as a ritual of ordinary inclusion of people with disabilities. Liberating our theology from biases against people with disabilities is a process that will require tremendous and continual commitment to identifying with the disabled God in our midst. Even in the process of developing the symbol of Jesus Christ, disabled deity, I have heard numerous objections. Individuals who are heavily invested in a belief in the transcendence of God constituted as radical otherness will undoubtedly find this representation disconcerting. The theological implications of the disabled God resist the notion of power as absolute control over human-divine affairs. For people with disabilities who have grasped divine healing as the only liberatory image the traditional church has offered, relinquishing belief in an all-powerful God who could heal, if He would, is painful. Yet who is this god whose attention we cannot get, whose inability to respond to our pain causes still more pain? This god is surely not Emmanuel—God for us. The second objection some have expressed is that the articulation of a model of God that incorporates disability signals runaway confusion in the church, and they insist that a halt should be called on all representational language for God. With the emergence of African American, feminist, gay-lesbian, and Latin American liberation theologies in recent history, models of God have proliferated. Yet this representational proliferation does not portend chaos; rather it is the corporate enactment of the Resurrection of God. The body of God is becoming alive, vivified by an insurrection of subjugated knowledges. This resurrection happens, however, only when these emerging models of God are more than simply new names for the same symbolic order. The challenge for the Christian is to engage one or more "names" of God and to follow these images into the worlds they open.

BEARING OUR BODIES

For me and, I hope, other people with disabilities, as well as for some able-bodied people, the presence of the disabled God makes it possible to bear a nonconventional body. This God enables both a struggle for justice among people with disabilities and an end to estrangement from our own bodies.

NOTES

1. Rebecca Chopp, *The Power to Speak* (New York: Crossroads, 1989), 117.
2. Clifford Geertz, *The Interpretation of Cultures: Selected Essays* (New York: Basic, 1973), 90.
3. Carol Christ, "Why Women Need the Goddess: Phenomenological, Psychological, and Political Reflections," in *Woman-spirit Rising: A Feminist Reader in Religion,* ed. C. Christ and J. Plaskow (San Francisco: Harper & Row, 1979), 275.

4. Iris Marion Young, *Justice and the Politics of Difference* (Princeton, N.J.: Princeton University Press, 1990), 148.

5. Erving Goffman, *Stigma: Notes on the Management of Spoiled Identity* (Englewood Cliffs, N.J.: Prentice-Hall, 1963).

6. Young, *Justice and the Politics of Difference,* 59.

7. Chopp, *The Power to Speak,* 7.

8. Young, *Justice and the Politics of Difference,* 147.

9. Nancy Mairs, *Carnal Acts* (New York: HarperCollins, 1990), 18.

10. Audre Lorde, *Sister Outsider* (Trumansburg, N.Y.: Crossing Press, 1984), 56–57.

11. Lorde, *Sister Outsider,* 57.

12. "Malnutrition Disables 100 Million," *One World* 62:13.

13. Quoted in R. Funk, "Disability Rights: From Caste to Class in the Context of Civil Rights" in *Images of the Disabled, Disabling Images,* ed. A. Gartner and T. Joe (New York: Praeger, 1987), 23.

14. In "Metaphor and Symbol," Ricoeur qualifies his earlier position. "Today I am less certain that one can attack the problem so directly without first having taken linguistics into account. Within the symbol, it now seems to me, there is something non-semantic." Paul Ricoeur, *Interpretation Theory: Discourse and the Surplus of Meaning* (Fort Worth: Texas Christian University Press, 1976), 45. Yet the approach employed here is consonant with Ricoeur's approach. Ricoeur understands the dynamic of reading the biblical text as a challenge for the reader to engage one or more "names" of God and to follow these epithets into "worlds" that the text then opens.

15. Orlando E. Costas, *Christ Outside the Gate: Mission Beyond Christendom* (Maryknoll, N.Y.: Orbis, 1989), 5.

16. Nancy Mairs, *Ordinary Time* (Boston: Beacon Press, 1993), 3.

17. Raymond Brown, *The Birth of the Messiah: A Commentary on the Infancy Narratives in Matthew and Luke* (Garden City, N.Y.: Doubleday, 1979), 26. Brown contends that the earliest Christian preaching about Jesus concerned his death and resurrection.

18. Carter Heyward, *Our Passion for Justice* (New York: Pilgrim Press, 1984), 215.

19. Jacquelyn Grant, *While Women's Christ and Black Women's Jesus: Feminist Christology and Womanist Response* (Atlanta: Scholars Press, 1989), 219.

20. Jürgen Moltmann, *The Church in the Power of the Spirit: A Contribution to Messianic Ecclesiology* (San Francisco: Harper & Row, 1977), 132.

VI

THE LIBERATION OF GENDER

The relation of Torah to women calls Torah itself into question. Where is the missing Commandment that sits in judgment on the world? Where is the Commandment that will say, from the beginning of history until now: Thou shalt not lessen the humanity of women?

—Cynthia Ozick, "Notes toward Finding the Right Question"

One can justify [gender] equality by using certain scriptures, but one is unlikely to do so if one is motivated only by conformation to the canon. Only when one accepts insights coming out of contemporary feminism is one likely to find that these are supported in scripture.

—John Cobb, *Reclaiming the Church*

The last forty years has witnessed an unprecedented expansion of women's rights throughout all of social life. Although women are still not equal to men in wealth or social position, virtually the entire developed world has lessened its legal and cultural constraints on their lives. This initially secular movement has had a decisive effect on religious life, leading to the development of feminist theology, woman-oriented rituals, and female power in religion's institutional life. It is a remarkable example of a nonreligious political movement transforming religion, of politics helping religions to become more holy.

Of course, many in religious life have not been won over by feminist arguments. Perhaps no other area of concern strikes as deeply into both our most personal sense of identity and the way we structure our public life. Feminism's challenges to long-held beliefs and practices have been responded to with passionate denunciation as well as passionate affirmation. Denominations have split over the issues confronted in this section, and many people believe that the liberation of gender is a threat to the Word of God rather than part of its fulfillment. What is decisively new is not the full accomplishment of women's equality, but the struggle for it.

The feminist challenge begins with the simple but profound observation that the world's dominant religions have been deeply patriarchal. Their founding texts were male authored and interpreted; men have held virtually all positions of institutional authority; and in numerous ways their theologies have bolstered the idea of male spiritual superiority. In response to these crucial insights, some women simply abandoned the tradition. Others, however, have been rebuilding—in a way that reflects their collective experiences and interests—what they insist are their own traditions. They are committed to changing their faiths even as they remain within them.

Such changes begin, as we see in the selections by Anne Clifford, Rosemary Ruether, Judith Plaskow, Elisabeth Schüssler Fiorenza, Asghar Ali Engineer, and Fernando Pagés Ruiz, with a fundamental reexamination of the content, history, and goal of the world's dominant religions.

These writers engage in three essential tasks: first, they criticize the sexism of the tradition, denying that the subordination or devaluation of women can ever be identified with the word of God. Second, they challenge existing interpretations of women's roles in religious history, arguing that patriarchy is often a later invention or a distortion of original teachings (see especially the pieces by Fiorenza and Engineer). Third, they offer new ideas of what a transformed tradition might look like: how recognition of women's equality before God and Spirit would not just mean that a male-oriented tradition opens to women, but that the actual content of the religion would be altered. This alteration, in turn, may involve a fundamental rethinking of the nature of God, religious community, and spiritual truth.

Issues of personal freedom and violence are at the heart of women's struggles for justice. Beverly Harrison here explores some of the complexities of what it means to support abortion rights from the perspective of feminist theology; and Susan Thistlethwaite discusses the moral and theological import of that most private and widespread of crimes, male violence against women.

The political and religious meanings of gender are enormously complex, not only because gender is central to human life, but also because male and female identity unfolds in relation to other identities: for instance, those of class and race. Shamara Riley and Cheryl Gilkes explore these connections, and indicate how commitment to women's equality within "the church" necessarily leads to a wider commitment to social justice, ecological wisdom, and a concern for other forms of oppression.

Finally, we should recognize that the liberation of gender includes, but is not limited to, the women's liberation. As Stephen Boyd writes, patriarchy wounds men even as it gives them privileges over women. Further, the liberation of gender incorporates the liberation of the choice to be gay or lesbian, and selections by Anita Hill and Leo Treadway and the Central Conference of American Rabbis show how contemporary writers and religious organizations are taking this freedom seriously.

from "The 'Why' and 'What' of Christian Feminist Theology"

⌘

Anne M. Clifford

Anne M. Clifford is professor of theology at Duquesne University. She is the author of numerous articles in the areas of feminist theology, ecofeminism, and science and religion. This essay sketches the fundamental concerns of feminist theology.

⌘

There is not the slightest doubt that women belong to the people of God and the human race as much as men and are not another species or dissimilar race.

—Christine de Pizan[1]

Christine de Pizan (1365–1430), poet, author, and invited member of the court of Charles V and Jeanne de Bourbon, king and queen of France, wrote these words of passionate conviction six hundred years ago. Why does she find it necessary to affirm that women are human beings? Apparently, the humanity of women was a question because being male was equated with being human. The prevailing thinking of the time regarded woman as "another [dissimilar] species."[2] To the reader today, Pizan's words are a simple affirmation of the obvious: women are human. Yet, the implication of her affirmation that women too belong to the "people of God" has profound implications, especially where the life of a Christian is concerned. Christine de Pizan lived in an era in which to be educated was virtually equated with being well-read in the texts of Western antiquity. In the writings of the ancients, particularly in the most frequently cited classics, some of which were written by highly revered, male Christian saints, women were judged to be deficient as human beings. That there could be a different conception of woman was beyond questioning. Women's deficient nature was even attributed to God's plan for creation.

Why was this so? The answer is simple: the judgment about what counts as the criteria for humanness was drawn exclusively from male experience. What was associated with being male was the standard for being human. Women were substandard humans, even, perhaps, a species different from men. Simone de Beauvoir's book title captures the position aptly: women were the *Second Sex,* not quite deserving of the word "human."[3] This judgment prevailed until women stepped forward and raised their voices in protest.

319

Pizan's words of protest draw attention to how long it is that women who were unwilling to accept the limits their societies prescribed for them have struggled to claim their full participation in "the human race" and the "people of God." Nearly six hundred years ago, Pizan listened to her own experience of being a woman and questioned deeply ingrained opinions about women's inferiority. This self-educated woman was exceptional for her time. Pizan herself was conscious of being an anomaly where women were concerned. Unlike her female contemporaries, not only could she read, but also she could write well enough to attract an audience, including the royal court of France, for what she had to say.

In *The Book of the City of Ladies,* Pizan engaged in a debate of great importance for women. Were women by nature more prone to vice and evil than were men? This was a serious question in an era in which women were blamed for a spectrum of evils, from sterility to deadly illnesses. Another common question was, Were the female descendants of Eve, the evil temptress of Adam, capable of thinking clearly and acting ethically? The common response was no. Was it not fitting, therefore, that men rule over women, the sex weaker in mind, body, and morality? Pizan pondered these questions and the arguments of many highly regarded male experts who claimed that women by nature were inferior in every way to men. After thinking intensely about these matters and praying for divine guidance, she decided to trust herself over male authorities. She notes,

> I began to examine my character and conduct as a natural woman, and similarly I considered other women whose company I frequently kept, princesses, great ladies, women of the middle and lower classes.[4]

What did Pizan conclude from her reflection on the experiences of these women? Without qualification, women are fully human and not in need of the protection and guidance of men. To prove her position, she drew on stories about women from the Bible, from history, and from her own time. She argued that women are not inferior to men because of their sex. It was women's inferior education and training that created the illusion of male superiority. If women were as well taught as men, they would understand the subtleties of the arts and sciences as well as men do.[5]

Long before the term "feminism" was coined, many characteristics commonly associated with contemporary feminist authors are found in Christine de Pizan's writing:

1. She gave attention and credence to her own experience. Listening to her experience and to the experiences of other women rather than uncritically accepting the opinions of male authorities is a hallmark of feminism today.

2. She critically analyzed attitudes about women. Like so many feminist authors today, her critique of prevailing attitudes that define woman as less than man was highly negative. This type of thinking conflicted with her own experience of being a woman.

3. Positively, Pizan did research on women from a variety of sources that enabled her to uncover the constructive contributions of women. She engaged in the type of research that feminists today often call a "search for a useable past." Her search pointed out stories and traditions that gave her a basis for envisioning in new ways what it means to be a woman.

4. The steps that Pizan took in uncovering the contributions of women also had a goal beyond mere research: she was committed to ending men defining "woman" in male terms. Women should begin to define what it means to be a woman for themselves. To achieve this, she wanted women to have the same educational and professional opportunities that learned men could enjoy.

Christine de Pizan never used the term "feminism" in reference to her work. It was not until the late nineteenth century that the term was coined. Another woman who made her home in France, Hubertine Auclert, is credited with first using the word "feminism" in 1882 to name the struggle of women to gain political rights.[6] The term "feminism" had a long period of gestation associated with history-making women. A century before Auclert penned the word "feminism," Mary Wollstonecraft wrote *A Vindication of the Rights of Woman* in England in 1792.[7] In the United States, women began to lift their voices to challenge the inferior status of women at the end of the 1830s. This chorus rose in the midst of women's active participation in the pre–Civil War abolitionist movement.

The Female Anti-Slavery Society, founded in 1833, was a natural setting for connecting the oppression of slaves with the subordination of women.[8] History records the emergence of a woman's movement in the United States in the words and actions of women such as the Grimké sisters, Sarah (1792–1873) and Angelina (1805–1879).[9] The Grimké sisters spent their childhood in the South on a slave-owning plantation and their adulthood in the North as Quaker abolitionists. They not only condemned the evils of slavery, but also championed why it was appropriate for women to speak publicly about this dehumanizing evil in Christian churches. Certainly, few women of this period are better known than the former slave Sojourner Truth (Belle Baumfree [1797–1883]), who, in her famous "And Ain't I a Woman" speech, drew attention not only to the degradation of being owned by another, but also to the burden of grief borne by female slaves who were separated from their children when they were sold and sent to unknown destinations. Elizabeth Cady Stanton (1815–1902), an active abolitionist, brought attention to the ways in which the Bible contributed to the subordination of women. She gathered female colleagues to create a biblical commentary, *The Woman's Bible*. Stanton, along with Lucretia Mott (1793–1880)[10] and Susan B. Anthony (1820–1906),[11] are the best-known champions for the legal and economic equality of women with men in the United States of this first wave of feminism. Due largely to the persistence of these women, women in the United States won the right to own property. These women paved the way for the success of women's suffrage. Carrie Chapman Catt (1859–1947)[12] and many others aided women in getting the right to vote through the passage of the Nineteenth Amendment to the U.S. Constitution in 1920. Elsewhere, women had already attained this right. New Zealand was the first country on record to give women the vote; the year was 1893, and Finland followed in 1906. Women in Russia and Canada were permitted to vote in 1918. In the same year, women over thirty could vote in Great Britain. A decade later, women in Great Britain over twenty-one were fully enfranchised. That same year (1928), Ecuador became the first Latin American country to permit women to vote. Gradually, many other countries granted women voting rights.

Providing an answer to why feminism emerged in Western Europe and the United States during the nineteenth century is complex. Prior to the nineteenth century, women in most societies were regarded as subordinate to and dependent on their male relatives. Like the women of Christine de Pizan's time, they were excluded from equal access to education and participation in public life. As men created new political and economic structures, they assigned to women the role of producing and raising male citizens who would lead society. Men exercised sovereignty in the city square, while women were charged with making a home for them and their children. In the nineteenth century, women were commonly said to be morally superior to men, yet too weak and delicate to be active in the public world of business and politics. This widely accepted cluster of attitudes, known as "the cult of true womanhood," was something that the women of the first wave of feminism used to their own advantage. They selectively conferred on the "cult of true womanhood" a significance that suited their cause, attributing a special status to women because they cared for children and were the guardians of Christian moral values, while rejecting that women were unsuited for politics.

The momentum for the cause of women's equality did not continue in the United States after voting rights were acquired by women. Since the first wave of feminism was so closely associated with getting access to voting booths, once women could vote, the feminist movement virtually ended in the United States. The worldwide economic depression and the many adjustments in societal life during and immediately after World War II also contributed to the movement's decline. It was not until the 1960s that a second and broader women's liberation movement emerged in the United States and Western Europe. In the United States, this new wave of feminism once again converged with the struggles of African Americans.[13] Women participants in the civil rights movement realized that not only were the black men and women not equal to white men and women, the women championing their cause were not equal to white males. A glaring disparity existed between the lofty ideals of the civil rights movement for blacks and women's own lived realities. Women such as Betty Friedan,[14] Gloria Steinem, Susan Brownmiller, and a host of others began to call for the expansion of women's rights. These women revived earlier dreams of political and economic equality of women with men. Some of these same women would also lend their voice in protest of the Vietnam War, forming or joining demonstrations for peace. At approximately the same time, women in Great Britain, France, and West Germany also were actively criticizing the gap between public rhetoric about women's roles and their own experience, between, in the words of Bonnie S. Anderson and Judith P. Zinsser, "what they were told they had achieved and their private perceptions of their own situation."[15]

In the late 1970s a new development in feminism arose, one that drew attention to differences in race and social class of women. Historians of feminism now call this the "third wave" of feminism. It emerged in the United States with "women of color" taking that name to expose the whiteness of the interests of second-wave feminism. Difference was given center stage at an international feminist conference held in New York in 1979 with these challenging words from the African American poet Audre Lorde:

> If white American feminist theory need not deal with the differences between us (black women and all women of color), and the resulting difference in our oppressions, then how do you deal with the fact that women who clean your houses and tend your children while you attend conferences on feminist theory are, for the most part, poor women and women of color? What is the theory of racist feminism?[16]

In response to challenges such as Lorde's from women of color, many Euro-American feminists became attuned to the difference that race and class make to feminist identities, challenges, and goals.

[...]

TYPES OF FEMINIST THEOLOGY

Attentive to experiences, which are personal yet profoundly affected by social location, feminist theologies are not privatized exercises. Feminist theologies have a public and communal character. Obviously, there are many publics and communities from which and for which theologians do their work. Part of the public situatedness of feminist theologians is their relationship to the secular feminisms that exist today. These relationships account, in part, for the different types of feminist theologies. At the risk of oversimplification, the major forms of feminist theology can be grouped under three major headings: revolutionary, reformist, and reconstructionist.[17] In the treatment of each that follows, it is important to keep in mind that this analysis is intended to sketch the landscape of the major forms of feminist theology. The shortcoming of this sketch is that it does not sufficiently address the many differences in feminist theologies. No categorical analysis can fully account for the enormous diversity in feminist theology today.

Revolutionary feminist theology is affected most by radical feminists, especially by those who advocate woman-centered culture. Many radical feminist theologians can accurately be described as post-Christian. Many of these women originally participated in Christian churches, but their own feminist consciousness led them to conclude that Christianity is irredeemably patriarchal, even antiwoman. We can trace the beginnings of this line of argument in the United States to Matilda Joslyn Gage (1826–1893), a suffragist closely associated with Susan B. Anthony and Elizabeth Cady Stanton. Her considerable research on the cultures of the Near East and Egypt led her to propose worship of the Goddess as a key to female ascendancy in families and in religious and secular societies.[18] She insisted that if women ever hoped to be liberated, they must cast aside Christianity and the patriarchal legal codes influenced by the Christian Bible.

Gage remained a little-known figure until feminists involved in the second wave of feminism discovered her work and reprinted her *Woman, Church and State*. Her theory of matriarchy resonated with the positions of radical feminists. We can rightly call many of these women post-Christian feminists. Their major problem with Christianity is the centrality given to the revelation of a male God, whom they believe is used to legitimate the patriarchal oppression of women by Christian churches. In addition, they point out that Christians continue to subordinate women in their churches and in their marital relationships. Thus, these theologians have abandoned Christianity as oppressive to women. Many have turned to ancient Goddess traditions for their theology. They envision the Goddess to be an appropriate symbol for the creative power of women.[19]

Reformist Christian feminist theology has virtually nothing in common with the revolutionary model. The reformist theologian is not looking for sweeping changes that totally revolutionize Christianity. Reformist theologians do not want to replace the God revealed by Jesus Christ. They do not want to be part of a community that worships goddesses. They are looking for far more modest changes within existing church structures. Although unanimity among reformist feminist theologians does not exist, they do share in common their commitment to the Christian tradition. Their positions show commonalities with cultural feminism. Reformist feminists can be found in Protestant denominations and in Roman Catholicism.

In the Protestant denominations, the more conservative of the reformist feminists are the evangelicals or fundamentalists who are committed to the inerrancy of the Bible and to a literal interpretation of its texts, yet are also opposed to gender bias in the treatment of women in their families, churches, and civil societies. Proponents of this form of feminist theology believe that they can solve the problems of women's secondary status with measures such as better translations of the Bible and more emphasis on egalitarian passages in the Bible.

Roman Catholic women and men who espouse a deep respect for the Roman Catholic tradition and its institutional authority, yet hold that women need to be more included in the life and leadership of the church, are another example of reformist feminists. They are, for the most part, uncritical of the structures of the institutional church and are supportive of church teaching, such as limiting ordained ministries to males, yet they also champion having women involved in other church ministries and in theological education.

Reconstructionist Christian feminist theology, the third major type, shares with reformist feminism a commitment to Christianity, but does not find the positions of reformist feminism to be an adequate response to the subjugation and secondary status of women. Permitting women to hold church offices and do church-related ministries is not sufficient. Reconstructionist feminist theologians seek a liberating theological core for women within the Christian tradition, while also envisioning a deeper transformation, a true reconstruction, not only of their church structures but also of civil society. In company with the revolutionary feminist theologians, reconstructionist feminists share a critical appraisal of patriarchy, but they believe that reinterpreting the traditional symbols and ideas of Christianity without abandoning the God revealed in Jesus Christ is possible and desirable.

What makes a reconstructionist feminist theology Christian? The short answer is Jesus. The somewhat longer answer is the gospel vision of release from bondage for a new creation—the realization of the reign of God, proclaimed by Jesus, the Christ, in word and deed. Jesus' powerful social vision was incarnate in the inclusive community of women and men, drawn together and empowered by him to preach the good news of God's coming reign. Like the Jesus of Mark's Gospel, there is an urgency about the mission of this inclusive community for feminist theologians: "This is the time of fulfillment. The reign of God is at hand. Repent, and believe in the gospel" (Mark 1:15). The time of fulfillment is an age of shared commitment to the loving God of Jesus Christ in the Holy Spirit, the giver of life. The shared commitment in a discipleship of equals, embraced by Christian feminist theologians, transcends particular denominational affiliations. Christian feminist theologians, whether they are Episcopalian, Lutheran, Presbyterian, or Roman Catholic, may have doctrinal differences, but these usually take a distant second place to their shared partnership and liberating social vision. Interdenominational partnership emerged in the second wave of feminism and continues as new directions that constitute the third wave continue to unfold.

A powerful theme of the feminist theology of the second wave is that the reign of God, when rightly understood, liberates and empowers women for the fullness of life. Feminist theologians participating in the third wave seek to bring this theme to bear on the difference that social location makes in their theologies. Many reconstructionist feminist theologians envision feminist theology to be a form of liberation theology, a term first coined by Gustavo Gutiérrez in 1968, when he called for a theology that speaks from the life experience of the poor of Latin America and engages in praxis that liberates them from economic poverty and political oppression.[20]

The liberation sought by reconstructionist feminist theologians is not one dimensional, nor is it a "cheap grace" easily incarnated. It calls for repentance by righting wrongs. The wrongs of primary concern are the life-denying effects of patriarchy, a panoply of "isms": sexism, of course, but also racism, classism, and any other societal distortions of patriarchy—ageism, heterosexism, and naturism (the exploitation of the creatures of the earth). In the third wave of Christian feminist theology, partnership transcends more than denominational lines; it stretches across the lines of race, class, sexual orientation, and religion. Christian feminist solidarity envisions these lines not as ones of demarcation, but rather as respectful acknowledgment of difference. This extension of hands across the lines of race, ethnicity, and class honors difference, while creating a space for listening to the heartaches and hopes of persons who speak from diverse cultural and religious experiences. European and Euro-American feminists, womanists, *mujerista*, Latina, and Asian feminists are engaging in conversations—"hearing each other into speech"—becoming attuned to each other's experiences. For many European and Euro-American feminists, such conversations have been painful because they have meant facing the legacy of patriarchy from which they have benefited simply by being born white. Yet, without facing this truth, talk about respecting difference and commitment to a common struggle to resist subjugation can be merely hollow-sounding words.

What makes a theology reconstructionist from the standpoint of feminism? The term "reconstruction" rarely appears as a subtitle in feminist theological writing. Although the related term "revisionist" is used at times for this third type of feminist theology, "reconstructionist" is preferred because I believe that third-wave feminist theologies are doing more than revising and adjusting an already existing tradition by calling for renewed vision of Christianity. They are incorporating women's experiences of God in dialogue with primary theological sources. They recognize that male theologians in patriarchal societies have spoken about justice and peace, love and mercy, sin and forgiveness in meaningful ways. Yet, the application of these words to women and subordinate men has all too often been deficient. Therefore, a reconstructionist theology praises some theologies, critiques others, and draws into discussion the voices of women long ignored to forge not only new feminist theologies but also transformed societies marked by equality and mutuality of women and men. They are, in a sense, constructing a theology from multiple bricks and fresh mortar needed for our time.

To forge this construction in the era of the third wave of feminism, the methodology of Christian reconstructionist feminist theologies often incorporates these three basic steps:

1. Attending to experience(s) of patriarchy and androcentrism by listening attentively to one's own experience and that of other women and/or subjugated men;
2. Bringing these experiences into dialogue with a feminist reading of the Bible and/or other Christian texts;
3. Developing strategies for transformative action or praxis that are liberating.

1. Attending to experience is the first step in developing a reconstructionist feminist theology. This stage flows from a feminist recognition of the particular and the experiential. A feminist theology true to the word "feminist" cannot start from abstract theory about God and the things of God. Concrete experiences must be listened to and learned from. Human experience is particular because it is always embodied experience. It is profoundly affected by the life situation or social location in which one finds oneself. The effects of patriarchy on some women are far less extensive and debilitating than on others. To be born in certain countries immediately makes it more likely for a woman to struggle with poverty, experience violence, or enjoy only a limited number of civil rights.

In this first step of feminist theology, attention is given to one's own experience. Since most people engaged in doing reconstructionist feminist theology are in an academic setting, a location of privilege, to this personal reflection is added an important additional component: being receptive to women's experiences different from one's own, especially of women who have been abused, exploited, and impoverished. Patriarchy negatively affects all women's life experience, but its effects cannot be abstracted from social location.

The term often used for this type of attending to experience, especially by *mujerista* and Latina theologians is conscientization.[21] The purpose of conscientization is to encourage people to listen to and validate their experiences, especially experiences of subjugation, and to probe their causes. Why is conscientization needed? Experiences are usually interpreted in thought patterns that prevail in a given culture. Ideology created by the dominant voices in a society tends to be heard as if it is the way things are and are meant to be. Persons whose life choices are limited by patriarchy unthinkingly internalize the interpretations of them given by persons in power. They do this usually with an attitude of passive resignation. Burdened by patriarchal definitions and androcentric attitudes, subjugated persons tend to uncritically accept their "lot in life" as inevitable and unchangeable. Most of the history of women, with very few exceptions, is characterized by this picture to a greater or lesser degree. Patriarchy, like any reigning pattern of thought or ideology, uses distorted images to promote the internalization of inferiority in the group that is being dominated. This is key to those in power maintaining dominance. Androcentrism works with this distortion, assisting the domination of women by pushing their experiences to the periphery.

Reconstructionist feminist theology not only brings to consciousness the experiences of discrimination and subordination that patriarchy and androcentrism promote, but also unmasks them as not of God and therefore sinful. Suffering visited upon people because of their sex, race, class, age, sexual orientation, or disability can never be of God. Attending to culturally shaped interpretations of diminishment is an important hermeneutical strategy and a necessary first step in developing a recontructionist feminist theology.

It logically follows, therefore, that when you read a feminist theological work, the social location of the author and the people for whom she or he is writing is always significant. Third-wave feminist theology presumes that it is neither possible nor desirable to universalize women's experiences. There are enormous differences in experience in North America among white, black, Hispanic, and Asian American women. The differences are even more pronounced when North American experiences are examined in relationship to those of women in Latin America, Africa, and Asia. Reconstructionist feminist theologies, therefore, are not "value-neutral" thought experiments. They promote new thinking and forge societal patterns of action. An important guiding question to ask while reading them is, What experiences of patriarchy and androcentrism is the author of this text trying to remedy? Apart from remedying patriarchal abuses, reconstructionist feminist theologies also seek to broaden the theological horizon of their communities by attending to religious experiences, especially those relevant to the lives of women, that have been ignored.

2. Feminist interpretation of the Bible and church teachings requires that attention be given to what does and does not liberate women and men from the effects of patriarchy. If a biblical text, church teaching, or an interpretation of either does not liberate, then it either must not be true or has been misinterpreted. This insight is rooted in the words of Jesus, "You will know the truth, and the truth will set you free" (John 8:32). Getting at the freeing truth where the Bible, church teaching, and their interpretations are concerned is not an easy task. All three present some messages about women that are obviously patriarchal, but many more are ambivalent where women are concerned. Yet, for centuries women have drawn inspiration and guidance from biblical texts and the teachings of their churches, finding in them a freeing truth.

Feminist theological hermeneutics requires detecting patriarchy and androcentrism in biblical texts, church teachings, and their interpretations. Any talk about texts draws attention to the issue of language and the power of symbols. Words not only enable communication, but also condition our thinking. For a Christian feminist theology to be truly liberating for women and for subjugated men, the language of biblical texts and of church teachings that interpret them must be examined from the standpoint of whether they contribute to the diminishment of persons. Such examinations require carefully conceived criteria. One obvious criterion is whether a particular text promotes male advantage at the expense of women's dignity or of a certain group of men. The language in some texts makes them "period pieces," suffering under the limitations of historical patriarchal influences in form and content.

An additional strategy is to focus on biblical texts and Christian sources that illumine the struggles of women and subjugated men and provide a reason for hope in the God of life. Like the watchful sister of Moses in Exodus 2:3–4, feminist theologians guard these texts, many of which heretofore have received very little attention, lest the fragile baby of freeing truth perish in powerful currents of patriarchy. Part of this strategy is to develop interpretations that are liberating and empowering for women and for anyone whose life has been diminished by patriarchy. These components converge in the construction of guiding visions for liberation from those things that diminish the human dignity of any person. But it is important that there not be a gap between the language of liberation and the reality. Taking responsibility for bridging gaps is the final major step in a reconstructionist feminist theology.

3. Liberating action is the final step in a reconstructionist feminist theology. Reconstructionist feminism has a strong sense of the importance of concrete action that effectively embodies religious language that gives voice to truth and wisdom. It is therefore interested in more than raising awareness of the manifestations of patriarchy and of constructing a liberating interpretation of biblical revelation and church teachings; it seeks to make a difference in the Christian community and civil society. Creating societies that are more just and more in keeping with the reign of God proclaimed by Jesus in word and deed is the most important goal of Christian feminist theologies. This requires "transformative praxis." Since theology is a process in service of the faith-life of the people of God, Christian feminist theologies take up the love command of Jesus, recognizing that actively loving one's neighbors, especially those most in need, cannot be separated from love for God (Matt. 22:39; Mark 12:33; Luke 10:27). It is only through praxis, rooted in theological reflection, that the gap that has often existed between theological language and concrete reality can be closed.

NOTES

1. Christine de Pizan, *The Book of the City of Ladies*, original edition published in 1405, trans. Earl Jeffrey Richards (New York: Persea, 1982), 187. Christine de Pizan (also sometimes spelled "Pisan"), the daughter of an Italian astrologer brought to France to be a member of the court of King Charles V and Queen Jeanne de Bourbon, was a prolific writer who made her living from her works. She was the first woman known to have participated in literary and philosophical debates about women (*querelle des femmes*).

2. Prior to the late eighteenth century, the educated opinion was that women were a separate species. Gender differences were viewed in absolute terms.

3. Simone de Beauvoir, *The Second Sex*, trans. and ed. H. M. Parshley (New York: Knopf, 1952; reprint, New York: Random House, 1974).

4. Pizan, *City of Ladies*, 4.

5. Pizan, *City of Ladies*, 153–54.

6. Bonnie S. Anderson and Judith P. Zinsser, *A History of Their Own: Women in Europe from Prehistory to the Present*, vol. 2 (New York: Harper & Row, 1988); on 492 n. 1 the date for the first appearance of the word "feminism" is given as 1882.

7. Wollstonecraft argues in the introduction of this work that the whole of society suffers under the burden of a false education gathered from books written on the subject by men who consider "females as women rather than as human creatures"; apparently, Pizan's argument for the humanity of women had not yet taken hold! See Mary Wollstonecraft, *A Vindication of the Rights of Women* (1792; reprint, London: J. M. Dent; Rutland, Vt.: Charles E. Tuttle, 1995), 9.

8. Margaret Hope Bacon, *Mothers of Feminism: The Story of Quaker Women in America* (San Francisco: Harper & Row, 1986), 103–5.

9. Angelina became a persuasive orator, and Sarah published influential works on abolition (1836) and the equality of the sexes in the church (1838).

10. Mott was a Quaker lecturer for temperance and abolition. She aided fugitive slaves and helped form the Philadelphia Female Antislavery Society. When the World Antislavery Convention in London

(1840) refused to recognize women delegates, she joined Elizabeth Cady Stanton in organizing the first Women's Rights Convention, held in Seneca Falls, New York, in 1848.

11. Anthony organized the first women's temperance association, the Daughters of Temperance, and with Elizabeth Cady Stanton secured the first laws in New York guaranteeing women rights over their children and control of property and wages (1848). In 1863 she was coorganizer of the Women's Loyal League to support Lincoln's government, but after the Civil War she opposed granting suffrage to freedmen without also giving it to women. She was president of the National American Woman Suffrage Association (1892–1900).

12. Catt, an American suffragist, was the president of the National American Woman Suffrage Association (1900–1920). When the Nineteenth Amendment to the U.S. Constitution was passed, she organized the League of Women Voters. A woman of wealth, she traveled widely to network for women's rights.

13. Not only were some of the women who supported civil rights for African Americans feminist in their leanings, but also the Civil Rights Bill of 1964 prohibited discrimination on the basis of sex. "Sex" was added to a list that included race, color, religion, and national origin by Howard W. Smith, an eighty-one-year-old representative from Virginia and chair of the rules committee of the House. No feminist, this defender of the "Southern way of life" had voted against bills guaranteeing equal pay for equal work regardless of sex. He made the addition of the word "sex" as a joke—one that backfired. The bill passed on 9 February 1963. In April 1964 Senator Everett Dirksen, Republican majority leader, led a drive to have "sex" stricken from the bill, but was unsuccessful. See Caroline Bird, *Born Female: The High Cost of Keeping Women Down* (New York: Pocket, 1971), 1–15.

14. Betty Friedan wrote *The Feminine Mystique* (New York: Norton, 1963), in which she criticized the traditional notion that women find fulfillment only through childbearing and homemaking. This work is widely regarded as the book that launched the second wave of the women's movement. Instrumental in founding the National Organization of Women (1966), she served as its first president and also helped to organize the National Women's Political Caucus (1970).

15. Anderson and Zinsser, *A History of Their Own*, 407.

16. Audre Lorde, *Sister Outsider* (Trumansburg, N.Y.: Crossing Press, 1984), 112.

17. Carol Christ and Judith Plaskow, in their introduction to *Womenspirit Rising: A Feminist Reader in Religion* (San Francisco: Harper & Row, 1979), analyzed feminist theology under the headings "revolutionary" and "reformist" (4). In the introduction to a more recent collection of essays edited by Christ and Plaskow, *Weaving the Visions: New Patterns in Feminist Spirituality* (San Francisco: Harper & Row, 1989), they draw attention to the limitations of these categories where the enormous variety of feminist theology is concerned (3). I am using them with the addition of the typology "reconstructionist" to account for the major development since 1979. In making this addition, I realize that the three typologies do not completely account for the many distinctive nuances in the growing body of feminist theological literature. Some feminist theologians might prefer "revisionist" to "reconstructionist"; I have chosen the latter because I believe that it more adequately names what feminists are doing in their theologies.

18. Matilda Joslyn Gage, *Woman, Church and State* (1893; reprint, Watertown, Mass.: Persephone Press, 1980). Because of her negativity about Christianity, Gage lost most of her friends in the suffrage movement and her name was deleted from its annals.

19. More attention will be given to Goddess "thealogy" in chapters 3 and 6.

20. Gustavo Gutiérrez, *A Theology of Liberation: History, Politics, and Salvation*, trans. and ed. Sister Caridad Inda and John Eagleson (Maryknoll, N.Y.: Orbis, 1973; rev. ed., 1988). See also Leonardo Boff and Clodovis Boff, *Introducing Liberation Theology*, trans. Paul Burns (Maryknoll, N.Y.: Orbis, 1987), for a fine introduction to Latin American liberation theology.

21. Paulo Freire coined the term "conscientization" in *Pedagogy of the Oppressed* (New York: Herder and Herder, 1970).

"Prophetic Tradition and the Liberation of Women: A Story of Promise and Betrayal"

෴

Rosemary Radford Ruether

Rosemary Radford Ruether, professor of theology at the Graduate Theological Union, is among the most widely read feminist theologians in North America. Ruether has written or edited more than twenty books, including the classic *Sexism and God-Talk*. This essay examines the dual character of prophetic religion: liberating in many ways, but also oppressive to women.

෴

Are women today's prophets? This theme immediately begs the question, what is a prophet? And why should women see any particular connection between feminism as a theological and social movement and the figure of the prophet? I would like to argue that there are some compelling reasons to make special links between feminism and prophecy. The prophet in the biblical tradition is a figure who stands outside the institutionalized leadership—specifically the priesthood—of the religious tradition, but within the covenant of the community. The prophet speaks a judgmental word of God in order to call the community back to faithfulness to the radical foundations of biblical faith, contextualized in the contemporary situation.

Prophecy presupposes a relationship between religion and society that conflicts profoundly with established religion. Established religion sees religion as the sacred ideology of the established social order. It is the "handmaiden" of the ruling class. It pronounces the established social order to be created by God and to be a reflection of the divine will. Words for God resemble titles for the ruling class. God and the ruling class are called by the same names and imaged as having similar lifestyles, except God is raised to the immortal level. The ruling class therefore appears godly and is seen as having special closeness to the divine and as representing the divine on earth. By contrast, those lower classes who are to be ruled do not image the divine and obey God by obeying their social superiors. This is the way most religion has functioned, including most Christian religion. A certain stratum of the Bible, particularly the laws in the Old Testament and the household codes in the New, also presupposes such a relationship between religion and society.

Prophetic faith, by contrast, sets God in tension with the ruling class by having God speak through the prophet(ess) as the advocate of the poor and the oppressed. The word of God comes through the prophet(ess) to denounce the unjust practices of the rich and powerful who grind the faces of the poor and oppress the widow and the orphan. The prophet(ess) also denounces the corruption of biblical faith itself into a religious establishment that has become purely cultic and has turned away from the social substance of faith, which is justice and mercy. Thus the prophets in Hebrew Scripture and Jesus in the Gospels are figures in conflict with religious establishments, denouncers of the use of religion to sacralize unjust privilege and to ignore the needs of the people.

The prophetic tradition goes on to imagine God active in history as a power that will overthrow an unjust social order and transform the world into a new social order where there is no more war and no more injustice, where justice between human and human and harmony between human and nonhuman nature have been restored, and all creation is in communion with God. This vision in the prophetic tradition was not equated with immortality or life after death. It was thought of as an ideal state to be established on earth as the right relation between creation and its Creator. As Jesus put it succinctly in the Lord's Prayer: "God's Kingdom come, God's will be done on earth."

Early Christianity saw itself as having a particular affinity with the prophetic tradition. Not only was Jesus the ultimate messianic prophet, but in the dispensation of the Holy Spirit that founded the church on Pentecost, the prophetic spirit had been restored, as had been predicted by the prophet Joel. For first-generation Christians, and for some Christians well into the third century, the prophet was the normative leader of the local Christian community and the one empowered to bring down the power of the Holy Spirit upon the eucharistic gifts. Unlike the priesthood, from which women were excluded in the Old Testament and again excluded as this concept of leadership developed in patristic Christianity, women were never excluded from prophecy. Miriam, Deborah, and Huldah were prophets, and prophecy was seen as restored to women, as well as men, in the Pentecostal tradition. Patriarchal Christianity excluded women from the kind of leadership exercised by bishops and presbyters, although it retained a marginal place for women in the diaconate. It also waged a battle in the second and third centuries to suppress charismatic or prophetic traditions of leadership. But it never, in principle, denied that God might send contemporary prophets and that women could exercise prophecy equally. It simply tried to discount any actual prophets that came along as being true prophets, especially if those prophets were female. And if they were female, it also tried to prove that they were witches and agents of the devil.

Prophecy also has a close relationship with the renewal of women's ministry throughout church history. The Waldensians of the twelfth century included women in public preaching, on the basis of the sect's equation of preaching and prophecy. The same connection was made among Baptists in the Puritan Civil War, who included women as preachers. In the sermon at the ordination of Antoinette Brown, the first woman to be ordained in the Congregationalist tradition, Luther Lee argued in 1853 for women's ordination by equating preaching with the prophetic office. Christ himself, according to Lee, restored the prophetic office to women, and so the church had erred throughout history in excluding women from ordained ministry. Again and again through the centuries up to the present, women who claimed the right to public ministry did so by claiming the text of Acts 2:17: "Your sons and your daughters shall prophesy."[1]

Yet despite this continual tradition of the inclusion of women in prophecy, women have been betrayed by male-led prophetic movements. Such movements represent the rebellion of oppressed males against dominant males but have no intention of including in their rebellion the overthrow of male domination. These male-led movements typically welcome the enthusiastic participation of women in the work of the revolution. But when women try to include themselves in the revolution's ideology and program, the male leaders make clear that this is not the agenda, that women are being selfish and diversionary by bringing up questions of the emancipation of women from patriarchy.

We see this betrayal of women in the Exodus tradition of Hebrew Scripture. Here women begin the rebellion against Pharaoh by being the first to disobey his orders to kill the firstborn. Moses' mother and sister and Pharaoh's daughter establish a subversive conspiracy that not only saves Moses' life but also raises the leader of the rebellion in the court of Pharaoh. In the Exodus, Moses, Miriam, and Aaron are named as leaders, but in Num. 12:12–16, when Aaron and Miriam criticize Moses for betraying the people by marrying a Cushite woman, it is Miriam who is stricken with leprosy. It is said that she had become like a daughter whose father has spit in her face, that is, repudiated her totally. Thus Miriam is marginalized from coequal leadership in the Exodus. When the "people" of Israel assemble at Sinai to receive the Law, they are told to purify themselves for three days by "not going near a woman." So it becomes clear that the "people of Israel" means the males of Israel (Exod. 19:14–15).

Similarly, in the Gospels the church is seen as a new Exodus community. It is identified in the Magnificat with a servant-class woman who has been lifted up, as the mighty are put down from their thrones. The story line of all four Gospels is one in which the messianic prophet is rejected by successive groups. First he is betrayed by his family and the hometown folks, who try to kill him after his first sermon in Nazareth, when he identifies the coming of God's liberation to the poor with the lepers and poor widows among despised social groups living around Israel. Then he is betrayed by the established religious leadership—scribes and priests—and by the crowds who turn fickle when he is arrested for subversion in Jerusalem. Finally, he is betrayed by his own male disciples, led by Peter, when the crisis of impending crucifixion reaches its climax. Only the women disciples, led by Mary Magdalene, remain faithful at the cross. They are the first to receive the news of the Resurrection, which they carry back to the unbelieving male disciples.

However, Christian tradition marginalizes Mary Magdalene's role in apostolic leadership by identifying her as a prostitute and repentant sinner (an identification found nowhere in the New Testament) rather than as a leading disciple. Although Paul establishes a close connection between apostleship and witnessing the Resurrection, making himself the last such witness, he doesn't use the tradition that women were the first witnesses, instead identifying Peter as the first witness and hence first apostle. It is not accidental that we find in alternative early Christian gospels that were not included in the canon, such as the *Gospel of Mary*, a controversy between Peter and Mary Magdalene over women's apostleship. In these gospels Mary's apostleship is confirmed, while Peter is rebuked for denying the inclusion of women in the discipleship that Christ has established.

The same pattern of promise and betrayal of women appears in the Reformation—for example, in the conflict between Radical and Magisterial Puritanism. When Puritanism was a dissenting movement in England, it encouraged women to dissent against husbands, ministers, and magistrates and to act according to their own conscience when these authorities were Anglican. Research has shown that dissenting congregations often had a predominance of women, and women often played de facto leadership roles in gathering such congregations and securing an independently paid minister. As a result, New England Puritanism in the 1640s included a significant number of strong women who had become accustomed to independent thinking as a result of decades of leadership as dissenters against established authorities in England.

However, once the Puritan ministers and magistrates made themselves the new established church of the Massachusetts Bay Colony, they reverted to a patriarchal social order, which they regarded as the reflection of the order of creation. They distinguished between the covenant of grace and the covenant of works. In the covenant of grace, all humans were equal before God and were elected without regard to merit, including social status. However, in the covenant of works, God had established a social order of husband over wife, parents over children, masters over servants. Social subordinates obeyed God by obeying their divinely ordained social superiors. For women to dissent against the male authority of husband, minister, or magistrate now became heresy, a rejection of the law of God, and probably witchcraft as well, because only the devil could empower weak women so to rebel against their rightful place in God's order. Thus the Puritan male leadership occupied itself in the seventeenth century by suppressing strong, independent women in a series of campaigns: first against women as heretics in the antinomian controversy, led by Anne Hutchinson; then against the Quakers, who had developed the equalitarian traditions of Radical Puritanism and allowed female leadership; and finally, at the end of the century, against witches.

A similar pattern of promise and betrayal of women can also be found in modern male-led reform and revolutionary movements, such as liberalism, socialism, and antiracist and anticolonialist liberation movements. For example, in the American Declaration of Independence it is said to be a "self-evident" truth that God created "all men" equal and endowed them equally with the rights of life, liberty, and the pursuit of happiness. (Property, included among natural rights in the French Declaration of the Rights of Man and the Citizen, is pointedly not included as a natural right in the American Declaration.)

Women, organized in women's support work for the American Revolution, called themselves the Daughters of Liberty. However, it soon became clear that the male revolutionary merchants and planters had no intention of including their wives or daughters, much less their slaves, in those claims to natural equality that led, self-evidently, to the rights of the citizen. Abigail Adams, herself a leading Daughter of Liberty, wrote to her husband, John Adams, at the Constitutional Convention admonishing him to "Remember the Ladies" and to include them equally in the rights of citizenship, even threatening that if he did not do so, women would foment a rebellion, just as men had done, and would not hold themselves bound by any laws that they could not participate in making. She was brushed off with a laugh. John Adams confessed that the American Revolution had raised fears that all constituted order might be overthrown; that Indians had begun to slight their guardians, slaves their owners, and servants their masters, but that "your Letter was the first Intimation that another Tribe more numerous and more powerfull than all the rest were grown discontented."[2] Clearly, Adams thinks that women are easily mollified, although his letters to his male peers show that he is worried by the inconsistency of the universalist claims of equality with the maintenance of patriarchy, a social order assumed to include not only the domination of women, but of servants and slaves as well.

Promise and betrayal are also found in the socialist movement. In the Owenite and Fourierite movements of the 1830s, socialism not only included many women but also enunciated a clear relationship between socialism and the emancipation of women. Socialism was understood to mean not only the socialization of productive labor but also the socialization of reproductive labor, of the labor of women in the family, in a communal society owned and managed at the base. One of the strongest tracts on women's liberation ever to be written by a male feminist came from the collaboration of the Owenite socialists William Thompson and Anna Wheeler in England in 1825: *The Appeal of One Half of the Human Race, Women, against the Pretensions of the Other Half, Men, to Retain Them in Civil and Domestic Slavery.*

Marxist socialism, however, dismissed these ideas as mere utopianism, in contrast to truly "scientific socialism." Engels reaffirmed feminism as a part of socialism, but socialism was defined as a political movement that would seize and redefine the power relationships in the sphere of paid labor, not of domestic labor. Feminism apart from this context was dismissed as a "bourgeois" movement. Socialist women should reject feminism and give themselves solely to the emancipation of the worker, in whose cause they were automatically included. Thus the connection between women's inequality on the job and the unpaid labor that women did in the home was covered up. In Hilda Scott's study of Eastern European socialism, *Does Socialism Liberate Women?*[3] she shows that despite all commitments to equal civil rights, equal education and jobs, and some collectivized domestic services, such as nurseries, women are at the bottom of the economic and political hierarchies of socialist societies and receive less pay than men in the same jobs. The chief reason for this, she shows, is the four to six hours of unpaid labor that women do for the family in addition to the "equal" work roles with men in the paid labor force.

The pattern of promise and betrayal of women is also found in antiracist and anticolonial liberation movements today. This is especially true of cultural nationalist movements, such as is found in Muslim nationalism in Iran and in American black nationalism, which is modeled on Muslim nationalism. Here we find a need in the male nationalist to reassert the total subjugation of women. Women should be reduced to invisibility and total obedience to men. Any assertion of women's rights is defined as the corrupt influence of the decadent West, against the purity of the culture of the nation which is throwing off the shackles of Western colonialism.

One finds acted out here, in extreme form, the conflict between the patriarchal egoism of dominant and subordinate males. Dominant males act out their superiority to subjugated males not only by insulting them as a racial group but, above all, by insulting their masculinity, by treating them and referring to them as "boys." Thus, males in rebellion typically see themselves not only as asserting the autonomy of their people but also as vindicating their injured masculinity. They often act this out by rigid insistence on the resubordination of the women of their community, who are regarded as having lost their proper respect for their men as a result of colonialism. We may have here, in the ego conflict of dominant and subordinate males based on a shared model of male domination as normative, the key to the promise and betrayal of women in male-led exodus movements.

Liberation movements based on socialism rather than on cultural nationalism are generally more generous to women. They concede those aspects of feminism traditional to socialism: civil rights, equal education, incorporation into the paid labor force, and state nurseries for working mothers. But they are generally hostile to a feminism that goes beyond these limits and that organizes women autonomously to criticize the sexual, domestic, and psychocultural dimensions of patriarchy. Such feminism is regarded as bourgeois and antisocialist.

What is to be concluded from this history of promise and betrayal of women in male-led exodus movements? One should not conclude that women have no stake in the liberation of subjugated nations, classes, and races, nor that the prophetic tradition of biblical faith is irrelevant for women. Rather, what women must conclude is that they cannot entrust the definition of such prophetic and emancipatory movements exclusively to male liberators. They cannot believe that any liberation movement that does not define itself as liberation from patriarchy will truly include women.

Moreover, they have a right to suspect that any liberation movement that is not defined as liberation from patriarchy will not truly overthrow class domination between ruling and subordinate males. A reform or revolution not defined as emancipation from patriarchy leads inevitably to a new social order in which the former male revolutionaries set themselves up as a new ruling class of priests and kings, or ministers and magistrates, or merchants and politicians, or commandos and party apparatchiks. Patriarchy is once again declared the order of nature, as defined either by God or by science. Women are thanked very much for their help in bringing about the revolution and then sent back to their homes and neighborhoods to do the unpaid and low-paid labor that supports the new society's male hierarchy.

Can feminism do better than this as a prophetic and emancipatory movement? Feminism, as renewed in the last twenty years in Western Europe and particularly in the United States, has been very creative in reestablishing the interconnections between all relations of domination and violence. First, modern feminism has clearly enunciated the personal as political in patriarchal relations. Feminists have brought crimes against women out of the invisibility of the private world. The unpaid work of women in the household; the denial to women of reproductive self-determination; physical violence against women in the home and in the streets; mugging, battery, child abuse; sexual violence against women in the home, the streets, and the workplace; incest; marital and nonmarital rape; sexual harassment and the culture and practice of pornography and prostitution—feminists have shown that all these support a social structure built on the subjugation of women as sexual objects and exploited workers.

Modern feminism has also shown the interconnections between patriarchy and class and racial hierarchy. Feminists have shown that racial and class hierarchies include sexual hierarchy within all their stratifications and thus place poor women of color at the bottom of the whole system. These hierarchies are also characterized by the sexualizing of race and class domination. Subordinate males are portrayed either as sexual brutes who represent a threat to the virtue of ruling-class women or as overgrown children who lack adult male status. In this way, white women are split from black men, black men from black women, and black women from white women. The whole system is held in place by setting subordinate groups against each other, each nursing its wounds and protecting its privileges against the others, rather than uniting against the common master of all, the ruling-class white Western male system.

Modern feminism has also established the relationship between patriarchy and the global systems of destruction that threaten the survival of everyone on the planet: militarism and destruction of nature. Both of these systems of violence and destruction have been shown to operate on the sexual imagery of male domination of women. In military violence, the male soldier is taught to identify his weapon with his sexual organ and to repress all revulsion to killing another human being as an effeminate trait that threatens to deprive him of male status, to make him a "sissy" or a "fag." The right of ruling-class males to dominate nature and to deny their own roots in natural ecology is justified by imaging nature as a "virgin" who invites "rape" and as a sensuous courtesan who entices the scientist-technocrat to "bare her secret" and "penetrate her in-most recesses."[4]

Not only does patriarchy provide the cultural, symbolic, and psychological connections between male ruling-class egoism, militarism, and ecological destruction, it also provides the social structure that allows the rapacious use of the world's resources for the profit of the few to the impoverishment of the many. And it directs that this empire of wealth and power be defended even to the death of the last man, woman, and child on earth and of the planet itself.

In that sense I would claim that feminism is a most important prophetic movement in contemporary culture. It is the prophetic movement that attempts the most comprehensive analysis of the systems of oppression and evil that dehumanize us all and reaches for the most comprehensive vision of what is necessary to save our lives and our planet from the many injustices and threats that surround us.

Moreover, I would claim that this comprehensiveness, far from making feminism utopian (in the sense of a movement characterized by excessive demands and dreams that transcend realistic possibilities of change within the human condition), provides the only account that really gets at the root of the systems of domination. Any attempt to dismiss feminism as excessive or marginal is based finally on the assumption that male domination is itself the constitutive framework of what is called "the human condition." But this is a human condition defined by males who assume that maleness is normative humanness. This definition is, and has always been, dehumanizing to women. No movement to rehumanize our life on earth will succeed in making significant changes until men, as well as women, take seriously the need to root out patriarchy with all its works and pomps.

However, the fact that feminism contains the promise of being a most comprehensive prophetic movement today, a movement that gets at the root of the system of domination, does not mean that it will succeed in realizing this promise. Feminism may fail to realize its prophetic promise. It may fail, first and most important, because males refuse to take it seriously, continue either to try to ridicule it or to co-opt it into their systems of control, and disdain to imagine that they might include themselves in it, not just to liberate women, but also to liberate themselves from patriarchy. The refusal of males to include themselves in liberation from patriarchy has meant, as we have shown, that every male-led liberation movement has failed to get at the roots of social domination. As long as men continue to identify their masculinity with domination, there can be no real humanization of society.

Although male rejection is the most important reason feminism may fail as a prophetic movement and be gradually silenced with token changes, as it has been in the past, feminism may also fail because it succumbs to the internal contradictions and antagonisms that patriarchy sets up among women. A feminism that does not maintain both the radicality of its vision and compassionate outreach to all women is already providing the ammunition for its own suicide.

Feminism may commit suicide in one of several ways. First, it may remain a white, middle-class movement and fail to establish itself as a genuine interclass and interracial (interreligious, intercultural) movement. This danger was discerned in the socialist criticism of feminism as a bourgeois movement, but this criticism was used to dismiss feminism as an autonomous movement demanding its own organization and analysis of patriarchy. In order to be truly a women's liberation movement, feminism must include all women of all classes, races, and cultures. This means that black women, working-class women, Jewish women, Muslim women, Asian women, African women—all women in every social context—must form self-defined feminist movements that critique patriarchy from within their own situations. Feminism then would become a network of solidarity among all these movements, in which white and middle-class women (and we must remember that "middle class" is not synonymous with white or Western) define their own movement in solidarity with these movements of less privileged women, rather than define feminism only in terms of their own class and cultural context.

Feminism could also commit suicide by becoming merely the feminism of professional women, a more extreme version of middle-class feminism. Feminism would become primarily a vehicle for a small number of middle-class women who are seeking inclusion in male-defined, high-status professions and who bond with the few other women of their same professional group in order to win equality between themselves and their male colleagues. Feminism would mean women clergy, women lawyers, women doctors, and women politicians seeking equality with male clergy, lawyers, doctors, and politicians, while failing to establish solidarity, either in theory or practice, with other women—with women secretaries or maintenance workers in their own workplace or with housewives.

Such a feminism assures that it will remain the feminism of an elite and will achieve only token success in its own context, while awakening the animosity of the 90 percent of women who work as unpaid houseworkers and low-paid salaried workers. Very soon this feminism of the elite will become the struggle of each woman in the elite for herself, in a way that disavows any interest in women's issues either within her own profession or in relation to the vast body of other women. In other words, it ceases to be feminism at all and becomes sheer Jeane Kirkpatrick–ism.

Finally, feminism may commit suicide by distorting the radical critique of patriarchy into an in-group sectarianism of women who define their ideological purity by their disavowal of the humanity of all males and the repudiation of any women who have friendly intercourse with males in either sense of the word. Such sectarian feminism writes off the humanity not only of all males and all nonfeminist women but also of all feminist women who seek to reclaim traditions of male culture or who have social and sexual relations with males. Thus, feminists who also wish to be Christians (Jews, Muslims), feminists who are married or heterosexual, finally even feminists who are lesbian mothers raising male children, will come to feel uncomfortable in the feminist "sect." They will be made to feel guilty of crimes of ideological impurity through their social, sexual, or cultural complicity with the "enemy." Such a feminism not only fails to convert any men or any women who are not presently feminists, but manages to turn off many women who consider themselves feminists.

Thus, if feminism is to continue as a prophetic movement that can grow and attract increasing numbers of women, as well as men, into its alternative vision, it must clearly reject these ways of dividing women against each other. This does not mean muting the radicality of its criticism of patriarchy. It does mean constantly striving to communicate its criticism of patriarchy in a way that shows why it is in the self-interest of all women and most men. It does not mean pretending that there are no disagreements between feminists and nonfeminist women, much less antifeminist women. It means discussing those disagreements in ways that lead to clear insight into antifeminism as the defensive ideology of women trapped by patriarchy.[5]

It does not mean denying that women need to talk together without men and to establish autonomous groups not controlled by men. It certainly does not mean denying that lesbianism is a valid sexual and human relationship. It means not transforming lesbianism or the need for organizational autonomy into an ideological sectarianism that denies the humanity of all males and of male-friendly women. Finally, it does not mean that feminists don't dispute with each other. Rather, it means that one recognizes in differences among feminists evidence of contradictions in reality that call for clear and compassionate struggle that can lead to a new synthesis.

In short, to maintain its vision as a prophetic alternative to the historical reality of patriarchy, feminism must be comprehensive enough to embrace all women and to convince increasing numbers of males that their humanity, too, could be enhanced if they ceased to identify being a human of the male sex with social and sexual domination of others, particularly of women.

NOTES

1. This and other biblical citations are from the New Revised Standard Version.
2. See Alice S. Rossi, ed., *The Feminist Papers: From Adams to de Beauvoir* (New York: Bantam, 1974), 10, 11.
3. Hilda Scott, *Does Socialism Liberate Women?* (Boston: Beacon Press, 1974).
4. The development of this type of sexual language in modern science is explored in Brian Easlea, *Witchhunting, Magic, and the New Philosophy* (Atlantic Highlands, N.J.: Humanities Press, 1980).
5. For a model of this kind of radical, yet compassionate, insight into antifeminist women, see Andrea Dworkin, *Right Wing Women* (New York: Perigee, 1983).

from *Standing Again at Sinai: Judaism from a Feminist Perspective*

❧

Judith Plaskow

Judith Plaskow is a leading Jewish feminist theologian. She teaches at Manhattan College and has served as president of the American Academy of Religion. This essay describes some of the essential structures and concerns of Jewish feminist theology.

❧

GATHERING THE STRANDS: TOWARD A JEWISH FEMINIST UNDERSTANDING OF GOD

Where does all this leave us in terms of a Jewish feminist understanding of God? It should be clear from all I have said that one aspect of such an understanding would have to be advocacy and appreciation of a plurality of images for God, a plurality that includes some traditional metaphors but that also goes well beyond them in embracing the experience of those who have hitherto been excluded from the process of naming the sacred. Just as the feminist rethinking of Torah involves broadening Jewish memory, and the reconceptualization of Israel involves acknowledging and respecting the diversity of Jewish community, so the feminist reimaging of God entails reclaiming and shaping sufficient metaphors for God that the diversity of Jewish community is reflected in its naming of divinity and the commitment to communal diversity is grounded in an inclusive monotheism. If identifying God with a particular set of metaphors both limits God and supports a community in which some people have more value than others, using a broad and changing variety of metaphors brings home on the nonrational level on which images function that God has many guises, no one of which is final. When we feel free to try on and play with a range of images for God, then our speaking and praying becomes explicitly a "naming toward God,"[1] and all Jews are challenged to reach into the depths of our experience to speak out the names we find there.

The affirmation of multiple images for God is thus an essential aspect of Jewish feminist spirituality; yet it is not its center. Any particular community, even when it knows its symbols for God are tentative and open, is still likely to express itself through a set of images that reflect its own central experiences, experiences that become normative for sifting and creating imagery. We have seen that at the center of the women's spirituality movement, for example, is a

337

sense of connection to the natural world that controls the metaphors adopted for the sacred. In dethroning the white male God who is in the "white folks' white bible," Shug begins with "trees. Then air. Then birds." Only "then other people."[2] Goddess spirituality is rooted in the intuition that "the earth is holy," and that the Goddess is found in the elements that surround us: earth, ocean, stars, air, sky, moon, flowers, trees.[3] In this spirituality, people are part of the natural world, persons among others without holding a privileged position within the natural order.

This use of natural imagery for God is enormously important in a culture that has trampled on and violated the natural world and that threatens the whole biosphere with ecological and nuclear destruction. The affirmation that the earth is holy and that all parts of creation have intrinsic value provides a powerful corrective to the view that human beings are the measure of all things. Yet to my mind, the rediscovery of human connection with nature and the search for adequate metaphors to express it is just one aspect of a Jewish feminist spirituality. The other aspect—and one feminists have been less successful in translating into imagery—is the presence of God in empowered, egalitarian community. The emphasis on community that Judaism and feminism share means that the God who sustains the world is experienced not only in relation to nature, but also in the coming together of human beings who see their communal purpose as transparent to a larger purpose in which it is grounded. As I argued in discussing the spiritual dimension of community in the last chapter, community "can be the primary vehicle and place of religious experience," and "the divine presence rests in community in a uniquely powerful way."[4]

The centrality of human community to the Jewish religious experience is clear. Jews first found God in the midst of community, and, finding God, were constituted a community. But I would also maintain that insofar as women's experience of the holiness of nature has been named in a feminist context, in the feminist case too, it is the experience of community that has allowed the articulation and development of a nature spirituality. Feminism created a communal context in which women could identify and claim experiences that they might otherwise never have brought to full consciousness or might have regarded as purely personal. What Carol P. Christ has called "communal mysticism"—a form of mysticism in which "the great powers to which women awaken are experienced through social groups or movements"—would thus accompany and support the "nature mysticism" that is the more prominent theme in feminist spirituality.[5] My point is not to insist that the one form of spirituality is more fundamental or valid than the other; different emphases often reflect basic individual differences in religious experience. But I would argue that the relatively neglected human communal dimension of feminist spirituality requires far more attention—and that it is precisely in this dimension that Judaism and feminism converge.

From a critical perspective, of course, the centrality of human community in Jewish religious history may be taken simply as a sign of Jewish anthropocentrism. Yet even if we highlight those aspects of Judaism that recognize the intrinsic worth of nonhuman creation and seek to move the tradition further in this direction, I believe there are still aspects of human community that make it a particularly powerful locus for religious experience. Not only is human community the place and prerequisite of our coming to personhood, but also our relationships with other human beings involve the possibility of a reciprocity and mutuality of intention and commitment that is not available in other sorts of connection. Martin Buber, the philosopher of relation, remarks in his classic work *I and Thou* that there are three arenas of human life in which genuine relationships can arise: life with nature, life with other human beings, and life with "spiritual beings," by which he means ideas and cultural creations. Yet along with Buber's—often criticized—insistence that there can be dialogue with nature, he says that it is only in relation to the second sphere that true mutuality is possible. Relationships between human beings need not hover at the "threshold of mutuality" but can express themselves in language, so that acknowledgment of the other as a person can be both given and received.[6]

This capacity for mutuality in human relations is the foundation for the moral life that also finds expression in human community. Human responsibility for the well-being of the world never can be fulfilled simply through personal action. Human beings come to accountability in the midst of communities that interpret and set out where obligations lie, and community is the context for fulfilling our obligations. Moreover, in coming together with others in mutual commitment to ideas or causes, we ever and again form new communities through which to renew and carry on our purposes. It is as we join with others, in a way that only human beings can, in shared engagement to a common vision, that we find ourselves in the presence of another presence that is the final source of our hopes and intentions, and that undergirds and sustains them. Whether the substance of our cause be our lives as women, the fate of the earth, the pursuit of justice in human community, or some more narrowly religious purpose, it is through the struggle with others to act responsibly in history that we come to know our own actions as encompassed and empowered by a wider universe of action and thus come to know God in a profound and significant way.[7]

The feminist experience of finding in community both a new sense of personal empowerment and mission and connection with its sustaining source may not be so different from the early Israelite experience of discovering in community both a dawning national identity and a covenant with the God who gave it. In both cases, community is the location and vehicle for the experience of God and for the continuing enactment of its meaning. Nevertheless, neither Jews nor feminists have found a vocabulary for speaking about God that adequately reflects the presence of God in the midst of a responsive and responsible community. Feminist spirituality has developed a fuller range of natural imagery than imagery taken from feminist community. And the predominant Jewish language for speaking about God, while it supposedly elaborates the experience of covenant, in fact draws from community those images of dominance that dominate the liturgy. Images of God as lord and king evoke one who is over against community as its ruler and head, not one who is with it as partner, nourisher, and goad. The Jewish mystical tradition provides important alternative conceptions of God that emphasize human community and responsibility, but without translating these conceptions into a range of new images for *Ha-Kadosh Borukh Hu* (the holy one, blessed be he).[8] Jewish feminism, in seeking to draw together into a vision of empowered egalitarian community the Jewish and feminist affirmations of community, needs an understanding of God that emerges out of and is faithful to the place where its God is found.

Insofar as God is experienced in community, changes in communal structure and in the shape and forms of worship can of themselves contribute to a new understanding of God even in the absence of changes in metaphor. Women's religious leadership in many Jewish communities testifies to the presence of God within women. Feminist or havurah-style prayer, which favors small groups whose members face each other during worship and depends on the participation of all present, evokes a sense of God immanent in community. Communities that open themselves to the richness of Jewish diversity gain access to the spiritual resources present in that diversity. One need not explicitly name God for God to be found—a truth Marcia Falk tries to express in her blessings by varying their syntax so that God appears in unexpected or hidden places.[9] Indeed, the experience of God conveyed by the structure of a group can contradict or overpower the messages of a traditional liturgy.

Yet given the power of images and of the traditional liturgy in shaping conceptions of God for the Jewish community as a whole, feminists also cannot avoid the task of suggesting images that express the presence of God in a diverse and egalitarian community. In doing so, we will have to put new emphasis on traditional metaphors forgotten or slighted and bring to birth new metaphors that reflect the experiences of members of the community who heretofore have been subordinated or silenced. Birth is the appropriate image for this process, for naming new metaphors involves not simply invention, but the capacity to listen to what is already happening and to articulate communal experiences as they begin to emerge. It may be that truly satisfying communal images of God await the creation of new communities, for communal structures and communal metaphors are mutually related. One cannot create images in a vacuum; they arise out of new experiences and need time and nurturance to ripen and flower. Feminist images of God name the experience of people on the way, in the process of becoming—as, indeed, do *all* images of God, though this is often forgotten.

Recognizing, then, that the becoming of new images is in its early stages, I would suggest that there are (at least) two kinds of Jewish feminist God-naming that need to be taken together to produce a picture of God that reflects the experience of egalitarian community. The first kind of God-language is anthropomorphic language. Modern Jewish thinkers who have emphasized the importance of a lived relationship with God have tended to speak about God in philosophical language, avoiding anthropomorphisms that might objectify God and thus undermine the immediacy of relation.[10] Similarly, some feminists have sought to solve the problem of traditional male metaphors by using nonimagistic, or at least nonpersonal language. Some women have preferred to fill in names like "God" or "the Eternal" with new experiences, rather than create new images that would reify certain aspects of experience. Others have avoided personal imagery because it necessarily reinforces traditional anthropocentrism and because it implies that God is separable from the world.[11]

But while it is certainly true that anthropomorphic images can be dangerous, supporting patterns of dominance or substituting for the experiences they claim to communicate, such images also appeal to places in our nature that cannot be reached by abstract philosophical discourse or direct designations like "God" and "the Eternal." Even nonpersonal images, though they are important to feminist God-language, are not themselves sufficient, I would argue, to evoke the God of community. Nonanthropomorphic language threatens to leave intact old anthropomorphic images that can continue to coexist with and subvert neutral language. For the English speaker, it is quite possible to avoid pronouns for God and to refer to God as the Eternal or source of life and still picture that eternal source as male. Only deliberately disruptive—that is, female—metaphors can break the imaginative hold of male metaphors that have been used for millennia. For the Hebrew speaker, who has available nonpersonal female images, it is still difficult to convey the presence of God in community while excluding those images that come most directly from the web of interpersonal relations that constitute community. We are roused to remember the God of community and to value and create certain kinds of communities precisely by those images that most vividly evoke our real experiences of community. Just as feminists are struggling to find communal structures that do not involve hierarchy, so we need to find ways of speaking about God's presence in community that do not invoke metaphors of domination. Failing to use the images that emerge from our real-life struggles, we banish as a source of religious expression central aspects of our lives.[12]

To my mind, then, feminists cannot avoid the use of anthropomorphic imagery. Indeed, incorporating the appreciation of diversity that should characterize all feminist God-language, this kind of imagery would include a wide range of metaphors, from purposely disquieting female images, to female and nongendered images that express intimacy, partnership, and mutuality between humans and God. It may be important, for example, to use for a time images like

Queen of the Universe and Woman of War in order to jar worshipers, precipitate discussion, and raise questions about the meaning and effects of the imagery we use. What is the source of our attachment to male imagery? Is the image of a monarch—male or female—one we want to affirm? Do women need to claim the warrior within ourselves, and are there images of warrior that are not images of violent destruction?[13] While metaphors of queen and warrior are problematic and will not constitute the lasting contribution of feminism to Jewish God-language, they have an important bridge role to play in presenting images of female religious power to a community that has denied women this attribute.[14] Other, perhaps more enduring, images will try to combine female metaphors with a changed conception of God or use nongendered language drawn from human community. Sallie McFague, in her book *Models of God,* devotes extensive discussion to images of God as lover and friend.[15] These images, along with companion and cocreator, might well be taken up by Jewish feminists and developed conceptually and liturgically.

Images of God as lover and friend are present in the Jewish tradition, but they are greatly overshadowed by father and king and rarely appear in the liturgy. In midrashic parallels to the passage in *Pesikta Rabbati* that describes God's different guises, God as a young warrior at the Red Sea is identified with the lover of the Song of Songs who, at the moment of liberation, comes to Israel as her beautiful bridegroom. Although the image of God as lover-bridegroom later disappears, it and father-judge are the central rabbinic metaphors for the love of God.[16] In McFague's rendering, the image of God as lover validates the erotic element in spirituality and affirms the value of that which is loved. Unlike images of king, judge, and (one side of) father, which promise enduring love *despite* a community's sins, the notion of God as lover proclaims that God loves Israel *because of* who Israel is. The idea that we are loved for what is most valuable in us, that God sees our worth even when we cannot, is far more conducive to human empowerment and accountability than the idea that we are loved despite our worthlessness.[17] In traditional Jewish usage, of course, God as valuing lover is the comely young man wooing (the subordinate) Israel as his bride. Feminist use of the image of God as lover would need to break through this patriarchal model of love relations, envisioning the lover as both female and male. Israel is not "she"; *it* is a community of women and men, all of whom can be lovers and loved of God. The astonishingly mutual imagery of the Songs of Songs presents both male and female lovers as pursuer and pursued. There is no reason why, with this book as a model, only the male should be identified with God—except, of course, for the androcentric context of the history of its interpretation.

The image of God as friend also appears in rabbinic discussion and finds its way into the Yom Kippur liturgy in the multiple metaphors of *Ki Anu Amekhah.*[18] A striking contrast with symbols of God as Other, this image of free and reciprocal connection is a profound metaphor for the convenantal relation. As McFague sees it, the image of God as friend points to a common vision or commitment that brings friends together and that both unites them and turns them to the world. While friendship often implies an exclusive element, it is also possible for people of different backgrounds and abilities to join in friendship around a common undertaking. Friendship is a human possibility, moreover, irrespective of gender and across gender lines. Indeed, McFague suggests, since all of life is relational, friendship is possible even across ontological boundaries: We can be friends of the earth and friends of God.[19]

Closely related to the image of friend is the image of companion. While both images are ambiguous, and they are often used interchangeably, they can also represent different aspects of the experience of relation. If friendship entails a unique bond between two people that distinguishes their relationship from more casual connections, a companion is simply one who travels on the same way. The image of companion thus lacks the passion and specialness of friendship, but it provides the same sense of equality with a more communal metaphor. One can imagine many companions linked together by some shared task, laboring side by side for the achievement of their ends. Such companionship may be brief or can last throughout a lifetime, lightening shared work with the pleasure of human connection. Metaphors of God as friend and companion capture in different ways the closeness of God's relationship to Israel and the sense of striving toward a common goal. They suggest that God and Israel are mutually related and accountable as they join in the shared project of sanctifying and repairing the world.

Another, somewhat more awkward, image that suggests the shared responsibility of God and Israel has both feminist and Jewish roots. At the Grailville conference at which the participants used many "ing" words for God, they also suggested the term "cocreator" as evoking important aspects of their week together.[20] The prefix "co," which might in fact be used with a range of images, conjures the sense of personal empowerment and mutual responsibility that emerges out of speaking and acting in community with others. The feeling of possibility that comes with seeing the limits placed on women and envisioning a life beyond them fosters a sense of significant participation in the larger project of world-creation, a project that God and human beings share. To name the self and name the world in new ways is to enter with God into the act of creation. Insofar as human beings are cocreators with God, God is also a cocreator. Creation is not a discrete event completed by God in six days but a process that continues in dialogue with human beings who can carry forward or destroy the world that God has brought to be. This image of God as cocreator strongly accords with the sense of the Jewish mystical tradition that human beings are responsible for fulfilling the work of creation, uniting the separated aspects of divinity through the power of the deed.

These images of God—lover, friend, companion, cocreator—are more appropriate metaphors for the God of the covenant than traditional images of lord and king. Defining God's power not as domination but empowerment, they evoke a God who is with us instead of over us, a partner in dialogue who ever and again summons us to responsible action. Rather than reminding human beings of our frailty and nothingness, they call us to accountability as partners in a solemn compact that makes demands on us to which we can respond. It is not as we are subjugated, as we feel our worthlessness and culpability, that we can act most responsibly and effectively, but as we know our own value, mirrored in the constancy of God as friend and lover who calls us to enter into the task of creation. Responding responsibly,[21] we do so not because otherwise we are guilty, but because—as the Kabbalistic tradition reminds us—what we do or leave undone as cocreators makes a difference in the world.

Imagining God as friend and cocreator begins to name aspects of the deity lost in metaphors of domination, but it still provides only one stratum of a feminist understanding of God. Human beings become cocreators with God only after we come into being as part of a much larger web of existence—a web we now have the power to destroy but which we did not conceive or create. Moreover, the images I have suggested are still primarily dyadic; and while they can be applied to community, they do not in the first instance take us beyond the interpersonal plane. Anthropomorphic images must thus be supplemented by a second kind of language that can evoke the creative and sustaining power of God present throughout the world and in ever-widening circles of relation. This stratum of language will encompass an even wider range of images than the first—from natural and impersonal metaphors to conceptual terms that express God's relation to all being and becoming.

Images of God as fountain, source, wellspring, or ground of life and being remind us that God loves and befriends us as one who brings forth all being and sustains it in existence.[22] As cocreators with God for the brief span of our lives, we are responsible not just to the community of our fellow persons with whom we especially share the sense of God's presence, but to the larger community of creation that God also loves and befriends. Metaphors of ground and source continue the reconceptualization of God's power, shifting our sense of direction from a God in the high heavens who creates through the magical word to the very ground beneath our feet that nourishes and sustains us. As a tree draws up sustenance from the soil, so we are rooted in the source of our being that bears and maintains us even as it enables us to respond to it freely. Images of God as rock, tree of life, light, darkness, and myriad other metaphors drawn from nature, teach us the intrinsic value of this wider web of being in which we dwell. The God who is the ground of being is present and imaged forth in all beings, so that every aspect of creation shows us another face of God.

More conceptual images for God also have a role in feminist discourse. The traditional image of God as place (*makom*) evokes both the presence of the world in God and the extraordinary presence of God in particular places. As Rabbi Jose b. Halafta said, "We do not know whether God is the place of His world, or the world is His place."[23] Lacking personal communal images to refer to God, we can use this richly ambiguous term to point to community as a special place of God's self-manifestation. Community is a place we find ourselves in God; God dwells in this place. Also relevant here is the image of Shekhinah, which like the term God itself, cuts across the layers of anthropomorphic and nonpersonal language. Addressed in myriad personal guises, the Shekhinah is also the presence of God in the place called the world and the one who rests in a unique way in the midst of community.

There are, of course, many other metaphors that can be and have been evoked as part of the feminist naming of God. The images I mention here are just some of those that might convey the presence of God in a diverse, egalitarian community, replacing images of domination with a different understanding of the divine/human relation. Moreover, insofar as these images reflect the experience of a distinct community, they comprise only one of many communal namings of the experience and nature of the sacred. The connection between these different namings remains an important question, particularly as it pertains to the continuing place of traditional images of God in a feminist Judaism.

Certainly, the particular metaphors that emerge out of feminist experience are not meant to replace all other metaphors for God. Feminist metaphors call attention to important neglected aspects of the experience of God in community, and in doing so relativize and modify traditional metaphors by placing them in a different and larger context. Many traditional images of God can be altered in connotation or meaning by being seen in conjunction with feminist metaphors and with the changing social context out of which these metaphors arise. The image of God as father, for example, in a transformed social, and metaphoric nexus, is potentially simply a parental image, shedding its implications of patriarchal domination and control. The image of God as judge confronts us when we fail to live up to our own ideals of diversity and mutuality, thus remaining an important counterpart to friend and source of being. But while feminist metaphors are nonexclusive, the experience of God in diverse, egalitarian community is also normative from a feminist perspective and as such functions as a criterion for selecting and rejecting images of divinity. Traditional images like lord and king, for example, evoke by definition relations of domination. Since it is difficult to imagine how such images could be transformed by context, they need to be seen as injurious reflections and supports of a hierarchical social system, and excised from our religious vocabularies.[24]

The rejection of all metaphors of domination raises, finally, a question frequently asked of feminists: What becomes of the Otherness or "Godness" of God when the primary feminist metaphors for God are warm and intimate ones? If God is friend and lover—albeit also ground and source of being—does this not somehow make God less God, less utterly more than us in every way? This question can be answered only by distinguishing among very different meanings of the concept of Otherness. The sense of Otherness I have been criticizing throughout this chapter is the notion of God as a dominating sovereign manipulating the world from outside it and above. I have argued that metaphors that depict God as Other in this sense mirror and sustain destructive social relations that ought never to be sanctified by any religious usage. But rejecting such metaphors does not entail abandoning God's "moreness"; it simply challenges us to imagine that moreness in nonhierarchical terms. Just as a community is more than the sum of its members, for example, without necessarily controlling or dominating them, so God as the ultimate horizon of community and source of unity is more than all things—also without needing to control or dominate them. A second meaning of Otherness found frequently in this book refers to peoples or aspects of reality seen as different from and less than some dominant group, the nonnormative Other in a hierarchical system. Feminist God-language does not simply reject this sense of Otherness, but seeks actively to address and undermine it through finding divinity in what has hitherto been despised. In imaging God as female, as darkness, as nature, and as a myriad of other metaphors taken from realms devalued and spurned, we reexamine and value the many forms of Otherness, claiming their multiform particularity as significant and sacred.

The third meaning of Otherness points to God as mystery and adversary—the presence of God experienced not as friend but as devouring fire, and the relationship of God to the terrible aspects of human existence. Feminists, although we continually confront human evil in the form of patriarchy and other destructive structures of hierarchical relation, have not yet fully addressed the theological question of evil as a feminist issue.[25] This side of God, which we cannot neglect without introducing a fundamental dualism into our conception of the world, can be expressed through images of waning and death, pain and struggle, all of which are aspects of a complex and changing reality. God as source can also be experienced as abyss; God as friend can also appear as enemy.[26] But while we must speak about God as Other in this sense, it is unnecessary to do so using images of hierarchical domination. The hierarchies in our world are human creations. The God who brings to birth and destroys, gives forth and takes away, judges my limitations and calls me to struggle, is terrifying not for God's distance, but precisely for God's nearness. That which is awesome, painful, or evil appalls or bewilders me not because it is far away, but because it is all around and as near as my own heart. This Otherness is not incompatible with the intimacy of feminist metaphors, but is found alongside and within them as their difficult counterparts and companions.

We are left, then, with a picture of God as a God of many faces—as many as the 600,000 souls that stood at Sinai and the complexities and conflicts of Jewish and human existence. At the center of this picture stands the Jewish/feminist experience of a God encountered in the midst of community—a God revealed as the community and those within it discover their destiny and understand that destiny as part of a larger universe of action and response.[27] This God is male/female lover, friend, companion, cocreator, the one who, seeing what is best in us, lures us to be the most we can become. This God is ground and source of all life, creating, holding, sustaining the great web of existence and, as part of it, the human companions who labor to make the world a home for the divine presence. This God is the God of Israel, the God the nascent community experienced and acknowledged behind the wonderful events at the Red Sea. This is the God the people stood before at Sinai, coming to their identity as a people, responding with the myriad laws, institutions, and customs that have given form and substance to their communal life. This is the God to whom they found themselves tied in a covenant, reciprocally binding through good times and bad: friend, holy terror, persistent goad.

Jewish feminists, in seeking to name this God of our experience, search for images of God that convey God's power and presence in community, at the same time trying to undo that community's hierarchical distortions. Selecting metaphors for God that acknowledge the differences within a covenantal community, we are also aware of the many covenants and greater differences that lie beyond our particular naming. As feminists, as Jews, we come to respond to and speak of God in certain characteristic ways. So every community in its uniqueness imagines the power that surrounds and sustains it. The naming of God and Israel that would turn God into Israel's God and Israel into "his" chosen people is part of the dualistic, hierarchical misnaming of God and reality that emerges out of and supports a patriarchal worldview. In speaking of the moving, changing ground and source, our companion and our lover, we name toward the God known in community that cherishes diversity within and without, even as that diversity has its warrant in the God of myriad names.

NOTES

1. Mary Daly, *Beyond God the Father* (Boston: Beacon Press, 1973), 33.
2. Alice Walker, *The Color Purple* (New York: Pocket Books, 1990), 166–67.
3. Carol P. Christ, *Laughter of Aphrodite: Reflections on a Journey to the Goddess* (New York: Harper Collins, 1989), ix; Starhawk, *The Spiral Dance* (New York: Harper Collins, 1989), 77–78.
4. See chapter 3, 85–86.
5. Carol P. Christ, *Diving Deep and Surfacing: Women Writers on Spiritual Quest* (Boston: Beacon Press, 1995), 23; also passim.
6. Martin Buber, *I and Thou*, trans. Walter Kaufmann (New York: Scribner's, 1976), 56–57, 172–73, 180–81.
7. H. Richard Niebuhr, *The Responsible Self: An Essay in Christian Moral Philosophy* (New York: Harper & Row, 1963), 84–89.
8. Lawrence Fine, "The Contemplative Practice of Yihudim in Lurianic Kabbalah" and Louis Jacobs, "The Uplifting of Sparks in Later Jewish Mysticism," both in *Jewish Spirituality from the Sixteenth Century Revival to the Present*, ed. Arthur Green (New York: Crossroad, 1987), 65–70, 107–8, 115–25. For a fascinating image of communal spirituality within Hasidism, see J. G. Weiss, "R. Abraham Kalisker's Concept of Communion with God and Men," *Journal of Jewish Studies* 6 (1955): 87–99. Thanks to Martha Ackelsberg and Gershon Hundert for this last reference.
9. Marcia Falk, "Notes on Composing New Blessings: Toward a Feminist-Jewish Reconstruction of Prayer," in *Weaving the Visions*, ed. Judith Plaskow and Carol P. Christ (New York: Harper Collins 1989), 48.
10. Arthur Green, "The Children in Egypt and the Theophany at the Sea," *Judaism* 24 (fall 1975): 446.
11. Falk, "Notes on Composing New Blessings," 45, and "Toward a Feminist-Jewish Reconstruction of Monotheism," *Tikkun* 4 (July/August 1989); 53–54.
12. See Sallie McFague, *The Models of God: Theology for an Ecological, Nuclear Age* (Minneapolis, Minn.: Fortress, 1989), 79–84 for a very fine extended argument for personal God-language.
13. This last question comes out of a conversation with Marcia Falk, May 1988.
14. See Christ, *Laughter of Aphrodite*, 121–26.
15. Chapters 5 and 6. McFague also proposes the image of God as Mother. I do not discuss it here because it is an image drawn from family, and I want to focus on images that come from community.
16. Green, "The Children in Egypt," 453–55.

17. McFague, *Models of God*, 125–34. McFague talks about God as lover of the world as God's body; again, I want to focus on community. It may be no coincidence that the image of God as lover is important in the Jewish mystical tradition which also emphasizes human responsibility for the world.

18. Marmorstein, *The Old Rabbinic Doctrine of God*, vol. I (New York: McGraw-Hill, 1969), 86. *Ki Anu Amekhah* is a liturgical poem—my favorite since childhood—repeated many times on Yom Kippur that provides a long series of metaphors for the relationship between God and Israel. While almost all the metaphors are metaphors of domination, the prayer is an excellent spur to imagistic inventiveness.

19. McFague, *Models of God*, 163–64.

20. "Brainstorm: The Meaning of the Grailville Conference," in *Women Exploring Theology at Grailville* (Loveland, Ohio, 1972).

21. In *The Responsible Self*, H. R. Niebuhr takes "responsibility" as the fundamental metaphor for understanding human life before God.

22. Falk, "Notes on Composing New Blessings," 46. "Wellspring" is Falk's more recent translation of *eyn ha-khayyim* (conversation, May 1988).

23. Marmorstein, *The Old Rabbinic Doctrine of God*, vol. I, 91, 92–93, 149.

24. I am aware that the image of God as king has been used to question the authority of any earthly king. (See, for example, 1 Sam. 8:7 and Rosemary Ruether, *Sexism and God-Talk: Toward a Feminist Theology* [Boston: Beacon Press, 1983], 64.) But the image is still problematic in its hierarchical understanding of the divine/human relation and is too easily reversed politically.

25. See Catherine Madsen and respondents, "If God Is God She Is Not Nice," *Journal of Feminist Studies in Religion* 5 (spring 1989): 103–17.

26. H. Richard Niebuhr, *Radical Monotheism and Western Culture* (New York: Harper & Row, Harper Torchbooks, 1970), 122–24; Paul Tillich, *Systematic Theology*, 3 vols. (Chicago: University of Chicago Press, 1951–1963), 1: 110.

27. Niebuhr, *The Responsible Self*, 83, 86–87.

"In Search of Women's Heritage"

❧

Elisabeth Schüssler Fiorenza

Elisabeth Schüssler Fiorenza's groundbreaking work on women in early Christianity has been translated into twelve languages. She teaches theology at Harvard Divinity School and was the first woman president of the Society of Biblical Literature. Here she describes the feminist task of reclaiming Christianity from patriarchy.

❧

In the passion account of Mark's Gospel three disciples figure prominently: on the one hand, two of the twelve—Judas who betrays Jesus and Peter who denies him—and on the other, the unnamed woman who anoints Jesus. But while the stories of Judas and Peter are engraved in the memory of Christians, the story of the woman is virtually forgotten. Although Jesus pronounces in Mark: "And truly I say to you, wherever the gospel is preached in the whole world, what she has done will be told in memory of her" (14:9), the woman's prophetic sign-action did not become a part of the gospel knowledge of Christians. Even her name is lost to us. Wherever the gospel is proclaimed and the eucharist celebrated another story is told: the story of the apostle who betrayed Jesus. The name of the betrayer is remembered, but the name of the faithful disciple is forgotten because she was a woman.

Although the story of the anointing is told in all four Gospels,[1] it is obvious that the redactional retelling of the story seeks to make the story more palatable to a patriarchal Greco-Roman audience. Whereas the Fourth Gospel identifies the woman as Mary of Bethany who as faithful friend of Jesus shows her love by anointing him, Luke shifts the focus of the story from woman as disciple to woman as sinner. Whether Luke used Mark's text or transmits a different tradition is disputed. But this exegetical dispute does not matter much since we are used to reading the Markan story in the light of Luke. In the process the woman becomes a great sinner who is forgiven by Jesus.

Despite their differences, all four Gospels reflect the same basic story: a woman anoints Jesus. This incident causes objections which Jesus rejects by approving of the woman's action. If the original story had been just a story about the anointing of a guest's feet, it is unlikely that such a commonplace gesture would have been remembered and retold as the proclamation of the gospel. Therefore, it is much more likely that in the original story the woman anointed Jesus' head. Since the prophet in the Old Testament anointed the head of the Jewish king, the anointing of Jesus' head must have been understood immediately as the prophetic recognition of Jesus, the Anointed, the Messiah, the Christ. According to the tradition it was a woman who named Jesus by and through her prophetic sign-action. It was a politically dangerous story.[2]

In Mark's Gospel the story is sandwiched between the statement that the leaders of Jesus' people wanted to arrest him and the announcement of Jesus' betrayal by Judas for money. Mark thus depoliticizes the story of Jesus' passion: first, by shifting the blame for his death from the Romans to the Jewish establishment; and second, by theologically defining Jesus' messiahship as one of suffering and death. Whereas according to Mark the leading male disciples do not understand this suffering messiahship of Jesus, reject it, and finally abandon him, the women disciples who have followed Jesus from Galilee to Jerusalem suddenly emerge as the true disciples in the passion narrative. They are Jesus' true followers (*akolouthein*) who have understood that his ministry was not rule and kingly glory but *diakonia*, "service" (Mark 15:41). Thus the women emerge as the true Christian ministers and witnesses. The unnamed woman who names Jesus with a prophetic sign-action in Mark's Gospel is the paradigm for the true disciple. While Peter had confessed, without truly understanding it, "you are the anointed one," the woman anointing Jesus recognizes clearly that Jesus' messiahship means suffering and death.

Both Christian feminist theology and biblical interpretation are in the process of rediscovering that the Christian gospel cannot be proclaimed if the women disciples and what they have done are not remembered. They are in the process of reclaiming the supper at Bethany as women's Christian heritage in order to correct symbols and ritualizations of an all-male Last Supper that is a betrayal of true Christian discipleship and ministry.[3] Or, in the words of the artist Judy Chicago: "All the institutions of our culture tell us through words, deeds, and even worse silence that we are insignificant. But our heritage is our power."[4]

The explorations of this book have two goals: they attempt to reconstruct early Christian history as women's history in order not only to restore women's stories to early Christian history but also to reclaim this history as the history of women and men. I do this not only as a feminist historian but also as a feminist theologian. The Bible is not just a historical collection of writings but also Holy Scripture, gospel, for Christians today. As such it informs not only theology but also the commitment of many women today. Yet as long as the stories and history of women in the beginnings of early Christianity are not theologically conceptualized as an integral part of the proclamation of the gospel, biblical texts and traditions formulated and codified by men will remain oppressive to women.

Such a reconstruction of early Christian history as women's history and of biblical-historical theology as feminist theology presupposes historical and theological critical analysis as well as the development of a feminist biblical-historical hermeneutics. Since I am trained in New Testament exegesis, I will limit my explorations to the beginnings of Christianity but not include all of biblical history. Methodologically, however, it will be necessary to go beyond the limits of the New Testament canon since it is a product of the patristic church, that is, a theological document of the "historical winners." To forego such an undertaking because historical critical scholarship and hermeneutics are "male" but not feminist does an intellectual disservice to women. Since it reinforces male-female role stereotypes, such an assumption is not capable of naming the particular oppressive assumptions and androcentric components of such scholarship.

Reconstruction of early Christian history in a feminist perspective raises difficult hermeneutical, textual, and historical problems. Since feminism has developed different theoretical perspectives and models, this reconstruction must also include the formulation of a feminist heuristic framework or model that allows for the oppression as well as for the historical agency of women in early Christianity.

1. A fundamental methodological insight of historical criticism of the Bible was the realization that the *Sitz im Leben* or life setting of a text is as important for its understanding as its actual formulation. Biblical texts are not verbally inspired revelation nor doctrinal principles but historical formulations within the context of a religious community. Although this insight is

challenged today by literary formalism as well as textual biblicism, it nevertheless remains basic to any historical reconstruction. Studies of the social world of Israel and early Christianity are in the process of developing heuristic models that comprehend more fully the social-historical context of the biblical texts.

Similarly, feminist theory insists that all texts are products of an androcentric patriarchal culture and history. The current feminist movement has therefore engendered an explosion of scholarly works in all areas of scientific inquiry and research.[5] Historians, philosophers, and anthropologists have emphasized that current scholarly theory and research are deficient because they neglect women's lives and contributions and construe humanity and human history as male. Feminist scholarship in all areas, therefore, seeks to construct heuristic models and concepts that allow us to perceive the human reality articulated insufficiently in androcentric texts and research.

The explorations of this book begin therefore with the hope of moving away from the pervasive apologetic that characterizes most treatments of women in the Bible, to a historical-critical reconstruction of women's history and women's contributions to early Christian beginnings. Moreover, I have assumed that the new questions raised by feminist scholarship will enhance our understanding of early Christian history. The attempt to "write women back into early Christian history" should not only restore early Christian history to women but also lead to a richer and more accurate perception of early Christian beginnings. If scholars employ philosophical, sociological, or psychological analyses for constructing new interpretative models of early Christian development, nothing should prevent us from utilizing feminist heuristic concepts as well, in order to reconstruct an early Christian history in which women are not hidden and invisible. While an androcentric model cannot do justice to those texts that positively mention women's leadership in early Christianity, a feminist model can positively integrate them.

Biblical scholars, however, do not perceive the question as a serious historical problem of great significance for the reconstruction of early Christian history and theology. As a "woman's issue" it is trivial or marginal to the academic enterprise. Seen as a "woman's problem" the issue belongs to books and symposia on "woman" but not in the program of exegetical conferences or in the pages of an exegetical *Festschrift*. Usually, anyone identified with the "feminist cause" is ideologically suspect and professionally discredited. As one of my colleagues remarked about a professor who had written a moderate article on women in the Old Testament: "It is shame, she may have ruined her scholarly career."

The tacit assumption underlying such expressed or unexpressed reservations is that scholars who do not reflect or articulate their political allegiances are "objective," free from bias, nonpartisan and scientific. Yet, anyone even slightly familiar with problems raised by the sociology of knowledge or by critical theory will have difficulty asserting such scholarly objectivity on scientific grounds. In a brilliant analysis of slavery in antiquity the eminent scholar Moses Finley has explored the ways in which current ideological and societal interests have deeply affected the historiography of ancient slavery. He sums up his explorations:

> Nevertheless, other contemporary ideological considerations are active in that seemingly remote field of historical study—active in the sense that they underlie, and even direct, what often appears to be a purely "factual," "objective" presentation. . . . I believe that a full, open account of how modern interest in ancient slavery has manifested itself is a necessary prerequisite to the substantive analysis of the institution itself, and I have therefore begun with that theme.[6]

Since historical knowledge is inferential (Collingwood), historians have to construct some frame of reference within which to discuss the available historical evidence. Such a frame of reference is always determined by their own philosophical perspective and values. Historians who pretend to record nothing but pure facts while refusing to acknowledge their own presuppositions and theoretical perspectives succeed only in concealing from themselves the ideologies upon which their historiography is based. All historiography is a selective view of the past. Historical interpretation is defined by contemporary questions and horizons of reality and conditioned by contemporary political interests and structures of domination. Historical "objectivity" can only be approached by reflecting critically on and naming one's theoretical presuppositions and political allegiances.

Interest in legitimization, as well as in opening up future possibilities, is a major motif in biblical interpretation. As James Robinson states:

> New Testament scholarship as an intellectual activity is a modern science reflecting as well as molding the modern understanding of reality, a reciprocity it shares with the humanities in general. . . . Every scholar or scientist who deals with a subject matter from the past does so in terms of his present grasp of reality and the results of his research in turn flow into the current body of knowledge from which the continual modification of our understanding of reality emerges.[7]

If this is the case—and I believe it is—then it must be asked whether the reluctance of scholars to investigate the present topic might be sustained by an unconscious or conscious refusal to modify our androcentric grasp of reality and religion rather than by a legitimate concern for the integrity of biblical-historical scholarship. The dictum of Simone de Beauvoir about scholarship on women in general applies also to studies of women in the Bible: "If the 'woman's question' seems trivial it is because masculine arrogance has made it a 'quarrel' and when quarrelling one no longer reasons well."[8]

2. While it is hard to dislodge the intellectual misgivings of my colleagues in the academy, I have found it even more difficult to sustain my biblical interests in the face of feminist objections. Questions and misgivings expressed by women in response to my lectures and publications have taught me how to phrase problems more clearly and how to keep in mind the structural obstacles to a feminist historiography or theology. Such exchanges have also compelled me to explore more deeply how a "feminist hermeneutics" can be formulated. The first part of this book—which might to many women seem strange and too academic at first glance—owes its conception to feminist rather than to academic theoretical questions.

When I attempt to explore the history of women who became Christians in the beginnings of Christianity this should not be misunderstood as an attempt to save the Bible from its feminist critics. I simply mean to raise the question: how can early Christian origins be reconstructed in such a way as to be understood as "women's affairs"? In other words, is early Christian history "our own" history or heritage? Were women as well as men the initiators of the Christian movement?

While theologians in the academy refuse to discuss publicly their own political allegiance and preconceived bias and function, many postbiblical feminists are prepared to relinquish their historical roots and their solidarity with women in biblical religion. Recognizing that androcentric Western language and patriarchal religion have "erased" women from history and made them "non-beings," such feminists argue that biblical religion (and theology) is sexist to the core. It is not retrievable for women, since it ignores women's experience, speaks of the godhead in male terms, legitimizes women's subordinate positions of powerlessness, and promotes male dominance and violence against women. Therefore, feminists must move beyond the boundaries of biblical religion and reject the patriarchal authority of biblical revelation.

Revisionist interpretations of the Bible are at best a waste of time and at worst a legitimization of the prevailing sexism of biblical religion—therefore, a co-optation of women and the feminist movement. Feminist praxis is rooted in the religious experience of contemporary women but does not derive its inspiration from the Christian past.

Yet such a postbiblical feminist stance is in danger of becoming ahistorical and apolitical. It too quickly concedes that women have no authentic history within biblical religion and too easily relinquishes women's feminist biblical heritage. Nor can such a stance do justice to the positive experiences of contemporary women within biblical religion. It must either neglect the influence of biblical religion on women today or declare women's adherence to biblical religion as "false consciousness." Insofar as biblical religion is still influential today, a cultural and social feminist transformation of Western society must take into account the biblical story and the historical impact of the biblical tradition. Western women are not able to discard completely and forget our personal, cultural, or religious Christian history. We will either transform it into a new liberating future or continue to be subject to its tyranny whether we recognize its power or not.

Feminists cannot afford such an ahistorical or antihistorical stance because it is precisely the power of oppression that deprives people of their history. This is perceived by both black and Latin American theologians. In his book *Roots,* Alex Haley traces the history of his people from its slave days. He does so in the hope "that this story of our people can alleviate the legacies of the fact that preponderantly the histories are written by the winners."[9] In a similar mode Gustavo Gutiérrez states:

> Human history has been written by a white hand, a male hand, from the dominating social class. The perspective of the defeated in history is different. Attempts have been made to wipe from their minds the memories of their struggles. This is to deprive them of a source of energy, of an historical will to rebellion.[10]

Among feminists, artist Judy Chicago has underlined the importance of women's heritage as a source for women's power. She created the *Dinner Party* as a symbolic history of women's past "pieced together" from the scanty information gleaned from cultural-religious channels. She observes:

> Sadly most of the 1,038 women included in the Dinner Party are unfamiliar, their lives and achievements unknown to most of us. To make people feel worthless, society robs them of their pride: this has happened to women. All the institutions of our culture tell us—through words, deeds and even worse silence—that we are insignificant. But our heritage is our power.[11]

Thus to reclaim early Christian history as women's own past and to insist that women's history is an integral part of early Christian historiography imply the search for roots, for solidarity with our foresisters, and finally for the memory of their sufferings, struggles, and powers as women.

If history in general, and early Christian history in particular, is one way in which androcentric culture and religion have defined women, then it must become a major object for feminist analysis. Such an analysis of history and the Bible must critically reveal patriarchal history for what it is and, at the same time, reconstruct the history of women in early Christianity as a challenge to historical-religious patriarchy. Therefore, a feminist reconstruction of early Christian history has not only a theoretical but also a practical goal: it aims at both cultural-religious critique and at reconstruction of women's history as women's story within Christianity.

It seeks not just to undermine the legitimization of patriarchal religious structures but also to empower women in their struggle against such oppressive structures. In other words, a feminist reconstruction of early Christian beginnings seeks to recover the Christian heritage of women because, in the words of Judy Chicago, "our heritage is our power."

Yet such a recovery of women's history in early Christianity must not only restore women to history, it must also restore the history of Christian beginnings to women. It claims the Christian past as women's own past, not just as a male past in which women participated only on the fringes or were not active at all. The New Testament sources provide sufficient indicators for such a history of early Christian beginnings, since they mention that women are both followers of Jesus and leading members of the early Christian communities. Moreover, in the second and third centuries Christianity was still defending itself against the accusation that it was a religion of women and uncultured people. The task, therefore, involves not so much rediscovering new sources as rereading the available sources in a different key. The goal is an increase in "historical imagination."

3. The debate between feminist "engaged" and androcentric academic "neutral" scholarship indicates a shift in interpretative paradigms.[12] Whereas traditional academic scholarship has identified humanness with maleness and understood women only as a peripheral category in the "human" interpretation of reality, the new field of women's studies not only attempts to make "women's" agency a key interpretative category but also seeks to transform androcentric scholarship and knowledge into truly human scholarship and knowledge, that is, inclusive of *all* people, men and women, upper and lower classes, aristocracy and "common people," different cultures and races, the powerful and the weak.

Thomas Kuhn's notion of scientific paradigms and heuristic interpretative models[13] can help us to understand this shift in interpretation and to map out a new feminist paradigm that has as its scientific goal an inclusive "human" reconstruction of early Christian history. According to Kuhn, a paradigm represents a coherent research tradition created and sustained by a scientific community. A paradigm defines the type of problems to be researched, interpretations to be given, and interpretative systems to be constructed. Thus a scientific paradigm determines all aspects of scientific research: observations, theories and interpretative models, research traditions and exemplars, as well as the philosophical-theoretical assumptions about the nature of the world and its total world view. All data and recorded observations are theory laden, no bare uninterpreted data and sources exist. Equally there are no criteria and research models that are not dependent on the scientific paradigm in which they were developed.

The shift from an androcentric to a feminist interpretation of the world implies a revolutionary shift in scientific paradigm, a shift with far-reaching ramifications not only for the interpretation of the world but also for its change. Since paradigms determine how scholars see the world and how they conceive of theoretical problems, a shift from an androcentric to a feminist paradigm implies a transformation of the scientific imagination. It demands an intellectual conversion that cannot be logically deduced but is rooted in a change of patriarchal-social relationships. Such an intellectual conversion engenders a shift in commitment that allows the community of scholars to see old "data" in a completely new perspective. The debate between androcentric scholarship and feminist scholarship does more than indicate the intellectual limitations of the scholars involved in the argument. In fact, it shows a competition between rival paradigms that may exist alongside each other in the phase of transition, but ultimately are exclusive of each other.

According to Kuhn, such a transition can only be accomplished when the emerging paradigm has produced its own institutional structures and support-systems. While the androcentric paradigm of scholarship is rooted in the patriarchal institutions of the academy, the feminist paradigm has created its own institutional basis in the alternative institutions of women's centers, academic institutes, and study programs. Yet the patriarchial dependencies and hierarchical institutions of the academy guarantee structural perpetuation of the androcentric scientific paradigm. The issue is not just a problem of feminist reconstruction of history and of a renaming of the world, but a fundamental change of both scholarship and the academy. Feminist studies are therefore primarily accountable to the women's movement for societal-ecclesial change rather than to the academy. Or in the words of Michelle Russel:

> The question is this: How will you refuse to let the academy separate the dead from the living, and then yourself declare allegiance to life? As teachers, scholars, and students, how available will you make your knowledge to others as tools for their own liberation? This is not a call for mindless activism, but rather for engaged scholarship.[14]

While a critical feminist reconstruction of women's early Christian history is in the interest of all women who are affected by the influence of biblical religion in Western societies, it nevertheless owes its special allegiance to Christian women of the present and of the past. In my opinion, feminist biblical scholarship and historical biblical scholarship share as their common hermeneutical perspective a critical commitment to the Christian community and its traditions. Although historical-critical analysis of the Bible has developed over and against a doctrinal understanding of Scripture and has challenged clerical control of theology, it nevertheless has as its hermeneutical presupposition a theological engagement insofar as it operates theoretically within the boundaries of the canon as well as institutionally within Christian schools of theology. The Bible is not just a document of past history but functions as Scripture in present-day religious communities. Therefore, like women's studies, exegetical-biblical studies are by definition already "engaged." Insofar as biblical studies are canonical studies they are conditioned by and related to their *Sitz im Leben* in the Christian past and present. Like feminist studies, historical-critical interpretations of the Bible cannot abstract from the presuppositions, commitments, beliefs, or cultural and institutional structures influencing the questions they raise and the models they choose for interpreting their data. Historical biblical studies, like historical studies in general, are a selective view of the past whose scope and meaning is limited not only by the extant sources and materials but also by the interests and perspectives of the present.

Similarly feminist theology as a critical theology of liberation[15] has developed over and against symbolic androcentrism and patriarchal domination within biblical religion, while at the same time seeking to recover the biblical heritage of women for the sake of empowering women in the struggle for liberation. Feminist historical analyses, therefore, share both the impetus of historical biblical studies and an explicit commitment to a contemporary group of people, women, who, either religiously or culturally, are impacted by the traditions of the Bible. Critical-historical analysis and a clearly specified commitment serve as the common ground between academic biblical scholarship and a feminist critical theology of liberation. The explorations of this book, therefore, begin with the hope that this common ground might engender a hermeneutical perspective and method for reconstructing early Christian history in such a way that it overcomes the chasm between historical-critical studies and the contemporary church of women.

Feminist analysis and consciousness raising enables one to see the world and human lives, as well as the Bible and tradition, in a different light and with different "glasses." It has as its goal a new feminist engagement and way of life, a process traditionally called conversion. The discussions of the first part of the book seek to provide new lenses that enable one to read the biblical sources in a new feminist light, in order to engage in the struggle for women's liberation inspired by the Christian feminist vision of the discipleship of equals.

NOTES

1. For an extensive discussion of the exegetical literature, see Robert Holst, "The Anointing of Jesus: Another Application of the Form-Critical Method," *JBL* 95 (1976): 435–46.

2. Cf. J. K. Elliott, "The Anointing of Jesus," *Exp Tim* 85 (1974): 105–7.

3. Cf. also Elizabeth E. Platt, "The Ministry of Mary of Bethany," *Theology Today* 34 (1977): 29–39.

4. Judy Chicago, *The Dinner Party: A Symbol of Our Heritage* (New York: Doubleday, 1979), 246–49.

5. *Signs: Journal of Women in Culture and Society,* which was founded in 1975, has regular reviews of scholarship in various areas. Of equal importance are the *Women's Studies International Quarterly and Feminist Studies.* See also Dale Spender, ed., *Men's Studies Modified: The Impact of Feminism on the Academic Disciplines* (Oxford: Pergamon Press, 1981).

6. Moses I. Finley, *Ancient Slavery and Modern Ideology* (New York: Viking Press, 1980), 9f.

7. James M. Robinson and Helmut Koester, *Trajectories through Early Christianity* (Philadelphia: Fortress, 1971), 1f.

8. See the introduction in Simone de Beauvoir, *The Second Sex* (New York: Knopf, 1953), 18ff.

9. Alex Haley, *Roots: The Saga of an American Family* (New York: Doubleday, 1976), 687f.

10. Gustavo Gutiérrez, "Where Hunger Is, God Is Not," *The Witness* (April 1976): 6.

11. Judy Chicago, *The Dinner Party,* 241–51.

12. For a discussion of this shift, cf. Elizabeth Janeway, "Who Is Sylvia? On the Loss of Sexual Paradigms," *Signs* 5 (1980): 573–89.

13. See Thomas S. Kuhn, *The Structure of Scientific Revolutions* (Chicago: University of Chicago Press, 1962); Ian G. Barbour, *Myth Models, and Paradigms* (New York: Harper & Row, 1974).

14. Michelle Russell, "An Open Letter to the Academy," *Quest* 3 (1977): 77f.

15. See my articles "Feminist Theology as a Critical Theology of Liberation," *Theological Studies* 36 (1975): 605–26; "Towards a Liberating and Liberated Theology," *Concilium* 15 (1979): 22–32; "To Comfort or To Challenge: Theological Reflections," in *New Woman, New Church, New Priestly Ministry,* ed. M. Dwyer (Rochester, N.Y.: Women's Ordination Conference, 1980), 43–60.

from "Islam, Women, and Gender Justice"

❧

Asghar Ali Engineer

Asghar Ali Engineer is a prolific Indian Moslem writer and activist for peace and interrelgious understanding. He has received the Government of India's National Communal Harmony Award for his work for promoting communal harmony. Here he challenges conventional understandings of the relation between gender and Islam.

❧

THEORY OF JUSTICE IN ISLAM

Before we critique the existing gender laws it is important to say a few words about the theory of justice in Islam. There is a great deal of emphasis on justice in the Qur'anic teachings. Qur'an uses words like 'adl and qist for emphasizing the concept of justice. According to Imam Raghib Isfahani 'adl in Shari'ah means "equal retaliation" and to substantiate his point he said: "And the recompense of evil is punishment like it. . . ." (Raghib 1971, 676–77; 40:42). But the Qur'an also uses it in a loftier moral sense when it says further in the same verse: ". . . but whoever forgives and amends, his reward is with Allah. He loves not wrong doers." The Qur'an also uses repeatedly the words 'adl and 'ihsan, that is, "justice" and "benevolence" in a moral sense. Thus according to the Qur'an, retaliation for "justice" may be considered necessary but "forgiving" and "benevolence" are higher ideals. Allah enjoins upon all believers to be just and to do good to others (16:90). Thus, according to the Qur'an one must be quite just in trade transactions. One should weigh justly, not letting selfishness interfere (170:35, 260:182, 55:6, etc.).

In fact, economic justice in Islamic law embodies high ideals, ideals that offer moral challenges to many contemporary capitalist practices. The Qur'an strongly condemns accumulation of wealth and its unjustly uneven distribution or its limited circulation among the rich only (see 107:1–7, chap. 104, 9:34, 59:7, etc.). Also, Islamic justice insists on treating one's enemies justly. Animosity with people should not provoke one to be unjust to them. "Be just, it is closest to observance of duty" (5:8).

Similarly, gender justice is also integral to the theory of justice in Islam (2:228, 33:35). Both of these verses leave no doubt that gender justice is highly crucial to Qur'anic teachings. These verses also make it abundantly clear that gender justice cannot be realized without gender equality. "The rights of the wives (with regard to their husbands) are equal to the (husbands') rights with regard to them . . ." (2:228). According to the Qur'an, it's always necessary to favor the less powerful groups of society (and women in a patriarchal social structure also belong in this category). The Qur'an shows its preference for the poor and the disempowered (28:5).

This in short is the rich Qur'anic concept of justice. Thus all gender-based laws evolved by the Muslim jurists must be reviewed today in the light of this theory of justice. This theory is far more important than the interpretations of the Qur'anic verses under the influence of patriarchal values.

ISLAM AND WOMEN

It is widely thought that Islam treats women unfairly and gender justice is not possible within the Islamic law. This assertion is partly true and partly untrue. It is true as far as the existing shari'ah laws are concerned; untrue, as the existing laws were codified during the second and third centuries of Islam when the general view of women's rights was very different from today's perspective. The Qur'anic verses that are quite fundamental to the Islamic law, were interpreted so as to be in conformity with the views about gender rights prevailing at this time.

Thus it will be seen that the most fundamental values in Islam, as expounded by the Qur'an are justice, benevolence, and compassion. The Qur'anic terminology for these values is '*adl, ihsan,* and *rahmah.* The Qur'an places these values in the imperative category. Another Qur'anic verse testifies to this. "And surely Allah enjoins justice and benevolence (to others)" (16:90). Thus it will be seen that justice is very central to the Islamic value system—as central as love to the Christian ethics and Tsedaqah in the Jewish tradition. No legislation in Islam that ignores this value can be valid. The meaning of this for men's obligations to women should be clear.

It is because of this concern for justice that the Qur'an shows deep concern for the weaker sections of society." And We desire to bestow a favour upon those who were deemed weak in the land, and to make them the leaders, and to make them the heirs" (28:5). The Qur'an desires to bestow the mantle of leadership of this earth upon the weak. Islamic jurisprudence has to imbibe this compassionate spirit toward the weaker sections of society. And, again, women certainly belong to this category as far as the patriarchal society is concerned.

SCRIPTURES AND SITUATIONAL CONSTRAINTS

It is important to note that scriptural injunctions are always mediated through the prevailing social ethos. Also, and it is fundamental in the framing of laws based on Scriptures, that Scriptures both reflect the given situation and also transcend it. There cannot be any Scripture—revealed or otherwise—which is unidimensional, that is, merely descriptive, reflecting only the given situation. Scripture is normative. Every Scripture tries to go beyond what is given, pointing to a better, more just society. Of course, it faces stiff opposition from those who lose out if these transcendental and challenging perspectives are spelled out and enforced. The Scriptures condemn prevailing social evils and provide a new vision. Those who benefit from the new vision embrace the new faith. Those who lose privileges oppose it tooth and nail. But, the vested interests and those who want to perpetuate the old order have their own strategies. Soon they find ways and means to hijack the religious tradition to their own benefit. This is done in a number of ways:

1. They capture political power, and religion becomes part of the political establishment and loses its initial revolutionary thrust as it is appropriated by the ruling classes.
2. They convert religion itself into an institutionalized establishment and a power structure develops around it; religion is then used more for the distribution of favors than for spiritual enrichment.
3. Intellectual resources are used to resist the judgments of true justice, and this is done chiefly by interpreting the Scriptures in a way that robs it of its transcendental thrust.

Thus a theology is developed that is supportive of the status quo.

One must distinguish between what the basic scriptural pronouncements are and what the theology is that is woven around it. Scriptural pronouncements are divinely inspired and hence transcendental, and theological formulations are human and hence often contradict divine intentions. Scriptural pronouncements are a source of hope for the weaker and disempowered peoples, whereas theological formulations are weapons in the hands of powerful interests. It is therefore necessary that theological formulations be continuously challenged by scriptural pronouncements. One must strive to build up creative tension between the theological and the scriptural. While Scripture remains immutable with its transcendental spirit, theology must change, facing new challenges and newly emergent situations.

THEOLOGIANS AND OPPOSITION TO CHANGE

Those who oppose any change in theological formulations and in Shari'ah laws are those who would lose their dominant position. This is also true for the priesthood who monopolize theology since religion for them is instrumental in promoting their interests rather than the spiritual source of inner enrichment. The priesthood, while monopolizing theology, projects it as divine and immutable. The run-of-the-mill faithfuls' understanding of religion is mediated through the priesthood and hence they are made to believe that theology as formulated by the priesthood or by their predecessors is divine and hence immutable. Any change will amount to changing the divine will.

IS SHARI'AH IMMUTABLE?

In Islam, it is widely believed that the Shari'ah is divine and hence immutable. Whenever any measures for gender justice are proposed one meets with this stock argument. It is important to note that Shari'ah, though undoubtedly based on the Holy Qur'an, is a human endeavor to understand the divine will. It is an approach to, rather than divine will itself. The priesthood, that is, the community of *'ulama* projects it as a divine end itself and hence refuse to admit any change. "The Shari'ah is divine" has become a commonly accepted position. Thus what was thought of women's rights during the early period of Islamic history has come to be final and immutable. Even to think of changing it, much less actually changing it, is presented as interfering with the divine, and hence is an unpardonable sin.

As just pointed out, there is a big gap between the scriptural, that is, the Qur'anic pronouncements, and Shari'ah formulations. While the Qur'anic pronouncements are purely transcendental in spirit, the Shari'ah formulations have been influenced by various human situations and interests as well as by human thinking on all related issues. Women were in a subordinate position in the patriarchal societies and this relationship came to be reflected in the Shari'ah laws relating to women's rights. The transcendental divine spirit was conveniently ignored, and the prevailing situation was rationalized through contextual Qur'anic pronouncements. As was just pointed out, there is always a creative tension between what is and what ought to be in Scriptures. However, this tension is often resolved in favor of the prevalent rather than the emergent, and the prevalent is eternalized by rationalizing certain divine pronouncements.

ON THE METHODOLOGY OF CREATING ISLAMIC LEGAL STRUCTURE

If we want to effect necessary changes in the Shari'ah laws, it is important to understand the methodology of creating Islamic law. The Islamic legal corpus is known as "Shari'ah." As Shari'ah is, after all, a human approach to divine will as reflected through the Scripture, that is, the holy Qur'an, it is not uniform but has several variants. In Sunni Islam itself there are four different schools of jurisprudence, that is, *Hanafi, Shafi'i, Hanbali,* and *Maliki*. Besides these schools there is what is known as the *Zahiri* school. Also, there are several schools in the Shi'ah Islam as well, the *Ja'fari* or the *Ithna 'Ashari,* the *Isma'ili,* and the *Zaidi* schools.

Sunni Islam bases Shari'ah—besides the Qur'an—on *Sunna* (i.e., the sayings and doings of the Holy Prophet), *qiyas* (analogy) and finally *ijma'* (consensus). However, except for the Qur'an, the remaining three sources, that is, *Sunna, qiyas,* and *ijma'* are controversial. Some *ahadith* (sayings of the Prophet) are accepted by some while they are rejected by others. Some *ahadith* are considered weak (*da'if*), some of doubtful origin, and some appear to be outright forgeries. Also, *qiyas,* analogical reasoning, varies from jurist to jurist. There is controversy about *ijma'* as well. The crucial question is, Whose *ijma'*? Is it a consensus of the jurists and the 'Ulama, or of the entire community? Also, has the determination of *ijma'* ever been possible? Have all 'Ulama, let alone the entire community, ever developed consensus on any issue? There are hardly any instances of this nature in the history of Islamic jurisprudence. Thus it will be seen that except for the Qur'an that is divine (i.e., the belief of all Muslims), the three other fundamental sources, that is, *Sunna, qiyas,* and *ijma'* are human and hence controversial.

It is also important to point out here that there is controversy about the Prophet's pronouncements, that is, the Prophet's *ahadith,* about whether they should be considered as divine or human. The Ahl-e-Hadith (i.e., the followers of *Hadith*) consider *hadith* as divine like the Qur'an, while many others do not give it that status and consider it as human and hence not eternal.

THE SHI'AH JURISPRUDENCE

The Shi'i jurisprudence (Shari'ah) is based on the Qur'an and on the Prophet's sayings as reported by Imams, that is, the male descendants of the Prophet's daughter Hazrat Fatima and her husband 'Ali. The Qur'an as interpreted by these Imams is considered the only right interpretation, while every other interpretation is considered mere conjecture or opinion (*ra'i*). And *tafsir bi'r ra'i* (i.e., Qur'anic interpretation or exegesis through human opinion) is rejected outright in the Shi'a Islam. But there is controversy in the Shi'ah Islam as to who is rightfully appointed Imam. The Ithna 'Asharis ("twelvers"), the Isma'ilis (also referred to as "seveners"), Zaidis, the Qaramitas, and the Alavids, all differ on this issue. All of these sects have Imams of their own and consider others as not rightfully appointed and hence have no legitimacy. Also, at times, the juridical pronouncements of these Imams differ from each other even on matters of principle.

Thus the important conclusion is this: had it been immutable the Shari'ah would not have differed from one school to the other and from sect to sect. The Qur'an, being divine, does not differ and is immutable. It admits of no change. However, its interpretation differs from sect to sect and from one school to the other. Thus the Qur'an is divine and its interpretations are human, and what is human admits of change. The Shari'ah, being based on human interpretations of divine word, can and does admit change.

What was thought to be just in respect to women's rights in medieval ages is no longer so. The idea of justice also changes with changing consciousness; what is just in one age may not necessarily be just in the other. We will throw more light on this aspect a little later. This is in fact a very important aspect as far as the Qur'anic concept of law is concerned.

HADITH AND SHARI'AH

There are two types of controversies about *hadith* and Sunna:

1. Whether *hadith* is divine or human;
2. Whether it is authentic, weak, or forged.

The Qur'an is unanimously accepted as divine and there is no controversy about it. Also, its contents are accepted with unanimity and without any controversy. No one maintains that this or that verse of the Qur'an is inauthentic, or added later, or of doubtful origin. But it is not so as far as *hadith* literature is concerned. There are several *ahadith* that are controversial. Either they are considered of doubtful origin, or weak, or outright forgery. It is said that Imam Abu Hanifa, the founder of the Hanafi School of Law, accepted only seventeen *ahadith* as true and authentic and yet he used many more while giving his juridical opinions.

There are Muslims who maintain that *ahadith* (Prophet's sayings) are divine like the Qur'an. They believe that the Qur'anic verse: "Nor does he speak out of desire. It is naught but revelation that is revealed" (53:34) applies to all of the Prophet's pronouncements, including his *ahadith.* These Muslims believe that *ahadith*, too, are divine and hence above any human controversy. Thus this source of Shari'ah also becomes equally divine for them. However, there is no unanimity about it. Many Muslims do not believe that *hadith* is divine. *Hadith* is not above controversy as to its origin. Imam Bukhari, one of the greatest collectors of *ahadith*, is said to have collected more than six hundred thousand *ahadith* of which he accepted only four thousand and rejected others as of doubtful origin or outright forgeries. This clearly shows how some people with special interests were producing *hadith* literature to serve their own ends. Unfortunately, many of these *ahadith* went into juridical formulations in general, and formulations about women, in particular. These formulations reflect the prejudices and dominant thinking of the time rather than the Qur'anic principles. These formulations, therefore, cannot be treated as immutable.

Also, there is yet another problem about *hadith* literature. And this problem remains, even if *hadith* literature is treated as divine and immutable. The Qur'an, which is unanimously held to be divine by all Muslims, contains many sayings that are directly related to the then prevailing Arab social structure. These pronouncements also reflect social norms or social problems as they existed then. They cannot be of universal application in other societies and cultures; for example, there was a practice called *zihar* among Arabs that is mentioned in the Qur'an (33:4 and 58:2–3). It was a practice among Arabs to declare their wives like their mothers and to abandon them. "Allah has not made for any man two hearts within him; nor has He made your wives whom you desert by *Zihar*, your mothers. . . ." (33:4). Edward William Lane defines *Zihar* in his Arabic-English Lexicon as a husband telling his wife "thou art to me as the back of my mother." "Those of you who put away their wives by calling them their mothers—they are not their mothers. None are their mothers save those who give them birth, and they utter indeed a hateful word and a lie. . . ." (58:2). "And those who put away their wives by calling them their mothers, then go back on that which they said, must free a captive before they touch one another. To this you are exhorted. . . ." (58:3).

From these two verses we come to know that Arabs used to desert their wives, saying they were now like their mothers, and some used to go back on that vow and wanted to touch their wives again. The Qur'an prescribed that they free a captive (i.e., a slave) before breaking their vow. This practice was unique to the Arab society of that time. We do not find such practices in other societies. Also, today there is no institution of slavery. It has already been abolished. If an Arab today pronounces *Zihar* on his wife and wants to take back his vow, there are no slaves available to free. Thus such verses in the Qur'an should be treated as contextual, that is, revealed in the context of that society, and are no more valid because social practices have changed. Similarly, there are several pronouncements about slaves and slavery in the holy Qur'an but they are no longer applicable as the institution itself does not exist anymore. But in Shari'ah, as formulated in the second and third century *Hijrah* (Islamic calendar), these practices prevailed and hence elaborate laws were made by the jurists based on Qur'an or *hadith*. But they are totally irrelevant today. Thus the proposition that Shari'ah laws are immutable is not maintainable.

CATEGORIES OF QUR'ANIC VERSES

The Qur'anic verses thus should be divided into two categories, contextual and normative. The normative pronouncements of the Qur'an are eternal and while rethinking issues in Islamic Shari'ah, particularly pertaining to women's rights, the normative pronouncements will have precedence over the contextual. But during the early centuries contextual often had precedence over normative and it was quite "normal" then. And hence these formulations became widely acceptable in that society. These laws were thought to be normative then and hence struck deep roots in society as well as in the hearts and minds of the people. They came to acquire the status of immutability with the passage of time.

Thus even if *ahadith* is accepted as divine, its contextuality will have to be kept in mind. It is also said, and rightly so, that the Prophet explained the Qur'anic verses through his words and deeds, and who knew the meaning and import of the Qur'anic verses better than the Prophet? Quite true. But the question of contextuality remains. The holy Prophet, while dealing with the given society, could not have gone beyond its context in explaining and practicing the Qur'anic pronouncements. It can best be illustrated with an example of women's status in that society. While explaining the cause of revelation of the Qur'anic verse 4:34, all classical commentators like Tabari and Fakhruddin Razi maintain that the Prophet allowed a woman (daughter of his companion) the right to retaliate against her husband who had unjustly slapped her but, because of the prevailing social ethos, it led to unrest among the men and the Qur'an reversed the Prophet's decision. This once again shows that the question of contextuality is highly relevant in all judicial pronouncements be they those of the Prophet or of other Islamic jurists. There is room for change and growth.

Another example in this respect is that of *milk-e-yamin*, that is, legitimizing sexual relations with a slave girl. There was near unanimity among the ancient Islamic jurists that it was permissible to have sexual relations with slave girls and that the Prophet himself had such relations with a Coptic Christian slave girl. The modernists and some other commentators, of course, challenge this formulation and maintain that the Prophet had married her. But Maulana Maududi, a contemporary Islamic thinker and founder of the Jam'at-e-Islami, maintains in his commentary on the Qur'an (*Tafhim al Qur'an*) that the Prophet had relations with the slave girl without marrying her. Most of the eminent medieval jurists concur with this. But this view that sexual relations with a slave girl is permissible could not be approved by contemporary society. Thus the Prophet's Sunna cannot be seen as acceptable outside of its social context.

SCHOOLS OF LAW IN ISLAM

There were four great jurists in Sunni Islam who founded four different schools of jurisprudence. All four differ from each other on many issues. The modern scholars maintain that one important reason was their differing social situations. Imam Hanbal and Imam Malik lived in Medina and thus were quite close to the social ethos of the society in which the Prophet himself lived. They were closer in their juridical formulations to what the Prophet said and did in that society. Imam Shafi'i and Imam Abu Hanifa, on the other hand, lived in Egypt and Iraq, respectively. There were confluences of many cultures in these countries and thus writers were seen as unorthodox in the method they used to arrive at juridical opinions. While Imam Malik and Hanbal mainly relied on *Hadith*, Imam Sahfi'i and Abu Hanifa used *qiyas* and *ijma'* more liberally, apart from *Hadith*. Thus while the former two Imams' formulations were closer to Arab practices in Mecca and Medina, the latter two Imams' formulations had been largely influenced by other practices. This clearly shows that Shari'ah is influenced by human situations and can incorporate situational changes. The Arab '*adat* (customary law) also became an integral part of the Shari'ah law.

Applying all this to women, it can be seen that the then prevailing opinions about women in Arab society greatly influenced the Shari'ah laws pertaining to women. The Arab '*adat* cannot certainly be considered as divine injunction and hence immutable. In fact, the Arab '*adat* had great relevance as long as Islam was confined to Arab society. But once it spread out to far off areas, the need to incorporate other practices also became equally important. And now the changed consciousness about women's rights can also not be ignored. This is an important conclusion.

PROBLEMS OF HADITH LITERATURE

There is yet another problem about the *hadith* literature that is, as just pointed out, an important ingredient of Shari'ah. The *ahadith* were generally passed on by the Prophet's companions. In this respect even the most authentically reported *ahadith* present different kinds of problems.

First, most of the *ahadith* reported by the companions were not the exact words of the Prophet but the overall meaning of what he said. There are few *ahadith* that can be said to be the exact words of the Prophet. Second, the *hadith* literature also incorporates the reports about what the companions saw the Prophet doing. Thus the prophetic Sunna includes both what the Prophet said as well as reports about what he did in different situations.

Now among the Prophet's companions there were all kinds of people. There were companions who had sharp memories and good comprehension of the problems. There were companions who had very poor understanding of the complex issues, and also there were companions who had poor memories. And there were companions who spent several years with the Prophet and there were companions who spent only a few hours with him, and there were those who saw and heard him from a distance. All that these companions reported having heard from the Prophet became part of *hadith* corpus that then was used for formulating Shari'ah laws.

Not only that. There is yet another problem. The *ahadith* have been reported by people who heard it from the companions of the companions (*tab'i tabi'in*) and from the companions of the companions of the companions of the Prophet. Thus there is a whole chain of narrators known as *rijal* (narrating men or women). The collectors of *ahadith* did try to develop the science of *rijal* (i.e., *'ilm al-rijal*) criteria to judge the honesty and integrity of the narrators. But this criteria judged the honesty and integrity of the narrators rather than his or her comprehension or intelligence. Moreover, there were often missing links. Also there were cases wherein much was not known about one or more of the narrators in the chain. Many narrators were of totally different cultural backgrounds—some narrators being Arabs and others non-Arabs not properly acquainted with Arab affairs. Also, many narrators had their own biases for or against women (also about other matters), and these biases definitely affected their narratives or reports.

It was for this reason that the Prophet had strictly prohibited his followers from compiling his sayings. He knew very well that his sayings may not be reported faithfully to future generations for various reasons. Also, he was fully aware of the fact that future generations would insist on strictly following what reached them as the sayings of Allah's Messenger though they may be facing different circumstances. Even the first caliph Hazrat Abu Bakr did not permit compilation of *ahadith* for similar reasons. Still, people did compile these *ahadith*, though much later. And by the time they were compiled, spurious ones had mixed up with authentic ones.

Thus it will be seen that *hadith* literature, even if entirely authentic, presents several problems. It cannot be considered a highly reliable source of Islamic legislation. But the Islamic *juris corpus* is as much based on the problematic *hadith* literature as on the holy Qur'an. Still, the 'Ulama present it as unquestionably divine and hence immutable. They refuse to admit any change even though sweeping changes are taking place in the social, cultural, economic, and political circumstances. The doctrine of *taqlid* (mechanical imitation) is emphasized by many contemporary jurists in the world of Islam. They maintain that rethinking the formulations of the great Imams is not permissible. In fact, these formulations are treated as divine. Also, most of the 'Ulama do not even permit taking more favorable views of women drawn from other schools of law. They insist that only one school should be followed in its entirety. Some 'Ulama follow such a rigid approach but they are fewer in numbers today. Now, more and more 'Ulama are coming around to permitting this approach that has given some relief to women. The Ottoman rulers had adopted this approach in the nineteenth century, but still it is not widely accepted. The rigid *Taqlid* is the more generally established rule. This is causing a great deal of hardship to Muslim women everywhere.

CONCEPT OF *IJTIHAD*

The holy Prophet had anticipated the problems that would arise in the future. He took care to leave some guidance in this respect. First, he encouraged what is known as *ijtihad* (i.e., exerting oneself to solve newly arising problems if no precise guidance was available in the Qur'an and in the Prophet's Sunnah). The *hadith* regarding Ma'adh bin Jabal is a good example of this. When the Prophet appointed Ma'adh as governor of the Yemen, he asked him how he would govern. "According to the Qur'an," Ma'adh replied. And if it is not in the Qur'an? the Prophet asked him. "According to the Prophet's Sunnah," replied Ma'adh. And if he does not find anything of the sort in the Sunnah? the Prophet inquired. "Then I will exert myself to solve the problem" (*Ana ajtahedo*). The Prophet patted his back in approval. Also, the Prophet is reported to have said that even if one makes a mistake in doing *ijtihad* he or she will earn one merit and if one does not err he or she will earn two merits. The Prophet did this to encourage Muslims to solve problems that were likely to arise in the future. This would be very helpful in treating the status of women today.

Many modern scholars argue that we should use *ijtihad* to solve new problems and issues, including women's issues. However, the orthodox 'Ulama argue that the gates of *ijtihad* were closed long ago and that now there are no qualified persons to do *ijtihad*. They feel that the great Imams and some of their followers had the requisite qualifications and none today has such impressive merits. Some 'Ulama do feel the need for *ijtihad* but they too stop short of resorting to it for fear of the consequences. Some who did faced the wrath of the fellow jurists and were even ostracized. The debate is raging in the Islamic world for and against *ijtihad*. And when it comes to women's issues and rights, the resistance to change and to rethinking is much greater in the male-dominated Islamic world.

Dr. Muhammad Iqbal, a noted Urdu poet and thinker from India (d. 1938), was greatly in favor of *ijtihad*. He wrote in his *Reconstruction of Religious Thought in Islam*: "The ultimate spiritual basis of all life, as conceived by Islam, is eternal and reveals itself in variety and change. A society based on such a conception of reality must reconcile, in its life, the categories of permanence and change. But eternal principles when they are understood to exclude all possibilities of change which, according to the Qur'an, is one of the greatest 'signs' of God, tend to immobilize what is essentially mobile in its nature" (Iqbal n.d., 147–48).

Iqbal also stated very boldly: "The only alternative open to us, then, is to tear off from Islam the hard crust which has immobilized an essentially dynamic outlook on life, and to rediscover the original verities of freedom, equality, and solidarity with a view to rebuild our moral, social and political ideas out of their original simplicity and universality" (156). Iqbal thus maintains that *ijtihad* is necessary to rebuild the law of Shari'ah in the light of modern insights and experience in the realm of morality.

My own position is that *ijtihad* is even more necessary today in respect to Shari'ah laws pertaining to women. It is highly regrettable that the Shari'ah laws are neglected in many other respects (e.g., property and contract laws, criminal laws, financial transactions) but when it comes to women's issues, these laws are strictly applied. In several Muslim majority and minority countries, modern secular laws are applied in respect to all other things except laws pertaining to marriage, divorce, maintenance, and inheritance, in the sphere of what is called "personal law." The greatest resistance, in the name of Shari'ah, is manifested by men when it comes to according better status to women. In this respect the Shari'ah becomes sacred and immutable and arouses great passions. The Islamic world, if it will ever come to understand the dynamic spirit of Qur'an, and to enact it in real life, will have to enact changes in the Shari'ah laws and accord women an equal status. In fact, the time has come to put the grand Qur'anic vision of sexual equality in practice.

BASIC ISLAMIC TEACHINGS

Permit me here to set out certain values that are fundamental to the Islamic teachings. Any legislation that ignores these fundamental values would be anything but Islamic. It is necessary to understand that the classical jurists did not ignore these fundamental values, but the application of these values was constrained by the social ethos of the age.

It is important to note that values like justice and compassion cannot be applied abstractly and independently. In the medieval period the very understanding of the concept of justice was very different from what it is today. Our era is a democratic era and justice in our era is not a condition of society if equality of all humans irrespective of sex, race, and creed, is not ensured. Discrimination between one and another human being on any ground, including the sexual one, will be perceived as injustice. But in medieval ages these discriminations were thought to be quite natural and nonviolative of the concept of justice. Even slavery was thought to be natural and in keeping with the principles of justice. In fact, if a slave ran away from the master it was thought to be an unjust act. Today, slavery, bonded labor, and child labor are considered as grossly violative of justice. Thus the concept of justice varies greatly in a democratic era from that of a feudal one. And yet justice as a value remains important in both ages. The expression of the concept of justice in a particular era will vary but justice as the ideal of giving to each person what is his or her due perdures. However, religious traditions, including those of Islam, may give permanent status to expressions of justice from the past, expressions that do not do justice to our understanding of what justice entails in our time. What was thought to be just during the classical period of Islam is thought to be just even today. Because of this, some of the orthodox think the contemporary expression of the notion of justice is violative of divine will. It is this attitude that impedes a change in Islamic legislation so as to accord women equality with men.

GENDER JUSTICE IN THE QUR'AN

One finds in the Qur'an full support for sexual equality in several verses. The Qur'an was certainly mindful of what was just in the era when it was revealed and what ought to be just in the transcendental sense. When the Prophet permitted a Muslim wife retaliation against her husband as a measure of justice, the Qur'an overruled him and permitted a measure of conditional male domination (see 4:34). It would have been thought to be unjust if the Qur'an had permitted the wife to retaliate against her husband; it would not have found acceptability in that society.

However, the Qur'an also did not intend to eternalize the then acceptable notion of justice. The dynamics of "is" and "ought" or interaction between history and eternity informs the whole spirit of the Qur'an. Unfortunately, the orthodox miss this very spirit while reading the Qur'an from their own perspective. The Qur'an is much more fundamental in this respect as it clearly accords women equality with men in all respects (33:35). Another verse is informed by the spirit of that era (4:34); another verse deals with the eternal dimension (33:34). The orthodox, however, do not wish to go beyond the divine injunction (4:34). They have frozen their minds in the classical age of Islam. What was temporal has become permanent for them, and what is permanent is just brushed aside as of no consequence.

The Qur'an must be reread and reinterpreted in today's context as the classical jurists read and interpreted it in their own context. Otherwise no reformation is possible. The real intention of the Qur'an—that of sexual equality—comes through several verses. Those verses need to be reemphasized. . . . The rights of the wives (with regard to their husbands) are equal to (husbands') rights with regard to them . . . (2:228) is quite definitive in this respect. It hardly needs any comment. Maulana Muhammad Ali, a noted Pakistani commentator, says of this verse that it must have caused a stir in a society that never recognized any rights for women. He notes that this was a truly revolutionary change since, to that point, Arabs had regarded women as chattel. This Qur'anic verse gave women a position equal to that of men. This change not only affected Arabia but the whole world since the equality of women with men had never been recognized by any nation or reformer. A woman could no longer be discarded by her husband, and she could now claim equality and even demand a divorce (Muhammad Ali 1973, 97).

However, much of this spirit of justice and equality was lost when the Islamic doctors legislated under the influence of their own social ethos. The Qur'anic categorical imperatives were ignored, as pointed out before, in favor of those verses that were actually concessions to the mores of that age. There are many instances of this. Polygamy is an example. First, it was seen as a protective measure in some circumstances (there were large numbers of war widows and orphans to be taken care of as many men perished fighting in the battle of Uhud) and there was great emphasis on justice to all the wives (their number not to exceed four). It was a great advance over the pre-Islamic practice of marrying an unlimited number of women without any obligation toward the wives. Second, the verse on polygamy (4:3) is preceded by a verse that emphasizes sexual equality in these words: ". . . the Lord Who created you from a single being (*min nafsin wahidatin*) and created its mate of the same (kind) and spread from these two many men and women . . ." (4:1). There is a reference to justice for orphans and widows (4:2). Polygamy is permitted provided one marries widows and orphans (and not just any woman). And when one was permitted to marry more than one woman, there had to be true justice for all the wives. If one could not meet the demands of justice for all wives, then one must marry only one. No one before had insisted on such moral conditionalities regarding a plurality of wives. Third, and more importantly yet, another verse states that even if you desire to do justice to all your wives, you cannot do it (4:129). The verse says that you cannot do justice between or among the wives. There will be disinclination toward one and a preference for the other, leaving the first in suspense. If two of these verses (4:3 and 4:129) are read together, the implications are clear: *polygamy is as good as not permissible*. But the jurists, in order to avoid the implications of reading the two verses together invented various explanations and resorted to *hadith* to keep the possibility of polygamy open. And, much worse, in practicing it, the claims of justice toward the wives were hardly enforced. In today's conditions, polygamy should be done away with in order to implement the Qur'anic conditions required by justice. Abolition of polygamy will serve the end of justice far better than its practice today. The various arguments (men are more sexual, or there are more women than men and so we should permit polygamous marriages to avoid immoral relations, etc.) are all attempts at human rationalization rather than expressions of divine intention. These arguments do not hold much water as there may be an excess of women over men in one country and an excess of men over women in another. And prostitution and immoral sex thrived even when men could marry any number of wives and also keep slave girls without limit.

RIGHTS OF WOMEN IN ISLAM

Normatively speaking, the Qur'an concedes all rights to women that were available earlier only to men. They could exercise their rights to divorce their husbands as men could divorce them at will. The Prophet permitted a woman called Jamila to divorce her husband—against his will and without consulting him—just because she did not approve of his looks! While a woman was permitted to liberate herself from an unsatisfactory marriage by suitable compensation to her husband (i.e., returning the dower amount; 2:229), she had the right to appoint an arbiter of her own to settle the marital dispute or agree to divorce (4:35). Also, the Qur'an requires men to keep their wives in a goodly manner and to leave them, if it is necessary, in a benevolent manner. And another verse lays down the law that women could not be inherited or taken as wives against their will (4:19). Men are also exhorted in this verse not to take a portion of what they have given to their wives and to treat them kindly. It was also emphasized that believing men and women are each others' friends, they enjoin good and forbid evil (9:71). Thus both enjoy equal obligations. From this verse, jurists like Abu Hanifa have concluded that a woman can become *Qadi*, that is, a judge, as it is also her obligation to enjoin good and forbid evil.

It is argued that a daughter inherits only half that of a son and hence this shows that man is superior (4:11). Some modern commentators also argue on the basis of this verse that this shows injustice to a daughter as she has been given half that of the son and hence it is bias against the female sex. Neither interpretation is correct. What can be said is that this verse was a cautious reform in favor of daughters. In pre-Islamic society daughters did not inherit at all, and now they were given the right to inherit half that of a son. From another perspective it could be argued that it was not bias against the daughter to be given only half that of the son because daughters were duly compensated by *mehr* (dower amount at the time of marriage) whereas sons had to lose out by paying dowers to their wives. Also, they argue, wives do not have to spend anything by way of maintenance as it is enjoined upon the husbands to maintain their wives. Also, a woman inherited as both a wife and a mother. Moreover, she did not contribute to family wealth in those days by way of earning but now she does and her portion could be increased in view of the changed conditions. Thus, the Qur'an properly understood has done no injustice to her even in matters of inheritance.

Another question is of *hijab* (veil). *There is no injunction in the Qur'an that women should veil their faces.* It only lays down the law that women should not display their adornment and fineries publicly and that they should cover their breasts (tribal women in those days used to leave their breasts uncovered) and that they should not cover their ankles with ornate anklets in public so as to draw attention to their adornments. In these verses both men and women have been asked to lower their gaze (24:31 and 4:30–31) and to restrain their sexual passions. As for what constitutes adornment and what should and should not be displayed, there are sharp differences of opinion. These differences are human and every commentator has his views. But Abi Ja'far Muhammad bin Jami'-al-Bayan Tabari, the noted classical commentator, has summarized the views of many eminent jurists in his *Jami'-al-Bayan*. According to Tabari adornment means:

1. adornment of dress or the clothes that a woman wears—in other words, she is not required to cover the clothes she wears;
2. adornment which the woman is not required to cover, such as collyria, rings, bracelets, and her face.

This is more lenient than the veiling regulations in some Muslim countries.

CULTURE AND MODE OF DRESSING

What to cover and what to reveal and what to wear is highly culture-sensitive and culturally conditioned. There can be no universal norm in this respect. The mode of dressing that is quite acceptable in the West may be rejected by the people of the East. And what is considered a sexually exciting mode of dressing in one society may not be so in another society. Even in Islamic countries, mode of dressing (for women) varies greatly. What is acceptable to Indonesian or Thai Muslims by way of dressing for women may be scandalous for Arabs. Dress and sexual stimulation are certainly culturally conditioned.

The opinions of theologians have varied over the ages. Today the sensibilities in this respect are very different and the scope of the exception can be made much wider, subject to—and that is the intention behind it—restraint of sexual passion and protection of one's chastity. To prevent extramarital sex is the responsibility of both men and women and not of women alone, as per the Qur'an. Also, both should avoid wearing sexually stimulating dress. They should wear dignified dress. Covering of the face by women is not required in the Qur'an at all. It was a cultural practice of some post-Islamic societies. The Qur'an also does not require women to be confined to their homes. On the contrary, they could earn and what they earned was theirs alone (4:32); thus women can benefit from what they earn. The cultural practices like confining women to home were sought to be legitimized later by inventing suitable *ahadith* or by farfetched interpretations of the Qur'an.

CONCLUSION

In conclusion, it should be said that if one goes by those verses of the Qur'an that belong to the normative category or that are of the nature of laying down principles and basic values, *men and women should enjoy equal rights in every respect*. It would be necessary to reread and reinterpret many verses that were used for centuries to subjugate women in Muslim societies. This subjugation was more cultural and patriarchal than genuinely Islamic or Qur'anic. The whole *corpus juris* of Islam relating to women needs to be seriously rethought on the basis of the Qur'an and understood in the light of the powerful Qur'anic sense of compassionate justice. When this is done, the genuine beauty at the heart of Islam would be more visible to all.

REFERENCES

al-Tabari, Abi Ja'far Muhammad bin Jarir. 1988. *Jami'-al-Bayan 'An Ta'wil Aya al-Qur'an*, Beirut, Lebanon: Dar al-Fikr.

Holy Qur'an. 1973. Trans. by Maulana Muhammad Ali. Lahore, Pakistan.

Iqbal Muhammad. *Reconstruction of Religious Thought in Islam.* Lahore, Pakistan.

Isfahani, Imam Raghib. 1971. *Mufradat al-Qur'an.* Lahore, Pakistan: Ahl-e-Hadith Academy.

The Message of the Qur'an. 1980. Trans. by Muhammad Asad. Gibraltar: Dar Al-Andalus.

"The Feminine Critique"

❧

Fernando Pagés Ruiz

Fernando Pagés Ruiz is a health and fitness writer and yoga student in Lincoln, Nebraska. His interview with two leading yoga teachers explores the gender dimensions of this ancient spiritual and meditative practice.

❧

By tradition, only the males of India's upper castes could study the sacred texts. These were written expressly for Brahmins and kings, whose duty required they learn scripture and practice yoga. A woman's duty, regardless of caste, was to tend to her family. Nowadays, however, things have changed, and Western women have embraced the sacred traditions of India. How can modern, liberated yoginis relate to the obvious male slant in yogic classics like the *Bhagavad Gita*, which unfolds as a battlefield dialogue between the warrior-prince Arjuna and Lord Krishna? To find out, we asked Esther Myers and Nischala Joy Devi how they deal with sexism in yoga scripture.

Esther Myers holds a B.A. in philosophy from the University of Toronto. She studied Iyengar Yoga and worked closely with teacher Vanda Scaravelli. The author of *Yoga and You* (Shambhala Publications, 1997), Myers leads yoga workshops internationally and recently released the video *Gentle Yoga for Breast Cancer Survivors* (reviewed in "Mixed Media," Jan/Feb '02).

Nischala Joy Devi, best known for developing the yoga portion of Dean Ornish's Program for Reversing Heart Disease, lived almost eighteen years as a traditional *sannyasin* (renunciate). Cofounder of Commonweal Cancer Self-Help Program, she now teaches and directs Yoga of the Heart, a training program for yoga teachers and health-care professionals working with cardiac and cancer patients, and is the author of *The Healing Path of Yoga* (Three Rivers Press, 2000).

Yoga Journal:	Can an ancient scripture like the *Bhagavad Gita*, written by and for men, provide a universal message that includes modern women?
Nischala Joy Devi:	The *Gita* did not speak to women directly because women weren't allowed to read it. Great wisdom abounds in the story, but when a woman keeps hearing the word "he," it becomes very difficult to swim through the metaphors and find it.
Esther Myers:	We need our own expression of what yoga means to us today more than we need to look backward. The *Gita* offers an extremely male, militaristic, and sexist approach, while the majority of those practicing yoga in North America are women.

YJ: Is it just the pronoun "he" that causes trouble?

NJD: Changing the words would be a good start. But the problem runs deeper. In the first chapter, Arjuna clearly doesn't want to fight his kin. These are the people he loves and respects. Yet Krishna tells him to repress his feelings and charge. The message is very masculine. A woman approaches her feelings in a different way: not as an obstacle but as a guiding force to honor just as deeply as her social obligations.

EM: While most of us interpret the *Gita*'s central metaphor as an internal struggle and not a "real" war, I'm not sure I want to use war, in any form, as a metaphor for spiritual practice. A metaphor colors your perspective. War has become a way of solving problems: There's a war on cancer, a war on drugs, a war on illiteracy, and a war on terrorism. The way war permeates our culture shuts out other kinds of solutions. I prefer the language of nurturing and compassion. It's the search for well-being that brings people to yoga class, not combat.

NJD: The Taliban considered September 11 a righteous attack, which, in a sense, paraphrases Krishna's message to Arjuna. At a certain point we have to question whether it really helps to approach a spiritual practice with the idea of conquest. Even if we set out to conquer our own mind, shouldn't we try becoming friends first?

YJ: Many interpret the *Gita*'s message as suggesting a way to fulfill worldly obligations while keeping a spiritual outlook. Doesn't this relate to modern women engaged in politics and the workplace?

NJD: Many women have embraced masculine principles to get ahead. I'm hoping we can begin to also honor the feminine principles and still get ahead.

EM: For me, yoga practice represents a time to say: I don't have to override my emotions or my body's needs; I don't have to take on a role and maintain it because it's my "duty." Women are already conditioned to disregard their own needs and not value themselves. Of course, the *Gita*'s message of karma yoga and selfless service is hard to argue with, but if you consider a woman's reality, many of us still need to learn how to take care of ourselves. That's why I cringe when I hear talk of denying the ego. It took me a long time to build a healthy one, and now I'm in much better shape to be kind to myself and to others.

YJ: Does sexism go beyond Hindu scriptures and affect asana practice?

EM: I have had to acknowledge that my own practice was driven and judgmental. These attitudes are very patriarchal, and the realization of it created a paradox in my career. Working with Vanda Scaravelli, I adopted a more feminine style of yoga—a more expressive, fluid, and sensual approach, which offers a change in texture that speaks to a feminine power. I now see spiritual practice as a form of playful exploration, not conquest. I love the notion of meditation as pure pleasure, not pain.

NJD: The most basic precept of yoga is *ahimsa*, which is nonharming. Somehow, this principle was overturned, and suffering became more important than compassion. Perhaps male pride got involved—"I can do this even if it hurts." Some teachers emphasized this commando attitude: If your back hurts, too bad; if you're cold, too bad. I know this "no pain, no gain" approach well because I spent eighteen years in the monastery, and discipline was emphasized. Eventually, though, I realized suffering was not the point. The world is suffering enough, so why reproduce this in your yoga practice?

EM: In the past few years, I've finally given myself permission to be as restless as I feel in my meditation practice. Every time I feel like fidgeting, I fidget. Now, when I'm sitting still and quiet, it's because I'm actually feeling quiet—not because I am determined not to move.

NJD: I have a friend who went to study at a Zen monastery. After a time, she returned and I asked her, "Why did you come back?" She replied, "Most of the disciplines they taught were made for the male ego, and I don't have one." It's not that women can't have a masculine-type ego; they can. It's just that in a lot of the yoga I see there's an attitude of conquest. While there's nothing inherently wrong with this attitude, you should understand that all physical progress is temporary. The body gets ill, it gets old, and one day you may not be able to bend at all. Will you feel like a failure then? Your spiritual practice has to go deeper. If your model is physical perfection, you'll lose. Whereas, if you focus on how you feel, yoga breeds compassion instead of competition.

YJ: How would you reform yoga on a feminine model?

EM: By giving validation to our own stories and our own experiences. Women need to be validated in their knowledge and learn to trust and give voice to that unique understanding. The very first verse of the *Yoga Sutra* reads something like, "This is the authoritative teaching of yoga." Yet my and other women's experiences do not correlate with Patanjali's.

NJD: I taught the *Sutra* literally for years, and I could see the bewilderment in my student's faces—especially the women. Slowly I began to interject teachings that sprang from my heart and my own understanding. I became bold enough to change things that supposedly should not change. A person named Patanjali spoke to a particular group of people at a given time. As the teachers of our time, we address a particular group too. I hope we can bring yoga to life in a contemporary way that our students can relate to. Yoga represents much more than "control of the movements of the mind." It goes through the heart too.

YJ: What about karma yoga and bhakti yoga—don't these speak to the heart?

EM: Values like selfless service and surrender are a counterbalance to the highly empowered position of the typical Indian male. For contemporary women, it seems the more important values are relatedness, interconnectedness, support, and integration.

NJD: Most of us practice bhakti and karma yoga because we're devoted to our families. But there's a difference between the masculine concept of work as a daily battle and the mothering attitude of nurturing life day by day.

YJ: If Arjuna had been a woman, what would Krishna have said to her?

EM: "Trust your own experience. Trust your own values and your own needs." Arjuna still might have come to the realization that, yes, she does need to fight this battle. But then again, maybe not.

NJD: First, I would cast Devi, not Krishna, as the deity. The Goddess would tell Arjuna to wait. Waiting is a very feminine quality. In our society, we're told the opposite: "Don't just stand there, *do* something!" While waiting, you can listen to the voice in your heart. It's not that Arjuna should stop thinking and acting, but rather that she should lead her thoughts and actions by means of a loving heart. My version of the story would not unfold on a battlefield, but rather in a fertile field, the field of love and growth.

"A Theology of Pro-Choice: A Feminist Perspective on Abortion"

Beverly W. Harrison

Beverly W. Harrison is professor of Christian Ethics at Union Theological Seminary. She has been a leading feminist theologian for decades and has written *Our Right to Choose* and *Making the Connections*. This essay confronts the complex and difficult issue of abortion, an issue on which even those who agree with much of the progressive political agenda can disagree.

Much discussion of abortion betrays the heavy hand of misogyny, or the hatred of women. We all have a responsibility to recognize this bias, sometimes subtle, when ancient negative attitudes toward women intrude into the abortion debate. It is morally incumbent upon us to convert the Christian position to a teaching more respectful of women's history and experience.

My professional peers who are my opponents on this question feel that they own the Christian tradition in this matter and recognize no need to rethink their positions in the light of this claim. As a feminist, I cannot sit in silence when women's right to determine how procreative power is to be used is under challenge. That right is being withdrawn by the State even before its moral basis has been fully elaborated. Those who deny that women deserve to control procreative power claim the right to do so out of "moral sensibility," in the name of the "sanctity of human life." We have a long way to go before the sanctity of human life will include genuine regard and concern for every female already born, and no social policy which obscures that fact deserves to be called "moral."

I believe the human wisdom which informs our ethics about abortion comes from what earlier Catholic moral theologians meant by "natural law" more than from quoting the Bible alone. Unfortunately, however, natural law reflection in a Roman Catholic context has been every bit as awful as Protestant biblicism on any subject that involves human sexuality, including discussion of women's "nature" and women's "divine vocation" in relation to procreative power.

Protestants who oppose procreative choice either tend to follow Roman Catholic moral theology or ground their positions in Biblicist anti-intellectualism, claiming that "God's word" requires no justification other than their claim that it (God's word) says what it says. Against such irrationalism, no rational objections have a chance. If Protestant fundamentalists do give reasons why they believe that abortion is evil, they too revert to traditional natural law assumptions about women, sex, and procreation. Therefore, it is against the claims of traditional Catholic natural law thinking on the subject of sexuality, procreation, and women's power of rational choice that objection must be registered.

Any treatment of a moral problem is inadequate if it fails to question the morality of the act in a way which represents the concrete experience of the agent who faces a decision with respect to that act. Misogyny in Christian discussions of abortion is evidenced in that the decision is never treated as an integral part of the female agent's life process. Abortion is treated as an abstractable act, rather than as what it always is—a possible way to deal with a pregnancy.

Those who uphold the immorality of abortion are wise to obscure the fact that it is a fully living human female who is the moral agent in the decision. In the case of pregnancy, the woman's life is deeply, irrevocably affected.

Where the question of abortion might arise, a woman finds herself facing an *unwanted* pregnancy. Consider the actual circumstances which may precipitate this. One is the situation in which a woman did not intend to be sexually active or did not enter into the act voluntarily. Since women are frequently victims of sexual violence, numerous cases of this type arise because of rape, incest, or forced marital coitus. Many morally sensitive opponents of abortion will concede that in such cases it may be morally justifiable. I would insist that in such cases it is a moral good, because it is not rational to treat a newly fertilized ovum as though it had the same value as the existent, pregnant, female person, and because it is morally wrong to make the victim of sexual violence suffer the further agonies of unwanted pregnancy.

Another, more frequent case results when a woman—or usually a young girl—participates in heterosexual activity without clear knowledge of how pregnancy occurs and without intention to conceive. A girl who became pregnant in this manner would, by traditional natural law morality, be held to be in a state of "invincible ignorance" and therefore not morally culpable. I once met a scholarly Roman Catholic nun who argued, quite seriously, that her church should not consider the abortions of young Catholic girls as morally culpable since the church was "overprotective" of them, which prevented them from understanding procreation and the sexual pressures which contemporary society puts on girls.

A related type of pregnancy occurs when a woman runs risks by not using contraceptives, perhaps because taking precautions is not "ladylike" or requires her to be "unspontaneous" about sex. However, when pregnancies occur because women are skirting the edges of knowledge and running risks, is enforced motherhood a desirable solution? Such pregnancies could be minimized by eradicating childish myths, embedded in natural law teaching, about female sexuality.

In likelihood, the largest number of abortions arise because mature women who are sexually active with men and who understand the consequences experience contraceptive failure. Schizophrenia in this area is exhibited in that many who believe that women have more responsibility than men to practice contraception, and that family planning is a moral good, rule out abortion altogether. Such a split consciousness ignores the fact that there is no inexorable biological line between prevention of conception and abortion. More important, this ignores genuine risks involved in female contraceptive methods. The reason we do not have more concern for finding safer contraceptive methods for men and women is that matters relating to women's health and well-being are *never* urgent in this society. Moreover, many failures are due to the irresponsibility of the producers of contraceptives rather than to "bad luck." Given these facts, should a woman who actively attempts to avoid pregnancy be punished for contraceptive failure when it occurs?

THEOLOGICAL CONTEXT

In the history of Christian theology, the central metaphor for understanding life, including human life, is as a gift of God. Creation itself is seen primarily under this metaphor. In this context, it follows that procreation itself takes on special meaning when expressed within a patriarchal society in which it is the male's power which is enhanced by this "divine gift."

Throughout history, women's power of procreation stands in definite tension with male control. In fact, ancient historical evidence suggests that what we call patriarchy derives from the need of men, and later of male-dominated political institutions such as tribes and states, to control women's procreative power. We must assume, then, that many of the efforts at social control—including church teaching on contraception and abortion—were part of an overall system. The perpetuation of patriarchal control itself depended on wresting the power of procreation from women. Another critical point is that in the last four centuries the entire Christian story has had to undergo dramatic accommodations to new and emergent world conditions grounded in the scientific revolution. As the older theological metaphors for creation encountered a new human self-understanding, Christian theology had either to incorporate this new reality in its story or to become obscurantist.

The range of human freedom to shape and enhance creation is now celebrated theologically up to the point of changes in sexuality or ways of seeing women's nature. Around these issues a barrier has been drawn which declares: *No Freedom Here!* The only difference between mainline Protestant and Catholic theologians is on the question of contraception. That Protestant male clergy are usually married does have a positive experiential effect on their dealing with this issue; generally they have accepted the moral appropriateness of contraception. Most Protestants and nearly all Catholics, however, draw back from recognizing abortion as a defensible exercise of human freedom or self-determination.

The problem, then, is that Christian theology everywhere else celebrates the power of human freedom to shape and determine the quality of human life, except when the issue of abortion arises. The power of *man* to shape creation radically is never rejected. When one stops to consider the awesome power over nature which males take for granted and celebrate, including the power to alter the conditions of human life in myriad ways, the suspicion dawns that the near hysteria that prevails about the immorality of women's right to choose abortion derives its force from misogyny rather than from any passion for the sacredness of human life. The refusal of male theologians to incorporate the full range of human power to shape creation into their theological worldview when that power relates to the quality of women's lives and women's freedom and women's role as full moral agents is an index of the continuing misogyny in Christian tradition.

By contrast, a feminist theological approach recognizes that nothing is more urgent, in light of the changing circumstances of human beings on Planet Earth, than to recognize that the entire natural-historical context of human procreative power has shifted. We desperately need a "desacralization" of our biological power to reproduce, and at the same time, a real concern for human dignity and the social conditions for personhood and the values of human relationship. And note that "desacralization" does not mean complete devaluation of the worth of procreation. It means that we must shift away from the notion that the central metaphors for divine blessing are expressed at the biological level to the recognition that social values bear the image of what is most holy. The best statement I know on this point comes from a

Roman Catholic feminist who is also a distinguished sociologist of religion, Marie Augusta Neal:

> As long as the central human need called for was continued motivation to propagate the race, it was essential that religious symbols idealize that process above all others. Given the vicissitudes of life in a hostile environment, women had to be encouraged to bear children and men to support them; child-bearing was central to the struggle for existence. Today, however, the size of the base population, together with knowledge already accumulated about artificial insemination, sperm banking, cloning, make more certain a peopled world.
>
> The more serious human problems now are who will live, who will die and who will decide.

ALTERNATIVE READING OF HISTORY

Between persons who oppose all abortions on moral grounds and those who believe that abortion is sometimes or frequently morally justifiable, *there is no difference of moral principle*. Pro-choice advocates and antiabortion advocates share the ethical principle of respect for human life, which is probably why the debate is so acrimonious. I have already indicated that one major source of disagreement is the way in which the theological story is appropriated in relation to the changing circumstances of history. In addition, we should recognize that whenever strong moral disagreement is encountered, we simultaneously confront a different reading of history. The way we interpret the past is already laden with a sense of what the "moral problem" is.

For example, professional male Christian ethicists tend to assume that the history of the morality of abortion can best be traced by studying the teaching of the now best-remembered theologians. Looking at the matter this way, one can find plenty of proof-texts to show that *some* of the "church fathers" (as we call them) condemned abortion and some even equated abortion with either homicide or murder. However, when a "leading" churchman equated abortion with homicide or murder, he also *and simultaneously* equated *contraception* with homicide or murder as well. This reflects the then almost hysterical antisexual bias of the Christian tradition.

However, this antisexual tradition is *not* universal, even among theologians and canon lawyers. On the subject of sexuality and its abuse, many well-known theologians had nothing to say and abortion was not even mentioned. An important, untold chapter in Christian history is the great struggle that took place in what we call the medieval period, when clerical celibacy came to be *imposed*, and the rules of sexual behavior rigidified.

By contrast, my thesis is that there is a relative disinterest in the question of abortion overall in Christian history. Occasionally, Christian theologians picked up the issue, *especially when those theologians were "state-related theologians,"* i.e., articulating policy not only for the church but for the political authority. Demographer Jean Meyer, himself a Catholic, insists that the Christian tradition took over "expansion by population growth" from the Roman Empire. Christians only opposed abortion strongly when Christianity was closely identified with the state or when the theologians repudiated sexuality except in the reluctant service of procreation.

The "Holy Crusade" quality of present teaching on abortion is quite new and related to cultural shifts which are requiring the Christian tradition to choose sides in ideological struggle and to rethink its entire attitude to women and sexuality. No Protestant clergy gave early support for proposed nineteenth-century laws banning abortion in the United States. It is my impression that Protestant clergy, usually married and often poor, were aware that romanticizing "nature's bounty" with respect to procreation resulted in a great deal of human suffering. The

Protestant clergy who finally did join the antiabortion crusade in the nineteenth century were racist, classist, white clergy, who feared that America's strength was being threatened because white, middle-class, "respectable" women had a lower birthrate than black and ethnic women. Sound familiar?

One other point must be stressed. Until the late nineteenth century, the natural law tradition, and biblicism following it, always tended to define the act of abortion as interruption of pregnancy after ensoulment, or the coming of the breath of God to the fetus. The point at which ensoulment was said to take place varied, but most typically it was at quickening. Quickening was important because knowledge about embryology was terribly primitive until the last half century. As a result, where abortion was condemned, it was understood to refer to the termination of pregnancy well into the process of that pregnancy after ensoulment. Until the late nineteenth century, then, abortion in ecclesiastical teaching applied only to termination of prenatal life in more advanced stages of pregnancy.

Another distortion in the male-generated history of this issue derives from failure to note that, until the development of safe, surgical, elective abortion, the "act of abortion" frequently referred to something done to the woman, with or without her consent (see Exodus 22), as an act of violence. Now, in recent discussion, it is the woman who does the "wrongful" act. When "to do an abortion" meant terminating a pregnancy against the woman's wishes, grounds for moral objections were clear.

Furthermore, whether the act was done with or without the woman's consent, until recent decades abortion always endangered the woman as much as it did the prenatal life in her womb. No one has a right to discuss the morality of abortion today without recognizing that one of the traditional moral reasons for objection to abortion was concern for women's well-being.

Beyond all this, however, the deepest moral flaw in the pro-life position's historical view is that none of its proponents have attempted to reconstruct the all but desperate struggle by sexually active women to gain some proximate control over nature's profligacy in conception. Under the most adverse conditions, women have had to try to control their fertility—everywhere, always. Even when women are infertile, their relationship to procreation irrevocably marks and shapes their lives. Those who have sought to avoid sexual contacts with males, through celibacy or through lesbian love, have been potential, even probable, victims of male sexual violence or have had to bear heavy social stigma for refusing the centrality of dependence on men and of procreation in their lives. Women's lack of social power, in all recorded history, has made this struggle to control procreation a life-bending, often life-destroying one.

So women have had to do whatever they could to avoid too numerous pregnancies. In most societies and cultures, procreation has been in the hands of women's culture. Some primitive birth control techniques have proven rather effective. Increasingly, anthropologists are gaining hints of how procreative control occurred in some premodern societies. A woman often has chosen to risk her life in order not to have that extra child that would destroy the family's ability to cope or that would bring about a crisis unmanageable within her life.

We have to concede that modern medicine, for all *its* misogyny, has replaced some rather ghastly practices still widely used where surgical abortion is unavailable. In the light of these gains, more privileged Western women must not lose the ability to imagine the real-life pressures which lead women in other cultures to submit to ground-glass douches, reeds inserted in the uterus, etc., to induce labor. The radical nature of methods women resort to bespeaks the desperation involved in unwanted pregnancy.

Nor should we suppress the fact that a major means of birth control now is, as it was in earlier times, *infanticide*. And let no one imagine that women made decisions to expose or kill newborn infants casually. Women understand what many men cannot seem to grasp—that the birth of a child requires that some person must be prepared to care, without interruption, for that infant, to provide material resources and energy-draining amounts of time and attention. It seems to me that men, especially celibate men, romanticize the total and uncompromising dependency of the newly born infant upon the already existing human community. This dependency is even greater in a fragmented, centralized urban-industrial modern culture than in a rural culture, where another pair of hands often increased an extended family unit's productive power. No historical interpretation of abortion as a moral issue which ignores these matters deserves moral standing in the present debate.

In drawing this section to a close, I want to stress that if present efforts to criminalize abortion succeed we will need a state apparatus of massive proportions to enforce compulsory childbearing. In addition, withdrawal of legal abortion will create one more massively profitable underworld economy in which the Mafia and other sections of quasi-legal capitalism may and will profitably invest. The radical right promises to get the state out of regulation of people's lives, but what they really mean is that they will let economic activity go unrestrained. What their agenda signifies for the personal lives of women is quite another matter.

An adequate historical perspective on abortion recognizes the long struggle women have waged for some degree of control over fertility and of their efforts to regain control of procreative power from patriarchal and state-imperial culture and institutions. Such a perspective also takes into account that more nearly adequate contraceptive methods and the existence of safe, surgical, elective abortion represent positive historic steps toward full human freedom and dignity for women. While the same gains in medical knowledge also open the way to sterilization abuse and to social pressures against some women's use of their power of procreation, I know of no woman who would choose to return to a state of lesser knowledge about these matters.

There has been an objective gain in the quality of women's lives for those fortunate enough to possess procreative choice. That millions of women do not possess even the rudimentary conditions for such a choice is obvious. Our moral goal should be to struggle against those real barriers—poverty, racism, and cultural oppression—which prevent authentic choice from being a reality for every woman.

"Every Two Minutes: Battered Women and Feminist Interpretation"

❧

Susan Brooks Thistlethwaite

Susan Brooks Thistlethwaite is president and professor of theology at Chicago Theological Seminary. She has written *Sex, Race, and God: Christian Feminism in Black and White*. Here she examines violence against women as simultaneously a moral, political, and religious issue.

❧

All day long, every day, women are verbally intimidated, battered, injured, and killed by the men they live with. If, as Susan Brownmiller has said, "rapists are the shock troops of patriarchy," then batterers are the army of occupation. This essay is concerned with the way in which this climate of violence that touches women's lives affects biblical interpretations.

All women live with male violence. A survey conducted by the National Division of the United Methodist Church's Program of Ministries with Women in Crisis in 1980 and 1981 indicates that one in every twenty-seven United Methodist women had been raped, one in every thirteen had been physically abused by her husband, one in every four had been verbally or emotionally abused. Of the respondents, both male and female, one in nine knew of a close friend or relative who had been raped, one in six knew of physical abuse, one in five knew of emotional abuse.[1]

While the authors are aware of the limitations of their survey, as a random sampling of Protestants the survey seems to indicate that even scratching the surface of women's lives reveals the daily presence of violence.

The authors also observed, "Denial runs deep." Their report has met with "disbelief and an amazing capacity to rationalize the findings."[2] Denial is the way to the continuation of the abuse of women. Consciousness of the violence against women with which we all live every day is the beginning of its end.

A feminist biblical interpretation must have this consciousness at its center. The Christian scriptures are inextricably interwoven with this history of the belief systems that support the view of women as scapegoats. In *Violence against Wives*, Emerson Dobash and Russell Dobash have a chapter on the relationship of biblical material to the problem of spouse abuse, in which they call women "the appropriate victim." They believe this problem requires intensive examination of history for the structures that support the legitimization of wife as victim.

The seeds of wife beating lie in the subordination of females and in their subjection to male authority and control. This relationship between women and men has been institutionalized in the structure of the patriarchal family and is supported by the economic and political institutions and by a belief system, *including a religious one*, that makes such relationships seem natural, morally just, sacred.[3]

There is apparent division over the question of whether the location of the authority (warrant, cause, justification) of a feminist interpretation of the Bible is in the text or in women's experience. I believe it is impossible to make this distinction with any clarity because women's experience in Western culture has been shaped by the biblical materials, and the biblical materials were shaped by a patriarchal culture.

Following a presentation I gave on the Bible and battered women in New York in October 1982, one member of the audience raised the question, "Why deal with the Bible at all?" But as anyone who works with abused women knows, this is not an option. Battered women frequently bring their religious beliefs to the process of working through a battering relationship. Phone calls to shelters often begin with the phrase, "I'm a Bible-believing Christian, but. . . ." We begin to develop a feminist interpretation because the Bible is a part of the fabric of the oppression of battered women.

In the early 1970s I became involved as a pastor counseling abused women. I received calls from some women who were experiencing abuse but were reluctant to try to change their situation because they had been told the teaching of the Bible prohibited their protest. I organized Bible studies with some of these women, and I have continued this work in several locations. Many of the examples that follow are from such groups.

FEMINIST METHOD

A feminist method does not always come first chronologically. In Elisabeth Schüssler Fiorenza's landmark work *In Memory of Her: A Feminist Theological Reconstruction of Christian Origins*, method appears first in the volume, but it does not come first in the development of her thought. It was living with the texts themselves in the midst of the contemporary women's movement that shaped her method of investigation. Precisely because it is a method of investigation, it is a process for discovery of what has been hidden.

Moreover, a history of the *use* of biblical materials must become a part of the interpretation. John Cobb has noted that critical study recognizes, and indeed emphasizes, the sociohistorical context in which the text functioned in the early church.[4] Feminist biblical interpretation has added a recognition of the patriarchal context in which the text functioned. But the text is still functioning, so to speak, and the patriarchal view that formed part of the formulation of the text is in turn supporting and supported by the text. All that history must become part of a feminist interpretation of the Bible.

Likewise, the origin of women's suspicions of the biblical interpretation of their situation is *both* the text *and* their life experience. Method emerges in this process of interrogation between text and experience. The key is that this process of interrogation proceeds over time.

Work with abused women is a process of support in which women who are physically safe, perhaps for the first time in many years, find self-esteem through affirmations of the gifts of women, through taking control of their lives, and through claiming their anger and finding in that anger a source of strength to act and to change. This process takes time. It cannot happen overnight.

Likewise, the development of a feminist method of biblical interpretation takes time. In Western philosophy, thought has been deemed a timeless, eternal absolute. But if that were the case, nothing new would ever emerge from human consciousness, because it would have to emerge full-blown. Plato wrestled with this problem in the *Meno* and decided that the way we come to know anything new is by remembering it from a formerly perfect state of knowledge before birth. Today we follow an investigative, scientific model of deduction that holds that thoughts proceed from first principles toward a logical conclusion. This is the grip of positivism that has held us in obeisance to science for more than two centuries.

In fact, it appears more likely that we think by analogy. When we want to ask about the unknown, we ask, "What is it like?" We learn something new both from the similarity and from the dissimilarity. The tension of the dissimilarity probes us to ask again. Thought moves by analogy and it moves through time. We have to live with something for awhile before we can move on.

Over time, women come to varying levels of interpretation of biblical materials. Each of these levels is possible with the whole corpus, and all are necessary in order to deal with the varying attitudes toward women within the Bible.

THE LIBERATION IN THE TEXT: FINDING SELF-ESTEEM

The support given by programs and shelters is essential so that an abused woman can begin to see her life in a new way. Through her research, Lenore Walker has described the battered woman as follows:

1. Has low self-esteem.
2. Believes all the myths about battering relationships.
3. Is a traditionalist about the home, with strong beliefs in family unity and the prescribed feminine sex-role stereotype.
4. Accepts responsibility for the batterer's action.
5. Suffers from guilt, yet denies the terror and anger she feels.
6. Presents a passive face to the world but has the strength to manipulate her environment enough to prevent further violence.
7. Has severe stress reactions, with psychophysiological complaints.
8. Uses sex as a way to establish intimacy.
9. Believes no one will be able to help her resolve her predicament except herself.[5]

Abused women who receive support begin to learn that they have self-worth and to experience their anger as legitimate. Yet these women believe what they have been taught the Bible says about their situations: that women are inferior in status before husband and God and deserving of a life of pain. One woman said, "God punished women more" (see Gen. 3:16).

Frequently, women with strong religious backgrounds have the most difficulty in accepting that the violence against them is wrong. They believe what they have been taught, that resistance to this injustice is unbiblical and unchristian. Christian women are supposed to be meek, and claiming rights for oneself is committing the sin of pride. But as soon as battered women who hold rigidly traditional religious beliefs begin to develop an ideological suspicion that this violence against them is wrong, they react against it.

In workshops for persons who work with abused women, I have found that most social workers, therapists, and shelter personnel view religious beliefs as uniformly reinforcing passivity and tend to view religion, both traditional Christianity and Judaism, as an obstacle to a woman's successful handling of abuse. Unfortunately, they also say that many strongly religious women cease attending shelters and groups for abused women when these beliefs are attacked.

For women whose religious beliefs include extremely literal interpretations of the Bible as the norm, no authority except that of the Bible itself can challenge the image contained in these texts of woman as silent, subordinate, bearing her children in pain, and subject to the absolute authority of her husband. Yet in Bible study groups, these women can learn that the scriptures are much more on their side than they dared hope. They can become suspicious of a biblical exegesis that is a power play used against them. The process of critical interpretation is often painful and wrenching, because new ways of looking at the Bible have to be learned. But it is also affirming, because one is telling abused women, "You have a right both to your religious beliefs and to your self-esteem."

The core insight with which to begin such a process of interpretative suspicion is that the Bible is written from the perspective of the powerless.[6] The people of Israel, God's chosen, are a ragged band of runaway slaves. God, by identifying *this* people as chosen, is revealed as a God who sides with those who are out of power. It may be that to be out of power is a continuing metaphor in scripture for those who are especially valued by God.

Several types of texts have proved especially helpful to abused women. The theme of God's care for widows and orphans can be helpful in demonstrating that those who are oppressed by societal structures are especially dear to God. A widow in Israel was effectually without economic support and a nonperson in the eyes of that society. The children of a widow, because they lacked this economic support, were considered orphans. God's judgment on those who would afflict any woman or child was especially severe (Ex. 22:2–24).

Yet this does not mean that the impoverished condition of widows and orphans is legitimated because of God's care. God's identification with the oppressed helps them to value themselves as God values them and to recognize that their oppression is unjust. God does not want meek acceptance of oppression.

In *Liberation Preaching,* Justo and Catherine Gonzalez note, "God seems to choose those who have been made to feel like outcasts and then gives them a new sense of self-worth. God vindicates them in the eyes of their former oppressors."[7] This theme of the vindication of the powerless is a constant one in the Hebrew scriptures (see 1 Sam. 2:1–10). It is to be contrasted with the sinful arrogance of the powerful, who believe themselves secure in their own strength (see Psalm 73).

It is essential to see that the ministry of Jesus of Nazareth continued this identification of the chosen of God with the poor. Jesus announced his ministry as one who proclaimed "release to the captives, and recovering of sight to the blind, to set at liberty those who are oppressed, to proclaim the acceptable year of the Lord" (Luke 4:18–20).

Jesus included women in his ministry and ministered to their distress, both spiritual and socioeconomic. The striking amount of biblical material that recounts Jesus' special regard for women, despite androcentric reaction, was the beginning point for the development of a feminist interpretation of the Bible.

Examples of Jesus' care for women are seen in the story of the widow's mite (Luke 21:1–4; 15:8–10), the forgiveness of the prostitute who has faith (Mark 14:3–9), the healing of the woman with the bloody flux (Luke 8:43–48), and the defense of Mary's right to discipleship (John 4:16–30).

Raymond E. Brown has entertained the idea that the crucial role women play in discipleship and apostolic witness is evidence of female leadership in the Johannine community. Jesus' public ministry begins and ends with a story about women: Mary, the mother of Jesus, and Mary Magdalene. Several times, stories of the discipleship of women and that of men are paired: the faithfulness of Nicodemus is paired with the insight of the Samaritan woman; the Christological confession of Peter is paralleled by that of Martha. Women's roles in the Fourth Gospel placed them as intimate disciples, those whom Jesus loved (Martha and Mary).

> In researching the evidence of the Fourth Gospel, one is still surprised to see to what extent in the Johannine community women and men were already on an equal level in the Good Shepherd. This seems to have been a community where in the things that really mattered in the following of Christ there was no difference between male and female—a Pauline dream (Gal. 3:28) that was not completely realized in the Pauline communities.[8]

Yet the text with which many abused women find the most identification is John 7:53–8:11. Jesus' defense of the woman who would have been stoned (abused) for adultery, omitted in many manuscripts, including the earliest ones, appears to be an authentic incident in the life of Jesus. Some interpreters have argued that this pericope was not originally part of the Gospel of John. Yet the extraordinary position of women in this Gospel may be a reason for its later inclusion.

Whether or not the woman has already been tried, she is on the verge of execution, having been caught in the act of adultery. Adultery for Jewish women could consist merely in speaking to a male alone. Her crime is not specified beyond that text. But somehow she has transgressed patriarchal grounds.

Textual interpretation usually overlooks the woman's situation and stresses that the scribes and Pharisees wanted to put Jesus to the test and were looking for grounds on which to accuse him.[9] But women who have suffered physical violence hear that whatever human law or custom may legitimate violence against women, it cannot stand face to face with the revelation of God's affirmation of all humanity. Many abused women would echo the joy of the woman who exclaimed, "That's right! He [Jesus] broke the law for her!"

THE LIBERATION OF THE TEXT: TAKING CONTROL

Some biblical material that appears not to address women, or even appears hostile to them, can be reworked to bring out liberating themes for abused women. The opinion of women that prevailing androcentric interpretation of the Bible is wrong, coupled with the emphasis in a major portion of the biblical materials themselves on God's identification with the oppressed, creates critical interpretation. Consciousness-raising for these women has provided the essential catalyst: the insight that women are included in the category of the poor, the oppressed, and the outcast. Moving from that critical standpoint, women can begin to examine and reinterpret these texts, imagining new relationships between the texts and their experience.

An especially useful text is Luke 9:1–5, which ends, "And wherever they do not receive you, when you leave [there] shake off the dust from your feet as a testimony against them." One of the crucial issues for abused women is the psychological and physical intimidation they experience that prevents them from leaving. Shelters and safe houses can begin to help with the fear of destitution and further violence faced by a woman who contemplates leaving. But there are psychological factors as well that include religious sanctions against a woman's "breaking up the home."

> What kind of people are my children going to become, seeing us or hearing us live this way? Will my son abuse his wife or girlfriend as he's seen his father do? Will my daughter live in fear and dread of every man she meets? For *them,* if not for me, I've got to do something. But instead, I stay, and stay, and stay for what seems like an eternal hell. I can't see my way out. I'm fearful of losing family respect for my failed marriage, *afraid of censure about my religious convictions,* fearful of a terrible reputation with my own friends (the few who are left). Finally I become obsessed with a fear of losing my respect for myself, and for my sanity—what's left of it.[10]

Because abused women experience themselves as out of control of their lives, part of working with them involves attempts to take control. One of the major obstacles to women's hearing the permission to leave where they are not valued is that they do not identify themselves with the disciples.

Disciples are followers of Jesus who hear the Word and do it (Mark 8:34–35). By this definition, the Synoptic Gospels agree that women were among the most faithful of Jesus' disciples, remaining at the foot of the cross even when others had fled. Jesus appeared first to women and commissioned them to tell of his resurrection, the central fact of the "good news," to the other disciples (Matt. 28:10; Mark 16:7; Luke 24:8–9).

The Roman Catholic Church has emphasized the absence of women among the twelve as indicative of Jesus' preference for male leadership.[11] While the New Testament authors are not uniformly in agreement on the role of the twelve, the theological function of the twelve is to represent the twelve tribes of Israel. In this way they provide a bridge between the Israelite past and the hoped-for future in which all Jews and Gentiles would be united as the People of God. The twelve thus have a largely symbolic role, not an administrative one, as evidenced by the fact that they were not replaced by the church after their deaths.[12]

Much of the New Testament material leads one to believe that the circle around Jesus was in fact quite fluid and did include women. Another title for Jesus' followers throughout his ministry is apostles. Generally, the term "apostle" is thought to refer to the twelve, a point of view held by the framers of the Vatican Declaration. On the contrary: it is a much wider circle, according to some New Testament writers. Junia, considered a woman by John Chrysostom, is named by Paul as "outstanding among the apostles" (Rom. 16:7, NIV). The "apostle" Paul, of course, was not a member of the twelve at all (see Gal. 1:1–24).

It is therefore quite reasonable to decide that women were included in the most intimate circle around Jesus and that their inclusion was deliberate on his part. We begin to see how this text can be heard as addressing women. Power and authority are given to those who hear the Word of God and do it, the disciples. Women can claim this power and authority to heal their situation. One woman, reading the text in this way, remarked, "I thought that you always had to turn the other cheek."

For too long we have neglected the healing and casting out of demons that occurs so frequently in biblical materials in favor of discussions focused solely around the miraculous. But for abused women, women who study the Bible with bloodied noses, bruised ribs, and broken limbs, healing has a concrete and immediate reference. Likewise, the demonic has a concrete reference for those who have experienced the cycle of violence that builds in the home of an abuser.[13]

Women are not named in scripture as among the twelve. But women can learn to imagine themselves in the text on the basis of other textual material that does affirm women (such as women's discipleship) and on the basis of their own experience, which shows that they have been the ones to hear the Word of God and do it. This type of imagining challenges traditional interpretation, which has ignored women who are actually in the text or whose presence is implied by the text, and moves interpretation to a new level of engagement with the contemporary life of the church.

THE LIBERATION FROM THE TEXT: CLAIMING ANGER

Recently I have been conducting Bible study groups composed primarily of Catholic women over forty. Biblical material has not formed the religious framework for their acceptance of battering. Rather, it has been the church and its teaching about the role of women, divorce, and contraception that has provided religious legitimation for battering. Biblical study with these women has proceeded in a different manner because they did not regard the text as the primary religious authority in their lives. Rather, they were willing to enter into a suspicion of the many texts we examined that seemed to legitimize violence against women. These women found that they could not always trust the text or its traditional interpretations and that some of the texts are "harmful to their health."

Ephesians 5:21–23 is a very difficult passage for abused women struggling to find self-respect and some control over their lives. A preliminary study of this passage modifies extreme misinterpretation by demonstrating that to be "subject" (v. 21) does not mean specifically subject to physical violence: "For no man ever hates his own flesh, but nourishes and cherishes it, as Christ does the church" (v. 29). Husbands are admonished to love their wives "as their own bodies" (v. 28).

But physical violence is not the only form of abuse. Verbal intimidation, economic deprivation, and deliberate humiliation also characterize the violent relationship. One woman reported that her husband would deliberately keep her from arriving at family parties on time and then make her apologize to her relatives for being so late. This type of subjection appears compatible with the Ephesians passage, since only wives are admonished to "respect" their spouses.

Liberation from this text requires a recognition of its location within the biblical materials and of the function this particular emphasis in Ephesians played in the history of the church. In the pseudo-Pauline epistles, a shift away from the egalitarian ethos of the Jesus movement can be observed. Ephesians was written about the same time as Colossians, another epistle where the subjection of wives to husbands is emphasized. This is the first of the household duty codes, a series of exhortations to obedience in the households of the early Christian communities.

In Colossians 3:11, women are left out of the otherwise complete repetition of the baptismal formula of Galatians 3:28: "Here there cannot be Greek and Jew, circumcised and uncircumcised, barbarian, Scythian, slave, free man, but Christ is all, and all in all." "Neither male nor female" seems to belong to an earlier vision of human equality in Christ.

In Ephesians the household duty codes are limited to the relation of husbands and wives, combined with a theology of Christ and the church. This tends to reinforce the cultural notion of submission contained in the household duty codes with a theological legitimation of dominance and submission in the household of God. While the negative exhortation of Colossians ("Do not be harsh" to your wives) is softened ("Love" your wives), the inferior position of both wives and the church is cemented.

This is not the only pattern for divine-human relationships in the scripture. It is a pattern developed in response to social criticism of the newfound freedom of Christians, especially as this was reflected in the behavior of Christian wives and slaves. Other patterns exist, such as

Galatians 3:28, and these can be drawn upon to critique patriarchal patterns such as Ephesians 5:21–23. The religious sanction in the household codes for the submission of women is a primary legitimation of wife abuse and must be challenged by women in order for them to gain some control over their own lives. A woman relates the traditional response of clergy:

> Well, he spoke to both of us and he sat down for about an hour and he spoke about our financial situation and how having a child affected a marriage and things like that. Then he would bring in the vows of marriage—" to love, honor, and obey until death do us part." And I argued on the point of obeying because I feel, I felt at that time, to obey, it's all right in certain principles but you cannot obey all your life. I mean, if I asked him to stop gambling he would not obey me, but I have to obey all his rules. The minister would not talk about that fact.[14]

On the contrary, we must begin to talk about obedience and the role it has played in the cultural accommodation of religion to social mores, particularly to patriarchy. We must find strength to reject this notion of obedience to male authority in claiming our anger at the suffering that women have experienced in obedience.

A final text to consider within this rubric of liberation from the text involves a more subtle perception of the patriarchal violence against women that is in the biblical material. Genesis 2:21–24 is such a text.

Although Phyllis Trible has dealt with this text creatively in suggesting ways it can be understood as a basis of equality between woman and man, feminist interpretation must also recognize that the history of control of women's bodies is at stake in this text and must become part of its interpretation.[15] In the development of patriarchy, a very important issue has been control of women's abilities to procreate. The ability of women's bodies to create life has resulted in awe, fear, and the desire to control this power. While Freud may have discovered penis envy, womb envy has also played a role in human history.

This story is apparent in Genesis 2. A woman is born from a man in contrast to every other human birth. Perhaps, too, this interpretation of the first birth is also meant to symbolize control over woman's abilities to make decisions about whether to bear a child. From an early period the church has attempted to curtail knowledge of contraception and abortion. Puritanical Protestants led a late-nineteenth-century campaign to pass laws making contraceptive knowledge a crime. The current "Right to Life" movement is ecumenical in that its adherents are both Catholics and Evangelical/Fundamental Protestants. These movements are attacks on female autonomy that threatens patriarchal power at its core.

A Maryland woman who was severely abused over many years told me that when she complained after some attacks that she had sustained injuries, her husband would retort that "your bones are my bones—just like it says in the Bible." Less explicit reinforcement of patterns of domination and submission that legitimate violence against women can be found in inter-pretations of this text. Walter Brueggemann argues in the *Catholic Biblical Quarterly* that this text "suggests nothing of the superiority of the male as is often suggested." But Brueggemann correctly connects this text to marriage metaphors for divine-human relationship, such as "the Image of God and his [*sic*] bride Israel."[16] He then rightly draws the important analogy between Genesis 2:18–23 and Ephesians 5:21–33:

> The same imagery in Paul [Ephesians 5:21–23] is illuminated. The relation of Christ and his bride-church is grounded in a commonality of concern, loyalty, and responsibility which is pledged to endure through weakness and strength.[17]

But the metaphor of patriarchal marriage for divine-human relationship is not one of mutuality; it is an image of dominance and subordination in that cultural context. Likewise, tying marriage to the divine-human relationship clearly divinizes male superiority in that relationship.

Brueggemann's interpretation of Genesis 2:18–23 illustrates the limits of a biblical interpretation that does not take a nuanced approach to the materials. There is much affirmation of women within the biblical materials, but grounds for violence against women exist as well, along with much material in between. This material has shaped cultural attitudes toward women. But contemporary experience also shapes our interpretation of the text.

Feminist biblical interpretation for women who live with male violence is a healing process that develops over time. It involves claiming self-esteem, taking control, and owning one's anger. Women's relationships to biblical materials need to undergo the same type of healing process. As Adrienne Rich has observed, "We have lived with violence far too long."[18]

NOTES

1. *Crisis: Women's Experience and the Church's Response. Final Report of a Crisis Survey of United Methodists,* The United Methodist Church (March 1982), 4–9.

2. *Crisis,* 4–9.

3. R. Emerson Dobash and Russell Dobash, *Violence against Wives* (New York: Free Press, 1979), 33–34. My emphasis.

4. John B. Cobb Jr., *Process Theology as Political Theology* (Philadelphia: Westminster Press, 1982), 23.

5. Lenore E. Walker, *The Battered Woman* (New York: Harper & Row, 1979), 31.

6. Juan Luis Segundo, *The Liberation of Theology* (Maryknoll, N.Y.: Orbis, 1976), 9.

7. Justo L. Gonzalez and Catherine G. Gonzalez, *Liberation Preaching* (Nashville, Tenn.: Abingdon Press, 1980).

8. Raymond E. Brown, "Roles of Women in the Fourth Gospel," *Theological Studies* 36 (1975): 688–89, reprinted in Brown's *Community of the Beloved Disciple* (Ramsey, N.J.: Paulist Press, 1979), 183–98.

9. Rudolf Schnackenburg, *The Gospel According to St. John* (New York: Seabury Press, 1980), 165.

10. Quoted from *Introduction to Battered Women: One Testimony* (Southwest Community Mental Health Center, Columbus, Ohio). My emphasis.

11. "Declaration on the Question of Admission of Women to the Priesthood," in *Women Priests: Catholic Commentary on the Vatican Declaration,* ed. Leonard Swidler and Arlene Swidler (Ramsey, N.J.: Paulist Press, 1977).

12. Elisabeth Schüssler Fiorenza, "The Twelve," in *Women Priests,* ed. Leonard Swidler and Arlene Swidler (Ramsey, N.J.: Paulist Press, 1977), 138.

13. Lenore Walker has identified a three-stage cycle to the violence in homes of batterers: the "tension-building stage," the "acute battering incident," the "kindness and contrite, loving behavior" stage. Walker notes that women who kill their abusers do so in stage three (*The Battered Woman,* 55–70).

14. Dobash and Dobash, *Violence against Wives,* 205.

15. Phyllis Trible, *God and the Rhetoric of Sexuality* (Philadelphia: Fortress Press, 1978), 95–102.

16. Walter Brueggemann, "Of the Same Flesh and Bone, Genesis 2:23a," *Catholic Biblical Quarterly* 32 (1969): 532.

17. Brueggemann, "Flesh and Bone," 541.

18. Adrienne Rich, "Natural Resources," in her *Dream of a Common Language: Poems 1974–1977* (New York: Norton, 1978), 64.

from "Ministry to Women: Hearing and Empowering 'Poor' Black Women"

❧

Cheryl Townsend Gilkes

Cheryl Townsend Gilkes is professor of sociology and African-American studies and director of African American Studies at Colby College. This essay explores the interplay of class and race in religious contexts.

❧

"POOR" BLACK WOMEN

James Cone and others have pointed to the tripartite reality of institutional racism in the United States: economic exploitation, political exclusion, and cultural humiliation. African-American response to that racism has manifested itself in part in an adaptive self-hatred that accepts models defined by the dominant society as normative for their community. Existence in this society has involved a twofold struggle. One part consists of constantly challenging the dominant society; the other is an internal contest over roles, values, and strategies for survival as well as for social change. Women have been central to both sides of this struggle. Indeed it has been argued that the legal and cultural statuses of African women and their descendants have been central to the peculiarities of slavery and its aftermath in the United States.[1] Among women there exists a "multiple consciousness" in response to this "multiple jeopardy" that has been ever present in the history of African-American women in the United States.

In spite of the centrality of women's reality and roles and in spite of the legendary "sheroes,"[2] such as Harriet Tubman, Sojourner Truth, Ellen Craft, Milla Granson, and others, who emerge from slavery, African-American churches have not consistently empowered the voices of women. Perhaps it was in the slave churches where their voices were heeded most attentively. Although white society recognized and empowered the black male preacher, even when he was a bondsman, it mostly ignored the women. Accounts of the slave community indicate that enslaved men and women did not ignore women. Deborah Gray White points to several instances where powerful women arose as spiritual leaders who were able to exercise authority over the community.[3] Webber argues that slave communities exhibited a real lack of sexism in their allocation of leadership, authority, and respect.[4]

The church's voice during slavery was a clear and unwaveringly prophetic one. It was a voice that insisted simultaneously on the overthrow of slavery and the humanity of enslaved women and men. Occasionally, that voice was found in the themes that undergird the slave revolts, most notably Nat Turner's. Webber points to the centrality of women in constructing, maintaining, and transmitting a world view whose cultural themes emphasized solidarity and religious faith. "Even women preachers appear often enough, though admittedly less frequently than male preachers, to suggest that there was no community prohibition against their filling this crucial role."[5] Biographies of nineteenth-century evangelists and Toni Morrison's 1987 novel, *Beloved,* in the person of Baby Suggs, Holy, remind us that the voice of the preaching woman has been a significant force for psychic survival. Yet it was all too often ignored and hindered from attaining authority after Emancipation.

The suppression of women's voices within African-American churches coincides with what Gayraud Wilmore calls "the deradicalization of the Black Church" as the prophetic voices of people like Henry McNeal Turner and Harriet Tubman died out.[6] Around the beginning of the twentieth century, women lost ground in their access to platforms and pulpits. Churches were urged to "regularize" and regularized churches had male pastors in their pulpits. Some churches accommodated the religious zeal of women allowing them to lead worship and pray "from the floor" as missionaries and evangelists. According to Evelyn Brooks Higginbotham, a "feminist theology" emerged among Baptist women between 1885 and 1900 as they contested the masculinism that threatened them with silence and marginality.[7] Apparently, the work of these women as equals, first within the American National Baptist Convention and later within the National Baptist Convention, was delegitimized. Once they were, in the words of Nannie Helen Burroughs, "hindered from helping," these women formed the Women's Auxiliary Convention of the National Baptist Convention from which they wielded tremendous influence within the church and the community at large.[8] A number of women found places for their voices in the Holiness Movement of the late nineteenth century, and in the Pentecostal Movement of the early twentieth. Baptist and African Methodist women were recruited and "converted," became the pioneer educators of these new churches, and were also powerful evangelists and revivalists who "dug out" or founded urban churches when women and their work moved to the cities.

As their suppression within their churches progressed and the church became less prophetic and more priestly in its response to political realities, African-American Christian women created other avenues for their "ministry." One of these was a women's movement that culminated in the formation of the National Association of Colored Women. It is important *not* to view this club movement of the late nineteenth and early twentieth centuries primarily as secular. It is more accurately viewed as a movement of prophetic Christian women who fulfilled their calling in their responses to social issues and in their demands for social change. The club movement's motto, "Lifting as We Climb," reflected their sense of shared suffering and mission. These women rejected the notion of competitive American individualism in favor of a corporate mobility designed to liberate. Throughout the papers of these movements one repeatedly finds Christian themes. Often the women's church work and community work overlapped significantly. Mary McLeod Bethune, for instance, was a graduate of Moody Bible Institute and an experienced street preacher. When she was denied a missionary post in Africa, she claimed her Africa to be right next door and founded what is now Bethune-Cookman College.[9] Other black women's narratives, such as that of Mamie Garvin Fields, describe similar missionary motives.[10] Leaders such as Mary Church Terrell traveled the country exhorting church women to act on behalf of their communities. Others expressed a biblical hermeneutic that undergirded their worldviews and actions. In her novel *Iola Leroy or the Shadows Uplifted,* Frances Ellen Watkins Harper points to the church as a place to reconstitute the African-American community and to formulate strategies and ethics for social change.[11]

These women were part of a leadership class of "preachers and teachers."[12] In addition to being heroic educators, Lucie Campbell's hymn, "Something Within," hints that these "teachers" were also carriers of the gospel. "If anything characterizes the role of black women in religion in America, it is the successful extension of their individual sense of regeneration, release, redemption, and spiritual liberation to a collective ethos of struggle for and with the entire black community."[13] Historically, African-American women have argued for a collective approach to the community's suffering. Their advocacy has focused on the experience of men and children sometimes giving their own specific concerns less emphasis than they deserve. Yet every dimension of black women's experience cries out for a specific response from the church that needs to hear and empower the voices of "poor" black women.[14]

Novelist Alice Walker has offered the term *womanist,* along with a definition that organizes and interprets the heroic historical experience of African-American women with reference to their femaleness, their relationship to community, their strategies for change, and their cultural emphases.[15] What Walker has identified as holistic and universalist commitment to the community's survival, Patricia Hill Collins has described as a "recurrent humanist vision" among black women activists and writers.[16] Both Walker and Collins illuminate a consciousness that emerges from suffering and recognizes the suffering of others. Given the pivotal place of African-American women in the racial-ethnic, class, and gender hierarchies of American culture, a ministry that concentrates on their empowerment should benefit the entire community.

ECONOMIC EMPOWERMENT

African-American women's work history is linked inextricably with their religious history. Their roles as workers defined their history and status in the United States. Many of their responses to that history have been dependent on their religious opportunities and spiritual resources. As enslaved and free women, their work has been inseparable from the well-being of the entire African-American community. As wage earners, they have been the poorest, least protected, and most insurgent group of workers. Slave or free, these vulnerable women have been among the staunchest supporters and most enterprising participants in the religious life of their communities.

As enslaved women they were subjected to the same violence and exploitative working conditions as men. Angela Davis points out that the work roles of enslaved women set the foundations for a "new standard of womanhood" and established a different relationship between black women and the labor force. As a result:

> [p]roportionately, more Black women have always worked outside their homes than have their white sisters. The enormous space that work occupies in Black women's lives today follows a pattern established during the very earliest days of slavery. As slaves, compulsory labor overshadowed every other aspect of women's existence. It would seem, therefore, that the starting point for any exploration of Black women's lives under slavery would be an appraisal of their role as workers.[17]

Their combined role as workers and mothers was pivotal to the formation of African-American consciousness. Men were often the chroniclers of exploitations specific to women. One such memoirist described his mother's impact by simply saying, "my mother was *much* of a woman."[18]

These working women were also expected to reproduce the African labor force in America. As the demand for slave labor rose, the system depended more and more upon natural increase and unparalleled legal repression to maintain itself. Deborah Gray White points out that force, fraud, and other inducements were used to make enslaved women the most fertile population in the world (at that time). Central to their situation was a need for more humane conditions for mothering. These concerns provided the basis for an extensive network of mutual-aid among women that was, she argues, the base upon which the legendary strength of slave women rested. By helping each other, they were able to cope with work and motherhood in ways that became enshrined in folklore. The network's mutual-aid included prayer meetings and religious leaders who healed, prayed, exhorted, and prophesied, displaying remarkable amounts of influence and authority within slave communities.[19]

At the end of slavery, people sought liberation from the sexual and material oppression of the rural South. Women were eager to work for themselves and their families. To do this they educated their daughters as well as their sons. The educational ethic among freed women and men contributed institutions and policies that benefited the entire South. On occasion, black southerners in some areas had higher school attendance rates than their white neighbors. Part of the community's educational strategy was to free women from the sexual exploitation that came with agricultural and domestic work. Educated daughters, they hoped, would not have to work in "the white man's kitchen." Even with this work ethic, black women disappeared from the fields immediately after slavery. Their former owners accused them of "playing the lady." Some have argued, however, that fear of sexual exploitation prompted this disappearance.[20]

Some of the most poignant descriptions of the work orientation of African-American women are found with reference to their religious and educational orientations. Women worked and saved and ran farms to educate husbands called to the ministry.[21] Women also found enterprising ways to earn extra money to educate children in church-related schools and to support the missionaries who taught them. White female employers complained about the precedence church activities sometimes took over their own needs.[22] The investments of "Negro washer-women," according to Carter G. Woodson, were the foundations of the great black insurance companies in the South. The economic enterprise of African-American women, when successful, as in the cases of Maggie Lena Walker, Madame C. J. Walker, and Mary Ellen ("Mammy") Pleasants, benefited the entire community. Pleasants, a Catholic, financially supported the founding of several black Protestant congregations in California. Woodson insisted that the least educated and hardest working women were the ones most eager to invest in religiously suffused mutual-aid associations, community uplift projects, and new small businesses.[23]

Black women's work in the South moved to the cities before the demand for male rural labor declined. This transformation was a significant force in urbanization. Women outnumbered men in the cities. These migrant women and eventually their families became the nuclei around which new urban congregations formed. Many of these new late nineteenth- and early twentieth-century churches were part of the Holiness and Pentecostal movements. Many congregations were organized by the women who then sent "home" for male pastors. At the same time that sociologists, such as E. Franklin Frazier, decried the cities as places of "destruction,"[24] women were transforming the organizational and cultural matrix of the African-American church. The urbanization of women's work not only produced new churches but also new music, contributing to another cultural transformation in which women's voices are significant, the emergence of gospel music. Urban churches represented a substantial economic investment on the part of women. That investment was so prominent that, according to Taylor Branch, Montgomery Improvement Association founder E. D. Nixon defined the civic responsibilities of Montgomery's pastors in terms of what they "owed" the "washerwomen." For Nixon, it was obvious that the religious leadership derived its salaries and prestige from working women.[25] The centrality of churchwomen to the Montgomery bus boycott movement and to the civil rights movement overall is a story that is only beginning to be told.[26]

In spite of their hard work and sustained participation in the labor force, black women remain poorly remunerated and, as an aggregate, fall behind white men, black men, and white women. Only college-educated black women, a disproportionately small group, approach or surpass white women's income levels. This seeming anomaly is a consequence of black women's continuous labor force participation and the disincentive to remain in the labor force that married college-educated white women experience because of the economic opportunities available to their husbands.[27] Currently, according to Rothenberg, the poverty rate of all *working* black mothers *equals* the poverty rate of white men who are *not* in the labor force (13 percent).[28] Elderly black women represent one of the poorest groups. And it is elderly African-American women who are responsible for the organizational integrity of black religious organizations.

African-American churches need to be in the forefront of movements and strategies to uplift African Americans economically. African-American women and their communities stand to benefit from advocacy for economic justice more than any other group of women. Assuming the role of advocate for economic justice for African-American women is essential to the ministry of churches. Recently some churches have confused the roles of evangelism and prophecy. In the zeal to attract men, these churches ignore their mission to call social institutions to account for their failures to people. The most glaring economic failure (of many) in this society is the historical failure to secure economic justice for black women. Nannie Helen Burroughs and other churchwomen in the club movement recognized this contradiction and saw the call to secure economic justice as an essential task for creating an ideal society for everyone.[29] This task still awaits the full energies of the church.

POLITICAL EMPOWERMENT

It is in the area of political empowerment that the institutional discrimination of African-American churches most directly excludes women. "Get to the ministers!" is still an American political ethic, according to Charles V. Hamilton, when most white politicians are seeking the "black vote."[30] In urban politics, ministers are most likely to be approached when officials are seeking to represent the "voice" of the black community on civic boards and in appointive political office. The refusal of African-American churches, particularly Baptist churches, to include women in ordained and authoritative leadership directly excludes women from participating in the decision-making process affecting the communities in which they comprise the majority population.

Today, women do not accept such exclusion. The traditions of women's community work have provided alternative pathways for women to public leadership. Sometimes the path involves a highly public secular career in human services or electoral politics. While black women, as congresswomen, mayors, state representatives, agency heads, and city or town council members, and as Republican and Democratic Party workers, make a substantial contribution to what political empowerment black communities achieve, they are often isolated from the male religious enclaves that are accorded special privileges of access to white political powers. Since black churches remain the most important site for working- and middle-class people who vote and otherwise participate in traditional politics, women's exclusion from church leadership dilutes their influence in other public spaces.

Historically, African-American women have insisted upon participating in the political destiny of black people. The nineteenth and twentieth centuries are full of examples of such participation. One of black America's earliest political writers and the first woman of any race to speak publicly and leave existing manuscripts, Maria Stewart, offered incisive political-theological perspectives on the plight of black people.[31] Harriet Tubman and Sojourner Truth both framed their activism in religious terms. Sojourner Truth once challenged Frederick Douglass by asking, "Is God dead, Frederick?" Her challenge reminded Douglass and their listeners that, regardless of how hostile the society, African Americans were not totally alone in their struggle. She also underscored the significance black people attached to biblical-theological frameworks of social justice. Mary McLeod Bethune's missionary zeal moved her from higher education to the political arena during the Depression. She became, as convenor of Roosevelt's black cabinet, head of the National Youth Administration, and president of the National Council of Negro Women, the most powerful black leader since Booker T. Washington.

The activities of African-American women during the Civil Rights movement, although extensive and crucial, have not been adequately documented or assessed. However, two women, Ella Baker and Fannie Lou Hamer, both exude a common spirituality in spite of their radically different social origins. Ella Baker, the daughter of a minister, became a traveling prophet for the National Association for the Advancement of Colored People (NAACP) as a field secretary before becoming the executive director of Southern Christian Leadership Conference (SCLC) and the organizer of Student Nonviolent Coordinating Committee (SNCC). Her speaking schedule, as portrayed in a film biography, provides documentation of the extensive network of churches open to organizers from the NAACP.[32] Hamer was explicitly theological in her calls for participation in the Civil Rights movement. The same energy and assertiveness that made her an effective song leader in her church made her an effective public speaker and advocate for black people's political empowerment.[33] White women feminists point to women like Hamer as catalysts for their own assertiveness and political growth.[34]

These specific examples highlight the models of political participation that women often provide for the community. Although churchwomen can be as hierarchical and authoritarian as any human beings, they are more willing to "mother" others toward developing effective political participation and leadership skills. My own research on urban community workers uncovered networks and other organized settings in which women who became empowered actively recruited and trained others for similar kinds of participation and leadership. One may argue that women are more willing to do this because they have been so often forced to do this, but my observation of women's organizations leads me to conclude that black women enjoy exercising power by guiding others in its exercise. Both church mothers and community mothers utilize this model of influence in their organizations.[35]

If the church follows through in its advocacy for women's political empowerment, as in economics, such empowerment would be another source of benefit for the entire community. W. E. B. Du Bois recognized this during his campaigns for woman suffrage from the pages of *The Crisis*. We now know that African-American women vote in patterns that contradict their actual socioeconomic position in the society, in spite of their structural and social alienation. The enhanced empowerment of African-American women holds prophetic possibilities for the entire community. Including women in the institutional life of the church in such a way as to enhance their access to public power would enable the church to benefit from their skills and talents in a way that others outside the church and outside the black community already do. Many activist women who do not attend church regularly explain their absence in terms of the discrimination they perceive. The inclusion of women would also represent a significant affirmation to women and a balance for the demands that the dominant culture often places on the male role—demands that enhance the individual career sometimes at the expense of the community's collective interests.

CULTURAL EMPOWERMENT

The attainment of economic and political justice are really matters of "simple justice." Addressing the cultural humiliation of African-American women is a challenge to the church that is perhaps the most complex, most significant, and least understood emergency, cultural humiliation and its consequences for self-esteem. *Cultural humiliation* is a term that addresses the way in which African-American images, traditions, values, and symbols are devalued and regarded as deviant by the dominant (white) society. Some have argued that the low self-esteem of African-American women and girls contributes to the behaviors that choke off their most significant opportunities. Where the male supremacist dimensions of the society provide a few opportunities for black men that support a positive self-esteem, that same male supremacist ethic exacerbates the alienation of African-American women.

African-American women, by choice and by chance, violate nearly every dimension of American gender norms. Edwin Schur has pointed to the importance of "gender norms" in defining the position of women in our society.[36] These include meeting certain standards of beauty, a model of marriage and motherhood that enforces economic dependence, and social deference. Violation of these norms brings about the exclusion and punishment of women in a variety of ways. Schur describes the failure to meet society's beauty norms as "visual deviance." African-American women, in terms of their color alone, stand out from and against the culture's idolatry of whiteness. Not only are they assaulted from outside their communities, but African-American women who are too dark face an outrageous complex of attitudes and behaviors from within their own communities. Often the behavior of men and their stated preferences for lighter women reflect black men's own self-hatred, but in spite of changes brought about by the black power movement, Alice Walker is still able to lament, "If the present looks like the past, what does the future look like?"[37]

Ironically, black churches are often pastored by men who are the most fiercely committed to the dominant culture's notions of beauty and do not see these notions as white, male supremacist. Those notions are affirmed and reaffirmed from the pulpit to the door, often in quite subtle ways. The prettiest and lightest little girls in the church are often encouraged in ways that allow them to discover that their visual status is a resource for success; they are socialized to be "cute" and to grow up to be beautiful. In contrast the darker and plumper girls are encouraged to be serious, develop leadership skills, and, above all, do well in school. Some black women have called this the "pretty/ugly" syndrome in black culture.[38] Although poets and black feminists have vocalized this issue, churches have been strangely silent on the "pretty-ugly" ethic that abounds in our communities. Both strategies hurt! Many "pretty" black women are intellectually underdeveloped in a community that offers relatively little protection to its girls. Unless they are specially protected by middle-class organizations, such girls/women are subjected to inordinate amounts of sexual aggression. Michelle Wallace, though in my opinion expressing it badly, tries to point to this phenomenon in *Black Macho and the Myth of the Superwoman*, complaining that the "prettiest" little girls in ghettoes or inner cities seemed to be the most likely candidates for teenage pregnancy.[39] At the same time, many "dark" black women are excluded from feeling good about themselves by the withholding of those acts of ceremonial deference within their own communities which "honor" their womanhood.

Issues of beauty represent just one of the rocky areas of a complex and dangerous course that African-American women must negotiate in American culture. Issues of body image, sexuality, white and black cultural definitions of work and family roles, and the way in which black women's deviation from dominant cultural definitions reflects on the total community all combine to place an inordinate amount of pressure on black women. The "Mammy" image, particularly, as expressed in literature, movies, and television is an assault on black women's work roles. The highly publicized attempt of a crack-addicted mother in St. Louis, Missouri, to sell her infant for twenty dollars worth of crack cocaine may be a singular but dramatic indicator of the damage wrought through cultural humiliation. As Paula Giddings has noted, in the history of the community, black women have been materially worse off and at the same time exhibited far less social pathology.[40]

The church must take seriously its prophetic role in regard to women's self-esteem. Drug abuse, violence, and teenage pregnancy are all related to issues of low self-esteem. In many ways, both subtle and overt, the vast majority of females in African America are assaulted by stereotypes and ideologies that humiliate them (and, incidentally, humiliate by reflection those who use them in their dealings with black women). Although I personally find the sexism and patriarchalism of Islam objectionable, particularly in its African-American varieties, Islam is currently the only corporate religious voice that states categorically and loudly that American standards of beauty and fashion "shame" and humiliate African-American women. Without reverting to a more primitive and restrictive view of women, African-American churches must address the cultural humiliation of women.

Barbara Andolsen identifies four major areas where white feminists and black feminists disagree. Besides work, rape, and male-female solidarity, the issue of beauty and the racial privilege associated with it stands out as a source of tension. She notes that while the images of black males in the media have changed and become more diverse, the images of black women have not.[41] The Mammy and the Jezebel still dominate the culturally acceptable images of black women. Actresses who refuse to participate in roles which reinforce stereotypes and culturally demean simply do not work often and do not reap the economic rewards of those who do. How often do we see Ruby Dee, Esther Rolle, and Cicely Tyson in large budget motion pictures? How often do we see African-American actresses featured in nonstereotypical roles?

Refashioning social meanings and cultural definitions is an essential task for changing society. It is also one of the most controversial and difficult as the political correctness backlash of the 1990s demonstrates. Critiques of culture depend, for their thoroughness and prophetic insight, on the standpoints or points of view of their authors. If the church thoroughly carries through its challenge to the cultural humiliation of women, the Afro-Christian critique of culture should be the most penetrating and the most prophetic. The production of a humane cultural experience for all African-American women depends upon a radical cultural critique. The church must work to produce that humane experience. The uplift of the downtrodden involves an aggressive campaign to redefine those aspects of culture which demean and exclude and humiliate. Such a prophetic stance involves the call to black women, issued in Alice Walker's in her definition of a *womanist,* to be self-loving *"regardless."*[42]

CONTEMPORARY ISSUES AND SPIRITUAL EMPOWERMENT

If confusion over mission and identity are of any importance in the ability of any group of people to resist oppression, the last decades of the twentieth century may be the worst for African Americans. In spite of the misery and suffering of slavery and the wholesale terror and assault that characterized the Jim Crow era, there was a unity of purpose and a sense of shared suffering that helped to mediate the conflicts between women and men. Within the current context of social fragmentation, underclass isolation, and theological diversity, the economic and political issues confronting women are compounded by confusion and conflict over scripturally prescribed roles for women and misperceptions about the actual status of African-American women in society. Many male pastors and other spokespersons believe falsely that African-American women are doing better than the men in their communities. It is an unfortunate distortion of the situation of a small proportion of professional women to argue this. The cultural context of the United States has consistently assaulted and punished the economic roles of black women and, through various public policies, engineered blame for the disadvantage of black men in the direction of black women.

The distorted images of African-American women's professional and economic successes provide further fuel to many men's belief that the ministry is still the only place where African-American men have access to influence and authority. As a result, resistance to women's ordination is still quite fierce among many African-American ministers. Currently, the largest black denomination (National Baptist Convention, U.S.A., Inc. [NBC]) does not recognize the ordination of women at a level of national policy. Although the NBC leaves the issue of ordination to the local church and its associations, the overwhelming sentiment expressed by delegates has rejected efforts of leaders to encourage the acceptance of women's ordination. Contrary to the Baptist legacy of congregational autonomy and freedom of conscience, local and regional Baptist associations will go to great lengths to restrain churches and pastors from ordaining women. At times the struggle to maintain denominational power and public prominence seems to overshadow the response of these organizations to the current emergencies of public life. The black Methodist denominations, African Methodist Episcopal, African Methodist Episcopal Zion, and Christian Methodist Episcopal Churches, all ordain women. However, they elected no women bishops until the year 2000, when the Rev. Dr. Vashti Murphy McKenzie was elected a bishop of the African Methodist Episcopal Church. Several Pentecostal denominations, including the largest, the Church of God in Christ, do not officially ordain women, while other denominations do. Several of those denominations have presiding bishops who are women. The picture for women in the ordained ministry *within the historically African-American denominations* is not good.

Ironically, there are two contradictions at work among black professionals and white churches. Other black professional men, particularly in male-dominated professions such as medicine and law, have had no problem affirming the leadership of black women, electing them to the presidencies of the National Medical Association and the National Bar Association, as well as to the presidencies of other professional, clinical, and academic associations. Most mainstream white Protestant denominations, with the exception of the Southern Baptist Convention, do affirm white and black women in professional ministry. Episcopalians, United Methodists, Congregationalists, Presbyterians, and Disciples of Christ, Christian, ordain women without significant conflict. Episcopalians and United Methodists have elected women bishops. American Baptists and Presbyterians have elected black women as moderator or presiding officer. Ironically, the denominations most associated with upper- and middle-class white people or with poor and marginalized black people in the United States have provided the greatest access to ecclesiastical authority for black women. These churches are also more flexible in their approach to biblical interpretation. The churches with the greatest mass appeal in black communities facing great crises have thrown up the greatest barriers to women's empowerment in their national bodies and local congregations.

Churches in black communities are more female than their white counterparts. The more "mass" the church, the more female has been the congregation. Regardless of this skewing, Theressa Hoover offers us the overall figure of 75 percent to describe women's participation.[43] This figure masks a range that reaches past 90 percent in some congregations of the Sanctified Church. The full empowerment of the church to speak to the needs of all African-American people cannot be accomplished without the full empowerment of women at every level.

CONCLUSION

This chapter cannot answer all of our questions about the church's mission to African-American women. One aim has been to identify several key ideas or themes that will make it possible not only to serve the needs of African-American women in a changing society but also to contribute to the solution of national problems from a strong, viable, and flexible religious tradition. I believe, in precisely the ways in which the black Christian club women—ministers truly—of the late nineteenth and early twentieth centuries believed when they adopted the motto, "Lifting as We Climb," that to struggle and push from the bottom of our communities will mean that the whole community will rise. Listening to and empowering "poor colored women"—economically, politically, or culturally "poor"—is essential to the material and spiritual redemption of African-American communities.

Our communities sit literally on the edge of cultural, political, and economic destruction. Significant segments of the African-American community are experiencing a relentless economic genocide.[44] Our central challenge is this: If the "Black Church" or the "African-American religious experience" or the "Afro-Christian tradition" (whatever we may wish to call it) is as strong as our sagas, legends, and sermons insist that it is, then the church must, in its best historical tradition, respond to this crisis with an internal ministry that addresses the needs of those who are suffering at the same time it projects an uncompromising prophetic force outward that demands and effects significant social, economic, political, and cultural change. In an 1886 speech before the colored clergy of the Protestant Episcopal Church at Washington, D.C., Anna Julia Cooper, insisted:

> "*I am my Sister's keeper!*" should be the hearty response of every man and woman of the race, and this conviction should purify and exalt the narrow, selfish and petty personal aims of life into a noble and sacred purpose.[45]

We still have not answered Cooper's challenge to become, as a community and as a nation and, most importantly, as a church, our "sister's keeper." The echo of that call to ministry still stands unanswered. Harriet Tubman, Alice Walker's "Celie," and Anna Julia Cooper all challenge us to heed the voices of "poor" colored women. It may not be an overstatement to say that the community's response to the historical roles of black women, particularly active/activist black

Christian women within and outside of their churches may be the key to the moral and historical contributions of the entire black community to the twenty-first century.

NOTES

1. Paula Giddings, *When and Where I Enter: The Impact of Black Women on Race and Sex in America* (New York: Morrow, 1984), 35; Anna Julia Cooper, *A Voice from the South by a Woman of the South* (New York: Negro Universities Press, 1969 [Xenia, Ohio: Aldine, 1892]), 31.

2. This is a term offered by Katie G. Cannon.

3. Deborah Gray White, *Ar'n't I a Woman? Female Slaves in the Plantation South* (New York: W. W. Norton, 1999), 119–41.

4. Thomas L. Webber, *Deep like the Rivers: Education in the Slave Quarter Community, 1831–1865* (New York: Norton, 1978).

5. Webber, *Deep like the Rivers,* 149.

6. Gayraud Wilmore, *Black Religion and Black Radicalism: An Interpretation of the Religious History of Afro-American People,* 2d ed. (Maryknoll, N.Y.: Orbis, 1983).

7. Evelyn Brooks Higginbotham, *Righteous Discontent: The Women's Movement in the Black Baptist Church, 1880–1920* (Cambridge, Mass.: Harvard University Press, 1993).

8. Higginbotham, *Righteous Discontent.*

9. Rackham Holt, *Mary McLeod Bethune: A Biography* (Garden City, N.Y.: Doubleday, 1964).

10. Mamie Garvin Fields with Karen E. Fields, *Lemon Swamp and Other Places: A Carolina Memoir* (New York: Macmillan, 1983).

11. Frances Ellen Watkins Harper, *Iola Leroy or the Shadows Uplifted* (Boston: Beacon Press, 1987 [1893]).

12. Evelyn Brooks Higginbotham in *Righteous Discontent* calls the women of this group the female half of the talented tenth.

13. Jualynne Dodson and Cheryl Townsend Gilkes, "'Something Within': Social Change and Collective Endurance in the Sacred World of Black Christian Women," in *Women and Religion in America,* vol. 3, *The Twentieth Century,* ed. Rosemary Radford Ruether and Rosemary Keller (San Francisco: Harper & Row, 1986), 80–130.

14. I use the term "poor" not only as a designation for those whose incomes place them below the poverty line, but in a way similar to the way in which James Cone uses the term "black"—as a label designating those who stand in solidarity with the least of these, and, for the purposes of this discussion, the least of these are "poor" black women.

15. Alice Walker, *In Search of Our Mother's Gardens* (New York: Harcourt, 1983), xi–xii.

16. Patricia Hill Collins, "The Social Construction of Black Feminist Thought," *Signs: Journal of Women in Culture and Society* 14, no. 4 (1989).

17. Angela Davis, *Women, Race, and Class* (New York: Random House, 1981), 5.

18. Jacqueline Jones, *Labor of Love, Labor of Sorrow: Black Women, Work and the Family from Slavery to the Present* (New York: Basic, 1985).

19. White, *Ar'n't I a Woman?*

20. For extended discussions of this phenomenon, see Nell Irvin Painter, *The Exodusters: Black Migration to Kansas after Reconstruction* (New York: Random House, 1977), and Jones, *Labor of Love.*

21. Dorothy Sterling, *We Are Your Sisters: Black Women in the Nineteenth Century* (New York: W. W. Norton, 1984).

22. Jones, *Labor of Love.*

23. Carter G. Woodson, "The Negro Washerwoman," *Journal of Negro History* 15, no. 3 (1930): 269–77. See also, Giddings, *When and Where I Enter.*

24. E. Franklin Frazier, *The Negro Family in the United States* (Chicago: University of Chicago Press, 1939).

25. Taylor Branch, *Parting the Waters: America in the King Years, 1954–63* (New York: Simon and Schuster, 1988).

26. Jo Ann Gibson Robinson, *The Montgomery Bus Boycott and the Women Who Started It: The Memoir of Jo Ann Gibson Robinson* (Knoxville, Tenn.: University of Tennessee Press, 1987).

27. Deborah K. King, "Multiple Jeopardy, Multiple Consciousness: The Context of Black Feminist Ideology," *Signs: Journal of Women in Culture and Society* 14, no. 1 (1988): 42–72.

28. Paula S. Rothenberg, *Racism and Sexism: An Integrated Study* (New York: St. Martin's Press, 1988).

29. For fuller discussions of the role of Nannie Helen Burroughs within and outside of the National Baptist Convention, see also Evelyn Brooks, "Religion, Politics, and Gender: The Leadership of Nannie Helen Burroughs," *Journal of Religious Thought* 44 (winter/spring 1988): 7–22; and Evelyn Brooks Barnett, "Nannie Burroughs and the Education of Black Women," in *The Afro-American Woman: Struggles and Images,* ed. Sharon Harley and Rosalyn Terborg-Penn (Port Washington, N.Y.: Kennikat Press, 1978), 97–108.

30. Charles V. Hamilton, *The Black Preacher in America* (New York: William Morrow and Co., 1972).

31. Marilyn Richardson, ed., *Maria W. Stewart, America's First Black Woman Political Writer* (Bloomington: Indiana University Press, 1987).

32. Joanne Grant, "Fundi: The Story of Ella Baker" (New York: Icarus Films, 1986).

33. Kay Mills, *This Little Light of Mine: The Life of Fannie Lou Hamer* (New York: Dutton, 1993).

34. Mary King, *Freedom Song; A Personal Story of the 1960s Civil Rights Movement* (New York: Morrow, 1987).

35. I provide more extended discussion of community workers and church mothers in Cheryl Townsend Gilkes, "'Together and in Harness': Women's Traditions in the Sanctified Church," *Signs: Journal of Women in Culture and Society* 11, no. 4 (1985): 80–130; and idem, "The Roles of Church and Community Mothers: Ambivalent American Sexism or Fragmented African Familyhood?" *Journal of Feminist Studies in Religion* 2 (spring 1986): 41–59.

36. Edwin Schur, *Labeling Women Deviant: Gender, Stigma and Social Control* (New York: Random House, 1984).

37. Walker, *In Search of Our Mother's Gardens,* 290.

38. One of the most helpful discussions of this I have experienced was at a black feminist panel discussion on racism and self-hatred held at Simmons College in Boston, Massachusetts, in the early 1980s. The exact date and conference escape me now.

39. Michelle Wallace, *Black Macho and the Myth of the Superwoman* (New York: Dial Press, 1979).

40. Giddings, *When and Where I Enter.*

41. Barbara Andolsen, *"Daughters of Jefferson, Daughters of Bootblacks": Racism and American Feminism* (Macon, Ga.: Mercer University Press, 1986).

42. Walker, *In Search of Our Mother's Gardens,* xii.

43. Theressa Hoover, "Black Women and the Churches: Triple Jeopardy," in *Black Theology: A Documentary History, 1966–1979,* ed. Gayraud S. Wilmore and James H. Cone (Maryknoll, N.Y.: Orbis, 1980), 377–88.

44. Although left out of many of the current discussions of the underclass, I think that Sydney Wilhelm's volume *Who Needs the Negro* (Garden City, N.Y.: Doubleday, 1971) provides an important and provocative context that needs reexamination. He argued that any group that became economically useless became prime targets for genocide. He used the Native American experience as a historical example. He also pointed to the fact that "equally" could now be asserted since economic discrimination would maintain the same essential state of white over black.

45. Cooper, *A Voice from the South,* 32.

"Ecology Is a Sistah's Issue Too: The Politics of Emergent Afrocentric Ecowomanism"

❧

Shamara Shantu Riley

Shamara Shantu Riley is a political scientist who writes on the intersection of environmentalism, race, and gender. This essay connects those three concerns.

❧

Black womanists, like everyone in general, can no longer overlook the extreme threat to life on this planet and its particular repercussions on people of African descent.[1] Because of the race for increased "development," our world continues to suffer the consequences of such environmental disasters as the Chernobyl nuclear meltdown and Brazil's dwindling forests. Twenty percent of all species are at risk of extinction by the year 2000, with the rate of plant and animal extinction likely to reach several hundred per day in the next ten to thirty years (Worldwatch 1987, 3). Manufacturing chemicals and other abuses to the environment continue to weaken the ozone layer. We must also contend with the phenomenon of climate change, with its attendant rise in sea levels and changes in food production patterns.

Along with these tragic statistics, however, are additional environmental concerns that hit far closer to home than many Black people realize. In the United States, poor people of color are disproportionately likely to be the victims of pollution, as toxic waste is being consciously directed at our communities. The nation's largest hazardous-waste dump, which has received toxic material from forty-five states, is located in predominantly black Sumter County, Alabama (de la Pena and Davis 1990, 34). The mostly African-American residents in the eighty-five-mile area between Baton Rouge and New Orleans, better known as Cancer Alley, live in a region which contains 136 chemical companies and refineries. A 1987 study conducted by the United Church of Christ's Commission for Racial Justice found that two-thirds of all Blacks and Latinos in the United States reside in areas with one or more unregulated toxic-waste sites (Riley 1991, 15). The CRJ report also cited race as the most significant variable in differentiating communities with such sites from those without them. Partly as a result of living with toxic waste in disproportionate numbers, African-Americans have higher rates of cancer, birth defects, and lead poisoning than the United States population as a whole.[2]

On the African continent, rampant deforestation and soil erosion continue to contribute to the hunger and poverty rates in many countries. The elephant population is rapidly being reduced as poachers kill them to satisfy industrialized nations' ivory trade demands (Joyce 1989, 22).

Spreading to a dozen African nations, the Green Belt Movement is seeking to reverse the environmental damage created by the European settlers during colonialism, when the settlers brought nonindigenous trees on the continent. As with U.S. communities of color, many African nations experience "economic blackmail," which occurs when big business promises jobs and money to "impoverished areas in return for these areas' support of or acquiescence to environmentally undesirable industries" (Meyer 1992, 32).

The extinction of species on our ancestral continent, the "mortality of wealth," and hazardous-waste contamination in our backyards ought to be reasons enough for Black womanists to consider the environment as a central issue of our political agendas.[3] However, there are other reasons the environment should be central to our struggles for social justice. The global environmental crisis is related to the sociopolitical systems of fear and hatred of all that is natural, nonwhite, and female that has pervaded dominant Western thought for centuries.[4] I contend that the social constructions of race, gender, class, and nonhuman nature in mainstream Western thought are interconnected by an ideology of domination. Specific instances of the emergent Afrocentric ecowomanist activism in Africa and the United States, as well as West African spiritual principles that propose a method of overcoming dualism, will be discussed in this paper.

THE PROBLEM OF NATURE FOR BLACK WOMANISM

Until recently, few Black womanists gave more than token attention to environmental issues. At least in the United States, the origins of such oversight stem from the traditional Black association of environmentalism as a "white" concern. The resistance by many U.S. Blacks to the environmental movement may partly originate from a hope of revenge. Because of our acute oppression(s), many Blacks may conclude that if the world comes to an end because of willful negligence, at least there is the satisfaction that one's oppressors will also die. In "Only Justice Can Stop a Curse," author Alice Walker discusses how her life experiences with the Eurocentric, masculinist ideology of domination have often caused her to be indifferent to environmental issues:

> I think . . . *Let the earth marinate in poisons. Let the bombs cover the ground like rain. For nothing short of total destruction will ever teach them anything.* (A. Walker 1983, 341)

However, Walker later articulates that since environmental degradation doesn't make a distinction between oppressors and the oppressed, it should be very difficult for people of color to embrace the thought of extinction of all life forms simply for revenge.

In advocating a reformulation of how humans view nonhuman nature, ecofeminist theorist Ynestra King states that from the beginning, women have had to grapple with the historical projection of human concepts onto the natural, which were later used to fortify masculinist notions about females' nature (King 1989, 118). The same problem is applicable to people of color, who have also been negatively identified with the natural in white supremacist ideologies.

Black women in particular have historically been associated with animality and subsequently objectified to uphold notions of racial purity. bell hooks articulates that since the 1500s,

Western societies have viewed Black women's bodies as objects to be subdued and controlled like nonhuman nature:

> From slavery to the present day, the Black female body has been seen in Western eyes as the quintessential symbol of a "natural" female presence that is organic, closer to nature, animalistic, primitive. (hooks and West 1991, 153)

Patricia Hill Collins asserts that white exploitation of Black women as breeders during the Slave Era "objectified [Black women] as less than human because only animals can be bred against their will" (Collins 1990, 167). Sarah Bartmann, an African woman also known as the Hottentot Venus, was prominently displayed at elite Parisian parties. While being reduced to her sexual parts, Bartmann's protruding buttocks were often offered as "proof" that Blacks were closer to animals than whites. After her death in 1815, Bartmann was dissected, and her genitalia and buttocks remain on display in Paris (Gilman 1985). Bartmann's situation was similar to the predicament of Black female slaves who stood on auction blocks as masters described their productive body parts as humans do cattle. The historical dissection of Black women, be it symbolic or actual, to uphold white supremacist notions is interconnected with the consistent human view of nonhuman animals as scientific material to be dissected through an ideology that asserts both groups are inferior.

Because of the historical and current treatment of Blacks in dominant Western ideology, Black womanists must confront the dilemma of whether we should strive to sever or reinforce the traditional association of Black people with nature that exists in dominant Western thought. However, what we need is not a total disassociation of people from nature, but rather a reformulation of *everyone's* relationship to nature by socially reconstructing gender, class, and ethnic roles.

Environmentalism is a women's issue because females (especially those of color) are the principal farm laborers around the world, as well as the majority of the world's major consumers of agricultural products (Bizot 1992, 36). Environmentalism is also an important issue for people of color because we disproportionately bear the brunt of environmental degradation. For most of the world's population, reclaiming the Earth is not an abstract state of affairs but rather is inextricably tied to the survival of our peoples.

Womanism and ecology have a common theoretical approach in that both see all parts of a matrix as having equal value. Ecology asserts that without each element in the ecosystem, the biosphere as a whole cannot function properly. Meanwhile, womanism asserts the equality of races, genders, and sexual preferences, among other variables. There is no use in womanists advocating liberation politics if the planet cannot support people's liberated lives, and it is equally useless to advocate saving the planet without addressing the social issues that determine the structure of human relations in the world. If the planet as a whole is to survive, we must all begin to see ourselves as interconnected with nonhuman nature and with one another.

THE POLITICS OF NATURE-CULTURE DUALISM

At the foundation of dominant Western thought exists an intense ambivalence over humankind's place in the biosphere, not only in relation to one another, but also in relation to nonhuman nature. The systematic denigration of men of color, women, and nonhuman nature is interconnected through a nature-culture dualism. This system of interconnectedness, which bell hooks labels "the politic of domination," functions along interlocking axes of race, gender, species, and class oppression. The politic of domination "refers to the ideological ground that [the axes] share, which is a belief in domination, and a belief in the notions of superior and inferior, which are components of all those systems" (hooks 1989, 175). Although groups encounter different dimensions of this matrix based on such variables as species or sexual orientation, an overarching relationship nevertheless connects all of these socially constructed variables.

In discussing the origins of Western dualism, Dona Richards articulates the influence of dominant Jewish and Christian thought on Western society's conceptions about its relationship to nonhuman nature:

> Christian thought provides a view of man, nature, and the universe which supports not only the ascendancy of science, but of the technical order, individualism and relentless progress. Emphasis within this world view is placed on humanity's dominance over all other beings, which become "objects" in an "objectified" universe. Humanity is separated from nature. (Richards 1980, 69)

With dualistic thinking, humans, nonhuman nature, and ideas are categorized in terms of their difference from one another. However, one part is not simply deemed different from its counterpart; it is also deemed intrinsically *opposed* to its "Other" (Collins 1990, 69). For instance, speciesists constantly point to human neocortical development and the ensuing civilization that this development constructs as proof of human superiority over nonhuman animals. Women's position as other in Western patriarchies throughout the histories of both psychological theory and Christian thought has resulted in us being viewed as defective men.

Women, the nonelite, and men of color are not only socially constructed as the "Others," but the elite, white, male-controlled global political structure also has the power—through institutions such as the international media and politics—to extensively socialize us to view ourselves as others to be dominated. By doing so, the pattern of domination and subjugation is reinforced. Objectification is also central to the process of oppositional difference for all entities cast as other. Dona Richards claims that in dominant Western thought, intense objectification is a "prerequisite for the despiritualization of the universe and through it the Western cosmos was made ready for ever increasing materialization" (Richards 1980, 72). Since one component is deemed to be the other, it is simultaneously viewed as an object to be controlled and dominated, particularly through economic means.

Because nature-culture dualism conceives of nature as an other that (male) human undertakings transcend and conquer, women, nonhuman nature, and men of color become symbolically linked in Eurocentric, masculinist ideology. In this framework, the objectification of the other also serves as an escape from the anxiety of some form of mortality. For instance, white supremacists fear that it will be the death of the white race if people of color, who comprise the majority of the world's population, successfully resist the current global relations of power. Objectifying nonhuman nature by technology is predicated on an intense fear of the body, which reminds humans of death and our connection with the rest of nature. By making products that make tasks easier, one seeks to have more opportunities to live one's life, with time and nature converted into commodities.

World history can be seen as one in which human beings inextricably bind the material domination of nonhuman nature with the economic domination of other human beings. The Eurocentric, masculinist worldview that dominates Western thought tends to only value the parts of reality that can be exploited in the interest of profit, power, and control. Not only is that associated with nature deemed amenable to conquest, but it is also a conquest that requires no moral self-examination on the part of the prospective conqueror. For instance, there is very little moral examination by research laboratories that test cosmetics on animals, or by men who assault women. There was also very little moral examination on the part of slave owners on the issue of slavery or by European settlers on colonialism in "Third World" nations.

By defining people of color as more natural and animalistic, a political economy of domination has been historically reinforced. An example of this phenomenon is the founding of the United States and the nation's resultant slave trade. In order for the European colonialists to exploit the American land for their economic interests, they first needed to subjugate the Native American groups who were inhabiting the land. While this was being accomplished, the colonists dominated Blacks by utilizing Africans as slave labor (and simultaneously appropriating much of Mexico) in order to cultivate the land for profit and expand the new capitalist nation's economy. Meanwhile, the buffalo almost became extinct in the process of this nation building "from sea to shining sea."

A salient example of the interconnectedness of environmental degradation and male supremacy is the way many societies attach little value to that which can be exploited without (economic) cost. Because nonhuman nature has historically been viewed by Westerners as a free asset to be possessed, little value has been accredited to it. Work traditionally associated with women via cultural socialization has similarly often been viewed as having little to no value. For instance, in calculating the Gross Domestic Product, no monetary value is attached to women's contributions to national economies through reproduction, housework, or care of children.

THE ROLE OF THE ENVIRONMENTAL-ISMS IN PROVIDING THE FOUNDATION FOR AN AFROCENTRIC WOMANIST AGENDA

While serving as executive director of the United Church of Christ's Commission for Racial Justice in 1987, Reverend Benjamin Chavis Jr., coined the term environmental racism to explain the dynamics of socioeconomic inequities in waste-management policies. Peggy Shephard, the director of West Harlem Environmental Action, defines U.S. environmental racism as "the policy of siting potentially hazardous facilities in low-income and minority communities" (Day and Knight 1991, 77). However, environmental racism, which is often intertwined with classism, doesn't halt at the boundaries of poor areas of color. Blacks in Africa and the United States often have to contend with predominantly white environmental groups that ignore the connection between their own values and the struggles of people of color to preserve our future, which is a crucial connection in order to build and maintain alliances to reclaim the earth. For instance, because the Environmental Protection Agency is often seen as another institution that perceives elite white communities' complaints as more deserving of attention than poor communities of color, many U.S. social activists are accusing the EPA of "environmental apartheid" (Riley 1991, 15).

In "Granola Boys, Eco-Dudes, and Me," Elizabeth Larsen articulates how race, class, and gender politics are interconnected by describing the overwhelmingly white middle-class male leadership of mainstream U.S. environmental groups. In addition to being indifferent to the concerns of people of color and poor whites, the mainstream organizations often reinforce male supremacy by distributing organizational tasks along traditional gender roles (Larsen 1991, 96). The realization that only we can best represent our interests, an eco-identity politics, so to speak, lays the foundation for an Afrocentric ecowomanist agenda.[5] Even though many Black women have been active in the environmental movement in the past, there appears not to be much *published* analysis on their part about the role of patriarchy in environmental degradation. The chief reason for this sentiment may stem from perceiving race as the "primary" oppression. However, there is an emergent group of culturally identified Black women in Africa and the United States who are critically analyzing the social roles of white supremacy, patriarchy, and classism in environmental degradation.

EMERGENT AFROCENTRIC ECOWOMANISM ON THE NECESSITY OF SURVIVAL

There are several differences between ecofeminism and Afrocentric ecowomanism. While Afrocentric ecowomanism also articulates the links between male supremacy and environmental degradation, it lays far more stress on other distinctive features, such as race and class, that leave an impression markedly different from many ecofeminists' theories.[6]

Many ecofeminists, when analyzing the links between human relations and ecological degradation, give primacy to gender and thus fail to thoroughly incorporate (as opposed to mere tokenism) the historical links between classism, white supremacy, and environmental degradation in their perspectives. For instance, they often don't address the fact that in nations where such variables as ethnicity and class are a central organizing principle of society, many women are not only viewed in opposition to men under dualism, but also to other women. A salient example of this blind spot is Mary Daly's *Gyn/Ecology*, where she implores women to identify with nature against men and live our lives separately from men. However, such an essentialist approach is very problematic for certain groups of women, such as the disabled and Jews, who must ally themselves with men (while simultaneously challenging them on their sexism) in order to combat the isms in their lives. As writer Audre Lorde stated, in her critique of Daly's exclusion of how Black women use Afrocentric spiritual practices as a source of power against the isms while connecting with nonhuman nature:

> to imply, however, that women suffer the same oppression simply because we are women, is to lose sight of the many varied tools of patriarchy. It is to ignore how these tools are used by women without awareness against each other. (Lorde 1983, 95)

Unlike most white women, Black women are not limited to issues defined by our femaleness but are rather often limited to questions raised about our very humanity.

Although they have somewhat different priorities because of their different environments, Afrocentric ecowomanists in the United States and Africa nevertheless have a common goal—to analyze the issues of social justice that underlie environmental conflict. Not only do Afrocentric ecowomanists seek to avoid detrimental environmental impacts, we also seek to overcome the socioeconomic inequalities that led to the injustices in the first place.

Emergent U.S. Afrocentric Ecowomanist Activism

Contrary to mainstream U.S. media claims, which imply that African-Americans are not concerned about ecology, there has been increased environmental activism within Black communities since the early 1980s. Referred to as the environmental equity movement by Robert Bullard, predominantly Black grassroots environmental organizations tend to view environmentalism as an extension of the 1960s Civil Rights movement. In *Yearning*, bell hooks links environmentalism with social justice while discussing Black radicals and revolutionary politics:

> We are concerned about the fate of the planet, and some of us believe that living simply is part of revolutionary political practice. We have a sense of the sacred. The ground we stand on is shifting, fragile, and unstable. (hooks 1990, 19)

On discussing how the links between environmental concerns and civil rights encouraged her involvement with environmentalism, arts writer and poet Esther Iverem states:

> Soon I began to link civil rights with environmental sanity. . . . Because in 1970 Black folks were vocally fighting for their rightful share of the pie, the logical question for me became "What kind of shape will that pie be in?" (Iverem 1991, 38)

Iverem's question has been foremost in many African-American women's minds as we continue to be instrumental in the Black communities' struggle to ensure that the shape of the social justice pie on our planet will not be increasingly carcinogenic. When her neighborhood started to become dilapidated, Hattie Carthan founded the Magnolia Tree Earth Center of Bed-Stuy in Brooklyn in 1968, to help beautify the area. She planted more than 1,500 trees before her death in 1974. In 1986, the city council of Los Angeles decided that a thirteen-acre incinerator, which would have burned 2,000 tons of city waste daily, was to be built in a low-income Black and Latino neighborhood in South Central Los Angeles. Upon hearing this decision, residents, mostly women, successfully organized in opposition by forming Concerned Citizens of South Central Los Angeles. While planning direct actions to protest the incinerator, the grass roots organization didn't have a formal leadership structure for close to two years. Be it a conscious or unconscious decision, Concerned Citizens accepted a relatively nonhierarchical, democratic process in their political activism by rotating the chair's position at meetings, a form of decision making characteristic of many ecofeminist groups.[7]

The Philadelphia Community Rehabilitation Corporation (PCRC), founded by Rachel E. Bagby, operates a village community to maintain a nonhierarchical relationship between human and nonhuman nature for its working-class-to-poor urban Black residents. About 5,000 reside in the community, and there is communalistic living, like that of many African villages. PCRC has a "repeopling" program that renovates and rents more than fifty previously vacant homes and also created a twelve-unit shared house. PCRC also takes vacant lots and recycles them into gardens to provide food, and oversees literacy and employment programs. Hazel and Cheryl Johnson founded People for Community Recovery (PCR), which is operated from a storefront at the Altgeld Gardens housing project, after they became aware that their community sits atop a landfill and has the greatest concentration of hazardous waste in the nation. In its fight against environmental racism, PCR has insisted that the Chicago Housing Authority remove all asbestos from the Altgeld homes and has helped lobby city government to declare a moratorium on new landfill permits. PCR also successfully prevented the establishment of another landfill in Altgeld Gardens.

One Black women's organization that addresses environmental issues is the National Black Women's Health Project (NBWHP). The NBWHP expresses its Afrocentric ecowomanist sentiment primarily through its SisteReach program, which seeks to connect the NBWHP with various Black women's organizations around the world. On urging African-American women to participate in the environmental movement and analyze the connections between male supremacy and environmental degradation, Dianne J. Forte, the SisteReach coordinator, makes the following statement:

> At first glance and with all the major problems demanding our energy in our community we may be tempted to say, "this is not my problem." If however, we look at the ominous connection being made between environmental degradation and population growth; if we look at the same time at trends which control women's bodies and lives and control the world's resources, we realize that the same arguments are used to justify both. (Forte 1992, 5)

For instance, women are increasingly being told that we should not have control over our own bodies, while the Earth is simultaneously deemed feminine by scientists who use sexual imagery to articulate their plans to take control over the Earth. Meanwhile, dominant groups often blame environmental degradation on overpopulation (and with their privileged status, usually point at poor women of color), when industrial capitalism and patriarchal control over women's reproduction are among the most pronounced culprits.

The most salient example of practical U.S. Afrocentric ecowomanism combating such claims is Luisah Teish, a voodoo priestess. In connecting social justice issues with spiritual practices rooted in the West African heritage, Teish articulates the need for everyone to actively eliminate patriarchy, white supremacy, and classism, along with the domination of nonhuman nature. Members of Teish's altar circle have planned urban gardening projects both to supply herbs for their holistic healing remedies and to assist the poor in feeding themselves. They have also engaged in grassroots organizing to stop gentrification in various communities.

Emergent Afrocentric Ecowomanist Activism in Africa

On the African continent, women have been at the forefront of the movement to educate people about environmental problems and how they affect their lives. As with much of the African continent, environmental problems in Kenya particularly influence rural women's lives, since they comprise 80 percent of that nation's farmers and fuel gatherers (Maathai 1991, 74). Soil erosion directly affects the women, because they depend on subsistence agriculture for their families' survival. The lack of firewood in many rural areas of Kenya because of deforestation disproportionately alters the lives of women, who must walk long distances to fetch firewood. The lack of water also makes a negative imprint on Kenyan women's lives, because they have to walk long distances to fetch the water.

However, many Kenyan women are striving to alter these current realities. The most prominent Afrocentric ecowomanist in Africa is Wangari Maathai, a Kenyan microbiologist and one of Africa's leading activists on environmental issues. Maathai is the founder and director of the Green Belt Movement (GBM), a fifteen-year-old tree-planting project designed to help poor Kenyan communities stop soil erosion, protect their water systems, and overcome the lack of firewood and building materials.

Launched under the auspices of the National Council of Women of Kenya, the majority of the GBM's members are women. Since 1977, these women have grown ten million trees, 80 percent of which have survived, to offset Kenya's widespread deforestation.[8] Although the GBM's primary practical goal is to end desertification and deforestation, it is also committed to promoting public awareness of the relationship between environmental degradation and social problems that affect the Kenyan people—poverty, unemployment, and malnutrition. However, one of the most significant accomplishments of the GBM, Maathai asserts, is that its members are "now independent; had acquired knowledge, techniques; had become empowered" (Maathai 1991, 74).

Another Kenyan dedicated to environmental concerns is Wagaki Mwangi, the founder and coordinator of the International Youth Development and Environment Network. When she visited the University of Illinois at Urbana-Champaign, Mwangi discussed how Kenya suffers economic and environmental predicaments primarily because her homeland is trying to imitate Western cultures. "A culture has been superimposed on a culture," Mwangi said, but there are not enough resources for everyone to live up to the new standards of the neocolonial culture (Schallert 1992, 3). She asserted that in attempts to be more Western, "what [Kenyans] valued as our food has been devalued, and what we are valuing is what they value in the West" (Schallert 1992, 3). For instance, Kenyans used to survive by eating a variety of wild foods, but now many don't consider such foods as staples because of Western influences. In the process, many areas of Kenya are deemed to be suffering from food shortages as the economy has been transformed to consumer capitalism with its attendant mechanization of agriculture.

In Kourfa, Niger, women have been the primary force behind preventing the village from disappearing, a fate that many surrounding villages have suffered because of the Sahel region's desertification. Reduced rainfall and the drying up of watering places and vegetation, combined with violent sandstorms, have virtually deprived Kourfa of harvests for the past five years. As a result, the overwhelming majority of Kourfa's men have had to travel far away for long periods of time to find seasonal work.

With the assistance of the Association of Women of Niger and an agricultural advisor, the women have laid out a small marketgarden around the only well in Kourfa. Despite the few resources at their disposal, the Kourfa women have succeeded in supporting themselves, their children, and the village elders. In response to the survival of the village since these actions, the Kourfa women are now calling for increased action to reverse the region's environmental degradation so "the men won't go away" from the village (Ouedraogo 1992, 38).

Afrocentric Ecomotherists: Ecowomanist Potential?

The environmental activism of some Black women brings up the question of whether community-oriented Black women who are addressing environmental issues are genuinely Afrocentric ecowomanists or possibly Afrocentric ecomotherists.[9] According to Ann Snitow, motherists are women who, for various reasons, "identify themselves not as feminists but as militant mothers, fighting together for survival" (Snitow 1989, 48). Snitow also maintains that motherism usually arises when men are absent or in times of crisis, when the private sphere role assigned to women under patriarchy makes it impossible for the collective to survive. Since they are faced with the dictates of traditional work but face a lack of resources in which to fulfill their socially prescribed role, motherists become a political force.

Since they took collective action to secure the survival of the village's children and elders only after the necessary absence of Kourfa's men, the activism of the Kourfa women may possibly be based on a motherist philosophy. One can only conjecture whether the Kourfa women criticized the social role of motherhood in Niger as they became a political force, or if womanist consciousness emerged after their political experiences. Because of their potential to transform into ecowomanists after they enter the political realm, Afrocentic ecomotherists shouldn't be discounted in an analysis of Black women's environmental activism. For instance, Charlotte

Bullock contends that she "did not come to the fight against environmental problems as an intellectual but rather as a concerned mother" (Hamilton 1990, 216). However, she and other women in Concerned Citizens of South Central Los Angeles began to notice the sexual politics that attempted to discount their political activism while they were protesting. "I noticed when we first started fighting the issue how the men would laugh at the women . . . they would say, 'Don't pay no attention to them, that's only one or two women . . . they won't make a difference.' But now since we've been fighting for about a year the smiles have gone" (Hamilton 1990, 215). Robin Cannon, another member of Concerned Citizens, asserts that social relations in her home, specifically gender roles on caretaking, were transformed after she began participating in the group's actions (Hamilton 1990, 220).

MOVING BEYOND DUALISM: AN AFROCENTRIC APPROACH

In utilizing spiritual concepts to move beyond dualism, precolonial African cultures, with their both/and perspectives, are useful forms of knowledge for Afrocentric ecowomanists to envision patterns toward interdependence of human and nonhuman nature. Traditional West African cultures, in particular, which also happen to be the ancestral roots of the overwhelming majority of African-Americans, share a belief in nature worship and view all things as being alive on varying levels of existence (Haskins 1978, 30). One example of such an approach in West African traditions is the *Nyam* concept. A root word in many West African languages, *Nyam* connotes an enduring power and energy possessed by all life (Collins 1990, 220). Thus, all forms of life are deemed to possess certain rights, which cannot be violated at will.

In *Jambalaya*, Luisah Teish writes of the *Da* concept, which originates from the Fon people of Western Africa. *Da* is "the energy that carries creation, the force field in which creation takes place" (Teish 1985, 61). In the Fon view, all things are composed of energy provided by *Da*. For example, "the human is receptive to the energy emanating from the rock and the rock is responsive to human influence" (Teish 1985, 62). Because West Africans have traditionally viewed nonhuman nature as sacred and worthy of praise through such cultural media as song and dance, there is also a belief in *Nommo*. *Nommo* is "the physical-spiritual life force which awakens all 'sleeping' forces and gives physical and spiritual life" (Jahn 1961, 105).

However, with respect for nonhuman nature comes a different understanding of *Ache*, the Yoruba term for human power. *Ache* doesn't connote "power over" or domination, as it often does in mainstream Western thought, but rather power *with* other forms of creation. With *Ache*, Teish states that there is "a regulated kinship among human, animal, mineral, and vegetable life" (Teish 1985, 63). Humans recognize their *Ache* to eat and farm, "but it is also recognized that they must give back that which is given to them" (Teish 1985, 63). In doing so, we respect the overall balance and interdependence of human and nonhuman nature.

These concepts can be useful for Afrocentric ecowomanists not only in educating our peoples about environmental issues, but also in reclaiming the cultural traditions of our ancestors. Rachel Bagby states the positivity of humans connecting with nonhuman nature, a view that is interwoven in her organization's work:

> If you can appreciate the Earth, you can appreciate the beauty of yourself. The same creator created both. And if I learned to take care of that I'll also take care of myself and help take care of others. (Bagby 1990, 242)

Illustrating an outlook of planetary relations that is parallel to the traditional West African worldview, Bagby simultaneously reveals the continuous link between much of the African-American religious tradition and African spirituality.

In light of the relations of power and privilege that exist in the world, the appropriation of indigenous cultures by some ecofeminists must be addressed. Many womanists, such as Andy Smith and Luisah Teish, have criticized cultural feminists for inventing earth-based feminist spiritualities that are based on the exploitation of our ancestral traditions, while we're struggling to reclaim and defend our cultures from white supremacy. In "For All Those Who Were Indian in Another Life," Smith asserts that this appropriation of non-Western spiritual traditions functions as a way for many white women to avoid taking responsibility for being simultaneously oppressive as well as oppressed (see her article, 168–71). White ecofeminists can reclaim their own pre-Christian European cultures, such as the Wiccan tradition, for similar concepts of interconnectedness, community, and immanence found in West African traditions.[10]

Adopting these concepts would transform humans' relationship to nonhuman nature in a variety of ways. By seeing all components of the ecosystem affecting and being affected by one another, such a world perspective demonstrates a pattern of living in harmony with the rest of nature, instead of seeking to disconnect from it. By viewing ourselves as a part of nature, we would be able to move beyond the Western disdain for the body and therefore not ravage the Earth's body as a result of this disdain and fear. We would realize that the Earth is not merely the source of our survival, but also has intrinsic value and must be treated with respect, as it is our elder.

The notion of community would help us to appreciate the biological and cultural diversity that sustains life. Because every entity is viewed as embodying spirituality under immanence, culture wouldn't be viewed as separate from, and superior to, nature, as it is seen in mainstream Western religions. Communalism would also aid us in reformulating the social constructions of race, gender, species, class (among other variables), which keep groups separate from one another. And finally, the environmental movement in particular would view politics as rooted in community and communally take actions to reclaim the Earth and move toward a life of interdependence for generations to come.

NOTES

I would like to acknowledge the help that Carol Adams has given me with this essay. Her reading suggested valuable changes in the structure of the essay as well as clearing up minor flaws in writing. She also suggested some references that would augment my claims.

1. Alice Walker's definition of womanist is a feminist of color who is "committed to the survival and wholeness of entire people, male *and* female" (A. Walker 1983, xi–xii). University of Ibadan (Nigeria) English senior lecturer Chikwenye Okonjo Ogunyemi contends that "black womanism is a philosophy that celebrates black roots. . . . It concerns itself as much with the black sexual power tussle as with the world power structure that subjugates blacks" (Ogunyemi 1985, 72). Since feminism often gives primacy to gender, and race consciousness often gives primacy to race, such limitations in terminology have caused many women of color to adopt the term *womanist,* which both Walker and Ogunyemi independently coined in the early 1980s. Although some of the women in this paper refer to themselves as feminists rather than womanists, or use both terms interchangeably, I am using the term *womanist* in an interpretative sense to signify a culturally identified woman of color who also critically analyzes the sexual politics within her respective ethnic group.

2. For a discussion of how toxic waste has affected the environmental health of U.S. Black communities, see Day and Knight (1991).

3. Robert Bullard (1990) contends that the mortality of wealth involves toxic-waste dumping to pursue profits at the expense of others, usually low-income people of color in the United States. Because this demographic group is less likely to have economic resources and political clout, it can't fight back as easily as more affluent communities that possess white skin privileges. I think this term is also applicable to the economic nature of toxic dumping in "Third World" countries, which are basically disempowered in the global political process.

4. For an ecofeminist text that makes a similar claim, see King (1989).

5. My definition of an Afrocentric ecowomanist is a communalistic-oriented Black woman who understands and articulates the interconnectedness of the degradation of people of color, women, and the environment. In addition to articulating this interconnectedness, an Afrocentric ecowomanist also strives to eradicate this degradation. For an extensive discussion of Afrocentrism, see Myers (1988).

6. An example of this distinction can be seen in Davies (1988). In her article, Davies only discusses the interconnections between gender and nature and completely avoids analyzing how such variables as ethnicity and class influence the experience of gender in one's life.

7. For several descriptions of the political decision making within feminist peace organizations, see the essays in Harris and King (1989).

8. It is noteworthy that the seedlings come from over 1,500 tree nurseries, 99 percent of which are operated by women. In addition, the women are given a small payment for the trees that survive.

9. In comparison to an Afrocentric ecowomanist, I define an Afrocentric ecomotherist as a communalistic-oriented Black woman who is involved in saving the environment and challenging white supremacy, but who does not challenge the fundamental dynamics of sexual politics in women's lives.

10. For instance, Starhawk, a practitioner of the Wiccan tradition, has written about her spiritual beliefs (1990).

BIBLIOGRAPHY

Bagby, Rachel. 1990. "Daughters of Growing Things." In *Reweaving the World: The Emergence of Ecofeminism*, ed. Irene Diamond and Gloria Feman Orenstein. San Francisco: Sierra Club Books.

Bullard, Robert. 1990. *Dumping in Dixie: Race, Class and Environmental Quality*. Boulder, Colo.: Westview Press.

Collins, Patricia Hill. 1990. *Black Feminist Thought: Knowledge, Consciousness, and the Politics of Empowerment*. Boston: Unwin Hyman.

Davies, Katherine. 1988. "What Is Ecofeminism?" *Women and Environments* 10 (3): 4–6.

Day, Barbara, and Kimberly Knight. 1991. "The Rain Forest in Our Back Yard."*Essence* 21 (Jan.): 75–77.

de la Pena, Nonny, and Susan Davis. 1990. "The Greens Are White: And Minorities Want In." *Newsweek* 116 (Oct. 15): 34.

Forte, Dianne J. 1992. "SisteReach . . . Because 500 Years Is Enough." *Vital Signs: News from the National Black Women's Health Project* 1 (spring): 5.

Gilman, Sander L. 1985. "Black Bodies, White Bodies: Toward an Iconography of Female Sexuality in Late Nineteenth-Century Art, Medicine and Literature." *Critical Inquiry* 12 (autumn): 205–43.

Hamilton, Cynthia. 1990. "Women, Home and Community: The Struggle in an Urban Environment." In *Reweaving the World: The Emergence of Ecofeminism*, ed. Irene Diamond and Gloria Feman Orenstein. San Francisco: Sierra Club Books.

Harris, Adrienne, and Ynestra King, eds., 1989. *Rocking the Ship of State: Toward a Feminist Peace Politics*. Boulder, Colo.: Westview Press.

hooks, bell. 1989. *Talking Back: Thinking Feminist, Thinking Black*. Boston: South End Press.

———. 1990. *Yearning: Race, Gender and Cultural Politics*. Boston: South End Press.

hooks, bell, and Cornell West. 1991. *Breaking Bread: Insurgent Black Intellectual Life*. Boston: South End Press.

Iverem, Esther. 1991. "By Earth Obsessed." *Essence* 22 (Sept.): 37–38.

Jahn, Janheinz. 1961. *Muntu: The New African Culture*. New York: Grove Press.

Joyce, Christopher. 1989. "Africans Call for End to the Ivory Trade." *New Scientist* 122 (June 10): 22.

King, Ynestra. 1989. "Healing the Wounds: Feminism, Ecology, and the Nature/Culture Dualism." In *Gender/Body/Knowledge: Feminist Reconstructions of Being and Knowing*, ed. Alison M. Jaggar and Susan R. Bordo. New Brunswick, N.J.: Rutgers University Press.

Larsen, Elizabeth. 1991. "Granola Boys, Eco-Dudes, and Me." *Ms.* 2 (July/Aug.), 96–97.

Lorde, Audre. 1983. "An Open Letter to Mary Daly." In *This Bridge Called My Back: Writings by Radical Women of Color*, ed. Cherríe Moraga and Gloria Anzaldua. New York: Kitchen Table Press.

Maathai, Wangari. 1991. "Foresters without Diplomas." *Ms.* 1 (Mar./Apr.), 74–75.

Meyer, Eugene L. 1992. "Environmental Racism: Why Is It Always Dumped in Our Backyard? Minority Groups Take a Stand." *Audubon* 94 (Jan./Feb.): 30–32.

Myers, Linda James. 1988. *Understanding an Afrocentric Worldview: Introduction to an Optimal Psychology*. Dubuque, Iowa: Kendall/Hunt.

Ogunyemi, Chikwenye Okonjo. 1985. "Womanism: The Dynamics of the Contemporary Black Female Novel in English." *Signs: Journal of Women in Culture and Society* 11 (autumn): 63–80.

Ouedraogo, Josephine. 1992. "Sahel Women Fight Desert Advance." *UNESCO Courier* 45 (March): 38.

Richards, Dona. 1980. "European Mythology: The Ideology of 'Progress.'" In *Contemporary Black Thought*, ed. Molefi Kete Asante and Abdulai Sa Vandi. Beverly Hills, Calif.: Sage.

Riley, Shay. 1991. "Eco-Racists Use Fatal Tactics." *Daily Illini* 121 (Sept. 4): 15.

Schallert, K. L. 1992. "Speaker Examines Impact of the West on Africa" (Wagaki Mwangi). *Daily Illini* 121 (April 3): 3.

Smith, Andy. 1991. "For All Those Who Were Indian in Another Life." *Ms.* (Nov./Dec.): 44–45.

Snitow, Ann. 1989. "A Gender Diary." In *Rocking the Ship State: Towards a Feminist Peace Politics*, ed. Adrienne Harris and Ynestra King. Boulder, Colo.: Westview Press.

Starhawk. 1990. "Power, Authority, and Mystery: Ecofeminism and Earth-Based Spirituality." In *Reweaving the World: The Emergence of Ecofeminism*, ed. Irene Diamond and Gloria Feman Orenstein. San Francisco: Sierra Club Books.

Teish, Luisah. 1985. *Jambalaya: The Natural Woman's Book of Personal Charms and Practical Rituals*. San Francisco: Harper & Row.

Walker, Alice. 1983. *In Search of Our Mothers' Gardens: Womanist Prose*. New York: Harcourt Brace Jovanovich.

Walker, Barbara, 1983. *The Woman's Encyclopedia of Myths and Secrets*. San Francisco: Harper & Row.

Worldwatch. 1987. "On the Brink of Extinction." Quoted in *World Development Forum* 5 (Nov.): 3.

from *The Men We Long to Be: Beyond Lonely Warriors and Desperate Lovers*

❧

Stephen B. Boyd

Stephen B. Boyd teaches history of Christianity at Wake Forest University and has been a leader of the profeminist Christian men's movement. He searches here for an understanding of masculinity that celebrates men without the limitations or privileges of patriarchy.

❧

CHRISTIAN THEOLOGY IN AN OBJECTIFIED PARADIGM

My claim here is not that Christianity, as such, has done that or must do that or that Christianity is inherently antithetical to men's psychic and spiritual growth and health; in fact, I believe just the opposite. Rather, I believe that many men have been hurt by internalizing interpretations of Christianity that have been distorted by the structures of oppression I have sketched up to this point (sexism, heterosexism, racism, classism, anti-Semitism, and the oppression of men). In the language of the New Testament, the good news of Jesus, the Christ, has been, particularly since the time of Constantine, distorted by the "principalities and powers" of this world. They have shaped interpretations of Christianity in an "objectified paradigm."

By objectified paradigm I mean a framework for understanding the world in which one person is ever the subject and the other person, or group, is ever the object of the first person's knowledge or action.[1] Because human beings have a profound need to know and be known by others, we can be satisfied and most fully human only when we stand in a dual relation to others. We must be the active subject of knowledge about them and the receptive object of their knowledge about us:

I		Other
Subject	→	Object
Object	←	Subject

The problem in oppressive situations is that one group attempts to affect another group, or individual members of that group, without being affected by them. There is an attempt by members of the oppressor group to freeze members of the oppressed group exclusively in the role of object (S→O). In other words, members of oppressed groups are *objectified* by members of oppressor groups. There is an attempt to rob them of their inherent dignity as human subjects and their ability to affect others. I call *domination* this attempt to affect others without being affected by them, or to stand exclusively in a subject→object relation. This attempt to dominate others leads to a zero-sum understanding of power in this paradigm. That is the belief that there is only so much power in the world to go around and if someone has more, someone else has less. So, we are essentially competitors for power, or influence (to impose our will or to protect ourselves).

The form of masculinity I have been describing in this book is a socialization and conditioning to domination. Men are expected, even required, to try to affect others without being adversely affected by them. Christianity, interpreted in a model that assumes objectification, not only requires this kind of domination by men, but also sanctifies it. I give here a brief sketch of some major Christian doctrines as seen in such a paradigm.

God is seen as the ultimate Subject, or Affecter, who is not affected by anyone or anything else. Aquinas said that God is *actus purus*, pure act, with no potentiality. That is, God is ever what he is and does not become; he is not acted upon. Thus, he is absolute (literally: all relations that might affect him are absolved) and transcends, or is completely other than (*totaliter aliter* in medieval scholastic terms), everything else. God's other attributes follow from this view. God is omnipotent, meaning that he has ultimate power to affect everything and everyone.[2] And God is omniscient, knowing all things, with no need of input from anyone or anything else.

I say "he" because, in this paradigm, God is masculine—in fact, hypermasculine. Men are supposed to be in control, or dominant; God is omnipotent. Men are supposed to be experts; God is omniscient. Men are supposed to restrict their emotionality and sexuality; God is impassible.

If one takes H. Richard Niebuhr's definition of God as one's center of value, one could argue that this view of God leads to a "cult of masculinity," at the center of which is a hypermasculine image of God.[3] Rather than healing men of the strains and self- and other-destructiveness inherent in many masculine norms, this view of God reinforces them. In traditional theological terms, this view of God leads not to life and salvation but to death and perdition. To explore how that works, I will refer to the effects on men of several of the doctrines I discussed earlier.

In this paradigm, God is believed to have ordained an order to things—an order that is hierarchical. For example, the author of the Letter to the Ephesians advises:

> Wives, be subject to your husbands, as to the Lord. For the husband is the head of the wife as Christ is the head of the church.... Children, obey your parents in the Lord, for this is right.... Slaves, be obedient to those who are your earthly masters, with fear and trembling, in singleness of heart, as to Christ; ... Masters, do the same to them, and forbear threatening, knowing that he who is both their Master and yours is in heaven, and that there is no partiality with him. (Ephesians 5:22–6:9)

When we add other aspects of the world to this hierarchy, what we get looks like this:

God
↓
Christ
↓
Man
↓
Woman
↓
Children; Slaves
↓
Animals
↓
Plants
↓
Minerals

Those at the top of the hierarchy affect those underneath them without being affected by them. That is, the top members "objectify" the lower members. There is a unilateral flow of action or influence; that is why the arrows point in only one direction.

Justice, in this paradigm, is understood as the maintenance of this God-ordained, hierarchical order. Authority, which comes from the Latin word *auctoritas*, meaning power, is the coercive means by which this order is maintained. Authority is viewed as coming from the top down, which legitimates the unidirectional nature of the influence of those higher up the hierarchy on those lower down.

If we were to add the other objectified relationships shaped by the "principalities and powers," the hierarchy would look like this:

God			
↓			
Christ			
↓			
Man	Heterosexual	White/Gentile	Owners
↓	↓	↓	↓
Woman	Homosexual	Black/Jewish	Workers
↓			
Children; Slaves			
↓			
Animals			
↓			
Plants			
↓			
Minerals			

And justice is construed as maintaining these oppressive hierarchies.

Sin, in this paradigm, is the refusal to submit oneself to this ordering. For example, for a woman, it is to refuse to submit to the rule of men; sin is the rejection of sexism. For a man, sin is the refusal to take his place in this hierarchy and carry out his ruling function of keeping everyone else in their places. Said another way, sin for a man is the refusal to fill public offices in a dominating way and the rejection of the dual masculine identity of the lonely warrior and the desperate lover. In other words, sin is the attempt to integrate one's soul and body.

The doctrine of Christ's saving work is, then, seen in this context. Because human beings stepped out of the order ordained by God, or disobeyed God, we have incurred a debt and must pay a penalty for this disobedience. Since God does nothing more justly than uphold his order, he must exact a price for that disobedience. That price, as he ordained it (Genesis 2:17), was death. But, according to some readings of Saint Anselm of Canterbury, it would be unfitting if God, after having created human beings, simply allowed us to go to ruin without doing anything about it; it would show weakness in an omnipotent God. In addition, the dishonor we did to our Infinite Creator God is greater than anything finite creatures can redress. So, though human beings incurred the debt, or penalty, of sin, we cannot pay it. What is needed is a God-man, who because of his humanity can experience death, but because of his divinity can overcome it. That God-man was Jesus, the Christ—God's only-begotten Son. Christ undid our disobedience by his obedient submission to death—the just penalty imposed by God—on our behalf. In the resurrection he wins a victory over death. By doing so, he pays our penalty and shares with us his victory over death.[4]

If we have faith in Christ we are forgiven and redeemed (bought back) from death. We then step back into our proper place in God's order by accepting Christ, not only as Savior, but as Lord of our lives. We submit to his authority and express our love to others by becoming a conduit of his authority to others below us in God's order.

Grace in the dominating, or objectified, paradigm enables the man to deal with the strains consequent to the masculine role without changing the role. For example, grace gives men the ability to limit their yearning for intimacy and sexual/sensual expressions to one woman in the context of marriage and to endure the ensuing isolation and powerlessness; to dominate women, children, and the earth without abusing them; and to neglect or even punish their bodies and still believe that those same bodies are temples of God.

Love is understood to be selfless service in maintaining this order for the good of all. "[Love] does not insist on its own way; . . . [love] bears all things, believes all things, hopes all things, and endures all things" (1 Corinthians 13:5–7). For men, love is the acceptance of the dual identity—the tight control of our own emotionality and sexuality and of others through public offices.[5] Spirituality becomes any discipline or practice that enables us to imitate Christ's selfless love in submitting to God's hierarchy of obedience.

DOMINATIVE MASCULINE MEN AND KENOTIC MASCULINE MEN

I believe that this kind of theology both reflects and shapes the distortion of our characters as men.[6] As an illustration of that, I will look at the two predominant responses—defensive denial and guilty silence—that men in the church have given to women's objection to their objectification and exclusion from positions of leadership.

DOMINATIVE MASCULINITY AND DEFENSIVE DENIAL

In 1984 the Southern Baptist Convention, the largest Protestant denomination in America, passed a resolution excluding "women from pastoral leadership . . . to preserve a submission God requires because the man was first in creation and the woman was first in the Edenic fall." Brought to the floor by an all-male committee, the resolution makes clear how such questions are to be determined—*not* by "modern cultural, sociological, and ecclesiastical trends or by emotional factors" but by "the final authority of Scripture." It is this "final authority" that also attests to "God's delegated order of authority (God the head of Christ, Christ the head of man, man the head of woman)."[7] A motion made to extend the time for discussion of the resolution to ten minutes failed—a refusal to listen to the voices of those who opposed the resolution.

In the Roman Catholic Church, the Vatican, on the basis of the 1976 *Inter Insigniores* document, claims that since God in Christ determined the specific nature of the sacramental sign, the church has no right or authority to change it and admit women to the priestly order. The argument then runs: since sacramental signification requires a natural resemblance between the sign and thing signified; and since the priest, in the specific and unique act of presiding at the Eucharist is a sign; and since Christ was and remains a man, therefore it is fitting that priestly ordination be reserved to men. The reason that God chose to incarnate God's Word in a male is a mystery beyond the competence of the "human sciences"; it is simply a fact of God's revealed will to which the church (read: the church hierarchy) humbly submits. Since the church has received "charge and control" of the priesthood, the pastoral office is "not granted by people's spontaneous choice . . . ; it is the laying on of hands and the prayer of the successors of the Apostles which guarantee God's choice." One cannot give oneself access to it; the priestly vocation "cannot be reduced to a mere personal attraction, which can remain purely subjective."[8] It must be given to males by the exclusively male hierarchy, which listens not to the human heart or mind but to the immutable will of God, and to which the laity must humbly submit.

In both of these responses, there is a denial that the church and its authoritative structures are harmful to women, much less to men, and an unwillingness to listen to evidence that suggests otherwise. To the contrary, the hierarchical structure must be good for all involved, including women; it is the will of God. In both, an exclusively male authority structure is speaking without listening. In fact, any listening to human voices is ruled out because that would violate the immutable voice of God, the integrity of which the authority structure must protect. For many of the "conservative" men of the Southern Baptist Convention, the source is an inerrant Bible that contains the unassailable pronouncement of a perfect, omniscient Supersubject who needs no input from human beings. In fact, one must ignore the human mind and heart, that is, "modern cultural and sociological trends," as well as "emotional factors." For the Vatican, God's mysterious will is revealed in the Scriptures and protected by the male successors of the apostles—protected from "personal attraction" and "pure subjectivity." In both cases, the authoritative transmission of truth is unidirectional—from the top down. An implicit assumption seems to be that, though the authoritative structures are not harmful to women, women would be harmful to those structures.

It seems to me that these men tend to work out of internalized domination patterns and therefore manifest active distortions of our inherent capacities—tyranny, sadism, manipulation, addiction. Because God requires order-keeping and is the ultimate Order-keeper himself, our behavior has to be controlling, domineering, and judgmental. We must be aggressive, even to the point of violence, because people's selfishness is so deeply rooted and resistant to change. If we are calculating and manipulative, it is because so many people have been misled and are confused about the proper order of things. And we find ourselves, because of all this, a bit obsessive-compulsive about our very important work and other things that might compensate us for the energy we expend and the pleasures we forgo in those quite strenuous tasks. We believe that this behavior does not stem from our sinful selfishness, but rather from our selfless love. Obedience is the cardinal Christian virtue, and we preach it to others and to ourselves.

[. . .]

I believe one of the most debilitating effects of sexism in Western Christianity is the distortion it has caused in the ways we image and think about God. I think that our splitting off of those vulnerable aspects of ourselves as bad, debilitating, or counterproductive to our roles as protectors and providers contributed to the predominance of this image of God as omniscient, omnipotent, and disconnected from us. Those things we feared, including our own bodies, became identified with femininity. This, in turn, became identified with an immanent God, or Goddess—a God with or in us. That which we constructed to deal with our fear— invulnerability—became identified with masculinity; this, in turn, became identified with a transcendent God—a God completely separate from us. We, consequently, tend to emphasize those aspects of God when we find them in the Bible or in tradition. We highlight male images of God and tend to suppress female images of God.[9]

A perennial issue in the history of theology is how to develop ways of talking about God that integrate both God's transcendence, or distinctiveness, and God's immanence, or withness. The reason for that is that salvation—whether one views that by means of a juridical or a medicinal model—makes no sense without both. If God is completely other and apart from humanity, what good does that do us? If God is completely identified with us, what hope do we have of emerging out of the destruction in which we find ourselves?[10] So, we must find ways of holding the otherness of God together with God's withness—God's transcendence with God's immanence. Without one, the other is distorted. Without God's transcendence, God's immanence becomes petty and idolatrous; our God becomes too small. Without immanence, God's transcendence becomes distant, cold, even cruel.

Because there has been such an overemphasis on the transcendence of God in Western Christianity, I think we are in a historical period where an emphasis on the immanence of God is needed to balance our views. Dietrich Bonhoeffer, a Lutheran pastor and member of the German resistance movement, saw such a need during his imprisonment for his participation in a plot on Hitler's life. Reflecting on the passivity of many German Christians in the face of the horrors of the Nazi regime, he imagined a "world come of age" in which Christians practiced a "religionless" or "this-worldly" Christianity. For ethical reasons, he saw the need for Christians to reject a deus ex machina, or a false notion of a God who steps in when our justice, strength, intelligence, and compassion give out and saves us, in the next or "other" world, from the consequences of our fini- tude, weakness, and confusion in this one. In contrast, these "religionless" Christians do not en- gage in escapism or denial; they participate in the "powerlessness of God in the world."[11] They are

> summoned to share in God's suffering at the hands of a godless world. [They] must therefore really live in a godless world, without attempting to gloss over or explain its ungodliness in some religious way or other. [They] must live a "secular" life, and thereby share in God's sufferings. [They] may live a "secular" life. . . . It is not the religious act that makes the Christian, but participation in the sufferings of God in the secular life. That is metanoia [conversion]: not in the first place thinking about one's own needs, problems, sins, and fears, but allowing oneself to be caught up into the way of Jesus Christ, into the messianic event.[12]

That is, these "religionless Christians" don't wait for an utterly transcendent God to do something extraordinary to save us from deadly things, like sexism, heterosexism, racism, classism, or the oppression of men; they act.

What Bonhoeffer means by becoming "godless," I think, is to give up that distorted notion of God that has been produced by exaggerating God's distinctiveness, transcendence, or activity and ignoring God's withness, immanence, or vulnerability. It is that notion of an utterly transcendent God that contributes to the distortion of our sense of justice and our own strength. God is just, so we don't have to be; we can remain naive. "He" is strong, so we don't have to be; we can remain passive. This is just one of the ways such a notion of God hurts men and, by extension, others and the earth. It also means, I think, that we must stop splitting off our finitude, mortality, sensuousness, bodiliness, and desire for pleasure and projecting them exclusively onto our mothers, other women, and the Goddess. We need to stop splitting off our need for self-direction, self-definition, and boundary setting and projecting them exclusively onto our fathers, other men, and the Father God. Changing such a notion of God is extremely painful; as I have said, that notion has been very comforting and reassuring.[13] We can, however, take comfort in the fact that God is behind and in the painful process. As H. R. Niebuhr said, God is the "slayer" of all other gods.[14] That is, God is in the process of slaying that distorted notion we have of God. I'll say more about this in chapter 5.

Bonhoeffer believed that in moving out of denial and into honesty—in becoming "more godless"—we draw "nearer to God." God is the "beyond in the midst of our life. . . . The church stands, not at the boundaries where human powers give out, but in the middle of the village."[15] We are called to act out of more mature expressions of our first natures and to participate with others in the cocreation of more just, intelligent, and connected relations. God's power draws us into that maturation and empowers it. As we think more clearly and act more decisively in order to relate more justly, we experience the power of the God whose transcendence is found in the midst of us.

This is the God revealed to us in Christ; this is the God to whom Christ reconciles us. This is a God who is beyond us and within us; a God who is powerful and vulnerable; a God whom we need and who needs us. We need to be reconciled with God—not the distorted image that legitimates oppression, but the real God. The writer of the Gospel of John believed that Jesus provided that reconciliation: "On that day you will know that I [Jesus] am in my Father, and you in me, and I in you" (14:20). In Christ, knowledge of God is restored to us. We need, therefore, images of God that are less objectified and more mutual. We must stop objectifying God and believing the distorted stereotypes about God that are not true.[16]

Part of what it means, then, to be reconciled with God is to pay attention to images of God that express both God's transcendence and God's immanence. We have historically ascribed one set of human characteristics to men and then associated those with transcendence, and we have ascribed another set of characteristics to women and associated those with immanence. Consequently, since we have emphasized the transcendence of God, we have associated God with masculinity, or maleness. Few Christians, if asked, would say God is male, and many would say that God transcends gender, or sex. Nevertheless, when feminine images or language are used for God, many of us are disturbed. Part of the reason for that discomfort is, I think, because we have so overemphasized God's transcendence that female, or feminine, images suggest to us immanence and, thus, seem inappropriate. Further, because we have split human qualities into polarized masculine and feminine characteristics, and projected only one set onto God, we have a stunted sense of God's fullness. The answer to these difficulties is not to attempt to balance God's transcendence with God's immanence by using both masculine and feminine images.

Rather, since men are both active and vulnerable and women are both active and vulnerable, we need to distinguish maleness from distorted notions of masculinity and femaleness from distorted notions of femininity.[17] Consequently, male images and female images can convey both transcendence and immanence, and we need to use both.[18]

One understanding of God, or the center of value, in the mutual paradigm is as the ground of our right, or just, mutual relation, whose nature is love.[19] The trinitarian affirmation of God is that God is a plural, dynamic reality, not a singular, static one.[20] Within God's self, there is giving and receiving, affecting and being affected—mutuality. And there is mutuality between God and human beings. God desires to be known by us. In the Gospel of John (17:3), the author writes, "And this is eternal life, that they know you the only true God, and Jesus Christ whom you have sent." We can know God as God speaks to us through Scripture and tradition, as well as through our own bodies, through the earth, through the lives of women, gay men and lesbians, African-Americans, Jewish people, persons of different classes, and all others.

Authority in this paradigm is not perceived to be the coercive power to keep people in their proper places in a divine hierarchy; rather, it is the openness of one person to be affected by another because one is drawn to that person and trusts him or her. We are most deeply moved toward transformation not by someone's insistence or threats, but by our attraction to aspects of someone's life that we find compelling. In other words, authority is not something exacted from us, but an openness we freely give, because we know that something about that person will enhance our lives, or, in the words of Catherine of Siena, "fatten our souls." We are most deeply formed by our attractions—by our erotic desire to know and be known. As Augustine said, if you want to know who someone is, look at what that person loves; we become like what we love.

In the objectified paradigm, because of the hierarchical valuing of the soul over the body, issues of authority usually focus on the realm of ideas. Which ideas are right; which ideas are wrong? Which ideas serve to uphold the hierarchy; which ideas serve to upset it? So, the term *truth* comes to have a decidedly intellectual connotation. In the mutual paradigm, truth is a more inclusive term. We are attracted to and allow ourselves to be affected by more than people's ideas. We find ourselves attracted to their bodies, to their expressions of their emotional lives, to the just ways in which they live their lives, to the powerful ways they act on what they believe, and to the ways they relate to others. My sense is that our first natures are profoundly attracted to expressions of others' first natures. In fact, I think we are often open to other people's ideas because we find something in these other areas we admire.

Augustine believed truth (*veritas*) was the integration and harmony of the soul and body made possible by our attraction to the supreme Good, or God. For him, it was unreasonable to pursue truth by reason alone and unpleasurable to pursue truth by pleasure alone. Our reason and our bodily pleasure are drawn toward integration and fulfillment by our love of God (*amor dei*).

NOTES

1. For a discussion of paradigms and shifts from one paradigm to another, see Hans Küng, "Paradigm Change in Theology: A Proposal for Discussion," in *Paradigm Change in Theology: A Symposium for the Future*, trans. Margaret Kohl, ed. Hans Küng and David Tracy (New York: Crossroad, 1989), 7.

2. Charles Hartshorne, *Omnipotence and Other Theological Mistakes* (Albany: State University of New York Press, 1984).

3. Dinnerstein might give us at least one clue as to why many of us—men and women—have an investment in seeing God as a "he." She argues that the seeming omnipotence of the mother in the

"mother-involved" family is balanced by our projection of our split-off need for differentiation, autonomy, and independence onto the father. An absolute, utterly transcendent, self-sufficient Father offers us a cosmic emotional and psychological counterbalance to the perceived omnipotence of the mother.

4. This view is often called the Latin theory of the atonement, or the substitutionary view of Christ's work. Based on the scriptural language of sacrifice, it came to be a predominant view in Western Christianity, particularly in Reformed (Calvinist) circles. Many advocates of this viewpoint to Saint Anselm's *Cur Deus Homo* (Why God became man), in *A Scholastic Miscellany: Anselm to Ockham*, ed. Eugene R. Fairweather (New York: Macmillan, 1970), 100–183, as the clearest articulation of this formulation. This view employs early medieval political metaphors and Latin legal theory (e.g., God as lord, human beings as vassals) to express the relationship between God and humanity. Robert D. Crouse, "The Augustinian Background of St. Anselm's Concept of *Iustitia,*" *Canadian Journal of Theology* 4 (April 1958): 111–19, argues that Anselm's notion of justice is best understood aesthetically—as God's right ordering of the world. This tends toward a less juridical and more medicinal or remedial reading of Anselm's theory.

5. This may explain the investment many traditional, male theologians have had in separating *agape* and *eros*. If God is male, in fact hypermasculine, and we men are supposed to love God (and our neighbors as ourselves), given the strong homophobic aspect of masculinity, men's love for God cannot have an erotic component. Consequently, men assert that God's love doesn't either. Men are thus encouraged, even required, to keep their bodies, emotions, and sexual passion out of their relation to God. See Howard Eilberg-Schwartz, *God's Phallus: And Other Problems for Men and Monotheism* (Boston: Beacon Press, 1994), for a helpful treatment of some of these issues.

6. Portions of this discussion first appeared in print in the *Journal of Men's Studies* (1993): 323–45.

7. *Annual of the Southern Baptist Convention* (Nashville, Tenn., 1985), 65.

8. *Partners in the Mystery of Redemption: A Pastoral Response to Women's Concerns for Church and Society* (Washington, D.C.: National Conference of Catholic Bishops, March 23, 1988).

9. For help on this, see Ruether, *Sexism and God-Talk*; Sallie McFague, *Models of God: Theology for an Ecological, Nuclear Age* (Philadelphia: Fortress Press, 1987); and McFague, *The Body of God: An Ecological Theology* (Minneapolis: Fortress Press, 1993).

10. The development of the doctrines of the Trinity (three persons and one substance) at the Councils of Nicaea and Constantinople (A.D. 325 and 381) and of the twofold nature of Christ (two natures and one person) at the Council of Chalcedon (A.D. 451) were, I believe, attempts at holding those two aspects of God together.

11. Dietrich Bonhoeffer, *Letters and Papers from Prison*, ed. Eberhard Bethge (New York: Macmillan, 1973), 362.

12. Bonhoeffer, *Letters and Papers*, 361–62.

13. I think that the acrimonious responses to the November 1993 ecumenical conference held in Minneapolis, "RE-imagining: The Ecumenical Decade/Churches in Solidarity with Women," bear witness to this pain.

14. H. Richard Niebuhr, *Radical Monotheism and Western Culture* (New York: Harper & Row, 1943), 114ff.

15. Bonhoeffer, *Letters and Papers*, 282.

16. Carter Heyward, *The Redemption of God: A Theology of Mutual Relation* (Washington, D.C.: University Press of America, 1982), argues that a liberation, or redemption, of God is needed.

17. I agree here with Sallie McFague. See her "God as Mother," in *Weaving the Visions*, 139–50, for a fuller argument.

18. For help here, see Elizabeth Johnson, *She Who Is: The Mystery of God in Feminist Disclosure* (New York: Crossroad, 1994); Gail Ramshaw, *God Beyond Gender: Feminist Christian God-Language* (Minneapolis, Minn.: Augsburg Fortress Press, 1994); Brian Wrenn, *What Language Shall I Borrow? God-Talk in Worship: A Male Response to Feminist Theology* (New York: Crossroad, 1989); and Eilberg-Schwartz, *God's Phallus*.

19. I am indebted to Heyward's work, *Touching Our Strength*, for this notion of God—what she calls "our power in relation."

20. See Authur McGill, *Suffering: A Test of Theological Method* (Philadelphia: Westminster Press, 1982).

"Rituals of Healing: Ministry with and on Behalf of Gay and Lesbian People"

Anita C. Hill and Leo Treadway

Anita C. Hill, a Lutheran pastor, is on the staff of the Wingspan Ministry in St. Paul, Minnesota. Wingspan is a ministry of pastoral care, education, advocacy, and support for gay, lesbian, bisexual, and transgendered (GLBT) people. This essay explores the religious dimension of their particular situation. Leo Treadway has been a ministry associate with St. Paul-Reformation Lutheran Church, in St. Paul, Minnesota. He is an educator who developed a program in support of GLBT students, teachers, staff, and families in the Minneapolis public schools, a community organizer, and activist.

CONTEXT AND COMMITMENT

From a Lesbian Perspective

Why do you stay involved in organized religion? How do you survive in that patriarchal institution? These are questions I am often asked, especially by members of the lesbian community. The queries are understandable. Through the years, organized religion has, by and large, *not* been friend or advocate of gay and lesbian involvement in church and society. In fact, our communities have faced outright rejection and oppression from churches claiming to follow Jesus Christ, who, oddly enough, came with a message of love for all and freedom for the oppressed.

There are several approaches one can take to bring about change in institutions. One is to leave the institution and attempt to change it from the outside. Another is to ignore the organization by developing competing alternative systems. A third is to struggle from the inside to change the structure and essence of the institution. Each of these approaches has positive and negative aspects. Unfortunately, at times within the lesbian community, more energy is expended in arguing the importance of supporting *one* "politically correct" and unified method of action than is expended toward effecting change.

It is my firm belief that the combined efforts of many-sided attacks against a problem can best produce the changes we desire. I salute the creativity and courage of lesbians who abandon traditional churches to explore more women-centered spirituality and ways of worship. In similar fashion, I support the efforts of lesbians who critique organized religion from outside its often male-guarded gates. It takes yet another form of strength and fortitude to carry on the struggle for lesbian and gay rights inside religious institutions. I believe lesbians and gay men need to give each other and ourselves the flexibility and support required to connect with the spirituality and advocacy approaches best suited to our individual needs and circumstances.

I work inside the traditional church structures (as an openly lesbian ministry associate of a congregation in the Evangelical Lutheran Church of America) for two major reasons. First, organized religion in our society holds much control over the mind-set and functioning of many people. It seems an appropriate tactical stance to attempt to influence and change the views of the church's power base from its core. My role vacillates from that of revolutionary to conciliator depending on the situation, but the vision of a church and society that is accepting of diversity in its midst remains foremost.

The second reason is related to my feeling called by God/dess to a ministry of reconciliation and advocacy on behalf of lesbian and gay people and their family members. In a world that has become so removed from spiritual connections, many people find it strange to hear me speak of having a call to this ministry. Straight people tend to discount it as "another lesbian trying to justify her lifestyle," while lesbians and gay men discredit it as "a sellout to a straight oppressive institution." Nevertheless, I do what I must with God/dess guidance to move us toward an inclusive vision in a diverse world.

As a lesbian woman who has learned both the gift and the struggle inherent in being different in a culture that too often describes normal as monocultural, I acknowledge the bicultural reality that is mine as a member of the lesbian/gay subculture. I am committed to breaking the stereotypes and invisibility barrier faced by lesbian women. I am constantly reevaluating whether I can best impact the system (religious or secular) for change from inside or out. Naming and validating the reality of myself and my lesbian sisters is the starting place for change toward growth and life, and ultimately toward God and interconnectedness.

From the Perspective of a Gay Man

"Loving People, Loving God." That's what it said on the button I wore. The middle-aged woman with whom I spoke, following the adult forum, maintained that my button was ludicrous, there was no way that I could be a gay man and a Lutheran. Yet that is exactly who I am. Unable to accept myself as a child of God if I were gay, I spent many years living my life and faith on the margins, never really allowing myself to fit in. But something remarkable happened when I finally understood that my life as a gay man was a profound gift from a very caring God. I began to move away from the marginal existence I had led and found myself engaged in a life dedicated to bridging between groups, most specifically between gay men, lesbians, and the heterosexual majority which made up the institutional church.

That "coming out" experience was one of the most profoundly spiritual experiences of my life, and the excitement of knowing myself to be deeply loved and accepted by God was something I wanted to help others find and share. As I worked with, loved, and supported others I began to find a sense of my own spiritual journey. I knew that my life and faith had been sharpened and shaped by my own experience of being different, and being different in a way that evoked the intense hostility of many people in both church and society. They were also shaped by, but more importantly, rooted in my love for other men. This was not a condition in life I had chosen, but rather one which was given. Underneath all the storm and strife, I knew that if my being was rooted in love, then it must also be rooted in God.

But I labored long and hard under the oppressive understandings of the so-called traditional biblical material. I needed to be able to find my story in God's story, if I was to continue in the community of faith. I set myself to a process of intensive study. Imagine my surprise when I discovered that I did not know everything I always thought I knew about the Bible and homosexuality. The traditional material continued to speak to me, but also to others in a different way. I found people like myself in the scriptural stories. I discovered material in which I could find my own experiences and struggles. And I found that I had not been so wrong to trust that my love was also from God.

Simply finding myself in God's story was suddenly not enough, because it prompted me to continue my own journey in faith, and to become involved in caring for others and doing justice. My faith prompted me to begin active ministry with other gay men, lesbians, family members, and friends. I often reflected on an experience I had early in my process of coming out. Despite my bumbling and clumsiness, another young man took me under his wing. He was my first real contact with other men like myself. I must have tried his patience sorely, but his support and encouragement continued until I could walk by myself. I like to think of this man, whose name I cannot even recall, as a messenger from God, sent to me in the form of a human being who could show me that God did care. He came into my life, wrought a miracle, then disappeared. I owe my imaging of "servanthood" to this man.

Finding myself, and finding my place in God's heart, suddenly became the lens through which I could finally understand all those earlier lessons from Sunday school and church. With a very special gift from God, and knowing that there was nothing which could ever separate me from the love of God, I knew that my ministry was beginning. In a very tender scene during the movie *Outrageous*, a drag queen character said it most succinctly: "We were put here on this earth to love and take care of one another." I have tried to follow that commandment ever since. And I do that by trying to bridge the fears that separate us, and by working for justice. I continue to ask God to help and guide me . . . and the "angels" still come when needed.

CONSTRUCTION

Understanding gay and lesbian Christians presents a challenge for growth in faith to both clergy and laity today. Old models of working with the homosexual community began with the premise that all homosexuals needed to be cured or saved from their illness, which prompted ministry models of counseling for change to heterosexuality or sexual abstinence. Although homosexuality was removed as a diagnosis of illness in medicine and psychiatry in 1973, the notion of same-gender sexual orientation as inherently sinful has persisted in much of the religious community.

This chapter will critique the old models and provide examples of how healing grace and reconciliation have become hallmarks in the new models of ministry with and on behalf of gay and lesbian people and their family members. Key to the new model is listening to the voices of gay and lesbian people regarding their faith and life experiences. Hearing these voices challenges us to a new ministry of response and advocacy with people too often excluded from the Christian community.

A conspiracy of silence about lesbians and gay men has set the tone for an inadequate or absent sociopolitical response to the needs of these individuals in church and society.

Misinformation fills the void left by silence and perpetuates myths and stereotypes. Gay and lesbian people have been castigated by the church and have been the victims of violence and oppression in our society. Yet even in the face of others' denial of their common humanity and repudiation of their Christian faith, many lesbians and gay men have remained faithful people seeking Christian community. Because of their presence and witness, the conspiracy of silence which has surrounded gay and lesbian people in Christian communities is beginning to be broken.

At this time in history we are still faced with conflicting views regarding homosexuality. Materials which advocate acceptance can be located in both secular and religious realms, as can materials which hold a rejecting or punishing view toward homosexuality. Given a homophobic culture, it is not surprising to find confusion among helpful professionals (teachers, pastors, therapists, and physicians) regarding approaches. It is a curious time to be involved in ministry with gay and lesbian people. While many nongays remain uninformed about the realities of gay and lesbian lives, others are learning with a growing openness and finding lesbians and gay men to be "real people."

The two psychological and theological approaches to homosexuality in use today may be characterized broadly as: 1) a sickness/cure psychological model, paralleled by a sin/salvation theological model (the old ministry model); and 2) a health/integration psychological model, paralleled by a wholeness/acceptance theological model (the new ministry model).

Sickness/Cure Model

"The view that homosexuality is a disease originated in the 'organic' approach characteristic of the nineteenth century."[1] Since then researchers have sought causes of the "disease" in the areas of physiology, endocrinology, heredity, environment, and parenting.

Psychological studies have also proposed variables which may cause homosexuality. Irving Bieber's research findings on male homosexuals in psychoanalytic treatment have been the basis for much recent support of the sickness/cure model. His 1962 study laid the "blame" for homosexuality on disturbed parent-child interactions, labeling the child's resulting adaptation (homosexuality) "necessarily pathologic." Bieber maintained that through psychoanalytic treatment "a heterosexual shift is a possibility for all homosexuals who are strongly motivated to change."[2] Albert Ellis reported similar results with both male and female homosexuals in psychotherapy.[3]

Sigmund Freud's work on homosexuality stands in contrast to this. He and his followers assumed more than one mechanism was involved in the etiology of homosexuality and emphasized the concept of bisexuality, noting that the homosexual component may be dominant for some. They also denied homosexuality was a vice or an illness and insisted that the results of treatment were not predictable.[4]

The movement from Freud's position to that of Bieber and Ellis represents a shift from viewing homosexuality as a (nearly) unchangeable part of an individual to a belief that it is a pathologic condition which *must* be changed. The conviction of some psychoanalysts of the necessity for change to heterosexuality has produced such "treatment" techniques as systematic desensitization, moral persuasion, shaming, guilt, emetic persuasion, shock therapy, and brain surgery.[5] Although the sickness/cure model of psychotherapy with gay and lesbian individuals continues to be used today, homosexuality was removed from the list of mental disorders of the American Psychiatric Association in 1973 and the American Psychological Association in 1975.[6]

Sin/Salvation Model

The theological model which parallels the sickness/cure model assumes that homosexuality is a departure from the God-created heterosexual order of nature and therefore inherently sinful. Salvation is repentance from homosexuality and reorientation to heterosexuality or celibacy. Gay and lesbian persons are heretics who have turned away from the true faith, characterized by heterosexuality.

The church's traditional understanding of homosexuality is that it is a sin against nature. As Augustine argued, since homosexual acts cannot lead to procreation, they run counter to the Creator's intent. Thomas Aquinas added that homosexual acts are more grievous than adultery or rape "because homosexual practices 'are always an injury done to the Creator, whether or not any offense is at the same time committed against one's neighbor,' since they violate His creative intent for human behavior and destroy the beauty of His work."[7]

The sin/salvation model has led to church exclusion and condemnation of homosexuals. It is a theologically bankrupt model for gay and lesbian persons. The "love the sinner, but hate the sin" variation of this model can be defended in the abstract, but "in the concrete is a cop-out. 'Sin' is an abstraction which exists only when someone does something. In practice, it is the sinner who is hated and violated."[8] This model discounts the societal context of homophobia in which it arose and has, more often than not, been an instrument of harm rather than healing.

The term homophobia was coined in 1973 by Dr. George Weinberg, who defined it as "irrational fear on the part of heterosexuals of being in close proximity to a homosexual."[9] Current dictionary listings provide two definitions of homophobia: 1) fear, dislike, or hatred of gay men and lesbians, and 2) discrimination against lesbians and gay men. An insidious homophobia filters through all our interactions whether one is homosexual or heterosexual in orientation. Homophobic attacks on gay or lesbian individuals leave the entire community afraid and perhaps appropriately paranoid about "coming out of the closet" (acknowledging one's same-gender sexual orientation), thus perpetuating the conspiracy of silence. Lesbians and gay men must also overcome an internalized homophobia in which we devalue ourselves and our contributions by believing the untruths told about us by society at large. A circular trap exists in which we stay hidden to avoid discrimination and persecution while the very hiddenness which means survival perpetuates the stereotypes and fear about us.

The pervasive nature of our society's homophobia has recently been highlighted as a result of the AIDS (Acquired Immune Deficiency Syndrome) crisis. AIDS is a deadly disease which has struck a group of people whom many in our society presume are deviant, morally destitute, criminal, and ultimately disposable. It is commonplace to hear scapegoating of persons with AIDS because they are gay or bisexual men or intravenous drug users. Pronouncements of AIDS as God's judgment upon homosexuals leave us aware of the homophobic levels in our society. Gay and bisexual men have increasingly become the targets of violent acts, discrimination, and hate- or fear-motivated crimes. The National Gay/Lesbian Task Force indicates a twofold increase in reported acts of violence and victimization against lesbians and gay men across the United States from 1985 to 1986.[10]

The old models of ministry to homosexuals were based on a system that viewed heterosexuality as the *only* and the superior sexual orientation. This heterosexist system presumed further that since there was only one true orientation, homosexuality was obviously a deviant and sinful choice which should be changed at any cost. Homosexuality was viewed as illness or sinfulness in need of cure or salvation.

Health/Integration Model

The health/integration psychological model has an underlying premise that homosexuality is not an illness, but one orientation on the scale of human sexuality, no more or less valid than heterosexuality. In this model the caregiver's focus moves away from an exclusive preoccupation with the sexual activity of gay and lesbian persons to assisting the individual to integrate a same-gender sexual orientation into one's life. The terms "gay man and lesbian woman" and "gay/lesbian persons" replace the exclusive use of the term "homosexual(s)." George Weinberg (1973) proposed that "a homosexual person is gay [lesbian] when [s]he regards [her]himself as happily gifted with whatever capacity [s]he has to see people as romantically beautiful. It is to be free of shame, guilt, regret over the fact that one is homosexual. . . . To be gay [lesbian] is to view one's sexuality as the healthy heterosexual views his [hers]."[11]

The health/integration model supports Weinberg's idea that a gay or lesbian person can integrate his or her sexual orientation into a healthy, mature life. Sexual orientation is viewed as being as inherently natural to an individual as eye and skin color. Homosexuality is not afforded any special meaning. It is seen as "a fact of life; the rest is interpretation and consequence."[12] The task of the health/integration psychological approach is to assist gay and lesbian persons in accepting themselves and integrating their sexuality into mature lifestyles. Acknowledging societal homophobia and oppression of gay and lesbian people is an integral part of the process.

Ann and Barry Ulanov discuss the effect of societal rigidity: "If the effort to rid him[her]self of all impulses that contradict the ethical code is unconscious, then the person will probably resort—unconsciously—to repression of those defiant sides of him[her]self, and action with perilous consequences for those around him[her]self."[13] This sort of repression finds release in some other way, such as "projection onto a substitute enemy, a scapegoat who carries in one's place all that one identifies as immoral and shuns. One can then persecute the scapegoat who evokes no sympathy."[14] In our insidiously homophobic culture, gay and lesbian persons become the scapegoats which evoke no sympathy. "Hence, [a gay or lesbian person] can be only a victim, never a martyr."[15]

Relief in a therapeutic experience "comes when the sufferer sees the truth about [her]himself, the causes and the meaning of this suffering. Psychoanalysis aims to uncover and piece together the truth for the person to see, to feel, to ponder. What one wants to be true or needs to be true, what moral rules say should be true, mean nothing. Only the actual truth—unvarnished, self-evident, open to conscious and unconscious inspection—heals or can be endured."[16] Gay and lesbian people, through coming out, are stating what they know to be true about themselves and are bringing their reality to the attention of both psychology and theology to be considered in light of their truth.

Wholeness/Acceptance Model

The wholeness/acceptance model presents the theological possibility of full acceptance and affirmation of gay and lesbian people. As James B. Nelson has said, "Those who affirm this position most often make the assumption that homosexual orientation is more of a given than a free choice. More fundamentally, however, this position rests on the conviction that same-sex relationships can richly express and be the vehicle of God's humanizing intentions."[17]

Once homosexuality is considered a variation in the realm of human sexuality (no better or worse than heterosexuality), gay and lesbian life and faith experience can be taken seriously. "In the past, many gay people simply said, 'Your theory is wrong. So is your religion. Who needs it?'

and left the churches. Now, more and more gay people are saying, 'Your theory does not fit our experience. Religion and the church are important to us, and we are not going to go away.' "[18]

Coming out is a profound spiritual experience in the individual and community lives of gay and lesbian people. To name the truths about one's own reality in the world is to make the connections which end isolation, form community, and lead to an experience of liberating grace. Coming out, naming and claiming one's self even in the face of adversity and homophobia, is a freeing revelation which helps us feel God's presence in our midst. It is to know inside that even when we feel too scared or shamed to utter our own stories, God knows the story and is with us offering acceptance and a nonjudgmental listening ear.

The wholeness/acceptance model of ministry challenges Christians to follow Jesus Christ, who cared about "the most hated, discredited persons in the society in which He lived. . . . He felt their pain, knew their hunger and thirst, recognized their humanity, saw the image of God in them. In short, He loved them."[19] In the wholeness/acceptance model gay and lesbian people, recognized as an unjustly stigmatized, ostracized group, are accepted as whole persons receiving God's grace and concern.

Biblical themes used to support the wholeness/acceptance position include: injunctions against self-righteous judging of others and against bearing false witness against one's neighbors; the call to inclusivity in the church of the diversity of God's creation; and Jesus' example of love, concern, and action on behalf of the outcasts of society. Further support of this model may be seen in Fr. John McNeill's emphasis on contributions which acceptance of gay and lesbian people can make to church and society: "The objective acceptance of the homosexual community will potentially leave both communities (homosexual and heterosexual) free from the need to conform to narrow stereotypes, and positively free to develop all the qualities that belong to the fullness of the human personality."[20] The prophetic role of the gay and lesbian community is also seen as a gift of grace in the wholeness/acceptance model. "The future of gay/lesbian liberation lies not only in its ability unitedly to pursue justice for homosexual people, but also in its ability to embrace in love the outcry for freedom among all people."[21]

WINGSPAN MINISTRY MODEL

Background and Mission

Few congregations or denominations have taken seriously the challenges of the new models and opened themselves to dialogue with lesbian and gay Christians or carried out intentional ministry with and on behalf of these individuals. To do so is to acknowledge that "we don't know everything we always thought we knew about this" and to live with an openness to the voice of the Spirit. Wingspan Ministry with and on behalf of gay and lesbian people and their families at St. Paul-Reformation Lutheran Church in St. Paul, Minnesota, is one place where the challenge of the wholeness/acceptance model has been engaged. Since its inauguration by St. Paul-Reformation's church council in 1982, Wingspan Ministry has existed as a beacon of hope to lesbian and gay persons, their families and friends—a sign that the church can be a sanctuary and advocate for them.

St. Paul-Reformation Lutheran Church is a diverse community of faith, including elderly people, Black people, married people, young people, gay and lesbian people, white people, deaf people, Asian people, single people, handicapped people, Ethiopian people, families with children, middle-aged people, and more. It is intentionally a community which takes seriously the call to be an avenue of advocacy and Christian concern for those often excluded in our society and a sign that our differences can be a gift, not a barrier, to human relationships.

The major goal of Wingspan Ministry in this congregation is to welcome lesbians and gay men who are creative, gifted people, children of God, back into the church community through congregational involvement. Two tasks are central to this: 1) serving as a bridge between gay men and lesbians, their families, friends, communities, and the greater church to create an open door facilitating the "coming home" of people generally excluded from the church; and 2) improving the quality of life for gay men and lesbians through education, advocacy, and pastoral care, especially in the areas of wholeness and human justice.

Wingspan has been intentionally staffed by both an openly gay man and lesbian woman to provide access to both gay male and lesbian communities, which have often been quite separate from each other. It is important that as staff for a ministry with and on behalf of gay and lesbian people, we be open about ourselves and be clearly gay- and lesbian-identified. Being open about our experiences as lesbian and gay Christians has been a crucial aspect of our efforts to bring healing and reconciliation into congregational settings. Lesbian and gay people are active in leadership roles in congregation worship.

Being grounded in a diverse congregation which is concerned that language inclusive of women and symbolism representative of all of humanity be lifted up has helped to connect or reconnect lesbian women to the church as much as being open to different orientations and lifestyles. We are faced with two different evangelism scenarios regarding gay men and lesbian women. It is one thing to set aside judgment about homosexuality and welcome gay men back into a church with a male Godhead, as that presents a wonderfully empowering image for men who love men. It is quite another thing to attempt to reach out to lesbian women by inviting them to return to a sexist and patriarchal institution.

A Ministry of Empowerment and Advocacy

Wingspan was established as a ministry "with and on behalf of" gay and lesbian people, not "to" or "for" them. This distinction is important, for it indicates a ministry of support and empowerment of individuals, families, and groups; and a ministry of advocacy on behalf of lesbian and gay people both in church and society.

This ministry recognizes that homosexuality is not the problem; homophobia is the problem. Homophobia is a spiritual affliction which alienates and separates people from themselves, each other, and God. Antihomophobia presentations and workshops form a basis for much of the educational efforts of Wingspan.

Intentional dialogue is another central educational effort. Hearing from gay and lesbian people, listening to their life and faith stories is a way to interrupt the "them" and "us" naming of a group we fear as totally other, alien, or inhuman. Making personal the human connections through our stories helps nongay people recognize that the 10 percent of the population who are gay or lesbian are people just like themselves. People of faith need to get past the debate about "them" and whether "they" are acceptable to "us" or to "our" God or "our" church. We need to reframe the questions themselves. A more appropriate way of posing the question is: "What is the role of gay and lesbian people in the midst of this congregation, this place of community?"

An advertisement for Wingspan states that "Christ was not freed from the tomb to keep you locked in the closet." For some church people this message seems startling, shocking, even irreverent. For many gay and lesbian people, it means a new connection with their Savior. It means that the freedom from death promised in Christ's Resurrection also extends the promise of freedom from other fears and bondage in their lives. For many, embracing this message means freedom from the desperation of a closeted isolation.

Wingspan and St. Paul-Reformation congregation provide an atmosphere of acceptance and trust which helps gay and lesbian people to come out, to break through the barrier of invisibility which entraps us in our homophobic culture. Wingspan staff developed a service of preparation for coming out to parents and family in which the community names itself as family in solidarity with individuals grappling with coming out concerns. Just as coming out breaks the invisibility barrier so that people must see and respond to gay and lesbian existence, services of blessing of relationship call the church to examine the mixed messages it gives to gay and lesbian people. When the church is unable to support relationships and even discourages them, it seems not only to expect promiscuity from gay and lesbian people (whom it assumes cannot maintain committed, convenantal relationships), but to demand promiscuity (named as life-long abstinence).

Theologizing arises out of our human experience. For the most part, the church has denied the experience of lesbians and gay men in drawing its conclusions. Relationships are key to knowing the presence of God in our lives. Carter Heyward states "that the experience of relation is fundamental and constitutive of human being; that it is good and powerful; and it is only within this experience . . . that we may realize that the power in relation is God."[22] There is an ontological component which is an essential element of human relationships beneath the visible reality; it is an issue of transcendental "being." To deny the blessing which comes through gay and lesbian relationships is to deny God. By holding blessing of relationship services for gay and lesbian couples, Wingspan Ministry moves toward a goal of enabling each individual to relate, including sexual relating, in ways which are life-giving, creative, and whole.

Reclaiming scripture and establishing new parameters in which to engage our discussions about biblical material has provided a solid footing for Wingspan Ministry. Biblical witness is important to the lives and development of lesbian and gay people. It has been healing to set aside as the starting point the "seven troublesome passages" so often raised in the debate about homosexuality. Setting aside the passages generally used as a "biblical bludgeon" against gay and lesbian people has given us the freedom to allow the voices of the people to give insights about the scriptures that keep them connected to God, Christ, and Christian community in spite of the oppression within the church.

Too often, gay and lesbian people are put on the defensive by the demands that we justify our lifestyle by giving our responses to the story of Sodom and Gomorrah, the holiness codes in Leviticus, and the writings of St. Paul in Romans and Timothy which are usually translated to read homosexuality in modern versions. Putting those aside, rich imagery has been raised up by gay and lesbian interpreters of biblical material who find guidance for their lives recorded in the other stories found there. Like others involved in liberation theology movements, gay and lesbian people find in Jesus of Nazareth, one who came to bring freedom to the captives—in our case captives to homophobia and the resultant isolation and invisibility needed to survive. We hear in the good shepherd stories that "there are sheep who are not in this pen, who Christ will bring in so there will be one flock with one Shepherd." Jesus' message to Lazarus to "come out" takes on new meaning for gay and lesbian people who hear the message that there is freedom from our closet/tombs in life, resurrection, and the message of our Savior.

Wingspan has convened groups on Bible study and faith development and has held healing services in which a diverse group of congregation members participated. These times of sharing our life experiences have created a deeper understanding and bonding among community members. Weekend conferences provide the context for faith explorations in many arenas. Further work with biblical study will add to our communal understanding of the role of lesbian and gay persons in the church. "Embrace Hope" healing services are held regularly to help people prepare themselves spiritually in response to the AIDS crisis.

Building safe places of community among gay and lesbian persons, their family members, and friends has been a strength of the Wingspan Ministry. Wingspan staff act as liaisons for several groups which meet at St. Paul-Reformation: Parents and Friends of Lesbians and Gays, Lutherans Concerned/Twin Cities (the gay/lesbian caucus of Lutheran denominations), Gay Fathers' Support Group, Non-gay Spouses Support Group. Lesbian and Gay Youth Together is one example of groups with which Wingspan maintains a close working relationship. Facilitation is done in a supportive manner, and Wingspan does not run the programs or claim ownership of them. Giving people permission and space to explore their own needs and responses around gay and lesbian experience has been an important part of this evolving ministry of empowerment.

In contrast to ethnic minority groups, gay and lesbian people and their family members are isolated and invisible. Since there is no way to be sure of another person's affectional orientation until s/he acknowledges it for us, lesbian women and gay men may have a difficult time identifying others with whom they can feel safe to share their experiences and expectations. Family members live in the closet, too, and many actually feel more isolated than the lesbian or gay family member who has found support and friends in the lesbian or gay community.

The intergenerational sharing which provides history, continuity, perspective, and insight into the oppression felt by members of a minority community has been a virtual impossibility for lesbian and gay people, because so many have had to hide for so long. In situations where a Black, Hispanic, or Native American person might turn to family members for guidance about how to cope with a world that seemingly doesn't want them, lesbian and gay people often have nowhere to turn. The logical choice of family for another group could mean a painful rejection or disinheritance for gay men and lesbian women. Coming out to family members is often more difficult than telling strangers.

The concept of lesbian and gay elders who might provide such a familial role of continuity and education for younger gay and lesbian people is nearly unknown. Our culture has so closely connected active sexual involvement to the stereotype of what it means to be lesbian or gay that we virtually have no images of the elderly and few of adolescents or children who identify themselves as gay or lesbian people. It is a matter of conflicting stereotypes: gay and lesbian people are falsely labelled as totally sexual beings and adolescents and elders as asexual beings.

CONCLUSION

Breaking the conspiracy of silence which shrouds lesbian and gay existence is central to liberation theology for lesbian and gay people. The key lies in hearing the stories of gay and lesbian life and faith experience and responding to the needs raised by them. Some church communities have begun to realize the powerful impact of listening to the pain of hurting people. Gay and lesbian people are invited to share their stores in a forty-five-minute adult forum on a Sunday morning.

But simply hearing the stories is not enough. Without a component of advocacy and standing in a position of solidarity with gay and lesbian people in our pain about the injustice we face in society, the listening becomes an empty form of "churchly voyeurism" in which gay and lesbian people are further victimized. It is crucial to combat the homophobia, prejudice, and discrimination against gay men and lesbian women in our church and society, to break the conspiracy of silence supporting the status quo, and to extend a clear word of welcome in God's house for all peoples. To advocate with and on behalf of gay and lesbian persons in this manner is to extend to them the best that can be offered in pastoral care from a congregation.

RECOMMENDED READING

Edwards, George R. *Gay/Lesbian Liberation: A Biblical Perspective*. New York: Pilgrim, 1984.

Fortunado, John E. *Embracing the Exile: Healing Journeys of Gay Christians*. San Francisco: Harper & Row, 1982.

Heyward, Carter. *Touching Our Strength*. San Francisco: Harper & Row, 1989.

McCaffrey, Joseph A., ed. *The Homosexual Dialectic*. Englewood Cliffs, NJ: Prentice-Hall, 1972.

McNeill, John J., S.J. *The Church and the Homosexual*. Boston: Beacon Press, 1988.

Nugent, Robert, ed. *A Challenge to Love*. New York: Crossroad, 1978.

Scanzoni, Letha, and Virginia R. Mollenkott. *Is the Homosexual My Neighbor?* San Francisco: Harper & Row, 1980.

NOTES

1. Irving Bieber, *Homosexuality: A Psychoanalytical Study of Male Homosexuals* (New York: Random House, 1965), 12.

2. Bieber, *Homosexuality*, 319.

3. Albert Ellis, "The Effectiveness of Psychotherapy with Individuals Who Have Severe Homosexual Problems," in *The Problem of Homosexuality in Modern Society*, ed. Hendrik Ruitenbeek (New York: Dutton, 1963).

4. Bieber, *Homosexuality*, 4.

5. George Weinberg, *Society and the Healthy Homosexual* (New York: Anchor Press, 1973), chap. 3.

6. George R. Edwards, *Gay/Lesbian Liberation: A Biblical Perspective* (New York: Pilgrim, 1984), 16.

7. Richard Lovelace, *Homosexuality and the Church* (Old Tappan, N.J.: Revell, 1978), 19.

8. Michael Guinan, "Homosexuals: A Christian Pastoral Response Now," in *A Challenge to Love*, ed. Robert Nugent (New York: Crossroad, 1978), 69.

9. Weinberg, *Healthy Homosexual*.

10. *Open Hands, Journal of Reconciling Congregation Program*, Affirmation: United Methodists for Lesbian/Gay Concerns (fall 1987): 9.

11. Weinberg, *Healthy Homosexual*, 70; authors added female referents.

12. C. A. Tripp, *The Homosexual Matrix* (New York: New American Library, 1975), 253.

13. Ann Ulanov and Barry Ulanov, *Religion and the Unconscious* (Philadelphia: Westminster, 1975), 165.

14. Ulanov, *Religion and the Unconscious*, 165.

15. Thomas Szasz, "The Product Conversion—From Heresy to Illness," in *The Homosexual Dialectic*, ed. Joseph A. McCaffrey (Englewood Cliffs, N.J.: Prentice-Hall, 1972), 110.

16. Ulanov, *Religion and the Unconscious*, 143.

17. James B. Nelson, *Embodiment* (Minneapolis, Minn.: Augberg, 1978), 197.

18. Guinan, "Homosexuals," in *Challenge to Love*, 73

19. Letha Scanzoni and Virginia R. Mollenkott, *Is the Homosexual My Neighbor?* (San Francisco: Harper & Row, 1980), 135.

20. As quoted by Nelson, *Embodiment*, 198.

21. Edwards, *Gay/Lesbian Liberation*, 129.

22. Carter Heyward, *The Redemption of God* (Lanham, Md.: University Press of America, 1982), 1–2.

"Resolution on Same-Gender Officiation"

༄

Central Conference of American Rabbis

The Central Conference of American Rabbis was founded in 1889. Its members consider themselves and are considered to be the organized rabbinate of Reform Judaism. This brief document reveals a bit of the fascinating history of positions taken on gay issues by Reform Jews.

༄

RESOLUTION ADOPTED AT THE 111ᵀᴴ CONVENTION OF THE CENTRAL CONFERENCE OF AMERICAN RABBIS, MARCH 2000

Background

Over the years, the Central Conference of American Rabbis has adopted a number of positions on the rights of homosexuals, on homosexuality in the rabbinate, and advocating changes in civil law pertaining to same-gender relationships.

In 1977, the CCAR adopted a resolution calling for legislation decriminalizing homosexual acts between consenting adults, and calling for an end to discrimination against gays and lesbians. The resolution called on Reform Jewish organizations to develop programs to implement this stand.

In 1990, the CCAR endorsed the report of the Ad Hoc Committee on Homosexuality and the Rabbinate. This position paper urged that "all rabbis, regardless of sexual orientation, be accorded the opportunity to fulfill the sacred vocation that they have chosen." The committee endorsed the view that "all Jews are religiously equal regardless of their sexual orientation." The committee expressed its agreement with changes in the admissions policies of the Hebrew Union College-Jewish Institute of Religion, which stated that the "sexual orientation of an applicant [be considered] only within the context of a candidate's overall suitability for the rabbinate," and reaffirmed that all rabbinic graduates of the HUC-JIR would be admitted into CCAR membership upon application. The report described differing views within the committee as to the nature of *kiddushin*, and deferred the matter of rabbinic officiation.

A 1996 resolution resolved that the CCAR "support the right of gay and lesbian couples to share fully and equally in the rights of civil marriage," and voiced opposition to governmental efforts to ban gay and lesbian marriages.

In addition to these resolutions, two CCAR committees have addressed the question of same-gender officiation. The CCAR Committee on Responsa addressed the question of whether homosexual relationships can qualify as *kiddushin* (which it defined as "Jewish marriage"). By a committee majority of 7 to 2, the committee concluded that "homosexual relationships, however exclusive and committed they may be, do not fit within this legal category; they cannot be called *kiddushin.* We do not understand Jewish marriage apart from the concept of *kiddushin.*" The committee acknowledged its lack of consensus on this question.

The Ad Hoc Committee on Human Sexuality issued a report in 1998 which included its conclusion, by a committee majority of 11 with 1 abstention, that "kedushah may be present in committed same gender relationships between two Jews and that these relationships can serve as the foundation of stable Jewish families, thus adding strength to the Jewish community." The report called upon the CCAR to support all colleagues in their choices in this matter, and to develop educational programs.

RESOLUTION

WHEREAS justice and human dignity are cherished Jewish values, and

WHEREAS, in March of 1999 the Women's Rabbinic Network passed a resolution urging the Central Conference of American Rabbis to bring the issue of honoring ceremonies between two Jews of the same gender to the floor of the convention plenum, and

WHEREAS, the institutions of Reform Judaism have a long history of support for civil and equal rights for gays and lesbians, and

WHEREAS, North American organizations of the Reform Movement have passed resolutions in support of civil marriage for gays and lesbians, therefore

WE DO HEREBY RESOLVE, that the relationship of a Jewish, same-gender couple is worthy of affirmation through appropriate Jewish ritual, and

FURTHER RESOLVED, that we recognize the diversity of opinions within our ranks on this issue. We support the decision of those who choose to officiate at rituals of union for same-gender couples, and we support the decision of those who do not, and

FURTHER RESOLVED, that we call upon the CCAR to support all colleagues in their choices in this matter, and

FURTHER RESOLVED, that we also call upon the CCAR to develop both educational and liturgical resources in this area.

VII

THE WHOLENESS OF PEACE

All I knew then was that I believed that most people, regardless of race or any other distinction, were kind and had a conscience—or were capable of being kind and having a conscience. . . . I pity those filled with anger and hate because they are victims just as much as the people they attack.

—John Lewis, *Walking with the Wind*

You cannot really be frightened of people you do not hate. Hate and fear go hand in hand.

—Aung San Suu Kyi, *Voice of Hope*

If there is one value that seems to be held without exception by every religious and spiritual tradition, it is that of peace. The concept of peace, however, should not be thought to refer simply to an absence of war. Rather, it has to do with a sense of wholeness, completion, and fulfillment—even as a precondition for and essential aspect of that wholeness is the nonviolent resolution of interpersonal conflict.

The religious contribution to political life in this dimension has to do with its capacity—a capacity, sadly, which believers may too often fail to exercise—to concentrate on our universally human need for peace and the universally shared concerns which make peace so important. All of us have families we love and personal concerns we seek to fulfill. Each of us would like to "sit under his vine and fig tree and not be afraid" and to "beat our swords into ploughshares"—the better to plow our lands and feed our communities. Progressive political traditions compel us to see human beings as socially and historically situated—holders of rights, members of social classes, genders, nations, or ethnic groups. Religions teach our universally shared characteristics: all are equally made in the image of God, and all are equally liable to suffering, delusion, loss, and pain.

Thus this aspect of what might roughly be called the "culture of religion"—an emphasis on certain values often associated with but not requiring a belief in God or spiritual Reality—can be an essential element in resolving conflict peacefully and avoiding the scourges of war and needless, bitter conflict.

As these selections indicate, conflict among human beings takes a wide variety of forms. Religious voices have called for peace not only in place of war between nations, but also as an alternative to religious violence aimed at unbelievers or heretics, in the context of political struggles, and even among comrades in the same political organizations.

R. Scott Appleby begins with a brief description of some activist religious peacemaking efforts, efforts all the more striking because of the contrast they make to the constant headlines describing global religious violence. Working from Christianity and Buddhism, Walter Wink and Thich Nhat Hanh provide models of how essential religious teachings aim toward peace in place of violence or coercion. Religious peacefulness, they emphasize, is quite distinct from any form of passivity; and requires that we treat other people respectfully in all ways, not merely refrain from physical assault. Its foundation is the cultivation of a peaceful heart and a fundamental attitude of respect for everyone, even one's opponents.

Nafram Ateek and John Paul Lederach explore the challenges of maintaining this attitude in the face of histories of suffering and oppression: the Israeli-Palestinian struggle and government repression in Central America. Each context demands that religious peacemakers find a way to balance peace with justice and truth with reconciliation. As these authors make clear, doing so requires a simultaneous transformation of both our most personal state of mind and our largest collective institutions. The brief founding statement of the Student Nonviolent Coordinating Committee indicates how that critically important civil rights organization drew its initial inspiration from a religious commitment to nonviolence.

Humanity has a bleak history of war, wars that are themselves often motivated by religion. Over the last several decades, however, religious voices have spoken, sometimes with great force and to some effect, for peace in place of military action. "Speak Truth to Power" is a simple and eloquent affirmation of the traditional Quaker rejection of force in human affairs. Writings from American Catholic Henri Nouen focus on the general issue of resistance to violence, especially the truly unprecedented threat of nuclear war, and also remind us of the large religious presence in the movement against the Vietnam War. Thomas Merton explores the role of love in a violent world, and cautions especially against choosing love and nonviolence while accepting the reigning structures of injustice.

Stanley Hauerwas's passionate essay in response to the terror of September 11, 2001, reminds us that a principled religious pacifist must always be willing to speak his or her truth, even when he or she may be surrounded by a society convulsed by rage, fear, and loss. Finally, Abraham Heschel warns that the existence of war and violence of all kinds reflects not just on the perpetrators but on all of us. If evil men make war and commit genocide, he tells us, it is only because the rest of us have been passive and timid in our commitment to the good.

"Religion and Conflict Transformation"

❧

R. Scott Appleby

R. Scott Appleby is professor of history at Notre Dame University, director of the Cushwa Center for the Study of American Catholicism, and fellow of the Institute for International Peace Studies. He has been active in recent efforts to heal—and change—the American Catholic Church in the wake of its sex abuse scandals.

❧

1.

In the spring of 1998 representatives of the Organization of the Islamic Conference (OIC), the United Nations, and the warring factions in Afghanistan laid the groundwork for a cease-fire and talks between the Taliban and the forces of the Afghan Muslim leader, Ahmed Shah Masud. The Taliban, an extremist movement led by Muslim religious scholars (ulema) from the rural southern region around the city of Kandahar, occupied two-thirds of the country, having driven Masud's army from Kabul in October 1996.

By defeating the "Northern Alliance" of Muslim leaders, the Sunni Taliban had alarmed Shi'ite hard-liners within Iran, delighted Sunni Islamists within the Pakistani government, and posed a dilemma for the Clinton administration. Russia and the Muslim nations of Kazakhstan, Kyrgyzstan, Uzbekistan, Tajikistan, and Turkmenistan feared that the Taliban might export extremist Islam across the Amu-Darya River, Afghanistan's northern border. Moreover, the Clinton administration joined most of the world in deploring the Taliban's brutally chauvinistic treatment of women and its imposition of a penal code, drawn from the Shari'a, that provided for the amputation of thieves' hands and the stoning to death of adulterers. On the other hand, the Taliban victory raised the prospect of an end to a costly civil war that would leave a counterweight to Shi'ite Iran in power and enhance the possibility of building a pipeline through Afghanistan to link Pakistan to the gas fields of Turkmenistan.

The Taliban victory was incomplete, however. The forces of Masud had staged a comeback in the summer of 1997, aided in part by the Tajik, Uzbek, and Hazara ethnic groups of the north, who resented the Taliban's version of radical Islam and its Pashtun way of life. During negotiations in the spring of 1998 the two sides exchanged prisoners and agreed to appoint a commission of forty ulema, twenty to be selected by each side. The Muslim religious scholars

435

would serve as mediators of the conflict, their expertise in the Shari'a and Islamic norms of warfare providing a common framework for negotiations between the rival Islamist parties.[1] On May 3, however, the peace talks broke down after the Taliban refused to lift a blockade of Hazarajat, the central region where tens of thousands of Afghans were threatened by food shortages, until the commission of religious scholars was in place. Fighting between the two sides resumed on May 20.[2]

2.

Several Filipino priests and nuns, drawn from the ranks of a new generation of Catholic social justice advocates and enjoying the status that accompanied their position as official representatives of the Roman Catholic Church, served as monitors in the 1986 national election that President Ferdinand Marcos fraudulently claimed as a victory over Corazon Aquino. As a result of the monitors' reports of widespread vote tampering, the Catholic Bishops' Conference—one of the few remaining Filipino institutions with credibility among the people—denounced the election in its immediate aftermath and declared publicly that the Marcos regime had lost its mandate to govern. Shortly thereafter, in February 1986, two million Filipinos amassed on EDSA, the main boulevard in Manila, to provide a cordon of protection around soldiers rebelling against the Marcos regime. Many of the protesters had come in response to a call by Cardinal Jaime Sin, the ranking Roman Catholic prelate in the Philippines. As the four-day People's Power revolution unfolded, the Catholic-owned Radio Veritas was instrumental in mobilizing the popular defense of the military that proved decisive in expelling Marcos nonviolently and bringing Aquino to power. Shortly after the EDSA revolution a "Victory of the People" mass, attended by millions, was held at the Luneta, a huge park in downtown Manila. Aquino led a prayer of thanks for the success of the campaign of civil disobedience. Like most outside observers, she acknowledged the central role of the Catholic Church in guiding the nonviolent revolution that ousted Marcos.[3]

3.

A delegation of U.S. religious leaders appointed by President Clinton—the principals being Dr. Don Argue, the president of the National Association of Evangelicals; the Most Reverend Theodore E. McCarrick, the Roman Catholic archbishop of Newark, New Jersey; and Rabbi Arthur Schneier, president and founder of the Appeal of Conscience Foundation—visited the People's Republic of China in February 1998 at the invitation of President Jiang Zemin in order to discuss the subject of religious freedom. The delegation, which received significant media coverage in the United States and in the official Chinese press, toured temples, churches, a mosque, monasteries, a nunnery, and Catholic and Protestant seminaries. Unlike previous delegations, however, this was not a fact-finding mission but a process designed to establish a high-level dialogue between Chinese and U.S. religious leaders, scholars and individual believers, and Chinese government and party officials. Thus, the delegates spent much of their time raising concerns related to religious freedom and advocating on behalf of "specific situations, individuals, and groups requiring special attention, especially religious leaders detained as prisoners of conscience."

At issue was China's narrow concept of religious freedom (the state recognized only Buddhism, Taoism, Islam, Catholicism, and Protestantism; restricted their worship; and forbade religious education, social service, and other forms of practice); the government's requirement that religious sites and activities register with and be regulated by the Religious Affairs Bureau; and the Chinese state's "administrative procedure" of "education through labor" for religious believers who participated in unauthorized activities. The delegates produced documentation of a local government's directive to "eliminate" unregistered churches and handed Chinese officials a list of thirty pastors, evangelists, bishops, Buddhist monks, and others who had been detained or harassed because of their religious activities. They made special pleas on behalf of several religious bodies: the large underground Catholic Church (in dissent from the official Patriotic Catholic Church); the Orthodox Christian communities in Beijing, Harbin, and Shanghai; the ethnically divided Muslim community; and the historic Jewish community of Shanghai. Finally, the delegates visited Tibet, where they inquired into the policies of the Democratic Management Committees that selected the "leaders" of the Buddhist monasteries and temples; and they registered objections to the Patriotic Education Campaigns that the Chinese government imposed on monks and nuns.

Although no prisoners of conscience were released as a result of its importunations, the delegation garnered some modest concessions from Shanghai and Tibetan government officials, reported a willingness on the part of Chinese officials to continue the process, and formulated six recommendations for enhancing the dialogue and strengthening religious freedom in China.[4]

4.

Until 1990 the Yugoslavian province of Kosovo, where Albanian Muslims constituted 90 percent of the population, enjoyed a statute of autonomy within the Yugoslav Federation. That year, however, the Yugoslav government in Belgrade abolished the statute and imposed the mandatory teaching of the Serbian language in the schools of Kosovo. In vehement response, the Albanian-speaking majority abandoned the public school and university system and created their own parallel educational institutions. In September 1996, as tensions reached a flashpoint, the Community of Sant'Egidio, active as a provider of social services in Albania since 1990 and having established a relationship with Yugoslav President Slobodan Milosevic, brokered an agreement between the Serbian government in Belgrade and the Albanian community in Kosovo. Signed by Milosevic and Ibrahim Rugova, the Albanian leader of Kosovo, the Agreement on Education restored the teaching of Albanian in Kosovo's schools and university and created a joint educational administrative team whose members were to be drawn from Kosovo's Albanian and Serb communities. Andrea Riccardi, founder of the Sant'Egidio movement, said that he hoped to build on the progress toward resolving this "highly explosive and contentious issue" by negotiating agreements to restore peaceful relations to the health and recreation sectors.[5]

On March 23, 1998, Serbian and Albanian officials endorsed a measure that gave Sant'Egidio significant responsibility for implementing the provisions of the Agreement on Education. It appointed Sant'Egidio representatives to a joint Serbian-Albanian committee charged with reintegrating the elementary and high schools of Kosovo, as well as the faculty and students of Pristina University, and with overcoming the remaining obstacles to the normalization of the educational system (e.g., funding, administration, languages, programs, diplomas, and employee status questions).[6]

5.

The Accord for a Firm and Lasting Peace, which brought an end to the civil war in Guatemala in 1996, was the product of nearly six years of UN-supervised negotiations between the government and the insurgent leftist rebels of the Unidad Revolucionaria Nacional Guatemalteca (URNG). During the thirty-six years of fighting, more than 150,000 unarmed civilians were killed, and a million more were driven from their homes or into exile. The war's origins lay in a 1954 coup, backed by the Central Intelligence Agency (CIA), that toppled an elected leftist president. The military dictatorship that came to power and ruled until 1985 was responsible for the near genocidal slaughter of Guatemala's Mayan Indian majority and the perpetuation and deepening of radical social inequalities: 2 percent of Guatemalans owned 70 percent of the land, Mayan women attended school for an average of less than two years and had little or no access to health care, and one in ten Mayan infants died in their first year.[7]

In 1977 Juan José Gerardi Conedera, the Catholic bishop of El Quiché, the large north-central province of Guatemala, publicly denounced both the state-sponsored death squads and the URNG rebels for their murderous ambushes and conquest of towns. "We could not bless the guerrillas," he later remarked. "I don't think [insurrectionist violence] is the answer to our problems." After surviving two subsequent assassination attempts Bishop Gerardi repaired to Costa Rica. Following his return in 1984 as auxiliary bishop and vicar-general of Guatemala City, Gerardi became coordinator of the new Archdiocesan Office of Human Rights established by Archbishop Próspero Penados; in 1988 his fellow bishops selected him as one of their representatives on the Committee on National Reconciliation.

These experiences prepared Bishop Gerardi for his final appointment, in 1995, as director of the Project for the Recovery of Historical Memory, a three-year church-sponsored study of the most egregious assassinations, massacres, and "disappearances" of the civil war. Conducted by 600 investigators who used fifteen Mayan dialects in interviewing 6,500 witnesses to the atrocities, the project was modeled on Argentina's similar "truth-telling" commission. It produced a 1,400-page document entitled *Guatemala: Never Again*, which traced 80 percent of the 55,000 deaths it described to the military, police, and death squads and 10 percent to the guerrilla movement. The report, prepared in the spirit of the 1996 peace accord, called for the appointment of international observers to monitor its enforcement. Going beyond the accord, it recommended reform of the judiciary, stronger measures to curtail the political influence of the military, economic restitution and psychological counseling for the victims' families, and full public acknowledgment by the government, the army, and paramilitary groups of the human rights violations they committed during the war. Delivering the report on April 24, 1998, Bishop Gerardi declared that "the search for truth does not end here.... It must support the role of memory as an instrument for social reconstruction." Two days later, the seventy-five-year-old bishop was attacked and beaten to death by unidentified assailants.[8]

TOWARD A TYPOLOGY OF RELIGIOUS CONFLICT TRANSFORMATION

These five vignettes, along with the cases introduced in earlier chapters, suggest a range of peacemaking activities that fall within the sphere of religious influence: preventive diplomacy, education and training, election monitoring, conflict mediation, nonviolent protest and advocacy for structural reform, and withdrawing or providing moral legitimacy for a government in times of crisis. It is important to recognize the interrelatedness of religious involvement in peacemaking at every phase of a conflict and at various levels of society.

Indeed, there is a certain "logic" to religious peacemaking that is not captured by terminology that divides it into self-contained temporal phases. Thus I use the term *religious peacebuilding* to comprehend the various phases, levels, and types of activity, by religious actors and others, that strengthen religion's role in creating tolerant and nonviolent societies.[9]

In this usage religious peacebuilding includes not only conflict transformation on the ground and postconflict structural reform (the standard connotation of the term *peacebuilding*) but also the efforts of people working at a remove from actual sites of deadly conflict, such as legal advocates of religious human rights, scholars conducting research relevant to cross-cultural and interreligious dialogue, and theologians and ethicists who are probing and strengthening their religious communities' traditions of nonviolent militance. The efforts of these human rights advocates, theologians, and ecumenists are the subject of the next chapter.

At the heart of peacebuilding is *conflict transformation*, the replacement of violent with nonviolent means of settling disputes. In what follows I suggest elements of a typology of religious conflict transformation, the fuller elaboration of which will depend on the growth of empirical research and case studies in this inchoate field of inquiry.[10]

On the basis of the available evidence, we can make several assertions. First, in the decades since the end of World War II, and with a special intensity in the years surrounding the end of the Cold War, religious militants, religious nongovernmental organizations (NGOs), national and transnational religious hierarchies and offices, ecumenical and interreligious bodies, and local religious communities, assuming a variety of critical roles, participated vigorously in conflict transformation in its three dimensions: *conflict management, conflict resolution*, and *structural reform*. Conflict management entails the prevention of conflict from becoming violent or expanding to other arenas. Conflict resolution entails removing, to the extent possible, the inequalities between the disputants by means of mediation, negotiation, and/or advocacy and testimony on behalf of one or more parties to a conflict. These processes, when successful, result in cease-fires and peace accords designed to contain the conflict in lieu of (and, ideally, in anticipation of) structural reform—efforts to address the root causes of the conflict and to develop long-term practices and institutions conducive to peaceful, nonviolent relations in the society.[11]

Finally, religious actors participated in conflict transformation under three different sets of sociopolitical circumstances—what I call the crisis mode, the saturation mode, and the intervention mode. Religious actors, as we will see, were engaged most frequently in the crisis mode, where their impact was significant but short term. In each mode, however, religious individuals and organizations collaborated effectively with government, nongovernment, and other religious actors; indeed, "religious peacebuilding" is a misnomer if it leads one to believe that religious actors were able to transform dimensions of modern conflict by functioning independently of government and other secular and religious actors.

NOTES

1. Olivier Roy describes the Taliban as a "conservative fundamentalist movement" rather than an Islamist party, the former being "traditional, calling for the implementation of Shari'a as the basis for an Islamic state," while the latter see Islam as a political ideology as well as a legal and religious system (Olivier Roy, "Islam and the Rise of the Taliban," *Muslim Politics Report* 11 [January/February 1997]: 5).

2. The Taliban resumed the fighting after withdrawing its proposal to allow the commission of ulema to discuss peace terms to end the civil war. The decision was conveyed to a UN mission visiting the Taliban's headquarters in Kandahar. See "Fighting Resumes in Afghanistan," *New York Times*, May 21, 1998, A11; "Afghan Peace Talks Break off, Bringing Fear of New Fighting," *New York Times*, May 4, 1998, A5; and "Afghans Hold Peace Talks; Signs of Hope and Pessimism," *New York Times*, April 27, 1998, A6. For background on Masud, Gulbuddin Hikmatyar, and the "Muslim Youth" movement that emerged from the State Faculty of Sciences or Polytechnic School in Kabul in the 1970s and provided the guerrilla leadership that opposed the Soviet Union's armies and eventually took Kabul, see Olivier Roy, *Islam and Resistance in Afghanistan* (Cambridge: Cambridge University Press, 1992), and "Afghanistan: An Islamic War of Resistance," in *Fundamentalisms and the State: Remaking Polities, Economies and Militance*, ed. Martin E. Marty and R. Scott Appleby (Chicago: University of Chicago Press, 1993), 495–500. On the Taliban military victories leading to the cease-fire or "halt in major military operations," see John Burns, "In Newly Won Afghan Region, Taliban Consolidate Their Hold," *New York Times*, May 26, 1997, A6.

3. Henry Wooster, "Faith at the Ramparts: The Philippine Catholic Church and the 1986 Revolution," in *Religion: The Missing Dimension of Statecraft*, ed. Douglas Johnston and Cynthia Sampson (New York: Oxford University Press, 1994), 163; see also Gordon Wise and Alice Cardel, "The Cardinal and the Revolution," *For a Change* 4 (April 1991): 4.

4. Dr. Don Argue, the Most Reverend Theodore E. McCarrick, and Rabbi Arthur Schneier, "Religious Freedom: A Report of the U.S. Religious Leaders Delegation to the People's Republic of China," February 1998, 2.

5. "Sant'Egidio Brokers Kosovo Deal," *The Tablet*, September 14, 1996, 12.

6. "Agreed Measures for the Implementation of the Agreement on Education in the Serbian Province of Kosovo and Metohija," 2; Andrea Riccardi, *Sant'Egidio, Rome and the World*, trans. Peter Heinegg (London and Maynooth: St. Paul's, 1999), 93–95.

7. Editorial Desk, "Peace by Piece in Guatemala," *New York Times*, September 23, 1997, A14.

8. Quoted in Stephen Privett, "Guatemala Report: A Bishop–Martyr Is Buried," *Commonweal* 215, no. 10 (May 22, 1998): 9–10.

9. See the similar definition in John Paul Lederach, *Building Peace: Sustainable Reconciliation in Divided Societies* (Washington, D.C.: U.S. Institute of Peace Press, 1997), 20.

10. The typology is limited by the current state of knowledge regarding the question. While there have been numerous instances of religious actors and institutions contributing in constructive ways to the prevention, mediation, peaceful resolution, and postsettlement transformation of conflict, the historical and social scientific study of the phenomenon is a relatively recent undertaking. Scholars have not yet produced a critical mass of case studies and nuanced comparative statements that might provide a reliable basis for a comprehensive typology of religious conflict transformation.

11. Compare the definitions provided in I. William Zartman, "Toward the Resolution of International Conflicts," in *Peacemaking in International Conflict: Methods and Techniques*, ed. I. William Zartman and J. Lewis Rasmussen (Washington, D.C.: U.S. Institute of Peace Press, 1997), 11. Zartman uses other peace-related terms as they are defined by their UN usage; hence, *peacemaking* refers to diplomatic efforts to resolve conflict according to Chapter VI of the UN Charter, and *peacekeeping* refers to forces positioned to monitor a peace agreement. I have used these terms throughout the text in a more general sense. By the UN usage, *peace-building* refers to what I am calling *structural transformation*, namely, the provision of structural measures to preclude a relapse into conflict. As mentioned, I use the term *religious peace-building* to comprehend all the elements of religious work for peace.

"Jesus' Third Way"

❧

Walter Wink

Walter Wink is a professor at Auburn Theological Seminar. He has been a peace fellow at the United States Institute of Peace and has written *Naming the Powers* and *Engaging the Powers*. This essay explores some of the hidden strengths of religious nonviolence as a guiding principle in social change.

❧

Many who have committed their lives to working for change and justice in the world simply dismiss Jesus' teachings about nonviolence as impractical idealism. And with good reason. "Turn the other cheek" suggests the passive, Christian doormat quality that has made so many Christians cowardly and complicit in the face of injustice. "Resist not evil" seems to break the back of all opposition to evil and counsel submission. "Going the second mile" has become a platitude meaning nothing more than "extend yourself." Rather than fostering structural change, such attitudes encourage collaboration with the oppressor.

Jesus never behaved in such ways. Whatever the source of the misunderstanding, it is neither Jesus nor his teaching, which, when given a fair hearing in its original social context, is arguably one of the most revolutionary political statements ever uttered.

> You have heard that it was said, "An eye for an eye and a tooth for a tooth." But I say to you, Do not resist one who is evil. But if anyone strikes you on the right cheek, turn to him the other also; and if anyone would sue you and take your coat, let him have your cloak as well; and if any one forces you to go one mile, go with him two miles. (Matt. 5:38–41, RSV)

When the court translators working in the hire of King James chose to translate *antistenai* as "*Resist* not evil," they were doing something more than rendering Greek into English. They were translating nonviolent resistance into docility. Jesus did *not* tell his oppressed hearers not to resist evil. That would have been absurd. His entire ministry is at odds with such a preposterous idea. The Greek word is made up of two parts: *anti*, a word still used in English for "against," and *histemi*, a verb which in its noun form (*stasis*) means violent rebellion, armed revolt, sharp dissension. Thus Barabbas is described as a rebel "who had committed murder in the *insurrection*" (Mark 15:7; Luke 23:19, 25), and the townspeople in Ephesus "are in danger of being charged with *rioting*" (Acts 19:40). The term generally refers to a potentially lethal disturbance or armed revolution.[1]

A proper translation of Jesus' teaching would then be, "Do not strike back at evil (or one who has done you evil) in kind. Do not give blow for blow. Do not retaliate against violence with violence." Jesus was no less committed to opposing evil than the anti-Roman resistance fighters. The only difference was over the means to be used. The issue was *how*—not whether—one should fight evil.

There are three general responses to evil: (1) passivity, (2) violent opposition, and (3) the third way of militant nonviolence articulated by Jesus. Human evolution has conditioned us for only the first two of these responses: fight or flight.

Fight had been the cry of Galileans who had abortively rebelled against Rome only two decades before Jesus spoke. Jesus and many of his hearers would have seen some of the two thousand of their countrymen crucified by the Romans along the roadsides. They would have known some of the inhabitants of Sepphoris (a mere three miles north of Nazareth) who had been sold into slavery for aiding the insurrectionists' assault on the arsenal there. Some also would live to experience the horrors of the war against Rome in 66–70 C.E., one of the ghastliest in history. If the option *fight* had no appeal to them, their only alternative was *flight*: passivity, submission, or, at best, a passive-aggressive recalcitrance in obeying commands. For them no third way existed. Submission or revolt spelled out the entire vocabulary of their alternatives to oppression.

Now we are in a better position to see why King James' servants translated antistenai as "resist not." The king would not want people concluding they had any recourse against his or any other sovereign's unjust policies. Therefore the populace must be made to believe there were two and only two alternatives: flight or fight. Either we resist not, or we resist. And Jesus commands us, according to these king's men, to resist not. Jesus appears to authorize monarchical absolutism. Submission is the will of God. Most modern translations have meekly followed the King James path.

Neither of the invidious alternatives of flight/fight is what Jesus is proposing. It is important to be clear about this point before going on: *Jesus abhors both passivity and violence as responses to evil*. His is a third alternative not even touched by these options. Antistenai may be translated variously as "Do not take up arms against evil," "Do not react reflexively to evil," "Do not let evil dictate the terms of your opposition." The *Scholars Version* translates it brilliantly: "Don't react violently against someone who is evil." The word cannot be construed to mean submission.

Jesus clarifies his meaning by three brief examples. "If anyone strikes you on the right cheek, turn to him the other also." Why the *right* cheek? How does one strike another on the right cheek anyway? Try it. A blow by the right fist in that right-handed world would land on the *left* cheek of the opponent. To strike the right cheek with the fist would require using the left hand, but in that society the left hand was used only for unclean tasks. Even to gesture with the left hand at Qumran carried the penalty of ten days penance (*The Dead Sea Scrolls*, 1 QS 7). The only way one could strike the right cheek with the right hand would be with the *back of the hand*.

What we are dealing with here is unmistakably an insult, not a fistfight. The intention is not to injure but to humiliate, to put someone in his or her place. One normally did not strike a peer in this way, and if one did the fine was exorbitant (four *zuz* was the fine for a blow to a peer with a fist, four hundred zuz for backhanding him; but to an underling, no penalty whatever; *Mishna, Baba Kamma* 8:1–6). A backhand slap was the normal way of admonishing inferiors. Masters backhanded slaves; husbands, wives; parents, children; men, women; Romans, Jews. One black South African told me that during his youth white farmers still gave the backhand to disobedient workers.

We have here a set of unequal relations, in each of which retaliation would be suicidal. The only normal response would be cowering submission. It is important to ask who Jesus' audience is. In every case, Jesus' listeners are not those who strike, initiate lawsuits, or impose forced labor. Rather, Jesus is speaking to their victims ("If anyone strikes *you* . . . would sue *you* . . . forces *you* to go one mile . . ."). There are among his hearers people who have been subjected to these very indignities. They have been forced to stifle their inner outrage at the dehumanizing treatment meted out to them by the hierarchical system of caste and class, race and gender, age and status, and by the guardians of imperial occupation.

Why then does Jesus counsel these already humiliated people to turn the other cheek? Because this action robs the oppressor of power to humiliate them. The person who turns the other cheek is saying, in effect, "Try again. Your first blow failed to achieve its intended effect. I deny you the power to humiliate me. I am a human being just like you. Your status (gender, race, age, wealth) does not alter that. You cannot demean me."

Such a response would create enormous difficulties for the striker. Purely logistically, how can he now hit the other cheek? He cannot backhand it with his right hand. If he hits with a fist, he makes himself an equal, acknowledging the other as a peer. But the whole point of the back of the hand is to reinforce the caste system and its institutionalized inequality. Even if the master orders the person flogged, the point has irrevocably been made. He has been forced, against his will, to regard that person as an equal human being. He has been stripped of his power to dehumanize the other.

The second example Jesus gives is set in a court of law. Someone is being sued for his outer garment.[2] Who would do that and under what circumstances? The Old Testament provides the clues:

> If you lend money to any of my people with you *who is poor*, you shall not be to him as a creditor, and you shall not exact interest from him. If ever you take your neighbor's garment in pledge, you shall restore it to him before the sun goes down; for that is his only covering, it is his mantle for his body; in what else shall he sleep? And if he cries to me, I will hear, for I am compassionate. (Exod. 22:25–27, emphasis added)

> When you make your neighbor a loan of any sort, you shall not go into his house to fetch his pledge. You shall stand outside, and the man to whom you make the loan shall bring the pledge out to you. And *if he is a poor man*, you shall not sleep in his pledge; when the sun goes down, you shall restore to him the pledge that he may sleep in his cloak and bless you. . . . You shall not . . . take a widow's garment in pledge. (Deut. 24:10–13, 17, emphasis added)

> They that trample the head of the poor into the dust of the earth . . . lay themselves down beside every altar on garments taken in pledge. (Amos 2:7–8)

Only the poorest of the poor would have nothing but an outer garment to give as collateral for a loan. Jewish law strictly required its return every evening at sunset, for that was all the poor had in which to sleep. The situation to which Jesus alludes is one with which his hearers would have been too familiar: the poor debtor has sunk ever deeper into poverty, the debt cannot be repaid, and his creditor has hauled him into court to wring out repayment.

Indebtedness was the most serious social problem in first-century Palestine. Jesus' parables are full of debtors struggling to salvage their lives. The situation was not, however, a natural calamity that had overtaken the incompetent. It was the direct consequence of Roman imperial policy. Emperors had taxed the wealthy so vigorously to fund their wars that the rich began seeking nonliquid investments to secure their wealth. Land was best, but there was a problem: it was not bought and sold on the open market as today but was ancestrally owned and passed down over generations. Little land was ever for sale, at least in Palestine. Exorbitant interest, however, could be used to drive landowners into ever deeper debt until they were forced to sell their land. By the time of Jesus we see this process already far advanced: large estates (*latifundia*) are owned by absentee landlords, managed by stewards, and worked by servants, sharecroppers, and day laborers. It is no accident that the first act of the Jewish revolutionaries in 66 C.E. was to burn the temple treasury, where the record of debts was kept.

It is in this context that Jesus speaks. His hearers are the poor ("if anyone would sue *you*"). They share a rankling hatred for a system that subjects them to humiliation by stripping them of their lands, their goods, finally even their outer garments.

Why then does Jesus counsel them to give over their inner garment as well? This would mean stripping off all their clothing and marching out of court stark naked! Put yourself in the debtor's place; imagine the chuckles this saying must have evoked. There stands the creditor, beet red with embarrassment, your outer garment in one hand, your underwear in the other. You have suddenly turned the tables on him. You had no hope of winning the trial; the law was entirely in his favor. But you have refused to be humiliated. At the same time you have registered a stunning protest against a system that spawns such debt. You have said, in effect, "You want my robe? Here, take everything! Now you've got all I have except my body. Is that what you'll take next?"

Nakedness was taboo in Judaism. Shame fell not on the naked party but the person viewing or causing one's nakedness (Gen. 9:20–27). By stripping you have brought the creditor under the same prohibition that led to the curse of Canaan. As you parade into the street, your friends and neighbors, startled, aghast, inquire what happened. You explain. They join your growing procession, which now resembles a victory parade. The entire system by which debtors are oppressed has been publicly unmasked. The creditor is revealed to be not a "respectable" moneylender but a party in the reduction of an entire social class to landlessness and destitution. This unmasking is not simply punitive, however; it offers the creditor a chance to see, perhaps for the first time in his life, what his practices cause—and to repent.

Jesus in effect is sponsoring clowning. In so doing he shows himself to be thoroughly Jewish. A later saying of the Talmud runs, "If your neighbor calls you an ass, put a saddle on your back."[3]

The Powers That Be literally stand on their dignity. Nothing takes away their potency faster than deft lampooning. By refusing to be awed by their power, the powerless are emboldened to seize the initiative, even where structural change is not possible. This message, far from being a counsel of perfection unattainable in this life, is a practical, strategic measure for empowering the oppressed. It provides a hint of how to take on the entire system in a way that unmasks its essential cruelty and to burlesque its pretensions to justice, law, and order. Here is a poor man who will no longer be treated as a sponge to be squeezed dry by the rich. He accepts the laws as they stand, pushes them to the point of absurdity, and reveals them for what they really are. He strips nude and walks out before his compatriots, leaving stark naked the creditor and the whole economic edifice he represents.

Jesus' third example, the one about going the second mile, is drawn from the enlightened practice of limiting the amount of forced labor that Roman soldiers could levy on subject peoples. Jews would have seldom encountered legionnaires except in time of war or insurrection. They interacted primarily with auxiliaries headquartered in Judea who were paid at half the rate of legionnaires; they were rather a scruffy bunch.

In Galilee, Herod Antipas maintained an army patterned after Rome's; presumably it also had the right to impose labor. Mile markers were placed regularly beside the highways. A soldier could impress a civilian to carry his pack one mile only; to force the civilian to go further carried with it severe penalties under military law. In this way Rome tried to limit the anger of the occupied people and still keep its armies on the move. Nevertheless, this levy was a bitter reminder to the Jews that they were a subject people even in the Promised Land.

To this proud but subjugated people Jesus does not counsel revolt. One does not "befriend" the soldier, draw him aside, and drive a knife into his ribs. Jesus was keenly aware of the futility of armed revolt against Roman imperial might. He minced no words about it, though it must have cost him support from the revolutionary factions.

But why walk the second mile? Is this not to rebound to the opposite extreme: aiding and abetting the enemy? Not at all. The question here, as in the two previous instances, is how the oppressed can recover the initiative, how they can assert their human dignity in a situation that cannot for the time being be changed. The rules are Caesar's but not how one responds to the rules. The response is God's, and Caesar has no power over that.

Imagine then the soldier's surprise when, at the next mile marker, he reluctantly reaches to assume his pack (sixty-five to eighty-five pounds in full gear). You say, "Oh no, let me carry it another mile." Why would you do that? What are you up to? Normally he has to coerce your kinsmen to carry his pack; now you do it cheerfully and will not stop! Is this a provocation? Are you insulting his strength? Being kind? Trying to get him disciplined for seeming to make you go farther then you should? Are you planning to file a complaint? To create trouble?

From a situation of servile impressment, you have once more seized the initiative. You have taken back the power of choice. The soldier is thrown off-balance by being deprived of the predictability of your response. He has never dealt with such a problem before. Now you have forced him into making a decision for which nothing in his previous experience has prepared him. If he has enjoyed feeling superior to the vanquished, he will not enjoy it today.

Imagine the hilarious situation of a Roman infantryman pleading with a Jew, "Aw, come on, please give me back my pack!" The humor of this scene may escape those who picture it through sanctimonious eyes. It could scarcely, however, have been lost on Jesus' hearers, who must have delighted in the prospect of thus discomfiting their oppressors.

Some readers may object to the idea of discomfiting the soldier or embarrassing the creditor. But can people engaged in oppressive acts repent unless made uncomfortable with their actions? There is, admittedly, the danger of using nonviolence as a tactic of revenge and humiliation. There is also, at the opposite extreme, an equal danger of sentimentality and softness that confuses the uncompromising love of Jesus with being nice. Loving confrontation can free both the oppressed from docility and the oppressor from sin.

Even if nonviolent action does not immediately change the heart of the oppressor, it does affect those committed to it. As Martin Luther King Jr. attested, it gives them new self-respect and calls on strength and courage they did not know they had. To those with power, Jesus' advice to the powerless may seem paltry. But to those whose lifelong pattern has been to cringe, bow, and scrape before their masters, to those who have internalized their role as inferiors, this small step is momentous.

These three examples amplify what Jesus means in his thesis statement: "Do not react violently against the one who is evil." Instead of the two options ingrained in us by millions of years of unreflective, brute response to biological threats from the environment, instead of flight or fight, Jesus offers a third way. This new way marks a historic mutation in human development: the revolt against the principle of natural selection.[4] With Jesus a way emerges by which evil can be opposed without being mirrored.

JESUS' THIRD WAY

- ❧ Seize the moral initiative.
- ❧ Find a creative alternative to violence.
- ❧ Assert your own humanity and dignity as a person.
- ❧ Meet force with ridicule or humor.
- ❧ Break the cycle of humiliation.
- ❧ Refuse to submit or to accept the inferior position.
- ❧ Expose the injustice of the system.
- ❧ Take control of the power dynamic.
- ❧ Shame the oppressor into repentance.
- ❧ Stand your ground.
- ❧ Force the Powers into decisions for which they are not prepared.
- ❧ Recognize your own power.
- ❧ Be willing to suffer rather than retaliate.
- ❧ Force the oppressor to see you in a new light.
- ❧ Deprive the oppressor of a situation where force is effective.
- ❧ Be willing to undergo the penalty of breaking unjust laws.
- ❧ Die to fear of the old order and its rules.

- ❧ Avoid

Flight	and	**Fight**
submission		armed revolt
passivity		violent rebellion
withdrawal		direct retaliation
surrender		revenge

It is too bad Jesus did not provide fifteen or twenty more examples since we do not tend toward this new response naturally. Some examples from political history might help engrave it more deeply in our minds.

In Alagamar, Brazil, a group of peasants organized a long-term struggle to preserve their lands against attempts at illegal expropriation by national and international firms (with the connivance of local politicians and the military). Some of the peasants were arrested and jailed in town. Their companions decided they were all equally responsible. Hundreds marched to town. They filled the house of the judge, demanding to be jailed with those who had been arrested. The judge was finally obliged to send them all home, including the prisoners.[5]

During the Vietnam War, one woman claimed seventy-nine dependents on her U.S. income tax, all Vietnamese orphans, so she owed no tax. They were not legal dependents, of course, so were disallowed. No, she insisted, these children have been orphaned by indiscriminate U.S. bombing; we are responsible for their lives. She forced the Internal Revenue Service to take her to court. That gave her a larger forum for making her case. She used the system against itself to unmask the moral indefensibility of what the system was doing. Of course she "lost" the case, but she made her point.

Another story Jesus himself must have known and which may have served as a model for his examples: In 26 C.E., when Pontius Pilate brought the imperial standards into Jerusalem and displayed them at the Fortress Antonio overlooking the temple, all Jerusalem was thrown into a tumult. These "effigies of Caesar which are called standards" not only infringed on the commandment against images but were the particular gods of the legions. Jewish leaders requested their removal. When Pilate refused, a large crowd of Jews "fell prostrate around his house and for five whole days and nights remained motionless in that position." On the sixth day, Pilate assembled the multitude in the stadium with the apparent intention of answering them. Instead, his soldiers surrounded the Jews in a ring three deep. As Josephus tells it,

> Pilate, after threatening to cut them down, if they refused to admit Caesar's images, signaled to the soldiers to draw their swords. Thereon the Jews, as by concerted action, flung themselves in a body on the ground, extended their necks, and exclaimed that they were ready rather to die than to transgress the law. Overcome with astonishment at such intense religious zeal, Pilate gave orders for the immediate removal of the standards from Jerusalem.[6]

During World War II, when Nazi authorities in occupied Denmark promulgated an order that all Jews had to wear yellow armbands with the Star of David, the king made it a point to attend a celebration in the Copenhagen synagogue. He and most of the population of Copenhagen donned yellow armbands as well. His stand was affirmed by the Bishop of Sjaelland and other Lutheran clergy.[7] The Nazis eventually had to rescind the order.

It is important to repeat such stories to extend our imaginations for creative nonviolence. Since it is not a natural response, we need to be schooled in it. We need models, and we need to rehearse nonviolence in our daily lives if we ever hope to resort to it in crises.

Sadly, Jesus' three examples have been turned into laws, with no reference to the utterly changed contexts in which they were being applied. His attempt to nerve the powerless to assert their humanity under inhuman conditions has been turned into a legalistic prohibition on schoolyard fistfights between peers. Pacifists and those who reject pacifism alike have tended to regard Jesus' infinitely malleable insights as iron rules. The one group urges that they be observed inflexibly; the other treats them as impossible demands intended to break us and catapult us into the arms of grace. The creative, ironic, playful quality of Jesus' teaching has thus been buried under an avalanche of humorless commentary. And as always, the law kills.

How many a battered wife has been counseled, on the strength of a legalistic reading of this passage, to "turn the other cheek." This when what she needs, according to the spirit of Jesus' words, is to find a way to restore her own dignity and end the vicious circle of humiliation, guilt, and bruising. She needs to assert some sort of control in the situation and force her husband to regard her as an equal—or get out of the relationship altogether. The victim needs to recover her self-worth and seize the initiative from her oppressor. And he needs to be helped to overcome his violence. The most creative and loving thing she could do, at least in the American setting, might be to have him arrested.

As such an example suggests, "Turn the other cheek" is not intended as a legal requirement to be applied woodenly in every situation. Rather, it is the impetus for discovering creative alternatives that transcend the only two we are conditioned to perceive: submission or violence, flight or fight.

Shortly after I was promoted from the "B" team to the varsity basketball squad in high school, I noticed that Ernie, the captain, was missing shot after shot from the corner because he was firing the ball like a bullet. So—helpfully, I thought—I shouted, "Arch it, Ernie, arch it." His best friend Ham thought advice from a greenhorn impertinent. From that day on he sniped at me without letup. I had been raised a Christian, so I "turned the other cheek." To each sarcastic jibe I answered with a smile or soft words. This confused Ham somewhat; by the end of the season he lost his taste for taunts.

It was not until four years later that I suddenly woke to the realization that I had not loved Ham into changing. The fact was, *I hated his guts*. It might have been far more creative for me to have challenged him to a fistfight. Then he would have had to deal with me as an equal. But I was *afraid* to fight him, though the fight would probably have been a draw. I was scared I might get hurt. I was hiding behind the Christian "injunction" to "turn the other cheek." Instead I could have been asking, what is the most creative, transformative response to this situation? Perhaps I had done the right thing for the wrong reason, but I suspect that creative nonviolence can never be a genuinely moral response unless we are capable of first entertaining the possibility of violence and consciously saying no. Otherwise our nonviolence may actually be a mask for cowardice.

Oppressed people are justifiably suspicious that those with wealth or power are more concerned to avoid violence than bring about justice. Nobel Peace Prize laureate Adolfo Perez Esquivel comments, "What has always caught my attention is the attitude of peace movements in Europe and the United States, where nonviolence is envisioned as the final objective. Nonviolence is a lifestyle. The final objective is humanity. It is life."[8]

[. . .]

Today we can draw on the cumulative historical experience of nonviolent social struggle over the centuries and employ newer tools for political and social analysis. But the spirit, the thrust, the surge for creative transformation which is the ultimate principle of the universe—this is the same one we see incarnated in Jesus. Freed from literalistic legalism, his teaching reads like a practical manual for empowering the powerless to seize the initiative even in situations impervious to change. It seems almost as if his teaching has only now, in this generation, become an inescapable task and practical necessity.

To people dispirited by the enormity of the injustices which crush us and the intractability of those in positions of power, Jesus' words beam hope across the centuries. We need not be afraid. We can assert our human dignity. We can lay claim to the creative possibilities that are still ours, burlesque the injustice of unfair laws, and force evil out of hiding from behind the facade of legitimacy.

To risk confronting the Powers with such clownlike vulnerability, to affirm at the same time our own humanity and that of those we oppose, to dare to draw the sting of evil by absorbing it—such behavior is unlikely to attract the faint of heart. But I am convinced a host of people are waiting for the Christian message to challenge them, for once, to a heroism worthy of their lives. Has Jesus not given us that word?

NOTES

1. *Anthistemi* is the Greek word most frequently used in the Septuagint to translate the Hebrew *qum* and often carries the sense of "to rise up" against someone in revolt or war (Gen. 4:8; Num. 16:2; Judg. 9:35, 43; 20:33; 2 Chron. 13:6; Ps. 94:16 [93:16 LXX]; Isa. 14:22; Amos 7:9; Obad. 1; Hab. 2:7). *Epanistemi* is used synonymously: Deut. 19:11; 22:26; 33:11; Judg. 9:18; Job 20:27; 27:7; 30:12; Ps. 27:3; Isa. 31:2; Mic. 7:6. So also *katephistamai* (Acts 18:12—"made insurrection," KJV; "made a united attack," RSV); and *akatastasia* (Luke 21:9—"revolutions," JB; "insurrections," KJV, NEB). *Anthistemi* is also used of armed, violent warfare in 3 Macc. 6:19; Rom. 13:2; and Eph. 6:13. Liddell and Scott define it as "to set against, especially in battle." We can be virtually assured that it is used in Matt. 5:39 in the sense of "to resist forcibly" because the Jesus tradition elsewhere cites Mic. 7:6—"For the son treats the father with contempt, the daughter *rises up* against her mother, the daughter-in-law against her mother-in-law; a man's enemies are the men of his own house" (see Matt. 10:34–36; Luke 12:53). And Jesus may have

formulated the statement about debtors giving their clothing to creditors in contrast to Hab. 2:7, where the wealthy are threatened with visions of debtors suddenly *rising up* in bloody revolt. Both passages use a form of *qum*.

2. Matthew and Luke are at odds on whether the outer garment (Luke) or the inner garment (Matthew) is being taken. But the Jewish practice of giving the outer garment as collateral for a loan makes it clear that Luke is correct.

3. *Babylonian Talmud, Babba Kamma* 92b.

4. Gerd Thiessen, *Biblical Faith: An Evolutionary Approach* (Philadelphia: Fortress Press, 1985), 122.

5. Therese de Coninck, ed., *Essays on Nonviolence* (Nyack, N.Y.: Fellowship of Reconciliation, n.d.), 38.

6. Josephus, *War* 2.172–74; *Antiquities* 18.55–59. Despite the similarity to a wolf's baring his throat to show he is overmastered, the two acts are polar opposites. The wolf is surrendering; these Jews were being defiant. The wolf seeks to save its life; these Jews were prepared to die for their faith. The Jews later tried the same tactic against the Emperor Gaius (Caligula) and again prevailed, aided by the providential death of the emperor (*Ant.* 18.257–309).

7. William Robert Miller, *Nonviolence* (New York: Schocken, 1966), 252.

8. "An Interview with Adolfo Perez Esquivel," *Fellowship* 51 (July/August 1985): 10.

"The Fourteen Mindfulness Trainings of the Order of Interbeing"

&

Thich Nhat Hanh

Thich Nhat Hanh is an internationally known Vietnamese Buddhist monk, who was active in resisting war in his country and in support for its refugees. Author of dozens of books on spirituality, Buddhism, and bringing peace into the social life, he is one of the creators of Engaged Buddhism. Here he describes some guiding commitments for a life of peace, commitments that are to be followed both in the larger society and within any particular organization or small community. Hanh's lessons are particularly valuable for social activists, who are themselves liable to fall victim to a consciousness dominated by self-righteousness and anger.

&

First: Do not be idolatrous about or bound to any doctrine, theory, or ideology, even Buddhist ones. All systems of thought are guiding means; they are not absolute truth.

This precept is the roar of the lion. Its spirit is characteristic of Buddhism. It is often said that the Buddha's teaching is only a raft to help you cross the river, a finger pointing to the moon. Don't mistake the finger for the moon. The raft is not the shore. If we cling to the raft, if we cling to the finger, we miss everything. We cannot, in the name of the finger or the raft, kill each other. Human life is more precious than any ideology, any doctrine.

The Order of Interbeing was born in Vietnam during the war, which was a conflict between two world ideologies. In the name of ideologies and doctrines, people kill and are killed. If you have a gun, you can shoot one, two, three, five people; but if you have an ideology and stick to it, thinking it is the absolute truth, you can kill millions. This precept includes the precept of not killing in its deepest sense. Humankind suffers very much from attachment to views. "If you don't follow this teaching, I will cut off your head." In the name of the truth we kill each other. The world now is stuck in that situation. Many people think that Marxism is the highest product of the human mind, that nothing can compare with it. Other people think that it's crazy, and that we have to destroy those people. We are caught in this situation.

Buddhism is not like that. One of the most basic teachings of Shakyamuni is that life is the most precious. It is an answer to our main problem of war and peace. Peace can only be achieved when we are not attached to a view, when we are free from fanaticism. The more you decide to practice this precept, the deeper you will go into reality and understand the teaching of Buddhism.

Second: Do not think that the knowledge you presently possess is changeless, absolute truth. Avoid being narrow-minded and bound to present views. Learn and practice nonattachment from views in order to be open to receive others' viewpoints. Truth is found in life and not merely in conceptual knowledge. Be ready to learn throughout your entire life and to observe reality in yourself and in the world at all times.

This precept springs from the first one. Remember the young father who refused to open the door to his own son, thinking the boy was already dead. The Buddha said, "If you cling to something as the absolute truth and you are caught in it, when the truth comes in person to knock on your door, you will refuse to let it in." A scientist with an open mind, who can question the present knowledge of science, will have more of a chance to discover a higher truth. A Buddhist, also, in her meditation, in her quest for higher understanding has to question her present view concerning reality. The technique of understanding is to overcome views and knowledge. The way of nonattachment from views is the basic teaching of Buddhism concerning understanding.

Third: Do not force others, including children, by any means whatsoever, to adopt your views, whether by authority, threat, money, propaganda, or even education. However, through compassionate dialogue, help others renounce fanaticism and narrowness.

This also springs from the first precept. It is the spirit of free inquiry. I think Westerners can accept this, because you understand it. If you can find a way to organize it globally, it will be a happy event for the world.

Fourth: Do not avoid contact with suffering or close your eyes before suffering. Do not lose awareness of the existence of suffering in the life of the world. Find ways to be with those who are suffering by all means, including personal contact and visits, images, sound. By such means, awaken yourself and others to the reality of suffering in the world.

The first Dharma Talk given by the Buddha was on the Four Noble Truths. The first truth is the existence of suffering. This kind of contact and awareness is needed. If we don't encounter pain, ills, we won't look for the causes of pain and ills to find a remedy, a way out of the situation.

America is somehow a closed society. Americans are not very aware of what is going on outside of America. Life here is so busy that even if you watch television and read the newspaper, and the images from outside flash by, there is no real contact. I hope you will find some way to nourish the awareness of the existence of suffering in the world. Of course, inside America there is also suffering, and it is important to stay in touch with that. But much of the suffering in the West is "useless" and can vanish when we see the real suffering of other people. Sometimes we suffer because of some psychological fact. We cannot get out of our self, and so we suffer. If we get in touch with the suffering in the world, and are moved by that suffering, we may come forward to help the people who are suffering, and our own suffering may just vanish.

Fifth: Do not accumulate wealth while millions are hungry. Do not take as the aim of your life fame, profit, wealth, or sensual pleasure. Live simply and share time, energy, and material resources with those who are in need.

The *Eight Realizations of Great Beings Sutra* says, "The human mind is always searching for possessions, and never feels fulfilled. Bodhisattvas move in the opposite direction and follow the principle of self-sufficiency. They live a simple life in order to practice the Way, and consider the realization of perfect understanding as their only career." In the context of our modern society, simple living also means to remain as free as possible from the destructive social and economic machine, and to avoid stress, depression, high blood pressure, and other modern diseases. We should make every effort to avoid the pressures and anxieties that fill most modern lives. The only way out is to consume less. Once we are able to live simply and happily, we are better able to help others.

Sixth: Do not maintain anger or hatred. As soon as anger and hatred arise, practice the meditation on compassion in order to deeply understand the persons who have caused anger and hatred. Learn to look at other beings with the eyes of compassion.

We have to be aware of irritation or anger as it arises, and try to understand it. Once we understand, we are better able to forgive and love. Meditation on compassion means meditation on understanding. If we do not understand, we cannot love.

"Learn to look at other beings with the eyes of compassion" is directly quoted from *The Lotus Sutra*, the chapter on Avalokitesvara. You might like to write this down and put it in your sitting room. The original Chinese is only five words: "compassionate eyes looking living beings." The first time I recited *The Lotus Sutra*, when I came to these five words, I was silenced. I knew that these five words are enough to guide my whole life.

Seventh: Do not lose yourself in dispersion and in your surroundings. Learn to practice breathing in order to regain composure of body and mind, to practice mindfulness, and to develop concentration and understanding.

This precept is in the middle. It is the heart of the fourteen precepts, the most important precept: to live in awareness. Without this precept, without mindfulness, the other precepts cannot be observed completely. It is like a carrying pole. In Asia they used to carry things with a pole, and put the middle of the pole on their shoulders. This precept is like the middle of the pole that you carry on your shoulders.

Eighth: Do not utter words that can create discord and cause the community to break. Make every effort to reconcile and resolve all conflicts, however small.

We now come to the second set of precepts, concerning speech. The first seven precepts deal with mind, then two with speech, and five with body. This precept is about reconciliation, the effort to make peace, not only in your family, but in society as well. In order to help reconcile a conflict, we have to be in touch with both sides. We must transcend the conflict; if we are still in the conflict, it is difficult to reconcile. We have to have a nondualistic viewpoint in order to listen to both sides and understand. The world needs persons like this for the work of reconciliation, persons with the capacity of understanding and compassion.

Ninth: Do not say untruthful things for the sake of personal interest or to impress people. Do not utter words that cause division and hatred. Do not spread news that you do not know to be certain. Do not criticize or condemn things that you are not sure of. Always speak truthfully and constructively. Have the courage to speak out about situations of injustice, even when doing so may threaten your own safety.

The words we speak can create love, trust, and happiness around us, or create a hell. We should be careful about what we say. If we tend to talk too much, we should become aware of it and learn to speak less. We must become aware of our speech and the results of our speaking. There is a gatha which can be recited before picking up the telephone:

> Words can travel across thousands of miles.
> They are intended to build up understanding and love.
> Each word should be a jewel,
> A beautiful tapestry.

We should speak constructively. In our speech we can try not to cause misunderstanding, hatred, or jealousy, rather to increase understanding and mutual acceptance. This may even help reduce our telephone bills. The ninth precept also requires frankness and courage. How many of us are brave enough to denounce injustice in a situation where speaking the truth might threaten our own safety?

Tenth: Do not use the Buddhist community for personal gain or profit, or transform your community into a political party. A religious community should, however, take a clear stand against oppression and injustice, and should strive to change the situation without engaging in partisan conflicts.

This does not mean that we must be silent about injustice. It just means we should do it with awareness and not take sides. We should speak the truth and not just weigh the political consequences. If we take sides, we will lose our power to help mediate the conflict.

During one visit to America, I met with a group of people who wanted to raise funds to help the government of Vietnam rebuild the country. I asked whether they would also like to do something for the boat people, and they said no. They thought that politically it is not good to talk about the boat people, because that would discredit the government of Vietnam. In order to succeed in one thing, they have to refrain from doing something that they think is right.

Eleventh: Do not live with a vocation that is harmful to humans and nature. Do not invest in companies that deprive others of their chance to life. Select a vocation which helps realize your ideal of compassion.

This is an extremely hard precept to observe. If you are lucky enough to have a vocation that helps you realize your ideal of compassion, you still have to understand more deeply. If I am a teacher, I am very glad to have this job helping children. I am glad that I am not a butcher who kills cows and pigs. Yet the son and the daughter of the butcher come to my class, and I teach them. They profit from my right livelihood. My son and daughter eat the meat that the butcher prepares. We are linked together. I cannot say that my livelihood is perfectly right. It cannot be. Observing this precept includes finding ways to realize a collective right livelihood.

You may try to follow a vegetarian diet, to lessen the killing of animals, but you cannot completely avoid the killing. When you drink a glass of water, you kill many tiny living beings. Even in your dish of vegetables, there are quite a lot of them, boiled or fried. I am aware that my vegetarian dish is not completely vegetarian, and I think that if my teacher, the Buddha, were here, he could not avoid that either. The problem is whether we are determined to go in the direction of compassion or not. If we are, then can we reduce the suffering to a minimum? If I lose my direction, I have to look for the North Star, and I go to the north. That does not mean I expect to arrive at the North Star. I just want to go in that direction.

Twelfth: Do not kill. Do not let others kill. Find whatever means possible to protect life and to prevent war.

The defense budgets in Western countries are enormous. Studies show that by stopping the arms race, we will have more than enough money to erase poverty, hunger, illiteracy, and many diseases from the world. This precept applies not only to humans, but to all living beings. As we have seen, no one can observe this precept to perfection; however, the essence is to respect and protect life, to do our best to protect life. This means not killing, and also not letting other people kill. It is difficult. Those who try to observe this precept have to be working for peace in order to have peace in themselves. Preventing war is much better than protesting against the war. Protesting the war is too late.

Thirteenth: Possess nothing that should belong to others. Respect the property of others but prevent others from enriching themselves from human suffering or the suffering of other beings.

Bringing to our awareness the pain caused by social injustice, the thirteenth precept urges us to work for a more livable society. This precept is linked with the fourth precept (the awareness of suffering), the fifth precept (lifestyle), the eleventh precept (right livelihood), and the twelfth precept (the protection of life). In order to deeply comprehend this precept, we must also meditate on these four precepts.

To develop ways to prevent others from enriching themselves on human suffering and the suffering of other beings is the duty of legislators and politicians. However, each of us can also act in this direction. To some degree, we can be close to oppressed people and help them protect their right to life and defend themselves against oppression and exploitation. Letting people enrich themselves from human suffering or the suffering of other beings is something we cannot do. As a community we must try to prevent this. How to work for justice in our own city is a problem that we have to consider. The Bodhisattvas's vows—to help all sentient beings—are immense. Each of us can vow to sit in their rescue boats.

Fourteenth: Do not mistreat your body. Learn to handle it with respect. Do not look on your body as only an instrument. Preserve vital energies (sexual, breath, spirit) for the realization of the Way. Sexual expression should not happen without love and commitment. In sexual relationships be aware of future suffering that may be caused. To preserve the happiness of others, respect the rights and commitments of others. Be fully aware of the responsibility of bringing new lives into the world. Meditate on the world into which you are bringing new beings.

You may have the impression that this precept discourages having children, but it is not so. It only urges us to be aware of what we are doing. Is our world safe enough to bring in more children? If you want to bring more children into the world, then do something for the world.

This precept also has to do with celibacy. Traditionally, Buddhist monks were celibate for at least three reasons. The first is that the monks in the time of the Buddha were urged to practice meditation for most of the day. They had to be in contact with the people in the village in order to teach them the Dharma, and in order to ask for some food for the day. If a monk had to support a family, he would not be able to perform his duties as a monk.

The second reason is that sexual energy had to be preserved for meditation. In the religious and medical traditions of Asia, the human person was said to have three sources of energy: sexual, breath, and spirit. Sexual energy is what you spend during sexual intercourse. Breath energy is the kind of energy you spend when you talk too much and breathe too little. Spirit energy is energy that you spend when you worry too much, and do not sleep well. If you spend these three sources of energy, your body is not strong enough for the realization of the Way and a deep penetration into reality. Buddhist monks observed celibacy, not because of moral admonition, but for conservation of energy. Someone on a long fast knows how important it is to preserve these three sources of energy.

The third reason Buddhist monks observed celibacy is the question of suffering. At that time, and even today, if we go to India we see many children without food, so many children sick without medicine, and one woman can give birth to ten, twelve children, without being able to feed two or three properly. "Life is suffering" is the first truth in Buddhism. To bring a child into the world is a great responsibility. If you are wealthy, maybe you can do it with no problem. But if you are poor, this is a real concern. To be reborn means first to be reborn in your children. Your children are a continuation of yourself. You are reborn in them. You continue the cycle of suffering. Aware that having more children in his society would be to make them suffer, the Buddha urged the monks not to have children. I think that during the past 2,500 years, Buddhist monks in many countries have helped curb the birth rate. That is quite important.

The fourteenth precept urges us to respect our own body, to maintain our energy for the realization of the Way. Not only meditation, but any kind of efforts that are required to change the world require energy. We should take good care of ourselves.

In my opinion, the liberation of sexual behavior in the West has caused a number of good results, but has also caused some problems. The liberation of women, because of modern birth control methods, has been something very real. In the past, young girls, in Asia as well as Europe, had enormous problems and some even committed suicide when they became pregnant. Since the discovery of birth control, these kinds of tragedies have lessened considerably. But the liberation of sexual behavior has also caused much stress, much trouble. I think the fact that many people suffer from depression is partly because of that. Please meditate on the problem. It is a very important problem for Western society.

If you wish to have children, please do something for the world you bring them into. That will make you someone who works for peace, in one way or another.

"The Christian Challenge: Love Your Enemies"

❦

Naim Stifan Ateek

Canon Naim Ateek is a Palestinian Anglican cleric whose family lost its home and lands when Israel was established in 1948. Here he seeks to find a way to peace and coexistence with Israel, a way in which Christian principles of love can triumph over bitterness and hate. If there is ever to be peace in that tortured region, it will only come with the help of voices such as Ateek's on both sides.

❦

My final plea, however, is directed to my own people, the Palestinians. Let me introduce it with a story.

It happened after ten o'clock one cold night in February 1988, in one of the suburbs of East Jerusalem. Their two little girls were already asleep, and my friend Issa and his wife were watching TV in their pajamas, when they heard a loud banging on their front door. The soldiers did not wait for the door to be opened; they had started breaking the glass windows on the front porch when Issa, frightened, opened the door. The troops shoved him aside and dashed into the house, searching it. The little girls awoke and clung to their parents. The soldiers broke a few things in their wild search, but they did not find whatever they were looking for. Worst of all, they were using very bad language. They ordered my friend to go with them, not even allowing him to change into his street clothes. So Issa went with them, in his pajamas. His wife managed to quickly give him his identity card. Then, shocked and scared, she called her relatives, who hurried over to stay with her and the children.

Issa was taken to a dark open area where dozens of other people, young and old, were detained. They, too, had been grabbed from their homes during the cold winter night. They were ordered to sit there and wait. Their identity cards were taken from them. Every few minutes one of the soldiers would come, scream at them, threaten them, curse at them, and then leave. This scene was repeated often until two o'clock in the morning, when one soldier came, flung all the ID cards into the dark night air, and told the gathered men to each look for his card and walk home. In the early hours of the morning, my friend reached his house.

A few days later, Issa came to my office and told me his story. I have known him for a number of years, and he has always struck me as a peaceful and gentle man, a hard worker who tries to make a good living for his young family. He has never been involved in politics and has never belonged to a political party. He loves his country and his people. He is honest and truthful. I listened very carefully to him while he told me his story. I remember him saying at the end, "I never hated the Jews; even after they occupied the West Bank, I never felt much hate for them. But now it is different. Hate is building up in me. I hate them. I know it is wrong to hate, but they are making me hate them."

This young man is not anti-Semitic; he is, after all, a Semite himself. His ancestors have lived in the Jerusalem area for hundreds of years. He was expressing a phenomenon of hate that, since the *Intifada*, is slowly spreading to engulf most of the Palestinian community on the West Bank and in Gaza.

Neither in 1948 nor in 1967 has so much hatred and resentment been generated as since the beginning of the *Intifada*. The Israeli army feels helpless in the face of rioting Palestinians and it has turned brutal. Every change in the military policy takes a turn for the worse—beatings, tear gassing, crushing of bones, live ammunition . . . the iron-fist policies generate more and more hatred. And the Palestinians stand unshaken in their determination to resist the occupation. People who are oppressed and have no freedom easily learn to hate.

In *The Yellow Wind,* David Grossman tells the story of a thirty-year-old man who lives in the Balata refugee camp near Nablus on the West Bank. The man spent ten years of his life in jail for belonging to one of the PLO organizations. This man's Palestinian identity was awakened and strengthened while in jail. "Before I went to jail, I didn't even know I was a Palestinian. There they taught me who I am. Now I have opinions. Don't believe the ones who tell you that the Palestinians don't really hate you. Understand: the average Palestinian is not the fascist and hating type, but you and the life under your occupation push him into hatred."[1]

In the face of such mounting hatred, what should be the attitude of the Palestinian Christian? Some Christians would deny the possibility of love and forgiveness in such circumstances. They would say that the hatred that is being bred is too much for the human spirit to endure and deal with constructively. So they succumb to hatred. And hatred, when used as a weapon, destroys its users as well as their victims.

Others would pronounce pious platitudes about love and forgiveness. Their words are unreal and superficial. They have not suffered themselves, and so they can detach themselves from the suffering of others and live in their own spiritual realm while repeating those sweet words from the New Testament.

I believe that neither of these two groups is being faithful to the true Christian calling. Christians are conscious of their full and real life in the world. They do not live a shadowy existence, pretending that they are not affected by what is going on around them. Life is real. In fact, for Christians, life should be as real as it can be. Jesus said, "I came that they may have life, and have it abundantly."[2] Christians are supposed to have a heightened level of consciousness, sensitive to all that is going on around them in the world. They recognize that this is God's world and that they are called to be faithful stewards of it. Furthermore, they are their brothers' and sisters' keepers. To be sensitive is to care, to be concerned, and to become involved in the real world of people. On the one hand, Christians know the depth and extent of sin and evil in the world. Therefore, nothing comes as a shock or a surprise to them when people are living without God; when people allow their selfish desires to control them; when, guided by greed, people manipulate and subjugate others. On the other hand, Christians should try not to dilute or compromise the Christian way of life, which is in essence the truly human life—the human values of the good life as they have come to be understood through Christ. They do not succumb to generalities. The ideal remains lifted up and not watered down. They will constantly aspire to that ideal and try to live up to it. It should not create frustration, because they should be realistic in their life with God. Indeed, they are conscious of their weak and frail humanity, but very much aware of the power of God at work in them. Therefore, in the midst of so much hate and bitterness, they cannot forget the words of Jesus: "You have heard that it was said, 'You shall love your neighbor and hate your enemy.' But I say to you, Love your enemies and pray for those who persecute you, so that you may be sons of your Father who is in heaven. . . ."[3]

Christians know how difficult these words are. But they are fully cognizant that the words of Jesus reflect the genuinely human, and they should remain for them the standard of the truly authentic life.

Therefore, the challenge to the Palestinian Christians, and indeed of all Christians faced with situations of bitterness and hate, is to keep up the struggle and never to succumb to despair and hate. I am speaking out of my own experience with Israel since 1948. I have learned much from my father, who had to come to terms with the hate and resentment in his life after he lost everything to the Israelis in Beisan. His struggle was real but he did not succumb to hate. For when people hate, its power engulfs them and they are totally consumed by their hatred. So I consider the challenge to my fellow Palestinians to be threefold:

Keep struggling against hate and resentment. Always confess that the struggle goes on and the battle is not over. At times you will have the upper hand, at times you will feel beaten down. Although it is extremely difficult, never let hatred completely overtake you. By the power of God the struggle will go on until the day comes when you begin to count more victories than defeats.

Never stop trying to live the commandment of love and forgiveness. Do not dilute the strength of Jesus' message: do not shun it, do not dismiss it as unreal and impractical. Do not cut it to your size, trying to make it more applicable to real life in the world. Do not change it so that it will suit you. Keep it as it is; aspire to it, desire it, and work with God for its achievement.

Remember that so often it is those who have suffered most at the hands of others who are capable of offering forgiveness and love.

NOTES

1. David Grossman, *The Yellow Wind* (New York: Picador, 2002), 11.
2. John 10:10.
3. Matt. 5:43–45a.

from *The Journey toward Reconciliation*

❧

John Paul Lederach

John Paul Lederach is one of several hundred professional peacemakers trained and supported by the Mennonite Church. He has worked in Africa, Central America, and the Middle East. He is Professor of International Peacebuilding at Notre Dame University and Distinguished Scholar at Eastern Mennonite University. In this poignant selection he explores his own struggles with peacefulness and his own tendency to dehumanize the enemy.

❧

ENCOUNTERING AN EPIPHANY

Early in 1987, I was traveling in Honduras near the border with Nicaragua. The Contra war was still raging. Along this border, particularly in the outskirts of the remote village of Danli, Honduran Mennonite brothers and sisters had been displaced from their homes. This happened because Nicaraguan resistance troops occupied the region as their military base. They were opposing the Sandinista government. Some Hondurans hailed the troops as freedom fighters, and others counted them as counterrevolutionaries.

At that time, the Honduran government claimed there were no Nicaraguan fighters based in Honduras. It was a hidden war of great cost. I had traveled with Carmen and Luke Schrock-Hurst, who were working with the displaced families. These people had the pain of lost time, homes, and family members etched in their faces. They were victims in a war for freedom that was not theirs.

After that trip, I stood at the large plateglass window and was looking out over the airport tarmac at Tegucigalpa, the capital of Honduras. There I first saw the colonel. I had checked in two hours early and was alone in the departure room, absorbed in my thoughts about the day's travels.

The words of the young Honduran mother ran through my mind. "Nonexistent soldiers" occupied her family's house. "How do you take it?" I had asked, expecting some bitterness. Her answer surprised me: "I feel pain for them. They are so young. They have so little hope. They know only death."

I was trying to sort through her experience, which I could barely understand, when the sirens in the airport went off. There was instant action. Soldiers hustled across the runway to a

459

fleet of helicopters, which slowly rose and filed off toward the mountains bordering Nicaragua. From my spot at the window, I could see it all. *Is this a drill or the real thing?* I wondered.

The helicopters would quickly arrive at the areas I had just traveled, probably to support Contra fighters. A little less than an hour later, the helicopters started flying back. One by one they came over the crest of the hill, flying low, floating a few feet above the ground. One of the war birds peeled off and came directly toward the terminal. The wind from its rotor slammed the door shut a few feet from where I stood. The noise was deafening.

The chopper settled down a few yards from the window, so close that I could see the pilot. His face was taut, his eyes hidden behind dark Ray-Bans. The side door of the helicopter flew open, and out jumped a passenger. He wore civilian clothes and carried a small duffel bag.

The passenger ran to the terminal door, joked a bit with the customs officials, and then jumped across the customs table. Just then I sat down, and he sat beside me. He was American. He did not pay taxes or show a passport or ticket.

The Honduran pilot took the helicopter to join the fleet across the runway. About an hour later, his American passenger left on a flight to San Salvador.

My Tan-Sahsa flight was late arriving from New Orleans. I waited and watched as people slowly filled up the seats around me. A truck pulled up past the window, and a Honduran military official stepped out. He was dressed in a green fatigue jumpsuit, black boots, and dark glasses. The official walked right past the window, and I recognized him as the pilot of the helicopter I had seen earlier. He was a big man, well muscled, almost exploding out of his suit.

A perfect Rambo! I thought. *Who is this man? Does he really believe in what he is doing? What did he just do on the border, this very afternoon? Whose lives did he take?* My mind was racing with the images I had just seen in Danli.

As he entered, customs officials smiled and called him "*mi Coronel.*" He spoke briefly with them, then went back out the door. There he stood, waiting for the flight to arrive from the United States, the same one that I would take to Costa Rica.

Within minutes that plane pulled up to the terminal. As we waited to board, the arriving passengers filed past the window on their way to the immigration and customs room. The colonel was waiting for someone on that flight.

This should be interesting, I thought. *Who are you picking up this time, mi Coronel? What mercenary for freedom will you escort this time?* A righteous disdain floated in my pacifist mind as I positioned myself to get a better look at the coming encounter. *What secrets are held in your mind? Who are your contacts? Is this not the very evil of the war itself? American and Honduran militaries ganging up against oppressed Nicaraguans!*

The colonel moved toward the plane to meet his friend and disappeared from my sight. A few minutes later, he reappeared. His arm was around a ten-year-old girl. Metal braces supported her thin legs. She was smiling and waving and trying to walk all at once.

The muscular body of the colonel seemed engulfed by her enthusiasm. He tried to find a way to help her. First he tried to take her hand and then awkwardly put his arm behind her to support her back.

They slowly made their way past my window. His Ray-Ban glasses were off. For a moment he looked through the window at me, and our eyes met. What I saw startled me. *The colonel is a father like me!* It was a metaphorical moment of stunning insight.

To this day, I carry that image of the colonel with me. I still try to understand and learn from what happened in those moments. I never spoke with the colonel. I never shook his hand. I do not know who he was or what involvement he had in the war. But I do know that in the space of a short time, I had created the image of an enemy.

CREATING ENEMIES

In thinking about my own process, I have concluded that enemies are created. Lay aside all the other factors, from social conditioning to real physical threat. In the end, an enemy is rooted and constructed in our hearts and minds and takes on social significance as others share in the construction. From my own experience, I have learned that critical steps need to be taken to construct an enemy. Each step is in the story of the colonel.

First, to construct an image of the enemy, I must *separate* myself from another. In my mind and rooted in my heart, I begin to see in another person, not the sameness we share, but the differences between us that I identify as negative. I attach to those differences a negative judgment, a projection that this person is a threat to me and is wrong.

Inside, hidden, unexplored, and unrecognized, is a question about myself, who I am, and what I believe. In a subtle but critical way, the enemy is connected to my own self-view and identity. Who I am is defined by who I am not. The origin of enmity lies in a self-definition built on a negative projection about another. I imagine that the other person is completely bad and that I am completely good.

A *second* phenomenon goes hand in hand with separation. I see myself as *superior*. Superiority is the qualitative opposite of what we see in the example of Jesus emptying himself (Phil. 2:7). Jesus, though in the form of God, did not regard his position as superior. Instead, he humbled himself to take the form of a common person, even a slave. In other words, he sought to bring compassion by being like others. He recognized and embraced his sameness. He chose to take his place as a servant.

When I feel superior, I believe I am not only different from but better than the other person. It is the incarnation story in reverse. Though I am in the form of a common person, the same as others, I raise myself above them and take the position of God. To construct an enemy, we must both lose sight of our sameness and create a sense that we are superior.

Third, separation and superiority lead to *dehumanizing* the other person(s). I dehumanize when I deprive people of the qualities that make them humans. I rob them of being created in the image of God. I lose the sight of God in their faces. I no longer see "that of God" in them (see chapter 8). To construct an enemy, I must both dehumanize the other and deface the image of God in that person.

What I did in a matter of minutes with the colonel carried these elements and dynamics. I separated myself from him. I saw myself as morally superior. I felt a certain righteousness about myself. I saw myself as good. I saw him as evil. My own identity as a pacifist and peacemaker became more impermeable to the degree that I cast him as my opposite, a militarist and warmaker. He was less than I was. Morally, I stood above him.

What shook my very foundation was the unexpected reentry of human sameness and God. I saw myself in the colonel. I was shaken by this surprise from God: the colonel and I were so much alike.

In the second chapter, I said that a theology of the enemy must face the dilemma of embracing the righteous cry for justice and incarnating the sacrificial love of God.

Here is another paradox of reconciliation. We must learn how to develop a positive identity of self and group that is not based on criticizing or feeling superior to another person or group.

In Christian circles we claim to hate the sin but love the sinner (cf. Jude 23). I believe this is much more complex than it appears on the surface. It is filled with intricate trappings of self-deception and superiority. I have found it more honest within myself to say, "Be careful about what you hate. You may find that like a blindfold it removes your ability to see. Look first for what you see of yourself in others. Love the sinners, and see yourself in them. There you will find God."

My encounter with the colonel was an internal holy ground, a place I have marked on my journey toward reconciliation. That day outside the Tegucigalpa airport, God was in the burning bush. The encounter still has the power to shake me. It represents one of the things I find most scary about my work.

I have lived and talked with people who have been both victims of violence and creators of violence. I have shaken the hands of convicted terrorists and people who have tortured others. I have sat with warlords who seem merciless in their pursuit of power. I have listened to freedom fighters who cry out against injustice and pick up weapons to defend their cause. What scares me the most is not how different I am, but rather how I can see and feel a bit of myself in each of them.

Every time I come away with the reminder of the colonel in my mind and with the search to find God present in everyone. It may seem easy to understand, but I find it hard to practice. Nonetheless, this is my belief: I cannot create an enemy when I look for and find that of God in another.

This is a short chapter on a complex subject. However, writing about my personal journey toward reconciliation would be incomplete without this story. In the search to build peace, I set out to bring enemies together and to practice peace and reconciliation. The encounter with the colonel reminds me of a hard lesson. I am capable of quickly and easily creating enemies.

"Founding Statement"

☙

Student Nonviolent Coordinating Committee

The Student Nonviolent Coordinating Committee emerged from the Nashville sit-ins against segregation in 1960. While Martin Luther King and the Southern Christian Leadership Congress were mired in organizational difficulties, SNCC took the lead in pushing the civil rights movement toward direct, nonviolent confrontations with segregation. Leaders of SNCC included John Lewis, James Lawson, Diane Nash, and Robert Moses.

☙

We affirm the philosophical or religious ideal of nonviolence as the foundation of our purpose, the presupposition of our belief, and the manner of our action.

Nonviolence, as it grows from the Judeo-Christian tradition, seeks a social order of justice permeated by love. Integration of human endeavor represents the crucial first step toward such a society.

Through nonviolence, courage displaces fear. Love transcends hate. Acceptance dissipates prejudice; hope ends despair. Faith reconciles doubt. Peace dominates war. Mutual regards cancel enmity. Justice for all overthrows injustice. The redemptive community supersedes immoral social systems.

By appealing to conscience and standing on the moral nature of human existence, nonviolence nurtures the atmosphere in which reconciliation and justice become actual possibilities.

Although each local group in this movement must diligently work out the clear meaning of this statement of purpose, each act or phase of our corporate effort must reflect a genuine spirit of love and goodwill.

from "Speak Truth to Power"

❧

American Friends Service Committee

The American Friends Service Committee (AFSC) is a Quaker organization that includes people of various faiths who are committed to social justice, peace, and humanitarian service. This excerpt from a 1955 document is, regrettably, as appropriate to contemporary conflict as to the Cold War, the context for which it was written. One need only replace "communism" with "terrorism" (and alter the dated sexist usage) for it to be as contemporary as tomorrow's headlines.

❧

Most Americans accept without question the assumption that winning the peace depends upon a simultaneous reliance upon military strength and long-range programs of a positive and constructive character. They accept also that totalitarian communism is the greatest evil that now threatens men and that this evil can be met only by violence, or at least by the threat of violence. We believe these assumptions cannot be sustained, and therefore that the policies based on them are built upon sand. We have here attempted to suggest another and less widely considered alternative built on a different assumption, namely, that military power in today's world is incompatible with freedom, incapable of providing security, and ineffective in dealing with evil.

Our title, Speak Truth to Power, taken from a charge given to eighteenth-century Friends, suggests the effort that is made to speak from the deepest insight of the Quaker faith. We speak to power in three senses:

To those who hold high places in our national life and bear the terrible responsibility of
    making decisions for war or peace.
To the American people who are the final reservoir of power in this country.
To the idea of Power itself, and its impact on twentieth-century life.

Our truth is an ancient one; that love endures and overcomes; that hatred destroys; that what is obtained by love is retained, but what is obtained by hatred proves a burden. This truth, fundamental to the position which rejects reliance on the method of war, is ultimately a religious perception, a belief that stands outside of history.

FACING EVIL

What is this nonviolent method that we suggest offers new hope? Its simplest and most obvious statement is found in the religious literature of many faiths, most familiarly to Christians in the

Sermon on the Mount. At its heart, it is the effort to maintain unity among men. It seeks to knit the break in the sense of community whose fracture is both a cause and a result of human conflict. It relies upon love rather than hate, and though it involves a willingness to accept rather than inflict suffering, it is neither passive nor cowardly. It offers a way of meeting evil without relying on the ability to cause pain to the human being through whom evil is expressed. It seeks to change the attitude of the opponent rather than to force his submission through violence. It is in short, the practical effort to overcome evil with good.

THE INSIGHTS OF NONVIOLENCE

Today an increasing amount of research is focused on the problem of individual and group conflict, and nonviolent insights are being established as valid for the successful treatment of specific situations. What are these insights?

a. The oneness of man. An essential component of the nonviolent philosophy, and indeed of most religious traditions, is the belief that in the sight of God, all men are one. Without this sense of oneness, real community is not possible.

b. The sacredness of human personality. This is the religious perception from which springs the belief in the innate worth and dignity of every human being. It sustains also the insistence on loving treatment of all men that is a second element of the nonviolent philosophy.

c. The creative nature of love. If belief in man's divine quality has been the foundation of much religious witness, faith in the positive power of love has been its dynamic. Indeed, the whole public case of the nonviolent method of resolving conflict rests ultimately on demonstrating the power of love. Unless love proves itself by overcoming fear and vanquishing evil, it will be rejected, for men are bound to resist evil.

d. The necessity for self-examination. Still another insight inherent in every religious tradition and integral to the nonviolent method is the importance of honest and candid self-examination whenever conflict arises. Unless each party to a dispute is prepared to search himself first to discover his own measure of responsibility, the chance of peaceful resolution will be diminished.

REASON AND RIGHT

The American Friends Service Committee is deeply rooted in the faith that there is that of God in every man which gives him inalienable worth and dignity. He may not therefore be exploited or expended by any man for any purpose. We have been and we continue to be opposed to all wars, but we are not among those who deny the reality of evil, or assume that peace is merely the absence of war.

We have tried to face the hard facts; to put the case for nonviolence in terms of common sense. Yet, we are aware that the man who chooses in these terms alone cannot sustain himself against the mass pressures of an age of violence. If ever truth reaches power, if ever it speaks to the individual citizen, it will not be the argument that convinces. Rather it will be his own inner sense of integrity that impels him to say, "Here I stand. Regardless of relevance or consequence, I can do no other."

This is not "reasonable": the politics of eternity is not ruled by reason alone, but by reason ennobled by right. Reason alone may dictate destroying an enemy who would destroy liberty, but conscience balks. We do not end violence by compounding violence, nor conquer evil by destroying the evildoer. Evil cannot overcome evil, and the end does not justify the means. Rather, we are convinced that evil means corrupt good ends; and we know with a terrible certainty demonstrated by two world wars in our time, that when we undertake to overcome evil with evil, we ourselves tend to become the evil that we seek to overcome.

WE MUST TURN ABOUT

Community is built on trust and confidence, which some say is not possible now because the communist cannot be trusted. The politics of eternity do not require that we trust him. They require us to love him and to trust God. We call for no calculated risk on behalf of national interest or preservation; rather for an uncalculated risk in living by the claims of the Kingdom, on behalf of the whole family of man conceived as a divine-human society.

The politics of eternity work not by might but by spirit; a Spirit whose redemptive power is released among men through suffering endured on behalf of the evildoers, and in obedience to the divine command to love all men. Such love is worlds apart from the expedient of loving those who love us, of doing good to those who have done good to us. It is the essence of such love that it does not require an advance guarantee that it will succeed, will prove easy or cheap, or that it will be met with swift answering love.

To act on such a faith, the politics of eternity demand of us, first, repentance. As individuals and as a nation we must literally turn about. We must turn from our self-righteousness and arrogance, and confess that we do that which is evil in the sight of the Lord. We must turn from the substitution of material for spiritual values; we must turn not only from our use of mass violence but from what is worse, our readiness to use this violence whenever it suits our purpose, regardless of the pain it inflicts on others. We must turn about.

The race is on; it may be almost run. The weak are impotent, the strong dictate. Claims of national interest or group loyalty are made to justify the crushing of human personality. There is an arrogance that identifies self-interest with virtue, and deafens men to the needs and voices of others outside their own group or nation. Men strive for security in a world where security cannot exist. The more we cling to security the less secure we feel; the more we cling to armaments and economic privilege the more frightened we become. How shall man be released from his besetting fears, and from his prevailing sense of futility?

To risk all may be to gain all. We do not fear death, but we want to live and we want our children to live and fulfill their lives. There can hardly be a greater cause than the release of man from the terror and hate that now enslave him. Each man has the source of freedom within himself. He can say "No" to the war machine and to immoral claims of power wherever they exist and whatever the consequences may be. We call on all men to say "Yes" to courageous nonviolence, which alone can overcome injustice, persecution, and tyranny.

The early Friends realized only too clearly that the Kingdom of God had not come, but they had an inward sense that it would never come until somebody believed in its principles enough to try them in actual operation. They resolved to go forward then, and make the experimental trial, and take the consequences. So we believe and so we advise.

"Resisting the Forces of Death" and "'No' to the Vietnam War"

 ❧

Henri Nouen

Henri Nouen was one of the most beloved Catholic writers of the twentieth century. He was ordained a priest in 1957, served the L'Arche community for people with mental disabilities, and taught at several different universities. In the first of these essays, he explores the connections between our political resistance to war and our personal commitment to lives of peace. In the second, a speech given at Yale in 1972, he offers eloquent spiritual testimony for resistance to the Vietnam War.

❧

RESISTING THE FORCES OF DEATH

When the Second World War came to an end, I was only thirteen years old. Although my parents had skillfully protected me and my brother from the horror of the Nazis in my native Holland, they couldn't prevent me from seeing how our Jewish neighbors were led away, and from hearing about concentration camps to which they were deported and from which they never returned. Only in the years after the war did I become aware of the demonic dimensions of the Jewish persecution and learn the word *holocaust*. And now, forty years later, I often ask myself: "Why was there not a massive popular uprising? Why weren't there marches of thousands of people protesting the genocide that was taking place? Why did the millions of religious people not invade the camps and tear down the gas chambers and ovens that were being built to annihilate the Jewish people? Why did those who pray, sing hymns, and go to church not resist the powers of evil so visible in their own land?"

It is important to find answers for these questions. But today I am no longer a thirteen-year-old boy who does not fully understand what is going on. Today I am an adult living only a few miles from the place where the Trident submarine is being built, a weapon able to destroy in one second more people than were gassed in Nazi Germany during the long years of the Hitler regime. Today I am a well-informed person fully aware of the genocide in Guatemala and the murderous terror in El Salvador. Today I am a well-educated teacher who is able to show clearly and convincingly that the costly arms race between the super powers means starvation for millions of people all over the globe. Today I am a Christian who has heard the words of

467

Christ many times and knows that the God of Israel and Jesus Christ is the God of the living in whom there is no shadow of death.

Today I am asking myself the question: "Does my prayer, my communion with the God of life become visible in acts of resistance against the power of death surrounding me? Or will those who are thirteen years old today raise the same question about me forty years from now that I am raising about the adult Christians of my youth?" I have to realize that my silence or apathy may make it impossible for anyone to raise any questions forty years from today. Because what is being prepared is not a holocaust to extinguish a whole people, but a holocaust that puts an end to humanity itself—that will make not only giving answers but also raising questions a total impossibility.

These thoughts are constantly on my mind. These concerns keep me wondering how to be a peacemaker today and every day of my life. I will never be able to say: "I didn't know what was going on." I do know with frightening accuracy what will happen when nothing is done. Being a peacemaker today requires that my prayer become visible in concrete actions.

As I travel through life from day to day, I meet so many fellow travelers who see what I see, hear what I hear, and read what I read, and who are torn in their innermost selves by the same concerns that have come to me during the last decades. They, as I, are tempted to say: "We can't do much else but pray because we have our jobs, our families, our social obligations, and there is just no time left to work for peace. You can only do so much, and you have to accept your limitations." But in the face of nuclear weapons that threaten the very existence of jobs, family, and social obligations, they, as well as I, know that these excuses are groundless. Peacemaking is not an option any longer. It is a holy obligation for all people whatever their professional or family situation. Peacemaking is a way of living that involves our whole being all the time.

The word that I want to make central in these reflections on the daily life of the peacemaker is the word "resistance." As peacemakers we must resist resolutely all the powers of war and destruction and proclaim that peace is the divine gift offered to all who affirm life. Resistance means saying "No" to all the forces of death wherever they may be and, as a corollary, saying a clear "Yes" to all of life in whatever form we encounter it.

To work for peace is to work for life. But, more than ever before in history, we are surrounded by the powers of death. The rapidly escalating arms race has created a death-mood that pervades our thoughts and feelings in ways that we are only vaguely aware of. We try to live and work as if all is normal, but we hardly succeed in keeping the voice of death away from us. It is the voice that says: "Why work when all you create may soon be destroyed? Why study when you doubt that you ever will be able to use your gifts? Why bring forth children when you cannot promise them a future? Why write, make music, paint, dance, and celebrate when existence itself is in doubt?"

We know that in the case of a full-scale Russian nuclear attack 140 million Americans will probably die within days, and a U.S. retaliatory attack would take the lives of at least 100 million Russians. The fact that we can even think about such an event already does great harm to our minds and hearts. That human beings are considering saving their lives by killing millions of their fellow human beings is so preposterous that the words "saving life" have lost their meaning.

One of the most tragic facts of our century is that the "No" against the nuclear arms race has been spoken so seldom, so softly, and by so few. As I try to explain to myself my own lack of resistance against these dark forces of evil, it strikes me that I have always thought of the United States as the land of refuge for those who are persecuted—as the land of freedom, endless opportunity, democracy, and the land that came to the help of the victims of Nazism. Yes, as the land that liberated my own country. These perceptions are so strong that even after the sinister assassinations of John F. Kennedy, Robert Kennedy, and Martin Luther King Jr., the misery of

Vietnam, and the scandal of Watergate, I have kept thinking of the United States as a country in which such events are painful exceptions. While such events are signs of an increasing betrayal of the ideals this country proclaims, I still have a very hard time believing that anything similar to what happened during the Hitler years in Germany can possibly take place here. After all, the United States won a crusade against Nazi tyranny. How could such a tyranny move to this side of the ocean?

Yet many of my friends who have gone to prison for saying "No" to the arms race that causes millions of people to spend their lives in the service of destructive weapons and other millions to suffer starvation are slowly opening my eyes to another America that I do not really want to see, but that can no longer be ignored. It is the America that prepared itself for "first-strike capability," the ability not simply to prevent a nuclear attack by the threat of counterattack, but the ability to strike first and thus kill before being killed.

These friends have reminded me that the plans to fight and win a nuclear war are so completely contrary to Jesus' commandment of love and his own disarmed death on the cross that not saying "No" is a sign of faithlessness. They have made me see that those who prepare for the death of millions of people and are willing to start a nuclear war are doing nothing illegal, while those whose conscience calls them symbolically to hammer down these present-day Auschwitzes and Dachaus are put in prison as criminals.

It is very hard for me to convert my thoughts and feelings to such a degree that I am willing to defend those who "break the law" in order to proclaim the higher law—a commandment of love to which I have dedicated my life. But if I truly believe in Jesus Christ as the man of peace who did not choose to appeal to his Father "who would promptly send more than twelve legions of angels to his defense" (Mt. 26:53–54), but who chose to die on a cross in total disarmament, how can I not be a man of peace? How can I allow the power of death to destroy the physical and moral life of millions, now as well as in the future, while remaining a passive and thus guilty bystander? Nonresistance makes us accomplices of a nuclear holocaust.

The nuclear threat has created a situation that humanity has never faced before. History is filled with violence, cruelties, and atrocities committed by people against people. Cities, countries, and whole civilizations have been erased from this planet and millions of people have become the victims of hatred and revenge. But never before has it been possible for humanity to commit collective suicide, to destroy the whole planet and put an end to all of history. This awesome capability was not even within our reach during the Second World War. The bombing of Hiroshima and Nagasaki at the end of the war gave us an inkling of what a next war might look like. But a future world war cannot be compared with any previous war. It will be a war that not only ends all war but also all peace.

It is this totally original situation that makes a "No" to war a universal necessity. It can no longer be seen as a necessity only for certain people at certain times. Because the being or not-being of humanity itself is at stake, the nuclear threat overarches all other threats as cause for resistance. The small groups of "disobedient" people who jump the fences around nuclear weapons facilities, climb onboard nuclear submarines, or put their bodies in front of nuclear transports are trying to wake us up to a reality we continue to ignore or deny. Their small numbers should not mislead us.

Throughout history the truth has seldom been spoken by majorities. Statistics are not the way truth becomes known. The prophets of Israel, Jesus and his few disciples, and the small bands of holy men and women throughout history are there to make us wonder if "these crazy peaceniks" might after all not be as important for our conversion today as St. Francis and his followers were seven centuries ago. Their loud, clear, and often dramatic "No" has to make us wonder what kind of "No" we are called to speak.

When I try to come to terms with the effect of the nuclear threat on me, I realize that it not only brings me face to face with a completely new—and original—situation, but also makes me see in a new way the old and all-pervasive fascination with death that is an integral part of our daily lives. The confrontation with universal death has forced me to wonder about the more subtle ways in which death has us in its grip.

The Trident submarine, whose missiles can destroy many cities and countless people in one attack, is indeed the most insidious death machine human beings have ever created. But if we start saying "No" to this monster of destruction made by human hands, don't we also have to say "No" to the much less spectacular ways in which we play our death games? We are not simply victims of the power of death, for we are making Trident submarines and other nuclear weapons systems. The powers of death are far more intimate and pervasive than we are willing to confess.

Our ability to entertain even the possibility of a nuclear war is part of a much wider and deeper domination by death. We will never become true peacemakers until we are willing to unmask these death forces wherever and whenever they operate. An honest "No" against the nuclear arms race requires a "No" to the death hidden in the smallest corners of our minds and hearts. Peace in the world and peace of heart can never be separated. We need not answer the question: "Which is more important, peace in your heart or peace in the world?" Nor should we be distracted by arguments as to whether peace starts within or without. Inner and outer peace must never be separated. Peace work is a spectrum stretching from the hidden corners of our innermost selves to the most complex international deliberations.

Not long ago I visited an exclusive American preparatory school. Most of the boys and girls came from well-to-do families, most were well educated, and all were very bright. They were friendly, well-mannered, and ambitious; it was not hard for me to imagine many of them eventually holding important positions, driving big cars, and living in large homes.

One evening I joined these students in watching a movie in the school's auditorium. It was *The Blues Brothers*. I could not believe what I was seeing and hearing. The screen was filled with the wild destruction of supermarkets, houses, and cars, while the auditorium was filled with excited shouts coming from the mouths of these well-mannered, bright young people. While they were watching the total devastation of all the symbols of their own prosperous lives, they yelled and screamed as if their team had won a championship. As cars were being smashed, houses put on fire, and highrises pulled down, my excited neighbor told me that this was one of the most expensive "funny" movies ever made. Millions of dollars had been spent to film a few hours of what I considered to be death. No human beings were killed. It was supposed to bring a good laugh. But nothing human beings had made was left untouched by the destructive activities of *The Blues Brothers*.

What does it mean that ambitious young Americans are being entertained by millions of dollars worth of destruction in a world in which many people die from fear, lack of food, and ever-increasing violence? Are these the future leaders of a generation whose primary task is to prevent a nuclear war and stop the arms race?

I report this seemingly innocent event to point to the fact that much contemporary entertainment is designed to feed our fascination with violence and death. Long hours of our lives are spent filling our minds with images not only of disintegrating skyscrapers and cars, but also of shootings, torture scenes, and other manifestations of human violence. Once I met a Vietnam veteran on an airplane. He told me that as a youngster he had seen so many people being killed on TV that once he got to Vietnam it had been hard for him to believe that those whom *he* killed would not stand up again and act in the next program. Death had become an unreal act. Vietnam woke him up to the truth that death is real and final and very ugly.

When I am honest with myself I have to confess that I, too, am often seduced by the titillating power of death. I bite my nails in fascinated excitement when I see trapeze artists making somersaults without a safety net beneath them. I look with open eyes and mouth at stunt pilots, motorcyclists, and race car drivers who put their lives at risk in their desire to break a record or perform a dazzling feat. In this respect, I am little different from the Romans who were entertained by the death games of the gladiators, or from the crowds who in the past and even the present are attracted to places of public execution.

Any suggestion that these real or imagined death games are healthy ways to deal with our "death-instincts" or "aggressive fantasies" needs to be discarded as unfounded, unproved, or simply irresponsible. Acting out death wishes either in fact or in the imagination can never bring us any closer to peace, whether it is peace of heart or peace in our life together.

Our preoccupation with death, however, goes far beyond real or imagined involvement in physical violence. We find ourselves engaged over and over again in much less spectacular but no less destructive death games. During my visit to Nicaragua and my subsequent lectures and conversations in the United States about the Nicaraguan people, I became increasingly aware of how quick judgments and stereotypes can transform people and nations into distorted caricatures, thus offering a welcome excuse for destruction and war. By talking one-dimensionally about Nicaragua as a land of Marxist-Leninist ideology, totalitarianism, and atheism we create in our minds a monster that urgently needs to be attacked and destroyed. Whenever I spoke about the people of Nicaragua, their deep Christian faith, their struggles for some economic independence, their desire for better health care and education, and their hope that they might be left alone to determine their own future, I found myself confronted with deadening stereotypes. People would say: "But shouldn't we be aware that Russia is trying to get a foothold there and that we are increasingly being threatened by Communism?" Such remarks made me see that long before we start a war, kill people, or destroy nations, we have already killed our enemies mentally, by making them into abstractions with which no real, intimate human relationship is possible. When men, women, and children who eat, drink, sleep, play, work, and love each other as we do have been perverted into an abstract Communist evil that we are called—by God—to destroy, then war has become inevitable.

The Nazis were able to make the concrete human beings we call Jews into abstractions. They made them into "the Jewish problem." And for abstract problems there are abstract solutions. The solution to the Jewish problem was the gas chamber. And on the way to the gas chamber, there were many stages of dehumanizing abstraction: isolation from non-Jews, labeling with yellow stars, and deportation to faraway concentration camps. Thus the Jew became less and less one-of-us and more and more the stranger, the xxx, and finally, simply, "the problem."

As I reflect on the horrors of the Second World War, I realize how much violence was mental before it was physical. Today, again, it seems that a similar process is taking place. We have "made up our mind" about the Nicaraguans, the Cubans, the Russians, and these abstract creations of the mind are the first products of the powers of death.

Saying "No" to death therefore starts much earlier than saying "No" to physical violence, whether in war or entertainment. It requires a deep commitment to the words of Jesus: "Do not judge" (Mt. 7:1). It requires a "No" to all the violence of heart and mind. I personally find it one of the most difficult disciplines to practice.

Constantly I find myself "making up my mind" about somebody else: "He cannot be taken seriously. She is really just asking for attention. They are rabble-rousers who only want to cause trouble." These judgments are indeed a form of moral killing. I label my fellow human beings, categorize them, and put them at a safe distance from me. By judging others I take false burdens upon myself. By my judgments I divide my world into those who are good and those who are evil, and thus I play God. But everyone who plays God ends up acting like the demon.

Judging others implies that somehow we stand outside of the place where weak, broken, sinful human beings dwell. It is an arrogant and pretentious act that shows blindness not only toward others but also toward ourselves. Paul says it clearly: "...No matter who you are, if you pass judgment you have no excuse. For in judging others you condemn yourself, since you behave no differently from those you judge. We know God condemns that sort of behavior impartially" (Rom. 2:1–2).

I am moved by the idea that the peacemaker never judges anybody—neither his neighbor close by, nor his neighbor far away; neither her friend nor her enemy. It helps me to think of peacemakers as persons whose hearts are so anchored in God that they do not need to evaluate, criticize, or weigh the importance of others. They can see their neighbors—whether they are North Americans or Russians, Nicaraguans or South Africans—as fellow human beings, fellow sinners, fellow saints, men and women who need to be listened to, looked at, and cared for with the love of God and who need to be given the space to recognize that they belong to the same human family as we do.

I vividly remember encountering a man who never judged anyone. I was so used to being around people who are full of opinions about others and eager to share them that I felt somewhat lost at the beginning. What do you talk about when you have nobody to discuss or judge? But, discovering that he also did not judge me, I gradually came to experience a new inner freedom within myself. I realized that I had nothing to defend, nothing to hide, and could be myself in his presence without fear. Through this true peacemaker, a new level of conversation opened up, based not on competing or comparing but on celebrating together the love of the One who is "sent into the world not to judge the world, but so that through him the world might be saved" (Jn. 3:17). Through this man I came to realize that for Jesus, to whom God has entrusted all judgment (see John 5:22), the other name of judgment is mercy.

This encounter continues to change my life. For a long time I had simply assumed that I needed to have opinions about everyone and everything in order to participate in ordinary life. But this man made me see that I am allowed to live without the heavy burden of judging others and can be free to listen, look, care, and fearlessly receive the gifts offered to me. And the more I become free from the inner compulsion to make up my mind quickly about who the other "really" is, the more I feel part of the whole human family stretched out over our planet from east to west and from north to south. Indeed, saying "No" to the violence of judgments leads me into the nonviolence of peacemaking which allows me to embrace all who share life with me as my brothers and sisters.

But there is more. As peacemakers we must have the courage to see the powers of death at work even in our innermost selves because we find these powers in the way we think and feel about ourselves. Yes, our most intimate inner thoughts can be tainted by death.

When I reflect on my own inner struggles I must confess that one of the hardest struggles is to accept myself, to affirm my own person as being loved, to celebrate my own being alive. Sometimes it seems that there are evil voices deeply hidden in my heart trying to convince me that I am worthless, useless, and even despicable. It might sound strange, but these dark inner voices are sometimes most powerful when family and friends, students and teachers, and supporters and sympathizers cover me with praise. Precisely then there are these voices who say: "Yes, but they really do not know me, they really cannot see my inner ugliness. If they could know and see they would discover how impure and selfish I am and they would withdraw their praise quickly." This self-loathing voice is probably one of the greatest enemies of the peacemaker. It is a voice that seduces us to commit spiritual suicide.

The central message of the Gospel is that God sent his beloved Son to forgive our sins and make us new people, able to live in this world without being paralyzed by self-rejection, remorse, and guilt. To accept that message in faith and truly believe that we are forgiven is probably one of the most challenging spiritual battles we have to face. Somehow we cannot let go of our self-rejections. Somehow we cling to our guilt, as if accepting forgiveness fully would call us to a new and ominous task we are afraid to accept. Resistance is an essential element of peacemaking, and the "No" of the resisters must go all the way to the inner reaches of their own hearts to confront the deadly powers of self-hate.

I often think that I am such a hesitant peacemaker because I still have not accepted myself as a forgiven person, a person who has nothing to fear and is truly free to speak the truth and proclaim the kingdom of peace. It sometimes seems to me that the demonic forces of evil and death want to seduce me into believing that I do not deserve the peace I am working for. I then become self-accusing, apologetic, even self-defeating, always hesitant to claim the grace I have been given and say clearly: "As a forgiven person I call forth the peace which is the fruit of forgiveness!"

My own inner struggles are not just my own. I share them with millions of others. Underneath much self-assured behavior and material success, many people think little of themselves. They might not show it—since that is socially unacceptable—but they suffer from it no less. Feelings of depression, inner anxiety, spiritual lostness, and (most painfully) guilt over past failures and past successes are often constant companions of highly respected men and women. These feelings are like small rodents slowly eating up the foundations of our lives.

Personally I believe that the battle against these suicidal inner powers is harder than any other spiritual battle. If those who believe in Jesus Christ were able to believe fully that they are forgiven people, loved unconditionally, and called to proclaim peace in the name of the forgiving Lord, our planet would not be on the verge of self-destruction.

It might seem contrived to extend the "No" of the peacemakers against nuclear war to a "No" against violent public entertainment, destructive stereotyping, and even self-loathing. But when we are trying to develop a spirituality of peacemaking we cannot limit ourselves to one mode of resistance. All levels need to be considered, even when it might seem that we are stretching things too far. I am deeply convinced that we have to keep all these forms of resistance together as parts of the great work of resistance. Peace activists who are willing to risk their freedom to prevent a nuclear holocaust, but who at the same time feed their imaginations with violent scenes, stereotype their fellow human beings, or nurture an inner disgust for themselves cannot be witnesses to life for very long. Full spiritual resistance requires a "No" to death wherever it operates.

Wherever there is life there is movement and growth. Wherever life manifests itself we have to be prepared for surprises, unexpected changes, and constant renewal. Nothing alive is the same from moment to moment. To live is to face the unknown over and over again. We never know exactly how we will feel, think, and behave next week, next year, or in a decade. Essential to living is trust in an unknown future that requires a surrender to the mystery of the unpredictable.

At a time such as ours, in which everything has become unhinged and there is little to hold onto, uncertainty has become so frightening that we are tempted to prefer the certainty of death over the uncertainty of life. It seems that many people say in words or actions: "It is better to be sure of your unhappiness than to be unsure of your happiness." Translated into different situations this reads: "It is better to have clear-cut enemies than to have to live with people of whose lasting friendship you cannot be sure"; or, "It is better to ask people to accept your weaknesses than to be constantly challenged to overcome them"; or, "It is better to be defined as a bad person than to have to be good in constantly changing circumstances." It is shocking to see how many people choose the certainty of misery in order not to have to deal with the uncertainty of joy. This is a choice for death, a choice that is increasingly attractive when the future no longer seems trustworthy.

As I reflect on my childhood experiences of fear, I remember a time in which I was tempted to fail even before I had seriously tried to succeed. Somewhere I was saying to myself: "Why not run back from the diving board and cry so that you can be sure of pity, since you are not so sure of praise." Such childhood memories offer me an image of the temptation that faces all of us on a worldwide scale. It is the temptation to choose the satisfaction of death when the satisfaction of life seems too precarious. When the future has become a dark, fearful unknown that repulses me more and more, isn't it then quite attractive to opt for the satisfactions that are available in the present, even when these satisfactions are very partial, ambiguous, and tainted with death?

The nuclear situation in which the future itself has become not only dark and fearful but also uncertain has made the temptation to indulge ourselves in brief pleasures of the present greater than ever. It is therefore quite possible that we will see an increasingly death-oriented self-indulgence going hand-in-hand with increasing doubt about a livable future. Fascination with death and hedonism are intimately connected, because both lust and death keep our eyes away from the anxiety-provoking future and imprison us in the pleasurable certainties of the moment.

Peacemaking requires clear resistance to death in all its manifestations. We cannot say "No" to nuclear death if we are not also saying "No" to the less visible but no less hideous forms of death, such as abortion and capital punishment. As peacemakers we have to face the intimate connection between the varied forms of our contemporary fascination with death and the deaths caused by a nuclear holocaust. By recognizing in our own daily lives our many "innocent" death games, we gradually come to realize that we are part of that complex network of war making that finds its most devastating expression in a nuclear holocaust.

Real resistance requires the humble confession that we are partners in the evil that we seek to resist. This is a very hard and seemingly endless discipline. The more we say "No," the more we will discover the all pervasive presence of death. The more we resist, the more we recognize how much more there is to resist. The world—and we are an intimate part of the world—is indeed Satan's territory. When the demon shows Jesus all the kingdoms of the world and their splendor, he says: "I will give you all these, if you fall at my feet and worship me" (Mt. 4:9). Jesus never disputes that these kingdoms are Satan's; he only refuses to worship him. The world and its kingdoms are under the destructive power of the evil spirit, the spirit of destruction and death. The nuclear threat reveals the ultimate implication of this truth. It is not that God—who created the world out of love—will destroy it, but that *we* will destroy it when we allow the satanic power of death to rule us. This is what makes saying "No" to death in all its manifestations such an urgent spiritual task.

"NO" TO THE VIETNAM WAR[1]

We are trying to do a very difficult thing. We are trying to say *NO* to war, *NO* to the indiscriminate killing of men, women, and children, *NO* to the horrendous destruction of villages, cities, and fertile lands, in short, *NO* to all the evil powers that sow death instead of life. Why is this such a difficult task? Because we want to say *NO* in such a way that the possibility of peace becomes visible in our words, hands, and eyes. When our words are only angry curses, our hands only clenched fists, and our eyes filled with hostile gazes, then we are trying to end a war with a war, and we add narrow-mindedness to narrow-mindedness, hostility to hostility, fear to fear, and violence to violence.

When we walk downtown with empty hands and return with candles instead of guns, we want to express not only our deep sadness, but also our expectation that sadness will lead to repentance, that repentance will lead to compassion, and that compassion will lead to peace.

If we want to respond to the incredible violence in our world with a credible nonviolence, we have to be willing to realize that nonviolence is not a technique to conquer peace, but a deep personal attitude which makes it possible to receive peace as a gift. Therefore we are called today to confess that the evil we are protesting against is alive in our own selves, to repent with contrite hearts for the sins of the world, to witness to the possibility and desirability of peace in the midst of a war-ridden society, to show a deep compassion not only for our friends but also for those we have called our enemies, and to work with hope for the liberation that frees both the oppressor and the oppressed from the tyrannical automation of violence.

Let us therefore go forth in the peace which the world cannot give, a peace we want to share with each other and with everyone we meet on our way.

NOTE

1. A speech given at a moratorium rally against the Vietnam War on May 4, 1972, at Yale University, New Haven, Connecticut.

"Toward a Theology of Resistance"

❧

Thomas Merton

Thomas Merton became a Trappist monk in 1941, committing himself to an intense and highly structured life of prayer, meditation, study, and manual labor. His many books on spiritual life, the place of religion in society, and the fruitful connections between Christianity and other religions are classics of twentieth-century religious thought. Here, Merton addresses the demands of nonviolence and love in the modern age, especially in the face of violence that can stem as much from bureaucracy as from passion.

❧

Theology today needs to focus carefully upon the crucial problem of violence. The commandment "Thou shalt not kill" is more than a mere matter of academic or sentimental interest in an age when man not only is more frustrated, more crowded, more subject to psychotic and hostile delusion than ever, but also has at his disposition an arsenal of weapons that make global suicide an easy possibility. But the so-called "nuclear umbrella" has not simplified matters in the least: it may (at least temporarily) have caused the nuclear powers to reconsider their impulses to reduce one another to radioactive dust. But meanwhile "conventional" wars go on with unabated cruelty, and already more bombs have been exploded on Vietnam than were dropped in the whole of World War II. The population of the affluent world is nourished on a steady diet of brutal mythology and hallucination, kept at a constant pitch of high tension by a life that is intrinsically violent in that it forces a large part of the population to submit to an existence which is humanly intolerable. Hence murder, mugging, rape, crime, corruption. But it must be remembered that the crime that breaks out of the ghetto is only the fruit of a greater and more pervasive violence: the injustice which forces people to live in the ghetto in the first place. The problem of violence, then, is not the problem of a few rioters and rebels, but the problem of a whole social structure which is outwardly ordered and respectable, and inwardly ridden by psychopathic obsessions and delusions.

It is perfectly true that violence must at times be restrained by force: but a convenient mythology which simply legalizes the use of force by big criminals against little criminals—whose small-scale criminality is largely *caused* by the large-scale injustice under which they live—only perpetuates the disorder.

Pope John XXIII in *Pacem in Terris* quoted, with approval, a famous saying of St. Augustine: "What are kingdoms without justice but large bands of robbers?" The problem of violence today must be traced to its root: not the small-time murderers but the massively organized bands of murderers whose operations are global.

This book is concerned with the defense of the dignity and rights of man against the encroachments and brutality of massive power structures which threaten either to enslave him or to destroy him, while exploiting him in their conflicts with one another.

The Catholic moral theology of war has, especially since the Renaissance, concerned itself chiefly with casuistical discussion of how far the monarch or the sovereign state can justly make use of force. The historic context of this discussion was the struggle for a European balance of power, waged for absolute monarchs by small professional armies. In a new historical context we find not only a new struggle on a global scale between mammoth nuclear powers provided with arsenals capable of wiping out the human race, but also the emergence of scores of small nations in an undeveloped world that was until recently colonial. In this Third World we find not huge armed establishments but petty dictatorships (representing a rich minority) armed by the great powers, opposed by small, volunteer guerilla bands fighting for "the poor." The Great Powers tend to intervene in these struggles, not so much by the threat and use of nuclear weapons (with which however they continue to threaten one another) but with armies of draftees and with new experimental weapons which are sometimes incredibly savage and cruel and which are used mostly against helpless noncombatants. Although many Churchmen, moved apparently by force of habit, continue to issue mechanical blessings upon these draftees and upon the versatile applications of science to the art of killing, it is evident that this use of force does not become moral just because the government and the mass media have declared the cause to be patriotic. The cliche "My country right or wrong" does not provide a satisfactory theological answer to the moral problems raised by the intervention of American power in all parts of the Third World. And in fact the Second Vatican Council, following the encyclical of John XXIII, *Pacem in Terris,* has had some pertinent things to say about war in the nuclear era. (See below, Chapter V).

To assert that conflict resolution is one of the crucial areas of theological investigation in our time is not to issue an a priori demand for a theology of pure pacifism. To declare that *all* use of force in any way whatever is by the very fact immoral is to plunge into confusion and unreality from the very start, because, as John XXIII admitted, "unfortunately the law of fear still reigns among peoples" and there are situations in which the only way to protect human life and rights effectively is by forcible resistance against unjust encroachment. Murder is not to be passively permitted, but resisted and prevented—and all the more so when it becomes mass-murder. The problem arises not when theology admits that force can be necessary, but when it does so in a way that implicitly favors the claims of the powerful and self-seeking establishment against the common good of mankind or against the rights of the oppressed.

The real moral issue of violence in the twentieth century is obscured by archaic and mythical presuppositions. We tend to judge violence in terms of the individual, the messy, the physically disturbing, the personally frightening. The violence we want to see restrained is the violence of the hood waiting for us in the subway or the elevator. That is reasonable, but it tends to influence us too much. It makes us think that the problem of violence is limited to this very small scale, and it makes us unable to appreciate the far greater problem of the more abstract, more global, more organized presence of violence on a massive and corporate pattern. Violence today is *white-collar violence, the systematically organized bureaucratic and technological destruction of man.*

The theology of violence must not lose sight of the real problem which is not the individual with a revolver but *death and even genocide as big business.* But this big business of death is all the more innocent and effective because it involves a long chain of individuals, each of whom can feel himself absolved from responsibility, and each of whom can perhaps salve his conscience by contributing with a more *meticulous efficiency* to his part in the massive operation.

We know, for instance, that Adolf Eichmann and others like him felt no guilt for their share in the extermination of the Jews. This feeling of justification was due partly to their absolute obedience to higher authority and partly to the care and efficiency which went into the details of their work. This was done almost entirely on paper. Since they dealt with numbers, not with people, and since their job was one of abstract bureaucratic organization, apparently they could easily forget the reality of what they were doing. The same is true to an even greater extent in modern warfare in which the real moral problems are not to be located in rare instances of hand-to-hand combat, but in the remote planning and organization of technological destruction. The real crimes of modern war are committed not at the front (if any) but in war offices and ministries of defense in which no one ever has to see any blood unless his secretary gets a nosebleed. Modern technological mass murder is not directly visible, like individual murder. It is abstract, corporate, businesslike, cool, free of guilt-feelings and therefore a thousand times more deadly and effective than the eruption of violence out of individual hate. It is this polite, massively organized white-collar murder machine that threatens the world with destruction, not the violence of a few desperate teenagers in a slum. But our antiquated theology myopically focused on *individual* violence alone fails to see this. It shudders at the phantasm of muggings and killings where a mess is made on our own doorstep, but blesses and canonizes the antiseptic violence of corporately organized murder because it is respectable, efficient, clean, and above all profitable.

In another place I have contrasted, in some detail, the mentality of John XXIII on this point with the mentality of Macchiavelli (see *Seeds of Destruction*, Part III). Macchiavelli said: "There are two methods of fighting, one by law and the other by force. The first method is that of men, the second of beasts; but as the first method is often insufficient, one must have recourse to the second." I submit that a theology which merely seeks to justify the "method of beasts" and to help it disguise itself as law—since it is after all a kind of "prolongation of law"—is not adequate for the problems of a time of violence.

On the other hand we also have to recognize that when oppressive power is thoroughly well established, it does not always need to resort openly to the "method of beasts" because its laws are already powerful—perhaps also bestial—enough. In other words, when a system can, without resort to overt force, *compel* people to live in conditions of abjection, helplessness, wretchedness that keeps them on the level of beasts rather than of men, it is plainly violent. To make men live on a subhuman level against their will, to constrain them in such a way that they have no hope of escaping their condition, is an unjust exercise of force. Those who in some way or other concur in the oppression—and perhaps profit by it—are exercising violence even though they may be preaching pacifism. And their supposedly peaceful laws, which maintain this spurious kind of order, are in fact instruments of violence and oppression. If the oppressed try to resist by force—which is their right—theology has no business preaching nonviolence to them. Mere blind destruction is, of course, futile and immoral: but who are we to condemn a desperation we have helped to cause!

However, as John XXIII pointed out, the "law of fear" is not the only law under which men can live, nor is it really the normal mark of the human condition. To live under the law of fear and to deal with one another by "the methods of beasts" will hardly help world events "to follow a course in keeping with man's destiny and dignity." In order for us to realize this, we must remember that "one of the profound requirements of (our) nature is this: . . . it is not fear that should reign but love—a love that tends to express itself in mutual collaboration."

"Love" is unfortunately a much misused word. It trips easily off the Christian tongue—so easily that one gets the impression it means others ought to love us for standing on their necks.

A theology of love cannot afford to be sentimental. It cannot afford to preach edifying generalities about charity, while identifying "peace" with mere established power and legalized violence against the oppressed. A theology of love cannot be allowed merely to serve the interests of the rich and powerful, justifying their wars, their violence and their bombs, while exhorting the poor and underprivileged to practice patience, meekness, longsuffering and to solve their problems, if at all, nonviolently.

The theology of love must seek to deal realistically with the evil and injustice in the world, and not merely to compromise with them. Such a theology will have to take note of the ambiguous realities of politics, without embracing the specious myth of a "realism" that merely justifies force in the service of established power. Theology does not exist merely to appease the already too untroubled conscience of the powerful and the established. A theology of love may also conceivably turn out to be a theology of revolution. In any case, it is a theology of *resistance*, a refusal of the evil that reduces a brother to homicidal desperation.

On the other hand, Christian faith and purity of intention—the simplicity of the dove— are no guarantee of political acumen, and theological insight is no substitute for the wisdom of the serpent which is seldom acquired in Sunday school. Should the theologian or the priest be too anxious to acquire that particular kind of wisdom? Should he be too ambitious for the achievements of a successful political operator? Should he be more careful to separate authentic Christian witness from effectiveness in political maneuvering? Or is the real place of the priest the place which Fr. Camilo Torres took, with the Colombian guerillas?

This book cannot hope to answer such questions. But it can at least provide a few materials for a theology, not of pacifism and nonviolence in the sense of *nonresistance*, but for a theology of resistance which is at the same time *Christian* resistance and which therefore emphasizes reason and humane communication rather than force, but which also admits the possibility of force in a limit-situation when everything else fails.

Such a theology could not claim to be Christian if it did not retain at least some faith in the meaning of the Cross and of the redemptive death of Jesus who, instead of using force against his accusers, took all the evil upon himself and overcame that evil by his suffering. This is a basic Christian pattern, but a realistic theology will, I believe, give a new practical emphasis to it. Instead of preaching the Cross *for others* and advising them to suffer patiently the violence which we sweetly impose on them, with the aid of armies and police, we might conceivably recognize the right of the less fortunate to use force, and study more seriously the practice of nonviolence and humane methods on our own part when, as it happens, we possess the most stupendous arsenal of power the world has ever known.

"September 11, 2001: A Pacifist Response"

❧

Stanley Hauerwas

Currently professor of theological ethics at Duke University, Stanley Hauerwas's work cuts across disciplinary lines and includes the widely respected *A Community of Character: Toward a Constructive Christian Social Ethic*. In this essay, Hauerwas argues forcefully for a Christian pacifist response to September 11.

❧

I want to write honestly about September 11, 2001. But it is not easy. Even now, some months after that horrible event, I find it hard to know what can be said or, perhaps more difficult, what should be said. Even more difficult, I am not sure for what or how I should pray. I am a Christian. I am a Christian pacifist. Being Christian and being a pacifist are not two things for me. I would not be a pacifist if I were not a Christian, and I find it hard to understand how one can be a Christian without being a pacifist. But what does a pacifist have to say in the face of terror? Pray for peace? I have no use for sentimentality.

Indeed some have suggested pacifists have nothing to say in a time like the time after September 11, 2001. The editors of the magazine *First Things* assert that "those who in principle oppose the use of military force have no legitimate part in the discussion about how military force should be used."[1] They make this assertion because according to them the only form of pacifism that is defensible requires the disavowal by the pacifist of any political relevance. That is not the kind of pacifism I represent. I am a pacifist because I think nonviolence is the necessary condition for a politics not based on death. A politics that is not determined by the fear of death means no strong distinction can be drawn between politics and military force.

Yet I cannot deny that September 11, 2001, creates and requires a kind of silence. We desperately want to "explain" what happened. Explanation domesticates terror, making it part of "our" world. I believe attempts to explain must be resisted. Rather, we should learn to wait before what we know not, hoping to gain time and space sufficient to learn how to speak without lying. I should like to think pacifism names the habits and community necessary to gain the time and place that is an alternative to revenge. But I do not pretend that I know how that is accomplished.

Yet I do know that much that has been said since September 11, 2001, has been false. In the first hours and days following the fall of the towers, there was a stunned silence. President Bush flew from one safe haven to another, unsure what had or was still to happen. He was quite literally in the air. I wish he might have been able to maintain that posture, but he is the leader of the "free world." Something must be done. Something must be said. We must be in control.

The silence must be shattered. He knew the American people must be comforted. Life must return to normal.

So he said, "We are at war." Magic words necessary to reclaim the everyday. War is such normalizing discourse. Americans know war. This is our Pearl Harbor. Life can return to normal. We are frightened, and ironically war makes us feel safe. The way to go on in the face of September 11, 2001, is to find someone to kill. Americans are, moreover, good at killing. We often fail to acknowledge how accomplished we are in the art of killing. Indeed we, the American people, have become masters of killing. In our battles, only the enemy has to die. Some in our military are embarrassed by our expertise in war making, but what can they do? They are but following orders.

So the silence created by destruction was soon shattered by the need for revenge—a revenge all the more unforgiving because we cannot forgive those who flew the planes for making us acknowledge our vulnerability. The flag that flew in mourning was soon transformed into a pride-filled thing; the bloodstained flag of victims transformed into the flag of the American indomitable spirit. We will prevail no matter how many people we must kill to rid ourselves of the knowledge Americans died as victims. Americans do not die as victims. They have to be heroes. So the stock trader who happened to work on the seventy-second floor becomes as heroic as the policemen and the firemen who were doing their jobs. No one who died on September 11, 2001, gets to die a meaningless death. That is why their deaths must be revenged.

I am a pacifist, so the American "we" cannot be my "me." But to be alienated from the American "we" is not easy. I am a neophyte pacifist. I never really wanted to be a pacifist. I had learned from Reinhold Niebuhr that if you desire justice you had better be ready to kill someone along the way. But then John Howard Yoder and his extraordinary book *The Politics of Jesus* came along. Yoder convinced me that if there is anything to this Christian "stuff," it must surely involve the conviction that the Son would rather die on the cross than for the world to be redeemed by violence. Moreover, the defeat of death through resurrection makes possible as well as necessary that Christians live nonviolently in a world of violence. Christian nonviolence is not a strategy to rid the world of violence, but rather the way Christians must live in a world of violence. In short Christians are not nonviolent because we believe our nonviolence is a strategy to rid the world of war, but rather because faithful followers of Christ in a world of war cannot imagine being anything else than nonviolent.

But what does a pacifist have to say in the face of the terror September 11, 2001, names? I vaguely knew when I first declared I was a pacifist that there might be some serious consequences. To be nonviolent might even change my life. But I do not really think I understood what that change might entail until September 11. For example after I declared I was a pacifist, I quit singing the "Star-Spangled Banner." I will stand when it is sung, particularly at baseball games, but I do not sing. Not to sing the "Star-Spangled Banner" is a small thing that reminds me that my first loyalty is not to the United States but to God and God's church. I confess it never crossed my mind that such small acts might over the years make my response to September 11 quite different from that of the good people who sing "God Bless America"—so different that I am left in saddened silence.

That difference, moreover, haunts me. My father was a bricklayer and a good American. He worked hard all his life and hoped his work would not only support his family, but also make some contribution to our common life. He held a war-critical job in World War II, so he was never drafted. Only one of his five bricklaying brothers was in that war, but he was never exposed to combat. My family was never militarized, but as Texans they were good Americans. For most of my life I, too, was a good American, assuming that I owed much to the society that enabled me, the son of a bricklayer, to gain a Ph.D. at Yale—even if the Ph.D. was in theology.

Of course there was Vietnam. For many of us Vietnam was extended training necessary for the development of a more critical attitude toward the government of the United States. Yet most of us critical of the war in Vietnam did not think our opposition to that war made us less loyal Americans. Indeed the criticisms of the war were based on an appeal to the highest American ideals. Vietnam was a time of great tension, but the politics of the antiwar movement did not require those opposed to the war to think of themselves as fundamentally standing outside the American mainstream. Most critics of Vietnam (just as many that now criticize the war in Afghanistan) based their dissent on their adherence to American ideals that they felt the war was betraying. That but indicates why I feel so isolated even among the critics of the war in Afghanistan. I do not even share their allegiance to American ideals.

So I simply did not share the reaction of most Americans to the destruction of the World Trade Center. Of course I recoil from murder on such a scale, but I hope I remember that one murder is too many. That Americans have hurried to call what happened "war" strikes me as self-defeating. If this is war, then bin Laden has won. He thinks he is a warrior not a murderer. Just to the extent the language of war is used, he is honored. But in their hurry to call this war, Americans have no time for careful discriminations.

Where does that leave me? Does it mean, as an estranged friend recently wrote me, that I disdain all "natural loyalties" that bind us together as human beings, even submitting such loyalties to a harsh and unforgiving standard? Does it mean that I speak as a solitary individual, failing to acknowledge that our lives are interwoven with the lives of others, those who have gone before, those among whom we live, those with whom we identify, and those with whom we are in Christian communion? Do I refuse to acknowledge my life is made possible by the gifts of others? Do I forsake all forms of patriotism, failing to acknowledge that we as a people are better off because of the sacrifices that were made in World War II? To this I can only answer, "Yes." If you call patriotism "natural," I certainly do disavow that connection. Such a disavowal, I hope, does not mean I am inattentive to the gifts I have received from past and present neighbors.

In response to my friend I pointed out that because he, too, is a Christian I assumed he also disdained some "natural loyalties." After all he had his children baptized. The "natural love" between parents and children is surely reconfigured when children are baptized into the death and resurrection of Christ. Paul says:

> Do you not know that all of us who have been baptized into Christ Jesus were baptized into his death? Therefore we have been buried with him by baptism into death, so that, just as Christ was raised from the dead by the glory of the Father, so we too might walk in the newness of life. For if we have been united with him in a death like his, we will certainly be united with him in a resurrection like his.[2]

Christians often tend to focus on being united with Christ in his resurrection, forgetting that we are also united with him in his death. What could that mean if it does not mean that Christians must be ready to die, indeed have their children die, rather than betray the Gospel? Any love not transformed by the love of God cannot help but be the source of the violence we perpetrate on one another in the name of justice. Such a love may appear harsh and dreadful from the perspective of the world, but Christians believe such a love is life-giving not life-denying.

Of course living a life of nonviolence may be harsh. Certainly you have to imagine, and perhaps even face, that you will have to watch the innocent suffer and even die for your convictions. But that is no different from those that claim they would fight a just war. After all, the just warrior is committed to avoiding any direct attack on noncombatants, which might well mean that more people will die because the just warrior refuses to do an evil that a good may come. For example, on just-war grounds the bombings of Hiroshima and Nagasaki were clearly murder. If you are serious about just war, you must be ready to say that it would be better that more people died on the beaches of Japan than to have committed one murder, much less the bombing of civilian populations.

This last observation may suggest that when all is said and done, a pacifist response to September 11, 2001, is just one more version of the anti-American sentiments expressed by what many consider to be the American Left. I say "what many consider" because it is very unclear if there is a Left left in America. Nowhere is that more apparent than in the support to the war on terrorism given by those who identify as the "Left." Yet much has been made of the injustice of American foreign policy that lends a kind of intelligibility to the hatred given form on September 11. I am no defender of American foreign policy, but the problem with such lines of criticism is that no matter how immoral what the American government may have done in the world, such immorality cannot explain or justify the attack on the World Trade Center.

American imperialism, often celebrated as the new globalism, is a frightening power. It is frightening not only because of the harm such power inflicts on the innocent, but because it is difficult to imagine alternatives. Pacifists are often challenged after an event like September 11 with the question, "Well, what alternative do you have to bombing Afghanistan?" Such a question assumes that pacifists must have an alternative foreign policy. My only response is I do not have a foreign policy. I have something better—a church constituted by people who would rather die than kill.

Indeed I fear that absent a countercommunity to challenge America, bin Laden has given Americans what they so desperately needed—a war without end. America is a country that lives off the moral capital of our wars. War names the time we send the youth to kill and die (maybe) in an effort to assure ourselves the lives we lead are worthy of such sacrifices. They kill and die to protect our "freedom." But what can freedom mean if the prime instance of the exercise of such freedom is to shop? The very fact that we can and do go to war is a moral necessity for a nation of consumers. War makes clear we must believe in something even if we are not sure what that something is, except that it has something to do with the "American way of life."

What a gift bin Laden has therefore given America. Americans were in despair because we won the Cold War. Americans won by outspending the USSR, proving that we can waste more money on guns than they can or did. But what do Americans do after they have won a war? The war was necessary to give moral coherence. We had to cooperate with one another because we were at war. How can America make sense of what it means for us to be "a people" if we have no common enemy? We were in a dangerous funk having nothing better to do than entertain ourselves with the soap opera Bill Clinton was. Now we have something better to do. We can fight the war against terrorism.

The good thing, moreover, about the war on terrorism is it has no end, which makes it very doubtful that this war can be considered just. If a war is just, your enemy must know before the war begins what political purpose the war is to serve. In other words, they need to know from the beginning what the conditions are if they choose to surrender. So you cannot fight a just war if it is "a war to end all wars" (World War I) or for "unconditional surrender" (World War II). But a "war on terrorism" is a war without limit. Americans want to wipe this enemy off the face of the earth. Moreover, America even gets to decide who counts and does not count as a terrorist.

Which means Americans get to have it any way they want it. Some that are captured, for example, are prisoners of war; some are detainees. No problem. When you are the biggest kid on the block, you can say whatever you want to say, even if what you say is nonsense. We all know the first casualty in war is truth. So the conservatives who have fought the war against "post-modernism" in the name of "objective truth," the same conservatives that now rule us, assume they can use language any way they please.

That Americans get to decide who is and who is not a terrorist means that this is not only a war without clear purpose, but also a war without end. From now on we can be in a perpetual state of war. America is always at her best when she is on permanent war footing. Moreover, when our country is at war, it has no space to worry about the extraordinary inequities that constitute our society, no time to worry about poverty or those parts of the world that are ravaged by hunger and genocide. Everything—civil liberties, due process, the protection of the law—must be subordinated to the one great moral enterprise of winning the unending war against terrorism.

At the heart of the American desire to wage endless war is the American fear of death. The American love of high-tech medicine is but the other side of the war against terrorism. Americans are determined to be safe, to be able to get out of this life alive. On September 11, Americans were confronted with their worst fear—a people ready to die as an expression of their profound moral commitments. Some speculate such people must have chosen death because they were desperate or, at least, they were so desperate that death was preferable to life. Yet their willingness to die stands in stark contrast to a politics that asks of its members in response to September 11 to shop.

Ian Buruma and Avishai Margalit observe in their article "Occidentalism" that lack of heroism is the hallmark of a bourgeois ethos.[3] Heroes court death. The bourgeois is addicted to personal safety. They concede that much in an affluent, market-driven society is mediocre, "but when contempt for bourgeois creature comforts becomes contempt for life itself you know the West is under attack." According to Buruma and Margalit, the West (which they point out is not just the geographical West) should oppose the full force of calculating antibourgeois heroism, of which Al-Qaeda is but one representative, through the means we know best—cutting off their money supply. Of course, Buruma and Margalit do not tell us how that can be done, given the need for oil to sustain the bourgeois society they favor.

Christians are not called to be heroes or shoppers. We are called to be holy. We do not think holiness is an individual achievement, but rather a set of practices to sustain a people who refuse to have their lives determined by the fear and denial of death. We believe by so living we offer our non-Christian brothers and sisters an alternative to all politics based on the denial of death. Christians are acutely aware that we seldom are faithful to the gifts God has given us, but we hope the confession of our sins is a sign of hope in a world without hope. This means pacifists do have a response to September 11, 2001. Our response is to continue living in a manner that witnesses to our belief that the world was not changed on September 11, 2001. The world was changed during the celebration of Passover in A.D. 33.

Mark and Louise Zwick, founders of the Houston Catholic Worker House of Hospitality, embody the life made possible by the death and resurrection of Jesus. They know, moreover, that Christian nonviolence cannot and must not be understood as a position that is no more than being "against violence." If pacifism is no more than "not violence," it betrays the form of life to which Christians believe they have been called by Christ. Drawing on Nicholas Berdyaev, the

Zwicks rightly observe that "the split between the Gospel and our culture is the drama of our times," but they also remind us that "one does not free persons by detaching them from the bonds that paralyze them: one frees persons by attaching them to their destiny." Christian nonviolence is but another name for the friendship we believe God has made possible and constitutes the alternative to the violence that grips our lives.

I began by noting that I am not sure for what I should pray. But prayer often is a form of silence. The following prayer I hope does not drown out silence. I wrote the prayer as a devotion to begin a Duke Divinity School general meeting. I was able to write the prayer because of a short article I had just read in the *Houston Catholic Worker* by Jean Vanier.[4] Vanier is the founder of the L'arche movement—a movement that believes God has saved us by giving us the good work of living with and learning to be friends with those the world calls retarded. I end with this prayer because it is all I have to give.

Great God of surprise, our lives continue to be haunted by the spectre of September 11, 2001. Life must go on and we go on keeping on—even meeting again as the Divinity School Council. Is this what Barth meant in 1933 when he said we must go on "as though nothing has happened"? To go on as though nothing has happened can sound like a counsel of despair, of helplessness, of hopelessness. We want to act, to do something to reclaim the way things were. Which, I guess, is but a reminder that one of the reasons we are so shocked, so violated, by September 11 is the challenge presented to our prideful presumption that we are in control, that we are going to get out of life alive. To go on "as though nothing has happened" surely requires us to acknowledge you are God and we are not. It is hard to remember that Jesus did not come to make us safe, but rather he came to make us disciples, citizens of your new age, a kingdom of surprise. That we live in the end times is surely the basis for our conviction that you have given us all the time we need to respond to September 11 with "small acts of beauty and tenderness," which Jean Vanier tells us, if done with humility and confidence "will bring unity to the world and break the chain of violence." So we pray give us humility that we may remember that the work we do today, the work we do every day, is false and pretentious if it fails to serve those who day in and day out are your small gestures of beauty and tenderness.

NOTES

1. Editorial, "In a Time of War," *First Things* (December 2001), http://www.firstthings.com/ftissues/ft0112/opinion/editorial.html.

2. Rom. 6:3–5.

3. Ian Buruma and Avishai Margalit, "Occidentalism," *New York Review of Books* 49, no. 1 (January 17, 2002): 4–7.

4. Jean Vanier, "L'arche Founder Responds to Violence," *Houston Catholic Worker*, November 16, 2001.

"The Meaning of This Hour"

❦

Abraham Joshua Heschel

Born in Europe, Abraham Joshua Heschel served as professor of Jewish ethics and mysticism at the Jewish Theological Seminary of America from 1945 to 1972. His many writings combined careful scholarship with a passionate attempt to reveal the heart and soul of religious life to an American culture in which Jews had achieved religious freedom but seemed to have lost any sense of spiritual vitality. This selection, written after the Holocaust, reflects on our collective responsibility for a world seemingly gone mad with hate and violence. It remains, sadly, as relevant now as it was then.

❦

Emblazoned over the gates of the world in which we live is the escutcheon of the demons. The mark of Cain in the face of man has come to overshadow the likeness of God. There has never been so much guilt and distress, agony, and terror. At no time has the earth been so soaked with blood. Fellow men turned out to be evil ghosts, monstrous and weird. Ashamed and dismayed, we ask: Who is responsible?

History is a pyramid of efforts and errors; yet at times it is the Holy Mountain on which God holds judgment over the nations. Few are privileged to discern God's judgment in history. But all may be guided by the words of the Baal Shem: If a man has beheld evil, he may know that it was shown to him in order that he learn his own guilt and repent; for what is shown to him is also within him.

We have trifled with the name of God. We have taken the ideals in vain. We have called for the Lord. He came. And was ignored. We have preached but eluded Him. We have praised but defied Him. Now we reap the fruits of our failure. Through centuries His voice cried in the wilderness. How skillfully it was trapped and imprisoned in the temples! How often it was drowned or distorted! Now we behold how it gradually withdraws, abandoning one people after another, departing from their souls, despising their wisdom. The taste for the good has all but gone from the earth. Men heap spite upon cruelty, malice upon atrocity.

The horrors of our time fill our souls with reproach and everlasting shame. We have profaned the word of God, and we have given the wealth of our land, the ingenuity of our minds and the dear lives of our youth to tragedy and perdition. There has never been more reason for man to be ashamed than now. Silence hovers mercilessly over many dreadful lands. The day of the Lord is a day without the Lord. Where is God? Why didst Thou not halt the trains loaded with Jews being led to slaughter? It is so hard to rear a child, to nourish and to educate. Why dost Thou make it so easy to kill? Like Moses, we hide our face; for we are afraid to look upon

Elohim, upon His power of judgment. Indeed, where were we when men learned to hate in the days of starvation? When raving madmen were sowing wrath in the hearts of the unemployed?

Let modern dictatorship not serve as an alibi for our conscience. We have failed to fight *for* right, *for* justice, *for* goodness; as a result we must fight *against* wrong, *against* injustice, *against* evil. We have failed to offer sacrifices on the altar of peace; thus we offered sacrifices on the altar of war. A tale is told of a band of inexperienced mountain climbers. Without guides, they struck recklessly into the wilderness. Suddenly a rocky ledge gave way beneath their feet and they tumbled headlong into a dismal pit. In the darkness of the pit they recovered from their shock only to find themselves set upon by a swarm of angry snakes. For each snake the desperate men slew, ten more seemed to lash out in its place. Strangely enough, one man seemed to stand aside from the fight. When indignant voices of his struggling companions reproached him for not fighting, he called back: "If we remain here, we shall be dead before the snakes. I am searching for a way of escape from the pit for all of us."

Our world seems not unlike a pit of snakes. We did not sink into the pit in 1939, or even in 1933. We had descended into it generations ago, and the snakes have sent their venom into the bloodstream of humanity, gradually paralyzing us, numbing nerve after nerve, dulling our minds, darkening our vision. Good and evil, that were once as real as day and night, have become a blurred mist. In our everyday life we worshiped force, despised compassion, and obeyed no law but our unappeasable appetite. The vision of the sacred has all but died in the soul of man. And when greed, envy, and the reckless will to power came to maturity, the serpents cherished in the bosom of our civilization broke out of their dens to fall upon the helpless nations.

The outbreak of war was no surprise. It came as a long expected sequel to a spiritual disaster. Instilled with the gospel that truth is mere advantage and reverence weakness, people succumbed to the bigger advantage of a lie—"the Jew is our misfortune"—and to the power of arrogance— "tomorrow the whole world shall be ours," "the peoples' democracies must depend upon force." The roar of bombers over Rotterdam, Warsaw, London, was but the echo of thoughts bred for years by individual brains, and later applauded by entire nations. It was through our failure that people started to suspect that science is a device for exploitation; parliaments pulpits for hypocrisy, and religion a pretext for a bad conscience. In the tantalized souls of those who had faith in ideals, suspicion became a dogma and contempt the only solace. Mistaking the abortions of their conscience for intellectual heroism, many thinkers employ clever pens to scold and to scorn the reverence for life, the awe for truth, the loyalty to justice. Man, about to hang himself, discovers it is easier to hang others.

The conscience of the world was destroyed by those who were wont to blame others rather than themselves. Let us remember. We revered the instincts but distrusted the prophets. We labored to perfect engines and let our inner life go to wreck. We ridiculed supersitition until we lost our ability to believe. We have helped to extinguish the light our fathers had kindled. We have bartered holiness for convenience, loyalty for success, love for power, wisdom for information, tradition for fashion.

We cannot dwell at ease under the sun of our civilization as our ancestors thought we could. What was in the minds of our martyred brothers in their last hours? They died with disdain and scorn for a civilization in which the killing of civilians could become a carnival of fun, for a civilization which gave us mastery over the forces of nature but lost control over the forces of our self.

Tanks and planes cannot redeem humanity, nor the discovery of guilt by association nor suspicion. A man with a gun is like a beast without a gun. The killing of snakes will save us for the moment but not forever. The war has outlasted the victory of arms as we failed to conquer the infamy of the soul: the indifference to crime, when committed against others. For evil is indivisible. It is the same in thought and in speech, in private and in social life. The greatest task of our time is to take the souls of men out of the pit. The world has experienced that God is involved. Let us forever remember that the sense for the sacred is as vital to us as the light of the sun. There can be no nature without spirit, no world without the Torah, no brotherhood without a father, no humanity without attachment to God.

God will return to us when we shall be willing to let Him in—into our banks and factories, into our Congress and clubs, into our courts and investigating committees, into our homes and theaters. For God is everywhere or nowhere, the Father of all men or no man, concerned about everything or nothing. Only in His presence shall we learn that the glory of man is not in his will to power, but in his power of compassion. Man reflects either the image of His presence or that of a beast.

Soldiers in the horror of battle offer solemn testimony that life is not a hunt for pleasure, but an engagement for service; that there are things more valuable than life; that the world is not a vacuum. Either we make it an altar for God or it is invaded by demons. There can be no neutrality. Either we are ministers of the sacred or slaves of evil. Let the blasphemy of our time not become an eternal scandal. Let future generations not loathe us for having failed to preserve what prophets and saints, martyrs and scholars have created in thousands of years. The apostles of force have shown that they are great in evil. Let us reveal that we can be as great in goodness. We will survive if we shall be as fine and sacrificial in our homes and offices, in our Congress and clubs, as our soldiers are on the fields of battle.

There is a divine dream which the prophets and rabbis have cherished and which fills our prayers, and permeates the acts of true piety. It is the dream of a world, rid of evil by the grace of God as well as by the efforts of man, by his dedication to the task of establishing the kingship of God in the world. God is waiting for us to redeem the world. We should not spend our life hunting for trivial satisfactions while God is waiting constantly and keenly for our effort and devotion.

The Almighty has not created the universe that we may have opportunities to satisfy our greed, envy, and ambition. We have not survived that we may waste our years in vulgar vanities. The martyrdom of millions demands that we consecrate ourselves to the fulfillment of God's dream of salvation. Israel did not accept the Torah of their own free will. When Israel approached Sinai, God lifted up the mountain and held it over their heads, saying: "Either you accept the Torah or be crushed beneath the mountain."

The mountain of history is over our heads again. Shall we renew the covenant with God?

VIII

THIS SACRED EARTH:
RELIGION AND ENVIRONMENTALISM

The natural world is the larger sacred community to which we belong. To be alienated from this community is to become destitute in all that makes us human.

—Thomas Berry

Sacred places are the foundation of all other beliefs and practices because they represent the presence of the sacred in our lives. They properly inform us that we are not larger than nature and that we have responsibilities to the rest of the natural world that transcend our own personal desires and wishes.

—Vine DeLoria, "Sacred Places and Moral Responsibility"

In the sphere of environmental concern, religious social activism reaches, I believe, its most important and complete fulfillment. Sparked by an initially secular movement, the world's dominant religions—as well as many people who identify with the "spiritual" rather than with established faiths—have come to see that the environmental crisis involves much more than assaults on human health, leisure, or convenience. Rather, humanity's war on nature is at the same time a deep affront to one of the essentially divine aspects of existence. Whether nature is seen as God's creation or as something holy in its own right, religious environmentalists now teach that destroying it is, quite simply, a sin. The addition of religious language to our ecological concern expresses, many feel, the gravity of our situation, and deepens our sense that there is something fundamentally wrong with the basic structures of our civilization.

For this reason religious environmentalism, while it may begin with new forms of theology (or the recovery of ecological concern found in earlier traditions) is necessarily driven to embrace and utilize many of the insights of secular political theory. If we ask, for instance, why the juggernaut of industrial development is so hard to stop, it is necessary to engage with Marxist accounts of the dynamics of capitalist development. If we ask why African American communities in the United States or indigenous peoples worldwide bear a disproportionate share of the burdens of toxic waste or disastrous mineral extraction, we will have to examine the social role of racism. If we want to understand the cavalier, dismissive, and exploitative attitudes toward nature that are essential to the current crisis, we will have to study ecofeminism's analysis of the connections between patriarchy's attitudes toward women and its attitudes toward nature.

In short, in religious environmentalism we have a convergence of the spiritual and the political to such an extent that it may in some cases be hard to tell them apart.

My essay develops in detail the claims just made, and provides an overview of the characteristics and importance of religious environmentalism. The essays by Winona LaDuke and Stan McKay are prompted by the experience, and draw on the wisdom, of indigenous traditions. These traditions have never lost touch with the divinity of the earth, and the communities that hold them are most at risk when industrial civilization treats nature purely as resources to meet our ever-expanding wants. Eric Katz, Stephanie Kaza, Sallie McFague, Thomas Berry, Andrew Linzey, and Nawal H. Ammar face a different task. Whatever the original intent of most of the world's dominant religions, in actual practice they have been blind to the consequences of unrestrained industrial development and ecological devastation. Consequently, these traditions now face tasks of reconstruction and retrieval. Neglected resources need to be recovered, and theology, ritual, and social involvement must engage with a new, and deeply troubling, reality.

Ivone Gebara, Vandana Shiva, and Jonna Higgins-Freese and Jeff Tomhave examine different concrete contexts of religious environmentalism: the role of feminism in Latin American environmentalism, the interconnections between women's social position and the struggle to save the forest in India, and the particular position of Native Americans in environmental thought.

Finally, a series of institutional statements gives a tiny sampling of the enormous range of organizational commitment and public action. A great deal is happening in the world of religious environmentalism. Whether it will be enough, and soon enough, only God knows.

"Saving the World: Religion and Politics in the Environmental Movement"

꩜

Roger S. Gottlieb

In this essay I argue that religious environmentalism is the fulfillment of religion's attempt to come to grips with modernity and that environmentalism is, by the nature of its concerns, driven toward a somewhat spiritual attitude toward politics.

꩜

Christians are joining together to save the world's rainforests in Jesus' name.

—Target Earth[1]

Bishops Say Dealing with Global Warming a Moral Imperative

—Boston Globe, June 16, 2001

We must learn to . . . recognize the interconnectedness of all living creatures, and to respect the value of each thread in the vast web of life. This is a spiritual perspective, and it is the foundation of all Green politics.

—Petra Kelly, *Thinking Green*[2]

Two short stories:

March 25, 2000. Over 1,000 people crowded the halls of the urban campus of Boston's Northeastern University. This was, in terms reminiscent of the 1960s, a teach-in. It was called Biodevastation—in ironic parody of the simultaneous Boston gathering of high-tech entrepreneurs, scientists, and policy wonks of the genetic engineering industry. Public demonstrations and civil disobedience actions were planned for the next day. Calls would be made for an end to the commercialization of genetically engineered products, corporate control over food and health, and ownership of forms of life (patenting of seeds, and so on); and for tighter public regulations of potentially dangerous biotechnologies.[3]

As one of the day's many workshops, I had been asked to give a talk about the role of spirituality in environmental politics. Because the crowd seemed heavily political, I wasn't sure anyone would show up. Much to my gratified surprise, the medium-size lecture hall held a standing-room-only crowd, with bearded activists, student leaders, and passionate organizers sprawled on the floor and spilling out into the hallway. Although I would have liked to believe it was my vast fame that had brought folks to hear me, I was well aware that most of them didn't know me from Adam, but were drawn by the topic. Like me, they intuited that resistance to the interconnected issues of global environmental crisis, genetic engineering of organisms, and centralized international power of institutions like the World Bank and the International Monetary Fund necessitate a new spiritual and political vision. Concern for humanity's place in the cosmos will have to join resistance to the inequalities of race and class; a moral commitment to future generations of human beings will be matched by care for other species; a deep distrust in the wisdom of markets will be balanced by an emerging faith in ordinary people's knowledge of their own lands and lives.

March 1998. In my own community of Jamaica Plain, a racially and economically mixed section of Southwest Boston, people are banding together to protect our treasured Jamaica Pond: an actual lake—one and one-half miles around—within the city limits! The pond is bordered by a thin belt of trees and graced by seagulls, Canada geese, ducks, mysterious looking cormorants, snapping turtles, and imported swans. Its marvelously clear water attracts joggers, baby carriages, dog walkers, drummers on hot summer nights, old Chinese ladies doing Tai Chi, and couples of various sexual persuasions dreamily holding hands. On brilliant weekends in July or sweltering August afternoons, city-owned rowboats and sailboats allow the city dwellers to feel like they've gone away to their country estates.

When you stand at the little boathouse where popsicles and popcorn are sold, you can look across the water and see the sun set over wooded hills. These hills, which border the park but are not actually part of it, had been sold to a builder seeking to replace the old trees with luxury condos—so that proud owners can enjoy the vista of the pond while the rest of us can view the sun setting over expensive apartments. On the coldest night of the winter of 1998, 350 people jammed a local church to express their disagreement. After a variety of audience members spoke their piece, I approached the mike and said, quite gently, that I was going to use a word rarely heard in political circles but that I hoped people would understand. "The pond," I declared quietly, "is sacred space."

Although this was not a particularly religious crowd, a stunned silence soon gave way to a rising murmur of agreement that soon swept the room and culminated in sustained applause. In thirty years of university teaching and of public speaking in a wide variety of contexts, I had never sensed such an immediate, visceral, and heartfelt response. I had voiced my truth, and it seemed to serve virtually everyone in the room.

These two stories illustrate the theme of this chapter, that in the environmental movement there is a dramatic confirmation of the major ideas of this book. World-making politics and emancipatory religion have joined in environmental politics and ecological spirituality. Theology has been transformed by political awareness and action. And political ideology has transcended the constraints of individual rights and group self-interest. If the civil rights struggle shows religion transforming the world of politics and feminist theology demonstrates the political transformation of religion, then the environmental movement reveals the two working together in critically important ways, at times virtually fusing to form a historically unprecedented phenomenon.

Modern environmentalism has challenged and changed religion throughout the world. Awakened by environmental activists, religious institutions have been moved by the seriousness of pollution, climate change, endangered species issues, resource depletion, and overpopulation. Religious leaders, theologians, and local clergy have signed on to the recognition that the earth as a whole is in an unprecedented predicament. Even if this response is not uniform and absolute, it is still extremely widespread.

Using language that would not be out of place in a Greenpeace broadside, Rabbi Arthur Hertzberg, vice president of the World Jewish Congress, has warned: "Now when the whole world is in peril, when the environment is in danger of being poisoned, and various species, both plant and animal, are becoming extinct, it is our Jewish responsibility to put the defense of the whole of nature at the very center of our concern."[4] In 1990, Pope John Paul II spoke of the worldwide threat caused by "*a lack of due respect for nature . . .* the plundering of natural resources and . . . the widespread destruction of the environment."[5] The Dalai Lama, in his foreword to the first major anthology of writings on Buddhism and ecology, wrote: "The Earth, our Mother, is telling us to behave. All around, signs of nature's limitations abound. Moreover, the environmental crisis currently underway involves all of humanity, making national boundaries of secondary importance."[6]

Yet claims that we are in ecological hot water do not, in themselves, make for a particularly religious contribution to environmentalism. Part of what is so important about that contribution is that it brings to the context a new language, expressing a distinct point of view. For instance, Bartholomew I, ecumenical patriarch of the Eastern Orthodox Church's more than 100 million members, wrote in 1997:

> To commit a crime against the natural world is a sin. For humans to cause species to become extinct and to destroy the biological diversity of God's creation . . . to degrade the integrity of Earth by causing changes in its climate, by stripping the Earth of its natural forests . . . to contaminate the Earth's waters, its land, its air, and its life, with poisonous substances: these are sins.[7]

Conversely, as a Protestant theologian and environmental activist puts it: "The specter of ecocide raises the risk of deicide: to wreak environmental havoc on the earth is to run the risk that we will do irreparable, even fatal harm to the mystery we call God."[8]

A religious perspective applied to the earth, to a "nature" that because of human action has become the "environment," offers insights and prompts emotions that a purely secular story cannot. Spiritual language offers the environmental movement a means to express its passion, hope, and love, regardless of whether activists accept the explicit details of one theology or another. Instead of a large rock with vegetation growing on it, the world becomes "creation" or "the goddess." We experience the world as "holy"—and mean we believe in a God who created it, or that it is of "ultimate concern," or simply that it is heartbreakingly beautiful and infinitely worth cherishing and preserving. Commonplace processes—the coevolution of a rainforest plant with its pollinating insect partners, how wetlands clean water, the murmur of whale songs—become "daily miracles."

When religion engages in environmental concerns, the customary boundaries of "religious issues" in political life are decisively broken. Asserting that environmental degradation is not only a health danger, an economic catastrophe, or an aesthetic blight but also *sacrilegious, sinful*, and an *offense against God* catapults religions directly into questions of political power, social policy, and the overall direction of secular society. Religious organizations now take it as given that their voices deserve to be heard on issues such as energy, economic development, population, transportation, industrial production, and agriculture. These topics are, to put it mildly, a far cry from the usual public religious concern with abortion, school prayer, tax exemptions for churches, Holocaust memorials, national Christmas trees, or even pornography in the media.

For example, in March 2001, six senior Christian and Jewish religious leaders wrote to President George W. Bush asking for a meeting with him about his environmental policy, especially around issues of climate change. In a fascinating combination of scriptural references, quotes from the Environmental Protection Agency (EPA), and appeals to scientific expertise, representatives of conservative Judaism (the chancellor of its major rabbinical school), the head of the National Council of the Churches of Christ, and senior officers of the Presbyterian Church, the United Methodist Church, the Disciples of Christ, and the African Methodist Episcopal Church sought to use religious authority to influence national politics.

In another instance, we find that the World Council of Churches (WCC), an international Christian umbrella organization representing 340 churches in 122 countries, has tied its environmental concerns to a deep suspicion of globalization. In doing so, it has challenged the globe's dominant institutions, from the International Monetary Fund and the World Bank to corporations whose budgets are larger than most countries. Globalization is intimately linked to environmentalism because the new global institutions consistently preempt local efforts to control pollution or create sustainable economies. Their tribunals have ruled against clean air legislation in the United States, Canadian restrictions on toxic gasoline additives, attempts to protect marine mammals, European rejection of hormone-injected beef, and efforts to support indigenous, organic farmers rather than Chiquita bananas.[9]

> Recent developments have reinforced our perception that issues of justice, peace and creation need to be seen together. One such development is globalization. Globalization impacts not only national and regional economies, causing ever-greater social and economic injustice. It also destroys relationships between individuals, groups, communities, nations, causing conflicts, wars and violence. And it affects the environment of our whole inhabited earth.[10]

The secular left, too, has begun to realize that religious organizations are part of the environmental movement. In the May 2001 issue of *The Nation*, environmentalist David Helvarg has listed actions by the National Council of Churches, the Evangelical Environmental Network, and the Jewish Council of Public Affairs in an article titled, "Bush Unites the Enviros."[11] Over the past several years, all of the major environmental magazines—including *Sierra, Audubon, Amicus Journal*, and *E Magazine*—have run features on the rise of religious environmentalism.[12] They have recognized that from the National Religious Partnership for the Environment, with constituent groups numbering 100 million Americans, to the New England Friends's recent collective commitment to "speak truth to power" in protecting human healths and the environment, self-defined religious groups are now major players on the environmental stage.

On the religious side, the environmental crisis is seen by some thinkers as the critical test of their faith's contemporary relevance. As Catholic priest and cultural historian Thomas Berry, whose own attempt to offer a new understanding of humanity's place in the cosmos has been enormously influential, says: "The future of the Catholic church in America, in my view, will depend above all on its capacity to assume a religious responsibility for the fate of the earth."[13] Bearing this out, the website of the Lutheran Church offers study material on "health and the environment." One situation offered for reflection asks what a "Christian response" would be to a family whose children are suffering from environmentally caused asthma and who cannot move because no one will buy their house, which is surrounded by polluting industries.[14] For Lutherans, in other words, the interlocking contexts of health, the economy, and pollution are now part of their ministry—as much as sexual ethics or the discipline of prayer.

These few instances of the extremely numerous meetings between religion and environmentalism further exemplify modern religion's political transformation. Historically, the dominant attitudes of religious leaders toward modern industrialism—that is, to the immediate source of the environmental crisis—was positive. Once it was clear that capitalism and democracy were here to stay, most churches saw increases in scientific knowledge and technical expertise as promising a better life. Provided that industrial workers achieved a reasonable standard of living, technology meant progress. Challenges to the modern economy came from poets like Blake and Wordsworth, anti-Communist Western Marxists like Max Horkheimer and Herbert Marcuse, philosophers like Martin Heidegger, and imaginative nature lovers like Thoreau and John Muir. As in the case of feminism, it was only after a political movement brought global ecological crisis to the fore of public discussion that religion jumped on board.[15] Yet jump on board it did, and with an energy and acumen that has, so far, outpaced corporations, organized labor, the academic community, and such professionals as doctors or lawyers.

Besides an acknowledgment of the severity of the crisis, new theologies have been devised in which the earth, or nature, or our fellow creatures are recognized as carrying a divine and sacred meaning. Such theologies are in stark contrast to what has been the dominant position of world religions, especially those of the West. Despite the presence of occasional dissenting voices, Western religions long stressed the gap between humans and the rest of creation, espousing ethical systems in which concern for the nonhuman was peripheral at best. Just as feminism has required a new valuation of women, so the ecological crisis has led to a new—or at least a revised—sense of our proper relationship to nature.

These new theologies sometimes originate in attempts to recover the few nature-respecting elements that can be found in tradition. Thus, Lynn White, whose 1967 essay criticizing the "anthropocentrism" (human-centeredness) of Western religions helped initiate a dialogue on the subject that continues to this day, did not suggest a total rejection of Christianity. Rather, he proposed St. Francis's love of animals and the whole of physical creation as an alternative to the reigning Christian attitudes.[16] Similarly, essayist and farmer Wendell Berry challenged dominant interpretations of the biblical passage often cited as divine justification for human dominion, God's command to Adam: "Go forth, subdue the earth, and master it" (Genesis 1:28). By stressing the importance of other passages of the Torah, especially Deuteronomy 8:10 ("Thou shalt bless the lord thy God for the good land which He has given you"), Berry teaches that biblical ethics requires us to live "knowingly, lovingly, skillfully, reverently" rather than "ignorantly, greedily, clumsily, destructively." In the first case, our use of Creation will be a "sacrament," in the latter, a "desecration."[17] Jewish writers have recovered biblical and Talmudic doctrines stressing the sinfulness of squandering resources (*bal tashchit* ["do not waste"]), holidays celebrating the birthday of the trees, and biblical restrictions on the exploitation of animals (if your ox is threshing your grain, you can't muzzle him, even if he ends up eating some of it!). These traditions are then applied to a host of contemporary ecological issues, such as recycling, carpooling, the disposal of toxics, the waste of food, factory farming, and the protection of old-growth forests.[18]

Buddhist teacher Thich Nhat Hanh has adapted the mindfulness practice of Buddhist *gathas* (short prayers or poems used to focus attention) to include ecological awareness. For instance, while planting trees, one may recite: "I entrust myself to Buddha; / Buddha entrusts himself to me. / I entrust myself to Earth; / Earth entrust herself to me."[19] The National Council of Churches offers the following prayer to be included in First Sunday after Easter as part of a service called "Witnessing to the Resurrection: Caring for God's Creation":

> We pursue profits and pleasures that harm the land and pollute the waters.
>   We have squandered the earth's gifts on technologies of destruction.
>   The land mourns, and all who live in it languish; together with the wild animals and the birds of the air, even the fish of the sea are perishing.[20]

Or in the words of the general secretary of the United Methodist Church: "Our biblical tradition affirms that God calls people of faith to defend and protect all of God's creation, both human and non-human."[21]

Feminist versions of Christianity and Judaism may, in good conscience, focus their efforts on creating inclusive God language, getting women into positions of power in religious organizations, and criticizing the sexism of past doctrine. By contrast, the new theologies of nature necessarily involve their adherents in political life. Once religions assert that "ecology and justice, stewardship of creation and redemption are interdependent"[22] or that "[w]here human life and health are at stake, economic gain must not take precedence,"[23] they are—like it or not—headed for a confrontation with the dominant powers of economics and politics.

In this confrontation, religious discourse has and will continue to play a significant role. If this is not a universal religious response, it is an extremely widespread one. As one journalist puts it: "More and more it appears religion and ecology are walking hand-in-hand. The sermon titles are the Kyoto treaty on global warming and endangered species protection."[24] For example, there is the 1997–1999 campaign of the "Redwood Rabbis," a group of rabbis and lay Jewish environmental activists who struggled to protect an ancient redwood grove in Northern California. Working with the local Sierra Club, the group invoked biblical principles and contemporary ecological values to try to influence Charles Hurwitz, a visible leader of the Houston Jewish community and head of the corporation that was clear-cutting the site. The Redwood Rabbis received backing from the Coalition on the Environment and Jewish Life—which is itself supported by mainstream Jewish groups such as Hillel, Hadassa, and B'nai Brith—and engaged in civil disobedience by planting redwood seedlings in defiance of Hurwitz's orders.[25]

Buddhists in both the United States and Japan have actively resisted the storage and transportation of dangerous nuclear material, while in Germany, Buddhists have challenged both the ethics and the environmental consequences of factory farming.[26] Christian groups have formed coalitions to reduce global warming, have held religious services to celebrate lakes, and have authorized study groups to reduce the environmental impact of church buildings. National and international organizations have formed to radically transform theological education to take account of the environmental crisis.[27]

In these and thousands more examples, it is clear that to be ethical in relation to environmental issues is also to be political. The economy, the government, the military, health care, transportation, and just about everything else are called into question. Believers may still pray for a pure heart and train their awareness mindfully, but environmental problems simply cannot be solved though individual action. In just this way, environmental issues are a direct confirmation of the claims I made in chapters 1 and 3 about how the modern world politicizes ethics. Through the work we do and the taxes we pay, what we buy and what we drive, our personal moral lives have a global meaning. When any serious religious group talks about the environment, it necessarily expresses support for certain concrete political policies: for instance, the need to monitor and restrict market forces, limit the prerogatives of corporations, make the government responsive to the interests of ecosystems and the socially powerless, limit military expenditures, and direct technology toward sustainability.

As they confront the environmental crisis, many religious groups throughout the world advocate not only the values of "ecotheology" but the pursuit of "ecojustice," i.e., the seamless blending of concern for earth's creation and human beings, the biotically marginalized and the socially powerless, endangered species and endangered human communities. This blending includes issues of class, race, gender, and indigenous rights, alongside more familiar concern with "nature." It requires—and is achieving—a comprehensive understanding of political life that joins religious visionaries with the most sophisticated and principled of secular political movements.

Consider the comprehensive notions of environmental racism and environmental justice, phrases that refer to the fact that racial minorities and the poor in the United States, just like indigenous peoples worldwide, are exposed to a great deal more pollution than are the racially and economically dominant groups. Lacking social power, their lives are held as less valuable; the environmental crisis is written on—and in—their bodies.[28] During the last thirty years, a comprehensive concern with environmental justice developed with the constant input of black religious social activists.[29] The historic 1987 report *Toxic Wastes and Race*, the first comprehensive account of environmental racism, was researched and written by the commission for racial justice of the United Church of Christ.[30] This report detailed the fundamental racial and class inequality in the siting and cleanup of hazardous wastes in the United States. Its lead investigator, Reverend Benjamin Chavis, was instrumental in connecting the civil rights, religious, and environmental communities of the South. Four years later, in 1991, the very first principle of the historic National People of Color Environmental Leadership Summit proclaimed that "environmental justice affirms the sacredness of mother Earth, ecological unity and the interdependence of all species, and the right to be free from ecological destruction."[31] A few years later, President Clinton ordered government agencies to take environmental justice issues into account in their programs.

Alongside racial and class issues, an ecojustice perspective focuses on the ways in which Western thought has historically equated women and nature and devalued both. The initial justification for this dual subordination was found in the claim that both lacked the holiness or closeness to God of men. Later, it was men's (self-proclaimed) rationality that was thought to justify masculine social privileges. In terms of concrete social policy, contemporary Western schemes of economic development for poor countries often have disastrous effects on Third World women, whose lives and livelihood are tied to their immediate surroundings. For example, in poorer countries men plant cash crops, but women plant subsistence crops. When export agriculture promoting a single agricultural commodity takes over, women in the local community are hurt more than men. Awareness of the combination of the cultural devaluation of women with their economic subordination helps create an "ecofeminism" that has powerful religious and political implications.[32]

The religious presence in environmental politics, like a good deal of the entire environmental movement, not only breaks barriers between religion and politics, theology, and social activism but also helps develop a world-making *political* agenda that may avoid being limited to one or another particular social group. Religions have a powerful contribution to make here. Insofar as they have a mandate, it is, after all, from God: a God who is not tied, one hopes, to the valid but inevitably partial concerns of one political group or another. Of course, in the past much of traditional religion was rabidly sectarian, racist, colonialist, or just downright nasty. But religions that have been deeply affected by the liberal and radical politics of the last two centuries have moved beyond those moral failings, or at least are trying to.

Ecojustice is, thus, a comprehensive political and spiritual vision. In the words of the Eco-justice Ministries, a Denver-based Protestant activist organization, part of that vision involves "Confronting Power Relationships":

> Faithful and ethical living is not confined to personal choices. Moses and the prophets all spoke to, and about, the power structures of their communities. Jesus and Paul dealt with the realities of political power. An eco-justice perspective recognizes that the power relationships of each situation must be analyzed and addressed. In our globalized economy, it is absurd to suggest that personal choices alone can address the crises we face. Various forms of power—economic, political, military, intellectual and personal—must be taken into account in the ways that we understand the world and live within it.
>
> Eco-justice is not one "issue" out of the many from which congregations can pick and choose: hunger, housing, guns, abortion, militarism, morality, globalization, families, wilder-ness, affirmative action, civil rights, economic justice, education, immigration, hunger, health care—and the list goes on and on. Rather, eco-justice is a theological perspective that shapes the way that we approach each of these issues.[33]

The religious participation in the environmental justice movement is not simply a matter of pious statements. There are many places where religious organizations play an active role in the movement itself. For instance, The White Violet Center for Eco-Justice of Indiana is staffed by Catholics and focuses on a range of justice and environmental issues, including wetlands preservation, organic agriculture, and preservation of endangered bird species. It "exists to foster a way of living that recognizes the interdependence of all creation" and "seeks to create systems that support justice and sustainability, locally and globally."[34]

The Social Action Organization of Queensland, Australia, is also centered in the Catholic Church. It has an annual budget of $A160,000 and employs one full-time coordinator and four part-time employees. One of its main areas is "ecojustice," in the pursuit of which it prepared a detailed and technically sophisticated account of the human and environmental affects of a prospective development of the Brisbane harbor. It also encourages readers to boycott Exxon, and its website provides links to both church statements on environmental issues and secular political groups like Greenpeace.[35]

When in 2001 a Boston coalition was formed to confront environmental justice issues in the local distribution of toxic materials, the Greater Boston Coalition on the Environment and Jewish Life played a critical role.[36] When the first resistance to dumping of PCBs in predomi-nantly poor and black Warren County, North Carolina, got underway in 1982, it was the black religious community that took the lead. Worldwide, indigenous peoples resist environmentally destructive "development" of their land in part because they have religious bonds to the land that are essential to their culture and community.[37]

These examples are a tiny fraction of the whole picture. But the essential point is clear. It is simply no longer true of religions, as political radicals have been claiming for nearly two centuries: "They concentrate on the individual and not social institutions; they are unwilling to envision radical social changes; they cannot see the links among different moral and political concerns; they seek changes in attitudes or values rather than in basic social institutions; they are unwilling to learn from the insights of world-making political theory." Such criticisms may well continue to apply to some groups, but they have become completely inapplicable to others. The great divide between religion and progressive politics, weakened by Protestant abolitionism, the social teachings of the Catholic Church, and the social gospel of the late nineteenth century, cracked by Gandhi and King and the religious presence in the peace and antiapartheid movements, has in the global environment movement finally been decisively overcome.

If religions have to some extent turned Green, Green politics are in some important ways religious. In the contemporary environmental movement, even those groups totally unconnected to religiously identified organizations are often practicing a new kind of politics, one in which a religious or spiritual sensibility is present. It is this simultaneous transformation of both religion and political activism that helps make environmental politics dramatically new and historically important.

The politics I have in mind here include but are not limited to government programs and laws. Politics, as political scientist Paul Wapner says, also "takes place in the home, office, and marketplace."[38] At one end of the spectrum of activities and concerns that make up Green politics, we find direct actions aimed at stopping some particular instance of "development" or some concrete industrial practice. When the women of India's Chipka movement physically encircle the trees of their beloved forest (which provides herbs, fodder for animals, and firewood) to prevent them from being chopped down, when Greenpeace plugs the outflow pipe of a chemical factory, when thousands protest "free trade" agreements that would cripple communities' rights to limit ecological degradation, environmental politics means putting your body on the line to protect both other species and human beings. At the other end of the spectrum, we find attempts to influence world culture through teaching, writing, films, Internet sites, poetry, and art. In between these two poles are a host of governmental and nongovernmental policies, institutions, and activities: from government regulation of pesticide use to the creation of wildlife refuges, from lobbying to protect wetlands to resisting environmental racism, from researching the duplicity of the chemical industry to organizing neighbors to clean up a local river. In this light, nongovernmental organizations like transnational environmental groups "contribute to addressing global environmental problems by heightening world-wide concern for the environment. They persuade vast numbers of people to care about and take actions to protect the earth's ecosystems."[39]

What gives this wide spectrum of Green politics a religious or spiritual dimension? Well, in some cases this dimension will not be present. If we seek to preserve a forest so that we can hunt big game in it (one of the original motivations for wildlife preservation efforts)[40] or if our sole concern with pesticides is their effect on human health, then our approach to environmental issues is purely "instrumental." It is, we might say, simply a continuation of the "anthropocentric" attitudes that have marked Western culture for at least 3,000 years, attitudes resting on the belief that only human beings are morally valuable. In this form, caring for a river or an endangered species is little different from concern over auto safety or tennis elbow—valuable and important, to be sure, but not historically new or spiritually significant.

If however, we are at least partly motivated by "ecocentric" or biocentric values, if there is an element of "deep ecology" in our passion, if we see nature as a mother, a lover, or a partner, then the situation is different[41]—for then we are expressing a distinct vision of the value of our surroundings and a new and powerful sense of the meaning of human identity itself.[42] When environmental politics are motivated by a concern for life as a whole or ecosystems above and beyond the human, I believe, they are profoundly spiritual and, in a deep and general sense, *religious*.

Whether known as deep ecology, ecofeminism, bioregionalism, the land ethic, or simply the special place that some beach, forest, or mountain has in our hearts, this sensibility involves a passionate communion with the earth. What is "deep" about this perspective is the experience—and the conviction—that our surroundings are essential to who we are. And this is not just because they are useful, but because we are tied to them by invisible threads of inspiration, memory, esthetic delight, emotional connection, and simple wonder. Sky and earth, bird and fish, each leaf on each tree—without them, we could not be ourselves. As one of the architects of modern environmental politics, David Brower, wrote: "To me, God and Nature are synonymous."[43] Poisoning nature thus not only leads to the concrete suffering of soaring cancer rates and our children's asthma but creates the emotional and spiritual crisis comparable to what would happen if our families were murdered, our cathedrals bombed, or our holy books burned.

In contrast to the precisely formulated content of ecotheology, with its biblical references, new models of God, and creative applications of traditional concepts to environmental issues, some of the new environmental spirituality is diffuse and at times hard to capture. As Christopher Childs, longtime Greenpeace activist and spokesperson says, "[T]here is broad acceptance among Greenpeace staff that the work is quintessentially spiritual, though definitions of what is meant by the term vary."[44]

When this sensibility enters environmental politics, it takes a variety of forms. One element is the simple faith in the political power of a moral statement. For instance, the Quaker-inspired practice of "bearing witness" is "central to Greenpeace's well-publicized actions in the face of pollution or mammal killing."[45] The goal is to reveal the damaging actions to the world and to help encourage an alternative perception of reality that might lead to massive resistance or at least a shift in public sentiment. Similar elements can be found in Buddhist and feminist resistance to the production and transport of radioactive materials. In these settings ecoactivism calls on a quasi-religious sense of the ultimate imperative of moral action, a sense that hopes for victory but does not depend on it. As I indicated in chapter 4, it is one of religion's gifts to assign to moral acts an abiding importance in and of themselves, an importance that can keep us going even when (as almost always seems the case in environmental politics) we have no certainty of getting the results we seek.

This spiritual vision of environmental politics also provides a crucial alternative to the destructive values of the global marketplace, values that privilege economic growth, rising exports, and individual autonomy above all else. The "religion" of modernity demands control over nature and a model of development that turns every meadow and village into the same old mall. Nature is thought of as a thing, an element to be used. Selfhood is defined by consumption, and there is a widespread attempt to broadcast excessive styles of consumption throughout the world.

Sulak Sivaraksa, Buddhist environmental activist from Thailand, writes that "Western consumerism is the dominant ethic in the world today. . . . The new 'spiritual advisors' are from Harvard Business School, Fletcher School of Law and Diplomacy, and London School of Economics. . . . The department stores have become our shrines, and they are constantly filled with people. For the young people, these stores have replaced the Buddhist temples."[46] The drive toward globalization, says a Third World Christian theologian, is often seen as a sort of new religion: "it has its God: profit and money. It has it high priests: GATT [General Agreement on Tariffs and Trade], WTO [World Trade Organization], IMF-WB. It has its doctrines and dogmas: import liberalization, deregulation. . . . It has its temples: the super megamalls. It has its victims on the altar of sacrifice: the majority of the world—the excluded and marginalized poor."[47]

Referring to the conflict between native peoples and economic development over the proposed building of a massive, ecosystem-destroying and native-people-uprooting hydroelectric dam in James Bay, Ontario, David Kinsley argues:

> If hunting animals is a sacred occupation among the Mistassini Cree, building dams to harness power for electricity is equally sacred for many members of modern industrial society...the conflict between the Cree and [Ontario political leader] Bourassa, then, is not so much a conflict between a religious view and a secular view as it is a conflict between two contrasting visions of the nature of human beings and human destiny, that is, two conflicting myths about the place of human beings in the natural order, two contrasting ecological visions.[48]

Charlene Spretnak describes the difference between these two visions: "Modern culture... is based on mechanistic analysis and control of human systems as well as Nature... nationalistic chauvinism, sterile secularism, and monoculture shaped by mass media.... Green values, by contrast, seek a path of 'ecological wisdom' and attempt to integrate freedom *and* tradition, the individual *and* the community, science *and* Nature, men *and* women."[49] To accomplish that goal, said leader of the German Green Party Petra Kelly, "We must learn to...recognize the interconnectedness of all living creatures, and to respect the value of each thread in the vast web of life. This is a spiritual perspective, and it is the foundation of all Green politics."[50] Or as Earth First! activist Mark Davis said, in explaining why he broke the law in trying to prevent the further expansion of a ski resort into mountains revered by the Hopi and Navajo, "[T]he bottom line is that those mountains are sacred, and that what has occurred there, despite our feeble efforts, is a terrible spiritual mistake."[51]

In fact, spiritual values in general and the value(s) of nature in particular give us a way out of the ecocidal cul-de-sac of the endless mall. They help us to develop an alternative sense of self that acknowledges dependence, mutuality, and happiness *without* requiring endless "development," soulless gadgetry, and the elimination of other life forms. This alternative allows the withdrawal of psychic energy from a cultural and economic system that threatens the earth and people alike. In the same vein, a spiritual relationship with the natural world allows us to orient political struggle in a direction not tied (or at least less tied) by psychic addiction to the very social system that destroys us. Greens have, some observers believe, "moved beyond materialist values while at the same time embracing some preindustrial values derived from indigenous non-European cultures. These value shifts have been tied to specific issues that are crucial for the Greens but often ignored by the Democratic Left."[52] The interface of spiritual and Green values has helped create the emerging discipline of "ecopsychology," which is oriented to understanding the psychic costs of our alienation from the rest of the earth, and the psychologically and spiritually healing experiences that come from lessening that alienation.[53]

Sociologist Manuel Castells describes a deep Green perspective as one in which:

> The holistic notion of integration between humans and nature...does not refer to a naive worshipping of pristine natural landscapes, but to the fundamental consideration that the relevant unit of experience is not each individual, or for that matter, historically existing human communities. To merge ourselves with our cosmological self we need first to change the notion of time, to feel "glacial time" run through our lives, to sense the energy of stars flowing in our blood, and to assume the rivers of our thoughts endlessly merging in the boundless oceans of multiform living matter.[54]

Such a perspective, Castells believes, leads environmentalism to be in fundamental opposition to the dominant values of multinational corporate power, transnational economic institutions like the IMF and the World Bank, and placeless cultural and economic icons like MTV and Nike.

When Green values inform the best of Green politics, "we are a long way from the instrumentalist perspective that has dominated the industrial era, in both its capitalist and statist [i.e., socialist] versions. And we are in direct contradiction with the dissolution of meaning in the flows of faceless power that constitute the network society."[55]

It is environmentalism, more than any other political setting, that unites the "cultural creatives" described in chapter 2; the nonviolent spiritual resistance of the Civil Rights movement, feminist theology, and spirituality of chapter 6, and in fact the comprehensive notion that religion has something specific and precious to add to political life. In environmentalism, liberal support for individual rights and the socialist concern with economic rationality can meet each other and join forces with the non-Western emphasis on community and responsibility.

Environmentalists can be dramatically different from each other. They include those who long nostalgically for a hunter-gatherer lifestyle, those who support Aldo Leopold's call for "an individual responsibility for the health of the land,"[56] as well as hard-headed city planners eager to replace cars with bikes, integrate communities with an ecofriendly Internet, and design apartment complexes with organic rooftop gardens. Yet the comprehensive values referred to by Spretnak, Kelly, and Castells resonate throughout much of the movement. These include a distrust of uncontrolled economic growth and thoughtless technological innovation, in combination with the belief that both the market and technology should serve collective rather than narrowly human interests. There is a corresponding belief that has clear spiritual overtones: the idea that human life has other purposes than the acquisition of power and wealth. It is stressed, rather, that we live for the development of wisdom, peacefulness, harmonious coexistence with the earth, and the quiet (itself a radical demand in these deafening times) enjoyment of life. Journalist Mark Dowie suggests that despite the enormous diversity of the environmental movement, a number of common principles can be found. Along with familiar political goals, these include an ethical and spiritual redefinition of human beings as part of nature and not its master or the only part that really matters.[57]

What applying these values would mean is often far from clear. Since the ecological crisis is a product of our entire civilization, broader in scope and more universally threatening than any other form of political injustice or collective irrationality, the transformation called for is correspondingly large. We might take as a hopeful example the enormous social success of Kerala, India's southernmost state, which has dramatically increased literacy and education, reduced infant mortality, raised life expectancy to nearly Western levels, improved women's social position, and cultivated a culture of intellectual and artistic engagement *without* high levels of industrialization or the raising of per capita income. We might consider Columbia's village of Gaviotas, where appropriate technology has led to a sustainable life in the midst of a formerly barren wasteland, sustainable crops help regenerate a rain forest, and children's swings power the water pumps.[58] We might notice how the citizens of Maine, who suffer each year through several weeks of highly annoying and virtually impossible-to-stop black flies, reject the use of potentially dangerous chemical pesticides, even if it will cost them tourist income. "If people can't live with the flies," some say, "they just shouldn't come here."[59]

We can see the new sensibility expressed in political campaigns aimed at inclusive goals of protecting endangered species, preserving the culture and ecosystems of indigenous peoples, and preventing industrial pollution. In one powerful example, international activity mobilized in response to the Narmada River Valley Project in India.[60] Called by critics the "world's greatest planned environmental disaster," the project envisaged 30 major, 135 medium, and 3,000 minor dams throughout Central India. If completed as planned, it would have displaced close to 400,000 people, destroyed wildlife habitat, and flooded some of the last remaining tropical forests in India. As early as 1977, local opposition formed when people realized that there was in fact no land available for the residents who were to be displaced—that they would simply join the tens of millions of other "refugees from development." During the next decade and a half, opposition grew and took a variety of forms: road blockades, hunger fasts, demonstrations at state capitals, and massive gatherings at sites that were to be flooded. A ring of international solidarity formed. Japanese environmentalists persuaded their government not to advance money to it, while American activists pressured the World Bank. The San Francisco–based International Rivers Project organized financial and technical aid. In 1992, facing reports that the entire project was marked by fraud and incompetence, legislators in Finland, Sweden, and the United States asked the World Bank not to lend any more money. In this heartening case, the more familiar dimension of human rights mixed with concern for other species; citizens of different countries and continents gave time, energy, and money to support those of another. A vital mix of personal and group self-interest, abstract political principle, and transpersonal celebration of the earth took shape.

Such principles can be found anywhere environmental struggles emerge. In an attempt to protect their village from predatory commercial fishing, a Brazilian group stresses values connected to Catholic liberation theology: "group solidarity, the participation and inclusion of all in . . . group decisions and . . . a suspicion if not of material wealth itself at least a distrust of what wealth acquisition requires in terms of . . . oppressive and unjust structures."[61] In resistance to ecologically damaging mining and timber practices in India, local groups have combined concern for health, local communities, and the sacred status of forests or rivers.[62]

In all these struggles, environmentalism is not simply interest-group politics applied to forests and toxic incinerators. Rather, it is informed by a comprehensive vision of human identity and of how that identity is interrelated with the universe as a whole. This vision deserves to be considered, in the broadest sense, religious.

When the United Church of Christ talks about racism in citing toxic waste sites, when religious organizations instruct the president of the United States on global warming, when Buddhist monks protest globalization, they show how contemporary religious and spiritual voices have adopted some of the conceptual tools of progressive political theory. Broad orientations toward human identity (we are kin to the rain forest); or to moral values (we have obligations to other species and to humans injured by our industrial practices); or to the meaning of life or the cosmos (our task is to be part of life, we are to be loving stewards to the earth) have always been part of religion. However, when the critique of dams, the diagnosis of racism in the placing of Superfund sites, and analysis of the economic and human costs of globalization are added in, something new is afoot.

For example, consider the Dalai Lama's suggestion that "[w]hen we talk about preservation of the environment, it is related to many other things. Ultimately, the decision must come from the human heart. The key point is to have a genuine sense of universal responsibility, based on love and compassion, and clear awareness."[63] This statement correctly points out that each person who opposes the juggernaut of industrialism must make a personal commitment, with no guarantee of "success," to a daunting task. However, the statement ignores the fact that *personal* awareness, love, and compassion are extremely limited if they are not joined by an understanding of—and an attempt to change—our collective institutions. The Dalai Lama—exactly like the author of this book and, in all probability, the reader as well—plugs into the same electronic grid as everyone else, burns fossil fuels to fly from place to place, and employs the resources of our environmentally unsustainable society in his struggle to save some vestige of his people's national identity. His personal love and compassion, in short, do not keep him from contributing to the mess! Understanding the problems, criticizing them fully, and offering alternatives requires a "social" ecology whose nuts-and-bolts account of the economic and political sources of ecocrisis take their place alongside appeals to personal love, compassion, and awareness.

To take another example, one of the most ambitious descriptions of what an ecological society might look like, *For the Common Good: Redirecting the Economy Toward Community, the Environment and a Sustainable Future* is—significantly—the joint product of a Protestant theologian (John Cobb) and a professor of economics and former senior economist for the World Bank (Herman Daly). Daly and Cobb propose a rich combination of policy and value changes. They challenge existing economies of scale and current trade policies, suggest new ways to cultivate local communities, and redesign educational priorities. And they address the cosmic meaning of human existence and the ethical standards that should guide it. Similarly, when theologian Dorothy Soelle confronts the prospects of religion in the twenty-first century, she must diagnose the political ills of globalization along with the more familiar problems of Christian complacency or arrogance.[64]

What we are witnessing, then, is a double movement: the entry of spiritual values into world-making political perspectives and religion's assimilation of analytic tools for understanding the logic of ecological destruction. Here, despite the moral, political, and economic institutional failures of Communist nations, it is not hard to see how much of Marxist theory is in fact extremely useful. And despite the fact that many claim to have left Marxism in the dustbin of history, its general understanding of capitalism is widely used.

Marx's original theory correctly predicted much of the economic future of capitalism: the expansion and development of productive technology, the ascendancy of corporate power in politics and culture, the evolution of larger and more concentrated forms of wealth, and the worldwide spread of social relationships based on money. Since Marx, theorists under his influence have described an economy dominated by national and global megacorporations, the role of the government in organizing and stabilizing the economy, and the manner in which the international market economy leads to the internationalization of poverty and ecological destruction. We have not "outgrown" Marxist insights in our age of global capitalism, corporations larger than many nations, and frequently unrestrained state power in the service of big business.[65]

Let us examine, for example, the replacement of subsistence agriculture with large plantations producing a single crop for export. This pattern has been repeated countless times throughout Asia, Latin America, and Africa, almost always with disastrous results. Basic Marxist premises provide a straightforward explanation. Land oriented toward local production for use has been converted to production for profitable export. Because the land is no longer directly connected to a self-subsistent community, its distant owners have no compunctions about using techniques that degrade both land (now overburdened by unsustainable pesticides, chemical fertilizers, and water use) *and* the human community (now turned into poverty-stricken "masses," usually forced to join the unemployed in overburdened urban centers). If enough profits are made, it does not matter whether much is left of the land (or people) when the capital is transferred to some other investment. In this way international *trade* in sugar and bananas, coffee and cotton, degrades agricultural *communities and land* throughout the world. And the situation is only made worse when genetic engineering further reduces the diversity of seeds, farming techniques, and input from traditional farming communities.[66]

Another problem that can be easily understood in broadly Marxist terms concerns the way corporations can treat the pollution they cause as "external" to the cost of the commodities they sell.[67] Production, sale, and profits are typically the business of the company in question; cleanup and health costs are borne by society—and the ecosystem—as a whole. What looks like "freedom of the market" is really the privilege to acquire wealth while impoverishing the human (and nonhuman) community.

In cases such as these, abstractions about our "attitudes toward nature" may be relevant, but not nearly so much as is an understanding of the capitalist globalization of agriculture or the vital need for some collective control of productive life.

For a Marxist political orientation, the ultimate question is whether this control can be realized. Even though most religious environmentalists do not call for complete nationalization of the forces of production, the vast majority of them do demand serious social constraints on the productive activity of private corporations. This Marxian goal, though rarely acknowledged as such, is common to all but the most timid and conservative forms of religious environmentalism. In many other instances, more direct condemnations of the imperatives of capitalism are present.

What I have just described in reference to Marxism could be repeated in relation to religious environmentalists' use of a feminist critique of patriarchy, antiracism theory, and postcolonial perspectives on the pernicious effects of globalization. The United Church of Christ report, after all, was about a structural racism that had little or nothing to do with emotional racial antagonism, traditional segregation, or minorities refused jobs or mortgages. Religious voices concerned with environmental justice focus on contrasting real estate values, differences in the capacity of communities for self-defense, and lack of personal connections to motivate institutional concern.

Whether those who use such language to describe social problems needing religious attention are ministers, professors of political science, or paid organizers, the language itself is the stuff of progressive political theory and originates in secular political movements. Without these perspectives, the new values of environmental theology simply cannot comprehend the real world.

Just as the pressure of a historically unprecedented environmental crisis transforms traditional religion and nondenominational spirituality, so political theory has had to change as well. For a start, Western liberals and radicals, like their religious comrades, have had to question their own anthropocentric premises. Democratic theory, rooted in the notion of the autonomous, "rational" individual, has been extended to discussions of the rights of animals, trees, and ecosystems. Marxism, in many ways functioning under the same human-centered premises as liberalism, has similarly had to ask whether the liberation of the working class and the fulfillment of human goals were the sole purposes of political movements. All progressive political positions have been challenged to answer new questions about what they mean by happiness, freedom, justice, and human fulfillment. As Andrew MacLaughlin has argued, and many Greens have agreed, the problem is not simply capitalism, but an "industrialism" that privileges human consumption, unchecked technological innovation, and a mindless popular culture over tradition, community, and ties to other species.[68] If traditional religion was not up to the demands of the environmental crisis, most world-making political theories weren't either. Just as the nonviolent activists of biodevastation were eager to think about the spiritual roots of their passion for the earth and my Jamaica Plain neighbors understood the pond as sacred, so it is that many hardheaded accounts of the death of forests or toxic air quality indicate a fundamental concern that is spiritual in terms of its transcendence of purely instrumental interest.

I've argued throughout this book that the religious spirit can add something to political life. In particular, we often find in world-making religious social activists certain values typically absent in the secular left. These values include compassion, empathy even for the guilty, self-awareness, and some reflective distance from the typical pursuit of status and power within the movement.

Such virtues are especially important for environmentalism. One reason this is true is that the universality and severity of the ecological crisis offer environmental activists an enormous range of potential allies. Harshness, unforgiving self-righteousness, and uncontrolled anger will alienate many who might join the cause. Self-destructive infighting, arrogance, aggression, name-calling, and factionalism can—once again—only lead to failure. These were, according to its most well-known leader, the source of the downfall of the once-powerful German Green Party.[69]

For environmental politics, simple pieties like those of Thich Nhat Hanh about how it is important to smile, breathe, and be pleasant to adversaries become critically important. The spiritually rooted practice of moral self-examination, the awareness of the near-universal tendency toward egotism (or "sin"), and the trust that others act badly only out of ignorance can lead spiritual social activists to a more human, inclusive, and ultimately successful politics. Often, environmental struggles involve fundamental shifts in community life: Jobs are at stake, freedom to use private property is curtailed, cultural values such as hunting are challenged. In the face of the inevitable emotional pain such struggles create, activists need all the resources of empathy and compassion that spiritual traditions—at their best—can offer.

Similarly, the environmentalists' concern for nature is a value that can provide the basis for a new kind of social solidarity. We might remember that whatever else divides us as human beings, we all need air and water; and virtually all of our hearts rejoice in the sounds of spring. These commonalties may save us when the divisions of race, class, gender, ethnicity, or sexuality leave us deeply suspicious of each other. Emphasizing what we share is a particular gift of spiritual social activists.[70] Such activists cultivate respect for each person's essential spiritual worth and not just condemnation of the "bad guys"; and this attitude is stressed as much within the movement as on the outside. As an example of detailed thought on this matter, consider the "Fourteen Precepts for the Order of Interbeing," which Thich Nhat Hanh wrote as a kind of guidebook for Buddhist social activists. These precepts stress humility, peacefulness, and integrity in the pursuit of political change. "Do not force others," one precept teaches, "to accept your views, whether by authority, threat, money, propaganda or even education. However, through compassionate dialogue, help others renounce fanaticism and narrowness."[71] Of course, one person's peaceful pursuit of ecological wisdom might be another's fanaticism. Guidelines of this kind cannot end all the tensions of political life. However, even a casual examination of the history of world-making political organizations reveals how much more successful political groups might have been if they had even been aware such principles existed! The environmental movement has had its share of bitterness, infighting, careerism, and energy wasted on internal hostility. We might remember how the career of David Brower, perhaps the single most important architect of modern activist environmentalism, was marked by situations of unnecessary conflict.[72]

Because activists are struggling against a system in which they themselves take part, spiritual values of humility and self-awareness seem particularly appropriate. In the more familiar contexts of racism or sexism, one can overcome prejudicial attitudes, refuse to support stereotyping or discrimination, and promote the interests of the oppressed group; and, in the case of men and feminism, a man can do his share of the housework and make respect for women a basic masculine virtue. However, when it comes to the environment, it is unlikely that we will stop using electricity, consuming food transported from thousands of miles away, or driving. To be sure, everyone is not equally responsible. Only a tiny percentage of us control energy policy, displace peasants to create pesticide-drenched export farming, or support political candidates who will lessen restrictions on automobile fuel efficiency. But we all consume the fruits of industrial civilization and contribute to the mess.

Also, environmental movements from developing nations, particularly those of Asia, offer an emphasis on collective well-being and communal values that is an important counterweight to the Western stress on individual rights. Having been catapulted into a global economy without the centuries-long development of extreme forms of individualism, Buddhist and indigenous groups can remind the rest of us that concern for the village, the tribe, the community, the clan, and the people are as essential to the creation of a just and rational social order as is the "individual." These are political concerns that focus on peoplehood, on shared culture, and on ties to a particular place rather than on issues of economic class or generalized race or ethnicity.[73]

Further, unlike movements keyed solely to economic gain or group interests, environmentalism must counter the reigning belief that the "good life" is defined by high consumption. It must propose alternative models of human goodness, fulfillment, and happiness.

Most secular political viewpoints have ignored this task. Liberalism, after all, was concerned with untrammeled personal freedom in social and economic life. Marxism sought to liberate exploited classes. Most of the dominant social movements of the last two centuries have focused on equal treatment for their constituents and raising standards of living. As products of the Enlightenment, they carried its strengths and its weaknesses.

Although certain elements of the 1960s counterculture and feminism did challenge some of modernity's basic principles, these elements have come to full flower in environmentalism— especially environmentalism that is infused with some spiritual values. These radically new perspectives ask: What is the ultimate worth of this construction project, these jobs, that commodity? Whose needs or wants deserve to be satisfied? Which desires are or are not healthy? Rational? Spiritually fulfilling? How might they be altered? If we truly suffer, as writers from David Abram to Stephanie Kaza have insisted, from a great loneliness for the "more-than-human," what do we need to change to encounter its mystery once again?[74] Asking these questions goes to the core of both our broad cultural values and our hard-edged institutions. They allow us to confront inner-city toxic incinerators and wildlife preservation, the commodification of agriculture and saving the redwoods. For example, deep ecology's emphasis on the value of the nonhuman offers a measure of and a limit to what we are seeking when we pursue an improved "standard of living." The notion of a "sustainable" form of life begins to condition what we are after, becoming an essential defining element along with "justice," "freedom," and even "community."

Buttressing these challenges to our way of life with a religious vocabulary gives us a leg to stand on when so much that is familiar is being criticized. Perhaps only the divine right of God is powerful enough to challenge what many take to be the divine right of the economy! As Max Oelschlaeger suggests:

> [R]eligious discourse, expressing itself in the democratic forum, offers the possibility of overcoming special interest politics—especially those which are narrowly economic—on environmental issues. . . . Biblical language has been a vital part of our nation's public debate over the structure and texture of the good society. There is no reason that it cannot play a role in determining an environmental agenda.[75]

In this line of thought, there is a clear overlap between ecological activists and the religious traditions, for many elements of both share a love of simplicity, an appreciation for life, and a long-term, nonmonetary definition of "success."[76] As world-making movements, religion and politics now converge.

Finally, as I argued at the end of chapter 4, religious traditions can offer social activists the practical techniques of moral and emotional self-transformation found in prayer, meditation, and ritual. Such resources are particularly needed in the environmental movement. The scope of the problem, the daunting resources of the adversary, the awareness of how much has been lost already—all these make ecological activism rife with grief, anger, and despair. Yet as the Dalai Lama said, when asked why he did not hate the Chinese for what they had done to Tibet, "They have taken so much else from me, I will not give them my peace of mind."[77] In fact, a spiritual perspective on our successes and failures can help sustain us in hard times. Prayers of thanksgiving, beseeching pleas to a Great Spirit (of whatever form) to help us along the way, rituals to mourn for the dead and take joy in what remains—all these are the common stuff of religion, easily adapted to the great task of coming to a sane and sustainable relation with the rest of the planet. As necessary counterbalances to a constant focus on rising cancer rates, clear-cut ancient forests, and extinguished species, rituals of celebration and joy allow activists to feel some happiness no matter what. Such rituals, however, do not come easily to most great traditions of social struggle. The lifestyle of secular radicalism rarely has a place for moments of silence, prayers for peace, candles lit in memory of the fallen, or—as Thich Nhat Hanh puts it—moments of delight in the trees that have not yet been stricken by acid rain.

We can now return to the question of religious pluralism, of how politically oriented religious groups can function in modern society without undermining the enlightenment values of religious freedom, free speech, and a reasonable separation of church and state.

Religious participation in environmental politics, it seems to me, has solved this problem: if not by addressing it theoretically then—more important—in practice. The common bond of love of the earth and the use of the vocabulary of divinity, sacredness, and ultimate concern far outweighs the names of gods, the holidays celebrated, or the precise form of prayer. In interfaith partnerships for environmental reform and programmatic statements, religious environmentalists have realized the goal I described in chapter 2: to hold fast to ethics while allowing for a pluralism of metaphysics.

Consider, for example, these excerpts from a remarkable statement on global warming and climate change by the North Carolina Interfaith Coalition on Climate Change:

> As witnesses of the serious climate changes the earth is now undergoing, we leaders of North Carolina's *various spiritual traditions* join together to voice our concerns about the health of the planet we share with all species. We acknowledge the need to commit ourselves to a course of action that will help us recognize our part in the devastating effects on much of our planet brought about by increasingly severe weather events. We declare the necessity for North Carolina's *spiritual communities* to be leaders in *turning human activities in a new direction* for the well-being of the planet. . . .
>
> We believe that global warming is a challenge to all people but particularly to the spiritual communities that recognize the *sacredness of preserving all eco-systems* that sustain life. . . .
>
> Global warming *violates that sacredness*. Already we see people dying from extreme weather conditions exacerbated by climate change, including record-breaking storms, heat waves, floods, and droughts. The burdens of a degraded environment fall disproportionately upon the most vulnerable of the planet's people: *the poor, sick, elderly,* and those who will face still greater threats in future generations. . . .
>
> We pledge ourselves to . . . organize our communities to meet with local and state political leaders, and members of Congress, to encourage their participation and support.[78]

The thirty-six signers listed on the group's website include rabbis, Buddhist priests, Roman Catholic and Episcopal bishops, and ministers from the Lutheran, Unitarian Universalist,

Quaker, Baptist, Methodist, and United Church of Christ denominations. If we examine the language of the document, we see what appears to be a self-conscious attempt to put in practice a conception of religious life that prizes finding common ground on which different groups can work together. The frequent use of the term "spiritual" signals an acceptance of the variety of paths to God; the acknowledgment of the sacredness of the earth announces an end to theological anthropocentrism; naming the special vulnerability of the poor opens the way for an account of irrational and unjust social institutions and for common work with secular liberal to leftist organizations. The challenge to existing political and economic arrangements is direct and serious.

In another example, we find that in 1986, the World Wide Fund for Nature celebrated its twenty-fifth anniversary by bringing together representatives of five major world religions to focus on how their respective faiths understood and could respond to the environmental crisis. Catholic priest Lanfranco Serrini declared: "We are convinced of the inestimable value of our respective traditions and what they can offer to re-establish ecological harmony; but, at the same time, *we are humble enough to desire to learn from each other.* The very richness of our diversity lends strength to our shared concern and responsibility for our planet earth."[79]

In these two illustrative cases, the Gordian knot of pluralism—how religions can coexist despite their different beliefs—is undone. And if that is undone, then our fear that any serious religion is necessarily fanatical and undemocratic should be similarly assuaged. Facing the enormous implications of the environmental crisis, believers have shown that they are capable of actively working with people whose theologies are different from their own. But that was always the key question: Could the faithful function respectfully with people who held contradictory beliefs? Contrary to the secular left's belief that religion is inherently antidemocratic, religious environmentalists have shown both a broad spiritual openness and a deep civic concern. More than this, surely, is not necessary. Religions become—like the AFL-CIO, the World Trade Organization, General Motors, and Ralph Nader's Green Party—one more group that seeks to realize its particular vision in social life. Each vision promotes certain values and institutions rather than others—whether those are the rights of private property, higher wages, the SUV, or sustainable agriculture. The demands of religion are no more irrational, partial, or exclusive than those of any other group in our uneasy democracy. That some leaders or groups are bigoted or tyrannical may be true, but which secular movement doesn't have its share of the same? Given this similarity, the task is to oppose bigotry and tyranny, and not world-making religion or politics.

Religions now enter the modern world as legitimate and authentic partners in the political drama of making—and remaking—the world. Further, their values now color the world's most important political movement. Surprisingly, as time progresses it is getting harder and harder to tell the two of them apart.

NOTES

1. A Christian organization devoted to "love our neighbors as ourselves and to care for the earth," at www.targetearth.org.

2. Petra Kelly, *Thinking Green: Essays on Feminism, Environmentalism, and Nonviolence* (Berkeley, Calif.: Parallax Press, 1964), 37.

3. See http://www.biodev.org/index2.htm.

4. In Libby Bassett, ed., *Earth and Faith: A Book of Reflection for Action* (New York: United National Environmental Programme, 2000), 11.

5. Pope John Paul II, "The Ecological Crisis: A Common Responsibility," in *This Sacred Earth*, ed. Roger S. Gottlieb (New York: Routledge, 1995), 230. Emphasis in original.

6. Foreword to *Dharma Gaia: A Harvest of Essays in Buddhism and Ecology,* ed. Allan Hunt Badiner (Berkeley, Calif.: Parallax Press, 1990).

7. Bassett, *Earth and Faith*, 52.

8. Mark Wallace, *Fragments of the Spirit* (New York: Continuum, 1996), 141.

9. The antiglobalization literature is now very large. For informative recent treatments, see Jerry Mander, "Economic Globalization and the Environment," *Tikkun* (September-October 2001); Mark Weisbrot, "Tricks of Free Trade," *Sierra* (September-October 2001); the International Foundation on Globalization, www.ifg.org; and Global Exchange, www.globalexchange.org.

10. See www.wcc-coe.org.

11. David Helvarg, "Bush Unites the Enviros," *Nation*, May 7, 2001.

12. For example, *Sierra* (November-December 1998).

13. Thomas Berry, "Ecology and the Future of Catholicism," in *Embracing Earth: Catholic Approaches to Ecology*, ed. Albert P. LaChance and John E. Carroll (Maryknoll, N.Y.: Orbis, 1994), xi.

14. See www.elca.org.

15. A range of information and sources can be found in Gottlieb, *This Sacred Earth.*

16. Lynn White, "The Historical: Roots of Our Ecological Crisis," *Science* 155 (March 10, 1967).

17. Wendell Berry, *The Gift of Good Land* (San Francisco: North Point Press, 1981), 317–18.

18. Ellen Bernstein and Dan Fink, *Let the Earth Teach You Torah* (Philadelphia: Shomrei Adama, 1992).

19. Quoted in Gottlieb, *This Sacred Earth*, 449.

20. National Council of Churches website, www.nccusa.org.

21. See www.umc.org.

22. American Baptist Churches, "Creation and the Covenant of Caring," in *This Sacred Earth*, ed. Gottlieb, 239.

23. "Safety and Health in Workplace and Community," *United Methodist Book of Resolutions,* 1996, www.umc.org.

24. Justin Torres, "Religion and Environmentalism: Match Made in Heaven?" January 19, 2000, www.cns.com.

25. Seth Zuckerman, "Redwood Rabbis," *Sierra* (November-December 1998).

26. For a range of political activities of Buddhists see Christopher S. Queen, ed., *Engaged Buddhism in the West* (Boston: Wisdom, 2000).

27. For example, Theological Education to Meet the Environmental Challenge, www.webofcreation.org, has organized dozens of major conferences and offers resources to seminaries, divinity schools, and so on.

28. Of the now enormous literature on environmental racism and environmental justice, one might start with Robert D. Bullard, *Unequal Protection: Environmental Protection and Communities of Color* (San Francisco: Sierra Club, 1994); and James Lester, David Allen, and Kelly Hill, *Environmental Injustice in the United States: Myths and Realities* (Boulder: Westview Press, 2001).

29. Deeohn Ferris and David Hahn-Baker, "Environmentalists and Environmental Justice Policy," in *Environmental Justice: Issues, Policies, and Solutions,* ed. Bunyan Bryant (Washington, D.C.: Island Press, 1995).

30. Commission for Racial Justice, *Toxic Wastes and Race in the United States* (New York: United Church of Christ, 1987).

31. Reprinted in Gottlieb, *This Sacred Earth*, 634.

32. See discussion in Peter Wenz, *Environmental Ethics Today* (New York: Oxford University Press, 2001), 200–208. Also, Vandana Shiva, *The Violence of the Green Revolution* (Atlantic Highlands, N.J.: Zed, 1991). For a useful overview of the by now large ecofeminist literature, see Victoria Dayton, "Ecofeminism," in *A Companion to Environmental Philosophy*, ed. Dale Jamieson (London: Blackwell, 2001).

33. See www.eco-justice.org.

34. See www.sai.ciriq.org.au/eco.

35. See www.sao.cirq.org.au/eco.

36. Daniel Faber, director of the coalition, personal communication, September 2, 2001.

37. See essays in Barbara Rose Johnston, ed., *Who Pays the Price: The Sociocultural Context of Environmental Crisis* (Washington, D.C.: Island Press, 1994); and Aubrey Wallace, ed., *Eco-Heroes: Twelve Tales of Environmental Victory* (San Francisco: Mercury House, 1993).

38. Paul Wapner, *Environmental Activism and World Civic Politics* (Albany: State University of New York Press, 1996), 41.

39. Wapner, *Environmental Activism*, 42.

40. Raymond Bonner, *At the Hand of Man: Peril and Hope for Africa's Wildlife* (New York: Knopf, 1993).

41. Joanna Macy, *World as Lover, World as Self*; Carolyn Merchant, *Earthcare: Women and the Environment* (New York: Routledge, 1999); Riane Eisler, *The Chalice and the Blade: Our History, Our Future* (San Francisco: Harper and Row, 1988).

42. Of many sources, see George Sessions, ed., *Deep Ecology for the Twenty-First Century* (Boston: Shambala, 1994). For connections with traditional religions, see David Barnhill and Roger S. Gottlieb, eds., *Deep Ecology and World Religions: New Essays on Common Ground* (Albany: State University of New York Press, 2001).

43. David Brower, *Let the Mountains Talk, Let the Rivers Run* (New York: Harper Collins, 1995), 176.

44. Christopher Childs, *The Spirit's Terrain: Creativity, Activism, and Transformation* (Boston: Beacon Press, 1999), 50.

45. Wapner, *Environmental Activism*, 50.

46. Sulak Sivaraksa, "The Religion of Consumerism," in *Dharma Rain: Sources of Buddhist Environmentalism*, ed. Kenneth Kraft and Stephanie Kaza (Boston: Shambhala, 2000), 178–79.

47. Mary John Mananzan, "Globalization and the Perennial Question of Justice," in *Spiritual Question for the Twenty-First Century*, ed. Mary Hembrow Snyder (Maryknoll, N.Y.: Orbis, 2001), 157.

48. David Kinsley, *Ecology and Religion: Ecological Spirituality in Cross-Cultural Perspective* (Englewood Cliffs, N.J.: Prentice-Hall, 1995).

49. Charlene Spretnak, "The Spiritual Dimension of Green Politics," in *This Sacred Earth*, ed. Gottlieb, 532–35.

50. Kelly, *Thinking Green*, 37.

51. Bron Taylor, "Earth First! From Primal Spirituality to Ecological Resistance," in *This Sacred Earth*, ed. Gottlieb, 545–46.

52. Daniel Neal Graham, "The Theory of a Transformational Political Movement: Green Political Theory," in *Transformational Politics: Theory, Study, and Practice*, ed. Stephen Wolpert, Christ Slaton, and E. W. Schwerin (Albany: State University of New York Press, 1998), 75.

53. Theodore Roszak, Mary E. Gomes, and Allen D. Kanner, eds., *Ecopsychology: Restoring the Earth, Healing the Mind* (San Francisco: Sierra Club, 1995).

54. Manuel Castells, *The Information Age*, vol. 2, *The Power of Identity*, 125–26.

55. Castells, *The Information Age*, 126.

56. Aldo Leopold, *A Sand County Almanac* (New York: Oxford University Press, 1949), 258.

57. Mark Dowie, *Losing Ground: American Environmentalism at the Close of the Twentieth Century* (Cambridge: MIT Press, 1996), 226.

58. See Bill McKibben, *Hope, Human and Wild*; Alan Richman, *Gaviotas: A Village to Invent the World* (Chelsea, Vt.: Chelsea Green, 1999).

59. Sue Hubbell, *Broadsides from the Other Orders: A Book of Bugs* (New York: Random House, 1993), 74–89.

60. See accounts of this in Bruce Rich, *Mortgaging the Earth*, 251–53; and Madhava Gadgil and Ramachandra Guha, "Ecological Conflicts and the Environmental Movement in India," in *Development and Environment: Sustaining People and Nature*, ed. Dharam Ghai (Oxford and Cambridge: Blackwell, 1994).

61. Heidi Hadsell, "Profits, Parrots, Peons: Ethical Perplexities in the Amazon," in *Ecological Resistance Movements: The Global Emergence of Radical and Popular Environmentalism*, ed. Bron Taylor (Albany: State University of New York Press, 1995), 77.

62. Vikram K. Akula, "Grassroots Environmental Resistance in India," in *Ecological Resistance Movements*, ed. Bron Taylor (Albany: State University of New York, 1995).

63. Bassett, *Earth and Faith*, 144.

64. Dorothee Soelle, *The Silent Cry: Mysticism and Resistance* (Minneapolis, Minn.: Fortress Press, 2001), esp. 191–207.

65. For an accessible survey of nineteenth- and twentieth-century Marxism, see Roger S. Gottlieb, *Marxism 1844–1990* (New York: Routledge, 1992). For some recent Marxist work on ecological issues, see the journal *Capitalism, Nature, Socialism*; James O'Connor, *Natural Causes: Essays in Ecological Marxism* (New York: Guilford Press, 1997). And, for an area study, see Daniel Faber, *Environment under Fire: Imperialism and the Ecological Crisis in Central America* (New York: Monthly Review Press, 1993).

66. Among many treatments of this theme, see Shiva, *Violence of the Green Revolution*; Tom Athanasiou, *Divided Planet: The Ecology of Rich and Poor* (Athens: University of Georgia Press, 1998); and the journal *Ecologist*.

67. See Mike Jacobs, *The Green Economy: Environment, Sustainable Development, and the Politics of the Future* (London: Pluto Press, 1993).

68. See Andrew MacLaughlin, *Regarding Nature: Industrialism and Deep Ecology* (Albany: State University of New York Press, 1993); as well as the well-known Green self-description: "We're neither left nor right, but out in front."

69. Kelly, *Thinking Green*, 123.

70. For an inspiring account of individual leaders, see Catherine Ingram, *In the Footsteps of Gandhi: Conversations with Spiritual Social Activists* (Berkeley, Calif.: Parallax Press, 1990). For responses to current events, see publications such as *Fellowship Magazine, Tikkun,* and *Reconciliation.*

71. Thich Nhat Hanh, *Being Peace*, 91. See a commentary on these principles applied to environmental politics: Joan Halifax and Marty Peale, "Interbeing: Precepts and Practices of an Applied Ecology," in *Cultural and Spiritual Values of Biodiversity*, ed. Darrell Posey (London: United Nations Environment Programme, 1999), 475–80.

72. See accounts in John McPhee, *Encounters with the Archdruid* (New York: Farrar, Straus & Giroux, 1971); and David Brower, *For Earth's Sake: The Life and Times of David Brower* (Salt Lake City, Utah: Peregrine Smith, 1990).

73. For one brief but precise statement of these issues, see George Tinker, "The Full Circle of Liberation: An American Indian Theology of Place," in *Ecotheology: Voices from South and North*, ed. David G. Hallman (Maryknoll, N.Y.: Orbis, 1994).

74. David Abram, *The Spell of the Sensuous: Language and Perception in a More Than Human World* (New York: Pantheon, 1997); Stephanie Kaza, *The Attentive Heart: Conversations with Trees* (New York: Fawcett Columbine, 1993).

75. Max Oelschlaeger, *Caring for Creation: An Ecumenical Approach to the Environmental Crisis* (New Haven: Yale University Press, 1994), 57, 68.

76. Robert Paehlke, *Environmentalism and the Future of Progressive Politics* (New Haven: Yale University Press, 1988), 3.

77. I heard him say this during an interview on television, many years ago.

78. See www.webofcreation.org. Comparable groups exist in close to twenty other states.

79. Bassett, *Earth and Faith*, 8. My emphasis.

"Traditional Ecological Knowledge and Environmental Futures"

❧

Winona LaDuke

Winona LaDuke is a leading Native American activist and writer and was Ralph Nader's running mate on the Green Party ticket in 1996 and 2000. Author of the novel *Last Standing Woman* as well as many books and essays on Native American traditions, environmental struggles, and the politics of racism, she here reminds us that a serious environmentalism has always been essential to Native American traditions, not something that must be invented or rediscovered.

❧

Traditional ecological knowledge is the culturally and spiritually based way in which indigenous peoples relate to their ecosystems. This knowledge is founded on spiritual-cultural instructions from "time immemorial" and on generations of careful observation within an ecosystem of continuous residence. I believe that this knowledge represents the clearest empirically based system for resource management and ecosystem protection in North America, and I will argue that native societies' knowledge surpasses the scientific and social knowledge of the dominant society in its ability to provide information and a management style for environmental planning. Frankly, these native societies have existed as the only example of sustainable living in North America for more than three hundred years.

This essay discusses the foundation of traditional ecological knowledge and traditional legal systems, the implications of colonialism on these systems, and the challenges faced by the environmental movement and native peoples in building a common appreciation for what is common ground—Anishinaabeg Akiing—the people's land.

> I had a fish net out in a lake and at first I was getting quite a few fish in it. But there was an otter in the lake and he was eating the fish in the net. After a while, fish stopped coming into the net. They knew there was a predator there. So similarly game know about the presence of hunters as well. The Cree say, "all creatures are watching you. They know everything you are doing. Animals are aware of your activities." In the past, animals talked to people. In a sense, there is still communication between animals and hunters. You can predict where the black bear is likely to den. Even though the black bear zigzigs before retreating into his den to hibernate, tries to shake you off his trail, you can still predict where he is likely to go to. When he approaches his den entrance, he makes tracks backwards, loses his tracks in the bush, and makes a long detour before coming into the den. The hunter tries to think what the bear is thinking. Their minds touch. The hunter and the bear have parallel knowledge, and they share that knowledge. So in a sense they communicate.[1]

To be secure that one will be able to harvest enough involves more than skill; it also involves careful observation of the ecosystem and careful behavior determined by social values and cultural practices.

"Minobimaatisiiwin,"[2] or the "good life," is the basic objective of the Anishinaabeg and Cree[3] people who have historically, and to this day, occupied a great portion of the north-central region of the North American continent. An alternative interpretation of the word is "continuous rebirth." This is how we traditionally understand the world and how indigenous societies have come to live within natural law. Two tenets are essential to this paradigm: cyclical thinking and reciprocal relations and responsibilities to the Earth and creation. Cyclical thinking, common to most indigenous or land-based cultures and value systems, is an understanding that the world (time, and all parts of the natural order—including the moon, the tides, women, lives, seasons, or age) flows in cycles. Within this understanding is a clear sense of birth and rebirth and a knowledge that what one does today will affect one in the future, on the return. A second concept, reciprocal relations, defines responsibilities and ways of relating between humans and the ecosystem. Simply stated, the resources of the economic system, whether they be wild rice or deer, are recognized as animate and, as such, gifts from the Creator. Within that context, one could not take life without a reciprocal offering, usually tobacco or some other recognition of the Anishinaabeg's reliance on the Creator. There must always be this reciprocity. Additionally, assumed in the "code of ethics" is an understanding that "you take only what you need, and you leave the rest."

Implicit in the concept of Minobimaatisiiwin is a continuous inhabitation of place, an intimate understanding of the relationship between humans and the ecosystem, and the need to maintain that balance. These values and basic tenets of culture made it possible for the Cree, Ojibway, and many other indigenous peoples to maintain economic, political, religious, and other institutions for generations in a manner that would today be characterized as sustainable.[4]

A MODEL

By its very nature, "development"—or, concomitantly, an "economic system" based on these ascribed indigenous values—must be decentralized, self-reliant, and very closely based on the carrying capacity of that ecosystem. By example, the nature of northern indigenous economies has been a diversified mix of hunting, harvesting, and gardening, all utilizing a balance of human intervention or care, in accordance with these religious and cultural systems' reliance upon the wealth and generosity of nature. Because by their very nature indigenous cultures are not in an adversarial relationship with nature, this reliance is recognized as correct and positive.

> A hunter always speaks as if the animals are in control of the hunt. The success of the hunt depends on the animals: the hunter is successful if the animal decides to make himself available. The hunters have no power over the game, animals have the last say as to whether they will be caught.[5]

The Anishinaabeg or Ojibway nation, for example, encompasses people and land within four Canadian provinces and five U.S. states. This nation has a shared common culture, history, governance, language, and land base—the five indicators, according to international law[6] of the existence of a nation of people. This nation historically and correctly functions within a decentralized economic and political system, with much of the governance left to local bands (like villages or counties) through clan and extended family systems. The vast natural wealth of this region and the resource management systems of the Anishinaabeg have enabled people to prosper for many generations. In one study of Anishinaabeg harvesting technologies and systems, a scientist noted:

> Economically, these family territories in the Timiskaming band were regulated in a very wise and interesting manner. The game was kept account of very closely, proprietors knowing about how abundant each kind of animal was. Hence they could regulate the killing so as not to deplete the stock. Beaver was made the object of the most careful "farming," an account being kept of the numbers of occupants old and young to each "cabin."[7]

The killing of game was regulated by each family.[8]

The Anishinaabeg employed a resource management system that used techniques for sustained yield. Such systems show a high degree of unification of conception and execution (possible because the "scientist" is the "resource manager"). There has only been limited imitation of this system by the scientific community.[9]

This system has allowed traditional land-based economies to prosper. Conceptually, the system provides for both domestic production and production for exchange or export. Hence, whether the resource is wild rice or white fish, the extended family as a production unit harvests within a social and resource management code that insures sustained yield. Traditional management practices have often been dismissed by North American settlers as useless in the current circumstances of more significant populations. However, it is important to note that previous North American indigenous populations were substantially higher than they are now. This indicates that these management practices were applied in greater population densities, an argument which is useful in countering the perceptions that all Native American practices have occurred with very low populations. I believe there is a more substantial question meriting discussion: Can North American society craft the social fabric to secure a traditional management practice, based on consensual understanding and a collective process?

COLONIALISM AND UNDERDEVELOPMENT

The governance of this land by traditional ecological knowledge has been adversely affected by genocide, colonialism, and subsequent circumstances that need to be considered in the current dialogue on North American resource management, the role of the environmental movement, and indigenous peoples. The holocaust of America is unmatched on a world scale, and its aftermath caused the disruption necessary to unseat many of our indigenous economic and governmental systems. There can be no accurate estimate of the number of people killed since the invasion, but one estimate provides for 112,554,000 indigenous people in the western hemisphere in 1492 and an estimated 28,554,000 in 1980. Needless to say, this is a significant depopulation.[10] This intentional and unintentional genocide facilitated a subsequent process of colonialism, which served to establish a new set of relations between indigenous nations and colonial or "settler" nations in the Americas.

Three basic concepts govern relations between colonial "settlers" and indigenous nations. Colonialism has been extended through a set of "center periphery relations" in which the center has expanded through: (1) the cultural practice spreading Christianity and, later, Western science and other forms of Western thought; (2) the socioeconomic practice of capitalism; and (3) the military-political practice of colonialism.[11]

These practices have resulted in the establishment of a set of relations between indigenous economies and peoples and the North American colonial economy that are characterized by dependency and underdevelopment. Underdevelopment—or, more accurately, "underdeveloping," because it is an ongoing practice—is the process by which the economy both loses wealth and undergoes the structural transformation which accentuates and institutionalizes this process.[12] This process, underway for at least the past two hundred years, is characterized by the appropriation of land and resources from indigenous nations for the purpose of "developing" the U.S. and Canadian economies and, subsequently, the "underdeveloping" of indigenous economies. The resulting loss of wealth (closely related to loss of control over traditional territories) has created a situation in which most indigenous nations are forced to live in circumstances of material poverty. It is no coincidence that Native Americans and Native Hawaiians (as well as First Nations in Canada) are the poorest people both in the United States and on the continent as a whole. As a consequence, indigenous peoples are subjected to an array of socioeconomic and health problems that are a direct consequence of poverty.[13]

In this process of colonialism, and later marginalization, indigenous nations become peripheral to the colonial economy and eventually are involved in a set of relations characterized by dependency. As Latin American scholar Theotonio Dos Santos notes: "By dependence we mean a situation in which the economy of certain countries is conditioned by the development and expansion of another economy to which the former is subjected."[14] These circumstances— and indeed, the forced underdevelopment of sustainable indigenous economic systems for the purpose of colonial exploitation of land and resources—are an essential backdrop for any discussion of existing environmental circumstances in the North American community and of any discussion of sustainable development in a North American context. Perhaps most alarming is the understanding that even today this process continues, because a vast portion of the remaining natural resources on the North American continent are still under native lands or, as in the case of the disposal of toxic wastes on Indian reservations, the residual structures of colonialism make native communities focal points for dumping the excrement of industrial society.

INDIGENOUS NATIONS TODAY

On a worldwide scale, there are more than 5,000 nations and just over 170 states. "Nations" are defined under international law as those in possession of a common language, land base, history, culture, and territory, while "states" are usually recognized and seated at the United Nations.[15] North America similarly contains a series of nations, known as "First Nations" in Canada and, with few exceptions, denigrated in the United States by the term "tribes." Demographically, indigenous nations represent the majority population north of the 55th Parallel in Canada (the 50th Parallel in the eastern provinces) and occupy approximately two-thirds of the Canadian landmass.

Although the United States has ten times the population it had during colonial times, Indian people do not represent the majority, except in a few areas, particularly the "Four Corners" region of the United States (so named because four states—Arizona, Utah, New Mexico, and Colorado—all meet at one point) where Ute, Apache, Navajo, and Pueblo people reside. However, inside our reservations, which occupy approximately 4 percent of our original land base in the United States, Indian people remain the majority population.

In our territories and our communities a mix of old and new coexist, sometimes in relative harmony and at other times in a violent disruption of the traditional way of life. In terms of economic and land tenure systems, the material basis for relating to the ecosystem, most indigenous communities are a melange of colonial and traditional structures and systems. Although U.S. or Canadian laws may restrict and allocate resources and land on reservations (or aboriginal territory), the indigenous practice of "usufruct rights" is often still maintained and, with it, traditional economic and regulatory institutions like the trapline, "rice boss," and family hunting, grazing (for peoples who have livestock), or harvesting territories.

These subsistence lifestyles continue to provide a significant source of wealth for domestic economies on the reservation, whether for nutritional consumption or for household use, as in the case of firewood. They also, in many cases, provide the essential ingredients of foreign exchange; wild rice, furs, woven rugs, and silverwork. These native economic and land tenure systems, which are specific to each region, are largely invisible to U.S. and Canadian government agencies' economic analysts who consistently point to native "unemployment" with no recognition of the traditional economy. The Bureau of Indian Affairs labor statistics are categorized by sector, as is most employment data available from the U.S. Census Bureau.

In many northern communities, over half of local food and a significant amount of income is garnered from this traditional economic system. In other cases, for instance on the Northern Cheyenne Reservation in Montana, over 90 percent of the land is held by Cheyenne and is used primarily for ranching. Although they do not represent formal "wage work" in the industrial system, these land-based economies are essential to native communities. The lack of recognition for indigenous economic systems, although it has a long history in the North American colonial view of native peoples, is particularly frustrating in terms of the current debate over development options.

Resource extraction plans or energy mega projects proposed for indigenous lands do not consider the current significance of these economic systems nor their value for the future, as demonstrating what remains of sustainable ways of living in North America. A direct consequence is that environmentally destructive development programs ensue, many times foreclosing the opportunity to continue the lower-scale, intergenerational economic practices that had been underway in the native community.

INDIGENOUS ENVIRONMENTAL ISSUES

The conflict between two paradigms—industrial thinking and indigenous thinking—becomes central to the North American and, indeed to the worldwide, environmental and economic crisis. As native communities struggle to survive, issues of sovereignty and control over natural resources become central to North American resource politics and the challenge for North Americans of conscience. Consider these facts:

- More than fifty million indigenous peoples inhabit the world's remaining rain forests.
- More than one million indigenous people will be relocated to allow for the development of hydroelectric dam projects in the next decade.
- The United States has detonated all its nuclear weapons in the lands of indigenous people, more than six hundred of those tests within land legally belonging to the Shoshone nation.
- One-half of all uranium resources within the borders of the United States lay under native reservations. In 1974, Indians produced 100 percent of all federally controlled uranium.[16]

- One-third of all low-sulfur coal in the western United States is on Indian land, with four of the ten largest coal strip mines in these same areas.[17]
- Over forty billion board feet of timber stands on Indian reservations—trees now coveted by U.S. timber interests.[18]
- Fifteen of the eighteen recipients of phase one nuclear waste research grants, so-called Monitored Retrievable Nuclear Storage sites, are Indian communities.
- The largest hydroelectric project on the continent, the James Bay Project, is on Cree and Inuit lands in northern Canada.[19]

For many indigenous peoples, the reality is as sociologist Ivan Illich has suggested: development practices are in fact a war on subsistence.

NOTES

1. Fikret Berkes, "Environmental Philosophy of the Chisasibi Cree People of James Bay," in *Traditional Knowledge and Renewable Resource Management in Northern Regions,* ed. Milton M. R. Freeman and Ludwig N. Carbyn (Edmonton, Alberta, Canada: IUCN Commission on Ecology; Boreal Institute for Northern Studies, 1988), 7, 10.

2. "Minobimaatisiiwin" can be literally translated as the "good life"—"mino" means "good" and "Bimatisiiwin" means "life" in the language of the Anishinaabeg people.

3. Anishinaabeg, which means "the people," are also called the Ojibway or Chippewa, and are an Algonkin-speaking people who reside in the Great Lakes region. The Cree or Ecyou, which can be translated as "the people" in their language, are close relatives of the Anishinaabeg.

4. For discussion, see generally, Colin Scott, "Knowledge Discussion among Cree Hunters: Metaphors and Literal Understanding," *Journal De Societe Anthropologic* 75 (1989): 193–208.

5. Berkes, "Environmental Philosophy," 10.

6. Jason W. Clay, "What's a Nation?" *Mother Jones,* Nov.–Dec. 1990, 28.

7. Frank G. Speck, "The Family Hunting Band as the Basis of Algonkian Social Organization," *American Anthropologist* 17 (1915): 289, 296

8. See generally, Speck, "The Family Hunting Band," 289–305.

9. Peter J. Usher, "Property Rights: The Basis of Wildlife Management," in *National and Regional Interests in the North* (Ottawa, Ontario, Canada: Canadian Arctic Resources Commission, 1984), 389, 408–9.

10. Robert Venables, "The Cost of Columbus: Was There a Holocaust?" *Northeast Indian Quarterly* (fall 1990): 29, 30 n.7.

11. Johan Galtung, "Self Reliance: Concepts, Practice and Rationale," in *Self Reliance: A Strategy for Development,* ed. Johan Galtung, Peter O' Brien, and Roy Preiswerk (London: Bogle-L'Ouverture Publications, 1980), 19, 20.

12. Samir Amin, *Unequal Development: An Essay on the Social Formations of Peripheral Capitalism,* trans. Brian Pearce (New York: Monthly Review Press, 1976), 201–3.

13. *American Indian Policy Review Commission, Final Report Submitted to Congress May 17, 1977* (Washington, D.C.: U.S. Government Printing Office, 1977).

14. Theotonio Dos Santos, "The Structure of Dependence," in *Readings in U.S. Imperialism,* ed. K. T. Fann and Donald C. Hodges (Boston: Porter Sargent, 1971), 225, 226 n. 1.

15. Clay, "What's a Nation?" 6.

16. Winona LaDuke, "Native America: The Economics of Radioactive Colonialism," *Review of Radical Political Economics* (fall 1983): 9, 10.

17. Winona LaDuke, "Native America," 9, 10.

18. Interview with Marshall Cutsforth, Bureau of Indian Affairs Office of Trust Responsibility (August 10, 1993).

19. See Boyce Richardson, *Strangers Devour the Land* (New York: Random House, 1976).

"An Aboriginal Perspective on the Integrity of Creation"

❧

Stan McKay

Reverend Stan McKay, former moderator of the United Church of Canada, is currently working as codirector of the Dr. Jessie Saulteaux Resource Centre. An aboriginal educator, in this selection he presents some basic features of the aboriginal view of humanity's relation to the natural world.

❧

Aboriginal culture is passed from one generation to the next by storytelling. The philosophy of life is passed on to the young mainly by their observation of the elders. Many of the most profound teachings are passed on without words.

Our elders say that when our thoughts and dreams are put into written form they lose life. We are people of the oral tradition and it is a struggle to put our teachings into written form. Thus there is a sense of compromise in writing an article which seeks to reflect our spiritual insights on paper. But the turmoil of these days has brought us to the point that our elders advise us to share the insights and even to risk writing them. It is urgent for all people to come together for a healing vision for the earth, our mother.

Art Solomon, an Annishinabe (Ontario, Canada) spiritual elder, wrote the following prayer for a 1983 World Council of Churches meeting in Mauritius which brought together people representing various faith communities to prepare for the WCC's sixth assembly in Vancouver:

> Grandfather, look at our brokenness.
>
> Now we must put the sanctity of life as the most sacred principle of power, and renounce the awesome might of materialism.
>
> We know that in all creation, only the family of man has strayed from the sacred way.
>
> We know that we are the ones who are divided, and we are the ones who must come back, together to worship and walk in a sacred way, that by our affirmation we may heal the earth and heal each other.
>
> Now we must affirm life for all that is living or face death in a final desecration with no reprieve.
>
> We hear the screams of those who die for want of food, and whose humanity is aborted and prevented.
>
> Grandfather, the sacred one, we know that unless we love and have compassion the healing cannot come.
>
> Grandfather, teach us how to heal our brokenness.

What Art Solomon has shared in this prayer allows the reader to ponder how simple our spiritual world view is—and how profound. The purpose of this paper is to develop some themes that support the renewed ecumenical emphasis on the creation, particularly in the World Council of Churches. Much of this does affirm a Native North American view of creation, but there are also some areas which have not been developed that I could add to the scope of the discussion. Moreover, there are subtle differences in terminology and emphasis which can be confusing and at times contradictory.

"ALL MY RELATIONS" (OR ANTS AND UNCLES)

For those who come from a Judaeo-Christian background it might be helpful to view Aboriginal peoples as an "Old Testament people." Like them, we come out of an oral tradition rooted in the creator and the creation. We, like Moses, know about the sacredness of the earth and the promise of land. Our creation stories also emphasize the power of the creator and the goodness of creation. We can relate to the vision of Abraham and the laughter of Sarah. We have dreams like Ezekiel and have known people like the Pharaoh. We call ourselves "the people" to reflect our sense of being chosen.

Indigenous spirituality around the world is centered on the notion of relationship to the whole creation. We call the earth our mother and the animals are our brothers and sisters. Those parts of creation which biologists describe as inanimate we call our relatives. This naming of creation into our family is an imagery of substance, but it is more than that, because it describes a relationship of love and faithfulness between human persons and the creation. This unity as creatures in the creation cannot be expressed exclusively, since it is related to the interdependence and connectedness of all life.

The next logical reflection is that because of our understanding of the gift of creation we are called to share in the fullness of life. It is difficult to express individual ownership within the Native spiritual understanding. If the creatures and the creation are interdependent, it follows that it is not faithful to speak of ownership. Life is understood as a gift, and it makes no sense to claim ownership of any part of the creation. Our leaders have often described how nonsensical it is to lay claim to the air, the water or the land; because these are related to all life. Chief Dan George expresses it this way in *My Heart Soars:* "Of all the teachings we receive, this one is the most important: Nothing belongs to you of what there is; what you take, you must share."

Reference to the earth in our culture is not individualistic so as to indicate ownership. Our words indicate sharing and belonging to the earth. The coming of Europeans to the land which we used in North America meant a conflict of understanding which centers on the ownership of land. The initial misunderstanding is not surprising, since the first immigrants thought of themselves as coming to take "possession" of a "vacant, pagan land." The incredible fact is that this perception continues after five centuries. Equally surprising has been the historical role of the Christian church in this process of colonization, which basically was a dividing up of the earth so it could be a possession.

The developments of our own generation may alter the pattern of noncommunication with indigenous peoples about the earth and life. It may be that we have entered into a time of survival which will not allow people to pursue ownership of the earth without perceiving that this path leads to destruction of life, including their own. The most obvious example has been the nuclear threat, but more important for Native people are the depletion of resources and pollution of the environment. We understand this activity to be insane, since we live in an environment which gives life but is sensitive to abuse.

Our elders have told stories about the destruction of mother earth. In their dreams and visions they have known from time immemorial about a deep caring and reverence for life. Living in very natural environments they taught that we are to care for all life or we may die. The elders say: "If you see that the top of the tree is sick you will know that it is dying. If the trees die, we too will die." The earth is our life. It is to be shared, and we know the creator intends it for generations yet unborn.

The process in political circles and in government that has come to be known as "land claims" is devastating to our cultural values. In order for us to participate in the process, our statements become sterile and technical. Our documents must be in language suggested by lawyers and understood by judges. This legal jargon contains concepts of ownership which do not carry our spiritual sense of life. As marginalized peoples, forced to live on tiny plots of land, we encounter the worldview of the wealthy and powerful and are forced to compromise or to die.

Yet we maintain the earth is to be shared, and we continue to challenge faceless corporations to be faithful to their humanity. Even as we are being pushed into the "land claims" process, we maintain our heritage and are motivated by a love of the earth and a concern for the survival of the creation. Our earth mother is in a time of pain and she sustains many thoughtless children.

The Circle of Life

My remarks thus far may not make sufficiently clear what the spiritual relationships to earth are for us. It is necessary to say that we feel a sense of "Amen" to the psalmist's words, "The earth is the Lord's and all that is in it" (Ps. 24:1). The value that informs the spirituality of my people is one of wholeness. It is related to a view of life which does not separate or compartmentalize. The relationship of health with ourselves, our community, and with all creation is a spiritual relationship. The need of the universe is the individual need to be in harmony with the creator. This harmony is expressed by living in the circle of life.

There is an awareness that the Spirit moves through all of life. The Great Spirit is in fact the "cosmic order." Aboriginal North American spirituality draws this cosmic order together with human life in a very experiential way. Our view of the creation and the creator is thus an attempt to unify the worldview of human beings who are interdependent. We are a part of all life. Dogmatic statements are not relevant, since the spiritual pilgrimage is one of unity in which there are many truths from a variety of experiences.

I find the image of living on the earth in harmony with the creation and therefore the creator a helpful one. It means that "faithful" living on the earth will be moving in the rhythm of the creation. It means vibrating to the pulse of life in a natural way without having to "own" the source of the music. It is our experience that the creator reveals truth to the creation and all may share in it. We have ceremonies and symbols of what may be true for us. We have developed myths and rituals which remind us of the centrality of the earth in our experience of the truth about the creator. We seek to integrate life so that there will not be boundaries between the secular and religious. For us, the Great Spirit is in the daily earthly concerns about faithful living in a relationship with the created order.

Each day we are given is for thanksgiving for the earth. We are to enjoy it and share it in service of others. This is the way to grow in unity and harmony. Central to the movement into harmony with other communities is the idea of respect. Respect allows for diversity within the unity of the creator. Dialogue can then take place in a global community which does not develop defensive arguments to protect some truth. The situation will be one of sharing stories instead of dogmatic statements and involves listening as well as talking.

Mending the Hoop

Many teachings of the aboriginal North American nations use the symbol of the circle. It is the symbol of the inclusive caring community, in which individuals are respected and interdependence is recognized.

The Christian church has been unclear in its relationship to the creation. The church's earliest understanding of the second coming of Christ was that it was imminent, so that we should disconnect ourselves from the things of creation. Apocalyptic thought becomes part of a philosophy of "hatred of the world," which holds up spiritual salvation as the goal. The result has been a Christology from Europe which interprets biblical references to God's love for the world as being *only* about human salvation. The North American refinement of this incomplete Christology has been to explain that this is a teaching about *individual* human salvation. This entire message of hope is detached from the creation which in the beginning was "good" and which is a part of the world that God "so loved."

The Industrial Revolution and recent technological development have brought us into a mind-set which fits our theology. Economic gain is more important than caring for the creation. The pursuit of short-term gain renders the created order disposable. Materialism and militarism are served by science and technology. There is a critical imbalance in the circle of life when our lifestyle does not reflect a holistic and inclusive vision of the creation.

Aboriginal teachers speak of our individual wholeness which is discovered in a balance of body, mind, and spirit. The discovery of the self leads to an understanding of our interdependence with the whole creation. The integrity of creation is a faith statement about our intention to live in balance and harmony with creation. The elders say "you do what you believe." Anthropocentric philosophies and theologies cannot accommodate a holistic balanced approach. They describe the natural order as enemy and seek to destroy the mystery of hope itself.

"To Save All Beings:
Buddhist Environmental Activism"

❧

Stephanie Kaza

Stephanie Kaza is professor of environmental studies at University of Vermont and a widely acknowledged expert on Buddhism and ecology. She has written *The Attentive Heart: Conversations with Trees* and coedited *Dharma Rain*. Here she provides a theological, practical, and political account of Buddhist Environmental activism.

❧

Meditators form a circle at the base camp of the Headwaters Forest. All are invited to join the Buddhists sitting still in the flurry of activity. While others drum, talk, dance, and discuss strategy, the small group of ecosattvas—Buddhist environmental activists—focus on their breathing and intention amidst the towering trees. They chant the *Metta Sutta* to generate a field of loving-kindness. Here in volatile timber country they renew their pledges to the most challenging task of Buddhist practice—to save all beings.

In this action, old-growth redwoods are the beings at risk, slated for harvest on the Maxxam company property in northern California. Until recently the sixty-thousand-acre ecosystem was logged slowly and sustainably by a small family company. Then in 1985 logging accelerated dramatically following a hostile corporate buyout. Alarmed by the loss of irreplaceable giants, forest defenders have fought tirelessly to halt clear-cutting and preserve these ancient stands of redwoods. They have been joined by Hollywood stars, rock singers, and Jewish rabbis, many willing to practice civil disobedience in protest. How is it that Buddhists have become involved with this effort?

Motivated by ecological concerns, the ecosattvas formed as an affinity group at Green Gulch Zen Center in Marin County, California. As part of their practice they began exploring the relationship between Zen training and environmental activism. They wanted to know: What does it mean to take the bodhisattva vow as a call to save endangered species, decimated forests, and polluted rivers? What does it mean to engage in environmental activism from a Buddhist perspective?[1] The ecosattvas are part of an emerging movement of ecospiritual activism, backed by a parallel academic development which has become the field of Religion and Ecology.[2] Christian scholars, Jewish social justice groups, Hindu tree-planting projects, and Islamic resistance to usurious capitalism are all part of this movement. Buddhist efforts in the United States like those of the ecosattvas are matched by monks in Thailand protesting the oil pipeline from Burma and Tibetans teaching environmental education in Dharamsala.[3]

Activist scholar Joanna Macy suggests these actions are all part of the "third turning of the wheel [of Dharma]," her sense that Buddhism is undergoing a major evolutionary shift at the turn of the millennium.[4] In today's context, one of the oldest teachings of the Buddha— *paticca samuppada* or dependent co-arising—is finding new form in the ecology movement. If ecosystem relationships are the manifestation of interdependence, then protecting ecosystems is a way to protect the Dharma: "with the Third Turning of the Wheel, we see that everything we do impinges on all beings."[5] Acting with compassion in response to the rapidly accelerating environmental crisis can be seen as a natural fruit of Buddhist practice.

Is there a Buddhist ecospiritual movement in North America? Not in any obvious sense, at least not yet. No organizations have been formed to promote Buddhist environmentalism; no clearly defined environmental agenda has been agreed upon by a group of self-identified American Buddhists. However, teachers are emerging, and Buddhist students of all ages are drawn to their writings and ideas. Writers Joanna Macy and Gary Snyder have made ecological concerns the center of their Buddhist practice. Teachers Thich Nhat Hanh and His Holiness the Dalai Lama have frequently urged mindful action on behalf of the environment. Activists John Seed, Nanao Sakaki, and others are beginning to define a Buddhist approach to environmental activism. There is a strong conversation developing among Western and Eastern Buddhists, asking both practical and philosophical questions from this emerging perspective. With environmental issues a mounting global concern, Buddhists of many traditions are creatively adapting their religious heritage to confront these difficult issues.

In this chapter, I begin the preliminary work of documenting the scope of Buddhist environmentalism in the late 1990s, gathering together the historical and philosophical dimensions of what has been called "green Buddhism." This study will be necessarily limited to Western Buddhism, in keeping with the focus of this volume. However, it is important to note the strong relationship with other global initiatives. Buddhist tree-ordaining in Thailand, for example, has inspired similar ceremonies in California.[6] Environmental destruction by logging and uranium mining in Tibet has prompted the formation of the U.S.-based Eco-Tibet group.[7] Environmental issues in Buddhist countries have been a natural magnet for Buddhist activists in the West. But Western Buddhists have taken other initiatives locally, bringing their Buddhist and environmental sensibilities to bear on nuclear waste, consumerism, animal rights, and forest defense.[8] Out of these impulses Buddhist environmental activism is taking shape, based on distinct principles and practices.

One of the most challenging aspects of documenting these developments is finding the hidden stories. In the United States today, environmentalism has grown so strong as a political and cultural force that it is suffering the impact of "brownlash," as biologists Paul and Anne Ehrlich call it. Christian fundamentalism is often allied with the wing of the conservative right that promulgates antienvironmental views. Taking a strong environmental position as a self-proclaimed Buddhist can be doubly threatening. My personal experience is that the environmental arena is a place to act as a small "b" Buddhist. This means concentrating on the message of the Buddha by cultivating awareness, tolerance, and understanding, and acting from a loving presence. "In Buddhism, we say that the presence of one mindful person can have great influence on society and is thus very important."[9] Mindful Buddhist practitioners engaging difficult environmental issues may not proclaim their Buddhism to help solve the problem at hand. Yet they can bring inner strength and moral courage to the task at hand, drawing on the teachings of the Buddha as a basic framework for effective action.

LOOKING BACK

When Buddhism arrived in the West in the mid-1800s, there was little that could be called an environmental movement. Although Henry David Thoreau had written *Walden* in 1854, it was not until the end of the century that a serious land conservation movement coalesced. Advocates recognizing the unique heritage of such landforms as Yellowstone, Yosemite, and the Grand Canyon pressed for the establishment of the National Park system. Conservationists alert to the ravaging of eastern forests and the rush to cut the West spurred the formation of the National Forest Service. But serious concern about overpopulation, air and water pollution, and endangered species did not ignite until the 1960s. Since then the list of dangerous threats has only increased—toxic wastes, ozone depletion, global climate change, genetic engineering, endocrine disrupters—fires are burning on all fronts.

The most recent Western wave of interest in Buddhism coincides almost exactly with the expansion of the environmental movement.[10] Young people breaking out of the constrictions of the 1950s took their curiosity and spiritual seeking to India, Southeast Asia, and Japan; some discovered Buddhist meditation and brought it back to the United States.[11] During this period, Gary Snyder was probably the most vocal in spelling out the links between Buddhist practice and ecological activism. His books of poetry, *Turtle Island* (1974) and *Axe Handles* (1983), expressed a strong feeling for the land, influenced by his seven years of Zen training in Japan. His 1974 essay "Four Changes" laid out the current conditions of the world in terms of population, pollution, consumption, and the need for social transformation. Core to his analysis was the Buddhist perspective "that we are interdependent energy fields of great potential wisdom and compassion."[12] Snyder's ideas were adopted by the counterculture through his affiliation with beat writers Jack Kerouac and Allen Ginsberg and then further refined in his landmark collection of essays, *The Practice of the Wild.*[13]

Interest in Buddhism increased steadily through the 1970s along with the swelling environmental, civil rights, and women's movements. While Congress passed such landmark environmental laws as the Marine Mammal Protection Act, the Endangered Species Act, and the National Environmental Protection Act, Buddhist centers and teachers were becoming established on both coasts. San Francisco Zen Center, for example, expanded to two additional sites—a wilderness monastery at Tassajara, Big Sur, and a rural farm and garden temple in Marin County. By the 1980s the Buddhist Peace Fellowship was well along in its activist agenda and a number of Buddhist teachers were beginning to address the environmental crisis in their talks. In his 1989 Nobel Peace Prize acceptance speech His Holiness the Dalai Lama proposed making Tibet an international ecological reserve.[14] Thich Nhat Hanh, the influential Buddhist peace activist and Vietnamese Zen monk, referred often to ecological principles in his writings and talks on "interbeing," the Buddhist teaching of interdependence.[15]

The theme was picked up by Buddhist publications, conferences, and retreat centers. Buddhist Peace Fellowship featured the environment in *Turning Wheel* and produced a substantial packet and poster for Earth Day 1990.[16] The first popular anthology of Buddhism and ecology writings, *Dharma Gaia*, was published by Parallax Press that same year, following the more scholarly collection, *Nature in Asian Traditions of Thought.*[17] World Wide Fund for Nature brought out a series of books on five world religions, including *Buddhism and Ecology.*[18] *Tricycle* magazine examined green Buddhism and vegetarianism in 1994;[19] *Shambhala Sun* interviewed Gary Snyder and Japanese antinuclear poet-activist Nanao Sakaki.[20] The Vipassana newsletter *Inquiring Mind* produced an issue on "coming home"; *Ten Directions* of Zen Center

Los Angeles, *Mountain Record* of Zen Mountain Monastery, and *Blind Donkey* of Honolulu Diamond Sangha also took up the question of environmental practice.

Some retreat centers confronted ecological issues head on. Green Gulch Zen Center in northern California had to work out water use agreements with its farming neighbors and the Golden Gate National Recreation Area. Zen Mountain Monastery in New York faced off with the Department of Environmental Conservation over a beaver dam and forestry issues. In earlier days when vegetarianism was not such a popular and commercially viable choice, most Buddhist centers went against the social grain by refraining from meat-eating, often with an awareness of the associated environmental problems. Several Buddhist centers made some effort to grow their own organic food.[21] Outdoor walking meditation gained new stature through backpacking and canoeing retreats on both coasts.

By the 1990s, spirituality and the environment had become a hot topic. The first "Earth and Spirit" Conference was held in Seattle in 1990, and Buddhist workshops were part of the program. Middlebury College in Vermont hosted a "Spirit and Nature" conference that same year with the Dalai Lama as keynote speaker, sharing his Buddhist message for protection of the environment.[22] More interfaith conferences followed and Buddhism was always represented at the table. By 1993, human rights, social justice, and the environment were top agenda items at the Parliament of the World's Religions in Chicago. Buddhists from all over the world gathered with Christians, Hindus, pagans, Jews, Jains, and Muslims to consider the role of religion in responding to the environmental crisis.

Parallel sparks of interest were ignited in the academic community. Though both environmental studies and religious studies programs were well established in the academy, very few addressed the overlap between the two fields. In 1992 religion and ecology scholars formed a new group in the American Academy of Religion and began soliciting papers on environmental philosophy, animal rights, Gaian cosmology, and other environmental topics. Out of this initiative, colleagues generated campus interreligious dialogues and new religion and ecology courses. In the spring of 1997, Mary Evelyn Tucker and John Grimm of Bucknell University convened the first of a series of academic conferences with the aim of defining the field of religion and ecology.[23] The first of these addressed Buddhism and Ecology; the volume of collected papers was the first publication in the series.[24] The spring 1998 meeting of the International Buddhist-Christian Theological Encounter also focused on the environment, looking deeply at the impacts of consumerism.[25]

For the most part, the academic community did not address the *practice* of Buddhist environmentalism. This was explored more by socially engaged Buddhist teachers such as Thich Nhat Hanh, Bernie Glassman, the Dalai Lama, Sulak Sivaraksa, Christopher Titmuss, John Daido Loori, and Philip Kapleau.[26] One leader in developing a Buddhist ecological perspective for activists was Joanna Macy. Her doctoral research explored the significant parallels and distinctions between Western general systems theory and Buddhist philosophy.[27] In her sought-after classes and workshops, Macy developed a transformative model of experiential teaching designed to cultivate motivation, presence, and authenticity.[28] Her methods were strongly based in Buddhist meditation techniques and the Buddhist law of dependent co-arising. She called this "deep ecology work," challenging participants to take their insights into direct action. Working with John Seed, a Buddhist Australian rainforest activist, she developed a ritual "Council of All Beings" and other guided meditations to engage the attention and imagination on behalf of all beings.[29] Thousands of councils have now taken place in Australia, New Zealand, the United States, Germany, Russia, and other parts of the Western world.

Following in the footsteps of these visionary thinkers, a number of Buddhist activists organized groups to address specific issues—nuclear guardianship, factory farming, and forest protection. Each initiative has had its own history of start-up, strategizing, attracting interest, and, in some cases, fading enthusiasm. When these groups work with well-established environmental groups, they seem to be more successful in accomplishing their goals. Some Buddhist environmental activists have been effective in helping shape the orientation of an existing environmental group. The Institute for Deep Ecology, for example, which offers summer training for activists, has had many Buddhists among its faculty, especially on the West Coast.

Though the history of Buddhist environmentalism is short, it has substance: bright minds suggesting new ways to look at things, teachers and writers inspiring others to address the challenges, and fledgling attempts to practice ecospiritual activism based in Buddhist principles. As Western interest in Buddhism grows, it affects wider social and political circles. As other Buddhist activists take up the task of defining the principles and practices of socially engaged Buddhism, environmental Buddhism can play a vital role. As Buddhist teachers come to see the "ecosattva" possibilities in the bodhisattva vows, they can encourage such practice-based engagement. The seeds for all this are well planted; the next ten years of environmental disasters and activist responses will indicate whether Buddhist environmental activism will take its place among other parallel initiatives.

PHILOSOPHICAL GROUND

During its two-thousand-year-old history, Buddhism has evolved across a wide range of physical and cultural geographies. From the Theravada traditions in tropical South and Southeast Asia, to the Mahayana Schools in temperate and climatically diverse China and Japan, to the Vajrayana lineages in mountainous Tibet—Buddhist teachings have been received, modified, and elaborated in many ecological contexts. Across this history the range of Buddhist understandings about nature and human–nature relations has been based on different teachings, texts, and cultural views. These have not been consistent by any means; in fact, some views directly contradict each other.

Malcolm David Eckel, for example, contrasts the Indian view with the Japanese view of nature.[30] Indian Buddhist literature shows relatively little respect for wild nature, preferring tamed nature instead; Japanese Buddhism reveres the wild but engages it symbolically through highly developed art forms. Tellenbach and Kimura take this up in their investigation of the Japanese concept of nature, "what-is-so-of-itself"; Ian Harris discusses the difficulties in comparing the meaning of the word "nature" in different Asian languages.[31] When Harris reviews traditional Buddhist texts, he does not find any consistent philosophical orientation toward environmental ethics. He also challenges claims that Buddhist philosophies of nature led to any recognizable ecological awareness among early Buddhist societies, citing some evidence to the contrary. Lambert Schmithausen points out that according to early Buddhist sources, most members of Buddhist societies, including many monks, preferred the comforts of village life over the threats of the wild.[32] Images of Buddhist paradises are generally quite tame, not at all untrammeled wilderness. Only forest ascetics chose the hermitage path with its immersion in wild nature.

Even with these distinctions, Buddhist texts do contain many references to the natural world, both as inspiration for teachings and as source for ethical behavior. For Westerners tasting the Dharma in the context of the environmental crisis, all the Buddhist traditions are potential sources for philosophical and behavioral guidelines toward nature. The newest cultural form of Buddhism in the West will be different from what evolved in India, Thailand, China, and Japan. In seeking wisdom to address the world as it is now, Westerners are eagerly, if sometimes clumsily, looking for whatever may be helpful. From the earliest guidelines for forest monks to the hermitage songs of Milarepa, from the Jataka tales of compassion to Zen teachings on mountains and rivers, the inheritance is rich and diverse.[33] In this section, I lay out the principal teachings identified by leading Buddhist environmental thinkers in the late twentieth century as most relevant to addressing the current environmental situation.

Interdependence

In the canonical story of the Buddha's enlightenment, the culminating insight comes in the last hours of his long night of deep meditation. According to the story, he first perceived his previous lives in a continuous cycle of birth and death, then saw the vast universe of birth and death for all beings, gaining understanding of the workings of karma. Finally he realized the driving force behind birth and death, and the path to release from it. Each piece of the Buddha's experience added to a progressive unfolding of a single truth about existence—the law of mutual causality or dependent origination (in Sanskrit *pratityasamutpada*, in Pali *paticca samuppada*). According to this law, all phenomena, that is, all of nature, arise from complex sets of causes and conditions, each set unique to the specific situations. Thus, the simple but penetrating Pali verse:

> This being, that becomes;
> from the arising of this, that arises;
> this not being, that becomes not;
> from the ceasing of this, that ceases.[34]

Ecological understanding of natural systems fits very well within the Buddhist description of interdependence. This law has been the subject of much attention in the Buddhism and Ecology literature because of its overlapping with ecological principles.[35] Throughout all cultural forms of Buddhism, nature is perceived as relational, each phenomenon dependent on a multitude of causes and conditions. From a Buddhist perspective these causes include not only physical and biological factors but also historical and cultural factors, that is, human thought forms and values.

The Hua-Yen School of Buddhism, developed in seventh-century China, placed particular emphasis on this principle, using the jewel net of Indra as a teaching metaphor. This cosmic net contains a multifaceted jewel at each of its nodes. "Because the jewels are clear, they reflect each other's images, appearing in each other's reflections upon reflections, ad infinitum, all appearing at once in one jewel."[36] To extend the metaphor, if you tug on any one of the lines of the net—for example, through loss of species or habitat—it affects all the other lines. Or, if any of the jewels become cloudy (toxic or polluted), they reflect the others less clearly. Likewise, if clouded jewels are cleared up (rivers cleaned, wetlands restored), life across the web is enhanced. Because the web of interdependence includes not only the actions of all beings but also their thoughts, the intention of the actor becomes a critical factor in determining what happens. This, then, provides a principle of both explanation for the way things are, and a path for positive action.

Modern eco-Buddhists working with this principle have taken various paths. Using the term "interbeing," Thich Nhat Hanh emphasizes nonduality of view, encouraging students to "look at reality as a whole rather than to cut it into separate entities."[37] Gary Snyder takes up the interdependence of eater and eaten, acknowledging the "simultaneous path of pain and beauty of this complexly interrelated world."[38] Feminist theologian Rita Gross looks at the darker implications of cause and effect in the growing human population crisis.[39] Activist Joanna Macy leads people through their environmental despair by steadily reinforcing ways to work together and build more functional and healing relationships with the natural world.[40]

The law of interdependence suggests a powerful corollary, sometimes noted as "emptiness of separate self." If all phenomena are dependent on interacting causes and conditions, nothing exists by itself, autonomous and self-supporting. This Buddhist understanding (and experience) of self directly contradicts the traditional Western sense of self as a discrete individual. Alan Watts called this assumption of separateness the "skin-encapsulated ego"—the very delusion that Buddhist practices seek to cut through. Based on the work of Gregory Bateson and other systems theorists, Macy describes a more ecological view of the self as part of a larger flow-through.[41] She ties this to Arne Naess's deep ecology philosophy, derived from a felt shift of identification to a wider, more inclusive view of self. Buddhist rainforest activist John Seed described his experience of no-self in an interview with *Inquiring Mind:* "All of a sudden, the forest was inside me and was calling to me, and it was the most powerful thing I have ever felt."[42] Gary Snyder suggests this emptiness of self provides a link to "wild mind," or access to the energetic forces that determine wilderness. These forces act outside of human influence, setting the historical, ecological, and even cosmological context for all life. Thus "emptiness" is dynamic, shape-shifting, energy in motion—"wild" and beyond human imagination.[43]

The Path of Liberation

The Buddhist image of the Wheel of Life contains various realms of beings; at the center are three figures representing greed, hate, and delusion. They chase each other around, generating endless suffering, perpetrating a false sense of self or ego. Liberation from attachment to this false self is the central goal in Buddhist practice. The first and second of the four noble truths describe the very nature of existence as suffering, due to our instincts to protect our own individual lives and views. The third and fourth noble truths lay out a path to liberation from this suffering of self-attachment, the eight-fold path of morality, awareness, and wisdom.

Buddhist scholar Alan Sponberg argues that green Buddhism has overemphasized interdependence or the relational dimension almost to the exclusion of the developmental aspect of practice.[44] By working to overcome ego-based attachments and socially conditioned desires, students cultivate the capacity for insight and compassion. This effort, he says, is crucial to displacing the hierarchy of oppression that undermines the vision of an ecologically healthy world. Sponberg suggests that a Buddhist environmental ethic is a virtue ethic, based fundamentally on development of consciousness and a sense of responsibility to act compassionately for the benefit of all forms of life. This is the basis for the Mahayana archetype of the bodhisattva, committed to serving others until suffering is extinguished. Macy argues that this responsibility need not be some morally imposed self-righteous action (often characteristic of environmentalists) but rather an action that "springs naturally from the ground of being."[45]

The path of liberation includes the practice of physical, emotional, and mental awareness. Such practice can increase one's appreciation for the natural world; it can also reveal hidden cultural assumptions about privilege, comfort, consumption, and the abuse of nature.

When one sees one's self as part of a mutually causal web, it becomes obvious that there is no such thing as an action without effect. Through the practice of green virtue ethics, students are encouraged to be accountable for all of their actions, from eating food to using a car to buying new clothes. Likewise, they can investigate the reigning economic paradigm and see how deeply it determines their choices. Through following the fundamental precepts, environmentally oriented Buddhists can practice moderation and restraint, simplifying needs and desires to reduce suffering for others. For Westerners this may mean withdrawal from consumer addictions to products with large ecological impacts, such as coffee, cotton, computers, and cars.

Practice in Action

Buddhist environmental teachers and writers point to three primary arenas of practice that can serve the environment: compassion, mindfulness, and nonharming. In the Theravada tradition, one practices loving-kindness, wishing that all beings be free from harm and blessed by physical and mental well-being. In the Mahayana tradition one takes up the bodhisattva path, vowing to return again and again to relieve the suffering of all sentient beings—the life work of an environmentalist! Both practices are impossible challenges if interpreted literally; the environmental implications of these prayers or vows can be overwhelming. Yet the strength of intention offers a substantial foundation for Buddhist environmental activism. Budding eco-Buddhists struggle with the application of these spiritual vows in the very real contexts of factory farms, pesticide abuse, genetic engineering, and loss of endangered species habitat.

Mindfulness practice, a natural support to Buddhist environmentalism, can take a range of forms. Thich Nhat Hanh teaches the basic principles of the *Satipatthana Sutta* or the mindfulness text, practicing awareness of breath, body, feelings, and mind. Walking and sitting meditation generate a sense of grounded presence and alertness to where one actually is. Environmental educators stress mindfulness through nature appreciation exercises and rules of respect toward the natural world. Environmental strategists use promotional campaigns to generate awareness of threatened species and places. These efforts take mindfulness practice off the cushion and out into the world where alarming situations of great suffering require strong attention.

The practice of *ahimsa* or nonharming derives naturally from a true experience of compassion. All the Buddhist precepts are based fundamentally on nonharming or reducing the suffering of others. Practicing the first precept, not killing, raises ethical dilemmas around food, land use, pesticides, pollution, and cultural economic invasion. The second precept, not stealing, suggests considering the implications of global trade and corporate exploitation of resources. Not lying brings up issues in advertising and consumerism. Not engaging in abusive relations covers a broad realm of cruelty and disrespect for nonhuman others. As Gary Snyder says, "The whole planet groans under the massive disregard of ahimsa by the highly organized societies and corporate economies of the world."[46] Thich Nhat Hanh interprets the precept prohibiting drugs and alcohol to include the toxic addictions of television, video games, and junk magazines.[47] Practicing restraint and nonharming is a way to make Buddhist philosophy manifest in the context of rapidly deteriorating global ecosystems. Zen teacher Robert Aitken offers this vow:

> With resources scarcer and scarcer, I vow with all beings—
> To reduce my gear in proportion even to candles and carts.[48]

BUDDHIST ENVIRONMENTAL ACTIVISM

How is green Buddhism being practiced? What is the evidence of green Buddhism on the front lines? Macy suggests three types of activism that characterize environmentalism today: 1) holding-actions of resistance, 2) analysis of social structures and creation of new alternatives, and 3) cultural transformation.[49] Some of the best examples of Buddhist environmentalism come from outside the West, but here I report only on local efforts in North America.

Holding-actions aim primarily to stop or reduce destructive activity, buying time for more effective long-term strategies. The small group of ecosattvas protesting the logging of old growth redwood groves is part of the holding-actions in northern California. They draw on local support from Buddhist deep ecologist Bill Devall and his ecosangha in Humboldt County as well as support from the Green Gulch Zen community and the Buddhist Peace Fellowship. For the big 1997 demonstration, the ecosattvas invited others to join them in creating a large prayer flag covered with human handprints of mud. This then served as visual testimony of solidarity for all those participating in Headwaters actions. Six months after the protest, several ecosattvas made a special pilgrimage deep into the heart of the Headwaters, carrying a Tibetan treasure vase. Activists used the vase to bring attention to the threatened trees at various Bay Area sangha meetings. People were invited to offer their gifts and prayers on behalf of the redwoods. On a rainy winter's day, the vase was ceremonially buried beneath one of the giants to strengthen spiritual protection for the trees.[50]

Resistance actions by Buddhists Concerned for Animals were initiated by Brad Miller and Vanya Palmers, two Zen students in the San Francisco area. Moved by the suffering of animals in cages, on factory farms, and in export houses, they joined the animal rights movement, educating other Buddhists about the plight of monkeys, beef cattle, and endangered parrots. Vanya has continued this work in Europe, where he now lives, focusing on the cruelty in large-scale hog farming.[51]

When the federal government proposed burial of nuclear waste deep under Yucca Mountain, a group of Buddhists and others gathered together under Joanna Macy's leadership and met as a study group for several years. They took the position that nuclear waste was safer above ground where it could be monitored, and they developed an alternate vision of nuclear guardianship based in Buddhist spiritual practices.[52] At about the same time, Japan arranged for several shipments of plutonium to be reprocessed in France and then shipped back to Japan. Zen student and artist Mayumi Oda helped to organize Plutonium-Free Future and the Rainbow Serpents to stop these shipments of deadly nuclear material. One ship was temporarily stopped, and although shipments resumed, the actions raised awareness in Japan and the United States, affecting Japanese government policies.[53]

The second type of activism, undertaking structural analysis and creating alternative green visions, has also engaged twentieth-century Buddhists. Small "b" Buddhist Rick Klugston directs the Washington, D.C.-based Center for Respect of Life and the Environment, an affiliate of the Humane Society of the United States. He and his staff work on sustainability criteria for humane farming, basing their work in religious principles of nonharming. In 1997 the Soka Gakkai-affiliated group, Boston Research Center for the 21st Century, held a series of workshops addressing the people's earth charter, an internationally negotiated list of ethical guidelines for human–earth relations. The center published a booklet of Buddhist views on the charter's principles for us in discussions leading up to United Nations adoption.[54] A subgroup of the International Network of Engaged Buddhists and the Buddhist Peace Fellowship, called the

"Think Sangha," is engaged in structural analysis of global consumerism. Collaborating between the United States and Southeast Asia, they have held conferences in Thailand on alternatives to consumerism, pressing for moderation and lifestyle simplification.[55] One of the boldest visions is the Dalai Lama's proposal that the entire province of Tibet be declared an ecological reserve. Sadly, this vision, put forth in his Nobel Peace Prize acceptance speech, is nowhere close to actualization.[56]

Scholars have offered structural analyses using Buddhist principles to shed light on environmental problems. Rita Gross, Buddhist feminist scholar, has laid out a Buddhist framework for considering global population issues.[57] I have compared ecofeminist principles of activism with Buddhist philosophy, showing a strong compatibility between the two.[58] Through Buddhist-Christian dialogue, process theologian and meditator Jay McDaniel has developed spiritual arguments for compassionate treatment of animals as a serious human responsibility.[59] Sociologist Bill Devall integrated Buddhist principles into his elaboration of Arne Naess's Deep Ecology philosophy urging simplification of needs and wants.[60] Joanna Macy likewise draws on Buddhist philosophy and practices to analyze the paralyzing states of grief, despair, and fear that prevent people from acting on behalf of the environment.

As for the third type of activism, transforming culture, these projects are very much in progress and sometimes met with resistance. Two Buddhist centers in rural northern California, Green Gulch Zen Center and Spirit Rock, already demonstrate a serious commitment to the environment through vegetarian dining, land and water stewardship efforts, an organic farm and garden at Green Gulch, and ceremonies that include the natural world.[61] On Earth Day 1990, the abbot led a tree-ordaining precepts ceremony and an animal memorial service. Other environmental rituals include special dedications at the solstices and equinoxes, a Buddha's birthday celebration of local wildflowers, Thanksgiving altars from the farm harvest, and participation in the United Nations Environmental Sabbath in June. The ecosattvas meet regularly to plan restoration projects that are now part of daily work practice. When people visit Green Gulch, they can see ecological action as part of a Buddhist way of life. Similar initiatives have been undertaken at Spirit Rock Meditation Center, also in the San Francisco Bay area.

In the Sierra foothills, Gary Snyder has been a leader in establishing the Yuba River Institute, a bioregional watershed organization working in cooperation with the Bureau of Land Management. They have done ground survey work, controlled burns, and creek restoration projects, engaging the local community in the process. "To restore the land one must live and work in a place. To work in a place is to work with others. People who work together in a place become a community, and a community, in time, grows a culture."[62] Snyder models the level of commitment necessary to reinhabit a place and build community that might eventually span generations. Zen Mountain Center in Southern California is beginning similar work, carrying out resource management practices such as thinning for fire breaks, restoring degraded forest, and limiting human access to some preserve areas.[63] Applying Buddhist principles in an urban setting, Zen teacher Bernard Glassman has developed environmentally oriented small businesses that employ local street people, sending products to socially responsible companies such as Ben and Jerry's.[64]

As the educational element of cultural transformation, several Buddhist centers have developed lecture series, classes, and retreats based on environmental themes. Zen Mountain Monastery in the Catskills of New York offers "Mountains and Rivers" retreats based on the center's commitment to environmental conservation. These feature backpacking, canoeing, nature photography, and haiku as gateways to Buddhist insight. Ring of Bone Zendo at Kitkitdizze, Gary Snyder's community, has offered backpacking *sesshins* in the Sierra Mountains since its inception. Green Gulch Zen Center cohosts a "Voice of the Watershed" series each year with Muir Woods National Monument, including talks and walks across the landscape of the two valleys. At Manzanita Village in southern California, Caitriona Reed and Michele Benzamin-Masuda include deep ecology practices, gardening, and nature observation as part of their Thich Nhat Hanh-style mindfulness retreats.

Most of these examples represent social change agents working within Buddhist or non-Buddhist institutions to promote environmental interests. But what about isolated practitioners, struggling to consider the implications of their lifestyles in consumer America and other parts of the West? Independent of established groups, a number of Buddhists are taking small steps of activism as they try to align their actions with their Buddhist practice. One growing area of interest is ethical choices in food consumption, prompted both by health and environmental concerns. Many people, Buddhists included, are turning to vegetarianism and veganism as more compassionate choices for animals and ecosystems. Others are committing to eat only organically grown food, in order to support pesticide-free soil and healthy farming. Thich Nhat Hanh has strongly encouraged his students to examine their consumption habits, not only around food and alcohol, but also television, music, books, and magazines. His radical stance is echoed by Sulak Sivaraksa in Thailand, who insists the Western standard of consumption is untenable if extended throughout the world. Some Buddhists have participated in "International Buy Nothing" Day, targeted for the busiest shopping day right after Thanksgiving. Others have joined support groups for reducing credit card debt, giving up car dependence, and creating work cooperatives. Because Buddhism is still so new in the Western world, the extent of Buddhist lifestyle activism is very hard to gauge. But for many students, environmental awareness and personal change flow naturally from a Buddhist practice commitment

ELEMENTS OF GREEN BUDDHIST ACTIVISM

What makes Buddhist environmentalism different from other environmental activism or from other ecoreligious activism? The answer in both cases lies in the distinctive orientation of Buddhist philosophy and practice. Buddhist environmentalists turn to principles of nonharming, compassion, and interdependence as core ethics in choosing activism strategies. They aim to serve all beings through equanimity and loving-kindness. Though activists may not fulfill the highest ideals of their Buddhist training, they at least struggle to place their actions in a spiritual context. This reflects an underlying premise that good environmental work should also be good spiritual work, restoring both place and person to wholeness.

To be sure, there are significant challenges. Engaged Buddhist scholar Kenneth Kraft outlines four dilemmas a generic American Buddhist environmentalist ("Gabe") might encounter.[65] First, he or she would likely encounter some gaps between the traditional teachings and current political realities. Most of the Buddha's advice to students deals with individual morality and action; but today's environmental problems require *collective* action and a conscious sense of group responsibility. It is not so easy to find guidelines for global structural change within these ancient teachings. Second, Gabe must make some tough decisions about how to use his or her time. Meditate or organize a protest? When political decisions are moving at a rapid rate, activists must respond very quickly for effective holding action. Yet cultivating equanimity, patience, and loving-kindness requires regular hours of practice on the cushion. The yearning for time dedicated to Buddhist retreats can compete with time needed for soul-renewing wilderness.

Third, Gabe may question the effectiveness of identifying his or her efforts as specifically Buddhist. It may be easier just to "blend in" with others working on the same issue. Fourth, Gabe may also begin to wonder about the effectiveness of some forms of practice forms in combatting environmental destruction. How can meditation or ceremony stop clear-cut logging? Can spiritually oriented activists make a difference in the high pressure political world? Given these and other challenges, green Buddhists nonetheless try to carry out their work in a manner consistent with Buddhist practice and philosophy.

Characteristic ideals for green Buddhism can be described in terms of the Three Jewels: the Buddha, Dharma, and Sangha. The Buddha exemplified a way of life based on spiritual practice, including meditation, study, questioning and debate, ceremony and ritual. Each Buddhist lineage has its own highly evolved traditional practice forms that encourage the student to "act like Buddha." At the heart of the Buddha's path is reflective inquiry into the nature of reality. Applying this practice in today's environmental context, ecoactivists undertake rigorous examination of conditioned beliefs and thought patterns regarding the natural world. This may include deconstructing the objectification of plants and animals, the stereotyping of environmentalists, dualistic thinking of enemy-ism, the impacts of materialism, and environmental racism.

In addition, the green Buddhist would keep his or her activist work grounded in regular engagement with practice forms—for example, saying the precepts with other activists, as Thich Nhat Hanh has encouraged, or reciting sutras that inspire courage and loving-kindness (that is, the *Metta Sutta* for example, or the Zen chant to Kanzeon). Ring of Bone Zen students chant Dogen's "Mountains and Rivers" treatise on their backpacking retreats. Mindfulness practice with the breath can help sustain an activist under pressure, during direct political action or in the workplace. Green Buddhist ceremonies are evolving, often as variations on standard rituals—for example, the Earth Day precepts at Green Gulch, and the earth relief ceremony at Rochester Zen Center.[66] If the Buddha's path is foundational to Buddhist environmental activism, it means each engaged person undertakes some form of spiritual journey toward insight and awakening. Activism is the context in which this happens, but the Buddha's way serves as the model.

Of the Buddha's teachings, or Dharma, several core principles contribute to a green Buddhist approach. First, it is based on a relational understanding of interdependence and no-self. This may mean, for example, assessing the relationships of the players in an environmental conflict from a context of historical and geographical causes and conditions. It may also mean acknowledging the distribution of power across the human political relationships, as well as learning about the ecological relationships that are under siege. Second, green Buddhist activism could reflect the teachings of ahimsa, nonharming, with compassion for the suffering of others. For the Buddhist environmentalist this may extend to oppression based on race, class, or gender discrimination as well as to environmental oppression of plants, animals, rivers, rocks, and mountains. This recognition of suffering in the nonhuman world is rarely acknowledged by the capitalist economy. Voicing it as a religious point of view may open some doors to more humane policies. This green Buddhist teaching is congruent with many schools of ecophilosophy that respect the intrinsic value and capacity for experience of each being.

A third Buddhist teaching applicable to activism is the *nondualistic* view of reality. Most political battles play out as confrontations between sworn enemies: loggers vs. spotted owl defenders, housewives vs. toxic polluters, birdlovers vs. pesticide producers. From a Buddhist perspective, this kind of hatred destroys spiritual equanimity; thus, it is much better to work from an inclusive perspective, offering kindness to all parties involved, even while setting firm moral boundaries against harmful actions. This approach is quite rare among struggling, discouraged, battle-weary environmentalists who, in fact, are being attacked by government officials, sheriffs, or the media. A Buddhist commitment to nondualism can help to stabilize a volatile situation and establish new grounds for negotiation.

A fourth Buddhist teaching reinforces the role of *intention*. Buddhist texts emphasize a strong relationship between intention, action, and karmic effects of an action. If a campaign is undertaken out of spite, revenge, or rage, that emotional tone will carry forth into all the ripening of the fruits of that action (and likely cause a similar reaction in response). However, if an action is grounded in understanding that the other party is also part of Indra's jewel net, then things unfold with a little less shoving and pushing.

Perhaps the most significant teaching of the Dharma relevant to Buddhist activism is the practice of detachment from the ego-generating self. Thus, a green Buddhist approach is not motivated primarily by the need for ego identity or satisfaction. Strong intention with less orientation to the self relieves the activist from focusing so strongly on results.[67] One does what is necessary in the situation, not bound by the need for it to reinforce one's ideas or to turn out a certain way. By leaning into the creative energies moving through the wider web but holding to a strong intention, surprising collaborative actions take place. Small "b" Buddhists have been able to act as bridge-builders in hostile or reactive situations by toning down the need for personal recognition.

Sangha, the third of the Three Jewels, is often the least recognized or appreciated by American Buddhists. As newcomers to the practice in a speedy, product-driven society, most students are drawn to the calming effects of meditation practice and the personal depth of student-teacher relationships. Practicing with community can be difficult for students living away from Buddhist centers. Building community among environmental Buddhists is even harder, since they are even more isolated geographically from each other and sometimes marginalized even by their own peers in Buddhist centers. From a green Buddhist perspective, sangha work presents not only the challenges of personal and institutional relations, but also ecological relations. Some of the leading green Buddhist thinkers have suggested ways to move toward this work in an integrated way.

Gary Snyder brings his sangha work home through the framework of bioregional thinking and organizing. His foundation for this is more than ecological; it is aesthetic, economic, and practice-based. He suggests that "by being in place, we get the largest sense of community." The bioregional community "does not end at the human boundaries; we are in a community with certain trees, plants, birds, animals. The conversation is with the whole thing."[68] He models and encourages others to take up the practice of *reinhabitation*, learning to live on the land with the same respect and understanding as the original indigenous people. He expects this will take a number of generations, so the wisdom gathered now must be passed along to the young ones. Spiritual community on the land offers one place to do this.

Others can participate in ecosangha through supporting and lobbying for ecological practices at their local Buddhist centers. The hundreds of people who come to Green Gulch Zen Center or Spirit Rock Meditation Center, for example, follow the centers' customs regarding water conservation, recycling, vegetarianism, and land protection. With each step toward greater ecological sustainability, local community culture takes on a greener cast. These actions need not be only a painful commitment to restraint, rather they can become a celebration of environmental awareness. Printed materials such as the booklet on environmental practices at Green Gulch can help to educate visitors about institutional commitments.

Joanna Macy recommends sangha-building as central to deep ecology work. Through trust-building exercises, brainstorming, and contract-making, Macy helps people find ways to support each other in their activist efforts. Learning networks of Buddhists and non-Buddhists often stay together after her workshops for mutual support and prevention of activist burnout. Macy helps people taste the power of *kalyana mitta,* or spiritual friendship—acting together in the web to help others practice the Dharma and take care of this world.

CONCLUSION

How might Buddhist environmentalism affect the larger environmental movement and how might it influence Western Buddhism in general? Will Buddhist environmentalism turn out to be more environmental than Buddhist?[69] The answers to these questions must be largely speculative at this time, since green Buddhism is just finding its voice. It is possible that this fledgling voice will be drowned in the brownlash against environmentalists, or in the Western resistance to engaged Buddhism. Environmental disasters of survival proportions may overwhelm anyone's capacity to act effectively. The synergistic combination of millennialism and economic collapse may flatten green Buddhism as well as many other constructive social forces.

But if one takes a more hopeful view, it seems possible to imagine that green Buddhism will grow and take hold in the minds and hearts of young people who are creating the future. Perhaps some day there will be ecosattva chapters across the world affiliated with various practice centers. Perhaps Buddhist ecoactivists will be sought out for their spiritual stability and compassion in the face of extremely destructive forces. Buddhist centers might become models of ecological sustainability, showing other religious institutions ways to encourage ecological culture. More Buddhist teachers may become informed about environmental issues and raise these concerns in their teachings, calling for moderation and restraint. Perhaps the next century will see Buddhist practice centers forming around specific ecological commitments.

Making an educated guess from the perspective of the late 1990s, I predict that the influence of green Buddhism may be small in numbers, but great in impact. Gary Snyder, for example, is now widely read by college students in both literature and environmental studies classes. Joanna Macy has led workshops for staff at the White House and the Hanford nuclear reactor in Washington State. Thich Nhat Hanh has shared his commentaries on the interbeing of paper, clouds, trees, and farmers with thousands of listeners on lecture tours throughout the West. Some practicing Buddhists already hold influential positions in major environmental groups such as the Natural Resources Defense Council, Rainforest Action Network, and Greenpeace. Perhaps in the near future they will also hold cabinet positions or Congressional committee chairs or serve as staff for environmental think tanks.

Buddhist centers and thinkers will not drive the religious conversation in the West for quite some time, if ever. The Judeo-Christian heritage of the West is still a prominent force in Western thinking, laws, and religious customs. However, Buddhists are already significant participants in interfaith dialogue regarding the environment. This could have an increasing impact on public conversations by raising ethical questions in a serious way. Right now, decisions that affect the health and well-being of the environment are often made behind closed doors. To challenge these in a public way from a religious perspective could shed some much needed light on ecologically unethical ways of doing business.

What happens next lies in the hands of those who are nurturing this wave of enthusiasm for green Buddhism and those who will follow. It may be religious leaders, writers, teachers, or elders; it may be the younger generations, full of energy and passion for protecting the home they love. Because the rate of destruction is so great now, with major life systems threatened, any and all green activism is sorely needed. Buddhists have much to offer the assaulted world. It is my hope that many more step forward boldly into the melee of environmental conflict. Side by side with other bodhisattvas, may they join the global effort to stop the cruelty and help create a more respectful and compassionate future for all beings.

NOTES

1. For information on ecosattva activity, see "Universal Chainsaw, Universal Forest," *Turning Wheel* (winter 1998): 31–33.

2. See, for example, such recent volumes as Steven C. Rockefeller and John C. Elder, *Spirit and Nature: Why the Environment Is a Religious Issue* (Boston: Beacon Press, 1992); Mary Evelyn Tucker and John A. Grim, eds., *Worldviews and Ecology* (Lewisburg, Pa.: Bucknell University Press, 1993); Fritz Hull, ed., *Earth and Spirit: The Spiritual Dimensions of the Environmental Crisis* (New York: Continuum, 1993); David Kinsley, *Ecology and Religion: Ecological Spirituality in Cross-Cultural Perspective* (Englewood Cliffs, N.J.: Prentice Hall, 1995); Dieter T. Hessel, ed., *Theology for Earth Community: A Field Guide* (Maryknoll, N.Y.: Orbis, 1996); Roger Gottlieb, ed., *This Sacred Earth: Religion, Nature, and Environment* (New York: Routledge, 1996).

3. Parvel Gmuzdek, "Kalayanamitra's Action on the Yadana Pipeline," *Seeds of Peace* 13, no. 3 (September–December 1997): 23–26.

4. Joanna Macy, "The Third Turning of the Wheel," *Inquiring Mind* 5, no. 2 (winter 1989): 10–12.

5. Macy, *Inquiring Mind,* 11.

6. Wendy Johnson and Stephanie Kaza, "Earth Day at Green Gulch," *Journal of the Buddhist Peace Fellowship* (summer 1990): 30–33.

7. See reports on their activities in Bay Area Friends of Tibet newsletters.

8. Stephanie Kaza and Kenneth Kraft, eds., *Dharma Rain: Sources of Buddhist Environmentalism* (Boston: Shambhala, 1999).

9. Sulak Sivaraksa, "Buddhism with a Small 'b,'" *Seeds of Peace* (Berkeley, Calif.: Parallax Press, 1992), 69.

10. Peter Timmerman, "It Is Dark Outside: Western Buddhism from the Enlightenment to the Global Crisis," in *Buddhism and Ecology,* ed. Martine Batchelor and Kerry Brown (London: Cassell, 1992), 65–76.

11. See Rick Fields, *How the Swans Came to the Lake: A Narrative History of Buddhism in America* (Boston: Shambhala, 1986), for a thorough history of these and earlier forays to the East by Westerners.

12. Gary Snyder, *A Place in Space* (Washington, D.C.: Counterpoint Press, 1995), 41.

13. Gary Snyder, *The Practice of the Wild* (San Francisco: North Point Press, 1990).

14. "The Nobel Peace Prize Lecture," in *The Dalai Lama: A Policy of Kindness,* ed. Sidney Piburn (Ithaca, New York: Snow Lion, 1990), 15–27.

15. Thich Nhat Hanh, *Love in Action* (Berkeley, Calif.: Parallax Press, 1993).

16. Issues on the theme of environmental activism were published in spring 1990, spring 1994, and spring 1997.

17. Alan Hunt-Badiner, ed., *Dharma Gaia* (Berkeley, Calif.: Parallax Press, 1990); J. Baird Callicott and Roger T. Ames, eds., *Nature in Asian Traditions of Thought* (Albany: State University of New York Press, 1989).

18. The other four books in the series address Christianity, Hinduism, Islam, Judaism, and Ecology.

19. See *Tricycle* 4, no. 2 (winter 1994): 2, 49–63.

20. For Gary Snyder interviews, see "Not Here Yet" 2, no. 4 (March 1994): 19–25; "The Mind of Gary Snyder" 4, no. 5 (May 1996): 19–26; for Nanao Sakaki, see "Somewhere on the Water Planet" 4, no. 2 (November 1995): 45–47.

21. For a detailed study of two Buddhist centers see Stephanie Kaza, "American Buddhist Response to the Land: Ecological Practice at Two West Coast Retreat Centers," in *Buddhism and Ecology: The*

Interconnectedness of Dharma and Deeds, ed. Mary Evelyn Tucker and Duncan Ryuken Williams (Cambridge: Harvard University Press, 1997), 219–48.

22. See conference talks in Rockefeller and Elder, eds., *Spirit and Nature*.

23. Mary Evelyn Tucker, "The Emerging Alliance of Ecology and Religion," *Worldviews: Environment, Culture, and Religion* 1, no. 1 (1997): 3–24.

24. Tucker and Williams, eds., *Buddhism and Ecology*.

25. See one of the lead papers from the meeting: Stephanie Kaza, "Overcoming the Grip of Consumerism," forthcoming in *Journal of Buddhist-Christian Studies*.

26. See, for example, such works as Thich Nhat Hanh, "The Individual, Society, and Nature," in *The Path of Compassion*, ed. Fred Eppsteiner (Berkeley, Calif.: Parallax Press, 1988), 40–46; Dalai Lama, "The Ethical Approach to Environmental Protection," in *The Dalai Lama: A Policy of Kindness*, ed. Piburn (Ithaca, N.Y.: Snow Lion, 1990), 118–28; Sulak Sivaraksa, *Seeds of Peace* (Berkeley, Calif.: Parallax Press, 1992); Christopher Titmuss, "A Passion for the Dharma," *Turning Wheel* (fall 1991): 19–20; John Daido Loori, "River Seeing River," in *Mountain Record* 14, no. 3 (spring 1996): 2–10; and Philip Kapleau, *To Cherish All Life: A Buddhist Case for Becoming Vegetarian* (San Francisco: Harper and Row, 1982).

27. Joanna Macy, *Mutual Causality in Buddhism and General Systems Theory: The Dharma of Natural Systems* (Albany: State University of New York Press, 1991).

28. Joanna Macy, *Despair and Personal Power in the Nuclear Age* (Philadelphia: New Society, 1983).

29. John Seed, Joanna Macy, Pat Fleming, and Arne Naess, *Thinking Like a Mountain: Towards a Council of All Beings* (Philadelphia: New Society, 1988).

30. Malcolm David Eckel, "Is There a Buddhist Philosophy of Nature?" in *Buddhism and Ecology*, ed. Tucker and Williams, 327–50.

31. Ian Harris, "Buddhism and the Discourse of Environmental Concern: Some Methodological Problems Considered," in *Buddhism and Ecology*, ed. Tucker and Williams, 377–402; and Hubertus Tellenbach and Bin Kimura, "The Japanese Concept of 'Nature,'" in *Nature in Asian Traditions of Thought*, ed. J. Baird Callicott and Roger T. Ames (Albany: State University of New York Press, 1989).

32. Lambert Schmidthausen, "The Early Buddhist Tradition and Ecological Ethics," *Journal of Buddhist Ethics* 4 (1997): 1–42.

33. Represented in Stephanie Kaza and Kenneth Kraft, eds., *Dharma Rain*.

34. *Samyutta Nikaya* II.28, 65; *Majjhima Nikaya* II.32.

35. See, for example, Francis H. Cook, "The Jewel Net of Indra," in *Nature in Asian Traditions of Thought*, ed. Callicott and Ames, 213–30; Bill Devall, "Ecocentric Sangha," in *Dharma Gaia*, ed. Hunt-Badiner, 155–64; Paul O. Ingram, "Nature's Jeweled Net: Kukai's Ecological Buddhism," *The Pacific World* 6 (1990): 50–64; Joanna Macy, *Mutual Causality in Buddhism;* and Gary Snyder, *A Place in Space*.

36. Tu Shun, in Thomas Cleary, *Entry into the Inconceivable: An Introduction to Hua-Yen Buddhism* (Honolulu: University of Hawaii Press, 1983), 66.

37. Thich Nhat Hanh, "The Individual, Society, and Nature," in *The Path of Compassion*, ed. Fred Eppsteiner, 40.

38. Snyder, *A Place in Space*, 70.

39. Rita Gross, "Buddhist Resources for Issues of Population, Consumption, and the Environment," in *Buddhism and Ecology*, ed. Tucker and Williams, 291–312.

40. Joanna Macy and Molly Young Brown, *Coming Back to Life: Practices to Reconnect Our Lives, Our World* (Gabriola Island, British Columbia: New Society, 1998).

41. Macy, *Mutual Causality in Buddhism*.

42. Interview with John Seed, "The Rain Forest as Teacher," *Inquiring Mind* 8, no. 2 (spring 1992): 1.

43. Gary Snyder, "The Etiquette of Freedom," in *The Practice of the Wild*, 10.

44. Alan Sponberg, "Green Buddhism and the Hierarchy of Compassion," in *Buddhism and Ecology*, ed. Tucker and Williams, 351–76.

45. Joanna Macy, "Third Turning of the Wheel," *Inquiring Mind* 5, no. 2 (winter 1989): 10–12.

46. Snyder, *A Place in Space*, 73.

47. See his discussion of the fifth precept in Thich Nhat Hanh, *For a Future to Be Possible* (Berkeley, Calif.: Parallax Press, 1993).

48. Robert Aitken, *The Dragon Who Never Sleeps* (Berkeley, Calif.: Parallax Press, 1992), 62.

49. Macy and Brown, *Coming Back to Life*.

50. Wendy Johnson, "A Prayer for the Forest," *Tricycle* 8, no. 1 (fall 1998): 84–85.

51. Vanya Palmers, "What Can I Do," *Turning Wheel* (winter 1993): 15–17.

52. Joanna Macy, "Guarding the Earth," *Inquiring Mind* 7, no. 2 (spring 1991): 1, 4–5, 12.

53. Kenneth Kraft, "Nuclear Ecology and Engaged Buddhism," in *Buddhism and Ecology*, ed. Tucker and Williams, 269–90.

54. Amy Morgante, ed., *Buddhist Perspectives on the Earth Charter* (Cambridge, Mass.: Buddhist Research Center for the 21st Century, November 1997).

55. See 1998–1999 issues of *Seeds of Peace* for reports and announcements of these events.

56. Tenzin Gyatso, "The Nobel Peace Prize Lecture," in *The Dalai Lama: A Policy of Kindness*, ed. Piburn, 15–27.

57. Gross, *Buddhism and Ecology*.

58. Stephanie Kaza, "Acting with Compassion: Buddhism, Feminism, and the Environmental Crisis," in *Ecofeminism and the Sacred*, ed. Carol Adams (New York: Continuum, 1993).

59. Jay B. McDaniel, *Earth, Sky, Gods, and Mortals: Developing an Ecological Spirituality* (Mystic, Conn.: Twenty-Third Publications, 1990).

60. Bill Devall, *Simple in Means, Rich in Ends: Practicing Deep Ecology* (Salt Lake City: Peregrine Smith, 1988).

61. Stephanie Kaza, "American Buddhist Response to the Land: Ecological Practice at Two West Coast Retreat Centers," in *Buddhism and Ecology*, ed. Tucker and Williams, 219–48.

62. Snyder, *A Place in Space*, 250. See also David Barnhill, "Great Earth Sangha: Gary Snyder's View of Nature as Community," in *Buddhism and Ecology*, ed. Tucker and Williams, 187–217.

63. Jeff Yamauchi, "The Greening of Zen Mountain Center: A Case Study," in *Buddhism and Ecology*, ed. Tucker and Williams, 249–65.

64. Interviewed by Alan Senauke and Sue Moon, "Monastery in the Streets: A Talk with Tetsugen Glassman," *Turning Wheel* (fall 1996): 22–25.

65. Kenneth Kraft, "Nuclear Ecology and Engaged Buddhism," in *Buddhism and Ecology*, ed. Tucker and Williams, 280–83.

66. A selection of such evolving practice forms are presented in the forthcoming anthology by Kaza and Kraft, *Dharma Rain*.

67. See Christopher Titmuss, "A Passion for the Dharma," *Turning Wheel* (fall 1991): 19–20; also Chogyam Trungpa, *Shambhala: The Sacred Path of the Warrior* (Boston: Shambhala, 1988).

68. David Barnhill, "Great Earth Sangha: Gary Snyder's View of Nature as Community," in *Buddhism and Ecology*, ed. Tucker and Williams, 192.

69. As Ian Harris suggests in "Buddhism and the Discourse of Environmental Concern: Some Methodological Problems Considered," in *Buddhism and Ecology*, ed. Tucker and Williams, 377–402.

"Faith, God, and Nature: Judaism and Deep Ecology"

❧

Eric Katz

Eric Katz is professor of philosophy at New Jersey Institute of Technology and one of the leading writers on contemporary environmental ethics. This essay explores the connections—and tensions—between Judaism and ecology, as well as the relation of both to the Holocaust.

❧

GOD'S ANSWER

In the book of Job we find some of the most troubling verses in the Hebrew Bible. Near the end of the book, Job is able to question God about the misfortunes that have befallen him, and God answers him out of the whirlwind:

> Where wast thou when I laid the foundations of the earth? Declare, if thou hast understanding.
>
> Who hath laid the measures thereof, if thou knowest? or who hath stretched the line upon it?
>
> ... Who hath divided a watercourse for the overflowing of waters, or a way for the lightning of thunder;
>
> To cause it to rain on the earth, where no man is; on the wilderness, wherein there is no man;
>
> To satisfy the desolate and waste ground; and to cause the bud of the tender herb to spring forth? (Job 38:4–5; 25–27)

The meaning of these verses is chilling. Job seeks an explanation of his troubles, and instead God delivers a lecture about the creation and the operation of the natural world. Although the Lord's tirade goes on for four chapters (a total of 129 verses), these five verses are especially important. The Lord is reminding Job that humanity was not present when God created the universe. The world was not created *for* humanity. The events of the natural world—rain, for example—do not take place for the benefit of humanity. Rain falls on the wilderness where no man is; it is thus a mistake to see the rain as God's contribution to human agriculture and livestock.[1]

These verses are disturbing because they question the idea that human purpose, human good, and human reason lie at the heart of divine activity. Human beings are finite; we are not omniscient. We want to believe that although God may act in mysterious ways, these actions are for a purpose and a good that do not lie outside of human interests. We want to believe that everything that happens in the world is for the best. We have a faith that the universe is rational, ordered, and essentially benign, ruled by a caring omnipotent God. God's answer to Job undermines that faith. Although the universe may be rationally ordered, this rational order may not at all be connected to human interests and concerns.

These lines from the Book of Job, I believe, provide a framework for a comparison of a Jewish response to the meaning of the environmental crisis and the philosophy of deep ecology. The key idea expressed here in Job is nonanthropocentrism, the removal of human interests from the center of value in our understanding of the operation of the natural world. Over the last twenty-five years, much of environmental philosophy has emphasized the need for, and the possibility of, a nonanthropocentric revolution in our thought toward the natural world. An adequate environmental ethic, it has been argued, will only be possible from a perspective of nonanthropocentrism.[2] But does the nonanthropocentrism expressed in these lines from the book of Job represent the basic perspective of Judaism? What are the nonanthropocentric elements in the Jewish philosophy of the ethics of nature? And can the nonanthropocentric themes in Jewish thought be seen as similar to the central ideas in the philosophy of deep ecology? I must admit that I am skeptical: I have profound misgivings that traditional Judaism can be understood as an ally of deep ecology, that Jewish ideas about the nonhuman natural world can be seen as an expression of deep ecological principles. This essay is an attempt to confront my skepticism: here I offer my personal reflections on the problem of reconciling a Jewish philosophy of nature with the philosophy of deep ecology.

First, consider two central commands in the environmental ethics of Judaism: *tza'ar ba'alei chayim* ["the pain of living creatures"] and *bal tashchit* ["do not destroy"]. Anyone searching for a basic nonanthropocentrism in Jewish thought will find these two principles a useful starting point.[3] *Tza'ar ba'alei chayim* is perhaps the most important principle in Judaism concerning the human relationship with animals: it requires an attitude of compassion for all animal life. In particular, humans have a special obligation to care for and consider the pain of the domesticated animals that live within the larger human community. Thus, the fourth commandment concerning the Sabbath requires rest for one's livestock as well as for humanity (Exodus 20:10 and Deuteronomy 5:14). There is also the law forbidding the yoking together of animals of unequal strength (Deuteronomy 22:10), for this would cause pain to the weaker animal. And one is not permitted to muzzle an ox during the threshing of the grain (Deuteronomy 25:4). All of these commandments are based on a compassion for animal suffering, and thus demonstrate that Judaism extends the realm of moral consideration beyond the limits of the human community, at least into the realm of domesticated animal life.

Judaism, of course, does not advocate an absolute reverence for all life, nor does it require vegetarianism. Genesis 1:29 *does* prohibit meat-eating—"And God said, Behold, I have given you every herb bearing seed, which is upon the face of all the earth, and every tree, in which is the fruit of a tree yielding seed; to you it shall be for meat"—but this prohibition was rescinded for Noah and his descendants after the flood—"Every thing that liveth shall be meat for you; even as the green herb have I given you all things" (Genesis 9:3). And yet the freedom to eat meat comes with an obligation to treat the animal food source with a certain amount of respect, for the next verse places a limit on the methods and kind of meat to be eaten: "But the flesh with the life thereof, which is the blood thereof, shall ye not eat" (Genesis 9:4). This limitation on the eating of blood, the eating of life itself, became the basis for the laws of kosher slaughtering, laws designed to minimize the pain of the animals being killed. Although eating meat was thought essential for human survival, it did not nullify an obligation for compassion for all living animals.

The principle of *bal tashchit* concerns the prohibition against the wanton destruction of natural entities, living beings (plants and animals) and even human artifacts. Its source is a passage from Deuteronomy 20:19–20:

> When you besiege a city for a long time ... you shall not destroy its trees by wielding an ax against them. You may eat of them, but you may not cut them down. Are the trees in the field men that they should be besieged by you? Only the trees which you know are not trees for food you may destroy and cut down, that you may build siege-works against the city.

The point here appears to be that the trees may be destroyed only if they are not food-producing and only if their destruction will be useful for the war effort. To destroy trees that produce food will ultimately be harmful to all humans; similarly, to destroy trees for no useful purpose is pointless and counterproductive.

Bal tashchit becomes, in Jewish thought, a general principle against vandalism. For example, in the *Sefer Hahinukh* (529) is written this comment on *bal tashchit*: "In addition [to the cutting down of trees] we include the negative commandment that we should not destroy anything, such as burning or tearing clothes, or breaking a utensil—without purpose." But this raises the fundamental issue of what constitutes a good or justifiable purpose for the destruction of something, and in particular, for the destruction of a natural entity, such as a tree. Judaism does not exclude the consideration of economic motives. In the Talmud (*Baba Kama* 91b–92a) there is an extended discussion on the permissibility of cutting down trees based on their economic worth: a fruit-bearing tree may be destroyed if the value of its crop is less than the value of the lumber the tree would produce; moreover, the tree may be destroyed if the land is needed for the construction of a house, or if there are more productive trees in the same area. These exceptions to *bal tashchit* are not permitted for purely aesthetic reasons, such as landscaping.[4] Thus, the commentator Eric G. Freudenstein concludes: "[T]he standards of bal tashchit are relative rather than absolute. The law is interpreted in the Talmud as limited to purposeless destruction and does not prohibit destruction for the sake of economic gain."[5]

Although this analysis is far from complete, it is clear that *bal tashchit* requires some consideration of the social implications of actions that harm nonhuman entities. It concerns, in part, the proper human response to the nonhuman environment. Similarly, *tza'ar ba'alei chayim* concerns the proper human response to animal life and animal suffering. But do these principles express what contemporary environmental philosophers would call nonanthropocentric values? Can they be the basis of a robust nonanthropocentric environmental ethic? Are these principles similar to basic ideas in the philosophy of deep ecology? To answer these questions, we need to look closely at the fundamental principles of deep ecology.

What is the philosophy of deep ecology? This is a difficult question to answer, because there are a large number of different positions that are called deep ecology, and many other environmental philosophies that are deep ecological even though they do not use the label. So what is the *real* deep ecology? Does it make sense to ask this question?

In an essay of this limited scope, I cannot pretend to give a full account of the meaning of deep ecology as an environmental philosophy. Instead, I will present what I consider to be the most important features of deep ecological thought as a general worldview, i.e., as a philosophical system regarding the environment. As is now well known, the terminology was introduced in a rough outline by the Norwegian philosopher Arne Naess in 1972 where he contrasted the political and social movement of "deep ecology" from that of "shallow ecology."[6] Naess claimed that shallow ecology developed policies that merely reformed human practices regarding the environment—such as pollution abatement or energy conservation—and that mainly affected the well-being of those people in the more affluent nations. Deep ecology, in contrast, was concerned with rethinking the fundamental human relationship with the natural world. Deep ecology was truly a *philosophical* outlook on the environmental crisis, for it asked us to develop, not environmental policies per se, but rather basic principles about the meaning of human life.

In this initial formulation, deep ecology is essentially an approach, a strategy—a *methodology*—for thinking about the human relationship with the natural world and the environmental crisis. But the merely methodological framework of questioning basic principles soon developed a substantive content of its own. These substantive ideas perhaps can be traced to the Platform of Deep Ecology, written down in 1984 by Naess and the American philosopher George Sessions. It must be emphasized that the platform expresses the basic ideas of the deep ecology *movement*, not the basic ideas of the *philosophy* of deep ecology. Nevertheless, Andrew McLaughlin has called the platform "the heart of deep ecology,"[7] and thus it is a useful place to begin to tease out its central philosophical ideas. Here is the platform as it appears in Naess's *Ecology, Community, and Lifestyle*:

1. The flourishing of human and nonhuman life on Earth has intrinsic value. The value of nonhuman life forms is independent of the usefulness these may have for narrow human purposes.
2. Richness and diversity of life forms are values in themselves and contribute to the flourishing of human and nonhuman life on Earth.
3. Humans have no right to reduce this richness and diversity except to satisfy vital needs.
4. Present human interference with the nonhuman world is excessive, and the situation is rapidly worsening.
5. The flourishing of human life and cultures is compatible with a substantial decrease of the human population. The flourishing of nonhuman life requires such a decrease.
6. Significant change of life conditions for the better requires change in policies. These affect basic economic, technological, and ideological structures.
7. The ideological change is mainly that of appreciating *life quality* (dwelling in situations of intrinsic value) rather than adhering to a high standard of living. There will be a profound awareness of the difference between big and great.
8. Those who subscribe to the forgoing points have an obligation directly or indirectly to participate in the attempt to implement the necessary changes.[8]

From the perspective of a philosophical system, what is most important about this platform is the emphasis on nonhuman intrinsic or inherent value. Nonhuman life must flourish even if this reduces human affluence or human population. In addition, the ideas of richness and diversity play a significant role here, not only as a value-principle for the evaluation of the natural environment as a whole, but also as a guiding principle in the evaluation and reexamination of the ends of human life. In many ways, deep ecology is a philosophy as old as Western civilization, for it reinforces a critique of the single-minded pursuit of material abundance. Human activity, in and of itself, and in relation to the natural environment, will be guided by a respect for all life forms, noninterference in natural processes, and a resistance to the homogenization and simplification of both natural and human systems.

The ideas of the platform are expressed quite broadly, so as not to exclude any potential sympathizers to the political and social movement of deep ecology. But two specific philosophical ideas have been omitted from the platform, even though almost all versions of deep ecology include them in some fashion—these are the ideas of identification and Self-realization.[9] By identification, the philosophy of deep ecology means that each human individual identifies with all other entities in the natural world. This is not an identification of actual personal identity—I do not believe that I am literally the tree in my garden. It is an identification of *interests*. A human being who identifies with the entities of the natural world considers the interests of all other living beings as closely connected to his or her own interests. This identification leads directly into the notion of Self-realization as the ultimate goal of the philosophy of deep ecology, where the upper case "S" in Self implies that there is a larger, more comprehensive, Self than the self (with a lower case "s") of the individual ego. Because I identify with the rest of the natural world, I care for the rest of creation. I expand myself outward to include an interest in the value and flourishing of the entire natural environment. I come to understand that I can only fully realize myself through the flourishing—the Self-realization—of the entire natural universe.

In sum, the basic principles of the philosophy of deep ecology include: a respect for and identification with all natural entities, a deemphasis on human interests as the focal point of moral evaluation, and the understanding that the maximization of good involves the fullest realization of all forms of life. These philosophical ideals lead to practical principles of action: a policy of noninterference in nature (or at least a policy of minimal intervention) and a desire to restructure human society to be more in harmony with natural processes. Two philosophers of deep ecology, David Rothenberg and George Sessions, have summarized this philosophical position with the term *ecocentrism*—i.e., the idea that the ecological system or the ecosphere is the center of value. Rothenberg comments: "The whole designation 'ecocentrism' is closer to an equivalent for what Naess means by 'deep ecology': centering on the ecosphere."[10] And Sessions sees ecocentrism as the essential point of the platform: "The philosophy of the Deep Ecology movement is characterized essentially by ecocentrism, as outlined in the 1984 Deep Ecology platform."[11] Deep ecology values the ecosphere—the ecological systems and the natural entities that comprise the living and developing natural world. Deep ecology values the ecosphere in itself, not merely for human purposes. Its chief practical concern is for the ecosphere to continue to develop and flourish with a minimal amount of human interference, degradation, and destruction. To accomplish this task, human social institutions must be reoriented so that they can exist in harmony with the processes and life forms of the natural world.

THE MATTER OF ANTHROPOCENTRISM

At this point in the exposition, it should be easy to compare the philosophy of deep ecology with those principles of Jewish environmental thought that were examined above, *tza'ar ba'alei chayim* and *bal tashchit*, for both Jewish ideas stress that humans should be concerned for entities and life forms that are nonhuman. *Tza'ar ba'alei chayim* and *bal tashchit*, may be expressions of a kind of nonanthropocentric thought in the Jewish tradition. If so, there would be at least a prima facie similarity between the central ideas of deep ecology and important principles of Judaism regarding the nonhuman natural world, even if there were differences in practical activity and policy.

Yet I hesitate to make this facile comparison. Two problems appear significant. First, in my desire to find resonances of nonanthropocentrism in Jewish thought, I may have overemphasized

Judaism's concern for the nonhuman. *Tza'ar ba'alei chayim* and *bal tashchit* may not be fundamentally nonanthropocentric ethical principles. Second, questions can be raised about the standard interpretation of deep ecology that I have outlined above. It may be that deep ecology itself is fundamentally an anthropocentric point of view. These problems, as we will see below, reintroduce a consideration of the lessons from the book of Job with which I began this essay.

First, we must reexamine the nonanthropocentrism of *tza'ar ba'alei chayim* and *bal tashchit*. Does *tza'ar ba'alei chayim* really demonstrate a universal moral concern for the pain of all living creatures? Notice that virtually all of the examples used to demonstrate the human concern for animal suffering involve domesticated animals, livestock—animals that exist in a community with human beings. There is one possible exception to this, one place where the suffering of a wild creature is considered: in Deuteronomy 22:6–7 one is warned not to take a mother bird along with the eggs from its nest, but to let the mother fly away. But the passage actually makes no mention of the suffering of the mother bird, and whether or not the suffering of the mother is the main reason for the divine command is a controversial issue in the intellectual history of the passage.[12] In general, Judaism does not prescribe principles of action regarding wild nature, the environment outside of human institutions and community. Wild nature, as we discover in God's answer to Job, is beyond human comprehension and human influence. The beings of the wild are quite different from the domesticated animals that are part of the broader human community. By virtue of the human power over domesticated animals, we have ethical obligations to them—thus, we must consider animal pain as stated in *tza'ar ba'alei chayim*. But the human power over wild nature is much more limited, and so it is possible to see that *tza'ar ba'alei chayim* does not extend to wild creatures. *Tza'ar ba'alei chayim*, in sum, does not seem to be primarily a nonanthropocentric principle of moral evaluation—it is best understood as an ethical precept regarding the organization and treatment of animal life within the human community.

What of *bal tashchit*? Here the case for nonanthropocentrism is even more problematic, for the ban on destroying fruit trees appears to be tied directly to the future potential use of the trees for human good. Human interests and human value are the basis of the ethical command. Thus, the expansion of the prohibition to create a ban on wanton destruction is also connected to artifacts of use to humans. Maimonides is explicit on the importance of human interests. He first notes that one is permitted to cut down nonfruit-bearing trees, "even if one does not need" the tree for any purpose. Moreover, the commandment of *bal tashchit* applies, in Maimonides's list, to household goods, clothing, food, buildings, and a spring—all objects of human utility.[13] A later commentator, Baruch Halevi Epstein, supports Maimonides's view: "[O]ne is permitted to destroy both trees or other things when there is bodily need for them . . . [i.e.,] whenever a person's need is fulfilled through this destruction."[14] Thus, *bal tashchit* prohibits purposeless destruction, but purpose is dependent on human needs and human good.

In a recent survey of the literature on *bal tashchit*, Eilon Schwartz demonstrates that Jewish thought concerning this commandment has developed in two opposing traditions. In the minimalist tradition, "human needs and wants take precedence over the rest of creation"—as in the passage by Maimonides cited above. In the maximalist tradition, human wants are "counterbalanced with the legitimate claims of the natural world," primarily in the sense that destruction is not permitted merely for the sake of human *luxury* goods.[15] But Schwartz concludes that neither the minimalist nor the maximalist position can be understood as endorsing contemporary ideas about nonanthropocentrism in environmental ethics. The Jewish tradition explicitly denies a holistic ecocentrism, a concern for the extensive system of nature outside of the human realm. *Bal tashchit's* "concern was domesticated nature, nature in contact with day-to-day living,"[16] just as we saw in *tza'ar ba'alei chayim*. Even more problematic for a comparison with deep ecology, Judaism is opposed to a neoromantic notion that humans can reconnect with a truer, more natural reality by increasing their respect and care for the natural environment. As Schwartz concludes, there is "a strong preference in Jewish ethical philosophy to see morality as transcendent of the natural world and not immanent within it."[17] *Bal tashchit*, in short, is not a step on the path to the deep ecological identification with nature and human Self-realization. Neither *bal tashchit* nor *tza'ar ba'alei chayim* appear to be primarily nonanthropocentric.

The second problem concerns the interpretation of deep ecology. Perhaps the philosophy of deep ecology is itself an anthropocentric view.[18] Consider the interconnected goal of Self-realization and the process of identification, two central ideas in the deep ecology position. On closer examination, both appear to be fundamentally anthropocentric—i.e., they both acquire meaning through their connection to human ideals, human thought, and human value. According to the philosophy of deep ecology, human individuals will only realize themselves, achieve the highest levels of satisfaction and fulfillment, by the complementary realization of all other living and natural beings. The realization of the individual ego, self-realization with a lower case "s," is only possible through Self-realization, the fulfillment, actualization, and flourishing of the larger nonegoistic Self, all living beings in the world (or ecosphere). Each individual human is to conceive of himself or herself as part of the more comprehensive Self that comprises the whole world. We achieve this Self-realization, in the main, through the process of identification: we identify the interests of the nonhuman natural world with our own human interests. We come to see that we and all other living things share a commonality of interests. In practice, then, we will work to preserve the flourishing of the natural world because in doing so, we act to preserve ourselves—human individuals—and our own flourishing. In harming the interests of the natural world, we harm ourselves. The focus of the preservation of natural processes is the maximization of human interests.

It seems clear, as Richard Sylvan points out in his criticism of deep ecology, that we should be wary of the entire notion of self-realization, for it has an anthropocentric history and pedigree.[19] The goal of self-realization "emerges direct from the humanistic Enlightenment; it is linked to the modern celebration of the individual human, freed from service to higher demands, and also typically from ecological constraints." Sylvan reminds us that the concept involves the maximization of egos, individual selves, or, at best, the privileged class of humanlike selves. Even the attempt to escape egoism, with the notion of a capital "S" Self as a holistically extended superself, only succeeds because we are identifying ourselves with the universe through an anthropocentric notion, a comparison to ourselves as individual human beings.

The anthropocentric character of the idea of self-realization is actually only one version of a more general problem in the methodology of environmental ethics, a problem originally discussed by John Rodman but elaborated by Sylvan.[20] In the attempt to ascribe value to entities in the universe, we human evaluators select features of these entities, and generalize these features as the standard or the criterion for possessing value, or being in the class of morally considerable entities. But "no simple species or subspecies, such as humans or superhumans, no single feature, such as sentience or life, serves as a reference benchmark, a base class, for determining moral relevance and other ethical dimensions." Any such feature we select is "arbitrary" and "loaded"— i.e., it is inherently biased toward characteristics possessed by the elite human class. A truly unbiased environmental ethic must be based on a notion of "eco-impartiality" in which none of the characteristics of any particular class of entities is used as the sole determining factor of moral value.[21] Deep ecology, with its emphasis on self-realization—and to a lesser extent, the goal of all living entities to flourish and blossom—fails this test.[22] Deep ecology selects as a fundamental value the fulfillment, flourishing, and realization of the Self—but this realization-value is based on characteristics of human life and human experience. Thus, the processes of identification and Self-realization are clearly anthropocentric in character, structure, and goal.

It is in considering the problems inherent in the deep ecological ideas of identification and self-realization that we once again encounter the challenge of the book of Job. Quite simply, the challenge is this: can we *identify* with the processes of nature? God's speech to Job suggests that we cannot, for God tells Job that the operations of the divinely created natural world are beyond the understanding of the individual human mind. "Where wast thou when I laid the foundations of the earth? Declare if thou has understanding" (Job 38:4). God causes it to rain where no humans will benefit (Job 38:26). He brings into existence wild beasts such as the behemoth and the leviathan whose power dwarfs that of humankind (Job 40:15 and 41:1). How is it possible for humans to identify with a natural, wild, and inhuman world such as this? Does the deep ecological principle of identifying with the interests of the nonhuman world make any sense in a universe that lies beyond the comprehension of humanity? And if we are unable to understand or to identify the interests of the natural world, and feel their compatibility with our own interests, then what sense is there to the idea of Self-realization? How can my fulfillment be based on the flourishing of nonhuman entities whose interests and goals, ordained by God, are beyond my limited understanding? How do I become fully realized by protecting the wild natural processes of the ecosphere, when only God understands these processes?

Perhaps the answer lies in accepting God's understanding of the natural order, without imposing a human framework—human categories—on the divine creation. As E. L. Allen wrote about the Book of Job fifty years ago, long before there was an ecological crisis to consider: "The untamed world beyond the frontiers of human society is fraught with the numinous, it is a constant reminder that man is not master in the world but only a privileged and therefore responsible inhabitant of it."[23] God's message to Job is that the universe does not exist for human benefit. It is God's world, a theocentric universe, and at best humans will be fulfilled if they accede to the interests and demands of God.

Judaism offers us a theocentric universe, a world that is fundamentally divine because it is literally God's world: it belongs to God. "The earth is the Lord's, and the fullness thereof; the world, and they that dwell therein" (Psalms 24:1). Once we acknowledge that the world belongs to God, the ambiguities and complexities of *tza'ar ba'alei chayim* and *bal tashchit* tend to be resolved. The point of *tza'ar ba'alei chayim* is to care for the living creatures that are part of the divine creation, that belong to no one but God. The principle emphasizes domesticated animals that are part of the human community because those are the animals that are most clearly affected by human action. The pain of wild animals is of little concern to humans—at least during the time the Hebrew Bible was composed—because the lives of wild animals were so removed from the daily lives of humans. The basis of *bal tashchit* also now becomes obvious. The prohibition against wanton or purposeless destruction does not revolve around the presence or absence of merely human goods—it concerns the destruction of worldly entities that belong to God. Humans must care and preserve all that exists in the universe, for all that exists is divine—it was created by God and it belongs to God.

The essential tension between the philosophy of deep ecology and the Jewish tradition regarding the natural world is now apparent. Deep ecology is, at best, an attempt to blend the anthropocentric self-interest of humans with the ecocentric interests of entities in the natural order. Deep ecology encourages individual humans to identify their interests with the interests of natural entities, and thus to protect the natural environment because it is in their wider interest to do so. Deep ecology is a type of ecocentric world view in which human individuals and human institutions are understood as part of the totality of the ecosphere. But Judaism is not an ecocentric view—it is a theocentric view. In Judaism, value, purpose, and meaning all emerge from God and his divine creative activity. The world exists because God has created it thus. The value of natural processes lies not in their usefulness for humanity but in their existence as part of the divine plan. This is the message of Job: do not believe that the rain falls for you.

POSTSCRIPT

Perhaps this discussion of Judaism and deep ecology should end here. But permit me a few personal reflections, a concluding unreligious postscript. I am uncomfortable with the uncompromising theocentrism that has concluded the previous section. I lack the faith.

In the autumn of 1995, I traveled to Eastern Europe to witness firsthand the sites of the Holocaust, the planned extermination by Nazi Germany of European Jewry. I do not know if every Jew should make this trip, but I knew that it was necessary for me, in order to come to terms with my history and the history of my people.

One of my stops was the Jewish cemetery in Warsaw, across the street from the downtown area that once was the Warsaw Ghetto. The Jewish cemetery is a remarkably beautiful and serene place. Because of neglect for decades after World War II the cemetery has been overwhelmed by the growth of trees and unchecked plant life. I visited the cemetery on a rainy day, and through the mist and fog it was difficult to see the tombstones, for the trees and underbrush have grown almost everywhere. A path led to a clearing, a clearing of grave stones, not trees. Here was the mass grave of the Jews who died in the Warsaw Ghetto before the deportations to Treblinka began in July 1942. The mass grave appeared as a meadow under a canopy of tree branches. Dozens of memorial candles were flickering there, remaining lit despite the light rain. The beauty of this mass grave surprised and shocked me. It is a monument to human evil, but it nevertheless demonstrates the power of nature to create beauty and peace in the universe.[24]

The Holocaust, of course, is the defining event for Jews in the twentieth century, and it surely represents the supreme crisis of faith for any individual Jew. When we view the destruction and evil of the Holocaust, are we like Job seeking a reason from God for his suffering? Can there be a rational explanation for the extent of the evil that surrounds us? Or must we accept the answer from the whirlwind, as Job did, that God alone can comprehend the meaning of events in a universe that God created. Is the explanation for the Holocaust only understandable to God?

The theocentrism of the book of Job leaves me with nothing but despair. It is impossible for me to accept an incomprehensible divinity as a guide to human action. The eminent Jewish scholar, Robert Gordis, in discussing the Jewish response to the environmental crisis, argued that humans need to do more than merely preserve the natural environment. Humanity is the "copartner of God in the work of creation" and thus we have a duty to enhance and improve the world.[25] But how can we be a partner with a divine being that we do not understand?

The processes of nature, however, I can understand. I can see in the Warsaw cemetery that nature heals the remnants of one of the most absolute evils of human history. God offers me no explanation, but I have faith in the healing presence of natural processes. That faith is the foundation of my abiding belief in ecocentrism. I can be a partner with nature, and work for the preservation and flourishing of all the natural entities of the universe.[26]

NOTES

1. I was initially inspired to think seriously about Job by reading Bill McKibben's discussion in his book, *The End of Nature* (New York: Random House, 1989), 75–80.

2. Most environmental philosophers trace the position of nonanthropocentrism from Aldo Leopold's "The Land Ethic," in *A Sand County Almanac* (New York: Oxford University Press, 1949). Other major texts that espouse a nonanthropocentric environmental ethic are: J. Baird Callicott, *In Defense of the Land Ethic: Essays in Environmental Philosophy* (Albany: State University of New York Press, 1989); Holmes Rolston III, *Environmental Ethics: Duties to and Values in the Natural World* (Philadelphia: Temple University Press, 1988); Paul Taylor, *Respect for Nature: A Theory of Environmental Ethics* (Princeton: Princeton University Press, 1986); and Andrew Brennan, *Thinking about Nature: An Investigation of Nature, Value, and Ecology* (Athens: University of Georgia Press, 1988). My own work also examines and defends a nonanthropocentric environmental ethic. See Eric Katz, *Nature as Subject: Human Obligation and Natural Community* (Lanham, Md.: Rowman and Littlefield, 1997).

3. The discussion of these two principles is taken from my essay, "Judaism and the Ecological Crisis," in *Nature as Subject*, 205–20.

4. See Norman Lamm, "Ecology and Jewish Law and Theology," in *Faith and Doubt* (New York: KTAV, 1971), 170, and Eilon Schwartz, "*Bal Tashchit:* A Jewish Environmental Precept," *Environmental Ethics* 19 (1997): 360.

5. Eric G. Freudenstein, "Ecology and the Jewish Tradition," *Judaism* 19 (1970): 411.

6. Arne Naess, "The Shallow and the Deep, Long-Range Ecology Movement. A Summary," *Inquiry* 16 (1973): 95–100.

7. Andrew McLaughlin, "The Heart of Deep Ecology," in *Deep Ecology for the Twenty-first Century,* ed. George Sessions (Boston: Shambhala), 95.

8. Arne Naess, *Ecology, Community, and Lifestyle,* translated and edited by David Rothenberg (Cambridge: Cambridge University Press, 1989), 29.

9. These two ideas are most closely identified with Naess and his personal version of deep ecology, what he calls Ecosophy T. See *Ecology, Community, and Lifestyle,* 63–212.

10. Rothenberg, "Introduction," in *Ecology, Community, and Lifestyle,* 15.

11. Sessions, *Twenty-first Century,* xiii.

12. Maimonides, for example, does think the main issue is the pain of the mother (*Guide for the Perplexed* 3:48), while Nachmanides (Commentary on Deuteronomy 22:6) does not.

13. Maimonides, *Mishnah Torah,* "The Book of Judges," Kings 6:9–10.

14. Baruch Halevi Epstein, *Torah Temimah* to Deuteronomy 20:19. I wish to thank Rabbi David Kraemer of the Jewish Theological Seminary for this reference.

15. Schwartz, "*Bal Tashchit:* A Jewish Environmental Precept," 371. A detailed explanation of two positions can be found on pages 365–71.

16. Schwartz, "*Bal Tashchit,*" 372.

17. Schwartz, "*Bal Tashchit,*" 372.

18. See my essay, "Against the Inevitability of Anthropocentrism," in *Beneath the Surface: Critical Essays in the Philosophy of Deep Ecology,* ed. Eric Katz, Andrew Light, and David Rothenberg (Cambridge, Mass.: MIT Press, 2000).

19. Richard Sylvan and David Bennett, *The Greening of Ethics* (Tucson: University of Arizona Press, 1994), 154. Although this volume is coauthored, it is clear that most of the criticisms of deep ecology derive from the work of Sylvan. Most of the arguments critical of deep ecology in this book are taken from Sylvan's 1985 essay "A Critique of Deep Ecology," published in two parts in *Radical Philosophy* 40 (summer 1985): 2–11 and *Radical Philosophy* 41 (autumn 1985): 10–22. With apologies to David Bennett, I will refer only to Sylvan. Another important criticism of deep ecology can be found in William Grey, "Anthropocentrism and Deep Ecology," *Australasian Journal of Philosophy* 71:4 (December 1993): 463–73.

20. See John Rodman, "The Liberation of Nature?" *Inquiry* 20 (1977): 83–131, and Sylvan and Bennett, *Greening,* 140ff.

21. Sylvan and Bennett, *Greening,* 142.

22. For more, see Sylvan's criticism of biocentrism in "A Critique" Part I, 8–10.

23. E. L. Allen, "The Hebrew View of Nature," *Journal of Jewish Studies* 2, no. 2 (1951): 103.

24. For a more complete discussion of my experiences with Holocaust sites, see Eric Katz, "Nature's Presence: Reflections on Healing and Domination," in *Nature as Subject*, 189–201.

25. Robert Gordis, "Judaism and the Environment," *Congress Monthly* 57, no. 6 (September-October 1990): 10. Gordis cites *Talmud B. Shabbat* 10a.

26. I owe a great deal of thanks to Rabbi Steven Shaw of the Jewish Theological Seminary. Without his inspiration and advice, I would never have begun an examination of the Jewish philosophical tradition regarding the natural environment.

"Islam and Deep Ecology"

☙

Nawal H. Ammar

Nawal H. Ammar is associate dean of Kent State University. He has published widely in the areas of women's rights, Islam, Middle Eastern politics, and ecology. Here, he explores the relationship between Islam and the philosophical and spiritual perspective of "deep ecology," which argues that nature is both essential to who we are and possesses its own inherent value.

☙

In the last decade of the twentieth century my conversations with colleagues about Islam and ecology often resulted in suggestions about a need for a new theology or a reformation of the religion to provide a vision of a new earth.[1] With more than half of the forty armed conflicts in the world taking place in Islamic countries, the crude birth rate of Muslim countries being 1 percent higher than that of the developing world as a whole, and Cairo, the Islamic capital with one thousand minarets, being the second most polluted city in the world, the anxiety about the role of Muslims in protecting the environment is reasonable.[2]

Islam, however, like all religions and ideologies, can be misconceived and misinterpreted, and hence, instead of a new theology we need to retrieve the fundamentals of Islam, and in so doing seek the spirit of the progressive theological elements that the Prophet Muhammad brought to Arabia in the seventh century. In a progressive Islam the connection and linkage between nature and other creations of God lie at the center of the theology and social existence. Nature in Islam, notes al Faruqi, is not "an enemy. It is not a demonic force challenging and inciting humanity to conquer and subdue it. . . . Nature is a perfectly fitted theater where humanity is to do good deeds."[3] This connection is based on three premises: everything on earth is created by God, everything that God creates reflects His sacredness, and that everything on earth worships the same God.[4] As such humans have to respect and protect nature not because it is sacred, but because it is a reflection of God's glory, power, and might. Many verses in the Qur'an speak of respecting and reflecting on God's glory in His creations (for example see 50:6–8; 21:30; 13:2; 6:73).[5] One verse of the Qur'an clearly states God's supremacy over creation: "Don't you know that to God belongs the skies and the earth; Without him you have neither a patron nor a supporter" (2:107).[6]

In Islam the central concept of *Tawhid*, Oneness of God as a creator, links His creation to His sacredness, but does not make creation sacred in and of itself. *Tawhid* requires a dependency on the one source of life, God, and links His creation together in an ephemeral relationship of interdependency and respect.

In this chapter, I examine Islam's teachings about *Tawhid* and how they translate into an ecological ethic and action that are "deep" and not "shallow." Islam has a complex view of humans, the universe, and their relationship to God. At one level such a relationship may be viewed as "shallow" ecology in that Islam is not an aesthetic religion: it does not view nature as sacred. In the Islamic vision, "(Hu)man(s) are a distinct part of the universe and have a special position among the other parts of the universe." Nature is seen as being of use for human fulfillment and utilization. Yet at another level, humans are part of this universe, "whose elements are complementary to one another in an integrated whole."[7] Hence, if Islam's view of nature is examined from one perspective it can be misconstrued. It is, therefore, important to understand the Islamic view in its totality and complexity, especially the *Tawhid* perspective, in order to understand how as a religion it respects the universe and nature, and in turn how this reflects a deep relational perspective on natural and social ecology.

In Islam the relationship between humans and nature is one of use as well as contemplation, worship, appreciation of beauty, moral responsibility toward protection, prohibition of destruction and revival. This relationship is a moral destiny; if fulfilled it will lead humans to their desired Gardens in Heaven.

It is worth noting, however, that the one vision presented here in this chapter will have both supporters and opponents. As it is well known, there are more than one billion Muslims in the world today who live in more than eighty-three countries, and I make no claims to speak on behalf of all of them. Yet, "at any point of history each individual Muslim wishing to respond to his/her awareness of God's guidance may do so"[8] and not until Judgment Day can its appropriateness be evaluated.

TAWHID (ONENESS) AND DEEP ECOLOGY IN ISLAM

The Creator and the Created: The Duality of Holism

Tawhid refers to the belief in the absolute oneness of God, Lord and Master of all things. In the *Shahadah*, the first pillar of Islam, Muslims are to declare that there is no God but Allah and that Muhammad is the Prophet of God, *la ilaha illa Allah wa Muhammad Rasul Allah*. This oneness of God is the essence of Islamic civilization and religion.[9] *Tawhid* is a belief that sees God as one who stands in a dual relationship with what He creates. It is an article of faith that connects and diverts everything created to the divinity of God; it also binds the parameters of responsibility for God's creation to humans.[10]

> al Faruqi and al Faruqi note about *Tawhid* that the duality in Islam is of, God and non-God; Creator and creature. The first order has but one member, Allah the Absolute and Almighty. He alone is God, eternal, Creator, transcendent. Nothing like unto Him; He remains forever absolutely unique and devoid of partners or associates. The second is the order of space-time, of experience, of creation. It includes all creatures, the world of things, plants and animals, humans, jinn and angles, heaven and earth, paradise and hell and all their becoming since they came into beings. The two orders of creator and creation are utterly and absolutely disparate.... Neither can the Creator be ontologically transformed so as to become the creature, nor can the creature transcend and transfigure itself so as to become in any way or sense Creator.[11]

The *Tawhid* perspective, which creates a duality between God and the creatures, renders all created equal and alike. At the same time, however, none of the created are sacred except in their relationship to God and in fulfilling the purpose of God's creation. It is at this level that the Islamic vision may be mistaken for a naturalistic one. It is essential to underscore the issue that in Islam to consider nature or other creatures as sacred is in direct opposition of the *Tawhid* perspective, which views only God as sacred and only Allah to be worthy of worship. The created are considered equal in their relationship to God. This relationship is one of obedience, worship of, reverence to, and dependence on God. It is a relationship that makes the created subservient to and followers of God's commands. The Prophet repeatedly stated that all God's creation is dependent and supported by God and, "He loveth the most, those who are beneficent to His family."[12]

The Unity of the Created within a Tawhid *Perspective*

The *Tawhid* perspective in Islam renders nature a creation of God by a sheer commandment, for God's creation is not a generative act. As such the Qur'anic verse notes, "Say: He is Allah, the One and Only. Allah, the Eternal, Absolute; He begetteth not, nor is He begotten; and there is none unto Him" (112:1–4); "He just has to say to it 'Be' and it evolves into 'Being'" (2:117). Nature itself is not sacred. It is sacred insofar as it is a reflection of the will of God. Hence the Qur'anic verse, "To Him belongs what is in the heavens and on earth and all between, and all beneath the soil" (20:6); "Do they not look at the Camels how they are created?, and the Sky how it is raised high, and the Mountains how they are fixed firm and the earth how it is spread" (88:17–20). Islam has a transcendental view of nature. To attribute sacredness to nature is to associate other beings with God and that is against *Tawhid* and the Oneness of God, *shirk*. This transcendental vision, however, does not relegate nature to the secular or profane. It is not a duality of separate domains of God the Creator as sacred and the creation as profane. It is rather a totality, a dependency where nature reflects the glory of sacredness but is not itself sacred. Such a unified vision renders the deep ecologists' call for "the sacredness of nature/creation" an impossible task for Muslims. At the same time, however, it coincides with the deep ecologists' call for respect and glorification of nature.

Islam postulates that God owns all the universe (*al mulk lilah*), and nature is a blessed gift of God, granted to humans to do good deeds. The Qur'anic verse says, "It is God who created heaven and earth . . . that you may distinguish yourselves by your better deeds" (11:7).

The duality of the Creator and created renders the latter in Islam (e.g., nature, animals, humans and other creatures) a unified class of God's creation. The Prophet in regard to God's creation said, "[A]ll creatures are God's dependents and the most beloved to God among them is the one that does good to God's dependents." These dependents, though diverse, still have many characteristics in common. First, all creation is a reflection of God's sacredness, glory, and power. The Qur'anic verse notes about such creation, "Whithersoever you turn there is the Face of God" (11:115). Second, God's creation is orderly, has purpose, and exists with function. The Qur'anic verses say, "And the earth we have spread out; set therein mountains firm and immovable; and produced therein all kinds of things in due balance" (15:19); and "Verily, all things have been created with measure" (59:49).

Third, the created category is all actualized to worship and obey God. Hence, the Qur'anic verse states, "Sees thou not that to Allah bow down in worship all things that are in the heavens and earth, the sun, the moon, the stars; the hills, the trees, the animals; and a great number among humankind" (22:18).

Fourth, the created have all been created from the same element, water.[13] The Qur'anic verse states, "We made from water every living thing" (12:30), and continues in another verse by stating, "And God has created every animal from water of them there are some that creep on their bellies; some that walk on two legs; and some that walk on four.... It is he who has created humans from water" (24:45).

Fifth, the unity of God's creation as a category is also exemplified in Islam in terms of the social structure.[14] The Qur'an states that all that God created He created in communities by stating, "There is not an animal (that lives) on earth. Nor a being that flies on its wings, but (forms a part) of a community like you" (6:38).

The likeness and unity of all creatures created by God is also exemplified in certain *Hadiths* and *Sunnah,* Prophet's Sayings and tradition. The Prophet spent his early days of contemplation in a cave where he saw himself close to nature. It is also reported that the Prophet said about the mountain Uhud, close to Mecca: "It is a mountain that loves us and we love it," and he also spoke to this mountain after an earthquake saying: "Be calm, Uhud."[15]

Islam, in considering all God's creation as having common characteristics and divine reflections, echoes views of deep ecology. The whole universe is one single system created and united by Allah. Looking at the universe with such a perspective where all creatures are connected reveals common principles in Islam and deep ecology. Humans and other creations here have a relationship with each other and the universe reflecting kinship, admiration, respect, contemplation, adoration, and consideration, but not sacredness.

This unity of God's creation and the relationship of its components, however, becomes more complicated at the level of using and protecting nature as well as the role of humans in such endeavors. Although Islam's final teachings parallel the objectives of deep ecology, it nevertheless approaches the details of such objectives differently because the *Tawhid* perspective views the various components of nature as engaged in an order of interdependence for the final objective of glorification of God. As such the respect for nature is an outcome of mutual respect among the elements in nature, not because nature is sacred or because nature should be respected by itself, but because of its link to the One God, Creator of all.

Tawhid, *the Human Responsibility, and the Ecology: A Devotional-Moral Dimension*

Tawhid views only God, the Creator, as having the special quality of independence, while the created as being interdependent on each other and dependent on God. In this relationship of interdependence among the created, Islam places the keeping of the earth and heavens under the hands of humans, as the *Khalifah* (vice-regents) on earth. The Qur'anic verse states, "I am setting on the earth a vice-regent" (2:30). The *Khalifah* is a manager not a proprietor, a keeper for all generations. The Qur'anic verse (2:22) stating, "Who has made the earth your couch and the heavens your canopy and sent rains from the heavens, and brought forthwith fruits for your sustenance, *then set not up rivals unto Allah when you know,*" clearly ends with a plural "you," carrying the message that the universe is not for one generation but for every generation past, present, and future.

Humans were given the responsibility for managing the earth because they possess special qualities, and not because they have better qualities. Raisail II notes,

> All creatures are alike.... Plants are superior to minerals in being able to absorb nourishment, to grow and feed, animals in addition to these powers have one or more of the five senses, and (hu)man(s), while of the animal kingdom in other respects and possessing all senses, also speaks and reasons.[16]

These special qualities attributed to humans, notes Izzi Dien (1992:27–28), include their ability to speak and know the names of the creation, an independent will to know good from evil, and their ability to prevent evil. The Qur'anic verses state,

> *And He taught Adam all the names;* (2:31)
> *By the Soul, and the proportion and order given to it, and its*
> *enlightenment as to its wrong and its right.* (91:7–8)

Additionally, humans are the managers of earth because in His search, God found that only humans agreed to take on the responsibility. The Qur'anic verse notes, "God offered his trust to heaven and earth and mountain, but they shied away in fear and rejected it, Humans only carried it" (33:72). For these reasons the universe is given to humans as a "trust," *ammanah,* which they accepted when they bore witness to God in their covenant of *Tawhid.* There is no God but *Allah.* According to the Qur'an this covenant was renewed throughout the years (7:65,69,87; 10:73; 11:56,61) until it reached Muslims in verses such as "Generations before you we destroyed when they did wrong" (10:13); "Then we made you heirs in the land after them to see how ye would behave" (10:14).

The role of humans as *Khalifah,* vice-regent, on earth is to better it and improve it and not to spread evil and destruction. The Qur'an is full of injunctions concerning such behaviors and states clearly that this responsibility of improving the earth will be checked by God to see how it has been accomplished, "And follow not the bidding of those who are extravagant" (26:152); "O my people! Serve Allah, and fear the Last day: nor commit evil on the earth, with intent to do mischief" (29:36); "But they strive to make mischief on earth and Allah loveth not those who do mischief" (5:64); "And look for his Creation for any discrepancy! And look again! Do you find any gap in its system? Look again! Your sight, having found none, will return to you humbled" (67:3–4); "He it is who created the heavens and the earth. . . . That He might try you, which of you is best in conduct" (11:7); "That which is on earth we have made but as a glittering show for the earth in order that we may test them as to which of them are best in conduct" (18:7).

Scholars of Islam[17] note that God created humankind for the purpose of protecting the universe. Purpose, as al Faruqi and al Faruqi put it, "pervades the whole creation without exception."[18] Humans are an integral part of this purpose, hence, note the Qur'anic verses, "We have not created heaven and earth and all that stands between them in sport . . . we have created them in righteousness . . . for the purpose of confuting evil and error with truth and value" (44:38; 21:16). God did not create earth in vain, but as a test for humans to do good. It is the purpose and the moral duty of humans to act on the responsibility placed in their hands. al Faruqi notes this protection is human destiny (purpose) to show their moral and devotional abilities and if they fail in fulfilling it they displease God the Creator.[19]

Muslims, however, are left with another duty, namely to enjoy and use the bounties of the earth. Humans in Islam have a dual relationship with nature/earth/universe. On the one hand they are their manager, but they are also their user. The Qur'anic verse notes, "Do you not see that Allah has subjected to your (use) all things on the heavens and on earth, and has made his bounties flow to you in exceeding measure, both seen and unseen" (31:20); "It is He who made the earth manageable for you, so traverse ye through its tracts and enjoy of the sustenance which he furnishes" (67:15). Islam has a clear view that encourages the use of the bounties of earth, and the engagement in other human pleasures. The Qur'anic verse states, "Wealth and children are *zinat* (beauty, decoration) of this worldly life." Islam does not tolerate abstinence, thus the absence of priests and nuns in the mainstream religious hierarchy. One of the sayings, *Hadiths,* of the Prophet reports that three believers came to his home to declare their piety and belief in and love of God. One of the believers said, "I want to show my belief in God that I will abstain from food." The second one said, "I will show my belief in God by not sleeping nights." The third one said, "I will show my belief in God by not touching my wife." The Prophet stopped them and recommended, "that God does not tolerate the extremes of abstentions and that moderation is the best path to piety."

This dual role of the *Khalifah,* vice-regent, creature of God and user of earth, poses the theological test for Muslims. Central to reaching the Gardens of Heaven is the issue of keeping the equilibrium between having been charged with managing the earth and bettering it, while at the same time using its bounties for their fulfillment. The Qur'anic verse states, "Thus we have made of you an Ummah (a community) justly balanced" (2:143). The Qur'an speaks of God's trust in human ability to maintain the balance and do well, "Behold God said to the angels I will create a viceregent on earth. They said will You place one who will make mischief and shed blood? While we celebrate your praises and glorify your holiness, He said, I know what you know not?" (2:30). The Qur'an warns Muslims throughout of the consequences of doing mischief (not fulfilling their role as vice-regents who maintain justly balance):

> When he turns his back his aim everywhere is to spread mischief throughout the earth and destroy crops and populations; (2:205)

> And Allah loveth not those who do mischief; (5:60)

> Fear Allah and obey me and follow not the bidding of those who are extravagant who make mischief in the land and mend not their ways. (26:150–152)

Islam recommends a clear path to achieving the equilibrium between use and protection, namely action. The balance of this chapter discusses some of the actions taken by Muslims to maintain the balance, and also explores the contemporary ecological crisis in light of such action.

TAWHID, DEEP ECOLOGY, AND DEVOTIONAL ACTION

Islam is often defined as the total submission to God, and portrayed as the religion of pre-destination. As such the role of humans is often relegated to little free will and choice. The discussion of free will and predestination in Islam is a long, protracted, unresolved, and highly volatile issue.[20] Islam, however, has prescribed rationalism and the ability of humans to know right from wrong, hence the Qur'an notes, "Say (unto them Muhammad): Are those who know equal to those who know not?" In terms of action to better life and to attain the moral purpose, Islam clearly sees a place for human action and good deeds. As such the Qur'an states, "Let there be among you a group of people who order good, *almaruf* and prohibit evil, *almunkar*" (3:104). This ordering of good and prohibition of evil in Islam is an important form of action and it includes various verbal and other components, hence the Prophet's saying, "Anyone who witnesses evil should remonstrate upon it by his hand, his mouth or his heart, the last is the weakest of faith." This order of *maruf* and prohibition of *munkar* does not differentiate between actions toward humans or other creatures of God. Within the perspective of *Tawhid* it is all good deeds performed by the created to please the Creator. As such a saying of the Prophet notes, "A good deed done to a beast is as good as doing good to a human being; while an act of cruelty to a beast is as bad as an act of cruelty to a human being."[21] The ordering of good and prohibition of evil according to Islam is not only done for the Day of Judgment, but should be done for the here and now. Hence, the Prophet enjoined Muslims to "work in this world as though you are living forever and work for the hereafter as though you are dying tomorrow." The commandment of *maruf* and prohibition of *munkar* in Islam is an essential part of the continuity of life. In the Qur'an Muslims are warned that if they do not perform good deeds and act against evil they will perish: "Generations before you were destroyed when they did wrong" (10:13).

There is ample evidence both in the Qur'an and in tradition about how action (both in negating evil and performing good deeds) is required for Muslims to maintain the equilibrium of use and protection. The Qur'anic verse says, "Do no mischief on the Earth after it has been set in order" (7:85). This call, however, is not of a hands-off approach but rather of engagement, and those who do not act or engage will be at a loss, according to the Qur'anic verse, "Verily humans are at a loss, except those who have faith, and *do righteous deeds* and (together they join) *in the mutual teaching of truth*" (103:1–2, my emphasis).

The Prophet's tradition and sayings also reveal action toward performing good deeds and averting evil, with more particular reference to nature and earth. Many of the Prophet's sayings speak of acting to improve and protect nature (including animals, and resources). In relation to plants the Prophet has said,

> if anyone plants a tree or sows a field and humans, beasts or birds eat from it, he should consider it a charity on his part;

> Whoever plants a tree and looks after it with care until it matures and becomes productive, will be rewarded in the hereafter.

The Prophet has also claimed the need to protect animals (including humans). The Prophet has said, "[W]hoever is kind to the creatures of God is kind to himself." The Prophet has forbidden the beating of animals on the face, and prohibited the throwing of stones at animals. He has recommended that every care should be taken when slaughtering animals. It is forbidden to make animals the object of human sports or entertainment. The Prophet asks humans to feel within their souls the pain animals feel and avoid all practices that torture and frighten living beings. The Prophet says about using animals in game, "A sparrow that was used just for entertainment would on the day of judgment complain to [God] against the person who did so just for fun."[22]

There is evidence throughout the early history of Islam that action toward protecting the environment by doing good deeds and averting evil continued. Hence, it is reported that the first Muslim Caliph ordered his army "not to cut down trees, not to abuse a river, not to harm animals and be always kind and gentle to God's creation, even to your enemies." It is reported that the fourth Caliph and the cousin of the Prophet said to a man digging a canal and reclaiming a land, "[P]artake of it with joy, so long as you are a benefactor, not a corrupter, a cultivator not a destroyer."[23]

Performing good deeds and averting evil as devotional actions in Islam toward attaining equilibrium between use and protection of the earth have taken many forms throughout Islamic history. I will discuss two of them, namely, legal and educational actions.

LEGAL FORMS TO PROTECT THE ENVIRONMENT

Muslims throughout history have to strive to fulfill their moral obligation to God toward being protectors and users of earth. As such they have developed rules and regulations that protect nature. Such rules can be subsumed under five general regulations:

1. Use nature and its resources in a balanced, not excessive manner;
2. Treat nature and its resources with kindness;
3. Do not damage, abuse, or distort nature in any way;
4. Share natural resources;
5. Conserve.[24]

To many, the above rules sound like a World Bank report for a sustainable development project and in many ways they could. It is, however, the Islamic sense of theology in its devotional morality and action that underlies these rules and that differentiates them from sustainable development. Themes mentioned above such as the likeness of all creatures, the accountability of humans to God, and the subservience of nature as part of God's will render these regulations the essence of life on earth and the afterlife in Heaven. Muslims ought to tremble in fear from the catastrophic consequences of pollution, ozone depletion, famines, extinction of species, disease and epidemics, since such signs indicate *fasad,* corruption on earth, which they will be held responsible for during Judgment Day.[25] As such, acting on rules and regulations that reduce the corruption of the earth has a theological and spiritual resonance imposed and, unlike the effect of those that come from development and aid institutions such as the World Bank, emanates from within to serve the higher authority, the Creator, God.

Additionally, the points of departure of Islamic regulations are different from those of sustainable development. As mentioned above, humans are not here to make nature or resources subservient to their needs and utilization. Nature has already been made subservient by God and not by humans or other creatures. The aim is not to use nature by controlling it, but rather to use it by managing it for devotional purposes, i.e., to attain the Garden of Heaven in the hereafter.

Islamic Regulations and the Notion of Use

The issue of use here is an important one to underscore. Islam provides a basis for an economic system of use, ownership, exchange, and production. The general system has been set in the Qur'an, and legal scholars have worked its details.[26] The rules revolve around three principles. The reduction of waste, exchange, or consumption through use value and partnership in use.[27] All these principles work to reduce overconsumption by humans, one important source of corruption of and harm to nature.

Reduction of Waste

The reduction of waste is a very clear principle in the Islamic economic system. The rule that defines waste is one that states, "the merit of utilization in the benefit it yields, in proportion to its harm." If the harm in use exceeds the benefit then it is wasteful. The Qur'anic verse clearly admonishes against waste by stating, "Eat and drink but waste not in indulging in excess, surely God does not approve" (7:31). The Prophet's *hadiths,* sayings, also show Islamic concern about waste and hence, overconsumption. It is reported that the Prophet said to someone who was using water in excess while performing *wudu'*, ablution, to pray, "do not waste." He was then asked if there can be waste of water during a sacred ritual such as ablution. He replied, "[T]here can be waste in anything."

Use Value

Islamic exchange is based on the transfer of goods and services for another equivalent in value, and exchange determined by other forces such as supply/demand is considered usury. Usury is seen as unjust exchange that exploits resources (both human and natural). The Qur'an warns, "That which you lay out for increase through the property of [other] people, will have no increase with God: but that which you lay out for charity seeking the countenance of God, [will increase], it is these who will get a recompense multiplied" (30:39).

Partnership

Islam sees partnership as the essence of use. The Prophet has said, "people are partners in water, pasture land and fire." Partnership implies permission in using the elements as well as equality in the distribution of use patterns. For one group to use resources without permission or to use more than its share implies transgression and could result in losing its right of use completely. The Qur'an for example says regarding water, "And tell them the water is to be divided amongst them" (54:86).

EDUCATION AND ECOLOGY IN ISLAM

Muslims have consistently been engaged in action to perform good deeds and avoid evil ones in nature and the universe through education. We can find in Islamic history scientists who were concerned with nature, such as vegetal pharmacologist Ibn Bytar (who lived in the middle thirteenth century C.E.) who translated and added to the works from Persia, India, and the Mediterranean about plants and medicine.[28] Ibn Bytar mentioned in his books more than fourteen hundred natural medicinal drugs to cure humans and animals.[29] The medical botanist al Razi (who lived in the ninth century C.E.) used to collect flowers, leaves, and roots from nature and mix them to prepare medicines. Jabir Ibn Hayyan, the father of chemistry, was concerned about pollution and its effects on humans and the rest of the environment. The Arab Muslim thinker, al-Jahiz wrote in the eighth century C.E. of the effects of environmental changes on animal behavior. Al-Izz bin 'abd al-Salam who lived in the thirteenth century C.E. wrote about the rights of animals.[30]

In other parts of the Islamic world there are many names that are associated with teaching and learning about the linkage between humans and nature and its preservation. In Saudi Arabia, the Kingdom's Meteorology and Environmental Protection Administration (MEPA) has funded good research about Islamic principles and the environment.[31] There is also an Islamic environmental organization in the U.K. headed by Fazlun Khaled that produces very good educational books and materials.[32]

Muslim countries have created ministries of the environment to educate about and protect it. The campaigns have gone as far as, for example, some scholars in Egypt urging that harming the environment should be considered a criminal act, while other policy makers have urged that loans should not be given to companies that do not protect the environment.[33]

Ecological activism through education within the Islamic faith is not a difficult responsibility. In addition to the theological implications for protecting, bettering, and improving the conditions of God's creation, Muslims follow rituals that make them close to all God's creations. To pray, Muslims need clean water and surroundings free of communicable disease for their communal prayers on Fridays. To fast and celebrate the feasts they need to have a sky clear from pollutants to be able to see the crescent moon. To fulfill the duty of pilgrimage and for it to be accepted, they need to be strong (hence free of disease) and to protect God's creation. Educating Muslims about the relationship between humans and other creations of God is not a complicated theological task, and its practical aspects are clear and easy for all Muslims to understand. The difficult task, however, is to convince Muslims that their activism is required and that they are contributing to the devastation of the environment. It is to this that now I want to turn.

MUSLIM ACTIVISM, ACTION, AND ECOLOGY

The dilemma for those who would awaken Muslim activism to protect the environment does not dwell in the clarity of the spiritual and theological teachings. The quandary lies in providing a persuasive argument demonstrating that some Muslims are contributing to the devastation of the universe, and hence motivating their individual and collective activism as incumbent on them as Muslims. Muslims in both the distant and recent history see themselves as having lost their Golden Age, a time when their actions were respected. Since the time of European colonialism, Muslims have had a vision of themselves as the colonized, oppressed, demonized, and disabled within the larger global perspective. They see the harm that is done to God's creation as being the consequence of the non-Muslims. Dangers that threaten the environment such as industrial and chemical pollution, overconsumption, inequality between the poor and rich, new infectious diseases such as HIV, and even wars are caused by the non-Muslims' having lost sight of the sacred, their greed, and their hunger for power. As such, Muslims regard the destruction of nature as not their doing and believe that God will punish those who are destroying his creation.

Additionally, secular/Western suggestions (including deep ecology) for protecting nature are unacceptable to many Muslim scholars and leaders. This was best exemplified at the United Nations International Conference on Population and Development (ICPD) held in Cairo in 1994, when the official Islamic position opposed the Cairo Platform of Action on slowing population growth to raise the quality of life. Such a call was seen as a "foreign" intervention that has no relevance to the Islamic scheme of life. The entire argument about how the empowered role of women (through education, employment, reduction and spacing of births, etc.) contributes to the welfare of the ecosystem has been perceived as a Western notion that encroaches on the Islamic way of life. As a result the activism of Muslims has taken the form of protecting themselves from the non-Muslims' encroachment on their way of life.

The failure of Muslims to avoid evil and perform good deeds regarding environmental depletion goes against the core of Qur'an and tradition, and in many ways contributes to the corrupted state of the earth. Regardless of who is corrupting and destroying the earth and God's creation, action to protect and improve the environment is incumbent on Muslims. Islam is very clear about the unity—oneness—of God's creation. The Qur'an emphasizes the common origin (and hence the common responsibility) of human creation by stating, "O humankind! We created you male and female and made you into nations and tribes that ye may know each other (not to despise each other). The most honored of you in the sight of Allah is the most Righteous of you" (49:13). This oneness does not differentiate among nationalities or languages. Hence, the Prophet in his last Sermon stated, "People: your God is one, you all belong to Adam and Adam to earth . . . the most honored is the most pious and there is no difference between an Arab and a foreigner." The Qur'an clearly states that all humans are God's creation by saying, "And among His Signs is the creation of the heavens and the earth and the variations in your languages and colors, verily in that are signs for those who know" (30:2).

Additionally, the empowerment of women (and its related problem of family planning) is not a Western encroachment on Islam. Islam sees women as equal to men. The Qur'an states, "O humankind! Reverence your God who created you from a single soul, created of like nature its mate" (4:1). Part of the Qur'anic vision about women acknowledges the fact that they have been historically (prior to Islam) a disadvantaged group that was treated badly and inhumanely. The Qu'ran never describes women as the seductresses who caused the expulsion from Heaven, but rather it was the devil, *al-Shitan,* who led to such a fate. As such the Qur'an addresses both men and women, "the self surrendering men and the self surrendering women, the believing men and believing women, the obedient men and obedient women (33:35)." It also sees them both as protectors of each other: "[Y]ou are their garments and you are their garments" (2:187); and both are rewarded and responsible for their own actions, "to men allotted what they earn and to women what they earn" (4:32).

The inaction of Muslims can also be seen in the largest world war we have witnessed since World War II, the 1990 "Desert Shield/Desert Storm." More than thirty Muslim nations were involved in this war. It would seem that by adopting a war ethic of negotiations first, Muslims should have been at the forefront of averting a war that environmentalist have dubbed the "Nuclear Winter," because the inaccurate Scud missiles, germ warfare, and the oil fires reduced sunlight and temperatures throughout the region.[34] Unlike Buddhism's nonviolent struggle, Gandhi's concept of nonharm (*satyagraha*), or Christ's dictum "to turn the other cheek," Islam considers war as a viable form of struggle against injustice or oppression. One Qur'anic verse says, "[A]nd fight them on until there is no more tumult or oppression, and there prevail justice and faith in God, altogether and everywhere" (8:39). Nonetheless, as a form of struggle in Islam, war is seen as a last resort. Persuasion and patience should be employed first. According to the Qur'an, first "invite (all) to the way of thy lord with wisdom, and beautiful preaching and argue with them in ways that are best and most gracious" (16:127). If gracious words and arguments do not improve the oppression and distress, another form of nonviolent reaction is recommended, namely, emigration. According to the Qur'an: "He who forsakes his home in the name of God, finds in the earth many refuges, wide and spacious" (4:100).

If nonviolent modes of struggle fail to eliminate tumult and oppression, the Qur'an calls the "Prophet, [to] rouse the faithful to arms" (8:65), "[m]uster against them [the enemies] all the men and cavalry at your disposal" (8:60), and "turn them [the enemies] out from where they turned you out" (2:191). At this stage of war, all Muslims are ordered to join the war in all their capacities. According to the Qur'an: "[F]ighting is obligatory for you, much as you dislike it" (3:200). However, in many wars Muslims fail to follow such steps and often call for war as a first resort. Muslims during the Desert Storm war not only neglected to avert evil and perform good, but they went against clear theological commands of warring.[35]

It is thus important to underscore that Muslims will only be able to perform their role as God's vice-regents who know right from wrong and good from evil if they participate actively in use and protection of the earth/nature. In the last quarter of a century the problem for Muslims has been their acceptance of a hands-off approach regarding a very clear duty toward fulfilling their moral devotional destiny, namely pleasing the one God, Allah.

SUMMARY AND CONCLUSION

Islam has in common with deep ecology its respect for nature and earth. Both Islam and deep ecology view humans as part of this creation and not superior to it. Beyond this commonality the Islamic vision of linking humans to nature, nature and humans to God, and the protection of nature become complex and at many points difficult to compare with deep ecology. Islam, for example does not view creation as sacred in itself. Rather, it is respected as a reflection of sacredness, because it is the creation of God. The distinction of creation from sacredness lies at the heart of the Islamic profession of faith, *Tawhid*. The *Tawhid*, Oneness of God, principle allows for only one sacred entity, namely, Allah. The rest of the entities are created by God and they reflect His sacredness. The fact that nature reflects God's sacredness removes it from the secular domain and places it within the realm of respect and devotion. Yet, this devotion is not of nature itself but of the source of nature, God the Almighty.

Within these devotional layers of linkages between God and nature, humans are appointed as the vice-regents, *Khalifahs*, of God on earth to protect it. They are appointed because they can distinguish between good and evil (91:7–8), are capable of knowing and judging good from evil (90:8–9), and can control harm and corruption (79:40). Humans were also appointed because they were the only ones who accepted such a role. In addition to their appointment as protectors of the earth, humans are asked to use the bounties of the earth as part of their devotion to God's creation. Humans are asked to balance the role of use and protection of the earth as a test of their devotional abilities.

In contrast to some deep ecologists who view action in nature as undesired intervention and corruption, I argue that in Islam action is the only course that fulfills the charge humans were given by God, namely to keep the equilibrium of use and protection of earth. Islam views action to avert evil and do good as the solution to save the corruption of the earth. Although there have been both historical and contemporary actions to avert evil and perform good, there is a need for a more systematic and comprehensive activity to save the environment. The problem in the past quarter century in Islamic countries and with Muslims has been their hesitation to act against the corruption of the earth, namely because they perceive that they are disempowered, that the corruption is not their own doing, and that they need to protect their own culture from Western encroachment. Such views, however, are in direct opposition to the core teachings of the Qur'an that view all humanity as the creation of God, that call for avoidance of excess, and that mandate respect for women as God's creations. It is the inaction and complacency of Muslims toward protecting the environment that has contributed to such levels of devastation. A retrieval of the action-oriented ethic toward the environment and a systematic program to achieve it would contribute to protecting the earth as a trust, *ammanah*, for the next generations of Muslims and non-Muslims.

NOTES

1. See a new book edited by Harold Coward and Daniel C. Maguire, *Visions of a New Earth: Religious Perspectives on Population, Consumption, and Ecology* (Albany: State University of New York Press, 2000). Initially the book was entitled "A New Theology." However, as the Islamic scholar I argued that there is a clear environmental ethic in Islam and all that is needed is to retrieve it and not to invent it. Most other scholars agreed with my viewpoint and hence the new title.

2. "The Effects of Armed Conflict on Girls," *World Vision Report,* 1997.

3. I. al Faruqi, *Islam* (Brentwood, Md.: International Graphics, 1984), 53.

4. I use the words *nature, universe, environment,* and *earth* interchangeably. The Qur'an and Arabic generally use earth to denote our universe (the globe) including the natural and social, and also use the word *Muhit,* which denotes human surroundings. I reflect the linguistic diversity in the Islamic context by using different words at different times in my chapter.

5. The Qur'anic references are cited by chapter and then verse.

6. I have sometimes used Abdullah Yusuf Ali, Holy Qur'an translation. Often, however, I found the generic word *Insan* or *Nas* translated as Man. Instead, I translated it as Humankind or People, a more accurate translation and more inclusive.

7. Abou Bakr Ahmad Ba Kader, et al., *Basic Paper on the Islamic Principles for the Conservation of the Natural Environment* (Gland, Switzerland: IUCN and the Kingdom of Saudi Arabia, 1983), 13.

8. Nawal Ammar, "Islam, Population, and the Environment: A Textual and Juristic View," in *Population, Consumption, and The Environment: Religious and Secular Responses,* ed. Harold Coward (Albany: State University of New York Press, 1995), 123, 124.

9. I. al Faruqi and L. al Faruqi, *The Cultural Atlas of Islam* (New York: Macmillan, 1986).

10. al Faruqi and al Faruqi, *The Cultural Atlas of Islam;* M. Abul-Fadl, "Revisiting the Woman Question: An Islamic Perspective," *The Chicago Theological Seminary Register* 83 (1993): 28–61.

11. al Faruqi and al Faruqi, *The Cultural Atlas of Islam,* 74.

12. Quoted in A. H. Masri, "Islam and Ecology," in *Islam and Ecology,* ed. F. Khalid and J. O'Brien (London: Cassell, 1992), 18.

13. Ammar, "Islam, Population, and the Environment," 128; S. A. Ismail, *Environment: An Islamic Perspective,* 1993. http://www.igc.apc.org/elaw/mideast/palestine/islamenviro.html.

14. Ammar, "Islam, Population, and the Environment," 129.

15. Ammar, "Islam, Population, and the Environment," 129.

16. Quoted in M. Rafiq and M. Ajmal, "Islam and the Present Ecological Crisis," in *World Religions and the Environment,* ed. O. P. Dwivedi (New Delhi: Gitanjali, 1989), 123.

17. al Faruqi and al Faruqi, *The Cultural Atlas of Islam;* M. Izzi Dien, "Islamic Ethics and the Environment," in *Islam and Ecology,* 25–35; and Izzi Dien, *Shari'a and the Environment,* 1993. http://www.igc.apc.org/elaw/mideast/palestine/shariaenviro.html.

18. al Faruqi and al Faruqi, *The Cultural Atlas of Islam,* 316.

19. al Faruqi, *Islam.*

20. For a discussion of free will and predestination with regard to the environment see Ammar, "An Islamic Response to the Manifest Ecological Crisis: Issues of Justice," in *Visions of a New Earth: Religious Perspectives on Population, Consumption, and Ecology,* ed. Harold Coward and Daniel C. Maguire (Albany: State University of New York Press, 2000), 131–46.

21. Quoted in Masri, "Islam and Ecology," 18.

22. These sayings are commonly known, being among those memorized by Muslims as part of their education.

23. Ammar, "Islam, Population, and the Environment," 130–31.

24. Ammar, "Islam, Population, and the Environment," 130–33.

25. Izzi Dien, *Shari'a and the Environment.*

26. Ammar, "An Islamic Response to the Manifest Ecological Crisis," 135.

27. See my "An Islamic Response to the Manifest Ecological Crisis."

28. al Faruqi and al Faruqi, *The Cultural Atlas of Islam,* 327.

29. Ammar, "Islam, Population, and the Environment," 133.

30. He stated that the rights of animals upon humans are as follows:

Spend on it (time, money and effort), even if it is aged or diseased such that no benefit is expected from it. The spending should be equal to that on a similar animal useful;

Do not overburden it;

Should not place with it whatsoever what may cause it harm, be it of the same kind or a different species;

Do not slaughter their young within their sight;
Give them different resting shelters and watering places which should all be cleaned regularly;
Should put the male and female in the same place during their mating season.
Should not hunt a wild animal with a tool that breaks bones. (Quoted in Izzi Dien, 5)

31. See A. H. Ba Kader, A. T. S. al Sabbagh, M. S. al-Glejd, and M. U. S. Izzi Dien, *Islamic Principles for the Conservation of the Natural Environment* (MEPA: Saudi Arabia, 1983), 1–25.

32. Fazlun Kahled and Joanne O'Brien have edited a very good book entitled *Islam and Ecology* (New York: Cassell Publishers, 1992).

33. Egypt, for example, created a Ministry of the Environment in the 1990s and it was headed by a woman minister. Indonesia in the summer of 1993 announced that its banks will not grant aide to any industry, firm, or individual that pollutes natural resources.

34. Ammar, "An Islamic Response to the Manifest Ecological Crisis," 133.

35. This war's environmental consequences were grave, including more than two hundred thousand people killed or injured, more than ten thousand Kurds displaced, and many soldiers afflicted with germ warfare ailments.

"The Universe Story: Its Religious Significance"

✒

Thomas Berry

Cultural historian and ecotheologian Thomas Berry is one of the most important writers on religious environmentalism. He taught at several universities and wrote *The Dream of the Earth*. This essay continues his work of attempting to redefine our sense of the universe for an ecological age.

✒

I write these words in the hill country of the northern Appalachians, at the eastern edge of the North American continent, some miles inland from the North Atlantic Ocean, during what might be considered the terminal phase of the Cenozoic period in the geobiological history of the earth. To get some understanding of the nature and order of magnitude of what is happening just now, it might be helpful to situate our thinking within this Cenozoic period, which can be dated roughly as the past sixty-five million years of earth history.

This is the lyric period in the entire history of the planet. During this period the flowers and birds and forests and all the mammals, such as we know them, came into being. As this continent drifts westward away from Africa and the great Eurasian continent, we are opening the North Atlantic Ocean ever wider as we move across the Pacific Ocean and approach the Eurasian continent on its eastward borders.

We need to think of these things, of where we are and what is happening on this larger scale as well as on the smaller scale of the territory we occupy and the times in which we live. We need to think of the northern Appalachian Mountains that surround us. We need to think of hardwood forests and the magnificent white pines that once covered this region, the region with perhaps the greatest display of deciduous trees on the planet. The more we think of these things, the more we are caught up in the wonder and mystery of the world about us, the more evident it is that we live amid a vast celebratory process, a kind of colorful pageant beyond anything that we as humans could ever have imagined.

The more we consider all this, the more evident it is that the universe throughout its vast extent in space and its long sequence of transformations in time can be seen as a single multiform celebratory event. Our human role, it would appear, is to be that being in whom the universe reflects on and celebrates itself and its numinous origins in a special mode of conscious self-awareness.

While this pertains primarily to the universe itself, it pertains in a special manner to our experience of the planet Earth, one of the nine planets in our solar system. All of these were originally the same, composed of exactly the same material, yet only Earth came to express itself in such color and form and life and movement, in such taste and fragrance as we observe about us. Only Earth of all the planets in our solar system was able to burst forth into such magnificence.

Mars turned to rock because the gravitational pressures could not produce the inner heat required to create the turbulence needed for air and water and life development. Jupiter remained the turbulent fiery mass of gases that it was in the beginning. Its gravitational pressure was such that nothing firm could take shape. Jupiter has no surface such as we find on Earth. Of all the planets only Earth had the proper balance between turbulence and restraint that enabled the planet to bring forth the amino acids, the living cells, all the superb organisms that inhabit the earth, and finally ourselves.

Earth, too, was just the proper distance from the Moon so that the tides could keep the seas in motion. Otherwise, if the Moon were closer to Earth, the tides would overwhelm the continents. If the Moon were somewhat more distant, there would be no tides, the seas would be stagnant, and life could not come. So in relation to the Sun, Earth is situated so that the appropriate differences of temperature could exist between the arctic and the tropics, and the vast variety of other climatic conditions could exist to shape the diversity of life as we find it.

There is something wild and unfathomable throughout this entire process, something that evokes awe and wonder at the source from which all this came into being, something that invites us to participate in this vast celebratory process. From earliest times humans in the temperate parts of the world have sought to enter into the ever-renewing cycle of the seasons through ritual celebration of the springtime renewal, when new life appears throughout the plant and animal kingdoms. Spring is especially significant for the mammals whose cycle of gestation has taken place throughout the winter months and who are ready to bring forth their young. Spring is the time that mating rituals take place, especially the gorgeous rituals of the birds.

These human celebrations became ever more sophisticated as the great urban civilizations developed and the ceremonies were elaborated. I mention all this as integral with the Cenozoic period, for it seems that the human could come into being only at a period when the planet was at such a gorgeous moment in its expression of itself and also at a moment when the human could enter into the larger functioning of the universe through some form of ritual celebration coordinated with the great liturgy of the universe itself.

It would seem that the coming of the human mode of consciousness could have occurred only when a world with the brilliance of the advanced Cenozoic period had set the stage. Perhaps this was needed to awaken human intelligence, imagination, sensitivity. Yet if this brilliance was needed to excite wonder, it was needed also as a healing for the sorrow of life that would inevitably result from the burden of the human form of intelligence and freedom of choice in actions. The human had to shape itself to a degree far beyond that of other modes of being.

While other modes of life are guided in their self-expression through their genetic coding, with relatively little further teaching or acculturation, there is a further self-formation of the human, a cultural coding mandated by our genetic coding. This required a special mode of self-invention on the part of the human. Once the human was brought into being, there was a several-million-year period when the earliest forms of intelligence were elaborated in the shaping of implements, in the discovery of fire-making, in the shaping of social order, in learning the arts of dealing with the nonhuman world, especially in dealing with all the spirit powers perceived throughout the surrounding world. It was a world of person presences. Every being was to be addressed as a "thou" rather than an "it." Finally, there was the invention of spoken language, which begins we know not when. We know only that this greatest of human inventions most likely occurred within the past hundred thousand years, perhaps as recently as the past fifty thousand years.

We need not go through the long narrative of the period leading up to the Neolithic village life of some twelve thousand years ago nor to the shaping of the great urban literate civilizations of the past five thousand years. These civilizations continued in the pattern of earlier human development. The discovery of writing was decisive in its consequences, for the various traditions fixed their revealed texts in written language that then came to control the greater part of the human venture over these past several thousand years.

In the past few centuries, however, since the time of Copernicus, a new area of consciousness has awakened in Western intelligence. We began to look more intently at the universe in its material structure, both the forces that swing the starry heavens through their orbit and the structure and functioning of forces that govern life on Earth. Suddenly, we discovered that the heavens did not move in circular but in elliptical order, that neither the heavens nor the earth were formed of eternal matter, that the smallest particles composing the material world contained immense quantities of energy. But above all, we discovered that the universe came into being through a vast period of time, through a sequence of transformations leading from the simpler to the more complex, from lesser to greater manifestation of consciousness, from lesser to greater freedom of action.

These discoveries gave to the human a range of power over the functioning of earth such as was never dreamed of in former times. We discovered that we could use earth for our own indulgent purposes. Soon we turned the entire human venture into an assault on those planetary processes that have over the millennia brought about all these wonders that we have outlined here. It is such a poignant moment as we look about us and observe that we are terminating this period of immense creativity, the Cenozoic era, the period that has for sixty-five million years brought about the grandeur of the world about us. We generally talk about our times in more limited terms, saying that we are at the end of the Enlightenment period or at the end of the medieval period or terminating Western civilization. We even think at times of the ending of the human mode of being due to the degradation of life conditions.

Yet we must consider that what is happening now is not some change such as occurred in the transition from the classical Mediterranean phase of Western civilization to the medieval period or from the medieval to the commercial-industrial civilization of the past two hundred years. Nor is the present situation something that pertains to the survival or destiny of simply the human. We are apparently at the end of a geobiological period. We are altering the chemistry of the planet, the biosystems of the planet, even the geological structure of the planet, all in a deleterious manner.

For the most part this has happened in my generation. When I was born in 1914, the planet and the North American continent were severely damaged but perhaps in a manner that could have been recovered from to an extensive degree. Now the planet has been damaged far beyond what occurred in the earlier part of the century, so damaged that the children of the immediate future will live amid the ruined infrastructures of the industrial world and amid the ruins of the natural world itself.

When I ask myself how to explain what has happened, I can only answer that my generation has been austitic. My generation had no effective capacity for communicating with the nonhuman world. Earth was seen as an inexhaustible resource of materials for human use and consumption. The nonhuman world had neither honor nor rights nor any sacred mode of its being.

Here in America we were heirs to the English tradition of jurisprudence, which is deeply concerned with life, liberty, and pursuit of happiness for humans at the expense of the natural world. Humans were protected in their liberty to own and exploit property for whatever purposes they wished. Yet mountains had no rights to their grandeur, rivers had no rights to remain free of pollution, the salmon had no rights to their spawning places, birds had no rights to their habitat nor to protected access along their migratory paths.

The rights we enjoy are determined by the Constitution. Yet nothing in the Constitution or in the Bill of Rights recognizes any rights possessed by natural modes of being. The National Geographic Survey was instituted early in the history of the nation, not for the purpose of a more profound communion with the natural wonders of the North American continent but for the purpose of distributing the land to private ownership, with no inherent responsibilities other than not to infringe on the rights of other humans dwelling in the same region. That land should be owned in accord with the nature of the land and the integral mode of its functioning was never a question.

Exploitation was the preordained way for humans to bear themselves toward the surrounding world: the continent must in some sense be reengineered and its power appropriated; otherwise it was simply wasted. Not to dam the western rivers—the Colorado, the Columbia, the Snake, or the river that flowed through the Hetch Hetchy valley of California—was wasteful. Not to exploit the Tennessee with a long series of dams was to refuse the power and the water offered there. Not to force the soil with fertilizer was to deny ourselves an increased harvest. Not to pave the roads was neglect. Not to take the petroleum from the earth was to reject a God-given opportunity for bettering human life, despite the fact that nature had stored the carbon in the petroleum and in the forests so that the chemical constitution of the air and the water and the soil could be worked out in some effective manner. That humans had rights to do what they pleased was self-evident, not to be contested.

To explain such autism it is not sufficient simply to go back to nineteenth-century industrialization or to Newtonian physics or even to Francis Bacon or Descartes. The origin of such autism requires a more profound explanation that would push our inquiry back into the anthropocentrism of the Hellenic world; back also to the biblical world and the scriptural foundations of our Western life formation; back to the two great commandments, love of God and love of neighbor; the fulfillment of the Law and the Prophets with no reference of any relation with the world about us.

That our religious traditions, our humanistic traditions, our educational programs, our jurisprudence, and the other shaping forces of our society all contributed equally to this autism might be too heavy a position to propose, but to note that none of these traditions was able to prevent this autism and the destruction emanating from within our Western civilization seems entirely appropriate. To say that all of these traditions were excessively committed to anthropocentrism also seems a proper conclusion. To say that they all favored processes that led to the present disastrous situation may even be defensible.

Certainly, none of these traditions has protested the devastation in any comprehensive manner, nor has it altered its basic orientation in any substantial manner. That is the difficult side of our present situation. There seems to be a stand-off attitude, an attitude of noninvolvement, even what might be considered a pervasive denial of the real magnitude of the difficulty.

Here we might consider just where we go from here. I propose that we need to go from the terminal Cenozoic to an emerging "Ecozoic" period, defined as the period when humans would be present to the earth in a mutually enhancing manner. This is the clearest way that I can express my own sense of the possibilities that are before us.

I prefer the term *ecozoic* to *ecological* since this enables us to place the coming geobiological period in its proper context in the sequence from the Palcozoic (from 600 to 220 million years ago), to the Mesozoic (from 220 to 65 million years ago), to the Cenozoic (the past 65 million years), and what now might be termed the Ecozoic period. This might now be accepted as the proper sequence in articulating the ages of the earth.

The term *ecozoic* is appropriate because it indicates that we are concerned with life forms themselves, not simply with our understanding of the life forms. But most of all, the term *ecozoic* gives some feel for the order of magnitude of what we are about. Our greatest failure at present would be to underestimate the exact magnitude of the issues that are before us.

What I miss most at present is the realism needed in evaluating the nature and order of severity in the challenge we face. Despite all the renewal of the Earth Movements, our society generally is still, it seems, in a period of denial. What is before us is too overwhelming. We are still reacting in a manner similar to that of the autistic child, who because of some psychic trauma has closed itself off from communication with the outer world. So we have closed ourselves off from any intimate feeling rapport with or even any rational understanding of our relation to the outer world. Indeed, if we were not so closed off, if we had some rapport with other modes of being, we would not be able to do what we are doing.

Yet we are beginning to listen when the soil tells us that it will grow our food if only we will assist it in functioning according to its own rhythms and in accord with its own needs. So too we begin to understand the infinite abundance of marine life in the seas that could feed us forever if only we permit the abundant marine life to multiply in accord with its inherent nature. We are finally learning when the natural world tells us that it cannot fulfill its role in sustaining us if we interfere with its proper modes of functioning.

We would expect the universities and the religious establishments to have guided us long ago, for these carry the humanistic and the religious wisdom of our traditions in their most exalted form. Yet even when biologists such as E. O. Wilson indicate that the extinctions of life occurring now have not been experienced on the planet since the termination of the Mesozoic era, even with such validation of the severity of what is happening, the universities have shown almost no willingness to shape their academic and professional programs to meet such a situation, thus leaving the students in a certain ignorance of the real-life context in which they must function in their professional lives. As with the professions generally, the move from the terminal Cenozoic to the ecozoic mode of functioning is a transformation beyond their capacities for adaptation, even though it is increasingly clear each day that the present modes of functioning of all the professions are leading us ever deeper into a tragic impasse.

But while we have used our modern knowledge in destructive ways, we find that the knowledge itself is valid and has given us a new story of the universe. This is the supreme achievement of modern intelligence, even though it has given us this knowledge as secular, materialistic, without inherent meaning. Yet once we realize that the universe has had a psychic-spiritual as well as a physical-material aspect from the beginning, once we realize that the human story is inseparable from the universe story, then we can see that this story of the universe is in a special manner our sacred story, the story that reveals the divine, the story that illumines every aspect of our religious and spiritual lives as well as our economic and imaginative lives.

Once we recognize this mystical dimension of the universe, we can appreciate the unity of every being out of this same primordial origin; we can see that every being in the universe is cousin to every other being in the universe. This is especially true of living beings who are descended through the same life process. Whatever the causes of our present situation, our need now is for a program that would enable us to manage the transition into the Ecozoic period in an effective manner. There are a number of conditions that must be fulfilled if we are to make this transition to a period in which humans would be present to the earth in a mutually enhancing manner.

First, we must understand that the universe is a communion of subjects, not a collection of objects. This implies that we recover our primordial intimacy with the entire natural world. We belong here. Our home is here. The excitement and fulfillment of our lives is here. However we think of eternity, it can only be another aspect of the present. The urgency of this psychic identity with the larger universe about us can hardly be exaggerated. We are fulfilled in our communion with the larger community to which we belong. It is our role to articulate a dimension of the universe. In a corresponding manner our smaller individual self is fulfilled in our larger self, in our family self, our community self, our earth self, our universe self. That is why we are drawn so powerfully to inquire into and understand and appreciate the stars in the heavens and the wonders of the earth. Every being is needed, for every being shares in the great community of existence. The comprehensive community is the supreme value in the phenomenal order.

Nothing substantial can be done until we withdraw from our attitude that every other mode of being attains its identity and value simply in being used by the human. Every being has its identity, its honor, and its value through its role in the universe. The universe is the normative reference, for as Saint Thomas tells us in his *Summa Theologica*, part I, question 47, article I, "the entire universe of beings participates in and manifests the divine more than any single being whatsoever." Within the larger universe the planet Earth constitutes a single integral community of existence. It lives or dies, is honored or degraded, as a single interrelated reality. As regards the future, it can be said quite simply that the human community and the natural world will go into the future as a single sacred community or we will both experience disaster on the way.

That the human is a subsystem of the earth system is most evident in the economic order. To advance the human economy by subverting the earth economy is an obvious absurdity, and yet our entire commercial-industrial system of the present is based on this absurdity. Only now is a new consciousness emerging in the economic institutions of our society.

Most difficult is jurisprudence. There already exists in the natural world a governance of the earth, a governance too subtle for us to understand. This governance enables the earth to bring forth the immense variety of its living forms that interact so intimately and so extensively with each other that the well-being of each is fulfilled in the well-being of the whole. This governance has capacities far beyond anything that humans are capable of. Yet this must remain the context into which we assert our human governance. Our human governance needs to function within the context of earth governance, just as our economic functioning needs to be an extension of the earth economy.

As regards healing, we begin to appreciate that the earth is a self-healing community just as it is a self-sustaining community and a self-governing community. It becomes clearer each day that there can be little hope for human healing except through the assistance of an integral natural world. When the earth becomes toxic, humans become toxic. We lose the only context in which we can hope for that vigorous mode of well-being that should be ours.

The next condition for our entering effectively into the Ecozoic era is that we accept our new story of the universe as our sacred story, with a special role to fulfill in this transition moment from the terminal Cenozoic to the emerging Ecozoic. This story enhances rather than negates the other stores of the universe that have over the years guided the course of human affairs among the indigenous peoples of the world as well as in the classical civilizations that have presided over the greater volume of human expression over the centuries. We are, however, at a time when these earlier traditions can no longer, out of their own resources, provide adequate guidance in the task that is before us.

Assuredly, we cannot do without the guidance of these traditions of the past. They provide understanding and guidance that is not available from this story of the universe that we are presenting here. Yet we are faced with vast realms of knowledge and power that require the new range of understanding available to us from this new insight into the structure and functioning of the world that surround us.

We need the story and the dream. We need the story to understand where we are in the unfolding reality of the universe. But we also need the dream, for the dream drives the action; the dream creates the future. The Ecozoic era must first be dreamed. Through the dream comes the guidance, the energy, and the endurance that we will need. For the transition that is before us will cost an immense effort and a wisdom beyond anything that we have known before. Our greatest encouragement just now is that we have begun to dream the ecozoic dream.

Here it is necessary to note that our planet will never again in the future function in the manner that it has functioned in the past. Until the present the magnificence splashed throughout the vast realms of space, the songs that resonate throughout the earth, the luxuriance of the tropical rain forests, the movement of the great blue whale through the sea, the autumn colors of the eastern woodlands—all this and so much else came into being entirely apart from any human design or deed. We did not even exist when all this came to be. But now, in the foreseeable future, almost nothing will happen that we will not be involved in. We cannot make a blade of grass, but there is liable not to *be* a blade of grass unless we accept it, protect it, and foster it. Even the wildnerness must now be protected by us. On occasion the wild animals need our care. So too there is an infinite amount of healing that must take place throughout the planet, healing that will at times require assistance from us; although, for the most part, the natural world will bring about its own healing if only we will permit it to function within the dynamism of its own genius.

Just now we are a transition moment such as neither we nor any other present living being, nor the earth itself, has ever experienced before. We are in the early hours of dusk as night settles over the land. Day is over, and night moves quietly over the land with its healing power. Dawn, when the eastern sky reveals itself in its faint purple glow, night when the sun sinks over the horizon and reflects its light in a colorful spectrum on the clouds of the western sky—these are the sacred moments of the day, the mystical moments, the moments of transformation.

So with sacred moments generally. Our moments of grace are our moments of transformation. In human life our greatest transformation moment is the moment of our birth, a sacred moment indeed, followed through the years with the sacred moment of adulthood and marriage and then the moment of death, itself such an awesome, such a sacred moment.

But if such moments of transformation—in the day and night, in autumn and springtime, in birth and death—are sacred moments, we must believe also that those vast cosmological transformation moments that enable the universe, Earth, and all its living beings to come into existence are sacred moments. Such a moment we observe in the sacrificial collapse of that first-generation star, which formed, in the intense heat of its collapse, the ninety-some elements that were needed for the formation of our solar system and especially the planet Earth, elements needed for the emergence of life. These elements were formed and then scattered with infinite abandon out into space, to be gathered and shaped into our Sun and its nine planets.

This was, I suggest, a cosmological moment of grace, for only through this event did Earth or life or the human form of consciousness become possible. So too, there are other cosmological moments of grace, such as the moment when photosynthesis was invented. These moments are indeed moments of grace, moments of divine manifestation, on a scale that we seldom think about. Such I would propose is the moment in which we find ourselves just now at the terminal phase of the Cenozoic era. We are in a transition moment, a transformation moment on an immense scale, as we experience the decline of the Cenozoic era and begin to shape some idea of what the emerging Ecozoic era might be. This, we must believe, is a moment of grace on a scale we have never thought of previously.

We begin to recognize in a dim and distant manner what is before us. Yet before my generation moves from the scene and the new generations take over their role in the immense drama of these centuries, we might communicate to them at least that encouragement and that faint glimmer of wisdom that we have attained in these recent decades and provide them with some assurance that the task before them is not simply their task. It is the task of the entire earth community, for only this community is capable of the transformation that is needed.

Finally, I would note that this transition to the Ecozoic era is the great work that we are about at present and for the immediate future. It would appear that each age has some great work that provides for the age its life purpose. This great work enables societies and civilizations to endure the agonies inherent in fulfilling any significant role in the larger historical process. We have, it seems, an immediate, particular work or profession whereby we fulfill our role in the social order, obtain our living, and support our families. Within this context we carry on the great work to be done in the larger historical order; inventing the Neolithic period, building a civilization, establishing a religious tradition, founding a nation, building the medieval cathedrals—these are among the great works of the past.

In more recent times the great work of the scientists has been to discover the large-scale as well as the small-scale structure and functioning of the universe and of the planet Earth. The pathos of our times is that the commercial-industrial establishment of this century thought of itself also as doing a good and great and noble work. Even when it was devastating the planet and bringing the Cenozoic period down into ruins, it thought that it was introducing the human community into a millennial age. Such is the deep cultural pathology that we are called upon to heal. Such a poignant moment. We already had a glorious world; but we did not recognize it or know how to relate to it.

History has chosen us to begin the great work of the twenty-first century, to initiate the Ecozoic era as a remedy for the cultural pathology of the present and to initiate the period when humans would be present to the earth in a mutually enhancing manner.

"The Trinity and Human Experience:
An Ecofeminist Approach"

❧

Ivone Gebara

Ivone Gebara, one of Latin America's leading theologians, is a Brazilian Sister of Our Lady, and the author of *Mary: Mother of God, Mother of the Poor,* and *Trinity.* This essay provides a deeply political and deeply religious view of the cosmic and moral meaning of human existence.

❧

Human beings are a part of the whole we call the Universe, a small region in time and space. They regard themselves, their ideas and their feelings as separate and apart from all the rest. It is something like an optical illusion in their consciousness. This illusion is a sort of prison; it restricts us to our personal aspirations and limits our affective life to a few people very close to us. Our task should be to free ourselves from this prison, opening up our circle of compassion in order to embrace all living creatures and all of nature in its beauty.

—Albert Einstein

When we hear the word Trinity, we immediately associate it with unfathomable mystery. It is part of our faith, but we have trouble relating to it. We've been told that our God is a Trinity who has overcome all loneliness and isolation. We've heard that it is the communion among Father, Son, and Holy Spirit, a beautiful and perfect sharing that we should imitate in our own relationships. Today, this "imitation" seems more and more difficult to understand. It seems to take place so far from ourselves: from our own flesh, our concerns, our limitations. In the final analysis it is a sharing among "persons" who are totally spiritual and perfect. It is, after all, a divine communion.

There is a real fear in all of us of daring to doubt certain ideas, of raising questions about things we were taught that have been set forth as truths we have to accept. Religious institutions often create this fear in us, fettering our ability to think critically about faith issues. The Trinity, and the words Father, Son, and Holy Spirit are like a code that needs to be broken and translated anew. They are symbols that refer to life experiences, but their symbolism has grown hazy and has been absolutized within a closed, eminently masculine and arcane theoretical system. I invite you to *dare to think,* above all because this is a decisive moment in our history, a moment full of difficult questions and institutional crises, a moment in which the very survival of life is at stake.

For all these reasons, the perspective I adopt in this reflection is *ecofeminism*. In simple and practical terms, I'd like to show that there is a need to rediscover and reflect on the truly universal aspects of life, on dimensions that reflect what the earth and the cosmos are telling us about themselves, and the things women are vehemently affirming with regard to their own dignity and that of all humanity.

Before I speak of the Trinity I'd like to say a few words about the wonder of being human. I want to remind you that human beings are a fruit of a long process, the evolution of life itself. Life evolved for thousands and thousands of years before the creation of the species to which we belong and which we call human. Within us, life continues to be created: it develops, folds back, and reveals itself in differing cultures and economic, political, social, and cultural organizations. Life itself led humanity to arise from within the whole creative evolutionary process, which is both earthly and cosmic.

The human race carries on this creative expression of life both in itself and in its works. Participating in the creative evolution of life, we re-create ourselves. This is manifest in our ability to reflect and love, in our ethical behavior, and in all the other capabilities that make us what we are.

Living within the context of nature as a whole, we have gradually accumulated significant learnings. We have responded, for example, to the challenge of rivers that stretched before us, separating one place from another: we learned to build bridges. To move on water we built boats, then ships. To cross great distances we built airplanes, and so on. We learned to closely examine our human experience, as well as the lives of insects, animals, and plants; and thus we found ways of living and developing our creativity as we responded to the challenges posed by each situation.

Our learning led us to discover the social causes of poverty, and then to formulate hypotheses aimed at explaining and interpreting history and responding with concrete actions. Our learning also led us to cultivate a sense of wonder and perplexity in the face of the astounding order that marks all of reality.

We ourselves continually re-create the life that is in us. Human culture, in its multiple artistic and literary expressions, bears witness to our admirable creativity. This creativity also exists, albeit in a different form, in the vegetable and animal worlds. We have often been taught, however, that these "other worlds" have little creativity. The real reason for this attitude is that we always think of creativity in human terms and judge everything else on that basis. It would be good, however, if human beings would stop once in a while and reflect on the creativity that is manifest in an orange seed: the memory present in this small, vital center; its ability to develop when conditions are favorable; its ability to adapt to different soils and situations; to become a tree; to produce flowers and fruit, and then once again seeds. The seed's creativity is surely not the same as human creativity, but it clearly participates in the ongoing and awesome creativity of the universe.

The seed planted in the depths of the earth goes through a complex process of transformation, of changes in life and in death, before it breaks through the soil's surface. And when we discover that the seed has become a small plant, we do not remember the entire, arduous process it went through in the bowels of the earth and in its own innermost recesses; neither do we remember its multiple interactions with all the forces of nature.

The same is true of human beings. The things we produce, even the most precious among them, sublime creations such as our religious beliefs, emanate from a long maturation process in which our concern for our immediate needs has always been present. Our extraordinary creativity acquired the ability to produce meanings capable of helping us live out this or that situation. But these meanings are not static realities; they are part of the dynamism of life, and thus they change as well. Of necessity, they undergo transformations in order to respond to life's demands and adapt to new situations as they arise.

The important thing, if we are going to be able to take the next step in our reflection, is to get a clear sense that the *human* meanings of things come from ourselves, as does the human meaning of the entire universe. It is we ourselves who construct our interpretations, our science, our wisdom, our knowledge. It is we ourselves who today affirm one thing and tomorrow correct what we have said. It is we who affirm the image of God as warrior-avenger or as tender and compassionate. It is we, in our ancestors and traditions, who have construed the Trinity as three distinct persons in one God; so too, we can change our way of portraying it as we develop new perceptions.

The Trinity is an expression of our history, of human history, which is both tragic and challenging; but it is a unified Trinity, as if in that unity we were expressing our own desire for harmony and communion with all that exists. It is a communion to which we aspire in the midst of tears, of the experience of pain and suffering, as if that Holy Trinity of which we speak was the expression of a world that is both plural and transformed, harmonized, in which all suffering and pain are overcome, separation and division overcome, every tear wiped away; and in the end God, that is, the One, Love, is all in all.

The Trinity brings multiplicity and the desire for unity into one single and unique movement, as if they were moments within the same breath. Trinity is a name we give to ourselves, a name that is the synthesis of our perception of our own existence. Trinity is a language we build in an attempt to express our awareness of being a multitude and at the same time a unity. Trinity is a word that points to our common origin, our shared substance, our universal breathing within the immense diversity that surrounds each and every one of us, each a unique and original creation, a path along the great road of life. Trinity is also a word about ourselves, about what we know and live out in our own flesh-and-blood life stories.

A baptism of fire is one we go through as a result of our inner faithfulness to ourselves. It is a reality that envelops us by virtue of our rediscovery of our deepest self. Within that rediscovery we are reborn in God; we are reborn to the earth, to the cosmos, to history, and to service in the construction of human relationships grounded in justice and mutual respect.

Today, if we are to recover the dynamism of the Trinity, we need to recover the dynamism of our own existence—even at the risk of not managing to formulate our ideas in clear and precise terms. Our great challenge is to accept the insecurity involved in discussing what is real and to seek only the security that comes from dealing with the here and now, with daily life, with our own experiences and with our questions, heeding that wise phrase from the Hebrew world, "sufficient to the day is its own task."

The Trinity, then, is not three separate persons living in a heaven we cannot locate. It is not three persons different from one another the way we differ as persons. The Father, Son, and Holy Spirit are not of divine stuff as opposed to our human stuff; rather, they are *relationships*, that is, relationships we human beings experience. These relationships are expressed in anthropomorphic style; but the expression is metaphorical and not primarily metaphysical. Within Christian experience, Father, Son, and Holy Spirit are symbolic expressions we use to speak of the profound intuition that all of us share, along with everything that exists, in the same divine breath of life.

RECONSTRUCTING THE MEANING OF THE TRINITY

We speak of "reconstruction" when a human relationship, a piece of land, a city, or even a society needs to remake itself, re-create itself, renew its relational life. Something has happened that has weakened an edifice, a relationship, a bond of friendship. In this sense I'd like to offer a somewhat tentative effort at rebuilding Trinitarian meanings—a reconstruction demanded by the present historical situation. I'd like to propose five reflections on this reconstruction: the Trinity in the cosmos; the Trinity on earth; the Trinity in relationships among peoples and cultures; the Trinity in human relationships; and the Trinity in every person.

The Trinity in the Cosmos

"This universe is a single multiform energetic unfolding of matter, mind, intelligence and life."[1] So says Brian Swimme, a North American astrophysicist who has worked hard to tell the story of the universe in empirical language. He tries to show that as we approach the end of this century, humanity has acquired the ability to tell the story of the universe itself. This is a fundamental step in coming to understand our shared history and in the effort to create a new relationship with the earth, the cosmos, and with all peoples.

At this point I merely want to draw your attention to the unique and multiform structure of the universe that in symbolic and metaphorical terms we could call a "Trinitarian" structure. By Trinitarian structure I mean the reality that constitutes the entire cosmos and all life forms, a reality marked at the same time by multiplicity and by unity, by the differences among all things and their interdependence.

Stars, galaxies, heavenly bodies, planets, satellites, the atmosphere, the seas, rivers, winds, rain, snow, mountains, volcanos—all are expressions of the multiple creativity of the universe; they are profoundly interdependent and interrelated. They are diversity and unity, existing and interrelating in a unique and single movement of continual creativity.

The Trinity on Earth

Plants, animals, forests, mountains, rivers, and seas form the most diverse combinations in the most remote and varied places. They attract one another, couple with one another, blend with one another, destroy one another, and re-create themselves in species of pale or exuberant colors. They grow and feed on one another's lives, transforming and adapting to one another, dying and rising in many ways within the complex life process to which we all belong. In its stunning mutations, the earth sometimes threatens us and sometimes awes us, sometimes makes us shiver and at other times inspires cries of joy. Spinning around the sun and on its own axis, the earth creates days and seasons and brings forth the most varied forms of life.

The Earth as Trinity: The Trinitarian earth is a movement of continuous creativity, unfolding processes of creation and destruction that are expressions of a single vital process. To grasp the immense creative force in which we are immersed and of which we are an integral part, we need only think of the succession of geological eras, the birth of the continents, the transformation of seas into deserts, the flowering of forests, and the emergence of manifold expressions of vegetable and animal life.

The Trinity in Relationships among Peoples and Cultures

Whites, blacks, indigenous peoples, Asiatics, and *mestizos,* all with different languages, customs, statures, and sexes, make up the awesome and diverse human symphony in which, once again, multiplicity and unity are constitutive expressions of the single vital process that sustains us all. Life, in its complex process of evolution, brings about the variety of human groups and invites us to contemplate the luxuriance of our diversity.

If we accept this diversity as part of the Trinitarian structure itself and take it seriously as the basic make-up of all beings, there is no way to justify the idea of any being's superiority or inferiority. What we have now is cosmic citizenship. We are merely "cosmics," terrestrials, members of the cosmos and of the earth; we need one another, and can exist only on the basis of a community of being, of interdependence among our differences.

I am convinced that if we were to try to develop this idea of cosmic citizenship, we could more easily overcome the different strains of racism, antiracism, xenophobia, exclusion, violence, and sexism that are rife in our culture. A new sense of citizenship needs to be born and grow in us, without denying the national affiliations that are still part of our history.

The pluralism that makes us a human species is Trinity: it is the symbolic expression of a single and multiple reality that is an essential component of our living tissue. This plurality is essential if human life itself is to continue on, if the different races and cultures are to develop, support one another, and enter into communion.

The Trinity in Human Relationships

The Trinitarian mystery is also found in intimate I–thou relationships. We are I–thou and mystery—the mystery of our presence to the world, to the universe, to ourselves. We are the mystery of our stories, our traditions, our questions. We are I, thou, and mystery, and therefore Trinity, in the closeness and allure of a profound relationship that leads us to a deeper level of intimacy, of desire to know one another, of tender sharing. For this reason, knowing one another requires not only time, patience, and dialogue but a constant and challenging investment of ourselves. We are challenged to enter into a process of shared self-revelation, of unmasking ourselves, of manifesting an ever greater part of ourselves. We will find that what we reveal is drawn from those things that are known and unknown to ourselves, and therefore to others.

The Trinity in Every Person

Our own personal being is Trinitarian: it is mysteriously multiple at the same time that it is one. And most important, this extraordinary reality can be seen in the lives of all peoples; it is present in all biological functions, in all cultural and religious processes. This vision gives us a new worldview and a different anthropology, on the basis of which we see ourselves as persons who are *of* the earth and *of* the cosmos, participants in the extraordinary process of life's evolution. "The new heavens and the new earth" are always on the way: they were coming to be yesterday, they are coming to be today, and they will be on the way tomorrow. Heaven is not opposed to earth; it does not present itself as something superior or as the final aim of our efforts, the place where we will at last enter into a state of divine peace and harmony.

THE CELEBRATION OF LIFE

By trying to understand the Trinity as a human experience, as an experience of the earth and of the cosmos, we are able to celebrate life in a new way. "In a new way" means we ourselves are celebrated as we celebrate life in the Trinity. It means, too, that we experience a broader oneness with the life processes that are beyond our own boundaries. We praise ourselves; we praise the earth; we praise all beings as we raise our voices in praise of the Trinity, using the symbolic language that is most dear to us. We include ourselves in the celebration. It is not just something apart from us; it starts with our own existential experience, in our communion with all forms of life and all the cosmic energies.

THE TRINITY AND THE PROBLEM OF EVIL

The ancient problem of evil is very much with us today, above all because, as I pointed out previously, we see an increase in the destruction of persons, of groups, and of the earth itself. Our society seems ever less capable of devising formulas that permit dignified human sharing and the possibility of survival on the earth. We have the impression that our present world, despite its theories, its analyses and its designs, has turned evermore often to violence and exclusion in order to solve its problems. This in turn has brought about a growing wave of destruction, greater than at any other time in history. The wretched of the earth, the hungry, the landless, the unemployed—those who thirst for justice—feel evermore acutely the silence of God even when, hoping beyond all hope, they continue to speak of God's justice.

A Trinitarian vision of the universe and of humanity does not identify evil, destruction, and suffering as realities that are outside ourselves and need to be eliminated through violence; neither does it say they should be accepted as God's will. Rather than point to "the other" as the source of evil, it recognizes that what we call evil is in ourselves; in a certain sense evil is also our body. Evil is a relationship we ourselves construct; it leads to the destruction not only of the individual but of the entire fabric of human life.

The Trinitarian view of the universe places us at the very energy source of all that exists. At the same time it makes a distinction: on the one hand is the creative-destructive process that is inherent in the evolution of life itself; on the other is moral evil, evil defined in ethical terms. The latter refers to human evil, the evil worked by ourselves: actions that, when combined with our inherent frailty, can make us murderers of life in all its multiple expressions.

When we speak of human beings, we always speak in terms of good and evil. But when we speak of the cosmos, of the universe, we need to speak of forces that are at once creative and destructive. This constitutive reality of the universe, these positive and negative poles (we use these terms with an awareness of the limitations of our language) are inseparable in all the life processes. The birth of our solar system required the destruction of others. The appearance of a desert region may mean the death of a river. The use of fish as food may require the destruction of many of them, and so on.

The fact that we are the "consciousness" or the thinking process of the universe leads us to label things good or evil according to the way they affect us. Today we need to have another look at these reflections in the light of our contemporary historical situation and our more global and articulated sense of the life processes.

Ethical evil is evil wrought by human beings. On the one hand, it arises from the dynamics of life itself and from our human condition of frailty, dependence, and interdependence. On the other, the Christian tradition has always taught that evil actions arise out of our selfishness and the excesses of our passions.

But ethical evil is also a result of our very limited understanding of ourselves and our relationship with all other beings. We have acquired a highly developed sense of our individuality, of our superiority or inferiority, but have relatively little sense of our collective nature, of the way in which our communion with everything else assures our survival and shared happiness.

Because of our narrow affirmation of our personal, racial, religious, and even class identity, we have created systems to protect ourselves from one another—the systems based on greed or on the perceived superiority of those who regard themselves as "the strongest" or "the finest." These systems do not allow us to perceive the ephemeral nature of our individual lives and projects. Instead, we exalt the individual and regard the most powerful, wealthy, or brilliant individuals as absolutes, quasidivinities to be protected against all the ebbs and flows of history.

From this perspective we developed the idea of a God who is above and presides over history. This in turn led us to construct an image of a just divinity outside our world—a powerful deity often fashioned in the image of the powerful of this world. This God, who is also an "individual," is always just, strong, and good—the very opposite of our fragility and depravity. This is the God of theodicy, a God who is very difficult to reconcile with the tragic reality of human history. It is a God whose goodness "in itself" must always be affirmed and defended, as if in defending the goodness of a supreme being we could guarantee our escape from our own tragic iniquity.

The poor continue to bend their knees before this deity, begging for mercy, clemency, and help in satisfying their most basic needs and harboring the spark of hope in their daily lives. They act toward this God much the way they act toward the powerful of this world, hoping to be treated with consideration and left with some prospect of earning their bread with dignity. The poor are slaves of many masters and, by analogy, also of a supreme master.

To leave behind this crude and highly patriarchal, hierarchical, materialistic, individualistic, dependent, and class-biased understanding of God and of the Trinity seems to me an essential step for the present and the future. Above all this is a spiritual path, a personal and collective empowerment that opens us to a wider and freer perspective. By "spiritual path" I mean a path that transforms our inner convictions, a demanding path that goes beyond adherence to a political party's program or obedience to a code of canon law. It is a spiritual path because it is the path of the Spirit, which blows freely where it will; no one can hold back its movement. It is a spiritual path because it is the path of God in each and all of us.

We are constantly being invited to return to our roots: to communion with the earth, with all peoples and with all living things; to realize that transcendence is not a reality "out there," isolated, "in itself," superior to all that exists, but a transcendence within us, among us, in the earth, in the cosmos, everywhere. That transcendence is here and now, among those who are similar to us and different from us, among plants and animals, rivers and seas. That transcendence invites us to reach beyond the limitations of our selfishness and respond to our call to a new collective ethic centered on saving all of life. That transcendence is a canticle, a symphony unceasingly played by the infinite creativity of *Life*.

What, then, is evil in this traditional yet novel perspective? Within this perspective, what we call evil is the unbalanced situation in which we find ourselves, our millennial thirst for individual power and our millennial hunger to eat more and more while preventing others from consuming their rightful share.

The basic evil propagated by our species originates in the desire to possess life and make it our own—selfishly. It is the appropriation of goods by individuals and groups—the self-appointed proprietors of the earth—of other persons and groups, whom the dominant regard as of secondary importance. Evil is the growing dysfunctionality in both personal and social life that leads me to the narcissistic cultivation of my own individuality and my ecclesiastical, political, or business interests.

Evil is the excess or abundance that is held back and hoarded, whether it be food, land, power, knowledge, or pleasure. It remains in the hands of the owners of capital: those who, with the support of their direct and indirect accomplices, present themselves as veritable gods upon the earth.

Evil is the idolatry of the individual, of the "pure" race, of the messianic people, of the empire that dominates by insinuating itself into everything, even into people's inner being, inducing them to believe in their own inferiority. Evil is the ascendancy of one sex over another, its domination over all personal, social, political, and economic realms.

Evil is the proclamation and imposition of my gods as eternal and exclusive, capable of saving all of humanity. Evil is the claim that some people know the will of God and are commissioned to teach it as irrefutable dogma, while others are obligated to humbly recognize and accept their own ignorance.

Human evil leaves us perplexed. It poses innumerable questions, many of them unanswerable. Cosmic "evil," on the other hand, is the creation-destruction process inherent in the universe, and it only frightens us when we suffer its consequences.

Cosmic evil has two faces: it is rooted in the Trinity we are and in the humanity and divinity we participate in. This evil is the negative aspect or, to use a different term, the emptiness found everywhere in the universe, on earth, and among human persons. This emptiness opens the way for opposition, conflict, tension, and destruction; but at the same time it bears extraordinary creative possibilities for the unfolding of our sensitivities and the opening of our inner being to that which is beyond ourselves.

In some way, too, things that appear negative have an energy capable of developing within us the capacity for loving others, bending to those who have fallen in the street, taking in an abandoned child, replanting a ravaged forest, cleaning up a polluted river, or feeding animals during a time of drought. Out of the garbage we accumulate, a flower can bloom; dry bones can return to life; the horror of war can become a cradle of compassion. We ourselves and the whole universe are made up of the same energy, an energy that is both positively and negatively charged. This very energy continually creates and re-creates the earth and human existence.

Human history bears witness to the fact that great gestures of mercy and tenderness are born of dramatic, life-threatening situations. When another's pain becomes unbearable, it becomes my pain and stimulates the birth of loving gestures. The Buddha, Jesus, Mohammed, the thousand Francises, Clares and Theresas, the ever-present unnamed saints turn pain into a source of compassion, mercy, and new prospects for life.

This new vision, which is present in our reflection on the Trinity, helps us leave behind the dualistic and confining anthropocentrism that has characterized our Western Christian tradition, a dualism that not only regards the dyad God and humanity as opposites but does the same to the dyads spirit and matter, man and woman, and good and evil. Throughout the course of our history, dualism has engendered a thousand and one antitheses.

The saying attributed to Jesus of Nazareth, "Love your neighbor as yourself," should be taken up by us and understood as the way back to a Trinitarian balance. If we have excessive love for ourselves, we will fall into a sort of unlimited narcissism and the virtually implacable destruction of others. We will continue to build empires: Nazism, fascism, racism, classism, *machismo,* and all kinds of excesses that end up turning back on us, and above all, on the poor. A balance between I and thou, I and we, we and they, ourselves and the earth is the way to turn around and allow the human, as well as plants and animals and all the creative energies of the earth, to flourish anew.

This new vision calls on us to see the universe as our body, the earth as our body, the variety of human groups as our body—a body that is in evolution, in creative ecstasy, in the midst of destructive and regenerative labor, of death and resurrection. Everything is our body, our

Trinitarian body: it is a continual tension and communion of multiplicity and unity, all within the ecstatic and mysterious adventure of Life.

CONCLUSION

In conclusion I want to express a hope-filled certainty. At the end of this millennium we are beginning to work together, as peoples from many parts of the earth, to build a new spirituality. It looks, in fact, like a new Pentecost; but it is a slow-moving Pentecost: patient, universal, at times almost imperceptible. It is an inner and outer Pentecost that bursts open our religious boundaries. It begins not only to change our understanding of the world and of ourselves, but to modify our behavior. All this is spirituality, that is, an energy that puts order in our lives, that gives meaning, that awakens in us the desire to help others to discover the "pearl of great price" hidden in our own bodies and in earth's body. We know that when people find their personal and collective "pearl," they "sell all they have" in order to obtain it. The pearl is the symbolic expression of the new spirituality that is growing in our own bodies, nourished by our human energies, by the earth, by the cosmos—in the last analysis, by the indissoluble one and multiple Trinitarian energy that is present in all that exists.

The Trinity is our primary creative reality, a constitutive reality, a reality that permeates all we do and are. A Trinity of things old and new, of stories and tales that evolve and are organized in many creative ways. The ecofeminist perspective, which is an intimate connection between feminist thought and ecology, opens us not only to the possibility of real equality between men and women of different cultures, but to a different relationship between ourselves, the earth, and the entire cosmos. This new relationship, which is still in its embryonic stages, aims at going beyond merely speculative discussions, which do not lead to a change in relationships.

We are tired of sterile religious-scientific discourse, of its powers grounded in an All-Powerful, One and Trinitarian God, distant and apart from ourselves. We are tired, to use the words of Arnaldo Jabor, of seeing the world "divided between those who bewail hell and those who live in it."[2] This refers to the hell of our society, which kills Indians, children, and entire peoples; but which can also produce individuals who designate themselves as the "conscience" of society and as critics of its ills, and who speak in the name of God but fail to recognize either the blasphemy they commit or the complicity that flaws their beliefs.

The important thing is to renew our lives daily, with tenderness, responsibility, keenness, and great passion, to experience daily our struggle to defend the extraordinary Life that is within us, in the unity in multiplicity of all things.

—Translated by David J. Molineaux

NOTES

An abridged version of a long essay originally published in Portuguese as *Trinidade, palavra sobre coisas velhas novas: uma perspectiva ecofeminista*. Sao Paulo: Paulinas, 1994.

1. Brian Swimme, *The Universe Is a Green Dragon* (Santa Fe: Bear & Co., 1984), 28.
2. Arnaldo Jabor, "Todos temos inveja da paz dos ianomamis," *Jornal do Commercio*, Recife: Aug. 25, 1993.

"The Chipko Women's Concept of Freedom"

Vandana Shiva

Vandana Shiva directs the Research Foundation for Science, Technology, and Natural Resource Policy in Dehradun, India, and is the author of *Staying Alive* and *Monocultures of the Mind*. In this essay she explores the intersection of environmentalism, gender, and religion in a women's group's struggle to protect the local forest in northern India.

On November 30, 1986, Chamundeyi, a woman of Nahi-Kala village in Doon Valley, was collecting fodder in the forest when she heard trucks climbing up the mountain toward the limestone quarry in the area. But since September 1986 there had been a Chipko camp on the road to the quarry set up by the village communities of the Thano region, to stop the mining operations which have created ecological havoc in the region; the trucks should not, therefore, have been there. The quarry workers had attacked the protesters, removed them from the blockade, and driven the trucks through. Chamundeyi threw down her sickle, raced down the slope and stood in front of the climbing trucks, telling the drivers that they could go only over her dead body. After dragging her for a distance, they stopped and reversed.

In April 1987 the people of Nahi-Kala were still protesting because the government had been tardy in taking action to close the mine although the lease had expired in 1982. The mining operations were also in total violation of the 1980 Forest Conservation Act. People's direct action to stop the mining was an outcome of the government's failure to implement its own laws. The quarry contractor meantime tried to take the law into his own hands. On March 20, 1987, he brought about two hundred hired thugs to the area who attacked the peaceful protesters with stones and iron rods. But the children, women, and men did not withdraw from the blockade. They are their own leaders, their own decision makers, their own source of strength.

The myth that movements are created and sustained by charismatic leaders from outside is shattered by the nonviolent struggle in Nahi-Kala in which ordinary women like Itwari Devi and Chamundeyi have provided local leadership through extraordinary strength. It is the invisible strength of women like them that is the source of the staying power of Chipko—a movement whose activities in its two decades of evolution have been extended from embracing trees to embracing living mountains and living waters. Each new phase of Chipko is created by invisible women. In 1977, Bachni Devi of Advani created Chipko's ecological slogan: "What do the forests bear? Soil, water and pure air."

A decade later, in Doon Valley, Chamundeyi inspired the Chipko poet Ghanshyam "Shailani" to write a new song:

A fight for truth has begun
At Sinsyaru Khala
A fight for rights has begun
In Malkot Thano
Sister, it is a fight to protect
Our mountains and forests.
They give us life
Embrace the life of the living trees
And streams to your hearts
Resist the digging of mountains
Which kills our forests and streams
A fight for life has begun at
Sinsyaru Khala

On March 29, during a meeting of friends of Chipko, I spent a day with Chamundeyi and Itwari Devi—to learn about their hidden strengths, to learn from them about the hidden strengths of nature. Here are some extracts from our exchange of experiences:

Vandana: *What destruction has been caused by limestone mining in Nahi-Kala?*

Chamundeyi: When I came to Nahi seventeen years ago, the forests were rich and dense with ringal, tun, sinsyaru, gald, chir, and banj. Gujral's mine has destroyed the ringal, the oak, the sinsyaru. Our water sources which are nourished by the forests have also dried up. Twelve springs have gone dry. Two years ago, the perennial waterfall, Mande-ka-Chara which originates in Patali-ka-Dhar and feeds Sinsyaru Khala went dry. Mining is killing our forests and streams, our sources of life. That is why we are ready to give up our lives to save our forests and rivers.

Itwari: Sinsyaru-ka-Khala was a narrow perennial stream full of lush sinsyaru bushes. Today it is a wide barren bed of limestone boulders. With the destruction caused by mining our water, mills, forests, and paddy fields have been washed away. When Gujral first came he was in rags. I remember I had come to the water mill to get flour ground. Gujral had come with a dilapidated truck, and his lunch was a dry chappati, with raw onion. Today, after having robbed our mountain for twenty-six years, Gujral is a rich man with twelve trucks who can hire armies of thugs to trouble and attack us, as he hired armies of labor to dig our mountain. We have been camping on the road for seven months now to stop his mine, and his efforts to hurt us and threats to kill us keep increasing.

First, he started picking limestone boulders from the river bed. Then he climbed the mountain. He has done ten years of very intensive mining and turned our rich and productive mountain into a desert. The source of Sinsyaru has become a desert. We decided then that the mine must be closed if our children were to survive.

The young boys of the Yuvak Mandal who are working with our Mahila Mandal to get the mine closed, were six months to one year old when Gujral first came to our village. They have spent a lifetime watching him treat our land and resources as his private property. The Chipko protest was precipitated when the boys went to demand royalty payment for the mining in Gram Sabha land. Gujral said to them, "You have grown on crumbs I have thrown to you—how dare you demand royalty from me." The boys said, "We have grown with the nurturance of our mothers—and the mountains and forests and streams which are like our mothers—and we will no longer let you destroy our sources of sustenance. We will not let your trucks go to the mine.

C: On March 20, we saw Gujral's truck come. They pushed out the five people who were at the Satyagraha camp—meantime the women rushed down to the camp. We held on to the trucks and said, "Please stop, listen to us." They had hired women from the Dehra Dun slums to assault us—they pushed us aside and went to the line. Eight thugs stayed with us and said, "Listen, mothers and sisters, you have been sitting on a Chipko protest for six months now with the Chipko activists. What facilities have they created for you in six months?" I said, "Listen brothers, Gujral has been digging our mountain for twenty-six years, what has he done for us? The Chipko people have been with us for only six months of struggle—come back in twenty-six years and find out what they helped us create." Gujral's people said, "Ask for whatever you need—we will provide it." We replied, "We have only one need and one demand, that the mine be closed." They said they would stop mining and only take what has already been mined. We told them, "No, those stones came from the mountain and we will put them back to stabilize it. We will make check-dams with them. We will protect our forests and mountain with the boulders. These boulders are the flesh of *Dharti Ma* (Mother Earth). We will return them to where they belong, and heal her wounds." Then they said, "For each trip we make, we will give you earnings from our truckload of limestone." We continued to insist that we wanted the mine closed, that nothing could tempt us. They said "We will give you a truck for transport. Bahuguna cannot give you that." We answered "We are our own transport, our feet are our most dependable transport. We do not need your trucks. We only want the mine closed."

V: *This is the third time they have attacked you; what happened in the November [1986] incident?*

C: I had just fed my children and was going to the forest for fodder with my sons Suraj Singh and Bharat Singh. I saw a truck coming. I sent Suraj Singh to inform the Satyagrahis at the Camp, but they had already been attacked and removed from the road. I met the trucks half way up the mine and put myself in front of them and said, "The trucks can go only over my dead body." They finally turned back.

V: *What are the three most important things in life you want to conserve?*

C: Our freedom and forests and food. Without these, we are nothing, we are impoverished. With our own food production we are prosperous—we do not need jobs from businessmen and governments—we make our own livelihood—we even produce crops for sale like rajma and ginger; two quintals of ginger can take care of all our needs. Forests are central as sources of fertilizer and fodder. Our freedom to work in the forests and to farm is very important. Gujral's mine is destroying our work and our prosperity while they talk of mining and "creating" work and prosperity.

V: *Do you feel tempted by his bribes?*

I: Gujral offered my son Rs.500,000 if he would remove me from the Chipko protest. My son replied, "Money I can get anywhere, but my mother's dignity and respect comes from the village community, and we can never sacrifice that."

C: They went to my brother and said, "Get your sister away." Gujral himself came and said he would make a school and hospital for us. We asked him why it had taken him twenty-six years to think of all this? Now it was too late. We are determined to close his mine and protect ourselves.

V: *What is your source of strength (shakti)? What is Chipko's strength?*

I: *Shakti* comes to us from these forests and grasslands, we watch them grow, year in and year out through their internal *shakti* and we derive our strength from it. We watch our streams renew themselves and we drink their clear, sparkling water, that gives us *shakti*. We drink fresh milk, we eat ghee, we eat food from our own fields. All this gives us not just nourishment for the body but a moral strength, that we are our own masters, we control and produce our own wealth. That is why it is "primitive," "backward" women who do not buy their needs from the market but produce for themselves, who are leading Chipko. Our power is nature's power. Our power against Gujral comes from these inner sources and is strengthened by his attempts to oppress and bully us with his false power of money. We have offered ourselves, even at the cost of our lives, for a peaceful protest to close this mine, to challenge and oppose the power that Gujral represents. Each attempt to violate us has strengthened our integrity. They stoned us on March 20, when they returned from the mine. They stoned our children and hit them with iron rods, but they could not destroy our *shakti*.

"Race, Sacrifice, and Native Lands"

☙

Jonna Higgins-Freese and Jeff Tomhave

Jonna Higgins-Freese is environmental outreach coordinator at Prairiewoods Franciscan Spirituality Center in Hiawatha, Iowa, and a fellow of the Environmental Leadership Program. Jeff Tomhave is an enrolled member of the Three Affiliated Tribes in North Dakota and the founder of Effective Self-Determination Solutions, an organization that trains Indian people to be their own advocates; and a fellow of the Environmental Leadership Program. This essay describes the intersection of Native American concerns with the use (and misuse) of Native American culture.

☙

Across the United States, nonnative peoples' interest in shamanic and indigenous-based spiritual practices is strong, as can be seen by the large number of sweat lodges, drum circles, dream catchers, references to quotes from Chief Seattle—even the fact that shamanism is the theme for this issue of EarthLight.

This interest in native ecospiritual practices contrasts sharply with the actual state of the environment in native communities. For example, the most polluted site under the Environmental Protection Agency's (EPA) Superfund program is at Tar Creek, Oklahoma. Toxic contamination from lead and zinc mines at Tar Creek has had significant impact on seven Indian tribes and three states. Acid mine drainage and wind-blown dust have poisoned many of the tribes' sacred and ceremonial sites. The dust blows off the mine tailing piles, which stand like gray mountains hundreds of feet high above the flat plains. The underground mine system reaches into the aquifer, leaching heavy metals, and depositing them to the surface water of Tar Creek.

Tar Creek is only one example of how places and communities have been "sacrificed" for the American way of life. This sacrifice has been recognized by the U.S. government in a National Academy of Sciences study, which concluded that some areas of the country could be used for national priorities irrespective of the resulting permanent environmental damage. Such places are designated "National Sacrifice Areas."

Many of these areas are on native land and are open to resource extraction and defense activities. The Four Corners area of the Navajo Nation and the Black Hills of South Dakota, sacred to the Lakota Nations, have been officially designated as "national sacrifice areas." Seventy-five percent of the U.S. national uranium reserve is on Indian land under the control of the major oil companies. In fact, most of the armaments and munitions that supplied American forces in both World Wars and Korea came out of the Tar Creek minefields.

In secular terms, a sacrifice occurs when a person or group gives up something in order to achieve another, greater good. In this context, it is important to ask what "greater good" is being aimed for—and to note that no one should have the ability to give up another person's land or health for any reason.

A closer look at the western religious origins of the term is even more disturbing. The "sacrificial lamb" or "scapegoat" is symbolically understood to take on the weight of the community's sins, and is then either exiled from the community or killed as an act of atonement. In that sense, the designation of many Indian lands as National Sacrifice Areas is a disturbingly accurate recognition of present reality.

Native communities are the scapegoats for Western consumer culture, bearing the burdens of the sins of the community. Indian communities have hosted toxic waste, a by-product of white middle-class consumer lifestyles, without ever having benefited from those lifestyles. Government officials and community leaders have even claimed that native communities are good hosts for such toxic materials precisely because of their concern for the Earth. This is not a problem of politicians far away, but of the way white privilege still provide benefits—including the leisure to study shamanic practices.

Given the history of exploiting the natural resources of native communities, it is important to be careful that native spiritual traditions are not appropriated and used in the same way. Any ecospiritual tradition that draws upon shamanic or indigenous practices must be careful not to become yet another way that native traditions are used to the detriment of the Earth and native people.

The first step is to overcome any tendency to romanticize native cultures or to see them as "spiritual resources" rather than complex, vibrant, living traditions within communities that have suffered grave abuse. As George Tinker has written, "Euro-Americans and their elected officials seem to engage in a behavior pattern well-known in alcohol and drug addiction therapies: denial. Too many churches and too many politicians have lived out such a denial, as if such eco-devastation and national injustice and immorality cannot possibly affect them, living in the protected comfort zones of American society. [In this context], it becomes all too easy to think of Indian reservations as 'National Sacrifice Areas.'"[1]

The truth of Tinker's analysis was demonstrated recently when one of the cowriters of this piece, Jonna Higgins-Freese, led an ecotheology training for a group of Episcopal priests who have been designated as leaders within their communities. When they were shown a video about the environmental and health effects of the acid mine drainage at Tar Creek, one of them commented, "Well, this is interesting, but I wonder if it's really effective to play the 'race card'—is there a reason to make this into a race issue? Won't people be put off by thinking of environmental problems in racial terms? And what's the link to religion and spirituality?"

This is a clear example of denial, of the conviction that as long as we don't use racial epithets or specifically and consciously set out to harm people of a particular race, the actual harmful outcome is irrelevant. It demonstrates a cultural conviction that as long as we don't talk about the racial dimensions of environmental problems, they won't exist. And it demonstrates the all-too-common belief that spiritual practice is individual and other-worldly—that it is separate from real communities, present realities, and the mess of politics.

What, then, are our responsibilities if we want to turn to shamanic ecospiritual practices as a resource? The first step is to overcome our denial and squarely face the truth of the way native people and people of color have been sacrificed and made scapegoats for the toxic by-products of the American consumerist lifestyle. Across the United States, race is the determining factor for a number of environmental quality indicators.

Once called environmental racism, "environmental justice" is typically perceived to be an urban issue, and for good reason. In 1987 the United Church of Christ's Commission for Racial Justice issued the landmark study "Toxic Wastes and Race in the United States." The study found race to be the single most important factor (more important than income, home ownership, property value, etc.) in the location of abandoned toxic waste sites.

The study also found that:

1. Sixty percent of African Americans live in communities with one or more abandoned toxic waste sites.
2. Three of the five largest commercial hazardous waste landfills are located in predominantly African American or Latino communities and account for 40 percent of the nation's total estimated landfill capacity.
3. African Americans are heavily overrepresented in the population of cities with the largest number of abandoned waste sites.

In 1998, a cursory EPA survey of tribal lands found over 180 off-reservation air pollution sources, scores of federally built schools and houses with lead paint and asbestos, and over 1,000 leaking underground storage tanks impacting the health and environment of Indian tribes. Smokestack dioxins impact the tribes of the Northeast and Great Lakes. Military dumpsites dot the landscape surrounding Alaska Native Villages. Bombing ranges continually threaten western tribes.

Until recently, there has not been empirical data documenting the various environmental threats which impact Indian communities and tribal peoples. However, Jeff Tomhave, the other cowriter of this piece, is currently shepherding a three-year research project unprecedented in its scope. The project marks the first time ever that tribes are being asked to supply information as to what they know or suspect to be hazardous waste contamination from manufacturing, municipal landfills, mining, and defense and energy activities on or near their land (see www.taswer.org/ for more information on the tribal hazardous contamination study).

Nationally, only about 44 percent of African Americans own their homes compared to over two-thirds of the nation as a whole. Homeowners are the strongest advocates of the "not in my backyard" positions taken against locally unwanted land uses such as the construction of garbage dumps, landfills, incinerators, sewer treatment plants, recycling centers, prisons, drug treatment units, and public housing projects. Generally, affluent white communities have greater access than communities of color when it comes to influencing land use and environmental decision making. The ability of individual families to escape a health-threatening physical environment is directly related to affluence.

For tribal communities, home ownership is a foreign concept. Tribes don't actually own their land; the federal government does. Without land as collateral, private lending doesn't extend to tribal communities. The idea that tribal people could mount a public campaign against an unwanted land use is next to impossible. The idea that tribal people would move, even if they could, away from the last remnant of their land is similarly improbable.

However, simple awareness of the problem is not enough. As George Tinker says, "we need to move beyond the mere naming of ecological devastations that are affecting Indian peoples and other indigenous and poor peoples today. . . . Changing individual patterns of behavior has failed us as a strategy. We need more holistic and systemic solutions" (Tinker, 166).

Any ecospiritual tradition that draws upon native traditions or shamanic practices should properly include justice and alliance-building as central elements of the spiritual practice. Many people have a deep love for Native cultures and a sense that the history of their treatment in the U.S. is shameful and wrong. We must move beyond guilt to practical action—to become allies with Native people as they work for justice.

One way to engage in such action is to support tribal organizations that engage in work to protect the health and environment of Indian communities. Effective Self-Determination Solutions (ESDS) is one such organization. ESDS is based on the age-old knowledge that the best form of charity is to help people help themselves. ESDS deploys multidisciplinary teams (law, science, health, finance, and media) to work with individual tribes at a time until the tribe's specific environmental problem is solved. These individual tribes benefit because they attain the skills, experience, and resources necessary to protect their own health and environment in a culturally appropriate way that benefits tribal and nontribal people alike.

Many native spiritual practices include the recognition that every place on Earth is sacred. Our spiritual practices—including work for environmental justice—must also be locally based.

We can begin with examining our daily lives and noticing the connections between what happens here and what happens far away. For example, the proposed permanent nuclear waste storage site at Yucca Mountain has recently been in the news; the site is near the Western Shoshone tribe, and they are concerned about its potential health impacts. All of us use electricity; some portion of it likely comes from nuclear power plants. From an ecospiritual perspective, we must actively support and promote alternatives to nuclear power, including energy conservation and renewable energy.

Finally, any healthy ecospiritual practice should include engagement with these issues in our own communities. Look around at the people who live in your community. Find out what issues are of concern to them and ask whether there is an environmental link—are there unusual rates of asthma or other illnesses? Is the problem simply that there is inadequate health care, so that it is impossible to know if disproportionate health problems exist? Are there brownfields or abandoned toxic waste sites near these communities? If so, ask yourself what you can do to be an ally to these communities as they address the problem. To do so should be as central to our ecospiritual practice as drumming or attending sweat lodges.

NOTE

1. George E. Tinker, "An American Indian Theological Response to Ecojustice," in *Defending Mother Earth: Native American Perspectives on Environmental Justice,* ed. Jace Weaver (Maryknoll, N.Y.: Orbis, 1996), 166–67.

The Earth Charter

✍

In 1987 the United Nations World Commission on Environment and Development issued a call for creation of a new charter that would set forth fundamental principles for sustainable development. In 1994 Maurice Strong, the Secretary General of the Earth Summit and Chairman of the Earth Council, and Mikhail Gorbachev, President of Green Cross International, launched a new Earth Charter initiative with support from the Dutch government. An Earth Charter Commission was formed in 1997 to oversee the project and an Earth Charter Secretariat was established at the Earth Council in Costa Rica.

✍

PREAMBLE

We stand at a critical moment in Earth's history, a time when humanity must choose its future. As the world becomes increasingly interdependent and fragile, the future at once holds great peril and great promise. To move forward we must recognize that in the midst of a magnificent diversity of cultures and life forms we are one human family and one Earth community with a common destiny. We must join together to bring forth a sustainable global society founded on respect for nature, universal human rights, economic justice, and a culture of peace. Towards this end, it is imperative that we, the peoples of Earth, declare our responsibility to one another, to the greater community of life, and to future generations.

EARTH, OUR HOME

Humanity is part of a vast evolving universe. Earth, our home, is alive with a unique community of life. The forces of nature make existence a demanding and uncertain adventure, but Earth has provided the conditions essential to life's evolution. The resilience of the community of life and the well-being of humanity depend upon preserving a healthy biosphere with all its ecological systems, a rich variety of plants and animals, fertile soils, pure waters, and clean air. The global environment with its finite resources is a common concern of all peoples. The protection of Earth's vitality, diversity, and beauty is a sacred trust.

THE GLOBAL SITUATION

The dominant patterns of production and consumption are causing environmental devastation, the depletion of resources, and a massive extinction of species. Communities are being undermined. The benefits of development are not shared equitably and the gap between rich and poor is widening. Injustice, poverty, ignorance, and violent conflict are widespread and the cause of great suffering. An unprecedented rise in human population has overburdened ecological and social systems. The foundations of global security are threatened. These trends are perilous—but not inevitable.

THE CHALLENGES AHEAD

The choice is ours: form a global partnership to care for Earth and one another or risk the destruction of ourselves and the diversity of life. Fundamental changes are needed in our values, institutions, and ways of living. We must realize that when basic needs have been met, human development is primarily about being more, not having more. We have the knowledge and technology to provide for all and to reduce our impacts on the environment. The emergence of a global civil society is creating new opportunities to build a democratic and humane world. Our environmental, economic, political, social, and spiritual challenges are interconnected, and together we can forge inclusive solutions.

UNIVERSAL RESPONSIBILITY

To realize these aspirations, we must decide to live with a sense of universal responsibility, identifying ourselves with the whole Earth community as well as our local communities. We are at once citizens of different nations and of one world in which the local and global are linked. Everyone shares responsibility for the present and future well-being of the human family and the larger living world. The spirit of human solidarity and kinship with all life is strengthened when we live with reverence for the mystery of being, gratitude for the gift of life, and humility regarding the human place in nature.

We urgently need a shared vision of basic values to provide an ethical foundation for the emerging world community. Therefore, together in hope we affirm the following interdependent principles for a sustainable way of life as a common standard by which the conduct of all individuals, organizations, businesses, governments, and transnational institutions is to be guided and assessed.

PRINCIPLES

I. RESPECT AND CARE FOR THE COMMUNITY OF LIFE
    1. Respect Earth and life in all its diversity.
        a. *Recognize that all beings are interdependent and every form of life has value regardless of its worth to human beings.*

b. *Affirm faith in the inherent dignity of all human beings and in the intellectual, artistic, ethical, and spiritual potential of humanity.*

2. Care for the community of life with understanding, compassion, and love.

a. *Accept that with the right to own, manage, and use natural resources comes the duty to prevent environmental harm and to protect the rights of people.*

b. *Affirm that with increased freedom, knowledge, and power comes increased responsibility to promote the common good.*

3. Build democratic societies that are just, participatory, sustainable, and peaceful.

a. *Ensure that communities at all levels guarantee human rights and fundamental freedoms and provide everyone an opportunity to realize his or her full potential.*

b. *Promote social and economic justice, enabling all to achieve a secure and meaningful livelihood that is ecologically responsible.*

4. Secure Earth's bounty and beauty for present and future generations.

a. *Recognize that the freedom of action of each generation is qualified by the needs of future generations.*

b. *Transmit to future generations values, traditions, and institutions that support the long-term flourishing of Earth's human and ecological communities.*

In order to fulfill these four broad commitments, it is necessary to:

II. Ecological Integrity

5. Protect and restore the integrity of Earth's ecological systems, with special concern for biological diversity and the natural processes that sustain life.

a. *Adopt at all levels sustainable development plans and regulations that make environmental conservation and rehabilitation integral to all development initiatives.*

b. *Establish and safeguard viable nature and biosphere reserves, including wild lands and marine areas, to protect Earth's life support systems, maintain biodiversity, and preserve our natural heritage.*

c. *Promote the recovery of endangered species and ecosystems.*

d. *Control and eradicate non-native or genetically modified organisms harmful to native species and the environment, and prevent introduction of such harmful organisms.*

e. *Manage the use of renewable resources such as water, soil, forest products, and marine life in ways that do not exceed rates of regeneration and that protect the health of ecosystems.*

f. *Manage the extraction and use of non-renewable resources such as minerals and fossil fuels in ways that minimize depletion and cause no serious environmental damage.*

6. Prevent harm as the best method of environmental protection and, when knowledge is limited, apply a precautionary approach.

a. *Take action to avoid the possibility of serious or irreversible environmental harm even when scientific knowledge is incomplete or inconclusive.*

b. *Place the burden of proof on those who argue that a proposed activity will not cause significant harm, and make the responsible parties liable for environmental harm.*

c. *Ensure that decision making addresses the cumulative, longterm, indirect, long distance, and global consequences of human activities.*

d. *Prevent pollution of any part of the environment and allow no build-up of radioactive, toxic, or other hazardous substances.*

e. *Avoid military activities damaging to the environment.*

7. Adopt patterns of production, consumption, and reproduction that safeguard Earth's regenerative capacities, human rights, and community well-being.

a. *Reduce, reuse, and recycle the materials used in production and consumption systems, and ensure that residual waste can be assimilated by ecological systems.*

b. *Act with restraint and efficiency when using energy, and rely increasingly on renewable energy sources such as solar and wind.*

c. *Promote the development, adoption, and equitable transfer of environmentally sound technologies.*

d. *Internalize the full environmental and social costs of goods and services in the selling price, and enable consumers to identify products that meet the highest social and environmental standards.*

e. *Ensure universal access to health care that fosters reproductive health and responsible reproduction.*

f. *Adopt lifestyles that emphasize the quality of life and material sufficiency in a finite world.*

8. ***Advance the study of ecological sustainability and promote the open exchange and wide application of the knowledge acquired.***

a. *Support international scientific and technical cooperation on sustainability, with special attention to the needs of developing nations.*

b. *Recognize and preserve the traditional knowledge and spiritual wisdom in all cultures that contribute to environmental protection and human well-being.*

c. *Ensure that information of vital importance to human health and environmental protection, including genetic information, remains available in the public domain.*

III. Social and Economic Justice

9. ***Eradicate poverty as an ethical, social, and environmental imperative.***

a. *Guarantee the right to potable water, clean air, food security, uncontaminated soil, shelter, and safe sanitation, allocating the national and international resources required.*

b. *Empower every human being with the education and resources to secure a sustainable livelihood, and provide social security and safety nets for those who are unable to support themselves.*

c. *Recognize the ignored, protect the vulnerable, serve those who suffer, and enable them to develop their capacities and to pursue their aspirations.*

10. ***Ensure that economic activities and institutions at all levels promote human development in an equitable and sustainable manner.***

a. *Promote the equitable distribution of wealth within nations and among nations.*

b. *Enhance the intellectual, financial, technical, and social resources of developing nations, and relieve them of onerous international debt.*

c. *Ensure that all trade supports sustainable resource use, environmental protection, and progressive labor standards.*

d. *Require multinational corporations and international financial organizations to act transparently in the public good, and hold them accountable for the consequences of their activities.*

11. ***Affirm gender equality and equity as prerequisites to sustainable development and ensure universal access to education, health care, and economic opportunity.***

a. *Secure the human rights of women and girls and end all violence against them.*

b. *Promote the active participation of women in all aspects of economic, political, civil, social, and cultural life as full and equal partners, decision makers, leaders, and beneficiaries.*

c. *Strengthen families and ensure the safety and loving nurture of all family members.*

12. Uphold the right of all, without discrimination, to a natural and social environment supportive of human dignity, bodily health, and spiritual well-being, with special attention to the rights of indigenous peoples and minorities.

   a. *Eliminate discrimination in all its forms, such as that based on race, color, sex, sexual orientation, religion, language, and national, ethnic or social origin.*

   b. *Affirm the right of indigenous peoples to their spirituality, knowledge, lands and resources and to their related practice of sustainable livelihoods.*

   c. *Honor and support the young people of our communities, enabling them to fulfill their essential role in creating sustainable societies.*

   d. *Protect and restore outstanding places of cultural and spiritual significance.*

IV. Democracy, Non-violence and Peace

13. Strengthen democratic institutions at all levels, and provide transparency and accountability in governance, inclusive participation in decision making, and access to justice.

   a. *Uphold the right of everyone to receive clear and timely information on environmental matters and all development plans and activities which are likely to affect them or in which they have an interest.*

   b. *Support local, regional and global civil society, and promote the meaningful participation of all interested individuals and organizations in decision making.*

   c. *Protect the rights to freedom of opinion, expression, peaceful assembly, association, and dissent.*

   d. *Institute effective and efficient access to administrative and independent judicial procedures, including remedies and redress for environmental harm and the threat of such harm.*

   e. *Eliminate corruption in all public and private institutions.*

   f. *Strengthen local communities, enabling them to care for their environments, and assign environmental responsibilities to the levels of government where they can be carried out most effectively.*

14. Integrate into formal education and life-long learning the knowledge, values, and skills needed for a sustainable way of life.

   a. *Provide all, especially children and youth, with educational opportunities that empower them to contribute actively to sustainable development.*

   b. *Promote the contribution of the arts and humanities as well as the sciences in sustainability education.*

   c. *Enhance the role of the mass media in raising awareness of ecological and social challenges.*

   d. *Recognize the importance of moral and spiritual education for sustainable living.*

15. Treat all living beings with respect and consideration.

   a. *Prevent cruelty to animals kept in human societies and protect them from suffering.*

   b. *Protect wild animals from methods of hunting, trapping, and fishing that cause extreme, prolonged, or avoidable suffering.*

   c. *Avoid or eliminate to the full extent possible the taking or destruction of non-targeted species.*

16. Promote a culture of tolerance, nonviolence, and peace.

   a. *Encourage and support mutual understanding, solidarity, and cooperation among all peoples and within and among nations.*

   b. *Implement comprehensive strategies to prevent violent conflict and use collaborative problem solving to manage and resolve environmental conflicts and other disputes.*

    c. *Demilitarize national security systems to the level of a nonprovocative defense posture, and convert military resources to peaceful purposes, including ecological restoration.*

    d. *Eliminate nuclear, biological, and toxic weapons and other weapons of mass destruction.*

    e. *Ensure that the use of orbital and outer space supports environmental protection and peace.*

    f. *Recognize that peace is the wholeness created by right relationships with oneself, other persons, other cultures, other life, Earth, and the larger whole of which all are a part.*

THE WAY FORWARD

As never before in history, common destiny beckons us to seek a new beginning. Such renewal is the promise of these Earth Charter principles.

To fulfill this promise, we must commit ourselves to adopt and promote the values and objectives of the Charter.

This requires a change of mind and heart. It requires a new sense of global interdependence and universal responsibility. We must imaginatively develop and apply the vision of a sustainable way of life locally, nationally, regionally, and globally. Our cultural diversity is a precious heritage and different cultures will find their own distinctive ways to realize the vision. We must deepen and expand the global dialogue that generated the Earth Charter, for we have much to learn from the ongoing collaborative search for truth and wisdom.

Life often involves tensions between important values. This can mean difficult choices. However, we must find ways to harmonize diversity with unity, the exercise of freedom with the common good, short-term objectives with long-term goals. Every individual, family, organization, and community has a vital role to play. The arts, sciences, religions, educational institutions, media, businesses, nongovernmental organizations, and governments are all called to offer creative leadership. The partnership of government, civil society, and business is essential for effective governance.

In order to build a sustainable global community, the nations of the world must renew their commitment to the United Nations, fulfill their obligations under existing international agreements, and support the implementation of Earth Charter principles with an international legally binding instrument on environment and development.

Let ours be a time remembered for the awakening of a new reverence for life, the firm resolve to achieve sustainability, the quickening of the struggle for justice and peace, and the joyful celebration of life.

"The Cochabamba Declaration on Water: Globalization, Privatization, and the Search for Alternatives"

❦

The Cochabamba Declaration on Water was a collective statement issued after the privatization of water supplies in this Columbian city led to drastic increases in the cost of water, privation for the city's poor, resistance, and government repression.

❦

On December 8, 2000, several hundred people gathered in Cochabamba, Bolivia, for a seminar on the global pressure to turn water over to private water corporations. For many of those who attended it was the first time they had come together since the mass uprising at the beginning of the year when the people of Cochabamba took back their water from the private water company. Also in attendance was an international delegation of water activists. The result of that meeting was the following declaration that captures the essence of their struggle and the struggle of more and more communities around the world. If you agree please sign below. This declaration is a rallying call to join the struggle to protect the planet and human rights.

DECLARATION

We, citizens of Bolivia, Canada, United States, India, Brazil:

Farmers, workers, indigenous people, students, professionals, environmentalists, educators, nongovernmental organizations, retired people, gather together today in solidarity to combine forces in the defense of the vital right to water.

Here, in this city which has been an inspiration to the world for its retaking of that right through civil action, courage and sacrifice standing as heroes and heroines against corporate, institutional and governmental abuse, and trade agreements which destroy that right, in use of our freedom and dignity, we declare the following:

For the right to life, for the respect of nature and the uses and traditions of our ancestors and our peoples, for all time the following shall be declared as inviolable rights with regard to the uses of water given us by the earth:

1. Water belongs to the earth and all species and is sacred to life, therefore, the world's water must be conserved, reclaimed and protected for all future generations and its natural patterns respected.

2. Water is a fundamental human right and a public trust to be guarded by all levels of government, therefore, it should not be commodified, privatized or traded for commercial purposes. These rights must be enshrined at all levels of government. In particular, an international treaty must ensure these principles are noncontrovertible.

3. Water is best protected by local communities and citizens who must be respected as equal partners with governments in the protection and regulation of water. Peoples of the earth are the only vehicle to promote democracy and save water.

"Evangelical Declaration on the Care of Creation"

❧

Evangelical Environmental Network

The Evangelical Environmental Network is an evangelical ministry whose purpose is to "declare the Lordship of Christ over all creation" and to promote recognition of the fact that many environmental problems are fundamentally spiritual problems. The following declaration was signed by hundreds of ministers, institutional leaders, educators, and laypeople.

❧

The earth is the Lord's, and the fullness thereof (Psalm 24:1)

The cosmos, all its beauty, wildness, and life-giving bounty, is the work of our personal and loving Creator. As followers of Jesus Christ, committed to the full authority of the Scriptures, and aware of the ways we have degraded creation, we believe that biblical faith is essential to the solution of our ecological problems.

Because we worship and honour the Creator, we seek to cherish and care for creation.

Because we have sinned, we have failed in our stewardship of creation. Therefore we repent of the way we have polluted, distorted, or destroyed so much of the Creator's work.

Because in Christ God has healed our alienation from God and extended to us the first fruits of the reconciliation of all things, we commit ourselves to working in the power of the Holy Spirit to share the Good News of Christ in word and deed, to work for the reconciliation of all people in Christ, and to extend Christ's healing to suffering creation.

Because we await the time when even the groaning creation will be restored to wholeness, we commit ourselves to work vigorously to protect and heal that creation for the honour and glory of the Creator—whom we know dimly through creation, but meet fully through Scripture and in Christ. We and our children face a growing crisis in the health of the creation in which we are embedded, and through which, by God's grace, we are sustained.

Yet we continue to degrade that creation. These degradations of creation can be summed up as: land degradation; deforestation; species extinction; water degradation; global toxification; the alteration of atmosphere; human and cultural degradation.

Many of these degradations are signs that we are pressing against the finite limits God has set for creation. With continued population growth, these degradations will become more severe. Our responsibility is not only to bear and nurture children, but to nurture their home on earth. We respect the institution of marriage as the way God has given to ensure thoughtful procreation of children and their nurture to the glory of God.

We recognize that human poverty is both a cause and a consequence of environmental degradation. Many concerned people, convinced that environmental problems are more spiritual than technological, are exploring the world's ideologies and religions in search of non-Christian spiritual resources for the healing of the earth.

As followers of Jesus Christ, we believe that the Bible calls us to respond in four ways:

First, God calls us to confess and repent of attitudes which devalue creation, and which twist or ignore biblical revelation to support our misuse of it. Forgetting that "the earth is the Lord's," we have often simply used creation and forgotten our responsibility to care for it.

Second, our actions and attitudes toward the earth need to proceed from the center of our faith, and be rooted in the fullness of God's revelation in Christ and the Scriptures. We resist both ideologies which would presume the Gospel has nothing to do with the care of nonhuman creation and also ideologies which would reduce the Gospel to nothing more than the care of that creation.

Third, we seek carefully to learn all that the Bible tells us about the Creator, creation, and the human task. In our life and words we declare that full good news for all creation which is still waiting "with eager longing for the revealing of the children of God" (Rom. 8:19).

Fourth, we seek to understand what creation reveals about God's divinity, sustaining presence, and everlasting power, and what creation teaches us of its God-given order and the principles by which it works.

Thus we call on all those who are committed to the truth of the Gospel of Jesus Christ to affirm the following principles of biblical faith, and to seek ways of living out these principles in our personal lives, our churches, and society.

Our creating God is prior to and other than creation, yet intimately involved with it, upholding each thing in its freedom, and all things in relationships of intricate complexity. God is transcendent, while lovingly sustaining each creature, and immanent, while wholly other than creation and not to be confused with it. God the Creator is relational in very nature, revealed as three persons in One. Likewise, the creation which God intended is a symphony of individual creatures in harmonious relationship.

The Creator's concern is for all creatures. God declares all creation "good" (Gen. 1:31); promises care in a covenant with all creatures (Gen. 9:9-17); delights in creatures which have no human apparent usefulness (Job 39–41); and wills in Christ, "to reconcile all things to himself" (Col. 1:20).

Men, women, and children, have a unique responsibility to the Creator; at the same time we are creatures, shaped by the same processes and embedded in the same systems of physical, chemical, and biological interconnections which sustain other creatures. Men, women, and children, created in God's image, also have a unique responsibility for creation. Our actions should both sustain creation's fruitfulness and preserve creation's powerful testimony to its Creator.

Our God-given, stewardly talents have often been warped from their intended purpose: that we know, name, keep and delight in God's creatures; that we nourish civilisation in love, creativity and obedience to God; and that we offer creation and civilisation back in praise to the Creator. We have ignored our creaturely limits and have used the earth with greed, rather than care.

The earthly result of human sin has been a perverted stewardship, a patchwork of garden and wasteland in which the waste is increasing. "There is no faithfulness, no love, no acknowledgement of God in the land. Because of this the land mourns, and all who live in it waste away" (Hosea 4:1, 3). Thus, one consequence of our misuse of the earth is an unjust denial of God's created bounty to other human beings, both now and in the future.

God's purpose in Christ is to heal and bring to wholeness not only persons but the entire created order. "For God was pleased to have all his fullness dwell in him, and through him to reconcile to himself all things, whether things on earth or things in heaven, by making peace through his blood shed on the cross" (Col. 1:19–20).

In Jesus Christ, believers are forgiven, transformed and brought into God's kingdom. "If anyone is in Christ, there is a new creation" (2 Cor. 5:17). The presence of the kingdom of God is marked not only by renewed fellowship with God, but also by renewed harmony and justice between people, and by renewed harmony and justice between people and the rest of the created world. "You will go out in joy and be led forth in peace; the mountains and the hills will burst into song before you, and all the trees of the field will clap their hands" (Isa. 55:12). We believe that in Christ there is hope, not only for men, women and children, but also for the rest of creation which is suffering from the consequences of human sin.

Therefore we call upon all Christians to reaffirm that all creation is God's; that God created it good; and that God is renewing it in Christ.

We encourage deeper reflection on the substantial biblical and theological teaching which speaks of God's work of redemption in terms of the renewal and completion of God's purpose in creation.

We seek a deeper reflection on the wonders of God's creation and the principles by which creation works. We also urge a careful consideration of how corporate and individual actions respect and comply with God's ordinances for Creation. We encourage Christians to incorporate the extravagant creativity of God into their lives by increasing the nurturing role of beauty and the arts in their personal, ecclesiastical, and social patterns.

We urge individual Christians and churches to be centres of creation's care and renewal, both delighting in creation as God's gift, and enjoying it as God's provision, in ways which sustain and heal the damaged fabric of the creation which God has entrusted to us.

We recall Jesus' words that our lives do not consist in the abundance of our possessions, and therefore we urge followers of Jesus to resist the allure of wastefulness and overconsumption by making personal lifestyle choices that express humility, forbearance, self restraint and frugality.

We call on all Christians to work for godly, just, and sustainable economics which reflect God's sovereign economy and enable men, women and children to flourish along with all the diversity of creation. We recognise that poverty forces people to degrade creation in order to survive; therefore we support the development of just, free economies which empower the poor and create abundance without diminishing creation's bounty. We commit ourselves to work for responsible public policies which embody the principles of biblical stewardship of creation.

We invite Christians—individuals, congregations and organizations—to join with us in this evangelical declaration on the environment, becoming a covenant people in an ever-widening circle of biblical care for creation.

We call upon Christians to listen to and work with all those who are concerned about the healing of creation, with an eagerness both to learn from them and also to share with them our conviction that the God whom all people sense in creation (Acts 17:27) is known fully only in the Word made flesh in Christ the living God who made and sustains all things.

We make this declaration knowing that until Christ returns to reconcile all things, we are called to be faithful stewards of God's good garden, our earthly home.

Address of His Holiness Ecumenical Patriarch Bartholomew

❧

Ecumenical Patriarch Bartholomew is the formal leader of Eastern Orthodox Christianity. This speech makes clear in no uncertain terms the moral and religious meaning of environmental destruction. The speech was given on November 8, 1997, at the Environmental Symposium at the Santa Barbara Greek Orthodox Church in Santa Barbara, California.

❧

The Ecumenical Throne of Orthodoxy, as a preserver and herald of the ancient Patristic tradition and of the rich liturgical experience of the Orthodox Church, today renews its long-standing commitment to healing the environment. We have followed with great interest and sincere concern, the efforts to curb the destructive effects that human beings have wrought upon the natural world. We view with alarm the dangerous consequences of humanity's disregard for the survival of God's creation.

It is for this reason that our predecessor, the late Patriarch Dimitrios, of blessed memory, invited the whole world to offer, together with the Great Church of Christ, prayers of thanksgiving and supplications for the protection of the gift of creation. Since 1989, every September 1, the beginning of the ecclesiastical calendar has been designated as a day of prayer for the protection of the environment, throughout the Orthodox world.

Since that time, the Ecumenical Throne has organized an Inter-Orthodox Conference in Crete in 1991, and convened annual Ecological Seminars at the historic Monastery of the Holy Trinity on Halki, as a way of discerning the spiritual roots and principles of the ecological crisis. In 1995, we sponsored a symposium, sailing the Aegean to the island of Patmos. The symposium on Revelation and the Environment, A.D. 95 to 1995, commemorated the 1900th anniversary of the recording of the Apocalypse. We have recently convened a transnational conference on the Black Sea ecological crisis, that included participation of all the nations that border the sea.

In these and other programs, we have sought to discover the measures that may be implemented by Orthodox Christians worldwide, as leaders desiring to contribute to the solution of this global problem. We believe that through our particular and unique liturgical and ascetic ethos, Orthodox Spirituality may provide significant moral and ethical direction toward a new generation of awareness about the planet.

We believe that Orthodox liturgy and life hold tangible answers to the ultimate questions concerning salvation from corruptibility and death. The Eucharist is at the very center of our worship. And our sin toward the world, or the spiritual root of all our pollution, lies in our refusal to view life and the world as a sacrament of thanksgiving, and as a gift of constant communion with God on a global scale.

We envision a new awareness that is not mere philosophical posturing, but a tangible experience of a mystical nature. We believe that our first task is to raise the consciousness of adults who most use the resources and gifts of the planet. Ultimately, it is for our children that we must perceive our every action in the world as having a direct effect upon the future of the environment. At the heart of the relationship between man and environment is the relationship between human beings. As individuals, we live not only in vertical relationships to God, and horizontal relationships to one another, but also in a complex web of relationships that extend throughout our lives, our cultures, and the material world. Human beings and the environment form a seamless garment of existence; a complex fabric that we believe is fashioned by God.

People of all faith traditions praise the Divine, for they seek to understand their relationship to the cosmos. The entire universe participates in a celebration of life, which St. Maximos the Confessor described as a "cosmic liturgy." We see this cosmic liturgy in the symbiosis of life's rich biological complexities. These complex relationships draw attention to themselves in humanity's self-conscious awareness of the cosmos. As human beings, created "in the image and likeness of God" (Gen. 1:26), we are called to recognize this interdependence between our environment and ourselves. In the bread and the wine of the Eucharist, as priests standing before the altar of the world, we offer the creation back to the creator in relationship to Him and to each other. Indeed, in our liturgical life, we realize by anticipation, the final state of the cosmos in the Kingdom of Heaven. We celebrate the beauty of creation, and consecrate the life of the world, returning it to God with thanks. We share the world in joy as a living mystical communion with the Divine. Thus it is that we offer the fullness of creation at the Eucharist, and receive it back as a blessing, as the living presence of God.

Moreover, there is also an ascetic element in our responsibility toward God's creation. This asceticism requires from us a voluntary restraint, in order for us to live in harmony with our environment. Asceticism offers practical examples of conservation.

By reducing our consumption, in Orthodox Theology "encratia" or self-control, we come to ensure that resources are also left for others in the world. As we shift our will we demonstrate a concern for the third world and developing nations. Our abundance of resources will be extended to include an abundance of equitable concern for others.

We must challenge ourselves to see our personal, spiritual attitudes in continuity with public policy. Encratia frees us of our self-centered neediness, that we may do good works for others. We do this out of a personal love for the natural world around us. We are called to work in humble harmony with creation and not in arrogant supremacy against it. Asceticism provides an example whereby we may live simply.

Asceticism is not a flight from society and the world, but a communal attitude of mind and way of life that leads to the respectful use, and not the abuse of material goods. Excessive consumption may be understood to issue from a worldview of estrangement from self, from land, from life, and from God. Consuming the fruits of the earth unrestrained, we become consumed ourselves, by avarice and greed. Excessive consumption leaves us emptied, out-of-touch with our deepest self. Asceticism is a corrective practice, a vision of repentance. Such a vision will lead us from repentance to return, the return to a world in which we give, as well as take from creation.

We invite Orthodox Christians to engage in genuine repentance for the way in which we have behaved toward God, each other, and the world. We gently remind Orthodox Christians that the judgment of the world is in the hands of God. We are called to be stewards, and reflections of God's love by example. Therefore, we proclaim the sanctity of all life, the entire creation being God's and reflecting His continuing will that life abound. We must love life so that others may see and know that it belongs to God. We must leave the judgment of our success to our Creator.

We lovingly suggest to all the people of the earth, that they seek to help one another to understand the myriad ways in which we are related to the earth, and to one another. In this way, we may begin to repair the dislocation many people experience in relation to creation.

We are of the deeply held belief, that many human beings have come to behave as materialistic tyrants. Those that tyrannize the earth are themselves, sadly, tyrannized. We have been called by God, to "be fruitful, increase and have dominion in the earth" (Gen. 1:28). Dominion is a type of the Kingdom of Heaven. Thus it is that St. Basil describes the creation of man in paradise on the sixth day, as being the arrival of a king in his palace. Dominion is not domination, it is an eschatological sign of the perfect Kingdom of God, where corruption and death are no more.

If human beings treated one another's personal property the way they treat their environment, we would view that behavior as antisocial. We would impose the judicial measures necessary to restore wrongly appropriated personal possessions. It is therefore appropriate for us to seek ethical, legal recourse where possible, in matters of ecological crimes.

It follows that, to commit a crime against the natural world, is a sin. For humans to cause species to become extinct and to destroy the biological diversity of God's creation . . . for humans to degrade the integrity of Earth by causing changes in its climate, by stripping the Earth of its natural forests, or destroying its wetlands . . . for humans to injure other humans with disease . . . for humans to contaminate the Earth's waters, its land, its air, and its life, with poisonous substances . . . these are sins.

In prayer, we ask for the forgiveness of sins committed both willingly and unwillingly. And it is certainly God's forgiveness, which we must ask, for causing harm to His Own Creation.

Thus we begin the process of healing our worldly environment which was blessed with Beauty and created by God. Then we may also begin to participate responsibly, as persons making informed choices in both the integrated whole of creation, and within our own souls.

In just a few weeks the world's leaders will gather in Kyoto, Japan, to determine what, if anything, the nations of the world will commit to do, to halt climate change. There has been much debate back and forth about who should, and should not have to change the way they use the resources of the earth. Many nations are reluctant to act unilaterally. This self-centered behavior is a symptom of our alienation from one another, and from the context of our common existence.

We are urging a different and, we believe, a more satisfactory ecological ethic. This ethic is shared with many of the religious traditions represented here. All of us hold the earth to be the creation of God, where He placed the newly created human "in the Garden of Eden to cultivate it and to guard it" (Gen. 2:15). He imposed on humanity a stewardship role in relationship to the earth. How we treat the earth and all of creation defines the relationship that each of us has with God. It is also a barometer of how we view one another. For if we truly value a person, we are careful as to our behavior toward that person. The dominion that God has given humankind over the Earth does not extend to human relationships. As the Lord said, "You know that the rulers of the Nations lord it over them, and their great ones are tyrants over them. It will not be so among you; but whoever wishes to be great among you must be your servant, and whoever wishes to be first among you must be your slave; just as the Son of Man came not to be served but to serve, and to give his life as a ransom for many" (Matt. 20:25–28).

It is with that understanding that we call on the world's leaders to take action to halt the destructive changes to the global climate that are being caused by human activity. And we call on all of you here today, to join us in this cause. This can be our important contribution to the great debate about climate change. We must be spokespeople for an ecological ethic that reminds the world that it is not ours to use for our own convenience. It is God's gift of love to us and we must return his love by protecting it and all that is in it.

[. . .]

The Lord suffuses all of creation with His Divine presence in one continuous legato from the substance of atoms to the Mind of God. Let us renew the harmony between heaven and earth, and transfigure every detail, every particle of life. Let us love one another, and lovingly learn from one another, for the edification of God's people, for the sanctification of God's creation, and for the glorification of God's most holy Name. Amen.

"The Theological Basis of Animal Rights"

❧

Andrew Linzey

Andrew Linzey teaches theology and animal rights at Oxford. His books include *Animal Rights, Christianity and the Rights of Animals,* and *Political Theory and Animal Rights.* This essay challenges us all to ask how moral we can consider ourselves if we take part in the commonplace exploitation, torture, and consumption of beings who can suffer.

❧

Secretary of Health and Human Services Louis Sullivan recently told a Vatican conference that animal rights "extremists" threaten the future of health research and that churches "cannot remain on the periphery in this struggle.... Any assertion of moral equivalence between humans and animals is an issue that organized religion must refute vigorously and unambiguously." Sullivan went on to say that world religious leaders possess the authority to "affirm the necessity of appropriate and humane uses of animals in biomedical research."

At first sight, Sullivan has backed a winner. What better than conservative theology and who better than conservative churches to respond to the rallying call for human superiority over animals—even and especially if this "superiority" involves inflicting pain and suffering? Christian theology has, it must be admitted, served long and well the oppressors of slaves, women, and animals. Only 131 years ago, William Henry Holcombe wrote confidently of slavery as the "Christianization of the dark races." It took nineteen hundred years for theologians to question seriously the morality of slavery, and even longer the oppression of women. Keith Thomas reminds us that over the centuries theologians debated "half frivolously, half seriously, whether or not the female sex had souls, a discussion which closely paralleled the debate about animals." Apparently the Quaker George Fox encountered some who thought women had "no souls, no more than a goose."

Who better to look to then but the Roman Catholic Church, which in its approved *Dictionary of Moral Theology* of 1962 confidently proclaims that "Zoophilists often lose sight of the end for which animals, irrational creatures, were created by God, viz., the service and use of man.... In fact, Catholic moral doctrine teaches that animals have no rights on the part of man"? In practice, Catholic countries are among the worst in the world as far as animals are concerned. Bullfighting and the Spanish fiestas in which animals are gratuitously mutilated (with the compliance of priests and nuns) are examples of how historical theology lives on. Surely Sullivan could not have chosen a more agreeable ally in his fight against "extremists" who believe that animals have rights.

And yet, there are signs that Christian theology and Christian churches cannot be so easily counted upon to support the standard line that humans are morally free to do as they like with animals. Anglican Archbishop Donald Coggan in 1977 stated the unthinkable: "Animals, as part of God's creation, have rights which must be respected. It behooves us always to be sensitive to their needs and to the reality of their pain." Archbishop Robert Runcie went further in 1988 and specifically contradicted historical anthropocentrism. His words deserve to be savored:

> The temptation is that we will usurp God's place as Creator and exercise a *tyrannical* dominion over creation. . . . At the present time, when we are beginning to appreciate the wholeness and interrelatedness of all that is in the cosmos, preoccupation with humanity will seem distinctly parochial. . . . Too often our theology of creation, especially, here in the so-called "developed" world, has been distorted by being too man-centered. We need to maintain the value, the preciousness of the human by affirming the preciousness of the nonhuman also—of all that is. For our concept of God forbids the idea of a *cheap creation,* of a throwaway universe in which everything is expendable save human existence. . . . The value, the worth of natural things is not found in Man's view of himself but in the goodness of God who made all things good and precious in his sight. . . . As Barbara Ward used to say, "We have only one earth." Is it not worth our love? ["Address to the Global Forum of Spiritual and Parliamentary Leaders on Human Survival" (his emphases).]

Even at the very center of conservative theology there are indications of movement. The pope's 1984 encyclical *Solicitudo Rei Socialis* speaks of the need to respect "the nature of each being" within creation. It underlines the modern view that the "dominion granted to man . . . is not an absolute power, nor can one speak of a freedom to use and misuse or to dispose of things as one pleases."

It would be silly to pretend that Pope John Paul II and Archbishops Coggan and Runcie are card-carrying members of the animal rights movement (there are no membership cards in any case). Yet for Sullivan, desperately hoping for moral assurance in the face of animal rights "extremists," these cannot be encouraging signs. Is the ecclesiastical bastion of human moral exclusivity really going to tumble? Might there be, in fifty or one hundred years, a Roman encyclical defending the worth, dignity, and rights of the nonhuman world? The *National Catholic Reporter* noted that Pope John Paul II had only "cautiously" defended animal experimentation. In 1982, the paper recalled, the pope argued that "the diminution of experimentation on animals, which has progressively been made ever less necessary, corresponds to the plan and well-being of all creation." The true reading of Sullivan's overture might be not confidence but desperation. Perhaps the most worrying thing for Sullivan is that the churches *won't* remain on the periphery in this struggle.

Sullivan has a counterpart in the United Kingdom: agriculture minister and fellow Anglican John Selwyn Gummer, who tried to bolster the meat trade by asserting that vegetarianism is a "wholly unnatural" practice. Like Sullivan he thought Christian theology would be of some help—in his case, against five million British vegetarians. "I consider meat to be an essential part of the diet," argued Gummer. "The Bible tells us that we are masters of the fowls of the air, and the beasts of the field and we very properly eat them."

Alas, biblical theology cannot be so easily wheeled in to rescue the minister of agriculture. The creation saga in Genesis 1 does indeed give humans dominion over animals (v. 28) but just one verse later commands vegetarianism (vv. 29–31). As Karl Barth observed: "Whether or not we find it practicable and desirable, the diet assigned to men and beasts by God the Creator is vegetarian" (*Church Dogmatics*, III/1, 208). Bystanders may marvel at how Gummer could in all innocence hurl himself not at the weakest but the strongest part of his enemy's armor.

Sullivan and Gummer seem united in the view that if theology is to speak on animal rights, it will speak not on the side of the oppressed but on behalf of the oppressor. Indeed, the view somehow seems to have got about that there can be no mainstream theological basis for animal rights. As well as accusing the movement of being "philosophically flawed and obscurantistic—based on ignorance and emotion, not reason and knowledge—and antihuman and even antianimal," the magazine *Eternity* produced by Evangelical Ministries Inc., claimed in 1985 that "the true religious underpinning of animal-rights consists is a kind of vague neopantheism" (Lloyd Billingsley, "Save the Beasts, Not the Children? The Dangerous Premises of the Animal-Rights Crusade," February 1985).

To begin to construct an adequate theological understanding of animals, we should recall Runcie's statement about the "value, the preciousness of the nonhuman." Secular thinkers are free to be agnostic about the value of the nonhuman creation. They could argue, for example, that creation has value only insofar as humankind is benefited or insofar as other creatures can be classed as utilities. Not so, however, for Christians. If, as Runcie observes, "our concept of God forbids the idea of a cheap creation" because "the whole universe is a work of love" and "nothing which is made in love is cheap," Christians are precluded from a purely humanistic, utilitarian view of animals. This point will sound elementary, but its implications are profound.

At its most basic it means that animals must not be viewed simply as commodities, resources, tools, utilities for human use. If we are to grapple with real theology, we must abandon purely humanocentric perspectives on animals. What may be the use of animals to us is a totally separate question from what their value is to almighty God. To argue that the value and significance of animals in the world can be circumscribed by their value and significance to human beings is simply untheological. I make the point strongly because there seems to be the misconception— even and especially prevalent among the doctrinal advocates of Christian faith—that theological ethics can be best expressed by a well-meaning, ethically enlightened humanism. Not so. To attempt a theological understanding must involve a fundamental break with humanism, secular and religious. God alone is the source of the value of all living beings.

This argument is usually countered in one of two ways. The first is to say that if this is so, it should follow that all creation has value, so we cannot rate animals of greater value than rocks or vegetables, let alone insects or viruses. Increasingly this argument seems to be made by "conservationists" and "green thinkers" who want to exclude animals from special moral consideration. They argue that the value of animals, and therefore what we owe them, is really on a par with the value of natural objects such as trees or rivers. One can immediately see how this view falls in neatly with the emerging green view of "holistic interdependence" and holistic appeals to respect "earth as a whole." God loves the whole creation holistically, so it is claimed.

But is it true that God loves everything equally? Not so, I think, Christian tradition clearly makes a distinction between humans and animals, and also between animals and vegetables. Scholars eager to establish the preeminence of humans in Scripture have simply overlooked ways in which animals exist alongside humans within the covenant relationship. The Spirit is itself the "breath of life" (Gen. 1:30) of both humans and animals. The Torah delineates animals within its notion of moral community. After having surveyed the ways in which animals are specifically associated, if not identified, with humans themselves, Barth concludes: "'O Lord, thou preservest man and beast' (Ps. 36:6) is a thread running through the whole of the Bible; and it first emerges in a way which is unmistakable when the creation of man is classified in Gen. 1:24f with that of the land animals" (*Church Dogmatics*, III/1, 181n).

The second way in which my argument may be countered is by proposing that while animals have some value, it is incontestably less than the special value of humans. But this objection only adds fuel to my thesis. I, for one, do not want to deny that humans are unique, superior, even, in a sense, of "special value" in creation. Some secular animal rightists, it is true, have argued in ways that appear to eclipse the uniqueness of humanity. But Christian animal rights advocates are not interested in dethroning humanity. On the contrary, the animal rights thesis requires the reenthroning of humanity.

The key question is, What kind of king is to be reenthroned? Gummer's utterances show only too well how "dominion" has come to mean little more than despotism. But the kingly rule of which we are, according to Genesis, the vice-regents or representatives is not the brutalizing regime of a tyrant. Rather, God elects humanity to represent and actualize the loving divine will for all creatures. Humanity is the one species chosen to look after the cosmic garden (Gen. 2:15). This involves having power over animals. But the issue is not whether we have power over animals but how we are to use it.

It is here that we reach the Christological parting of the ways. Secularists may claim that power is itself the sufficient justification for our use of it. But Christians are not so free. No appeal to the power of God can be sufficient without reference to the revelation of that power exemplified in Jesus Christ. Much of what Jesus said or did about slaves, women, or animals remains historically opaque. But we know the contours even if many of the details are missing. The power of God is Jesus is expressed in *katabasis*, humility, self-sacrifice, powerlessness. The power of God is redefined in Jesus as practical costly service extending to those who are beyond the normal boundaries of human concern: the diseased, the poor, the oppressed, the outcast. If humans claim a lordship over creation, then it can only be a lordship of service. There can be no lordship without service.

According to the theological doctrine of animal rights, then, humans are to be the servant species: the species given power, opportunity, and privilege to give themselves, nay sacrifice themselves, for the weaker, suffering creatures. According to Sullivan, the churches must refute "any assertion of moral equivalence between humans and animals." But I, for one, have never claimed any strict moral equality between humans and animals. I have always been a bit worried by Peter Singer's view that animal liberation consists in accepting "equal consideration of interests" between humans and animals. In my view, what we owe animals is more than equal consideration, equal treatment, or equal concern. The weak, the powerless, the disadvantaged, the oppressed should not have equal moral priority but greater moral priority. When we minister to the least of all we minister to Christ himself. To follow Jesus is to accept axiomatically that the weak have moral priority. Our special value as a species consists in being of special value for others.

No one has enumerated this doctrine better than that nineteenth-century pioneer of social reform for both humans and animals, the seventh earl of Shaftesbury:

> I was convinced that God had called me to devote whatever advantages He might have bestowed upon me to the cause of the weak, the helpless, both man and beast, and those who had none to help them.... What I have done has been given to me; what I have done I was enabled to do; and all happy results (if any there be) must be credited, not to the servant, but to the great Master, who led and sustained him.

The relevance of such theology to animal rights should be clear. Readers will have noticed I have assiduously used the term "animal rights" rather than "animal welfare" or "animal protection." Some Christians are still apt to regard "rights" terminology as a secular import into moral theology. They are mistaken. The notion of rights was first used in explicitly theological contexts. Moreover, animal rights is explicitly a problem of Christian moral theology for this reason: Catholic scholasticism has specifically and repeatedly repudiated animal rights. It is the tradition, not its so-called modern detractors, that insists on the relevance of the concept of rights. The problem is only now compounded because, unaware of history, Christians want to talk boldly of human rights yet quibble about the language when it comes to animals. For me the theological basis of rights is compelling. God is the source of rights, and indeed the whole debate about animals is precisely about the rights of the Creator. For this reason in *Christianity and the Rights of Animals* (New York: Crossroad, 1987) I used the ugly but effective term "theos-rights." Animal rights language conceptualizes what is objectively owed the Creator of animals. From a theological perspective, rights are not something awarded, granted, won, or lost but something recognized. To recognize animal rights is to recognize the intrinsic value of God-given life.

I do not deny that the rights view involves a fundamental reorientation. This is one of its merits. The value of living beings is not something to be determined by human beings alone. Part of the reason rights language is so controversial is that people sense from the very outset that recognizing animal rights must involve personal and social change. Whatever else animal rights means it cannot mean that we can go on consuming their flesh, destroying their habitats, wearing their dead skins, and inflicting suffering. Quite disingenuously some church people say that they do not "know" what "animal rights" are. Meanwhile, by steadfastly refusing to change their lifestyles, they show a precise understanding of what animal rights are.

Earlier I compared the oppression of slaves and women to that of animals. Some may regard that comparison as exaggerated, even offensive. But at the heart of each movement of reform has been a simple yet fundamental change of perception. Slaves should not be thought of as property but as human beings with dignity and rights. Women should not be regarded as second-class humans but as humans with dignity and rights. At the heart of the animal rights movement is a change of moral perception, simple, yet profound: animals are not our property or utilities but living beings with dignity and rights.

To recognize animal rights is a spiritual experience and a spiritual struggle. One homely example may suffice. The university where I work is situated amid acres of eighteenth-century parkland. Wildlife abounds. From my study window I observe families of wild rabbits. Looking up from my word processor from time to time, I gaze in wonder, awe, and astonishment at these beautiful creatures. I sometimes say half-jokingly, "It is worth coming to the university for the rabbits." Occasionally I invite visitors to observe them. Some pause in conversation and say something like, "Oh yes," as though I had pointed out the dust on my bookshelves or the color of my carpet. What they see is not rabbits. Perhaps they see machines on four legs, "pests" that should be controlled, perhaps just other "things." It is difficult to believe that such spiritual blindness and impoverishment is the best that the superior species can manage.

Sullivan makes free with calling animal rightists "extremists." The reality is, however, that moral theology would hardly advance at all without visionaries and extremists, people who see things differently from others and plead God's cause even in matters that others judge insignificant. I don't think there are many moderates in heaven.

IX

FROM THE HEART:
RITUALS, PRAYERS, CELEBRATIONS

Prayer is naught else but a yearning of soul . . . when it is practiced with the whole heart, it has great power.

—Mechthild of Magdeburg

In the depth of my soul there is a wordless song.
—Kahil Gibran

Something opens our wings.
Something makes boredom and hurt disappear.
Someone fills the cup in front of us:
We taste only sacredness.

—Rumi

Much of the power of religion lies in its ability to touch our hearts: to help us celebrate, mourn, quietly reflect, and joyously praise the Lord. The attraction to ritual may be as old as human culture itself and is clearly an essential part of every civilization of which we have knowledge.

Sometimes the power of ritual is bound up with its ability to trigger an emotional response by the medium it employs: Music, sacred objects, poetic language—these literally activate a different part of the brain than do rigorous theology or ethical argument. By activating our emotional selves, rituals allow us to connect our deepest sense of personhood to the concerns and values of religious life. We feel, as well as intellectually acknowledge, the sacredness of nature, or of peace, or of justice. Also, participating in rituals connects us to our present community of faith, and to communities over time. It means something that we may be saying a particular prayer or engaging in a rite that people have performed for centuries.

Perhaps most important, rituals can motivate us to act. They surround and underline our good intentions with a special kind of seriousness, consecrating our goals and our commitment. A longing for peace becomes, at least sometimes and to some degree, more momentous—and therefore more motivating—when it has been celebrated as part of a religious service, when it is tied to our faith in God, or when we contemplate it for long periods of absorbing meditation. Our understanding of justice resonates more deeply when we feel that it is connected to the underlying principles of the universe, and when we celebrate those principles in song and story.

611

Finally, the emotional technology of religion provides spiritual social activists with a bit of emotional nurturing. Political activism is often boring, sometimes dangerous, frequently frustrating, and always—if we are aware—something that arouses grief, fear, and anger. A spirited hymn, a traditional ceremony, the joys of a Sabbath meal, or the celebration of the miracle of resurrection—such things can give us a peace and light so that we can return to the struggle once again. As Thich Nhat Hanh said, even if nine out of ten trees are dying from acid rain, we still must celebrate the beauty of the one that is not.

As religion encounters and joins with secular political movements, its prayers and rituals take new forms. Buddhists learn to meditate on our relations to nature, Christians ask forgiveness for anti-Semitism, Jewish celebrations of Passover focus on contemporary oppression as well as the Israelite slavery in Egypt. The selections which follow can only provide a glimpse into this rich world or spiritual creativity. Inbal Kashtan describes how lesbians, people marginalized and pretty much invisible in traditional Judaism, can adapt the tradition's wedding ceremony to consecrate their own love and commitment. The National Council of Churches and the Episcopal Peace Fellowship offer prayers and services oriented to serious political struggles. Their words make concrete the traditional Christian concern with moral virtue by embodying that concern in the actual life struggles of contemporary societies.

As we become politically aware, grounding ourselves in the collective pursuit of justice, peace, and ecological wisdom, our prayers change. We learn to ask for different things: both from the Great Spirit, and for our own spirits. The prayers written by Anwar Fazal, Judy Chicago, the Dalai Lama, Diane Ackerman, and an anonymous Lutheran are examples of how our awareness of the tasks of prayer have been transformed.

Dee Smith brings a sparkling sensibility to our spiritual relation to Nature, reminding us that prayers can come from the whole body, and need not be restricted to words.

Finally, the "Peace Seeds," adapted from many of the world's religious traditions, bring us back to the ethical foundation of religious participation in political life. While all these prayers are from established faiths, they were published and recited together. If the words are old, the spirit that brings them all together is new. It is the spirit, we might say, of a Liberating Faith.

"Breaking Ground: A Traditional Jewish Lesbian Wedding"

❧

Inbal Kashtan

Inbal Kashtan is parenting project coordinator at the Center for Nonviolent Communication and has written on parenting. Part of what is striking about this essay is how Kashtan refuses to leave a tradition—Judaism—that has no place for her, but demands the right to transform that tradition in accordance with her own conception of love.

❧

Kathy and I had a sense before, during, and after our wedding that we were making history—breaking ground in positioning lesbian weddings within traditional Judaism. We wanted to record this history, and so along with our thank-you cards, we sent out a request for guests to write us a note about their experience of our wedding. We received numerous responses, most from people who were deeply moved by the ceremony and who felt in some way transformed by it. One of our guests, a heterosexual modern Orthodox woman, wrote:

> I was quite impacted by my sense of the courage it required of you both to stand so boldly in your love and commitment to one another. It seemed to me, given the innovative and "untraditional" nature of your "traditional" wedding, that there were few places for the two of you to hide.

Another friend expressed his difficulty in grappling with the image of two women in a traditional Jewish ceremony. He wrote: "The lesbian piece shook me up a little. It was just totally new to see a traditional Jewish wedding [in which] my eyes kept seeing . . . two dresses, two pairs of breasts . . . A challenging new image." Another heterosexual friend, who had been a vocal supporter of gay and lesbian rights for years, understood the event differently from how she expected to. "I get it now," she wrote. "It wasn't just a wedding; it was a political rally." And a relative wrote: "Your wedding was truthfully one of the deepest and most beautiful I've seen. Every little bit of exposure I get to gays and lesbians expands my vision of what is 'normal.'"

In different ways, each of these responses captured something of the essence of our traditional Jewish wedding. The first two responses reflected the dichotomy of tradition and innovation, the shock of "two pairs of breasts" at the most traditional locus of heterosexual union. The third response grasped the radical political statement still inherent in the act of lesbian and gay marriage. The fourth response and a number of others like it attested to the way our wedding resonated for Jews—many of an older generation—connecting it with their own heterosexual experience. All of these responses confirmed that our attempt to create a recognizably "normal" Eastern-European Jewish wedding had succeeded; these people were able to resonate with the sacredness and power of the day in a way that profoundly affected their understanding of the meaning of a "lesbian" and a "Jewish" wedding.

In creating a traditional Jewish lesbian wedding, Kathy and I joined a generation of Jews who are seeking a more meaningful relationship with Judaism. Many contemporary Jews are seeking to connect to Judaism by turning to older traditions, ancient texts, and spiritual practices. However, our unique relationship to Judaism as queer Jews presents a poignant paradox: the deeper we delve into tradition, the more it seems to reject our sexualities, our loves, our unions, our families.

How, then, do we struggle with this seeming rejection and still fulfill our yearning for tradition and connection to Judaism? Kathy's and my response to this question was to stake our relationship at the center of Jewish ritual by creating a wedding utterly grounded in Jewish tradition, yet boldly asserting our queerness. For us, this meant taking a traditional Orthodox wedding and wrestling with every ritual and text that we could uncover, taking our wedding beyond the realm of a "political rally" and squarely into the sphere of cultural transformation. Choosing any framework other than traditional Judaism for our wedding was unthinkable for us, because the particular rituals of our tradition are the ones we find most meaningful for marking our important life-cycle events.

One of the reasons that our lesbian wedding resonated so powerfully for our mostly heterosexual guests is that it took them not only into their own experience but, more profoundly, *beyond* their experience, touching on their own yearning for a spiritual connection with Jewish tradition. Our wedding looked like an Orthodox wedding—aside from the two pairs of breasts. Yet because it was a wedding of two women, it was an inclusive Orthodoxy, one that held a promise to queer *and* straight Jews of the possibility of finding themselves in the tradition.

Figuring out how to create a traditional Jewish lesbian wedding was a bittersweet challenge. We struggled with how to capture in the texts of the ceremony two of the deep truths about the day. First, that this was a wedding like the countless weddings that had gone before it in the history of our people, in the sense that it publicly expressed, in Jewish idiom, a commitment to a life together. Second, that this wedding was something new and different and radical and traditionally inconceivable.

Originally, the *halachic* requirements that made a wedding Jewish were simple: "the bride accepts an object worth more than a dime from the groom, the groom recites a ritual formula of acquisition and consecration, and these two actions must be witnessed."[1] The other rituals familiar to most Jews, such as the wedding canopy (*huppa*), having a rabbi officiate, and even breaking the glass, are customs that developed over centuries, and that varied between locations and times, suggesting that the tradition has been flexible and open to interpretation and modification. We relied on this understanding of the imperative to interpret texts and make them relevant to contemporary Jews in the design of our wedding.

Our interpretive work varied with each element of the traditional Jewish wedding. Some texts we were able to keep with very few changes, some required a great deal of work to make them both relevant to our particular situation and still clearly resonant with the original text. The text of *Birkat Erusin* (engagement blessing), for example, praises God for creating marriage as a vehicle for intimacy, but also records the teachings regarding forbidden marriages (such as those between siblings). We chose to abbreviate the text slightly to emphasize the delight over the very existence of rituals to sanctify a relationship, and cut completely the section on forbidden marriages. This was one of the easiest choices for us.

One very brief yet key text we changed was the spoken formula during the exchange of rings, the key text marking the union: "You are hereby sanctified unto me, with this ring, *according to the religious law of Moses and Israel.*" Kathy and I wrestled with the question of whether we can, with full integrity, claim this wedding as falling within our people's explicit legal framework. We ended up deciding that we could not make such a claim, and so we changed the wording to reflect what we felt we could claim. We said to each other, and wrote in our ketubah, the wedding contract: "You are hereby sanctified unto me, with this ring, *in the tradition of the Jewish people.*" This was the one choice we made that we later regretted. In retrospect, we wished we had made the claim of legality, because our wedding was so profoundly an expression of Jewish life and tradition that it made more clear to us the imperative to chart a path toward making it legal. As our rabbi and friend Rona Shapiro said at the wedding, it marked the direction that Jewish law *should* follow:

> If *halachic* principles, followed strictly, yield unjust conclusions, then it is our duty according to *halacha* to exercise civil disobedience. At such times brave individuals and communities must be willing to stand in front of the *halacha,* to walk as Abraham did in front of God, and to say, "this is where we're going," trusting that *halacha* will catch up with us. We stand on the edge of a *halachic* limb and assert stubbornly that this limb is part of the tree. We say, *this* is *halacha, this* is Torah, and we wait for the rest of the community to join us.

Other texts presented different challenges. We almost entirely rewrote the text of the ketubah. Written in Aramaic (Jews's lingua franca when the text was being formulated in the early centuries C.E.), the ketubah was essentially a legal contract in which the woman's dowry and her monetary settlement in case of divorce or the death of the husband were specified. The different branches of Judaism have devised alternate, more egalitarian ketubot; some couples create their own. Since we could not find great meaning in the original text, we did not want to use it as a base for creating a same-sex ketubah. Instead, we chose to retain the text's framing structure while constructing a new document composed of quotations from Jewish texts. The first paragraph follows the traditional text stating the facts of the marriage—with an embellishment at the end. The second paragraph begins as a quotation from the last of the wedding ceremony's seven blessings, while our commitments to one another are primarily amended quotations of verses from the books of Hosea and Ruth. And in keeping with the Jewish tradition of not making explicit vows—as well as with our own understanding of human nature—we stated our commitments as intentions rather than promises. The text of the ketubah follows:

> On Monday, the fourth of Elul in the year 5756, August 19, 1996, in Berkeley, California, Katherine Grace Simon, daughter of Anna, of blessed memory, and Jerome, and Inbal Kashtan, daughter of Rivka and Mordechai, of blessed memory, entered into a covenant of kiddushin, according to the traditions of the Jewish people, and as is the practice of lovers in all the nations of the world.
>
> In joy and happiness, gladness and delight, love and companionship, mindfulness and seriousness, Inbal and Kathy committed to one another to do their utmost to continue cultivating their shared and unique paths, deepening their love, and renewing their relationship.
>
> Inbal and Kathy said to one another: You are hereby sanctified unto me, with this ring, in the tradition of the Jewish people. I sanctify you unto me for life; I sanctify you unto me

in justice and righteousness, in loving kindness and compassion; I sanctify you unto me in faithfulness. Where thou goest I will go, where thou dwellest I will dwell.

All this was done and said under God's wings and with the support and presence of family and friends.

All this is valid and binding.

A pastiche of biblical and rabbinic verses and framed by the traditional structure of the ketubah the text is more *midrash,* or textual interpretation, than contemporary marriage agreement.

Unlike the ketubah, which we crafted ourselves, the text of the Seven Blessings we were able to retain almost entirely, struggling principally with producing a clear translation and gleaning the different blessings' themes. We asked seven different people to "bless" us by reading the texts. Most simply, where the blessings traditionally speak of "the bridegroom and the bride," we used alternate constructions. Other changes reflected more theological and political concerns. In order to highlight God's many manifestations, we used alternate names for God in addition to the traditional, "Lord, our God, King of the Universe." After much discussion, we replaced "the cities of Judah" with "the cities of Israel and the hearts of the world" to acknowledge our sadness about continued Israeli occupation of Palestinian land in the Judean Hills and our wishes for peace and joy for all peoples.

In addition to the original blessings, we also suggested a theme that the people giving each blessing might use as the basis of a brief personal blessing for us. We derived these themes from traditional commentaries, which explain why these particular blessings are used at wedding ceremonies, as well as our own interpretations:

First blessing
Blessed are you, Adonai our God, ruler of the universe, creator of the fruit of the vine.
Theme: Abundance, sweetness, joy.[2]

Second blessing
Blessed are you, Shchina, creator of the universe, who created all for your glory.
Theme: Creating relationships adds to the glory of creation.

Third blessing
Blessed are you, source of life, creator of the first human beings.
Theme: A new relationship is like a fresh creation of humanity.

Fourth blessing
Blessed are you, spring of life, who created human beings in her image, humanity in the image of divinity, and patterned for humanity the perpetuation of life. Blessed are you, spring of life, creator of humanity.
Theme: The divinity in human beings, and the ability to give life through procreation and nurturing.

Fifth blessing
May the barren one rejoice in the ingathering of her children in gladness and peace. Blessed are you, righter of the world, who brings Tzion joy in her children.
Theme: Hope that those who are separated will come together and unite in peace and joy, and that we may return to a whole relationship with the earth.

Sixth blessing
Delight these beloved companions as you delighted your creations in the Garden of Eden of yore. Blessed are you, heart of the world, delighter of beloved companions.
Theme: This union is a little glimpse of the delight of the Garden of Eden.

Seventh blessing
Blessed are you, embracer of the world, who created joy and happiness, bride and bride, mirth, merriment, gladness, delight, love and companionship, peace and partnership. Quickly, embracer of the world, may there be heard in the cities of Israel and in the hearts of nations the voice of joy and the voice of happiness, the voice of the bride and the voice of the bride, the mirthful shouts of beloveds under their *huppas*, of young women and men feasting and singing. Blessed are you, Adonai our God, delighter of the beloved companions.
Theme: Through the union of loving people, the possibility of joy and healing in the world is increased.

We framed the ceremony with rituals that also reflected the melding of tradition and radical innovation. We appropriated the custom of a *tish*, in which (traditionally) the groom takes a few minutes before the ceremony to speak some words of Torah, known as *dvar Torah* (with his male guests seated with him around a table—*tish* in Yiddish). Traditionally, too, the groom is nervous, and not much in the mood to teach, so his friends interrupt his talk with teasing and song. At our wedding, we declared ourselves teachers and transmitters of Jewish tradition by having two separate *tishes* (we were separate so as not to see each other until the ceremony began), where we each gave a *dvar Torah* and were each joyously interrupted. After the ceremony, our wedding turned into a raucous celebration, with guests partaking in the traditional Eastern European *freilakh*—lifting us up in chairs, dancing in whirling circles, and sitting us down to watch mirthful acrobatics, a rap song, a rhyme on our relationship, and impromptu merrymaking.

As Jews who grew up disconnected from traditional Judaism because of our sexual orientation, we have the challenge of making our connection to Judaism meaningful and personally authentic. In order to build a significant and meaningful relationship with traditional Judaism we had to wrestle with the tradition. What we saw at our wedding was that, although as queer Jews, we are *forced* to struggle with tradition, every Jew who wishes to engage with Judaism, to make meaning out of Judaism *should* struggle, because the tradition does not lend itself readily to our modern sensibilities. Many Jews feel alienated by their tradition, and queer Jews have the tools to make it meaningful for *everyone*. The gift some queer Jews have is that we come into this engagement with Judaism from a feminist and queer critical awareness. We have experience with teasing meaning out of history that has traditionally felt exclusive and alienating to us. If we can harness this awareness with an impulse for finding connection, love, and meaning in these traditions and texts rather than abdicating what is uncomfortable to us, we can actually find the threads of dissent and internal critique. Our tradition has been built on interpretation and multivocality. And therein lies the true paradox: the more we delve into a tradition that seems to exclude us, the more we find embedded within it the principles and voices we can use to transform it. Daniel Boyarin, an Orthodox professor of talmudic culture, writes:

> My endeavor is to justify my love [of rabbinic texts and culture], that is, both to explain it and to make it just. . . . I cannot . . . paper over, ignore, explain away, or apologize for the oppressions of women and lesbigay people that this culture has practiced, and therefore I endeavor . . . to render it just by presenting a way of reading the tradition that may help it surmount or expunge—in time—that which I and many others can no longer live with.[3]

As queer Jews who wish to participate in Judaism's ritual traditions, we must engage in cultural transformation. Through our endeavor we forge a path for other Jews seeking to make their relationships to Judaism fully engaged and meaningful. Mining our tradition for meaning—contemporary, relevant, and deeply rooted—we open it up to all Jews who do not see themselves reflected in an unexamined Judaism.

NOTES

1. Anita Diamant, *The New Jewish Wedding* (New York: Simon & Schuster, 1985), 18–19. While the book's title suggests a break from tradition, Diamant convincingly argues that customizing the tradition is in fact part of the traditional Jewish wedding.

2. Kathy's father gave us this blessing, which many of our guests found particularly moving. He said:

In trying to think of what I could say to bless the two of you on the theme of abundance, sweetness, and joy, it finally occurred to me that the most sincere and deepest thing I could say to you is to remind you that I, in my lifetime, was blessed with marriage with two wonderful people. And I enjoyed with each of my wives the sweetness and the abundance and the joy in such measure that if I could wish it for you, it would be the most wonderful thing of all. And that's what I wish for you.

3. Daniel Boyarin, *Unheroic Conduct: The Rise of Heterosexuality and the Invention of the Jewish Man* (Berkeley: University of California Press, 1997), xvii. For more on the multivocality of talmudic Judaism, see his *Intertextuality and the Reading of Midrash* (Bloomington: Indiana University Press, 1990), and *Carnal Israel: Reading Sex in Talmudic Culture* (Berkeley: University of California Press, 1993).

Worship Resources Earth Day Sunday

❧

National Council of Churches

The National Council of Churches (NCC), founded in 1950, is the leading force for ecumenical cooperation among Christians in the United States. The NCC's thirty-six Protestant, Anglican, and Orthodox member denominations include more than 50 million people in 140,000 local congregations.

❧

The celebration of Earth Day provides a uniquely visible time for churches to draw attention to the Christian's call to care for all God's creation.

Call to Worship (Based on Hymn #555, "Forward Through the Ages")
Leader: Forward through the ages in an unbroken line, move the faithful spirits at the call divine.
People: We gather today in the presence of God and in communion with those who have gone before us and those who will come after.
Leader: On this Earth Sabbath, we open our minds to learn about ecological threats to the health of present and future generations and to the whole community of life.
People: We open our hearts to the message of hope that comes to us through Jesus Christ.
Leader: We reach out our hands to bring healing and change, for the sake of the children of the earth—past, present, and future.
People: And we raise our voices to join with the rest of creation in singing praise to God, whose steadfast love and faithfulness endures to all generations.

Opening Hymn: #555 "Forward Through the Ages"

A Litany of Confession and Grace
Reader 1: John Wesley said: Sin is the refusal to acknowledge our dependence on God for life and breath and all things.
Reader 2: God of life, we confess that we often forget that we are utterly dependent upon you and interdependent with the rest of your creation.
People: Forgive us, O God, and inspire us to change.
Reader 1: Jesus quoted the prophet Isaiah when he challenged the people, saying: This people's hearts have grown dull. They have eyes, but do not see; ears, but do not hear; hearts, but do not understand.

Reader 2:   God of love, we confess that at times we would rather stay in denial than see, hear, and understand how our lifestyles affect our world.

People: Forgive us, O God, and inspire us to change.

Reader 1:   The prophets Isaiah and Hosea said: The land lies polluted under its inhabitants. The beasts of the field, the birds of the air, even the fish of the sea are dying.

Reader 2:   God of mercy, we confess that we are damaging the earth, the home that you have given us. We buy and use products that pollute our air, land, and water, harming wildlife and endangering human health.

People: Forgive us, O God, and inspire us to change.

Reader 1:   Chief Seattle said: Whatever we do to the web of life we do to ourselves.

Reader 2:   God of justice, we confess that we have not done enough to protect the web of life. We have failed to insist that our government set standards based on precaution. We allow companies to release dangerous toxins that destroy fragile ecosystems and harm human beings, especially those among us who are most vulnerable.

People: Forgive us, O God, and inspire us to change.

All: God of compassion, today we acknowledge our dependence upon you and our interconnectedness with the whole web of life. We open our eyes, ears, and hearts to the pain of the earth, that we may be open to your truth, see your way of hope, and walk with courage in your way.

Reader 1:   So be it. You are beloved children of God, forgiven, renewed, and sent out into the world to work for healing and justice, hope and wholeness, in faithfulness to God.

Hymn: #140 "Great Is Thy Faithfulness"

Pastoral Prayer (from Genesis 9, Genesis 17, and Deuteronomy 30)

Gracious God, your amazing love extends through all time and space, to all parts of your creation, which you created and called good. You made a covenant with Noah and his family, putting a rainbow in the sky to symbolize your promise of love and blessing to every living creature, and to all successive generations. You made a covenant with Abraham and Sarah, blessing them and their descendants throughout the generations. You made a covenant with Moses and the Israelite people to all generations, giving them the ten commandments and challenging them to choose life. In Jesus, you invite us to enter into a new covenant, in communion with all who seek to be faithful to you.

As people of faith, we are called into covenant. Your covenant of faithfulness and love extends to the whole creation. We pray for the healing of the earth, that present and future generations may enjoy the fruits of creation, and continue to glorify and praise you.

Offertory Prayer

Generous God, you have blessed us with the resources to share the good news of your love for all creation. We dedicate these gifts and pray that they may bring healing, wholeness, and hope to the world, that future generations may also know your graciousness and love. Amen.

Responsive Benediction (Hebrews 12)

Leader: Certainly God is raising up people even today to bring us through this dark time.

People: Life-giving God, we offer ourselves in service to you, supported by a great cloud of witnesses who urge us on.

Leader: We are connected to other people of faith and conscience around the world who are working for a peaceful, just, and sustainable world.

People: This global community supports us—we support each other.

Leader: We are connected with those who have gone before us: the martyrs and heroes, all the ancestors who invested themselves for the sake of future generations, and we are connected with those who will come after us.

People: Our ancestors and descendents support us—we are their champions.

Leader: We are related to the earth and all its creatures in a web that cannot be broken without injury to all.

People: The earth and our fellow creatures support us—we are their advocates.

Leader: We are connected to Jesus Christ, who reveals God to us, sends us the Spirit, and sends us out in his name.

People:

Leader: Therefore, let us lay aside every weight and sin that clings so closely, and let us run with perseverance the race that is set before us, looking to Jesus, the pioneer and perfecter of our faith, resisting all powers that destroy, bringing healing and hope to the world.

People: O God, Creator, Redeemer, Sustainer, we offer our lives in service to you.

Closing Hymn: #581 "Lord, Whose Love Through Humble Service"

Other Hymns for Earth Day: #126 "Sing Praise to God Who Reigns Above," #311 "Now the Green Blade Riseth," #92 "For the Beauty of the Earth," and Hymns #145 to #152. All hymn numbers are from the *United Methodist Hymnal* (1989).

"Dance to Heal the Earth"

❧

Dee Smith

Dee Smith is a Native American activist and writer.

❧

Whenever you dance, wherever you dance, dance to heal the earth!
Dancing is power. Dancing is prayer. Some say that all is dance. Maybe. Now there's a big dance coming, a dance to heal the earth. If you're reading this, you're probably part of it. You take part whenever you do whatever you do to help heal the earth. When you recycle. When you choose to show love, to fight for justice, to bring healing, to bring out what is good in others. When you avoid cruelty and dishonesty and waste. When you are outraged. When you speak out. When you give. When you consider the generations to come. When you protest to the oppressors and encourage those who feel the cutting edge of injustice. And, of course, when you dance. There is a tree that all the prophets see, and whenever you let your love show, you make the flowers grow.

Soon this dance will be done in a big way, in the old way, on sacred ground. All living things will take part. If you want to, you can take part. No one is twisting your arm. You can stop any time you need to, and start up again whenever you're ready. If you've read this far, you probably know what I'm talking about. You've probably been doing it in one way or another for a good while. Soon will be the time to make no bones about it! Cut loose!

Anytime you dance, anywhere, whether at a party or in church, dance to heal the earth! Let your feet beat a healing rhythm into the earth. Let your feet beat a strengthening rhythm for those who struggle the hardest. Let your feet beat a life-giving rhythm for all peoples, regardless of race or national boundary, regardless of whether we're human or whether we're the trees, the air, the fish, the birds, the buffalo, the bear, the crow. We come out of hiding, we come back from the dead, and we dance, and our dance is a prayer, and our songs and our rhythms and our breath give life.

Is the music they're playing some mindless jingle? Never mind, as long as it's not bad music, and you can dance to the beat! Make your own words, and make the words a prayer. A prayer for the end of exploitation, a prayer for the end of lies, a prayer for healing, for justice, for life. Remember your prayer-song, feed it and let it get strong and pass it along. Dance and pray, whenever you dance, dance to heal the earth.

Have you seen anything? Wear it out! Make it so that all can see what you see! Take a white T-shirt and mark it with your dreams. Is there anything you'd like to tell the world? Take your shirt and mark it with your song! This is the way it has been done, so you can do it too. Use any color except black (there are reasons for that that will become clearer later), and you'll probably find that a loose, pure cotton T is most comfortable for dancing in. Cos this is an actual dance, you dance hard, you sing and breathe hard and sweat. Wear it when you plan to go out dancing, to dance to heal the earth.

Some people do this dance while fasting, and dance for several days straight. But even a few minutes of dancing helps, and joins with all the other dancing going on, everywhere on Earth. Not everyone can fast these days. Besides, you never know when you're gonna dance, and you have to eat sometimes! But if you plan to dance, hold off eating till later, or just have a little. It's easier to dance if you don't have a hotdog weighing you down.

Some people say, do not do sacred things where people are drinking and partying. But all the universe is a sacred place. It really doesn't matter what others are doing, you can make a place sacred wherever you are, with your intention and your prayers. Some people use smoke to make a place sacred; a cigarette or incense stick will do fine. You can dance to heal the earth anywhere, even a party or a bar! The earth is everywhere, so you can dance anywhere to heal her. Only one thing. Please hold off drinking or using any other intoxicants till you're done. It works better that way.

The Lie has gone far enough. It spreads and makes everyone sick. Now is the time for this dance to begin. It, too, will spread, and it will bring healing to all. In the beginning, they say, God put a rainbow in the sky, to let us know that Spirit never forgets. Now is the time for us to put a rainbow across the earth, to let God know that we, too, remember.

Dance to heal the earth. Not just when you're dancing, but always. Live the dance, whenever you move, in all you do, dance to heal the earth.

"Peace Prayers of the People"

❧

Episcopal Peace Fellowship

The Chicago–based Episcopal Peace Fellowship has worked since 1939 in opposition to war and, more recently, in opposition to the death penalty.

❧

PEACE PRAYERS OF THE PEOPLE

Lead Us into Your Peace

Lord we pray that you will lead us into your LOVE—
You sent Jesus as a token of that love.
Lord we pray that you will lead us into your JUSTICE.
You sent the Prophets and gave us The Law to show us your justice.
Lord we pray that you will lead us into your RECONCILIATION.
You showed us how to forgive and reconcile.
Lord we pray that you will lead us into your PEACE.
Your LOVE and JUSTICE and your way of RECONCILIATION.
Amen.

—Bishop William Davidson, past chair of EPF

A Prayer for the Bombed Out, Burned Out, Driven Out

Lord God, we pray for all the bombed out, burned out, driven out, relocated, wondering, wandering, unwilling pilgrims in this world. Forgive us for our part in uprooting them. Restore their lives, make us partners with in the rebuilding of their lives. We pray in the name of the Son of Man, who had no place to lay His head.

—Arnold Kenseth and Richard Unsworth, in *Prayers for Worship Leaders*

Open Our Eyes

Take all hate from our hearts, O God, and teach us how to take it from the hearts of others. Open our eyes and show us what things make it easy for hatred to flourish and hard for us to conquer it. Then help us to change these things.

—Alan Paton

A Christian Prayer of Confession

Spirit of God, forgive us. For 2000 years, we Christians have failed to live the Gospel message of Jesus Christ.

Instead of sharing with our sisters and brothers, instead of feeding the hungry, clothing the naked, and healing the sick; we have stored up treasures and sent the vulnerable, sick, hungry and homeless from our door.

Instead of forgiving, we have sought vengeance retribution, harsh punishment and death. We have asked the state to kill in our name.

Instead of crying out against injustice, we have dominated, discriminated and demeaned; and we have benefited from the economic oppression of our neighbors.

Instead of holding your Creation in sacred trust, instead of respecting the interconnectedness and beauty of our universe; we have wasted and polluted, disrupted the balance, and ignored our responsibility to those who come after us.

Instead of loving our enemies, we have demonized them. Instead of peace, nonviolence, and reconciliation; we Christians have unleashed in your name, violent crusades, slavery, the Holocaust, and nuclear war. We have killed through landmines, depleted uranium, bombing runs, smart weapons, and economic sanctions.

We confess that we have neglected our prayer life and community building. We have lost our way and are not the people you called us to be. Accept our prayer and restore us. In your mercy, forgive us. Forgive us. Forgive us. Amen.

—Janet Chisholm, vice chair of EPF

O Lord Jesus Christ, whose perfect love met death by violence and was not extinguished; so enter the hearts and minds of those affected by violence that frailty may give way to your strength, loss to gain, bitterness to your total and victorious love.

—Susan Williams

A Prayer of Intercession

O God, who called the peacemakers your children, we beseech you that as you did send Your Son with the heavenly voice of peace on earth to be the Prince of Peace to men, so you will keep our hearts and minds in his peace, and make us both to love and defend the same. Guide the counsels of the President and of all leaders, in equity and steadfastness, to establish unity and concord among the nations, that all mankind may render you the fruits of peace and righteousness; through Jesus Christ our Lord. Amen.

—Diocese of Canterbury

Love Is Stronger Than Hate

Oh God, we stand before you with so many fears and uncertainties—imagined and real. Come into us and all people who truly seek your way. Bring into creation the chaos that is war and use us as your sons and daughters to show and live the way of peace and love. For we take our stand on your promise that love is stronger than hate, kindness greater than revenge. Turn our hearts, ever convert us to this truth and make us more whole as your Body in the world. Through your child, Jesus, who overcame violence and death with love and reigns with you and the Holy Spirit now and for eternity. Amen.

—Rev. T. Scott Allen, EPF Board

Gift of Shalom/Salaam

Gracious God, after the Resurrection Jesus bestowed upon the disciples the gift of Peace by proclaiming "My Peace I leave with you, my Peace I give to you." Inspire us with that hope in the gift of shalom and salaam, the gift of wholeness and the promise of your presence. Give us wisdom to seek nonviolence as an answer to the violence of our lives and world. Give us courage to seek wholeness in a fractured and divided world, to find reconciliation rather than revenge, to interfere with the madness of militarism and war. May your presence fill us and others with the thirst for unity, wholeness, and a desire to see all people valued as created in your image. May we and others receive your shalom and salaam, that we might be instruments of your love. Blessed be your name forever. Amen.

—Rev. David Selzer, chair of EPF

World Peace Prayer

Lead us from death to life
Lead us from falsehood to truth
Lead us from despair to hope
Lead us from fear to trust
Lead us from hate to love
Lead us from war to peace
Let peace fill our hearts, our world, our Universe.

Pax Christi Prayer to End the War against Iraq

Loving God,

We beg your forgiveness for the war that the U.S. is waging against the Iraqi people, for destroying Iraq's infrastructure by massive bombings, for using highly toxic weapons that contaminate Iraqi land and water, and are causing major increases in cancers among children.

Forgive us for imposing economic sanctions that have killed over one million Iraqis, mostly children.

Forgive us for placing oil interests above human welfare.

Heal us of our moral blindness and fill our hearts with love.

Help us to renounce all killing, to stop demonizing our adversaries, to value all life as sacred, and to see the Iraqi people as our brothers and sisters.

Empower us to engage in nonviolent action to end this slaughter of the innocents. O God, make us channels of your peace and reconciliation. Amen.

—Art Laffin

Calm Our Angry Hearts

Christ, no one on earth really wants the pain and horror of war. We do not want to kill or be killed, to hurt or be hurt. But we all see injustice, and sometimes it makes us angry and we see no other way to right the wrong except by war. Christ, teach us the ways of peace! Calm our angry hearts and grant to all peoples and their leaders patience in the search for peace and justice. Help us to be ready to give up some of our comforts and power and pride, so that war will leave the face of the earth and we may work for you in peace.

—Avery Brooks, in *Plain Prayers in a Complicated World*

Two Prayers for Peace

Eternal God, the Creator of all, we commit to you the needs of the whole world: where there is hatred, give love; where there is injury, pardon; where there is distrust, faith; where there is darkness, light. We pray for those who out of the bitter memories of strife and loss are seeking a more excellent way for the nations of the world, whereby justice and order may be maintained and the differences of people be resolved in equity. Bestow your blessings, we pray You, upon all who labor for peace and righteousness among the peoples, that the day may be hastened when war shall be no more and Your will only shall govern the nations upon earth; through Jesus Christ our Lord. Amen.

Almighty God, Creator of all people upon the earth, most heartily we pray that you will deliver your children from the cruelties of war and lead all the nations into the way of peace. Teach us to put away all bitterness and misunderstanding, both in Church and State; that we, with all the people may draw together as one community of peoples and dwell evermore in the fellowship of that Prince of Peace, who lives and reigns with You in the unity of the Holy Spirit, now and ever. Amen.

Prudence, Wisdom, and Humaneness

Grant us prudence in proportion to our power,
wisdom in proportion to our science,
humaneness in proportion to our wealth and might.
And bless all races and peoples
who travel in friendship along the road to justice,
liberty and lasting peace.
—Conference of European Churches, *Gloria Deo Worship Book,* 1986

Christian Prayer Book of Hope

Beloved God, we give you thanks for the life and message of Jesus, Jesus the Rebel, who remains our guide and inspiration and the promise of Hope in our time.

For Jesus calls us to love in a time of indifference, to nonviolence in a time of injustice, and to life in a time of death. He teaches us not only how to live, but how to die; how to transform not only the world but our own broken hearts, as well. His revolution transcends all our dreams for a better world and declares your reign here and now, at this very moment in human history.

In Jesus, we meet you, our beloved God. We see your true face. From now on we know that you are not a god of despair but of hope, not a god of wrath but of mercy; not a god of condemnation but of compassion; not a god of imperial power but of suffering; not a god of domination but of loving service; not a god of oppression but of liberation; not a god who blesses injustice but the God of justice; not a god of war but of peace; not a god of violence but of nonviolence; not a god of death but of Life. From now on we know that we all have been created to share in the fullness of life, in your love and unending mercy.

We step forward into the future, supporting each other, building community, making peace, practicing nonviolence, resisting the forces of war, and reconciling with our enemies, come what may. We have met Jesus the Rebel. He is alive and goes before us, summoning us to carry on the mission of nonviolence. We have been changed forever. Beloved God, you have begun the revolution within us.

Our hearts burn with the fire of Hope. Amen.

—Janet Chisholm, adapted from and inspired by "Jesus the Rebel" by John Dear

"Remember We Are One"

Anwar Fazal

Malaysian–born Anwar Fazal has received international recognition for his work on consumer rights, conservation, health, and the rights of migrant workers.

We all drink from one water
We all breathe from one air
We rise from one ocean
And we live under one sky

Remember
We are one

The newborn baby cries the same
The laughter of children is universal
Everyone's blood is red
And our hearts beat the same song

Remember
We are one

We are all brothers and sisters
Only one family, only one earth
Together we live
And together we die

Remember
We are one

Peace be on you
Brothers and Sisters
Peace be on you

"All That Has Divided Us Will Merge"

❧

Judy Chicago

Judy Chicago is an artist, author, feminist, educator, and intellectual whose internationally known work has focused on women's history and the Holocaust.

❧

And then all that has divided us will merge
Ant then compassion will be wedded to power
And then softness will come to a world
   that is harsh and unkind
And then both men and women will be gentle
And then both women and men will be strong
And then no person
   will be subject to another's will
And then all will be rich and free and varied
And then the greed of some
   will give way to the needs of many
And then all will share equally
   in the earth's abundance
And then all will care
   for the sick and the weak and the old
And then all will cherish life's creatures
And then all will live
   in harmony with each other and the earth.
And then everywhere
   will be called Eden once again.

"Please"

✺

Dalai Lama

His Holiness the fourteenth Dalai Lama Tenzin Gyatso is the head of state and spiritual leader of the Tibetan people. He is known throughout the world as an advocate of peaceful conflict resolution and the use of Buddhist teachings to reduce suffering.

✺

Please pacify the uninterrupted miseries
and unbearable fears,
such as famines and sicknesses,
that torment powerless beings
completely oppressed by inexhaustable
and violent evils,
and henceforth lead us from suffering states
and place us in an ocean of happiness and joy.

Those who, maddened by the demons of delusion,
commit violent negative actions
that destroy both themselves and others
should be the object of our compassion.
May the hosts of undisciplined beings
fully gain the eye that knows
what to abandon and practice,
and be granted a wealth
of loving-kindness and friendliness.

Through the force of dependent-arising,
which by nature is profound
and empty of appearances,
the force of the Words of Truth,
the power of the kindness of the Three Jewels
and the true power of nondeceptive actions
and their effects;
may my prayer of truth
be accomplished quickly and without hindrance.

"School Prayer"

Diane Ackerman

Diane Ackerman is a naturalist, poet, and essayist whose books include *The Rarest of the Rare* and *A Natural History of the Senses*.

In the name of daybreak
and the eyelids of morning
and the wayfaring moon
and the night when it departs,

I swear I will not dishonor
my soul with hatred,
but offer myself humbly
as a guardian of nature,
as a healer of misery,
as a messenger of wonder,
as an architect of peace.

In the name of the sun and its mirrors
and the day that embraces it
and the cloud veils drawn over it
and the uttermost night
and the male and the female
and the plants bursting with seed
and the crowning seasons
of the firefly and the apple,

I will honor all life—
wherever and in whatever form
it may dwell—on Earth my home,
and in the mansions of the stars.

"When Did We See You Hungry?"

❧

Anonymous Lutheran Prayer from France

Our gratitude to this anonymous poet.

❧

Lord, when did we see you hungry?

I was hungry and you were flying around the moon.
I was hungry and you told me to wait.
I was hungry and you formed a committee.
I was hungry and you talked about other things.

I was hungry and you told me:
    "There is no reason."
I was hungry
    and you had bills to pay for weapons.
I was hungry and you told me:
    "Now machines do that kind of work."
I was hungry and you said:
    "Law and order come first."
I was hungry and you said:
    "There are always poor people."
I was hungry and you said:
    "My ancestors were hungry too."
I was hungry and you said:
    "After age fifty, no one will hire you."
I was hungry and you said:
    "God helps those in need."
I was hungry and you said:
    "Sorry, stop by again tomorrow."

—Translated by Mary-Theresa McCarthy

Peace Seeds

❧

Peace Seeds represent the twelve prayers for peace prayed in Assisi, Italy, on the Day of Prayer for World Peace during the United Nations International Year of Peace, 1986. The prayers were brought to the United States and entrusted to the children at The Life Experience School in Sherborn, Massachusetts, under the care and direction of The Peace Abbey, an interfaith center for spiritual social activism and pacifism.

❧

1. THE HINDU PRAYER FOR PEACE

Oh God, lead us from the unreal to the Real. Oh God, lead us from darkness to light. Oh God, lead us from death to immortality. Shanti, Shanti, Shanti unto all. Oh Lord God almighty, may there be peace in celestial regions. May there be peace on earth. May the waters be appeasing. May herbs be wholesome, and may trees and plants bring peace to all. May all beneficent beings bring peace to us. May thy Vedic Law propagate peace all through the world. May all things be a source of peace to us. And may thy peace itself, bestow peace on all, and may that peace come to me also.

2. THE BUDDHIST PRAYER FOR PEACE

May all beings everywhere plagued with sufferings of body and mind quickly be freed from their illnesses. May those frightened cease to be afraid, and may those bound be free. May the powerless find power, and may people think of befriending one another. May those who find themselves in trackless, fearful wildernesses—the children, the aged, the unprotected—be guarded by beneficent celestials, and may they swiftly attain Buddhahood.

3. THE JAINIST PRAYER FOR PEACE

Peace and Universal Love is the essence of the Gospel preached by all the Enlightened Ones. The Lord has preached that equanimity is the Dharma. Forgive do I the creatures all, and let all creatures forgive me. Unto all have I amity, and unto none enmity. Know that violence is the root cause of all miseries in the world. Violence, in fact, is the knot of bondage. "Do not injure any living being." This is the eternal, perennial, and unalterable way of spiritual life. A weapon howsoever powerful it may be, can always be superseded by a superior one; but no weapon can, however, be superior to nonviolence and love.

4. THE MUSLIM PRAYER OF PEACE

In the name of Allah, the beneficent, the merciful. Praise be to the Lord of the Universe who has created us and made us into tribes and nations, that we may know each other, not that we may despise each other. If the enemy incline towards peace, do thou also incline towards peace, and trust in God, for the Lord is the one that heareth and knoweth all things. And the servants of God, Most Gracious are those who walk on the Earth in humility, and when we address them, we say "PEACE."

5. THE SIKH PRAYER FOR PEACE

"God adjudges us according to our deeds, not the coat that we wear": that Truth is above everything, but higher still is truthful living. "Know that we attaineth God when we loveth, and only that victory endures in consequence of which no one is defeated."

6. THE BAHAI' PRAYER FOR PEACE

Be generous in prosperity, and thankful in adversity. Be fair in thy judgment, and guarded in thy speech. Be a lamp unto those who walk in darkness, and a home to the stranger. Be eyes to the blind, and a guiding light unto the feet of the erring. Be a breath of life to the body of humankind, a dew to the soil of the human heart, and a fruit upon the tree of humility.

7. THE SHINTO PRAYER FOR PEACE

"Although the people living across the ocean surrounding us, I believe, are all our brothers and sisters, why are there constant troubles in this world? Why do winds and waves rise in the ocean surrounding us? I only earnestly wish that the wind will soon puff away all the clouds which are hanging over the tops of the mountains."

8. THE NATIVE AFRICAN PRAYER FOR PEACE

Almight God, the Great Thumb we cannot evade to tie any knot; the Roaring Thunder that splits mighty trees: the all-seeing Lord up on high who sees even the footprints of an antelope on a rockmass here on Earth. You are the one who does not hesitate to respond to our call. You are the cornerstone of peace.

9. THE NATIVE AMERICAN PRAYER FOR PEACE

O Great Spirit of our Ancestors, I raise my pipe to you. To your messengers the four winds, and to Mother Earth who provides for your children. Give us the wisdom to teach our children to love, to respect, and to be kind to each other so that they may grow with peace in mind. Let us learn to share all the good things that you provide for us on this Earth.

10. THE ZOROASTRIAN PRAYER FOR PEACE

We pray to God to eradicate all the misery in the world: that understanding triumph over ignorance, that generosity triumph over indifference, that trust triumph over contempt, and that truth triumph over falsehood.

11. THE JEWISH PRAYER FOR PEACE

Come let us go up to the mountain of the Lord, that we may walk the paths of the Most High. And we shall beat our swords into ploughshares, and our spears into pruning hooks. Nation shall not lift up sword against nation—neither shall they learn war any more. And none shall be afraid, for the mouth of the Lord of Hosts has spoken.

12. THE CHRISTIAN PRAYER FOR PEACE

Blessed are the PEACEMAKERS, for they shall be known as the Children of God. But I say to you that hear, love your enemies, do good to those who hate you, bless those who curse you, pray for those who abuse you. To those who strike you on the cheek, offer the other also, and from those who take away your cloak, do not withhold your coat as well. Give to everyone who begs from you, and of those who take away your goods, do not ask them again. And as you wish that others would do to you, do so to them.

Further Study

Nearly two thousand years ago the Jewish sage Hillel was asked if he could sum up the Torah's wisdom while standing on one foot: "Whatever is hateful to you," he replied, "do not do unto your neighbor. The rest is commentary. Now go and study." It is a mark of Hillel's spiritual genius that he combined the short version with an injunction for further learning, knowing that our understanding of that simple but profound commandment would benefit from a great deal of additional elaboration.

As wonderful as the material is in this book, it too requires further elaboration. Since a bibliography of three pages would be far too selective and inadequate, and one of thirty would still leave out great stuff and take up too much space, I will make no pretense at either objectivity or completeness and instead offer some personal suggestions for authors, publishers, websites, areas of inquiry, and other resources to enable the reader to "go and study." I'll add contacts for the (at least!) equally important arena of religious social action as well. Since just about everyone who will read this book will also be able to use the Internet, amazon.com, libraries, Google, and so forth, I will just mention names or titles, and trust that publishing details can easily be found.

To begin with, all the authors in *Liberating Faith* have written a great deal more than you see here. Study their other writings to get a fuller sense of the richness and complexity of their ideas. Further, for the important historical figures, biography and autobiography show you how, as Gandhi said of himself, "My life is my message." One could begin with Louis Fisher's biography of Gandhi, the many accounts of Martin Luther King's life (by Taylor Branch and David Garrow, for instance), or James Forest's life of Dorothy Day, *Love is the Measure*. Catherine Ingram's wonderful collection of interviews, *In the Footsteps of Gandhi*, offers insight into the lives and beliefs of more than a dozen inspiring figures.

More generally, any good historical account of political movements that includes a religious dimension can teach us a good deal. John Lewis's wonderful autobiography (*Walking with the Wind*) offers a wealth of information about the Civil Rights movement. Peter Ackerman and Jack Duvall's *A Force More Powerful* describes nonviolence in over a dozen contexts, almost all of which have a religious dimension.

Unfortunately, there are a number of important authors who were not included here. Archbishop Oscar Romero, martyred in El Salvador, and Buddhist leader of the Burmese pro-democracy movement Aung San Suu Kyi are perhaps the most important. One could start with Romero's *The Violence of Love*, while Suu Kyi's ideas can be found in *Voice of Hope* and *Freedom from Fear*. Bishop Desmond Tutu has written on the importance of reconciliation.

In the realm of feminist theology, it would be rewarding to explore books by several vital thinkers besides the ones included here. Mary Daly began as a radical Catholic, but then moved outside the boundaries of Christianity entirely. Rebecca Adler and Rita Gross have written challenging rethinkings of Judaism and Buddhism respectively. Marija Gimbutas provided much of the research for new understandings of earth-centered goddess spirituality, and Starhawk has helped popularize the Wicca perspective on the spiritual and political implications of recognizing the divinity of the earth.

For insights into peace and social justice, the works of Dietrich Bonhoeffer, a German theologian killed for opposing Hitler, are both demanding and rewarding. John Cobb Jr. and H. R. Niebuhr are American Protestant theologians who concentrate on the limitations of the institutional church and ecumenism. Cobb was also an early voice in ecotheology. Seyyed Nasr is a progressive Islamic theologian who challenges both other Moslems and Westerners alike. A. T. Ariyratne, a Sri Lankan Buddhist, offers searching criticisms of globalization from both spiritual and political perspectives. African American philosopher Cornel West draws on resources from American philosophy, the black historical experience, Christianity, and Marxism.

For sources on religious environmentalism beyond those cited in Part VIII, I particularly recommend the writings of Arthur Waskow, especially his important work on liturgy and celebrations. Matthew Fox, ex-Dominican priest who was silenced by the Vatican, has proposed a "creation theology" which focuses on the mysteries and wonder of life rather than on sin. The Forum on Religion and Ecology has produced several collections on ecotheology from different religious traditions (*Buddhism and Ecology, Christianity and Ecology,* etc.) that contain cutting-edge accounts of the theory and practice of religious environmentalism. The Forum also has a comprehensive website (www.environment.harvard.edu/religion/).

On the rather abstract level of theology and philosophy, it is important to seek out views of religious life that stress personal passion over doctrinal proof and mystery over certainty. In this regard my own views have been most influenced by Søren Kierkegaard, particularly his *Concluding Unscientific Postscript,* and by Elie Wiesel, whose novel *Dawn* and several books of commentary on biblical and postbiblical Jewish sources are spiritually and intellectually rewarding.

There are a number of contexts in which the connections between religion and political action have long been central. I must make special mention of one particular publisher, Orbis Books, which is to my mind America's most consistent, principled, and creative publisher of this material. Beacon Press, Fortress, Herald Press, New Society Publishers, Jewish Lights, Rowman and Littlefield, and Parallax Press are other important sources, ones sometimes overlooked because they are not as large, widely known, or well funded as other publishers.

Two American magazines are particularly committed to progressive religious political activism. *Tikkun* is a bimonthly Jewish critique of politics, religion, and culture; *Sojourners,* edited by Jim Wallis, has its roots in Evangelical Christianity. They both have websites as well: www.tikkun.org and www.sojo.net. I recommend also *Reconciliation,* the publication of the Fellowship of Reconciliation, the oldest interfaith peace and justice activist group in the United States. Both the organization and the magazine can be reached at www.forusa.org, which also has links to "Peace Fellowships" formed by Jews, Buddhists, Baptists, Moslems, and others. *Earthlight* (www.Earthlight.org) emphasizes nondenominational connections between spirituality and ecology. More scholarly treatments of a wide range of issues can be found in the *Journal of Religious Ethics,* the *Journal of Feminist Studies in Religion, Feminist Theology,* and *Worldviews: Environment, Culture, Religion.*

After we study (as well as before!), we should act, and the web also makes it easy to connect to action-oriented groups of virtually every type of religion. The National Council of Churches (www.nccusa.org) and the Conference of Catholic Bishops, (www.usccb.org), for instance, have their own committees working on, or have links to, dozens of groups concerned with social justice, peace, the environment, reconciliation, women's rights, antiracism, workers' rights, occupational health and safety, and more. Similar connections can be found at the websites of every particular denomination. Jews, Methodists, Lutherans, Baptists, Unitarians, Moslems, Hindus, and Buddhists (to name just some!) throughout the world offer politically committed material for religious education and worship, are engaging in political action in hundreds of communities, and seek to be progressive voices in national and international affairs. Wonderful resources can also be found at the site of the Indigenous Environmental Network (www.ienearth.org), including information, essays, prayers, and links to action groups. Finally, we should remember that Quakers (www.quaker.org) and Mennonites (www.mennonites.org) have for a very long time been pioneers in using religious resources to support peace and women's rights, and to question modernity's individualism and consumerism.

Permissions

"Feminist Theology, 1880–1900"

Reprinted by permission of the publisher from *Righteous Discontent: The Women's Movement in the Baptist Church 1880–1920* by Evelyn Brooks Higginbotham, Cambridge, Mass.: Harvard University Press, copyright © 1993 by the President and Fellows of Harvard College.

PART III

Selections from His Writings

From Ragavan Iyer (ed), "The Moral and Political Writings of Mahatma Gandhi," Vol. I (1986). Reprinted by permission of Oxford University Press.

From M. K. Gandhi, *Non-Violent Resistance*. New York: Schocken Books, 1951. Reprinted by permission of Navajivan Trust.

From Jack Homer, *The Gandhi Reader*. Indianapolis: Indiana University Press, 1956. Reprinted by permission of Navajivan Trust.

"Gandhi in the Twenty-First Century"

From Ronald J. Terchek, "Gandhi in the Twenty-First Century," from *Gandhi: Struggling for Autonomy*, Rowman & Littlefield, 1998. Reprinted by permission of the publisher.

PART IV

"The Struggle between Two Voices of God in Torah"

From *Jewish Renewal: A Path to Healing and Transformation* by Michael Lerner, copyright © 1994 by Michael Lerner. Used by permission of Grosset & Dunlap, Inc., a division of Penguin Group (USA) Inc.

"The Justice of Transcendence and the Transcendence of Justice"

From Roger S. Gottlieb, "The Justice of Transcendence and the Transcendence of Justice," *Journal of the American Academy of Religion*, 1999, vol. 67, no. 1, pp. 149–66. Reprinted by permission of Oxford University Press.

from The Silent Cry: Mysticism and Resistance

From Dorothee Soelle, *The Silent Cry: Mysticism and Resistance*, pp. 195–99: Fortress Press, 2001. Reprinted by permission of Hoffman und Campe Verlag.

from Qur'an, Liberation, and Pluralism: An Islamic Perspective of Interreligious Solidarity against Oppression

From *Qur'an, Liberation, and Pluralism*, copyright © 1997 by Farid Esack. Reproduced by permission of Oneworld Publications.

"The Social Teachings of the Buddha"

From "The Social Teachings of the Buddha" by Walpola Rahula. Reprinted from *The Path of Compassion: Writings on Socially Engaged Buddhism* (1985) edited by Fred Eppsteiner with permission of Parallax Press, Berkeley, California, www.parallax.org.

from Moral Man and Immoral Society

From Reinhold Niebuhr, *Moral Man and Immoral Society,* pp. 52–54, 60–62, 71–73: Scribners, 1953. Reprinted by permission of the estate of Reinhold Niebuhr.

from "Jesus of Nazareth/Christ of Faith: Foundations of a Reactive Christology"

From Carter Heyward, "Wrong Relation in Christological Epistemology: False Knowing," *Speaking of Christ: A Lesbian Feminist Voice,* Ellen C. Davis, ed. (New York: The Pilgrim Press, 1989), 18–20. Copyright © 1989, The Pilgrim Press. Used by permission.

"How Christians Become Socialists"

Philip Berryman, "How Christians Become Socialists," from *Churches in Struggle: Liberation Theologies and Social Change in North America,* edited by William K. Tabb, copyright © 1986 by Monthly Review Press. Reprinted by permission of Monthly Review Foundation.

"Beyond the Enlightenment Mentality"

Tu Weiming, "Beyond Enlightenment," from *Confucianism and Ecology: The Interrelation of Heaven, Earth, and Humans,* edited by Mary Evelyn Tucker and John Berthong, Harvard University Press, 1998. Reprinted by permission of Associated University Presses.

PART V

"Letter from a Birmingham Jail"

Martin Luther King Jr., "Letter from a Birmingham Jail," reprinted by arrangement with the Estate of Martin Luther King Jr., c/o Writers House as agent for the proprietor, New York, NY. Copyright © 1963 Dr. Martin Luther King Jr., copyright renewed 1991 by Coretta Scott King.

from Black Theology and Black Power

James H. Cone, "Violence" and "Preface to the 1989 Edition," from *Black Theology and Black Power,* Orbis, 1997. Reprinted by permission of Orbis Books.

from A Theology of Liberation

Gustavo Gutiérrez, *A Theology of Liberation,* pp. 272–79: Orbis, 1973. Reprinted by permission of Orbis Books (North America) and Canterbury Press Ltd. (world outside North America).

"Toward the 'Rights of the Poor': Human Rights in Liberation Theology"

Mark Engler, "Toward the 'Rights of the Poor': Human Rights in Liberation Theology," from *Journal of Religious Ethics,* Vol. 28, No. 3, Fall 2000, pp. 339–66. Reprinted by permission of Blackwell Publishing Ltd.

"The Martyrs' Living Witness: A Call to Honor and Challenge"

From the April 1990 issue of *Sojourners.* Reprinted with permission from Sojourners. (800) 714-7474, www.sojo.net.

"Love Is the Measure" and "Our Brothers, the Communists"

Dorothy Day, "Love Is the Measure" and "Our Brothers, the Communists." From *Dorothy Day: Selected Writings,* edited by Robert Ellsberg: Orbis, 1998. Reprinted by permission of Orbis Books.

from Disarmed and Dangerous: The Radical Life and Times of Daniel and Philip Berrigan

From *Disarmed and Dangerous: The Radical Life and Times of Daniel and Philip Berrigan* by Murray Polner and Jim O'Grady. Copyright © by Murray Polner and Jim O'Grady. Reprinted by permission of Basic Books, a member of Perseus Books, L.L.C.

"Faith Takes a Seat at the Bargaining Table"

Rich Barlow, "Faith Takes a Seat at the Bargaining Table," October 12, 2002. Boston: *The Boston Globe.* Reprinted by permission of the author.

"Religion and the Fall of Communism"

Michael Bourdeaux, "Religion and the Fall of Communism," from *Catholic World Report,* January 22, 1997. Reprinted by permission.

"A Catholic Rural Ethic for Agriculture, Environment, Food, and Earth"

Used by permission of the chairperson of the National Catholic Rural Life Conference, http://www.ncric.com.

"Globalization and the Perennial Question of Justice"

Mary John Mananzan, "Globalization and the Perennial Question of Justice," from *Spiritual Questions for the Twenty-First Century: Essays in Honor of Joan D. Chittister,* by Mary Hembrow Snyder: Orbis 2001. Reprinted by permission of Orbis Books.

"Mammon and the Culture of the Market: A Socio-Theological Critique"

Harvey Cox, "Mammon and the Culture of the Market: A Socio-Theological Critique," from *Meaning and Modernity: Religion, Polity and Self,* edited by Richard Madsen et al., University of California Press, 2002. Reprinted by permission.

"Sarvodaya"

Reprinted from *Mindfulness in the Marketplace* (2002), edited by Allan Hunt Badiner with permission of Parallax Press, Berkeley, California, www.parallax.org.

"Alternatives to Consumerism"

Reprinted from *Mindfulness in the Marketplace* (2002), edited by Allan Hunt Badiner with permission of Parallax Press, Berkeley, California, www.parallax.org.

"Islamic Banking"

Rami G. Khouri, "Islamic Banking," from *Seeds of Peace,* Vol. 5, No. 1, January 1989. Reprinted by permission of the author.

"Statement of Indigenous Nations, Peoples, and Organizations"

"Statement of Indigenous Nations, Peoples, and Organizations," from http://www.yvwiiusdinvnohii.net/political/state.htm. Reprinted by permission.

"Voices of the Peoples—Voices of the Earth: Indigenous Peoples—Subjugation or Self-Determination?"

Michael Dodson, "Voices of the Peoples—Voices of the Earth: Indigenous Peoples—Subjugation or Self-Determination?" from *Voices of the Earth: Indigenous Peoples, New Partners and the Right to Self-Determination in Practice,* edited by Leo van der Vilst, International Books/NCIV, 1994. Reprinted by permission.

from The Disabled God: Toward a Liberatory Theology of Disability

Nancy L. Eiesland, *The Disabled God: Toward a Liberatory Theology of Disability,* Abindon, 1994. Used by permission.

PART VI

from "The 'Why' and 'What' of Christian Feminist Theology"

Anne M. Clifford, *Introducing Feminist Theology,* Orbis, 2001. Reprinted by permission of Orbis Books.

"Ecology Is a Sistah's Issue Too: The Politics of Emergent Afrocentric Ecowomanism"

"Ecology Is a Sistah's Issue Too: The Politics of Emergent Afrocentric Ecowomanism" by Shamara Shantu Riley. From *Ecofeminism and the Sacred* edited by Carol J. Adams. Copyright © 1993 by The Continuum Publishing Company. Reprinted by permission of the publisher.

from The Men We Long to Be: Beyond Lonely Warriors and Desperate Lovers

Pages 87–97, 115–19 from *The Men We Long to Be* by Stephen B. Boyd. Copyright © 1995 by Stephen B. Boyd. Reprinted by permission of HarperCollins Publishers Inc.

"Rituals of Healing: Ministry with and on Behalf of Gay and Lesbian People"

Anita C. Hill and Leo Treadway, "Rituals of Healing: Ministry with and on Behalf of Gay and Lesbian People" from *Lift Every Voice: Constructing Christian Theologies from the Underside*, edited by Susan Brooks Thistlethwaite and Mary Potter Engel: Harper & Row, 1990. Reprinted by permission of Orbis Books.

PART VII

"Religion and Conflict Transformation"

R. Scott Appleby, "Religion and Conflict Transformation," from *The Ambivalence of the Sacred: Religion, Violence, and Reconciliation*, by Scott Appleby, Rowman & Littlefield, 2000. Reprinted by permission.

"Jesus' Third Way"

Walter Wink, "Jesus' Third Way," from *Transforming Violence: Linking Local and Global Peacemaking*, edited by Robert Herr and Judy Herr, Herald Press, 1998, Scottdale, PA 15683. All rights reserved.

"The Fourteen Mindfulness Trainings of the Order of Interbeing"

Reprinted from *Being Peace* (1987) by Thich Nhat Hanh with permission of Parallax Press, Berkeley, California, www.parallax.org.

"The Christian Challenge: Love Your Enemies"

Naim Stifan Ateek, "The Christian Challenge: Love Your Enemies," from *Justice and Only Justice: A Palestinian Theology of Liberation*, Orbis, 1990. Reprinted by permission of Orbis Books.

from The Journey toward Reconciliation

John Paul Lederach, *The Journey toward Reconciliation*, Herald Press, 1999, Scottdale, PA 15683. Used by permission.

from "Speak Truth to Power"

"Speak Truth to Power" ed. by Susan Furry. *Peacework,* December 2001/January 2002.

"Resisting the Forces of Death" and "'No' to the Vietnam War"

Henri Nouen, "Resisting the Forces of Death" and "'No' to the Vietnam War" from *The Road to Peace,* edited by John Dear, Orbis, 1998. Reprinted by permission of Orbis Books.

"Toward a Theology of Resistance"

From *Faith and Violence* by Thomas Merton. Copyright © 1984 by University of Notre Dame Press. Notre Dame, IN 46556. Used by permission.

"September 11, 2001: A Pacifist Response"

Stanley Hauerwas, "September 11, 2001: A Pacifist Response," in *South Atlantic Quarterly,* Vol. 101, No. 2, pp. 425–33, 2002. Copyright © 2002, Duke University Press. All rights reserved. Used by permission of the publisher.

"The Meaning of This Hour"

Abraham Joshua Heschel, "The Meaning of This Hour," from *Man's Quest for God,* pp. 147–51. New York: Scribner's, 1954.

PART VIII

"Saving the World: Religion and Politics in the Environmental Movement"

From *Joining Hands: Politics and Religion Together for Social Change* by Roger Gottlieb. Copyright © by Westview Press. Reprinted by permission of Westview Press, a member of Perseus Books, L.L.C.

"Traditional Ecological Knowledge and Environmental Futures"

Winona LaDuke, "Traditional Ecological Knowledge and Environmental Futures," in *The Winona LaDuke Reader,* Voyageur Press, 2002. Reprinted by permission of the author.

The Earth Charter

"Earth Charter" reprinted by permission of the Earth Charter Initiative.

"The Cochabamba Declaration on Water: Globalization, Privatization, and the Search for Alternatives"

"The Cochabamba Declaration on Water: Globalization, Privatization, and the Search for Alternatives," from *Global Backlash*, edited by Robin Broad, Rowman & Littlefield, 2002. Reprinted by permission.

"Evangelical Declaration on the Care of Creation"

Evangelical Environmental Network, "Evangelical Declaration on the Care of Creation." Permission given by the Evangelical Environmental Network. http://www.creationcare.org/.

Address of His Holiness Ecumenical Patriarch Bartholomew

Address of His Holiness Ecumenical Patriarch Bartholomew at the Environmental Symposium at the Santa Barbara Greek Orthodox Church, Santa Barbara, California, November 8, 1997. Used by permission of His All Holiness.

"The Theological Basis of Animal Rights"

Andrew Linzey, "The Theological Basis of Animal Rights." Copyright © 1991 Christian Century Foundation. Reprinted with permission from the October 9, 1991 issue of the *Christian Century*.

PART IX

"Breaking Ground: A Traditional Jewish Lesbian Wedding"

Inbal Kashtan, "Breaking Ground: A Traditional Jewish Lesbian Wedding." Copyright © 2002. From *Queer Jews* by David Shneer and Caryn Aviv. Reproduced by permission of Routledge, Inc., part of The Taylor & Francis Group.

Worship Resources Earth Day Sunday

National Council of Churches, Worship Resources Earth Day Sunday, fourth Sunday after Easter, April 21, 2002.

"Peace Prayers of the People"

From the Episcopal Peace Fellowship, www.episcopalpeacefellowship.org.

About the Editor

Roger S. Gottlieb, professor of philosophy at Worcester Polytechnic Institute, is the author or editor of twelve books and dozens of articles on subjects including political philosophy, ethics, spiritual life, modern religion, environmental politics, ecotheology, disability, and the Holocaust. Among his recent books are *This Sacred Earth: Religion, Nature, Environment; A Spirituality of Resistance: Finding a Peaceful Heart and Protecting the Earth;* and *Joining Hands: Politics and Religion Together for Social Change.* Gottlieb is the "Reading Spirit" columnist for *Tikkun Magazine;* serves on the editorial boards of *Social Theory and Practice; Capitalism, Nature, Socialism;* and *Worldviews;* and edits several academic book series on radical politics, religion, and environmental issues.